373

214 Sing, sweet
harp

W
273 When Midst
The Gay I meet

383 -
The hooded
falcon

391
The past, the
future, two
eternities.

394
Wind proceeding
from the throne
of God

547 The Sceptic

254
MUSIC - A short
strain

360

Thomes Moore

THOMAS MOORE'S

COMPLETE POETICAL WORKS

COLLECTED BY HIMSELF

WITH EXPLANATORY NOTES

AND

BIOGRAPHICAL INTRODUCTION

NEW YORK: 46 EAST FOURTEENTH STREET

THOMAS Y. CROWELL & COMPANY

BOSTON: 100 PURCHASE STREET

TYPOGRAPHY BY C. J. PETERS & SON,
BOSTON.

BIOGRAPHICAL SKETCH.

THOMAS MOORE was born at No. 12 Little Longford Street, Dublin, on the 28th of May, 1779.[1]

His father originally kept a small wine shop or grocery store, and afterwards was raised to the dignity of barrack-master. His mother's name was Anastasia Codd; his maternal grandfather a gouty Tom Codd. They were Roman Catholics. Both of his parents were amiable; his father not remarkable in any other way; his mother rather superior in wit and intelligence. They took great pride in their boy and made a show child of him. He early displayed a talent for recitation and music; his mother predicted that he would go on the stage.

When he was eleven he wrote an epilogue for a private exhibition at a summer bathing-place, and won great applause by his singing of the songs of Patrick in O'Keefe's farce, "The Poor Soldier." Long before that he had "lisped in numbers, for the numbers came." When he was fourteen his first published verses appeared in the *Anthologia Hibernica*, a Dublin magazine, creditable, but short lived.

In 1793 the University and the Bar were thrown open to Roman Catholics, and the following summer Moore entered at Trinity College. He followed his tastes, and only by his natural quickness escaped the disgrace of failure. He became an intimate friend of Robert Emmett and other young conspirators, and narrowly evaded the judicial inquisition which made martyrs of so many of his friends.

He was eighteen when he took his degree of Bachelor of Arts. He had already made a large part of his translation, or rather paraphrase, of Anacreon, and the Provost of the University advised him to publish it.

He went to London in the spring of 1799, and there entered the Middle Temple as a law student. Lord Moira was the first of the long list of his titled friends. Through him Moore made other fashionable acquaintances, and when the publisher to whom he submitted the Anacreon refused to publish the work without a guarantee, Moore easily secured a large number of influential subscribers, including the Marquis of Lansdowne, and — what was still more important — permission to dedicate it to the Prince of Wales. It was published in 1800, and brought him fame. His law studies suffered under the burden of his popularity; he often had six invitations for an evening, dined with bishops and lords; everywhere happy, gay, and Irish-careless.

The next year he published a volume of original poems under the title: "The Poetical Works of the Late Thomas Little." He lived long enough to be ashamed of the indecencies which marred them, but he did not at the time hesitate to dedicate the second edition over his initials to a Dublin friend.

Lord Moira got Moore appointed Poet Laureate, but his only official work in that capacity was one birthday ode. He quickly resigned it, and accepted the office of Registrar of the Admiralty Court of Bermuda. He left England in September,

[1] A baptismal register extant gives the date as 1780. The doubt is of small moment.

iii

1803, but he found the duties of the place uncongenial, and he undoubtedly longed for the gay society of London. He appointed a deputy, and, after spending four months in travelling in the United States and Canada, he returned home with a volume of poems completed. The new volume of " Epistles, Odes, and other Poems" appeared early in 1806, and that same year he began the composition of his " Irish Melodies."

Jeffrey contemptuously reviewed Moore's poems in *The Edinburgh Review,* and called them " a public nuisance." Moore challenged Jeffrey, and just as the parties were about to fire off their pistols, which were charged blank, the police arrested them. This duel resulted in a warm friendship. Lord Byron made an allusion to " Little's leadless pistol," and the fiery young poet sent out a challenge to Byron. This also led to a life-long friendship. Moore was disappointed in not receiving high political preferment on the death of Pitt. He lived for several years at Lord Moira's house at Donington Park, writing his songs and going into the finest society, where his fascinating manners and his delightful talent for music made him the cynosure of all.

In 1802 a private theatre had been established at Kilkenny. The female parts were filled by professional actresses ; the male characters by amateurs. Moore was frequently called upon to exercise his talent on that stage.

In 1809 a Miss Elizabeth Dyke was performing the part of " Lady Godiva " to Moore's " Peeping Tom." She was only seventeen, and extremely pretty. Moore fell in love with her, and married her clandestinely in March, 1811.

It proved to be a happy marriage. Moore's London friends received her cordially, and the parents of both the young people quickly forgave them the imprudent step. Moore was receiving from the publishers of his songs £500 a year, and that with a prospect of the engagement continuing indefinitely.

In 1812 Moore began his satirical attacks on the Prince Regent and other political personages. Naturally they ruined his chances of obtaining office, though they diverted the Whig society of Holland House, and were popular in town. For twenty years he glibly poured out pasquinades, squibs, epigrams, and satires, full of audacious wit, not seldom vulgar and scurrilous, but as a rule marked by good temper. In 1813 appeared "The Twopenny Post Bag," which, incredible as it may seem at the present day, went through fourteen editions in a few months. In March of that year his second daughter Anastasia was born, and he moved to Ashburne in Derbyshire, where, during the following three years, he wrote his romance of "Lalla Rookh." Even before he had put pen to paper he received £3000 from the Longmans. But it was some time after the arrangement was made before he actually got to work on the poems. The only sorrow that touched the young couple at their Ashburne cottage was the loss of their third daughter, Olivia, who died when only seven months old.

"Lalla Rookh " was published in May, 1817. A second edition was printed within a fortnight, and six or seven were exhausted within the year. He was enabled to pay off his debts, and to pension his father, who had lost his place as barrack-master.

He then accepted the banker-poet Rogers's invitation to visit Paris, and was so delighted with the gay city that he proposed to live there for several years. That little plan was abandoned, owing to the death of his oldest daughter, Barbara, a beautiful little girl of five. He took his family to Sloperton Cottage, near the estate of his friend, Lord Lansdowne. The rent was only £40 a year. That was his home during the rest of his life. He soon began the composition of his "Fudge Family in Paris," which turned out to be a satire on Lord Castlereagh and Sidmouth rather than what he had at first intended — an *exposé* of the absurdities of the English tourists visiting Paris after the war. Five editions came out in quick succession, and Moore's share of the profits was £350. But whatever success he had in poetry and the products of his muse was absolutely counter-balanced by a great misfortune that now overwhelmed him. He still held his Bermuda office. It proved to be for him "the vex'd Bermoothes." His deputy, who sent him occasional remittances, was apparently left to his own unguided will. In April, 1818, he was found to be a defaulter and embezzler, and Moore was called upon to make good the £6000 missing.

The matter was carried into the courts, and while the suit dragged its slow length along Moore kept up his usual round of gay and innocent dissipations.

Now began that minute diary of his actions and sayings which fills so large a part of Earl Russell's portentous and ill-digested "Life of Moore."

At the end of a year, during which a son was born to him, he received word that the case was likely to go against him. Moore, for the first time in his life, confessed to feeling blue, and "wished he had a good cause to die in."

The adverse decision was rendered in July, and though hosts of his friends offered to help him out, and his publishers gladly volunteered to advance on account whatever sum he needed, he declined all such aid and — ran off to the Continent in company with Lord John Russell. He spent ten days in Paris, then went to visit Lord Byron near Venice. After spending three months in Italy he returned to Paris, and wrote his wife to join him. He and his family settled in a pleasant cottage near the Champs Elysées. He tried hard to work and refrain from expensive society, but temptations were too much for him. His promised poems, "The Fudge Family in Italy," and his long delayed "Life of Sheridan" were suspended, and the only result of his labors was the first letter of Alciphron and a dozen melodies.

In 1821 he disguised himself with a pair of false mustaches and went to London under the name of Dyke. He called on his publishers and authorized them to offer the American claimant 1000 guineas. Then he ran across to Dublin and visited his parents. On his return he found the arrangements made. Lord Lansdowne advanced the greater part of the needed sum, an uncle of the absconded deputy contributed £300, and Moore was a free man.

Moore, during his visit to Italy, had received as a gift Byron's Autobiographical Memoirs. He offered them to Murray, who agreed to pay Moore 2000 guineas as editor of the memoirs and historian of Byron's life. A second agreement was made whereby Byron or Moore might, during Lord Byron's life, repay Murray the 2000 guineas advanced, and recover the manuscript. Otherwise Murray was free to publish the Memoirs within three months after Byron's death.

Shortly after this Moore finished his "Loves of the Angels," which was published in December, 1822, about a month after his final return to England.

The following May appeared the "Fables for the Holy Alliance." The two volumes together reduced his indebtedness to Murray by the handsome sum of £1500. The same month his second son, the last of his children, was born.

In April, 1824, Lord Byron died. Moore claimed the manuscript of the memoirs. The story of the final destruction of the manuscript is told most interestingly in the recently published life of Murray the publisher. Moore certainly in this matter showed a very noble and lofty sense of honor.

In 1825 his life of Sheridan, on which he had been so long engaged, was published. During the last months of its preparation he wrote many songs for Powers, who was glad to renew the engagement. In October he made a trip to Scotland, spending three or four days with Scott at Abbotsford, and nine or ten with Jeffrey. He was innocently delighted to find himself the greatest man in Scotland. At the theatre the whole pit rose and cheered him vociferously.

His principal occupation on his return was in writing "The Epicurean," which he had planned while in France. It was published in June, 1827, and four editions were sold in eight months, bringing him in £700. Meantime he was adding to his precarious and varying income by writing songs and satires, as pot-boilers, which sold readily.

In February, 1828, he arranged with Murray to write the life of Byron. Besides putting a large amount of material in his hands, Murray offered him £4000, advancing for the Longmans upwards of £3000, settling Moore's debts in that quarter.

The task occupied Moore three years: the first volume was issued in January, 1830; the second in the following December. The publishers lost on it, owing principally to the popular dislike of Byron.

In 1830, he wrote a life of Lord Edward Fitzgerald, which was published in midsummer, 1831; and the following year a subscription was set on foot for the purchase on his behalf of an estate in Limerick, the electors of that place having expressed a desire to return him to Parliament. He was also proposed as a member to represent Trinity College. But Moore wisely declined.

The latter part of Moore's life was saddened by misfortunes. In 1832 his mother died, saying with her dying breath: "Tom, you have from the first to the last done your duty, and far more than your duty, by me and all connected with you." When he was fifty-five the arrangement for furnishing songs to Powers came to an end. The following year he was given a government pension of £300. In 1840–41 the ten volumes of his poetical works were published. The only other literary work of consequence was his history of Ireland, which had dragged along unsatisfactorily for years. The first volume was published in 1835: he received £750 for it; for the three other volumes he got £500 apiece.

Moore's sons brought him sorrow and disappointment: 't was a sad story of illness and premature death, of unworthy behavior and reckless extravagance.

Moore himself gradually lost the use of his faculties, and died on the 26th of February, 1852. During his feeble condition his wife, by patient economy, paid his debts, and when he died, with the £3000 which Longmans had paid for his diary and letters, and a crown pension, she was enabled to end her days in comfort.

Tom Moore was a little man: Gerald Griffin thus described him in 1835: —

"A little man, but full of spirits, with eyes, hands, feet, and frame forever in motion, looking as if it would be a feat for him to sit for three minutes quiet in his chair. I am no great observer of proportions, but he seemed to me to be a neat-made little fellow, tidily buttoned up, young as fifteen at heart, though with hair that reminded me of Alps in the sunset; not handsome, perhaps, but without an actor's affectation; easy as a gentleman, but without *some* gentlemen's formality."

N. P. Willis, who met him in 1834, declared himself surprised at the diminutiveness of his person: —

"He is much below the middle size, and with his white hat and long chocolate frock coat, was far from prepossessing in appearance."

He was "near-sighted, and had the frank, merry manner of a confident favorite." He thus describes meeting him at Lady Blessington's: —

"Moore's head is distinctly before me while I write, but I shall find it difficult to describe his hair, which curled once all over it in long tendrils, unlike any body else's in the world, and which, probably, suggested his sobriquet of 'Bacchus,' is diminished now to a few curls, sprinkled with gray, and scattered in a single ring above his ears. His forehead is wrinkled, with the exception of a most prominent development of the organ of gayety, which, singularly enough, shines with the lustre and smooth polish of a pearl, and is surrounded by a semicircle of lines drawn close about it, like intrenchments against Time. His eyes still sparkle like a champagne bubble, though the invader has drawn his pencillings about the corners, and there is a kind of wintry red, of the tinge of an October leaf, that seems enamelled on his cheek, the eloquent record of the claret his wit has brightened. His mouth is the most characteristic feature of all. The lips are delicately cut, slight and changeable as an aspen; but there is a set-up look about the lower lip — a determination of the muscles to a particular expression, and you fancy that you can almost see wit astride upon it. It is written legibly, with the imprint of political success. It is arch, confident, and half diffident, as if he were disguising his pleasure at applause, while another bright gleam of fancy was breaking on him. The slightly tossed nose confirms the fun of the expression, and altogether it is a face that sparkles, beams, radiates."

Leigh Hunt said : —

" His forehead is long and full of character, with 'bumps' of wit, large and radiant enough to transport a phrenologist. His eyes are as dark and fine as you would wish to see under a set of vine leaves; his mouth generous and good-humored, with dimples; his nose sensual, prominent, and at the same time the reverse of aquiline. There is a very peculiar character in it, as if it were looking forward, and scenting a feast or an orchard. The face, upon the whole, is bright, not unruffled with care and passion; but festivity is the predominant expression."

He was born and bred a Catholic, and generally attended the Roman Catholic chapel in Wardour Street, but no one could have been more liberal. He often went to the churches of other denominations, and his children were educated as Protestants.

Every one was fond of Moore. Byron said:—

" Moore is a very noble fellow in all respects."

And again:—

" There is nothing Moore may not do if he will but seriously set about it. In society he is gentleman, gentle, and, altogether, more pleasing than any individual with whom I am acquainted. For his honor, principle, and independence, his conduct to Hunt speaks 'trumpet-tongued.' "

Scott says:—

" There is a manly frankness with perfect ease and good breeding about him which is delightful. Not the least touch of the poet or the pedant. A little, very little man, . . . his countenance is plain, but the expression is very animated, especially in speaking or singing."

But the pleasantest testimony as to Moore's character is what Miss Godfrey wrote him: —

" You have contrived, God knows how! amidst the pleasures of the world to preserve all your home fireside affections true and genuine as you brought them out with you; and this is a trait in your character that I think beyond all praise: it is a perfection that never goes alone; and I believe you will turn out a saint or an angel after all."

And this is confirmed by Earl Russell's words: —

" Rightly did Mr. Moore understand the dignity of the laurel. He never would barter his freedom away for any favor from any quarter."

And he adds: —

" Never did he make his wife and family a pretext for political shabbiness; never did he imagine that to leave a disgraced name as an inheritance to his children was his duty as a father. Neither did he, like many a richer man, with a negligence amounting to crime, leave his tradesmen to suffer for his want of fortune. Mingling careful economy with an intense love of all the enjoyments of society, he managed, with the assistance of his excellent wife, who carried on for him the details of his household, to struggle through all the petty annoyances attendant on narrow means, to support his father, mother, and sister, besides his own family; and at his death he left no debt behind him."

Much of Moore's poetry is of course of ephemeral interest. He had the fatal gift of fluency; but at his best he was a born singer, and his sweetest songs will never pass from the memory of men. One may almost agree with Byron, who said, " some of his Irish melodies are worth all the epics ever composed."

NATHAN HASKELL DOLE.

BOSTON, July 26, 1895.

CONTENTS.

CONTENTS.

ODES OF ANACREON

(1800).

TRANSLATED INTO ENGLISH VERSE.

WITH

NOTES.

TO

HIS ROYAL HIGHNESS

THE PRINCE OF WALES.

Sir, — In allowing me to dedicate this Work to Your Royal Highness, you have conferred upon me an honor which I feel very sensibly: and I have only to regret that the pages which you have thus distinguished are not more deserving of such illustrious patronage.

Believe me, Sir,

With every sentiment of respect,

Your Royal Highness's

Very grateful and devoted Servant,

THOMAS MOORE.

ADVERTISEMENT.

It may be necessary to mention, that, in arranging the Odes, the Translator has adopted the order of the Vatican MS. For those who wish to refer to the original, he has prefixed an Index, which marks the number of each Ode in Barnes and the other editions.

INDEX.

For the order of the rest, see the Notes.

AN ODE BY THE TRANSLATOR.

'ΕΠΙ ῥοδίνοις τάπησι,
Τήϊός ποτ' ὁ μελιστὴς
ἱλαρὸς γελῶν ἔκειτο,
μεθύων τε καὶ λυρίζων·
ἀμφὶ αὐτὸν οἱ δ' ἔρωτες
ἁπαλοὶ συνεχόρευσαν·
ὁ βέλη τὰ τῆς Κυθήρης
ἐπύει, ψυχῆς ὄϊστούς·
ὁ δὲ λευκὰ πορφυροῖσι
κρίνα σὺν ῥόδοισι πλέξας,
ἐφίλει στέφων γέροντα·
ἡ δὲ θεάων ἄνασσα,
ϹΟΦΙΗ ποτ' ἐξ' Ὀλύμπου
ἐσορῶσ' Ἀνακρέοντα,
ἐσορῶσα τοὺς ἔρωτας,
ὑπομειδιάσσας εἶπε·
σόφε, δ' ὡς Ἀνακρέοντα
τὸν σοφώτατον ἁπάντων,
καλέουσιν οἱ σοφισταί,
τί, γέρων, τέον βίον μὲν
τοῖς ἔρωσι, τῷ Λυαίῳ,

κ' οὐκ ἐμοὶ κρατεῖν ἐδώκας ;
τί φίλημα τῆς Κυθήρης,
τί κύπελλα τοῦ Λυαίου,
αἰεὶ γ' ἐτρυφήσας ἄδων,
οὐκ ἐμοὺς νόμους διδάσκων,
οὐκ ἐμὸν λαχὼν ἄωτον ;
ὁ δὲ Τήϊος μελιστὴς
μήτε δυσχέραινέ, φησι,
ὅτι, θεά, σου γ' ἄνευ μέν,
ὁ σοφώτατος ἁπάντων
παρὰ τῶν σοφῶν καλοῦμαι·
φιλέω, πίω, λυρίζω,
μετὰ τῶν καλῶν γυναικῶν·
ἀφελῶς δὲ τερπνὰ παίζω,
ὡς λύρη γὰρ, ἐμὸν ἦτορ
ἀναπνεῖ μόνους ἔρωτας·
ὧδε βιότου γαλήνην
φιλέων μάλιστα πάντων,
οὐ σοφὸς μελῳδός εἰμι ;
τίς σοφώτερος μέν ἐστι ;

CORRECTIONS OF THE PRECEDING ODE

SUGGESTED BY

AN EMINENT GREEK SCHOLAR.

ἘΠΙ πορφυρέοις τάπησι
Τήϊός ποτ' ᾠδοποιὸς
ἱλαρὸς γελῶν ἔκειτο,
μεθύων τε καὶ λυρίζων·
περὶ δ' αὐτὸν ἀμφ' Ἔρωτες 5
τρομεροῖς ποσὶν χόρευον.
τὰ βέλεμν' ὁ μὲν Κυθήρης
ἐποίει καλῆς, ὀϊστοὺς
πυρόεντας, ἐκ κεραυνοῦ·
ὁ δὲ λευκὰ καλλιφύλλοις 10
κρίνα σὺν ῥόδοισι πλέξας,
ἐφίλει στέφων γέροντα.
κατὰ δ' εὐθὺς ἐξ Ὀλύμπου }
Σοφίη θέαινα βᾶσα,
ἐσορῶσ' Ἀνακρέοντα, 15
ἐσορῶσα τοὺς Ἔρωτας,
ὑπομειδιῶσά φησι·
Σόφ',— ἐπεὶ βροτῶν σὲ τοῦτο

Ἐπὶ ῥοδίνοις τάπησι
Τήϊός ποτ' ὃ μελιστὴς

ἀμφὶ αὐτὸν οἱ δ' Ἔρωτες
ἁπαλοὶ συνέχόρευσαν

ἐποίει, ψυχῆς ὀϊστοὺς

ἡ δὲ θεάων ἄνασσα

ὑπομειδιάσσᾱς εἶπε
τ'ὸν σοφώτατὸν ἁπάντων

1 πορφυρέοις *vox trisyllbica.* Anacr. Fragm. xxix. 3. ed. Fischer. πορφυρέη τ' Ἀφροδίτη. Id. Fragm. xxxvi. 1. σφαίρη δεῦτέ με πορφυρέῃ, *ut legendum plane ex Athenæo.* Ἁλιπορφύροις τάπησι *dixit* Pseud-Anacreon, Od. viii. 2. Theocr. Id. xv. 125. πορφύρεοι δὲ τάπητες ἄνω, μαλακώτεροι ὕπνω.
5 *Tmesis pro* ἀμφεχόρευσαν. Theocr. Id. vii. 142. πωτῶντο ξουθαὶ περὶ πίδακας ἀμφὶ μέλισσαι, h. e. ἀμφεπωτῶντο.
6 Pseud-Anacr. Od. lii. 12. τρομεροῖς ποσὶν χορεύει.
7, 10 ὁ μὲν, *hic* — ὁ δὲ, *ille.* Bion. Id. i. 82. χὠ μὲν ὀϊστὼς, | ὅς δ' ἐπὶ τόξον ἔβαιν', κ. τ. λ. *itidem de Amoribus.*
8, 9 ἐποίει — ἐκ κεραυνοῦ. Pseud-Anacr. Od. xxviii. 18. τὸ δὲ βλέμμα νῦν ἀληθῶς | ἀπὸ τοῦ πυρὸς ποίησον.
10, 11 καλλιφύλλοις — ῥόδοισι. Pseud-Anacr. Od. v. 3. τὸ ῥόδον τὸ καλλίφυλλον.
13 *Tmesis pro* καταβᾶσα. Pseud-Anacr. Od. iii. 15. ἀνὰ δ' εὐθὺ λύχνον ἄψας, *h. e.* ἀνάψας.
18 *Supple* ὄνομα, *quo* τοῦτο *referatur.* Eurip. Phœn. 12. τοῦτο γὰρ πατὴρ | ἔθετο. *h. e.* τοῦτο ὄνομα. βροτῶν φῦλα πάντα *Adumbratum ex* Pseud-Anacr. Od. iii. 4. μερόπων δὲ φῦλα πάντα.

καλέουσι φῦλα πάντα,
καλέουσιν οἱ σοφισταί, —   20
τί, γέρων, μάτην ὁδεύεις
βιότου τρίβον τεοῦ μὲν
μετὰ τῶν καλῶν Ἐρώτων,
μετὰ τοῦ καλοῦ Λυαίου,   τοῖς Ἔρωσι, τῷ Λυαίῳ
ἐμὲ δ' ὧδε λὰξ ἀτίζεις;   25   κ' οὐκ ἐμοὶ κρατεῖν ἐδώκας
τί φίλημα τῆς Κυθήρης,
τί κύπελλα τοῦ Λυαίου,
ἐσαεὶ τρυφῶν ἀείδεις,   αἰεὶ ῖ γ' ἐτρυφήσας ᾄδων
ἐμὰ θέσμι' οὒ διδάσκων,   οὐκ ἐμοὺς νομοὺς διδάσκων
ἐμὸν οὐ λαχὼν ἄωτον;   30   οὐκ ἐμὸν λαχὼν ἄωτον
ὁ δὲ Τήϊος μελιηδὴς,
σὺ παρὲκ νόον γε μή μοι   ⎫   μῆτε δυσχέραινέ, φησι
χαλέπαινε, φήσ', ἄνευθε   ⎬
ὅτι σεῦ σοφὸς καλοῦμαι   ὅτι, θὲ ᾶ σοῦ γ' ἄνευ μὲν
παρὰ τῶν σοφῶν ἁπάντων. 35   ὁ σοφώτατός ἁπάντων
φιλέω, πίω, λυρίζω,
μετὰ τῶν καλῶν γυναικῶν,
ἀφελῶς δὲ τερπνὰ παίζω·
κιθάρη γὰρ, ὡς κέαρ μεῦ,   ὣς λύρη γὰρ, ἐμὸν ἦτορ
ἀνυμνεῖ μόνους Ἔρωτας.   40
βιότου δὲ τὴν γαλήνην   ὧδε βιότου γαλήνην
φιλέων μάλιστα πάντων,
σοφὸς οὐ μελῳδός εἰμι;   οὗ σοφὸς μελῳδός εἰμι
τί σοφώτερον γένοιτ' ἄν;
ἐμέθεν σοφώτερος τίς;   45   τίς σοφώτερος μέν ἐστι;

---

21 Pseud-Anacr. Od. XXIV. 2.   βιότου τρίβον ὁδεύειν.

25 Æsch. Eumen. 538.   μηδέ νιν, | κέρδος ἰδὼν, ἀθέῳ ποδὶ λὰξ ἀτί- | σῃς.

32 παρὲκ νόον γε μή μοι χαλέπαινε, ne præter rationem in me sævi. Il. Υ. 133. Ἥρη, μὴ χαλέπαινε παρὲκ νόον. Similem positionem particularum μή μοι exhibet Pseud-Anac. Od. XXVIII. 13.

REMARKS ON ANACREON.

THERE is but little known with certainty of the life of Anacreon. Chamæleon Heracleotes,[1] who wrote upon the subject, has been lost in the general wreck of ancient literature. The editors of the poet have collected the few trifling anecdotes which are scattered through the extant authors of antiquity, and, supplying the deficiency of materials by fictions of their own imagination, have arranged what they call a life of Anacreon. These specious fabrications are intended to indulge that interest which we naturally feel in the biography of illustrious men; but it is rather a dangerous kind of illusion, as it confounds the limits of history and romance,[2] and is too often supported by unfaithful citation.[3]

Our poet was born in the city of Teos,[4] in the delicious region of Ionia, and the time of his birth appears to have been in the sixth century before Christ.[5] He flourished at that remarkable period when, under the polished tyrants Hipparchus and Polycrates, Athens and Samos were become the rival asylums of genius. There is nothing certain known about his family; and those who pretend to discover in Plato that he was a descendant of the monarch Codrus, show much more of zeal than of either accuracy or judgment.[6]

The disposition and talents of Anacreon recommended him to the monarch of Samos, and he was formed to be the friend of such a prince as Polycrates. Susceptible only to the pleasures, he felt not the corruptions, of the court; and while Pythagoras fled from the tyrant, Anacreon was celebrating his praises on the lyre. We are told, too, by Maximus Tyrius, that, by the influence of his amatory songs, he softened the mind of Polycrates into a spirit of benevolence towards his subjects.[7]

1 He is quoted by Athenæus "ἐν τῷ περὶ τοῦ Ἀνακρέοντος."
2 The History of Anacreon, by Gaçon (*le Poète sans fard*, as he styles himself), is professedly a romance; nor does Mademoiselle Scudéri, from whom he borrowed the idea, pretend to historical veracity in her account of Anacreon and Sappho. These, then, are allowable. But how can Barnes be forgiven, who, with all the confidence of a biographer, traces every wandering of the poet, and settles him at last, in his old age, at a country villa near Teos?
3 The learned Bayle has detected some infidelities of quotation in Le Fèvre. ("Dictionnaire Historique," etc.) Madame Dacier is not more accurate than her father: they have almost made Anacreon prime minister to the monarch of Samos.
4 The Asiatics were as remarkable for genius as for luxury. "*Ingenia Asiatica inclyta per gentes fecère Poetæ, Anacreon, inde Mimnermus et Antimachus, etc.*" — SOLINUS.
5 I have not attempted to define the particular Olympiad, but have adopted the idea of Bayle, who says: "*Je n'ai point marqué d'Olympiade; car, pour un homme qui a vécu quatre-vingt-cinq ans, il me semble que l'on ne doit point s'enfermer dans des bornes si étroites.*"
6 This mistake is founded on a false interpretation of a very obvious passage in Plato's "Dialogue on Temperance;" it originated with Madame Dacier, and has been received implicitly by many. Gail, a late editor of Anacreon, seems to claim to himself the merit of detecting this error; but Bayle had observed it before him.
7 Ἀνακρέων Σαμίοις Πολυκράτην ἡμέρωσε. Maxim. Tyr. § 21. Maximus Tyrius mentions this among other instances of the influence of poetry. If Gail had read Maximus Tyrius, how could he ridicule this idea in Moutonnet as unauthenticated?

The amours of the poet, and the rivalship of the tyrant,[1] I shall pass over in silence; and there are few, I presume, who will regret the omission of most of those anecdotes, which the industry of some editors has not only promulged, but discussed. Whatever is repugnant to modesty and virtue is considered, in ethical science, by a supposition very favorable to humanity, as impossible; and this amiable persuasion should be much more strongly entertained where the transgression wars with nature as well as virtue. But why are we not allowed to indulge in the presumption ? Why are we officiously reminded that there have been really such instances of depravity?

Hipparchus, who now maintained at Athens the power which his father Pisistratus had usurped, was one of those princes who may be said to have polished the fetters of their subjects. He was the first, according to Plato, who edited the poems of Homer, and commanded them to be sung by the rhapsodists at the celebration of the Panathenæa. From his court, which was a sort of galaxy of genius, Anacreon could not long be absent. Hipparchus sent a barge for him; the poet readily embraced the invitation, and the Muses and the Loves were wafted with him to Athens.[2]

The manner of Anacreon's death was singular. We are told that in the eighty fifth year of his age he was choked by a grape-stone;[3] and however we may smile at their enthusiastic partiality who see in this easy and characteristic death a peculiar indulgence of Heaven, we cannot help admiring that his fate should have been so emblematic of his disposition. Cælius Calcaginus alludes to this catastrophe in the following epitaph on our poet:[4]—

> Those lips, then, hallowed sage, which poured along
> A music sweet as any cygnet's song,
> The grape hath closed for ever!
> Here let the ivy kiss the poet's tomb,
> Here let the rose he loved with laurels bloom,
> In bands that ne'er shall sever.
> But far be thou, oh! far, unholy vine,
> By whom the favorite minstrel of the Nine
> Lost his sweet vital breath;
> Thy God himself now blushes to confess,
> Once hallowed vine! he feels he loves thee less,
> Since poor Anacreon's death.

1 In the romance of Clelia, the anecdote to which I allude is told of a young girl, with whom Anacreon fell in love while she personated the god Apollo in a mask. But here Mademoiselle Scudéri consulted nature more than truth.

2 There is a very interesting French poem founded upon this anecdote, imputed to Desyvetaux, and called "Anacréon Citoyen."

3 Fabricius appears not to trust very implicitly in this story. *" Uvæ passæ acino tandem suffocatus, si credimus Suidæ in* οἰνοπότης *; alii enim hoc mortis genere periisse tradunt Sophoclem."* — "Fabricii Bibliothec. Græc." lib. ii. cap. 15. It must be confessed that Lucian, who tells us that Sophocles was choked by a grape-stone, in the very same treatise mentions the longevity of Anacreon, and yet is silent on the manner of his death. Could he have been ignorant of such a remarkable coincidence, or, knowing, could he have neglected to remark it? See Regnier's introduction to his Anacreon.

> 4 *At te, sancte senex, acinus sub Tartara misit ;*
> *cygneæ clausit qui tibi vocis iter.*
> *Vos, hederæ, tumulum, tumulum vos cingite, lauri:*
> *hoc rosa perpetuo vernet odora loco ;*
> *at vitis procul hinc, procul hinc odiosa facessat,*
> *quæ causam diræ protulit, uva, necis,*
> *creditur ipse minus vitem jam Bacchus amare,*
> *in vatem tantum quæ fuit ausa nefas.*

The author of this epitaph, Cælius Calcaginus, has translated or imitated the epigrams εἰς τὴν Μύρωνος Βοῦν, which are given under the name of Anacreon.

It has been supposed by some writers that Anacreon and Sappho were contemporaries; and the very thought of an intercourse between persons so congenial, both in warmth of passion and delicacy of genius, gives such play to the imagination that the mind loves to indulge in it. But the vision dissolves before historical truth; and Chamæleon and Hermesianax, who are the source of the supposition, are considered as having merely indulged in a poetical anachronism.[1]

To infer the moral dispositions of a poet from the tone of sentiment which pervades his works, is sometimes a very fallacious analogy; but the soul of Anacreon speaks so unequivocally through his odes, that we may safely consult them as the faithful mirrors of his heart.[2] We find him there the elegant voluptuary, diffusing the seductive charm of sentiment over passions and propensities at which rigid morality must frown. His heart, devoted to indolence, seems to have thought that there is wealth enough in happiness, but seldom happiness in mere wealth. The cheerfulness, indeed, with which he brightens his old age is interesting and endearing; like his own rose, he is fragrant even in decay. But the most peculiar feature of his mind is that love of simplicity, which he attributes to himself so feelingly, and which breathes characteristically throughout all that he has sung. In truth, if we omit those few vices in our estimate which religion, at that time, not only connived at, but consecrated, we shall be inclined to say that the disposition of our poet was amiable; that his morality was relaxed, but not abandoned; and that Virtue, with her zone loosened, may be an apt emblem of the character of Anacreon.[3]

Of his person and physiognomy time has preserved such uncertain memorials, that it were better, perhaps, to leave the pencil to fancy; and few can read the

---

1 Barnes is convinced (but very gratuitously) of the synchronism of Anacreon and Sappho. In citing his authorities, he has strangely neglected the line quoted by Fulvius Ursinus, as from Anacreon, among the testimonies to Sappho : —

Εἰμὶ λαβὼν εἰσαρὰς Σαπφὼ πάρθενον ἀδύφωνον.

Fabricius thinks that they might have been contemporary, but considers their amour as a tale of imagination. Vossius rejects the idea entirely; as do also Olaus Borrichius and others.

2 An Italian poet, in some verses on Belleau's translation of Anacreon, pretends to imagine that our bard did not feel as he wrote : —

> Lyæum, Venerem, Cupidinemque
> senex lusit Anacreon poeta.
> Sed quo tempore nec capaciores
> rogabat cyathos, nec inquietis
> urebatur amoribus, sed ipsis
> tantum versibus et jocis amabat,
> nullum præ se habitum gerens amantis.

> To Love and Bacchus ever young
> While sage Anacreon touched the lyre,
> He neither felt the loves he sung,
> Nor filled his bowl to Bacchus higher.
> Those flowery days had faded long,
> When youth could act the lover's part;
> And passion trembled in his song,
> But never, never, reached his heart.

3 Anacreon's character had been variously colored. Barnes lingers on it with enthusiastic admiration; but he is always extravagant, if not sometimes also a little profane. Baillet runs too much into the opposite extreme, exaggerating also the testimonies which he has consulted ; and we cannot surely agree with him when he cites such a compiler as Athenæus, as "*un des plus savans critiques de l'antiquité.*" — " Jugement des Savans," M.CV.

Barnes could hardly have read the passage to which he refers, when he accuses Le Fèvre of having censured our poet's character in a note on Longinus ; the note in question being manifest irony, in allusion to some censure passed upon Le Fèvre for his Anacreon. It is clear, indeed, that praise rather than censure is intimated. See Johannes Vulpius (" de Utilitate Poëtices "), who vindicates our poet's reputation.

with that language.[1] The Anacreontics of Scaliger, however, scarcely deserve the name; as they glitter all over with conceits, and, though often elegant, are always labored. The beautiful fictions of Angerianus[2] preserve more happily than any others the delicate turn of those allegorical fables, which, passing so frequently through the mediums of version and imitation, have generally lost their finest rays in the transmission. Many of the Italian poets have indulged their fancies upon the subjects; and in the manner of Anacreon, Bernardo Tasso first introduced the metre, which was afterwards polished and enriched by Chabriera and others.

To judge by the references of Degen, the German language abounds in Anacreontic imitations; and Hagedorn[3] is one among many who have assumed him as a model. La Farre, Chaulieu, and the other light poets of France, have also professed to cultivate the muse of Teos; but they have attained all her negligence, with little of the simple grace that embellishes it. In the delicate bard of Schiras[4] we find the kindred spirit of Anacreon: some of his gazelles, or songs, possess all the character of our poet.

We come now to a retrospect of the editions of Anacreon. To Henry Stephen we are indebted for having first recovered his remains from the obscurity in which, so singularly, they had for many ages reposed. He found the seventh ode, as we are told, on the cover of an old book, and communicated it to Victorius, who mentions the circumstance in his "Various Readings." Stephen was then very young; and this discovery was considered by some critics of that day as a literary imposition.[5] In 1554, however, he gave Anacreon to the world,[6] accompanied with annotations and a Latin version of the greater part of the odes. The learned still hesitated to receive them as the relics of the Teian bard, and suspected them to be the fabrication of some monks of the sixteenth century. This was an idea from which the classic muse recoiled; and the Vatican manuscript, consulted by Scaliger and Salmasius, confirmed the antiquity of most of the poems. A very inaccurate copy of this MS. was taken by Isaac Vossius, and this is the authority which Barnes has followed in his collation. Accordingly he misrepresents almost as often

1 Thus too Albertus, a Danish poet: —

Fidii tui minister
gaudebo semper esse,,
gaudebo semper illi
litare thure mulso ;
gaudebo semper illum
laudare pumilillis
anacreonticillis.

See the "Danish Poets" collected by Rostgaard.

These pretty diminutives defy translation. A beautiful Anacreontic by Hugo Grotius, may be found Lib. i. "Farraginis."

2 To Angerianus Prior is indebted for some of his happiest mythological subjects.

3 "*L'aimable Hagedorn vaut quelquefois Anacréon.*" — DORAT· "*Idée de la Poësie Allemande.*"

4 See Toderini on the learning of the Turks, as translated by de Cournard. Prince Cantemir has made the Russians acquainted with Anacreon. See his Life, prefixed to a translation of his Satires, by the Abbé de Guasco.

5 Robertullus, in his work "De Ratione corrigendi," pronounces these verses to be the triflings of some insipid Græcist.

6 Ronsard commemorates this event: —

Je vay boire à Henrie Étienne
Qui des enfers nous a rendu,
Du vieil Anacréon perdu,
La douce lyre Téienne.   Ode xv. book 5.

I fill the bowl to Stephen's name,
  Who rescued from the gloom of night
The Teian bard of festive fame,
  And brought his living lyre to light.

as he quotes; and the subsequent editors, relying upon his authority, have spoken of the manuscript with not less confidence than ignorance. The literary world, however, has at length been gratified with this curious memorial of the poet, by the industry of the Abbé Spaletti, who published at Rome, in 1781, a facsimile of those pages of the Vatican manuscript which contained the odes of Anacreon.[1]

A catalogue has been given by Gail of all the different editions and translations of Anacreon. Finding their number to be much greater than I could possibly have had an opportunity of consulting, I shall here content myself with enumerating only those editions and versions which it has been in my power to collect; and which, though very few, are, I believe, the most important.

The edition by Henry Stephen, 1554, at Paris; the Latin version is attributed by Colomesius to John Dorat.[2]

The old French translations, by Ronsard and Belleau,— the former published in 1555, the latter in 1556. It appears from a note of Muretus upon one of the sonnets of Ronsard, that Henry Stephen communicated to this poet his manuscript of Anacreon, before he promulgated it to the world.[3]

The edition by Le Fèvre, 1660.

The edition by Madame Dacier, 1681, with a prose translation.[4]

The edition by Longepierre, 1684, with a translation in verse.

The edition by Baxter; London, 1695.

A French translation by la Fosse, 1704.

" L'Histoire des Odes d'Anacreon," by Gaçon; Rotterdam, 1712.

A translation in English verse, by several hands, 1713, in which the odes by Cowley are inserted.

The edition by Barnes; London, 1721.

The edition by Dr. Trapp, 1733, with a Latin version in elegiac metre.

A translation in English verse, by John Addison, 1735.

A collection of Italian translations of Anacreon, published at Venice, 1736, consisting of those by Corsini, Regnier, Salvini, Marchetti, and one by several anonymous authors.[5]

A translation in English verse, by Fawkes and Doctor Broome, 1760.[6]

Another, anonymous, 1768.

The edition by Spaletti, at Rome, 1781; with the fac-simile of the Vatican MS.

The edition by Degen, 1786, who published also a German translation of Anacreon, esteemed the best.

A translation in English verse, by Urquhart, 1787.

The edition by Gail, at Paris, 1799, with a prose translation.

---

1 This manuscript, which Spaletti thinks as old as the tenth century, was brought from the Palatine into the Vatican library; it is a kind of anthology of Greek epigrams.

2 " Le même (M. Vossius) m'a dit qu'il avoit possédé un Anacréon, où Scaliger avoit marqué de sa main, qu' Henri Étienne n'était pas l'auteur de la version latine des odes de ce poète, mais Jean Dorat." — PAULUS COLOMESIUS, " Particularités."

Colomesius, however, seems to have relied too implicitly on Vossius; almost all these Particularités begin with " M. Vossius m'a dit."

3 " La fiction de ce sonnet comme l'auteur même m'a dit, est prise d'une ode d'Anacréon, encore non imprimée, qu'il a depuis traduit, Σὺ μὲν φίλη χελιδών."

4 The author of " Nouvelles de la Répub. des Lett." bestows on this translation much more praise than its merits appear to me to justify.

5 I find in Haym's " Notizia de' Libri rari," Venice, 1670, an Italian translation by Cappone, mentioned.

6 This is the most complete of the English translations.

ODES OF ANACREON.

ODE I.[1]

I SAW the smiling bard of pleasure,
The minstrel of the Teian measure;
'T was in a vision of the night,
He beamed upon my wondering sight.
I heard his voice, and warmly prest
The dear enthusiast to my breast.
His tresses wore a silvery dye,
But beauty sparkled in his eye;
Sparkled in his eyes of fire,[2]
Through the mist of soft desire.
His lip exhaled, whene'er he sighed,
The fragrance of the racy tide;
And, as with weak and reeling feet
He came my cordial kiss to meet,
An infant, of the Cyprian band,
Guided him on with tender hand.

1 This ode is the first of the series in the Vatican manuscript, which attributes it to no other poet than Anacreon. They who assert that the manuscript imputes it to Basilius, have been mislead by the words Τοῦ αὐτοῦ βασιλικῶς in the margin, which are merely intended as a title to the following ode. Whether it be the production of Anacreon or not, it has all the features of ancient simplicity, and is a beautiful imitation of the poet's happiest manner.

2 Sparkled in his eyes of fire,
Through the mist of soft desire.

"How could he know at the first look (says Baxter) that the poet was φίλεννος [fond of the marriage-bed]?" There are surely many tell-tales of this propensity; and the following are the indices which the physiognomist gives, describing a disposition perhaps not unlike that of Anacreon: Ὀφθαλμοὶ κλυζόμενοι, κυμαίνοντες ἐν αὐτοῖς, εἰς ἀφροδίσια καὶ εὐπάθειαν ἐπτόηνται, οὔτε δὲ ἄδικοι οὔτε κακούργοι, οὔτε φύσεως φαύλης, οὔτε ἄμουσοι. — ADAMANTIUS. "The eyes that are humid and fluctuating show a propensity to pleasure and love; they bespeak, too, a mind of integrity and beneficence, a generosity of disposition, and a genius for poetry."

Baptista Porta tells us some strange opinions of the ancient physiognomists on this subject, their reasons for which were curious, and perhaps not altogether fanciful. Vide "Physiognom. Johan. Baptist. Portæ."

Quick from his glowing brows he drew
His braid, of many a wanton hue;
I took the wreath, whose inmost twine
Breathed of him and blushed with wine.[3]
I hung it o'er my thoughtless brow,
And ah! I feel its magic now:[4]
I feel that even his garland's touch
Can make the bosom love too much.

ODE II.

GIVE me the harp of epic song,
Which Homer's finger thrilled along;
But tear away the sanguine string,
For war is not the theme I sing.
Proclaim the laws of festal right,[5]

3 I took the wreath whose inmost twine
Breathed of him, etc.

Philostratus has the same thought in one of his Ἐρωτικά, where he speaks of the garland which he had sent to his mistress. Εἰ δὲ βούλει τι φίλῳ χαρίζεσθαι, τὰ λείψανα ἀντιπέμψον, μηκέτι πνέοντα ῥόδων μόνον ἀλλὰ καὶ σοῦ. "If thou art inclined to gratify thy lover, send him back the remains of the garland, no longer breathing of roses only, but also of thee!" Which pretty conceit is borrowed (as the author of the "Observer" remarks) in a well-known little song of Ben Jonson's: —

"But thou thereon didst only breathe,
And sent it back to me;
Since when it looks and smells, I swear,
Not of itself, but thee!"

4 And ah! I feel its magic now:
This idea, as Longepierre remarks, occurs in an epigram of the seventh book of the "Anthologia": —

Ἐξότε μοι πίνοντι συνεστιάουσα Χαρίκλῳ
λάθρῃ τοὺς ἰδίους ἀμφέβαλε στεφανούς,
πῦρ ὀλοὸν δάπτει με.

While I unconscious quaffed my wine,
'T was then thy fingers slily stole
Upon my brow that wreath of thine,
Which since has maddened all my soul.

5 Proclaim the laws of festal rite.
The ancients prescribed certain laws of drinking at their festivals, for an account of which see the commentators. Anacreon here acts the sym-

I 'm monarch of the board to-night;
And all around shall brim as high,
And quaff the tide as deep as I.
And when the cluster's mellowing dews
Their warm enchanting balm infuse,
Our feet shall catch the elastic bound,
And reel us through the dance's round.
Great Bacchus! we shall sing to thee,
In wild but sweet ebriety;
Flashing around such sparks of thought,
As Bacchus could alone have taught.

Then, give the harp of epic song,
Which Homer's finger thrilled along;
But tear away the sanguine string,
For war is not the theme I sing.

ODE III.[1]

LISTEN to the Muse's lyre,
Master of the pencil's fire!
Sketched in painting's bold display,
Many a city first portray;
Many a city, revelling free,
Full of loose festivity.
Picture then a rosy train,
Bacchants straying o'er the plain;
Piping, as they roam along,
Roundelay or shepherd-song.
Paint me next, if painting may
Such a theme as this portray,
All the earthly heaven of love
These delighted mortals prove.

ODE IV.[2]

VULCAN! hear your glorious task;
I do not from your labors ask
In gorgeous panoply to shine,
For war 'was ne'er a sport of mine.
No — let me have a silver bowl,
Where I may cradle all my soul;
But mind that, o'er its simple frame
No mimic constellations flame;
Nor grave upon the swelling side,
Orion, scowling o'er the tide.

I care not for the glittering wain,
Nor yet the weeping sister train.
But let the vine luxuriant roll
Its blushing tendrils round the bowl,
While many a rose-lipped bacchant maid [3]
Is culling clusters in their shade.
Let sylvan gods, in antic shapes,
Wildly press the gushing grapes,
And flights of Loves, in wanton play,
Wing through the air their winding way;
While Venus, from her arbor green,
Looks laughing at the joyous scene,
And young Lyæus by her side
Sits, worthy of so bright a bride.

ODE V.[4]

SCULPTOR, wouldst thou glad my soul,
Grave for me an ample bowl,
Worthy to shine in hall or bower,
When spring-time brings the reveller's hour.
Grave it with themes of chaste design,
Fit for a simple board like mine.
Display not there the barbarous rites
In which religious zeal delights;
Nor any tale of tragic fate
Which History shudders to relate.
No — cull thy fancies from above,
Themes of heaven and themes of love.
Let Bacchus, Jove's ambrosial boy,
Distil the grape in drops of joy,
And while he smiles at every tear,
Let warm-eyed Venus, dancing near,

---

posiarch, or master of the festival. I have translated according to those who consider κύπελλα θεσμῶν as an inversion of θεσμοὺς κυπέλλων.

1 La Fosse has thought proper to lengthen this poem by considerable interpolations of his own, which he thinks are indispensably necessary to the completion of the description.

2 This ode, Aulus Gellius tells us, was performed at an entertainment where he was present.

3 While many a rose-lipped bacchant maid, etc.

   I have availed myself here of the additional lines given in the Vatican manuscript, which have not been accurately inserted in any of the ordinary editions: —

> Ποίησον ἀμπέλους μοι
> καὶ βότρυας κατ' αὐτῶν
> καὶ μαινάδας τρυγώσας.
> ποιεῖ δε λῆνον οἴνου,
> ληνοβάτας πατοῦντας,
> τοὺς σατύρους γελῶντας,
> καὶ χρυσοὺς τοὺς ἔρωτας,
> καὶ Κυθέρην γελῶσαν;
> ὁμοῦ καλῷ Λυαίῳ,
> Ἔρωτα κ' Ἀφροδίτην.

4 Degen thinks that this ode is a more modern imitation of the preceding. There is a poem by Cælius Calcagninus, in the manner of both, where he gives instructions about the making of a ring: —

> *Tornabis annulum mihi*
> *et fabre, et apte, et commode*, etc., etc.

With spirits of the genial bed,
The dewy herbage deftly tread.
Let Love be there, without his arms,[1]
In timid nakedness of charms;
And all the Graces, linked with Love,
Stray, laughing, through the shadowy
    grove;
While rosy boys disporting round,
In circlets trip the velvet ground.
But ah! if there Apollo toys,[2]
I tremble for the rosy boys.

ODE VI.[3]

As late I sought the spangled bowers,
To cull a wreath of matin flowers,
Where many an early rose was weeping,
I found the urchin Cupid sleeping.[4]

1 Let Love be there, without his arms, etc.
    Thus Sannazaro in the eclogue of "Gallicio
nell' Arcadia:"—

> *Vegnan li vaghi Amori*
> *Senza fiammelle, ò strali,*
> *Scherzando insieme pargoletti e nudi.*

> Fluttering on the busy wing,
>   A train of naked Cupids came,
> Sporting around in harmless ring,
>   Without a dart, without a flame.

And thus in the "Pervigilium Veneris:"—

> *Ite nymphæ, posuit arma, feriatus est amor.*

> Love is disarmed —ye nymphs, in safety stray,
> Your bosoms now may boast a holiday!

2 But ah! if there Apollo toys,
    I tremble for the rosy boys.

An allusion to the fable that Apollo had killed
his beloved boy Hyacinth, while playing with him
at quoits. "This (says M. La Fosse) is assuredly
the sense of the text, and it cannot admit of any
other."
    The Italian translators, to save themselves the
trouble of a note, have taken the liberty of making Anacreon himself explain this fable. Thus
Salvini, the most literal of any of them:—

> *Ma con lor non giuochi Apollo;*
> *Che in fiero risco*
> *Col duro disco*
> *A Giacinto fiaccò il collo.*

3 This beautiful fiction, which the commentators have attributed to Julian, a royal poet, the
Vatican MS. pronounces to be the genuine offspring of Anacreon. It has, indeed, all the
features of the parent:—

> *et facile insciis*
> *Noscitetur ab omnibus.*

4 Where many an early rose was weeping,
    I found the urchin Cupid sleeping.
    This idea is prettily imitated in the following
epigram by Andreas Naugerius:—

> *Florentes dum forte vagans mea Hyella per*
>   *hortos*

I caught the boy, a goblet's tide
Was richly mantling by my side,
I caught him by his downy wing,
And whelmed him in the racy spring.
Then drank I down the poisoned bowl,
And Love now nestles in my soul.
Oh, yes, my soul is Cupid's nest,
I feel him fluttering in my breast.

ODE VII.[5]

THE women tell me every day
That all my bloom has past away.
"Behold," the pretty wantons cry,
"Behold this mirror with a sigh;
The locks upon thy brow are few,
And like the rest, they 're withering too!"
Whether decline has thinned my hair,
I'm sure I neither know nor care;[6]

> *texit odoratis lilia cana rosis,*
> *ecce rosas inter latitantem invenit Amorem*
> *et simul annexis floribus implicuit.*
> *Luctatur primo, et contra nitentibus alis*
>   *indomitus tentat solvere vincla puer:*
> *mox ubi lacteolas et dignas matre papillas*
>   *vidit et ora ipsos nuta movere Deos,*
> *impositosque comæ ambrosios ut sentit odores*
>   *quosque legit diti messe beatus Arabs;*
> *"I (dixit) mea, quære novum tibi, mater,*
>   *Amorem,*
>   *imperio sedes hæc erit apta meo."*

> As fair Hyella, through the bloomy grove,
> A wreath of many mingled flowerets wove,
> Within a rose a sleeping Love she found,
> And in the twisted wreaths the baby bound
> Awhile he struggled, and impatient tried
> To break the rosy bonds the virgin tied;
> But when he saw her bosom's radiant swell,
> Her features, where the eye of Jove might dwell;
> And caught the ambrosial odors of her hair,
> Rich as the breathings of Arabian air;
> "Oh! mother Venus," (said the raptured child,
> By charms, of more than mortal bloom, beguiled,)
> "Go, seek another boy, thou 'st lost thine own,
> Hyella's arms shall now be Cupid's throne!"

This epigram of Naugerius is imitated by
Lodovico Dolce in a poem, beginning—

> *Mentre raccoglie hor uno, hor altro fiore*
> *Vicina a un rio di chiare et lucid' onde,*
> *Lidia,* etc., etc.

5 Alberti has imitated this ode in a poem,
beginning—

> *Nisa mi dice e Clori*
> *Tirsi, tu se' pur veglio.*

6 Whether decline has thinned my hair,
    I'm sure I neither know nor care;
    Henry Stephen very justly remarks the ele-
gant negligence of the expression in the original
here:—

> Ἐγὼ δὲ τὰς κόμας μέν,
> εἴτ' εἰσὶν, εἴτ' ἀπῆλθον,
> οὐκ οἶδα.

And Longepierre has adduced from Catullus

But this I know, and this I feel,
As onward to the tomb I steal,
That still as death approaches nearer,
The joys of life are sweeter, dearer;[1]
And had I but an hour to live,
That little hour to bliss I 'd give.

ODE VIII.[2]

I CARE not for the idle state
Of Persia's king, the rich, the great:[3]
I envy not the monarch's throne,
Nor wish the treasured gold my own.
But oh! be mine the rosy wreath,
Its freshness o'er my brow to breathe;
Be mine the rich perfumes that flow,
To cool and scent my locks of snow.[4]

what he thinks a similar instance of this simplicity of manner: —

*Ipse quis sit, utrum sit, an non sit, id quoque
nescit.*

Longepierre was a good critic; but perhaps
the line which he has selected is a specimen of
a carelessness not very commendable. At the
same time I confess that none of the Latin poets
have ever appeared to me so capable of imitating
the graces of Anacreon as Catullus, if he had not
allowed a depraved imagination to hurry him so
often into mere vulgar licentiousness.

1 *That still as death approaches nearer,
The joys of life are sweeter, dearer;*

Pontanus has a very delicate thought upon the
subject of old age: —

*Quid rides, Matrona? senem quid temnis
amantem?
Quisquis amat nullâ est conditione senex.*

Why do you scorn my want of youth,
And with a smile my brow behold?
Lady dear! believe this truth,
That he who loves cannot be old.

2 "The German poet Lessing has imitated
this ode. Vol. i. p. 24." — DEGEN; "Gail de
Editionibus."

Baxter conjectures that this was written upon
the occasion of our poet's returning the money to
Polycrates, according to the anecdote in Stobæus.

3 *I care not for the idle state
Of Persia's king, etc.*

"There is a fragment of Archilochus in Plutarch, ' De tranquillitate animi,' which our poet
has very closely imitated here; it begins, —

Οὔ μοι τὰ Γύγεω τοῦ πολυχρύσου μέλει."
                                            BARNES.

In one of the monkish imitators of Anacreon
we find the same thought: —

Ψυχὴν ἐμὴν ἐρωτῶ,
τί σοι θέλεις γένεσθαι;
Θέλεις Γύγεω τὰ καὶ τά;

4 *Be mine the rich perfumes that flow,
To cool and scent my locks of snow.*

In the original, μύροισι καταββρέχειν ὑπήνην.
On account of this idea of perfuming the beard,

To-day I 'll haste to quaff my wine,
As if to-morrow ne'er would shine;
But if to-morrow comes, why then —
I 'll haste to quaff my wine again.
And thus while all our days are bright,
Nor time has dimmed their bloomy light,
Let us the festal hours beguile
With mantling cup and cordial smile;
And shed from each new bowl of wine
The richest drop on Bacchus' shrine.
For Death may come, with brow un-
    pleasant,
May come, when least we wish him
    present,
And beckon to the sable shore,
And grimly bid us — drink no more!

ODE IX.[5]

I PRAY thee, by the gods above,
Give me the mighty bowl I love,
And let me sing, in wild delight,
"I will — I will be mad to-night!"
Alcmæon once, as legends tell,
Was frenzied by the fiends of hell;
Orestes, too, with naked tread,
Frantic paced the mountain-head;

Cornelius de Pauw pronounces the whole ode to
be the spurious production of some lascivious
monk, who was nursing his beard with unguents.
But he should have known that this was an
ancient eastern custom, which, if we may believe
Savary, still exists: " *Vous voyez, Monsieur*
(says this traveller), *que l'usage antique de se
parfumer la tête et la barbe,* * *célébré par le
prophète Roi, subsiste encore de nos jours.*"
Lettre 12. Savary likewise cites this very ode of
Anacreon. Angerianus has not thought the idea
inconsistent, having introduced it in the following
lines: —

*Hæc mihi cura, rosis et cingere tempora myrto,
    Et curas multo delapidare mero.
Hæc mihi cura, comas et barbam tingere succo
    Assyrio et dulces continuare jocos.*

This be my care, to wreath my brow with flowers,
    To drench my sorrows in the ample bowl;
To pour rich perfume o'er my beard in showers,
    And give full loose to mirth and joy of soul!

5 The poet is here in a frenzy of enjoyment,
and it is, indeed, "*amabilis insania ;*"—

*Furor di poesia,
Di lascivia, e di vino,
Triplicato furore,
Bacco, Apollo, et Amore.
    Ritratti del Cavalier Marino.*

This is truly, as Scaliger expresses it,

—— *Insanire dulce
et sapidum furere furorem.*

* "*Sicut unguentum in capite quod descendit
in barbam Aaronis.*"— Psaume 133.

And why? a murdered mother's shade
Haunted them still where'er they strayed.
But ne'er could I a murderer be,
The grape alone shall bleed for me;
Yet can I shout, with wild delight,
" I will — I will be mad to-night."

Alcides' self, in days of yore,
Imbrued his hands in youthful gore,
And brandished, with a maniac joy,
The quiver of the expiring boy:
And Ajax, with tremendous shield,
Infuriate scoured the guiltless field.
But I, whose hands no weapon ask,
No armor but this joyous flask;
The trophy of whose frantic hours
Is but a scattered wreath of flowers,
Ev'n I can sing with wild delight,
" I will — I will be mad to-night ! "

ODE X.[1]

How am I to punish thee,
For the wrong thou 'st done to me,
Silly swallow, prating thing [2] —
Shall I clip that wheeling wing?
Or, as Tereus did, of old,[3]
(So the fabled tale is told,)
Shall I tear that tongue away,
Tongue that uttered such a lay?
Ah, how thoughtless hast thou been!
Long before the dawn was seen,

1 This ode is addressed to a swallow. I find
from Degen and from Gail's index, that the German poet Weisse has imitated it, " Sherz. Lieder." *lib.* ii. *carm.* 5.; that Ramler also has
imitated it, " Lyr. Blumenlese," *lib.* iv. p. 335.;
and some others. See " Gail de Editionibus."

We are here referred by Degen to that dull
book, " The Epistles of Alciphron," tenth epistle, third book; where Iophon complains to
Eraston of being wakened by the crowing of
a cock, from his vision of riches.

2 Silly swallow, prating thing, etc.

The loquacity of the swallow was proverbialized; thus Nicostratus : —

Εἰ τὸ συνεχῶς καὶ πόλλα καὶ ταχέως λαλεῖν
ἦν τοῦ φρονεῖν παράσημον, αἱ χελιδόνες
ἐλέγοντ' ἂν ἡμῶν σωφρονέστεραι πολύ.

If in prating from morning till night,
A sign of our wisdom there be,
The swallows are wiser by right,
For they prattle much faster than we.

3 Or, as Tereus did, of old, etc.

Modern poetry has confirmed the name of
Philomel upon the nightingale; but many respectable authorities among the ancients assigned
this metamorphose to Progne, and made Philomel the swallow, as Anacreon does here.

When a dream came o'er my mind,
Picturing her I worship, kind,
Just when I was nearly blest,
Loud thy matins broke my rest!

ODE XI.[4]

"TELL me, gentle youth, I pray thee,
What in purchase shall I pay thee
For this little waxen toy,
Image of the Paphian boy?"
Thus I said, the other day,
To a youth who past my way:
" Sir," (he answered, and the while
Answered all in Doric style,)
" Take it, for a trifle take it;
'T was not I who dared to make it;
No, believe me, 't was not I;
Oh, it has cost me many a sigh,
And I can no longer keep
Little gods, who murder sleep ! " [5]
" Here, then, here," (I said with joy,)
" Here is silver for the boy:
He shall be my bosom guest,
Idol of my pious breast ! "

Now, young Love, I have thee mine,
Warm me with that torch of thine;
Make me feel as I have felt,
Or thy waxen frame shall melt:
I must burn with warm desire,
Or thou, my boy — in yonder fire.[6]

ODE XII.

THEY tell how Atys, wild with love,
Roams the mount and haunted grove; [7]

4 It is difficult to preserve with any grace the
narrative simplicity of this ode, and the humor
of the turn with which it concludes. I feel, indeed, that the translation must appear vapid, if
not ludicrous, to an English reader.

5 And I can no longer keep
Little gods, who murder sleep !

I have not literally rendered the epithet παντόρεκτα; if it has any meaning here, it is one,
perhaps, better omitted.

6 I must burn with warm desire,
Or thou, my boy — in yonder fire.

From this Longepierre conjectures, that, whatever Anacreon might say, he felt sometimes the
inconveniences of old age, and here solicits from
the power of Love a warmth which he could no
longer expect from Nature.

7 They tell how Atys, wild with love,
Roams the mount and haunted grove.

There are many contradictory stories of the
loves of Cybele and Atys. It is certain that he
was mutilated, but whether by his own fury, or

Cybele's name he howls around,[1]
The gloomy blast returns the sound!
Oft too, by Claros' hallowed spring,[2]
The votaries of the laurelled king
Quaff the inspiring, magic stream,
And rave in wild, prophetic dream.
But frenzied dreams are not for me,
Great Bacchus is my deity!
Full of mirth, and full of him,
While floating odors round me swim,[3]
While mantling bowls are full supplied,
And you sit blushing by my side,
I will be mad and raving too —
Mad, my girl, with love for you!

ODE XIII.

I WILL, I will, the conflict's past,
And I 'll consent to love at last.
Cupid has long, with smiling art,
Invited me to yield my heart;
And I have thought that peace of mind
Should not be for a smile resigned;
And so repelled the tender lure,
And hoped my heart would sleep se-
cure.

But, slighted in his boasted charms,
The angry infant flew to arms;
He slung his quiver's golden frame,
He took his bow, his shafts of flame,
And proudly summoned me to yield,
Or meet him on the martial field.
And what did I unthinking do?

Cybele's jealousy, is a point upon which authors
are not agreed.

1 Cybele's name he howls around, etc.

I have here adopted the accentuation which
Elias Andreas gives to Cybele: —

*In montibus Cybèlen
magno sonans boatu.*

2 Oft too, by Claros' hallowed spring, etc.

This fountain was in a grove, consecrated to
Apollo, and situated between Colophon and Le-
bedos, in Ionia. The god had an oracle there.
Scaliger thus alludes to it in his Anacreontica:—

*Semel ut concitus æstro,
veluti qui Clarias aquas
ebibere loquaces,
quo plus canunt, plura volunt.*

3 While floating odors, etc.

Spaletti has quite mistaken the import of κο-
ρεσθείς, as applied to the poet's mistress— "*Meâ
fatigatus amicâ;*"—thus interpreting it in a
sense which must want either delicacy or gallantry; if not, perhaps, both.

I took to arms, undaunted, too;[4]
Assumed the corslet, shield, and spear,
And, like Pelides, smiled at fear.
Then (hear it, all ye powers above!)
I fought with Love! I fought with Love!
And now his arrows all were shed,
And I had just in terror fled —
When, heaving an indignant sigh,
To see me thus unwounded fly,
And, having now no other dart,
He shot himself into my heart![5]
My heart — alas the luckless day!

4 And what did I unthinking do?
I took to arms, undaunted, too.

Longepierre has here quoted an epigram from
the Anthologia, in which the poet assumes Reason as the armor against Love.

Ὥπλισμαι πρὸς ἔρωτα περὶ στέρνοισι λογισμόν,
οὐδέ με νικήσει, μόνος ἐὼν πρὸς ἕνα·
θνατὸς δ' ἀθανάτῳ συνελεύσομαι· ἢν δὲ βοηθὸν
Βάκχον ἔχῃ, τί μόνος πρὸς δυ' ἐγὼ δύναμαι;

With Reason I cover my breast as a shield,
And fearlessly meet little Love in the field;
Thus fighting his godship, I 'll ne'er be dismayed;
But if Bacchus should ever advance to his aid,
Alas! then, unable to combat the two,
Unfortunate warrior, what should I do?

This idea of the irresistibility of Cupid and
Bacchus united, is delicately expressed in an
Italian poem, which is so truly Anacreontic, that
its introduction here may be pardoned. It is an
imitation, indeed, of our poet's sixth ode.

*Lavossi Amore in quel vicino fiume
Ove giuro (Pastor) che bevend' io
Bevei le fiamme, anzi l'istesso Dio,
Ch'or con l'humide piume
Lascivetto mi scherza al cor intorno.
Ma che sarei s'io lo bevessi un giorno,
Bacco, nel tuo liquore?
Sarei, piu che non sono ebro d'Amore.*

The urchin of the bow and quiver
Was bathing in a neighboring river,
Where, as I drank on yester-eve,
(Shepherd-youth, the tale believe,)
'T was not a cooling, crystal draught,
'T was liquid flame I madly quaffed;
For Love was in the rippling tide,
I felt him to my bosom glide;
And now the wily, wanton minion
Plays round my heart with restless pinion.
A day it was of fatal star,
But ah, 't were even more fatal far,
If, Bacchus, in thy cup of fire,
I found this fluttering, young desire:
Then, then indeed my soul would prove,
Ev'n more than ever, drunk with love!

5 And, having now no other dart,
He shot himself into my heart!

Dryden has parodied this thought in the following extravagant lines: —

—— I 'm all o'er Love;
Nay, I am Love, Love shot, and shot so fast,
He shot himself into my breast at last.

Received the God, and died away.
Farewell, farewell, my faithless shield!
Thy lord at length is forced to yield.
Vain, vain, is every outward care,
The foe 's within, and triumphs there.

ODE XIV.[1]

COUNT me, on the summer trees,
Every leaf that courts the breeze;[2]

1 The poet, in this catalogue of his mistresses,
means nothing more, than by a lively hyperbole,
to inform us, that his heart, unfettered by any
one object, was warm with devotion towards the
sex in general. Cowley is indebted to this ode
for the hint of his ballad, called "The Chronicle;" and the learned Menage has imitated it in
a Greek Anacreontic, which has so much ease and
spirit, that the reader may not be displeased at
seeing it here: —

ΠΡῸΣ ΒΙΩΝΑ.

Εἰ ἀλσέων τὰ φύλλα,
λειμωνίους τε ποίας,
εἰ νυκτὸς ἄστρα πάντα,
παρακτίους τε ψάμμους,
ἁλός τε κυματώδη,
δύνῃ, Βίων, ἀριθμεῖν,
καὶ τοὺς ἐμοὺς ἔρωτας
δύνῃ, Βίων, ἀριθμεῖν.
κόρην, γυναῖκα, χήραν,
σμικρὴν, μῆσην, μεγίστην,
λευκήν τε καὶ μέλαιναν,
ὀρειάδας, ναπαίας,
νηρηΐδας τε πάσας
ὃ σὸς φίλος φίλησε.
Πάντων κόρος μέν ἐστιν,
αὐτὴν νέων Ἐρώτων,
δέσποιναν Ἀφροδίτην,
χρυσῆν, καλὴν, γλυκεῖαν,
ἐράσμιαν, ποθεινήν,
ἀεὶ μόνην φιλῆσαι
ἔγωγε μὴ δυναίμην.

Tell the foliage of the woods,
Tell the billows of the floods,
Number midnight's starry store,
And the sands that crowd the shore,
Then, my Bion, thou mayst count
Of my loves the vast amount.
I 've been loving, all my days,
Many nymphs, in many ways;
Virgin, widow, maid, and wife —
I 've been doting all my life.
Naiads, Nereids, nymphs of fountains,
Goddesses of groves and mountains,
Fair and sable, great and small,
Yes, I swear I 've loved them all!
Soon was every passion over,
I was but the moment's lover;
Oh! I 'm such a roving elf,
That the Queen of Love herself,
Though she practised all her wiles,
Rosy blushes, wreathed smiles,
All her beauty's proud endeavor
Could not chain my heart for ever.

2 Count me, on the summer trees,
Every leaf, etc.

Count me, on the foamy deep,
Every wave that sinks to sleep;
Then, when you have numbered these
Billowy tides and leafy trees,
Count me all the flames I prove,
All the gentle nymphs I love.
First, of pure Athenian maids
Sporting in their olive shades,
You may reckon just a score,
Nay, I 'll grant you fifteen more.
In the famed Corinthian grove,
Where such countless wantons rove,[3]
Chains of beauties may be found,
Chains, by which my heart is bound;
There, indeed, are nymphs divine,
Dangerous to a soul like mine.[4]
Many bloom in Lesbos' isle;

This figure is called, by rhetoricians, the Impossible (ἀδύνατον), and is very frequently made
use of in poetry. The amatory writers have exhausted a world of imagery by it, to express the
infinite number of kisses which they require from
the lips of their mistresses: in this Catullus led
the way: —

—— *Quam sidera multa, cum tacet nox,*
furtivos hominum vident amores;
tam te basia multa basiare
vesano satis, et super, Catullo est:
quæ nec pernumerare curiosi
possint, nec mala fascinare lingua.
Carm. 7.

As many stellar eyes of light,
As through the silent waste of night,
Gazing upon this world of shade,
Witness some secret youth and maid,
Who fair as thou, and fond as I,
In stolen joys enamoured lie, —
So many kisses, while I slumber,
Upon those dew-bright lips I 'll number;
So many kisses we shall count,
Envy can never tell the amount.
No tongue shall blab the sum, but mine;
No lips shall fascinate, but thine!

3 In the famed Corinthian grove,
Where such countless wantons rove, etc.

Corinth was very famous for the beauty and
number of its courtesans. Venus was the deity
principally worshipped by the people, and their
constant prayer was, that the gods should increase the number of her worshippers. We may
perceive from the application of the verb κοριν-
θιάζειν, in Aristophanes, that the lubricity of the
Corinthians had become proverbial.

4 There, indeed, are nymphs divine,
Dangerous to a soul like mine!

"With justice has the poet attributed beauty
to the women of Greece."— DEGEN.
M. de Pauw, the author of "Dissertations
upon the Greeks," is of a different opinion; he
thinks, that by a capricious partiality of nature,
the other sex had all the beauty; and by this supposition endeavors to account for a very singular
depravation of instinct among that people.

Many in Ionia smile;
Rhodes a pretty swarm can boast;
Caria too contains a host.
Sum them all — of brown and fair
You may count two thousand there.
What, you stare? I pray you, peace!
More I 'll find before I cease.
Have I told you all my flames,
'Mong the amorous Syrian dames?
Have I numbered every one,
Glowing under Egypt's sun?
Or the nymphs, who blushing sweet
Deck the shrine of Love in Crete;
Where the God, with festal play,
Holds eternal holiday?
Still in clusters, still remain
Gades' warm, desiring train; [1]
Still there lies a myriad more
On the sable India's shore;
These, and many far removed,
All are loving — all are loved!

ODE XV.[2]

TELL me, why, my sweetest dove,
Thus your humid pinions move,
Shedding through the air in showers
Essence of the balmiest flowers?
Tell me whither, whence you rove,
Tell me all, my sweetest dove.

---

1   Gades' warm, desiring train.

The Gaditanian girls were like the Baladières of India, whose dances are thus described by a French author: " *Les danses sont presque toutes des pantomimes d'amour ; le plan, le dessein, les attitudes, les mesures, les sons et les cadences de ces ballets, tout respire cette passion et en exprime les voluptés et les fureurs.*" — " Histoire du Commerce des Europ. dans les deux Indes." RAYNAL.

The music of the Gaditanian females had all the voluptuous character of their dancing, as appears from Martial: —

Cantica qui Nili, qui Gaditana susurrat.
              Lib. iii. epig. 63.

Lodovico Ariosto had this ode of our bard in his mind, when he wrote his poem " De diversis amoribus." See the " Anthologia Italorum."

2 The dove of Anacreon, bearing a letter from the poet to his mistress, is met by a stranger, with whom this dialogue is imagined.

The ancients made use of letter-carrying pigeons, when they went any distance from home, as the most certain means of conveying intelligence back. That tender domestic attachment which attracts this delicate little bird through every danger and difficulty till it settles in its native nest, affords to the author of " The

---

Curious stranger, I belong
To the bard of Teian song;
With his mandate now I fly
To the nymph of azure eye; —
She, whose eye has maddened many,[3]
But the poet more than any.
Venus, for a hymn of love,
Warbled in her votive grove,[4]
('T was in sooth a gentle lay,)
Gave me to the bard away.
See me now his faithful minion, —
Thus with softly-gliding pinion,
To his lovely girl I bear
Songs of passion through the air.
Oft he blandly whispers me,
" Soon, my bird, I 'll set you free."
But in vain he 'll bid me fly,
I shall serve him till I die.
Never could my plumes sustain
Ruffling winds and chilling rain,
O'er the plains, or in the dell,
On the mountain's savage swell,
Seeking in the desert wood
Gloomy shelter, rustic food.

Pleasures of Memory " a fine and interesting exemplification of his subject.

   Led by what chart, transports the timid dove
   The wreaths of conquest, or the vows of love?

See the poem. Daniel Heimsius, in speaking of Dousa, who adopted this method at the siege of Leyden, expresses a similar sentiment.

Quo patriæ non tendit amor ? Mandata referre postquam hominem nequiit mittere, misit avem.

Fuller tells us that, at the siege of Jerusalem, the Christians intercepted a letter, tied to the legs of a dove, in which the Persian Emperor promised assistance to the besieged. — " Holy War," cap. 24. book i.

3 She, whose eye has maddened many, etc.

For τύραννον, in the original, Zeune and Schneider conjecture that we should read τυράννου, in allusion to the strong influence which this object of his love held over the mind of Polycrates. See DEGEN.

4 Venus, for a hymn of love,
Warbled in her votive grove, etc.

" This passage is invaluable, and I do not think that anything so beautiful or so delicate has ever been said. What an idea does it give of the poetry of the man, from whom Venus herself, the mother of the Graces and the Pleasures, purchases a little hymn with one of her favorite doves ! " — LONGEPIERRE.

De Pauw objects to the authenticity of this ode, because it makes Anacreon his own panegyrist; but poets have a license for praising themselves, which, with some indeed, may be considered as comprised under their general privilege of fiction.

Now I lead a life of ease,
Far from rugged haunts like these.
From Anacreon's hand I eat
Food delicious, viands sweet;
Flutter o'er his goblet's brim,
Sip the foamy wine with him.
Then, when I have wantoned round
To his lyre's beguiling sound;
Or with gently-moving wings
Fanned the minstrel while he sings:
On his harp I sink in slumbers,
Dreaming still of dulcet numbers!

This is all — away — away —
You have made me waste the day.
How I 've chattered! prating crow
Never yet did chatter so.

ODE XVI.[1]

Thou, whose soft and rosy hues
Mimic form and soul infuse,[2]
Best of painters, come portray
The lovely maid that 's far away.[3]

Far away, my soul! thou art,
But I 've thy beauties all by heart.
Paint her jetty ringlets playing,
Silky locks, like tendrils straying;[4]
And, if painting hath the skill
To make the spicy balm distil,[5]
Let every little lock exhale
A sigh of perfume on the gale.
Where her tresses' curly flow
Darkles o'er the brow of snow,
Let her forehead beam to light,
Burnished as the ivory bright.
Let her eyebrows smoothly rise
In jetty arches o'er her eyes,
Each, a crescent gently gliding,
Just commingling, just dividing.

But, hast thou any sparkles warm,
The lightning of her eyes to form?
Let them effuse the azure rays
That in Minerva's glances blaze,
Mixt with the liquid light that lies

---

1 This ode and the next may be called companion-pictures; they are highly finished, and give us an excellent idea of the taste of the ancients in beauty. Franciscus Junius quotes them in his third book "De Pictura Veterum."

This ode has been imitated by Ronsard, Giuliano Goselini, etc. Scaliger alludes to it thus in his Anacreontica: —

> *Olim lepore blando,*
> *litis versibus*
> *candidus Anacreon*
> *quam pingeret amicus*
> *descripsit Venerem suam.*

The Teian bard, of former days,
Attuned his sweet descriptive lays,
And taught the painter's hand to trace
His fair beloved's every grace.

In the dialogue of Caspar Barlæus, entitled "An formosa sit ducenda," the reader will find many curious ideas and descriptions of womanly beauty.

2 Thou, whose soft and rosy hues
Mimic form and soul infuse.

I have followed here the reading of the Vatican MS. ῥοδέης. Painting is called "the rosy art," either in reference to coloring, or as an indefinite epithet of excellence, from the association of beauty with that flower. Salvini has adopted this reading in his literal translation: —

> *Della rosea arte signore.*

3 The lovely maid that 's far away.

If this portrait of the poet's mistress be not merely ideal, the omission of her name is much

to be regretted. Meleager, in an epigram on Anacreon, mentions "the golden Eurypyle" as his mistress: —

βεβληκὼς χρυσέην χεῖρας ἐπ' Εὐρυπύλην.

4 Paint her jetty ringlets playing,
Silky locks, like tendrils straying.

The ancients have been very enthusiastic in their praises of the beauty of hair. Apuleius, in the second book of his Milesiacs, says that Venus herself, if she were bald, though surrounded by the Graces and the Loves, could not be pleasing even to her husband Vulcan.

Stesichorus gave the epithet καλλιπλόκαμος to the Graces, and Simonides bestowed the same upon the Muses. See Hadrian Junius's "Dissertation upon Hair."

To this passage of our poet, Selden alluded in a note on the "Polyolbion" of Drayton, Song the Second, where observing, that the epithet "black-haired" was given by some of the ancients to the goddess Isis, he says, "Nor will I swear, but that Anacreon (a man very judicious in the provoking motives of wanton love), intending to bestow on his sweet mistress that one of the titles of woman's special ornament, well-haired (καλλιπλόκαμος), thought of this when he gave his painter direction to make her black-haired."

5 And, if painting hath the skill
To make the spicy balm distil, etc.

Thus Philostratus, speaking of a picture: ἐπαινῶ καὶ τὸν ἐνδροσον τῶν ῥόδων, καί φημι γέγραφθαι αὐτὰ μετὰ τῆς ὀσμῆς. "I admire the dewiness of these roses, and could say that their very smell was painted."

In Cytherea's languid eyes.[1]
O'er her nose and cheek be shed
Flushing white and softened red;
Mingling tints, as when there glows
In snowy milk the bashful rose.[2]
Then her lip, so rich in blisses,
Sweet petitioner for kisses,[3]
Rosy nest, where lurks Persuasion,

> 1 Mixt with the liquid light that lies
> In Cytherea's languid eyes.

Marchetti explains thus the ὑγρόν of the
original : —

> *Dipingili umidetti*
> *Tremuli e lascivetti,*
> *Quai gli ha Ciprigna l' alma Dea d' Amore.*

Tasso has painted in the same manner the
eyes of Armida : —

> *Qual raggio in onda le scintilla un riso*
> *Negli umidi occhi tremulo e lascivo.*

> Within her humid, melting eyes
> A brilliant ray of laughter lies,
> Soft as the broken solar beam,
> That trembles in the azure stream.

The mingled expression of dignity and tenderness, which Anacreon requires the painter to
infuse into the eyes of his mistress, is more
amply described in the subsequent ode. Both
descriptions are so exquisitely touched, that the
artist must have been great indeed, if he did not
yield in painting to the poet.

> 2 Mingling tints, as when there glows
> In snowy milk the bashful rose.

Thus Propertius, eleg. 3. lib. ii.

> *Utque rosæ puro lacte natant folia.*

And Davenant, in a little poem called "The
Mistress," —

> Catch as it falls the Scythian snow,
> Bring blushing roses steept in milk.

Thus too Taygetus : —

> *Quæ lac atque rosas vincis candore rubenti.*

These last words may perhaps defend the
"flushing white" of the translation.

> 3 Then her lip, so rich in blisses,
> Sweet petitioner for kisses.

The "lip, provoking kisses," in the original,
is a strong and beautiful expression. Achilles
Tatius speaks of χείλη μαλθακὰ πρὸς τὰ φιλήματα, "Lips soft and delicate for kissing." A
grave old commentator, Dionysius Lambinus, in
his notes upon Lucretius, tells us with the appar-
ent authority of experience, that "*Suavius viros
osculantur puellæ labiosæ, quam quæ sunt brevi-
bus labris.*" And Æneas Sylvius, in his tedious
uninteresting story of the loves of Euryalus and
Lucretia, where he particularizes the beauties of
the heroine (in a very false and labored style of
latinity), describes her lips thus : "*Os parvum
decensque, labia corallini coloris ad morsum ap-
tissima.*" — *Epist.* 114. *lib.* i.

Mutely courting Love's invasion.
Next, beneath the velvet chin,
Whose dimple hides a Love within,[4]
Mould her neck with grace descending,
In a heaven of beauty ending;
While countless charms, above, below,
Sport and flutter round its snow.
Now let a floating, lucid veil,
Shadow her form, but not conceal;[5]
A charm may peep, a hue may beam,
And leave the rest to Fancy's dream.
Enough — 't is she ! 't is all I seek;
It glows, it lives, it soon will speak !

ODE XVII.[6]

AND now with all thy pencil's truth,
Portray Bathyllus, lovely youth !
Let his hair, in masses bright,
Fall like floating rays of light;[7]
And there the raven's die confuse
With the golden sunbeam's hues.

> 4 Next, beneath the velvet chin,
> Whose dimple hides a Love within, etc.

Madame Dacier has quoted here two pretty
lines of Varro : —

> *Sigilla in mento impressa Amoris digitulo*
> *vestigio demonstrant mollitudinem.*

> In her chin is a delicate dimple,
> By Cupid's own finger imprest;
> There Beauty, bewitchingly simple,
> Has chosen her innocent nest.

> 5 Now let a floating, lucid veil,
> Shadow her form, but not conceal; etc.

This delicate art of description, which leaves
imagination to complete the picture, has been
seldom adopted in the imitations of this beautiful poem. Ronsard is exceptionally minute; and
Politianus, in his charming portrait of a girl, full
of rich and exquisite diction, has lifted the veil
rather too much. The "*questo che tu m' intendi*"
should be always left to fancy.

> 6 The reader, who wishes to acquire an accu-
rate idea of the judgment of the ancients in
beauty, will be indulged by consulting Junius's
"De Pictura Veterum," *lib.* 3. *cap.* 9., where he
will find a very curious selection of descriptions
and epithets of personal perfections. Junius
compares this ode with a description of Theo-
doric, king of the Goths, in the second epistle,
first book, of Sidonius Apollinaris.

> 7 Let his hair, in masses bright,
> Fall like floating rays of light; etc.

He here describes the sunny hair, the *flava
coma*, which the ancients so much admired. The
Romans gave this color artificially to their hair.
See STANISL. KOBIENZYCK, "De Luxu Romanorum."

Let no wreath, with artful twine,[1]
The flowing of his locks confine;
But leave them loose to every breeze,
To take what shape and course they
    please.
Beneath the forehead, fair as snow,
But flushed with manhood's early glow,
And guileless as the dews of dawn,[2]
Let the majestic brows be drawn,
Of ebon hue, enriched by gold,
Such as dark, shining snakes unfold.
Mix in his eyes the power alike,
With love to win, with awe to strike;[3]
Borrow from Mars his look of ire,
From Venus her soft glance of fire;
Blend them in such expression here,
That we by turns may hope and fear!

Now from the sunny apple seek
The velvet down that spreads his cheek;
And there, if art so far can go,
The ingenuous blush of boyhood show.
While, for his mouth — but no, — in
    vain
Would words its witching charm explain.
Make it the very seat, the throne,

That Eloquence would claim her own;[4]
And let the lips, though silent, wear
A life-look, as if words were there.[5]

Next thou his ivory neck must trace,
Moulded with soft but manly grace;
Fair as the neck of Paphia's boy,
Where Paphia's arms have hung in joy.
Give him the winged Hermes' hand,[6]
With which he waves his snaky wand;
Let Bacchus the broad chest supply,
And Leda's son the sinewy thigh;
While, through his whole transparent
    frame,
Thou show'st the stirrings of that flame,

Oh! tell me, brightly beaming eye,
Whence in your little orbit lie
So many different traits of fire,
Expressing each a new desire.
Now with pride or scorn you darkle,
Now with love, with gladness, sparkle,
While we who view the varying mirror,
Feel by turns both hope and terror.

Chevreau, citing the lines of our poet, in his critique on the poems of Malherbe, produces a Latin version of them from a manuscript which he had seen, entitled " Joan. Falconis Anacreontici Lusus."

1 Let no wreath, with artful twine, etc.

If the original here, which is particularly beautiful, can admit of any additional value, that value is conferred by Gray's admiration of it. See his letters to West.

Some annotators have quoted on this passage the description of Photis's hair in Apuleius; but nothing can be more distant from the simplicity of our poet's manner, than that affectation of richness which distinguishes the style of Apuleius.

2 But flushed with manhood's early glow,
And guileless as the dews of dawn, etc.

Torrentius, upon the words "*insignem tenui fronte,*" in Horace, Od. 33., lib. 1., is of opinion, incorrectly, I think, that "*tenui*" here bears the same meaning as the word ἀπαλόν.

3 Mix in his eyes the power alike,
With love to win, with awe to strike; etc.

Tasso gives a similar character to the eyes of Clorinda: —

Lampeggiar gli occhi, e folgorar gli sguardi
Dolci nell' ira.

Her eyes were flashing with a heavenly heat,
A fire that, even in anger, still was sweet.

The poetess Veronica Cambara is more diffuse upon this variety of expression: —

Occhi lucenti e belli,
Come esser puo ch' in un medesmo istante
Nascan de voi si nuove forme et tante?
Lieti, mesti, superbi, humil', altieri,
Vi mostrate in un punto, onde di speme,
Et di timor, de empiete, etc.

4 That Eloquence would claim her own.

In the original, in the preceding ode, Peitho, the goddess of persuasion, or eloquence. It was worthy of the delicate imagination of the Greeks to deify Persuasion, and give her the lips for her throne. We are here reminded of a very interesting fragment of Anacreon, preserved by the scholiast upon Pindar, and supposed to belong to a poem reflecting with some severity on Simonides, who was the first, we are told, that ever made a hireling of his muse: —

Οὐδ' ἀργυρέη ποτ' ἔλαμψε Πείθω.

Nor yet had fair Persuasion shone
In silver splendors, not her own.

5 And let the lips, though silent, wear
A life-look, as if words were there.

In the original λαλῶν σιοπῇ. The mistress of Petrarch *parla con silenzio*, which is perhaps the best method of female eloquence.

6 Give him the winged Hermes' hand, etc.

In Shakespeare's "Cymbeline" there is a similar method of description: —

—— this is his hand,
His foot mercurial, his martial thigh,
The brawns of Hercules.

We find it likewise in "Hamlet." Longepierre thinks that the hands of Mercury are selected by Anacreon on account of the graceful gestures which were supposed to characterize the god of eloquence; but Mercury was also the patron of thieves, and may perhaps be praised as a light-fingered deity.

Which kindles, when the first love-sigh
Steals from the heart, unconscious why.

But sure thy pencil, though so bright,
Is envious of the eye's delight,
Or its enamoured touch would show
The shoulder, fair as sunless snow,
Which now in veiling shadow lies,
Removed from all but Fancy's eyes.
Now, for his feet — but hold — for-
    bear —
I see the sun-god's portrait there;[1]
Why paint Bathyllus? when, in truth,
There, in that god, thou'st sketched the
    youth.
Enough — let this bright form be mine,
And send the boy to Samos' shrine;
Phœbus shall then Bathyllus be,
Bathyllus then, the deity!

ODE XVIII.

Now the star of day is high,
Fly, my girls, in pity fly,
Bring me wine in brimming urns,[2]
Cool my lip, it burns, it burns!
Sunned by the meridian fire,
Panting, languid I expire.
Give me all those humid flowers,[3]

1 —— but hold — forbear —
    I see the sun-god's portrait there.

The abrupt turn here is spirited, but requires
some explanation. While the artist is pursuing
the portrait of Bathyllus, Anacreon, we must
suppose, turns round and sees a picture of Apollo,
which was intended for an altar at Samos. He
then instantly tells the painter to cease his work;
that this picture will serve for Bathyllus; and
that, when he goes to Samos, he may make an
Apollo of the portrait of the boy which he had
begun.

"Bathyllus" (says Madame Dacier) "could
not be more elegantly praised, and this one passage does him more honor than the statue, however beautiful it might be, which Polycrates
raised to him."

2 Bring me wine in brimming urns, etc.

Original πιεῖν ἀμυστί. The amystis was a
method of drinking used among the Thracians.
Thus Horace, *Threiciâ vincat amystide.* Mad.
Dacier, Longepierre, etc.

Parrhasius, in his twenty-sixth epistle (" The-
saur. Critic." vol. i.), explains the amystis as a
draught to be exhausted without drawing breath,
uno haustu. A note in the margin of this epistle
of Parrhasius says, *Politianus vestem esse puta-
bat,* but adds no reference.

3 Give me all those humid flowers, etc.

According to the original reading of this line,
the poet says, " Give me the flower of wine " —

Drop them o'er my brow in showers.
Scarce a breathing chaplet now
Lives upon my feverish brow;
Every dewy rose I wear
Sheds its tears, and withers there.[4]
But to you, my burning heart,[5]
What can now relief impart?
Can brimming bowl, or flowret's dew,
Cool the flame that scorches you?

Date flosculos Lyæi, as it is in the version of
Elias Andreas; and —

*Deh porgetimi del fiore
Di quel almo e buon liquore,*

as Regnier has it, who supports the reading.
The word ἄνθος would undoubtedly bear this
application, which is somewhat similar to its
import in the epigram of Simonides upon
Sophocles: —

ἐσβέσθης γέραιε Σοφόκλεες, ἄνθος ἀοιδῶν·

and *flos* in the Latin is frequently applied in the
same manner — thus Cethegus is called by En-
nius, *Flos inlibatus populi, suadæque medulla,*
" The immaculate flower of the people, and the
very marrow of persuasion." See these verses
cited by Aulus Gellius, lib. xii., which Cicero
praised, and Seneca thought ridiculous.

But in the passage before us, if we admit
ἐκείνων, according to Faber's conjecture, the
sense is sufficiently clear, without having recourse to such refinements.

4 Every dewy rose I wear
    Sheds its tears, and withers there.

There are some beautiful lines, by Angerianus,
upon a garland, which I cannot resist quoting
here : —

*Ante fores madidæ sic sic pendete corollæ,
mane orto imponet Cælia vos capiti ;
at quum per niveam cervicem influxerit humor.
dicite, non roris aqua hæc lacrimæ.*

By Celia's arbor all the night
    Hang, humid wreath, the lover's vow ;
And haply, at the morning light,
    My love shall twine thee round her brow.

Then, if upon her bosom bright
    Some drops of dew shall fall from thee,
Tell her, they are not drops of night,
    But tears of sorrow shed by me!

In the poem of Mr. Sheridan's, " Uncouth is
this moss-covered grotto of stone," there is an
idea very singularly coincident with this of Angerianus : —

And thou, stony grot, in thy arch may'st preserve
    Some lingering drops of the night-fallen dew ;
Let them fall on her bosom of snow, and they 'll
    serve
As tears of my sorrow entrusted to you.

5 But to you, my burning heart, etc.

The transition here is peculiarly delicate and
impassioned ; but the commentators have per-
plexed the sentiment by a variety of readings
and conjectures.

ODE XIX.[1]

Here recline you, gentle maid,[2]
Sweet is this embowering shade;
Sweet the young, the modest trees,
Ruffled by the kissing breeze;
Sweet the little founts that weep,
Lulling soft the mind to sleep;
Hark! they whisper as they roll,
Calm persuasion to the soul;
Tell me, tell me, is not this
All a stilly scene of bliss?
Who, my girl, would pass it by?
Surely neither you nor I.[3]

1 The description of this bower is so natural
and animated, that we almost feel a degree
of coolness and freshness while we peruse it.
Longepierre has quoted from the first book of
the "Anthologia" the following epigram, as
somewhat resembling this ode: —

ἔρχεο καὶ κατ' ἐμὰν ἵζευ πίτυν ἅ τὸ μελιχρὸν
    πρὸς μαλακοὺς ἠχεῖ κεκλιμένα ζεφύρους.
ἠνίδε καὶ κρυόντι μα μελιστραγές, ἔνθα μελίσδων
    ἡδὺν ἐρημαίοις ὕπνον ἄγω καλάμοις.

Come, sit by the shadowy pine
    That covers my sylvan retreat;
And see how the branches incline
    The breathing of zephyr to meet.

See the fountain, that, flowing, diffuses
    Around me a glittering spray;
By its brink, as the traveller muses,
    I soothe him to sleep with my lay.

2 Here recline you, gentle maid, etc.

The Vatican MS. reads βαθύλλου, which renders the whole poem metaphorical. Some commentator suggests the reading of βαθύλλον, which
makes a pun upon the name; a grace that Plato
himself has condescended to in writing of his
boy Ἀστήρ. See the epigram of this philosopher,
which I quote on the twenty-second ode.
There is another epigram by this philosopher,
preserved in Laertius, which turns upon the same
word.

Ἀστὴρ πρὶν μὲν ἔλαμπες ἐνὶ ζώοισιν ἐῶος,
    νῦν δὲ θανὼν λάμπεις ἕσπερος ἐν φθιμένοις.

In life thou wert my morning star,
    But now that death has stolen thy light,
Alas! thou shinest dim and far,
    Like the pale beam that weeps at night.

In the Veneres Blyenburgicæ, under the head
of "Allusiones," we find a number of such frigid
conceits upon names, selected from the poets of
the middle ages.

3 Who, my girl, would pass it by?
    Surely neither you nor I.

The finish given to the picture by this simple
exclamation τίς ἂν οὖν ὁρῶν παρέλθοι, is inimitable. Yet a French translator says on the passage, "This conclusion appeared to me too

ODE XX.[4]

One day the Muses twined the hands
Of infant Love with flowery bands;
And to celestial Beauty gave
The captive infant for her slave.
His mother comes, with many a toy,

trifling after such a description, and I thought
proper to add somewhat to the strength of the
original."

4 The poet appears, in this graceful allegory,
to describe the softening influence which poetry
holds over the mind, in making it peculiarly susceptible to the impressions of beauty. In the
following epigram, however, by the philosopher
Plato (Diog. Laert. lib. 3.), the Muses are represented as disavowing the influence of Love.

ἁ Κύπρις Μούσαισι, κοράσια τὰν Ἀφροδίταν
    τίματ', ἢ τὸν Ἔρωτα ὕμμιν ἐφοπλίσομαι.
αἱ Μοῦσαι ποτὶ Κύπριν, Ἄρει τὰ στωμύλα ταῦτα·
    ἡμῖν οὐ πέταται τοῦτο τὸ παιδάριον.

"Yield to my gentle power, Parnassian maids;"
    Thus to the Muses spoke the Queen of
        Charms —
"Or Love shall flutter through your classic
        shades,
    And make your grove the camp of Paphian
        arms!"

"No," said the virgins of the tuneful bower,
    "We scorn thine own and all thy urchin's art;
Though Mars has trembled at the infant's power,
    His shaft is pointless o'er a Muse's heart!"

There is a sonnet by Benedetto Guidi, the
thought of which was suggested by this ode: —

Scherzava dentro all' auree chiome Amore
    Dell' alma donna della vita mia:
E tanta era il piacer ch' ei ne sentia,
    Che non sapea, nè volea uscirne fore.

Quando ecco ivi annodar si sente il core,
    Sì, che per forza ancor convien che stia:
Tai lacci alta beltate orditi avia
    Del crespo crin, per farsi eterno onore.

Onde offre infin dal ciel degna mercede,
    A chi scioglie il figliuol la bella dea
Da tanti nodi, in ch' ella stretti il vede.
Ma ei vinto a due occhi l' arme cede:
    Et t' affatichi indarno, Citerea;
Che s' altri'l scioglie, egli a legar si riede

Love, wandering through the golden maze
    Of my beloved's hair,
Found, at each step, such sweet delays,
    That rapt he lingered there.

And how, indeed, was Love to fly
    Or how his freedom find,
When every ringlet was a tie,
    A chain, by Beauty twined.

In vain to seek her boy's release,
    Comes Venus from above:
Fond mother, let thy efforts cease,
    Love's now the slave of Love.
And, should we loose his golden chain,
The prisoner would return again!

To ransom her beloved boy; [1]
His mother sues, but all in vain, —
He ne'er will leave his chains again.
Even should they take his chains away,
The little captive still would stay.
" If this," he cries, " a bondage be;
Oh, who could wish for liberty?"

ODE XXI. [2]

OBSERVE when mother earth is dry,
She drinks the droppings of the sky;

    1 His mother comes, with many a toy,
To ransom her beloved boy, etc.

    In the first idyl of Moschus, Venus thus proclaims the reward for her fugitive child : —

      ὁ μανυτὰς γέρας ἕξει,
μισθός τοι, τὸ φίλαμα τὸ Κύπριδος· ἢν δ', ἀγάγῃς
    νιν
οὐ γυμνὸν τὸ φίλαμα, τὺ δ', ὦ ξένε, καὶ πλέον
    ἕξεις.

On him, who the haunts of my Cupid can show,
A kiss of the tenderest stamp I 'll bestow;
But he, who can bring back the urchin in chains,
Shall receive even something more sweet for his
    pains.

    Subjoined to this ode, we find in the Vatican MS. the following lines, which appear to me to boast as little sense as metre, and which are most probably the interpolation of the transcriber : —

      ἡδυμελὴς Ἀνακρέων
      ἡδυμελὴς δὲ Σάπφω
      πινδαρικὸν τὸ δέ μοι μέλος
      συγκεράσας τις ἐγχέοι
      τὰ τρία ταῦτά μοι δόκει
      καὶ Διόννυσος εἰσελθὼν
      καὶ Παφίη παράχροος
      καὶ αὐτὸς Ἔρως κἂν ἐπίευν.

    2 Those critics who have endeavored to throw the chains of precision over the spirit of this beautiful trifle, require too much from Anacreontic philosophy. Among others, Gail very sapiently thinks that the poet uses the epithet μελαίνη, because black earth absorbs moisture more quickly than any other ; and accordingly he indulges us with an experimental disquisition on the subject. — See Gail's Notes.
    One of the Capilupi has imitated this ode, in an epitaph on a drunkard : —

Dum vixi sine fine bibi, sic imbrifer arcus
   sic tellus pluvias sole perusta bibit.
Sic bibit assiduè fontes et flumina Pontus,
   sic semper sitiens Sol maris haurit aquas.
Ne te igitur jactes plus me, Silene, bibisse ;
   et mihi da victas tu quoque, Bacche, manus.
             HIPPOLYTUS CAPILUPUS.

While life was mine, the little hour
   In drinking still unvaried flew ;
I drank as earth imbibes the shower,
   Or as the rainbow drinks the dew ;
As ocean quaffs the rivers up,
   Or flushing sun inhales the sea :
Silenus trembled at my cup,
   And Bacchus was outdone by me!

And then the dewy cordial gives
To every thirsty plant that lives.
The vapors, which at evening weep,
Are beverage to the swelling deep;
And when the rosy sun appears,
He drinks the ocean's misty tears.
The moon too quaffs her paly stream
Of lustre, from the solar beam.
Then, hence with all your sober thinking !
Since Nature's holy law is drinking;
I 'll make the laws of nature mine,
And pledge the universe in wine.

ODE XXII.

THE Phrygian rock, that braves the storm,
Was once a weeping matron's form; [3]
And Progne, hapless, frantic maid,
Is now a swallow in the shade.
Oh ! that a mirror's form were mine,
That I might catch that smile divine;
And like my own fond fancy be,
Reflecting thee, and only thee ;

    I cannot omit citing those remarkable lines of Shakspeare, where the thoughts of the ode before us are preserved with such striking similitude : —

    " I 'll example you with thievery.
The sun 's a thief, and with his great attraction
Robs the vast sea. The moon 's an arrant thief,
And her pale fire she snatches from the sun.
The sea 's a thief, whose liquid surge resolves
The mounds into salt tears. The earth 's a thief,
That feeds, and breeds by a composture stolen
From general excrements."
    "Timon of Athens," act iv. sc. 3.

    3 —— a weeping matron's form.

    Niobe. — Ogilvie, in his " Essay on the Lyric Poetry of the Ancients," in remarking upon the Odes of Anacreon, says, " In some of his pieces there is exuberance and even wildness of imagination ; in that particularly, which is addressed to a young girl, where he wishes alternately to be transformed to a mirror, a coat, a stream, a bracelet, and a pair of shoes, for the different purposes which he recites ; this is mere sport and wantonness."
    It is the wantonness, however, of a very graceful Muse ; *ludit amabiliter.* The compliment of this ode is exquisitely delicate, and so singular for the period in which Anacreon lived, when the scale of love had not yet been graduated into all its little progressive refinements, that if we were inclined to question the authenticity of the poem, we should find a much more plausible argument in the features of modern gallantry which it bears, than in any of those fastidious conjectures upon which some commentators have presumed so far. Degen thinks it spurious, and De Pauw pronounces it to be miserable. Longepierre and Barnes refer us to several imitations of this ode, from which I

Or could I be the robe which holds
That graceful form within its folds;
Or, turned into a fountain, lave
Thy beauties in my circling wave.
Would I were perfume for thy hair,
To breathe my soul in fragrance there;
Or, better still, the zone, that lies
Close to thy breast, and feels its sighs![1]
Or even those envious pearls that show

shall only select the following epigram of Dionysius:

εἴθ' ἄνεμος γενόμην, σὺ δέ γε στείχουσα παρ'
αὐγάς,
στήθεα γυμνώσαις, καί με πνέοντα λάβοις.
εἴθε ῥόδον γενόμην ὑποπόρφυεον, ὄφρα με χερσὶν
ἀραμένη, κομίσαις στέθεσι χιονέοις.
εἴθε κρίνον γενόμην λευκόχροον, ὄφρα με χερσὶν
ἀραμένη, μάλλον σῆς χρότιης κορέσης.

I wish I could like zephyr steal
To wanton o'er thy mazy vest;
And thou wouldst ope thy bosom-veil,
And take me panting to thy breast!

I wish I might a rose-bud grow,
And thou wouldst cull me from the bower,
To place me on that breast of snow,
Where I should bloom, a wintry flower.

I wish I were the lily's leaf,
To fade upon that bosom warm;
Content to wither, pale and brief,
The trophy of thy fairer form!

I may add, that Plato has expressed as fanciful a wish in a distich preserved by Laertius: —

ἀστέρας εἰσαθρεῖς, Ἀστὴρ ἐμός. εἴθε γενοίμην
οὐρανός, ὡς πολλοῖς ὄμμασιν εἰς σὲ βλέπω.

TO STELLA.

Why dost thou gaze upon the sky?
Oh! that I were that spangled sphere,
And every star should be an eye,
To wonder on thy beauties here!

Apuleius quotes this epigram of the divine philosopher, to justify himself for his verses on Critias and Charinus. See his "Apology," where he also adduces the example of Anacreon: *"Fecere tamen et alii talia, et si vos ignoratis, apud Græcos Teius quidam,"* etc.

1 Or, better still, the zone, that lies
Close to thy breast, and feels its sighs!

This ταινίη was a riband, or band, called by the Romans *fascia* and *strophium,* which the women wore for the purpose of restraining the exuberance of the bosom. *Vide* "Polluc. Onomast." Thus Martial: —

Fascia crescentes dominæ compesce papillas.

The women of Greece not only wore this zone, but condemned themselves to fasting, and made use of certain drugs and powders for the same purpose. To these expedients they were compelled, in consequence of their inelegant fashion of compressing the waist into a very narrow compass, which necessarily caused an excessive tumidity in the bosom. See "Dioscorides," lib. v.

So faintly round that neck of snow —
Yes, I would be a happy gem,
Like them to hang, to fade like them.
What more would thy Anacreon be?
Oh, any thing that touches thee;
Nay, sandals for those airy feet —
Even to be trod by them were sweet![2]

ODE XXIII.[3]

I OFTEN wish this languid lyre,
This warbler of my soul's desire,
Could raise the breath of song sublime,
To men of fame, in former time.
But when the soaring theme I try,
Along the chords my numbers die,
And whisper, with dissolving tone,
"Our sighs are given to love alone!"
Indignant at the feeble lay,
I tore the panting chords away,

2 Nay, sandals for those airy feet —
Even to be trod by them were sweet!

The sophist Philostratus, in one of his love-letters, has borrowed this thought; ὦ ἄδετοι πόδες, ὦ κάλλος ἐλευθερος, ὦ τρισευδαίμων ἐγὼ καὶ μακάριος ἐὰν πατήσετέ με. — "Oh lovely feet! oh excellent beauty! oh! thrice happy and blessed should I be, if you would but tread on me! In Shakspeare, Romeo desires to be a glove: —

Oh! that I were a glove upon that hand,
That I might kiss that cheek!

And, in his "Passionate Pilgrim," we meet with an idea somewhat like that of the thirteenth line: —

He, spying her, bounced in, where as he stood,
"O Jove!" quoth she, "why was not I a flood?"

In Burton's "Anatomy of Melancholy," that whimsical farrago of "all such reading as was never read," we find a translation of the ode made before 1632. — "Englished by Mr. B. Holiday, in his 'Technog.' act i. scene 7."

3 According to the order in which the odes are usually placed, this (Θέλω λέγειν Ἀτρείδας) forms the first of the series; and is thought to be peculiarly designed as an introduction to the rest. It however characterizes the genius of the Teian but very inadequately, as wine, the burden of his lays, is not even mentioned in it: —

— *cum multo Venerem confundere mero
precepit Lyrici Teia Musa senis.* — OVID.

The twenty-sixth Ode, Σὺ μὲν λέγεις τὰ Θήβης, might, with just as much propriety, be placed at the head of his songs.

We find the sentiments of the ode before us expressed by Bion with much simplicity in his fourth idyl. The above translation is, perhaps, too paraphrastical; but the ode has been so frequently translated, that I could not otherwise avoid triteness and repetition.

Attuned them to a nobler swell,
And struck again the breathing shell;
In all the glow of epic fire,
To Hercules I wake the lyre,[1]
But still its fainting sighs repeat,
" The tale of love alone is sweet ! " [2]
Then fare thee well, sēductive dream,
That madest me follow Glory's theme;
For thou my lyre, and thou my heart,
Shall never more in spirit part;
And all that one has felt so well
The other shall as sweetly tell !

ODE XXIV.[3]

To all that breathe the air of heaven,
Some boon of strength has Nature given.
In forming the majestic bull,
She fenced with wreathed horns his skull;
A hoof of strength she lent the steed,
And winged the timorous hare with speed.
She gave the lion fangs of terror,
And, o'er the ocean's crystal mirror,
Taught the unnumbered scaly throng
To trace their liquid path along;

1 In all the glow of epic fire,
   To Hercules I wake the lyre.

Madame Dacier generally translates λύρη into
a lute, which I believe is inaccurate. " *D'ex-
pliquer la lyre des anciens* [says M. Sorel] *par
un luth, c'est ignorer la différence qu'il y a entre
ces deux instrumens de musique*." — " Bibliothèque Françoise."

2 But still its fainting sighs repeat,
   " The tale of love alone is sweet ! "

The word ἀντεφώνει in the original, may imply that kind of musical dialogue practised by the
ancients, in which the lyre was made to respond
to the questions proposed by the singer. This
was a method which Sappho used, as we are
told by Hermogenes ; " ὅταν τὴν λύραν 'ερωτᾶ
Σάπφω, καὶ ὅταν αὐτὴ ἀποκρίνηται." — Περὶ
'Ιδεῶν, τόμ. δεύτ.

3 Henry Stephen has imitated the idea of this
ode in the following lines of one of his poems : —

*Provida dat cunctis Natura animantibus arma,
et sua fœmineum possidet arma genus,
ungulâque ut defendit equum, atque ut cornua
   taurum,
armata est formâ fœmina pulchra suâ.*

And the same thought occurs in those lines
spoken by Corisca in " Pastor Fido : " —

*Cosi noi la bellezza
   Ch' è vertù nostra cosi propria, come
La forza del leone,
   E l'ingegno de l' huomo.*

The lion boasts his savage powers,
And lordly man his strength of mind ;
But beauty's charm is solely ours,
   Peculiar boon, by Heav'n assigned.

While for the umbrage of the grove,
She plumed the warbling world of love.

To man she gave, in that proud hour,
The boon of intellectual power.[4]
Then, what, oh woman, what, for thee,
Was left in Nature's treasury?
She gave thee beauty — mightier far
Than all the pomp and power of war.[5]
Nor steel, nor fire itself hath power
Like woman, in her conquering hour.
Be thou but fair, mankind adore thee,
Smile, and a world is weak before thee ! [6]

ODE XXV.[7]

ONCE in each revolving year,
Gentle bird ! we find thee here.
When Nature wears her summer-vest,

4 To man she gave, in that proud hour,
   The boon of intellectual power.

In my first attempt to translate this ode, I
had interpreted φρόνημα, with Baxter and Barnes,
as implying courage and military virtue; but I do
not think that the gallantry of the idea suffers
by the import which I have now given to it. For,
why need we consider this possession of wisdom
as exclusive ? and in truth, as the design of Anacreon is to estimate the treasure of beauty,
above all the rest which Nature has distributed,
it is perhaps even refining upon the delicacy of
the compliment, to prefer the radiance of female
charms to the cold illumination of wisdom and
prudence; and to think that women's eyes are —

—— the books, the academies,
From whence doth spring the true Promethean
fire.

5 She gave thee beauty — mightier far
   Than all the pomp and power of war.

Thus Achilles Tatius : κάλλος 'οξύτερον τιτρώ-
σκει βέλους, καὶ διὰ τῶν ὀφθαλμῶν εἰς τὴν ψυχὴν
καταρρεῖ. 'Οφθαλμὸς γὰρ ὁδὸς ἐρωτικῷ τραύματι.
" Beauty wounds more swiftly than the arrow,
and passes through the eye to the very soul; for
the eye is the inlet to the wounds of love."

6 Be thou but fair, mankind adore thee,
   Smile, and a world is weak before thee !

Longepierre's remark here is ingenious :
" The Romans," says he, " were so convinced
of the power of beauty, that they used a word
implying strength in the place of the epithet
beautiful. Thus Plautus, act 2. scene 2. ' Bac-
chid.'

Sed Bacchis etiam fortis tibi visa.

' *Fortis, id est formosa,*' say Servius and
Nonius."

7 We have here another ode addressed to the
swallow. Alberti has imitated both in one
poem, beginning —

*Perch' io pianga al tuo canto,
   Rondinella importuna,* etc.

Thou comest to weave thy simple nest;
But when the chilling winter lowers,
Again thou seekest the genial bowers
Of Memphis, or the shores of Nile,
Where sunny hours for ever smile.
And thus thy pinion rests and roves, —
Alas! unlike the swarm of Loves,
That brood within this hapless breast,
And never, never change their nest! [1]
Still every year, and all the year,
They fix their fated dwelling here;
And some their infant plumage try,
And on a tender winglet fly;
While in the shell, impregned with fires,
Still lurk a thousand more desires;
Some from their tiny prisons peeping,
And some in formless embryo sleeping.
Thus peopled, like the vernal groves,
My breast resounds with warbling Loves;
One urchin imps the other's feather,
Then twin-desires they wing together,
And fast as they thus take their flight,
Still other urchins spring to light.
But is there then no kindly art,
To chase these Cupids from my heart;
Ah, no! I fear, in sadness fear,
They will for ever nestle here!

ODE XXVI.[2]

THY harp may sing of Troy's alarms,
Or tell the tale of Theban arms;

1 Alas! unlike the swarm of Loves,
   That brood within this hapless breast,
   And never, never change their nest!

Thus Love is represented as a bird, in an
epigram cited by Longepierre from the Anthologia: —

αἰεί μοι δύνει μὲν ἐν οὔασιν ἦχος ἔρωτος,
  ὄμμα δὲ σῖγα πόθοις τὸ γλυκὺ δάκρυ φέρει.
οὐδ' ἡ νύξ, οὐ φέγγος ἐκοίμισεν, ἀλλ' ὑπὸ φίλτρων
  ἤδέ που κραδίη γνωστὸς ἔνεστι τύπος.
ὦ πτανοί, μὴ καί ποτ' ἐφίπτασθαι μὲν ἔρωτες
  οἴδατ', ἀποπτῆναι δ' οὔθ' ὅσον ἰσχύετε,

'T is Love that murmurs in my breast,
  And makes me shed the secret tear;
Nor day nor night my soul hath rest,
  For night and day his voice I hear.

A wound within my heart I find,
  And oh! 't is plain where Love has been;
For still he leaves a wound behind,
  Such as within my heart is seen.

Oh, bird of Love! with song so drear,
  Make not my soul the nest of pain;
But, let the wing which brought thee here,
  In pity waft thee hence again!

2 "The German poet Uz has imitated this
ode. Compare also Weisse Scherz. Lieder, lib.
iii., 'Der Soldat.'" GAIL, DEGEN.

With other wars my song shall burn,
For other wounds my harp shall mourn.
'T was not the crested warrior's dart,
That drank the current of my heart;
Nor naval arms, nor mailed steed,
Have made this vanquished bosom bleed;
No — 't was from eyes of liquid blue,
A host of quivered Cupids flew; [3]
And now my heart all bleeding lies
Beneath that army of the eyes!

ODE XXVII.[4]

WE read the flying courser's name
Upon his side, in marks of flame;
And, by their turbaned brows alone,
The warriors of the East are known.
But in the lover's glowing eyes,
The inlet to his bosom lies;[5]
Through them we see the small faint
   mark,
Where Love has dropt his burning spark!

3 No — 't was from eyes of liquid blue,
  A host of quivered Cupids flew.

Longepierre has quoted part of an epigram
from the seventh book of the Anthologia, which
has a fancy something like this: —

οὐ μὲ λέληθας,
τόξοτα, Ζηνοφίλας ὄμμασι κρυπτόμενος.

Archer Love! though slily creeping,
  Well I know where thou dost lie;
I saw thee through the curtain peeping,
  That fringes Zenophelia's eye.

The poets abound with conceits on the archery
of the eyes, but few have turned the thought so
naturally as Anacreon. Ronsard gives to the
eyes of his mistress *un petit camp d'amours.*

4 This ode forms a part of the preceding in the
Vatican MS., but I have conformed to the editions in translating them separately.

5 But in the lover's glowing eyes,
  The inlet to his bosom lies.

"We cannot see into the heart," says Madame
Dacier. But the lover answers —

Il cor ne gli occhi et ne la fronte ho scritto.

M. La Fosse has given the following lines, as
enlarging on the thought of Anacreon: —

Lorsque je vois un amant,
  Il cache en vain son tourment,
A le trahir tout conspire,
  Sa langueur, son embarras,
Tout ce qu'il peut faire ou dire,
  Même ce qu'il ne dit pas.

In vain the lover tries to veil
  The flame that in his bosom lies;
His cheeks' confusion tells the tale,
  We read it in his languid eyes:
And while his words the heart betray,
His silence speaks even more than they.

ODE XXVIII.

As, by his Lemnian forge's flame,
The husband of the Paphian dame
Moulded the glowing steel, to form
Arrows for Cupid, thrilling warm;
And Venus, as he plied his art,
Shed honey round each new-made dart,
While Love, at hand, to finish all,
Tipped every arrow's point with gall;[1]
It chanced the Lord of Battles came
To visit that deep cave of flame.
'T was from the ranks of war he rushed,
His spear with many a life-drop blushed;
He saw the fiery darts, and smiled
Contemptuous at the archer-child.
" What! " said the urchin, " dost thou
smile?
Here, hold this little dart awhile,
And thou wilt find, though swift of flight,
My bolts are not so feathery light."

Mars took the shaft — and, oh, thy
look,
Sweet Venus, when the shaft he took! —
Sighing, he felt the urchin's art,
And cried, in agony of heart,
" It is not light — I sink with pain!
Take — take thy arrow back again."
" No," said the child, " it must not be;
That little dart was made for thee! "

1 While Love, at hand, to finish all,
Tipped every arrow's point with gall.

Thus Claudian : —

*Labuntur gemini fontes, hic dulcis, amarus
alter, et infusis corrumpit mella venenis,
unde Cupidineas armavit fama sagittas.*

In Cyprus' isle two rippling fountains fall,
And one with honey flows, and one with gall;
In these, if we may take the tale from fame,
The son of Venus dips his darts of flame.

See Alciatus, emblem 91., on the close connection which subsists between sweets and bitterness. *"Apes ideo pungunt* [says Petronius],
quia ubi dulce, ibi et acidum invenies."

The allegorical description of Cupid's employment, in Horace, may vie with this before us in
fancy, though not in delicacy : —

—— *ferus et Cupido
semper ardentes acuens sagittas
cote cruentâ.*

And Cupid, sharpening all his fiery darts,
Upon a whetstone stained with blood of hearts.

Secundus has borrowed this, but has somewhat softened the image by the omission of the
epithet *"cruentâ."*

Fallor an ardentes acuebat cote sagittas?
Eleg. 1.

ODE XXIX.

YES — loving is a painful thrill,
And not to love more painful still;[2]

2 Yes —loving is a painful thrill,
And not to love more painful still; etc.

The following Anacreontic, addressed by Menage to Daniel Huet, enforces, with much grace,
the " necessity of loving." —

περὶ τοῦ δεῖν φιλῆσαι.
πρὸς Πέτρον Δανιῆλα Ὕεττον.

μέγα θαῦμα τῶν ἀοιδῶν,
χαρίτων θάλος, Ὕεττε,
φιλέωμεν, ὦ ἑταῖρε.
φιλέησαν οἱ σοφισταί.
φιλέησε σεμνὸς ἀνήρ,
τὸ τέκνον τοῦ Σωφρονίσκου,
σοφίης πατὴρ ἁπάσης.
τί δ' ἄνευ γένοιτ' Ἔρωτος;
ἀκονὴ μὲν ἐστι ψυχῆς.*
πτερύγεσσιν εἰς Ὄλυμπον
κατακειμένους ἀναίρει.
βραδέας τετηγμένοισι
βελέεσι ἐξαγείρει.
πυρὶ λάμπαδος φαείνω
ῥυπαρωτέρους καθαίρει.
φιλέωμεν οὖν, Ὕεττε,
φιλέωμεν ὦ ἑταῖρε.
ἀδικῶς δὲ λαιδορούντι
ἀγίους ἔρωτας ἡμῶν
κακὸν εὔξομαι τὸ μοῦνον,
ἵνα μὴ δύναιτ' ἐκεῖνος
φιλέειν τε καὶ φιλεῖσθαι.

TO PETER DANIEL HUET.

Thou! of tuneful bards the first,
Thou! by all the Graces nurst;
Friend! each other friend above,
Come with me, and learn to love.
Loving is a simple lore,
Graver men have learned before;
Nay, the boast of former ages,
Wisest of the wisest sages,
Sophroniscus' prudent son,
Was by love's illusion won.
Oh! how heavy life would move
If we knew not how to love!
Love's a whetstone to the mind;
Thus 't is pointed, thus refined.
When the soul dejected lies,
Love can waft it to the skies;
When in languor sleeps the heart,
Love can wake it with his dart;
When the mind is dull and dark,
Love can light it with his spark!
Come, oh! come then, let us haste
All the bliss of love to taste;
Let us love both night and day,
Let us love our lives away!
And when hearts, from loving free,
(If indeed such hearts there be,)
Frown upon our gentle flame,
And the sweet delusion blame;

* This line is borrowed from an epigram by
Alpheus of Mitylene which Menage, I think, says
somewhere he was himself the first to produce to
the world : —

ψυχῆς ἐστιν Ἔρως ἀκονή.

But oh, it is the worst of pain,
To love and not be loved again!
Affection now has fled from earth,
Nor fire of genius, noble birth,
Nor heavenly virtue, can beguile
From beauty's cheek one favoring smile.
Gold is the woman's only theme,
Gold is the woman's only dream.
Oh! never be that wretch forgiven —
Forgive him not, indignant heaven!
Whose grovelling eyes could first adore,
Whose heart could pant for sordid ore.
Since that devoted thirst began,
Man has forgot to feel for man;
The pulse of social life is dead,
And all its fonder feelings fled!
War too has sullied Nature's charms,
For gold provokes the world to arms:
And oh! the worst of all its arts,
It rends asunder loving hearts.

ODE XXX.[1]

'T was in a mocking dream of night —
I fancied I had wings as light
As a young bird's, and flew as fleet;
While Love, around whose beauteous feet,
I knew not why, hung chains of lead,
Pursued me, as I trembling fled;
And, strange to say, as swift as thought,
Spite of my pinions, I was caught!
What does the wanton Fancy mean
By such a strange, illusive scene?
I fear she whispers to my breast,
That you, sweet maid, have stolen its rest;
That though my fancy, for a while,
Hath hung on many a woman's smile,
I soon dissolved each passing vow,
And ne'er was caught by love till now!

ODE XXXI.[2]

Armed with hyacinthine rod,
(Arms enough for such a god,)

> This shall be my only curse,
> (Could I, could I wish them worse?)
> May they ne'er the rapture prove,
> Of the smile from lips we love!

1 Barnes imagines from this allegory, that our poet married very late in life. But I see nothing in the ode which alludes to matrimony, except it be the lead upon the feet of Cupid; and I agree in the opinion of Madame Dacier, in her life of the poet, that he was always too fond of pleasure to marry.

2 The design of this little fiction is to intimate, that much greater pain attends insensibility than

Cupid bade me wing my pace,
And try with him the rapid race.
O'er many a torrent, wild and deep,
By tangled brake and pendent steep,
With weary foot I panting flew,
Till my brow dropt with chilly dew.[3]
And now my soul, exhausted, dying,
To my lip was faintly flying;[4]

can ever result from the tenderest impressions of love. Longepierre has quoted an ancient epigram which bears some similitude to this ode: —

Lacto compositus, vix prima silentia noctis
carpebam, et somno lumina victa dabam;
cum me sævus Amor prensum, sursumque capillis
excitat, et lacerum pervigilare jubet.
tu famulus meus, inquit, ames cum mille
puellas,
solus Io, solus, dure jacere potes?
exilio et pedibus nudis, tunicaque soluta,
omne iter impedio, nullum iter expedio.
nunc propero, nunc ire piget; rursumque redire
pænitet; et pudor est stare via media.
ecce tacent voces hominum, strepitusque fera-
rum,
et volucrum cantus, turbaque fida canum.
solus ego ex cunctis paveo somnumque torumque,
et sequor imperium, sæve Cupido, tuum.

Upon my couch I lay, at night profound,
My languid eyes in magic slumber bound,
When Cupid came and snatched me from my bed,
And forced me many a weary way to tread.
"What! (said the god) shall you, whose vows are known,
Who love so many nymphs, thus sleep alone?"
I rise and follow; all the night I stray,
Unsheltered, trembling, doubtful of my way;
Tracing with naked foot the painful track,
Loth to proceed, yet fearful to go back.
Yes, at that hour, when Nature seems interred,
Nor warbling birds, nor lowing flocks are heard,
I, I alone, a fugitive from rest,
Passion my guide, and madness in my breast,
Wander the world around, unknowing where,
The slave of love, the victim of despair!

3 Till my brow dropt with chilly dew.

I have followed those who read πείρεν ἱδρώς for πείρεν ὑδρος; the former is partly authorized by the MS. which reads πείρεν ἱδρώς.

4 And now my soul, exhausted, dying,
    To my lip was faintly flying; etc.

In the original, he says, his heart flew to his nose; but our manner more naturally transfers it to the lips. Such is the effect that Plato tells us he felt from a kiss, in a distich quoted by Aulus Gellius: —

τὴν ψυχὴν, Ἀγαθῶνα φιλῶν, ἐπὶ χείλεσιν ἔσχον.
ἦλθε γὰρ ἡ τλήμων ὡς διαβησομένη.

Whene'er thy nectared kiss I sip,
And drink thy breath, in trance divine,
My soul then flutters to my lip,
Ready to fly and mix with thine.

Aulus Gellius subjoins a paraphrase of this epigram, in which we find a number of those *mignardises* of expression, which mark the effemination of the Latin language.

And now I thought the spark had fled,
When Cupid hovered o'er my head,.
And fanning light his breezy pinion,
Rescued my soul from death's dominion;[1]
Then said, in accents half-reproving,
"Why hast thou been a foe to loving?"

ODE XXXII.[2]

STREW me a fragrant bed of leaves,
Where lotus with the myrtle weaves;
And while in luxury's dream I sink,
Let me the balm of Bacchus drink!
In this sweet hour of revelry
Young Love shall my attendant be —
Drest for the task, with tunic round
His snowy neck and shoulders bound,
Himself shall hover by my side,
And minister the racy tide!

Oh, swift as wheels that kindling roll,
Our life is hurrying to the goal:
A scanty dust, to feed the wind,
Is all the trace 't will leave behind.
Then wherefore waste the rose's bloom
Upon the cold, insensate tomb?
Can flowery breeze, or odor's breath,

1 And fanning light his breezy pinion,
    Rescued my soul from death's dominion.

"The facility with which Cupid recovers him,
signifies that the sweets of love make us easily
forget any solicitudes which he may occasion."
— LA FOSSE.

2 We here have the poet, in his true attributes, reclining upon myrtles, with Cupid for
his cup-bearer. Some interpreters have ruined
the picture by making Ἔρως the name of his slave.
None but Love should fill the goblet of Anacreon. Sappho, in one of her fragments, has
assigned this office to Venus. Ἐλθὲ, Κύπρι,
χρυσείαισιν ἐν κυλίκεσσιν ἁβροῖς συμμεμιγμέ-
νον θαλίαισι νέκταρ οἰνοχοῦσα τούτοισι τοῖς
ἑταίροις ἐμοῖς γε καὶ σοῖς.

Which may be thus paraphrased: —

    Hither, Venus, queen of kisses,
    This shall be the night of blisses;
    This the night, to friendship dear,
    Thou shalt be our Hebe here.
    Fill the golden brimmer high,
    Let it sparkle like thine eye;
    Bid the rosy current gush,
    Let it mantle like thy blush.
    Goddess, hast thou e'er above
    Seen a feast so rich in love?
    Not a soul that is not mine!
    Not a soul that is not thine!

"Compare with this ode [says the German
commentator] the beautiful poem in Ramler's
'Lyr. Blumenlese,' lib. iv. p. 296., 'Amor als
Diener.'"

Affect the still, cold sense of death?
Oh no; I ask no balm to steep
With fragrant tears my bed of sleep:
But now, while every pulse is glowing,
Now let me breathe the balsam flowing;
Now let the rose, with blush of fire,
Upon my brow in sweets expire;
And bring the nymph whose eye hath
        power
To brighten even death's cold hour.
Yes, Cupid! ere my shade retire,
To join the blest elysian choir,
With wine, and love, and social cheer,
I 'll make my own elysium here!

ODE XXXIII.[3]

'T WAS noon of night, when round the
        pole
The sullen Bear is seen to roll;
And mortals, wearied with the day,
Are slumbering all their cares away:
An infant, at that dreary hour,
Came weeping to my silent bower,
And waked me with a piteous prayer,
To shield him from the midnight air.
"And who art thou," I waking cry,
"That bid'st my blissful visions fly?"[4]
"Ah, gentle sire!" the infant said,
"In pity take me to thy shed;
Nor fear deceit: a lonely child
I wander o'er the gloomy wild.
Chill drops the rain, and not a ray
Illumes the drear and misty way!"

I heard the baby's tale of woe;
I heard the bitter night-winds blow;
And sighing for his piteous fate,
I trimmed my lamp and oped the gate.

3 M. Bernard, the author of "L'Art d'aimer,"
has written a ballet called "Les Surprises de
l'Amour," in which the subject of the third en-
trée is Anacreon, and the story of this ode suggests one of the scenes. — Œuvres de Bernard,
Anac. scene 4.

The German annotator refers us here to an
imitation by Uz, lib. iii., "Amor und sein
Bruder;" and a poem of Kleist, "Die Heil-
ung." La Fontaine has translated, or rather
imitated, this ode.

4 "And who art thou," I waking cry,
    "That bid'st my blissful visions fly?"

Anacreon appears to have been a voluptuary
even in dreaming, by the lively regret which he
expresses at being disturbed from his visionary
enjoyments. See the Odes x. and xxxvii.

'T was Love! the little wandering sprite,[1]
His pinion sparkled through the night.
I knew him by his bow and dart;
I knew him by my fluttering heart.
Fondly I take him in, and raise
The dying embers' cheering blaze;
Press from his dank and clinging hair
The crystals of the freezing air,
And in my hand and bosom hold
His little fingers thrilling cold.

And now the embers' genial ray
Had warmed his anxious fears away;
" I pray thee," said the wanton child,
(My bosom trembled as he smiled,)
" I pray thee let me try my bow,
For through the rain I 've wandered so,
That much I fear the midnight shower
Has injured its elastic power."
The fatal bow the urchin drew;
Swift from the string the arrow flew;
As swiftly flew as glancing flame,
And to my inmost spirit came!
" Fare thee well," I heard him say,
As laughing wild he winged away;
" Fare thee well, for now I know
The rain has not relaxt my bow;
It still can send a thrilling dart,
As thou shalt own with all thy heart!"

ODE XXXIV.[a]

Oh thou, of all creation blest,
Sweet insect, that delight'st to rest
Upon the wild wood's leafy tops,
To drink the dew that morning drops,

1 'T was Love! the little wandering sprite, etc.

See the beautiful description of Cupid, by
Moschus, in his first idyl.

2 In a Latin ode addressed to the grasshopper,
Rapin has preserved some of the thoughts of
our author: —

> *O quæ virenti graminis in toro,*
> *cicada, blande sidis, et herbidos*
>   *saltus oberras, otiosos*
>   *ingeniosa ciere cantus.*
> *seu forte adultis floribus incubas,*
> *cæli caducis ebria fletibus,* etc.

Oh thou, that on the grassy bed
Which Nature's vernal hand has spread,
Reclinest soft, and tunest thy song,
The dewy herbs and leaves among!
Whether thou lyest on springing flowers,
Drunk with the balmy morning-showers,
Or, etc.

See what Licetus says about grasshoppers,
cap. 93. and 185.

And chirp thy song with such a glee,[3]
That happiest kings may envy thee.
Whatever decks the velvet field,
Whate'er the circling seasons yield,
Whatever buds, whatever blows,
For thee it buds, for thee it grows.
Nor yet art thou the peasant's fear,
To him thy friendly notes are dear;
For thou art mild as matin dew;
And still, when summer's flowery hue
Begins to paint the bloomy plain,
We hear thy sweet prophetic strain;
Thy sweet prophetic strain we hear,
And bless the notes and thee revere!
The Muses love thy shrilly tone;[4]
Apollo calls thee all his own;
'T was he who gave that voice to thee,
'T is he who tunes thy minstrelsy.

Unworn by age's dim decline,
The fadeless blooms of youth are thine.
Melodious insect, child of earth,[5]
In wisdom mirthful, wise in mirth;
Exempt from every weak decay,
That withers vulgar frames away;

3 And chirp thy song with such a glee, etc.

" Some authors have affirmed [says Madame
Dacier], that it is only male grasshoppers which
sing, and that the females are silent; and on
this circumstance is founded a bon-mot of Xen-
archus, the comic poet, who says, εἶτ' εἰσὶν οἱ
τέττιγες οὐκ εὐδαίμονες, ὧν ταῖς γυναιξὶν οὐδ'
ὅτι οὖν φωνῆς ἔνι; ‘are not the grasshoppers
happy in having dumb wives?'" This note is
originally Henry Stephen's; but I choose
rather to make a lady my authority for it.

4 The Muses love thy shrilly tone; etc.

Phile, de Animal. Proprietat. calls this insect
Μούσαις φίλος, the darling of the Muses; and
Μουσῶν ὄρνιν, the bird of the Muses; and we
find Plato compared for his eloquence to the grasshopper, in the following punning lines of Timon,
preserved by Diogenes Laertius: —

τῶν πάντων δ' ἡγεῖτο πλατύστατος, ἀλλ' ἀγορήτης
ἡδυεπής τέττιξιν ἰσόγραφος, οἱ θ' Ἑκαδήμου
δένδρει ἐφεζόμενοι ὄπα λειριόεσσαν ἱεῖσι.

This last line is borrowed from Homer's Iliad,
γ, where there occurs the very same simile.

5 Melodious insect, child of earth.

Longepierre has quoted the two first lines of
an epigram of Antipater, from the first book of
the " Anthologia," where he prefers the grasshopper to the swan: —

ἀρκεῖ τέττιγας μεθύσαι δρόσος, ἀλλὰ πιόντες
ἀείδειν κύκνων εἰσὶ γεγωνότεροι.

In dew, that drops from morning's wings,
The gay Cicada sipping floats;
And, drunk with dew, his matin sings
Sweeter than any cygnet's notes.

With not a drop of blood to stain
The current of thy purer vein;
So blest an age is past by thee,
Thou seem'st — a little deity!

ODE XXXV.[1]

CUPID once upon a bed
Of roses laid his weary head;
Luckless urchin, not to see

1 Theocritus has imitated this beautiful ode
in his nineteenth idyl; but is very inferior, I
think, to his original, in delicacy of point and
naïveté of expression. Spenser, in one of his
smaller compositions, has sported more diffusely
on the same subject. The poem to which I
allude, begins thus: —

Upon a day, as Love lay sweetly slumbering
    All in his mother's lap;
A gentle bee, with his loud trumpet murmuring,
    About him flew by hap, etc.

In Almeloveen's collection of epigrams, there
is one by Luxorius, correspondent somewhat
with the turn of Anacreon, where Love complains
to his mother of being wounded by a rose.
The ode before us is the very flower of simplicity. The infantine complainings of the little
god, and the natural and impressive reflections
which they draw from Venus, are beauties of inimitable grace. I may be pardoned, perhaps,
for introducing here another of Menage's Anacreontics, not for its similitude to the subject of
this ode, but for some faint traces of the same
natural simplicity, which it appears to me to
have preserved: —

      Ἔρως ποτ' ἐν χορείαις
      τῶν παρθενῶν ἀωτον,
      τὴν μοι φιλὴν Κορίνναν,
      ὡς εἶδεν, ὡς πρὸς αὐτὴν
      προσέδραμε· τραχήλω
      διδύμας τε χείρας ἅπτων
      φιλεῖ με, μῆτερ, εἶπε.
      καλουμένη Κορίννα,
      μῆτηρ, ἐρυθριάζει,
      ὡς παρθένος μὲν οὖσα.
      κ' αὐτὸς δὲ δυσχεραίνων,
      ὡς ὄμμασι πλανηθείς,
      Ἔρως ἐρυθριάζει.
      ἐγὼ, δὲ οἱ παραστάς,
      μὴ δυσχέραινέ, φημι.
      Κύπριν τε καὶ Κορίνναν
      διαγνῶσαι οὐκ ἔχουσι
      καὶ οἱ βλέποντες ὀξύ.

As dancing o'er the enamelled plain,
The floweret of the virgin train,
My soul's Corinna lightly played,
Young Cupid saw the graceful maid;
He saw, and in a moment flew,
And round her neck his arms he threw;
Saying, with smiles of infant joy,
"Oh! kiss me, mother, kiss thy boy!"
Unconscious of a mother's name,
The modest virgin blushed with shame!
And angry Cupid, scarce believing
That vision could be so deceiving —
Thus to mistake his Cyprian dame!
It made even Cupid blush with shame.

Within the leaves a slumbering bee;
The bee awaked — with anger wild
The bee awaked, and stung the child.
Loud and piteous are his cries;
To Venus quick he runs, he flies;
"Oh mother!—I am wounded through —
I die with pain — in sooth I do!
Stung by some little angry thing,
Some serpent on a tiny wing —
A bee it was — for once, I know,
I heard a rustic call it so."
Thus he spoke, and she the while
Heard him with a soothing smile;
Then said, "My infant, if so much
Thou feel the little wild-bee's touch,
How must the heart, ah, Cupid! be,
The hapless heart that 's stung by thee!"

ODE XXXVI.[2]

IF hoarded gold possest the power
To lengthen life's too fleeting hour,
And purchase from the hand of death
A little span, a moment's breath,
How I would love the precious ore!
And every hour should swell my store;
That when Death came, with shadowy
          pinion,
To waft me to his bleak dominion,[3]
I might, by bribes, my doom delay,
And bid him call some distant day.
But, since, not all earth's golden store
Can buy for us one bright hour more,

    "Be not ashamed, my boy," I cried,
    For I was lingering by his side;
    "Corinna and thy lovely mother,
    Believe me, are so like each other,
    That clearest eyes are oft betrayed,
    And take thy Venus for the maid."

Zitto, in his "Cappriciosi Pensieri," has given
a translation of this ode of Anacreon.

2 Fontenelle has translated this ode, in his
dialogue between Anacreon and Aristotle in the
shades, where, on weighing the merits of both
these personages, he bestows the prize of wisdom upon the poet.
    "The German imitators of this ode are, Les-
sing, in his poem, 'Gestern Brüder,' etc.; Gleim,
in the ode, 'An den Tod;' and Schmidt, in 'Der
Poet.' Blumenl., Gotting. 1783, p. 7." — DEGEN.

3 That when Death came, with shadowy pinion,
    To waft me to his bleak dominion, etc.

The commentators, who are so fond of disputing *de lanâ caprinâ*, have been very busy on
the authority of the phrase ἱν' ἂν θανεῖν ἐπέλθῃ.
The reading of ἱν' ἂν Θάνατος ἐπέλθῃ, which
De Medenbach proposes in his "Amœnitates
Literariæ," was already hinted by Le Fèvre,
who seldom suggests any thing worth notice.

Why should we vainly mourn our fate,
Or sigh at life's uncertain date?
Nor wealth nor grandeur can illume
The silent midnight of the tomb.
No — give to others hoarded treasures —
Mine be the brilliant round of pleasures;
The goblet rich, the board of friends,
Whose social souls the goblet blends;[1]
And mine, while yet I 've life to live,
Those joys that love alone can give.

ODE XXXVII.[2]

'T was night, and many a circling bowl
Had deeply warmed my thirsty soul;
As lulled in slumber I was laid,
Bright visions o'er my fancy played.
With maidens, blooming as the dawn,
I seemed to skim the opening lawn;
Light, on tiptoe bathed in dew,
We flew, and sported as we flew!

Some ruddy striplings, who lookt on —
With cheeks, that like the wine-god's
    shone,

---

1 The goblet rich, the board of friends,
  Whose social souls the goblet blends.

This communion of friendship, which sweetened the bowl of Anacreon, has not been forgotten by the author of the following scholium,
where the blessings of life are enumerated with
proverbial simplicity. — 'ὑγιαίνειν μὲν ἄριστον
ἀνδρὶ θνητῷ. δεύτερον δὲ, καλὸν φυὴν γένεσθαι.
τὸ τρίτον δὲ, πλουτεῖν ἀδολώς. καὶ τὸ τέταρτον
συνέβαν μετὰ τῶν φίλων.

Of mortal blessing here the first is health,
And next those charms by which the eye we
  move;
The third is wealth, unwounding guiltless wealth,
And then, sweet intercourse with those we
  love!

2 " Compare with this ode the beautiful poem
' Der Traum ' of Uz." — DEGEN.

Le Fèvre, in a note upon this ode, enters into
an elaborate and learned justification of drunken-
ness; and this is probably the cause of the severe
reprehension which he appears to have suffered
for his Anacreon. "*Fuit olim fateor* [says he
in a note upon Longinus], *cum Sapphonem ama-
bam. Sed ex quo illa me perditissima fœmina
pene miserum perdidit cum sceleratissimo suo
congerrone,* (*Anacreontem dico, si nescis, Lec-
tor,*) *noli sperare,*" etc. He adduces on this ode
the authority of Plato, who allowed ebriety, at the
Dionysian festivals, to men arrived at their forti-
eth year. He likewise quotes the following line
from Alexis, which he says no one, who is not
totally ignorant of the world, can hesitate to
confess the truth of : —

οὐδεὶς φιλοπότης ἐστὶν ἄνθρωπος κακός.

" No lover of drinking was ever a vicious man."

Saw me chasing, free and wild,
These blooming maids, and slyly smiled;
Smiled indeed with wanton glee,
Though none could doubt they envied me.
And still I flew — and now had caught
The panting nymphs, and fondly thought
To gather from each rosy lip
A kiss that Jove himself might sip —
When sudden all my dream of joys,
Blushing nymphs and laughing boys,
All were gone![3] — " Alas!" I said,
Sighing for the illusion fled,
" Again, sweet sleep, that scene restore,
Oh! let me dream it o'er and o'er!"[4]

ODE XXXVIII.[5]

Let us drain the nectared bowl,
Let us raise the song of soul
To him, the god who loves so well
The nectared bowl, the choral swell;
The god who taught the sons of earth
To thrid the tangled dance of mirth;
Him, who was nurst with infant Love,
And cradled in the Paphian grove;
Him, that the snowy Queen of Charms
So oft has fondled in her arms.[6]

---

3 When sudden all my dream of joys,
  Blushing nymphs and laughing boys,
  All were gone!

" Nonnus says of Bacchus, almost in the same
words that Anacreon uses, —

ἐγρόμενος δὲ
παρθένον οὐκ ἐκίχησε, καὶ ἤθελεν αὖθις ἰαύειν."

Waking, he lost the phantom's charms,
The nymph had faded from his arms;
Again to slumber he essayed,
Again to clasp the shadowy maid.
           LONGEPIERRE.

4 " Again, sweet sleep, that scene restore,
  Oh! let me dream it o'er and o'er!"

Doctor Johnson, in his preface to Shakspeare,
animadverting upon the commentators of that
poet, who pretended, in every little coincidence
of thought, to detect an imitation of some ancient poet, alludes in the following words to the
line of Anacreon before us : " I have been told
that when Caliban, after a pleasing dream, says,
' I cried to sleep again,' the author imitates Anacreon, who had, like any other man, the same
wish on the same occasion."

5 " Compare with this beautiful ode to Bacchus the verses of Hagedorn, lib. v., ' Das Ge-
sellschaftliche;' and of Bürger, p. 51, etc. —
DEGEN.

6 Him, that the snowy Queen of Charms
  So oft has fondled in her arms.

Robertellus, upon the epithalamium of Catullus, mentions an ingenious derivation of Cythe-

Oh 't is from him the transport flows,
Which sweet intoxication knows;
With him, the brow forgets its gloom,
And brilliant graces learn to bloom.

Behold! — my boys a goblet bear,
Whose sparkling foam lights up the air.
Where are now the tear, the sigh?
To the winds they fly, they fly!
Grasp the bowl; in nectar sinking,
Man of sorrow, drown thy thinking!
Say, can the tears we lend to thought
In life's account avail us aught?
Can we discern with all our lore,
The path we 've yet to journey o'er?
Alas, alas, in ways so dark,
'T is only wine can strike a spark![1]

Then let me quaff the foamy tide,
And through the dance meandering glide;
Let me imbibe the spicy breath
Of odors chafed to fragrant death;
Or from the lips of love inhale
A more ambrosial, richer gale!
To hearts that court the phantom Care,
Let him retire and shroud him there;
While we exhaust the nectared bowl,
And swell the choral song of soul
To him, the god who loves so well
The nectared bowl, the choral swell!

ræa, the name of Venus, παρὰ τὸ κεύθειν τοὺς
ἔρωτας, which seems to hint that "Love's fairy
favors are lost, when not concealed."

[1] Alas, alas, in ways so dark,
   'T is only wine can strike a spark!

The brevity of life allows arguments for the
voluptuary as well as the moralist. Among
many parallel passages which Longepierre has
adduced, I shall content myself with this epigram from the " Anthologia ": —

λουσάμενοι, Προδίκη, πυκασώμεθα, καὶ τὸν
   ἄκρατον
ἕλκωμεν, κύλικας μείζονας ἀράμενοι.
ῥαῖος ὁ χαιρόντων ἐστὶ βίος. εἶτα τὰ λοῖπα
γῆρας κωλύσει, καὶ τὸ τέλος θάνατος.

Of which the following is a paraphrase : —

Let 's fly, my love, from noonday's beam,
To plunge us in yon cooling stream ;
Then, hastening to the festal bower,
We 'll pass in mirth the evening hour;
'T is thus our age of bliss shall fly,
As sweet, though passing as that sigh,
Which seems to whisper o'er your lip,
" Come, while you may, of rapture sip."
For age will steal the graceful form,
Will chill the pulse, while throbbing warm ;
And death — alas! that hearts, which thrill
Like yours and mine, should e'er be still!

ODE XXXIX.

How I love the festive boy,
Tripping through the dance of joy!
How I love the mellow sage,
Smiling through the veil of age!
And whene'er this man of years
In the dance of joy appears,
Snows may o'er his head be flung,
But his heart — his heart is young.[2]

ODE XL.

I know that Heaven hath sent me here,
To run this mortal life's career;
The scenes which I have journeyed o'er,
Return no more — alas! no more ;
And all the path I 've yet to go,
I neither know nor ask to know.
Away, then, wizard Care, nor think
Thy fetters round this soul to link;
Never can heart that feels with me
Descend to be a slave to thee![3]
And oh! before the vital thrill,
Which trembles at my heart, is still,

[2] Snows may o'er his head be flung,
   But his heart — his heart is young.

Saint Pavin makes the same distinction in a
sonnet to a young girl.

Je sais bien que les destinées
Ont mal compassée nos années ;
Ne regardez que mon amour ;
Peut-être en serez vous émue.
Il est jeune et n'est que du jour,
Belle Iris, que je vous ai vu.

Fair and young thou bloomest now,
   And I full many a year have told ;
But read the heart and not the brow,
   Thou shalt not find my love is old.

My love 's a child ; and thou canst say
   How much his little age may be,
For he was born the very day
   When first I set my eyes on thee!

[3] Never can heart that feels with me
   Descend to be a slave to thee!

Longepierre quotes here an epigram from the
" Anthologia," on account of the similarity of a
particular phrase. Though by no means Anacreontic, it is marked by an interesting simplicity
which has induced me to paraphrase it, and may
atone for its intrusion.

ἐλπὶς καὶ σὺ τύχη μέγα χαίρετε. τὸν λίμεν' εὗρον.
οὐδὲν ἐμοὶ χ' ὑμῖν, παίζετε τοὺς μετ' ἐμέ.

At length to Fortune, and to you,
Delusive Hope! a last adieu.
The charm that once beguiled is o'er,
And I have reached my destined shore.
Away, away, your flattering arts
May now betray some simpler hearts,
And you will smile at their believing,
And they shall weep at your deceiving!

I 'll gather Joy's luxuriant flowers,
And gild with bliss my fading hours;
Bacchus shall bid my winter bloom,
And Venus dance me to the tomb![1]

ODE XLI.

WHEN Spring adorns the dewy scene,
How sweet to walk the velvet green,
And hear the west wind's gentle sighs,
As o'er the scented mead it flies!
How sweet to mark the pouting vine,
Ready to burst in tears of wine;
And with some maid, who breathes but
love,
To walk, at noontide, through the grove,[2]
Or sit in some cool, green recess —
Oh, is not this true happiness?

ODE XLII.[3]

YES, be the glorious revel mine,
Where humor sparkles from the wine.
Around me, let the youthful choir
Respond to my enlivening lyre;

1 Bacchus shall bid my winter bloom,
And Venus dance me to the tomb!

The same commentator has quoted an epitaph,
written upon our poet by Julian, in which he
makes him promulgate the precepts of good fellowship even from the tomb.

πολλάκι μὲν τόδ' ἄεισα, καὶ ἐκ τύμβου δὲ βοήσω,
πίνετε, πρὶν ταύτην ἀμφιβάλησθε κόνιν.

This lesson oft in life I sung,
And from my grave I still shall cry,
" Drink, mortal, drink, while time is young,
Ere death has made thee cold as I."

2 And with some maid, who breathes but love,
To walk, at noontide, through the grove.

Thus Horace : —

> Quid habes illius, illius
> quæ spirabat amores,
> quæ me surpuerat mihi.
>   Lib. iv. Carm. 13.

And does there then remain but this,
And hast thou lost each rosy ray
Of her, who breathed the soul of bliss,
And stole me from myself away?

3 The character of Anacreon is here very
strikingly depicted. His love of social, harmonized pleasures, is expressed with a warmth,
amiable and endearing. Among the epigrams
imputed to Anacreon is the following; it is the
only one worth translation, and it breathes the
same sentiments with this ode : —

οὐ φίλος, ὃς κρητῆρι παρὰ πλέῳ οἰνοποτάζων,
νείκεα καὶ πολεμὸν δακρυόεντα λέγει.
ἀλλ' ὅστις Μουσεών τε, καὶ ἀγλαὰ δῶρ' Ἀφροδίτης
συμμίσγων, ἐρατῆς μνήσκεται εὐφροσύνης.

When to the lip the brimming cup is prest,
And hearts are all afloat upon its stream,

And while the red cup foams along,
Mingle in soul as well as song.
Then, while I sit, with flowerets crowned,
To regulate the goblet's round,
Let but the nymph, our banquet's pride,
Be seated smiling by my side,
And earth has not a gift or power
That I would envy, in that hour.
Envy! — oh never let its blight
Touch the gay hearts met here to-night.
Far hence be slander's sidelong wounds,
Nor harsh dispute, nor discord's sounds
Disturb a scene, where all should be
Attuned to peace and harmony.

Come, let us hear the harp's gay note
Upon the breeze inspiring float,
While round us, kindling into love,
Young maidens through the light dance
move.
Thus blest with mirth, and love, and
peace,
Sure such a life should never cease!

ODE XLIII.

WHILE our rosy fillets shed
Freshness o'er each fervid head,
With many a cup and many a smile
The festal moments we beguile.
And while the harp, impassioned, flings
Tuneful rapture from its strings, [4]

Then banish from my board the unpolished guest,
Who makes the feats of war his barbarous
theme.
But bring the man, who o'er his goblet wreathes
The Muse's laurel with the Cyprian flower;
Oh! give me him, whose soul expansive breathes
And blends refinement with the social hour.

4 And while the harp, impassioned, flings
Tuneful rapture from its strings, etc.

Respecting the barbiton a host of authorities
may be collected, which, after all, leave us ignorant of the nature of the instrument. There is
scarcely any point upon which we are so totally
uninformed as the music of the ancients. The
authors * extant upon the subject are, I imagine,
little understood ; and certainly if one of their
moods was a progression by quarter-tones, which
we are told was the nature of the enharmonic
scale, simplicity was by no means the characteristic of their melody ; for this is a nicety of
progression of which modern music is not susceptible.
The invention of the barbiton is, by Athenæus,
attributed to Anacreon. See his fourth book,
where it is called τὸ εὕρημα τοῦ Ἀνακρέοντος.
Neanthes of Cyzicus, as quoted by Gyraldus, as-

* Collected by Meibomius.

Some airy nymph, with graceful bound,
Keeps measure to the music's sound;
Waving, in her snowy hand,
The leafy Bacchanalian wand,
Which, as the tripping wanton flies,
Trembles all over to her sighs.
A youth the while, with loosened hair,
Floating on the listless air,
Sings, to the wild harp's tender tone,
A tale of woes, alas, his own;
And oh, the sadness in his sigh,
As o'er his lip the accents die! [1]
Never sure on earth has been
Half so bright, so blest a scene.
It seems as Love himself had come
To make this spot his chosen home; [2] —
And Venus, too, with all her wiles,
And Bacchus, shedding rosy smiles,
All, all are here, to hail with me
The Genius of Festivity! [3]

ODE XLIV.[4]

Buds of roses, virgin flowers,
Culled from Cupid's balmy bowers,

serts the same. *Vide* Chabot, in Horat. on the
words *Lesboum barbiton*, in the first ode.

1 And oh, the sadness in his sigh,
   As o'er his lip the accents die!

Longepierre has quoted here an epigram from
the "Anthologia" : —

κούρη τις μ' ἐφίλησε ποθέσπερα χείλεσιν ὑγροῖς.
νέκταρ ἔην τὸ φίλημα. τὸ γὰρ στόμα νέκταρος
   ἔπνει.
νῦν μεθύω τὸ φίλημα, πολὺν τὸν ἔρωτα πεπωκώς.

Of which the following paraphrase may give
some idea : —

The kiss that she left on my lip,
   Like a dew-drop shall lingering lie
'T was nectar she gave me to sip,
   'T was nectar I drank in her sigh.

From the moment she printed that kiss,
   Nor reason, nor rest has been mine;
My whole soul has been drunk with the bliss,
   And feels a delirium divine!

2 It seems as Love himself had come
   To make this spot his chosen home.

The introduction of these deities to the festival is merely allegorical. Madame Dacier thinks
that the poet describes a masquerade, where
these deities were personated by the company in
masks. The translation will conform with either
idea.

3 All, all are here, to hail with me
   The Genius of Festivity!

Κῶμος, the deity or genius of mirth. Philostratus, in the third of his pictures, gives a very
lively description of this god.

4 This spirited poem is a eulogy on the rose;

In the bowl of Bacchus steep,
Till with crimson drops they weep.
Twine the rose, the garland twine,
Every leaf distilling wine;
Drink and smile, and learn to think
That we were born to smile and drink.
Rose, thou art the sweetest flower
That ever drank the amber shower;
Rose, thou art the fondest child
Of dimpled Spring, the wood-nymph
   wild.
Even the Gods, who walk the sky,
Are amorous of thy scented sigh.
Cupid, too, in Paphian shades,
His hair with rosy fillet braids,
When with the blushing, sister Graces,
The wanton winding dance he traces.[5]
Then bring me, showers of roses bring,
And shed them o'er me while I sing,
Or while, great Bacchus, round thy
   shrine,
Wreathing my brow with rose and vine,
I lead some bright nymph through the
   dance,[6]
Commingling soul with every glance!

ODE XLV.

Within this goblet, rich and deep,
I cradle all my woes to sleep.
Why should we breathe the sigh of fear,
Or pour the unavailing tear?
For death will never heed the sigh,
Nor soften at the tearful eye;
And eyes that sparkle, eyes that weep,
Must all alike be sealed in sleep.

and again, in the fifty-fifth ode, we shall find our
author rich in the praises of that flower. In a
fragment of Sappho, in the romance of Achilles
Tatius, to which Barnes refers us, the rose is
fancifully styled "the eye of flowers;" and the
same poetess, in another fragment, calls the favors of the Muse "the roses of Pieria." See
the notes on the fifty-fifth ode.

"Compare with this ode [says the German
annotator] the beautiful ode of Uz, 'Die Rose.'"

5 When with the blushing, sister Graces,
   The wanton winding dance he traces.

"This sweet idea of Love dancing with the
Graces, is almost peculiar to Anacreon." —
Degen.

6 I lead some bright nymph through the dance,
   etc.

The epithet βαθύκολπος, which he gives to the
nymph, is literally "full-bosomed."

Then let us never vainly stray,[1]
In search of thorns, from pleasure's way;
But wisely quaff the rosy wave,
Which Bacchus loves, which Bacchus
  gave;
And in the goblet, rich and deep,
Cradle our crying woes to sleep.

ODE XLVI.[2]

BEHOLD, the young, the rosy Spring,
Gives to the breeze her scented wing;
While virgin Graces, warm with May;
Fling roses o'er her dewy way.[3]

1 Then let us never vainly stray,
In search of thorns, from pleasure's way; etc.

I have thus endeavored to convey the meaning of *τί δὲ τὸν βίον πλάνωμαι*; according to
Regnier's paraphrase of the line : —

  E che val, fuor della strada
  Del piacere alma e gradita,
  Vaneggiare in questa vita?

2 The fastidious affectation of some commentators has denounced this ode as spurious. Degen pronounces the four last lines to be the
patch-work of some miserable versificator, and
Brunck condemns the whole ode. It appears to
me, on the contrary, to be elegantly graphical;
full of delicate expressions and luxuriant imagery. The abruptness of *ἰδὲ πῶς ἔαρος φανέντος*
is striking and spirited, and has been imitated
rather languidly by Horace : —

  Vides ut alta stet nive candidum
  Soracte ——

The imperative *ἰδέ* is infinitely more impressive; as in Shakspeare, —

  But look, the morn, in russet mantle clad,
  Walks o'er the dew of yon high eastern hill.

There is a simple and poetical description
of Spring, in Catullus's beautiful farewell to Bithynia. Carm. 44.
Barnes conjectures, in his life of our poet,
that this ode was written after he had returned
from Athens, to settle in his paternal seat at
Teos; where, in a little villa at some distance
from the city, commanding a view of the Ægean
Sea and the islands, he contemplated the beauties
of nature and enjoyed the felicities of retirement.
Vide Barnes, in "Anac. Vita," § xxxv. This
supposition, however unauthenticated, forms a
pleasing association, which renders the poem
more interesting.
Chevreau says, that Gregory Nazianzenus
has paraphrased somewhere this description of
Spring; but I cannot meet with it. See Chevreau, "Œuvres Mêlées."
"Compare with this ode [says Degen] the
verses of Hagedorn, book fourth, 'Der Früh-
ling,' and book fifth, 'Der Mai.'"

3 While virgin Graces, warm with May,
Fling roses o'er her dewy way.

De Pauw reads, *Χάριτας ῥόδα βρύουσιν*, "the
roses display their graces." This is not unin-

The murmuring billows of the deep
Have languished into silent sleep;[4]
And mark ! the flitting sea-birds lave
Their plumes in the reflecting wave;
While cranes from hoary winter fly
To flutter in a kinder sky.
Now the genial star of day
Dissolves the murky clouds away;
And cultured field, and winding stream,[5]
Are freshly glittering in his beam.

Now the earth prolific swells
With leafy buds and flowery bells;
Gemming shoots the olive twine,
Clusters ripe festoon the vine;
All along the branches creeping,
Through the velvet foliage peeping,
Little infant fruits we see,
Nursing into luxury.

ODE XLVII.

'T IS true, my fading years decline,
Yet can I quaff the brimming wine,
As deep as any stripling fair,
Whose cheeks the flush of morning wear;
And if, amidst the wanton crew,
I 'm called to wind the dance's clue,
Then shalt thou see this vigorous hand,
Not faltering on the Bacchant's wand,
But brandishing a rosy flask,[6]
The only thyrsus e'er I 'll ask ![7]

Let those, who pant for Glory's
  charms,

genious; but we lose by it the beauty of the
personification, to the boldness of which Regnier
has rather frivolously objected.

4 The murmuring billows of the deep
Have languished into silent sleep ; etc.

It has been justly remarked, that the liquid
flow of the line *ἀπαλύνεται γαλήνη* is perfectly
expressive of the tranquillity which it describes.

5 And cultured field, and winding stream, etc.

By *βροτῶν ἔργα* "the works of men" (says
Baxter), he means cities, temples, and towns,
which are then illuminated by the beams of the
sun.

6 But brandishing a rosy flask, etc.

ἀσκός was a kind of leathern vessel for wine,
very much in use, as should seem by the proverb
ἀσκὸς καὶ θύλακος, which was applied to those
who were intemperate in eating and drinking.
This proverb is mentioned in some verses quoted
by Athenæus, from the Hesione of Alexis.

7 The only thyrsus e'er I 'll ask !

Phornutus assigns as a reason for the conse-

Embrace her in the field of arms;
While my inglorious, placid soul
Breathes not a wish beyond this bowl.
Then fill it high, my ruddy slave,
And bathe me in its brimming wave.
For though my fading years decay,
Though manhood's prime hath past away,
Like old Silenus, sire divine, .
With blushes borrowed from my wine,
I 'll wanton mid the dancing train,
And live my follies o'er again !

ODE XLVIII.

When my thirsty soul I steep,
Every sorrow 's lulled to sleep.
Talk of monarchs ! I am then
Richest, happiest, first of men;
Careless o'er my cup I sing,
Fancy makes me more than king;
Gives me wealthy Crœsus' store,
Can I, can I wish for more?
On my velvet couch reclining,
Ivy leaves my brow entwining,[1]
While my soul expands with glee,
What are kings and crowns to me?
If before my feet they lay,
I would spurn them all away !
Arm ye, arm ye, men of might,
Hasten to the sanguine fight;[2]
But let *me*, my budding vine !
Spill no other blood than thine.
Yonder brimming goblet see,
That alone shall vanquish me —
Who think it better, wiser far
To fall in banquet than in war.

ODE XLIX.[3]

When Bacchus, Jove's immortal boy,

cration of the thyrsus to Bacchus, that inebriety often renders the support of a stick very necessary.

    1 Ivy leaves my brow entwining, etc.

"The ivy was consecrated to Bacchus [says Montfaucon], because he formerly lay hid under that tree, or, as others will have it, because its leaves resemble those of the vine." Other reasons for its consecration, and the use of it in garlands at banquets, may be found in Longepierre, Barnes, etc.

    2 Arm ye, arm ye, men of might,
      Hasten to the sanguine fight.

I have adopted the interpretation of Regnier and others : —

    Altri segua Marte fero ;
    Che sol Bacco è 'l mio conforto.

    3 This, the preceding ode, and a few more of

The rosy harbinger of joy,
Who, with the sunshine of the bowl,
Thaws the winter of our soul[4] —
When to my inmost core he glides,
And bathes it with his ruby tides,
A flow of joy, a lively heat,
Fires my brain, and wings my feet,
Calling up round me visions known
To lovers of the bowl alone.

Sing, sing of love, let music's sound
In melting cadence float around,
While, my young Venus, thou and I
Responsive to its murmurs sigh.
Then, waking from our blissful trance,
Again we 'll sport, again we 'll dance.

ODE L.[5]

When wine I quaff, before my eyes
Dreams of poetic glory rise;[6]

the same character, are merely *chansons à boire*, — the effusions probably of the moment of conviviality, and afterwards sung, we may imagine, with rapture throughout Greece. But that interesting association, by which they always recalled the convivial emotions that produced them, can now be little felt even by the most enthusiastic reader; and much less by a phlegmatic grammarian, who sees nothing in them but dialects and particles.

    4 Who, with the sunshine of the bowl,
      Thaws the winter of our soul — etc.

Λυαίος is the title which he gives to Bacchus in the original. It is a curious circumstance, that Plutarch mistook the name of Levi among the Jews for Λέυι (one of the bacchanal cries), and accordingly supposed that they worshipped Bacchus.

    5 Faber thinks this ode spurious; but, I believe, he is singular in his opinion. It has all the spirit of our author. Like the wreath which he presented in the dream, "it smells of Anacreon."

The form of the original is remarkable. It is a kind of song of seven quatrain stanzas, each beginning with the line, —

    ὅτ' ἐγὼ πίω τὸν οἶνον.

The first stanza alone is incomplete, consisting of but three lines.

"Compare with this poem [says Degen] the verses of Hagedorn, lib. v., ' Der Wein,' where that divine poet has wantoned in the praises of wine."

    6 When wine I quaff, before my eyes
      Dreams of poetic glory rise.

"Anacreon is not the only one [says Longepierre] whom wine has inspired with poetry. We find an epigram in the first book of the "Anthologia," which begins thus : —

    οἶνός τοι χαρίεντι μέγας πέλει ἵππος ἀοιδῷ,
    ὕδωρ δὲ πίνων, καλὸν οὐ τέκοις ἔπος.

And freshened by the goblet's dews,
My soul invokes the heavenly Muse.
When wine I drink, all sorrow 's o'er;
I think of doubts and fears no more;
But scatter to the railing wind
Each gloomy phantom of the mind.
When I drink wine, the ethereal boy,
Bacchus himself, partakes my joy;
And while we dance through vernal bow-
ers,[1]
Whose every breath comes fresh from
flowers,
In wine he makes my senses swim,
Till the gale breathes of naught but him!

Again I drink, — and, lo, there seems
A calmer light to fill my dreams;
The lately ruffled wreath I spread
With steadier hand around my head;
Then take the lyre, and sing "how blest
The life of him who lives at rest!"
But then comes witching wine again,
With glorious woman in its train;
And, while rich perfumes round me rise,
That seem the breath of woman's sighs,
Bright shapes, of every hue and form,
Upon my kindling fancy swarm,
Till the whole world of beauty seems
To crowd into my dazzled dreams!
When thus I drink, my heart refines,
And rises as the cup declines;
Rises in the genial flow,
That none but social spirits know,
When, with young revellers, round the
bowl,

If with water you fill up your glasses,
  You 'll never write anything wise ;
For wine 's the true horse of Parnassus,
  Which carries a bard to the skies!

1 And while we dance through vernal bowers, etc.

If some of the translators had observed Doctor Trapp's caution, with regard to πολυάνθεσιν
μ' ἐν αὔραις, *Cave ne cœlum intelligas*, they would
not have spoiled the simplicity of Anacreon's
fancy, by such extravagant conceptions as the
following : —

Quand je bois, mon œil s'imagine
Que, dans un tourbillon plein de parfums divers,
Bacchus m'importe dans les airs,
  Rempli de sa liqueur divine.

Or this : —

  Indi mi mena
Mentre lieto ebro, deliro,
  Baccho in giro
    Per la vaga aura serena.

The old themselves grow young in soul![2]
Oh, when I drink, true joy is mine,
There 's bliss in every drop of wine.
All other blessings I have known,
I scarcely dared to call my own;
But this the Fates can ne'er destroy,
Till death o'ershadows all my joy.

ODE LI.[3]

FLY not thus my brow of snow,
Lovely wanton! fly not so.
Though the wane of age is mine,
Though youth's brilliant flush be thine,
Still I 'm doomed to sigh for thee,
Blest, if thou couldst sigh for me!
See, in yonder flowery braid,
Culled for thee, my blushing maid,[4]
How the rose, of orient glow,
Mingles with the lily's snow;
Mark, how sweet their tints agree,
Just, my girl, like thee and me!

2 When, with young revellers, round the bowl,
    The old themselves grow young in soul!

Subjoined to Gail's edition of Anacreon, we
find some curious letters upon the Θίασοι of the
ancients, which appeared in the French Journals.
At the opening of the Odéon in Paris, the managers of that spectacle requested Professor Gail
to give them some uncommon name for their
fêtes. He suggested the word "Thiase," which
was adopted ; but the *literati* of Paris questioned
the propriety of the term, and addressed their
criticisms to Gail through the medium of the
public prints.

3 Alberti has imitated this ode ; and Capi-
lupus, in the following epigram, has given a
version of it : —

Cur, Lalage, mea vita, meos contemnis amores ?
  cur fugis e nostro pulchra puella sinu ?
ne fugias, sint sparsa licet mea tempora canis,
  inque tuo roseus fulgeat ore color.
aspice ut intextas deceant quoque flore corollas
  candida purpureis lilia mista rosis.

Oh! why repel my soul's impassioned vow,
  And fly, belovèd maid, these longing arms ?
Is it, that wintry time has strewed my brow,
  While thine are all the summer's roseate
    charms?

See the rich garland culled in vernal weather,
  Where the young rosebud with the lily glows;
So, in Love's wreath we both may twine together,
  And I the lily be, and thou the rose.

4 See, in yonder flowery braid,
    Culled for thee, my blushing maid.

"In the same manner that Anacreon pleads
for the whiteness of his locks, from the beauty of
the color in garlands, a shepherd, in Theocritus, endeavors to recommend his black hair : —

ODE LII.[1]

AWAY, away, ye men of rules,
What have I to do with schools?
They 'd make me learn, they 'd make
    me think,
But would they make me love and drink?
Teach me this, and let me swim
My soul upon the goblet's brim;
Teach me this, and let me twine
Some fond, responsive heart to mine,[2]
For, age begins to blanch my brow,
I 've time for naught but pleasure now.

Fly, and cool my goblet's glow
At yonder fountain's gelid flow;
I 'll quaff, my boy, and calmly sink
This soul to slumber as I drink.
Soon, too soon, my jocund slave,
You 'll deck your master's grassy grave;
And there 's an end — for ah, you know
They drink but little wine below![3]

καὶ τὸ ἴον μέλαν ἐστὶ, καὶ ἅ γραπτὰ ὑάκινθος,
ἀλλ᾽ ἔμπας ἐν τοῖς στεφανοῖς τὰ πρῶτα λέγονται."
    LONGEPIERRE, BARNES, etc.

1 "This is doubtless the work of a more modern poet than Anacreon; for at the period when he lived rhetoricians were not known." — DEGEN.

Though this ode is found in the Vatican manuscript, I am much inclined to agree in this argument against its authenticity; for though the dawnings of the art of rhetoric might already have appeared, the first who gave it any celebrity was Corax of Syracuse, and he flourished in the century after Anacreon.

Our poet anticipated the ideas of Epicurus, in his aversion to the labors of learning, as well as his devotion to voluptuousness. Πᾶσαν παιδείαν μακάριοι φεύγετε, said the philosopher of the garden in a letter to Pythocles.

2 Teach me this, and let me twine
Some fond, responsive heart to mine.

By χρυσῆς Ἀφροδίτης here, I understand some beautiful girl, in the same manner that Λυαῖος is often used for wine. "Golden" is frequently an epithet of beauty. Thus in Virgil, *Venus aurea;* and in Propertius, *Cynthia aurea.* Tibullus, however, calls an old woman "golden."

The translation "d'Autori Anonimi," as usual, wantons on this passage of Anacreon : —

E m' insegni con piu rare
Forme accorte d' involare
A d amabile beltade
Il bel cinto d' onestade.

3 And there 's an end — for ah, you know
They drink but little wine below!

Thus Mainard : —

La Mort nous guette ; et quand ses lois
Nous ont enfermés une fois
Au sein d'une fosse profonde,
Adieu bons vins et bon répas ;

ODE LIII.

WHEN I behold the festive train
Of dancing youth, I 'm young again!
Memory wakes her magic trance,
And wings me lightly through the dance.
Come, Cybeba, smiling maid!
Cull the flower and twine the braid;
Bid the blush of summer's rose
Burn upon my forehead's snows;[4]
And let me, while the wild and young
Trip the mazy dance along,
Fling my heap of years away,
And be as wild, as young, as they.
Hither haste, some cordial soul!
Help to my lips the brimming bowl;
And you shall see this hoary sage
Forget at once his locks and age.
He still can chant the festive hymn,
He still can kiss the goblet's brim;[5]
As deeply quaff, as largely fill,
And play the fool right nobly still.

ODE LIV.[6]

METHINKS, the pictured bull we see
Is amorous Jove — it must be he!

Ma science ne trouve pas
Des cabarets en l'autre monde.

From Mainard, Gombauld, and De Cailly, old French poets, some of the best epigrams of the English language have been borrowed.

4 Bid the blush of summer's rose
Burn upon my forehead's snows; etc.

Licetus, in his "Hieroglyphica," quoting two of our poet's odes, where he calls to his attendants for garlands, remarks, "*Constat igitur floreas coronas poetis et potantibus in symposio convenire, non autem sapientibus et philosophiam affectantibus.*" — "It appears that wreaths of flowers were adapted for poets and revellers at banquets, but by no means became those who had pretensions to wisdom and philosophy." On this principle, in his 152d chapter, he discovers a refinement in Virgil, describing the garland of the poet Silenus, as fallen off; which distinguishes, he thinks, the divine intoxication of Silenus from that of common drunkards, who always wear their crowns while they drink. Such is the *labor ineptiarum* of commentators!

5 He still can kiss the goblet's brim; etc.

Wine is prescribed by Galen, as an excellent medicine for old men: "*Quod frigidos et humoribus expletos calefaciat,*" etc.; but Nature was Anacreon's physician.

There is a proverb in Eriphus, as quoted by Athenæus, which says, "that wine makes an old man dance, whether he will or not."

λόγος ἐστ᾽ ἀρχαῖος, οὐ κακῶς ἔχων,
οἶνον λέγουσι τοὺς γέροντας, ὦ πάτερ,
πείθειν χορέειν οὐ θέλοντας.

6 "This ode is written upon a picture which

How fondly blest he seems to bear
That fairest of Phœnician fair!
How proud he breasts the foamy tide,
And spurns the billowy surge aside!
Could any beast of vulgar vein,
Undaunted thus defy the main?
No: he descends from climes above,
He looks the God, he breathes of Jove![1]

ODE LV.[2]

WHILE we invoke the wreathed spring,

represented the rape of Europa." — MADAME
DACIER.

It may probably have been a description of
one of those coins, which the Sidonians struck
off in honor of Europa, representing a woman
carried across the sea by a bull. Thus Natalis
Comes, lib. VIII. cap. 23. "*Sidonii numismata
cum fœminâ tauri dorso insidente ac mare trans-
fretante cuderunt in ejus honorem.*" In the little treatise upon the goddess of Syria, attributed
very falsely to Lucian, there is mention of this
coin, and of a temple dedicated by the Sidonians
to Astarte, whom some, it appears, confounded
with Europa.

The poet Moschus has left a very beautiful
idyl on the story of Europa.

1 No: he descends from climes above,
He looks the God, he breathes of Jove!

Thus Moschus: —

κρύψε θεὸν καὶ τρέψε δέμας· καὶ γίνετο ταῦρος.

The God forgot himself, his heaven, for love,
And a bull's form belied the almighty Jove.

2 This ode is a brilliant panegyric on the rose.
" All antiquity [says Barnes] has produced nothing more beautiful."

From the idea of peculiar excellence, which
the ancients attached to this flower, arose a pretty
proverbial expression, used by Aristophanes, according to Suidas, ῥόδα μ' εἴρηκας, " You have
spoken roses," a phrase somewhat similar to the
dire des fleurettes of the French. In the same
idea of excellence originated, I doubt not, a very
curious application of the word ῥόδον, for which
the inquisitive reader may consult Gaulminus
upon the epithalamium of our poet, where it is
introduced in the romance of Theodorus. Muretus, in one of his elegies, calls his mistress his
rose: —

Jam te igitur rursus teneo, formosula, jam te
(*Quid trepidas?*) *teneo; jam, rosa, te teneo.*
Eleg. 8.

Now I again may clasp thee, dearest,
What is there now, on earth, thou fearest?
Again these longing arms infold thee,
Again, my rose, again I hold thee.

This, like most of the terms of endearment in
the modern Latin poets, is taken from Plautus;
they were vulgar and colloquial in his time, but
are among the elegancies of the modern Latinists.

Passeratius alludes to the ode before us, in
the beginning of his poem on the Rose: —

Resplendent rose! to thee we 'll sing;[3]
Resplendent rose, the flower of flowers,
Whose breath perfumes the Olympian
bowers;
Whose virgin blush, of chastened dye,
Enchants so much our mortal eye.
When pleasure's spring-tide season glows,
The Graces love to wreathe the rose;
And Venus, in its fresh-blown leaves,[4]
An emblem of herself perceives.
Oft hath the poet's magic tongue
The rose's fair luxuriance sung;[5]
And long the Muses, heavenly maids,
Have reared it in their tuneful shades.
When, at the early glance of morn,
It sleeps upon the glittering thorn,
'T is sweet to dare the tangled fence,
To cull the timid floweret thence,
And wipe with tender hand away
The tear that on its blushes lay!

*Carmine digna rosa est; vellem caneretur ut
illam*
Teius argutâ cecinit testudine vates.

3 Resplendent rose! to thee we 'll sing.

I have passed over the line σὺν ἑταίρει αὔξει
μέλπην, which is corrupt in this original reading,
and has been very little improved by the annotators. I should suppose it to be an interpola-
tion, if it were not for a line which occurs afterwards: φέρε δὴ φύσιν λέγωμεν.

4 And Venus, in its fresh-blown leaves, etc.

Belleau, in a note upon an old French poet,
quoting the original here ἀφροδισίων τ' ἄθυρμα,
translates it, *comme les délices et mignardises de
Venus.*

5 Oft hath the poet's magic tongue
The rose's fair luxuriance sung; etc.

The following is a fragment of the Lesbian
poetess. It is cited in the romance of Achilles
Tatius, who appears to have resolved the numbers into prose. Εἰ τοῖς ἄνθεσιν ἤθελεν ὁ Ζεὺς
ἐπιθεῖναι βασιλέα, τὸ ῥόδον ἂν τῶν ἀνθέων
ἐβασίλευε. γῆς ἐστι κόσμος, φυτῶν ἀγλάϊσμα,
ὀφθαλμὸς ἀνθέων, λείμωνος ἐρύθημα, κάλλος
ἄστραπτον Ἔρωτος πνεῖ, Ἀφροδίτην προξενεῖ,
εὐείδεσι φύλλοις κομᾷ, εὐκινήτοις πετάλοις
τρυφᾷ. τὸ πέταλον τῷ Ζεφύρῳ γελᾷ.

If Jove would give the leafy bowers
A queen for all their world of flowers,
The rose would be the choice of Jove,
And blush, the queen of every grove.
Sweetest child of weeping morning,
Gem, the vest of earth adorning,
Eye of gardens, light of lawns,
Nursling of soft summer dawns;
Love's own earliest sigh it breathes,
Beauty's brow with lustre wreathes,
And, to young Zephyr's warm caresses,
Spreads abroad its verdant tresses,
Till, blushing with the wanton's play,
Its cheek wears even a richer ray!

'T is sweet to hold the infant stems,
Yet dropping with Aurora's gems,
And fresh inhale the spicy sighs
That from the weeping buds arise.

When revel reigns, when mirth is high,
And Bacchus beams in every eye,
Our rosy fillets scent exhale,
And fill with balm the fainting gale.
There 's naught in nature bright or gay,
Where roses do not shed their ray.
When morning paints the orient skies,
Her fingers burn with roseate dyes; [1]
Young nymphs betray the rose's hue,
O'er whitest arms it kindles through.
In Cytherea's form it glows,
And mingles with the living snows.

The rose distils a healing balm,
The beating pulse of pain to calm;
Preserves the cold inurnèd clay, [2]
And mocks the vestige of decay: [3]

1 When morning paints the orient skies,
　Her fingers burn with roseate dyes; etc.

In the original here, he enumerates the many
epithets of beauty, borrowed from roses, which
were used by the poets, παρὰ τῶν σοφῶν. We
see that poets were dignified in Greece with the
title of sages: even the careless Anacreon, who
lived but for love and voluptuousness, was called
by Plato the wise Anacreon — *fuit hæc sapientia
quondam.*

2 Preserves the cold inurnèd clay, etc.

He here alludes to the use of the rose in embalming; and, perhaps (as Barnes thinks), to the
rosy unguent with which Venus anointed the
corpse of Hector. — Homer's Iliad ψ. It may
likewise regard the ancient practice of putting
garlands of roses on the dead, as in Statius,
Theb. lib. x. 782.

　　—— *hi sertis, hi veris honore soluto
　Accumulant artus, patriâque in sede reponunt
　Corpus odoratum.*

Where *veris honor,* though it mean every kind
of flowers, may seem more particularly to refer
to the rose, which our poet in another ode calls
ἔαρος μέλημα. We read, in the "Hieroglyphics"
of Pierius, lib. lv., that some of the ancients used
to order in their wills, that roses should be annually scattered on their tombs, and Pierius has
adduced some sepulchral inscriptions to this purpose.

3 And mocks the vestige of decay.

When he says that this flower prevails over
time itself, he still alludes to its efficacy in embalment (*tenerâ poneret ossa rosâ.* Propert. lib.
i. eleg. 17.), or perhaps to the subsequent idea of
its fragrance surviving its beauty; for he can
scarcely mean to praise for duration the *nimium
breves flores* of the rose. Philostratus compares

And when, at length, in pale decline,
Its florid beauties fade and pine,
Sweet as in youth, its balmy breath
Diffuses odor even in death! [4]
Oh! whence could such a plant have
　sprung?
Listen, — for thus the tale is sung.
When, humid, from the silvery stream,
Effusing beauty's warmest beam,
Venus appeared, in flushing hues,
Mellowed by ocean's briny dews;
When, in the starry courts above,
The pregnant brain of mighty Jove
Disclosed the nymph of azure glance,
The nymph who shakes the martial
　lance; —
Then, then, in strange eventful hour,
The earth produced an infant flower,
Which sprung, in blushing glories drest,
And wantoned o'er its parent breast.
The gods beheld this brilliant birth,
And hailed the Rose, the boon of earth!
With nectar drops, a ruby tide,
The sweetly orient buds they dyed, [5]

this flower with love, and says, that they both
defy the influence of time; χρόνον δὲ οὔτε Ἔρως,
οὔτε ῥόδα οἶδεν. Unfortunately the similitude
lies not in their duration, but their transience.

4 Sweet as in youth, its balmy breath
　Diffuses odor even in death!

Thus Casper Barlæus, in his "Ritus Nupti-
arum:" —

*Ambrosium late rosa tunc quoque spargit odo-
　rem,
　Cum fluit, aut multo languida sole jacet.*

Nor then the rose its odor loses,
　When all its flushing beauties die;
Nor less ambrosial balm diffuses,
　When withered by the solar eye.

5 With nectar drops, a ruby tide,
　The sweetly orient buds they dyed, etc.

The author of the "Pervigilium Veneris" (a
poem attributed to Catullus, the style of which
appears to me to have all the labored luxuriance
of a much later period) ascribes the tincture of
the rose to the blood from the wound of Adonis —

　　　—— *rosæ
　　Fuscæ aprino de cruore* —

according to the emendation of Lipsius. In the
following epigram this hue is differently accounted for: —

*Illa quidem studiosa suum defendere Adonim,
　gradivus stricto quem petit ense ferox,
affixit duris vestigia cæca rosetis,
　albaque divino picta cruore rosa est.*

While the enamoured queen of joy
Flies to protect her lovely boy,
On whom the jealous war-god rushes;

And bade them bloom, the flowers divine
Of him who gave the glorious vine;
And bade them on the spangled thorn
Expand their bosoms to the morn.

ODE LVI.[1]

HE, who instructs the youthful crew
To bathe them in the brimmer's dew,
And taste, uncloyed by rich excesses,
All the bliss that wine possesses;
He, who inspires the youth to bound
Elastic through the dance's round, —
Bacchus, the god again is here,
And leads along the blushing year;
The blushing year with vintage teems,
Ready to shed those cordial streams,
Which, sparkling in the cup of mirth,
Illuminate the sons of earth![2]

Then, when the ripe and vermil
    wine, —
Blest infant of the pregnant vine,
Which now in mellow clusters swells, —
Oh! when it bursts its roseate cells,
Brightly the joyous stream shall flow,
To balsam every mortal woe!
None shall be then cast down or weak,
For health and joy shall light each cheek;
No heart will then desponding sigh,
For wine shall bid despondence fly.
Thus — till another autumn's glow
Shall bid another vintage flow.

She treads upon a thorned rose,
And while she wound with crimson flows,
    The snowy floweret feels her blood, and blushes!

1 " Compare with this elegant ode the verses
of Uz, lib. i. ' Die Weinlese.' " — DEGEN.
This appears to be one of the hymns which
were sung at the anniversary festival of the vintage; one of the ἐπιλήνιοι ὕμνοι, as our poet himself terms them in the fifty-ninth ode. We cannot help feeling a sort of reverence for these
classic relics of the religion of antiquity. Horace may be supposed to have written the nineteenth ode of his second book, and the twenty-fifth
of the third, for some bacchanalian celebration of
this kind.

2 Which, sparkling in the cup of mirth,
    Illuminate the sons of earth!
In the original πότον ἄστονον κομίζων. Madame Dacier thinks that the poet here had the nepenthe of Homer in his mind. Odyssey, lib. iv.
This nepenthe was a something of exquisite
charm, infused by Helen into the wine of her
guests, which had the power of dispelling every
anxiety. A French writer, De Meré, conjectures
that this spell, which made the bowl so beguiling, was the charm of Helen's conversation.
See Bayle, art. Helène.

ODE LVII.[3]

WHOSE was the artist hand that spread
Upon this disk the ocean's bed?[4]
And, in a flight of fancy, high
As aught on earthly wing can fly,
Depicted thus, in semblance warm,
The Queen of Love's voluptuous form
Floating along the silvery sea
In beauty's naked majesty!
Oh! he hath given the enamoured sight
A witching banquet of delight,
Where, gleaming through the waters
    clear,
Glimpses of undreamt charms appear,
And all that mystery loves to screen,
Fancy, like Faith, adores unseen.[5]

Light as a leaf, that on the breeze
Of summer skims the glassy seas,
She floats along the ocean's breast,
Which undulates in sleepy rest;
While stealing on, she gently pillows
Her bosom on the heaving billows.

3 This ode is a very animated description of
a picture of Venus on a discus, which represented
the goddess in her first emergence from the
waves. About two centuries after our poet
wrote, the pencil of the artist Apelles embellished this subject, in his famous painting of the
Venus Anadyomene, the model of which, as
Pliny informs us, was the beautiful Campaspe,
given to him by Alexander; though, according
to Natalis Comes, lib. vii. cap. 16., it was Phryne
who sat to Apelles for the face and breast of
this Venus.
There are a few blemishes in the reading of
the ode before us, which have influenced Faber,
Heyne, Brunck, etc., to denounce the whole
poem as spurious. But, *non ego paucis offendar
maculis.* I think it is quite beautiful enough to
be authentic.

4 Whose was the artist hand that spread
    Upon this disk the ocean's bed?
The abruptness of ἄρα τίς τόρευσε πόντον, is
finely expressive of sudden admiration, and is
one of those beauties, which we cannot but
admire in their source, though, by frequent imitation, they are now become familiar and un-
impressive.

5 And all that mystery loves to screen,
    Fancy, like Faith, adores unseen, etc.
The picture here has all the delicate character
of the semi-reducta Venus, and affords a happy
specimen of what the poetry of passion *ought* to
be — glowing but through a veil, and stealing
upon the heart from concealment. Few of the
ancients have attained this modesty of description, which, like the golden cloud that hung over
Jupiter and Juno, is impervious to every beam
but that of fancy.

Her bosom, like the dew-washed rose,[1]
Her neck, like April's sparkling snows,
Illume the liquid path she traces,
And burn within the stream's embraces.
Thus on she moves, in languid pride,
Encircled by the azure tide,
As some fair lily o'er a bed
Of violets bends its graceful head.

Beneath their queen's inspiring glance,
The dolphins o'er the green sea dance,
Bearing in triumph young Desire,[2]
And infant Love with smiles of fire!
While, glittering through the silver waves,
The tenants of the briny caves
Around the pomp their gambols play,
And gleam along the watery way.

ODE LVIII.[3]

When Gold, as fleet as zephyr's pinion,
Escapes like any faithless minion,[4]

1 Her bosom, like the dew-washed rose, etc.

"'Ροδέων [says an anonymous annotator] is a whimsical epithet for the bosom." Neither Catullus nor Gray have been of his opinion. The former has the expression, —

En hic in roeis latet papillis.

And the latter,

Lo! where the rosy-bosomed hours, etc.

Crottus, a modern Latinist, might indeed be censured for too vague a use of the epithet "rosy," when he applies it to the eyes, — "*e roseis oculis.*"

2 —— young Desire, etc.

In the original Ἵμερος, who was the same deity with Jocus among the Romans. Aurelius Augurellus has a poem beginning : —

*Invitat olim Bacchus ad cœnam suos
Comon, Jocum, Cupidinem.*

Which Parnell has closely imitated : —

Gay Bacchus, liking Estcourt's wine,
A noble meal bespoke us;
And for the guests that were to dine,
Brought Comus, Love, and Jocus, etc.

3 I have followed Barnes's arrangement of this ode, which, though deviating somewhat from the Vatican MS., appears to me the more natural order.

4 When Gold, as fleet as zephyr's pinion,
Escapes like any faithless minion, etc.

In the original Ὁ δραπέτης ὁ χρυσός. There is a kind of pun in these words, as Madame Dacier has already remarked; for Chrysos, which signifies gold, was also a frequent name for a slave. In one of Lucian's dialogues, there is, I think, a similar play upon the word, where the followers of Chrysippus are called golden fishes.

And flies me (as he flies me ever),[5]
Do I pursue him? never, never!
No, let the false deserter go,
For who would court his direst foe?
But, when I feel my lightened mind
No more by grovelling gold confined,
Then loose I all such clinging cares,
And cast them to the vagrant airs.
Then feel I, too, the Muse's spell,
And wake to life the dulcet shell,
Which, roused once more, to beauty sings,
While love dissolves along the strings!

But, scarcely has my heart been taught
How little Gold deserves a thought,
When, lo! the slave returns once more,
And with him wafts delicious store
Of racy wine, whose genial art
In slumber seals the anxious heart.
Again he tries my soul to sever
From love and song, perhaps for ever!

Away, deceiver! why pursuing
Ceaseless thus my heart's undoing?
Sweet is the song of amorous fire,
Sweet the sighs that thrill the lyre;
Oh! sweeter far than all the gold
Thy wings can waft, thy mines can hold.
Well do I know thy arts, thy wiles —
They withered Love's young wreathèd smiles;
And o'er his lyre such darkness shed,
I thought its soul of song was fled!
They dashed the wine-cup, that, by him,

The puns of the ancients are, in general, even more vapid than our own; some of the best are those recorded of Diogenes.

5 And flies me (as he flies me ever), etc.

Ἀεὶ δ', ἀεί με φεύγει. This grace of iteration has already been taken notice of. Though sometimes merely a playful beauty, it is peculiarly expressive of impassioned sentiment, and we may easily believe that it was one of the many sources of that energetic sensibility which breathed through the style of Sappho. See Gyrald. Vet. Poet. Dial. 9. It will not be said that this is a mechanical ornament by any one who can feel its charm in those lines of Catullus, where he complains of the infidelity of his mistress, Lesbia : —

*Cœli, Lesbia nostra, Lesbia illa,
illa Lesbia, quam Catullus unam,
plus quam se atque suos amavit omnes,
nunc,* etc.

Si sic omnia dixisset ! — but the rest does not bear citation.

Was filled with kisses to the brim.[1]
Go — fly to haunts of sordid men,
But come not near the bard again.
Thy glitter in the Muse's shade,
Scares from her bower the tuneful maid;
And not for worlds would I forego
That moment of poetic glow,
When my full soul, in Fancy's stream,
Pours o'er the lyre its swelling theme.
Away, away! to worldlings hence,
Who feel not this diviner sense;
Give gold to those who love that pest, —
But leave the poet poor and blest.

ODE LIX.[2]

Ripened by the solar beam,
Now the ruddy clusters teem,
In osier baskets borne along
By all the festal vintage throng
Of rosy youths and virgins fair,
Ripe as the melting fruits they bear.
Now, now they press the pregnant grapes,
And now the captive stream escapes,
In fervid tide of nectar gushing,
And for its bondage proudly blushing!
While, round the vat's impurpled brim,
The choral song, the vintage hymn
Of rosy youths and virgins fair,
Steals on the charmed and echoing air.

1 They dashed the wine-cup, that, by him,
Was filled with kisses to the brim.

Original : —

φιλημάτων δε κεδνῶν,
πόθων κύπελλα κίρνης.

Horace has *Desiderique temperare poculum*,
not figuratively, however, like Anacreon, but im-
porting the love-philtres of the witches. By
"cups of kisses" our poet may allude to a
favorite gallantry among the ancients, of drinking when the lips of their mistresses had touched
the brim : —

" Or leave a kiss within the cup,
And I 'll not ask for wine."

As in Ben Jonson's translation from Philostratus ; and Lucian has a conceit upon the same
idea, "Ίνα καὶ πίνῃς ἅμα καὶ φιλῇς," "that you
may at once both drink and kiss."

2 The title Ἐπιλήνιος ὕμνος, which Barnes
has given to this ode, is by no means appropriate. We have already had one of those hymns
(ode 56), but this is a description of the vintage ;
and the title εἰς οἶνον, which it bears in the Vatican MS., is more correct than any that have
been suggested.

Degen, in the true spirit of literary scepticism, doubts that this ode is genuine, without
assigning any reason for such a suspicion ; — *non
amo te, Sabidi, nec possum dicere quare.* But
this is far from satisfactory criticism.

Mark, how they drink, with all their eyes,
The orient tide that sparkling flies,
The infant Bacchus, born in mirth,
While Love stands by, to hail the birth.

When he, whose verging years decline
As deep into the vale as mine,
When he inhales the vintage-cup,
His feet, new-winged, from earth spring
up,
And as he dances, the fresh air
Plays whispering through his silvery hair.
Meanwhile young groups whom love in-
vites,
To joys even rivalling wine's delights,
Seek, arm in arm, the shadowy grove,
And there, in words and looks of love,
Such as fond lovers look and say,
Pass the sweet moonlight hours away.[3]

ODE LX.[4]

Awake to life, my sleeping shell,
To Phœbus let thy numbers swell;
And though no glorious prize be thine,
No Pythian wreath around thee twine,
Yet every hour is glory's hour
To him who gathers wisdom's flower.
Then wake thee from thy voiceless slum-
bers,
And to the soft and Phrygian numbers,
Which, tremblingly, my lips repeat,
Send echoes from thy chord as sweet.
'T is thus the swan, with fading notes,
Down the Cayster's current floats,
While amorous breezes linger round,
And sigh responsive sound for sound.

Muse of the Lyre! illume my dream,
Thy Phœbus is my fancy's theme;

3 Those well acquainted with the original
need hardly be reminded that, in these few concluding verses, I have thought right to give only
the general meaning of my author, leaving the
details untouched.

4 This hymn to Apollo is supposed not to have
been written by Anacreon ; and it is undoubtedly
rather a sublimer flight than the Teian wing is accustomed to soar. But, in a poet of whose works
so small a proportion has reached us, diversity
of style is by no means a safe criterion. If we
knew Horace but as a satirist, should we easily
believe there could dwell such animation in his
lyre ? Suidas says that our poet wrote hymns,
and this perhaps is one of them. We can perceive in what an altered and imperfect state his
works are at present, when we find a scholiast

And hallowed is the harp I bear,
And hallowed is the wreath I wear,
Hallowed by him, the god of lays,
Who modulates the choral maze.
I sing the love which Daphne twined
Around the godhead's yielding mind;
I sing the blushing Daphne's flight
From this ethereal son of Light;
And how the tender, timid maid
Flew trembling to the kindly shade.[1]
Resigned a form, alas, too fair,
And grew a verdant laurel there;
Whose leaves, with sympathetic thrill,
In terror seemed to tremble still!
The god pursued, with winged desire;
And when his hopes were all on fire,
And when to clasp the nymph he thought,
A lifeless tree was all he caught;
And, 'stead of sighs that pleasure heaves,
Heard but the west-wind in the leaves!

But, pause, my soul, no more, no
    more —
Enthusiast, whither do I soar?
This sweetly-maddening dream of soul
Hath hurried me beyond the goal.
Why should I sing the mighty darts
Which fly to wound celestial hearts,
When ah, the song, with sweeter tone,
Can tell the darts that wound my own?
Still be Anacreon, still inspire
The descant of the Teian lyre:[2]

upon Horace citing an ode from the third book
of Anacreon.

1 And how the tender, timid maid
    Flew trembling to the kindly shade, etc.

Original: —

τὸ μὲν ἐκπέφευγε κέντρον,
φύσεως δ᾽ ἄμειψε μορφήν.

I find the word κέντρον here has a double force,
as it also signifies that *omnium parentem, quam
sanctus Numa*, etc. (See Martial.) In order to
confirm this import of the word here, those who
are curious in new readings may place the stop
after φύσεως, thus: —

τὸ μὲν ἐκπέφευγε κέντρον
φύσεως, δ᾽ ἄμειψε μορφήν.

2 Still be Anacreon, still inspire
    The descant of the Teian lyre.

The original is τὸ. Ἀνακρέοντα μίμου. I have
translated it under the supposition that the hymn
is by Anacreon; though, I fear, from this very
line, that his claim to it can scarcely be supported.
Τὸν Ἀνακρέοντα μίμου, "Imitate Anacreon."
Such is the lesson given us by the lyrist; and if,

Still let the nectared numbers float,
Distilling love in every note!
And when some youth, whose glowing
    soul
Has felt the Paphian star's control,
When he the liquid lays shall hear,
His heart will flutter to his ear,
And drinking there of song divine,
Banquet on intellectual wine![3]

ODE LXI.[4]

YOUTH'S endearing charms are fled;
Hoary locks deform my head;

in poetry, a simple elegance of sentiment, enriched by the most playful felicities of fancy,
be a charm which invites or deserves imitation,
where shall we find such a guide as Anacreon?
In morality, too, with some little reserve, we
need not blush, I think, to follow in his footsteps. For if his song be the language of his
heart, though luxurious and relaxed, he was artless and benevolent; and who would not forgive
a few irregularities, when atoned for by virtues
so rare and so endearing? When we think of
the sentiment in those lines: —

Away! I hate the slanderous dart,
Which steals to wound the unwary heart,

how many are there in the world, to whom we
would wish to say, τὸν Ἀνακρέοντα μίμου!

3 Here ends the last of the odes in the Vatican MS., whose authority helps to confirm the
genuine antiquity of them all, though a few have
stolen among the number, which we may hesitate in attributing to Anacreon. In the little essay prefixed to this translation, I observed that
Barnes has quoted this manuscript incorrectly,
relying upon an imperfect copy of it, which
Isaac Vossius had taken. I shall just mention
two or three instances of this inaccuracy — the
first which occur to me. In the ode of the Dove,
on the words πτέροισι συγκαλύψω, he says,
"*Vatican MS.* συσκιάζων, *etiam Prisciano in-
vito:*" but the MS. reads συνκαλύψω, with
συσκιάσω interlined. Degen too, on the same
line, is somewhat in error. In the twenty-second
ode of this series, line thirteenth, the MS. has
τενίη with αι interlined, and Barnes imputes to it
the reading of τένδη. In the fifty-seventh, line
twelfth, he professes to have preserved the reading of the MS. ἀλαλημένη δ᾽ επ᾽ αὐτή, while
the latter has ἀλαλημένος δ᾽ ἐπ᾽ αὐτά. Almost all
the other annotators have transplanted these
errors from Barnes.

4 The intrusion of this melancholy ode, among
the careless levities of our poet, reminds us of
the skeletons which the Egyptians used to hang
up in their banquet-rooms, to inculcate a thought
of mortality even amidst the dissipations of
mirth. If it were not for the beauty of its numbers, the Teian Muse should disown this ode.
"*Quid habet illius, illius quæ spirabat amores?*"
To Stobæus we are indebted for it.

Bloomy graces, dalliance gay,
All the flowers of life decay.[1]
Withering age begins to trace
Sad memorials o'er my face;
Time has shed its sweetest bloom,
All the future must be gloom.
This it is that sets me sighing;
Dreary is the thought of dying![2]
Lone and dismal is the road,
Down to Pluto's dark abode;
And, when once the journey 's o'er,
Ah! we can return no more![3]

ODE LXII.[4]

FILL me, boy, as deep a draught,
As e'er was filled, as e'er was quaffed;
But let the water amply flow,
To cool the grape's intemperate glow; [5]

1 Bloomy graces, dalliance gay,
  All the flowers of life decay.

Horace often, with feeling and elegance, deplores the fugacity of human enjoyments. See book ii. ode 11.; and thus in the second epistle, book ii. : —

Singula de nobis anni prædantur euntes;
eripuere jocos, venerem, convivia, ludum.

The wing of every passing day
Withers some blooming joy away;
And wafts from our enamoured arms
The banquet's mirth, the virgin's charms.

2 Dreary is the thought of dying.

Regnier, a libertine French poet, has written some sonnets on the approach of death, full of gloomy and trembling repentance. Chaulieu, however, supports more consistently the spirit of the Epicurean philosopher. See his poem, addressed to the Marquis de Lafare —

Plus j'approche du terme et moins je le redoute,
etc.

3 And, when once the journey 's o'er,
  Ah! we can return no more!

Scaliger, upon Catullus's well-known lines, "*qui nunc it per iter,*" etc. remarks, that Acheron, with the same idea, is called ἀνέξοδος by Theocritus, and δυσέκδρομος by Nicander.

4 This ode consists of two fragments, which are to be found in Athenæus, book x., and which Barnes, from the similarity of their tendency, has combined into one. I think this a very justifiable liberty, and have adopted it in some other fragments of our poet.
Degen refers us here to verses of Uz, lib. iv., "Der Trinker."

5 But let the water amply flow,
  To cool the grape's intemperate glow; etc.

It was Amphictyon who first taught the Greeks to mix water with their wine; in commemoration of which circumstance they erected altars to Bacchus and the nymphs. On this mythological allegory the following epigram is founded: —

Let not the fiery god be single,
But with the nymphs in union mingle.
For though the bowl 's the grave of sadness,
Ne'er let it be the birth of madness.
No, banish from our board to-night
The revelries of rude delight;
To Scythians leave these wild excesses,
Ours be the joy that soothes and blesses!
And while the temperate bowl we wreathe,
In concert let our voices breathe,
Beguiling every hour along
With harmony of soul and song.

ODE LXIII.[6]

To Love, the soft and blooming child,
I touch the harp in descant wild;
To Love, the babe of Cyprian bowers,
The boy, who breathes and blushes flowers;
To Love, for heaven and earth adore him,
And gods and mortals bow before him!

ODE LXIV.[7]

HASTE thee, nymph, whose well-aimed spear
Wounds the fleeting mountain-deer!

Ardentem ex utero Semeles lumère Lyæum
Naiades, extincto fulminis igne cacri;
cum nymphis igitur tractabilis, at sine nymphis
candenti rursus fulmine corripitur.
          PIERIUS VALERIANUS.

Which is, *non verbum verbo,* —

While heavenly fire consumed his Theban dame,
A Naiad caught young Bacchus from the flame,
  And dipt him burning in her purest lymph;
Hence, still he loves the Naiad's crystal urn,
And when his native fires too fiercely burn,
  Seeks the cool waters of the fountain-nymph.

6 "This fragment is preserved in Clemens Alexandrinus, Strom. lib. vi. and in Arsenius, Collect. Græc." — BARNES.
It appears to have been the opening of a hymn in praise of Love.

7 This hymn to Diana is extant in Hephæstion. There is an anecdote of our poet, which has led some to doubt whether he ever wrote any odes of this kind. It is related by the Scholiast upon Pindar (Isthmionic. od. ii. v. 1. as cited by Barnes) that Anacreon being asked why he addressed all his hymns to women, and none to the deities? answered, "Because women are my deities."
I have assumed, it will be seen, in reporting this anecdote, the same liberty which I have thought it right to take in translating some of the odes; and it were to be wished that these little infidelities were always allowable in interpreting

Dian, Jove's immortal child,
Huntress of the savage wild!
Goddess with the sun-bright hair!
Listen to a people's prayer.
Turn, to Lethe's river turn,
There thy vanquished people mourn! [1]
Come to Lethe's wavy shore,
Tell them they shall mourn no more.
Thine their hearts, their altars thine;
Must they, Dian — must they pine?

ODE LXV. [2]

LIKE some wanton filly sporting,
Maid of Thrace, thou flyest my courting.
Wanton filly! tell me why
Thou trip'st away, with scornful eye,
And seem'st to think my doating heart
Is novice in the bridling art?
Believe me, girl, it is not so;
Thou 'lt find this skilful hand can throw
The reins around that tender form,
However wild, however warm.
Yes — trust me I can tame thy force,
And turn and wind thee in the course.
Though, wasting now thy careless hours,
Thou sport amid the herbs and flowers,
Soon shalt thou feel the rein's control,
And tremble at the wished-for goal!

ODE LXVI. [3]

To thee, the Queen of nymphs divine,
Fairest of all that fairest shine;

the writings of the ancients; thus, when nature
is forgotten in the original, in the translation
tamen usque recurret.

1 Turn, to Lethe's river turn,
  There thy vanquished people mourn!

Lethe, a river of Ionia, according to Strabo,
falling into the Meander. In its neighborhood
was the city called Magnesia, in favor of whose
inhabitants our poet is supposed to have addressed this supplication to Diana. It was written (as Madame Dacier conjectures) on the
occasion of some battle, in which the Magne-
sians had been defeated.

2 This ode, which is addressed to some Thra-
cian girl, exists in Heraclides, and has been
imitated very frequently by Horace, as all the
annotators have remarked. Madame Dacier rejects the allegory, which runs so obviously through
the poem, and supposes it to have been addressed
to a young mare belonging to Polycrates.

Pierius, in the fourth book of his "Hieroglyphics," cites this ode, and informs us that the
horse was the hieroglyphical emblem of pride.

3 This ode is introduced in the Romance of
Theodorus Prodromus, and is that kind of epi-

To thee, who rulest with darts of fire
This world of mortals, young Desire!
And oh! thou nuptial Power, to thee
Who bearest of life the guardian key,
Breathing my soul in fervent praise,
And weaving wild my votive lays,
For thee, O Queen! I wake the lyre,
For thee, thou blushing young Desire,
And oh! for thee, thou nuptial Power,
Come, and illume this genial hour.

Look on thy bride, too happy boy,
And while thy lambent glance of joy
Plays over all her blushing charms,
Delay not, snatch her to thine arms,
Before the lovely, trembling prey,
Like a young birdling, wing away!
Turn, Stratocles, too happy youth,
Dear to the Queen of amorous truth,
And dear to her, whose yielding zone
Will soon resign her all thine own.
Turn to Myrilla, turn thine eye,
Breathe to Myrilla, breathe thy sigh.
To those bewitching beauties turn;
For thee they blush, for thee they burn.

Not more the rose, the queen of flowers,
Outblushes all the bloom of bowers,
Than she unrivalled grace discloses,
The sweetest rose, where all are roses.
Oh! may the sun, benignant, shed
His blandest influence o'er thy bed;
And foster there an infant tree,
To bloom like her, and tower like thee! [4]

thalamium which was sung like a scolium at the
nuptial banquet.

Among the many works of the impassioned
Sappho, of which time and ignorant superstition
have deprived us, the loss of her epithalamiums
is not one of the least that we deplore. The following lines are cited as a relic of one of those
poems: —

ὄλβιε γάμβρε, σοὶ μὲν δὴ γάμος ὡς ἄραο,
ἐκτέτελεστ', ἔχεις δὲ παρθένον ἂν ἄραο.

See Scaliger, in his Poetics, on the Epithalamium.

4 And foster there an infant tree,
  To bloom like her, and tower like thee!

Original Κυπάριττος δὲ πεφύκοι σευ ἐνὶ κήπῳ.
Passeratius, upon the words "*cum castum
amisit florem,*" in the Nuptial Song of Catullus,
after explaining "*flos*" in somewhat a similar
sense to that which Gaulminus attributes to ῥόδον
says, *Hortum quoque vocant in quo flos ille
carpitur, et Græcis* κῆπόν ἐστι τὸ ἐφήβαιον
γυναικῶν."

I may remark, in passing, that the author of

LXVII.[1]

RICH in bliss, I proudly scorn
The wealth of Amalthea's horn;
Nor should I ask to call the throne
Of the Tartessian prince my own; [2]
To totter through his train of years,
The victim of declining fears.
One little hour of joy to me
Is worth a dull eternity!

ODE LXVIII.[3]

Now Neptune's month our sky deforms,
The angry night-cloud teems with storms;
And savage winds, infuriate driven,
Fly howling in the face of heaven!
Now, now, my friends, the gathering
  gloom
With roseate rays of wine illume:
And while our wreaths of parsley spread
Their fadeless foliage round our head,
Let 's hymn the almighty power of wine,
And shed libations on his shrine!

ODE LXIX.[4]

THEY wove the lotus band to deck
And fan with pensile wreath each neck;
And every guest, to shade his head,
Three little fragrant chaplets spread; [5]

the Greek version of this charming ode of Catullus, has neglected a most striking and anacreontic beauty in those verses " *Ut flos in septis,*" etc., which is the repetition of the line, " *Multi illum pueri, multæ optavère puellæ,*" with the slight alteration of *nulli* and *nullæ.* Catullus himself, however, has been equally injudicious in his version of the famous ode of Sappho; having translated γελώσας ίμερόεν, but omitted all notice of the accompanying charm, άδὺ φωνούσας: Horace has caught the spirit of it more faithfully: —

Dulce ridentem Lalagen amabo,
  Dulce loquentem.

1 This fragment is preserved in the third book of Strabo.

2 Of the Tartessian prince my own.

He here alludes to Arganthonius, who lived, according to Lucian, an hundred and fifty years; and reigned, according to Herodotus, eighty. See Barnes.

3 This is composed of two fragments; the seventieth and eighty-first in Barnes. They are both found in Eustathius.

4 Three fragments form this little ode, all of which are preserved in Athenæus. They are the eighty-second, seventy-fifth, and eighty-third, in Barnes.

5 And every guest, to shade his head,
  Three little fragrant chaplets spread.

And one was of the Egyptian leaf,
The rest were roses, fair and brief:
While from a golden vase profound,
To all on flowery beds around,
A Hebe, of celestial shape,
Poured the rich droppings of the grape!

ODE LXX.[6]

A BROKEN cake, with honey sweet,
Is all my spare and simple treat:
And while a generous bowl I crown
To float my little banquet down,
I take the soft, the amorous lyre,
And sing of love's delicious fire:
In mirthful measures warm and free,
I sing, dear maid, and sing for thee!

ODE LXXI.[7]

WITH twenty chords my lyre is hung,
  And while I wake them all for thee,
Thou, O maiden, wild and young,
  Disportest in airy levity.

The nursling fawn, that in some shade
  Its antlered mother leaves behind,[8]
Is not more wantonly afraid,
  More timid of the rustling wind!

Longepierre, to give an idea of the luxurious estimation in which garlands were held by the ancients, relates an anecdote of a courtezan, who, in order to gratify three lovers, without leaving cause for jealousy with any of them, gave a kiss to one, let the other drink after her, and put a garland on the brow of the third; so that each was satisfied with his favor, and flattered himself with the preference.

This circumstance resembles very much the subject of one of the *tensons* of Savari de Mauléon, a troubadour. See " L'Histoire Littéraire des Troubadours." The recital is a curious picture of the puerile gallantries of chivalry.

6 Compiled by Barnes, from Athenæus, Hephæstion, and Arsenius. See Barnes, 80th.

7 This I have formed from the eighty-fourth and eighty-fifth of Barnes's edition. The two fragments are found in Athenæus.

8 The nursling fawn, that in some shade
  Its antlered mother leaves behind, etc.

In the original : —

ός έν ΰλη κεροέσσης
όπολειφθείς ύπὸ μητρός.

" Horned " here, undoubtedly, seems a strange epithet; Madame Dacier however observes, that Sophocles, Callimachus, etc., have all applied it in the very same manner, and she seems to agree in the conjecture of the scholiast upon Pindar, that perhaps horns are not always peculiar to the males. I think we may with more ease conclude

ODE LXXII.[1]

FARE thee well, perfidious maid,
My soul, too long on earth delayed,
Delayed, perfidious girl, by thee,
Is on the wing for liberty.
I fly to seek a kindlier sphere,
Since thou hast ceased to love me here!

ODE LXXIII.[2]

AWHILE I bloomed, a happy flower,
Till Love approached one fatal hour,
And made my tender branches feel
The wounds of his avenging steel.
Then lost I fell, like some poor willow
That falls across the wintry billow!

ODE LXXIV.[3]

MONARCH Love, resistless boy,
With whom the rosy Queen of Joy,
And nymphs, whose eyes have Heaven's
    hue,
Disporting tread the mountain-dew;
Propitious, oh! receive my sighs,
Which, glowing with entreaty, rise,
That thou wilt whisper to the breast
Of her I love thy soft behest;
And counsel her to learn from thee,
That lesson thou hast taught to me.
Ah! if my heart no flattery tell,
Thou 'lt own I 've learned that lesson
    well!

ODE LXXV.[4]

SPIRIT of Love, whose locks unrolled,
Stream on the breeze like floating gold;

it to be a license of the poet, "*jussit habere
puellam cornua.*"

1 This fragment is preserved by the scholiast
upon Aristophanes, and is the eighty-seventh in
Barnes.

2 This is to be found in Hephæstion, and is
the eighty-ninth of Barnes's edition.

I have omitted, from among these scraps, a
very considerable fragment imputed to our poet,
Ξανθῆ δ' Εὐρυπύλη μέλει, etc., which is preserved in the twelfth book of Athenæus, and is
the ninety-first in Barnes. If it was really Anacreon who wrote it, "*nil fuit unquam sic impar
sibi.*" It is in a style of gross satire, and
abounds with expressions that never could be
gracefully translated.

3 A fragment preserved by Dion Chrysostom.
Orat. ii. de Regno. See Barnes, 93.

4 This fragment, which is extant in Athenæus
(Barnes, 101.), is supposed, on the authority of
Chamæleon, to have been addressed to Sappho.

Come, within a fragrant cloud
Blushing with light, thy votary shroud;
And, on those wings that sparkling play,
Waft, oh, waft me hence away!
Love! my soul is full of thee,
Alive to all thy luxury.
But she, the nymph for whom I glow,
The lovely Lesbian mocks my woe;
Smiles at the chill and hoary hues,
That time upon my forehead strews.
Alas! I fear she keeps her charms,
In store for younger, happier arms!

ODE LXXVI.[5]

HITHER, gentle Muse of mine,
   Come and teach thy votary old
Many a golden hymn divine,
   For the nymph with vest of gold.

Pretty nymph, of tender age,
   Fair thy silky locks unfold;
Listen to a hoary sage,
   Sweetest maid with vest of gold!

ODE LXXVII.[6]

WOULD that I were a tuneful lyre,
   Of burnished ivory fair,
Which, in the Dionysian choir,
   Some blooming boy should bear!

We have also a stanza attributed to her, which
some romancers have supposed to be her answer
to Anacreon. "*Mais par malheur* [as Bayle
says], *Sappho vint au monde environ cent ou six
vingt ans avant Anacréon.*" — "Nouvelles de
la Rép. des Lett." tom. ii. de Novembre, 1684.
The following is her fragment, the compliment of
which is finely imagined; she supposes that the
Muse has dictated the verses of Anacreon : —

κεῖνον, ὦ χρυσόθρονε Μοῦσ' ἔνισπες
ὕμνον, ἐκ τῆς καλλιγυναικος ἐσθλᾶς
Τήϊος χώρας ὃν ἄειδε τερπνῶς
πρεσβὺς ἀγανός.

Oh Muse! who sit'st on golden throne,
Full many a hymn of witching tone
   The Teian sage is taught by thee;
But, Goddess, from thy throne of gold,
The sweetest hymn thou 'st ever told,
   He lately learned and sung for me.

5 Formed of the 124th and 119th fragments in
Barnes, both of which are to be found in Scaliger's "Poetics."
De Pauw thinks that those detached lines and
couplets, which Scaliger has adduced as examples in his "Poetics," are by no means authentic,
but of his own fabrication.

6 This is generally inserted among the remains
of Alcæus. Some, however, have attributed it
to Anacreon. See our poet's twenty-second ode,
and the notes.

Would that I were a golden vase,
 That some bright nymph might hold
My spotless frame, with blushing grace,
 Herself as pure as gold!

ODE LXXVIII.[1]

WHEN Cupid sees how thickly now,
 The snows of Time fall o'er my brow,
Upon his wing of golden light,
He passes with an eaglet's flight,
And flitting onward seems to say,
" Fare thee well, thou 'st had thy day! "

CUPID, whose lamp has lent the ray,
That lights our life's meandering way,
That God, within this bosom stealing,
Hath wakened a strange, mingled feeling,
Which pleases, though so sadly teasing,
And teases, though so sweetly pleasing![2]

LET me resign this wretched breath,
 Since now remains to me
No other balm than kindly death,
 To soothe my misery![3]

I KNOW thou lovest a brimming measure,
 And art a kindly, cordial host;
But let me fill and drink at pleasure —
 Thus I enjoy the goblet most.[4]

1 See Barnes, 173d. This fragment, to which
I have taken the liberty of adding a turn not to
be found in the original, is cited by Lucian in his
short essay on the Gallic Hercules.

2 Barnes, 125th. This is in Scaliger's " Poetics." Gail has omitted it in his collection of
fragments.

3 This fragment is extant in Arsenius and Hephæstion. See Barnes (69th), who has arranged
the metre of it very skilfully.

4 Barnes, 72d. This fragment, which is found

I FEAR that love disturbs my rest,
 Yet feel not love's impassioned care;
I think there 's madness in my breast,
 Yet cannot find that madness there![5]

FROM dread Leucadia's frowning steep,
I 'll plunge into the whitening deep:
And there lie cold, to death resigned,
Since Love intoxicates my mind![6]

MIX me, child, a cup divine,
Crystal water, ruby wine:
Weave the frontlet, richly flushing,
O'er my wintry temples blushing.
Mix the brimmer — Love and I
Shall no more the contest try.
Here — upon this holy bowl,
I surrender all my soul![7]

in Athenæus, contains an excellent lesson for the
votaries of Jupiter Hospitalis.

5 Found in Hephæstion (see Barnes, 95th),
and reminds one somewhat of the following: —

Odi et amo; quare id faciam fortasse requiris;
nescio: sed fieri sentio, et excrucior.

Carm. 53.

I love thee and hate thee, but if I can tell
 The cause of my love and my hate, may I die.
I can feel it, alas! I can feel it too well,
 That I love thee and hate thee, but cannot tell
 why.

6 This is also in Hephæstion, and perhaps is
a fragment of some poem, in which Anacreon
had commemorated the fate of Sappho. It is
the 123d of Barnes.

7 Collected by Barnes, from Demetrius Pha
lareus and Eustathius, and subjoined in his edition to the epigrams attributed to our poet. And
here is the last of those little scattered flowers,
which I thought I might venture with any grace
to transplant; — happy if it could be said of the
garland which they form, τὸ δ' ὡζ 'Ανακρέοντος.

AMONG the Epigrams of the " Anthologia," are found some panegyrics on Anacreon, which I had translated, and originally intended as a sort of Coronis to this work.   But I found upon consideration, that they wanted variety; and that a frequent recurrence, in them, of the same thought, would render a collection of such poems uninteresting. I shall take the liberty, however, of subjoining a few, selected from the number, that I may not appear to have totally neglected those ancient tributes to the fame of Anacreon. The four epigrams which I give are imputed to Antipater Sidonius. They are rendered, perhaps, with too much freedom; but designing originally a translation of all that are extant on the subject, I endeavored to enliven their uniformity by sometimes indulging in the liberties of paraphrase.

ΑΝΤΙΠΤΑΡΟΥ ΣΙΔΩΝΙΟΥ, ΕΙΣ ΑΝΑΚΡΕΟΝΤΑ.

θάλλοι τετρακόρυμβος, Ἀνάκρεον, ἀμφί σε κισσὸς
ἁβρά τε λειμώνων πορφυρέων πέταλα·
πηγαὶ δ' ἀπγινόεντος ἀναθλίβοιντο γάλακτος,
εὐῶδες δ' ἀπὸ γῆς ἡδὺ χέοιτο μέθυ,
ὄφρα κέ τοι σποδιή τε καὶ ὄστεα τέρψιν ἄρηται,
εἰ δέ τις φθιμένοις χρίμπτεται εὐφρόσυνα,
ὦ τὸ φίλον στέρξας, φίλε, βάρβιτον, ὦ σὺν ἀοιδᾷ
πάντα διαπλώσας καὶ σὺν ἔρωτι βίον.

ΤΟΥ ΑΥΤΟΥ, ΕΙΣ ΤΟΝ ΑΥΤΟΝ.

τύμβος Ἀνακρείοντος. Ὁ Τήιος ἐνθάδε κύκνος
εὕδει, χὴ παίδων ζωροτάτη μανίη.
ἀκμὴν λειριόεντι μελίζεται ἀμφὶ Βαθύλλῳ
Ἱμέρα καὶ κίσσου λευκὸς ὀδῶδε λίθος.
οὐδ' Ἀίδης σοι ἔρωτας ἀπέσβεσεν ἐν δ' Ἀχέροντος
ὤν, ὅλος ὠδίνεις Κύπριδι θερμοτέρῃ.

AROUND the tomb, oh, bard divine!
Where soft thy hallowed brow reposes,
Long may the deathless ivy twine,
  And summer spread her waste of roses!

And there shall many a fount distil,
  And many a rill refresh the flowers;
But wine shall be each purple rill,
  And every fount be milky showers.

Thus, shade of him, whom Nature taught
To tune his lyre and soul to pleasure,
Who gave to love his tenderest thought,
Who gave to love his fondest measure, —

Thus, after death, if shades can feel,
  Thou may'st, from odors round thee streaming,
A pulse of past enjoyment steal,
  And live again in blissful dreaming![1]

HERE sleeps Anacreon, in this ivied shade;
Here mute in death the Teian swan is laid.[1]
Cold, cold that heart, which while on earth it dwelt
All the sweet frenzy of love's passion felt.
And yet, oh Bard! thou art not mute in death,

imputed to another poet * of the same name, of whom Vossius gives us the following account : " *Antipater Thessalonicensis vixit tempore Augusti Cæsaris, ut qui saltantem viderit Pyladem, sicut constat ex quodam ejus epigrammate* Ἀνθολογίας, lib. iv. tit. εἰς ὀρχηστρίδας. *At eum ac Bathyllum primos fuisse pantomimos ac sub Augusto claruisse, satis notum ex Dione,*" etc. The reader, who thinks it worth observing, may find a strange oversight in Hoffman's quotation of this article from Vossius, " Lexic. Univers." By the omission of a sentence he has made Vossius assert that the poet Antipater was one of the first pantomime dancers in Rome. Barnes, upon the epigram before us, mentions a version of it by Brodæus, which is not to be found in that commentator; but he more than once confounds Brodæus with another annotator on the " Anthologia," Vincentius Obsopœus, who has given a translation of the epigram.

1 —— the Teian swan is laid.

Thus Horace of Pindar : —

Multa Dircæum levat aura cycnum.

A swan was the hieroglyphical emblem of a poet. Anacreon has been called the swan of Teos by another of his eulogists.

* *Pleraque tamen Thessalonicensi tribuenda videntur.* — BRUNCK, " Lectiones et Emendat."

1 Antipater Sidonius, the author of this epigram, lived, according to Vossius, " de Poetis Græcis," in the second year of the 169th Olympiad. He appears, from what Cicero and Quintilian have said of him, to have been a kind of improvisatore. See " Institut. Orat." lib. x. cap. 7. There is nothing more known respecting this poet, except some particulars about his illness and death, which are mentioned as curious by Pliny and others; — and there remain of his works but a few epigrams in the " Anthologia," among which are found these inscriptions upon Anacreon. These remains have been sometimes

Still do we catch thy lyre's luxurious
breath; [1]
And still thy songs of soft Bathylla
bloom,
Green as the ivy round thy mouldering
tomb.
Nor yet has death obscured thy fire of
love,
For still it lights thee through the Elysian grove;
Where dreams are thine, that bless the
elect alone,
And Venus calls thee even in death her
own!

ἐν τοῖς μελίχροις Ἱμέροισι σύντροφον
Ἀναῖος Ἀνακρέοντα, Τήϊον κύκνον,
ἐσψήλας ὑγρῇ νέκταρος μεθηδύνῃ.
    Εὐγενοὺς, Ἀνθολόγ.

God of the grape! thou hast betrayed
  In wine's bewildering dream,
The fairest swan that ever played
  Along the Muse's stream! —
The Teian, nurst with all those honeyed boys,
The young Desires, light Loves, and rose-lipt
  Joys!

1 Still do we catch thy lyre's luxurious breath.

Thus Simonides, speaking of our poet: —

μολπῆς δ' οὐ λήθη μελιτέρπεος ἀλλ' ἔτι κεῖνο
βάρβιτον οὐδὲ θανὼν εὔνασεν εἰν ἀΐδῃ.
    Σιμονίδου, Ἀνθολογ.

Nor yet are all his numbers mute,
  Though dark within the tomb he lies;
But living still, his amorous lute
  With sleepless animation sighs!

This is the famous Simonides, whom Plato styled
"divine," though Le Fèvre, in his "Poëtes
Grecs," supposes that the epigrams under his
name are all falsely imputed. The most considerable of his remains is a satirical poem upon
women, preserved by Stobæus, ψόγος γυναικῶν.
We may judge from the lines I have just
quoted, and the import of the epigram before us,
that the works of Anacreon were perfect in the
times of Simonides and Antipater. Obsopœus,
the commentator here, appears to exult in their
destruction, and telling us they were burned by
the bishops and patriarchs, he adds, "*nec sane
id necquicquam fecerunt*," attributing to this outrage an effect which it could not possibly have
produced.

2 The spirit of Anacreon is supposed to utter
these verses from the tomb, — somewhat "*mutatus ab illo*," at least in simplicity of expression.

3 —— if Anacreon's shell
  Has ever taught thy heart to swell, etc.

We may guess from the words ἐκ βίβλων ἐμῶν,
that Anacreon was not merely a writer of *billets-
doux*, as some French critics have called him.
Amongst these Mr. Le Fèvre, with all his professed admiration, has given our poet a character
by no means of an elevated cast: —

ξεῖνε, τάφον παρὰ λιτὸν Ἀνακρείοντος ἀμείβων,
  εἴ τί τοι ἐκ βίβλων ἦλθεν ἐμῶν ὄφελος,
σπεῖσον ἐμῇ σποδιῇ, σπεῖσον γάνος, ὄφρα κεν οἴνῳ
  ὀστέα γηθήσῃ τἀμὰ νοτιζόμενα,
ὡς ὁ Διονύσου μεμελημένος οὐασι κώμος,
  ὡς ὁ φιλακρήτου σύντροφος ἁρμονίης,
μηδὲ καταφθίμενος Βάκχου δίχα τοῦτον ὑποίσω
  τὸν γενεῇ μερόπων χῶρον ὀφειλόμενον.

OH stranger! if Anacreon's shell
Has ever taught thy heart to swell [3]
With passion's throb or pleasure's sigh,
In pity turn, as wandering nigh,
And drop thy goblet's richest tear [4]
In tenderest libation here!
So shall my sleeping ashes thrill
With visions of enjoyment still.
Not even in death can I resign
The festal joys that once were mine,
When Harmony pursued my ways,
And Bacchus wantoned to my lays. [5]

Aussi c'est pour cela que la postérité
L'a toujours justement d'âge en âge chanté
Comme un franc goguenard, ami de goinfrerie,
A mi billets-doux et de badinerie.

See the verses prefixed to his "Poëtes Grecs."
This is unlike the language of Theocritus, to
whom Anacreon is indebted for the following
simple eulogium: —

ΕΙΣ ΑΝΑΚΡΕΟΝΤΟΣ ΑΝΔΡΙΑΝΤΑ.

θᾶσαι τὸν ἀνδριάντα τοῦτον, ὦ ξένε,
  σπούδα, καὶ λέγ', ἐπὰν ἐς οἶκον ἔνθῃς·
Ἀνακρέοντος εἰκον εἶδον ἐν Τέῳ,
  τῶν πρόσθ' εἴ τι περισσὸν ᾠδοποιῶν.
προσθεὶς δὲ χὤτι τοῖς νέοισιν ἅβετο,
  ἐρεῖς ἀτρεκέως ὅλον τὸν ἄνδρα.

UPON THE STATUE OF ANACREON.

Stranger! who near this statue chance to roam,
Let it awhile your studious eyes engage;
That you may say, returning to your home,
  "I 've seen the image of the Teian sage,
Best of the bards who deck the Muse's page."
Then, if you add, "That striplings loved him
  well,"
You tell them all he was, and aptly tell.

I have endeavored to do justice to the simplicity
of this inscription by rendering it as literally, I
believe, as a verse translation will allow.

  4 And drop thy goblet's richest tear, etc.

Thus Simonides, in another of his epitaphs
on our poet: —

καί μιν ἀεὶ τέγγοι νοτερὴ δρόσος, ἧς ὁ γεραιὸς
  λαρότερον μαλακῶν ἔπνεεν ἐκ στομάτων.

Let wines, in clustering beauty wreathed,
  Drop all their treasures on his head,
Whose lips a dew of sweetness breathed,
  Richer than vine hath ever shed!

  5 And Bacchus wantoned to my lays, etc.

The original here is corrupted, the line ὡς ὁ
Διονύσου, etc., is unintelligible.

Oh! if delight could charm no more,
If all the goblet's bliss were o'er,
When fate had once our doom decreed,
Then dying would be death indeed;
Nor could I think, unblest by wine,
Divinity itself divine!

ΤΟΥ ΑΥΤΟΥ, ΕΙΣ ΤΟΝ ΑΥΤΟΝ.

εὕδεις ἐν φθιμένοισιν, Ἀνάκρεον, ἐσθλὰ πονήσας
εὕδει δ' ἡ γλυκερὴ νυκτιλάλος κιθάρα,
εὕδει καὶ Σμέρδις, τὸ Πόθων ἔαρ, ᾧ σὺ μελίσδων,
βάρβιτ', ἀνεκρούου νέκταρ ἐναρμόνιον·
ἠίθεων γὰρ Ἔρωτος ἐφὺς σκόπος· ἐς δέ σε μοῦνον
τόξα τε καὶ σκολιᾶς εἶχεν ἐκηβολίας.

At length thy golden hours have winged
their flight,
And drowsy death that eyelid steepeth;
Thy harp, that whispered through each
lingering night,[1]
Now mutely in oblivion sleepeth!
She too, for whom that harp profusely
shed
The purest nectar of its numbers,[2]
She, the young spring of thy desires,
hath fled,[3]
And with her blest Anacreon slumbers!

Brunck's emendation improves the sense, but
I doubt if it can be commended for elegance.
He reads the line thus : —

ὡς ὁ Διωνύσοιο λελασμένος οὔποτε κωμῶν.

See Brunck, "Analecta Veter. Poet. Græc."
vol. ii.

1 Thy harp, that whispered through each lingering night, etc.

In another of these poems, "the nightly-
speaking lyre" of the bard is represented as not
yet silent even after his death.

ὡς ὁ φιλάκρητός τε καὶ οἰνοβαρὴς φιλόκωμος
παννύχιος κρούοι * τὴν φιλόμαιδα χέλυν.
    Σιμωνίδου, εἰς Ἀνακρέοντα.

To beauty's smile and wine's delight,
  To joys he loved on earth so well,
Still shall his spirit, all the night,
  Attune the wild, aërial shell!

2 The purest nectar of its numbers, etc.

Thus, says Brunck, in the prologue to the
"Satires of Persius" : —

Cantare credas Pegaseium nectar.

"melos" is the usual reading in this line, and
Casaubon has defended it; but "nectar" is, I
think, much more spirited.

3 She, the young spring of thy desires, etc.

The original, τὸ Πόθων ἔαρ, is beautiful. We
regret that such praise should be lavished so pre-

* Brunck has ἀρούων ; but κρούοι, the common
reading, better suits a detached quotation.

Farewell! thou had'st a pulse for every
dart [4]
That mighty Love could scatter from
his quiver;
And each new beauty found in thee a
heart,[5]
Which thou, with all thy heart and
soul, didst give her!

posterously, and feel that the poet's mistress
Eurypyle would have deserved it better. Her
name has been told us by Meleager, as already
quoted, and in another epigram by Antipater.

ὑγρὰ δὲ δερκομένοισιν ἐν ὄμμασιν οὖλον ἀείδοις
αἰθύσσων λιπαρῆς ἄνθος ὕπερθε κόμης,
ἠὲ πρὸς Εὐρυπύλην τετραμμένος . . .

Long may the nymph around thee play,
  Eurypyle, thy soul's desire,
Basking her beauties in the ray
  That lights thine eyes' dissolving fire!

Sing of her smile's bewitching power,
  Her every grace that warms and blesses;
Sing of her brows' luxuriant flower,
  The beaming glory of her tresses.

The expression here, ἄνθος κόμης, "the
flower of the hair," is borrowed from Anacreon
himself, as appears by a fragment of the poet
preserved in Stobæus : ἀπέκειρας δ' ἀπαλῆς
ἄμομον ἄνθος.

4 Farewell! thou had'st a pulse for every dart,
etc.

ἐφὺς σκόπος, "scopus eras naturâ," not "spec-
ulator," as Barnes very falsely interprets it.

Vincentius Obsopœus, upon this passage, con-
trives to indulge us with a little astrological wisdom, and talks in a style of learned scandal
about Venus, "male posita cum Marte in domo
Saturni."

5 And each new beauty found in thee a heart, etc.

This couplet is not otherwise warranted by
the original, than as it dilates the thought which
Antipater has figuratively expressed.

Critias, of Athens, pays a tribute to the legitimate gallantry of Anacreon, calling him, with
elegant conciseness, γυναικῶν ἠπεροπευτα.

τὸν δὲ γυνακείων μελέων πλέξαντα πότ' ᾠδάς,
ἡδὺν Ἀνακρείοντα,† Τέως εἰς Ἑλλαδ' ἀνῆγεν,
συμποσίων ἐρέθισμα γυναικῶν ἠπερόπευμα.

Teos gave to Greece her treasure,
  Sage Anacreon, sage in loving;
Fondly weaving lays of pleasure
  For the maids who blush'd approving.

When in nightly banquets sporting,
  Where 's the guest could ever fly him?
When with love's seduction courting,
  Where 's the nymph could e'er deny him?

† Thus Scaliger, in his dedicatory verses to
Ronsard : —

blandus, suaviloquus, dulcis Anacreon.

SONGS

THE GREEK ANTHOLOGY.

HERE AT THY TOMB.[1]

BY MELEAGER.

HERE, at thy tomb, these tears I shed,
    Tears, which though vainly now they
        roll,
Are all love hath to give the dead,
    And wept o'er thee with all love's
        soul; —

Wept in remembrance of that light,
    Which naught on earth, without thee,
        gives,
Hope of my heart! now quenched in
        night,
    But dearer, dead, than aught that lives.

Where is she? where the blooming bough
    That once my life's sole lustre made?
Torn off by death, 't is withering now,
    And all its flowers in dust are laid.

Oh earth! that to thy matron breast
    Hast taken all those angel charms,
Gently, I pray thee, let her rest, —
    Gently, as in a mother's arms.

SALE OF CUPID.[2]

BY MELEAGER.

WHO 'LL buy a little boy? Look, yon-
        der is he,
Fast asleep, sly rogue, on his mother's
        knee;
So bold a young imp 't is n't safe to keep,

So I 'll part with him now, while he 's
        sound asleep.
See his arch little nose, how sharp 't is
        curled,
His wings, too, even in sleep unfurled;
And those fingers, which still ever ready
        are found
For mirth or for mischief, to tickle, or
        wound.

He 'll try with his tears your heart to
        beguile,
But never you mind — he 's laughing all
        the while;
For little he cares, so he has his own
        whim,
And weeping or laughing are all one to
        him.
His eye is as keen as the lightning's flash,
His tongue like the red bolt quick and
        rash;
And so savage is he, that his own dear
        mother
Is scarce more safe in his hands than an-
        other.

In short, to sum up this darling's praise,
He 's a downright pest in all sorts of ways;
And if any one wants such an imp to em-
        ploy,
He shall have a dead bargain of this lit-
        tle boy.
But see, the boy wakes — his bright tears
        flow —
His eyes seem to ask could I sell him?
        oh no,
Sweet child no, no — though so naughty
        you be,
You shall live evermore with my Lesbia
        and me.

---

1 Δάκρυά σοι καὶ νέρθε διὰ χθονὸς Ἡλιόδωρα.
                            Ap. BRUNCK.
2 Πωλείσθω, καὶ ματρὸς ἔτ' ἐν κόλποισι
    καχεύδων.
            Ap. BRUNCK, *Analect.* xcv.

TO WEAVE A GARLAND FOR THE ROSE.[1]

BY PAUL, THE SILENTIARY.

To weave a garland for the rose,
　And think thus crown'd 't would love-
lier be,
Were far less vain than to suppose
　That silks and gems add grace to thee.
Where is the pearl whose orient lustre
　Would not, beside thee, look less
bright?
What gold could match the glossy cluster
　Of those young ringlets full of light?

Bring from the land, where fresh it
　gleams,
　The bright blue gem of India's mine,
And see how soon, though bright its
　beams,
　'T will pale before one glance of thine:
Those lips, too, when their sounds have
　blest us
With some divine, mellifluous air,
Who would not say that Beauty's cestus
Had let loose all its witcheries there?[2]

Here, to this conquering host of charms
　I now give up my spell-bound heart,
Nor blush to yield even Reason's arms,
　When thou her bright-eyed conqueror
　art.
Thus to the wind all fears are given;
　Henceforth those eyes alone I see,
Where Hope, as in her own blue heaven,
　Sits beckoning me to bliss and thee!

WHY DOES SHE SO LONG DELAY?[3]

BY PAUL, THE SILENTIARY.

Why does she so long delay?
Night is waning fast away;
Thrice have I my lamp renewed,
Watching here in solitude.
Where can she so long delay?
　Where, so long delay?

Vainly now have two lamps shone;
See the third is nearly gone:[4]
Oh that Love would, like the ray
Of that weary lamp, decay!
But no, alas, it burns still on,
　Still, still, burns on.

Gods, how oft the traitress dear
Swore, by Venus, she 'd be here!
But to one so false as she
What is man or deity?
Neither doth this proud one fear, —
　No, neither doth she fear.

TWIN'ST THOU WITH LOFTY WREATH THY BROW?[5]

BY PAUL, THE SILENTIARY.

Twin'st thou with lofty wreath thy brow?
　Such glory then thy beauty sheds,
I almost think, while awed I bow,
　'T is Rhea's self before me treads.
Be what thou wilt, — this heart
Adores whate'er thou art!

Dost thou thy loosened ringlets leave,
　Like sunny waves to wander free?
Then, such a chain of charms they weave,
　As draws my inmost soul from me.
Do what thou wilt, — I must
Be charm'd by all thou dost!

Even when, enwrapt in silvery veils,[6]
　Those sunny locks elude the sight, —
Oh, not even then their glory fails
　To haunt me with its unseen light.
Change as thy beauty may,
It charms in every way.

For, thee the Graces still attend,
　Presiding o'er each new attire,
And lending every dart they send
　Some new, peculiar touch of fire.
Be what thou wilt, — this heart
Adores whate'er thou art!

---

1 οὔτε ῥόδων στεφάνων ἐπιδεύεσαι, οὔτε σὺ
　πέπλων.
　　　　　　Ap. Brunck, xvii.

2 —— καὶ ἡ μελίφυρτος ἐκείνη
　ἤθεος ἁρμονίη, κεστὸς ἔφυ Παφίης.

3 Δηθύνει Κλεόφαντις.
　　　　　　Ap. Brunck, xxviii.

4 　　　ὁ δὲ τρίτος ἄρχεται ἠδὲ
　λύχνος ὑποκλάζειν.

5 κεκρύφαλοι σφίγγουσι τεὴν τρίχα;
　　　　　　Ap. Brunck, xxxiv.

6 ἀργενναῖς ὀθόνῃσί κατήορα βόστρυχα κεύ-
　θεις.

WHEN THE SAD WORD.[1]
BY PAUL, THE SILENTIARY.

WHEN the sad word, "Adieu," from
my lip is nigh falling,
And with it, Hope passes away,
Ere the tongue hath half breathed it, my
fond heart recalling
That fatal farewell, bids me stay.
For oh! 't is a penance so weary
One hour from thy presence to be,
That death to this soul were less dreary,
Less dark than long absence from thee.

Thy beauty, like Day, o'er the dull world
breaking,
Brings life to the heart it shines o'er,
And, in mine, a new feeling of happi-
ness waking,
Made light what was darkness before.
But mute is the Day's sunny glory,
While thine hath a voice,[2] on whose
breath,
More sweet than the Syren's sweet story,[3]
My hopes hang, through life and
through death!

MY MOPSA IS LITTLE. [4]
BY PHILODEMUS.

MY Mopsa is little, my Mopsa is brown,
But her cheek is as smooth as the peach's
soft down,
And, for blushing, no rose can come
near her;
In short, she has woven such nets round
my heart,
That I ne'er from my dear little Mopsa
can part, —
Unless I can find one that 's dearer.

Her voice hath a music that dwells on
the ear,
And her eye from its orb gives a daylight
so clear,
That I 'm dazzled whenever I meet her;
Her ringlets, so curly, are Cupid's own
net,

And her lips, oh their sweetness I ne'er
shall forget —
Till I light upon lips that are sweeter.

But 't is not her beauty that charms me
alone,
'T is her mind, 't is that language whose
eloquent tone
From the depths of the grave could
revive one :
In short, here I swear, that if death were
her doom,
I would instantly join my dead love in
the tomb —
Unless I could meet with a live one.

STILL, LIKE DEW IN SILENCE FALLING.[5]
BY MELEAGER.

STILL, like dew in silence falling,
Drops for thee the nightly tear;
Still that voice the past recalling,
Dwells, like echo, on my ear,
Still, still!

Day and night the spell hangs o'er me,
Here for ever fixt thou art;
As thy form first shone before me,
So 't is graven on this heart,
Deep, deep!

Love, oh Love, whose bitter sweetness
Dooms me to this lasting pain,
Thou who camest with so much fleetness,
Why so slow to go again?[6]
Why? why?

UP, SAILOR BOY, 'T IS DAY.

UP, sailor boy, 't is day!
The west wind blowing,
The spring tide flowing,
Summon thee hence away.
Didst thou not hear yon soaring swallow
sing?
Chirp, chirp, — in every note he seemed
to say
'T is Spring, 't is Spring.
Up boy, away, —

---

1 σώζεο σοι μέλλων ἐνέπειν.
              Ap. BRUNCK, xxxix.

2 ἤματι γάρ σεο φέγγος ὁμοῖιον. ἀλλὰ τὸ μέν
    που ἄφθογγον.

3   σὺ δ' ἐμοὶ καὶ τὸ λάλημα φέρεις
  κεῖνο, τὸ Σειρήνων γλυκυερώτερον.

4 Μίκκη καὶ μελανεῦσα Φιλίννιον.
              Ap. BRUNCK, x.

5 αἰεί μοι δύνει μὲν ἐν οὔασιν ἦχος Ἔρωτος.
              Ap. BRUNCK, liii.

6 Ὦ πτανοί, μὴ καὶ πότ' ἐφίπτασθαι μὲν,
  Ἔρωτες,
  οἴδατ', ἀποπτῆναι δ' οὐδ ὅσον ἰσχύετε.

Who 'd stay on land to-day?
   The very flowers
    Would from their bowers
Delight to wing away !

Leave languid youths to pine
   On silken pillows;
   But be the billows
Of the great deep thine.
Hark, to the sail the breeze sings, " Let
   us fly;"
While soft the sail, replying to the breeze,
Says, with a yielding sigh,
" Yes, where you please."
Up, boy ! the wind, the ray,
   The blue sky o'er thee,
   The deep before thee,
All cry aloud, " Away ! "

IN MYRTLE WREATHS.

BY ALCÆUS.

IN myrtle wreaths my votive sword I 'll
   cover,

Like them of old whose one immortal
   blow
Struck off the galling fetters that hung
   over
   Their own bright land, and laid her
   tyrant low.
Yes, loved Harmodius, thou 'rt undying;
   Still midst the brave and free,
In isles, o'er ocean lying,
   Thy home shall ever be.

In myrtle leaves my sword shall hide its
   lightning,
   Like his, the youth, whose ever-glori-
   ous blade
Leapt forth like flame, the midnight ban-
   quet brightening,
   And in the dust a despot victim laid.
Blest youths, how bright in Freedom's
   story
   Your wedded names shall be ;
A tyrant's death your glory,
   Your meed, a nation free !

JUVENILE POEMS.

1801.

PREFACE BY THE EDITOR.[1]

THE Poems which I take the liberty of publishing, were never intended by the author to pass beyond the circle of his friends. He thought, with some justice, that what are called Occasional Poems must be always insipid and uninteresting to the greater part of their readers. The particular situations in which they were written; the character of the author and of his associates; all these peculiarities must be known and felt before we can enter into the spirit of such compositions. This consideration would have always, I believe, prevented the author himself from submitting these trifles to the eye of dispassionate criticism: and if their posthumous introduction to the world be injustice to his memory, or intrusion on the public, the error must be imputed to the injudicious partiality of friendship.

Mr. LITTLE died in his one and twentieth year; and most of these Poems were written at so early a period that their errors may lay claim to some indulgence from the critic. Their author, as unambitious as indolent, scarce ever looked beyond the moment of composition; but, in general, wrote as he pleased, careless whether he pleased as he wrote. It may likewise be remembered, that they were all the productions of an age when the passions very often give a coloring too warm to the imagination; and this may palliate, if it cannot excuse, that air of levity which pervades so many of them. The *"aurea legge, s' ei piace ei lice,"* he too much pursued, and too much inculcates. Few can regret this more sincerely than myself; and if my friend had lived, the judgment of riper years would have chastened his mind, and tempered the luxuriance of his fancy.

Mr. LITTLE gave much of his time to the study of the amatory writers. If ever he expected to find in the ancients that delicacy of sentiment, and variety of fancy, which are so necessary to refine and animate the poetry of love, he was much disappointed. I know not any one of them who can be regarded as a model in that style; Ovid made love like a rake, and Propertius like a schoolmaster. The mythological allusions of the latter are called erudition by his commentators; but such ostentatious display, upon a subject so simple as love, would be now esteemed vague and puerile, and was even in his own times pedantic. It is astonishing that so many critics should have preferred him to the gentle and touching Tibullus; but those defects, I believe, which a common reader condemns, have been regarded rather as beauties by those erudite men, the commentators; who find a field for their ingenuity and research, in his Grecian learning and quaint obscurities.

Tibullus abounds with touches of fine and natural feeling. The idea of his unexpected return to Delia, *"tunc veniam subito,"* [2] etc. is imagined with all the

---

[1] A portion of the Poems here included were published originally as the works of "the late Thomas Little," with this Preface prefixed to them. "Little," it will be understood, was Moore's pseudonym.

[2] *Lib.* i. *Eleg.* 3.

delicate ardor of a lover; and the sentiment of "*nec te posse carere velim,*" however colloquial the expression may have been, is natural, and from the heart. But the poet of Verona, in my opinion, possessed more genuine feeling than any of them. His life was, I believe, unfortunate; his associates were wild and abandoned; and the warmth of his nature took too much advantage of the latitude which the morals of those times so criminally allowed to the passions. All this depraved his imagination, and made it the slave of his senses. But still a native sensibility is often very warmly perceptible; and when he touches the chord of pathos, he reaches immediately the heart. They who have felt the sweets of return to a home from which they have long been absent will confess the beauty of those simple unaffected lines: —

> *O quid solutis est beatius curis !*
> *cum mens onus reponit, ac peregrino*
> *labore fessi venimus Larem ad nostrum*
> *desideratoque acquiescimus lecto.*
>
> Carm. xxix.

His sorrows on the death of his brother are the very tears of poesy; and when he complains of the ingratitude of mankind, even the inexperienced cannot but sympathize with him. I wish I were a poet; I should then endeavor to catch, by translation, the spirit of those beauties which I have always so warmly admired.[1]

It seems to have been peculiarly the fate of Catullus, that the better and more valuable part of his poetry has not reached us; for there is confessedly nothing in his extant works to authorize the epithet *doctus*, so universally bestowed upon him by the ancients. If time had suffered his other writings to escape, we perhaps should have found among them some more purely amatory; but of those we possess, can there be a sweeter specimen of warm, yet chastened description than his loves of Acme and Septimius? and the few little songs of dalliance to Lesbia are distinguished by such an exquisite playfulness, that they have always been assumed as models by the most elegant modern Latinists. Still, it must be confessed, in the midst of all these beauties,

> —— *medio de fonte leporum*
> *surgit amari aliquid, quod in ipsis floribus angat.*[2]

It has often been remarked, that the ancients knew nothing of gallantry; and we are sometimes told there was too much sincerity in their love to allow them to trifle thus with the semblance of passion. But I cannot perceive that they were any thing more constant than the moderns: they felt all the same dissipation of the heart, though they knew not those seductive graces by which gallantry almost teaches it to be amiable. Wotton, the learned advocate for the moderns, deserts them in considering this point of comparison, and praises the ancients for their ignorance of such refinements. But he seems to have collected his notions of gallantry from the insipid *fadeurs* of the French romances, which have nothing congenial with the graceful levity, the *grata protervitas*, of a Rochester or a Sedley.

As far as I can judge, the early poets of our own language were the models which Mr. LITTLE selected for imitation. To attain their simplicity ("*ævo rarissima nostro simplicitas*") was his fondest ambition. He could not have aimed at a grace more difficult of attainment;[3] and his life was of too short a date to allow

---

1 In the following Poems, will be found a translation of one of his finest Carmina ; but I fancy it is only a mere schoolboy's essay, and deserves to be praised for little more than the attempt.

2 Lucretius.

3 It is a curious illustration of the labor which simplicity requires, that the "Ramblers" of Johnson, elaborate as they appear, were written with fluency, and seldom required revision ; while the simple language of Rousseau, which seems to come flowing from the heart, was the slow production of painful labor, pausing on every word, and balancing every sentence.

him to perfect such a taste; but how far he was likely to have succeeded, the critic may judge from his productions.

I have found among his papers a novel, in rather an imperfect state, which, as soon as I have arranged and collected it, shall be submitted to the public eye.

Where Mr. LITTLE was born, or what is the genealogy of his parents, are points in which very few readers can be interested. His life was one of those humble streams which have scarcely a name in the map of life, and the traveller may pass it by without inquiring its source or direction. His character was well known to all who were acquainted with him; for he had too much vanity to hide its virtues, and not enough of art to conceal its defects. The lighter traits of his mind may be traced perhaps in his writings; but the few for which he was valued live only in the remembrance of his friends.   T. M.

To JOSEPH ATKINSON, Esq.

MY DEAR SIR,

I feel a very sincere pleasure in dedicating to you the Second Edition of our friend LITTLE's Poems. I am not unconscious that there are many in the collection which perhaps it would be prudent to have altered or omitted; and, to say the truth, I more than once revised them for that purpose; but, I know not why, I distrusted either my heart or my judgment; and the consequence is, you have them in their original form:

> *non possunt nostros multæ, Faustine, lituræ*
> *emendare jocos ; una litura potest.*

I am convinced, however, that, though not quite a *casuiste relâché*, you have charity enough to forgive such inoffensive follies: you know that the pious Beza was not the less revered for those sportive *Juvenilia* which he published under a fictitious name; nor did the levity of Bembo's poems prevent him from making a very good cardinal.

Believe me, my dear friend,
With the truest esteem,
Yours,
T. M.

April 19, 1802.

JUVENILE POEMS.

FRAGMENTS OF COLLEGE EXERCISES.

Nobilitas sola est atque unica virtus. — Juv.

Mark those proud boasters of a splendid line,
Like gilded ruins, mouldering while they shine,
How heavy sits that weight of alien show,
Like martial helm upon an infant's brow;
Those borrowed splendors whose contrasting light
Throws back the native shades in deeper night.

Ask the proud train who glory's shade pursue,
Where are the arts by which that glory grew?
The genuine virtues with that eagle-gaze
Sought young Renown in all her orient blaze!
Where is the heart by chymic truth refined,
The exploring soul whose eye had read mankind?
Where are the links that twined, with heavenly art,
His country's interest round the patriot's heart?

. . . . . .

Justum bellum quibus necessarium, et pia arma quibus nulla nisi in armis relinquitur spes. — Livy.

. . . . . .

Is there no call, no consecrating cause,
Approved by Heav'n, ordained by nature's laws,
Where justice flies the herald of our way,
And truth's pure beams upon the banners play?

Yes, there 's a call sweet as an angel's breath
To slumbering babes or innocence in death;

And urgent as the tongue of Heaven within,
When the mind's balance trembles upon sin.

Oh! 't is our country's voice, whose claim should meet
An echo in the soul's most deep retreat;
Along the heart's responding chords should run,
Nor let a tone there vibrate — but the one!

VARIETY.

Ask what prevailing, pleasing power
Allures the sportive, wandering bee
To roam, untired, from flower to flower,
He 'll tell you, 't is variety.

Look Nature round, her features trace,
Her seasons, all her changes see;
And own, upon Creation's face,
The greatest charm 's variety.

For me, ye gracious powers above!
Still let me roam, unfixt and free;
In all things, — but the nymph I love,
I 'll change, and taste variety.

But, Patty, not a world of charms
Could e'er estrange my heart from thee; —
No, let me ever seek those arms,
There still I 'll find variety.

TO A BOY, WITH A WATCH.

WRITTEN FOR A FRIEND.

Is it not sweet, beloved youth,
To rove through Erudition's bowers,
And cull the golden fruits of truth,
And gather Fancy's brilliant flowers?

And is it not more sweet than this,
To feel thy parents' hearts approving,
And pay them back in sums of bliss
The dear, the endless debt of loving?

64

It must be so to thee, my youth;
  With this idea toil is lighter;
This sweetens all the fruits of truth,
  And makes the flowers of fancy
    brighter.

The little gift we send thee, boy,
  May sometimes teach thy soul to pon-
    der,
If indolence or siren joy
  Should ever tempt that soul to wander.

'T will tell thee that the wingèd day
  Can ne'er be chain'd by man's en-
    deavor;
That life and time shall fade away,
  While heaven and virtue bloom for
    ever!

SONG.

IF I swear by that eye, you 'll allow,
  Its look is so shifting and new,
That the oath I might take on it now
  The very next glance would undo.

Those babies that nestle so sly
  Such thousands of arrows have got,
That an oath, on the glance of an eye
  Such as yours, may be off in a shot.

Should I swear by the dew on your lip,
  Though each moment the treasure re-
    news,
If my constancy wishes to trip,
  I may kiss off the oath when I choose.

Or a sigh may disperse from that flower
  Both the dew and the oath that are
    there;
And I 'd make a new vow every hour,
  To lose them so sweetly in air.

But clear up the heaven of your brow,
  Nor fancy my faith is a feather;
On my heart I will pledge you my vow,
  And they both must be broken to-
    gether!

TO . . . .

REMEMBER him thou leavest behind,
  Whose heart is warmly bound to thee,
Close as the tenderest links can bind
  A heart as warm as heart can be.

Oh! I had long in freedom roved,
  Though many seemed my soul to share;
'T was passion when I thought I loved,
  'T was fancy when I thought them fair.

Even she, my muse's early theme,
  Beguiled me only while she warmed;
'T was young desire that fed the dream,
  And reason broke what passion formed.

But thou — ah! better had it been
  If I had still in freedom roved,
If I had ne'er thy beauties seen,
  For then I never should have loved.

Then all the pain which lovers feel
  Had never to this heart been known;
But then, the joys that lovers steal,
  Should *they* have ever been my own?

Oh! trust me, when I swear thee this,
  Dearest! the pain of loving thee,
The very pain is sweeter bliss
  Than passion's wildest ecstasy.

That little cage I would not part,
  In which my soul is prisoned now,
For the most light and wingèd heart
  That wantons on the passing vow.

Still, my beloved! still keep in mind,
  However far removed from me,
That there is one thou leavest behind,
  Whose heart respires for only thee!

And though ungenial ties have bound
  Thy fate unto another's care,
That arm, which clasps thy bosom round,
  Cannot confine the heart that 's there.

No, no! that heart is only mine
  By ties all other ties above,
For I have wed it at a shrine
  Where we have had no priest but Love.

SONG.

WHEN Time who steals our years away
  Shall steal our pleasures too,
The memory of the past will stay,
  And half our joys renew.
Then, Julia, when thy beauty's flower
  Shall feel the wintry air,

Remembrance will recall the hour
  When thou alone wert fair.
Then talk no more of future gloom;
  Our joys shall always last;
For Hope shall brighten days to come,
  And Memory gild the past.

Come, Chloe, fill the genial bowl,
  I drink to Love and thee:
Thou never canst decay in soul,
  Thou 'lt still be young for me.
And as thy lips the tear-drop chase,
  Which on my cheek they find,
So hope shall steal away the trace
  That sorrow leaves behind.
Then fill the bowl — away with gloom!
  Our joys shall always last;
For Hope shall brighten days to come,
  And Memory gild the past.

But mark, at thought of future years
  When love shall lose its soul,
My Chloe drops her timid tears,
  They mingle with my bowl.
How like this bowl of wine, my fair,
  Our loving life shall fleet;
Though tears may sometimes mingle
    there,
  The draught will still be sweet.
Then fill the cup — away with gloom!
  Our joys shall always last;
For Hope will brighten days to come,
  And Memory gild the past.

SONG.

HAVE you not seen the timid tear,
  Steal trembling from mine eye?
Have you not marked the flush of fear,
  Or caught the murmured sigh?
And can you think my love is chill,
  Nor fixt on you alone?
And can you rend, by doubting still,
  A heart so much your own?

To you my soul's affections move,
  Devoutly, warmly true;
My life has been a task of love,
  One long, long thought of you.
If all your tender faith be o'er,
  If still my truth you 'll try;
Alas, I know but *one* proof more —
  I 'll bless your name, and die!

REUBEN AND ROSE.

A TALE OF ROMANCE.

THE darkness that hung upon Willumberg's walls
Had long been remembered with awe
  and dismay;
For years not a sunbeam had played in
  its halls,
And it seemed as shut out from the
  regions of day.

Though the valleys were brightened by
  many a beam,
  Yet none could the woods of that cas-
    tle illume;
And the lightning which flashed on the
  neighboring stream
  Flew back, as if fearing to enter the
    gloom!

"Oh! when shall this horrible darkness
  disperse!"
  Said Willumberg's lord to the Seer of
    the Cave; —
"It can never dispel," said the wizard
  of verse,
  "Till the bright star of chivalry sinks
    in the wave!"

And who was the bright star of chivalry
  then?
  Who *could* be but Reuben, the flower
    of the age?
For Reuben was first in the combat of
  men,
  Though Youth had scarce written his
    name on her page.

For Willumberg's daughter his young
  heart had beat, —
  For Rose, who was bright as the spirit
    of dawn,
When with wand dropping diamonds,
  and silvery feet,
  It walks o'er the flowers of the moun-
    tain and lawn.

Must Rose, then, from Reuben so fatally
  sever?
  Sad, sad were the words of the Seer
    of the Cave,

That darkness should cover that castle
    for ever,
  Or Reuben be sunk in the merciless
    wave!

To the wizard she flew, saying, "Tell
    me, oh, tell!
  Shall my Reuben no more be restored
    to my eyes?"
" Yes, yes — when a spirit shall toll the
    great bell
  Of the mouldering abbey, your Reuben
    shall rise!"

Twice, thrice he repeated "Your Reu-
    ben shall rise!"
  And Rose felt a moment's release from
    her pain;
And wiped, while she listened, the tears
    from her eyes,
  And hoped she might yet see her hero
    again.

That hero could smile at the terrors of
    death,
  When he felt that he died for the sire
    of his Rose;
To the Oder he flew, and there, plunging
    beneath,
  In the depth of the billows soon found
    his repose. —

How strangely the order of destiny
    falls! —
  Not long in the waters the warrior lay,
When a sunbeam was seen to glance over
    the walls,
  And the castle of Willumberg basked
    in the ray!

All, all but the soul of the maid was in
    light,
  There sorrow and terror lay gloomy
    and blank:
Two days did she wander, and all the
    long night,
  In quest of her love, on the wide river's
    bank.

Oft, oft did she pause for the toll of the
    bell,
  And heard but the breathings of night
    in the air;

Long, long did she gaze on the watery
    swell,
  And saw but the foam of the white
    billow there.

And often as midnight its veil would un-
    draw,
  As she looked at the light of the
    moon in the stream,
She thought 't was his helmet of silver
    she saw,
  As the curl of the surge glittered high
    in the beam.

And now the third night was begemming
    the sky;
  Poor Rose, on the cold dewy margent
    reclined,
There wept till the tear almost froze in
    her eye,
  When — hark! — 't was the bell that
    came deep in the wind!

She startled, and saw, through the glim-
    mering shade,
  A form o'er the waters in majesty
    glide;
She knew 't was her love, though his
    cheek was decayed,
  And his helmet of silver was washed
    by the tide.

Was this what the Seer of the Cave had
    foretold? —
  Dim, dim through the phantom the
    moon shot a gleam;
'T was Reuben, but, ah! he was deathly
    and cold,
  And fleeted away like the spell of a
    dream!

Twice, thrice did he rise, and as often
    she thought
  From the bank to embrace him, but
    vain her endeavor!
Then, plunging beneath, at a billow she
    caught,
  And sunk to repose on its bosom for
    ever!

DID NOT.

'T was a new feeling — something more
Than we had dared to own before,

Which then we hid not;
We saw it in each other's eye,
And wished, in every half-breathed sigh,
    To speak, but did not.

She felt my lips' impassioned touch —
'T was the first time I dared so much,
    And yet she chid not;
But whispered o'er my burning brow,
" Oh! do you doubt I love you now? "
    Sweet soul! I did not.

Warmly I felt her bosom thrill,
I prest it closer, closer still,
    Though gently bid not;
Till — oh! the world hath seldom heard
Of lovers, who so nearly erred,
    And yet, who did not.

TO . . . .

THAT wrinkle, when first I espied it,
    At once put my heart out of pain;
Till the eye, that was glowing beside it,
    Disturbed my ideas again.

Thou art just in the twilight at present,
    When woman's declension begins;
When, fading from all that is pleasant,
    She bids a good night to her sins.

Yet thou still art so lovely to me,
    I would sooner, my exquisite mother!
Repose in the sunset of thee,
    Than bask in the noon of another.

TO MRS. . . . .
ON SOME CALUMNIES AGAINST HER CHARACTER.

Is not thy mind a gentle mind?
Is not that heart a heart refined?
Hast thou not every gentle grace,
We love in woman's mind and face?
And, oh! art *thou* a shrine for Sin
To hold her hateful worship in?

No, no, be happy — dry that tear —
Though some thy heart hath harbored
    near,
May now repay its love with blame;
Though man, who ought to shield thy
    fame,

Ungenerous man, be first to shun thee;
Though all the world look cold upon thee,
Yet shall thy pureness keep thee still
Unharmed by that surrounding chill;
Like the famed drop, in crystal found,[1]
Floating, while all was frozen round, —
Unchilled unchanging shalt thou be,
Safe in thy own sweet purity.

ANACREONTIC.
—— *in* lachrymas *verterat omne merum.*
TIB. *lib.* i. *eleg.* 5.

PRESS the grape, and let it pour
Around the board its purple shower;
And, while the drops my goblet steep,
I 'll think in woe the clusters weep.

Weep on, weep on, my pouting vine!
Heaven grant no tears, but tears of wine.
Weep on; and, as thy sorrows flow,
I 'll taste the luxury of woe.

TO . . . .

WHEN I loved you, I can't but allow
    I had many an exquisite minute;
But the scorn that I feel for you now
    Hath even more luxury in it.

Thus, whether we 're on or we 're off,
    Some witchery seems to await you;
To love you was pleasant enough,
    And, oh! 't is delicious to hate you!

TO JULIA.
IN ALLUSION TO SOME ILLIBERAL CRITICISMS.

WHY, let the stingless critic chide
With all that fume of vacant pride

---

1 This alludes to a curious gem, upon which Claudian has left us some very elaborate epigrams. It was a drop of pure water enclosed within a piece of crystal. See Claudian. Epigram. " *de crystallo cui aqua inerat.*" Addison mentions a curiosity of this kind at Milan; and adds, " It is such a rarity as this that I saw at Vendôme in France, which they there pretend is a tear that our Saviour shed over Lazarus, and was gathered up by an angel, who put it into a little crystal vial, and made a present of it to Mary Magdalen. — ADDISON'S " *Remarks on several Parts of Italy.*"

Which mantles o'er the pedant fool,
Like vapor on a stagnant pool.
Oh! if the song, to feeling true,
Can please the elect, the sacred few,
Whose souls, by Taste and Nature taught,
Thrill with the genuine pulse of thought —
If some fond feeling maid like thee,
The warm-eyed child of Sympathy,
Shall say, while o'er my simple theme
She languishes in Passion's dream,
" He was, indeed, a tender soul —
" No critic law, no chill control,
" Should ever freeze, by timid art,
" The flowings of so fond a heart! "
Yes, soul of Nature! soul of Love!
That, hovering like a snow-winged dove,
Breathed o'er my cradle warblings wild,
And hailed me Passion's warmest child,
Grant me the tear from Beauty's eye,
From Feeling's breast the votive sigh;
Oh! let my song, my memory, find
A shrine within the tender mind;
And I will smile when critics chide,
And I will scorn the fume of pride
Which mantles o'er the pedant fool,
Like vapor round some stagnant pool!

TO JULIA.

MOCK me no more with Love's beguiling
　　dream,
　　A dream, I find, illusory as sweet:
One smile of friendship, nay, of cold es-
　　teem,
　　Far dearer were than passion's bland
　　　deceit!

I 've heard you oft eternal truth declare;
　　Your heart was only mine, I once be-
　　　lieved.
Ah! shall I say that all your vows were
　　air?
　　And *must* I say, my hopes were all de-
　　　ceived?

Vow, then, no longer that our souls are
　　twined,
　　That all our joys are felt with mutual
　　　zeal;
Julia! — 't is pity, pity makes you kind;
　　You know I love, and you would *seem*
　　　to feel.

But shall I still go seek within those arms
　　A joy in which affection takes no part?
No, no, farewell! you give me but your
　　charms,
　　When I had fondly thought you gave
　　　your heart.

THE SHRINE.

TO . . . . . .

MY fates had destined me to rove
A long, long pilgrimage of love;
And many an altar on my way
Has lured my pious steps to stay;
For, if the saint was young and fair,
I turned and sung my vespers there.
This, from a youthful pilgrim's fire,
Is what your pretty saints require:
To pass, nor tell a single bead,
With them would be profane indeed!
But, trust me, all this young devotion
Was but to keep my zeal in motion;
And, every humbler altar past,
I now have reached THE SHRINE at last!

TO A LADY,

WITH SOME MANUSCRIPT POEMS.

ON LEAVING THE COUNTRY.

WHEN, casting many a look behind,
　　I leave the friends I cherish here —
Perchance some other friends to find,
　　But surely finding none so dear —

Haply the little simple page,
　　Which votive thus I 've traced for thee,
May now and then a look engage,
　　And steal one moment's thought for
　　　me.

But, oh! in pity let not those
　　Whose hearts are not of gentle mould,
Let not the eye that seldom flows
　　With feeling's tear, my song behold.

For, trust me, they who never melt
　　With pity, never melt with love;
And such will frown at all I 've felt,
　　And all my loving lays reprove.

But if, perhaps, some gentler mind,
　　Which rather loves to praise than
　　　blame,

Should in my page an interest find,
  And linger kindly on my name;

Tell him — or, oh! if, gentler still,
  By female lips my name be blest:
For, where do all affections thrill
  So sweetly as in woman's breast? —

Tell her, that he whose loving themes
  Her eye indulgent wanders o'er,
Could sometimes wake from idle dreams,
  And bolder flights of fancy soar;

That Glory oft would claim the lay,
  And Friendship oft his numbers move;
But whisper then, that, "sooth to say,
  "His sweetest song was given to
    Love!"

TO JULIA.

THOUGH Fate, my girl, may bid us part,
  Our souls it can not, shall not sever;
The heart will seek its kindred heart,
  And cling to it as close as ever.

But must we, must we part indeed?
  Is all our dream of rapture over?
And does not Julia's bosom bleed
  To leave so dear, so fond a lover?

Does *she* too mourn? — Perhaps she may;
  Perhaps she mourns our bliss so fleeting:
But why is Julia's eye so gay,
  If Julia's heart like mine is beating?

I oft have loved that sunny glow
  Of gladness in her blue eye gleaming —
But can the bosom bleed with woe,
  While joy is in the glances beaming?

No, no! — Yet, love, I will not chide;
  Although your heart *were* fond of roving,
Nor that, nor all the world beside
  Could keep your faithful boy from loving.

You 'll soon be distant from his eye,
  And, with you, all that 's worth possessing.
Oh! then it will be sweet to die,
  When life has lost its only blessing!

TO . . . .

SWEET lady, look not thus again:
  Those bright deluding smiles recall
A maid remember'd now with pain,
  Who was my love, my life, my all!

Oh! while this heart bewildered took
  Sweet poison from her thrilling eye,
Thus would she smile and lisp and look,
  And I would hear and gaze and sigh!

Yes, I did love her — wildly love —
  She was her sex's best deceiver!
And oft she swore she'd never rove —
  And I was destined to believe her!

Then, lady, do not wear the smile
  Of one whose smile could thus betray;
Alas! I think the lovely wile
  Again could steal my heart away.

For, when those spells that charmed my
    mind,
  On lips so pure as thine I see,
I fear the heart which she resigned
  Will err again and fly to thee!

NATURE'S LABELS.
A FRAGMENT.

IN vain we fondly strive to trace
The soul's reflection in the face;
In vain we dwell on lines and crosses,
Crooked mouth or short proboscis;
Boobies have looked as wise and bright
As Plato or the Stagirite:
And many a sage and learned skull
Has peeped through windows dark and
    dull.
Since then, though art do all it can,
We ne'er can reach the inward man,
Nor (howsoe'er "learned Thebans"
    doubt)
The inward woman, from without,
Methinks 't were well if Nature could
(And Nature could, if Nature would)
Some pithy, short descriptions write,
On tablets large, in black and white,
Which she might hang about our throttles,
Like labels upon physic-bottles;
And where all men might read — but
    stay —

As dialectic sages say,
The argument most apt and ample
For common use is the example.
For instance, then, if Nature's care
Had not portrayed, in lines so fair,
The inward soul of Lucy Lindon,
This is the label she 'd have pinned on.

LABEL FIRST.

Within this form there lies enshrined
The purest, brightest gem of mind.
Though Feeling's hand may sometimes throw
Upon its charms the shade of woe,
The lustre of the gem, when veiled,
Shall be but mellowed, not concealed.

Now, sirs, imagine, if you 're able,
That Nature wrote a second label,
They 're her own words — at least suppose so —
And boldly pin it on Pomposo.

LABEL SECOND.

When I composed the fustian brain
Of this redoubted Captain Vain,
I had at hand but few ingredients,
And so was forced to use expedients.
I put therein some small discerning,
A grain of sense, a grain of learning;
And when I saw the void behind,
I filled it up with — froth and wind!

· · · · · · ·

TO JULIA.

ON HER BIRTHDAY.

WHEN Time was entwining the garland
of years,
Which to crown my beloved was given,
Though some of the leaves might be sullied with tears,
Yet the flowers were all gathered in heaven.

And long may this garland be sweet to the eye,
May its verdure for ever be new;
Young Love shall enrich it with many a sigh,
And Sympathy nurse it with dew.

A REFLECTION AT SEA.

SEE how, beneath the moonbeam's smile,
Yon little billow heaves its breast,
And foams and sparkles for awhile, —
Then murmuring subsides to rest.

Thus man, the sport of bliss and care,
Rises on time's eventful sea;
And, having swelled a moment there,
Thus melts into eternity!

CLORIS AND FANNY.

CLORIS! if I were Persia's king,
I 'd make my graceful queen of thee;
While FANNY, wild and artless thing,
Should but thy humble handmaid be.

There is but *one* objection in it —
That, verily, I 'm much afraid
I should, in some unlucky minute,
Forsake the mistress for the maid.

THE SHIELD.

SAY, did you not hear a voice of death!
And did you not mark the paly form
Which rode on the silvery mist of the heath,
And sung a ghostly dirge in the storm?

Was it the wailing bird of the gloom,
That shrieks on the house of woe all night?
Or a shivering fiend that flew to a tomb,
To howl and to feed till the glance of light?

'T was *not* the death-bird's cry from the wood,
Nor shivering fiend that hung on the blast;
'T was the shade of Helderic — man of blood —
It screams for the guilt of days that are past.

See, how the red, red lightning strays,
And scares the gliding ghosts of the heath!
Now on the leafless yew it plays,
Where hangs the shield of this son of death.

That shield is blushing with murderous
        stains;
    Long has it hung from the cold yew's
        spray;
    It is blown by storms and washed by
        rains,
    But neither can take the blood away!

Oft by that yew, on the blasted field,
    Demons dance to the red moon's light;
While the damp boughs creak, and the
        swinging shield
    Sings to the raving spirit of night!

TO JULIA WEEPING.

OH! if your tears are given to care,
    If real woe disturbs your peace,
Come to my bosom, weeping fair!
    And I will bid your weeping cease.

But if with Fancy's visioned fears,
    With dreams of woe your bosom thrill;
You look so lovely in your tears,
    That I must bid you drop them still.

DREAMS.

TO

. . . .

IN slumber, I prithee how is it
    That souls are oft taking the air,
And paying each other a visit,
    While bodies are heaven knows where?

Last night, 't is in vain to deny it,
    Your Soul took a fancy to roam,
For I heard her, on tiptoe so quiet,
    Come ask, whether *mine* was at home.

And mine let her in with delight,
    And they talked and they laughed the
        time through;
For, when souls come together at night,
    There is no saying what they may n't
        do!

And *your* little Soul, heaven bless her!
    Had much to complain and to say,
Of how sadly you wrong and oppress
        her
    By keeping her prisoned all day.

"If I happen," said she, "but to steal
    "For a peep now and then to her eye,
"Or, to quiet the fever I feel,
    "Just venture abroad on a sigh;

"In an instant she frightens me in
    "With some phantom of prudence or
        terror,
"For fear I should stray into sin,
    "Or, what is still worse, into error!

"So, instead of displaying my graces,
    "By daylight, in language and mien,
"I am shut up in corners and places,
    "Where truly I blush to be seen!"

Upon hearing this piteous confession,
    My Soul, looking tenderly at her,
Declared, as for grace and discretion,
    He did not know much of the matter;

"But, to-morrow, sweet Spirit!" he
        said,
    "Be at home after midnight, and then
"I will come when your lady 's in bed,
    "And we 'll talk o'er the subject
        again."

So she whispered a word in his ear,
    I suppose to her door to direct him,
And, just after midnight, my dear,
    Your polite little Soul may expect him.

TO ROSA.

WRITTEN DURING ILLNESS.

THE wisest soul, by anguish torn,
    Will soon unlearn the lore it knew;
And when the shrining casket 's worn,
    The gem within will tarnish too.

But love 's an essence of the soul,
    Which sinks not with this chain of clay;
Which throbs beyond the chill control
    Of withering pain or pale decay.

And surely, when the touch of Death
    Dissolves the spirit's earthly ties,
Love still attends the immortal breath,
    And makes it purer for the skies!

Oh Rosa, when, to seek its sphere,
    My soul shall leave this orb of men,

That love which formed its treasure here,
 Shall be its *best* of treasures then !

And as, in fabled dreams of old,
 Some air-born genius, child of time,
Presided o'er each star that rolled,
 And tracked it through its path sub-
 lime;

So thou, fair planet, not unled,
 Shalt through thy mortal orbit stray;
Thy lover's shade, to thee still wed,
 Shall linger round thy earthly way.

Let other spirits range the sky,
 And play around each starry gem;
I 'll bask beneath that lucid eye,
 Nor envy worlds of suns to them.

And when that heart shall cease to beat,
 And when that breath at length is free,
Then, Rosa, soul to soul we 'll meet,
 And mingle to eternity !

SONG.

THE wreath you wove, the wreath you
 wove
 Is fair — but oh, how fair,
If Pity's hand had stolen from Love
 One leaf to mingle there !

If every rose with gold were tied,
 Did gems for dewdrops fall,
One faded leaf where Love had sighed
 Were sweetly worth them all.

The wreath you wove, the wreath you
 wove
 Our emblem well may be;
Its bloom is yours, but hopeless Love
 Must keep its tears for me.

THE SALE OF LOVES.

I DREAMT that, in the Paphian groves,
 My nets by moonlight laying,
I caught a flight of wanton Loves,
 Among the rose-beds playing.
Some just had left their silvery shell,
 While some were full in feather;
So pretty a lot of Loves to sell,
 Were never yet strung together.

Come buy my Loves,
 Come buy my Loves,
Ye dames and rose-lipped misses ! —
 They 're new and bright,
 The cost is light,
For the coin of this isle is kisses.

First Cloris came, with looks sedate,
 The coin on her lips was ready;
" I buy," quoth she, " my Love by
 weight,
 " Full grown, if you please, and
 steady."
" Let mine be light," said Fanny,
 " pray —
 " Such lasting toys undo one;
" A light little Love that will last to-
 day, —
 " To-morrow I 'll sport a new one."
 Come buy my Loves,
 Come buy my Loves,
Ye dames and rose-lipped misses ! —
 There 's some will keep,
 Some light and cheap,
At from ten to twenty kisses.

The learned Prue took a pert young thing,
 To divert her virgin Muse with,
And pluck sometimes a quill from his
 wing,
 To indite her billet-doux with.
Poor Cloe would give for a well-fledged
 pair
 Her only eye, if you 'd ask it;
And Tabitha begged, old toothless fair,
 For the youngest Love in the basket.
 Come buy my Loves, etc.

But *one* was left, when Susan came,
 One worth them all together;
At sight of her dear looks of shame,
 He smiled and pruned his feather.
She wished the boy — t 'was more than
 whim —
 Her looks, her sighs betrayed it;
But kisses were not enough for him,
 I asked a heart and she paid it !
 Good-by, my Loves,
 Good-by, my Loves,
'T would make you smile to 've seen us
 First trade for this
 Sweet child of bliss,
And then nurse the boy between us.

TO . . . .

THE world had just begun to steal
  Each hope that led me lightly on;
I felt not as I used to feel,
  And life grew dark and love was gone.

No eye to mingle sorrow's tear,
  No lip to mingle pleasure's breath,
No circling arms to draw me near —
  'T was gloomy, and I wished for death.

But when I saw that gentle eye,
  Oh! something seemed to tell me then,
That I was yet too young to die,
  And hope and bliss might bloom again.

With every gentle smile that crost
  Your kindling cheek, you lighted home
Some feeling which my heart had lost
  And peace which far had learned to
    roam.

'T was then indeed so sweet to live,
  Hope looked so new and Love so kind,
That, though I mourn, I yet forgive
  The ruin they have left behind.

I could have loved you — oh, so well! —
  The dream, that wishing boyhood
    knows,
Is but a bright, beguiling spell,
  That only lives while passion glows:

But, when this early flush declines,
  When the heart's sunny morning fleets,
You know not then how close it twines
  Round the first kindred soul it meets.

Yes, yes, I could have loved, as one
  Who, while his youth's enchantments
    fall,
Finds something dear to rest upon,
  Which pays him for the loss of all.

TO . . . .

NEVER mind how the pedagogue proses,
  You want not antiquity's stamp;
A lip, that such fragrance discloses,
  Oh! never should smell of the lamp.

Old Cloe, whose withering kiss
  Hath long set the Loves at defiance,

Now, done with the science of bliss,
  May take to the blisses of science.

But for *you* to be buried in books —
  Ah, Fanny, they 're pitiful sages,
Who could not in *one* of your looks
  Read more than in millions of pages.

Astronomy finds in those eyes
  Better light than she studies above;
And Music would borrow your sighs
  As the melody fittest for Love.

Your Arithmetic only can trip
  If to count your own charms you en-
    deavor;
And Eloquence glows on your lip
  When you swear that you 'll love me
    for ever.

Thus you see, what a brilliant alliance
  Of arts is assembled in you; —
A course of more exquisite science
  Man never need wish to pursue.

And, oh! — if a Fellow like me
  May confer a diploma of hearts,
With my lip thus I seal your degree,
  My divine little Mistress of Arts!

ON THE DEATH OF A LADY.

SWEET spirit! if thy airy sleep
  Nor sees my tears nor hears my sighs,
Then will I weep, in anguish weep,
  Till the last heart's drop fills mine eyes.

But if thy sainted soul can feel,
  And mingles in our misery;
Then, then my breaking heart I 'll seal —
  Thou shalt not hear one sigh from me.

The beam of morn was on the stream,
  But sullen clouds the day deform:
Like thee was that young, orient beam,
  Like death, alas, that sullen storm!

Thou wert not formed for living here,
  So linked thy soul was with the sky;
Yet, ah, we held thee all so dear,
  We thought thou wert not formed to
    die.

INCONSTANCY.

AND do I then wonder that Julia deceives me,
    When surely there 's nothing in nature
        more common?
She vows to be true, and while vowing
        she leaves me —
    And could I expect any more from a
        woman?

Oh, woman! your heart is a pitiful treasure;
    And Mahomet's doctrine was not too
        severe,
When he held that you were but materials of pleasure,
    And reason and thinking were out of
        your sphere.

By your heart, when the fond sighing
        lover can win it,
    He thinks that an age of anxiety 's
        paid;
But, oh, while he 's blest, let him die at
        the minute —
    If he live but a *day*, he 'll be surely
        betrayed.

THE NATAL GENIUS.

A DREAM.

TO . . . . . ,

THE MORNING OF HER BIRTHDAY.

IN witching slumbers of the night,
I dreamt I was the airy sprite
    That on thy natal moment smiled;
And thought I wafted on my wing
Those flowers which in Elysium spring,
    To crown my lovely mortal child.

With olive-branch I bound thy head,
Heart's ease along thy path I shed,
    Which was to bloom through all thy
        years;
Nor yet did I forget to bind
Love's roses, with his myrtle twined,
    And dewed by sympathetic tears.

Such was the wild but precious boon
Which Fancy, at her magic noon,
    Bade me to Nona's image pay;

And were it thus my fate to be
Thy little guardian deity,
    How blest around thy steps I 'd play!

Thy life should glide in peace along,
Calm as some lonely shepherd's song
    That 's heard at distance in the grove;
No cloud should ever dim thy sky,
No thorns along thy pathway lie,
    But all be beauty, peace, and love.

Indulgent Time should never bring
To thee one blight upon his wing,
    So gently o'er thy brow he 'd fly;
And death itself should but be felt
Like that of daybeams, when they melt,
    Bright to the last, in evening's sky!

ELEGIAC STANZAS,

SUPPOSED TO BE WRITTEN BY JULIA,

ON THE DEATH OF HER BROTHER.

THOUGH sorrow long has worn my heart;
    Though every day I 've counted o'er
Hath brought a new and quickening smart
    To wounds that rankled fresh before;

Though in my earliest life bereft
    Of tender links by nature tied;
Though hope deceived, and pleasure left;
    Though friends betrayed and foes be-
        lied;

I still had hopes — for hope will stay
    After the sunset of delight;
So like the star which ushers day,
    We scarce can think it heralds night! —

I hoped that, after all its strife,
    My weary heart at length should rest,
And, fainting from the waves of life,
    Find harbor in a brother's breast.

That brother's breast was warm with
        truth,
    Was bright with honor's purest ray;
He was the dearest, gentlest youth —
    Ah, why then was he torn away?

He should have stayed, have lingered
        here
    To soothe his Julia's every woe;
He should have chased each bitter tear,
    And not have caused those tears to flow.

We saw within his soul expand
　The fruits of genius, nurst by taste;
While Science, with a fostering hand,
　Upon his brow her chaplet placed.

We saw, by bright degrees, his mind
　Grow rich in all that makes men
　　dear; —
Enlightened, social, and refined,
　In friendship firm, in love sincere.

Such was the youth we loved so well,
　And such the hopes that fate denied; —
We loved, but ah! could scarcely tell
　How deep, how dearly, till he died!

Close as the fondest links could strain,
　Twined with my very heart he grew;
And by that fate which breaks the chain,
　The heart is almost broken too.

TO THE LARGE AND BEAUTIFUL

MISS . . . . ,

IN ALLUSION TO SOME PARTNERSHIP IN A LOT-
TERY SHARE.

IMPROMPTU.

— *Ego pars* —— Virg.

In wedlock a species of lottery lies,
　Where in blanks and in prizes we deal;
But how comes it that you, such a capi-
　　tal prize,
　Should so long have remained in the
　　wheel?

If ever, by Fortune's indulgent decree,
　To me such a ticket should roll,
A sixteenth, Heaven knows! were suffi-
　　cient for me;
　For what could *I* do with the whole?

A DREAM.

I thought this heart enkindled lay
　On Cupid's burning shrine:
I thought he stole thy heart away,
　And placed it near to mine.

I saw thy heart begin to melt,
　Like ice before the sun;
Till both a glow congenial felt,
　And mingled into one!

TO . . . . . .

With all my soul, then, let us part,
　Since both are anxious to be free;
And I will send you home your heart,
　If you will send back mine to me.

We 've had some happy hours together,
　But joy must often change its wing;
And spring would be but gloomy weather,
　If we had nothing else but spring.

'T is not that I expect to find
　A more devoted, fond, and true one,
With rosier cheek or sweeter mind —
　Enough for me that she 's a new one.

Thus let us leave the bower of love,
　Where we have loitered long in bliss;
And you may down *that* pathway rove,
　While I shall take my way through
　　this.

ANACREONTIC.

" She never looked so kind before —
　" Yet why the wanton's smile recall?
" I 've seen this witchery o'er and o'er,
　" 'T is hollow, vain, and heartless all!"

Thus I said and, sighing, drained
　The cup which she so late had tasted;
Upon whose rim still fresh remained
　The breath, so oft in falsehood wasted.

I took the harp and would have sung
　As if t' were not of her I sang;
But still the notes on Lamia hung —
　On whom but Lamia *could* they hang?

Those eyes of hers, that floating shine,
　Like diamonds in some eastern river;
That kiss, for which, if worlds were mine,
　A world for every kiss I 'd give her.

That frame so delicate, yet warmed
　With flushes of love's genial hue; —
A mould transparent, as if formed
　To let the spirit's light shine through.

Of these I sung, and notes and words
　Were sweet, as if the very air
From Lamia's lip hung o'er the chords,
　And Lamia's voice still warbled there!

But when, alas, I turned the theme,
  And when of vows and oaths I spoke,
Of truth and hope's seducing dream —
  The chord beneath my finger broke.

False harp! false woman! — such, oh,
  such
Are lutes too frail and hearts too will-
  ing;
Any hand, whate'er its touch,
  Can set their chords or pulses thrilling.

And when that thrill is most awake,
  And when you think Heaven's joys
  await you,
The nymph will change, the chord will
  break —
Oh Love, oh Music, how I hate you!

TO JULIA.

I SAW the peasant's hand unkind
  From yonder oak the ivy sever;
They seemed in very being twined;
  Yet now the oak is fresh as ever!

Not so the widowed ivy shines:
  Torn from its dear and only stay,
In drooping widowhood it pines,
  And scatters all its bloom away.

Thus, Julia, did our hearts entwine,
  Till Fate disturbed their tender ties:
Thus gay indifference blooms in thine,
  While mine, deserted, droops and dies!

HYMN

OF

A VIRGIN OF DELPHI,

AT THE TOMB OF HER MOTHER.

OH, lost, for ever lost — no more
  Shall Vesper light our dewy way
Along the rocks of Crissa's shore,
  To hymn the fading fires of day;
No more to Tempe's distant vale
  In holy musings shall we roam,
Through summer's glow and winter's
  gale,
  To bear the mystic chaplets home.[1]

'T was then my soul's expanding zeal,
  By nature warmed and led by thee,
In every breeze was taught to feel
  The breathings of a Deity.
Guide of my heart! still hovering round,
  Thy looks, thy words are still my own—
I see thee raising from the ground
  Some laurel, by the winds o'erthrown,
And hear thee say, " This humble bough
  " Was planted for a doom divine;
" And, though it droop in languor now,
  " Shall flourish on the Delphic shrine!
" Thus, in the vale of earthly sense,
  " Though sunk awhile the spirit lies,
" A viewless hand shall cull it thence
  " To bloom immortal in the skies! "

All that the young should feel and know
  By thee was taught so sweetly well,
Thy words fell soft as vernal snow,
  And all was brightness where they
  fell!
Fond soother of my infant tear,
  Fond sharer of my infant joy,
Is not thy shade still lingering here?
  Am I not still thy soul's employ?
Oh yes — and, as in former days,
  When, meeting on the sacred mount,
Our nymphs awaked their choral lays,
  And danced around Cassotis' fount;
As then, 't was all thy wish and care,
  That mine should be the simplest mien,
My lyre and voice the sweetest there,
  My foot the lightest o'er the green:
So still, each look and step to mould,
  Thy guardian care is round me spread,
Arranging every snowy fold
  And guiding every mazy tread.
And, when I lead the hymning choir,
  Thy spirit still, unseen and free,
Hovers between my lip and lyre,
  And weds them into harmony.
Flow, Plistus, flow, thy murmuring wave
  Shall never drop its silvery tear
Upon so pure, so blest a grave,
  To memory so entirely dear!

---

1 The laurel, for the common uses of the temple, for adorning the altars and sweeping the
pavement, was supplied by a tree near the fountain of Castalia; but upon all important occasions,
they sent to Tempe for their laurel. We find, in

Pausanias, that this valley supplied the branches,
of which the temple was originally constructed;
and Plutarch says, in his Dialogue on Music,
" The youth who brings the Tempic laurel to
Delphi is always attended by a player on the
flute."

ἀλλὰ μὴν καὶ τῷ κατακομίζοντι παιδὶ τὴν Τεμπι-
κὴν δάφνην εἰς Δελφοὺς παρομάρτει αὐλήτης.

SYMPATHY.

TO JULIA.

—— *sine me sit nulla Venus.*

SULPICIA.

OUR hearts, my love, were formed to be
The genuine twins of Sympathy,
  They live with one sensation:
In joy or grief, but most in love,
Like chords in unison they move,
  And thrill with like vibration.

How oft I 've heard thee fondly say,
Thy vital pulse shall cease to play
  When mine no more is moving;
Since, now, to feel a joy *alone*
Were worse to thee than feeling none,
  So twined are we in loving!

THE TEAR.

ON beds of snow the moonbeam slept,
  And chilly was the midnight gloom,
When by the damp grave Ellen wept —
  Fond maid! it was her Lindor's tomb!

A warm tear gushed, the wintry air
  Congealed it as it flowed away:
All night it lay an ice-drop there,
  At morn it glittered in the ray.

An angel, wandering from her sphere,
  Who saw this bright, this frozen gem,
To dew-eyed Pity brought the tear
  And hung it on her diadem!

THE SNAKE.

MY love and I, the other day,
Within a myrtle arbor lay,
When near us, from a rosy bed,
A little Snake put forth its head.

" See," said the maid with thoughtful
    eyes —
" Yonder the fatal emblem lies!
" Who could expect such hidden harm
" Beneath the rose's smiling charm? "

Never did grave remark occur
Less *à-propos* than this from her.

I rose to kill the snake, but she,
Half-smiling, prayed it might not be.

" No," said the maiden — and, alas,
  Her eyes spoke volumes, while she
    said it —
" Long as the snake is in the grass,
  "One *may*, perhaps, have cause to
    dread it:
" But, when its wicked eyes appear,
  "And when we know for what they
    wink so,
" One must be *very* simple, dear,
  "To let it wound one — don't you
    think so? "

TO ROSA.

Is the song of Rosa mute?
Once such lays inspired her lute!
Never doth a sweeter song
Steal the breezy lyre along,
When the wind, in odors dying,
Woos it with enamour'd sighing.

Is my Rosa's lute unstrung?
Once a tale of peace it sung
To her lover's throbbing breast —
Then he was divinely blest!
Ah! but Rosa loves no more,
Therefore Rosa's song is o'er;
And her lute neglected lies;
And her boy forgotten sighs.
Silent lute — forgotten lover —
Rosa's love and song are over!

ELEGIAC STANZAS.

Sic juvat perire.

WHEN wearied wretches sink to sleep,
  How heavenly soft their slumbers lie!
How sweet is death to those who weep,
  To those who weep and long to die!

Saw you the soft and grassy bed,
  Where flowrets deck the green earth's
    breast?
'T is there I wish to lay my head,
  'T is there I wish to sleep at rest.

Oh, let not tears embalm my tomb, —
  None but the dews at twilight given!
Oh, let not sighs disturb the gloom, —
  None but the whispering winds of
    heaven!

LOVE AND MARRIAGE.

Eque brevi verbo ferre perenne malum.
    SECUNDUS, eleg. vii.

STILL the question I must parry,
    Still a wayward truant prove:
Where I love, I must not marry;
    Where I marry, can not love.●

Were she fairest of creation,
    With the least presuming mind;
Learned without affectation;
    Not deceitful, yet refined;

Wise enough, but never rigid;
    Gay, but not too lightly free;
Chaste as snow, and yet not frigid;
    Fond, yet satisfied with me:

Were she all this ten times over,
    All that heaven to earth allows,
I should be too much her lover
    Ever to become her spouse.

Love will never bear enslaving;
    Summer garments suit him best;
Bliss itself is not worth having,
    If we 're by compulsion blest.

ANACREONTIC.

I FILLED to thee, to thee I drank,
    I nothing did but drink and fill;
The bowl by turns was bright and blank,
    'T was drinking, filling, drinking still.

At length I bade an artist paint
    Thy image in this ample cup,
That I might see the dimpled saint,
    To whom I quaffed my nectar up.

Behold, how bright that purple lip
    Now blushes through the wave at me;
Every roseate drop I sip
    Is just like kissing wine from thee.

And still I drink the more for this;
    For, ever when the draught I drain,
Thy lip invites another kiss,
    And — in the nectar flows again.

So, here 's to thee, my gentle dear,
    And may that eyelid never shine
Beneath a darker, bitterer tear
    Than bathes it in this bowl of mine!

THE SURPRISE.

CHLORIS, I swear, by all I ever swore,
That from this hour I shall not love thee
    more. —
"What! love no more? Oh! why this
    altered vow?"
Because I *can not* love thee *more* — than
    now!

TO MISS . . . . . . ,

ON HER ASKING THE AUTHOR WHY SHE
HAD SLEEPLESS NIGHTS.

I 'LL ask the sylph who round thee flies,
    And in thy breath his pinion dips,
Who suns him in thy radiant eyes,
    And faints upon thy sighing lips:

I 'll ask him where 's the veil of sleep
    That used to shade thy looks of light;
And why those eyes their vigil keep
    When other suns are sunk in night?

And I will say — her angel breast
    Has never throbbed with guilty sting;
Her bosom is the sweetest nest
    Where Slumber could repose his wing!

And I will say — her cheeks that flush,
    Like vernal roses in the sun,
Have ne'er by shame been taught to
    blush,
    Except for what her eyes have done!

Then tell me, why, thou child of air!
    Does slumber from her eyelids rove?
What is her heart's impassioned care? —
    Perhaps, oh sylph! perhaps, 't is *love.*

THE WONDER.

COME, tell me where the maid is found,
    Whose heart can love without deceit,
And I will range the world around,
    To sigh one moment at her feet.

Oh! tell me where 's her sainted home,
    What air receives her blessed sigh,
A pilgrimage of years I 'll roam
    To catch one sparkle of her eye!

And if her cheek be smooth and bright,
    While truth within her bosom lies,

I 'll gaze upon her morn and night,
  Till my heart leave me through my
    eyes.

Show me on earth a thing so rare,
  I 'll own all miracles are true;
To make one maid sincere and fair,
  Oh, 't is the utmost Heaven can do!

LYING.

Che con le lor bugie pajon divini.
       MAURO D'ARCANO.

I DO confess, in many a sigh,
  My lips have breathed you many a lie;
And who, with such delights in view,
  Would lose them for a lie or two?

Nay, — look not thus, with brow re-
    proving;
Lies are, my dear, the soul of loving.
If half we tell the girls were true,
If half we swear to think and do,
Were aught but lying's bright illusion,
This world would be in strange confusion.
If ladies' eyes were, every one,
As lovers swear, a radiant sun,
Astronomy must leave the skies,
To learn her lore in ladies' eyes.
Oh, no — believe me, lovely girl,
When nature turns your teeth to pearl,
Your neck to snow, your eyes to fire,
Your amber locks to golden wire,
Then, only then can Heaven decree,
That you should live for only me,
Or I for you, as night and morn,
We 've swearing kist, and kissing sworn.
  And now, my gentle hints to clear,
For once I 'll tell you truth, my dear.
Whenever you may chance to meet
Some loving youth, whose love is sweet,
Long as you 're false and he believes you,
Long as you trust and he deceives you,
So long the blissful bond endures,
And while he lies, his heart is yours:
But, oh! you 've wholly lost the youth
The instant that he tells you truth.

ANACREONTIC.

FRIEND of my soul, this goblet sip,
  'T will chase that pensive tear;
'T is not so sweet as woman's lip,
  But, oh! 't is more sincere.

Like her delusive beam,
  'T will steal away thy mind:
But, truer than love's dream,
  It leaves no sting behind.

Come, twine the wreath, thy brows to
    shade;
  These flowers were culled at noon; —
Like woman's love the rose will fade,
  But, ah! not half so soon.
For though the flower 's decayed,
  Its fragrance is not o'er;
But once when love 's betrayed,
  Its sweet life blooms no more.

THE PHILOSOPHER ARISTIPPUS [1]

TO A LAMP

WHICH HAD BEEN GIVEN HIM BY LAIS.

Dulcis conscia lectuli lucerna.
    MARTIAL, *lib.* xiv. *epig.* 39.

"OH! love the Lamp" (my Mistress
    said),
  "The faithful Lamp that, many a night,
"Beside thy Lais' lonely bed
  "Has kept its little watch of light.

"Full often has it seen her weep,
  "And fix her eye upon its flame,
"Till, weary, she has sunk to sleep,
  "Repeating her beloved's name.

1 It does not appear to have been very difficult to become a philosopher amongst the ancients. A moderate store of learning, with a
considerable portion of confidence, and just wit
enough to produce an occasional apophthegm,
seem to have been all the qualifications necessary
for the purpose. The principles of moral science
were so very imperfectly understood that the
founder of a new sect, in forming his ethical
code, might consult either fancy or temperament,
and adapt it to his own passions and propensities;
so that Mahomet, with a little more learning,
might have flourished as a philosopher in those
days, and would have required but the polish of
the schools to become the rival of Aristippus in
morality. In the science of nature, too, though
some valuable truths were discovered by them,
they seemed hardly to know they were truths, or
at least were as well satisfied with errors; and
Xenophanes, who asserted that the stars were
igneous clouds, lighted up every night and extinguished again in the morning, was thought and
styled a philosopher, as generally as he who anticipated Newton in developing the arrangement
of the universe.

For this opinion of Xenophanes, see Plutarch.
"de Placit. Philosoph." lib. ii. cap. 13. It is
impossible to read this treatise of Plutarch, without alternately admiring the genius, and smiling
at the absurdities of the philosophers.

"Then love the Lamp —'t will often lead
    "Thy step through learning's sacred
        way;
"And when those studious eyes shall
        read,
    "At midnight, by its lonely ray,
        "Of things sublime, of nature's
            birth,
        "Of all that 's bright in heaven or
            earth,
"Oh, think that she, by whom 't was
        given,
    "Adores thee more than earth or
        heaven!"

Yes — dearest Lamp, by every charm
    On which thy midnight beam has
        hung;[1]
The head reclined, the graceful arm
    Across the brow of ivory flung;

The heaving bosom, partly hid,
    The severed lip's unconscious sighs,
The fringe that from the half-shut lid
    Adown the cheek of roses lies:

By these, by all that bloom untold,
    And long as all shall charm my heart,
I 'll love my little Lamp of gold —
    My Lamp and I shall never part.

And often, as she smiling said,
    In fancy's hour, thy gentle rays
Shall guide my visionary tread
    Through poesy's enchanting maze.
Thy flame shall light the page refined,
    Where still we catch the Chian's
        breath,
    Where still the bard, though cold in
        death,
Has left his soul unquenched behind.
Or, o'er thy humbler legend shine,
    Oh man of Ascra's dreary glades,[2]

To whom the nightly warbling Nine[3]
    A wand of inspiration gave,[4]
Plucked from the greenest tree, that
        shades
    The crystal of Castalia's wave.

Then, turning to a purer lore,
We 'll cull the sages' deep-hid store,
From Science steal her golden clue,
And every mystic path pursue,
Where Nature, far from vulgar eyes,
Through labyrinths of wonder flies.
'T is thus my heart shall learn to know
How fleeting is this world below,
Where all that meets the morning light,
Is changed before the fall of night![5]

I 'll tell thee, as I trim thy fire,
    "Swift, swift the tide of being runs,
    "And Time, who bids thy flame expire,
        "Will also quench yon heaven of
            suns."

Oh, then if earth's united power
Can never chain one feathery hour;
If every print we leave to-day
To-morrow's wave will sweep away;
Who pauses to inquire of heaven
Why were the fleeting treasures given,
The sunny days, the shady nights,
And all their brief but dear delights,
Which heaven has made for man to use,
And man should think it crime to lose?
Who that has culled a fresh-blown rose
Will ask it why it breathes and glows,
Unmindful of the blushing ray,
In which it shines its soul away;
Unmindful of the scented sigh,
With which it dies and loves to die.

Pleasure, thou only good on earth![6]
    One precious moment given to thee —

3 ἐννύχιαι στεῖχον, περικάλλεα ὄσσαν ἱεῖσαι. "Theog." v. 10.

4 καί μοι σκῆπτρον ἔδον, δάφνης ἐριθηλέα ὄζον. Id. v. 30.

5 ῥεῖν τὰ ὅλα ποταμοῦ δίκην, as expressed among the dogmas of Heraclitus the Ephesian, and with the same image by Seneca, in whom we find a beautiful diffusion of the thought. "*Nemo est mane, qui fuit pridie. corpora nostra rapiuntur fluminum more; quidquid vides currit cum tempore. nihil ex his quæ videmus manet. ego ipse, dum loquor mutari ipsa, mutatus sum,*" etc.

6 Aristippus considered motion as the principle of happiness, in which idea he differed from

1 The ancients had their *lucernæ cubiculariæ*, or bedchamber lamps, which, as the Emperor Galienus said, "*nil cras meminere*;" and, with the same commendation of secrecy, Praxagora addresses her lamp in Aristophanes, "'Εκκλης." We may judge how fanciful they were, in the use and embellishment of their lamps, from the famous symbolic Lucerna, which we find in the "Romanum Museum," Mich. Ang. Causei, p. 127.

2 Hesiod, who tells us in melancholy terms of his father's flight to the wretched village of Ascra. "'Εργ. καὶ 'Ημέρ." v. 251.

Oh! by my Lais' lip, 't is worth
    The sage's immortality.

Then far be all the wisdom hence,
    That would our joys one hour delay!
Alas, the feast of soul and sense
    Love calls us to in youth's bright day,
    If not soon tasted, fleets away.
Ne'er wert thou formed, my Lamp, to
    shed
    Thy splendor on a lifeless page; —
Whate'er my blushing Lais said
Of thoughtful lore and studies sage,
'T was mockery all — her glance of joy
Told me thy dearest, best employ.[1]
And, soon as night shall close the eye
    Of heaven's young wanderer in the
    west;
When seers are gazing on the sky,
    To find their future orbs of rest;
Then shall I take my trembling way,
    Unseen but to those worlds above,
And, led by thy mysterious ray,
    Steal to the night-bower of my love.

TO MRS. ———.

ON HER BEAUTIFUL TRANSLATION OF VOITURE'S KISS.

Mon âme sur mon lèvre étoit lors toute entière,
  Pour savourer le miel qui sur la vôtre étoit;
Mais en me retirant, elle resta derrière,
Tant de ce doux plaisir l'amorce l'a restoit.
               VOITURE.

How heavenly was the poet's doom,
    To breathe his spirit through a kiss;
And lose within so sweet a tomb
    The trembling messenger of bliss!

And, sure his soul returned to feel
    That it *again* could ravished be;
For in the kiss that thou didst steal,
    His life and soul have fled to thee.

RONDEAU.

"GOOD night! good night!" — And is
    it so?
And must I from my Rosa go?
Oh Rosa, say "Good night!" once more,
And I 'll repeat it o'er and o'er,
Till the first glance of dawning light
Shall find us saying, still, "Good night."

And still "Good night," my Rosa, say —
But whisper still, "A minute stay;"
And I will stay, and every minute
Shall have an age of transport in it;
Till Time himself shall stay his flight,
To listen to our sweet "Good night."

"Good night!" you 'll murmur with a
    sigh,
And tell me it is time to fly:
And I will vow, will swear to go,
While still that sweet voice murmurs
    "No!"
Till slumber seal our weary sight —
And then, my love, my soul, "Good
    night!"

SONG.

WHY does azure deck the sky?
    'T is to be like thy looks of blue
Why is red the rose's dye?
    Because it is thy blushes' hue.
All that 's fair, by Love's decree,
Has been made resembling thee!

Why is falling snow so white,
    But to be like thy bosom fair?
Why are solar beams so bright?
    That they may seem thy golden hair!
All that 's bright, by Love's decree,
Has been made resembling thee!

---

the Epicureans, who looked to a state of repose as the only true voluptuousness, and avoided even the too lively agitations of pleasure, as a violent and ungraceful derangement of the senses.

[1] Maupertuis has been still more explicit than this philosopher, in ranking the pleasures of sense above the sublimest pursuits of wisdom. Speaking of the infant man, in his production, he calls him, "*une nouvelle créature, qui pourra comprendre les choses les plus sublimes, et ce qui est bien au-dessus, qui pourra gouter les mêmes plaisirs.*" See his "Vénus Physique." This appears to be one of the efforts at Fontenelle's gallantry of manner, for which the learned President is so well and justly ridiculed in the "Akakia" of Voltaire.

Maupertuis may be thought to have borrowed from the ancient Aristippus that indiscriminate theory of pleasures which he has set forth in his "Essai de Philosophe Morale," and for which he was so very justly condemned. Aristippus, according to Laertius, held μὴ διαφερειν τε ἡδονὴν ἡδονῆς, which irrational sentiment has been adopted by Maupertuis: "*Tant qu'on ne considère que l'état présent, tous les plaisirs sont du même genre,*" etc.

Why are nature's beauties felt?
　Oh! 't is thine in her we see!
Why has music power to melt?
　Oh! because it speaks like thee.
All that 's sweet, by Love's decree,
Has been made resembling thee!

TO ROSA.

LIKE one who trusts to summer skies,
　And puts his little bark to sea,
Is he who, lured by smiling eyes,
　Consigns his simple heart to thee.

For fickle is the summer wind,
　And sadly may the bark be tost;
For thou art sure to change thy mind,
　And then the wretched heart is lost!

WRITTEN IN A COMMONPLACE BOOK,

CALLED

"THE BOOK OF FOLLIES;"

IN WHICH EVERY ONE THAT OPENED IT WAS
TO CONTRIBUTE SOMETHING.

TO THE BOOK OF FOLLIES.

THIS tribute 's from a wretched elf,
Who hails thee, emblem of himself.
The book of life, which I have traced,
Has been, like thee, a motley waste
Of follies scribbled o'er and o'er,
One folly bringing hundreds more.
Some have indeed been writ so neat,
In characters so fair, so sweet,
That those who judge not too severely,
Have said they loved such follies dearly!
Yet still, O book! the allusion stands;
For these were penned by *female* hands:
The rest — alas! I own the truth —
Have all been scribbled so uncouth
That Prudence, with a withering look,
Disdainful, flings away the book.
Like thine, its pages here and there
Have oft been stained with blots of care;
And sometimes hours of peace, I own,
Upon some fairer leaves have shone,
White as the snowings of that heaven
By which those hours of peace were
　given.
But now no longer — such, oh, such
The blast of Disappointment's touch! —
No longer now those hours appear;
Each leaf is sullied by a tear:

Blank, blank is every page with care,
Not even a folly brightens there.
Will they yet brighten? — never, never!
Then *shut the book*, O God, for ever!

TO ROSA.

SAY, why should the girl of my soul be
　in tears
　At a meeting of rapture like this,
When the glooms of the past and the
　sorrow of years
　Have been paid by one moment of
　bliss?

Are they shed for that moment of bliss-
　ful delight,
　Which dwells on her memory yet?
Do they flow, like the dews of the love-
　breathing night,
　From the warmth of the sun that has
　set?

Oh! sweet is the tear on that languishing
　smile,
　That smile, which is loveliest then;
And if such are the drops that delight
　can beguile,
　Thou shalt weep them again and again.

LIGHT SOUNDS THE HARP.

LIGHT sounds the harp when the com-
　bat is over,
　When heroes are resting, and joy is in
　bloom;
When laurels hang loose from the brow
　of the lover,
　And Cupid makes wings of the war-
　rior's plume.
　　But, when the foe returns,
　　Again the hero burns;
High flames the sword in his hand once
　more:
　　The clang of mingling arms
　　Is then the sound that charms,
And brazen notes of war, that stirring
　trumpets pour; —
Then, again comes the Harp, when the
　combat is over —
　When heroes are resting, and Joy is
　in bloom —
When laurels hang loose from the brow
　of the lover,
　And Cupid makes wings of the war-
　rior's plume.

Light went the harp when the War-God,
      reclining,
  Lay lulled on the white arm of Beauty
      to rest,
When round his rich armor the myrtle
      hung twining,
  And flights of young doves made his
      helmet their nest.
      But, when the battle came,
      The hero's eye breathed flame:
Soon from his neck the white arm was
      flung;
      While, to his wakening ear,
      No other sounds were dear
But brazen notes of war, by thousand
      trumpets sung.
But then came the light harp, when dan-
      ger was ended,
  And Beauty once more lulled the War-
      God to rest;
When tresses of gold with his laurels lay
      blended,
  And flights of young doves made his
      helmet their nest.

FROM

THE GREEK OF MELEAGER.[1]

FILL high the cup with liquid flame,
And speak my Heliodora's name.
Repeat its magic o'er and o'er,
And let the sound my lips adore,
Live in the breeze, till every tone,
And word, and breath, speaks her alone.

Give me the wreath that withers there,
  It was but last delicious night,
It circled her luxuriant hair,
  And caught her eyes' reflected light.
Oh! haste, and twine it round my
      brow,
'T is all of her that 's left me now.
And see — each rosebud drops a tear,
To find the nymph no longer here —
No longer, where such heavenly charms
As hers *should* be — within these arms.

---

1 ἐγχεῖ, καὶ πάλιν εἶπε, πάλιν, πάλιν, Ἡλιο-
      δώρας
  εἶπε, σὺν ἀκρήτῳ τὸ γλυκὺ μίσγ' ὄνομα.
καί μοι τὸν βρεχθέντα μύροις καὶ χθιζὸν ἐόντα,
  μναμόσυννον κείνας ἀμφιτιθεῖ στέφανον·
δακρύει φιλεραστὸν ἰδοῦ ρόδον, ὑ ηνεκα κείναν
  ἄλλοθι κ' οὐ κόλποις ἡμετέροις ἐσορᾷ.
      BRUNCK, "*Analect.*" *tom.* i. p. 28.

SONG.

FLY from the world, O Bessy! to me,
  Thou wilt never find any sincerer;
I 'll give up the world, O Bessy! for
      thee,
  I can never meet any that 's dearer.
Then tell me no more, with a tear and a
      sigh,
  That our loves will be censured by
      many;
All, all have their follies, and who will
      deny
  That ours is the sweetest of any?

When your lip has met mine, in commu-
      nion so sweet,
  Have we felt as if virtue forbid it? —
Have we felt as if heaven denied them
      to meet? —
  No, rather 't was heaven that did it.
So innocent, love, is the joy we then sip,
  So little of wrong is there in it,
That I wish all my errors were lodged on
      your lip,
  And I 'd kiss them away in a minute.

Then come to your lover, oh! fly to his
      shed,
  From a world which I know thou de-
      spisest;
And slumber will hover as light o'er our
      bed
  As e'er on the couch of the wisest.
And when o'er our pillow the tempest is
      driven,
  And thou, pretty innocent, fearest,
I 'll tell thee, it is not the chiding of
      heaven,
  'T is only our lullaby, dearest.

And, oh! while we lie on our deathbed,
      my love,
  Looking back on the scene of our er-
      rors,
A sigh from my Bessy shall plead then
      above,
  And Death be disarmed of his terrors.
And each to the other embracing will say,
  "Farewell! let us hope we 're for-
      given."
Thy last fading glance will illumine the
      way,
  And a kiss be our passport to heaven!

THE RESEMBLANCE.

—— *vo cercand' io,*
Donna, quant' e possibile, in altrui
La desiata vostra forma vera.
PETRARC. *Sonett.* 14.

YES, if 't were any common love,
That led my pliant heart astray,
I grant, there's not a power above,
Could wipe the faithless crime away.

But, 't was my doom to err with one
In every look so like to thee
That, underneath yon blessed sun,
So fair there are but thou and she.

Both born of beauty, at a birth,
She held with thine a kindred sway,
And wore the only shape on earth
That could have lured my soul to stray.

Then blame me not, if false I be,
'T was love that waked the fond ex-
cess;
My heart had been more true to thee,
Had mine eye prized thy beauty less.

FANNY, DEAREST.

YES! had I leisure to sigh and mourn,
Fanny, dearest, for thee I 'd sigh;
And every smile on my cheek should turn
To tears when thou art nigh.
But, between love, and wine, and sleep,
So busy a life I live,
That even the time it would take to weep
Is more than my heart can give.
Then bid me not to despair and pine,
Fanny, dearest of all the dears!
The Love that 's ordered to bathe in
wine,
Would be sure to take cold in tears.

Reflected bright in this heart of mine,
Fanny, dearest, thy image lies;
But, ah, the mirror would cease to shine,
If dimmed too often with sighs.
They lose the half of beauty's light,
Who view it through sorrow's tear;
And 't is but to see thee truly bright
That I keep my eye-beam clear.
Then wait no longer till tears shall flow,
Fanny, dearest — the hope is vain;
If sunshine cannot dissolve thy snow,
I shall never attempt it with rain.

THE RING.

TO

. . . .

No — Lady! Lady! keep the ring:
Oh! think, how many a future year,
Of placid smile and downy wing,
May sleep within its holy sphere.

Do not disturb their tranquil dream,
Though love hath ne'er the mystery
warmed;
Yet heaven will shed a soothing beam,
To bless the bond itself hath formed.

But then, that eye, that burning eye, —
Oh! it doth ask, with witching power,
If heaven can ever bless the tie
Where love inwreaths no genial
flower?

Away, away, bewildering look,
Or all the boast of virtue 's o'er;
Go — hie thee to the sage's book,
And learn from him to feel no more.

I cannot warn thee: every touch,
That brings my pulses close to thine,
Tells me I want thy aid as much —
Even more, alas, than thou dost mine.

Yet, stay, — one hope, one effort yet —
A moment turn those eyes away,
And let me, if I can, forget
The light that leads my soul astray.

Thou sayest, that we were born to meet,
That our hearts bear one common
seal; —
Think, Lady, think, how man's deceit
Can seem to sigh and feign to feel.

When, o'er thy face some gleam of
thought,
Like daybeams through the morning
air,
Hath gradual stole, and I have caught
The feeling ere it kindled there;

The sympathy I then betrayed,
Perhaps was but the child of art,
The guile of one, who long hath played
With all these wily nets of heart.

Oh! thine is not my earliest vow;
　　Though few the years I yet have told,
Canst thou believe I 've lived till now,
　　With loveless heart or senses cold?

No — other nymphs to joy and pain
　　This wild and wandering heart hath
　　　　moved;
With some it sported, wild and vain,
　　While some it dearly, truly, loved.

The cheek to thine I fondly lay,
　　To theirs hath been as fondly laid;
The words to thee I warmly say,
　　To them have been as warmly said.

Then, scorn at once a worthless heart,
　　Worthless alike, or fixt or free;
Think of the pure, bright soul thou art,
　　And — love not me, oh love not me.

Enough — now, turn thine eyes again;
　　What, still that look and still that sigh!
Dost thou not feel my counsel then?
　　Oh! no, beloved, — nor do I.

TO

THE INVISIBLE GIRL.

THEY try to persuade me, my dear little
　　sprite,
That you 're not a true daughter of ether
　　and light,
Nor have any concern with those fanci-
　　ful forms
That dance upon rainbows and ride upon
　　storms;
That, in short, you 're a woman; your
　　lip and your eye
As mortal as ever drew gods from the sky.
But I *will* not believe them — no, Sci-
　　ence, to you
I have long bid a last and a careless
　　adieu:
Still flying from Nature to study her laws,
And dulling delight by exploring its cause,
You forget how superior, for mortals be-
　　low,
Is the fiction they dream to the truth
　　that they know.
Oh! who, that has e'er enjoyed rapture
　　complete,
Would ask *how* we feel it, or *why* it is
　　sweet;

How rays are confused, or how particles
　　fly
Through the medium refined of a glance
　　or a sigh;
Is there one, who but once would not
　　rather have known it,
Than written, with Harvey, whole vol-
　　umes upon it?

As for you, my sweet-voiced and invis-
　　ible love,
You must surely be one of those spirits,
　　that rove
By the bank where, at twilight, the poet
　　reclines,
When the star of the west on his solitude
　　shines,
And the magical fingers of fancy have
　　hung
Every breeze with a sigh, every leaf with
　　a tongue.
Oh! hint to him then, 't is retirement
　　alone
Can hallow his harp or ennoble its tone;
Like you, with a veil of seclusion be-
　　tween,
His song to the world let him utter un-
　　seen,
And like you, a legitimate child of the
　　spheres,
Escape from the eye to enrapture the ears.

Sweet spirit of mystery! how I should
　　love,
In the wearisome ways I am fated to rove,
To have you thus ever invisibly nigh,
Inhaling for ever your song and your
　　sigh!
Mid the crowds of the world and the
　　murmurs of care,
I might sometimes converse with my
　　nymph of the air,
And turn with distaste from the clamor-
　　ous crew,
To steal in the pauses one whisper from
　　you.

Then, come and be near me, for ever
　　be mine,
We shall hold in the air a communion
　　divine,
As sweet as, of old, was imagined to
　　dwell
In the grotto of Numa, or Socrates' cell.

And oft, at those lingering moments of
  night,
When the heart's busy thoughts have
  put slumber to flight,
You shall come to my pillow and tell me
  of love,
Such as angel to angel might whisper
  above.
Sweet spirit! — and then, could you borrow the tone
Of that voice, to my ear like some fairy-
  song known,
The voice of the one upon earth, who
  has twined
With her being for ever my heart and
  my mind,
Though lonely and far from the light of
  her smile,
An exile, and weary and hopeless the
  while,
Could you shed for a moment her voice
  on my ear.
I will think, for that moment, that Cara
  is near;
That she comes with consoling enchantment to speak,
And kisses my eyelid and breathes on my
  cheek,
And tells me, the night shall go rapidly
  by,
For the dawn of our hope, of our heaven
  is nigh.

  Fair spirit! if such be your magical
  power,
It will lighten the lapse of full many an
  hour;
And, let fortune's realities frown as they
  will,
Hope, fancy, and Cara may smile for me
  still.

THE RING.[1]

A TALE.

Annulus ille viri.
OVID. "*Amor.*" *lib.* ii. *eleg.* 15.

THE happy day at length arrived
  When Rupert was to wed
The fairest maid in Saxony,
  And take her to his bed.

As soon as morn was in the sky,
  The feast and sports began;
The men admired the happy maid,
  The maids the happy man.

In many a sweet device of mirth
  The day was past along;
And some the featly dance amused,
  And some the dulcet song.

The younger maids with Isabel
  Disported through the bowers,
And decked her robe, and crowned her
  head
  With motley bridal flowers.

The matrons all in rich attire,
  Within the castle walls,
Sat listening to the choral strains
  That echoed through the halls.

Young Rupert and his friends repaired
  Unto a spacious court,
To strike the bounding tennis-ball
  In feat and manly sport.

The bridegroom on his finger wore
  The wedding-ring so bright,
Which was to grace the lily hand
  Of Isabel that night.

And fearing he might break the gem,
  Or lose it in the play,
He looked around the court, to see
  Where he the ring might lay.

Now, in the court a statue stood,
  Which there full long had been;
It might a Heathen goddess be,
  Or else, a Heathen queen.

Upon its marble finger then
  He tried the ring to fit;
And, thinking it was safest there,
  Thereon he fastened it.

1 I should be sorry to think that my friend
had any serious intentions of frightening the nursery by this story : I rather hope — though the
manner of it leads me to doubt — that his design
was to ridicule that distempered taste which prefers those monsters of the fancy to the "*speci-
osa miracula*" of true poetic imagination.
  I find, by a note in the manuscript, that he
met with this story in a German author, *From-
man upon Fascination*, book iii. part vi. ch. 18.
On consulting the work, I perceive that From-
man quotes it from Beluacensis, among many
other stories equally diabolical and interesting.
— E.

And now the tennis sports went on,
   Till they were wearied all,
And messengers announced to them
   Their dinner in the hall.

Young Rupert for his wedding-ring
   Unto the statue went;
But, oh, how shocked was he to find
   The marble finger bent!

The hand was closed upon the ring
   With firm and mighty clasp;
In vain he tried and tried and tried,
   He could not loose the grasp!

Then sore surprised was Rupert's mind —
   As well his mind might be;
" I 'll come," quoth he, " at night again,
   " When none are here to see."

He went unto the feast, and much
   He thought upon his ring;
And marvelled sorely what could mean
   So very strange a thing!

The feast was o'er, and to the court
   He hied without delay,
Resolved to break the marble hand
   And force the ring away.

But, mark a stranger wonder still —
   The ring was there no more,
And yet the marble hand ungrasped,
   And open as before!

He searched the base, and all the court,
   But nothing could he find;
Then to the castle hied he back
   With sore bewildered mind.

Within he found them all in mirth,
   The night in dancing flew:
The youth another ring procured,
   And none the adventure knew.

And now the priest has joined their hands,
   The hours of love advance:
Rupert almost forgets to think
   Upon the morn's mischance.

Within the bed fair Isabel
   In blushing sweetness lay,
Like flowers, half-opened by the dawn,
   And waiting for the day.

And Rupert, by her lovely side,
   In youthful beauty glows,
Like Phœbus, when he bends to cast
   His beams upon a rose.

And here my song would leave them both,
   Nor let the rest be told,
If 't were not for the horrid tale
   It yet has to unfold.

Soon Rupert, 'twixt his bride and him,
   A death cold carcass found;
He saw it not, but thought he felt
   Its arms embrace him round.

He started up, and then returned,
   But found the phantom still;
In vain he shrunk, it clipt him round,
   With damp and deadly chill!

And when he bent, the earthy lips
   A kiss of horror gave;
'T was like the smell from charnel vaults,
   Or from the mouldering grave!

Ill-fated Rupert! — wild and loud
   Then cried he to his wife,
" Oh! save me from this horrid fiend,
   " My Isabel! my life!"

But Isabel had nothing seen,
   She looked around in vain;
And much she mourned the mad conceit
   That racked her Rupert's brain.

At length from this invisible
   These words to Rupert came:
(Oh God! while he did hear the words
   What terrors shook his frame!)

" Husband, husband, I 've the ring
   " Thou gavest to-day to me;
" And thou 'rt to me for ever wed,
   " As I am wed to thee!"

And all the night the demon lay
   Cold-chilling by his side,
And strained him with such deadly grasp,
   He thought he should have died.

But when the dawn of day was near,
   The horrid phantom fled,
And left the affrighted youth to weep
   By Isabel in bed.

And all that day a gloomy cloud
  Was seen on Rupert's brows;
Fair Isabel was likewise sad,
  But strove to cheer her spouse.

And, as the day advanced, he thought
  Of coming night with fear:
Alas, that he should dread to view
  The bed that should be dear!

At length the second night arrived,
  Again their couch they prest;
Poor Rupert hoped that all was o'er,
  And looked for love and rest.

But oh! when midnight came, again
  The fiend was at his side,
And, as it strained him in its grasp,
  With howl exulting cried: —

" Husband, husband, I 've the ring,
  " The ring thou gavest to me;
" And thou 'rt to me for ever wed,
  " As I am wed to thee! "

In agony of wild despair,
  He started from the bed;
And thus to his bewildered wife
  The trembling Rupert said:

" Oh Isabel! dost thou not see
  " A shape of horrors here,
" That strains me to its deadly kiss,
  " And keeps me from my dear? "

" No, no, my love! my Rupert, I
  " No shape of horrors see;
" And much I mourn the fantasy
  " That keeps my dear from me."

This night, just like the night before,
  In terrors past away,
Nor did the demon vanish thence
  Before the dawn of day.

Said Rupert then, " My Isabel,
  " Dear partner of my woe,
" To Father Austin's holy cave
  " This instant will I go."

Now Austin was a reverend man,
  Who acted wonders maint —
Whom all the country round believed
  A devil or a saint!

To Father Austin's holy cave
  Then Rupert straightway went;
And told him all, and asked him how
  These horrors to prevent.

The father heard the youth, and then
  Retired awhile to pray;
And, having prayed for half an hour
  Thus to the youth did say:

" There is a place where four roads meet,
  " Which I will tell to thee;
" Be there this eve, at fall of night,
  " And list what thou shalt see.

" Thou 'lt see a group of figures pass
  " In strange disordered crowd,
" Travelling by torchlight through the
    roads,
  " With noises strange and loud.

" And one that 's high above the rest,
  " Terrific towering o'er,
" Will make thee know him at a glance,
  " So I need say no more.

" To him from me these tablets give,
  " They 'll quick be understood;
" Thou need'st not fear, but give them
    straight,
  " I 've scrawled them with my blood! "

The night-fall came, and Rupert all
  In pale amazement went
To where the cross-roads met, as he
  Was by the Father sent.

And lo! a group of figures came
  In strange disordered crowd,
Travelling by torchlight through the
    roads,
  With noises strange and loud.

And, as the gloomy train advanced,
  Rupert beheld from far
A female form of wanton mien
  High seated on a car.

And Rupert, as he gazed upon
  The loosely-vested dame,
Thought of the marble statue's look,
  For hers was just the same.

Behind her walked a hideous form,
  With eyeballs flashing death;
Whene'er he breathed, a sulphured smoke
  Came burning in his breath.

He seemed the first of all the crowd,
  Terrific towering o'er;
"Yes, yes," said Rupert, "this is he,
  "And I need ask no more."

Then slow he went, and to this fiend
  The tablets trembling gave,
Who looked and read them with a yell
  That would disturb the grave.

And when he saw the blood-scrawled
    name,
  His eyes with fury shine;
"I thought," cries he, "his time was out,
  "But he must soon be mine!"

Then darting at the youth a look
  Which rent his soul with fear,
He went unto the female fiend,
  And whispered in her ear.

The female fiend no sooner heard
  Than, with reluctant look,
The very ring that Rupert lost,
  She from her finger took.

And, giving it unto the youth,
  With eyes that breathed of hell,
She said, in that tremendous voice,
  Which he remembered well:

"In Austin's name take back the ring,
  "The ring thou gavest to me;
"And thou 'rt to me no longer wed,
  "Nor longer I to thee."

He took the ring, the rabble past,
  He home returned again;
His wife was then the happiest fair,
  The happiest he of men.

TO

. . . .

ON SEEING HER WITH A WHITE VEIL AND A
RICH GIRDLE.

μαργαρῖται δήλουσι δααρύων ρόον.
  Ἀρ. NICEPHOR. *in* "*Oneirocritico.*"

PUT off the vestal veil, nor, oh!
  Let weeping angels view it;
Your cheeks belie its virgin snow,
  And blush repenting through it.

Put off the fatal zone you wear;
  The shining pearls around it
Are tears, that fell from Virtue there,
  The hour when Love unbound it.

WRITTEN IN THE BLANK LEAF
OF
A LADY'S COMMONPLACE BOOK.

HERE is one leaf reserved for me,
From all thy sweet memorials free;
And here my simple song might tell
The feelings thou must guess so well.
But could I thus, within thy mind,
One little vacant corner find,
Where no impression yet is seen,
Where no memorial yet hath been,
Oh! it should be my sweetest care
To *write my name* for ever *there!*

TO
MRS. BL——.
WRITTEN IN HER ALBUM.

THEY say that Love had once a book
  (The urchin likes to copy you),
Where, all who came, the pencil took,
  And wrote, like us, a line or two.

'T was Innocence, the maid divine,
  Who kept this volume bright and fair,
And saw that no unhallowed line
  Or thought profane should enter there;

And daily did the pages fill
  With fond device and loving lore,
And every leaf she turned was still
  More bright than that she turned be-
    fore.

Beneath the touch of Hope, how soft,
  How light the magic pencil ran!
Till Fear would come, alas, as oft,
  And trembling close what Hope began.

A tear or two had dropt from Grief,
  And Jealousy would, now and then,
Ruffle in haste some snow-white leaf,
  Which Love had still to smooth again.

But, ah! there came a blooming boy,
  Who often turned the pages o'er,
And wrote therein such words of joy,
  That all who read them sighed for
    more.

And Pleasure was this spirit's name,
  And though so soft his voice and look,
Yet Innocence, whene'er he came,
  Would tremble for her spotless book.

For, oft a Bacchant cup he bore,
  With earth's sweet nectar sparkling
    bright;
And much she feared lest, mantling o'er,
  Some drops should on the pages light.

And so it chanced, one luckless night,
  The urchin let that goblet fall
O'er the fair book, so pure, so white,
  And sullied lines and marge and all!

In vain now, touched with shame, he
    tried
  To wash those fatal stains away;
Deep, deep had sunk the sullying tide,
  The leaves grew darker every day.

And Fancy's sketches lost their hue,
  And Hope's sweet lines were all ef-
    faced,
And Love himself now scarcely knew
  What Love himself so lately traced.

At length the urchin Pleasure fled,
  (For how, alas! could Pleasure stay?)
And Love, while many a tear he shed,
  Reluctant flung the book away.

The index now alone remains,
  Of all the pages spoiled by Pleasure,
And though it bears some earthly stains,
  Yet Memory counts the leaf a treasure.

And oft, they say, she scans it o'er,
  And oft, by this memorial aided,
Brings back the pages now no more,
  And thinks of lines that long have
    faded.

I know not if this tale be true,
  But thus the simple facts are stated;
And I refer their truth to you,
  Since Love and you are near related.

TO CARA,

AFTER AN INTERVAL OF ABSENCE.

CONCEALED within the shady wood
  A mother left her sleeping child,

And flew, to cull her rustic food,
  The fruitage of the forest wild.

But storms upon her pathway rise,
  The mother roams, astray and weeping;
Far from the weak appealing cries
  Of him she left so sweetly sleeping.

She hopes, she fears; a light is seen,
  And gentler blows the night wind's
    breath;
Yet no — 't is gone — the storms are
    keen,
  The infant may be chilled to death!

Perhaps, even now, in darkness shrouded,
  His little eyes lie cold and still; —
And yet, perhaps, they are not clouded,
  Life and love may light them still.

Thus, Cara, at our last farewell,
  When, fearful even thy hand to touch,
I mutely asked those eyes to tell
  If parting pained thee half so much:

I thought, — and, oh! forgive the
    thought,
For none was e'er by love inspired
Whom fancy had not also taught
  To hope the bliss his soul desired.

Yes, I *did* think, in Cara's mind,
  Though yet to that sweet mind un-
    known,
I left one infant wish behind,
  One feeling, which I called my own.

Oh blest! though but in fancy blest,
  How did I ask of Pity's care,
To shield and strengthen, in thy breast,
  The nursling I had cradled there.

And, many an hour, beguiled by pleasure,
  And many an hour of sorrow number-
    ing,
I ne'er forgot the new-born treasure,
  I left within thy bosom slumbering.

Perhaps, indifference has not chilled it,
  Haply, it yet a throb may give —
Yet, no — perhaps, a doubt has killed it;
  Say, dearest — *does* the feeling live?

TO CARA,

ON THE DAWNING OF A NEW YEAR'S
DAY.

WHEN midnight came to close the year,
　We sighed to think it thus should take
The hours it gave us — hours as dear
　As sympathy and love could make
Their blessed moments, — every sun
Saw us, my love, more closely one.

But, Cara, when the dawn was nigh
　Which came a new year's light to shed,
That smile we caught from eye to eye
　Told us, those moments were not fled:
Oh, no, — we felt, some future sun
Should see us still more closely one.

Thus may we ever, side by side,
From happy years to happier glide;
And still thus may the passing sigh
　We give to hours, that vanish o'er us,
Be followed by the smiling eye,
　That Hope shall shed on scenes before
　　us!

TO . . . . , 1801.

To be the theme of every hour
The heart devotes to Fancy's power,
When her prompt magic fills the mind
With friends and joys we 've left behind,
And joys return and friends are near,
And all are welcomed with a tear: —
In the mind's purest seat to dwell,
To be remembered oft and well
By one whose heart, though vain and wild,
By passion led, by youth beguiled,
Can proudly still aspire to be
All that may yet win smiles from thee: —
If thus to live in every part
Of a lone, weary wanderer's heart;
If thus to be its sole employ
Can give thee one faint gleam of joy,
Believe it, Mary, — oh! believe
A tongue that never can deceive,
Though, erring, it too oft betray
Even more than Love should dare to
　say, —
In Pleasure's dream or Sorrow's hour,
In crowded hall or lonely bower,
The business of my life shall be,
For ever to remember thee.
And though that heart be dead to mine,

Since Love is life and wakes not thine,
I 'll take thy image, as the form
Of one whom Love had failed to warm,
Which, though it yield no answering
　thrill,
Is not less dear, is worshipt still —
I 'll take it, wheresoe'er I stray,
The bright, cold burden of my way.
To keep this semblance fresh in bloom,
My heart shall be its lasting tomb,
And Memory, with embalming care,
Shall keep it fresh and fadeless there.

THE GENIUS OF HARMONY.

AN IRREGULAR ODE.

Ad harmoniam canere mundum.
　　CICERO, " de Nat. Deor." lib. iii.

THERE lies a shell beneath the waves,
　In many a hollow winding wreathed,
　　Such as of old
Echoed the breath that warbling sea-
　maids breathed;
　　This magic shell,
　From the white bosom of a syren fell,
　As once she wandered by the tide that
　　laves
　　　Sicilia's sands of gold.
　　　It bears
Upon its shining side the mystic notes
　Of those entrancing airs,[1]
The genii of the deep were wont to
　swell,
When heaven's eternal orbs their mid-
　night music rolled!
　Oh! seek it, whereso'er it floats;
　　And, if the power
　Of thrilling numbers to thy soul be
　　dear,

1 In the "Histoire Naturelle des Antilles,"
there is an account of some curious shells, found
at Curaçoa, on the back of which were lines,
filled with musical characters so distinct and perfect, that the writer assures us a very charming
trio was sung from one of them. " *On le nomme
musical, parce qu'il porte sur le dos des lignes
noirâtres pleines de notes, qui ont une espèce de
clé pour les mettre en chant, de sorte que l'on
diroit qu'il ne manque que la lettre à cette tabla-
ture naturelle. Ce curieux gentilhomme* (M. du
Montel) *rapporte qu'il en a vû qui avoient cinq
lignes, une clé, et des notes, qui formoient un ac-
cord parfait. Quelqu'un y avoit ajouté la lettre,
que la nature avoit oubliée, et la faisoit chanter
en forme de trio, dont l'air étoit fort agréable.*"
— Chap. xix. art. 11. The author adds, a poet
might imagine that these shells were used by the
syrens at their concerts.

Go, bring the bright shell to my
    bower,
And I will fold thee in such downy
    dreams
As lap the Spirit of the Seventh Sphere,
When Luna's distant tone falls faintly on
    his ear![1]
    And thou shalt own,
That, through the circle of creation's
    zone,
Where matter slumbers or where spirit
    beams;
From the pellucid tides,[2] that whirl
The planets through their maze of
    song,
To the small rill, that weeps along
    Murmuring o'er beds of pearl;
    From the rich sigh
Of the sun's arrow through an evening
    sky,[3]
To the faint breath the tuneful osier
    yields
    On Afric's burning fields;[4]

Thou 'lt wondering own this universe
    divine
    Is mine!
That I respire in all and all in me,
One mighty mingled soul of boundless
    harmony.

Welcome, welcome, mystic shell!
Many a star has ceased to burn,[5]
Many a tear has Saturn's urn
O'er the cold bosom of the ocean
    wept,[6]
Since thy aërial spell
Hath in the waters slept.
    Now blest I 'll fly
With the bright treasure to my choral
    sky,
Where she, who waked its early swell,
The Syren of the heavenly choir,
Walks o'er the great string of my Or-
    phic Lyre;[7]
Or guides around the burning pole
The winged chariot of some blissful
    soul:[8]
    While thou —
Oh son of earth, what dreams shall rise
    for thee!

---

1 According to Cicero, and his commentator, Macrobius, the lunar tone is the gravest and faintest on the planetary heptachord. *" Quam ob causam summus ille cœli stellifer cursus, cujus conversio est concitatior, acuto et excitato movetur sono; gravissimo autem hic lunaris atque infimus."* — *" Somn. Scip."* Because, says Macrobius, *" spiritu ut in extremitate languescente jam volvitur, et propter angustias quibus penultimus orbis arctatur impetu leniore convertitur."* — In *" Somn. Scip."* lib. ii. cap. 4. In their musical arrangement of the heavenly bodies, the ancient writers are not very intelligible. — See *Ptolem.* lib. iii.

Leone Hebrëo, pursuing the idea of Aristotle, that the heavens are animal, attributes their harmony to perfect and reciprocal love. *" Non pero manca fra loro il perfetto et reciproco amore : la causa principale, che ne mostra il loro amore, è la lor amicitia armonica et la concordanza, che perpetuamente si trova in loro."* — Dialog. ii. di Amore, p. 58. This *" reciproco amore"* of Leone is the φιλότης of the ancient Empedocles, who seems, in his Love and Hate of the Elements, to have given a glimpse of the principles of attraction and repulsion. See the fragment to which I allude in Laertius, ἄλλοτε μὲν φιλότητι, συνερχόμεν', κ. τ. λ., lib. viii. cap. 2. n. 12.

2 Leucippus, the atomist, imagined a kind of vortices in the heavens, which he borrowed from Anaxagoras, and possibly suggested to Descartes.

3 Heraclides, upon the allegories of Homer, conjectures that the idea of the harmony of the spheres originated with this poet, who, in representing the solar beams as arrows, supposes them to emit a peculiar sound in the air.

4 In the account of Africa which D'Ablancourt has translated, there is mention of a tree in

that country, whose branches, when shaken by the hand produce very sweet sounds. *" Le même auteur* (Abenzégar) *dit, qu'il y a un certain arbre, qui produit des gaules comme d'osier, et qu'en les prenant à la main et les branlant, elles font une espèce d'harmonie fort agréable,"* etc. — *"L'Afrique de Marmol."*

5 Alluding to the extinction, or at least the disappearance, of some of those fixed stars, which we are taught to consider as suns, attended each by its system. Descartes thought that our earth might formerly have been a sun, which became obscured by a thick incrustation over its surface. This probably suggested the idea of a central fire.

6 Porphyry says, that Pythagoras held the sea to be a tear, τὴν θάλατταν μὲν ἐκάλει εἶναι δάκρυον (*De Vitâ*); and some one else, if I mistake not, has added the planet Saturn as the source of it. Empedocles, with similar affectation, called the sea *"* the sweat of the earth:" ἱδρῶτα τῆς γῆς. See *Rittershusius upon Porphyry,* Num. 41.

7 The system of the harmonized orbs was styled by the ancients the Great Lyre of Orpheus, for which Lucian thus accounts: — ἡ δὲ Λύρη ἑπτάμιτος ἐοῦσα τὴν τῶν κινουμένων ἀστρῶν ἁρμονίαν συνεβάλλετο. κ. τ. λ. in *"Astrolog."*

8 διεῖλε ψύχας ἰσαρίθμους τοῖς ἀστροις, ἔνειμε θ' ἑκάστην πρὸς ἕκαστον, καὶ ἐμβιβάσας ΩΣ ΕΙΣ ΟΧΗΜΑ — *"* Distributing the souls severally among the stars, and mounting each soul upon a star as on its chariot." — *Plato, Timæus.*

Beneath Hispania's sun,
Thóu 'lt see a streamlet run,
Which I 've imbued with breathing
　melody; [1]
And there, when night-winds down the
　current die,
Thou 'lt hear how like a harp its waters
　sigh:
A liquid chord is every wave that flows,
An airy plectrum every breeze that
　blows. [2]

There, by that wondrous stream,
Go, lay thy languid brow,
And I will send thee such a godlike
　dream,
As never blest the slumbers even of him,[3]
Who, many a night, with his primordial
　lyre,[4]
Sate on the chill Pangæan mount,[5]
And, looking to the orient dim,
Watched the first flowing of that sacred
　fount,
From which his soul had drunk its fire.
Oh think what visions, in that lonely
　hour,
Stole o'er his musing breast;
　　　What pious ecstasy [6]
Wafted his prayer to that eternal Power,

Whose seal upon this new-born world
　imprest [7]
The various forms of bright divinity!
Or, dost thou know what dreams I
　wove,
Mid the deep horror of that silent
　bower,[8]
Where the rapt Samian slept his holy
　slumber?
　　　When, free
　From every earthly chain,
From wreaths of pleasure and from
　bonds of pain,
His spirit flew through fields above,
Drank at the source of nature's fontal
　number,[9]
And saw, in mystic choir, around him
　move
The stars of song, Heaven's burning
　minstrelsy!
　Such dreams, so heavenly bright,
　　　I swear
By the great diadem that twines my
　hair,
And by the seven gems that sparkle
　there,[10]

---

1 This musical river is mentioned in the romance of Achilles Tatius. ἐπεὶ ποταμοῦ . . . ἦν δὲ ἀκοῦσαι θέλῃς τοῦ ὕδατος λαλοῦντος. The Latin version, in supplying the hiatus which is in the original, has placed the river in Hispania. "*In Hispaniâ quoque fluvius est, quem primo aspectu,*" etc.

2 These two lines are translated from the words of Achilles Tatius. ἐὰν γὰρ ὀλίγος ἄνεμος εἰς τὰς δίνας ἐμπέσῃ, τὸ μὲν ὕδωρ ὡς χορδὴ κρούεται, τὸ δὲ πνεῦμα τοῦ ὕδατος πλῆκτρον γίνεται. τὸ ῥεῦμα δὲ ὡς κιθάρα λαλεῖ. — *Lib.* ii.

3 Orpheus.

4 They called his lyre ἀρχαιότροπον ἑπτάχορδον Ὀρφέως. See a curious work by a professor of Greek at Venice, entitled "*Hebdomades, sive septem de septenario libri.*" — *Lib.* iv. *cap.* 3. p. 177.

5 Eratosthenes, in mentioning the extreme veneration of Orpheus for Apollo, says that he was accustomed to go to the Pangæan mountain at day-break, and there wait the rising of the sun, that he might be the first to hail its beams. ἐπεγειρόμενός τε τῆς νυκτὸς, κατὰ τὴν ἑωθινὴν ἐπὶ τὸ ὄρος τὸ καλούμενον Παγγαῖον, προσέμενε τὰς ἀνατολὰς, ἵνα ἴδῃ τὸν Ἥλιον πρῶτον. — Καταστερίσμ. 24.

6 There are some verses of Orpheus preserved to us, which contain sublime ideas of the unity

and magnificence of the Deity. For instance, those which Justin Martyr has produced: —
οὗτος μὲν χάλκειον ἐς οὐρανὸν ἐστήρικται
χρυσείῳ ἐνὶ θρόνῳ, κ. τ. λ.
　　　"*Ad Græc. Cohortat.*"

It is thought by some, that these are to be reckoned amongst the fabrications, which were frequent in the early times of Christianity. Still, it appears doubtful to whom they are to be attributed, being too pious for the Pagans, and too poetical for the Fathers.

7 In one of the Hymns of Orpheus, he attributes a figured seal to Apollo, with which he imagines that deity to have stamped a variety of forms upon the universe.

8 Alluding to the cave near Samos, where Pythagoras devoted the greater part of his days and nights to meditation and the mysteries of his philosophy. "*Iamblich. de Vit.*" This, as Holstenius remarks, was in imitation of the Magi.

9 The tetractys, or sacred number of the Pythagoreans, on which they solemnly swore, and which they called παγάν ἀενάον φύσεως, "the fountain of perennial nature." Lucian has ridiculed this religious arithmetic very cleverly in his Sale of Philosophers.

10 This diadem is intended to represent the analogy between the notes of music and the prismatic colors. We find in Plutarch a vague intimation of this kindred harmony in colors and sounds. — ὄψις τε καὶ ἀκοὴ, μετὰ φωνῆς τε καὶ φωτὸς τὴν ἁρμονίαν ἐπιφαίνουσι. — "*De Musica.*"
Cassiodorus, whose idea I may be supposed to have borrowed, says, in a letter upon music to

Mingling their beams
In a soft iris of harmonious light,
Oh, mortal! such shall be thy radiant
dreams.

I FOUND her not — the chamber seemed
Like some divinely haunted place,
Where fairy forms had lately beamed,
And left behind their odorous trace!

It felt as if her lips had shed
A sigh around her, ere she fled,
Which hung, as on a melting lute,
When all the silver chords are mute,
There lingers still a trembling breath
After the note's luxurious death,
A shade of song, a spirit air
Of melodies which had been there.

I saw the veil, which, all the day,
Had floated o'er her cheek of rose;
I saw the couch, where late she lay
In languor of divine repose;
And I could trace the hallowed print
Her limbs had left, as pure and warm,
As if 't were done in rapture's mint,
And Love himself had stampt the form.

Oh my sweet mistress, where wert thou?
In pity fly not thus from me;
Thou art my life, my essence now,
And my soul dies of wanting thee.

TO MRS. HENRY TIGHE,
ON READING HER "PSYCHE."

TELL me the witching tale again,
For never has my heart or ear
Hung on so sweet, so pure a strain,
So pure to feel, so sweet to hear.

Say, Love, in all thy prime of fame,
When the high heaven itself was thine;
When piety confest the flame,
And even thy errors were divine;

Did ever Muse's hand, so fair,
A glory round thy temples spread?
Did ever lip's ambrosial air
Such fragrance o'er thy altars shed?

Boetius, "*Ut diadema oculis, varia luce gem-
marum, sic cythara diversitate soni, blanditur
auditui.*" This is indeed the only tolerable
thought in the letter. — *Lib.* ii. Variar.

One maid there was, who round her lyre
The mystic myrtle wildly wreathed; —
But all *her* sighs were sighs of fire,
The myrtle withered as she breathed.

Oh! you, that love's celestial dream,
In all its purity, would know,
Let not the senses' ardent beam
Too strongly through the vision glow.

Love safest lies, concealed in night,
The night where heaven has bid him
lie,
Oh! shed not there unhallowed light,
Or, Psyche knows, the boy will fly.[1]

Sweet Psyche, many a charmed hour,
Through many a wild and magic waste,
To the fair fount and blissful bower
Have I, in dreams, thy light foot traced!

Where'er thy joys are numbered now,
Beneath whatever shades of rest,
The Genius of the starry brow[3]
Hath bound thee to thy Cupid's breast;

Whether above the horizon dim,
Along whose verge our spirits stray, —

[1] See the story in Apuleius. With respect to
this beautiful allegory of Love and Psyche, there
is an ingenious idea suggested by the senator
Buonarotti, in his "*Osservazioni sopra alcuni
frammenti di vasi antici.*" He thinks the fable
is taken from some very occult mysteries, which
had long been celebrated in honor of Love; and
accounts, upon this supposition, for the silence
of the more ancient authors upon the subject, as
it was not till towards the decline of pagan superstition, that writers could venture to reveal or
discuss such ceremonies. Accordingly, observes
this author, we find Lucian and Plutarch treating,
without reserve, of the Dea Syria, as well as of
Isis and Osiris; and Apuleius, to whom we are
indebted for the beautiful story of Cupid and
Psyche, has also detailed some of the mysteries
of Isis. See the *Giornale di Litterati d'Italia,
tom.* xxvii. *articol.* 1. See also the observations
upon the ancient gems in the "Museum Florentinum," vol. i. p. 156.

I cannot avoid remarking here an error into
which the French Encyclopédistes have been led
by M. Spon, in their article Psyche. They say
"*Petrone fait un récit de la pompe nuptiale de
ces deux amans* (Amour et Psyche). *Déjà, dit-
il,*" etc. The Psyche of Petronius, however, is
a servant-maid, and the marriage which he describes is that of the young Pannychis. See
Spon's "*Recherches curieuses,*" etc. "*Dissertat.* 5.

[2] Allusions to Mrs. Tighe's Poem.

[3] Constancy.

Half sunk beneath the shadowy rim,
Half brightened by the upper ray, [1]—

Thou dwellest in a world, all light,
Or, lingering here, dost love to be,
To other souls, the guardian bright
That Love was, through this gloom, to
thee;

Still be the song to Psyche dear,
The song, whose gentle voice was given
To be, on earth, to mortal ear,
An echo of her own, in heaven.

FROM

THE HIGH PRIEST OF APOLLO
TO
A VIRGIN OF DELPHI.[2]

Cum digno digna ....
SULPICIA.

" WHO is the maid, with golden hair,
" With eye of fire, and foot of air,
" Whose harp around my altar swells,
" The sweetest of a thousand shells? "
'T was thus the deity, who treads
The arch of heaven, and proudly sheds
Day from his eyelids — thus he spoke,
As through my cell his glories broke.

Aphelia is the Delphic fair,[3]
With eyes of fire and golden hair,
Aphelia's are the airy feet,
And hers the harp divinely sweet;

1 By this image the Platonists expressed the
middle state of the soul between sensible and
intellectual existence.

2 This poem, as well as a few others in the
following volume, formed part of a work which
I had early projected, and even announced to
the public, but which, luckily, perhaps, for myself, had been interrupted by my visit to America
in the year 1803.
Among those impostures in which the priests
of the pagan temples are known to have indulged,
one of the most favorite was that of announcing
to some fair votary of the shrine, that the God
himself had become enamoured of her beauty, and
would descend in all his glory, to pay her a visit
within the recesses of the fane. An adventure of
this description formed an episode in the classic
romance which I had sketched out ; and the short
fragment, given above, belongs to an epistle by
which the story was to have been introduced.

3 In the 9th Pythic of Pindar, where Apollo,
in the same manner, requires of Chiron some
information respecting the fair Cyrene, the Centaur, in obeying, very gravely apologizes for

For foot so light has never trod
The laurelled caverns[4] of the god,
Nor harp so soft hath ever given
A sigh to earth or hymn to heaven.

" Then tell the virgin to unfold,
" In looser pomp, her locks of gold,
" And bid those eyes more fondly shine
" To welcome down a Spouse Divine ;
" Since He, who lights the path of years —
" Even from the fount of morning's tears
" To where his setting splendors burn
" Upon the western sea-maid's urn —
" Doth not, in all his course, behold
" Such eyes of fire, such hair of gold.
" Tell her, he comes, in blissful pride,
" His lip yet sparkling with the tide
" That mantles in Olympian bowls, —
" The nectar of eternal souls !
" For her, for her he quits the skies,
" And to her kiss from nectar flies.
" Oh, he would quit his star-throned
height,
" And leave the world to pine for light,
" Might he but pass the hours of shade,
" Beside his peerless Delphic maid,
" She, more than earthly woman blest,
" He, more than god on woman's
breast ! "

There is a cave beneath the steep,[5]
Where living rills of crystal weep
O'er herbage of the loveliest hue
That ever spring begemmed with dew:
There oft the greensward's glossy tint
Is brightened by the recent print
Of many a faun and naiad's feet, —
Scarce touching earth, their step so
fleet, —
That there, by moonlight's ray, had trod,
In light dance, o'er the verdant sod.
" There, there," the god, impassioned,
said,
" Soon as the twilight tinge is fled,

telling the God what his omniscience must know
so perfectly already :
εἰ δέ γε χρὴ καὶ πὰρ σοφὸν ἀντιφερίξαι,
ἐρέω.

4 ἀλλ' εἰς δαφνώδη γύαλα βήσομαι τάδε.
EURIPID. "*Ion.*" v. 76.

5 The Corycian Cave, which Pausanias mentions. The inhabitants of Parnassus held it
sacred to the Corycian nymphs, who were children of the river Plistus.

" And the dim orb of lunar souls [1]
" Along its shadowy pathway rolls —
" There shall we meet, — and not even
    He,
" The God who reigns immortally,
" Where Babel's turrets paint their pride
" Upon the Euphrates' shining tide,[2] —
" Not even when to his midnight loves
" In mystic majesty he moves,
" Lighted by many an odorous fire,
" And hymned by all Chaldæa's choir,—
" E'er yet, o'er mortal brow, let shine
" Such effluence of Love Divine,
" As shall to-night, blest maid, o'er
    thine."

Happy the maid, whom heaven allows
To break for heaven her virgin vows !
Happy the maid ! — her robe of shame
Is whitened by a heavenly flame,
Whose glory, with a lingering trace,
Shines through and deifies her race ! [3]

FRAGMENT.

PITY me, love ! I 'll pity thee,
If thou indeed has felt like me.
All, all my bosom's peace is o'er !
At night, which *was* my hour of calm,
When from the page of classic lore,
From the pure fount of ancient lay
My soul has drawn the placid balm,

Which charmed its every grief away,
Ah ! there I find that balm no more.
Those spells, which make us oft forget
The fleeting troubles of the day,
In deeper sorrows only whet
The stings they cannot tear away.
When to my pillow racked I fly,
With weary sense and wakeful eye.
While my brain maddens, where, oh,
    where
Is that serene consoling prayer,
Which once has harbingered my rest,
When the still soothing voice of Heaven

Hath seemed to whisper in my breast,
" Sleep on, thy errors are forgiven ! "
No, though I still in semblance pray,
My thoughts are wandering far away,
And even the name of Deity
Is murmured out in sighs for thee.

A NIGHT THOUGHT.

How oft a cloud, with envious veil,
   Obscures yon bashful light,
Which seems so modestly to steal
   Along the waste of night !

'T is thus the world's obtrusive wrongs
   Obscure with malice keen
Some timid heart, which only longs
   To live and die unseen.

THE KISS.

GROW to my lip, thou sacred kiss,
On which my soul's beloved swore
That there should come a time of bliss,
When she would mock my hopes no
    more.
And fancy shall thy glow renew,
In sighs at morn, and dreams at night,
And none shall steal thy holy dew
Till thou 'rt absolved by rapture's rite.
Sweet hours that are to make me blest,
Fly, swift as breezes, to the goal,
And let my love, my more than soul
Come blushing to this ardent breast,
Then, while in every glance I drink
The rich o'erflowings of her mind,
Oh ! let her all enamoured sink
In sweet abandonment resigned,
Blushing for all our struggles past,
And murmuring, " I am thine at last ! "

---

1 See a preceding note, p. 31. It should
seem that lunar spirits were of a purer order
than spirits in general, as Pythagoras was said
by his followers to have descended from the
regions of the moon. The heresiarch Manes, in
the same manner, imagined that the sun and
moon are the residence of Christ, and that the
ascension was nothing more than his flight to
those orbs.

2 The temple of Jupiter Belus, at Babylon ;
in one of whose towers there was a large chapel
set apart for these celestial assignations. " No
man is allowed to sleep here," says Herodotus ;
" but the apartment is appropriated to a female,
whom, if we believe the Chaldæan priests, the
deity selects from the women of the country, as
his favorite." *Lib.* i. *cap.* 181.

3 Fontenelle, in his playful *rifacimento* of
the learned materials of Van-Dale, has related in
his own inimitable manner an adventure of this
kind which was detected and exposed at Alexandria. See " *L'Histoire des Oracles*," dissert. 2. chap. vii. Crebillon, too, in one of his
most amusing little stories, has made the Génie
Mange-Taupes, of the Isle Jonquille, assert this
privilege of spiritual beings in a manner rather
formidable to the husbands of the island.

SONG.

THINK on that look whose melting ray
 For one sweet moment mixt with mine,
And for that moment seemed to say,
 " I dare not, or I would be thine ! "

Think on thy every smile and glance,
 On all thou hast to charm and move;
And then forgive my bosom's trance,
 Nor tell me it is sin to love.

Oh, *not* to love thee were the sin;
 For sure, if Fate's decrees be done,
Thou, thou art destined still to win,
 As I am destined to be won !

THE CATALOGUE.

" COME, tell me," says Rosa, as kissing
 and kist,
 One day she reclined on my breast;
" Come, tell me the number, repeat me
 the list
  " Of the nymphs you have loved and
  carest." —
Oh Rosa ! 't was only my fancy that roved,
 My heart at the moment was free;
But I 'll tell thee, my girl, how many
 I 've loved,
 And the number shall finish with thee.

My tutor was Kitty; in infancy wild
 She taught me the way to be blest;
She taught me to love her, I loved like
 a child,
 But Kitty could fancy the rest.
This lesson of dear and enrapturing lore
 I have never forgot, I allow:
I have had it *by rote* very often before,
 But never *by heart* until now.

Pretty Martha was next, and my soul
 was all flame,
But my head was so full of romance
That I fancied her into some chivalry
 dame,
 And I was her knight of the lance.
But Martha was not of this fanciful
 school,
 And she laughed at her poor little
 knight;
While I thought her a goddess, she
 thought me a fool,
 And I 'll swear *she* was most in the
 right.

My soul was now calm, till, by Cloris's
 looks,
 Again I was tempted to rove;
But Cloris, I found, was so learned in
 books
 That she gave me more logic than love.
So I left this young Sappho, and hastened
 to fly
 To those sweeter logicians in bliss,
Who argue the point with a soul-telling
 eye,
 And convince us at once with a kiss.

Oh ! Susan was then all the world unto
 me,
 But Susan was piously given ;
And the worst of it was, we could never
 agree
 On the road that was shortest to
 Heaven.
" Oh, Susan ! " I 've said, in the mo-
 ments of mirth,
 " What 's devotion to thee or to me ?
" I devoutly believe there 's a heaven
 on earth,
 " And believe that that heaven 's in
 thee ! "

IMITATION OF CATULLUS.

TO HIMSELF.

Miser Catulle, desinas ineptire, etc.

CEASE the sighing fool to play;
Cease to trifle life away;
Nor vainly think those joys thine own,
Which all, alas, have falsely flown.
What hours, Catullus, once were thine,
How fairly seemed thy day to shine,
When lightly thou didst fly to meet
The girl whose smile was then so sweet —
The girl thou lovedst with fonder pain
Then e'er thy heart can feel again.

Ye met — your souls seemed all in one,
Like tapers that commingling shone;
Thy heart was warm enough for both,
And hers, in truth, was nothing loath.

Such were the hours that once were
 thine;
But, ah ! those hours no longer shine.
For now the nymph delights no more
In what she loved so much before;
And all Catullus now can do,
Is to be proud and frigid too;

Nor follow where the wanton flies,
Nor sue the bliss that she denies.
False maid! he bids farewell to thee,
To love, and all love's misery;
The heyday of his heart is o'er,
Nor will he court one favor more.

Fly, perjured girl! — but whither fly?
Who now will praise thy cheek and eye?
Who now will drink the syren tone,
Which tells him thou art all his own?
Oh, none: — and he who loved before
Can never, never love thee more.

"*Neither do I condemn thee; go, and sin no more!*" — ST. JOHN, chap. viii.

OH woman, if through sinful wile
Thy soul hath strayed from honor's
track,
'T is mercy only can beguile,
By gentle ways, the wanderer back.

The stain that on thy virtue lies,
Washed by those tears, not long will
stay;
As clouds that sully morning skies
May all be wept in showers away.

Go, go, be innocent, — and live;
The tongues of men may wound thee
sore,
But Heaven in pity can forgive,
And bids thee " go, and sin no more!"

NONSENSE.

GOOD reader! if you e'er have seen,
When Phœbus hastens to his pillow,
The mermaids, with their tresses green,
Dancing upon the western billow:
If you have seen, at twilight dim,
When the lone spirit's vesper hymn
Floats wild along the winding shore,
If you have seen, through mist of eve,
The fairy train their ringlets weave,
Glancing along the spangled green: —
If you have seen all this, and more,
God bless me, what a deal you 've seen!

EPIGRAM,

FROM THE FRENCH.

" I NEVER gave a kiss (says Prue),
"To naughty man, for I abhor it."
She will not *give* a kiss, 't is true;
She 'll *take* one though, and thank you
for it.

ON A SQUINTING POETESS.

To no *one* Muse does she her glance
confine,
But has an eye, at once, to *all the Nine!*

TO . . . .

*Moria pur quando vuol, non è bisogna mutar
ni faccia ni voce per esser un Angelo.*[1]

DIE when you will, you need not wear
At Heaven's Court a form more fair
Than Beauty here on earth has given;
Keep but the lovely looks we see —
The voice we hear — and you will be
An angel *ready-made* for Heaven!

TO ROSA.

A far conserva, e cumulo d'amanti.
"*Past. Fid.*"

AND are you then a thing of art,
Seducing all, and loving none;
And have I strove to gain a heart
Which every coxcomb thinks his own?

Tell me at once if this be true,
And I will calm my jealous breast;
Will learn to join the dangling crew,
And share your simpers with the rest.

But if your heart be *not* so free, —
Oh! if another share that heart,
Tell not the hateful tale to me,
But mingle mercy with your art.

I 'd rather think you " false as hell,"
Than find you to be all divine,—
Than know that heart could love so well,
Yet know that heart would *not* be
mine!

TO PHILLIS.

PHILLIS, you little rosy rake,
That heart of yours I long to rifle:
Come, give it me, and do not make
So much ado about a *trifle!*

TO A LADY,

ON HER SINGING.

THY song has taught my heart to feel
Those soothing thoughts of heavenly
love,

---

[1] The words addressed by Lord Herbert of Cherbury to the beautiful Nun at Murano. — *See his Life.*

Which o'er the sainted spirits steal
  When listening to the spheres above!

When, tired of life and misery,
  I wish to sigh my latest breath,
Oh, Emma! I will fly to thee,
  And thou shalt sing me into death.

And if along thy lip and cheek
  That smile of heavenly softness play,
Which, — ah! forgive a mind that 's
    weak, —
  So oft has stolen my mind away;

Thou 'lt seem an angel of the sky,
  That comes to charm me into bliss:
I 'll gaze and die — Who would not die,
  If death were half so sweet as this?

SONG.

ON THE BIRTHDAY OF MRS. ——.

WRITTEN IN IRELAND. 1799.

OF all my happiest hours of joy,
  And even I have had my measure,
When hearts were full, and every eye
  Hath kindled with the light of pleasure,
An hour like this I ne'er was given,
  So full of friendship's purest blisses;
Young Love himself looks down from
    heaven,
  To smile on such a day as this is.
    Then come, my friends, this hour
      improve,
      Let 's feel as if we ne'er could
        sever;
    And may the birth of her we love
      Be thus with joy remembered ever!

Oh! banish every thought to-night,
  Which could disturb our soul's com-
    munion;
Abandoned thus to dear delight,
  We 'll even for once forget the Union!
On that let statesmen try their powers,
  And tremble o'er the rights they 'd
    die for;
The union of the soul be ours,
  And every union else we sigh for.
      Then come, my friends, etc.

In every eye around I mark
  The feelings of the heart o'erflowing;
From every soul I catch the spark
  Of sympathy, in friendship glowing.

Oh! could such moments ever fly;
  Oh! that we ne'er were doomed to
    lose 'em;
And all as bright as Charlotte's eye,
  And all as pure as Charlotte's bosom.
      Then come, my friends, etc.

For me, whate'er my span of years,
  Whatever sun may light my roving;
Whether I waste my life in tears,
  Or live, as now, for mirth and loving;
This day shall come with aspect kind,
  Wherever fate may cast your rover;
He 'll think of those he left behind,
  And drink a health to bliss that 's over!
      Then come, my friends, etc.

SONG.[1]

MARY, I believed thee true,
  And I was blest in thus believing;
But now I mourn that e'er I knew
  A girl so fair and so deceiving.
      Fare thee well.

Few have ever loved like me, —
  Yes, I have loved thee too sincerely!
And few have e'er deceived like thee, —
  Alas! deceived me too severely.

Fare thee well! — yet think awhile
  On one whose bosom bleeds to doubt
    thee;
Who now would rather trust that smile,
  And die with thee than live without
    thee.

Fare thee well! I 'll think of thee,
  Thou leavest me many a bitter token;
For see, distracting woman, see,
  My peace is gone, my heart is
    broken! —
      Fare thee well!

MORALITY.

A FAMILIAR EPISTLE.
ADDRESSED TO
J. ATKINSON, ESQ. M. R. I. A.

THOUGH long at school and college doz-
    ing,
O'er books of verse and books of prosing,

---

1 These words were written to the pathetic
Scotch air "Galla Water."

And copying from their moral pages
Fine recipes for making sages;
Though long with those divines at school,
Who think to make us good by rule;
Who, in methodic forms advancing,
Teaching morality like dancing,
Tell us, for Heaven or money's sake,
What *steps* we are through life to take:
Though thus, my friend, so long employed,
With so much midnight oil destroyed,
I must confess, my searches past,
I 've only learned *to doubt* at last.
I find the doctors and the sages
Have differed in all climes and ages,
And two in fifty scarce agree
On what is pure morality.
'T is like the rainbow's shifting zone,
And every vision makes its own.

The doctors of the Porch advise,
As modes of being great and wise,
That we should cease to own or know
The luxuries that from feeling flow: —
" Reason alone must claim direction,
" And Apathy 's the soul's perfection.
" Like a dull lake the heart must lie;
" Nor passion's gale nor pleasure's sigh,
" Though Heaven the breeze, the breath, supplied,
" Must curl the wave or swell the tide ! "

Such was the rigid Zeno's plan
To form his philosophic man;
Such were the modes *he* taught mankind
To weed the garden of the mind;
They tore from thence some weeds, 't is true,
But all the flowers were ravaged too !

Now listen to the wily strains,
Which, on Cyrene's sandy plains,
When Pleasure, nymph with loosened zone,
Usurped the philosophic throne, —
Hear what the courtly sage's [1] tongue
To his surrounding pupils sung : —
" Pleasure 's the only noble end
" To which all human powers should tend,
" And Virtue gives her heavenly lore,
" But to make Pleasure please us more.

1 Aristippus.

" Wisdom and she were both designed
" To make the senses more refined,
" That man might revel, free from cloying,
" Then most a sage when most enjoying ! "

Is this morality ? — Oh, no !
Even I a wiser path could show.
The flower within this vase confined,
The pure, the unfading flower of mind,
Must not throw all its sweets away
Upon a mortal mould of clay :
No, no, — its richest breath should rise
In virtue's incense to the skies.

But thus it is, all sects we see
Have watchwords of morality :
Some cry out Venus, others Jove;
Here 't is Religion, there 't is Love.
But while they thus so widely wander,
While mystics dream and doctors ponder;
And some, in dialectics firm,
Seek virtue in a middle term;
While thus they strive, in Heaven's defiance,
To chain morality with science;
The plain good man, whose actions teach
More virtue than a sect can preach,
Pursues his course, unsagely blest,
His tutor whispering in his breast;
Nor could he act a purer part,
Though he had Tully all by heart.
And when he drops the tear on woe,
He little knows or cares to know
That Epictetus blamed that tear,
By Heaven approved, to virtue dear !

Oh ! when I 've seen the morning beam
Floating within the dimpled stream;
While Nature, wakening from the night,
Has just put on her robes of light,
Have I, with cold optician's gaze,
Explored the *doctrine* of those rays?
No, pedants, I have left to you
Nicely to separate hue from hue.
Go, give that moment up to art,
When Heaven and nature claim the heart;
And, dull to all their best attraction,
Go — measure *angles of refraction*.
While I, in feeling's sweet romance,
Look on each daybeam as a glance
From the great eye of Him above,
Wakening his world with looks of love !

THE TELL-TALE LYRE.

I 'VE heard, there was in ancient days
    A Lyre of most melodious spell;
'T was heaven to hear its fairy lays,
    If half be true that legends tell.

'T was played on by the gentlest sighs,
    And to their breath it breathed again
In such entrancing melodies
    As ear had never drunk till then!

Not harmony's serenest touch
    So stilly could the notes prolong;
They were not heavenly song so much
    As they were dreams of heavenly song!

If sad the heart, whose murmuring air
    Along the chords in languor stole,
The numbers it awakened there
    Were eloquence from pity's soul.

Or if the sigh, serene and light,
    Was but the breath of fancied woes,
The string, that felt its airy flight,
    Soon whispered it to kind repose.

And when young lovers talked alone,
    If, mid their bliss that Lyre was near,
It made their accents all its own,
    And sent forth notes that heaven might
        hear.

There was a nymph, who long had loved,
    But dared not tell the world how well:
The shades, where she at evening roved,
    Alone could know, alone could tell.

'T was there, at twilight time, she stole,
    When the first star announced the
        night, —
With him who claimed her inmost soul,
    To wander by that soothing light.

It chanced that, in the fairy bower
    Where blest they wooed each other's
        smile,
This Lyre, of strange and magic power,
    Hung whispering o'er their heads the
        while.

And as, with eyes commingling fire,
    They listened to each other's vow,
The youth full oft would make the Lyre
    A pillow for the maiden's brow:

And, while the melting words she breathed
    Were by its echoes wafted round,
Her locks had with the chords so
        wreathed,
    One knew not which gave forth the
        sound.

Alas, their hearts but little thought,
    While thus they talked the hours away,
That every sound the Lyre was taught
    Would linger long, and long betray.

So mingled with its tuneful soul
    Were all their tender murmurs grown,
That other sighs unanswered stole,
    Nor words it breathed but theirs alone.

Unhappy nymph! thy name was sung
    To every breeze that wandered by;
The secrets of thy gentle tongue
    Were breathed in song to earth and sky.

The fatal Lyre, by Envy's hand
    Hung high amid the whispering groves,
To every gale by which 't was fanned,
    Proclaimed the mystery of your loves.

Nor long thus rudely was thy name
    To earth's derisive echoes given;
Some pitying spirit downward came,
    And took the Lyre and thee to heaven.

There, freed from earth's unholy wrongs,
    Both happy in Love's home shall be;
Thou, uttering naught but seraph songs,
    And that sweet Lyre still echoing thee!

PEACE AND GLORY.
WRITTEN ON THE APPROACH OF WAR.

WHERE is now the smile, that lightened
    Every hero's couch of rest?
Where is now the hope, that brightened
    Honor's eye and Pity's breast?
Have we lost the wreath we braided
    For our weary warrior men?
Is the faithless olive faded?
    Must the bay be plucked again?

Passing hour of sunny weather,
    Lovely, in your light awhile,
Peace and Glory, wed together,
    Wandered through our blessed isle.
And the eyes of Peace would glisten,
    Dewy as a morning sun,

When the timid maid would listen
　To the deeds her chief had done.
Is their hour of dalliance over?
Must the maiden's trembling feet
Waft her from her warlike lover
　To the desert's still retreat?
Fare you well! with sighs we banish
　Nymph so fair and guests so bright;
Yet the smile, with which you vanish,
　Leaves behind a soothing light; —

Soothing light, that long shall sparkle
　O'er your warrior's sanguined way,
Through the field where horrors darkle,
　Shedding hope's consoling ray.
Long the smile his heart will cherish,
　To its absent idol true;
While around him myriads perish,
　Glory still will sigh for you!

SONG.

TAKE back the sigh, thy lips of art
　In passion's moment breathed to me;
Yet, no — it must not, will not part,
'T is now the life-breath of my heart,
　And has become too pure for thee.

Take back the kiss, that faithless sigh
　With all the warmth of truth imprest;
Yet, no — the fatal kiss may lie,
Upon *thy* lip its sweets would die,
　Or bloom to make a rival blest.

Take back the vows that, night and day,
　My heart received, I thought, from
　　thine;
Yet, no — allow them still to stay,
They might some other heart betray,
　As sweetly as they 've ruined mine.

LOVE AND REASON.

"*Quand l'homme commence à raisonner, il cesse
de sentir.*" — J. J. ROUSSEAU.[1]

'T WAS in the summer time so sweet,
　When hearts and flowers are both in
　　season,
That — who, of all the world, should
　　meet,
　One early dawn, but Love and Reason!

[1] Quoted somewhere in St. Pierre's *Études
de la Nature.*

Love told his dream of yesternight,
　While Reason talked about the
　　weather;
The morn, in sooth, was fair and bright,
　And on they took their way together.

The boy in many a gambol flew,
　While Reason, like a Juno, stalked,
And from her portly figure threw
　A lengthened shadow, as she walked.

No wonder Love, as on they past,
　Should find that sunny morning chill,
For still the shadow Reason cast
　Fell o'er the boy, and cooled him still.

In vain he tried his wings to warm,
　Or find a pathway not so dim,
For still the maid's gigantic form
　Would stalk between the sun and him.

"This must not be," said little Love —
　"The sun was made for more than
　　you."
So, turning through a myrtle grove,
　He bid the portly nymph adieu.

Now gayly roves the laughing boy
　O'er many a mead, by many a stream;
In every breeze inhaling joy,
　And drinking bliss in every beam.

From all the gardens, all the bowers,
　He culled the many sweets they shaded,
And ate the fruits and smelled the flowers,
　Till taste was gone and odor faded.

But now the sun, in pomp of noon,
　Looked blazing o'er the sultry plains;
Alas! the boy grew languid soon,
　And fever thrilled through all his veins.

The dew forsook his baby brow,
　No more with healthy bloom he
　　smiled —
Oh! where was tranquil Reason now,
　To cast her shadow o'er the child?

Beneath a green and aged palm,
　His foot at length for shelter turning,
He saw the nymph reclining calm,
　With brow as cool as his was burning.

"Oh! take me to that bosom cold,"
  In murmurs at her feet he said;
And Reason oped her garment's fold,
  And flung it round his fevered head.

He felt her bosom's icy touch,
  And soon it lulled his pulse to rest;
For, ah! the chill was quite too much,
  And Love expired on Reason's breast.

NAY, do not weep, my Fanny dear;
  While in these arms you lie,
This world hath not a wish, a fear,
That ought to cost that eye a tear,
  That heart, one single sigh.

The world! — ah, Fanny, Love must
    shun
  The paths where many rove;
One bosom to recline upon,
One heart to be his only-one,
  Are quite enough for Love.

What can we wish, that is not here
  Between your arms and mine?
Is there, on earth, a space so dear
As that within the happy sphere
  Two loving arms entwine?

For me, there 's not a lock of jet
  Adown your temples curled,
Within whose glossy, tangling net,
My soul doth not, at once, forget
  All, all this worthless world.

'T is in those eyes, so full of love,
  My only worlds I see;
Let but *their* orbs in sunshine move,
And earth below and skies above
  May frown or smile for me.

ASPASIA.

'T WAS in the fair Aspasia's bower,
That Love and Learning, many an hour,
In dalliance met; and Learning smiled
With pleasure on the playful child,
Who often stole, to find a nest
Within the folds of Learning's vest.

There, as the listening statesman hung
In transport on Aspasia's tongue,
The destinies of Athens took
Their color from Aspasia's look.

Oh happy time, when laws of state
When all that ruled the country's fate,
Its glory, quiet, or alarms,
Was planned between two snow-white
    arms!

Blest times! they could not always
    last —
And yet, even now, they *are* not past.
Though we have lost the giant mould,
In which their men were cast of old,
Woman, dear woman, still the same,
While beauty breathes through soul or
    frame,
While man possesses heart or eyes,
Woman's bright empire never dies!

No, Fanny, love, they ne'er shall say,
That beauty's charm hath past away;
Give but the universe a soul
Attuned to woman's soft control,
And Fanny hath the charm, the skill,
To wield a universe at will.

THE GRECIAN GIRL'S DREAM
OF THE BLESSED ISLANDS.[1]
TO HER LOVER.

—— ἧχι τε καλὸς
Πυθαγόρης, ὅσσοι τε χόρον στήριξαν ἔρωτος.
Ἀπόλλων περὶ Πλωτίνου.
"*Oracul. Metric. a Joan.*
Opsop. collecta."

WAS it the moon, or was it morning's ray,
That call'd thee, dearest, from these arms
    away?
Scarce hadst thou left me, when a dream
    of night
Came o'er my spirit so distinct and bright,
That, while I yet can vividly recall
Its witching wonders, thou shalt hear
    them all.
Methought I saw, upon the lunar beam,
Two winged boys, such as thy muse might
    dream,
Descending from above, at that still hour,
And gliding, with smooth step, into my
    bower.

1 It was imagined by some of the ancients
that there is an ethereal ocean above us, and that
the sun and moon are two floating, luminous
islands, in which the spirits of the blest reside.
Accordingly we find that the word ὠκεανός was
sometimes synonymous with ἀήρ, and death was
not unfrequently called ὠκεανοῖο πόρος, or "the
passage of the ocean."

Fair as the beauteous spirits that, all day,
In Amatha's warm founts imprisoned
   stay,[3]
But rise at midnight, from the enchanted
   rill,
To cool their plumes upon some moonlight
   hill.

At once I knew their mission: — 't was
   to bear
My spirit upward, through the paths of
   air,
To that elysian realm, from whence stray
   beams
So oft, in sleep, had visited my dreams.
Swift at their touch dissolved the ties, that
   clung
All earthly round me, and aloft I sprung;
While, heavenward guides, the little genii
   flew
Thro' paths of light, refreshed by heaven's
   own dew,
And fanned by airs still fragrant with the
   breath
Of cloudless climes and worlds that know
   not death.

Thou knowest, that, far beyond our
   nether sky,
And shown but dimly to man's erring eye,
A mighty ocean of blue ether rolls,[2]

Gemmed with bright islands, where the
   chosen souls,
Who 've past in lore and love their earthly
   hours,
Repose for ever in unfading bowers.
That very moon, whose solitary light
So often guides thee to my bower at night,
Is no chill planet, but an isle of love,
Floating in splendor through those seas
   above,
And peopled with bright forms, aërial
   grown,
Nor knowing aught of earth but love
   alone.
Thither, I thought, we winged our airy
   way: —
Mild o'er its valleys streamed a silvery
   day,
While, all around, on lily beds of rest,
Reclined the spirits of the immortal
   Blest.[3]
Oh! there I met those few congenial
   maids,
Whom love hath warmed, in philosophic
   shades;
There still Leontium,[4] on her sage's
   breast,

---

1 Eunapius, in his life of Iamblichus, tells us of two beautiful little spirits or loves, which Iamblichus raised by enchantment from the warm springs at Gadara; " *dicens astantibus* (says the author of the " Dii Fatidici," p. 160) *illos esse loci Genios:* " which words, however, are not in Eunapius.

I find from Cellarius, that Amatha, in the neighborhood of Gadara, was also celebrated for its warm springs, and I have preferred it as a more poetical name than Gadara. Cellarius quotes Hieronymus. " *Est et alia villa in vicinia Gadaræ nomine Amatha, ubi calidæ aquæ erumpunt.*" — " *Geograph. Antiq.*" lib. iii. *cap.* 13.

2 This belief of an ocean in the heavens, or " waters above the firmament," was one of the many physical errors in which the early fathers bewildered themselves. Le P. Baltus, in his " *Défense des Saints Pères accusés de Platonisme*," taking it for granted that the ancients were more correct in their notions (which by no means appears from what I have already quoted), adduces the obstinacy of the fathers, in this whimsical opinion, as a proof of their repugnance to even truth from the hands of the philosophers. This is a strange way of defending the fathers, and attributes much more than they deserve to

the philosophers. For an abstract of this work of Baltus, (the opposer of Fontenelle, Van Dale, etc. in the famous Oracle controversy,) see " *Bibliothèque des Auteurs Ecclésiast. du 18me siècle, part 1. tom.* ii."

3 There were various opinions among the ancients with respect to their lunar establishment; some made it an elysium, and others a purgatory; while some supposed it to be a kind of *entrepôt* between heaven and earth, where souls which had left their bodies, and those that were on their way to join them, were deposited in the valleys of Hecate, and remained till further orders. τοῖς περὶ σελήνην ἀερι λέγειν αὐτὰς κατοικεῖν, καὶ ἀπ' αὐτῆς κάτω χωρεῖν εἰς τὴν περίγειον γένεσιν.—*Stob. lib.* i. "*Eclog. Physic.*"

4 The pupil and mistress of Epicurus, who called her his " dear little Leontium " (Λεοντάριον), as appears by a fragment of one of his letters in Laertius. This Leontium was a woman of talent; " she had the impudence (says Cicero) to write against Theophrastus; " and Cicero, at the same time, gives her a name which is neither polite nor translatable. " *Meretricula etiam Leontium contra Theophrastum scribere ausa est.*" — "*De Natur. Deor.*" She left a daughter called Danae, who was just as rigid an Epicurean as her mother; something like Wieland's Danae in Agathon.

It would sound much better, I think, if the name were Leontia, as it occurs the first time in Laertius; but M. Ménage will not hear of this reading.

Found lore and love, was tutored and
carest;
And there the clasp of Pythia's[1] gentle
arms
Repaid the zeal which deified her charms.
The Attic Master,[2] in Aspasia's eyes,
Forgot the yoke of less endearing ties;
While fair Theano,[3] innocently fair,
Wreathed playfully her Samian's flowing
hair,[4]
Whose soul now fixt, its transmigrations
past,
Found in those arms a resting-place, at
last;
And smiling owned, whate'er his dreamy
thought
In mystic numbers long had vainly sought,
The One that 's formed of Two whom
love hath bound,
Is the best number gods or men e'er found.

But think, my Theon, with what joy I
thrilled,
When near a fount, which through the
valley rilled,

My fancy's eye beheld a form recline,
Of lunar race, but so resembling thine
That, oh! 't was but fidelity in me,
To fly, to clasp, and worship it for thee.
No aid of words the unbodied soul re-
quires,
To waft a wish or embassy desires;
But by a power, to spirits only given,
A deep, mute impulse, only felt in heaven,
Swifter than meteor shaft through summer
skies,
From soul to soul the glanced idea flies.

Oh, my beloved, how divinely sweet
Is the pure joy, when kindred spirits meet!
Like him, the river-god,[5] whose waters
flow,
With love their only light, through caves
below,
Wafting in triumph all the flowery braids,
And festal rings, with which Olympic
maids
Have decked his current, as an offering
meet
To lay at Arethusa's shining feet.

Think, when he meets at last his foun-
tain-bride,
What perfect love must thrill the blended
tide!
Each lost in each, till, mingling into one,
Their lot the same for shadow or for
sun,
A type of true love, to the deep they run.
'T was thus —
But, Theon, 't is an endless theme,
And thou growest weary of my half-told
dream.

Oh would, my love, we were together
now,
And I would woo sweet patience to thy
brow,

<hr/>

1 Pythia was a woman whom Aristotle loved,
and to whom after her death he paid divine honors, solemnizing her memory by the same sacrifices which the Athenians offered to the Goddess
Ceres. For this impious gallantry the philosopher was, of course, censured; but it would be
well if certain of our modern Stagyrites showed
a little of this superstition about the memory of
their mistresses.

2 Socrates, who used to console himself in
the society of Aspasia for those "less endearing
ties" which he found at home with Xantippe.
For an account of this extraordinary creature,
Aspasia, and her school of erudite luxury at
Athens, see "*L'Histoire de l'Académie,*" etc.
tom. xxxi. p. 69. Ségur rather fails on the inspiring subject of Aspasia. — "*Les Femmes,*"
tom. i. p. 122.

The Author of the "*Voyage du Monde de
Descartes*" has also placed these philosophers
in the moon, and has alloted seigneuries to them,
as well as to the astronomers (part ii. p. 143.);
but he ought not to have forgotten their wives
and mistresses; "*curæ non ipsâ in morte relin-
quunt.*"

3 There are some sensible letters extant under
the name of this fair Pythagorean. They are addressed to her female friends upon the education
of children, the treatment of servants, etc. One,
in particular, to Nicostrata, whose husband had
given her reasons for jealousy, contains such truly
considerate and rational advice, that it ought to
be translated for the edification of all married
ladies. See Gale's Opuscul. Myth. Phys. p. 741.

4 Pythagoras was remarkable for fine hair, and
Doctor Thiers (in his "*Histoire des Perruques*")

seems to take for granted it was all his own; as
he has not mentioned him among those ancients
who were obliged to have recourse to the "*coma
apposititia.*" "*L'Hist. des Perruques,*" chap. i.

5 The river Alpheus, which flowed by Pisa
or Olympia, and into which it was customary
to throw offerings of different kinds, during the
celebration of the Olympic games. In the pretty
romance of Clitophon and Leucippe, the river is
supposed to carry these offerings as bridal gifts
to the fountain Arethusa. καὶ ἐπὶ τὴν Ἀρέθουσαν
οὕτω τὸν Ἀλφειὸν νυμφοστόλει. ὅταν οὖν ἦ τῶν
ὀλυμπίων ἑορτή, κ, τ. λ. *Lib.* i.

And make thee smile at all the magic
    tales
Of starlight bowers and planetary vales,
Which my fond soul, inspired by thee
    and love,
In slumber's loom hath fancifully wove.
But no; no more — soon as to-morrow's
    ray
O'er soft Ilissus shall have died away,
I 'll come, and, while love's planet in
    the west
Shines o'er our meeting, tell thee all the
    rest.

TO CLOE.

IMITATED FROM MARTIAL.

I COULD resign that eye of blue,
    Howe'er its splendor used to thrill
    me;
And even that cheek of roseate hue, —
    To lose it, Cloe, scarce would kill me.

That snowy neck I ne'er should miss,
    However much I 've raved about it;
And sweetly as that lip can kiss,
    I *think* I could exist without it.

In short, so well I 've learned to fast,
    That, sooth my love, I know not
    whether
I might not bring myself at last,
    To — do without you altogether.

THE WREATH AND THE CHAIN.

I BRING thee, love, a golden chain,
    I bring thee too a flowery wreath;
The gold shall never wear a stain,
    The flowerets long shall sweetly
    breathe.
Come, tell me which the tie shall be,
To bind thy gentle heart to me.

The Chain is formed of golden threads,
    Bright as Minerva's yellow hair,
When the last beam of evening sheds
    Its calm and sober lustre there.
The Wreath 's of brightest myrtle wove,
    With sunlit drops of bliss among it,
And many a rose-leaf, culled by Love,
    To heal his lip when bees have stung it.
Come, tell me which the tie shall be,
To bind thy gentle heart to me.

Yes, yes, I read that ready eye,
    Which answers when the tongue is
    loath,
Thou likest the form of either tie,
    And spreadest thy playful hands for
    both.
Ah! — if there were not something
    wrong,
    The world would see them blended oft;
The Chain would make the Wreath so
    strong!
    The Wreath would make the Chain so
    soft!
Then might the gold, the flowerets be
Sweet fetters for my love and me.

But, Fanny, so unblest they twine,
    That (heaven alone can tell the reason)
When mingled thus they cease to shine,
    Or shine but for a transient season.
Whether the Chain may press too much,
    Or that the Wreath is slightly braided,
Let but the gold the flowerets touch,
    And all their bloom, their glow is faded!
Oh! better to be always free,
Than thus to bind my love to me.

The timid girl now hung her head,
    And, as she turned an upward glance,
I saw a doubt its twilight spread
    Across her brow's divine expanse.
Just then, the garland's brightest rose
Gave one of its love-breathing sighs —
Oh! who can ask how Fanny chose,
    That ever looked in Fanny's eyes?
" The Wreath, my life, the Wreath shall
    be
" The tie to bind my soul to thee."

TO . . . .

AND hast thou marked the pensive shade,
    That many a time obscures my brow,
Midst all the joys, beloved maid,
    Which thou canst give, and only thou?

Oh! 't is not that I then forget
    The bright looks that before me shine;
For never throbbed a bosom yet
    Could feel their witchery, like mine.

When bashful on my bosom hid,
    And blushing to have felt so blest,

Thou dost but lift thy languid lid,
　Again to close it on my breast; —

Yes, — these are minutes all thine own,
　Thine own to give, and mine to feel;
Yet even in them, my heart has known
　The sigh to rise, the tear to steal.

For I have thought of former hours,
　When he who first thy soul possest,
Like me awaked its witching powers,
　Like me was loved, like me was blest.

Upon *his* name thy murmuring tongue
　Perhaps hath all as sweetly dwelt;
Upon his words thine ear hath hung,
　With transport all as purely felt.

For him — yet why the past recall,
　To damp and wither present bliss?
Thou 'rt now my own, heart, spirit, all,
　And heaven could grant no more than
　　this!

Forgive me, dearest, oh! forgive;
　I would be first, be sole to thee,
Thou shouldst have but begun to live,
　The hour that gave thy heart to me.

Thy book of life till then effaced,
　Love should have kept that leaf alone
On which he first so brightly traced
　That thou wert, soul and all, my own.

TO . . . . . . 'S PICTURE.

Go then, if she, whose shade thou art,
　No more will let thee soothe my pain;
Yet, tell her, it has cost this heart
　Some pangs, to give thee back again.

Tell her, the smile was not so dear,
　With which she made thy semblance
　　mine,
As bitter is the burning tear,
　With which I now the gift resign.

Yet go — and could she still restore,
　As some exchange for taking thee,
The tranquil look which first I wore,
　When her eyes found me calm and free;

Could she give back the careless flow,
　The spirit that my heart then knew —

Yet, no, 't is vain — go, picture, go —
　Smile at me once, and then — adieu!

FRAGMENT
OF
A MYTHOLOGICAL HYMN TO LOVE.[1]

BLEST infant of eternity!
Before the day-star learned to move,
In pomp of fire, along his grand career,
　Glancing the beamy shafts of light
From his rich quiver to the farthest
　　sphere,
　Thou wert alone, oh Love!
Nestling beneath the wings of ancient
　　Night,
　Whose horrors seemed to smile in shad-
　　owing thee.
No form of beauty soothed thine eye,
　As through the dim expanse it wan-
　　dered wide;
No kindred spirit caught thy sigh,
　As o'er the watery waste it lingering
　　died.

Unfelt the pulse, unknown the power,
　That latent in his heart was sleeping, —
Oh Sympathy! that lonely hour
　Saw Love himself thy absence weep-
　　ing.

But look, what glory through the dark-
　　ness beams!
Celestial airs along the water glide: —
What Spirit art thou, moving o'er the tide
So beautiful? oh, not of earth,
But, in that glowing hour, the birth
Of the young Godhead's own creative
　　dreams.
'T is she!
Psyche, the firstborn spirit of the air,
　To thee, oh Love, she turns,

1 Love and Psyche are here considered as the
active and passive principles of creation, and the
universe is supposed to have received its first
harmonizing impulse from the nuptial sympathy
between these two powers. A marriage is generally the first step in cosmogony. Timæus held
Form to be the father, and Matter the mother of
the World; Elion and Berouth, I think, are San-
choniatho's first spiritual lovers, and Manco-
capac and his wife introduced creation amongst
the Peruvians. In short, Harlequin seems to
have studied cosmogonies, when he said " *tutto
il mondo è fatto come la nostra famiglia.*"

On thee her eyebeam burns:
Blest hour, before all worlds or-
dained to be!
They meet —
The blooming god — the spirit fair
Meet in communion sweet.
Now, Sympathy, the hour is thine;
All Nature feels the thrill divine,
The veil of Chaos is withdrawn,
And their first kiss is great Creation's
dawn!

TO

HIS SERENE HIGHNESS
THE DUKE OF MONTPENSIER,
ON HIS
PORTRAIT OF THE LADY ADELAIDE
FORBES.

Donington Park, 1802.

To catch the thought, by painting's spell,
Howe'er remote, howe'er refined,
And o'er the kindling canvas tell
The silent story of the mind;

O'er nature's form to glance the eye,
And fix, by mimic light and shade,
Her morning tinges ere they fly,
Her evening blushes, ere they fade; —

Yes, these are Painting's proudest pow-
ers;
The gift, by which her art divine
Above all others proudly towers, —
And these, oh Prince! are richly thine.

And yet, when Friendship sees thee
trace,
In almost living truth exprest,
This bright memorial of a face
On which her eye delights to rest;

While o'er the lovely look serene,
The smile of peace, the bloom of youth,
The cheek, that blushes to be seen,
The eye that tells the bosom's truth;

While o'er each line, so brightly true,
Our eyes with lingering pleasure rove,
Blessing the touch whose various hue
Thus brings to mind the form we love;

We feel the magic of thy art,
And own it with a zest, a zeal,
A pleasure, nearer to the heart
Than critic taste can *ever* feel.

THE FALL OF HEBE.
A DITHYRAMBIC ODE.[1]

'T WAS on a day
When the immortals at their banquet lay;
The bowl
Sparkled with starry dew,
The weeping of those myriad urns of
light,
Within whose orbs, the almighty
Power,
At nature's dawning hour,
Stored the rich fluid of ethereal soul.[2]

1 Though I have styled this poem a Dithyrambic Ode, I cannot presume to say that it possesses, in any degree, the characteristics of that
species of poetry. The nature of the ancient
Dithyrambic is very imperfectly known. According to M. Burette, a licentious irregularity
of metre, an extravagant research of thought and
expression, and a rude embarrassed construction,
are among its most distinguishing features; and
in all these respects, I have but too closely, I
fear, followed my models. Burette adds, "*Ces
caractères des dityrambes se font sentir à ceux
qui lisent attentivement les odes de Pindare.*" —
"*Mémoires de l'Acad.*" vol. x. p. 306. The
same opinion may be collected from Schmidt's
dissertation upon the subject. I think, however,
if the Dithyrambics of Pindar were in our possession, we should find that, however wild and
fanciful they were by no means the tasteless jargon they are represented, and that even their
irregularity was what Boileau calls "*un beau
désordre.*" Chiabrera, who has been styled the
Pindar of Italy, and from whom all its poetry
upon the Greek model was called Chiabreresco
(as Crescimbeni informs us, *lib.* i. *cap.* 12.), has
given, amongst his Vendemmie, a Dithyrambic,
"*all' uso de' Greci;*" full of those compound
epithets, which, we are told, were a chief characteristic of the style (συνθέτους δὲ λέξεις ἐποίουν
— *Suid.* Διθυραμβοδιδ.) such as

*Briglindorato Pegaso
Nubicalpestator.*

But I cannot suppose that Pindar, even amidst
all the license of dithyrambics, would ever have
descended to ballad-language like the following:

*Bella Filli, e bella Clori,
Non più dar pregio a tue bellezze e taci,
Che se Bacco fa vezzi alle mie labbra
Fo le fiche a' vostri baci.
—— esser vorrei Coppier,
E se troppo desiro
Deh fossi io Bottiglier.*

Rime del CHIABRERA, part ii. p. 352.

2 This is a Platonic fancy. The philosopher
supposes, in his Timæus, that, when the Deity
had formed the soul of the world, he proceeded
to the composition of other souls, in which process, says Plato, he made use of the same cup,
though the ingredients he mingled were not quite
so pure as for the former; and having refined the
mixture with a little of his own essence, he distributed it among the stars, which served as res-

Around,
Soft odorous clouds, that upward wing
        their flight
    From eastern isles
(Where they have bathed them in the
        orient ray,
And with rich fragrance all their bosoms
        filled),
In circles flew, and, melting as they flew,
A liquid daybreak o'er the board distilled.

All, all was luxury!
All *must* be luxury, where Lyæus smiles.
    His locks divine
        Were crowned
        With a bright meteor-braid,
Which, like an ever-springing wreath of
        vine,
    Shot into brilliant leafy shapes,
And o'er his brow in lambent tendrils
        played:
    While mid the foliage hung,
        Like lucid grapes,
A thousand clustering buds of light,
Culled from the garden of the galaxy.

Upon his bosom Cytherea's head
Lay lovely, as when first the Syrens sung
        Her beauty's dawn,
And all the curtains of the deep, un-
        drawn,
Revealed her sleeping in its azure bed.
    The captive deity
Hung lingering on her eyes and lip,
        With looks of ecstasy.
        Now, on his arm,
        In blushes she reposed,
And, while he gazed on each bright
        charm,
To shade his burning eyes her hand in
        dalliance stole.

And now she raised her rosy mouth to sip
        The nectared wave
        Lyæus gave,
And from her eyelids, half-way closed,
    Sent forth a melting gleam,
    Which fell like sun-dew in the bowl:
While her bright hair, in mazy flow
        Of gold descending

ervoirs of the fluid. — ταῦτ᾽ εἶπε καὶ πάλιν ἐπὶ
τὸν πρότερον κρατῆρα ἐν ᾧ τὴν τοῦ πάντος ψυχὴν
κεραννὺς ἔμισγε, κ. τ. λ.

Adown her cheek's luxurious glow,
        Hung o'er the goblet's side,
And was reflected in its crystal tide,
        Like a bright crocus flower,
    Whose sunny leaves, at evening hour
        With roses of Cyrene blending,[1]
Hang o'er the mirror of some silvery
        stream.

        The Olympian cup
        Shone in the hands
Of dimpled Hebe, as she winged her
        feet
            Up
    The empyreal mount,
To drain the soul-drops at their stellar
        fount; [2]
        And still
        As the resplendent rill
Gushed forth into the cup with man-
        tling heat,
        Her watchful care
    Was still to cool its liquid fire
With snow-white sprinklings of that
        feathery air
The children of the Pole respire,
    In those enchanted lands,[3]
Where life is all a spring, and north
        winds never blow.

1 We learn from Theophrastus, that the roses
of Cyrene were particularly fragrant. — εὔοσματα
τὰ δὲ τὰ ἐν Κυρήνῃ ῥόδα.

2 Heraclitus (Physicus) held the soul to be a
spark of the stellar essence — " *scintilla stellaris
essentiæ.*" — MACROBIUS, in *Somn. Scip. lib.* i.
cap. 14.

3 The country of the Hyperboreans. These
people were supposed to be placed so far north
that the north wind could not affect them; they
lived longer than any other mortals; passed their
whole time in music and dancing, etc. But the
most extravagant fiction related of them is that
to which the two lines preceding allude. It was
imagined that, instead of our vulgar atmosphere,
the Hyperboreans breathed nothing but feathers!
According to Herodotus and Pliny, this idea was
suggested by the quantity of snow which was observed to fall in those regions; thus the former:
τὰ ὦν πτερὰ εἰκάζοντας τὴν χιόνα τοὺς Σκύθας
τε καὶ τοὺς περιοίκους δοκέω λέγειν. — HERODOT.
lib. iv. *cap.* 31. Ovid tells the fable otherwise:
see " Metamorph." *lib.* xv.

Mr. O'Halloran, and some other Irish Antiquarians, have been at great expense of learning
to prove that the strange country, where they
took snow for feathers, was Ireland, and that the
famous Abaris was an Irish Druid. Mr. Rowland, however, will have it that Abaris was a
Welshman, and that his name is only a corruption of Ap Rees!

But oh!
Bright Hebe, what a tear,
And what a blush were thine,
When, as the breath of every Grace
Wafted thy feet along the studded sphere,
With a bright cup for Jove himself to
drink,
Some star, that shone beneath thy tread,
Raising its amorous head
To kiss those matchless feet,
Checked thy career too fleet;
And all heaven's host of eyes
Entranced, but fearful all,
Saw thee, sweet Hebe, prostrate fall
Upon the bright floor of the azure
skies; [1]
Where, mid its stars, thy beauty lay,
As blossom, shaken from the spray
Of a spring thorn,
Lies mid the liquid sparkles of the morn.
Or, as in temples of the Paphian shade,
The worshippers of Beauty's queen behold
An image of their rosy idol, laid
Upon a diamond shrine.

The wanton wind,
Which had pursued the flying fair,
And sported mid the tresses unconfined
Of her bright hair,
Now, as she fell, — oh wanton breeze!
Ruffled the robe, whose graceful flow
Hung o'er those limbs of unsunned snow,
Purely as the Eleusinian veil
Hangs o'er the Mysteries! [2]

The brow of Juno flushed —
Love blest the breeze!
The Muses blushed;
And every cheek was hid behind a lyre,
While every eye looked laughing through
the strings.
But the bright cup? the nectared draught
Which Jove himself was to have quaffed?

1 It is Servius, I believe, who mentions this
unlucky trip which Hebe made in her occupation
of cup-bearer; and Hoffman tells it after him:
*cum Hebe pocula Jovi administrans, perque lu-
bricum minus cauté incedens, cecidisset,"* etc.
2 The arcane symbols of this ceremony were
deposited in the cista, where they lay religiously
concealed from the eyes of the profane. They
were generally carried in the procession by an
ass; and hence the proverb, which one may so
often apply in the world, *"asinus portat mysteria."* See "the Divine Legation," book ii.
sect. 4.

Alas, alas, upturned it lay
By the fallen Hebe's side;
While, in slow lingering drops, the ethe-
real tide,
As conscious of its own rich essence,
ebbed away.

Who was the Spirit that remembered
Man,
In that blest hour,
And, with a wing of love,
Brushed off the goblet's scattered
tears,
As, trembling near the edge of heaven
they ran,
And sent them floating to our orb be-
low? [3]
Essence of immortality!
The shower
Fell glowing through the spheres;
While all around new tints of bliss,
New odors and new light,
Enriched its radiant flow.

Now, with a liquid kiss,
It stole along the thrilling wire
Of Heaven's luminous Lyre, [4]
Stealing the soul of music in its flight:
And now, amid the breezes bland,
That whisper from the planets as they roll,
The bright libation, softly fanned
By all their sighs, meandering stole.
They who, from Atlas' height,
Beheld this rosy flame
Descending through the waste of night,
Thought 't was some planet, whose em-
pyreal frame
Had kindled, as it rapidly revolved
Around its fervid axle, and dissolved
Into a flood so bright!

3 In the "Geoponica," *lib.* ii. *cap.* 17, there
is a fable somewhat like this descent of the nectar to earth. ἐν οὐρανῷ τῶν θεῶν εὐωχουμένων,
καὶ τοῦ νέκταρος πολλοῦ παρακειμένου, ἀνασκιρ-
τῆσαι χορείᾳ τὸν Ἔρωτα καὶ συσσεῖσαι τῷ
πτερῷ τοῦ κρατῆρος τὴν βάσιν, καὶ περιτρέψαι
μὲν αὐτόν· τὸ δὲ νέκταρ εἰς τὴν γῆν ἐκχυθέν,
κ.τ.λ. *Vid. Autor. de "Re Rust." edit Cantab.*
1704.
4 The constellation Lyra. The astrologers
attribute great virtues to this sign in ascendenti,
which are enumerated by Pontano, in his "Ura-
nia:"

— *ecce novem cum pectine chordas
emodulans, mulcetque novo vaga sidera cantu,
quo captæ nascentum animæ concordia ducunt
pectora,* etc.

The youthful Day,
Within his twilight bower,
Lay sweetly sleeping
On the flushed bosom of a lotos-flower; [1]
When round him, in profusion weeping,
Dropt the celestial shower,
Steeping
The rosy clouds, that curled
About his infant head,
Like myrrh upon the locks of Cupid shed.
But, when the waking boy
Waved his exhaling tresses through the
        sky,
        O morn of joy! —
        The tide divine,
All glorious with the vermil dye
It drank beneath his orient eye,
Distilled, in dews, upon the world,
And every drop was wine, was heavenly
        WINE!
Blest be the sod, and blest the flower
On which descended first that shower,
All   fresh   from   Jove's   nectareous
        springs; —
Oh far less sweet the flower, the sod,
O'er which the Spirit of the Rainbow
        flings
The magic mantle of her solar God! [2]

RINGS AND SEALS.

ὥσπερ σφραγίδες τὰ φιλήματα.
                ACHILLES TATIUS, *lib.* ii.

" Go! " said the angry, weeping maid,
" The charm is broken! — once betrayed,
" Never can this wronged heart rely
" On word or look, on oath or sigh.
" Take back the gifts, so fondly given,
" With   promised   faith   and   vows   to
        heaven;

" That little ring which, night and morn,
" With wedded truth my hand hath worn;
" That seal which oft, in moments blest,
" Thou hast upon my lip imprest,
" And sworn its sacred spring should be
" A fountain sealed [3] for only thee :
" Take, take them back, the gift and vow,
" All sullied, lost and hateful now ! "

I took the ring — the seal I took,
While, oh, her every tear and look
Were such as angels look and shed,
When man is by the world misled.
Gently I whispered, " Fanny, dear!
" Not half thy lover's gifts are here:
" Say, where are all the kisses given,
" From morn to noon, from noon to
        even, —
" Those signets of true love, worth more
" Than Solomon's own seal of yore, —
" Where are those gifts, so sweet, so
        many?
" Come, dearest, — give back all, if any."

While thus I whispered, trembling too,
Lest all the nymph had sworn was true,
I saw a smile relenting rise
Mid the moist azure of her eyes,
Like daylight o'er a sea of blue,
While yet in mid-air hangs the dew.
She let her cheek repose on mine,
She let my arms around her twine;
One kiss was half allowed, and then —
The ring and seal were hers again.

TO MISS SUSAN BECKFORD. [4]

ON HER SINGING.

I MORE than once have heard at night
A song like those thy lip hath given,

---

1 The Egyptians represented the dawn of day by a young boy seated upon a lotos. εἴτε Αἰγύπτους ἑωρακὼς ἀρχὴν ἀνατολῆς παιδίον νεογνὸν γράφοντας ἐπὶ λωτῷ καθεζόμενον. — *Plutarch.* περὶ τοῦ μὴ χρᾶν ἐμμέτρ. See also his Treatise " *de Isid. et Osir.*" Observing that the lotos showed its head above water at sunrise, and sank again at his setting, they conceived the idea of consecrating this flower to Osiris, or the sun.

This symbol of a youth sitting upon a lotos is very frequent on the Abraxases, or Basilidian stones. See Montfaucon, *tom.* ii. *planche* 158., and the " Supplement," etc. *tom.* ii. *lib.* vii. *chap.* 5.

2 The ancients esteemed those flowers and trees the sweetest upon which the rainbow had appeared to rest; and the wood they chiefly burned in sacrifices, was that which the smile of

Iris had consecrated. Plutarch. " Sympos." *lib.* iv. *cap.* 2, where (as Vossius remarks) καίουσι, instead of καλοῦσι, is undoubtedly the genuine reading. See Vossius, for some curious particularities of the rainbow, " *De Origin. et Progress. Idololat.*" *lib.* iii. *cap.* 13.

3 " There are gardens, supposed to be those of King Solomon, in the neighbourhood of Bethlehem. The friars show a fountain, which, they say, is the 'sealed fountain' to which the holy spouse in the Canticles is compared; and they pretend a tradition, that Solomon shut up these springs and put his signet upon the door, to keep them for his own drinking." — *Maundrell's Travels.* See also the notes to Mr. Good's Translation of the Song of Solomon.

4 Afterward Duchess of Hamilton.

And it was sung by shapes of light,
  Who looked and breathed, like thee,
    of heaven.

But this was all a dream of sleep,.
  And I have said when morning
    shone : —
" Why should the night-witch, Fancy,
    keep
  " These wonders for herself alone? "

I knew not then that fate had lent
  Such tones to one of mortal birth;
I knew not then that Heaven had sent
  A voice, a form like thine on earth.

And yet, in all that flowery maze
  Through which my path of life has led,
When I have heard the sweetest lays
  From lips of rosiest lustre shed;

When I have felt the warbled word
  From Beauty's lip, in sweetness vying
With music's own melodious bird,
  When on the rose's bosom lying;

Though form and song at once combined
  Their loveliest bloom and softest thrill,
My heart hath sighed, my ear hath pined
  For something lovelier, softer still : —

Oh, I have found it all, at last,
  In thee, thou sweetest living lyre,
Through which the soul of song e'er past,
  Or feeling breathed its sacred fire.

All that I e'er, in wildest flight
  Of fancy's dreams, could hear or see
Of music's sigh or beauty's light
  Is realized, at once, in thee !

IMPROMPTU,

ON LEAVING SOME FRIENDS.

o dulces comitum valete cœtus !
                    CATULLUS.

No, never shall my soul forget
  The friends I found so cordial-hearted;
Dear shall be the day we met,
  And dear shall be the night we parted.

If fond regrets, however sweet,
  Must with the lapse of time decay,
Yet still, when thus in mirth you meet,
  Fill high to him that 's far away !

Long be the light of memory found
  Alive within your social glass;
Let that be still the magic round,
  O'er which Oblivion dares not pass.

A WARNING.

TO . . . .

OH fair as heaven and chaste as light !
Did nature mould thee all so bright,
That thou shouldst e'er be brought to
    weep
O'er languid virtue's fatal sleep,
O'er shame extinguished, honor fled,
Peace lost, heart withered, feeling dead?

No, no ! a star was born with thee,
Which sheds eternal purity.
Thou hast, within those sainted eyes,
So fair a transcript of the skies,
In lines of light such heavenly lore,
That man should read them and adore.
Yet have I known a gentle maid
Whose mind and form were both arrayed
In nature's purest light, like thine; —
Who wore that clear, celestial sign,
Which seems to mark the brow that 's fair
For destiny's peculiar care :
Whose bosom too, like Dian's own,
Was guarded by a sacred zone,
Where the bright gem of virtue shone;
Whose eyes had in their light a charm
Against all wrong and guile and harm.
Yet, hapless maid, in one sad hour
These spells have lost their guardian
    power;
The gem has been beguiled away;
Her eyes have lost their chastening ray;
The modest pride, the guiltless shame,
The smiles that from reflection came,
All, all have fled and left her mind
A faded monument behind;
The ruins of a once pure shrine,
No longer fit for guest divine.
Oh ! 't was a sight I wept to see —
Heaven keep the lost one's fate from
    thee !

TO . . . .

'T IS time, I feel, to leave thee now,
  While yet my soul is something free;
While yet those dangerous eyes allow
  One minute's thought to stray from
    thee.

Oh! thou becom'st each moment dearer;
  Every chance that brings me nigh thee,
Brings my ruin nearer, nearer, —
  I am lost, unless I fly thee.

Nay, if thou dost not scorn and hate me,
  Doom me not thus so soon to fall;
Duties, fame, and hopes await me, —
  But that eye would blast them all!

For, thou hast heart as false and cold
  As ever yet allured or swayed,
And couldst, without a sigh, behold
  The ruin which thyself had made.

Yet, — *could* I think that, truly fond,
  That eye but once would smile on me,
Even as thou art, how far beyond
  Fame, duty, wealth, that smile would
  be!

Oh! but to win it, night and day,
  Inglorious at thy feet reclined,
I 'd sigh my dreams of fame away,
  The world for thee forgot, resigned.

But no, 't is o'er, and — thus we part,
  Never to meet again, — no, never.
False woman, what a mind and heart
  Thy treachery has undone for ever!

WOMAN.

AWAY, away — you 're all the same,
  A smiling, fluttering, jilting throng;
And, wise too late, I burn with shame,
  To think I 've been your slave so long.

Slow to be won, and quick to rove,
  From folly kind, from cunning loath,
Too cold for bliss, too weak for love,
  Yet feigning all that 's best in both;

Still panting o'er a crowd to reign, —
  More joy it gives to woman's breast
To make ten frigid coxcombs vain,
  Than one true, manly lover blest.

Away, away — your smile 's a curse —
  Oh! blot me from the race of men,
Kind pitying Heaven, by death or worse,
  If e'er I love such things again.

TO . . . .

νοσεῖ τὰ φίλτατα.   EURIPIDES.

COME, take thy harp — 't is vain to muse
  Upon the gathering ills we see;
Oh! take thy harp and let me lose
  All thoughts of ill in hearing thee.

Sing to me, love! — Though death were
  near,
  Thy song could make my soul forget —
Nay, nay, in pity, dry that tear,
  All may be well, be happy yet.

Let me but see that snowy arm
  Once more upon the dear harp lie,
And I will cease to dream of harm,
  Will smile at fate, while thou art nigh.

Give me that strain of mournful touch,
  We used to love long, long ago,
Before our hearts had known as much
  As now, alas! they bleed to know.

Sweet notes! they tell of former peace,
  Of all that looked so smiling then,
Now vanished, lost — oh pray thee, cease,
  I cannot bear those sounds again.

Art *thou*, too, wretched? yes, thou art;
  I see thy tears flow fast with mine —
Come, come to this devoted heart,
  'T is breaking, but it still is thine!

A VISION OF PHILOSOPHY.

'T WAS on the Red Sea coast, at morn,
  we met
The venerable man; [1] a healthy bloom
Mingled its softness with the vigorous
  thought

1 In Plutarch's Essay on the Decline of the
Oracles, Cleombrotus, one of the interlocutors,
describes an extraordinary man whom he had
met with, after long research, upon the banks
of the Red Sea. Once in every year this supernatural personage appeared to mortals, and conversed with them; the rest of his time he passed
among the Genii and the Nymphs. περὶ τὴν
Ἐρυθρὰν Θάλασσαν εὗρον, ἀνθρώποις ἀνὰ πᾶν
ἔτος ἅπαξ ἐντυγχάνοντα, τ'ἄλλα δὲ σὺν ταῖς
νύμφαις, νόμασι καὶ δαίμοσι, ὡς ἔφασκε. He
spoke in a tone not far removed from singing,
and whenever he opened his lips, a fragrance
filled the place: φθεγγομένου δὲ τὸν τόπον εὐώδια
κατεῖχε, τοῦ στόματος ἥδιστον ἀποπνέοντος.
From him Cleombrotus learned the doctrine of
a plurality of worlds.

That towered upon his brow; and when
he spoke
'T was language sweetened into song —
such holy sounds
As oft, they say, the wise and virtuous
hear,
Prelusive to the harmony of heaven,
When death is nigh; [1] and still, as he
unclosed
His sacred lips, an odor, all as bland
As ocean-breezes gather from the flowers
That blossom in Elysium,[2] breathed
around,
With silent awe we listened, while he told
Of the dark veil which many an age had
hung
O'er Nature's form, till, long explored by
man,
The mystic shroud grew thin and lumi-
nous,
And glimpses of that heavenly form shone
through: —
Of magic wonders, that were known and
taught
By him (or Cham or Zoroaster named)
Who mused amid the mighty cataclysm,
O'er his rude tablets of primeval lore; [3]
And gathering round him, in the sacred
ark,
The mighty secrets of that former globe,
Let not the living star of science [4] sink

Beneath the waters, which ingulfed a
world! —
Of visions, by Calliope revealed
To him,[5] who traced upon his typic lyre
The diapason of man's mingled frame,
And the grand Doric heptachord of
heaven.
With all of pure, of wondrous and arcane,
Which the grave sons of Mochus, many
a night,
Told to the young and bright-haired
visitant
Of Carmel's sacred mount.[6] — Then, in
a flow

5 Orpheus. — Paulinus, in his "*Hebdom-
ades*," *cap.* 2. *lib.* iii. has endeavored to show,
after the Platonists, that man is a diapason, or
octave, made up of a diatesseron, which is his
soul, and a diapente, which is his body. Those
frequent allusions to music, by which the ancient
philosophers illustrated their sublime theories,
must have tended very much to elevate the character of the art, and to enrich it with associations
of the grandest and most interesting nature. See
a preceding note, for their ideas upon the harmony of the spheres. Heraclitus compared the
mixture of good and evil in this world, to the
blended varieties of harmony in a musical instrument (Plutarch, "*de Animæ Procreat.*"); and
Euryphamus, the Pythagorean, in a fragment
preserved by Stobæus, describes human life, in
its perfection, as a sweet and well tuned lyre.
Some of the ancients were so fanciful as to suppose that the operations of the memory were
regulated by a kind of musical cadence, and that
ideas occurred to it "*per arsin et thesin*," while
others converted the whole man into a mere harmonized machine, whose motion depended upon
a certain tension of the body, analogous to that
of the strings in an instrument. Cicero indeed
ridicules Aristoxenus for this fancy, and says,
"Let him teach singing, and leave philosophy
to Aristotle ;" but Aristotle himself, though decidedly opposed to the harmonic speculations
of the Pythagoreans and Platonists, could sometimes condescend to enliven his doctrines by
reference to the beauties of musical science ; as,
in the treatise "περὶ κόσμου" attributed to him,
καθάπερ δὲ ἐν χόρῳ, κορυφαίου κατάρξαντος,
κ. τ. λ.
The Abbé Batteux, in his inquiry into the
doctrine of the Stoics, attributes to those philosophers the same mode of illustration. "*L'âme
étoit cause active* ποιεῖν *αἴτιος ; le corps cause
passive* ἤδε τοῦ πάσχειν : — *l'une agissant dans
l'autre ; et y prenant, par son action même, un
caractère, des formes, des modifications, qu'elle
n'avoit pas par elle-même ; à peu près comme
l'air, qui, chassé dans un instrument de musique,
fait connoître, par les différentes modifications
qu'il y produit, les différentes modifications qu'il y reçoit.*"
See a fine simile founded upon this notion in
Cardinal Polignac's poem, *lib.* 5. v. 734.

6 Pythagoras is represented in Iamblichus
as descending with great solemnity from Mount

1 The celebrated Janus Dousa, a little before
his death, imagined that he heard a strain of
music in the air. See the poem of Heinsius "*in
harmoniam quam paulo ante obitum audire sibi
visus est Dousa.*" Page 501.

2 ―― ἔνθα μακάρων
νᾶσον ὠκεανίδες
αὖραι περιπνέουσιν· ἄν-
θεμα δὲ χρυσοῦ φλέγει.
PINDAR. "*Olymp.*" ii.

3 Cham, the son of Noah, is supposed to
have taken with him into the ark the principal
doctrines of magical, or rather of natural, science, which he had inscribed upon some very
durable substances, in order that they might resist the ravages of the deluge, and transmit the
secrets of antediluvian knowledge to his posterity. See the extracts made by Bayle, in his
article, Cham. The identity of Cham and Zoroaster depends upon the authority of Berosus
(or rather the impostor Annius), and a few
more such respectable testimonies. See Naudé's
"*Apologie pour les Grands Hommes*," etc., chap.
viii., where he takes more trouble than is necessary in refuting this gratuitous supposition.

4 *Chamum à posteris hujus artis admiratori-
bus Zoroastrum, seu vivum astrum, propterea
fuisse dictum et pro Deo habitum.* — *Bochart,
"Geograph. Sacr." lib.* iv. *cap.* 1.

Of calmer converse, he beguiled us on
Through many a maze of Garden and
   of Porch,
Through many a system, where the scat-
   tered light
Of heavenly truth lay, like a broken beam
From the pure sun, which, though re-
   fracted all
Into a thousand hues, is sunshine still,[1]

[1] Lactantius asserts that all the truths of
Christianity may be found dispersed through the
ancient philosophical sects, and that any one who
would collect these scattered fragments of orthodoxy might form a code in no respect differing

And bright through every change ! — he
   spoke of Him,
The lone,[2] eternal One, who dwells above,
And of the soul's untraceable descent
From that high fount of spirit, through
   the grades
Of intellectual being, till it mix
With atoms vague, corruptible, and dark;

from that of the Christian. "*si extitisset ali-
quis, qui veritatem sparsam per singulos per
sectasque diffusam colligeret in unum, ac redi-
geret in corpus, is profecto non dissentiret a
nobis.*" — "*Inst.*" *lib.* vi. c. 7.

[2] τὸ μόνον καὶ ἐρῆμον.

Carmel, for which reason the Carmelites have
claimed him as one of their fraternity. This
Mochus or Moschus, with the descendants of
whom Pythagoras conversed in Phœnicia, and
from whom he derived the doctrines of atomic
philosophy, is supposed by some to be the same
with Moses. Huett has adopted this idea, "*Dé-
monstration Évangélique,*" *Prop.* iv. *chap.* 2.
§ 7.; and Le Clerc, amongst others, has refuted
it. See "*Biblioth. Choisie,*" *tom.* i. p. 75. It
is certain, however, that the doctrine of atoms
was known and promulgated long before Epicurus. "With the fountains of Democritus,"
says Cicero, "the gardens of Epicurus were
watered ;" and the learned author of the Intellectual System has shown, that all the early
philosophers, till the time of Plato, were atom-
ists. We find Epicurus, however, boasting that
his tenets were new and unborrowed, and perhaps
few among the ancients had any stronger claim to
originality. In truth, if we examine their schools
of philosophy, notwithstanding the peculiarities
which seem to distinguish them from each other,
we may generally observe that the difference is
but verbal and trifling ; and that, among those
various and learned heresies, there is scarcely
one to be selected, whose opinions are its own,
original and exclusive. The doctrine of the
world's eternity may be traced through all the
sects. The continual metempsychosis of Pythagoras, the grand periodic year of the Stoics, (at
the conclusion of which the universe is supposed
to return to its original order, and commence a
new revolution,) the successive dissolution and
combination of atoms maintained by the Epicureans — all these tenets are but different intima-
tions of the same general belief in the eternity
of the world. As explained by St. Austin, the
periodic year of the Stoics disagrees only so far
with the idea of the Pythagoreans, that instead
of an endless transmission of the soul through a
variety of bodies, it restores the same body and
soul to repeat their former round of existence, so
that the "identical Plato, who lectured in the
Academy of Athens, shall again and again, at
certain intervals, during the lapse of eternity,
appear in the same Academy and resume the
same functions — " ――― *sic eadem tempora
temporaliumque rerum volumina repeti, ut v. g.
sicut in isto sæculo Plato philosophus in urbe
Atheniensi, in eâ scholâ quæ Academia dicta
est, discipulos docuit, ita per innumerabilia retro*

*sæcula, multum plexis quidem intervallis, sed
certis, et idem Plato, et eadem civitas, eademque
schola, iidemque discipuli repetiti et per innumerabilia deinde sæcula repetendi sint.* — "*De
Civitat. Dei,*" *lib.* xii. *cap.* 13. Vanini, in his
dialogues, has given us a similar explication of
the periodic revolutions of the world. "*eâ de
causâ, qui nunc sunt in usu ritus, centies millies
fuerunt, totiesque renascentur quoties cecide-
runt.*" 52.
   The paradoxical notions of the Stoics upon
the beauty, the riches, the dominion of their imaginary sage, are among the most distinguishing
characteristics of their school, and, according to
their advocate Lipsius, were peculiar to that sect.
"*Priora illa (decreta) quæ passim in philoso-
phantium scholis ferè obtinent, ista quæ peculia-
ria huic sectæ et habent contradictionem : i. e.
paradoxa.*"—"*Manuduct. ad Stoic. Philos.*"
lib. iii. *dissertat.* 2. But it is evident (as the
Abbé Garnier has remarked, "*Mémoires de
l'Acad.*" *tom.* xxxv.) that even these absurdities
of the Stoics are borrowed, and that Plato is the
source of all their extravagant paradoxes. We
find their dogma, "*dives qui sapiens,*" (which
Clement of Alexandria has transferred from the
Philosopher to the *Christian Pædagog. lib.* iii.
cap. 6.) expressed in the prayer of Socrates at
the end of the Phædrus. ὦ φίλε Πάν τε καὶ
ἄλλοι ὅσοι τῇδε θεοί, δοίητέ μοι καλῶ γένεσθαι
τἄνδοθεν· τἄξωθεν δὲ ὅσα ἔχω, τοῖς ἐντος εἶναί
μοι φίλια· πλούσιον δὲ νομίζοιμι τὸν σοφόν.
And many other instances might be adduced
from the "'Αντερασταί," the Πολιτικός, etc. to
prove that these weeds of paradox were all gathered among the bowers of the Academy. Hence
it is that Cicero, in the preface to his Paradoxes,
calls them Socratica ; and Lipsius, exulting in
the patronage of Socrates, says "*ille totus est nos-
ter.*" This is indeed a coalition, which evinces
as much as can be wished the confused similitude
of ancient philosophical opinions : the father of
scepticism is here enrolled amongst the founders
of the Portico ; he, whose best knowledge was
that of his own ignorance, is called in to authorize
the pretensions of the most obstinate dogmatists
in all antiquity.
   Rutilius, in his Itinerarium, has ridiculed the
sabbath of the Jews, as "*lassati mollis imago
Dei ;*" but Epicurus gave an eternal holiday to
his gods, and, rather than disturb the slumbers
of Olympus, denied at once the interference of a

Nor yet even then, though sunk in earthly
  dross,
Corrupted all, nor its ethereal touch
Quite lost, but tasting of the fountain
  still.

As some bright river, which has rolled
  along
Through meads of flowery light and
  mines of gold,
When poured at length into the dusky
  deep,
Disdains to take at once its briny
  taint,

Or balmy freshness, of the scenes it left.[1]
But keeps unchanged awhile the lustrous
  tinge,

And here the old man ceased — a
  winged train
Of nymphs and genii bore him from our
  eyes.
The fair illusion fled ! and, as I waked,

[1] This bold Platonic image I have taken from
a passage in Father Bouchet's letter upon the
Metempsychosis, inserted in Picart's "*Cérém.
Relig.*" tom. iv.

Providence. He does not, however, seem to
have been singular in this opinion. Theophilus
of Antioch, if he deserve any credit, imputes a
similar belief to Pythagoras: φησί (Πυθαγόρας)
τε των παντων θεους ανθρώπων μηθεν ψρυνίζειν.
And Plutarch, though so hostile to the followers
of Epicurus, has unaccountably adopted the very
same theological error. Thus, after quoting the
opinions of Anaxagoras and Plato upon divinity,
he adds, κοινως ουν αμαρτάνουσιν αμφότεροι, ότι
τον θεον εποίησαν επιστεφόμενον των ανθρωπίνων. — "*De Placit. Philosoph.*" *lib.* i. *cap.* 7.
Plato himself has attributed a degree of indifference to the gods, which is not far removed
from the apathy of Epicurus's heaven ; as thus,
in his Philebus, where Protarchus asks, ουκουν
εικός γε ουτε χαιρειν θεους, ουτε το εναντίον ; and
Socrates answers, πάνυ μεν ουν εικὸς, ασχημον
γουν αυτων εκάτερον γιγνόμενον εστιν ; — while
Aristotle supposes a still more absurd neutrality,
and concludes, by no very flattering analogy,
that the deity is as incapable of virtue as of vice.
και γαρ ώσπερ ουδεν θηρίου εστι κακία, ουδ'
αρετη, ουτως ουδε θεου. — "*Ethic. Nicomach.*"
lib. vii. *cap.* 1. In truth, Aristotle, upon the
subject of Providence, was little more correct
than Epicurus. He supposed the moon to be
the limit of divine interference, excluding of
course this sublunary world from its influence.
The first definition of the world, in his treatise
"Περι Κόσμου" (if this treatise be really the
work of Aristotle) agrees, almost *verbum verbo*,
with that in the letter of Epicurus to Pythocles ;
and both omit the mention of a deity. In his
Ethics, too, he intimates a doubt whether the
gods feel any interest in the concerns of mankind. — ει γάρ τις επιμέλεια των ανθρωπίνων υπὸ
θεων γίνεται. It is true, he adds ώσπερ δοκεί,
but even this is very sceptical.

In these erroneous conceptions of Aristotle,
we trace the cause of that general neglect which
his philosophy experienced among the early
Christians. Plato is seldom much more orthodox, but the obscure enthusiasm of his style allowed them to accommodate all his fancies to
their own purpose. Such glowing steel was
easily moulded, and Platonism became a sword
in the hands of the fathers.

The Providence of the Stoics, was vaunted in
their school, was a power as contemptibly in-
efficient as the rest. All was fate in the system
of the Portico. The chains of destiny were

thrown over Jupiter himself, and their deity was
like the Borgia of the epigrammatist, "*et Cæsar
et nihil.*" Not even the language of Seneca can
reconcile this degradation of divinity. "*ille ipse
omnium conditor ac rector scripsit quidam fata,
sed sequitur ; semper paret, semel jussit.*" —
"*Lib. de Providentiâ,*" *cap.* 5.

With respect to the difference between the
Stoics, Peripatetics, and Academicans, the following words of Cicero prove that he saw but
little to distinguish them from each other : —
"*Peripateticos et Academicos, nominibus dif-
ferentes, re congruentes ; a quibus Stoici ipsi
verbis magis quam sententiis dissenserunt.*"
— "*Academic.*" *lib.* ii. 5. ; and perhaps what Reid
has remarked upon one of their points of controversy might be applied as effectually to the
reconcilement of all the rest. "The dispute
between the Stoics and Peripatetics was probably all for want of definition. The one said
they were good under the control of reason, the
other that they should be eradicated." — *Essays*,
vol. iii. In short, it appears a no less difficult
matter to establish the boundaries of opinion
between any two of the philosophical sects, than
it would be to fix the landmarks of those estates
in the moon, which Ricciolus so generously alloted to his brother astronomers. Accordingly
we observe some of the greatest men of antiquity
passing without scruple from school to school,
according to the fancy or convenience of the
moment. Cicero, the father of Roman philosophy, is sometimes an Academician, sometimes
a Stoic ; and, more than once, he acknowledges
a conformity with Epicurus ; "*non sine causa
igitur Epicurus ausus est dicere semper in pluribus bonis esse sapientem, quia semper sit in volup-
tatibus.*" — "*Tusculan. Quæst.*" *lib.* v. Though
often pure in his theology, Cicero sometimes
smiles at futurity as a fiction ; thus, in his Oration
for Cluentius, speaking of punishments in the
life to come, he says, "*quæ si falsa sunt, id
quod omnes intelligunt, quid ei tandem aliud
mors eripuit, præter sensum doloris ?*" — though
here we should, perhaps, do him but justice, by
agreeing with his commentator Sylvius, who remarks upon this passage, "*hæc autem dixit, ut
causæ suæ subserviret.*" The poet, Horace,
roves like a butterfly through the schools, and
now wings along the walls of the Porch, now
basks among the flowers of the Garden ; while
Vergil, with a tone of mind strongly philosophi-

'T was clear that my rapt soul had
   roamed, the while,
To that bright realm of dreams, that
   spirit-world,
Which mortals know by its long track of
   light
O'er midnight's sky, and call the Galaxy.[1]

TO MRS. . . . . . .

To see thee every day that came,
And find thee still each day the same;
In pleasure's smile or sorrow's tear
To me still ever kind and dear; —
To meet thee early, leave thee late,
Has been so long my bliss, my fate,
That life, without this cheering ray,
Which came, like sunshine, every day,
And all my pain, my sorrow chased,
Is now a lone and loveless waste.

Where are the chords she used to touch?
The airs, the songs she loved so much?

1 According to Pythagoras, the people of
Dreams are souls collected together in the Galaxy. — δῆμος δὲ ὀνείρων, κατὰ Πυθαγόραν, αἱ
ψυχαὶ ἃς συνάγεσθαί φησιν εἰς τὸν γαλαξίαν. —
Porphyr. de Antro Nymph.

cal, has yet left us wholly uncertain as to the
sect which he espoused. The balance of opinion
declares him to have been an Epicurean, but the
ancient author of his life asserts that he was an
Academician; and we trace through his poetry
the tenets of almost all the leading sects. The
same kind of eclectic indifference is observable
in most of the Roman writers. Thus, Propertius, in the fine elegy to Cynthia, on his departure for Athens,

illic vel studiis animum emendare Platonis,
  incipiam, aut hortis, docte Epicure, tuis.
      Lib. iii. *Eleg.* 21.

Though Broeckhusius here reads, "*dux Epicure,*" which seems to fix the poet under the
banners of Epicurus. Even the Stoic Seneca,
whose doctrines have been considered so orthodox, that St. Jerome has ranked him amongst
the ecclesiastical writers, while Boccaccio doubts
(in consideration of his supposed correspondence
with St. Paul) whether Dante should have placed
him in Limbo with the rest of the Pagans — even
the rigid Seneca has bestowed such commendations on Epicurus, that if only those passages of
his works were preserved to us, we could not
hesitate, I think, in pronouncing him a confirmed
Epicurean. With similar inconsistency, we find
Porphyry, in his work upon abstinence, referring to Epicurus as an example of the most strict
Pythagorean temperance; and Lancelotti (the
author of "*Farfalloni degli antici Istorici*")
has been seduced by this grave reputation of
Epicurus into the absurd error of associating
him with Chrysippus, as a chief of the Stoic
school. There is no doubt, indeed, that however

Those songs are hushed, those chords are
   still,
And so, perhaps, will every thrill
Of feeling soon be lulled to rest,
Which late I waked in Anna's breast.
Yet, no — the simple notes I played
From memory's tablet soon may fade;
The songs, which Anna loved to hear,
May vanish from her heart and ear;
But friendship's voice shall ever find
An echo in that gentle mind,
Nor memory lose nor time impair
The sympathies that tremble there.

TO LADY HEATHCOTE,

ON AN

OLD RING FOUND AT TUNBRIDGE-WELLS.

  "*Tunnebridge est à la même distance de Lon-
dres, que Fontainebleau l'est de Paris. Ce qu'il
y a de beau et de galant dans l'un et dans l'autre
sexe s'y rassemble au tems des eaux. La com-
pagnie,*" etc. — See *Mémoires de Grammont,*
Second Part. chap. iii.

              Tunbridge Wells.

WHEN Grammont graced these happy
   springs,
  And Tunbridge saw, upon her Pantiles,

the Epicurean sect might have relaxed from its
original purity, the morals of its founder were as
correct as those of any among the ancient philosophers; and his doctrines upon pleasure, as
explained in the letter to Menœceus, are rational,
amiable, and consistent with our nature. A late
writer, De Sablons, in his "*Grands Hommes
vengés,*" expresses strong indignation against
the Encyclopédistes for their just and animated
praises of Epicurus, and discussing the question,
"*si ce philosophe étoit vertueux,*" denies it upon
no other authority than the calumnies collected
by Plutarch, who himself confesses that, on this
particular subject, he consulted only opinion and
report, without pausing to investigate their truth.
— ἀλλὰ τὴν δόξαν, οὐ τὴν ἀλήθειαν σκοποῦμεν.
To the factious zeal of his illiberal rivals, the
Stoics, Epicurus chiefly owed these gross misrepresentations of the life and opinions of himself and his associates, which, notwithstanding
the learned exertions of Gassendi, have still left
an odium on the name of his philosophy; and we
ought to examine the ancient accounts of this
philosopher with about the same degree of
cautious belief with which, in reading ecclesiastical
history, we yield to the invectives of the fathers
against the heretics, — trusting as little to Plutarch upon a dogma of Epicurus, as we would
to the vehement St. Cyril upon a tenet of Nes-
torius. (1801.)

  The preceding remarks, I wish the reader
to observe, were written at a time, when I
thought the studies to which they refer much
more important as well as more amusing
than, I freely confess, they appear to me at
present.

The merriest wight of all the kings
  That ever ruled these gay, gallant isles;

Like us, by day, they rode, they walked,
  At eve they did as we may do,
And Grammont just like Spencer talked,
  And lovely Stewart smiled like you.

The only different trait is this,
  That woman then, if man beset her,
Was rather given to saying " yes,"
  Because, — as yet, she knew no better.

Each night they held a coterie,
  Where, every fear to slumber charmed,
Lovers were all they ought to be,
  And husbands not the least alarmed.

Then called they up their school-day
    pranks,
  Nor thought it much their sense be-
    neath
To play at riddles, quips, and cranks,
  And lords showed wit, and ladies teeth.

As —" Why are husbands like the mint ? "
  Because, forsooth, a husband's duty
Is but to set the name and print
  That give a currency to beauty.

" Why is a rose in nettles hid
  " Like a young widow, fresh and
    fair ? "
Because 't is sighing to be rid
  Of *weeds*, that " have no business
    there ! "

And thus they missed and thus they hit,
  And now they struck and now they
    parried;
And some lay in of full grown wit,
  While others of a pun miscarried.

'T was one of those facetious nights
  That Grammont gave this forfeit ring
For breaking grave conundrum-rites,
  Or punning ill, or—some such thing;—

From whence it can be fairly traced,
  Through many a branch and many a
    bough,
From twig to twig, until it graced
  The snowy hand that wears it now.

All this I 'll prove, and then, to you
  Oh Tunbridge ! and your springs *iron-
    ical,*
I swear by Heathcote's eye of blue
  To dedicate the important chronicle.

Long may your ancient inmates give
  Their mantles to your modern lodgers,
And Charles's loves in Heathcote live,
  And Charles's bards revive in Rogers.

Let no pedantic fools be there;
  For ever be those fops abolished,
With heads as wooden as thy ware,
  And, heaven knows ! not half so pol-
    ished.

But still receive the young, the gay,
  The few who know the rare delight
Of reading Grammont every day,
  And acting Grammont every night.

THE DEVIL AMONG THE SCHOLARS,

A FRAGMENT.

τί κακὸν ὁ γέλως;
CHRYSOST. " *Homil. in Epist. ad Hebræos.*"

. . . .

BUT, whither have these gentle ones,
These rosy nymphs and black-eyed nuns,
With all of Cupid's wild romancing,
Led by truant brains a-dancing?
Instead of studying tomes scholastic,
Ecclesiastic, or monastic,
Off I fly, careering far
In chase of Pollys, prettier far
Than any of their namesakes are, —
The Polymaths and Polyhistors,
Polyglots and all their sisters.

So have I known a hopeful youth
Sit down in quest of lore and truth,
With tomes sufficient to confound him,
Like Tohu Bohu, heapt around him, —
Mamurra[1] stuck to Theophrastus,

1 Mamurra, a dogmatic philosopher, who never
doubted about anything, except who was his
father. — " *nullâ de re unquam præterquam de
patre dubitavit.*" — *In Vit.* He was very learned
— " *Là-dedans,* (that is, in his head when it was
opened,) *le Punique heurte le Persan, l'Hébreu
choque l'Arabique, pour ne point parler de la
mauvaise intelligence du Latin avec le Grec,*"
etc. — See " *L'Histoire de Montmaur.*" *tom.* ij
p. 91.

And Galen tumbling o'er Bombastus.[1]
When lo! while all that 's learned and
    wise
Absorbs the boy, he lifts his eyes,
And through the window of his study
Beholds some damsel fair and ruddy,
With eyes, as brightly turned upon him as
The angel's [2] were on Hieronymus.
Quick fly the folios, widely scattered,
Old Homer's laureled brow is battered,
And Sappho, headlong sent, flies just in
The reverend eye of St. Augustin.
Raptured he quits each dozing sage,
Oh woman, for thy lovelier page :
Sweet book ! — unlike the books of
    art, —
Whose errors are thy fairest part;
In whom the dear errata column
Is the best page in all the volume ! [3]
    But to begin my subject rhyme —
'T was just about this devilish time,

1 Bombastus was one of the names of that
great scholar and quack Paracelsus. — " *Philip-*
pus Bombastus latet sub splendido tegmine Au-
reoli Theophrasti Paracelsi," says *Stadelius de*
circumforaneâ Literatorum vanitate. — He used
to fight the devil every night with a broadsword,
to the no small terror of his pupil Oporinus, who
has recorded the circumstance. (*Vide Oporin.*
Vit. apud Christian. Gryph. Vit. Select. quo-
rundam Eruditissimorum, etc.) Paracelsus had
but a poor opinion of Galen : — " My very beard
(says he in his Paragrænum) has more learning in
it than either Galen or Avicenna."

2 The angel, who scolded St. Jerom for reading Cicero, as Gratian tells the story in his " *con-*
cordantia discordantium Canonum," and says,
that for this reason bishops were not allowed to
read the Classics : "*Episcopus gentilium libros*
non legat." — *Distinct.* 37. But Gratian is no-
torious for lying — besides, angels, as the illustrious pupil of Pantenus assures us, have got no
tongues. οὐχ᾽ ὡς ἡμῖν τὰ ὦτα, οὕτως ἐκείνοις ἡ
γλῶττα· οὐδ᾽ ἂν ὀργανά τις δώη φωνῆς ἀγγέλοις.
— *Clem. Alexand. Stromat.*

3 The idea of the Rabbins, respecting the
origin of woman, is not a little singular. They
think that man was originally formed with a tail,
like a monkey, but that the Deity cut off this
appendage, and made woman of it. Upon this
extraordinary supposition the following reflection
is founded : —

If such is the tie between women and men,
  The ninny who weds is a pitiful elf,
For he takes to his tail like an idiot again,
  And thus makes a deplorable ape of himself.

Yet, if we may judge as the fashions prevail,
  Every husband remembers the original plan,
And, knowing his wife is no more than his tail,
  Why he — leaves her behind him as much as
    he can.

When scarce there happened any frolics
That were not done by Diabolics,
A cold and loveless son of Lucifer,
Who woman scorned, nor saw the use of
    her,
A branch of Dagon's family,
(Which Dagon, whether He or She,
Is a dispute that vastly better is
Referred to Scaliger [4] *et cæteris,*)
Finding that, in this cage of fools,
The wisest sots adorn the schools,
Took it at once his head Satanic in,
To grow a great scholastic manikin, —
A doctor, quite as learned and fine as
Scotus John or Tom Aquinas,[5]
Lully, Hales Irrefragabilis,
Or any doctor of the rabble is.
In languages,[6] the Polyglots,
Compared to him, were Babel sots;
He chattered more than ever Jew did; —
Sanhedrim and Priest included,
Priest and holy Sanhedrim
Were one-and-seventy fools to him.
But chief the learned demon felt a
Zeal so strong for gamma, delta,
That, all for Greek and learning's glory,[7]

4 Scaliger. *de Emendat. Tempor.* — Dagon
was thought by others to be a certain sea-monster,
who came every day out of the Red Sea to teach
the Syrians husbandry. — See Jaques Gaffarel
(" *Curiosités Inouies,*" chap. i.), who says he
thinks this story of the sea-monster " carries little
show of probability with it."

5 I wish it were known with any degree of
certainty whether the Commentary on Boethius
attributed to Thomas Aquinas be really the work
of this Angelic Doctor. There are some bold
assertions hazarded in it : for instance, he says
that Plato kept school in a town called Academia, and that Alcibiades was a very beautiful
woman whom some of Aristotle's pupils fell in
love with : — " *Alcibiades mulier fuit pulcher-*
rima, quam videntes quidam discipuli Aristo-
telis," etc. — See *Freytag "Adparat. Litterar."*
art. 86. *tom.* i.

6 The following compliment was paid to Laurentius Valla, upon his accurate knowledge of
the Latin language : —

nunc postquam manes defunctus Valla petivit,
  non audet Pluto verba Latina loqui.

Since Val arrived in Pluto's shade,
  His nouns and pronouns all so pat in,
Pluto himself would be afraid
  To say his soul 's his own, in Latin !

See for these lines the " *Auctorum Censio* "
of Du Verdier (page 29.).

7 It is much to be regretted that Martin
Luther, with all his talents for reforming, should
yet be vulgar enough to laugh at Camerarius for

He nightly tippled "Græco more,"
And never paid a bill or balance
Except upon the Grecian Kalends: —
From whence your scholars, when they
  want tick,
Say, to be *At*tic 's to be *on* tick,
In logics, he was quite Ho Panu; [1]
Knew as much as ever man knew.
He fought the combat syllogistic
With so much skill and art eristic,
That though you were the learned Stagy-
  rite,
At once upon the hip he had you right.
In music, though he had no ears
Except for that amongst the spheres,
(Which most of all, as he averred it,
He dearly loved, 'cause no one heard it,)
Yet aptly he, at sight, could read
Each tuneful diagram in Bede,
And find, by Euclid's corollaria,
The ratios of a jig or aria.
But, as for all your warbling Delias,

Orpheuses and Saint Cecilias,
He owned he thought them much sur-
  past
By that redoubted Hyaloclast [2]
Who still contrived by dint of throttle,
Where'er he went to crack a bottle.

Likewise to show his mighty knowl-
  edge, he,
On things unknown in physiology,
Wrote many a chapter to divert us,
(Like that great little man Albertus,)
Wherein he showed the reason why,
When children first are heard to cry,
If boy the baby chance to be,
He cries O A ! — if girl, O E ! —
Which are, quoth he, exceeding fair hints
Respecting their first sinful parents;
" Oh Eve ! " exclaimeth little madam,
While little master cries " Oh Adam ! " [3]

But, 't was in Optics and Dioptrics,
Our dæmon played his first and top tricks.
He held that sunshine passes quicker
Through wine than any other liquor;
And though he saw no great objection
To steady light and clear reflection,
He thought the aberrating rays,
Which play about a bumper's blaze,
Were by the Doctors looked, in common,
  on,
As a more rare and rich phenomenon.
He wisely said that the sensorium
Is for the eyes a great emporium,
To which these noted picture-stealers
Send all they can and meet with dealers.
In many an optical proceeding
The brain, he said, showed great good
  breeding;
For instance, when we ogle women
(A trick which Barbara tutored him in),
Although the dears are apt to get in a
Strange position on the retina,
Yet instantly the modest brain
Doth set them on their legs again ! [4]

writing to him in Greek. " Master Joachim (says he) has sent me some dates and some raisins, and has also written me two letters in Greek. As soon as I am recovered, I shall answer them in Turkish, that he too may have the pleasure of reading what he does not understand." " *Græca sunt, legi non possunt,*" is the ignorant speech attributed to Accursius; but very unjustly: — for, far from asserting that Greek could not be read, that worthy juris-consult upon the Law 6. D. *de Bonor. Possess.* expressly says, " *Græcæ literæ possunt intelligi et legi.*" (*Vide* " *Nov. Libror. Rarior. Collection.*" *Fascic.* IV.) — Scipio. Carteromachus seems to have been of opinion that there is no salvation out of the pale of Greek Literature: " *via prima salutis Graiâ pandetur ab urbe :* " and the zeal of Laurentius Rhodomannus cannot be sufficiently admired, when he exhorts his countrymen, " *per gloriam Christi, per salutem patriæ, per reipublicæ decus et emolumentum,*" to study the Greek language. Nor must we forget Phavorinus, the excellent bishop of Nocera, who, careless of all the usual commendations of a Christian, required no further eulogium on his tomb than " Here lieth a Greek Lexicographer."

1 ὁ πάνυ. — The introduction of this language into English poetry has a good effect, and ought to be more universally adopted. A word or two of Greek in a stanza would serve as ballast to the most " light o' love " verses. Ausonius, among the ancients, may serve as a model : —

ού γάρ μοι θέμις έστίν in hac regione μένοντι
  άξιον ab nostris ἐπιδενέα esse καμήναις

Ronsard, the French poet, has enriched his sonnets and odes with many an exquisite morsel from the Lexicon. His " *chère Entelechie,*" in addressing his mistress, can only be equalled by Cowley's " Antiperistasis."

2 Or Glass-Breaker — Morhofius has given an account of this extraordinary man, in a work, published 1682, — " *De vitreo scypho fracto,*" etc.

3 Translated almost literally from a passage in Albertus de Secretis, etc.

4 Alluding to that habitual act of the judgment, by which, notwithstanding the inversion of the image upon the retina, a correct impression of the object is conveyed to the sensorium.

Our doctor thus, with "stuft suffi-
     ciency"
Of all omnigenous omnisciency,
Began (as who would not begin
That had, like him, so much within?)
To let it out in books of all sorts,
Folios, quartos, large and small sorts;
Poems, so very deep and sensible
That they were quite incomprehensible [1]
Prose, which had been at learning's Fair,
And bought up all the trumpery there,
The tattered rags of every vest,

In which the Greeks and Romans drest,
And o'er her figure swollen and antic
Scattered them all with airs so frantic,
That those, who saw what fits she had,
Declared unhappy Prose was mad!
Epics he wrote and scores of rebuses,
All as neat as old Turnebus's;
Eggs and altars, cyclopædias,
Grammars, prayer-books — oh! 't were
     tedious,
Did I but tell thee half, to follow me:
Not the scribbling bard of Ptolemy,
No — nor the hoary Trismegistus,
(Whose writings all, thank heaven! have
     missed us,)
E'er filled with lumber such a wareroom
As this great "*porcus literarum!* "

.   .   .   .

1 Under this description, I believe "the
Devil among the Scholars" may be included.
Yet Leibnitz found out the uses of incompre-
hensibility, when he was appointed secretary to a
society of philosophers at Nuremberg, chiefly
for his ingenuity in writing a cabalistical letter,
not one word of which either they or himself
could interpret. See the *Éloge Historique de
M. de Leibnitz, l'Europe Savante.* — People in
all ages have loved to be puzzled. We find
Cicero thanking Atticus for having sent him a
work of Serapion "*ex quo* (says he) *quidem ego
(quod inter nos liceat dicere) millesimam partem
vix intelligo.*" *Lib.* ii. *epist.* 4. And we know
that Avicen, the learned Arabian, read Aristotle's
Metaphysics forty times over for the mere pleasure of being able to inform the world that he
could not comprehend one syllable throughout
them. (Nicolas Massa in "*Vit. Avicen.*")

POEMS RELATING TO AMERICA.

TO

FRANCIS, EARL OF MOIRA,

GENERAL IN HIS MAJESTY'S FORCES, MASTER–GENERAL OF THE ORDNANCE, CON-
STABLE OF THE TOWER, ETC.

MY LORD,

It is impossible to think of addressing a Dedication to your Lordship without
calling to mind the well-known reply of the Spartan to a rhetorician, who proposed
to pronounce an eulogium on Hercules. "On Hercules!" said the honest Spartan,
"who ever thought of blaming Hercules?" In a similar manner the concurrence
of public opinion has left to the panegyrist of your Lordship a very superfluous
task. I shall, therefore, be silent on the subject, and merely entreat your indulgence to the very humble tribute of gratitude which I have here the honor to
present. I am, my Lord,

With every feeling of attachment and respect,
Your Lordship's very devoted Servant,
THOMAS MOORE.

27 Bury Street, St. James's,
April 10, 1806.

PREFACE.[1]

THE principal poems in the following collection were written during an absence
of fourteen months from Europe. Though curiosity was certainly not the motive
of my voyage to America, yet it happened that the gratification of curiosity was
the only advantage which I derived from it. Finding myself in the country of a
new people, whose infancy had promised so much, and whose progress to maturity
has been an object of such interesting speculation, I determined to employ the
short period of time, which my plan of return to Europe afforded me, in travelling
through a few of the States, and acquiring some knowledge of the inhabitants.

The impression which my mind received from the character and manners of
these republicans, suggested the Epistles which are written from the city of Washington and Lake Erie.[2] How far I was right, in thus assuming the tone of a
satirist against a people whom I viewed but as a stranger and a visitor, is a doubt
which my feelings did not allow me time to investigate. All I presume to answer
for is the fidelity of the picture which I have given; and though prudence might
have dictated gentler language, truth, I think, would have justified severer.

I went to America with prepossessions by no means unfavorable, and indeed rather

1 This Preface, as well as the Dedication which precedes it, were prefixed originally to the
miscellaneous volume entitled "Odes and Epistles," of which, hitherto, the poems relating to my
American tour have formed a part.

2 Epistles VI., VII., and VIII.

123

indulged in many of those illusive ideas, with respect to the purity of the government and the primitive happiness of the people, which I had early imbibed in my native country, where, unfortunately, discontent at home enhances every distant temptation, and the western world has long been looked to as a retreat from real or imaginary oppression; as, in short, the elysian Atlantis, where persecuted patriots might find their visions realized, and be welcomed by kindred spirits to liberty and repose. In all these flattering expectations I found myself completely disappointed, and felt inclined to say to America, as Horace says to his mistress, "*intentata nites.*" Brissot, in the preface to his travels, observes, that " freedom in that country is carried to so high a degree as to border upon a state of nature; " and there certainly is a close approximation to savage life, not only in the liberty which they enjoy, but in the violence of party spirit and of private animosity which results from it. This illiberal zeal imbitters all social intercourse; and, though I scarcely could hesitate in selecting the party, whose views appeared to me the more pure and rational, yet I was sorry to observe that, in asserting their opinions, they both assume an equal share of intolerance; the Democrats, consistently with their principles, exhibiting a vulgarity of rancor, which the Federalists too often are so forgetful of their cause as to imitate.

The rude familiarity of the lower orders, and indeed the unpolished state of society in general, would neither surprise nor disgust if they seemed to flow from that simplicity of character, that honest ignorance of the gloss of refinement which may be looked for in a new and inexperienced people. But, when we find them arrived at maturity in most of the vices, and all the pride of civilization, while they are still so far removed from its higher and better characteristics, it is impossible not to feel that this youthful decay, this crude anticipation of the natural period of corruption, must repress every sanguine hope of the future energy and greatness of America.

I am conscious that, in venturing these few remarks, I have said just enough to offend, and by no means sufficient to convince; for the limits of a preface prevent me from entering into a justification of my opinions, and I am committed on the subject as effectually as if I had written volumes in their defence. My reader, however, is apprised of the very cursory observation upon which these opinions are founded, and can easily decide for himself upon the degree of attention or confidence which they merit.

With respect to the poems in general, which occupy the following pages, I know not in what manner to apologize to the public for intruding upon their notice such a mass of unconnected trifles, such a world of epicurean atoms as I have here brought in conflict together.[1] To say that I have been tempted by the liberal offers of my bookseller, is an excuse which can hope for but little indulgence from the critic; yet I own that, without this seasonable inducement, these poems very possibly would never have been submitted to the world. The glare of publication is too strong for such imperfect productions: they should be shown but to the eye of friendship, in that dim light of privacy which is as favorable to poetical as to female beauty, and serves as a veil for faults, while it enhances every charm which it displays. Besides, this is not a period for the idle occupations of poetry, and times like the present require talents more active and more useful. Few have now the leisure to read such trifles, and I most sincerely regret that I have had the leisure to write them.

1 See the foregoing Note, p. 123.

POEMS RELATING TO AMERICA.

TO
LORD VISCOUNT STRANGFORD.

ABOARD THE PHAETON FRIGATE, OFF THE
AZORES, BY MOONLIGHT.

SWEET Moon! if, like Crotona's sage,[1]
  By any spell my hand could dare
To make thy disk its ample page,
  And write my thoughts, my wishes
    there;
How many a friend, whose careless eye
Now wanders o'er that starry sky,
Should smile, upon thy orb to meet
The recollection, kind and sweet,
  The reveries of fond regret,
  The promise, never to forget,
And all my heart and soul would send
To many a dear-loved, distant friend.

  How little, when we parted last,
I thought those pleasant times were past,
For ever past, when brilliant joy
Was all my vacant heart's employ:
When, fresh from mirth to mirth again,
  We thought the rapid hours too few;
Our only use for knowledge then
  To gather bliss from all we knew.
Delicious days of whim and soul!
  When, mingling lore and laugh to-
    gether,
We leaned the book on Pleasure's bowl,
  And turned the leaf with Folly's
    feather.
Little I thought that all were fled,
That, ere that summer's bloom was shed,
My eye should see the sail unfurled
That wafts me to the western world.

  And yet, 't was time; — in youth's
    sweet days,
To cool that season's glowing rays,

The heart awhile, with wanton wing,
May dip and dive in Pleasure's spring;
But, if it wait for winter's breeze,
The spring will chill, the heart will
    freeze.
And then, that Hope, that fairy Hope, —
  Oh! she awaked such happy dreams,
And gave my soul such tempting scope
  For all its dearest, fondest schemes,
That not Verona's child of song,
  When flying from the Phrygian shore,
With lighter heart could bound along,
  Or pant to be a wanderer more![2]

  Even now delusive hope will steal
Amid the dark regrets I feel,
  Soothing, as yonder placid beam
Pursues the murmurers of the deep,
And lights them with consoling gleam,
  And smiles them into tranquil sleep.
Oh! such a blessed night as this,
  I often think, if friends were near,
How we should feel, and gaze with
    bliss
  Upon the moon-bright scenery here!
The sea is like a silvery lake,
  And, o'er its calm the vessel glides
Gently, as if it feared to wake
  The slumber of the silent tides.
The only envious cloud that lowers
  Hath hung its shade on Pico's height,[3]
Where dimly, mid the dusk, he towers,
  And scowling at this heaven of light,
Exults to see the infant storm
Cling darkly round his giant form!

---

1 Pythagoras; who was supposed to have a
power of writing upon the Moon by the means
of a magic mirror. — See *Bayle*, art. *Pythag.*

2 Alluding to these animated lines in the 44th
Carmen of Catullus : —

  jam mens prætrepidans avet vagari,
  jam læti studio pedes vigescunt!

3 A very high mountain on one of the Azores,
from which the island derives its name. It is
said by some to be as high as the Peak of Ten-
eriffe.

Now, could I range those verdant isles,
    Invisible, at this soft hour,
And see the looks, the beaming smiles,
    That brighten many an orange bower;
And could I lift each pious veil,
    And see the blushing cheek it shades, —
Oh! I should have full many a tale,
    To tell of young Azorian maids.[1]
Yes, Strangford, at this hour, perhaps,
    Some lover (not too idly blest,
Like those, who in their ladies' laps
    May cradle every wish to rest,)
Warbles, to touch his dear one's soul,
    Those madrigals, of breath divine,
Which Camoens' harp from Rapture stole
    And gave, all glowing warm, to thine.[2]
Oh! could the lover learn from thee,
    And breathe them with thy graceful
        tone,
Such sweet, beguiling minstrelsy
    Would make the coldest nymph his
        own.

But, hark! — the boatswain's pipings
        tell
'T is time to bid my dream farewell:
Eight bells: — the middle watch is set;
Good night, my Strangford! — ne'er
        forget
That far beyond the western sea
Is one whose heart remembers thee.

STANZAS.

θυμὸς δὲ πότ' ἐμός ————
———— με προσφωνεῖ τάδε.
γίνωσκε τἀνθρώπεια μὴ σέβειν ἄγαν.
                    ÆSCHYL. *Fragment.*

A BEAM of tranquillity smiled in the west,
    The storms of the morning pursued us
        no more;
And the wave, while it welcomed the
        moment of rest,
    Still heaved, as remembering ills that
        were o'er.

Serenely my heart took the hue of the
        hour,
    Its passions were sleeping, were mute
        as the dead;

[1] I believe it is Guthrie who says, that the inhabitants of the Azores are much addicted to gallantry. This is an assertion in which even Guthrie may be credited.

[2] These islands belong to the Portuguese.

And the spirit becalmed but remembered
        their power,
    As the billow the force of the gale that
        was fled.

I thought of those days, when to pleasure
        alone
    My heart ever granted a wish or a sigh;
When the saddest emotion my bosom had
        known,
    Was pity for those who were wiser
        than I.

I reflected, how soon in the cup of Desire
    The pearl of the soul may be melted
        away;
How quickly, alas, the pure sparkle of
        fire
    We inherit from heaven, may be
        quenched in the clay;

And I prayed of that Spirit who lighted
        the flame,
    That Pleasure no more might its purity
        dim;
So that, sullied but little, or brightly the
        same,
    I might give back the boon I had bor-
        rowed from Him.

How blest was the thought! it appeared
        as if Heaven
    Had already an opening to Paradise
        shown;
As if, passion all chastened and error for-
        given,
    My heart then began to be purely its
        own.

I looked to the west, and the beautiful sky
    Which morning had clouded, was
        clouded no more:
"Oh! thus," I exclaimed, "may a
        heavenly eye
    "Shed light on the soul that was
        darkened before."

TO THE FLYING-FISH.[3]

WHEN I have seen thy snow-white wing
From the blue wave at evening spring,

[3] It is the opinion of St. Austin upon Genesis, and I believe of nearly all the Fathers, that birds, like fish, were originally produced from

And show those scales of silvery white,
So gayly to the eye of light,
As if thy frame were formed to rise,
And live amid the glorious skies;
Oh! it has made me proudly feel,
How like thy wing's impatient zeal
Is the pure soul, that rests not, pent
Within this world's gross element,
But takes the wing that God has given,
And rises into light and heaven!

But, when I see that wing, so bright,
Grow languid with a moment's flight,
Attempt the paths of air in vain,
And sink into the waves again;
Alas! the flattering pride is o'er;
Like thee, awhile, the soul may soar,
But erring man must blush to think,
Like thee, again the soul may sink.

Oh Virtue! when thy clime I seek,
Let not my spirit's flight be weak:
Let me not, like this feeble thing,
With brine still dropping from its wing,
Just sparkle in the solar glow
And plunge again to depths below;
But, when I leave the grosser throng
With whom my soul hath dwelt so
    long,
Let me, in that aspiring day,
Cast every lingering stain away,
And, panting for thy purer air,
Fly up at once and fix me there.

TO MISS MOORE.

FROM NORFOLK, IN VIRGINIA, NOVEMBER, 1803.

IN days, my Kate, when life was new,
When, lulled with innocence and you,
I heard, in home's beloved shade,
The din the world at distance made;
When, every night my weary head
Sunk on its own unthorned bed,
And, mild as evening's matron hour,
Looks on the faintly shutting flower,
A mother saw our eyelids close,
And blest them into pure repose;

the waters; in defence of which idea they have
collected every fanciful circumstance which can
tend to prove a kindred similitude between them;
συγγένειαν τοῖς πετομένοις πρὸς τὰ νηκτά. With
this thought in our minds, when we first see the
Flying-Fish, we could almost fancy, that we are
present at the moment of creation, and witness
the birth of the first bird from the waves.

Then, haply if a week, a day,
I lingered from that home away,
How long the little absence seemed!
How bright the look of welcome beamed,
As mute you heard, with eager smile,
My tales of all that past the while!

Yet now, my Kate, a gloomy sea
Rolls wide between that home and me;
The moon may thrice be born and die,
Ere even that seal can reach mine eye,
Which used so oft, so quick to come,
Still breathing all the breath of home, —
As if, still fresh, the cordial air
From lips beloved were lingering there.
But now, alas, — far different fate!
It comes o'er ocean, slow and late,
When the dear hand that filled its fold
With words of sweetness may lie cold.

But hence that gloomy thought! at
    last,
Beloved Kate, the waves are past:
I tread on earth securely now,
And the green cedar's living bough
Breathes more refreshment to my eyes
Than could a Claude's divinest dyes.
At length I touch the happy sphere
To liberty and virtue dear,
Where man looks up, and, proud to
    claim
His rank within the social frame,
Sees a grand system round him roll,
Himself its centre, sun, and soul!
Far from the shocks of Europe — far
From every wild, elliptic star
That, shooting with a devious fire,
Kindled by heaven's avenging ire,
So oft hath into chaos hurled
The systems of the ancient world.

The warrior here, in arms no more,
Thinks of the toil, the conflict o'er,
And glorying in the freedom won
For hearth and shrine, for sire and
    son,
Smiles on the dusky webs that hide
His sleeping sword's remembered pride.
While Peace, with sunny cheeks of
    toil,
Walks o'er the free, unlorded soil,
Effacing with her splendid share
The drops that war had sprinkled there.

Thrice happy land! where he who flies
From the dark ills of other skies,
From scorn, or want's unnerving woes,
May shelter him in proud repose:
Hope sings along the yellow sand
His welcome to a patriot land;
The mighty wood, with pomp, receives
The stranger in its world of leaves,
Which soon their barren glory yield
To the warm shed and cultured field;
And he, who came, of all bereft,
To whom malignant fate had left
Nor home nor friends nor country dear,
Finds home and friends and country
    here.

Such is the picture, warmly such,
That Fancy long, with florid touch,
Had painted to my sanguine eye
Of man's new world of liberty.
Oh! ask me not, if Truth have yet
Her seal on Fancy's promise set;
If even a glimpse my eyes behold
Of that imagined age of gold; —
Alas, not yet one gleaming trace! [1]
Never did youth, who loved a face
As sketched by some fond pencil's skill,
And made by fancy lovelier still,
Shrink back with more of sad surprise,
When the live model met his eyes,
Than I have felt, in sorrow felt,
To find a dream on which I 've dwelt
From boyhood's hour, thus fade and
    flee
At touch of stern reality!

But, courage, yet, my wavering heart!
Blame not the temple's meanest part, [2]
Till thou hast traced the fabric o'er: —
As yet, we have beheld no more
Than just the porch to Freedom's fane;

And, though a sable spot may stain
The vestibule, 't is wrong, 't is sin
To doubt the godhead reigns within!
So here I pause — and now, my Kate,
To you, and those dear friends, whose
    fate
Touches more near this home-sick soul
Than all the Powers from pole to pole,
One word at parting, — in the tone
Most sweet to you, and most my own.
The simple strain I send you here, [3]
Wild though it be, would charm your
    ear,
Did you but know the trance of thought
In which my mind its numbers caught.
'T was one of those half-waking dreams,
That haunt me oft, when music seems
To bear my soul in sound along,
And turn its feelings all to song.   •
I thought of home, the according lays
Came full of dreams of other days;
Freshly in each succeeding note
I found some young remembrance float,
Till following, as a clue, that strain,
I wandered back to home again.

Oh! love the song, and let it oft
Live on your lip, in accents soft.
Say that it tells you, simply well,
All I have bid its wild notes tell, —
Of Memory's dream, of thoughts that
    yet
Glow with the light of joy that 's set,
And all the fond heart keeps in store
Of friends and scenes beheld no more.
And now, adieu! — this artless air,
With a few rhymes, in transcript fair,
Are all the gifts I yet can boast
To send you from Columbia's coast;
But when the sun, with warmer smile,
Shall light me to my destined isle, [4]
You shall have many a cowslip-bell,
Where Ariel slept, and many a shell,
In which that gentle spirit drew
From honey flowers the morning dew.

---

1 Such romantic works as "The American
Farmer's Letters," and the account of Kentucky
by Imlay, would seduce us into a belief, that innocence, peace, and freedom had deserted the
rest of the world for Martha's Vineyard and the
banks of the Ohio. The French travellers, too,
almost all from revolutionary motives, have contributed their share to the diffusion of this flattering misconception. A visit to the country is,
however, quite sufficient to correct even the most
enthusiastic prepossession.

2 Norfolk, it must be owned, presents an unfavorable specimen of America. The characteristics of Virginia in general are not such as can

delight either the politician or the moralist, and
at Norfolk they are exhibited in their least attractive form. At the time when we arrived the
yellow fever had not yet disappeared, and every
odor that assailed us in the streets very strongly
accounted for its visitation.

3 A trifling attempt at musical composition
accompanied this Epistle.

4 Bermuda.

A BALLAD.

THE LAKE OF THE DISMAL SWAMP.

WRITTEN AT NORFOLK, IN VIRGINIA.

"They tell of a young man, who lost his mind upon the death of a girl he loved, and who, suddenly disappearing from his friends, was never afterwards heard of. As he had frequently said, in his ravings, that the girl was not dead, but gone to the Dismal Swamp, it is supposed he had wandered into that dreary wilderness, and had died of hunger, or been lost in some of its dreadful morasses." — *Anon.*

"La Poésie a ses monstres comme la nature."
D'ALEMBERT.

"THEY made her a grave, too cold and
    damp
  "For a soul so warm and true;
"And she 's gone to the Lake of the
    Dismal Swamp,[1]
"Where, all night long, by a fire-fly
    lamp,
  "She paddles her white canoe.

"And her fire-fly lamp I soon shall see,
  "And her paddle I soon shall hear;
"Long and loving our life shall be,
"And I 'll hide the maid in a cypress
    tree,
  "When the footstep of death is near."

Away to the Dismal Swamp he speeds —
  His path was rugged and sore,
Through tangled juniper, beds of reeds,
Through many a fen, where the serpent
    feeds,
  And man never trod before.

And, when on the earth he sunk to
    sleep,
  If slumber his eyelids knew,
He lay, where the deadly vine doth
    weep
Its venomous tear and nightly steep
  The flesh with blistering dew!

And near him the she-wolf stirred the
    brake,
  And the copper-snake breathed in his
    ear,
Till he starting cried, from his dream
    awake,

"Oh! when shall I see the dusky Lake,
  "And the white canoe of my dear?"

He saw the Lake, and a meteor bright
  Quick over its surface played —
"Welcome," he said, "my dear-one's
    light!"
And the dim shore echoed, for many a
    night,
  The name of the death-cold maid.

Till he hollowed a boat of the birchen
    bark,
  Which carried him off from shore;
Far, far he followed the meteor spark,
The wind was high and the clouds were
    dark,
  And the boat returned no more.

But oft, from the Indian hunter's camp
  This lover and maid so true
Are seen at the hour of midnight damp
To cross the Lake by a fire-fly lamp,
  And paddle their white canoe!

TO THE

MARCHIONESS DOWAGER OF DONEGALL.

FROM BERMUDA, JANUARY, 1804.

LADY! where'er you roam, whatever
    land
Woos the bright touches of that artist
    hand;
Whether you sketch the valley's golden
    meads,
Where mazy Linth his lingering current
    leads;[2]
Enamoured catch the mellow hues that
    sleep,
At eve, on Meillerie's immortal steep;
Or musing o'er the Lake, at day's decline,
Mark the last shadow on that holy shrine,[3]
Where, many a night, the shade of Tell
    complains
Of Gallia's triumph and Helvetia's
    chains;

---

1 The Great Dismal Swamp is ten or twelve miles distant from Norfolk, and the Lake in the middle of it (about seven miles long) is called Drummond's Pond.

2 Lady Donegall, I had reason to suppose, was at this time still in Switzerland, where the well-known powers of her pencil must have been frequently awakened.

3 The chapel of William Tell on the Lake of Lucerne.

Oh! lay the pencil for a moment by,
Turn from the canvas that creative eye,
And let its splendor, like the morning
   ray
Upon a shepherd's harp, illume my lay.

Yet, Lady, no — for song so rude as
   mine,
Chase not the wonders of your art
   divine;
Still, radiant eye, upon the canvas dwell;
Still, magic finger, weave your potent
   spell;
And, while I sing the animated smiles
Of fairy nature in these sun-born isles,
Oh, might the song awake some bright
   design,
Inspire a touch, or prompt one happy
   line,
Proud were my soul, to see its humble
   thought
On painting's mirror so divinely caught;
While wondering Genius, as he leaned
   to trace
The faint conception kindling into grace,
Might love my numbers for the spark
   they threw,
And bless the lay that lent a charm to
   you.

Say, have you ne'er, in nightly vision,
   strayed
To those pure isles of ever-blooming
   shade,
Which bards of old, with kindly fancy,
   placed
For happy spirits in the Atlantic waste?[1]
There listening, while, from earth, each
   breeze that came
Brought echoes of their own undying
   fame,
In eloquence of eye, and dreams of song,
They charmed their lapse of nightless
   hours along : —
Nor yet in song, that mortal ear might
   suit,

For every spirit was itself a lute,
Where Virtue wakened, with elysian
   breeze,
Pure tones of thought and mental harmonies.

Believe me, Lady, when the zephyrs
   bland
Floated our bark to this enchanted land,—
These leafy isles upon the ocean thrown,
Like studs of emerald o'er a silver zone,—
Not all the charm, that ethnic fancy
   gave
To blessed arbors o'er the western wave,
Could wake a dream, more soothing or
   sublime,
Of bowers ethereal, and the Spirit's clime.

Bright rose the morning, every wave
   was still,
When the first perfume of a cedar hill
Sweetly awaked us, and, with smiling
   charms,
The fairy harbor woo'd us to its arms.[2]
Gently we stole, before the whispering
   wind,
Through plaintain shades, that round,
   like awnings, twined
And kist on either side the wanton sails,
Breathing our welcome to these vernal
   vales;
While, far reflected o'er the wave serene,
Each wooded island shed so soft a green
That the enamoured keel, with whisper-
   ing play,
Through liquid herbage seemed to steal
   its way.

Never did weary bark more gladly
   glide,
Or rest its anchor in a lovelier tide !
Along the margin, many a shining dome,
White as the palace of a Lapland gnome,
Brightened the wave ; — in every myrtle
   grove
Secluded bashful, like a shrine of love,

---

1 M. Gébelin says, in his *Monde Primitif,*
"*Lorsque Strabon crût que les anciens théolo-
giens et poëtes plaçoient les champs élysées dans
les isles de l'Océan Atlantique, il n'entendit rien
à leur doctrine.*" M. Gébelin's supposition, I
have no doubt, is the more correct ; but that of
Strabo is, in the present instance, most to my
purpose.

2 Nothing can be more romantic than the
little harbor of St. George's. The number of
beautiful islets, the singular clearness of the
water, and the animated play of the graceful
little boats, gliding for ever between the islands,
and seeming to sail from one cedar-grove into
another, formed altogether as lovely a miniature
of nature's beauties as can well be imagined.

Some elfin mansion sparkled through the
    shade;
And, while the foliage interposing played,
Lending the scene an ever-changing
    grace,
Fancy would love, in glimpses vague, to
    trace
The flowery capital, the shaft, the porch,[1]
And dream of temples, till her kindling
    torch
Lighted me back to all the glorious days
Of Attic genius; and I seemed to gaze
On marble, from the rich Pentelic mount,
Gracing the umbrage of some Naiad's
    fount.

Then thought I, too, of thee, most
    sweet of all
The spirit race that come at poet's call,
Delicate Ariel! who, in brighter hours,
Lived on the perfume of these honied
    bowers,

In velvet buds, at evening, loved to lie,
And win with music every rose's sigh.
Though weak the magic of my humble
    strain
To charm your spirit from its orb again,
Yet, oh, for her, beneath whose smile I
    sing,
For her (whose pencil, if your rainbow
    wing
Were dimmed or ruffled by a wintry sky.
Could smooth its feather and relume its
    dye,)
Descend a moment from your starry
    sphere,
And, if the lime-tree grove that once was
    dear,
The sunny wave, the bower, the breezy
    hill,

The sparkling grotto can delight you still,
Oh cull their choicest tints, their softest
    light,
Weave all these spells into one dream of
    night,
And, while the lovely artist slumbering
    lies,
Shed the warm picture o'er her mental
    eyes;
Take for the task her own creative spells,
And brightly show what song but faintly
    tells.

TO GEORGE MORGAN, ESQ.

OF NORFOLK, VIRGINIA.[2]

FROM BERMUDA, JANUARY, 1804.

κείνη δ' ἠνεμόεσσα καὶ ἄτροπος οἷα θ' ἁλίπληξ,
αἰθυίης καὶ μᾶλλον ἐπίδρομος πέπερ ἵπποις,
πόντῳ ἐνεστήρικται.

CALLIMACH. *Hymn, in Del.* v. 11.

OH, what a sea of storm we 've past! —
    High mountain waves and foamy show-
        ers,
And battling winds whose savage blast
    But ill agrees with one whose hours
Have past in old Anacreon's bowers,
    Yet think not poesy's bright charm
Forsook me in this rude alarm:[3] —
    When close they reefed the timid sail,

1 This is an illusion which, to the few who are
fanciful enough to indulge in it, renders the scenery of Bermuda particularly interesting. In the
short but beautiful twilight of their spring evenings, the white cottages, scattered over the islands, and but partially seen through the trees
that surround them, assume often the appearance
of little Grecian temples; and a vivid fancy may
embellish the poor fisherman's hut with columns
such as the pencil of a Claude might imitate. I
had one favorite object of this kind in my walks,
which the hospitality of its owner robbed me of,
by asking me to visit him. He was a plain good
man, and received me well and warmly, but I
could never turn his house into a Grecian temple
again.

2 This gentleman is attached to the British
consulate at Norfolk. His talents are worthy of
a much higher sphere; but the excellent dispositions of the family with whom he resides, and the
cordial repose he enjoys amongst some of the
kindest hearts in the world, should be almost
enough to atone to him for the worst caprices of
fortune. The consul himself, Colonel Hamilton,
is one among the very few instances of a man,
ardently loyal to his king, and yet beloved by the
Americans. His house is the very temple of
hospitality, and I sincerely pity the heart of that
stranger who, warm from the welcome of such a
board, could sit down to write a libel on his host,
in the true spirit of a modern philosophist. See
the Travels of the Duke de la Rouchefoucault-
Liancourt, vol. ii.

3 We were seven days on our passage from
Norfolk to Bermuda, during three of which we
were forced to lay-to in a gale of wind. The
Driver sloop of war, in which I went, was built
at Bermuda of cedar, and is accounted an excellent sea-boat. She was then commanded by my
very regretted friend Captain Compton, who in
July last was killed aboard the Lilly in an action
with a French privateer. Poor Compton! he
fell a victim to the strange impolicy of allowing
such a miserable thing as the Lilly to remain in
the service; so small, crank, and unmanageable,
that a well-manned merchantman was at any time
a match for her.

When, every plank complaining loud,
We labored in the midnight gale,
And even our haughty main-mast
　bowed,
Even then, in that unlovely hour,
The Muse still brought her soothing
　power,
And, midst the war of waves and wind,
In song's Elysium lapt my mind.
Nay, when no numbers of my own
Responded to her wakening tone,
She opened, with her golden key,
　The casket where my memory lays
Those gems of classic poesy,
　Which time has saved from ancient
　　days.

Take one of these, to Lais sung, —
I wrote it while my hammock swung,
As one might write a dissertation
Upon " Suspended Animation ! "

Sweet [1] is your kiss, my Lais dear,
But, with that kiss I feel a tear
Gush from your eyelids, such as start
When those who 've dearly loved must
　part.
Sadly you lean your head to mine,
And mute those arms around me twine,
Your hair adown my bosom spread,
All glittering with the tears you shed.
In vain I 've kist those lids of snow,
For still, like ceaseless founts they
　flow,
Bathing our cheeks, whene'er they meet.
Why is it thus?　Do, tell me, sweet !
Ah, Lais ! are my bodings right?
Am I to lose you?　Is to-night
Our last ——go, false to heaven and me !
Your very tears are treachery.

SUCH, while in air I floating hung,
　Such was the strain, Morgante mio !
The muse and I together sung,
　With Boreas to make out the trio.
But, bless the little fairy isle !
How sweetly after all our ills,
We saw the sunny morning smile
　Serenely o'er its fragrant hills;
And felt the pure, delicious flow
Of airs that round this Eden blow
Freshly as even the gales that come
O'er our own healthy hills at home.

Could you but view the scenery fair,
　That now beneath my window lies,
You 'd think, that nature lavished there
　Her purest wave, her softest skies,
To make a heaven for love to sigh in,
For bards to live and saints to die in.
Close to my wooded bank below,
　In glassy calm the waters sleep,
And to the sunbeam proudly show
　The coral rocks they love to steep.[2]
The fainting breeze of morning fails;
　The drowsy boat moves slowly past,
And I can almost touch its sails
　As loose they flap around the mast.
The noontide sun a splendor pours
That lights up all these leafy shores;
While his own heaven, its clouds and
　　beams,
　So pictured in the waters lie,
That each small bark, in passing, seems
To float along a burning sky.

Oh for the pinnace lent to thee,[3]
　Blest dreamer, who, in vision bright,
Didst sail o'er heaven's solar sea
　And touch at all its isles of light.

1 This epigram is by Paul the Silentiary, and
may be found in the Analecta of Brunck, vol. iii.
p. 72.　As the reading there is somewhat different from what I have followed in this translation,
I shall give it as I had it in my memory at the
time, and as it is in Heinsius, who, I believe,
first produced the epigram.　See his "*Poemata.*"

ἡδὺ μέν ἐστι φίλημα τὸ Λαιδός· ἡδὺ δὲ αὐτῶν
　ἠπιοδινητῶν δάκρυ χέεις βλεφάρων,
καὶ πολὺ κιχλίζουσα σοβεῖς εὐβόστρυχον αἴγλην,
　ἡμέτερα κεφαλὴν δηρὸν ἐρεισαμένη.
μυρομένην δ' ἐφίλησα· τὰ δ' ὡς δροσερῆς ἀπὸ
　　πηγῆς,
　δάκρυα μιγνυμένων πίπτε κατὰ στομάτων·
εἶπε δ' ἀνειρομένῳ, τίνος οὕνεκα δάκρυα λείβεις;
　δείδια μή με λιπῇς· ἐστε γὰρ ὁρκαπάται.

2 The water is so clear around the island, that
the rocks are seen beneath to a very great depth;
and, as we entered the harbor, they appeared to
us so near the surface that it seemed impossible
we should not strike on them.　There is no
necessity, of course, for heaving the lead; and
the negro pilot, looking down at the rocks from
the bow of the ship, takes her through this difficult navigation, with a skill and confidence which
seem to astonish some of the oldest sailors.

3 In Kircher's "Ecstatic Journey to Heaven,"
Cosmiel, the genius of the world, gives Theodidactus a boat of asbestos, with which he embarks
into the regions of the sun.　" *Vides* (says Cosmiel) *hanc asbestinam naviculam commoditati
tuæ præparatam.*" — "*Itinerar.*" I. *Dial.* i.
cap. 5.　This work of Kircher abounds with
strange fancies.

Sweet Venus, what a clime he found
Within thy orb's ambrosial round![1] —
There spring the breezes, rich and
    warm,
  That sigh around thy vesper car;
And angels dwell, so pure of form
  That each appears a living star.[2]
These are the sprites, celestial queen!
  Thou sendest nightly to the bed
Of her I love, with touch unseen
  Thy planet's brightening tints to shed;
To lend that eye a light still clearer,
  To give that cheek one rose-blush
    more,
And bid that blushing lip be dearer,
  Which had been all too dear before.

But, whither means the muse to roam?
'T is time to call the wanderer home.
Who could have thought the nymph would
  perch her
Up in the clouds with Father Kircher?
So, health and love to all your mansion!
  Long may the bowl that pleasures
    bloom in,

The flow of heart, the soul's expansion,
  Mirth and song, your board illumine.
At all your feasts, remember too,
  When cups are sparkling to the brim,
That here is one who drinks to you,
  And, oh! as warmly drink to him.

1 When the Genius of the world and his fel-
low-traveller arrive at the planet Venus, they
find an island of loveliness, full of odors and intelligences, where angels preside, who shed the
cosmetic influence of this planet over the earth;
such being, according to astrologers, the "*vis
influxiva*" of Venus. When they are in this
part of the heavens, a casuistical question occurs
to Theodidactus, and he asks," Whether baptism
may be performed with the waters of Venus?"
— "*an aquis globi Veneris baptismus institui
possit?*" to which the Genius answers, "Certainly."

2 This idea is Father Kircher's: "*tot animatos
soles dixisses.*" — "*Itinerar.*" I. *Dial.* i. *cap.* 5.

LINES, WRITTEN IN A STORM AT SEA.

THAT sky of clouds is not the sky
To light a lover to the pillow
  Of her he loves —
The swell of yonder foaming billow
Resembles not the happy sigh
  That rapture moves.

Yet do I feel more tranquil far
Amid the gloomy wilds of ocean,
  In this dark hour,
Than when, in passion's young emotion,
I 've stolen, beneath the evening star,
  To Julia's bower.

Oh! there 's a holy calm profound
In awe like this, that ne'er was given
  To pleasure's thrill;
'T is as a solemn voice from heaven,
And the soul, listening to the sound,
  Lies mute and still.

'T is true, it talks of danger nigh,
Of slumbering with the dead to-morrow
  In the cold deep,
Where pleasure's throb or tears of sorrow
No more shall wake the heart or eye,
  But all must sleep.

Well! — there are some, thou stormy bed,
To whom thy sleep would be a treasure;
  Oh! most to him,
Whose lip hath drained life's cup of
    pleasure,
Nor left one honey drop to shed
  Round sorrow's brim.

Yes — *he* can smile serene at death:
Kind heaven, do thou but chase the
    weeping
  Of friends who love him;
Tell them that he lies calmly sleeping
Where sorrow's sting or envy's breath
  No more shall move him.

ODES TO NEA;

WRITTEN AT BERMUDA.

NEA τυραννεῖ.
EURIPID. " *Medea*," v. 967.

Nay, tempt me not to love again,
  There was a time when love was
    sweet;
Dear Nea! had I known thee then,
  Our souls had not been slow to meet.
But, oh, this weary heart hath run,
  So many a time, the rounds of pain,
Not even for thee, thou lovely one,
  Would I endure such pangs again.

If there be climes, where never yet
The print of beauty's foot was set,
Where man may pass his loveless nights,
Unfevered by her false delights,
Thither my wounded soul would fly,
Where rosy cheek or radiant eye
Should bring no more their bliss, or pain,
Nor fetter me to earth again.
Dear absent girl! whose eyes of light,
  Though little prized when all my own,
Now float before me, soft and bright
As when they first enamouring
    shone, —
What hours and days have I seen glide,
While fixt, enchanted, by thy side,
Unmindful of the fleeting day,
I 've let life's dream dissolve away.
O bloom of youth profusely shed!
O moments! simply, vainly sped,
Yet sweetly too — for Love perfumed
The flame which thus my life consumed;
And brilliant was the chain of flowers,
In which he led my victim-hours.

Say, Nea, say, couldst thou, like her,
When warm to feel and quick to err,
Of loving fond, of roving fonder,
This thoughtless soul might wish to wan-
    der, —
Couldst thou, like her, the wish reclaim,
  Endearing still, reproaching never,

Till even this heart should burn with
    shame,
  And be thy own more fixt than ever?
No, no — on earth there 's only one
  Could bind such faithless folly fast;
And sure on earth but one alone
  Could make such virtue false at last!

Nea, the heart which she forsook,
  For thee were but a worthless shrine —
Go, lovely girl, that angel look
  Must thrill a soul more pure than
    mine.
Oh! thou shalt be all else to me,
  That heart can feel or tongue can feign;
I 'll praise, admire, and worship thee,
  But must not, dare not, love again.

———

—— *tale iter omne cave.*
  PROPERT. *lib.* iv. *eleg.* 8.

I PRAY you, let us roam no more
Along that wild and lonely shore,
  Where late we thoughtless strayed;
'T was not for us, whom heaven intends
To be no more than simple friends,
  Such lonely walks were made.

That little Bay, where turning in
From ocean's rude and angry din,
  As lovers steal to bliss,
The billows kiss the shore, and then
Flow back into the deep again,
  As though they did not kiss.

Remember, o'er its circling flood
In what a dangerous dream we stood —
  The silent sea before us,
Around us, all the gloom of grove,
That ever lent its shade to love,
  No eye but heaven's o'er us!

I saw you blush, you felt me tremble,
In vain would formal art dissemble
  All we then looked and thought;
'T was more than tongue could dare re-
    veal,
'T was every thing that young hearts feel,
  By Love and Nature taught.

I stooped to cull, with faltering hand,
A shell that, on the golden sand,
  Before us faintly gleamed;
I trembling raised it, and when you
Had kist the shell, I kist it too —
  How sweet, how wrong it seemed!

Oh, trust me, 't was a place, an hour,
The worst that e'er the tempter's power
  Could tangle me or you in;
Sweet Nea, let us roam no more
Along that wild and lonely shore,
  Such walks may be our ruin.

YOU read it in these spell-bound eyes,
  And there alone should love be read;
You hear me say it all in sighs,
  And thus alone should love be said.

Then dread no more; I will not speak;
  Although my heart to anguish thrill,
I 'll spare the burning of your cheek,
  And look it all in silence still.

Heard you the wish I dared to name,
  To murmur on that luckless night,
When passion broke the bonds of shame,
  And love grew madness in your sight?

Divinely through the graceful dance,
  You seemed to float in silent song,
Bending to earth that sunny glance,
  As if to light your steps along.

Oh! how could others dare to touch
  That hallowed form with hand so
      free,
When but to look was bliss too much,
  Too rare for all but Love and me!

With smiling eyes, that little thought
  How fatal were the beams they threw,
My trembling hands you lightly caught,
  And round me, like a spirit, flew.

Heedless of all, but you alone, —
  And *you*, at least, should not condemn,
If, when such eyes before me shone,
  My soul forgot all eyes but them, —

I dared to whisper passion's vow, —
  For love had even of thought bereft
      me, —
Nay, half-way bent to kiss that brow,
  But, with a bound, you blushing left me.

Forget, forget that night's offence,
  Forgive it, if, alas! you can;
'T was love, 't was passion — soul and
    sense —
  'T was all that 's best and worst in man.

That moment, did the assembled eyes
  Of heaven and earth my madness view,
I should have seen, thro' earth and skies,
  But you alone — but only you.

Did not a frown from you reprove,
  Myriads of eyes to me were none;
Enough for me to win your love,
  And die upon the spot, when won.

A DREAM OF ANTIQUITY.

I JUST had turned the classic page,
  And traced that happy period over,
When blest alike were youth and age,
  And love inspired the wisest sage,
    And wisdom graced the tenderest lover.

Before I laid me down to sleep
  Awhile I from the lattice gazed
Upon that still and moonlight deep,
  With isles like floating gardens raised,
For Ariel there his sports to keep;
While, gliding 'twixt their leafy shores
The lone night-fisher plied his oars.

I felt, — so strongly fancy's power
  Came o'er me in that witching hour, —
As if the whole bright scenery there
    Were lighted by a Grecian sky,
And I then breathed the blissful air
    That late had thrilled to Sappho's sigh.

Thus, waking, dreamt I, — and when
    Sleep
  Came o'er my sense, the dream went
    on;

Nor, through her curtain dim and deep,
  Hath ever lovelier vision shone.
I thought that, all enrapt, I strayed
Through that serene, luxurious shade,[1]
Where Epicurus taught the Loves
  To polish virtue's native brightness, —
As pearls, we 're told, that fondling doves
  Have played with, wear a smoother
    whiteness.[2]
'T was one of those delicious nights
  So common in the climes of Greece,
When day withdraws but half its lights,
  And all is moonshine, balm, and peace.
And thou wert there, my own beloved,
And by thy side I fondly roved
Through many a temple's reverend gloom,
And many a bower's seductive bloom,
Where Beauty learned what Wisdom
    taught,
And sages sighed and lovers thought;
Where schoolmen conned no maxims
    stern,
  But all was formed to soothe or move,
To make the dullest love to learn,
  To make the coldest learn to love.

And now the fairy pathway seemed
  To lead us through enchanted ground,
Where all that bard has ever dreamed
  Of love or luxury bloomed around.
Oh! 't was a bright, bewildering scene —
Along the alley's deepening green
Soft lamps, that hung like burning flowers,
And scented and illumed the bowers,
Seemed, as to him, who darkling roves
Amid the lone Hercynian groves,
Appear those countless birds of light,
That sparkle in the leaves at night,
And from their wings diffuse a ray
Along the traveller's weary way.[3]

'T was light of that mysterious kind,
  Through which the soul perchance may
    roam,
When it has left this world behind,
  And gone to seek its heavenly home.
And, Nea, thou wert by my side,
Through all this heaven-ward path my
    guide.

But, lo, as wandering thus we ranged
That upward path, the vision changed;
And now, methought, we stole along
  Through halls of more voluptuous glory
Than ever lived in Teian song,
  Or wantoned in Milesian story.[4]

And nymphs were there, whose very eyes
Seemed softened o'er with breath of
    sighs;
Whose every ringlet, as it wreathed,
A mute appeal to passion breathed.
Some flew, with amber cups, around,
  Pouring the flowery wines of Crete;[5]
And, as they past with youthful bound,
  The onyx shone beneath their feet.[6]
While others, waving arms of snow
Entwined by snakes of burnished gold,[7]
And showing charms, as loath to show,
  Through many a thin, Tarentian fold,[8]
Glided among the festal throng
Bearing rich urns of flowers along.

---

1 Gassendi thinks that the gardens, which
Pausanias mentions, in his first book, were those
of Epicurus; and Stuart says, in his Antiquities
of Athens, " Near this convent (the convent of
Hagios Asomatos) is the place called at present
Kepoi, or the Gardens; and Ampelos Kepos,
or the Vineyard Garden : these were probably
the gardens which Pausanias visited." Vol. i.
chap. 2.

2 This method of polishing pearls, by leaving
them awhile to be played with by doves, is mentioned by the fanciful Cardanus, " *de Rerum
Varietat.*" *lib.* vii. *cap.* 34.

3 *In Hercynio Germaniæ saltu inusitata ge-
nera alitum accepimus, quarum plumæ, ignium
modo, colluceant noctibus.* — *Plin. lib.* x. *cap.* 47.

4 The Milesiacs, or Milesian fables, had their
origin in Miletus, a luxurious town of Ionia.
Aristides was the most celebrated author of these
licentious fictions. See *Plutarch* (in Crasso),
who calls them ἀκόλαστα βιβλία.

5 " Some of the Cretan wines, which Athenæus calls οἶνος ἀνθοσμίας, from their fragrancy
resembling that of the finest flowers." — *Barry
on Wines*, chap. vii.

6 It appears that in very splendid mansions,
the floor or pavement was frequently of onyx.
Thus Martial: " *calcatusque tuo sub pede lucet
onyx.*" Epig. 50. *lib.* xii.

7 Bracelets of this shape were a favorite ornament among the women of antiquity. οἱ ἐπι-
κάρπιοι ὄφεις καὶ αἱ χρυσαὶ πέδαι Θαιδὸς καὶ
Ἀρισταγόρας καὶ Λαιδὸς φάρμακα. — *Philostrat.
Epist.* xl. Lucian, too, tells us of the βραχίοισι
δράκοντες. See his Amores, where he describes
the dressing-room of a Grecian lady, and we
find the " silver vase," the rouge, the tooth-
powder, and all the " mystic order " of a modern
toilet.

8 Ταραντινίδιον, διαφανὲς ἔνδυμα, ὠνομασμέ-
νον ἀπὸ τῆς Ταραντίνων χρήσεως καὶ τρυφῆς. —
Pollux.

Where roses lay, in languor breathing,
And the young beegrape,[1] round them
    wreathing,
Hung on their blushes warm and meek,
Like curls upon a rosy cheek.

Oh, Nea! why did morning break
    The spell that thus divinely bound me?
Why did I wake? how *could* I wake
    With thee my own and heaven around
    me!

WELL — peace to thy heart, though an-
    other's it be,
And health to that cheek, though it
    bloom not for me!
To-morrow I sail for those cinnamon
    groves,[2]
Where nightly the ghost of the Carribee
    roves,
And, far from the light of those eyes, I
    may yet
Their allurements forgive and their splen-
    dor forget.

Farewell to Bermuda,[3] and long may the
    bloom
Of the lemon and myrtle its valleys per-
    fume;
May spring to eternity hallow the shade,
Where Ariel has warbled and Waller[4]
    has strayed.

1 Apiana, mentioned by Pliny, lib. xiv. and
"now called the Muscatell (*a muscarum telis*),"
says Pancirollus, book i. sect. 1. chap. 17.

2 I had, at this time, some idea of paying a
visit to the West Indies.

3 The inhabitants pronounce the name as if
it were written Bermooda. See the commentators on the words "still-vext Bermoothes," in
the Tempest. — I wonder it did not occur to some
of those all-reading gentlemen that, possibly, the
discoverer of this "island of hogs and devils"
might have been no less a personage than the
great John Bermudez, who, about the same period (the beginning of the sixteenth century),
was sent Patriarch of the Latin church to Ethi-
opia, and has left us most wonderful stories of
the Amazons and the Griffins which he encoun-
tered. — *Travels of the Jesuits*, vol. i. I am
afraid, however, it would take the Patriarch
rather too much out of his way.

4 Johnson does not think that Waller was
ever at Bermuda; but the "Account of the
European Settlements in America" affirms it
confidently. (Vol. ii.) I mention this work,
however, less for its authority than for the pleasure I feel in quoting an unacknowledged production of the great Edmund Burke.

And thou — when, at dawn, thou shalt
    happen to roam
Through the lime-covered alley that leads
    to thy home,
Where oft, when the dance and the revel
    were done,
And the stars were beginning to fade in
    the sun,
I have led thee along, and have told by
    the way
What my heart all the night had been
    burning to say —
Oh! think of the past — give a sigh to
    those times,
And a blessing for me to that alley of
    limes.

IF I were yonder wave, my dear,
    And thou the isle it clasps around,
I would not let a foot come near
    My land of bliss, my fairy ground.

If I were yonder conch of gold,
    And thou the pearl within it placed,
I would not let an eye behold
    The sacred gem my arms embraced.

If I were yonder orange-tree,
    And thou the blossom blooming there,
I would not yield a breath of thee
    To scent the most imploring air.

Oh! bend not o'er the water's brink,
    Give not the wave that odorous sigh,
Nor let its burning mirror drink
    The soft reflection of thine eye.

That glossy hair, that glowing cheek,
    So pictured in the waters seem,
That I could gladly plunge to seek
    Thy image in the glassy stream.

Blest fate! at once my chilly grave
    And nuptial bed that stream might be;
I'll wed thee in its mimic wave,
    And die upon the shade of thee.

Behold the leafy mangrove, bending
    O'er the waters blue and bright,
Like Nea's silky lashes, lending
    Shadow to her eyes of light.

Oh, my beloved! where'er I turn,
  Some trace of thee enchants mine eyes;
In every star thy glances burn;
  Thy blush on every floweret lies.

Nor find I in creation aught
  Of bright or beautiful or rare,
Sweet to the sense or pure to thought,
  But thou art found reflected there.

THE SNOW SPIRIT.

No, ne'er did the wave in its element
    steep
  An island of lovelier charms;
It blooms in the giant embrace of the
    deep,
  Like Hebe in Hercules' arms.
The blush of your bowers is light to the
    eye,
  And their melody balm to the ear;
But the fiery planet of day is too nigh,
  And the Snow Spirit never comes here.

The down from his wing is as white as
    the pearl
  That shines through thy lips when they
    part,
And it falls on the green earth as melt-
    ing, my girl,
  As a murmur of thine on the heart.
Oh! fly to the clime, where he pillows
    the death,
  As he cradles the birth of the year;
Bright are your bowers and balmy their
    breath,
  But the Snow Spirit cannot come here.

How sweet to behold him when borne
    on the gale,
  And brightening the bosom of morn,
He flings, like the priest of Diana, a veil
  O'er the brow of each virginal thorn.
Yet think not the veil he so chillingly
    casts
  Is the veil of a vestal severe;
No, no, thou wilt see, what a moment it
    lasts,
  Should the Snow Spirit ever come here.

But fly to his region — lay open thy zone,
  And he 'll weep all his brilliancy dim,
To think that a bosom, as white as his
    own,

Should not melt in the daybeam like
    him.
Oh! lovely the print of those delicate
    feet
  O'er his luminous path will appear —
Fly, my beloved! this island is sweet,
  But the Snow Spirit cannot come here.

ἐνταῦθα δὲ καθώρμισται ἡμῖν. καὶ ὅτι μὲν
ὄνομα τῇ νήσῳ, οὐκ οἶδα· χρυσῆ δ' ἂν πρός γε
ἐμοῦ ὀνομάζοιτο. — PHILOSTRAT. *Icon.* 17. *lib.* ii.

I STOLE along the flowery bank,
While many a bending seagrape [1] drank
The sprinkle of the feathery oar
That winged me round this fairy shore.

'T was noon; and every orange bud
Hung languid o'er the crystal flood,
Faint as the lids of maiden's eyes
When love-thoughts in her bosom rise.
Oh, for a naiad's sparry bower,
To shade me in that glowing hour!

A little dove, of milky hue,
Before me from a plantain flew,
And, light along the water's brim,
I steered my gentle bark by him;
For fancy told me, Love had sent
This gentle bird with kind intent
To lead my steps, where I should meet —
I knew not what, but something sweet.

And — bless the little pilot dove!
He had indeed been sent by Love,
To guide me to a scene so dear
As fate allows but seldom here;
One of those rare and brilliant hours,
That, like the aloe's [2] lingering flowers,
May blossom to the eye of man
But once in all his weary span.

Just where the margin's opening shade
A vista from the waters made,
My bird reposed his silver plume
Upon a rich banana's bloom.
Oh vision bright! oh spirit fair!
What spell, what magic raised her there?

1 The seaside or mangrove grape, a native of
the West Indies.

2 The Agave. This, I am aware, is an erroneous notion, but it is quite true enough for poetry.
Plato, I think, allows a poet to be "three re-
moves from truth;" τρίτατος ἀπὸ τῆς ἀληθείας.

'T was Nea! slumbering calm and mild,
And bloomy as the dimpled child,
Whose spirit in elysium keeps
Its playful sabbath, while he sleeps.

The broad banana's green embrace
Hung shadowy round each tranquil grace;
One little beam alone could win
The leaves to let it wander in,
And, stealing over all her charms,
From lip to cheek, from neck to arms,
New lustre to each beauty lent, —
Itself all trembling as it went!

Dark lay her eyelid's jetty fringe
Upon that cheek whose roseate tinge
Mixt with its shade, like evening's light
Just touching on the verge of night.
Her eyes, though thus in slumber hid,
Seemed glowing through the ivory lid,
And, as I thought, a lustre threw
Upon her lip's reflecting dew, —
Such as a night-lamp, left to shine
Alone on some secluded shrine,
May shed upon the votive wreath,
Which pious hands have hung beneath.

Was ever vision half so sweet!
Think, think how quick my heart-pulse
    beat,
As o'er the rustling bank I stole; —
Oh! ye, that know the lover's soul,
It is for you alone to guess,
That moment's trembling happiness.

A STUDY FROM THE ANTIQUE.

BEHOLD, my love, the curious gem
    Within this simple ring of gold;
'T is hallow'd by the touch of them
    Who lived in classic hours of old.

Some fair Athenian girl, perhaps,
    Upon her hand this gem displayed,
Nor thought that time's succeeding lapse
    Should see it grace a lovelier maid.

Look, dearest, what a sweet design!
    The more we gaze, it charms the more;
Come — closer bring that cheek to mine,
    And trace with me its beauties o'er.

Thou seest, it is a simple youth
    By some enamoured nymph em-
        braced —

Look, as she leans, and say in sooth
    Is not that hand most fondly placed?

Upon his curled head behind
    It seems in careless play to lie,[1]
Yet presses gently, half inclined
    To bring the truant's lip more nigh.

Oh happy maid! Too happy boy!
    The one so fond and little loath,
The other yielding slow to joy —
    Oh rare, indeed, but blissful both.

Imagine, love, that I am he,
    And just as warm as he is chilling;
Imagine, too, that thou art she,
    But quite as coy as she is willing:

So may we try the graceful way
    In which their gentle arms are twined,
And thus, like her, my hand I lay
    Upon thy wreathed locks behind:

And thus I feel thee breathing sweet,
    As slow to mine thy head I move;
And thus our lips together meet,
    And thus, — and thus, — I kiss thee,
        love.

—— λιβανωτῷ εἴκασεν, ὅτι ἀπολλύμενον
εὐφραίνει.
ARISTOT. *Rhetor. lib.* iii. *cap.* 4.

THERE's not a look, a word of thine,
    My soul hath e'er forgot;
Thou ne'er hast bid a ringlet shine,
Nor given thy locks one graceful twine
    Which I remember not.

There never yet a murmur fell
    From that beguiling tongue,
Which did not, with a lingering spell,
Upon my charmed senses dwell,
    Like songs from Eden sung.

Ah! that I could, at once, forget
    All that haunts me so —
And yet, thou witching girl, — and yet,
To die were sweeter than to let
    The loved remembrance go.

1 Somewhat like the symplegma of Cupid and
Psyche at Florence, in which the position of
Psyche's hand is finely and delicately expressive
of affection. See the *Museum Florentinum,
tom.* ii. *tab.* 43, 44. There are few subjects on
which poetry could be more interestingly employed than in illustrating some of these ancient
statues and gems.

No; if this slighted heart must see
Its faithful pulse decay,
Oh let it die, remembering thee,
And, like the burnt aroma, be
Consumed in sweets away.

TO JOSEPH ATKINSON, ESQ.

FROM BERMUDA.[1]

"THE daylight is gone — but, before
we depart,
"One cup shall go round to the friend
of my heart,
"The kindest, the dearest — oh! judge
by the tear
"I now shed while I name him, how
kind and how dear."

'T was thus in the shade of the Calabash-Tree,
With a few, who could feel and remember like me,
The charm that, to sweeten my goblet, I
threw
Was a sigh to the past and a blessing on
you.

1 Pinkerton has said that "a good history and
description of the Bermudas might afford a pleasing addition to the geographical library;" but
there certainly are not materials for such a work.
The island, since the time of its discovery, has experienced so very few vicissitudes, the people have
been so indolent, and their trade so limited, that
there is but little which the historian could am-
plify into importance; and, with respect to the
natural productions of the country, the few which
the inhabitants can be induced to cultivate are so
common in the West Indies, that they have been
described by every naturalist who has written
any account of those islands.

It is often asserted by the trans-Atlantic politicians that this little colony deserves more attention from the mother-country than it receives,
and it certainly possesses advantages of situation,
to which we should not be long insensible, if it
were once in the hands of an enemy. I was told
by a celebrated friend of Washington, at New
York, that they had formed a plan for its capture
towards the conclusion of the American War;
"with the intention (as he expressed himself) of
making it a nest of hornets for the annoyance of
British trade in that part of the world." And
there is no doubt it lies so conveniently in the
track to the West Indies, that an enemy might
with ease convert it into a very harassing impediment.

The plan of Bishop Berkeley for a college at
Bermuda, where American savages might be
converted and educated, though concurred in by
the government of the day, was a wild and useless speculation. Mr. Hamilton, who was governor of the island some years since, proposed,

Oh! say, is it thus, in the mirth-bring-
ing hour,
When friends are assembled, when wit,
in full flower,
Shoots forth from the lip, under Bacchus's dew,
In blossoms of thought ever springing
and new —
Do you sometimes remember, and hallow
the brim
Of your cup with a sigh, as you crown it
to him
Who is lonely and sad in these valleys
so fair,
And would pine in elysium, if friends
were not there!

Last night, when we came from the
Calabash-Tree,
When my limbs were at rest and my
spirit was free,
The glow of the grape and the dreams of
the day
Set the magical springs of my fancy in
play,
And oh, — such a vision as haunted me
then
I would slumber for ages to witness again.
The many I like, and the few I adore,
The friends who were dear and beloved
before,

if I mistake not, the establishment of a marine
academy for the instruction of those children of
West Indians, who might be intended for any
nautical employment. This was a more rational
idea, and for something of this nature the island
is admirably calculated. But the plan should be
much more extensive, and embrace a general
system of education; which would relieve the
colonists from the alternative to which they are
reduced at present, of either sending their sons
to England for instruction, or intrusting them to
colleges in the states of America, where ideas,
by no means favorable to Great Britain, are very
sedulously inculcated.

The women of Bermuda, though not generally
handsome, have an affectionate languor in their
look and manner, which is always interesting.
What the French imply by their epithet *aimante*
seems very much the character of the young
Bermudian girls — that predisposition to loving,
which, without being awakened by any particular
object, diffuses itself through the general manner in a tone of tenderness that never fails to
fascinate. The men of the island, I confess, are
not very civilized; and the old philosopher, who
imagined that, after this life, men would be
changed into mules, and women into turtle-doves,
would find the metamorphosis in some degree
anticipated at Bermuda.

But never till now so beloved and dear,
At the call of my Fancy, surrounded me
   here;
And soon, — oh, at once, did the light
   of their smiles
To a paradise brighten this region of
   isles;
More lucid the wave, as they looked on
   it, flowed,
And brighter the rose, as they gathered
   it, glowed.
Not the valleys Heræan (though watered
   by rills
Of the pearliest flow, from those pastoral
   hills,[1]
Where the Song of the Shepherd, pri-
   meval and wild,
Was taught to the nymphs by their mys-
   tical child,)
Could boast such a lustre o'er land and
   o'er wave
As the magic of love to this paradise gave.

Oh magic of love! unembellished by
   you,
Hath the garden a blush or the landscape
   a hue?
Or shines there a vista in nature or art,
Like that which Love opes thro' the eye
   to the heart?

Alas, that a vision so happy should fade!
That, when morning around me in brilliancy played,
The rose and the stream I had thought
   of at night
Should still be before me, unfadingly
   bright;
While the friends, who had seemed to
   hang over the stream,
And to gather the roses, had fled with
   my dream.

But look, where, all ready, in sailing
   array,
The bark that 's to carry these pages
   away,[2]

1 Mountains of Sicily, upon which Daphnis,
the first inventor of bucolic poetry, was nursed
by the nymphs. See the lively description of
these mountains in Diodorus Siculus, lib. iv.
Ἡραία γὰρ ὄρη κατὰ τὴν Σικελίαν ἐστίν, ἅ φασι
κάλλει, κ. τ. λ.

2 A ship, ready to sail for England.

Impatiently flutters her wing to the wind,
And will soon leave these islets of Ariel
   behind.
What billows, what gales is she fated to
   prove,
Ere she sleep in the lee of the land that
   I love!
Yet pleasant the swell of the billows
   would be,
And the roar of those gales would be
   music to me.
Not the tranquillest air that the winds
   ever blew,
Not the sunniest tears of the summer-eve
   dew,
Were as sweet as the storm, or as bright
   as the foam
Of the surge, that would hurry your
   wanderer home.

THE STEERSMAN'S SONG,

WRITTEN ABOARD THE BOSTON FRIGATE 28TH
APRIL.[3]

WHEN freshly blows the northern gale,
   And under courses snug we fly;
Or when light breezes swell the sail,
   And royals proudly sweep the sky;
'Longside the wheel, unwearied still
   I stand, and, as my watchful eye
Doth mark the needle's faithful thrill,
   I think of her I love, and cry,
         Port, my boy! port.

When calms delay, or breezes blow
   Right from the point we wish to steer;
When by the wind close-hauled we go,
   And strive in vain the port to near;
I think 't is thus the fates defer
   My bliss with one that 's far away,
And while remembrance springs to her,
   I watch the sails and sighing say,
         Thus, my boy! thus.

But see the wind draws kindly aft,
   All hands are up the yards to square,
And now the floating stu'n-sails waft
   Our stately ship thro' waves and air.

3 I left Bermuda in the Boston about the
middle of April, in company with the Cambrian
and Leander, aboard the latter of which was the
Admiral, Sir Andrew Mitchell, who divides his
year between Halifax and Bermuda, and is the
very soul of society and good-fellowship to both.
We separated in a few days, and the Boston after
a short cruise proceeded to New York.

Oh! then I think that yet for me
　Some breeze of fortune thus may spring,
Some breeze to waft me, love, to thee —
　And in that hope I smiling sing,
　　　　　　　Steady, boy! so.

TO THE FIRE-FLY.[1]

At morning, when the earth and sky
Are glowing with the light of spring,
We see thee not, thou humble fly!
　Nor think upon thy gleaming wing.

But when the skies have lost their hue,
　And sunny lights no longer play,
Oh then we see and bless thee too
　For sparkling o'er the dreary way.

Thus let me hope, when lost to me
　The lights that now my life illume,
Some milder joys may come, like thee,
　To cheer, if not to warm, the gloom!

TO
THE LORD VISCOUNT FORBES.
FROM THE CITY OF WASHINGTON.

If former times had never left a trace
Of human frailty in their onward race,
Nor o'er their pathway written, as they
　　ran,
One dark memorial of the crimes of man;
If every age, in new unconscious prime,
Rose, like a phenix, from the fires of time,
To wing its way unguided and alone,
The future smiling and the past unknown;
Then ardent man would to himself be new,
Earth at his foot and heaven within his
　　view:
Well might the novice hope, the sanguine
　　scheme
Of full perfection prompt his daring
　　dream,
Ere cold experience, with her veteran
　　lore,
Could tell him, fools had dreamt as much
　　before.
But, tracing as we do, through age and
　　clime,
The plans of virtue midst the deeds of
　　crime,

The thinking follies and the reasoning
　　rage
Of man, at once the idiot and the sage;
When still we see, through every varying
　　frame
Of arts and polity, his course the same,
And know that ancient fools but died, to
　　make
A space on earth for modern fools to take:
'T is strange, how quickly we the past
　　forget;
That Wisdom's self should not be tutored
　　yet,
Nor tire of watching for the monstrous
　　birth
Of pure perfection midst the sons of earth!

Oh! nothing but that soul which God
　　has given, ·
Could lead us thus to look on earth for
　　heaven;
O'er dross without to shed the light within,
And dream of virtue while we see but sin.

Even here, beside the proud Potow-
　　mac's stream,
Might sages still pursue the flattering
　　theme
Of days to come, when man shall conquer
　　fate,
Rise o'er the level of his mortal state,
Belie the monuments of frailty past,
And plant perfection in this world at last!
" Here," might they say, " shall power's
　　divided reign
" Evince that patriots have not bled in
　　vain.
" Here godlike liberty's herculean youth,
" Cradled in peace, and nurtured up by
　　truth
" To full maturity of nerve and mind,
" Shall crush the giants that bestride
　　mankind.[2]

*sur les orangers voisins, qu'ils mettoient tout en
feu, nous rendant la vue de leurs beaux fruits
dorés que la nuit avoit ravie,"* etc. -- See
" *L'Histoire des Antilles,"* art. 2. chap. 4. liv. i.

2 Thus Morse. " Here the sciences and the
arts of civilized life are to receive their highest
improvements: here civil and religious liberty
are to flourish, unchecked by the cruel hand of
civil or ecclesiastical tyranny: here genius, aided
by all the improvements of former ages, is to be
exerted in humanizing mankind, in expanding
and enriching their minds with religious and
philosophical knowledge," etc. — P. 569.

1 The lively and varying illumination, with
which these fire-flies light up the woods at night,
gives quite an idea of enchantment. " *Puis ces
mouches se developpant de l'obscurité de ces ar-
bres et s'approchant de nous, nous les voyions*

" Here shall religion's pure and balmy
draught
" In form no more from cups of state be
quaft,
" But flow for all, through nation, rank,
and sect,
" Free as that heaven its tranquil waves
reflect.
" Around the columns of the public shrine
" Shall growing arts their gradual wreath
intwine,
" Nor breathe corruption from the flower-
ing braid,
" Nor mine that fabric which they bloom
to shade.
" No longer here shall Justice bound her
view,
" Or wrong the many, while she rights
the few;
" But take her range through all the
social frame,
" Pure and pervading as that vital flame
" Which warms at once our best and
meanest part,
" And thrills a hair while it expands a
heart ! "

Oh golden dream ! what soul that loves
to scan
The bright disk rather than the dark of
man,
That owns the good, while smarting with
the ill,
And loves the world with all its frailty
still, —
What ardent bosom does not spring to
meet
The generous hope, with all that heavenly
heat,
Which makes the soul unwilling to resign
The thoughts of growing, even on earth,
divine !
Yes, dearest friend, I see thee glow to
think
The chain of ages yet may boast a link
Of purer texture than the world has
known,
And fit to bind us to a Godhead's throne.

But, is it thus? doth even the glorious
dream
Borrow from truth that dim, uncertain
gleam,

Which tempts us still to give such fancies
scope,
As shock not reason, while they nourish
hope?
No, no, believe me, 't is not so — even
now,
While yet upon Columbia's rising brow
The showy smile of young presumption
plays,
Her bloom is poisoned and her heart
decays.
Even now, in dawn of life, her sickly
breath
Burns with the taint of empires near their
death;
And, like the nymphs of her own withering clime,
She 's old in youth, she 's blasted in her
prime,[1]

Already has the child of Gallia's school
The foul Philosophy that sins by rule,
With all her train of reasoning, damning
arts,
Begot by brilliant heads on worthless
hearts,
Like things that quicken after Nilus' flood,
The venomed birth of sunshine and of
mud,
Already has she poured her poison here
O'er every charm that makes existence
dear;
Already blighted, with her blackening
trace,
The opening bloom of every social grace,
And all those courtesies, that love to
shoot
Round virtue's stem, the flowerets of her
fruit.
And, were these errors but the wanton
tide
Of young luxuriance or unchastened
pride;

1 " What will be the old age of this government, if it is thus early decrepit!" Such was
the remark of Fauchet, the French minister at
Philadelphia, in that famous despatch to his government, which was intercepted by one of our
cruisers in the year 1794. This curious memorial
may be found in Porcupine's Works, vol. i.
p. 279. It remains a striking monument of republican intrigue on one side and republican
profligacy on the other; and I would recommend
the perusal of it to every honest politician, who
may labor under a moment's delusion with respect to the purity of American patriotism.

The fervid follies and the faults of such
As wrongly feel, because they feel too
  much;
Then might experience make the fever
  less,
Nay, graft a virtue on each warm excess.
But no; 't is heartless, speculative ill,
All youth's transgression with all age's
  chill;
The apathy of wrong, the bosom's ice,
A slow and cold stagnation into vice.

Long has the love of gold, that mean-
  est rage,
And latest folly of man's sinking age,
Which, rarely venturing in the van of life,
While nobler passions wage their heated
  strife,
Comes skulking last, with selfishness and
  fear,
And dies, collecting lumber in the rear, —
Long has it palsied every grasping hand
And greedy spirit through this bartering
  land;
Turned life to traffic, set the demon gold
So loose abroad that virtue's self is sold,
And conscience, truth, and honesty are
  made
To rise and fall, like other wares of
  trade.[1]

Already in this free, this virtuous state,
Which, Frenchmen tell us, was ordained
  by fate,
To show the world, what high perfection
  springs
From rabble senators, and merchant
  kings, —
Even here already patriots learn to steal
Their private perquisites from public
  weal,
And, guardians of the country's sacred
  fire,
Like Afric's priests, let out the flame for
  hire.
Those vaunted demagogues, who nobly
  rose
From England's debtors to be England's
  foes,[2]

Who could their monarch in their purse
  forget,
And break allegiance, but to cancel debt,[3]
Have proved at length, the mineral's
  tempting hue,
Which makes a patriot, can unmake him
  too.[4]
Oh! Freedom, Freedom, how I hate thy
  cant!
Not Eastern bombast, not the savage
  rant
Of purpled madmen, were they num-
  bered all
From Roman Nero down to Russian Paul,
Could grate upon my ear so mean, so
  base,
As the rank jargon of that factious race,
Who, poor of heart and prodigal of words,
Formed to be slaves, yet struggling to
  be lords,
Strut forth, as patriots, from their negro-
  marts,
And shout for rights, with rapine in their
  hearts.

Who can, with patience, for a moment
  see
The medley mass of pride and misery,
Of whips and charters, manacles and
  rights,
Of slaving blacks and democratic whites,[5]

justify those arbitrary steps of the English government which the colonies found it so necessary
to resist; my only object here is to expose the
selfish motives of some of the leading American
demagogues.

3 The most persevering enemy to the interests
of this country, amongst the politicians of the
western world, has been a Virginian merchant,
who, finding it easier to settle his conscience
than his debts, was one of the first to raise the
standard against Great Britain, and has ever since
endeavored to revenge upon the whole country
the obligations which he lies under to a few of
its merchants.

4 See Porcupine's account of the Pennsyl-
vania Insurrection in 1794. In short, see Porcupine's works throughout, for ample corroboration
of every sentiment which I have ventured to express. In saying this, I refer less to the comments of that writer than to the occurrences
which he has related and the documents which
he has preserved. Opinion may be suspected of
bias, but facts speak for themselves.

5 In Virginia the effects of this system begin
to be felt rather seriously. While the master
raves of liberty, the slave cannot but catch the
contagion, and accordingly there seldom elapses
a month without some alarm of insurrection

1 "*Nous voyons que, dans les pays où l'on
n'est affecté que de l'esprit de commerce, on tra-
fique de toutes les actions humaines et de toutes
les vertus morales.*" — *Montesquieu, de l'Esprit
des Lois, liv.* xx. *chap.* 2.

2 I trust I shall not be suspected of a wish to

And all the piebald polity that reigns
In free confusion o'er Columbia's plains?
To think that man, thou just and gentle
    God!
Should stand before thee with a tyrant's
    rod
O'er creatures like himself, with souls
    from thee,
Yet dare to boast of perfect liberty;
Away, away — I 'd rather hold my neck
By doubtful tenure from a sultan's beck,
In climes, where liberty has scarce been
    named,
Nor any right but that of ruling claimed,
Than thus to live, where bastard Free-
    dom waves
Her fustian flag in mockery over slaves;
Where — motley laws admitting no de-
    gree
Betwixt the vilely slaved and madly
    free —
Alike the bondage and the license suit
The brute made ruler and the man made
    brute.

But, while I thus, my friend, in flow-
    erless song,
So feebly paint, what yet I feel so strong,
The ills, the vices of the land, where first
Those rebel fiends, that rack the world,
    were nurst,
Where treason's arm by royalty was
    nerved,
And Frenchmen learned to crush the
    throne they served —
Thou, calmly lulled in dreams of classic
    thought,
By bards illumined and by sages taught,
Pant'st to be all, upon this mortal scene,
That bard hath fancied or that sage hath
    been.
Why should I wake thee? why severely
    chase
The lovely forms of virtue and of grace,
That dwell before thee, like the pictures
    spread
By Spartan matrons round the genial bed,

Moulding thy fancy, and with gradual
    art
Brightening the young conceptions of
    thy heart.

Forgive me, Forbes — and should the
    song destroy
One generous hope, one throb of social
    joy,
One high pulsation of the zeal for man,
Which few can feel, and bless that few
    who can, —
Oh! turn to him, beneath those kindred
    eyes
Thy talents open and thy virtues rise,
Forget where nature has been dark or
    dim,
And proudly study all her lights in him.
Yes, yes, in him the erring world forget,
And feel that man *may* reach perfection
    yet.

TO THOMAS HUME, ESQ., M.D.

FROM THE CITY OF WASHINGTON.

διηγήσομαι διηγήματα ἴσως πιστα. κοινωνὰ ὧν
πέπονθα οὐκ ἔχων.

    XENOPHONT. *Ephes. Ephesiac. lib.* v.

'T IS evening now; beneath the western
    star
Soft sighs the lover through his sweet
    cigar,
And fills the ears of some consenting
    she
With puffs and vows, with smoke and
    constancy.
The patriot, fresh from Freedom's coun-
    cils come,
Now pleased retires to lash his slaves at
    home;
Or woo, perhaps, some black Aspasia's
    charms,
And dream of freedom in his bonds-
    maid's arms.[1]

In fancy now, beneath the twilight
    gloom,
Come, let me lead thee o'er this " sec-
    ond Rome! "[2]

---

amongst the negroes. The accession of Louisi-
ana, it is feared, will increase this embarrass-
ment; as the numerous emigrations, which are
expected to take place, from the southern states
to this newly acquired territory, will considerably diminish the white population, and thus
strengthen the proportion of negroes, to a degree
which must ultimately be ruinous.

1 The " black Aspasia " of the present * * *
* * * * * * of the United States, *inter Aver-
nales haud ignotissima nymphas,* has given rise
to much pleasantry among the anti-democrat wits
in America.

2 " On the original location of the ground now
allotted for the seat of the Federal City [says

Where tribunes rule, where dusky Davi
    bow,
And what was Goose-Creek once is Tiber
    now : [1] —
This embryo capital, where Fancy sees
Squares in morasses, obelisks in trees;
Which second-sighted seers, even now,
    adorn
With shrines unbuilt and heroes yet un-
    born,
Though naught but woods [2] and Jeffer-
    son they see,
Where streets should run and sages *ought*
    to be.

And look, how calmly in yon radiant
    wave,
The dying sun prepares his golden grave.
Oh mighty river ! oh ye banks of shade !
Ye matchless scenes, in nature's morning
    made,
While still, in all the exuberance of prime,
She poured her wonders, lavishly sublime,
Nor yet had learned to stoop, with hum-
    bler care,
From grand to soft, from wonderful to
    fair ; —
Say, were your towering hills, your bound-
    less floods,
Your rich savannas and majestic woods,

Where bards should meditate and heroes
    rove,
And woman charm, and man deserve her
    love, —
Oh say, was world so bright, but born to
    grace
Its own half-organized, half-minded race [3]
Of weak barbarians, swarming o'er its
    breast,
Like vermin gendered on the lion's crest?
Were none but brutes to call that soil
    their home,
Where none but demigods should dare to
    roam?
Or worse, thou wondrous world ! oh !
    doubly worse,
Did heaven design thy lordly land to nurse
The motley dregs of every distant clime,
Each blast of anarchy and taint of crime
Which Europe shakes from her perturbed
    sphere,
In full malignity to rankle here ?

But hold, — observe yon little mount of
    pines,
Where the breeze murmurs and the fire-
    fly shines.
There let thy fancy raise, in bold relief,
The sculptured image of that veteran
    chief [4]

Mr. Weld] the identical spot on which the capitol
now stands was called Rome. This anecdote is
related by many as a certain prognostic of the
future magnificence of this city, which is to be,
as it were, a second Rome." — *Weld's Travels*,
letter IV.

1 A little stream runs through the city, which,
with intolerable affectation, they have styled the
Tiber. It was originally called Goose-Creek.

2 "To be under the necessity of going through
a deep wood for one or two miles, perhaps, in
order to see a next-door neighbor, and in the
same city, is a curious and I believe, a novel
circumstance." — *Weld*, letter IV.

The Federal City (if it must be called a city)
has not been much increased since Mr. Weld
visited it. Most of the public buildings, which
were then in some degree of forwardness, have
been since utterly suspended. The hotel is already a ruin ; a great part of its roof has fallen
in, and the rooms are left to be occupied gratuitously by the miserable Scotch and Irish emi-
grants. The President's house, a very noble
structure, is by no means suited to the philosophical humility of its present possessor, who
inhabits but a corner of the mansion himself,
and abandons the rest to a state of uncleanly
desolation, which those who are not philosophers
cannot look at without regret This grand edifice

is encircled by a very rude paling, through which
a common rustic stile introduces the visitors of
the first man in America. With respect to all
that is within the house, I shall imitate the prudent forbearance of Herodotus, and say, τὰ δὲ ἐν
ἀπορρήτῳ.

The private buildings exhibit the same characteristic display of arrogant speculation and premature ruin ; and the few ranges of houses which
were begun some years ago have remained so
long waste and unfinished that they are now for
the most part dilapidated.

3 The picture which Buffon and De Pauw
have drawn of the American Indian, though
very humiliating, is, as far as I can judge, much
more correct than the flattering representations
which Mr. Jefferson has given us. See the
Notes on Virginia, where this gentleman endeavors to disprove in general the opinion maintained
so strongly by some philosophers that nature (as
Mr. Jefferson expresses it) *be-littles* her productions in the western world. M. de Pauw attributes the imperfection of animal life in America
to the ravages of a very recent deluge, from
whose effects upon its soil and atmosphere it has
not yet sufficiently recovered. — *Recherches sur
les Américains, part* i. *tom.* i. p. 102.

4 On a small hill near the capitol there is to
be an equestrian statue of General Washington.

Who lost the rebel's in the hero's name,
And climbed o'er prostrate loyalty to
  fame;
Beneath whose sword Columbia's patriot
  train
Cast off their monarch that their mob
  might reign.

How shall we rank thee upon glory's
  page?
Thou more than soldier and just less than
  sage!
Of peace too fond to act the conqueror's
  part,
Too long in camps to learn a statesman's
  art,
Nature designed thee for a hero's mould,
But, ere she cast thee, let the stuff grow
  cold.

While loftier souls command, nay, make
  their fate,
Thy fate made thee and forced thee to be
  great.
Yet Fortune, who so oft, so blindly sheds
Her brightest halo round the weakest
  heads,
Found *thee* undazzled, tranquil as before,
Proud to be useful, scorning to be more;
Less moved by glory's than by duty's
  claim,
Renown the meed, but self-applause the
  aim;
All that thou *wert* reflects less fame on
  thee,
Far less, than all thou didst *forbear to be.*
Nor yet the patriot of one land alone, —
For, thine 's a name all nations claim
  their own;
And every shore, where breathed the
  good and brave,
Echoed the plaudits thy own country gave.

Now look, my friend, where faint the
  moonlight falls
On yonder dome, and, in those princely
  halls, —
If thou canst hate, as sure that soul must
  hate,
Which loves the virtuous, and reveres the
  great, —
If thou canst loathe and execrate with me
The poisonous drug of French philosophy,

That nauseous slaver of these frantic
  times,
With which false liberty dilutes her
  crimes, —
If thou hast got, within thy freeborn
  breast,
One pulse that beats more proudly than
  the rest,
With honest scorn for that inglorious
  soul,
Which creeps and winds beneath a mob's
  control,
Which courts the rabble's smile, the
  rabble's nod,
And makes, like Egypt, every beast its
  god,
There, in those walls — but, burning
  tongue, forbear!
Rank must be reverenced, even the rank
  that 's there:
So here I pause — and now, dear Hume,
  we part:
But oft again, in frank exchange of
  heart,
Thus let us meet, and mingle converse
  dear
By Thames at home, or by Potowmac
  here.
O'er lake and marsh, through fevers and
  through fogs,
Midst bears and yankees, democrats and
  frogs,
Thy foot shall follow me, thy heart and
  eyes
With me shall wonder, and with me
  despise.[1]

[1] In the ferment which the French revolution
excited among the democrats of America, and
the licentious sympathy with which they shared
in the wildest excesses of jacobinism, we may
find one source of that vulgarity of vice, that hostility to all the graces of life, which distinguishes
the present demagogues of the United States,
and has become indeed too generally the characteristic of their countrymen. But there is another cause of the corruption of private morals,
which, encouraged as it is by the government,
and identified with the interests of the community, seems to threaten the decay of all honest
principle in America. I allude to those fraudulent
violations of neutrality to which they are indebted
for the most lucrative part of their commerce,
and by which they have so long infringed and
counteracted the maritime rights and advantages
of this country. This unwarrantable trade is
necessarily abetted by such a system of collusion,
imposture, and perjury, as cannot fail to spread
rapid contamination around it.

While I, as oft, in fancy's dream shall
　　rove,
With thee conversing, through that land
　　I love,
Where, like the air that fans her fields of
　　green,
Her freedom spreads, unfevered and
　　serene;
And sovereign man can condescend to
　　see
The throne and laws more sovereign still
　　than he.

LINES

WRITTEN ON LEAVING PHILADELPHIA.

—— τήνδε τὴν πόλιν φίλως
εἰπὼν᾽ ἐπάξια γάρ.
　　SOPHOCL. Œdip. Colon. v. 758.

ALONE by the Schuylkill a wanderer
　　roved,
　　And bright were its flowery banks to his
　　　eye;
But far, very far were the friends that he
　　loved,
　　And he gazed on its flowery banks with
　　　a sigh.

Oh Nature, though blessed and bright are
　　thy rays,
　　O'er the brow of creation enchantingly
　　　thrown,
Yet faint are they all to the lustre that
　　plays
　　In a smile from the heart that is fondly
　　　our own.

Nor long did the soul of the stranger
　　remain
　　Unblest by the smile he had languished
　　　to meet;
Though scarce did he hope it would soothe
　　him again,
　　Till the threshold of home had been
　　　prest by his feet.

But the lays of his boyhood had stolen to
　　their ear,
　　And they loved what they knew of so
　　　humble a name;
And they told him, with flattery welcome
　　and dear,
　　That they found in his heart something
　　　better than fame.

Nor did woman — oh woman! whose
　　form and whose soul
　　Are the spell and the light of each path
　　　we pursue;
Whether sunned in the tropics or chilled
　　at the pole,
　　If woman be there, there is happiness
　　　too : —

Nor did she her enamouring magic
　　deny, —
　　That magic his heart had relinquished
　　　so long, —
Like eyes he had loved was *her* eloquent
　　eye,
　　Like them did it soften and weep at
　　　his song.

Oh, blest be the tear, and in memory oft
　　May its sparkle be shed o'er the wan-
　　　derer's dream;
Thrice blest be that eye, and may passion
　　as soft,
　　As free from a pang, ever mellow its
　　　beam !

The stranger is gone — but he will not
　　forget,
　　When at home he shall talk of the toils
　　　he has known,
To tell, with a sigh, what endearments
　　he met,
　　As he strayed by the wave of the
　　　Schuylkill alone.

LINES

WRITTEN AT

THE COHOS, OR FALLS OF THE MOHAWK
RIVER.[1]

Gia era in loco ove s' udia 'l rimbombo
Dell' acqua.——　　　　　DANTE.

FROM rise of morn till set of sun
I 've seen the mighty Mohawk run;
And as I markt the woods of pine
Along his mirror darkly shine,
Like tall and gloomy forms that pass
Before the wizard's midnight glass;

1 There is a dreary and savage character in
the country immediately about these Falls, which
is much more in harmony with the wildness of
such a scene than the cultivated lands in the
neighborhood of Niagara. See the drawing of
them in Mr. Weld's book. According to him,
the perpendicular height of the Cohos Fall is

And as I viewed the hurrying pace
With which he ran his turbid race,
Rushing, alike untired and wild,
Through shades that frowned and flowers
    that smiled,
Flying by every green recess
That wooed him to its calm caress,
Yet, sometimes turning with the wind,
As if to leave one look behind, —
Oft have I thought, and thinking sighed,
How like to thee, thou restless tide,
May be the lot, the life of him
Who roams along thy water's brim;
Through what alternate wastes of woe
And flowers of joy my path may go;
How many a sheltered, calm retreat
May woo the while my weary feet,
While still pursuing, still unblest,
I wander on, nor dare to rest;
But, urgent as the doom that calls
Thy water to its destined falls,
I feel the world's bewildering force
Hurry my heart's devoted course
From lapse to lapse, till life be done,
And the spent current cease to run.

One only prayer I dare to make,
As onward thus my course I take; —
Oh, be my falls as bright as thine!
May heaven's relenting rainbow shine
Upon the mist that circles me,
As soft as now it hangs o'er thee!

SONG

OF

THE EVIL SPIRIT OF THE WOODS.[1]

qua via difficilis, quaque est via nulla.
    Ovid. *Metam. lib.* iii. v. 227.

Now the vapor, hot and damp,
Shed by day's expiring lamp,
Through the misty ether spreads
Every ill the white man dreads;

Fiery fever's thirsty thrill,
Fitful ague's shivering chill!

Hark! I hear the traveller's song,
As he winds the woods along; —
Christian, 't is the song of fear;
Wolves are round thee, night is near,
And the wild thou dar'st to roam —
Think, 't was once the Indian's home! [2]

Hither, sprites, who love to harm,
Wheresoe'er you work your charm,
By the creeks, or by the brakes,
Where the pale witch feeds her snakes,
And the cayman [3] loves to creep,
Torpid, to his wintry sleep:
Where the bird of carrion flits,
And the shuddering murderer sits,[4]
Lone beneath a roof of blood;
While upon his poisoned food,
From the corpse of him he slew
Drops the chill and gory dew.

Hither bend ye, turn ye hither,
Eyes that blast and wings that wither
Cross the wandering Christian's way,
Lead him, ere the glimpse of day,
Many a mile of maddening error
Through the maze of night and terror,
Till the morn behold him lying
On the damp earth, pale and dying.
Mock him, when his eager sight
Seeks the cordial cottage-light;
Gleam then, like the lightning-bug,

fifty feet; but the Marquis de Chastellux makes it seventy-six.

The fine rainbow, which is continually forming and dissolving, as the spray rises into the light of the sun, is perhaps the most interesting beauty which these wonderful cataracts exhibit.

1 The idea of this poem occurred to me in passing through the very dreary wilderness between Batavia, a new settlement in the midst of the woods, and the little village of Buffalo upon Lake Erie. This is the most fatiguing part of the route, in travelling through the Genesee country to Niagara.

2 "The Five Confederated Nations (of Indians) were settled along the banks of the Susquehannah and the adjacent country, until the year 1779, when General Sullivan, with an army of 4000 men, drove them from their country to Niagara, where, being obliged to live on salted provisions, to which they were unaccustomed, great numbers of them died. Two hundred of them, it is said, were buried in one grave, where they had encamped." — *Morse's American Geography.*

3 The alligator, who is supposed to lie in a torpid state all the winter, in the bank of some creek or pond, having previously swallowed a large number of pine-knots, which are his only sustenance during the time.

4 This was the mode of punishment for murder (as Charlevoix tells us) among the Hurons. "They laid the dead body upon poles at the top of a cabin, and the murderer was obliged to remain several days together, and to receive all that dropped from the carcass, not only on himself but on his food."

Tempt him to the den that 's dug
For the foul and famished brood
Of the she-wolf, gaunt for blood;
Or, unto the dangerous pass
O'er the deep and dark morass,
Where the trembling Indian brings
Belts of porcelain, pipes, and rings,
Tributes, to be hung in air,
To the Fiend presiding there![1]

Then, when night's long labor past,
Wildered, faint, he falls at last,
Sinking where the causeway's edge
Moulders in the slimy sedge,
There let every noxious thing
Trail its filth and fix its sting;
Let the bull-toad taint him over,
Round him let musquitoes hover,
In his ears and eyeballs tingling,
With his blood their poison mingling,
Till, beneath the solar fires,
Rankling all, the wretch expires!

TO

THE HONORABLE W. R. SPENCER.

FROM BUFFALO, UPON LAKE ERIE.

nec venit ad duros musa vocata Getas.

OVID. *ex Ponto, lib.* i. *ep.* 5.

THOU oft hast told me of the happy
hours
Enjoyed by thee in fair Italia's bowers,
Where, lingering yet, the ghost of an-
cient wit
Midst modern monks profanely dares to
flit,
And pagan spirits, by the Pope unlaid,
Haunt every stream and sing through
every shade.
There still the bard who (if his numbers
be
His tongue's light echo) must have talked
like thee, —

The courtly bard, from whom thy mind
has caught
Those playful, sunshine holidays of
thought,
In which the spirit baskingly reclines,
Bright without effort, resting while it
shines, —
There still he roves, and laughing loves
to see
How modern priests with ancient rakes
agree;
How, 'neath the cowl, the festal garland
shines,
And Love still finds a niche in Christian
shrines.

There still, too, roam those other souls
of song,
With whom thy spirit hath communed so
long,
That, quick as light, their rarest gems of
thought,
By Memory's magic to thy lip are brought.
But here, alas! by Erie's stormy lake,
As, far from such bright haunts my
course I take,
No proud remembrance o'er the fancy
plays,
No classic dream, no star of other days
Hath left that visionary light behind,
That lingering radiance of immortal mind,
Which gilds and hallows even the rudest
scene,
The humblest shed, where Genius once
has been!

All that creation's varying mass assumes
Of grand or lovely, here aspires and
blooms;
Bold rise the mountains, rich the gardens
glow,
Bright lakes expand, and conquering[2]
rivers flow;

1 "We find also collars of porcelain, tobacco,
ears of maize, skins, etc., by the side of difficult
and dangerous ways, on rocks, or by the side of
the falls; and these are so many offerings made
to the spirits which preside in these places."
— See *Charlevoix's Letter on the Traditions
and the Religion of the Savages of Canada.*

Father Hennepin too mentions this ceremony;
he also says, "We took notice of one barbarian,
who made a kind of sacrifice upon an oak at the
Cascade of St. Antony of Padua, upon the river
Mississippi." — See *Hennepin's Voyage into
North America.*

2 This epithet was suggested by Charlevoix's
striking description of the confluence of the Missouri with the Mississippi. "I believe this is the
finest confluence in the world. The two rivers
are much of the same breadth, each about half
a league; but the Missouri is by far the most
rapid, and seems to enter the Mississippi like
a conqueror, through which it carries its white
waves to the opposite shore, without mixing
them: afterwards it gives its color to the Mississippi, which it never loses again, but carries quite
down to the sea." — Letter xxvii.

But mind, immortal mind, without whose
   ray,
This world 's a wilderness and man but
   clay,
Mind, mind alone, in barren, still repose,
Nor blooms, nor rises, nor expands, nor
   flows.
Take Christians, Mohawks, democrats,
   and all
From the rude wigwam to the congress-
   hall,
From the savage, whether slaved or
   free,
To man the civilized, less tame than he, —
'T is one dull chaos, one unfertile strife
Betwixt half-polished and half-barbarous
   life;
Where every ill the ancient world could
   brew
Is mixt with every grossness of the new;
Where all corrupts, though little can en-
   tice,
And naught is known of luxury but its
   vice!

Is this the region then, is this the
   clime
For soaring fancies? for those dreams
   sublime,
Which all their miracles of light reveal
To heads that meditate and hearts that
   feel?
Alas! not so — the Muse of Nature
   lights
Her glories round; she scales the moun-
   tain heights,
And roams the forests; every wondrous
   spot
Burns with her step, yet man regards it
   not.
She whispers round, her words are in
   the air,
But lost, unheard, they linger freezing
   there,[1]
Without one breath of soul, divinely
   strong,
One ray of mind to thaw them into song.

Yet, yet forgive me, oh ye sacred few,
Whom late by Delaware's green banks
   I knew;

[1] Alluding to the fanciful notion of " words
congealed in northern air."

Whom, known and loved through many
   a social eve,
'T was bliss to live with, and 't was pain
   to leave.[2]
Not with more joy the lonely exile
   scanned
The writing traced upon the desert's sand,
Where his lone heart but little hoped to
   find
One trace of life, one stamp of human
   kind,
Than did I hail the pure, the enlightened
   zeal,
The strength to reason and the warmth
   to feel,
The manly polish and the illumined taste,
Which, — mid the melancholy, heartless
   waste
My foot has traversed, — oh you sacred
   few!
I found by Delaware's green banks with
   you.

Long may you loathe the Gallic dross
   that runs
Through your fair country and corrupts
   its sons;
Long love the arts, the glories which
   adorn
Those fields of freedom, where your sires
   were born.
Oh! if America can yet be great,
If neither chained by choice, nor doomed
   by fate
To the mob-mania which imbrutes her
   now,
She yet can raise the crowned, yet civic
   brow
Of single majesty, — can add the grace
Of Rank's rich capital to Freedom's
   base,

[2] In the society of Mr. Dennie and his friends,
at Philadelphia, I passed the few agreeable moments which my tour through the States afforded
me. Mr. Dennie has succeeded in diffusing
through this cultivated little circle that love for
good literature and sound politics which he feels
so zealously himself, and which is so very rarely
the characteristic of his countrymen. They will
not, I trust, accuse me of illiberality for the picture which I have given of the ignorance and corruption that surround them. If I did not hate,
as I ought, the rabble to which they are opposed,
I could not value, as I do, the spirit with which
they defy it; and in learning from them what
Americans *can be*, I but see with the more indignation what Americans *are*.

Nor fear the mighty shaft will feebler prove
For the fair ornament that flowers above; —
If yet released from all that pedant throng,
So vain of error and so pledged to wrong,
Who hourly teach her, like themselves, to hide
Weakness in vaunt and barrenness in pride,
She yet can rise, can wreathe the Attic charms
Of soft refinement round the pomp of arms,
And see her poets flash the fires of song,
To light her warriors' thunderbolts along ; —
It is to you, to souls that favoring heaven
Has made like yours, the glorious task is given : —
Oh ! but for *such*, Columbia's days were done ;
Rank without ripeness, quickened without sun,
Crude at the surface, rotten at the core,
Her fruits would fall, before her spring were o'er.

Believe me, Spencer, while I winged the hours
Where Schuylkill winds his way through banks of flowers,
Though few the days, the happy evenings few,
So warm with heart, so rich with mind they flew,
That my charmed soul forgot its wish to roam,
And rested there, as in a dream of home.
And looks I met, like looks I 'd loved before,
And voices too, which, as they trembled o'er
The chord of memory, found full many a tone
Of kindness there in concord with their own.
Yes, — we had nights of that communion free,
That flow of heart, which I have known with thee
So oft, so warmly; nights of mirth and mind,

Of whims that taught, and follies that refined.
When shall we both renew them ? when, restored
To the gay feast and intellectual board,
Shall I once more enjoy with thee and thine
Those whims that teach, those follies that refine ?
Even now, as, wandering upon Erie's shore,
I hear Niagara's distant cataract roar,
I sigh for home, — alas ! these weary feet
Have many a mile to journey, ere we meet.

Ω ΠΑΤΡΙΣ, 'ΩΣ ΣΟΥ ΚΑΡΤΑ ΝΥΝ ΜΝΕΙΑΝ ΕΧΩ.   EURIPIDES.

BALLAD STANZAS.

I KNEW by the smoke, that so gracefully curled
    Above the green elms, that a cottage was near,
And I said, " If there 's peace to be found in the world,
    " A heart that was humble might hope for it here ! "

It was noon, and on flowers that languished around
    In silence reposed the voluptuous bee;
Every leaf was at rest, and I heard not a sound
    But the woodpecker tapping the hollow beech-tree.

And, " Here in this lone little wood," I exclaimed,
    " With a maid who was lovely to soul and to eye,
" Who would blush when I praised her, and weep if I blamed,
    " How blest could I live, and how calm could I die !

" By the shade of yon sumach, whose red berry dips
    " In the gush of the fountain, how sweet to recline,
" And to know that I sighed upon innocent lips,
    " Which had never been sighed on by any but mine ! "

A CANADIAN BOAT SONG.
WRITTEN ON
THE RIVER ST. LAWRENCE.[1]

et remigem cantus hortatur.
QUINTILIAN.

FAINTLY as tolls the evening chime
Our voices keep tune and our oars keep
    time.
Soon as the woods on shore look dim,
We 'll sing at St. Ann's our parting hymn.[2]
Row, brothers, row, the stream runs fast,
The Rapids are near and the daylight 's
    past.

1 I wrote these words to an air which our
boatmen sung to us frequently. The wind was
so unfavorable that they were obliged to row all
the way, and we were five days in descending the
river from Kingston to Montreal, exposed to an
intense sun during the day, and at night forced
to take shelter from the dews in any miserable
hut upon the banks that would receive us. But
the magnificent scenery of the St. Lawrence re
pays all such difficulties.

Our *voyageurs* had good voices, and sung perfectly in tune together. The original words of
the air, to which I adapted these stanzas, appeared to be a long, incoherent story, of which
I could understand but little, from the barbarous
pronunciation of the Canadians. It begins

  Dans mon chemin j'ai rencontré
  Deux cavaliers très-bien montés ;

And the *refrain* to every verse was,

  À l'ombre d'un bois je m'en vais jouer,
  À l'ombre d'un bois je m'en vais danser.

I ventured to harmonize this air, and have
published it. Without that charm which association gives to every little memorial of scenes or
feelings that are past, the melody may, perhaps,
be thought common and trifling; but I remember
when we have entered, at sunset, upon one of
those beautiful lakes, into which the St. Lawrence so grandly and unexpectedly opens, I have
heard this simple air with a pleasure which the
finest compositions of the first masters have
never given me; and now there is not a note of
it which does not recall to my memory the dip of
our oars in the St. Lawrence, the flight of our
boat down the Rapids, and all those new and
fanciful impressions to which my heart was alive
during the whole of this very interesting voyage.

The above stanzas are supposed to be sung by
those *voyageurs* who go to the Grand Portage
by the Utawas River. For an account of this
wonderful undertaking, see Sir Alexander Mackenzie's General History of the Fur Trade,
prefixed to his Journal.

2 "At the Rapid of St. Ann they are obliged
to take out part, if not the whole, of their lading.
It is from this spot the Canadians consider they
take their departure, as it possesses the last
church on the island, which is dedicated to the
tutelar saint of voyagers." — *Mackenzie, General
History of the Fur Trade.*

Why should we yet our sail unfurl?
There is not a breath the blue wave to
    curl.
But, when the wind blows off the shore,
Oh! sweetly we 'll rest our weary oar.
Blow, breezes, blow, the stream runs fast,
The Rapids are near and the daylight 's
    past.

Utawas' tide! this trembling moon
Shall see us float over thy surges soon.
Saint of this green isle! hear our prayers,
Oh, grant us cool heavens and favoring
    airs.
Blow, breezes, blow, the stream runs fast,
The Rapids are near and the daylight 's
    past.

TO THE
LADY CHARLOTTE RAWDON.

FROM THE BANKS OF THE ST. LAWRENCE.

NOT many months have now been
    dreamed away
Since yonder sun, beneath whose evening
    ray
Our boat glides swiftly past these wooded
    shores,
Saw me where Trent his mazy current
    pours,
And Donington's old oaks, to every
    breeze,
Whisper the tale of by-gone centuries; —
Those oaks, to me as sacred as the groves,
Beneath whose shade the pious Persian
    roves,
And hears the spirit-voice of sire, or chief,
Or loved mistress, sigh in every leaf.[3]
There, oft, dear Lady, while thy lip hath
    sung
My own unpolished lays, how proud I 've
    hung
On every tuneful accent! proud to feel
That notes like mine should have the fate
    to steal,
As o'er thy hallowing lip they sighed
    along,
Such breath of passion and such soul of
    song.

3 " *Avendo essi per costume di avere in ve-
nerazione gli alberi grandi et antichi, quasi che
siano spesso ricettaccoli di anime beate.*" —
Pietro della Valle, part. second., lettera 16 *da i
giardini di Sciraz.*

Yes, — I have wondered, like some peas-
    ant boy
Who sings, on Sabbath-eve, his strains of
    joy,
And when he hears the wild, untutored
    note
Back to his ear on softening echoes float,
Believes it still some answering spirit's
    tone,
And thinks it all too sweet to be his own !

I dreamt not then that, ere the rolling
    year
Had filled its circle, I should wander
    here
In musing awe; should tread this won-
    drous world,
See all its store of inland waters hurled
In one vast volume down Niagara's steep,
Or calm behold them, in transparent
    sleep,
Where the blue hills of old Toronto shed
Their evening shadows o'er Ontario's
    bed;
Should trace the grand Cadaraqui, and
    glide
Down the white rapids of his lordly tide
Through massy woods, mid islets flower-
    ing fair,
And blooming glades, where the first
    sinful pair
For consolation might have weeping trod,
When banished from the garden of their
    God.
Oh, Lady ! these are miracles, which man,
Caged in the bounds of Europe's pigmy
    span,
Can scarcely dream of, — which his eye
    must see
To know how wonderful this world can
    be !

But lo, — the last tints of the west
    decline,
And night falls dewy o'er these banks of
    pine.
Among the reeds, in which our idle boat
Is rocked to rest, the wind's complaining
    note
Dies like a half-breathed whispering of
    flutes;
Along the wave the gleaming porpoise
    shoots,

And I can trace him, like a watery star,[1]
Down the steep current, till he fades afar
Amid the foaming breakers' silvery light,
Where yon rough rapids sparkle through
    the night.
Here, as along this shadowy bank I stray,
And the smooth glass-snake,[2] gliding o'er
    my way,
Shows the dim moonlight through his
    scaly form,
Fancy, with all the scene's enchantment
    warm,
Hears in the murmur of the nightly breeze
Some Indian Spirit warble words like
    these : —

From the land beyond the sea,
Whither happy spirits flee;
Where, transformed to   sacred
    doves,[3]
Many a blessed Indian roves
Through the air on wing, as white
As those wondrous stones of light,[4]
Which the eye of morning counts
On the Apalachian mounts, —
Hither oft my flight I take
Over Huron's lucid lake,
Where the wave, as clear as dew,
Sleeps beneath the light canoe,
Which, reflected, floating there,
Looks as if it hung in air.[5]

1 Anburey, in his Travels, has noticed this
shooting illumination which porpoises diffuse at
night through the river St. Lawrence. — Vol. i.
p. 29.

2 The glass-snake is brittle and transparent.

3 "The departed spirit goes into the Country
of Souls, where, according to some, it is trans-
formed into a dove." — *Charlevoix, upon the
Traditions and the Religion of the Savages of
Canada.* See the curious fable of the American
Orpheus in Lafitau, *tom.* i. p. 402.

4 " The mountains appeared to be sprinkled
with white stones, which glistened in the sun,
and were called by the Indians manetoe aseniah,
or spirit-stones." — *Mackenzie's Journal.*

5 These lines were suggested by Carver's description of one of the American lakes. "When
it was calm," he says, " and the sun shone bright,
I could sit in my canoe, where the depth was upwards of six fathoms, and plainly see huge piles
of stone at the bottom, of different shapes, some
of which appeared as if they had been hewn;
the water was at this time as pure and transparent as air, and my canoe seemed as if it hung
suspended in that element. It was impossible
to look attentively through this limpid medium,
at the rocks below, without finding, before many

Then, when I have strayed a while
Through the Manataulin isle,[1]
Breathing all its holy bloom,
Swift I mount me on the plume
Of my Wakon-Bird,[2] and fly
Where, beneath a burning sky,
O'er the bed of Erie's lake
Slumbers many a water-snake,
Wrapt within the web of leaves,
Which the water-lily weaves.[3]
Next I chase the floweret king
Through his rosy realm of spring;
See him now, while diamond hues
Soft his neck and wings suffuse,
In the leafy chalice sink,
Thirsting for his balmy drink;
Now behold him all on fire,
Lovely in his looks of ire,
Breaking every infant stem,
Scattering every velvet gem,
Where his little tyrant lip
Had not found enough to sip.

Then my playful hand I steep
Where the gold-thread[4] loves to
    creep,
Cull from thence a tangled wreath,
Words of magic round it breathe,
And the sunny chaplet spread
O'er the sleeping fly-bird's head.[5]

Till, with dreams of honey blest,
Haunted, in his downy nest,
By the garden's fairest spells,
Dewy buds and fragrant bells,
Fancy all his soul embowers
In the fly-bird's heaven of flowers.

Oft, when hoar and silvery flakes
Melt along the ruffled lakes,
When the gray moose sheds his horns,
When the track, at evening, warns
Weary hunters of the way
To the wigwam's cheering ray,
Then, aloft through freezing air,
With the snow-bird[6] soft and fair
As the fleece that heaven flings
O'er his little pearly wings,
Light above the rocks I play,
Where Niagara's starry spray,
Frozen on the cliff, appears
Like a giant's starting tears.
There, amid the island-sedge,
Just upon the cataract's edge,
Where the foot of living man
Never trod since time began,
Lone I sit, at close of day,
While, beneath the golden ray,
Icy columns gleam below,
Feathered round with falling snow,
And an arch of glory springs
Sparkling as the chain of rings
Round the neck of virgins hung, —
Virgins,[7] who have wandered young
O'er the waters of the west
To the land where spirits rest!

Thus have I charmed, with visionary
    lay,
The lonely moments of the night away;
And now, fresh daylight o'er the water
    beams!
Once more, embarked upon the glittering
    streams,
Our boat flies light along the leafy shore,
Shooting the falls, without a dip of oar
Or breath of zephyr, like the mystic bark

minutes were elapsed, your head swim and your eyes no longer able to behold the dazzling scene."

1 *Après avoir traversé plusieurs isles peu considérables, nous en trouvâmes le quatrième jour une fameuse nommée l'Isle de Manitoualin.* — *Voyages du Baron de Lahontan, tom.* i. *let.* 15. Manataulin signifies a Place of Spirits, and this island in Lake Huron is held sacred by the Indians.

2 "The Wakon-Bird, which probably is of the same species with the bird of Paradise, receives its name from the ideas the Indians have of its superior excellence ; the Wakon-Bird being, in their language, the Bird of the Great Spirit." — *Morse.*

3 The islands of Lake Erie are surrounded to a considerable distance by the large pond-lily, whose leaves spread thickly over the surface of the lake, and form a kind of bed for the water-snakes in summer.

4 "The gold thread is of the vine kind, and grows in swamps. The roots spread themselves just under the surface of the morasses, and are easily drawn out by handfuls. They resemble a large entangled skein of silk, and are of a bright yellow." — *Morse.*

5 " *L'oiseau mouche, gros comme un hanneton, est de toutes couleurs, vives et changeantes: il tire sa subsistence des fleurs commes les abeilles ; son nid est fait d'un cotton très-fin suspendu à*

une branche d'arbre." — *Voyages aux Indes Occidentales, par M. Bossu, seconde part, lett.* xx.

6 *Emberiza hyemalis.* — See *Imlay's Kentucky,* p. 280.

7 Lafitau supposes that there was an order of vestals established among the Iroquois Indians. — *Mœurs des Sauvages Américains,* etc. tom. i. p. 173.

The poet saw, in dreams divinely dark,
Borne, without sails, along the dusky
   flood,[1]
While on its deck a pilot angel stood,
And, with his wings of living light
   unfurled,
Coasted the dim shores of another world!

Yet, oh! believe me, mid this mingled
   maze
Of Nature's beauties, where the fancy
   strays
From charm to charm, where every
   floweret's hue
Hath something strange, and every leaf
   is new, —
I never feel a joy so pure and still,
So inly felt, as when some brook or hill,
Or veteran oak, like those remembered
   well,
Some mountain echo or some wild-flow-
   er's smell,
(For, who can say by what small fairy ties
The memory clings to pleasure as it flies?)
Reminds my heart of many a silvan dream
I once indulged by Trent's inspiring
   stream;
Of all my sunny morns and moonlight
   nights
On Donington's green lawns and breezy
   heights.

Whether I trace the tranquil moments
   o'er
When I have seen thee cull the fruits of
   lore,
With him, the polished warrior, by thy
   side,
A sister's idol and a nation's pride!
When thou hast read of heroes, trophied
   high
In ancient fame, and I have seen thine eye
Turn to the living hero, while it read,
For pure and brightening comments on
   the dead; —
Or whether memory to my mind recalls
The festal grandeur of those lordly halls,

1 *Vedi che sdegna gli argomenti umani;*
  Si che remo non vuol, ne altro velo,
  Che l' ale sue tra liti si lontani.

  Vedi come l' ha dritte verso 'l cielo
  Trattando l' aere con l' eterne penne;
  Che non si mutan, come mortal pelo.
         DANTE, *Purgator.* cant. ii.

When guests have met around the spark-
   ling board,
And welcome warmed the cup that luxury
   poured;
When the bright future Star of England's
   throne,
With magic smile, hath o'er the banquet
   shone,
Winning respect, nor claiming what he
   won,
But tempering greatness, like an evening
   sun
Whose light the eye can tranquilly admire,
Radiant, but mild, all softness, yet all
   fire; —
Whatever hue my recollections take,
Even the regret, the very pain they wake
Is mixt with happiness; — but, ah! no
   more —
Lady! adieu — my heart has lingered o'er
Those vanished times, till all that round
   me lies,
Stream, banks, and bowers have faded
   on my eyes!

IMPROMPTU,

AFTER A VISIT TO MRS. ——, OF MONTREAL.

'T WAS but for a moment — and yet in
   that time
   She crowded the impressions of many
     an hour:
Her eye had a glow, like the sun of her
   clime,
   Which waked every feeling at once into
     flower.

Oh! could we have borrowed from Time
   but a day,
   To renew such impressions again and
     again,
The things we should look and imagine
   and say
   Would be worth all the life we had
     wasted till then.

What we had not the leisure or language
   to speak,
   We should find some more spiritual
     mode of revealing,
And, between us, should feel just as much
   in a week
   As others would take a millennium in
     feeling.

WRITTEN
ON PASSING DEADMAN'S ISLAND,[1]
IN THE
GULF OF ST. LAWRENCE,
LATE IN THE EVENING, SEPTEMBER, 1804.

SEE you, beneath yon cloud so dark,
Fast gliding along a gloomy bark?
Her sails are full, — though the wind is
still,
And there blows not a breath her sails
to fill!

Say, what doth that vessel of darkness
bear?
The silent calm of the grave is there,
Save now and again a death-knell rung,
And the flap of the sails with night-fog
hung.

There lieth a wreck on the dismal shore
Of cold and pitiless Labrador;
Where, under the moon, upon mounts of
frost,
Full many a mariner's bones are tost.

Yon shadowy bark hath been to that
wreck,
And the dim blue fire, that lights her deck,
Doth play on as pale and livid a crew
As ever yet drank the churchyard dew.

To Deadman's Isle, in the eye of the
blast,
To Deadman's Isle, she speeds her fast;
By skeleton shapes her sails are furled,
And the hand that steers is not of this
world!

Oh! hurry thee on — oh! hurry thee on,
Thou terrible bark, ere the night be gone,
Nor let morning look on so foul a sight
As would blanch for ever her rosy light!

---

1 This is one of the Magdalen Islands, and,
singularly enough, is the property of Sir Isaac
Coffin. The above lines were suggested by a
superstition very common among sailors, who
call this ghost-ship, I think, "the flying Dutch-
man."

We were thirteen days on our passage from
Quebec to Halifax, and I had been so spoiled by
the truly splendid hospitality of my friends of
the Phaeton and Boston, that I was but ill prepared for the miseries of a Canadian vessel. The
weather, however, was pleasant, and the scenery
along the river delightful. Our passage through
the Gut of Canso, with a bright sky and a fair
wind, was particularly striking and romantic.

TO
THE BOSTON FRIGATE,[2]
ON
LEAVING HALIFAX FOR ENGLAND,
OCTOBER, 1804.

νόστου πρόφασις γλυκερου.
PINDAR. *Pyth.* 4.

WITH triumph this morning, oh Boston!
I hail
The stir of thy deck and the spread of
thy sail,
For they tell me I soon shall be wafted,
in thee,
To the flourishing isle of the brave and
the free,
And that chill Nova-Scotia's unpromis-
ing strand [2]
Is the last I shall tread of American land.
Well — peace to the land! may her sons
know, at length,
That in high-minded honor lies liberty's
strength,
That though man be as free as the fetter-
less wind,
As the wantonest air that the north can
unbind,
Yet, if health do not temper and sweeten
the blast,
If no harvest of mind ever sprung where
it past,
Then unblest is such freedom, and bale-
ful its might, —
Free only to ruin, and strong but to
blight!

Farewell to the few I have left with
regret;
May they sometimes recall, what I cannot forget,
The delight of those evenings, — too
brief a delight!
When in converse and song we have
stolen on the night;

---

2 Commanded by Captain J. E. Douglas, with
whom I returned to England, and to whom I am
indebted for many, many kindnesses. In truth,
I should not offend the delicacy of my friend
Douglas, and, at the same time, do injustice to
my own feelings of gratitude, did I attempt to
say how much I owe to him.

3 Sir John Wentworth, the Governor of Nova-
Scotia, very kindly allowed me to accompany
him on his visit to the College, which they have
lately established at Windsor, about forty miles
from Halifax, and I was indeed most pleasantly

When they 've asked me the manners,
    the mind, or the mien
Of some bard I had known or some chief
    I had seen,
Whose glory, though distant, they long
    had adored,
Whose name had oft hallowed the wine-
    cup they poured;
And still as, with sympathy humble but
    true,
I have told of each bright son of fame
    all I knew,
They have listened, and sighed that the
    powerful stream
Of America's empire should pass, like a
    dream,
Without leaving one relic of genius, to say
How sublime was the tide which had van-
    ished away!
Farewell to the few — though we never
    may meet
On this planet again, it is soothing and
    sweet
To think that, whenever my song or my
    name
Shall recur to their ear, they 'll recall me
    the same
I have been to them now, young, un-
    thoughtful, and blest,
Ere hope had deceived me or sorrow
    deprest.

But, Douglas! while thus I recall to
    my mind
The elect of the land we shall soon leave
    behind,
I can read in the weather-wise glance of
    thine eye,

As it follows the rack flitting over the
    sky,
That the faint coming breeze would be
    fair for our flight,
And shall steal us away, ere the falling
    of night.
Dear Douglas! thou knowest, with thee
    by my side,
With thy friendship to soothe me, thy
    courage to guide,
There is not a bleak isle in those sum-
    merless seas,
Where the day comes in darkness, or
    shines but to freeze,
Not a tract of the line, not a barbarous
    shore,
That I could not with patience, with
    pleasure explore!
Oh think then how gladly I follow thee
    now,
When Hope smooths the billowy path of
    our prow,
And each prosperous sigh of the west-
    springing wind
Takes me nearer the home where my
    heart is inshrined;
Where the smile of a father shall meet
    me again,
And the tears of a mother turn bliss into
    pain;
Where the kind voice of sisters shall
    steal to my heart,
And ask it, in sighs, how we ever could
    part? —

But see! — the bent top-sails are ready
    to swell —
To the boat — I am with thee — Colum-
    bia, farewell!

surprised by the beauty and fertility of the country which opened upon us after the bleak and
rocky wilderness by which Halifax is surrounded.
— I was told that, in travelling onwards, we
should find the soil and the scenery improve, and

it gave me much pleasure to know that the worthy
Governor has by no means such an "*inamabile
regnum*" as I was, at first sight, inclined to
believe.

IRISH MELODIES.

DEDICATION.

TO

THE MARCHIONESS DOWAGER OF DONEGAL.

It is now many years since, in a Letter prefixed to the Third Number of the Irish Melodies, I had the pleasure of inscribing the Poems of that work to your Ladyship, as to one whose character reflected honor on the country to which they relate, and whose friendship had long been the pride and happiness of their Author. With the same feelings of affection and respect, confirmed if not increased by the experience of every succeeding year, I now place those Poems in their present new form under your protection, and am,

With perfect sincerity,

Your Ladyship's ever attached friend,

THOMAS MOORE.

PREFACE.

Though an edition of the Poetry of the Irish Melodies, separate from the Music, has long been called for, yet, having, for many reasons, a strong objection to this sort of divorce, I should with difficulty have consented to a disunion of the words from the airs, had it depended solely upon me to keep them quietly and indissolubly together. But, besides the various shapes in which these, as well as my other lyrical writings, have been published throughout America, they are included, of course, in all the editions of my works printed on the Continent, and have also appeared, in a volume full of typographical errors, in Dublin. I have therefore readily acceded to the wish expressed by the Proprietor of the Irish Melodies, for a revised and complete edition of the poetry of the Work, though well aware that my verses must lose even more than the " *animæ dimidium* " in being detached from the beautiful airs to which it was their good fortune to be associated.

ADVERTISEMENT

PREFIXED TO

THE FIRST AND SECOND NUMBERS.

POWER takes the liberty of announcing to the Public a Work which has long been a *desideratum* in this country. Though the beauties of the National Music of Ireland have been very generally felt and acknowledged, yet it has happened, through the want of appropriate English words, and of the arrangement necessary to adapt them to the voice, that many of the most excellent compositions have hitherto remained in obscurity. It is intended, therefore, to form a Collection of the best Original Irish Melodies, with characteristic Symphonies and Accompaniments; and with Words containing, as frequently as possible, allusions to the manners and history of the country. Sir John Stevenson has very kindly consented to undertake the arrangement of the Airs; and the lovers of Simple National Music may rest secure, that in such tasteful hands, the native charms of the original melody will not be sacrificed to the ostentation of science.

In the poetical Part, Power has had promises of assistance from several distinguished Literary Characters; particularly from Mr. Moore, whose lyrical talent is so peculiarly suited to such a task, and whose zeal in the undertaking will be best understood from the following Extract of a Letter which he has addressed to Sir John Stevenson on the subject : —

"I feel very anxious that a work of this kind should be undertaken. We have too long neglected the only talent for which our English neighbors ever deigned to allow us any credit. Our National Music has never been properly collected;[1] and, while the composers of the Continent have enriched their Operas and Sonatas with Melodies borrowed from Ireland, — very often without even the honesty of acknowledgment, — we have left these treasures, in a great degree, unclaimed and fugitive. Thus our Airs, like too many of our countrymen, have, for want of protection at home, passed into the service of foreigners. But we are come, I hope, to a better period of both Politics and Music; and how much they are connected, in Ireland at least, appears too plainly in the tone of sorrow and depression which characterizes most of our early Songs.

"The task which you propose to me, of adapting words to these airs, is by no means easy. The Poet, who would follow the various sentiments which they express, must feel and understand that rapid fluctuation of spirits, that unaccountable mixture of gloom and levity, which composes the character of my countrymen, and has deeply tinged their Music. Even in their liveliest strains we find some melancholy note intrude, — some minor Third, or flat Seventh, — which throws its shade as it passes, and makes even mirth interesting. If Burns had been an Irishman (and I would willingly give up all our claims upon Ossian for him), his heart would have been proud of such music, and his genius would have made it immortal.

"Another difficulty (which is, however, purely mechanical) arises from the irregular structure of many of those airs, and the lawless kind of metre which it will in consequence be necessary to adapt to them. In these instances the Poet must write, not to the eye, but to the ear; and must be content to have his verses of that description which Cicero mentions, ' *quos si cantu spoliaveris nuda re-*

1 The writer forgot, when he made this assertion, that the public are indebted to Mr. Bunting for a very valuable collection of Irish Music; and that the patriotic genius of Miss Owenson has been employed upon some of our finest airs.

manebit oratio.' That beautiful Air, 'The Twisting of the Rope,' which has all the romantic character of the Swiss *Ranz des Vaches*, is one of those wild and sentimental rakes which it will not be very easy to tie down in sober wedlock with Poetry. However, notwithstanding all these difficulties, and the very moderate portion of talent which I can bring to surmount them, the design appears to me so truly National, that I shall feel much pleasure in giving it all the assistance in my power.

"*Leicestershire, Feb.* 1807."

ADVERTISEMENT TO THE THIRD NUMBER.

IN presenting the Third Number of this work to the Public, Power begs leave to offer his acknowledgments for the very liberal patronage with which it has been honored; and to express a hope that the unabated zeal of those who have hitherto so admirably conducted it, will enable him to continue it through many future Numbers with equal spirit, variety, and taste. The stock of popular Melodies is far from being exhausted; and there is still in reserve an abundance of beautiful Airs, which call upon Mr. Moore, in the language he so well understands, to save them from the oblivion to which they are hastening.

Power respectfully trusts he will not be thought presumptuous in saying, that he feels proud, as an Irishman, in even the very subordinate share which he can claim, in promoting a Work so creditable to the talents of the Country, — a Work which, from the spirit of nationality it breathes, will do more, he is convinced, towards liberalizing the feelings of society, and producing that brotherhood of sentiment which it is so much our interest to cherish, than could ever be effected by the mere arguments of well-intentioned but uninteresting politicians.

LETTER

TO

THE MARCHIONESS DOWAGER OF DONEGAL,

PREFIXED TO

THE THIRD NUMBER.

WHILE the publisher of these Melodies very properly inscribes them to the Nobility and Gentry of Ireland in géneral, I have much pleasure in selecting *one* from that number, to whom *my* share of the Work is particularly dedicated.   I know that, though your Ladyship has been so long absent from Ireland, you still continue to remember it well and warmly, — that you have not suffered the attractions of English society to produce, like the taste of the lotus, any forgetfulness of your own country, but that even the humble tribute which I offer derives its chief claim upon your interest and sympathy from the appeal which it makes to your patriotism.   Indeed, absence, however fatal to some affections of the heart, rather tends to strengthen our love for the land where we were born; and Ireland is the country, of all others, which an exile from it must remember with most enthusiasm. Those few darker and less amiable traits with which bigotry and misrule have stained her character, and which are too apt to disgust us upon a nearer intercourse, become at a distance softened, or altogether invisible.   Nothing is remembered but her virtues and her misfortunes, — the zeal with which she has always loved liberty, and the barbarous policy which has always withheld it from her, — the ease with which her generous spirit might be conciliated, and the cruel ingenuity which has been exerted to " wring her into undutifulness."[1]

It has been often remarked, and still oftener felt, that in our music is found the truest of all comments upon our history.   The tone of defiance, succeeded by the languor of despondency, — a burst of turbulence dying away into softness, — the sorrows of one moment lost in the levity of the next, — and all that romantic mixture of mirth and sadness, which is naturally produced by the efforts of a lively temperament to shake off, or forget, the wrongs which lie upon it.   Such are the features of our history and character, which we find strongly and faithfully reflected in our music; and there are even many airs, which it is difficult to listen to, without recalling some period or event to which their expression seems applicable.   Sometimes, for instance, when the strain is open and spirited, yet here and there shaded by a mournful recollection, we can fancy that we behold the brave allies of Montrose,[2] marching to the aid of the royal cause, notwithstanding all the perfidy of Charles and his ministers, and remembering just enough of past sufferings to enhance the generosity of their present sacrifice.   The plaintive melodies of Carolan takes us back to the times in which he lived, when our poor countrymen were driven to worship their God in caves, or to quit for ever the land of their birth, — like the bird that abandons the nest which human touch has violated.   In many of these mournful songs we seem to hear the last farewell of the exile,[3] mingling

---

1 A phrase which occurs in a Letter from the Earl of Desmond to the Earl of Ormond, in Elizabeth's time. — " *Scrinia Sacra,*" as quoted by Curry.

2 There are some gratifying accounts of the gallantry of these Irish auxiliaries in "The Complete History of the Wars in Scotland under Montrose " (1660).   See particularly, for the conduct of an Irishman at the battle of Aberdeen, chap. vi. p. 49.; and for a tribute to the bravery of Colonel O'Kyan, chap. vii. 55.   Clarendon owns that the Marquis of Montrose was indebted for much of his miraculous success to the small band of Irish heroes under Macdonnell.

3 The associations of the Hindu music, though more obvious and defined, were far less touching and characteristic.   They divided their songs according to the seasons of the year, by which

regret for the ties which he leaves at home, with sanguine hopes of the high honors that await him abroad, — such honors as were won on the field of Fontenoy, where the valor of Irish Catholics turned the fortune of the day, and extorted from George the Second that memorable exclamation, "Cursed be the laws which deprive me of such subjects!"

Though much has been said of the antiquity of our music, it is certain that our finest and most popular airs are modern; and perhaps we may look no further than the last disgraceful century for the origin of most of those wild and melancholy strains, which were at once the offspring and solace of grief, and were applied to the mind as music was formerly to the body, "*decantare loca dolentia.*" Mr. Pinkerton is of opinion [1] that none of the Scotch popular airs are as old as the middle of the sixteenth century; and though musical antiquaries refer us, for some of our melodies, to so early a period as the fifth century, I am persuaded that there are few, of a *civilized* description, (and by this I mean to exclude all the savage Ceanans, Cries,[2] etc.) which can claim quite so ancient a date as Mr. Pinkerton allows to the Scotch. But music is not the only subject upon which our taste for antiquity has been rather unreasonably indulged; and, however heretical it may be to dissent from these romantic speculations, I cannot help thinking that it is possible to love our country very zealously, and to feel deeply interested in her honor and happiness, without believing that Irish was the language spoken in Paradise; [3] that our ancestors were kind enough to take the trouble of polishing the Greeks,[4] or that Abaris, the Hyperborean, was a native of the North of Ireland.[5]

By some of these zealous antiquarians it has been imagined that the Irish were early acquainted with counterpoint; [6] and they endeavor to support this conjecture by a well-known passage in Giraldus, where he dilates with such elaborate praise upon the beauties of our national minstrelsy. But the terms of this eulogy are much too vague, too deficient in technical accuracy, to prove that even Giraldus himself knew any thing of the artifice of counterpoint. There are many expressions in the Greek and Latin writers which might be cited, with much more plausibility, to prove that they understood the arrangement of music in parts; [7] and it

---

(says Sir William Jones) "they were able to recall the memory of autumnal merriment, at the close of the harvest, or of separation and melancholy during the cold months," etc. — *Asiatic Transactions*, vol. iii. on the Musical Modes of the Hindus. — What the Abbé du Bos says of the symphonies of Lully, may be asserted, with much more probability, of our bold and impassioned airs: — "*Elles auroient produit de ces effets, qui nous paroissent fabuleux dans le récit des anciens, si on les avoit fait entendre à des hommes d'un naturel aussi vif que les Athéniens.*" — "*Réflex. sur la Peinture,*" etc. *tom.* i. sect. 45.

1 Dissertation, prefixed to the 2d volume of his Scottish Ballads.

2 Of which some genuine specimens may be found at the end of Mr. Walker's Work upon the Irish bards. Mr. Bunting has disfigured his last splendid volume by too many of these barbarous rhapsodies.

3 See Advertisement to the Transactions of the Gaelic Society of Dublin.

4 O'Halloran, vol. i. part iv. chap. vii.

5 Id. ib. chap. vi.

6 It is also supposed, but with as little proof, that they understood the diésis, or enharmonic interval. — The Greeks seem to have formed their ears to this delicate gradation of sound; and, whatever difficulties or objections may lie in the way of its *practical* use, we must agree with Mersenne, ("*Préludes de l'Harmonie,*" quest. 7.) that the *theory* of Music would be imperfect without it. Even in practice, too, as Tosi, among others, very justly remarks, (Observations on Florid Song, chap. i. sect. 16.) there is no good performer on the violin who does not make a sensible difference between D sharp and E flat, though, from the imperfection of the instrument, they are the same notes upon the piano-forte. The effect of modulation by enharmonic transitions is also very striking and beautiful.

7 The words ποικίλια and ἑτεροφωνία, in a passage of Plato, and some expressions of Cicero in Fragment, *lib.* ii. *de Republ.*, induced the Abbé Fraguier to maintain that the ancients had a knowledge of counterpoint. M. Burette, however, has answered him, I think, satisfactorily. (*Examen d'un Passage de Platon,* in the 3d vol. of "*Histoire de l'Acad.*") M. Huet is of opinion (*Pensées Diverses*), that what Cicero says of the music of the spheres, in his dream of Scipio, is

is in general now conceded, I believe, by the learned, that, however grand and pathetic the melody of the ancients may have been, it was reserved for the ingenuity of modern Science to transmit the " light of Song " through the variegating prism of Harmony.

Indeed, the irregular scale of the early Irish (in which, as in the music of Scotland, the interval of the fourth was wanting,[1]) must have furnished but wild and refractory subjects to the harmonist. It was only when the invention of Guido began to be known, and the powers of the harp[2] were enlarged by additional strings, that our airs can be supposed to have assumed the sweet character which interests us at present; and while the Scotch persevered in the old mutilation of the scale,[3] our music became by degrees more amenable to the laws of harmony and counterpoint.

While profiting, however, by the improvements of the moderns, our style still keeps its original character sacred from their refinements; and though Carolan, it appears, had frequent opportunities of hearing the works of Geminiani and other great masters, we but rarely find him sacrificing his native simplicity to any ambition of their ornaments, or affectation of their science. In that curious composition, indeed, called his Concerto, it is evident that he labored to imitate Corelli; and this union of manners, so very dissimilar, produces the same kind of uneasy sensation which is felt at a mixture of different styles of architecture. In general, however, the artless flow of our music has preserved itself free from all tinge of foreign innovation;[4] and the chief corruptions of which we have to complain arise from the unskilful performance of our own itinerant musicians, from whom,

sufficient to prove an acquaintance with harmony; but one of the strongest passages, which I recollect, in favor of this supposition, occurs in the Treatise (" Περι Κόσμου ") attributed to Aristotle — Μουσικὴ δὲ ὀξεῖς ἅμα καὶ βαρεῖς, κ. τ. λ.

1 Another lawless peculiarity of our music is the frequent occurrence of, what composers call, consecutive fifths; but this, I must say, is an irregularity which can hardly be avoided by persons not conversant with all the rules of composition. If I may venture, indeed, to cite my own wild attempts in this way, it is a fault which I find myself continually committing, and which has even, at times, appeared so pleasing to my ear, that I have surrendered it to the critic with no small reluctance. May there not be a little pedantry in adhering too rigidly to this rule? — I have been told that there are instances in Haydn, of an undisguised succession of fifths; and Mr. Shield, in his Introduction to Harmony, seems to intimate that Händel has been sometimes guilty of the same irregularity.

2 A singular oversight occurs in an Essay upon the Irish Harp, by Mr. Beauford, which is inserted in the Appendix to Walker's Historical Memoirs: — "The Irish [says he] according to Bromton, in the reign of Henry II. had two kinds of Harps, ' *Hibernici tamen in duobus musici generis instrumentis, quamvis præcipitem et velocem, suavem tamen et jucundum*: the one greatly bold and quick, the other soft and pleasing.' — How a man of Mr. Beauford's learning could so mistake the meaning, and mutilate the grammatical construction of this extract, is unaccountable. The following is the passage as I find it entire in Bromton; and it requires but little Latin to perceive the injustice which has been done to the words of the old Chronicler: — "*et cum Scotia, hujus terræ filia, utatur lyrâ, tympano et choro, ac Wallia cithara, tubis et choro Hibernici tamen in duobus musici generis instrumentis, q u a m v i s p r æ c i p i t e m e t v e l o c e m, s u a v e m t a m e n e t j u c u n d a m, crispatis modulis et intricatis notulis, e ffi c i u n t h a r m o n i a m.*" — "*Hist. Anglic. Script.*" page 1075. I should not have thought this error worth remarking, but that the compiler of the Dissertation on the Harp, prefixed to Mr. Bunting's last Work, has adopted it implicitly.

3 The Scotch lay claim to some of our best airs, but there are strong traits of difference between their melodies and ours. They had formerly the same passion for robbing us of our Saints, and the learned Dempster was for this offence called " The Saint Stealer." It must have been some Irishman, I suppose, who, by way of reprisal, stole Dempster's beautiful wife from him at Pisa. — See this anecdote in the " *Pinacotheca* " of Erythræus, part i. page 25.

4 Among other false refinements of the art, our music (with the exception perhaps of the air called " Mamma, Mamma," and one or two more of the same ludicrous description,) has avoided that puerile mimicry of natural noises, motions, etc., which disgraces so often the works of even Händel himself. D'Alembert ought to have had better taste than to have made the patron of this imitative affectation. — *Discours Préliminaire de l'Encyclopédie.* The reader may find some good remarks on the subject in Avison upon Musical Expression; a work which, though under the name of Avison, was written, it is said, by Dr. Brown.

too frequently, the airs are noted down, encumbered by their tasteless decorations, and responsible for all their ignorant anomalies. Though it be sometimes impossible to trace the original strain, yet, in most of them, "*auri per ramos aura refulget*,"[1] the pure gold of the melody shines through the ungraceful foliage which surrounds it, — and the most delicate and difficult duty of a compiler is to endeavor, by retrenching these inelegant superfluities, and collating the various methods of playing or singing each air, to restore the regularity of its form, and the chaste simplicity of its character.

I must again observe, that in doubting the antiquity of our music, my scepticism extends but to those polished specimens of the art, which it is difficult to conceive anterior to the dawn of modern improvement; and that I would by no means invalidate the claims of Ireland to as early a rank in the annals of minstrelsy, as the most zealous antiquary may be inclined to allow her. In addition, indeed, to the power which music must always have possessed over the minds of a people so ardent and susceptible, the stimulus of persecution was not wanting to quicken our taste into enthusiasm; the charms of song were ennobled with the glories of martyrdom, and the acts against minstrels, in the reigns of Henry VIII. and Elizabeth, were as successful, I doubt not, in making my countrymen musicians, as the penal laws have been in keeping them Catholics.

With respect to the verses which I have written for these Melodies, as they are intended rather to be sung than read, I can answer for their sound with somewhat more confidence than for their sense. Yet it would be affectation to deny that I have given much attention to the task, and that it is not through any want of zeal or industry, if I unfortunately disgrace the sweet airs of my country, by poetry altogether unworthy of their taste, their energy, and their tenderness.

Though the humble nature of my contributions to this work may exempt them from the rigors of literary criticism, it was not to be expected that those touches of political feeling, those tones of national complaint, in which the poetry sometimes sympathizes with the music, would be suffered to pass without censure or alarm. It has been accordingly said, that the tendency of this publication is mischievous,[2] and that I have chosen these airs but as a vehicle of dangerous politics, — as fair and precious vessels (to borrow an image of St. Augustin[3]), from which the wine of error might be administered. To those who identify nationality with treason, and who see, in every effort for Ireland, a system of hostility towards England, — to those, too, who, nursed in the gloom of prejudice, are alarmed by the faintest gleam of liberality that threatens to disturb their darkness, — like that Demophon of old, who, when the sun shone upon him, shivered,[4] — to such men I shall not condescend to offer an apology for the too great warmth of any political sentiment which may occur in the course of these pages.

But as there are many, among the more wise and tolerant, who, with feeling enough to mourn over the wrongs of their country, and sense enough to perceive all the danger of not redressing them, may yet be of opinion that allusions, in the least degree inflammatory, should be avoided in a publication of this popular description — I beg of these respected persons to believe, that there is no one who more sincerely deprecates than I do, any appeal to the passions of an ignorant and angry multitude; but that it is not through that gross and inflammable region of society, a work of this nature could ever have been intended to circulate. It looks

---

1 Vergil, Æneid, *lib.* vi. verse 204.

2 See Letters, under the signatures of Timæus, etc., in the *Morning Post, Pilot,* and other papers.

3 "*Non accuso verba, quasi vasa electa atque pretiosa; sed vinum erroris quod cum eis nobis propinatur.*" — *Lib.* i. *Confess. chap.* xvi.

4 This emblem of modern bigots was head-butler (τραπεζοποιός) to Alexander the Great. — *Sext. Empir. Pyrrh. Hypoth. Lib.* i.

much higher for its audience and readers, — it is found upon the piano-fortes of the rich and the educated, — of those who can afford to have their national zeal a little stimulated, without exciting much dread of the excesses into which it may hurry them; and of many whose nerves may be, now and then, alarmed with advantage, as much more is to be gained by their fears, than could ever be expected from their justice.

Having thus adverted to the principal objection, which has been hitherto made to the poetical part of this work, allow me to add a few words in defence of my ingenious coadjutor, Sir John Stevenson, who has been accused of having spoiled the simplicity of the airs by the chromatic richness of his symphonies, and the elaborate variety of his harmonies. We might cite the example of the admirable Haydn, who has sported through all the mazes of musical science, in his arrangement of the simplest Scottish melodies; but it appears to me, that Sir John Stevenson has brought to this task an innate and national feeling, which it would be vain to expect from a foreigner, however tasteful or judicious. Through many of his own compositions we trace a vein of Irish sentiment, which points him out as peculiarly suited to catch the spirit of his country's music; and, far from agreeing with those fastidious critics who think that his symphonies have nothing kindred with the airs which they introduce, I would say that, on the contrary, they resemble, in general, those illuminated initials of old manuscripts, which are of the same character with the writing which follows, though more highly colored and more curiously ornamented.

In those airs, which he has arranged for voices, his skill has particularly distinguished itself, and, though it cannot be denied that a single melody most naturally expresses the language of feeling and passion, yet often, when a favorite strain has been dismissed, as having lost its charm of novelty for the ear, it returns, in a harmonized shape, with new claims on our interest and attention; and to those who study the delicate artifices of composition, the construction of the inner parts of these pieces must afford, I think, considerable satisfaction. Every voice has an air to itself, a flowing succession of notes, which might be heard with pleasure, independently of the rest; — so artfully has the harmonist (if I may thus express it) *gavelled* the melody, distributing an equal portion of its sweetness to every part.

If your Ladyship's love of Music were not well known to me, I should not have hazarded so long a letter upon the subject; but as, probably, I may have presumed too far upon your partiality, the best revenge you now can take is to write me just as long a letter upon Painting; and I promise to attend to your theory of the art, with a pleasure only surpassed by that which I have so often derived from your practice of it. — May the mind which such talents adorn, continue calm as it is bright, and happy as it is virtuous!

Believe me, your Ladyship's

Grateful Friend and Servant,

THOMAS MOORE.

ADVERTISEMENT TO THE FOURTH NUMBER.

THIS Number of the Melodies ought to have appeared much earlier; and the writer of the words is ashamed to confess, that the delay of its publication must be imputed chiefly, if not entirely, to him. He finds it necessary to make this avowal, not only for the purpose of removing all blame from the Publisher, but in consequence of a rumor, which has been circulated industriously in Dublin, that the Irish Government had interfered to prevent the continuance of the Work.

This would be, indeed, a revival of Henry the Eighth's enactments against Minstrels, and it is flattering to find that so much importance is attached to our compilation, even by such persons as the inventors of the report. Bishop Lowth, it is true, was of opinion, that *one* song, like the *Hymn* to *Harmodius*, would have done more towards rousing the spirit of the Romans, than *all* the Philippics of Cicero. But we live in wiser and less musical times; ballads have long lost their revolutionary powers, and we question if even a " Lillibullero " would produce any very *serious* consequences at present. It is needless, therefore, to add, that there is no truth in the report; and we trust that whatever belief it obtained was founded more upon the character of *the Government* than of *the Work.*

The Airs of the last Number, though full of originality and beauty, were, in general, perhaps, too curiously selected to become all at once as popular as, we think, they deserve to be. The public are apt to be reserved towards new acquaintances in music, and this, perhaps, is one of the reasons why many modern composers introduce none but old friends to their notice. It is, indeed, natural that persons, who love music only by association, should be somewhat slow in feeling the charms of a new and strange melody; while those, on the other hand, who have a quick sensibility for this enchanting art, will as naturally seek and enjoy novelty, because in every variety of strain they find a fresh combination of ideas; and the sound has scarcely reached the ear, before the heart has as rapidly rendered it into imagery and sentiment. After all, however, it cannot be denied that the most popular of our National Airs are also the most beautiful; and it has been our wish, in the present Number, to select from those Melodies only which have long been listened to and admired. The least known in the collection is the Air of " *Love's Young Dream;* " but it will be found, I think, one of those easy and artless strangers whose merit the heart instantly acknowledges. **T. M.**

BURY STREET, ST. JAMES'S, *November*, 1811.

ADVERTISEMENT TO THE FIFTH NUMBER.

IT is but fair to those, who take an interest in this Work, to state that it is now very near its termination, and that the Sixth Number, which shall speedily appear, will, most probably, be the last of the series. Three volumes will then have been completed, according to the original plan, and the Proprietors desire me to say that a List of Subscribers will be published with the concluding Number.

It is not so much, I must add, from a want of materials, and still less from any abatement of zeal or industry, that we have adopted the resolution of bringing our task to a close; but we feel so proud, still more for our country's sake than our own, of the general interest which this purely Irish Work has excited, and so anxious lest a particle of that interest should be lost by too long a protraction of its existence, that we think it wiser to take away the cup from the lip, while its flavor is yet, we trust, fresh and sweet, than to risk any further trial of the charm, or give so much as not to leave some wish for more.

In speaking thus, I allude entirely to the Airs, which are, of course, the main attraction of these Volumes; and though we have still a great many popular and delightful Melodies to produce,[1] it cannot be denied that we should soon experience considerable difficulty in equalling the richness and novelty of the earlier numbers, for which, as we had the choice of all before us, we naturally selected only the most rare and beautiful. The Poetry, too, would be sure to sympathize with the decline of the Music; and, however feebly my words have kept pace with the *excellence* of the Airs, they would follow their *falling off*, I fear, with wonderful alacrity. Both pride and prudence, therefore, counsel us to come to a close, while yet our Work is, we believe, flourishing and attractive, and thus, in the imperial attitude, "*stantes mori*," before we incur the charge either of altering for the worse, or what is equally unpardonable, continuing too long the same.

We beg to say, however, that it is only in the event of our failing to find Airs as good as most of those we have given, that we mean thus to anticipate the natural period of dissolution (like those Indians who when their relatives become worn out, put them to death); and they who are desirous of retarding this Euthanasia of the Irish Melodies, cannot better effect their wish than by contributing to our collection, — not what are called curious Airs, for we have abundance of such, and they are, in general, *only* curious, — but any real sweet and expressive Songs of our Country, which either chance or research may have brought into their hands.

MAYFIELD COTTAGE, Ashbourne, *December*, 1813.   T. M.

ADVERTISEMENT TO THE SIXTH NUMBER.

IN presenting this Sixth Number to the Public as our last, and bidding adieu to the Irish Harp for ever, we shall not answer very confidently for the strength of our resolution, nor feel quite sure that it may not turn out to be one of those eternal farewells which a lover takes occasionally of his mistress, merely to enhance, perhaps, the pleasure of their next meeting. Our only motive, indeed, for discontinuing the Work was a fear that our treasures were nearly exhausted, and a natural unwillingness to descend to the gathering of mere seed-pearl, after the really precious gems it has been our lot to string together. The announcement, however, of this intention, in our Fifth Number, has excited a degree of anxiety in the lovers of Irish Music, not only pleasant and flattering, but highly useful to us; for the various contributions we have received in consequence, have enriched our collection with so many choice and beautiful Airs, that should we adhere to our present resolution of publishing no more, it would certainly furnish an instance of forbearance unexampled in the history of poets and musicians. To one Gentleman in particular, who has been for many years resident in England, but who has not forgot, among his various pursuits, either the language or the melodies of his native country, we beg to offer our best thanks for the many interesting communications with which he has favored us. We trust that neither he nor any other of our kind friends will relax in those efforts by which we have been so considerably assisted; for, though our work must now be looked upon as defunct, yet — as Réaumur found out the art of making the cicada sing after it was dead — it is just possible that we may, some time or other, try a similar experiment upon the Irish Melodies.   T. M.

MAYFIELD, Ashbourne, *March*, 1815.

1 Among these is *Savourna Deelish*, which I have been hitherto only withheld from selecting by the diffidence I feel in treading upon the same ground with Mr. Campbell, whose beautiful words to this fine Air have taken too strong possession of all ears and hearts, for me to think of following in his footsteps with any success. I suppose, however, as a matter of duty, I must attempt the air for our next Number.

ADVERTISEMENT TO THE SEVENTH NUMBER.

HAD I consulted only my own judgment, this Work would not have extended beyond the Six Numbers already published; which contain the flower, perhaps, of our national melodies, and have now attained a rank in public favor, of which I would not willingly risk the forfeiture, by degenerating, in any way, from those merits that were its source. Whatever treasures of our music were still in reserve, (and it will be seen, I trust, that they are numerous and valuable,) I would gladly have left to future poets to glean, and, with the ritual words "*tibi trado*," would have delivered up the torch into other hands, before it had lost much of its light in my own. But the call for a continuance of the work has been, as I understand from the Publisher, so general, and we have received so many contributions of old and beautiful airs,[1] — the suppression of which, for the enhancement of those we have published, would too much resemble the policy of the Dutch in burning their spices, — that I have been persuaded, though not without much diffidence in my success, to commence a new series of the Irish Melodies.

T. M.

DEDICATION

TO

THE MARCHIONESS OF HEADFORT,

PREFIXED TO

THE TENTH NUMBER.

IT is with a pleasure, not unmixed with melancholy, that I dedicate the last Number of the Irish Melodies to your Ladyship; nor can I have any doubt that the feelings with which you receive the tribute will be of the same mingled and saddened tone. To you, who, though but little beyond the season of childhood, when the earlier numbers of this work appeared, — lent the aid of your beautiful voice, and, even then, exquisite feeling for music, to the happy circle who met, to sing them together, under your father's roof, the gratification, whatever it may be, which this humble offering brings, cannot be otherwise than darkened by the mournful reflection, how many of the voices, which then joined with ours, are now silent in death!

I am not without hope that, as far as regards the grace and spirit of the Melodies, you will find this closing portion of the work not unworthy of what has preceded it. The Sixteen Airs, of which the Number and the Supplement consists, have been selected from the immense mass of Irish music, which has been for years past accumulating in my hands; and it was from a desire to include all that appeared most worthy of preservation, that the four supplementary songs which follow this Tenth Number have been added.

Trusting that I may yet again, in remembrance of old times, hear our voices together in some of the harmonized airs of this Volume, I have the honor to subscribe myself, Your Ladyship's faithful Friend and Servant,

THOMAS MOORE.

SLOPERTON COTTAGE, *May,* 1834.

---

1 One Gentleman, in particular, whose name I shall feel happy in being allowed to mention, has not only sent us nearly forty ancient airs, but has communicated many curious fragments of Irish poetry, and some interesting traditions current in the country where he resides, illustrated by sketches of the romantic scenery to which they refer; all of which, though too late for the present Number, will be of infinite service to us in the prosecution of our task.

IRISH MELODIES.

GO WHERE GLORY WAITS THEE.

Go where glory waits thee,
But while fame elates thee,
  Oh! still remember me.
When the praise thou meetest
To thine ear is sweetest,
  Oh! then remember me.
Other arms may press thee,
Dearer friends caress thee,
All the joys that bless thee,
  Sweeter far may be;
But when friends are nearest,
And when joys are dearest,
  Oh! then remember me!

When, at eve, thou rovest
By the star thou lovest,
  Oh! then remember me.
Think, when home returning,
Bright we 've seen it burning,
  Oh! thus remember me.
Oft as summer closes,
When thine eye reposes
On its lingering roses,
  Once so loved by thee,
Think of her who wove them,
Her who made thee love them,
  Oh! then remember me.

When, around thee dying,
Autumn leaves are lying,
  Oh! then remember me.
And, at night, when gazing
On the gay hearth blazing,
  Oh! still remember me.
Then should music, stealing
All the soul of feeling,
To thy heart appealing,
  Draw one tear from thee;
Then let memory bring thee
Strains I used to sing thee, —
  Oh! then remember me.

WAR SONG.

REMEMBER THE GLORIES OF BRIEN THE BRAVE.[1]

REMEMBER the glories of Brien the brave,
  Tho' the days of the hero are o'er;
Tho' lost to Mononia [2] and cold in the
    grave,
  He returns to Kinkora [3] no more.
That star of the field, which so often
    hath poured
  Its beam on the battle, is set;
But enough of its glory remains on each
    sword,
  To light us to victory yet.

Mononia! when Nature embellished the
    tint
  Of thy fields, and thy mountains so
    fair,
Did she ever intend that a tyrant should
    print
  The footstep of slavery there?
No! Freedom, whose smile we shall
    never resign,
  Go, tell our invaders, the Danes,
That 't is sweeter to bleed for an age at
    thy shrine,
  Than to sleep but a moment in chains.

Forget not our wounded companions,
    who stood [4]
  In the day of distress by our side;
While the moss of the valley grew red
    with their blood,

---

1 Brien Boromhe, the great monarch of Ireland, who was killed at the battle of Clontarf, in the beginning of the 11th century, after having defeated the Danes in twenty-five engagements.

2 Munster.

3 The palace of Brien.

4 This alludes to an interesting circumstance related of the Dalgais, the favorite troops of Brien, when they were interrupted in their return

They stirred not, but conquered and
died.
That sun which now blesses our arms
with his light,
Saw them fall upon Ossory's plain; —
Oh! let him not blush, when he leaves
us to-night,
To find that they fell there in vain.

ERIN! THE TEAR AND THE SMILE
IN THINE EYES.

ERIN, the tear and the smile in thine
eyes,
Blend like the rainbow that hangs in thy
skies!
Shining through sorrow's stream,
Saddening through pleasure's beam,
Thy suns with doubtful gleam,
Weep while they rise.

Erin, thy silent tear never shall cease,
Erin, thy languid smile ne'er shall in-
crease,
Till, like the rainbow's light,
Thy various tints unite,
And form in heaven's sight
One arch of peace!

OH! BREATHE NOT HIS NAME.

OH! breathe not his name, let it sleep
in the shade,
Where cold and unhonored his relics are
laid:
Sad, silent, and dark, be the tears that
we shed,
As the night-dew that falls on the grass
o'er his head.

But the night-dew that falls, tho' in silence it weeps,
Shall brighten with verdure the grave
where he sleeps;
And the tear that we shed, tho' in secret
it rolls,
Shall long keep his memory green in our
souls.

WHEN HE, WHO ADORES THEE.

WHEN he, who adores thee, has left but
the name
Of his fault and his sorrows behind,
Oh! say wilt thou weep, when they
darken the fame
Of a life that for thee was resigned?
Yes, weep, and however my foes may
condemn,
Thy tears shall efface their decree;
For Heaven can witness, tho' guilty to
them,
I have been but too faithful to thee.

With thee were the dreams of my earli-
est love;
Every thought of my reason was thine;
In my last humble prayer to the Spirit
above,
Thy name shall be mingled with mine.
Oh! blest are the lovers and friends who
shall live
The days of thy glory to see;
But the next dearest blessing that Heaven
can give
Is the pride of thus dying for thee.

THE HARP THAT ONCE THRO'
TARA'S HALLS.

THE harp that once thro' Tara's halls
The soul of music shed,
Now hangs as mute on Tara's walls,
As if that soul were fled. —
So sleeps the pride of former days,
So glory's thrill is o'er,
And hearts, that once beat high for praise,
Now feel that pulse no more.

No more to chiefs and ladies bright
The harp of Tara swells;
The chord alone, that breaks at night,
Its tale of ruin tells.
Thus Freedom now so seldom wakes,
The only throb she gives,
Is when some heart indignant breaks,
To show that still she lives.

from the battle of Clontarf, by Fitzpatrick, prince
of Ossory. The wounded men entreated that they
might be allowed to fight with the rest. — "*Let
stakes* [they said] *be stuck in the ground, and
suffer each of us, tied to and supported by one of
these stakes, to be placed in his rank by the side*
of a sound man." " Between seven and eight
hundred men [adds O'Halloran] pale, emaciated,
and supported in this manner, appeared mixed
with the foremost of the troops; — never was
such another sight exhibited." — " *History of
Ireland*," book xii. chap. i.

FLY NOT YET.

FLY not yet, 't is just the hour,
When pleasure, like the midnight flower
That scorns the eye of vulgar light,
Begins to bloom for sons of night,
   And maids who love the moon.
'T was but to bless these hours of shade
That beauty and the moon were made;
'T is then their soft attractions glowing
Set the tides and goblets flowing.
   Oh! stay, — Oh! stay, —
Joy so seldom weaves a chain
Like this to-night, that oh, 't is pain
   To break its links so soon.

Fly not yet, the fount that played
In times of old through Ammon's shade,[1]
Though icy cold by day it ran,
Yet still, like souls of mirth, began
   To burn when night was near.
And thus, should woman's heart and looks
At noon be cold as winter brooks,
Nor kindle till the night, returning,
Brings their genial hour for burning.
   Oh! stay, — oh! stay, —
When did morning ever break,
And find such beaming eyes awake
   As those that sparkle here?

OH! THINK NOT MY SPIRITS ARE ALWAYS AS LIGHT.

OH! think not my spirits are always as light,
   And as free from a pang as they seem to you now;
Nor expect that the heart-beaming smile of to-night
   Will return with to-morrow to brighten my brow.
No! — life is a waste of wearisome hours,
   Which seldom the rose of enjoyment adorns;
And the heart that is soonest awake to the flowers,
   Is always the first to be touched by the thorns.
But send round the bowl, and be happy awhile —
   May we never meet worse, in our pilgrimage here,

1 Solis Fons, near the Temple of Ammon.

Than the tear that enjoyment may gild with a smile,
   And the smile that compassion can turn to a tear.

The thread of our life would be dark, Heaven knows!
   If it were not with friendship and love intertwined;
And I care not how soon I may sink to repose,
   When these blessings shall cease to be dear to my mind.
But they who have loved the fondest, the purest,
   Too often have wept o'er the dream they believed;
And the heart that has slumbered in friendship securest,
   Is happy indeed if 't was never deceived.
But send round the bowl; while a relic of truth
   Is in man or in woman, this prayer shall be mine, —
That the sunshine of love may illumine our youth,
   And the moonlight of friendship console our decline.

THO' THE LAST GLIMPSE OF ERIN WITH SORROW I SEE.

THO' the last glimpse of Erin with sorrow I see,
Yet wherever thou art shall seem Erin to me;
In exile thy bosom shall still be my home,
And thine eyes make my climate wherever we roam.

To the gloom of some desert or cold rocky shore,
Where the eye of the stranger can haunt us no more,
I will fly with my Coulin, and think the rough wind
Less rude than the foes we leave frowning behind.

And I 'll gaze on thy gold hair as graceful it wreathes,
And hang o'er thy soft harp, as wildly it breathes;

Nor dread that the cold-hearted Saxon
will tear
One chord from that harp, or one lock
from that hair.[1]

RICH AND RARE WERE THE GEMS SHE WORE.[2]

RICH and rare were the gems she wore,
And a bright gold ring on her wand she
bore;
But oh! her beauty was far beyond
Her sparkling gems, or snow-white wand.

"Lady! dost thou not fear to stray,
"So lone and lovely through this bleak
way?
"Are Erin's sons so good or so cold,
"As not to be tempted by woman or
gold?"

"Sir Knight! I feel not the least alarm,
"No son of Erin will offer me harm:—
"For though they love woman and
golden store,
"Sir Knight! they love honor and virtue
more!"

On she went and her maiden smile
In safety lighted her round the green
isle;
And blest for ever is she who relied
Upon Erin's honor, and Erin's pride.

1 "In the twenty-eighth year of the reign of
Henry VIII. an Act was made respecting the
habits, and dress in general, of the Irish, whereby
all persons were restrained from being shorn or
shaven above the ears, or from wearing Glibbes,
or *Coulins* (long locks), on their heads, or hair on
their upper lip, called Crommeal. On this occasion a song was written by one of our bards, in
which an Irish virgin is made to give the preference to her dear *Coulin* (or the youth with the
flowing locks) to all strangers (by which the
English were meant), or those who wore their
habits. Of this song, the air alone has reached
us, and is universally admired."—*Walker's
"Historical Memoirs of Irish Bards,"* p. 134.
Mr. Walker informs us also, that, about the same
period, there were some harsh measures taken
against the Irish Minstrels.

2 This ballad is founded upon the following
anecdote:—"The people were inspired with
such a spirit of honor, virtue, and religion, by
the great example of Brien, and by his excellent
administration, that, as a proof of it, we are informed that a young lady of great beauty, adorned
with jewels and a costly dress, undertook a jour-

AS A BEAM O'ER THE FACE OF THE WATERS MAY GLOW.

As a beam o'er the face of the waters may
glow
While the tide runs in darkness and coldness below,
So the cheek may be tinged with a warm
sunny smile,
Though the cold heart to ruin runs darkly
the while.

One fatal remembrance, one sorrow that
throws
Its bleak shade alike o'er our joys and
our woes,
To which life nothing darker or brighter
can bring
For which joy has no balm and affliction
no sting—

Oh! this thought in the midst of enjoyment will stay,
Like a dead, leafless branch in the summer's bright ray;
The beams of the warm sun play round
it in vain,
It may smile in his light, but it blooms
not again.

THE MEETING OF THE WATERS.[3]

THERE is not in the wide world a valley
so sweet
As that vale in whose bosom the bright
waters meet;[4]
Oh! the last rays of feeling and life must
depart,
Ere the bloom of that valley shall fade
from my heart.

ney alone, from one end of the kingdom to the
other, with a wand only in her hand, at the top
of which was a ring of exceeding great value;
and such an impression had the laws and government of this Monarch made on the minds of all
the people, that no attempt was made upon her
honor, nor was she robbed of her clothes or
jewels."—*Warner's "History of Ireland,"*
vol. i. book x.

3 "The Meeting of the Waters" forms a part
of that beautiful scenery which lies between
Rathdrum and Arklow, in the county of Wicklow, and these lines were suggested by a visit
to this romantic spot, in the summer of the year
1807.

4 The rivers Avon and Avoca.

Yet it *was* not that nature had shed o'er
the scene
Her purest of crystal and brightest of
green ;
'T was *not* her soft magic of streamlet or
hill,
Oh ! no, — it was something more exquisite still.

'T was that friends, the beloved of my
bosom, were near,
Who made every dear scene of enchantment more dear,
And who felt how the best charms of
nature improve,
When we see them reflected from looks
that we love.

Sweet vale of Avoca ! how calm could I
rest
In thy bosom of shade, with the friends
I love best,
Where the storms that we feel in this cold
world should cease,
And our hearts, like thy waters, be min-
gled in peace.

HOW DEAR TO ME THE HOUR.

How dear to me the hour when daylight
dies,
  And sunbeams melt along the silent sea,
For then sweet dreams of other days arise,
  And memory breathes her vesper sigh
  to thee.

And, as I watch the line of light, that
plays
  Along the smooth wave toward the
  burning west,
I long to tread that golden path of rays,
  And think 't would lead to some bright
  isle of rest.

TAKE BACK THE VIRGIN PAGE.
WRITTEN ON RETURNING A BLANK BOOK.

TAKE back the virgin page,
  White and unwritten still;
Some hand, more calm and sage,
  The leaf must fill.
Thoughts come, as pure as light,
  Pure as even *you* require :
But, oh ! each word I write
  Love turns to fire.

Yet let me keep the book :
  Oft shall my heart renew,
When on its leaves I lcok,
  Dear thoughts of you.
Like you, 't is fair and bright;
  Like you, too bright and fair
To let wild passion write
  One wrong wish there.

Haply, when from those eyes
  Far, far away I roam,
Should calmer thoughts arise
  Towards you and home;
Fancy may trace some line,
  Worthy those eyes to meet,
Thoughts that not burn, but shine,
  Pure, calm, and sweet.

And as, o'er ocean far,
  Seamen their records keep,
Led by some hidden star
  Thro' the cold deep;
So may the words I write
  Tell thro' what storms I stray —
You still the unseen light,
  Guiding my way.

THE LEGACY.

WHEN in death I shall calmly recline,
  O bear my heart to my mistress dear ;
Tell her it lived upon smiles and wine
  Of the brightest hue, while it lingered
  here.
Bid her not shed one tear of sorrow
  To sully a heart so brilliant and light;
But balmy drops of the red grape borrow,
  To bathe the relic from morn till
  night.

When the light of my song is o'er,
  Then take my harp to your ancient
  hall;
Hang it up at that friendly door,
  Where weary travellers love to call.[1]
Then if some bard, who roams forsaken,
  Revive its soft note in passing along,
Oh ! let one thought of its master waken
  Your warmest smile for the child of
  song.

1 " In every house was one or two harps, free
to all travellers, who were the more caressed, the
more they excelled in music." — *O'Halloran.*

Keep this cup, which is now o'erflowing,
  To grace your revel, when I 'm at
    rest;
Never, oh! never its balm bestowing
  On lips that beauty hath seldom blest.
But when some warm devoted lover
  To her he adores shall bathe its brim,
Then, then my spirit around shall hover,
  And hallow each drop that foams for
    him.

HOW OFT HAS THE BANSHEE CRIED.

How oft has the Banshee cried,
How oft has death untied
  Bright links that Glory wove,
  Sweet bonds entwined by Love!
Peace to each manly soul that sleepeth;
Rest to each faithful eye that weepeth;
  Long may the fair and brave
  Sigh o'er the hero's grave.

We 're fallen upon gloomy days! [1]
Star after star decays,
  Every bright name, that shed
  Light o'er the land, is fled.
Dark falls the tear of him who mourneth
Lost joy, or hope that ne'er returneth;
  But brightly flows the tear,
  Wept o'er a hero's bier.

Quenched are our beacon lights —
Thou, of the Hundred Fights! [2]
  Thou, on whose burning tongue
  Truth, peace, and freedom hung! [3]
Both mute, — but long as valor shineth,
Or mercy's soul at war repineth,
  So long shall Erin's pride
  Tell how they lived and died.

1 I have endeavored here, without losing that
Irish character, which it is my object to preserve
throughout this work, to allude to the sad and
ominous fatality, by which England has been deprived of so many great and good men, at a
moment when she most requires all the aids of
talent and integrity.

2 This designation, which has been before applied to Lord Nelson, is the title given to a celebrated Irish Hero, in a Poem by O'Guive, the
bard of O'Niel, which is quoted in the " Philosophical Survey of the South of Ireland," page
433. " Con, of the hundred Fights, sleep in thy
grass-grown tomb, and upbraid not our defeats
with thy victories."

3 Fox, " *Romanorum ultimus.*"

WE MAY ROAM THROUGH THIS WORLD.

WE may roam thro' this world, like a
    child at a feast,
  Who but sips of a sweet, and then flies
    to the rest;
And, when pleasure begins to grow dull
    in the east,
  We may order our wings and be off to
    the west;
But if hearts that feel, and eyes that
    smile,
  Are the dearest gifts that heaven sup-
    plies,
We never need leave our own green isle,
  For sensitive hearts, and for sun-bright
    eyes.
Then remember, wherever your goblet is
    crowned,
  Thro' this world, whether eastward or
    westward you roam,
When a cup to the smile of dear woman
    goes round,
  Oh! remember the smile which adorns
    her at home.

In England, the garden of Beauty is kept
  By a dragon of prudery placed within
    call;
But so oft this unamiable dragon has
    slept,
  That the garden's but carelessly watched
    after all.
Oh! they want the wild sweet-briery
    fence,
  Which round the flowers of Erin
    dwells;
Which warns the touch, while winning
    the sense,
  Nor charms us least when it most repels.
Then remember, wherever your goblet is
    crowned,
  Thro' this world, whether eastward or
    westward you roam,
When a cup to the smile of dear woman
    goes round,
  Oh! remember the smile that adorns
    her at home.

In France, when the heart of a woman
    sets sail,
  On the ocean of wedlock its fortune
    to try,

Love seldom goes far in a vessel so frail,
But just pilots her off, and then bids
her good-by.
While the daughters of Erin keep the
boy,
Ever smiling beside his faithful oar,
Thro' billows of woe, and beams of joy,
The same as he looked when he left
the shore.
Then remember, wherever your goblet is
crowned,
Thro' this world, whether eastward or
westward you roam,
When a cup to the smile of dear woman
goes round,
Oh! remember the smile that adorns
her at home.

EVELEEN'S BOWER.

OH! weep for the hour,
When to Eveleen's bower
The Lord of the Valley with false vows
came;
The moon hid her light
From the heavens that night,
And wept behind her clouds o'er the
maiden's shame.

The clouds past soon
From the chaste cold moon,
And heaven smiled again with her vestal
flame;
But none will see the day,
When the clouds shall pass away,
Which that dark hour left upon Eveleen's
fame.

The white snow lay
On the narrow path-way,
When the Lord of the Valley crost over
the moor;
And many a deep print
On the white snow's tint
Showed the track of his footstep to
Eveleen's door.

The next sun's ray
Soon melted away
Every trace on the path where the false
Lord came;
But there's a light above,
Which alone can remove
That stain upon the snow of fair Eve-
leen's fame.

LET ERIN REMEMBER THE DAYS OF OLD.

LET Erin remember the days of old,
Ere her faithless sons betrayed her;
When Malachi wore the collar of gold,[1]
Which he won from her proud invader,
When her kings, with standard of green
unfurled,
Led the Red-Branch Knights to
danger; [2] —
Ere the emerald gem of the western
world
Was set in the crown of a stranger.

On Lough Neagh's bank as the fisher-
man strays,
When the clear cold eve's declining,
He sees the round towers of other days
In the wave beneath him shining;
Thus shall memory often, in dreams
sublime,
Catch a glimpse of the days that are
over;
Thus, sighing, look thro' the waves of
time
For the long-faded glories they cover.[3]

1 "This brought on an encounter between
Malachi (the Monarch of Ireland in the tenth
century) and the Danes, in which Malachi defeated two of their champions, whom he encoun-
tered successively, hand to hand, taking a collar
of gold from the neck of one, and carrying off the
sword of the other, as trophies of his victory."
— *Warner's "History of Ireland,"* vol. i.
book ix.

2 " Military orders of knights were very early
established in Ireland: long before the birth of
Christ we find an hereditary order of Chivalry in
Ulster, called *Curaidhe na Craiobhe ruadh*, or
the Knights of the Red Branch, from their chief
seat in Emania, adjoining to the palace of the Ulster kings, called *Teagh na Craiobhe ruadh,* or the
Academy of the Red Branch; and contiguous to
which was a large hospital, founded for the sick
knights and soldiers, called *Bronbhearg,* or the
House of the Sorrowful Soldier." — *O'Halloran's
Introduction,* etc., part i. chap. 5.

3 It was an old tradition, in the time of Giraldus, that Lough Neagh had been originally a
fountain, by whose sudden overflowing the country was inundated, and a whole region, like the
Atlantis of Plato, overwhelmed. He says that
the fishermen, in clear weather, used to point out
to strangers the tall ecclesiastical towers under
the water. *Piscatores aquæ illius turres ecclesi-
asticas, quæ more patriæ arctæ sunt et altæ,
necnon et rotundæ, sub undis manifeste sereno
tempore conspiciunt, et extraneis transeuntibus,
reique causas admirantibus, frequenter osten-
dunt.* — "*Topogr. Hib.*" dist. 2. c. 9.

THE SONG OF FIONNUALA.[1]

SILENT, oh Moyle, be the roar of thy
water,
Break not, ye breezes, your chain of
repose,
While, murmuring mournfully, Lir's
lonely daughter
Tells to the night-star her tale of woes.
When shall the swan, her death-note
singing,
Sleep, with wings in darkness furled?
When will heaven, its sweet bell ringing,
Call my spirit from this stormy world?

Sadly, oh Moyle, to thy winter-wave
weeping,
Fate bids me languish long ages away;
Yet still in her darkness doth Erin lie
sleeping,
Still doth the pure light its dawning
delay.
When will that day-star, mildly springing,
Warm our isle with peace and love?
When will heaven, its sweet bell ringing,
Call my spirit to the fields above?

COME, SEND ROUND THE WINE.

COME, send round the wine, and leave
points of belief
To simpleton sages, and reasoning
fools;
This moment 's a flower too fair and brief,
To be withered and stained by the dust
of the schools.
Your glass may be purple, and mine may
be blue,
But, while they are filled from the same
bright bowl,
The fool, who would quarrel for difference of hue,
Deserves not the comfort they shed o'er
the soul.

1 To make this story intelligible in a song
would require a much greater number of verses
than any one is authorized to inflict upon an
audience at once; the reader must therefore
be content to learn, in a note, that Fionnuala,
the daughter of Lir, was, by some supernatural
power, transformed into a swan, and condemned
to wander, for many hundred years, over certain
lakes and rivers in Ireland, till the coming of
Christianity, when the first sound of the mass-
bell was to be the signal of her release. — I found
this fanciful fiction among some manuscript translations from the Irish, which were begun under
the direction of that enlightened friend of Ireland,
the late Countess of Moira.

Shall I ask the brave soldier, who fights
by my side
In the cause of mankind, if our creeds
agree?
Shall I give up the friend I have valued
and tried,
If he kneel not before the same altar
with me?
From the heretic girl of my soul should I
fly,
To seek somewhere else a more orthodox kiss?
No, perish the hearts, and the laws that
try
Truth, valor, or love, by a standard
like this!

SUBLIME WAS THE WARNING.

SUBLIME was the warning that Liberty
spoke,
And grand was the moment when Span-
iards awoke
Into life and revenge from the con-
queror's chain.
Oh, Liberty! let not this spirit have rest,
Till it move, like a breeze, o'er the waves
of the west —
Give the light of your look to each sor-
rowing spot,
Nor, oh, be the Shamrock of Erin forgot
While you add to your garland the
Olive of Spain!

If the fame of our fathers, bequeathed
with their rights,
Give to country its charm, and to home
its delights,
If deceit be a wound, and suspicion a
stain,
Then, ye men of Iberia, our cause is the
same!
And oh! may his tomb want a tear and a
name,
Who would ask for a nobler, a holier
death,
Than to turn his last sigh into victory's
breath,
For the Shamrock of Erin and Olive
of Spain!

Ye Blakes and O'Donnels, whose fathers
resigned
The green hills of their youth, among
strangers to find

That repose which, at home, they had
sighed for in vain,
Join, join in our hope that the flame,
which you light,
May be felt yet in Erin, as calm, and as
bright,
And forgive even Albion while blushing
she draws,
Like a truant, her sword, in the long-
slighted cause
Of the Shamrock of Erin and Olive of
Spain!

God prosper the cause! — oh, it cannot
but thrive,
While the pulse of one patriot heart is
alive,
Its devotion to feel, and its rights to
maintain;
Then, how sainted by sorrow, its martyrs
will die!
The finger of Glory shall point where
they lie;
While, far from the footstep of coward
or slave,
The young spirit of Freedom shall shelter
their grave
Beneath Shamrocks of Erin and Olives
of Spain!

BELIEVE ME, IF ALL THOSE EN-
DEARING YOUNG CHARMS.

BELIEVE me, if all those endearing young
charms,
Which I gaze on so fondly to-day,
Were to change by to-morrow, and fleet
in my arms,
Like fairy-gifts fading away,
Thou wouldst still be adored, as this
moment thou art,
Let thy loveliness fade as it will,
And around the dear ruin each wish of
my heart
Would entwine itself verdantly still.

It is not while beauty and youth are thine
own,
And thy cheeks unprofaned by a tear,
That the fervor and faith of a soul can be
known,
To which time will but make thee more
dear;

No, the heart that has truly loved never
forgets,
But as truly loves on to the close,
As the sun-flower turns on her god, when
he sets,
The same look which she turned when
he rose.

ERIN, OH ERIN.

LIKE the bright lamp, that shone in
Kildare's holy fane,[1]
And burn'd thro' long ages of darkness
and storm,
Is the heart that sorrows have frowned
on in vain,
Whose spirit outlives them, unfading
and warm.
Erin, oh Erin, thus bright thro' the tears
Of a long night of bondage, thy spirit
appears.

The nations have fallen, and thou still
art young,
Thy sun is but rising, when others are
set;
And tho' slavery's cloud o'er thy morning
hath hung,
The full noon of freedom shall beam
round thee yet.
Erin, oh Erin, tho' long in the shade,
Thy star will shine out when the proudest shall fade.

Unchilled by the rain, and unwaked by
the wind,
The lily lies sleeping thro' winter's
cold hour,
Till Spring's light touch her fetters unbind,
And daylight and liberty bless the
young flower.[2]
Thus Erin, oh Erin, *thy* winter is past,
And the hope that lived thro' it shall
blossom at last.

1 The inextinguishable fire of St. Bridget, at
Kildare, which Giraldus mentions: —"*apud Kil-
dariam occurrit Ignis Sanctæ Brigidæ, quem
inextinguibilem vocant; non quod extingui non
possit, sed quod tam solicite moniales et sanctæ
mulieres ignem, suppentente materia, fovent et
nutriunt, ut a tempore virginis per tot annorum
curricula semper mansit inextinctus.*" — *Girald.
Camb. "de Mirabil. Hibern." dist.* 2. c. 34.

2 Mrs. H. Tighe, in her exquisite lines on the

DRINK TO HER.

DRINK to her, who long
   Hath waked the poet's sigh,
The girl, who gave to song
   What gold could never buy.
Oh! woman's heart was made
   For minstrel hands alone;
By other fingers played,
   It yields not half the tone.
Then here 's to her, who long
   Hath waked the poet's sigh,
The girl who gave to song
   What gold could never buy.

At Beauty's door of glass,
   When Wealth and Wit once stood,
They asked her, " *which* might pass?"
   She answered, "he, who could."
With golden key Wealth thought
   To pass — but 't would not do:
While Wit a diamond brought,
   Which cut his bright way through.
So here 's to her, who long
   Hath waked the poet's sigh,
The girl, who gave to song
   What gold could never buy.

The love that seeks a home
   Where wealth or grandeur shines,
Is like the gloomy gnome,
   That dwells in dark gold mines.
But oh! the poet's love
   Can boast a brighter sphere;
Its native home 's above,
   Tho' woman keeps it here.
Then drink to her, who long
   Hath waked the poet's sigh,
The girl, who gave to song
   What gold could never buy.

OH! BLAME NOT THE BARD.[1]

OH! blame not the bard, if he fly to the
      bowers,
   Where Pleasure lies, carelessly smiling
      at Fame;
He was born for much more, and in hap-
      pier hours
   His soul might have burned with a
      holier flame.

lily, has applied this image to a still more important object.

[1] We may suppose this apology to have been

The string, that now languishes loose
      o'er the lyre,
   Might have bent a proud bow to the
      warrior's dart;[2]
And the lip, which now breathes but the
      song of desire,
   Might have poured the full tide of a
      patriot's heart.

But alas for his country! — her pride is
      gone by,
   And that spirit is broken, which never
      would bend;
O'er the ruin her children in secret must
      sigh,
   For 't is treason to love her, and death
      to defend.
Unprized are her sons, till they 've learned
      to betray;
   Undistinguished they live, if they
      shame not their sires;
And the torch, that would light them
      thro' dignity's way,
   Must be caught from the pile, where
      their country expires.

Then blame not the bard, if in pleasure's
      soft dream,
   He should try to forget, what he never
      can heal:
Oh! give but a hope — let a vista but
      gleam
   Thro' the gloom of his country, and
      mark how he 'll feel!
That instant, his heart at her shrine
      would lay down
   Every passion it nurst, every bliss it
      adored;

uttered by one of those wandering bards, whom
Spenser so severely, and, perhaps, truly, describes
in his State of Ireland, and whose poems, he tells
us, " were sprinkled with some pretty flowers of
their natural device, which have good grace and
comeliness unto them, the which it is great pity
to see abused to the gracing of wickedness and
vice, which, with good usage, would serve to
adorn and beautify virtue."

[2] It is conjectured by Wormius, that the name
of Ireland is derived from *Yr*, the Runic for a
bow, in the use of which weapon the Irish were
once very expert. This derivation is certainly
more creditable to us than the following: " So
that Ireland, called the land of *Ire*, from the constant broils therein for 400 years, was now become
the land of concord." — *Lloyd's "State Worthies,"* art. *The Lord Grandison.*

While the myrtle, now idly entwined
    with his crown,
    Like the wreath of Harmodius, should
    cover his sword.[1]

But tho' glory be gone, and tho' hope
    fade away,
    Thy name, loved Erin, shall live in
    his songs;
Not even in the hour, when his heart is
    most gay,
    Will he lose the remembrance of thee
    and thy wrongs.
The stranger shall hear thy lament on his
    plains;
    The sigh of thy harp shall be sent o'er
    the deep,
Till thy masters themselves, as they rivet
    thy chains,
    Shall pause at the song of their cap-
    tive, and weep!

WHILE GAZING ON THE MOON'S LIGHT.

WHILE gazing on the moon's light,
    A moment from her smile I turned,
To look at orbs, that, more bright,
    In lone and distant glory burned.
            But *too* far
            Each proud star,
    For me to feel its warming flame;
            Much more dear
            That mild sphere,
    Which near our planet smiling came;[2]
Thus, Mary, be but thou my own;
    While brighter eyes unheeded play,
I 'll love those moonlight looks alone,
    That bless my home and guide my
    way.

The day had sunk in dim showers,
    But midnight now, with lustre meet,

Illumined all the pale flowers,
    Like hope upon a mourner's cheek.
    I said (while
    The moon's smile
    Played o'er a stream, in dimpling bliss,)
            "The moon looks
            "On many brooks,
    "The brook can see no moon but
    this;"[3]
And thus, I thought, our fortunes run,
    For many a lover looks to thee,
While oh! I feel there is but *one*,
    One Mary in the world for me.

ILL OMENS.

WHEN daylight was yet sleeping under
    the billow,
    And stars in the heavens still lingering
    shone,
Young Kitty, all blushing, rose up from
    her pillow,
    The last time she e'er was to press it
    alone.
For the youth whom she treasured her
    heart and her soul in,
    Had promised to link the last tie be-
    fore noon;
And when once the young heart of a
    maiden is stolen
    The maiden herself will steal after it
    soon.

As she looked in the glass, which a
    woman ne'er misses,
    Nor ever wants time for a sly glance
    or two,
A butterfly,[4] fresh from the night-flower's
    kisses,
    Flew over the mirror, and shaded her
    view.
Enraged with the insect for hiding her
    graces,
    She brushed him — he fell, alas; never
    to rise:
"Ah! such," said the girl, "is the pride
    of our faces,
    "For which the soul's innocence too
    often dies."

---

1 See the Hymn, attributed to Alcæus, ἐν
μύρτου κλαδὶ τὸ ξίφος φορήσω — " I will carry
my sword, hidden in myrtles, like Harmodius,
and Aristogiton," etc.

2 " Of such celestial bodies as are visible, the
sun excepted, the single moon, as despicable as
it is in comparison to most of the others, is much
more beneficial than they all put together." —
Whiston's Theory, etc.
    In the *Entretiens d'Ariste*, among other in-
genious emblems, we find a starry sky without
a moon, with these words, *non mille, quod absens.*

3 This image was suggested by the following
thought, which occurs somewhere in Sir William
Jones's works: " The moon looks upon many
night-flowers, the night-flower sees but one
moon."

4 An emblem of the soul.

While she stole thro' the garden, where
    heart's-ease was growing,
  She culled some, and kist off its night-
    fallen dew;
And a rose, further on, looked so tempt-
    ing and glowing,
  That, spite of her haste, she must
    gather it too:
But while o'er the roses too carelessly
    leaning,
  Her zone flew in two, and the heart's-
    ease was lost:
" Ah! this means," said the girl (and
    she sighed at its meaning),
  " That love is scarce worth the repose
    it will cost!"

BEFORE THE BATTLE.

By the hope within us springing,
  Herald of to-morrow's strife;
By that sun, whose light is bringing
  Chains or freedom, death or life —
Oh! remember life can be
No charm for him, who lives not free!
  Like the day-star in the wave,
  Sinks a hero in his grave,
Midst the dew-fall of a nation's tears.

Happy is he o'er whose decline
  The smiles of home may soothing shine
And light him down the steep of years: —
  But oh, how blest they sink to rest,
  Who close their eyes on victory's
    breast!

O'er his watch-fire's fading embers
  Now the foeman's cheek turns white,
When his heart that field remembers,
  Where we tamed his tyrant might.
Never let him bind again
A chain, like that we broke from then.
  Hark! the horn of combat calls —
  Ere the golden evening falls,
May we pledge that horn in triumph
    round! [1]

Many a heart that now beats high,
  In slumber cold at night shall lie,
Nor waken even at victory's sound: —
  But oh, how blest that hero's sleep,
  O'er whom a wondering world shall
    weep!

[1] " The Irish Corna was not entirely devoted

AFTER THE BATTLE.

Night closed around the conqueror's
    way,
  And lightnings showed the distant hill,
Where those who lost that dreadful day,
  Stood few and faint, but fearless still.
The soldier's hope, the patriot's zeal,
  For ever dimmed, for ever crost —
Oh! who shall say what heroes feel,
  When all but life and honor 's lost?

The last sad hour of freedom's dream,
  And valor's task, moved slowly by,
While mute they watcht, till morning's
    beam
  Should rise and give them light to die.
There 's yet a world, where souls are
    free,
  Where tyrants taint not nature's bliss; —
If death that world's bright opening be,
  Oh! who would live a slave in this?

'T IS SWEET TO THINK

'T is sweet to think, that, where'er we
    rove,
  We are sure to find something blissful
    and dear,
And that, when we 're far from the lips
    we love,
  We 've but to make love to the lips
    we are near. [2]
The heart, like a tendril, accustomed to
    cling,
  Let it grow where it will, can not flour-
    ish alone,
But will lean to the nearest and loveliest
    thing
  It can twine with itself and make
    closely its own.

Then oh! what pleasure, where'er we
    rove,
  To be sure to find something still that
    is dear,

to martial purposes. In the heroic ages, our
ancestors quaffed Meadh out of them, as the
Danish hunters do their beverage at this day." —
Walker.

[2] I believe it is Marmontel who says, "*Quand
on n'a pas ce que l'on aime, il faut aimer ce que
l'on a.*" — There are so many matter-of-fact
people, who take such *jeux d'esprit* as this defence of inconstancy, to be the actual and genuine
sentiments of him who writes them, that they

And to know, when far from the lips we
  love,
    We 've but to make love to the lips
    we are near.

'T were a shame, when flowers around
  us rise,
    To make light of the rest, if the rose
    is n't there;
And the world 's so rich in resplendent
  eyes,
    'T were a pity to limit one's love to a
    pair.
Love's wing and the peacock's are nearly
  alike,
    They are both of them bright, but
    they 're changeable too,
And, wherever a new beam of beauty
  can strike,
    It will tincture Love's plume with a
    different hue.
Then oh! what pleasure, where'er we
  rove,
    To be sure to find something still that
    is dear,
And to know, when far from the lips we
  love,
    We 've but to make love to the lips
    we are near.

THE IRISH PEASANT TO HIS MISTRESS.[1]

Thro' grief and thro' danger thy smile
  hath cheered my way,
Till hope seemed to bud from each thorn
  that round me lay;
The darker our fortune, the brighter our
  pure love burned,
Till shame into glory, till fear into zeal
  was turned;
Yes, slave as I was, in thy arms my spirit
  felt free,
And blest even the sorrows that made
  me more dear to thee.

compel one, in self-defence, to be as matter-of-
fact as themselves, and to remind them, that Democritus was not the worse physiologist, for
having playfully contended that snow was black;
nor Erasmus, in any degree, the less wise, for
having written an ingenious encomium of folly.

1 Meaning, allegorically, the ancient Church
of Ireland.

Thy rival was honored, while thou wert
  wronged and scorned,
Thy crown was of briers, while gold her
  brows adorned;
She wooed me to temples, while thou
  lay'st hid in caves,
Her friends were all masters, while thine,
  alas! were slaves;
Yet cold in the earth, at thy feet, I would
  rather be,
Than wed what I loved not, or turn one
  thought from thee.

They slander thee sorely, who say thy
  vows are frail —
Hadst thou been a false one, thy cheek
  had looked less pale.
They say, too, so long thou hast worn
  those lingering chains,
That deep in thy heart they have printed
  their servile stains —
Oh! foul is the slander, — no chain
  could that soul subdue —
Where shineth *thy* spirit, there liberty
  shineth too![2]

ON MUSIC.

When thro' life unblest we rove,
  Losing all that made life dear,
Should some notes we used to love,
  In days of boyhood, meet our ear,
Oh! how welcome breathes the strain!
  Wakening thoughts that long have
  slept;
Kindling former smiles again
  In faded eyes that long have wept.

Like the gale, that sighs along
  Beds of oriental flowers,
Is the grateful breath of song,
  That once was heard in happier hours;
Filled with balm, the gale sighs on,
  Tho' the flowers have sunk in death;
So, when pleasure's dream is gone,
  Its memory lives in Music's breath.

Music, oh how faint, how weak,
  Language fades before thy spell!
Why should Feeling ever speak,
  When thou canst breathe her soul so
  well?

2 "Where the Spirit of the Lord is, there is
liberty." — *St. Paul 2 Corinthians,* iii. 17.

Friendship's balmy words may feign,
　Love's are even more false than they;
Oh! 't is only music's strain
　Can sweetly soothe, and not betray.

IT IS NOT THE TEAR AT THIS MOMENT SHED.[1]

It is not the tear at this moment shed,
　When the cold turf has just been laid
　　o'er him,
That can tell how beloved was the friend
　that 's fled,
　Or how deep in out hearts we deplore
　him.
'T is the tear, thro' many a long day
　wept,
　'T is life's whole path o'ershaded;
'T is the one remembrance, fondly
　kept,
　When all lighter griefs have faded.

Thus his memory, like some holy light,
　Kept alive in our hearts, will improve
　them,
For worth shall look fairer, and truth
　more bright,
　When we think how he lived but to
　love them.
And, as fresher flowers the sod perfume
　Where buried saints are lying,
So our hearts shall borrow a sweetening
　bloom
　From the image he left there in dying!

THE ORIGIN OF THE HARP.

'T is believed that this Harp, which I
　wake now for thee,
Was a Siren of old, who sung under the
　sea;
And who often, at eve, thro' the bright
　waters roved,
To meet, on the green shore, a youth
　whom she loved.

But she loved him in vain, for he left her
　to weep,
And in tears, all the night, her gold
　tresses to steep;

1 These lines were occasioned by the loss of
a very near and dear relative, who had died lately
at Madeira.

Till heaven looked with pity on true-love
　so warm,
And changed to this soft Harp the sea-
　maiden's form.

Still her bosom rose fair — still her cheeks
　smiled the same —
While her sea-beauties gracefully formed
　the light frame;
And her hair, as, let loose, o'er her
　white arm it fell,
Was changed to bright chords uttering
　melody's spell.

Hence it came, that this soft Harp so
　long hath been known
To mingle love's language with sorrow's
　sad tone;
Till *thou* didst divide them, and teach the
　fond lay
To speak love when I 'm near thee, and
　grief when away.

LOVE'S YOUNG DREAM.

Oh! the days are gone, when Beauty
　bright
　　My heart's chain wove;
When my dream of life, from morn till
　night,
　　Was love, still love.
　New hope may bloom,
　And days may come,
Of milder, calmer beam,
But there 's nothing half so sweet in life
As love's young dream:
No, there 's nothing half so sweet in life
As love's young dream.

Tho' the bard to purer fame may soar,
　　When wild youth 's past;
Tho' he win the wise, who frowned
　before,
　　To smile at last;
　He 'll never meet
　A joy so sweet,
In all his noon of fame,
As when first he sung to woman's ear
His soul-felt flame,
And, at every close, she blushed to hear
The one lov'd name.

No, — that hallowed form is ne'er forgot
　　Which first love traced;

Still it lingering haunts the greenest spot
    On memory's waste.
    'T was odor fled
    As soon as shed;
  'T was morning's winged dream;
'T was a light, that ne'er can shine again
    On life's dull stream:
Oh! 't was light that ne'er can shine
    again
    On life's dull stream.

THE PRINCE'S DAY.[1]

THO' dark are our sorrows, to-day we 'll
    forget them,
    And smile thro' our tears, like a sun-
      beam in showers:
There never were hearts, if our rulers
    would let them,
    More formed to be grateful and blest
      than ours.
      But just when the chain
      Has ceased to pain,
  And hope has enwreathed it round
    with flowers,
      There comes a new link
      Our spirits to sink —
Oh! the joy that we taste, like the light
    of the poles,
  Is a flash amid darkness, too brilliant
    to stay;
But, tho' 't were the last little spark in
    our souls,
  We must light it up now, on our
    Prince's Day.

Contempt on the minion, who calls you
    disloyal!
    Tho' fierce to your foe, to your friends
      you are true;
And the tribute most high to a head that
    is royal,
    Is love from a heart that loves liberty
    too.
      While cowards, who blight
      Your fame, your right,
Would shrink from the blaze of the battle
    array,
      The Standard of Green
      In front would be seen, —

[1] This song was written for a *fête* in honor of the Prince of Wales's Birthday, given by my friend, Major Bryan, at his seat in the county of Kilkenny.

Oh, my life on your faith! were you
    summoned this minute,
    You 'd cast every bitter remembrance
      away,
And show what the arm of old Erin has
    in it,
    When roused by the foe, on her
      Prince's Day.

He loves the Green Isle, and his love is
    recorded
    In hearts, which have suffered too
      much to forget;
And hope shall be crowned, and attach-
    ment rewarded,
    And Erin's gay jubilee shine out yet.
      The gem may be broke
      By many a stroke,
  But nothing can cloud its native ray;
      Each fragment will cast
      A light, to the last, —
And thus, Erin, my country tho' broken
    thou art,
    There 's a lustre within thee, that ne'er
      will decay;
A spirit, which beams thro' each suffer-
    ing part,
    And now smiles at all pain on the
      Prince's Day.

WEEP ON, WEEP ON.

WEEP on, weep on, your hour is past;
    Your dreams of pride are o'er;
The fatal chain is round you cast,
    And you are men no more.
In vain the hero's heart hath bled;
    The sage's tongue hath warned in
      vain; —
Oh, Freedom! once thy flame hath
    fled,
    It never lights again.

Weep on — perhaps in after days,
    They 'll learn to love your name;
When many a deed may wake in praise
    That long hath slept in blame.
And when they tread the ruined isle,
    Where rest, at length, the lord and
      slave,
They 'll wondering ask, how hands so
    vile
    Could conquer hearts so brave?

" 'T was fate," they 'll say, " a wayward
    fate
  " Your web of discord wove;
" And while your tyrants joined in hate,
  " You never joined in love.
" But hearts fell off, that ought to twine,
  " And man profaned what God had
    given;
" Till some were heard to curse the shrine,
  " Where others knelt to heaven ! ' "

LESBIA HATH A BEAMING EYE.

LESBIA hath a beaming eye,
  But no one knows for whom it beameth;
Right and left its arrows fly,
  But what they aim at no one dreameth.
Sweeter 't is to gaze upon
  My Nora's lid that seldom rises;
Few its looks, but every one,
  Like unexpected light, surprises !
    Oh, my Nora Creina, dear,
  My gentle, bashful Nora Creina,
      Beauty lies
      In many eyes,
  But Love in yours, my Nora Creina.

Lesbia wears a robe of gold,
  But all so close the nymph hath laced it,
Not a charm of beauty's mould
  Presumes to stay where nature placed it.
Oh ! my Nora's gown for me,
  That floats as wild as mountain breezes,
Leaving every beauty free
  To sink or swell as Heaven pleases.
    Yes, my Nora Creina, dear,
  My simple, graceful Nora Creina,
      Nature's dress
      Is loveliness —
  The dress *you* wear, my Nora Creina.

Lesbia hath a wit refined,
  But, when its points are gleaming round
    us,
Who can tell if they 're design'd
  To dazzle merely, or to wound us?
Pillowed on my Nora's heart,
  In safer slumber Love reposes —
Bed of peace ! whose roughest part
  Is but the crumpling of the roses.
    Oh ! my Nora Creina dear,
  My mild, my artless Nora Creina !
      Wit, tho' bright,
      Hath no such light,
  As warms your eyes, my Nora Creina.

I SAW THY FORM IN YOUTHFUL PRIME.

I SAW thy form in youthful prime,
  Nor thought that pale decay
Would steal before the steps of Time,
  And waste its bloom away, Mary !
Yet still thy features wore that light,
  Which fleets not with the breath;
And life ne'er looked more truly bright
  Than in thy smile of death, Mary !

As streams that run o'er golden mines,
  Yet humbly, calmly glide,
Nor seem to know the wealth that shines
  Within their gentle tide, Mary !
So veiled beneath the simplest guise,
  Thy radiant genius shone,
And that, which charmed all other eyes,
  Seemed worthless in thy own, Mary !

If souls could always dwell above,
  Thou ne'er hadst left that sphere ;
Or could we keep the souls we love,
  We ne'er had lost thee here, Mary !
Though many a gifted mind we meet,
  Though fairest forms we see,
To live with them is far less sweet,
  Than to remember thee, Mary ! [1]

BY THAT LAKE, WHOSE GLOOMY SHORE.[2]

By that Lake, whose gloomy shore
Sky-lark never warbles o'er,[3]
Where the cliff hangs high and steep,
Young Saint Kevin stole to sleep.
" Here, at least," he calmly said,
" Woman ne'er shall find my bed."
Ah ! the good Saint little knew
What that wily sex can do.

'T was from Kathleen's eyes he flew, —
Eyes of most unholy blue !

1 I have here made a feeble effort to imitate
that exquisite inscription of Shenstone's, *"heu !
quanto minus est cum reliquis versari quam tui
meminisse !"*

2 This ballad is founded upon one of the
many stories related of St. Kevin, whose bed in
the rock is to be seen at Glendalough, a most
gloomy and romantic spot in the county of
Wicklow.

3 There are many other curious traditions con-
concerning this Lake, which may be found in
Giraldus, Colgan, etc.

She had loved him well and long,
Wished him hers, nor thought it wrong.
Wheresoe'er the Saint would fly,
Still he heard her light foot nigh;
East or west, where'er he turned,
Still her eyes before him burned.

On the bold cliff's bosom cast,
Tranquil now he sleeps at last;
Dreams of heaven, nor thinks that e'er
Woman's smile can haunt him there.
But nor earth nor heaven is free
From her power, if fond she be:
Even now, while calm he sleeps,
Kathleen o'er him leans and weeps.

Fearless she had tracked his feet
To this rocky, wild retreat;
And when morning met his view,
Her mild glances met it too.
Ah, your Saints have cruel hearts!
Sternly from his bed he starts,
And with rude, repulsive shock,
Hurls her from the beetling rock.

Glendalough, thy gloomy wave
Soon was gentle Kathleen's grave!
Soon the saint (yet ah! too late,)
Felt her love, and mourned her fate.
When he said, " Heaven rest her soul! "
Round the Lake light music stole;
And her ghost was seen to glide,
Smiling o'er the fatal tide.

SHE IS FAR FROM THE LAND.

SHE is far from the land where her young
hero sleeps,
And lovers are round her, sighing:
But coldly she turns from their gaze, and
weeps,
For her heart in his grave is lying.

She sings the wild song of her dear native plains,
Every note which he loved awaking; —
Ah! little they think who delight in her
strains,
How the heart of the Minstrel is
breaking.

He had lived for his love, for his country he died,
They were all that to life had entwined
him;

Nor soon shall the tears of his country
be dried,
Nor long will his love stay behind him.

Oh! make her a grave where the sun-
beams rest,
When they promise a glorious morrow;
They 'll shine o'er her sleep, like a smile
from the West,
From her own loved island of sorrow.

NAY, TELL ME NOT, DEAR.

NAY, tell me not, dear, that the goblet
drowns
One charm of feeling, one fond regret;
Believe me, a few of thy angry frowns
Are all I 've sunk in its bright wave yet.
Ne'er hath a beam
Been lost in the stream
That ever was shed from thy form or
soul;
The spell of those eyes,
The balm of thy sighs,
Still float on the surface, and hallow
my bowl.
Then fancy not, dearest, that wine can
steal
One blissful dream of the heart from
me;
Like founts that awaken the pilgrim's
zeal,
The bowl but brightens my love for
thee.

They tell us that Love in his fairy
bower
Had two blush-roses, of birth divine;
He sprinkled the one with a rainbow's
shower,
But bathed the other with mantling
wine.
Soon did the buds
That drank of the floods
Distilled by the rainbow, decline and
fade;
While those which the tide
Of ruby had dyed
All blushed into beauty, like thee,
sweet maid!
Then fancy not, dearest, that wine can
steal
One blissful dream of the heart from
me;

Like founts, that awaken the pilgrim's
zeal,
The bowl but brightens my love for
thee.

AVENGING AND BRIGHT.

AVENGING and bright fall the swift sword
of Erin [1]
On him who the brave sons of Usna
betrayed! —
For every fond eye he hath wakened a
tear in,
A drop from his heart-wounds shall
weep o'er her blade.

By the red cloud that hung over Conor's
dark dwelling,[2]
When Ullad's[3] three champions lay
sleeping in gore —
By the billows of war, which so often,
high swelling,
Have wafted these heroes to victory's
shore —

We swear to revenge them! — no joy
shall be tasted,
The harp shall be silent, the maiden
unwed,

[1] The words of this song were suggested by
the very ancient Irish story called "Deirdri, or
the Lamentable Fate of the Sons of Usnach,"
which has been translated literally from the
Gaelic, by Mr. O'Flanagan (see vol. i. of *Transactions of the Gaelic Society of Dublin*), and
upon which it appears that the "Darthula of
Macpherson" is founded. The treachery of
Conor, King of Ulster, in putting to death the
three sons of Usna, was the cause of a desolating
war against Ulster, which terminated in the destruction of Eman. "'This story [says Mr.
O'Flanagan] has been, from time immemorial,
held in high repute as one of the three tragic
stories of the Irish. These are 'The death of
the children of Touran;' 'The death of the
children of Lear' (both regarding Tuatha de
Danans), and this, 'The death of the children of
Usnach,' which is a Milesian story." It will be
recollected, that in the Second Number of these
Melodies, there is a ballad upon the story of the
children of Lear or Lir; "Silent, oh Moyle!"
etc.
    Whatever may be thought of those sanguine
claims to antiquity, which Mr. O'Flanagan and
others advance for the literature of Ireland, it
would be a lasting reproach upon our nationality,
if the Gaelic researches of this gentleman did
not meet with all the liberal encouragement they
so well merit.
    [2] "Oh Nasi! view that cloud that I here see
in the sky! I see over Eman-green a chilling
cloud of blood-tinged red." — *Deirdri's Song*.
    [3] Ulster.

Our halls shall be mute and our fields
shall lie wasted,
Till vengeance is wreaked on the
murderer's head.

Yes, monarch! tho' sweet are our home
recollections,
Tho' sweet are the tears that from tenderness fall;
Tho' sweet are our friendships, our hopes,
our affections,
Revenge on a tyrant is sweetest of all!

WHAT THE BEE IS TO THE FLOWERET.

HE.

WHAT the bee is to the floweret,
When he looks for honey-dew,
Thro' the leaves that close embower it,
That, my love, I 'll be to you.

SHE.

What the bank, with verdure glowing,
Is to waves that wander near,
Whispering kisses, while they 're going,
That I 'll be to you, my dear.

SHE.

But they say, the bee 's a rover,
Who will fly, when sweets are gone;
And, when once the kiss is over,
Faithless brooks will wander on.

HE.

Nay, if flowers *will* lose their looks,
If sunny banks *will* wear away,
'T is but right that bees and brooks
Should sip and kiss them while they
may.

LOVE AND THE NOVICE.

"HERE we dwell, in holiest bowers,
    "Where angels of light o'er our orisons
        bend;
"Where sighs of devotion and breathings
    of flowers
    "To heaven in mingled odor ascend.
        "Do not disturb our calm, oh Love!
        "So like is thy form to the cherubs
            above,
"It well might deceive such hearts as
    ours."

Love stood near the Novice and listened,
   And Love is no novice in taking a
     hint;
His laughing blue eyes soon with piety
   glistened;
   His rosy wing turned to heaven's own
     tint.
     " Who would have thought," the
      urchin cries,
     " That Love could so well, so gravely
      disguise
" His wandering wings and wounding
   eyes? "

Love now warms thee, waking and
   sleeping,
   Young Novice, to him all thy orisons
     rise.
He tinges the heavenly fount with his
   weeping,
He brightens the censer's flame with
   his sighs.
     Love is the Saint enshrined in thy
     breast,
     And angels themselves would admit
     such a guest,
If he came to them clothed in Piety's vest.

THIS LIFE IS ALL CHECKERED WITH PLEASURES AND WOES.

THIS life is all checkered with pleasures
   and woes,
   That chase one another like waves of
     the deep, —
Each brightly or darkly, as onward it
   flows,
   Reflecting our eyes, as they sparkle or
     weep.
So closely our whims on our miseries
   tread,
   That the laugh is awaked ere the tear
     can be dried;
And, as fast as the rain-drop of Pity is
   shed,
   The goose-plumage of Folly can turn
     it aside.
But pledge me the cup — if existence
   would cloy,
   With hearts ever happy, and heads
     ever wise,
Be ours the light Sorrow, half-sister to Joy,
   And the light, brilliant Folly that flashes
     and dies.

When Hylas was sent with his urn to the
   fount,
   Thro' fields full of light, and with heart
     full of play,
Light rambled the boy, over meadow
   and mount,
   And neglected his task for the flowers
     on the way.[1]
Thus many, like me, who in youth should
   have tasted
   The fountain that runs by Philosophy's
     shrine,
Their time with the flowers on the margin
   have wasted,
   And left their light urns all as empty
     as mine.
But pledge me the goblet; — while Idle-
   ness weaves
   These flowerets together, should Wis-
     dom but see
One bright drop or two that has fallen
   on the leaves
   From her fountain divine, 't is sufficient
     for me.

OH THE SHAMROCK.

   THRO' Erin's Isle,
     To sport awhile,
As Love and Valor wandered,
     With Wit, the sprite,
     Whose quiver bright
A thousand arrows squandered.
     Where'er they pass,
     A triple grass [2]
Shoots up, with dew-drops streaming,
     As softly-green
     As emeralds seen
Thro' purest crystal gleaming.
Oh the Shamrock, the green, immortal
   Shamrock !
     Chosen leaf,
     Of Bard and Chief,
   Old Erin's native Shamrock !

---

1 *proposito florem prætulit officio.*
       PROPERT. *lib.* i. *eleg.* 20.

2 It is said that St. Patrick, when preaching
the Trinity to the Pagan Irish, used to illustrate
his subject by reference to that species of trefoil
called in Ireland by the name of the Shamrock ;
and hence, perhaps, the Island of Saints adopted
this plant as her national emblem.   Hope, among
the ancients, was sometimes represented as a
beautiful child, standing upon tip-toes, and a trefoil or three-colored grass in her hand.

Says Valor, " See,
 " They spring for me,
" Those leafy gems of morning ! " —
Says Love, " No, no,
 " For *me* they grow,
" My fragrant path adorning."
 But Wit perceives
 The triple leaves,
And cries," Oh ! do not sever
 " A type, that blends
 " Three godlike friends,
" Love, Valor, Wit, for ever ! "
Oh the Shamrock, the green, immortal
 Shamrock !
 Chosen leaf
 Of Bard and Chief,
Old Erin's native Shamrock !

So firmly fond
 May last the bond,
They wove that morn together,
 And ne'er may fall
 One drop of gall
On Wit's celestial feather.
 May Love, as twine
 His flowers divine,
Of thorny falsehood weed 'em;
 May Valor ne'er
 His standard rear
Against the cause of Freedom !
Oh the Shamrock, the green, immortal
 Shamrock !
 Chosen leaf
 Of Bard and Chief,
Old Erin's native Shamrock !

AT THE MID HOUR OF NIGHT.

AT the mid hour of night, when stars
 are weeping, I fly
To the lone vale we loved, when life
 shone warm in thine eye;
And I think oft, if spirits can steal from
 the regions of air,
To revisit past scenes of delight, thou
 wilt come to me there,
And tell me our love is remembered,
 even in the sky.

Then I sing the wild song 't was once
 such pleasure to hear !
When our voices commingling breathed,
 like one, on the ear;

And, as Echo far off thro' the vale my
 sad orison rolls,
I think, oh my love ! 't is thy voice from
 the Kingdom of Souls,[1]
Faintly answering still the notes that
 once were so dear.

ONE BUMPER AT PARTING.

ONE bumper at parting ! — tho' many
 Have circled the board since we met,
The fullest, the saddest of any
 Remains to be crowned by us yet.
The sweetness that pleasure hath in it,
 Is always so slow to come forth,
That seldom, alas, till the minute
 It dies, do we know half its worth.
But come, — may our life's happy meas-
 ure
Be all of such moments made up;
They 're born on the bosom of Pleasure,
 They die midst the tears of the cup.

As onward we journey, how pleasant
 To pause and inhabit awhile
Those few sunny spots, like the present,
 That mid the dull wilderness smile !
But Time, like a pitiless master,
 Cries " Onward ! " and spurs the gay
 hours —
Ah, never doth Time travel faster,
 Than when his way lies among flowers.
But come — may our life's happy measure
Be all of such moments made up;
They 're born on the bosom of Pleasure,
 They die midst the tears of the cup.

We saw how the sun looked in sinking,
 The waters beneath him how bright;
And now, let our farewell of drinking
 Resemble that farewell of light.
You saw how he finished, by darting
 His beam o'er a deep billow's brim —
So, fill up, let 's shine at our parting,
 In full liquid glory, like him.
And oh ! may our life's happy measure
Of moments like this be made up,
 'T was born on the bosom of Pleasure,
 It dies mid the tears of the cup.

---

1 "There are countries," says Montaigne,
"where they believe the souls of the happy live
in all manner of liberty, in delightful fields ; and
that it is those souls, repeating the words we
utter, which we call Echo."

'T IS THE LAST ROSE OF SUM-
MER.

'T IS the last rose of summer
　Left blooming alone;
All her lovely companions
　Are faded and gone;
No flower of her kindred,
　No rose-bud is nigh,
To reflect back her blushes,
　Or give sigh for sigh.

I 'll not leave thee, thou lone one!
　To pine on the stem;
Since the lovely are sleeping,
　Go, sleep thou with them.
Thus kindly I scatter
　Thy leaves o'er the bed,
Where thy mates of the garden
　Lie scentless and dead.

So soon may *I* follow,
　When friendships decay,
And from Love's shining circle
　The gems drop away.
When true hearts lie withered,
　And fond ones are flown,
Oh! who would inhabit
　This bleak world alone?

THE YOUNG MAY MOON.

THE young May moon is beaming, love,
The glow-worm's lamp is gleaming, love,
　How sweet to rove
　Through Morna's grove,[1]
When the drowsy world is dreaming,
　love!
Then awake! — the heavens look bright,
　my dear,
'T is never too late for delight, my dear,
　And the best of all ways
　To lengthen our days,
Is to steal a few hours from the night,
　my dear!

Now all the world is sleeping, love,
But the Sage, his star-watch keeping,
　love,
　And I, whose star,
　More glorious far,

Is the eye from that casement peeping,
　love.
Then awake! — till rise of sun, my dear,
The Sage's glass we 'll shun, my dear,
　Or, in watching the flight
　Of bodies of light,
He might happen to take thee for one,
　my dear.

THE MINSTREL–BOY.

THE Minstrel-Boy to the war is gone,
　In the ranks of death you 'll find him;
His father's sword he has girded on,
　And his wild harp slung behind him. —
" Land of song! " said the warrior-bard,
　" Tho' all the world betrays thee,
" *One* sword, at least, thy rights shall
　　guard,
　" *One* faithful harp shall praise thee ! "

The Minstrel fell! — but the foeman's
　chain
Could not bring his proud soul under;
The harp he loved ne'er spoke again,
　For he tore its chords asunder;
And said, " No chains shall sully thee,
　" Thou soul of love and bravery !
" Thy songs were made for the pure and
　free,
　" They shall never sound in slavery."

THE SONG OF O'RUARK,
PRINCE OF BREFFNI.[2]

THE valley lay smiling before me,
　Where lately I left her behind;
Yet I trembled, and something hung o'er
　me,
　That saddened the joy of my mind.

whose death was as singularly melancholy and
unfortunate as his life had been amiable, honorable, and exemplary.

2 These stanzas are founded upon an event of
most melancholy importance to Ireland; if, as
we are told by our Irish historians, it gave England the first opportunity of profiting by our di-
visions and subduing us. The following are the
circumstances, as related by O'Halloran: — "The
king of Leinster had long conceived a violent
affection for Dearbhorgil, daughter to the king of
Meath, and though she had been for some time
married to O'Ruark, prince of Breffni, yet it
could not restrain his passion. They carried on
a private correspondence, and she informed him
that O'Ruark intended soon to go on a pilgrimage
(an act of piety frequent in those days), and con-

1 "Steals silently to Morna's grove." — See,
in Mr. Bunting's collection, a poem translated
from the Irish, by the late John Brown, one
of my earliest college companions and friends,

I looked for the lamp which, she told
 me,
  Should shine, when her Pilgrim re-
  turned;
But, tho' darkness began to infold me,
  No lamp from the battlements burned!

I flew to her chamber — 't was lonely,
  As if the loved tenant lay dead; —
Ah, would it were death, and death
  only!
  But no, the young false one had fled.
And there hung the lute that could soften
  My very worst pains into bliss;
While the hand, that had waked it so
  often,
  Now throbbed to a proud rival's kiss.

There *was* a time, falsest of women,
  When Breffni's good sword would have
  sought
That man, thro' a million of foemen,
  Who dared but to wrong thee *in*
  thought!
While now — oh degenerate daughter
  Of Erin, how fallen is thy fame!
And thro' ages of bondage and slaughter,
  Our country shall bleed for thy shame.

Already, the curse is upon her,
  And strangers her valleys profane;
They come to divide, to dishonor,
  And tyrants they long will remain.
But onward! — the green banner rearing,
  Go, flesh every sword to the hilt;
On *our* side is Virtue and Erin,
  On *theirs* is the Saxon and Guilt.

OH! HAD WE SOME BRIGHT LIT-
TLE ISLE OF OUR OWN.

OH! had we some bright little isle of
 our own,
In a blue summer ocean, far off and
 alone,
Where a leaf never dies in the still
 blooming bowers,
And the bee banquets on thro' a whole
 year of flowers;

Where the sun loves to pause
  With so fond a delay,
That the night only draws
  A thin veil o'er the day;
Where simply to feel that we breathe,
 that we live,
Is worth the best joy that life elsewhere
 can give.

There, with souls ever ardent and pure as
 the clime,
We should love, as they loved in the
 first golden time;
The glow of the sunshine, the balm of
 the air,
Would steal to our hearts, and make all
 summer there.
  With affection as free
   From decline as the bowers,
  And, with hope, like the bee,
   Living always on flowers,
Our life should resemble a long day of
 light,
And our death come on, holy and calm
 as the night.

FAREWELL! — BUT WHENEVER
YOU WELCOME THE HOUR.

FAREWELL! — but whenever you welcome the hour,
That awakens the night-song of mirth in
 your bower,
Then think of the friend who once welcomed it too,
And forgot his own griefs to be happy
 with you.
His griefs may return, not a hope may
 remain
Of the few that have brightened his
 pathway of pain,
But he ne'er will forget the short vision,
 that threw
Its enchantment around him, while lingering with you.

jured him to embrace that opportunity of conveying her from a husband she detested to a lover
she adored. MacMurchad too punctually obeyed
the summons, and had the lady conveyed to

his capital of Ferns." — The monarch Roder-
ick espoused the cause of O'Ruark, while Mac
Murchad fled to England, and obtained the assistance of Henry II.
" Such," adds Giraldus Cambrensis (as I find
him in an old translation), " is the variable and
fickle nature of woman, by whom all mischief
in the world (for the most part) do happen and
come, as may appear by Marcus Antonius, and
by the destruction of Troy."

And still on that evening, when pleasure
    fills up
To the highest top sparkle each heart
    and each cup,
Where'er my path lies, be it gloomy or
    bright,
My soul, happy friends, shall be with
    you that night;

Shall join in your revels, your sports, and
    your wiles,
And return to me, beaming all o'er with
    your smiles —
Too blest, if it tells me that, mid the gay
    cheer
Some kind voice had murmured, " I wish
    he were here ! "

Let Fate do her worst, there are relics
    of joy,
Bright dreams of the past, which she
    can not destroy;
Which come in the night-time of sorrow
    and care,
And bring back the features that joy
    used to wear.
Long, long be my heart with such memo-
    ries filled !
Like the vase, in which roses have once
    been distilled —
You may break, you may shatter the
    vase, if you will,
But the scent of the roses will hang
    round it still.

OH ! DOUBT ME NOT.

OH ! doubt me not — the season
    Is o'er, when Folly made me rove,
And now the vestal, Reason,
    Shall watch the fire awaked by Love.
Altho' this heart was early blown,
    And fairest hands disturbed the tree,
They only shook some blossoms down,
    Its fruit has all been kept for thee.
Then doubt me not — the season
    Is o'er, when Folly made me rove,
And now the vestal, Reason,
    Shall watch the fire awaked by Love.

And tho' my lute no longer
    May sing of Passion's ardent spell,
Yet, trust me, all the stronger
    I feel the bliss I do not tell.

The bee thro' many a garden roves,
    And hums his lay of courtship o'er,
But when he finds the flower he loves,
    He settles there, and hums no more.
Then doubt me not — the season
    Is o'er, when Folly kept me free,
And now the vestal, Reason,
    Shall guard the flame awaked by thee.

YOU REMEMBER ELLEN.[1]

YOU remember Ellen, our hamlet's pride,
    How meekly she blest her humble lot,
When the stranger, William, had made
    her his bride,
    And love was the light of their lowly
    cot.
Together they toiled through winds and
    rains,
    Till William, at length, in sadness said,
" We must seek our fortune on other
    plains; " —
    Then, sighing, she left her lowly shed.

They roamed a long and a weary way,
    Nor much was the maiden's heart at
    ease,
When now, at close of one stormy day,
    They see a proud castle among the
    trees.
"To-night," said the youth, " we 'll shel-
    ter there;
    " The wind blows cold, the hour is
    late : "
So he blew the horn with a chieftain's air,
    And the Porter bowed, as they past the
    gate.

" Now, welcome, Lady," exclaimed the
    youth, —
    " This castle is thine, and these dark
    woods all ! "
She believed him crazed, but his words
    were truth,
    For Ellen is Lady of Rosna Hall !
And dearly the Lord of Rosna loves
    What William the stranger wooed and
    wed;
And the light of bliss, in these lordly
    groves,
    Shines pure as it did in the lowly shed.

1 This ballad was suggested by a well-known
and interesting story told of a certain noble
family in England.

I 'D MOURN THE HOPES.

I 'D mourn the hopes that leave me,
  If thy smiles had left me too;
I 'd weep when friends deceive me,
  If thou wert, like them, untrue.
But while I 've thee before me,
  With heart so warm and eyes so
      bright,
No clouds can linger o'er me,
  That smile turns them all to light.

'T is not in fate to harm me,
  While fate leaves thy love to me;
'T is not in joy to charm me,
  Unless joy be shared with thee.
One minute's dream about thee
  Were worth a long, an endless
      year
Of waking bliss without thee,
  My own love, my only dear!

And tho' the hope be gone, love,
  That long sparkled o'er our way,
Oh! we shall journey on, love,
  More safely, without its ray.
Far better lights shall win me
  Along the path I 've yet to roam: —
The mind that burns within me,
  And pure smiles from thee at home.

Thus, when the lamp that lighted
  The traveller at first goes out,
He feels awhile benighted,
  And looks round in fear and doubt.
But soon, the prospect clearing,
  By cloudless starlight on he treads,
And thinks no lamp so cheering
  As that light which Heaven sheds.

COME O'ER THE SEA.

  COME o'er the sea,
  Maiden, with me,
Mine thro' sunshine, storm, and snows;
  Seasons may roll,
  But the true soul
Burns the same, where'er it goes.
Let fate frown on, so we love and part
    not;
'T is life where *thou* art, 't is death
    where thou art not.
      Then come o'er the sea,
      Maiden, with me,

Come wherever the wild wind blows;
  Seasons may roll,
  But the true soul
Burns the same, where'er it goes.

  Was not the sea
  Made for the Free,
Land for courts and chains alone?
  Here we are slaves,
  But, on the waves,
Love and Liberty 's all our own.
No eye to watch, and no tongue to
    wound us,
All earth forgot, and all heaven around
    us —
      Then come o'er the sea,
      Maiden, with me,
Mine thro' sunshine, storm, and snows;
  Seasons may roll,
  But the true soul
Burns the same, where'er it goes.

HAS SORROW THY YOUNG DAYS SHADED.

HAS sorrow thy young days shaded,
  As clouds o'er the morning fleet?
Too fast have those young days faded,
  That, even in sorrow, were sweet?
Does Time with his cold wing wither
  Each feeling that once was dear?
Then, child of misfortune, come hither,
  I 'll weep with thee, tear for tear.

Has love to that soul, so tender,
  Been like our Lagenian mine,[1]
Where sparkles of golden splendor
  All over the surface shine —
But, if in pursuit we go deeper,
  Allured by the gleam that shone,
Ah! false as the dream of the sleeper,
  Like Love, the bright ore is gone.

Has Hope, like the bird in the story,[2]
  That flitted from tree to tree
With the talisman's glittering glory —
  Has Hope been that bird to thee?

1 Our Wicklow Gold Mines, to which this
verse alludes, deserve, I fear, but too well the
character here given of them.

2 "The bird, having got its prize, settled not
far off, with the talisman in his mouth. The
prince drew near it, hoping it would drop it;
but, as he approached, the bird took wing, and
settled again," etc. — *"Arabian Nights."*

On branch after branch alighting,
　The gem did she still display,
And, when nearest and most inviting,
　Then waft the fair gem away?

If thus the young hours have fleeted,
　When sorrow itself looked bright;
If thus the fair hope hath cheated,
　That led thee along so light;
If thus the cold world now wither
　Each feeling that once was dear: —
Come, child of misfortune, come hither,
　I 'll weep with thee, tear for tear.

NO, NOT MORE WELCOME.

No, not more welcome the fairy numbers
　Of music fall on the sleeper's ear,
When half-awaking from fearful slumbers,
　He thinks the full choir of heaven is
　　near, —
Than came that voice, when, all forsaken,
　This heart long had sleeping lain,
Nor thought its cold pulse would ever
　waken
To such benign, blessed sounds again.

Sweet voice of comfort ! 't was like the
　stealing
　Of summer wind thro' some wreathed
　shell —
Each secret winding, each inmost feeling
　Of all my soul echoed to its spell.
'T was whispered balm — 't was sunshine
　spoken ! —
I 'd live years of grief and pain
To have my long sleep of sorrow broken
　By such benign, blessed sounds again.

WHEN FIRST I MET THEE.

WHEN first I met thee, warm and young,
　There shone such truth about thee,
And on thy lip such promise hung,
　I did not dare to doubt thee.
I saw thee change, yet still relied,
　Still clung with hope the fonder,
And thought, tho' false to all beside,
　From me thou couldst not wander.
　　But go, deceiver ! go,
　　　The heart, whose hopes could make it
　　Trust one so false, so low,
　　　Deserves that thou shouldst break it.

When every tongue thy follies named,
　I fled the unwelcome story;
Or found, in even the faults they blamed,
　Some gleams of future glory.
I still was true, when nearer friends
　Conspired to wrong, to slight thee;
The heart that now thy falsehood rends,
　Would then have bled to right thee.
　　But go, deceiver ! go, —
　　　Some day, perhaps, thou 'lt waken
　　From pleasure's dream, to know
　　　The grief of hearts forsaken.

Even now, tho' youth its bloom has
　shed,
　No lights of age adorn thee:
The few, who loved thee once, have
　fled,
　And they who flatter scorn thee.
Thy midnight cup is pledged to slaves,
　No genial ties enwreath it;
The smiling there, like light on graves,
　Has rank cold hearts beneath it.
　　Go — go — tho' worlds were thine,
　　　I would not now surrender
　　One taintless tear of mine
　　　For all thy guilty splendor !

And days may come, thou false one ! yet,
　When even those ties shall sever;
When thou wilt call, with vain regret,
　On her thou 'st lost forever;
On her who, in thy fortune's fall,
　With smiles had still received thee,
And gladly died to prove thee all
　Her fancy first believed thee.
　　Go — go —'t is vain to curse,
　　　'T is weakness to upbraid thee;
　　Hate cannot wish thee worse
　　　Than guilt and shame have made
　　　　thee.

WHILE HISTORY'S MUSE.

WHILE History's Muse the memorial was
　keeping
　Of all that the dark hand of Destiny
　weaves,
Beside her the Genius of Erin stood
　weeping,
　For hers was the story that blotted the
　leaves.
But oh ! how the tear in her eyelids grew
　bright,

When, after whole pages of sorrow and
    shame,
    She saw History write,
    With a pencil of light
That illumed the whole volume, her Wel-
    lington's name.

" Hail, Star of my Isle ! " said the Spirit,
    all sparkling
  With beams, such as break from her
    own dewy skies —
" Thro' ages of sorrow, deserted and
    darkling,
    " I 've watched for some glory like
    thine to arise.
" For, tho' heroes I 've numbered, un-
    blest was their lot,
" And unhallowed they sleep in the cross-
    ways of Fame;—
    " But oh ! there is not
    " One dishonoring blot
" On the wreath that encircles my Wel-
    lington's name.

" Yet still the last crown of thy toils is
    remaining,
    " The grandest, the purest, even *thou*
    hast yet known;
" Tho' proud was thy task, other nations
    unchaining,
    " Far prouder to heal the deep wounds
    of thy own.
" At the foot of that throne, for whose
    weal thou hast stood,
" Go, plead for the land that first cradled
    thy fame,
    " And, bright o'er the flood
    " Of her tears and her blood,
" Let the rainbow of Hope be her Wel-
    lington's name ! "

THE TIME I' VE LOST IN WOO-
ING.

THE time I 've lost in wooing,
In watching and pursuing
    The light, that lies
    In woman's eyes,
Has been my heart's undoing.
Tho' Wisdom oft has sought me,
I scorned the lore she brought me,
    My only books
    Were woman's looks,
And folly 's all they 've taught me.

Her smile when Beauty granted,
I hung with gaze enchanted,
    Like him the Sprite,[1]
    Whom maids by night
Oft meet in glen that 's haunted.
Like him, too, Beauty won me,
But while her eyes were on me,
    If once their ray
    Was turned away,
O ! winds could not outrun me.

And are those follies going?
And is my proud heart growing
    Too cold or wise
    For brilliant eyes
Again to set it glowing?
No, vain, alas ! the endeavor
From bonds so sweet to sever;
    Poor Wisdom's chance
    Against a glance
Is now as weak as ever.

WHERE IS THE SLAVE.

Oh, where 's the slave so lowly,
Condemned to chains unholy,
    Who, could he burst
    His bonds at first,
Would pine beneath them slowly?
What soul, whose wrongs degrade it,
Would wait till time decayed it,
    When thus its wing
    At once may spring
To the throne of Him who made it?

Farewell, Erin, — farewell, all,
Who live to weep our fall !

Less dear the laurel growing,
Alive, untouched and blowing,
    Than that, whose braid
    Is plucked to shade
The brows with victory glowing.
We tread the land that bore us,
Her green flag glitters o'er us,
    The friends we 've tried
    Are by our side,
And the foe we hate before us.

Farewell, Erin, — farewell, all,
Who live to weep our fall !

---

1 This alludes to a kind of Irish fairy, which
is to be met with, they say, in the fields at dusk.
As long as you keep your eyes upon him, he is

COME, REST IN THIS BOSOM.

Come, rest in this bosom, my own
stricken deer,
Tho' the herd have fled from thee, thy
home is still here;
Here still is the smile, that no cloud can
o'ercast,
And a heart and a hand all thy own to
the last.

Oh! what was love made for, if 't is not
the same
Thro' joy and thro' torment, thro' glory
and shame?
I know not, I ask not, if guilt 's in that
heart,
I but know that I love thee, whatever
thou art.

Thou hast called me thy Angel in moments of bliss,
And thy Angel I 'll be, mid the horrors
of this, —
Thro' the furnace, unshrinking, thy steps
to pursue,
And shield thee, and save thee, — or
perish there too!

'T IS GONE, AND FOR EVER.

'T is gone, and for ever, the light we
saw breaking,
Like Heaven's first dawn o'er the
sleep of the dead —
When Man, from the slumber of ages
awaking,
Looked upward, and blest the pure
ray, ere it fled.
'T is gone, and the gleams it has left of
its burning
But deepen the long night of bondage
and mourning,
That dark o'er the kingdoms of earth is
returning,
And darkest of all, hapless Erin, o'er
thee.

fixed, and in your power; — but the moment you
look away (and he is ingenious in furnishing some
inducement) he vanishes. I had thought that this
was the sprite which we call the Leprechaun; but
a high authority upon such subjects, Lady Morgan, (in a note upon her national and interesting
novel, O'Donnel), has given a very different account of that goblin.

For high was thy hope, when those
glories were darting
Around thee, thro' all the gross clouds
of the world;
When Truth, from her fetters indignantly
starting,
At once, like a Sun-burst, her banner
unfurled.[1]
Oh! never shall earth see a moment so
splendid!
Then, then — had one Hymn of Deliverance blended
The tongues of all nations — how sweet
had ascended
The first note of Liberty, Erin, from
thee!

But, shame on those tyrants, who envied
the blessing!
And shame on the light race, unworthy its good,
Who, at Death's reeking altar, like
furies, caressing
The young hope of Freedom, baptized
it in blood.
Then vanished for ever that fair, sunny
vision,
Which, spite of the slavish, the cold
heart's derision,
Shall long be remembered, pure, bright,
and elysian,
As first it arose, my lost Erin, on thee.

I SAW FROM THE BEACH.

I saw from the beach, when the morning was shining,
A bark o'er the waters move gloriously
on;
I came when the sun o'er that beach was
declining,
The bark was still there, but the waters
were gone.

And such is the fate of our life's early
promise,
So passing the spring-tide of joy we
have known;
Each wave, that we danced on at morning, ebbs from us,
And leaves us, at eve, on the bleak
shore alone.

1 "The Sun-burst" was the fanciful name
given by the ancient Irish to the Royal Banner.

Ne'er tell me of glories, serenely adorn-
 ing
 The close of our day, the calm eve of
 our night; —
Give me back, give me back the wild
 freshness of Morning,
 Her clouds and her tears are worth
 Evening's best light.

Oh, who would not welcome that moment's returning,
 When passion first waked a new life
 thro' his frame,
And his soul, like the wood, that grows
 precious in burning,
 Gave out all its sweets to love's exquisite flame.

FILL THE BUMPER FAIR.

FILL the bumper fair!
 Every drop we sprinkle
 O'er the brow of Care
 Smooths away a wrinkle.
Wit's electric flame
 Ne'er so swiftly passes,
 As when thro' the frame
 It shoots from brimming glasses.
Fill the bumper fair!
 Every drop we sprinkle
 O'er the brow of Care
 Smooths away a wrinkle.

Sages can, they say,
 Grasp the lightning's pinions,
And bring down its ray
 From the starred dominions: —
So we, Sages, sit,
 And, mid bumpers brightening,
From the Heaven of Wit
 Draw down all its lightning.

Wouldst thou know what first
 Made our souls inherit
This ennobling thirst
 For wine's celestial spirit?
It chanced upon that day,
 When, as bards inform us,
Prometheus stole away
 The living fires that warm us:

The careless Youth, when up
 To Glory's fount aspiring,
Took nor urn nor cup
 To hide the pilfered fire in. —

But oh his joy, when, round
 The halls of Heaven spying,
Among the stars he found
 A bowl of Bacchus lying!

Some drops were in that bowl,
 Remains of last night's pleasure,
With which the Sparks of Soul
 Mixt their burning treasure.
Hence the goblet's shower
 Hath such spells to win us;
Hence its mighty power
 O'er that flame within us.
Fill the bumper fair!
 Every drop we sprinkle
 O'er the brow of Care
 Smooths away a wrinkle.

DEAR HARP OF MY COUNTRY.

DEAR Harp of my Country! in darkness
 I found thee,
 The cold chain of silence had hung
 o'er thee long,[1]
When proudly, my own Island Harp, I
 unbound thee,
 And gave all thy chords to light, free-
 dom, and song!
The warm lay of love and the light note
 of gladness
 Have wakened thy fondest, thy liveli-
 est thrill;
But, so oft hast thou echoed the deep
 sigh of sadness,
 That even in thy mirth it will steal
 from thee still.
Dear Harp of my country! farewell to
 thy numbers,
 This sweet wreath of song is the last
 we shall twine!
Go, sleep with the sunshine of Fame on
 thy slumbers,

---

1 In that rebellious but beautiful song, "When
Erin first rose," there is, if I recollect right, the
following line : —
"The dark chain of Silence was thrown o'er the
 deep."
 The chain of Silence was a sort of practical figure of rhetoric among the ancient Irish. Walker
tells us of " a celebrated contention for precedence
between Finn and Gaul, near Finn's palace at
Almhaim, where the attending Bards, anxious, if
possible, to produce a cessation of hostilities,
shook the chain of Silence, and flung themselves
among the ranks." See also the *Ode to Gaul,
the Son of Morni, in* Miss Brooke's " *Reliques of
Irish Poetry.*".

Till touched by some hand less unworthy than mine;
If the pulse of the patriot, soldier, or
lover,
Have throbbed at our lay, 't is thy
glory alone;
I was *but* as the wind, passing heedlessly
over,
And all the wild sweetness I waked
was thy own.

MY GENTLE HARP.

My gentle Harp, once more I waken
The sweetness of thy slumbering strain;
In tears our last farewell was taken,
And now in tears we meet again.
No light of joy hath o'er thee broken,
But, like those Harps whose heavenly
skill
Of slavery, dark as thine, hath spoken,
Thou hang'st upon the willows still.

And yet, since last thy chord resounded,
An hour of peace and triumph came,
And many an ardent bosom bounded
With hopes — that now are turned to
shame.
Yet even then, while Peace was singing
Her halcyon song o'er land and sea,
Tho' joy and hope to others bringing,
She only brought new tears to thee.

Then, who can ask for notes of pleasure,
My drooping Harp, from chords like
thine?
Alas, the lark's gay morning measure
As ill would suit the swan's decline!
Or how shall I, who love, who bless
thee,
Invoke thy breath for Freedom's
strains,
When even the wreaths in which I dress
thee,
Are sadly mixt — half flowers, half
chains?

But come — if yet thy frame can borrow
One breath of joy, oh, breathe for
me,
And show the world, in chains and
sorrow,
How sweet thy music still can be;
How gaily, even mid gloom surrounding,

Thou yet canst wake at pleasure's
thrill —
Like Memnon's broken image sounding,
Mid desolation tuneful still ! [1]

IN THE MORNING OF LIFE.

In the morning of life, when its cares
are unknown,
And its pleasures in all their new lustre
begin,
When we live in a bright-beaming world
of our own,
And the light that surrounds us is all
from within;
Oh 't is not, believe me, in that happy time
We can love, as in hours of less transport we may; —
Of our smiles, of our hopes, 't is the
gay sunny prime,
But affection is truest when these fade
away.

When we see the first glory of youth
pass us by,
Like a leaf on the stream that will
never return;
When our cup, which had sparkled with
pleasure so high,
First tastes of the *other*, the dark-flow-
ing urn;
Then, then is the time when affection
holds sway
With a depth and a tenderness joy
never knew;
Love, nursed among pleasures, is faith-
less as they,
But the love born of Sorrow, like
Sorrow, is true.

In climes full of sunshine, tho' splendid
the flowers,
Their sighs have no freshness, their
odor no worth;
'T is the cloud and the mist of our own
Isle of showers,
That call the rich spirit of fragrancy
forth.
So it is not mid splendor, prosperity,
mirth,
That the depth of Love's generous
spirit appears;

1 *Dimidio magicæ resonant ubi Memnone
chordæ.* —*Juvenal.*

To the sunshine of smiles it may first owe
its birth,
But the soul of its sweetness is drawn
out by tears.

AS SLOW OUR SHIP.

As slow our ship her foamy track
Against the wind was cleaving,
Her trembling pennant still looked back
To that dear isle 't was leaving.
So loath we part from all we love,
From all the links that bind us;
So turn our hearts as on we rove,
To those we 've left behind us.

When, round the bowl, of vanished years
We talk, with joyous seeming, —
With smiles that might as well be tears,
So faint, so sad their beaming;
While memory brings us back again
Each early tie that twined us,
Oh, sweet 's the cup that circles then
To those we 've left behind us.

And when, in other climes, we meet
Some isle, or vale enchanting,
Where all looks flowery, wild, and
sweet,
And naught but love is wanting;
We think how great had been our bliss,
If Heaven had but assigned us
To live and die in scenes like this,
With some we 've left behind us!

As travellers oft look back at eve,
When eastward darkly going,
To gaze upon that light they leave
Still faint behind them glowing, —
So, when the close of pleasure's day
To gloom hath near consigned us,
We turn to catch one fading ray
Of joy that 's left behind us.

WHEN COLD IN THE EARTH.

When cold in the earth lies the friend
thou hast loved,
Be his faults and his follies forgot by
thee then;
Or, if from their slumber the veil be removed,
Weep o'er them in silence, and close
it again.

And oh! if 't is pain to remember how
far
From the pathways of light he was
tempted to roam,
Be it bliss to remember that thou wert
the star
That arose on his darkness and guided
him home.

From thee and thy innocent beauty first
came
The revealings, that taught him true
love to adore,
To feel the bright presence, and turn him
with shame
From the idols he blindly had knelt to
before.
O'er the waves of a life, long benighted
and wild,
Thou camest, like a soft golden calm
o'er the sea;
And if happiness purely and glowingly
smiled
On his evening horizon, the light was
from thee.

And tho', sometimes, the shades of past
folly might rise,
And tho' falsehood again would allure
him to stray,
He but turned to the glory that dwelt in
those eyes,
And the folly, the falsehood, soon
vanished away.
As the Priests of the Sun, when their
altar grew dim,
At the day-beam alone could its lustre
repair,
So, if virtue a moment grew languid in
him,
He but flew to that smile and re-
kindled it there.

REMEMBER THEE.

Remember thee? yes, while there 's life
in this heart,
It shall never forget thee, all lorn as thou
art;
More dear in thy sorrow, thy gloom, and
thy showers,
Than the rest of the world in their sunniest hours.

Wert thou all that I wish thee, great,
　　glorious, and free,
First flower of the earth, and first gem
　　of the sea,
I might hail thee with prouder, with
　　happier brow,
But oh! could I love thee more deeply
　　than now?

No, thy chains as they rankle, thy blood
　　as it runs,
But make thee more painfully dear to
　　thy sons —
Whose hearts, like the young of the
　　desert-bird's nest,
Drink love in each life-drop that flows
　　from thy breast.

WREATH THE BOWL.

WREATH the bowl
　　With flowers of soul,
The brightest wit can find us;
　　We 'll take a flight
　　Towards heaven to-night,
And leave dull earth behind us.
　　Should Love amid
　　The wreaths be hid,
That joy, the enchanter, brings us,
　　No danger fear,
　　While wine is near,
We 'll drown him if he stings us.
　　Then, wreath the bowl
　　With flowers of soul,
The brightest wit can find us;
　　We 'll take a flight
　　Towards heaven to-night,
And leave dull earth behind us.

'T was nectar fed
　　Of old, 't is said,
Their Junos, Joves, Apollos;
　　And man may brew
　　His nectar too,
The rich receipt 's as follows:
　　Take wine like this,
　　Let looks of bliss
Around it well be blended,
　　Then bring wit's beam
　　To warm the stream,
And there 's your nectar, splendid!
　　So wreath the bowl
　　With flowers of soul,

The brightest wit can find us;
　　We 'll take a flight
　　Towards heaven to-night,
And leave dull earth behind us.

　　Say, why did Time
　　His glass sublime
Fill up with sands unsightly,
　　When wine, he knew,
　　Runs brisker through,
And sparkles far more brightly?
　　Oh, lend it us,
　　And, smiling thus,
The glass in two we 'll sever,
　　Make pleasure glide
　　In double tide,
And fill both ends for ever!
　　Then wreath the bowl
　　With flowers of soul
The brightest wit can find us;
　　We 'll take a flight
　　Towards heaven to-night,
And leave dull earth behind us.

WHENE'ER I SEE THOSE SMIL-
ING EYES.

WHENE'ER I see those smiling eyes,
　　So full of hope, and joy, and light,
As if no cloud could ever rise,
　　To dim a heaven so purely bright —
I sigh to think how soon that brow
　　In grief may lose its every ray,
And that light heart, so joyous now,
　　Almost forget it once was gay.

For time will come with all its blights,
　　The ruined hope, the friend unkind,
And love, that leaves, where'er it lights,
　　A chilled or burning heart behind: —
While youth, that now like snow appears,
　　Ere sullied by the darkening rain,
When once 't is touched by sorrow's tears
　　Can never shine so bright again.

IF THOU 'LT BE MINE.

IF thou 'lt be mine, the treasures of air,
　　Of earth, and sea, shall lie at thy feet;
Whatever in Fancy's eye looks fair,
　　Or in Hope's sweet music sounds *most*
　　　sweet,
　　Shall be ours — if thou wilt be mine,
　　　love!

Bright flowers shall bloom wherever we
    rove,
    A voice divine shall talk in each stream;
The stars shall look like worlds of love,
    And this earth be all one beautiful
      dream
        In our eyes — if thou wilt be mine,
        love !

And thoughts, whose source is hidden
    and high,
    Like streams, that come from heaven-
      ward hills,
Shall keep our hearts, like meads, that lie
    To be bathed by those eternal rills,
    Ever green, if thou wilt be mine, love !

All this and more the Spirit of Love
    Can breathe o'er them, who feel his
      spells;
That heaven, which forms his home above,
    He can make on earth, wherever he
      dwells,
        As thou 'lt own, — if thou wilt be
        mine, love !

TO LADIES' EYES.

To Ladies' eyes around, boy,
    We can't refuse, we can't refuse,
Tho' bright eyes so abound, boy,
    'T is hard to choose, 't is hard to
      choose.
For thick as stars that lighten
    Yon airy bowers, yon airy bowers,
The countless eyes that brighten
    This earth of ours, this earth of ours.
But fill the cup — where'er, boy,
    Our choice may fall, our choice may
      fall,
We 're sure to find Love there, boy,
    So drink them all ! so drink them all !

Some looks there are so holy,
    They seem but given, they seem but
      given,
As shining beacons, solely,
    To light to heaven, to light to heaven.
While some — oh ! ne'er believe them —
    With tempting ray, with tempting ray,
Would lead us (God forgive them !)
    The other way, the other way.
But fill the cup — where'er, boy,
    Our choice may fall, our choice may
      fall,

We 're sure to find Love there, boy,
    So drink them all ! so drink them all !

In some, as in a mirror,
    Love seems portrayed, Love seems
      portrayed,
But shun the flattering error,
    'T is but his shade, 't is but his shade.
Himself has fixt his dwelling
    In eyes we know, in eyes we know,
And lips — but this is telling —
    So here they go ! so here they go !
Fill up, fill up — where'er, boy,
    Our choice may fall, our choice may
      fall,
We 're sure to find Love there, boy,
    So drink them all ! so drink them all !

FORGET NOT THE FIELD.

FORGET not the field where they perished,
    The truest, the last of the brave,
All gone — and the bright hope we cher-
      ished
    Gone with them, and quenched in their
      grave !

Oh ! could we from death but recover
    Those hearts as they bounded before,
In the face of high heaven to fight over
    That combat for freedom once more ; —

Could the chain for an instant be riven
    Which Tyranny flung round us then,
No, 't is not in Man, nor in Heaven,
    To let Tyranny bind it again !

But 't is past — and, tho' blazoned in
    story
    The name of our Victor may be,
Accurst is the march of that glory
    Which treads o'er the hearts of the
      free.

Far dearer the grave or the prison,
    Illumed by one patriot name,
Than the trophies of all, who have risen
    On Liberty's ruins to fame.

THEY MAY RAIL AT THIS LIFE.

THEY may rail at this life — from the
    hour I began it,
    I found it a life full of kindness and
      bliss;

And, until they can show me some hap-
　　pier planet,
　　More social and bright, I 'll content
　　me with this.
As long as the world has such lips and
　　such eyes,
　　As before me this moment enraptured
　　I see,
They may say what they will of their
　　orbs in the skies,
　　But this earth is the planet for you,
　　love, and me.

In Mercury's star, where each moment
　　can bring them
　　New sunshine and wit from the foun-
　　tain on high,
Tho' the nymphs may have livelier poets
　　to sing them,[1]
　　They 've none, even there, more en-
　　amoured than I.
And, as long as this harp can be wakened
　　to love,
　　And that eye its divine inspiration
　　shall be,
They may talk as they will of their Edens
　　above,
　　But this earth is the planet for you,
　　love, and me.

In that star of the west, by whose shadowy
　　splendor,
　　At twilight so often we 've roamed
　　thro' the dew,
There are maidens, perhaps, who have
　　bosoms as tender,
　　And look, in their twilights, as lovely
　　as you.[2]
But tho' they were even more bright than
　　the queen
　　Of that isle they inhabit in heaven's
　　blue sea,
As I never those fair young celestials
　　have seen,
　　Why — this earth is the planet for you,
　　love, and me.

As for those chilly orbs on the verge of
　　creation,
　　Where sunshine and smiles must be
　　equally rare,

Did they want a supply of cold hearts for
　　that station,
　　Heaven knows we have plenty on earth
　　we could spare.
Oh! think what a world we should have
　　of it here,
　　If the haters of peace, of affection and
　　glee,
Were to fly up to Saturn's comfortless
　　sphere,
　　And leave earth to such spirits as you,
　　love, and me.

OH FOR THE SWORDS OF FORMER TIME!

Oh for the swords of former time!
　Oh for the men who bore them,
When armed for Right, they stood sub-
　　lime,
　And tyrants crouched before them:
When free yet, ere courts began
　With honors to enslave him,
The best honors worn by Man
　Were those which Virtue gave him.
Oh for the swords, etc.

Oh for the kings who flourished then!
　Oh for the pomp that crowned them,
When hearts and hands of freeborn men
　Were all the ramparts round them.
When, safe built on bosoms true,
　The throne was but the centre,
Round which Love a circle drew,
　That Treason durst not enter.
Oh for the kings who flourished then!
　Oh for the pomp that crowned them,
When hearts and hands of freeborn men
　Were all the ramparts round them!

ST. SENANUS AND THE LADY.

ST. SENANUS. [3]

"Oh! haste and leave this sacred isle,
"Unholy bark, ere morning smile;
"For on thy deck, though dark it be,
　"A female form I see;
"And I have sworn this sainted sod
"Shall ne'er by woman's feet be trod."

1 *Tous les habitans de Mercure sont vifs.* —
"*Pluralité des Mondes.*"

2 *La Terre pourra être pour Vénus l'étoile du*
berger et la mère des amours, comme Vénus l'est
pour nous. — "*Pluralité des Mondes.*"

3 In a metrical life of St. Senanus, which is
taken from an old Kilkenny MS., and may be
found among the "*Acta Sanctorum Hiberniæ,*'
we are told of his flight to the island of Scattery,

THE LADY.

"Oh! Father, send not hence my bark,
  "Thro' wintry winds and billows dark:
  "I come with humble heart to share
    "Thy morn and evening prayer;
  "Nor mine the feet, oh! holy Saint,
  "The brightness of thy sod to taint."

The Lady's prayer Senanus spurned;
The winds blew fresh, the bark returned;
But legends hint, that had the maid
  Till morning's light delayed,
And given the saint one rosy smile,
She ne'er had left his lonely isle.

NE'ER ASK THE HOUR.

NE'ER ask the hour — what is it to us
  How Time deals out his treasures?
The golden moments lent us thus,
  Are not *his* coin, but Pleasure's.
If counting them o'er could add to their
    blisses,
  I 'd number each glorious second:
But moments of joy are, like Lesbia's
    kisses,
  Too quick and sweet to be reckoned.
Then fill the cup — what is it to us
  How time his circle measures?
The fairy hours we call up thus,
  Obey no wand but Pleasure's.

Young Joy ne'er thought of counting
    hours,
  Till Care, one summer's morning,
Set up, among his smiling flowers,
  A dial, by way of warning.
But Joy loved better to gaze on the sun,
  As long as its light was glowing,
Than to watch with old Care how the
    shadow stole on,
  And how fast that light was going.
So fill the cup — what is it to us
  How Time his circle measures?
The fairy hours we call up thus,
  Obey no wand but Pleasure's.

and his resolution not to admit any woman of
the party; he refused to receive even a sister
saint, St. Cannera, whom an angel had taken to
the island for the express purpose of introducing
her to him. The following was the ungracious
answer of Senanus, according to his poetical
biographer:

*cui Præsul, quid fæminis
commune est cum monachis?*

SAIL ON, SAIL ON.

SAIL on, sail on, thou fearless bark —
  Wherever blows the welcome wind,
It cannot lead to scenes more dark,
  More sad than those we leave behind.
Each wave that passes seems to say,
  "Tho' death beneath our smile may
    be,
"Less cold we are, less false than they,
  "Whose smiling wrecked thy hopes
    and thee."

Sail on, sail on, — thro' endless space —
  Thro' calm — thro' tempest — stop no
    more:
The stormiest sea 's a resting place
  To him who leaves such hearts on
    shore.
Or — if some desert land we meet,
  Where never yet false-hearted men
Profaned a world, that else were sweet,—
  Then rest thee, bark, but not till then.

THE PARALLEL.

YES, sad one of Sion,[1] if closely resem-
    bling,
  In shame and in sorrow, thy withered-
    up heart —
If drinking deep, deep, of the same "cup
    of trembling"
  Could make us thy children, our parent
    thou art.

Like thee doth our nation lie conquered
    and broken,
  And fallen from her head is the once
    royal crown;
In her streets, in her halls, Desolation
    hath spoken,
  And " while it is day yet, her sun hath
    gone down." [2]

*nec te nec ullam aliam
admittemus in insulam.*

See the "*Acta Sanct. Hib.*," page 610.
According to Dr. Ledwich, St. Senanus was
no less a personage than the river Shannon; but
O'Connor and other antiquarians deny the metamorphose indignantly.

1 These verses were written after the perusal
of a treatise by Mr. Hamilton, professing to
prove that the Irish were originally Jews.

2 "Her sun is gone down while it was yet
day." — *Jer.* xv. 9.

Like thine doth her exile, mid dreams of
  returning,
  Die far from the home it were life to
    behold;
Like thine do her sons, in the day of
  their mourning,
  Remember the bright things that blest
    them of old.

Ah, well may we call her, like thee "the
  Forsaken," [1]
  Her boldest are vanquished, her proud-
    est are slaves;
And the harps of her minstrels, when
  gayest they waken,
  Have tones mid their mirth like the
    wind over graves!

Yet hadst thou thy vengeance — yet came
  there the morrow,
  That shines out, at last, on the longest
    dark night,
When the sceptre, that smote thee with
  slavery and sorrow,
  Was shivered at once, like a reed, in
    thy sight.

When that cup, which for others the
  proud Golden City [2]
  Had brimmed full of bitterness,
    drenched her own lips;
And the world she had trampled on
  heard, without pity,
  The howl in her halls, and the cry
    from her ships.

When the curse Heaven keeps for the
  haughty came over
  Her merchants rapacious, her rulers
    unjust,
And, a ruin, at last, for the earthworm
  to cover, [3]
  The Lady of Kingdoms [4] lay low in the
    dust.

1 "Thou shalt no more be termed Forsaken."
— *Isaiah*, lxii. 4.

2 " How hath the oppressor ceased! the
golden city ceased!" — *Isaiah*, xiv. 4.

3 "Thy pomp is brought down to the grave
. . . and the worms cover thee." — *Isaiah*,
xiv. 11.

4 " Thou shalt no more be called the Lady of
Kingdoms." — *Isaiah*, xlvii. 5.

DRINK OF THIS CUP.

DRINK of this cup; — you 'll find there 's
  a spell in
  Its every drop 'gainst the ills of mor-
    tality;
Talk of the cordial that sparkled for
  Helen!
  Her cup was a fiction, but this is
    reality.

Would you forget the dark world we are
  in,
  Just taste of the bubble that gleams
    on the top of it;
But would you rise above earth, till akin
  To Immortals themselves, you must
    drain every drop of it;
Send round the cup — for oh there 's a
  spell in
  Its every drop 'gainst the ills of mor-
    tality;
Talk of the cordial that sparkled for
  Helen!
  Her cup was a fiction, but this is
    reality.

Never was philter formed with such
  power
  To charm and bewilder as this we are
    quaffing;
Its magic began when, in Autumn's rich
  hour,
  A harvest of gold in the fields it stood
    laughing.
There having, by Nature's enchantment,
  been filled
  With the balm and the bloom of her
    kindliest weather,
This wonderful juice from its core was
  distilled
  To enliven such hearts as are here
    brought together.
Then drink of the cup — you 'll find
  there's a spell in
  Its every drop 'gainst the ills of mor-
    tality;
Talk of the cordial that sparkled for
  Helen!
  Her cup was a fiction, but this is
    reality.

And tho' perhaps — but breathe it to no
  one —
  Like liquor the witch brews at mid-
    night so awful,

This philter in secret was first taught to
    flow on,
  Yet 't is n't less potent for being un-
    lawful.
And, even tho' it taste of the smoke of
    that flame,
  Which in silence extracted its virtue
    forbidden —
Fill up — there 's a fire in some hearts I
    could name,
  Which may work too its charm, tho'
    as lawless and hidden.
So drink of the cup — for oh there 's a
    spell in
  Its every drop 'gainst the ills of mor-
    tality;
Talk of the cordial that sparkled for
    Helen!
  Her cup was a fiction, but this is
    reality.

THE FORTUNE-TELLER.

Down in the valley come meet me to-
    night,
  And I 'll tell you your fortune truly
As ever 't was told, by the new-moon's
    light,
  To a young maiden, shining as newly.

But, for the world, let no one be nigh,
  Lest haply the stars should deceive me;
Such secrets between you and me and
    the sky
  Should never go farther, believe me.

If at that hour the heavens be not dim,
  My science shall call up before you
A male apparition, — the image of him
  Whose destiny 't is to adore you.

And if to that phantom you 'll be kind,
  So fondly around you he 'll hover,
You 'll hardly, my dear, any difference
    find
  'Twixt him and a true living lover.

Down at your feet, in the pale moon-
    light,
  He 'll kneel, with a warmth of devo-
    tion —
An ardor, of which such an innocent
    sprite
  You 'd scarcely believe had a notion.

What other thoughts and events may
    arise,
  As in destiny's book I 've not seen
    them,
Must only be left to the stars and your
    eyes
  To settle, ere morning, between them.

OH, YE DEAD!

OH, ye Dead! oh, ye Dead![1] whom we
    know by the light you give
From your cold gleaming eyes, tho' you
    move like men who live,
    Why leave you thus your graves,
    In far off fields and waves,
Where the worm and the sea-bird only
    know your bed,
    To haunt this spot where all
    Those eyes that wept your fall,
And the hearts that wailed you, like your
    own, lie dead?

It is true, it is true, we are shadows cold
    and wan;
And the fair and the brave whom we
    loved on earth are gone;
    But still thus even in death,
    So sweet the living breath
Of the fields and the flowers in our
    youth we wander'd o'er,
    That ere, condemned, we go
    To freeze mid Hecla's snow,
We would taste it awhile, and think we
    live once more!

O'DONOHUE'S MISTRESS.

Of all the fair months, that round the sun
In light-linked dance their circles run,
  Sweet May, shine thou for me;
For still, when thy earliest beams arise,
That youth, who beneath the blue lake
    lies,
  Sweet May, returns to me.

Of all the bright haunts, where daylight
    leaves
Its lingering smile on golden eves,

1 Paul Zealand mentions that there is a mountain in some part of Ireland, where the ghosts
of persons who have died in foreign lands walk
about and converse with those they meet, like
living people. If asked why they do not return
to their homes, they say they are obliged to go to
Mount Hecla, and disappear immediately.

Fair Lake, thou 'rt dearest to me;
For when the last April sun grows dim,
Thy Naïads prepare his steed [1] for him
    Who dwells, bright Lake, in thee.

Of all the proud steeds, that ever bore
Young plumed Chiefs on sea or shore,
    White Steed, most joy to thee;
Who still, with the first young glance of
    spring,
From under that glorious lake dost bring
    My love, my chief, to me.

While, white as the sail some bark unfurls,
When newly launched, thy long mane [2]
    curls,
    Fair Steed, as white and free;
And spirits, from all the lake's deep
    bowers,
Glide o'er the blue wave scattering
    flowers,
    Around my love and thee.

Of all the sweet deaths that maidens die,
Whose lovers beneath the cold wave lie,
    Most sweet that death will be,
Which, under the next May evening's
    light,
When thou and thy steed are lost to sight,
    Dear love, I 'll die for thee.

ECHO.

How sweet the answer Echo makes
    To music at night,
When, roused by lute or horn, she wakes,
And far away, o'er lawns and lakes,
    Goes answering light.

1 The particulars of the tradition respecting
O'Donohue and his White Horse, may be found
in Mr. Weld's Account of Killarney, or more
fully detailed in Derrick's Letters. For many
years after his death, the spirit of this hero is
supposed to have been seen on the morning of
May-day, gliding over the lake on his favorite
white horse, to the sound of sweet unearthly
music, and preceded by groups of youths and
maidens, who flung wreaths of delicate spring
flowers in his path.
    Among other stories, connected with this
Legend of the Lakes, it is said that there was
a young and beautiful girl whose imagination was
so impressed with the idea of this visionary chieftain, that she fancied herself in love with him,
and at last, in a fit of insanity, on a May-morning
threw herself into the lake.

2 The boatmen at Killarney call those waves
which come on a windy day, crested with foam,
" O'Donohue's white horses."

Yet Love hath echoes truer far,
    And far more sweet,
Than e'er beneath the moonlight's star,
Of horn or lute, or soft guitar,
    The songs repeat.

'T is when the sigh, in youth sincere,
    And only then, —
The sigh that 's breath'd for one to hear,
Is by that one, that only dear,
    Breathed back again !

OH BANQUET NOT.

OH banquet not in those shining bowers,
    Where Youth resorts, but come to me :
For mine 's a garden of faded flowers,
    More fit for sorrow, for age, and thee.
And there we shall have our feast of
    tears,
    And many a cup in silence pour;
Our guests, the shades of former years,
    Our toasts, to lips that bloom no more.

There, while the myrtle's withering
    boughs
    Their lifeless leaves around us shed,
We 'll brim the bowl to broken vows,
    To friends long lost, the changed, the
    dead.
Or, while some blighted laurel waves
    Its branches o'er the dreary spot,
We 'll drink to those neglected graves,
    Where valor sleeps, unnamed, forgot.

THEE, THEE, ONLY THEE.

THE dawning of morn, the daylight's
    sinking,
The night's long hours still find me
    thinking
    Of thee, thee, only thee.
When friends are met, and goblets
    crowned,
    And smiles are near, that once en-
    chanted,
Unreached by all that sunshine round,
    My soul, like some dark spot, is
    haunted
    By thee, thee, only thee.

Whatever in fame's high path could
    waken
My spirit once, is now forsaken
    For thee, thee, only thee.

Like shores, by which some headlong bark
    To the ocean hurries, resting never,
Life's scenes go by me, bright or dark,
    I know not, heed not, hastening ever
        To thee, thee, only thee.

I have not a joy but of thy bringing,
And pain itself seems sweet when springing
        From thee, thee, only thee.
Like spells, that naught on earth can break,
    Till lips, that know the charm, have spoken,
This heart, howe'er the world may wake
    Its grief, its scorn, can but be broken
        By thee, thee, only thee.

SHALL THE HARP THEN BE SILENT.

SHALL the Harp then be silent, when he who first gave
    To our country a name, is withdrawn from all eyes?
Shall a Minstrel of Erin stand mute by the grave,
    Where the first — where the last of her Patriots lies?

No — faint tho' the death-song may fall from his lips,
    Tho' his Harp, like his soul, may with shadows be crost,
Yet, yet shall it sound, mid a nation's eclipse,
    And proclaim to the world what a star hath been lost;[1] —

What a union of all the affections and powers
    By which life is exalted, embellished, refined,
Was embraced in that spirit — whose centre was ours,
    While its mighty circumference circled mankind.

1 These lines were written on the death of our great patriot, Grattan, in the year 1820. It is only the two first verses that are either intended or fitted to be sung.

Oh, who that loves Erin, or who that can see,
    Thro' the waste of her annals, that epoch sublime —
Like a pyramid raised in the desert — where he
    And his glory stand out to the eyes of all time;

That *one* lucid interval, snatched from the gloom
    And the madness of ages, when filled with his soul,
A Nation o'erleaped the dark bounds of her doom,
    And for *one* sacred instant, touched Liberty's goal?

Who, that ever hath heard him — hath drank at the source
    Of that wonderful eloquence, all Erin's own,
In whose high-thoughted daring, the fire, and the force,
    And the yet untamed spring of her spirit are shown?

An eloquence rich, wheresoever its wave
    Wandered free and triumphant, with thoughts that shone thro',
As clear as the brook's "stone of lustre," and gave,
    With the flash of the gem, its solidity too.

Who, that ever approached him, when free from the crowd,
    In a home full of love, he delighted to tread
'Mong the trees which a nation had given, and which bowed,
    As if each brought a new civic crown for his head —

Is there one, who hath thus, thro' his orbit of life
    But at distance observed him — thro' glory, thro' blame,
In the calm of retreat, in the grandeur of strife,
    Whether shining or clouded, still high and the same, —

Oh no, not a heart, that e'er knew him,
    but mourns
Deep, deep o'er the grave, where such
    glory is shrined —
O'er a monument Fame will preserve,
    'mong the urns
Of the wisest, the bravest, the best of
    mankind!

OH, THE SIGHT ENTRANCING.

OH, the sight entrancing,
When morning's beam is glancing
        O'er files arrayed
        With helm and blade,
And plumes, in the gay wind dancing!
When hearts are all high beating,
And the trumpet's voice repeating
        That song, whose breath
        May lead to death,
But never to retreating.
Oh the sight entrancing,
When morning's beam is glancing
        O'er files arrayed
        With helm and blade,
And plumes, in the gay wind dancing.

Yet, 't is not helm or feather —
For ask yon despot, whether
        His plumed bands
        Could bring such hands
And hearts as ours together.
Leave pomps to those who need 'em —
Give man but heart and freedom,
        And proud he braves
        The gaudiest slaves
That crawl where monarchs lead 'em.
The sword may pierce the beaver,
Stone walls in time may sever,
        'T is mind alone,
        Worth steel and stone,
That keeps men free for ever.
Oh that sight entrancing,
When the morning's beam is glancing,
        O'er files arrayed
        With helm and blade,
And in Freedom's cause advancing!

SWEET INNISFALLEN.

SWEET Innisfallen, fare thee well,
    May calm and sunshine long be thine!
How fair thou art let others tell, —
    To *feel* how fair shall long be mine.

Sweet Innisfallen, long shall dwell
    In memory's dream that sunny smile,
Which o'er thee on that evening fell,
    When first I saw thy fairy isle.

'T was light, indeed, too blest for one,
    Who had to turn to paths of care —
Through crowded haunts again to run,
    And leave thee bright and silent there;

No more unto thy shores to come,
    But, on the world's rude ocean tost,
Dream of thee sometimes, as a home
    Of sunshine he had seen and lost.

Far better in thy weeping hours
    To part from thee, as I do now,
When mist is o'er thy blooming bowers,
    Like sorrow's veil on beauty's brow.

For, though unrivalled still thy grace,
    Thou dost not look, as then, *too* blest,
But thus in shadow, seem'st a place
    Where erring man might hope to rest —

Might hope to rest, and find in thee
    A gloom like Eden's on the day
He left its shade, when every tree,
    Like thine, hung weeping o'er his way.

Weeping or smiling, lovely isle!
    And all the lovelier for thy tears —
For tho' but rare thy sunny smile,
    'T is heaven's own glance when it ap-
        pears.

Like feeling hearts, whose joys are few,
    But, when *indeed* they come, divine —
The brightest light the sun e'er threw
    Is lifeless to one gleam of thine!

'T WAS ONE OF THOSE DREAMS.[1]

'T WAS one of those dreams, that by
        music are brought,
Like a bright summer haze, o'er the poet's
        warm thought —
When, lost in the future, his soul wan-
        ders on,
And all of this life, but its sweetness, is
        gone.

---

[1] Written during a visit to Lord Kenmare, at
Killarney.

The wild notes he heard o'er the water
      were those
He had taught to sing Erin's dark bon-
      dage and woes,
And the breath of the bugle now wafted
      them o'er
From Dinis' green isle, to Glenà's wooded
      shore.

He listened — while, high o'er the eagle's
      rude nest,
The lingering sounds on their way loved
      to rest;
And the echoes sung back from their
      full mountain choir,
As if loath to let song so enchanting
      expire.

It seemed as if every sweet note, that died
      here,
Was again brought to life in some airier
      sphere,
Some heaven in those hills, where the
      soul of the strain
That had ceased upon earth was awaking
      again!

Oh forgive, if, while listening to music,
      whose breath
Seemed to circle his name with a charm
      against death,
He should feel a proud Spirit within him
      proclaim,
" Even so shalt thou live in the echoes of
      Fame:

" Even so, tho' thy memory should now
      die away,
" 'T will be caught up again in some
      happier day,
" And the hearts and the voices of Erin
      prolong,
" Through the answering Future, thy
      name and thy song.''

FAIREST! PUT ON AWHILE.

FAIREST! put on awhile
   These pinions of light I bring thee,
And o'er thy own green isle
   In fancy let me wing thee.
Never did Ariel's plume,
   At golden sunset hover
O'er scenes so full of bloom,
   As I shall waft thee over.

Fields, where the Spring delays
   And fearlessly meets the ardor
Of the warm Summer's gaze,
   With only her tears to guard her.
Rocks, thro' myrtle boughs
   In grace majestic frowning;
Like some bold warrior's brows
   That Love hath just been crowning.

Islets, so freshly fair,
   That never hath bird come nigh them,
But from his course thro' air
   He hath been won down by them; [1]
Types, sweet maid, of thee,
   Whose look, whose blush inviting,
Never did Love yet see
   From Heaven, without alighting.

Lakes, where the pearl lies hid, [2]
   And caves, where the gem is sleeping,
Bright as the tears thy lid
   Lets fall in lonely weeping.
Glens, [3] where Ocean comes,
   To 'scape the wild wind's rancor,
And harbors, worthiest homes
   Where Freedom's fleet can anchor.

Then, if, while scenes so grand,
   So beautiful, shine before thee,
Pride for thy own dear land
   Should haply be stealing o'er thee,
Oh, let grief come first,
   O'er pride itself victorious —
Thinking how man hath curst
   What Heaven had made so glorious!

QUICK! WE HAVE BUT A SECOND.

QUICK! we have but a second,
   Fill round the cup, while you may;
For Time, the churl, hath beckoned,
   And we must away, away!

1 In describing the Skeligs (islands of the
Barony of Forth), Dr. Keating says, "There is
a certain attractive virtue in the soil which draws
down all the birds that attempt to fly over it, and
obliges them to light upon the rock.''

2 " Nennius, a British writer of the ninth
century, mentions the abundance of pearls in
Ireland. Their princes, he says, hung them behind their ears: and this we find confirmed by a
present made A.C. 1094, by Gilbert, Bishop of
Limerick, to Anselm, Archbishop of Canterbury,
of a considerable quantity of Irish pearls.'' —
O'Halloran.

3 Glengariff.

Grasp the pleasure that 's flying,
  For oh, not Orpheus' strain
Could keep sweet hours from dying,
  Or charm them to life again.
    Then, quick! we have but a second,
      Fill round the cup, while you may;
    For Time, the churl, hath beckoned,
      And we must away, away!

See the glass, how it flushes,
  Like some young Hebe's lip,
And half meets thine, and blushes
  That thou shouldst delay to sip.
Shame, oh shame unto thee,
  If ever thou see'st that day,
When a cup or lip shall woo thee,
  And turn untouched away!
    Then, quick! we have but a second,
      Fill round, fill round, while you
        may;
    For Time, the churl, hath beckoned,
      And we must away, away!

AND DOTH NOT A MEETING LIKE THIS.

And doth not a meeting like this make
    amends,
  For all the long years I 've been wan-
    dering away —
To see thus around me my youth's early
    friends,
  As smiling and kind as in that happy
    day?
Tho' haply o'er some of your brows, as
    o'er mine,
  The snow-fall of time may be stealing
    — what then?
Like Alps in the sunset, thus lighted by
    wine,
  We 'll wear the gay tinge of youth's
    roses again.

What softened remembrances come o'er
    the heart,
  In gazing on those we 've been lost to
    so long!
The sorrows, the joys, of which once
    they were part,
  Still round them, like visions of yester-
    day, throng,
As letters some hand hath invisibly traced,
  When held to the flame will steal out
    on the sight,

So many a feeling, that long seemed
    effaced,
  The warmth of a moment like this
    brings to light.

And thus, as in memory's bark we shall
    glide,
  To visit the scenes of our boyhood
    anew,
Tho' oft we may see, looking down on
    the tide,
  The wreck of full many a hope shining
    thro';
Yet still, as in fancy we point to the
    flowers,
  That once made a garden of all the
    gay shore,
Deceived for a moment, we 'll think
    them still ours,
  And breathe the fresh air of life's
    morning once more.[1]

So brief our existence, a glimpse, at the
    most,
  Is all we can have of the few we hold
    dear;
And oft even joy is unheeded and lost,
  For want of some heart, that could
    echo it, near.
Ah, well may we hope, when this short
    life is gone,
  To meet in some world of more per-
    manent bliss,
For a smile, or a grasp of the hand,
    hastening on,
  Is all we enjoy of each other in this.[2]

But, come, the more rare such delights
    to the heart,
  The more we should welcome and
    bless them the more;

1 *Jours charmans, quand je songe à vos heureux
    instans,
  Je pense remonter le fleuve de mes ans ;
  Et mon cœur enchanté sur sa rive fleurie
  Respire encore l'air pur du matin de la vie.*

2 The same thought has been happily expressed by my friend Mr. Washington Irving, in
his "*Bracebridge Hall*," vol. i. p. 213. The
sincere pleasure which I feel in calling this gentleman my friend, is much enhanced by the
reflection that he is too good an American, to
have admitted me so readily to such a distinction,
if he had not known that my feelings towards the
great and free country that gave him birth, have
been long such as every real lover of the liberty
and happiness of the human race must entertain.

They 're ours, when we meet, — they are
    lost when we part,
  Like birds that bring summer, and fly
    when 't is o'er.
Thus circling the cup, hand in hand, ere
    we drink,
  Let Sympathy pledge us, thro' pleas-
    ure, thro' pain,
That, fast as a feeling but touches one
    link,
  Her magic shall send it direct thro'
    the chain.

THE MOUNTAIN SPRITE.

IN yonder valley there dwelt, alone,
A youth, whose moments had calmly
    flown,
'Till spells came o'er him, and, day and
    night,
He was haunted and watched by a
    Mountain Sprite.

As once, by moonlight, he wander'd o'er
The golden sands of that island shore,
A foot-print sparkled before his sight —
'T was the fairy foot of the Mountain
    Sprite!

Beside a fountain, one sunny day,
As bending over the stream he lay,
There peeped down o'er him two eyes of
    light,
And he saw in that mirror the Mountain
    Sprite.

He turned, but, lo, like a startled bird,
That spirit fled! — and the youth but
    heard
Sweet music, such as marks the flight
Of some bird of song, from the Mountain
    Sprite.

One night, still haunted by that bright
    look,
The boy, bewildered, his pencil took,
And, guided only by memory's light,
Drew the once-seen form of the Moun-
    tain Sprite.

"Oh thou, who lovest the shadow,"
    cried
A voice, low whispering by his side,

"Now turn and see," — here the youth's
    delight
Sealed the rosy lips of the Mountain
    Sprite.

"Of all the Spirits of land and sea,"
Then rapt he murmured, "there 's none
    like thee,
"And oft, oh oft, may thy foot thus light
"In this lonely bower, sweet Mountain
    Sprite!"

AS VANQUISHED ERIN.

As vanquished Erin wept beside
  The Boyne's ill-fated river,
She saw where Discord, in the tide,
  Had dropt his loaded quiver.
"Lie hid," she cried, "ye venomed
    darts,
  "Where mortal eye may shun you;
"Lie hid — the stain of manly hearts,
  "That bled for me, is on you."

But vain her wish, her weeping vain, —
  As Time too well hath taught her —
Each year the Fiend returns again,
  And dives into that water;
And brings, triumphant, from beneath
  His shafts of desolation,
And sends them, winged with worse than
    death,
  Through all her maddening nation.

Alas for her who sits and mourns,
  Even now, beside that river —
Unwearied still the Fiend returns,
  And stored is still his quiver.
"When will this end, ye Powers of
    Good?"
  She weeping asks for ever;
But only hears, from out that flood,
  The Demon answer, "Never!"

DESMOND'S SONG.[1]

By the Feal's wave benighted,
  No star in the skies,
To thy door by Love lighted,
  I first saw those eyes.

1 "Thomas, the heir of the Desmond family,
had accidentally been so engaged in the chase, that
he was benighted near Tralee, and obliged to take
shelter at the Abbey of Feal, in the house of one

Some voice whispered o'er me,
　As the threshold I crost,
There was ruin before me,
　If I loved, I was lost.

Love came, and brought sorrow
　Too soon in his train;
Yet so sweet, that to-morrow
　'T were welcome again.
Though misery's full measure
　My portion should be,
I would drain it with pleasure,
　If poured out by thee.

You, who call it dishonor
　To bow to this flame,
If you 've eyes, look but on her,
　And blush while you blame.
Hath the pearl less whiteness
　Because of its birth?
Hath the violet less brightness
　For growing near earth?

No — Man for his glory
　To ancestry flies;
But Woman's bright story
　Is told in her eyes.
While the Monarch but traces
　Thro' mortals his line,
Beauty, born of the Graces,
　Ranks next to Divine!

THEY KNOW NOT MY HEART.

THEY know not my heart, who believe
　there can be
One stain of this earth in its feelings for
　thee;
Who think, while I see thee in beauty's
　young hour,
As pure as the morning's first dew on the
　flower,
I could harm what I love, — as the sun's
　wanton ray
But smiles on the dew-drop to waste it
　away.

of his dependents, called Mac Cormac. Catherine, a beautiful daughter of his host, instantly
inspired the Earl with a violent passion, which he
could not subdue. He married her, and by this
inferior alliance alienated his followers, whose
brutal pride regarded this indulgence of his love
as an unpardonable degradation of his family." —
Leland, vol. ii.

No — beaming with light as those young
　features are,
There 's a light round thy heart which is
　lovelier far:
It *is* not that cheek — 't is the soul dawn-
　ing clear
Thro' its innocent blush makes thy beauty
　so dear;
As the sky we look up to, tho' glorious
　and fair,
Is looked up to the more, because Heaven
　lies there!

I WISH I WAS BY THAT DIM LAKE.

I WISH I was by that dim Lake,[1]
Where sinful souls their farewell take
Of this vain world, and half-way lie
In death's cold shadow, ere they die.
There, there, far from thee,
Deceitful world, my home should be;
Where, come what might of gloom and
　pain,
False hope should ne'er deceive again.

The lifeless sky, the mournful sound
Of unseen waters falling round;
The dry leaves, quivering o'er my head,
Like man, unquiet even when dead!
These, ay, these shall wean
My soul from life's deluding scene,
And turn each thought, o'ercharged with
　gloom,
Like willows, downward towards the
　tomb.

As they, who to their couch at night
Would win repose, first quench the light,
So must the hopes, that keep this breast
Awake, be quenched, ere it can rest.
Cold, cold, this heart must grow,
Unmoved by either joy or woe,
Like freezing founts, where all that 's
　thrown
Within their current turns to stone.

1 These verses are meant to allude to that ancient haunt of superstition, called Patrick's Purgatory. " In the midst of these gloomy regions
of Donegall (says Dr. Campbell) lay a lake, which
was to become the mystic theatre of this fabled
and intermediate state. In the lake were several
islands; but one of them was dignified with that
called the Mouth of Purgatory, which, during the

SHE SUNG OF LOVE.

SHE sung of Love, while o'er her lyre
  The rosy rays of evening fell,
As if to feed with their soft fire
  The soul within that trembling shell.
The same rich light hung o'er her cheek,
  And played around those lips that sung
And spoke, as flowers would sing and
    speak,
  If Love could lend their leaves a
    tongue.

But soon the West no longer burned,
  Each rosy ray from heaven withdrew;
And, when to gaze again I turned,
  The minstrel's form seemed fading too.
As if *her* light and heaven's were one,
  The glory all had left that frame;
And from her glimmering lips the tone,
  As from a parting spirit, came.[1]

Who ever loved, but had the thought
  That he and all he loved must part?
Filled with this fear, I flew and caught
  The fading image to my heart —
And cried, " Oh Love! is this thy doom?
  " Oh light of youth's resplendent day!
" Must ye then lose your golden bloom,
  " And thus, like sunshine, die away? "

SING—SING—MUSIC WAS GIVEN.

SING — sing — Music was given,
  To brighten the gay, and kindle the
    loving;
Souls here, like planets in Heaven,
  By harmony's laws alone are kept
    moving.

Beauty may boast of her eyes and her
    cheeks,
  But Love from the lips his true archery
    wings;
And she, who but feathers the dart when
    she speaks,
  At once sends it home to the heart
    when she sings.
    Then sing — sing — Music was given,
      To brighten the gay, and kindle the
        loving;
    Souls here, like planets in Heaven,
      By harmony's laws alone are kept
        moving.

When Love, rocked by his mother,
  Lay sleeping as calm as slumber could
    make him,
" Hush, hush," said Venus, "no other
  " Sweet voice but his own is worthy
    to wake him."
Dreaming of music he slumbered the while
  Till faint from his lip a soft melody
    broke,
And Venus, enchanted, looked on with
    a smile,
  While Love to his own sweet singing
    awoke.
    Then sing — sing — Music was given,
      To brighten the gay, and kindle the
        loving;
    Souls here, like planets in Heaven,
      By harmony's laws alone are kept
        moving.

THO' HUMBLE THE BANQUET.

THO' humble the banquet to which I in-
    vite thee,
  Thou 'lt find there the best a poor bard
    can command:
Eyes, beaming with welcome, shall throng
    round, to light thee,
  And Love serve the feast with his own
    willing hand.

And tho' Fortune may seem to have
    turned from the dwelling
  Of him thou regardest her favoring
    ray,
Thou wilt find there a gift, all her treas-
    ures excelling,
  Which, proudly he feels, hath ennobled
    his way.

dark ages, attracted the notice of all Christendom, and was the resort of penitents and pilgrims from almost every country in Europe."

" It was," as the same writer tells us, "one of the most dismal and dreary spots in the North, almost inaccessible, through deep glens and rugged mountains, frightful with impending rocks, and the hollow murmurs of the western winds in dark caverns, peopled only with such fantastic beings as the mind, however gay, is, from strange association, wont to appropriate to such gloomy scenes." — " *Strictures on the Ecclesiastical and Literary History of Ireland.*"

1 The thought here was suggested by some beautiful lines in Mr. Rogers's Poem of *Human Life*, beginning —
" Now in the glimmering, dying light she grows
  Less and less earthly."
I would quote the entire passage, did I not fear to put my own humble imitation of it out of countenance.

'T is that freedom of mind, which no
    vulgar dominion
      Can turn from the path a pure con-
      science approves;
Which, with hope in the heart, and no
    chain on the pinion,
      Holds upwards its course to the light
      which it loves.

'T is this makes the pride of his humble
    retreat,
      And, with this, tho' of all other treas-
      ures bereaved,
The breeze of his garden to him is more
    sweet
      Than the costliest incense that Pomp
      e'er received.

Then, come, — if a board so untempting
    hath power
      To win thee from grandeur, its best
      shall be thine;
And there 's one, long the light of the
    bard's happy bower,
      Who, smiling, will blend her bright
      welcome with mine.

SING, SWEET HARP.

Sing, sweet Harp, oh sing to me
    Some song of ancient days,
Whose sounds, in this sad memory,
    Long buried dreams shall raise;—
Some lay that tells of vanished fame,
    Whose light once round us shone;
Of noble pride, now turned to shame,
    And hopes for ever gone. —
Sing, sad Harp, thus sing to me;
    Alike our doom is cast,
Both lost to all but memory,
    We live but in the past.

How mournfully the midnight air
    Among thy chords doth sigh,
As if it sought some echo there
    Of voices long gone by;—
Of Chieftains, now forgot, who seemed
    The foremost then in fame;
Of Bards who, once immortal deemed,
    Now sleep without a name. —
In vain, sad Harp, the midnight air
    Among thy chords doth sigh;
In vain it seeks an echo there
    Of voices long gone by.

Couldst thou but call those spirits round,
    Who once, in bower and hall,
Sat listening to thy magic sound,
    Now mute and mouldering all;—
But, no; they would but wake to weep
    Their children's slavery;
Then leave them in their dreamless sleep,
    The dead, at least, are free!—
Hush, hush, sad Harp, that dreary tone,
    That knell of Freedom's day;
Or, listening to its death-like moan,
    Let me, too, die away.

SONG OF THE BATTLE EVE.

Time — the Ninth Century

To-morrow, comrade, we
On the battle-plain must be,
    There to conquer, or both lie low!
The morning star is up, —
But there 's wine still in the cup,
    And we 'll take another quaff, ere we
    go, boy, go;
    We 'll take another quaff, ere we go.

'T is true, in manliest eyes
A passing tear will rise,
    When we think of the friends we
    leave lone;
But what can wailing do?
See, our goblet 's weeping too!
    With its tears we 'll chase away our
    own, boy, our own;
    With its tears we 'll chase away our
    own.

But daylight 's stealing on; —
The last that o'er us shone
    Saw our children around us play;
The next — ah! where shall we
And those rosy urchins be?
    But — no matter — grasp thy sword
    and away, boy, away;
    No matter— grasp thy sword and away!

Let those, who brook the chain
Of Saxon or of Dane,
    Ignobly by their fire-sides stay;
One sigh to home be given,
One heartfelt prayer to heaven,
    Then, for Erin and her cause, boy,
    hurra! hurra! hurra!
    Then, for Erin and her cause, hurra!

THE WANDERING BARD.

WHAT life like that of the bard can be, —
The wandering bard, who roams as free
As the mountain lark that o'er him sings,
And, like that lark, a music brings
Within him, where'er he comes or goes, —
A fount that for ever flows!
The world 's to him like some play-
ground,
Where fairies dance their moonlight
round; —
If dimmed the turf where late they trod,
The elves but seek some greener sod;
So, when less bright his scene of glee,
To another away flies he!

Oh, what would have been young
Beauty's doom,
Without a bard to fix her bloom?
They tell us, in the moon's bright round,
Things lost in this dark world are found;
So charms, on earth long past and gone,
In the poet's lay live on. —
Would ye have smiles that ne'er grow
dim?
You 've only to give them all to him,
Who, with but a touch of Fancy's wand,
Can lend them life, this life beyond,
And fix them high, in Poesy's sky, —
Young stars that never die!

Then, welcome the bard where'er he
comes, —
For, tho' he hath countless airy homes,
To which his wing excursive roves,
Yet still, from time to time, he loves
To light upon earth and find such cheer
As brightens our banquet here.
No matter how far, how fleet he flies,
You 've only to light up kind young eyes,
Such signal-fires as here are given, —
And down he 'll drop from Fancy's
heaven,
The minute such call to love or mirth
Proclaims he 's wanting on earth!

ALONE IN CROWDS TO WANDER ON.

ALONE in crowds to wander on,
And feel that all the charm is gone
Which voices dear and eyes beloved
Shed round us once, where'er we
roved —

This, this the doom must be
Of all who 've loved, and lived to see
The few bright things they thought would
stay
For ever near them, die away.

Tho' fairer forms around us throng,
Their smiles to others all belong,
And want that charm which dwells alone
Round those the fond heart calls its own.
Where, where the sunny brow?
The long-known voice — where are they
now?
Thus ask I still, nor ask in vain,
The silence answers all too plain.

Oh, what is Fancy's magic worth,
If all her art can not call forth
One bliss like those we felt of old
From lips now mute, and eyes now cold?
No, no, — her spell is vain, —
As soon could she bring back again
Those eyes themselves from out the grave,
As wake again one bliss they gave.

I 'VE A SECRET TO TELL THEE.

I 'VE a secret to tell thee, but hush! not
here, —
Oh! not where the world its vigil
keeps:
I 'll seek, to whisper it in thine ear,
Some shore where the Spirit of Silence
sleeps;
Where summer's wave unmurmuring dies,
Nor fay can hear the fountain's gush;
Where, if but a note her night-bird sighs,
The rose saith, chidingly, "Hush,
sweet, hush!"

There, amid the deep silence of that
hour,
When stars can be heard in ocean dip,
Thyself shall, under some rosy bower,
Sit mute, with thy finger on thy lip:
Like him, the boy,[1] who born among
The flowers that on the Nile-stream
blush,
Sits ever thus, — his only song
To earth and heaven, "Hush, all,
hush!"

1 The God of Silence, thus pictured by the
Egyptians.

SONG OF INNISFAIL.

THEY came from a land beyond the sea,
　And now o'er the western main
Set sail, in their good ships, gallantly,
　From the sunny land of Spain.
" Oh, where 's the Isle we 've seen in
　　dreams,
　" Our destined home or grave? " [1]
Thus sung they as, by the morning's
　beams,
　They swept the Atlantic wave.

And, lo, where afar o'er ocean shines
　A sparkle of radiant green,
As tho' in that deep lay emerald mines,
　Whose light thro' the wave was seen.
" 'T is Innisfail [2] — 't is Innisfail ! "
　Rings o'er the echoing sea;
While, bending to heaven, the warriors
　hail
　That home of the brave and free.

Then turned they unto the Eastern
　wave,
　Where now their Day-God's eye
A look of such sunny omen gave
　As lighted up sea and sky.
Nor frown was seen thro' sky or sea,
　Nor tear o'er leaf or sod,
When first on their Isle of Destiny
　Our great forefathers trod.

THE NIGHT DANCE.

STRIKE the gay harp! see the moon is
　on high,
　And, as true to her beam as the tides
　　of the ocean,
Young hearts, when they feel the soft
　light of her eye,
　Obey the mute call and heave into
　　motion.
Then, sound notes — the gayest, the
　lightest,
　That ever took wing, when heaven
　　looked brightest!
　　　Again! Again!

1 " Milesius remembered the remarkable pre-
diction of the principal Druid, who foretold that
the posterity of Gadelus should obtain the possession of a Western Island (which was Ireland),
and there inhabit." — *Keating.*

2 The Island of Destiny, one of the ancient
names of Ireland.

Oh! could such heart-stirring music be
　heard
　In that City of Statues described by
　　romancers,
So wakening its spell, even stone would
　be stirred,
　And statues themselves all start into
　　dancers!

Why then delay, with such sounds in our
　ears,
　And the flower of Beauty's own garden
　　before us, —
While stars overhead leave the song of
　their spheres,
　And listening to ours, hang wondering
　　o'er us?
Again, that strain! — to hear it thus
　sounding
　Might set even Death's cold pulses
　　bounding —
　　　Again! Again!
Oh, what delight when the youthful and
　gay,
　Each with eye like a sunbeam and foot
　　like a feather,
Thus dance, like the Hours to the music
　of May,
　And mingle sweet song and sunshine
　　together!

THERE ARE SOUNDS OF MIRTH.

THERE are sounds of mirth in the night-
　air ringing,
　And lamps from every casement
　　shown;
While voices blithe within are singing,
　That seem to say " Come," in every
　　tone.
Ah! once how light, in Life's young
　season,
　My heart had leapt at that sweet lay;
Nor paused to ask of greybeard Reason
　Should I the syren call obey.

And, see — the lamps still livelier glitter,
　The syren lips more fondly sound;
No, seek, ye nymphs, some victim fitter
　To sink in your rosy bondage bound.
Shall a bard, whom not the world in arms
　Could bend to tyranny's rude control,
Thus quail at sight of woman's charms
　And yield to a smile his freeborn soul?

Thus sung the sage, while, slyly steal-
ing,
   The nymphs their fetters around him
     cast,
And, — their laughing eyes, the while,
concealing, —
   Led Freedom's Bard their slave at
     last.
For the Poet's heart, still prone to
loving,
   Was like that rock of the Druid race,[1]
Which the gentlest touch at once set
moving,
   But all earth's power could n't cast
     from its base.

OH! ARRANMORE, LOVED ARRANMORE.

OH! Arranmore, loved Arranmore,
How oft I dream of thee,
And of those days when, by thy shore,
I wandered young and free.
Full many a path I 've tried, since
then,
   Thro' pleasure's flowery maze,
But ne'er could find the bliss again
I felt in those sweet days.

How blithe upon thy breezy cliffs
At sunny morn I 've stood,
With heart as bounding as the skiffs
That danced along thy flood;
Or, when the western wave grew bright
With daylight's parting wing,
Have sought that Eden in its light
Which dreaming poets sing;[2] —

That Eden where the immortal brave
Dwell in a land serene, —
Whose bowers beyond the shining wave,
At sunset, oft are seen.
Ah dream too full of saddening truth!
Those mansions o'er the main
Are like the hopes I built in youth, —
As sunny and as vain!

1 The Rocking Stones of the Druids, some of
which no force is able to dislodge from their
stations.

2 "The inhabitants of Arranmore are still
persuaded that, in a clear day, they can see from
this coast Hy Brysail or the Enchanted Island,
the Paradise of the Pagan Irish, and concerning

LAY HIS SWORD BY HIS SIDE.

LAY his sword by his side,[3] — it hath
   served him too well
Not to rest near his pillow below;
To the last moment true, from his hand
   ere it fell,
   Its point was still turned to a flying
     foe.
Fellow-laborers in life, let them slumber
   in death,
   Side by side, as becomes the reposing
     brave, —
That sword which he loved still unbroke
   in its sheath,
   And himself unsubdued in his grave.

Yet pause — for, in fancy, a still voice I
   hear,
   As if breathed from his brave heart's
     remains; —
Faint echo of that which, in Slavery's
   ear,
   Once sounded the war-word, " Burst
     your chains ! "
And it cries from the grave where the
   hero lies deep,
   " Tho' the day of your Chieftain for
     ever hath set,
" Oh leave not his sword thus inglorious
   to sleep, —
   " It hath victory's life in it yet !

" Should some alien, unworthy such
   weapon to wield,
   " Dare to touch thee, my own gallant
     sword,
" Then rest in thy sheath, like a talisman
   sealed,
   " Or return to the grave of thy chain-
     less lord.
" But, if grasped by a hand that hath
   learned the proud use
   " Of a falchion, like thee, on the
     battle-plain, —
" Then, at Liberty's summons, like light-
   ning let loose,
   " Leap forth from thy dark sheath
     again ! "

which they relate a number of romantic stories."
—*Beaufort's "Ancient Topography of Ireland."*

3 It was the custom of the ancient Irish, in
the manner of the Scythians, to bury the favorite
swords of their heroes along with them.

OH, COULD WE DO WITH THIS WORLD OF OURS.

OH, could we do with this world of ours
As thou dost with thy garden bowers,
Reject the weeds and keep the flowers,
　What a heaven on earth we 'd make it !
So bright a dwelling should be our own,
So warranted free from sigh or frown,
That angels soon would be coming down,
　By the week or month to take it.

Like those gay flies that wing thro' air,
And in themselves a lustre bear,
A stock of light, still ready there,
　Whenever they wish to use it;
So, in this world I 'd make for thee,
Our hearts should all like fire-flies be,
And the flash of wit or poesy
　Break forth whenever we choose it.

While every joy that glads our sphere
Hath still some shadow hovering near,
In this new world of ours, my dear,
　Such shadows will all be omitted:—
Unless they 're like that graceful one,
Which, when thou 'rt dancing in the sun,
Still near thee, leaves a charm upon
　Each spot where it hath flitted!

THE WINE–CUP IS CIRCLING.

THE wine-cup is circling in Almhin's hall,[1]
And its Chief, mid his heroes reclining,
Looks up, with a sigh, to the trophied wall,
　Where his sword hangs idly shining.
　　When, hark ! that shout
　　From the vale without, —
" Arm ye quick, the Dane, the Dane is nigh ! "
　　Every Chief starts up
　　From his foaming cup,
And " To battle, to battle ! " is the Finian's cry.

The minstrels have seized their harps of gold,
And they sing such thrilling numbers,

'T is like the voice of the Brave, of old,
　Breaking forth from their place of slumbers !
　　Spear to buckler rang,
　　As the minstrels sang,
And the Sun-burst [2] o'er them floated wide;
　　While remembering the yoke
　　Which their fathers broke,
"On for liberty, for liberty ! " the Finians cried.

Like clouds of the night the Northmen came,
O'er the valley of Almhin lowering;
While onward moved, in the light of its fame,
　That banner of Erin, towering.
　　With the mingling shock
　　Rung cliff and rock,
While, rank on rank, the invaders die:
　　And the shout, that last
　　O'er the dying past,
Was " victory ! victory ! " — the Finian's cry.

THE DREAM OF THOSE DAYS.

THE dream of those days when first I sung thee is o'er,
Thy triumph hath stained the charm thy sorrows then wore;
And even of the light which Hope once shed o'er thy chains,
Alas, not a gleam to grace thy freedom remains.

Say, is it that slavery sunk so deep in thy heart,
That still the dark brand is there, tho' chainless thou art;
And Freedom's sweet fruit, for which thy spirit long burned,
Now, reaching at last thy lip, to ashes hath turned?

Up Liberty's steep by Truth and Eloquence led,
With eyes on her temple fixt, how proud was thy tread !

1 The Palace of Fin Mac-Cumhal (the Fingal of Macpherson) in Leinster. It was built on the top of the hill, which has retained from thence the name of the Hill of Allen, in the county of Kildare. The Finians, or Fenii, were the cele-brated National Militia of Ireland, which this Chief commanded. The introduction of the Danes in the above song is an anachronism common to most of the Finian and Ossianic legends.
2 The name given to the banner of the Irish.

Ah, better thou ne'er hadst lived that
   summit to gain
Or died in the porch than thus dishonor
   the fane.

FROM THIS HOUR THE PLEDGE IS GIVEN.

FROM this hour the pledge is given,
   From this hour my soul is thine:
Come what will, from earth or heaven,
   Weal or woe, thy fate be mine.
When the proud and great stood by thee,
   None dared thy rights to spurn;
And if now they 're false and fly thee,
   Shall I, too, basely turn?
No; — whate'er the fires that try thee,
   In the same this heart shall burn.

Tho' the sea, where thou embarkest,
   Offers now no friendly shore,
Light may come where all looks darkest,
   Hope hath life when life seems o'er.
And, of those past ages dreaming,
   When glory decked thy brow,
Oft I fondly think, tho' seeming
   So fallen and clouded now,
Thou 'lt again break forth, all beaming,—
   None so bright, so blest as thou!

SILENCE IS IN OUR FESTAL HALLS.[1]

SILENCE is in our festal halls, —
   Sweet Son of Song! thy course is o'er;

[1] It is hardly necessary, perhaps, to inform the reader, that these lines are meant as a tribute of sincere friendship to the memory of an old and valued colleague in this work, Sir John Stevenson.

In vain on thee sad Erin calls,
   Her minstrel's voice responds no
   more; —
All silent as the Eolian shell
   Sleeps at the close of some bright
   day,
When the sweet breeze that waked its
   swell
   At sunny morn hath died away.

Yet at our feasts thy spirit long
   Awaked by music's spell shall rise;
For, name so linked with deathless song
   Partakes its charm and never dies:
And even within the holy fane
   When music wafts the soul to heaven,
One thought to him whose earliest strain
   Was echoed there shall long be given.

But, where is now the cheerful day,
   The social night when by thy side
He who now weaves this parting lay
   His skilless voice with thine allied;
And sung those songs whose every tone,
   When bard and minstrel long have
   past,
Shall still in sweetness all their own
   Embalmed by fame, undying last.

Yes, Erin, thine alone the fame,
   Or, if thy bard have shared the
   crown,
From thee the borrowed glory came,
   And at thy feet is now laid down.
Enough, if Freedom still inspire
   His latest song and still there be,
As evening closes round his lyre,
   One ray upon its chords from thee.

NATIONAL AIRS.

ADVERTISEMENT.

It is Cicero, I believe, who says "*naturâ ad modos ducimur;*" and the abundance of wild, indigenous airs, which almost every country, except England, possesses, sufficiently proves the truth of his assertion. The lovers of this simple, but interesting kind of music, are here presented with the first number of a collection, which, I trust, their contributions will enable us to continue. A pretty air without words resembles one of those *half* creatures of Plato, which are described as wandering in search of the remainder of themselves through the world. To supply this other half, by uniting with congenial words the many fugitive melodies which have hitherto had none, — or only such as are unintelligible to the generality of their hearers, — is the object and ambition of the present work. Neither is it our intention to confine ourselves to what are strictly called National Melodies, but, wherever we meet with any wandering and beautiful air, to which poetry has not yet assigned a worthy home, we shall venture to claim it as an *estray* swan, and enrich our humble Hippocrene with its song.

T. M.

NATIONAL AIRS.

A TEMPLE TO FRIENDSHIP. [1]
(SPANISH AIR.)

"A TEMPLE to Friendship," said Laura,
enchanted,
"I 'll build in this garden, — the
thought is divine!"
Her temple was built and she now only
wanted
An image of Friendship to place on
the shrine.
She flew to a sculptor, who set down
before her
A Friendship, the fairest his art could
invent;
But so cold and so dull, that the youthful
adorer
Saw plainly this was not the idol she
meant.

"Oh! never," she cried, "could I think
of enshrining
"An image whose looks are so joyless
and dim; —
"But yon little god, upon roses reclining,
"We 'll make, if you please, Sir, a
Friendship of him."
So the bargain was struck; with the little
god laden
She joyfully flew to her shrine in the
grove:
"Farewell," said the sculptor, "you 're
not the first maiden
"Who came but for Friendship and
took away Love."

FLOW ON, THOU SHINING RIVER.
(PORTUGUESE AIR.)

FLOW on, thou shining river;
But ere thou reach the sea

<hr>

1 The thought is taken from a song by Le
Prieur, called "*La Statue de l'Amitié.*"

Seek Ella's bower and give her
The wreaths I fling o'er thee.
And tell her thus, if she 'll be mine
The current of our lives shall be,
With joys along their course to shine,
Like those sweet flowers on thee.

But if in wandering thither
Thou find'st she mocks my prayer,
Then leave those wreaths to wither
Upon the cold bank there;
And tell her thus, when youth is o'er,
Her lone and loveless charms shall be
Thrown by upon life's weedy shore,
Like those sweet flowers from thee.

ALL THAT 'S BRIGHT MUST FADE.
(INDIAN AIR.)

ALL that 's bright must fade, —
The brightest still the fleetest;
All that 's sweet was made,
But to be lost when sweetest.
Stars that shine and fall; —
The flower that drops in springing; —
These, alas! are types of all
To which our hearts are clinging.
All that 's bright must fade, —
The brightest still the fleetest;
All that 's sweet was made
But to be lost when sweetest!

Who would seek or prize
Delights that end in aching?
Who would trust to ties
That every hour are breaking?
Better far to be
In utter darkness lying,
Than to be blest with light and see
That light for ever flying.
All that 's bright must fade, —
The brightest still the fleetest;
All that 's sweet was made
But to be lost when sweetest!

221

SO WARMLY WE MET.

(Hungarian Air.)

So warmly we met and so fondly we
　　parted,
　　That which was the sweeter even I
　　　could not tell, —
That first look of welcome her sunny
　　eyes darted,
　　Or that tear of passion, which blest
　　　our farewell.
To meet was a heaven and to part thus
　　another, —
　　Our joy and our sorrow seemed rivals
　　　in bliss;
Oh! Cupid's two eyes are not liker each
　　other
　　In smiles and in tears than that mo-
　　　ment to this.

The first was like day-break, new,
　　sudden, delicious, —
　　The dawn of a pleasure scarce kindled
　　　up yet;
The last like the farewell of daylight,
　　more precious,
　　More glowing and deep, as 't is nearer
　　　its set.
Our meeting, tho' happy, was tinged by
　　a sorrow
　　To think that such happiness could not
　　　remain;
While our parting, tho' sad, gave a hope
　　that to-morrow
　　Would bring back the blest hour of
　　　meeting again.

THOSE EVENING BELLS.

(Air. — The Bells of St. Petersburgh.)

Those evening bells! those evening bells!
How many a tale their music tells,
Of youth and home and that sweet time
When last I heard their soothing chime.

Those joyous hours are past away;
And many a heart, that then was gay,
Within the tomb now darkly dwells,
And hears no more those evening bells.

And so 't will be when I am gone;
That tuneful peal will still ring on,
While other bards shall walk these dells,
And sing your praise, sweet evening bells!

SHOULD THOSE FOND HOPES.

(Portuguese Air.)

Should those fond hopes e'er forsake
　　thee,[1]
　　Which now so sweetly thy heart em-
　　　ploy;
Should the cold world come to wake thee
　　From all thy visions of youth and joy;
Should the gay friends, for whom thou
　　wouldst banish
　　Him who once thought thy young
　　　heart his own,
All, like spring birds, falsely vanish,
　　And leave thy winter unheeded and
　　　lone; —

Oh! 't is then that he thou hast slighted
　　Would come to cheer thee, when all
　　　seem'd o'er;
Then the truant, lost and blighted,
　　Would to his bosom be taken once
　　　more.
Like that dear bird we both can remem-
　　ber,
　　Who left us while summer shone round,
But, when chilled by bleak December,
　　On our threshold a welcome still found.

REASON, FOLLY, AND BEAUTY.

(Italian Air.)

Reason and Folly and Beauty, they say,
Went on a party of pleasure one day:
　　Folly played
　　Around the maid,
The bells of his cap rung merrily out;
　　While Reason took
　　To his sermon-book —
Oh! which was the pleasanter no one
　　need doubt,
Which was the pleasanter no one need
　　doubt.

Beauty, who likes to be thought very
　　sage,
Turned for a moment to Reason's dull
　　page,
　　Till Folly said,
　　"Look here, sweet maid!" —

1 This is one of the many instances among
my lyrical poems, — though the above, it must
be owned, is an extreme case, — where the metre
has been necessarily sacrificed to the structure of
the air.

The sight of his cap brought her back to
herself;
    While Reason read
    His leaves of lead,
With no one to mind him, poor sensible
elf!
No, — no one to mind him, poor sensible
elf!

Then Reason grew jealous of Folly's
gay cap;
Had he that on, he her heart might en-
trap —
    "There it is,"
    Quoth Folly, "old quiz!"
(Folly was always good-natured, 't is
said,)
    "Under the sun
    "There 's no such fun,
"As Reason with my cap and bells on
his head,
"Reason with my cap and bells on his
head!"

But Reason the head-dress so awkwardly
wore,
That Beauty now liked him still less than
before;
    While Folly took
    Old Reason's book,
And twisted the leaves in a cap of such
ton,
    That Beauty vowed
    (Tho' not aloud),
She liked him still better in that than his
own,
Yes, — liked him still better in that than
his own.

FARE THEE WELL, THOU
LOVELY ONE!

(Sicilian Air.)

FARE thee well, thou lovely one!
    Lovely still, but dear no more;
Once his soul of truth is gone,
    Love's sweet life is o'er.
Thy words, whate'er their flattering spell,
    Could scarce have thus deceived;
But eyes that acted truth so well
    Were sure to be believed.
Then, fare thee well, thou lovely one!
    Lovely still, but dear no more;

Once his soul of truth is gone,
    Love's sweet life is o'er.

Yet those eyes look constant still,
    True as stars they keep their light;
Still those cheeks their pledge fulfil
    Of blushing always bright.
'T is only on thy changeful heart
    The blame of falsehood lies;
Love lives in every other part,
    But there, alas! he dies.
Then, fare thee well, thou lovely one!
    Lovely still, but dear no more;
Once his soul of truth is gone,
    Love's sweet life is o'er.

DOST THOU REMEMBER

(Portuguese Air.)

DOST thou remember that place so
lonely,
A place for lovers and lovers only,
    Where first I told thee all my secret
    sighs?
When, as the moonbeam that trembled
o'er thee
Illumed thy blushes, I knelt before
thee,
    And read my hope's sweet triumph in
    those eyes?
Then, then, while closely heart was
  • drawn to heart,
Love bound us — never, never more to
part!

And when I called thee by names the
dearest [1]
That love could fancy, the fondest, nearest, —
    "My life, my only life!" among the
    rest;
In those sweet accents that still enthral
me,
Thou saidst, "Ah! wherefore thy life
thus call me?
    "Thy soul, thy soul 's the name I love
    best;
"For life soon passes, — but how blest
to be
"That Soul which never, never parts
from thee!"

1 The thought in this verse is borrowed from
the original Portuguese words.

OH, COME TO ME WHEN DAY-LIGHT SETS.

(VENETIAN AIR.)

OH, come to me when daylight sets;
Sweet! then come to me,
When smoothly go our gondolets
O'er the moonlight sea.
When Mirth 's awake, and Love begins,
Beneath that glancing ray,
With sound of lutes and mandolins,
To steal young hearts away.
Then, come to me when daylight sets;
Sweet! then come to me,
When smoothly go our gondolets
O'er the moonlight sea.

Oh, then 's the hour for those who love,
Sweet, like thee and me;
When all 's so calm below, above,
In Heaven and o'er the sea.
When maidens sing sweet barcarolles,[1]
And Echo sings again
So sweet, that all with ears and souls
Should love and listen then.
So, come to me when daylight sets;
Sweet! then come to me,
When smoothly go our gondolets
O'er the moonlight sea.

OFT, IN THE STILLY NIGHT.

(SCOTCH AIR.)

OFT in the stilly night,
Ere Slumber's chain has bound me,
Fond Memory brings the light
Of other days around me;
The smiles, the tears,
Of boyhood's years,
The words of love then spoken;
The eyes that shone,
Now dimmed and gone,
The cheerful hearts now broken!
Thus, in the stilly night,
Ere Slumber's chain has bound me,
Sad Memory brings the light
Of other days around me.

When I remember all
The friends, so linked together,
I 've seen around me fall,
Like leaves in wintry weather;

1 *Barcarolles, sorte de chansons en langue Vénitienne, que chantent les gondoliers à Venise.* — Rousseau, "*Dictionnaire de Musique.*"

I feel like one,
Who treads alone
Some banquet-hall deserted,
Whose lights are fled,
Whose garlands dead,
And all but he departed!
Thus, in the stilly night,
Ere Slumber's chain has bound me,
Sad Memory brings the light
Of other days around me.

HARK! THE VESPER HYMN IS STEALING.

(RUSSIAN AIR.)

HARK! the vesper hymn is stealing
O'er the waters soft and clear;
Nearer yet and nearer pealing,
And now bursts upon the ear:
Jubilate, Amen.
Farther now, now farther stealing,
Soft it fades upon the ear:
Jubilate, Amen.

Now, like moonlight waves retreating
To the shore, it dies along;
Now, like angry surges meeting,
Breaks the mingled tide of song:
Jubilate, Amen.
Hush! again, like waves, retreating
To the shore, it dies along:
Jubilate, Amen.

LOVE AND HOPE.

(SWISS AIR.)

AT morn, beside yon summer sea,
Young Hope and Love reclined;
But scarce had noon-tide come, when he
Into his bark leapt smilingly,
And left poor Hope behind.

"I go," said Love, "to sail awhile
"Across this sunny main;"
And then so sweet his parting smile,
That Hope, who never dreamt of guile,
Believed he 'd come again.

She lingered there till evening's beam
Along the waters lay;
And o'er the sands, in thoughtful dream,
Oft traced his name, which still the stream
As often washed away.

At length a sail appears in sight,
And toward the maiden moves!
'Tis Wealth that comes, and gay and
bright,
His golden bark reflects the light,
But ah! it is not Love's.

Another sail — 'twas Friendship showed
Her night-lamp o'er the sea;
And calm the light that lamp bestowed;
But Love had lights that warmer glowed,
And where, alas! was he?

Now fast around the sea and shore
Night threw her darkling chain;
The sunny sails were seen no more,
Hope's morning dreams of bliss were
o'er, —
Love never came again!

THERE COMES A TIME.
(GERMAN AIR.)

THERE comes a time, a dreary time,
To him whose heart hath flown
O'er all the fields of youth's sweet
prime,
And made each flower its own.
'T is when his soul must first renounce
Those dreams so bright, so fond;
Oh! then 's the time to die at once,
For life has naught beyond.

When sets the sun on Afric's shore,
That instant all is night;
And so should life at once be o'er,
When Love withdraws his light; —
Nor, like our northern day, gleam on
Thro' twilight's dim delay,
The cold remains of lustre gone,
Of fire long past away.

MY HARP HAS ONE UNCHAN-
GING THEME.
(SWEDISH AIR.)

MY harp has one unchanging theme,
One strain that still comes o'er
Its languid chord, as 't were a dream
Of joy that 's now no more.
In vain I try, with livelier air,
To wake the breathing string;
That voice of other times is there,
And saddens all I sing.

Breathe on, breathe on, thou languid
strain,
Henceforth be all my own;
Tho' thou art oft so full of pain
Few hearts can bear thy tone.
Yet oft thou 'rt sweet, as if the sigh,
The breath that Pleasure's wings
Gave out, when last they wantoned by,
Were still upon thy strings.

OH, NO — NOT EVEN WHEN
FIRST WE LOVED.
(CASHMERIAN AIR.)

OH, no — not even when first we loved,
Wert thou as dear as now thou art;
Thy beauty then my senses moved,
But now thy virtues bind my heart.
What was but Passion's sigh before,
Has since been turned to Reason's vow;
And, though I then might love thee *more*,
Trust me, I love thee *better* now.

Altho' my heart in earlier youth
Might kindle with more wild desire,
Believe me, it has gained in truth
Much more than it has lost in fire.
The flame now warms my inmost core,
That then but sparkled o'er my brow,
And, though I seemed to love thee more,
Yet, oh, I love thee better now.

PEACE BE AROUND THEE.
(SCOTCH AIR.)

PEACE be around thee, wherever thou
rov'st;
May life be for thee one summer's day,
And all that thou wishest and all that thou
lov'st
Come smiling around thy sunny way!
If sorrow e'er this calm should break,
May even thy tears pass off so lightly,
Like spring-showers, they 'll only make
The smiles that follow shine more
brightly.

May Time who sheds his blight o'er all
And daily dooms some joy to death
O'er thee let years so gently fall,
They shall not crush one flower beneath.
As half in shade and half in sun
This world along its path advances,
May that side the sun's upon
Be all that e'er shall meet thy glances!

COMMON SENSE AND GENIUS.
(French Air.)

While I touch the string,
  Wreathe my brows with laurel,
For the tale I sing
  Has, for once, a moral.
Common Sense, one night,
  Tho' not used to gambols,
Went out by moonlight,
  With Genius, on his rambles.
        While I touch the string, etc.

Common Sense went on,
  Many wise things saying;
While the light that shone
  Soon set Genius straying.
One his eye ne'er raised
  From the path before him;
T *'other* idly gazed
  On each night-cloud o'er him.
        While I touch the string, etc.

So they came, at last,
  To a shady river;
Common Sense soon past,
  Safe, as he doth ever;
While the boy, whose look
  Was in Heaven that minute,
Never saw the brook,
  But tumbled headlong in it!
        While I touch the string, etc.

How the Wise One smiled,
  When safe o'er the torrent,
At that youth, so wild,
  Dripping from the current!
Sense went home to bed;
  Genius, left to shiver
On the bank, 't is said,
  Died of that cold river!
        While I touch the string, etc.

THEN, FARE THEE WELL.
(Old English Air.)

Then, fare thee well, my own dear love,
  This world has now for us
No greater grief, no pain above
  The pain of parting thus,
        Dear love!
  The pain of parting thus.

Had we but known, since first we met,
  Some few short hours of bliss,

We might, in numbering them, forget
  The deep, deep pain of this,
        Dear love!
  The deep, deep pain of this.

But no, alas, we 've never seen
  One glimpse of pleasure's ray,
But still there came some cloud between,
  And chased it all away,
        Dear love!
  And chased it all away.

Yet, even could those sad moments last,
  Far dearer to my heart
Were hours of grief, together past,
  Than years of mirth apart,
        Dear love!
  Than years of mirth apart.

Farewell! our hope was born in fears,
  And nurst mid vain regrets;
Like winter suns, it rose in tears,
  Like them in tears it sets,
        Dear love!
  Like them in tears it sets.

GAYLY SOUNDS THE CASTANET.
(Maltese Air.)

Gayly sounds the castanet,
  Beating time to bounding feet,
When, after daylight's golden set,
  Maids and youths by moonlight meet.
Oh, then, how sweet to move
  Thro' all that maze of mirth,
Led by light from eyes we love
  Beyond all eyes on earth.

Then, the joyous banquet spread
  On the cool and fragrant ground,
With heaven's bright sparklers overhead,
  And still brighter sparkling round.
Oh, then, how sweet to say
  Into some loved one's ear,
Thoughts reserved thro' many a day
  To be thus whispered here.

When the dance and feast are done,
  Arm in arm as home we stray,
How sweet to see the dawning sun
  O'er her cheek's warm blushes play!
Then, too, the farewell kiss —
  The words, whose parting tone
Lingers still in dreams of bliss,
  That haunt young hearts alone.

LOVE IS A HUNTER-BOY.
(LANGUEDOCIAN AIR.)

LOVE is a hunter-boy,
  Who makes young hearts his prey,
And in his nets of joy
  Ensnares them night and day.
In vain concealed they lie —
  Love tracks them every where;
In vain aloft they fly —
  Love shoots them flying there.

But 't is his joy most sweet,
  At early dawn to trace
The print of Beauty's feet,
  And give the trembler chase.
And if, thro' virgin snow,
  He tracks her footsteps fair,
How sweet for Love to know
  None went before him there.

COME, CHASE THAT STARTING TEAR AWAY.
(FRENCH AIR.)

COME, chase that starting tear away,
  Ere mine to meet it springs;
To-night, at least, to-night be gay,
  Whate'er to-morrow brings.
Like sun-set gleams, that linger late
  When all is darkening fast,
Are hours like these we snatch from
    Fate —
  The brightest, and the last.
    Then, chase that starting tear, etc.

To gild the deepening gloom, if Heaven
  But one bright hour allow,
Oh, think that one bright hour is given,
  In all its splendor, now.
Let 's live it out — then sink in night,
  Like waves that from the shore
One minute swell, are touched with light,
  Then lost for evermore!
    Come, chase that starting tear, etc.

JOYS OF YOUTH, HOW FLEETING!
(PORTUGUESE AIR.)

WHISPERINGS, heard by wakeful maids,
  To whom the night-stars guide us;
Stolen walks thro' moonlight shades,
  With those we love beside us,
    Hearts beating,
    At meeting;

    Tears starting,
    At parting;
Oh, sweet youth, how soon it fades!
  Sweet joys of youth, how fleeting!

Wanderings far away from home,
  With life all new before us;
Greetings warm, when home we come,
  From hearts whose prayers watched
      o'er us.
    Tears starting,
    At parting;
    Hearts beating,
    At meeting;
Oh, sweet youth, how lost on some!
  To some, how bright and fleeting!

HEAR ME BUT ONCE.
(FRENCH AIR.)

HEAR me but once, while o'er the grave,
  In which our Love lies cold and dead,
I count each flattering hope he gave
  Of joys now lost and charms now fled.

Who could have thought the smile he wore
  When first we met would fade away?
Or that a chill would e'er come o'er
  Those eyes so bright thro' many a day?
    Hear me but once, etc.

WHEN LOVE WAS A CHILD.
(SWEDISH AIR.)

WHEN Love was a child, and went idling
      round,
  'Mong flowers the whole summer's day,
One morn in the valley a bower he found,
  So sweet, it allured him to stay.

O'erhead, from the trees, hung a garland
      fair,
  A fountain ran darkly beneath; —
'T was Pleasure had hung up the flowerets
      there;
  Love knew it, and jumped at the
      wreath.

But Love did n't know — and, at *his*
      weak years,
  What urchin was likely to know? —
That Sorrow had made of her own salt
      tears
  The fountain that murmured below.

He caught at the wreath — but with too
  much haste,
  As boys when impatient will do —
It fell in those waters of briny taste,
  And the flowers were all wet through.

This garland he now wears night and day;
  And, tho' it all sunny appears
With Pleasure's own light, each leaf,
    they say,
  Still tastes of the Fountain of Tears.

SAY, WHAT SHALL BE OUR SPORT TO-DAY ?

(SICILIAN AIR.)

SAY, what shall be our sport to-day?
  There 's nothing on earth, in sea, or air,
Too bright, too high, too wild, too gay
  For spirits like mine to dare !
'T is like the returning bloom
  Of those days, alas, gone by,
When I loved, each hour — I scarce knew
    whom —
  And was blest — I scarce knew why.

Ay — those were days when life had
    wings,
  And flew, oh, flew so wild a heigh,
That, like the lark which sunward springs,
  'T was giddy with too much light.
And, tho' of some plumes bereft,
  With that sun, too, nearly set,
I 've enough of light and wing still left
  For a few gay soarings yet.

BRIGHT BE THY DREAMS.

(WELSH AIR.)

BRIGHT be thy dreams — may all thy
    weeping
Turn into smiles while thou art sleeping.
  May those by death or seas removed,
The friends, who in thy spring-time knew
    thee,
  All, thou hast ever prized or loved,
In dreams come smiling to thee !

There may the child, whose love lay
    deepest,
Dearest of all, come while thou sleepest;
  Still as she was — no charm forgot —
No lustre lost that life had given;
  Or, if changed, but changed to what
Thou 'lt find her yet in Heaven !

GO, THEN — 'T IS VAIN.

(SICILIAN AIR.)

GO, then — 't is vain to hover
  Thus round a hope that 's dead ;
At length my dream is over ;
  'T was sweet — 't was false — 't is
    fled !
Farewell ! since naught it moves thee,
  Such truth as mine to see —
Some one, who far less loves thee,
  Perhaps more blest will be.

Farewell, sweet eyes, whose brightness
  New life around me shed ;
Farewell, false heart, whose lightness
  Now leaves me death instead.
Go, now, those charms surrender
  To some new lover's sigh —
One who, tho' far less tender,
  May be more blest than I.

THE CRYSTAL-HUNTERS.

(SWISS AIR.)

O'ER mountains bright
  With snow and light,
We Crystal-Hunters speed along;
    While rocks and caves,
    And icy waves,
  Each instant echo to our song ;
And, when we meet with store of gems,
We grudge not kings their diadems.
    O'er mountains bright
    With snow and light,
  We Crystal-Hunters speed along;
    While grots and caves,
    And icy waves,
  Each instant echo to our song.

Not half so oft the lover dreams
  Of sparkles from his lady's eyes,
As we of those refreshing gleams
  That tell where deep the crystal lies;
Tho', next to crystal, we too grant,
That ladies' eyes may most enchant.
    O'er mountains bright, etc.

Sometimes, when on the Alpine rose
  The golden sunset leaves its ray,
So like a gem the floweret glows,
  We thither bend our headlong way;
And, tho' we find no treasure there,
We bless the rose that shines so fair.

O'er mountains bright
With snow and light,
We Crystal-Hunters speed along ;
While rocks and caves,
And icy waves,
Each instant echo to our song.

ROW GENTLY HERE.
(VENETIAN AIR.)

Row gently here,
My gondolier,
So softly wake the tide,
That not an ear,
On earth, may hear,
But hers to whom we glide.
Had Heaven but tongues to speak, as well
As starry eyes to see,
Oh, think what tales 't would have to tell
Of wandering youths like me !

Now rest thee here,
My gondolier ;
Hush, hush, for up I go,
To climb yon light
Balcony's height,
While thou keep'st watch below.
Ah ! did we take for Heaven above
But half such pains as we
Take, day and night, for woman's love,
What Angels we should be !

OH, DAYS OF YOUTH.
(FRENCH AIR.)

OH, days of youth and joy, long clouded,
Why thus for ever haunt my view ?
When in the grave your light lay shrouded,
Why did not Memory die there too ?
Vainly doth Hope her strain now sing me,
Telling of joys that yet remain —
No, never more can this life bring me
One joy that equals youth's sweet pain.

Dim lies the way to death before me,
Cold winds of Time blow round my
brow ;
Sunshine of youth ! that once fell o'er me,
Where is your warmth, your glory now ?
'T is not that then no pain could sting
me ;
'T is not that now no joys remain ;
Oh, 't is that life no more can bring me
One joy so sweet as that worst pain.

WHEN FIRST THAT SMILE.
(VENETIAN AIR.)

WHEN first that smile, like sunshine,
blest my sight,
Oh what a vision then came o'er me !
Long years of love, of calm and pure de-
light,
Seemed in that smile to pass before me.
Ne'er did the peasant dream of summer
skies,
Of golden fruit, and harvests springing,
With fonder hope than I of those sweet
eyes,
And of the joy their light was bringing.

Where now are all those fondly-promised
hours ?
Ah ! woman's faith is like her brightness —
Fading as fast as rainbows or day-flowers,
Or aught that 's known for grace and
lightness.
Short as the Persian's prayer, at close of
day,
Should be each vow of Love's repeating ;
Quick let him worship Beauty's precious
ray
Even while he kneels, that ray is fleeting !

PEACE TO THE SLUMBERERS !
(CATALONIAN AIR.)

PEACE to the slumberers !
They lie on the battle-plain,
With no shroud to cover them ;
The dew and the summer rain
Are all that weep over them.
Peace to the slumberers !

Vain was their bravery ! —
The fallen oak lies where it lay,
Across the wintry river ;
But brave hearts, once swept away,
Are gone, alas ! for ever.
Vain was their bravery !

Woe to the conqueror !
Our limbs shall lie as cold as theirs
Of whom his sword bereft us,
Ere we forget the deep arrears
Of vengeance they have left us !
Woe to the conqueror !

WHEN THOU SHALT WANDER.
(SICILIAN AIR.)

WHEN thou shalt wander by that sweet
light
We used to gaze on so many an eve,
When love was new and hope was bright,
Ere I could doubt or thou deceive —
Oh, then, remembering how swift went by
Those hours of transport, even *thou*
may'st sigh.

Yes, proud one! even thy heart may own
That love like ours was far too sweet
To be, like summer garments, thrown
Aside, when past the summer's heat;
And wish in vain to know again
Such days, such nights, as blest thee then.

WHO 'LL BUY MY LOVE–KNOTS?
(PORTUGUESE AIR.)

HYMEN, late, his love-knots selling,
Called at many a maiden's dwelling:
None could doubt, who saw or knew them,
Hymen's call was welcome to them.
   " Who 'll buy my love-knots?
   " Who 'll buy my love-knots? "
Soon as that sweet cry resounded,
How his baskets were surrounded!

Maids, who now first dreamt of trying
These gay knots of Hymen's tying;
Dames, who long had sat to watch him
Passing by, but ne'er could catch him; —
   " Who 'll buy my love-knots?
   " Who 'll buy my love-knots? " —
All at that sweet cry assembled;
Some laughed, some blushed, and some
   trembled.

" Here are knots," said Hymen, taking
Some loose flowers, "of Love's own
   making;
" Here are gold ones — you may trust
   'em " —
(These, of course, found ready custom).
   " Come, buy my love-knots!
   " Come, buy my love-knots!
" Some are labelled ' Knots to tie men —
" Love the maker—Bought of Hymen.' "

Scarce their bargains were completed,
When the nymphs all cried, " We 're
   cheated!

" See these flowers — they 're drooping
   sadly;
" This gold-knot, too, ties but badly —
   " Who 'd buy such love-knots?
   " Who 'd buy such love-knots?
" Even this tie, with Love's name round
   it —
" All a sham — He never bound it."

Love, who saw the whole proceeding,
Would have laughed, but for good breed-
   ing;
While Old Hymen, who was used to
Cries like that these dames gave loose to—
   " Take back our love-knots!
   " Take back our love-knots ! "
Coolly said, " There 's no returning
" Wares on Hymen's hands — Good
   morning ! "

SEE, THE DAWN FROM HEAVEN.
(TO AN AIR SUNG AT ROME, ON CHRISTMAS EVE.)

SEE, the dawn from Heaven is breaking
      O'er our sight,
And Earth, from sin awaking,
      Hails the light!
See those groups of angels, winging
      From the realms above,
On their brows, from Eden, bringing
   Wreaths of Hope and Love.

Hark, their hymns of glory pealing
      Thro' the air,
To mortal ears revealing
      Who lies there!
In that dwelling, dark and lowly,
      Sleeps the Heavenly Son,
He, whose home 's above, — the Holy,
      Ever Holy One !

NETS AND CAGES.[1]
(SWEDISH AIR.)

COME, listen to my story, while
      Your needle's task you ply;
At what I sing some maids will smile,
      While some, perhaps, may sigh.
Though Love 's the theme, and Wisdom
      blames
      Such florid songs as ours,

1 Suggested by the following remark of
Swift's: — "The reason why so few marriages
are happy, is, because young ladies spend their
time in making nets, not in making cages."

Yet Truth sometimes, like eastern dames,
Can speak her thoughts by flowers.
Then listen, maids, come listen, while
Your needle's task you ply;
At what I sing there 's some may
smile,
While some, perhaps, will sigh.

Young Cloe, bent on catching Loves,
Such nets had learned to frame,
That none, in all our vales and groves,
E'er caught so much small game:
But gentle Sue, less given to roam,
While Cloe's nets were taking
Such lots of Loves, sat still at home,
One little Love-cage making.
Come, listen, maids, etc.

Much Cloe laughed at Susan's task;
But mark how things went on:
These light-caught Loves, ere you could
ask
Their name and age, were gone!
So weak poor Cloe's nets were wove,
That, tho' she charm'd into them
New game each hour, the youngest Love
Was able to break thro' them.
Come, listen, maids, etc.

Meanwhile, young Sue, whose cage was
wrought
Of bars too strong to sever,
One Love with golden pinions caught,
And caged him there for ever;
Instructing, thereby, all coquettes,
Whate'er their looks or ages,
That, tho' 't is pleasant weaving Nets,
'T is wiser to make Cages.

Thus, maidens, thus do I beguile
The task your fingers ply. —
May all who hear like Susan smile,
And not, like Cloe, sigh!

WHEN THROUGH THE PIAZZETTA.
(VENETIAN AIR.)

WHEN thro' the Piazzetta
Night breathes her cool air,
Then, dearest Ninetta,
I 'll come to thee there.
Beneath thy mask shrouded,
I' ll know thee afar,

As Love knows tho' clouded
His own Evening Star.

In garb, then, resembling
Some gay gondolier,
I 'll whisper thee, trembling,
" Our bark, love, is near:
" Now, now, while there hover
" Those clouds o'er the moon,
" 'T will waft thee safe over
" Yon silent Lagoon."

GO, NOW, AND DREAM.
(SICILIAN AIR.)

Go, now, and dream o'er that joy in thy
slumber —
Moments so sweet again ne'er shalt thou
number.
Of Pain's bitter draught the flavor ne'er
flies,
While Pleasure's scarce touches the lip
ere it dies.
Go, then, and dream, etc.

That moon, which hung o'er your parting, so splendid,
Often will shine again, bright as she then
did —
But, never more will the beam she saw
burn
In those happy eyes, at your meeting,
return.
Go, then, and dream, etc.

TAKE HENCE THE BOWL.
(NEAPOLITAN AIR.)

TAKE hence the bowl; — tho' beaming
Brightly as bowl e'er shone,
Oh, it but sets me dreaming
Of happy days now gone.
There, in its clear reflection,
As in a wizard's glass,
Lost hopes and dead affection,
Like shades, before me pass.

Each cup I drain brings hither
Some scene of bliss gone by; —
Bright lips too bright to wither,
Warm hearts too warm to die.
Till, as the dream comes o'er me
Of those long vanished years,
Alas, the wine before me
Seems turning all to tears!

FAREWELL, THERESA!
(Venetian Air.)

Farewell, Theresa! yon cloud that over
  Heaven's pale night-star gathering we
    see,
Will scarce from that pure orb have past
    ere thy lover
Swift o'er the wide wave shall wander
    from thee.

Long, like that dim cloud, I 've hung
    around thee,
  Darkening thy prospects, saddening
    thy brow;
With gay heart, Theresa, and bright
    cheek I found thee;
  Oh, think how changed, love, how
    changed art thou now!

But here I free thee: like one awaking
  From fearful slumber, thou break'st
    the spell;
'T is over — the moon, too, her bondage
    is breaking —
  Past are the dark clouds; Theresa,
    farewell!

HOW OFT, WHEN WATCHING STARS.
(Savoyard Air.)

Oft, when the watching stars grow pale,
  And round me sleeps the moonlight
    scene,
To hear a flute through yonder vale
  I from my casement lean.
"Come, come, my love!" each note
    then seems to say,
"Oh, come, my love! the night wears
    fast away!"
    Never to mortal ear
    Could words, tho' warm they be,
  Speak Passion's language half so
    clear
    As do those notes to me!

Then quick my own light lute I seek,
  And strike the chords with loudest
    swell;
And, tho' they naught to others speak,
  He knows their language well.
"I come, my love!" each note then
    seems to say,
"I come, my love!—thine, thine till
    break of day."

Oh, weak the power of words,
  The hues of painting dim,
Compared to what those simple
    chords
  Then say and paint to him!

WHEN THE FIRST SUMMER BEE.
(German Air.)

When the first summer bee
  O'er the young rose shall hover,
Then, like that gay rover,
  I 'll come to thee.
He to flowers, I to lips, full of sweets to
    the brim —
What a meeting, what a meeting for me
    and for him!
  When the first summer bee, etc.

Then, to every bright tree
  In the garden he 'll wander;
While I, oh, much fonder,
  Will stay with thee.
In search of new sweetness thro' thou-
    sands he 'll run,
While I find the sweetness of thousands
    in one.
  Then, to every bright tree, etc.

THO' 'T IS ALL BUT A DREAM.
(French Air.)

Tho' 't is all but a dream at the best,
  And still, when happiest, soonest o'er,
Yet, even in a dream, to be blest
  Is so sweet, that I ask for no more.
    The bosom that opes
    With earliest hopes,
  The soonest finds those hopes untrue;
    As flowers that first
    In spring-time burst
  The earliest wither too!
    Ay — 't is all but a dream, etc.

Tho' by friendship we oft are deceived,
  And find love's sunshine soon o'ercast,
Yet friendship will still be believed,
  And love trusted on to the last.
    The web 'mong the leaves
    The spider weaves
  Is like the charm Hope hangs o'er men;
    Tho' often she sees
    'T is broke by the breeze,
  She spins the bright tissue again.
    Ay — 't is all but a dream, etc.

WHEN THE WINE–CUP IS SMILING.

(ITALIAN AIR.)

WHEN the wine-cup is smiling before us,
  And we pledge round to hearts that
  are true, boy, true,
Then the sky of this life opens o'er us,
  And Heaven gives a glimpse of its
  blue.
Talk of Adam in Eden reclining,
  We are better, far better off thus, boy,
  thus;
For *him* but *two* bright eyes were
  shining —
See, what numbers are sparkling for
  us !

When on *one* side the grape-juice is
  dancing,
  While on t' other a blue eye beams,
  boy, beams,
'T is enough, 'twixt the wine and the
  glancing,
  To disturb even a saint from his dreams.
Yet, tho' life like a river is flowing,
  I care not how fast it goes on, boy, on,
So the grape on its bank is still grow-
  ing,
  And Love lights the waves as they run.

WHERE SHALL WE BURY OUR SHAME?

(NEAPOLITAN AIR.)

WHERE shall we bury our shame?
  Where, in what desolate place,
Hide the last wreck of a name
  Broken and stained by disgrace?
Death may dissever the chain,
  Oppression will cease when we 're
  gone;
But the dishonor, the stain,
  Die as we may, will live on.

Was it for this we sent out
  Liberty's cry from our shore?
Was it for this that her shout
  Thrilled to the world's very core?
Thus to live cowards and slaves ! —
  Oh, ye free hearts that lie dead,
Do you not, even in your graves,
  Shudder, as o'er you we tread?

NE'ER TALK OF WISDOM'S GLOOMY SCHOOLS.

(MAHRATTA AIR.)

NE'ER talk of Wisdom's gloomy schools;
  Give me the sage who 's able
To draw his moral thoughts and rules
  From the study of the table; —
Who learns how lightly, fleetly pass
  This world and all that 's in it,
From the bumper that but crowns his
  glass,
  And is gone again next minute !

The diamond sleeps within the mine,
  The pearl beneath the water;
While Truth, more precious, dwells in
  wine,
  The grape's own rosy daughter.
And none can prize her charms like him,
  Oh, none like him obtain her,
Who thus can, like Leander, swim
  Thro' sparkling floods to gain her !

HERE SLEEPS THE BARD.

(HIGHLAND AIR.)

HERE sleeps the Bard who knew so well
All the sweet windings of Apollo's shell;
Whether its music rolled like torrents
  near,
Or died, like distant streamlets, on the
  ear.
Sleep, sleep, mute bard; alike unheeded
  now
The storm and zephyr sweep thy lifeless
  brow; —
That storm, whose rush is like thy mar-
  tial lay;
That breeze which, like thy love-song,
  dies away !

DO NOT SAY THAT LIFE IS WANING.

Do not say that life is waning,
  Or that hope's sweet day is set;
While I 've thee and love remaining,
  Life is in the horizon yet.

Do not think those charms are flying,
  Tho' thy roses fade and fall;
Beauty hath a grace undying,
  Which in thee survives them all.

Not for charms, the newest, brightest,
That on other cheeks may shine,
Would I change the least, the slightest,
That is lingering now o'er thine.

THE GAZELLE.

Dost thou not hear the silver bell,
Thro' yonder lime-trees ringing?
'T is my lady's light gazelle,
To me her love thoughts bringing, —
All the while that silver bell
Around his dark neck ringing.

See, in his mouth he bears a wreath,
My love hath kist in tying;
Oh, what tender thoughts beneath
Those silent flowers are lying, —
Hid within the mystic wreath,
My love hath kist in tying!

Welcome, dear gazelle, to thee,
And joy to her, the fairest,
Who thus hath breathed her soul to
me,
In every leaf thou bearest;
Welcome, dear gazelle, to thee,
And joy to her the fairest!

Hail ye living, speaking flowers,
That breathe of her who bound ye;
Oh, 't was not in fields, or bowers,
'T was on her lips, she found ye;—
Yes, ye blushing, speaking flowers,
'T was on her lips she found ye.

NO — LEAVE MY HEART TO REST.

No — leave my heart to rest, if rest it
may,
When youth, and love, and hope, have
past away.
Couldst thou, when summer hours are
fled,
To some poor leaf that 's fallen and
dead,
Bring back the hue it wore, the scent it
shed?
No — leave this heart to rest, if rest it
may,
When youth, and love, and hope, have
past away.

Oh, had I met thee then, when life was
bright,
Thy smile might still have fed its tranquil
light;
But now thou comest like sunny skies,
Too late to cheer the seaman's eyes,
When wrecked and lost his bark before
him lies!
No — leave this heart to rest, if rest it
may,
Since youth, and love, and hope, have
past away.

WHERE ARE THE VISIONS.

" Where are the visions that round me
once hovered,
   " Forms that shed grace from their
shadows alone;
" Looks fresh as light from a star just
discovered,
   " And voices that Music might take
for her own?"

Time, while I spoke, with his wings
resting o'er me,
   Heard me say, " Where are those
visions, oh where?"
And pointing his wand to the sunset
before me,
   Said, with a voice like the hollow
wind, " There."

Fondly I looked, when the wizard had
spoken,
   And there, mid the dim-shining ruins
of day,
Saw, by their light, like a talisman
broken,
   The last golden fragments of hope
melt away.

WIND THY HORN, MY HUNTER BOY.

Wind thy horn, my hunter boy,
And leave thy lute's inglorious sighs;
Hunting is the hero's joy,
Till war his nobler game supplies.
Hark! the hound-bells ringing sweet,
While hunters shout and the woods
repeat,

Hilli-ho! Hilli-ho!

Wind again thy cheerful horn,
  Till echo, faint with answering, dies:
Burn, bright torches, burn till morn,
  And lead us where the wild boar lies.
Hark! the cry, "He's found, he's found,"
While hill and valley our shouts resound,
  Hilli-ho! Hilli-ho!

OH, GUARD OUR AFFECTION.

Oh, guard our affection, nor e'er let it feel
The blight that this world o'er the warmest will steal:
While the faith of all round us is fading or past,
Let ours, ever green, keep its bloom to the last.

Far safer for Love 't is to wake and to weep,
As he used in his prime, than go smiling to sleep;
For death on his slumber, cold death follows fast,
While the love that is wakeful lives on to the last.

And tho', as Time gathers his clouds o'er our head,
A shade somewhat darker o'er life they may spread,
Transparent, at least, be the shadow they cast,
So that Love's softened light may shine thro' to the last.

SLUMBER, OH SLUMBER.

"Slumber, oh slumber; if sleeping thou mak'st
" My heart beat so wildly, I 'm lost if thou wak'st."
  Thus sung I to a maiden,
  Who slept one summer's day,
  And, like a flower o'erladen
  With too much sunshine, lay.
  Slumber, oh slumber, etc.

" Breathe not, oh breathe not, ye winds, o'er her cheeks;
" If mute thus she charm me, I 'm lost when she speaks."

Thus sing I, while, awaking,
  She murmurs words that seem
As if her lips were taking
  Farewell of some sweet dream.
  Breathe not, oh breathe not, etc.

BRING THE BRIGHT GARLANDS HITHER.

Bring the bright garlands hither,
  Ere yet a leaf is dying;
If so soon they must wither,
  Ours be their last sweet sighing.
Hark, that low dismal chime!
'T is the dreary voice of Time.
Oh, bring beauty, bring roses,
  Bring all that yet is ours;
Let life's day, as it closes,
  Shine to the last thro' flowers.

Haste, ere the bowl's declining,
  Drink of it now or never;
Now, while Beauty is shining,
  Love, or she 's lost for ever.
Hark! again that dull chime,
'T is the dreary voice of Time.
Oh, if life be a torrent,
  Down to oblivion going,
Like this cup be its current,
  Bright to the last drop flowing!

IF IN LOVING, SINGING.

If in loving, singing, night and day
We could trifle merrily life away,
Like atoms dancing in the beam,
Like day-flies skimming o'er the stream,
Or summer blossoms, born to sigh
Their sweetness out, and die —
How brilliant, thoughtless, side by side,
Thou and I could make our minutes glide!
No atoms ever glanced so bright,
No day-flies ever danced so light,
Nor summer blossoms mixt their sigh,
So close, as thou and I!

THOU LOVEST NO MORE.

Too plain, alas, my doom is spoken,
  Nor canst thou veil the sad truth o'er;
Thy heart is changed, thy vow is broken,
  Thou lovest no more — thou lovest no more.

Tho' kindly still those eyes behold me,
  The smile is gone, which once they
    wore;
Tho' fondly still those arms enfold me,
  'T is not the same — thou lovest no
    more.

Too long my dream of bliss believing,
  I 've thought thee all thou wert before;
But now — alas! there 's no deceiving,
  'T is all too plain, thou lovest no more.

Oh, thou as soon the dead couldst waken,
  As lost affection's life restore,
Give peace to her that is forsaken,
  Or bring back him who loves no more.

WHEN ABROAD IN THE WORLD.

WHEN abroad in the world thou appearest,
  And the young and the lovely are there,
To my heart while of all thou 'rt the
    dearest,
  To my eyes thou 'rt of all the most fair.
    They pass, one by one,
    Like waves of the sea,
    That say to the Sun,
    " See, how fair we can be."
  But where 's the light like thine,
    In sun or shade to shine?
No — no, 'mong them all, there is noth-
    ing like thee,
    Nothing like thee.

Oft, of old, without farewell or warning,
  Beauty's self used to steal from the
    skies;
Fling a mist round her head, some fine
    morning,
  And post down to earth in disguise;
    But, no matter what shroud
    Around her might be,
    Men peeped through the cloud,
    And whispered, " 'T is She."
  So thou, where thousands are,
    Shinest forth the only star, —
Yes, yes, 'mong them all, there is noth-
    ing like thee,
    Nothing like thee.

KEEP THOSE EYES STILL PURELY
MINE.

KEEP those eyes still purely mine,
  Tho' far off I be:

When on others most they shine,
  Then think they 're turned on me.

Should those lips as now respond
  To sweet minstrelsy,
When their accents seem most fond,
  Then think they 're breathed for
    me.

Make what hearts thou wilt thy own,
  If when all on thee
Fix their charmed thoughts alone,
  Thou think'st the while on me.

HOPE COMES AGAIN.

HOPE comes again, to this heart long a
    stranger,
  Once more she sings me her flattering
    strain;
But hush, gentle syren — for, ah, there 's
    less danger
  In still suffering on, than in hoping
    again.

Long, long, in sorrow, too deep for
    repining,
  Gloomy, but tranquil, this bosom hath
    lain;
And joy coming now, like a sudden light
    shining
  O'er eyelids long darkened, would
    bring me but pain.

Fly then, ye visions, that Hope would
    shed o'er me;
  Lost to the future, my sole chance of
    rest
Now lies not in dreaming of bliss that 's
    before me,
  But, ah — in forgetting how once I
    was blest.

O SAY, THOU BEST AND
BRIGHTEST.

O SAY, thou best and brightest,
  My first love and my last,
When he, whom now thou slightest,
  From life's dark scene hath past,
Will kinder thoughts then move thee ?
  Will pity wake one thrill
For him who lived to love thee,
  And dying loved thee still?

If when, that hour recalling
 From which he dates his woes,
Thou feel'st a tear-drop falling,
 Ah, blush not while it flows:
But, all the past forgiving,
 Bend gently o'er his shrine,
And say, " This heart, when living,
 " With all its faults, was mine."

WHEN NIGHT BRINGS THE HOUR.

WHEN night brings the hour
 Of starlight and joy,
There comes to my bower
 A fairy-winged boy;
With eyes so bright,
 So full of wild arts,
Like nets of light,
 To tangle young hearts;
With lips, in whose keeping
 Love's secret may dwell,
Like Zephyr asleep in
 Some rosy sea-shell.
Guess who he is,
 Name but his name,
And his best kiss
 For reward you may claim.

Where'er o'er the ground
 He prints his light feet,
The flowers there are found
 Most shining and sweet:
His looks, as soft
 As lightning in May,
Tho' dangerous oft,
 Ne'er wound but in play:
And oh, when his wings
 Have brushed o'er my lyre,
You 'd fancy its strings
 Were turning to fire.
Guess who he is,
 Name but his name,
And his best kiss
 For reward you may claim.

LIKE ONE WHO, DOOMED.

LIKE one who, doomed o'er distant
 seas
His weary path to measure,
When home at length, with favoring
 breeze,
He brings the far-sought treasure;

His ship, in sight of shore, goes down,
 That shore to which he hasted ;
And all the wealth he thought his own
 Is o'er the waters wasted !

Like him, this heart, thro' many a track
 Of toil and sorrow straying,
One hope alone brought fondly back,
 Its toil and grief repaying.

Like him, alas, I see that ray
 Of hope before me perish,
And one dark minute sweep away
 What years were given to cherish.

FEAR NOT THAT, WHILE AROUND THEE.

FEAR not that, while around thee
 Life's varied blessings pour,
One sigh of hers shall wound thee,
 Whose smile thou seek'st no more.
No, dead and cold for ever
 Let our past love remain;
Once gone, its spirit never
 Shall haunt thy rest again.

May the new ties that bind thee
 Far sweeter, happier prove,
Nor e'er of me remind thee,
 But by their truth and love.
Think how, asleep or waking,
 Thy image haunts me yet ;
But, how this heart is breaking
 For thy own peace forget.

WHEN LOVE IS KIND.

WHEN Love is kind,
 Cheerful and free,
Love 's sure to find
 Welcome from me.

But when Love brings
 Heartache or pang,
Tears, and such things —
 Love may go hang !

If Love can sigh
 For one alone,
Well pleased am I
 To be that one,

But should I see
　　Love given to rove
To two or three,
　　Then — good-by Love !

Love must, in short,
　　Keep fond and true,
Thro' good report,
　　And evil too.

Else, here I swear,
　　Young Love may go,
For aught I care —
　　To Jericho.

THE GARLAND I SEND THEE.

THE Garland I send thee was culled from
　　those bowers
Where thou and I wandered in long van-
　　ished hours;
Not a leaf or a blossom its bloom here
　　displays,
But bears some remembrance of those
　　happy days.

The roses were gathered by that garden
　　gate,
Where our meetings, tho' early, seemed
　　always too late;
Where lingering full oft thro' a summer-
　　night's moon,
Our partings, tho' late, appeared always
　　too soon.

The rest were all culled from the banks
　　of that glade,
Where, watching the sunset, so often
　　we 've strayed,
And mourned, as the time went, that
　　Love had no power
To bind in his chain even one happy hour.

HOW SHALL I WOO?

IF I speak to thee in friendship's name,
　　Thou think'st I speak too coldly;
If I mention Love's devoted flame,
　　Thou say'st I speak too boldly.
Between these two unequal fires,
　　Why doom me thus to hover?
I 'm a friend, if such thy heart requires,
　　If more thou seek'st, a lover.
Which shall it be?　How shall I woo?
Fair one, choose between the two.

Tho' the wings of Love will brightly
　　play,
　　When first he comes to woo thee,
There 's a chance that he may fly away
　　As fast as he flies *to* thee.
While Friendship, tho' on foot she come,
　　No flights of fancy trying,
Will, therefore, oft be found at home,
　　When Love abroad is flying.
Which shall it be?　How shall I woo?
Dear one, choose between the two.

If neither feeling suits thy heart,
　　Let 's see, to please thee, whether
We may not learn some precious art
　　To mix their charms together;
One feeling, still more sweet, to form
　　From two so sweet already —
A friendship that like love is warm,
　　A love like friendship steady.
Thus let it be, thus let me woo,
Dearest, thus we 'll join the two.

SPRING AND AUTUMN.

EVERY season hath its pleasures;
　　Spring may boast her flowery prime,
Yet the vineyard's ruby treasures
　　Brighten Autumn's soberer time.
So Life's year begins and closes;
　　Days tho' shortening still can shine;
What tho' youth gave love and roses,
　　Age still leaves us friends and wine.

Phillis, when she might have caught
　　me,
　　All the Spring looked coy and shy,
Yet herself in Autumn sought me,
　　When the flowers were all gone by.
Ah, too late; — she found her lover
　　Calm and free beneath his vine,
Drinking to the Spring-time over,
　　In his best autumnal wine.

Thus may we, as years are flying,
　　To their flight our pleasures suit,
Nor regret the blossoms dying,
　　While we still may taste the fruit.
Oh, while days like this are ours,
　　Where 's the lip that dares repine?
Spring may take our loves and flowers,
　　So Autumn leaves us friends and
　　wine.

LOVE ALONE.

IF thou wouldst have thy charms enchant
  our eyes,
First win our hearts, for there thy empire
  lies:
Beauty in vain would mount a heartless
  throne,
Her Right Divine is given by Love alone.

What would the rose with all her pride
  be worth,
Were there no sun to call her brightness
  forth?
Maidens, unloved, like flowers in dark-
  ness thrown,
Wait but that light which comes from
  Love alone.

Fair as thy charms in yonder glass appear,
Trust not their bloom, they 'll fade from
  year to year:
Wouldst thou they still should shine as
  first they shone,
Go, fix thy mirror in Love's eyes
  alone.

SACRED SONGS.

TO

EDWARD TUITE DALTON, ESQ.

THIS FIRST NUMBER

OF

SACRED SONGS

IS INSCRIBED,

BY HIS SINCERE AND AFFECTIONATE FRIEND,

THOMAS MOORE.

Mayfield Cottage, Ashbourne,
May, 1816.

SACRED SONGS.

THOU ART, O GOD.

(Air. — Unknown.)[1]

"The day is thine, the night is also thine:
thou hast prepared the light and the sun.
"Thou hast set all the borders of the earth:
thou hast made summer and winter." — *Psalm*
lxxiv. 16, 17.

THOU art, O GOD, the life and light
Of all this wondrous world we see;
Its glow by day, its smile by night,
    Are but reflections caught from Thee.
Where'er we turn, thy glories shine,
And all things fair and bright are Thine!

When Day, with farewell beam, delays
    Among the opening clouds of Even,
And we can almost think we gaze
    Thro' golden vistas into Heaven —
Those hues, that make the Sun's decline
So soft, so radiant, LORD! are Thine.

When Night, with wings of starry gloom,
    O'ershadows all the earth and skies,
Like some dark, beauteous bird, whose plume
    Is sparkling with unnumbered eyes —
That sacred gloom, those fires divine,
So grand, so countless, LORD! are Thine.

When youthful Spring around us breathes,
    Thy Spirit warms her fragrant sigh;
And every flower the Summer wreathes
    Is born beneath that kindling eye.
Where'er we turn, thy glories shine,
And all things fair and bright are Thine.

THE BIRD, LET LOOSE.

(Air. — Beethoven.)

THE bird, let loose in eastern skies,[2]
    When hastening fondly home,

Ne'er stoops to earth her wing, nor flies
    Where idle warblers roam.
But high she shoots thro' air and light,
    Above all low delay,
Where nothing earthly bounds her flight,
    Nor shadow dims her way.

So grant me, GOD, from every care
    And stain of passion free,
Aloft, thro' Virtue's purer air,
    To hold my course to Thee!
No sin to cloud, no lure to stay
    My Soul, as home she springs; —
Thy Sunshine on her joyful way,
    Thy Freedom in her wings!

FALLEN IS THY THRONE.

(Air. — Martini.)

FALLEN is thy Throne, oh Israel!
    Silence is o'er thy plains;
Thy dwellings all lie desolate,
    Thy children weep in chains.
Where are the dews that fed thee
    On Etham's barren shore?
That fire from Heaven which led thee,
    Now lights thy path no more.

LORD! thou didst love Jerusalem —
    Once she was all thy own;
Her love thy fairest heritage,[3]
    Her power thy glory's throne.[4]
Till evil came, and blighted
    Thy long-loved olive-tree; [5] —
And Salem's shrines were lighted
    For other gods than Thee.

---

1 I have heard that this air is by the late Mrs.
Sheridan. It is sung to the beautiful old words,
" I do confess thou 'rt smooth and fair."

2 The carrier-pigeon, it is well known, flies
at an elevated pitch, in order to surmount every
obstacle between her and the place to which she
is destined.

3 " I have left mine heritage; I have given
the dearly beloved of my soul into the hands of
her enemies." — *Jeremiah*, xii. 7.

4 " Do not disgrace the throne of thy glory."
— *Jer.* xiv. 21.

5 " The LORD called thy name a green olive-
tree; fair, and of goodly fruit," etc. — *Jer.* xi. 16.

Then sunk the star of Solyma —
　Then past her glory's day,
Like heath that, in the wilderness,[1]
　The wild wind whirls away.
Silent and waste her bowers,
　Where once the mighty trod,
And sunk those guilty towers,
　While Baal reign'd as God.

" Go " — said the LORD — " Ye Con-
　querors !
" Steep in her blood your swords,
" And raze to earth her battlements,[2]
　" For they are not the LORD's.
" Till Zion's mournful daughter
　" O'er kindred bones shall tread,
" And Hinnom's vale of slaughter [3]
　" Shall hide but half her dead ! "

WHO IS THE MAID?

ST. JEROME'S LOVE.[4]

(AIR. — BEETHOVEN.)

WHO is the Maid my spirit seeks,
　Thro' cold reproof and slander's blight?
Has *she* Love's roses on her cheeks?
　Is *hers* an eye of this world's light?
No — wan and sunk with midnight prayer
　Are the pale looks of her I love;
Or if at times a light be there,
　Its beam is kindled from above.

I chose not her, my heart's elect,
　From those who seek their Maker's
　　shrine
In gems and garlands proudly decked,
　As if themselves were things divine.
No — Heaven but faintly warms the
　breast
That beats beneath a broidered veil;

And she who comes in glittering vest
　To mourn her frailty, still is frail.[5]

Not so the faded form I prize
　And love, because its bloom is gone;
The glory in those sainted eyes
　Is all the grace *her* brow puts on.
And ne'er was Beauty's dawn so bright,
　So touching as that form's decay,
Which, like the altar's trembling light,
　In holy lustre wastes away.

THIS WORLD IS ALL A FLEET-ING SHOW.

(AIR. — STEVENSON.)

THIS world is all a fleeting show,
　For man's illusion given;
The smiles of joy, the tears of woe,
Deceitful shine, deceitful flow —
　There 's nothing true but Heaven !

And false the light on glory's plume,
　As fading hues of even;
And love and hope, and beauty's bloom,
Are blossoms gathered for the tomb —
　There 's nothing bright but Heaven !

Poor wanderers of a stormy day,
　From wave to wave we 're driven,
And fancy's flash and reason's ray
Serve but to light the troubled way —
　There 's nothing calm but Heaven !

OH THOU WHO DRY'ST THE MOURNER'S TEAR.

(AIR. — HAYDN.)

　" He healeth the broken in heart, and bind-
eth up their wounds." — *Psalm* cxlvii. 3.

OH Thou who dry'st the mourner's tear,
　How dark this world would be,
If, when deceived and wounded here,
　We could not fly to Thee.
The friends who in our sunshine live,
　When winter comes, are flown;
And he who has but tears to give,
　Must weep those tears alone.

---

1 " For he shall be like the heath in the
desert." — *Jer.* xvii. 6.
2 " Take away her battlements; for they are
not the LORD's." — *Jer.* v. 10.
3 " Therefore, behold, the days come, saith
the LORD, that it shall no more be called Tophet,
nor the Valley of the Son of Hinnom; but the
Valley of Slaughter; for they shall bury in Tophet till there be no place." — *Jer.* vii. 32.
4 These lines were suggested by a passage in
one of St. Jerome's Letters, replying to some calumnious remarks that had been circulated respecting his intimacy with the matron Paula : —
" *numquid me vestes sericæ, nitentes gemmæ,
picta facies, aut auri rapuit ambitio? nulla*

*fuit alia Romæ matronarum, quæ meam possit
edomare mentem, nisi lugens atque jejunans,
fletu pene cæcata.*" — *Epist.*　" *si tibi putem.*"
5 οὐ γὰρ κρυσοφορεῖν τὴν δακρύουσαν δεῖ. —
Chrysost. Homil. 8, *in Epist. ad. Tim.*

But Thou wilt heal that broken heart,
  Which, like the plants that throw
Their fragrance from the wounded part,
  Breathes sweetness out of woe.

When joy no longer soothes or cheers,
  And even the hope that threw
A moment's sparkle o'er our tears
  Is dimmed and vanished too,
Oh, who would bear life's stormy doom,
  Did not thy Wing of Love
Come, brightly wafting thro' the gloom
  Our Peace-branch from above?
Then sorrow, touched by Thee, grows
    bright
  With more than rapture's ray;
As darkness shows us worlds of light
  We never saw by day!

WEEP NOT FOR THOSE.

(AIR. — AVISON.)

WEEP not for those whom the veil of the
    tomb,
  In life's happy morning, hath hid from
    our eyes,
Ere sin threw a blight o'er the spirit's
    young bloom,
  Or earth had profaned what was born
    for the skies.

Death chilled the fair fountain, ere sorrow
    had stained it;
  'T was frozen in all the pure light of
    its course,
And but sleeps till the sunshine of
    Heaven has unchained it,
  To water that Eden where first was
    its source.

Weep not for those whom the veil of the
    tomb,
  In life's happy morning, hath hid from
    our eyes,
Ere sin threw a blight o'er the spirit's
    young bloom,
  Or earth had profaned what was born
    for the skies.

Mourn not for her, the young Bride of
    the Vale,[1]
  Our gayest and loveliest, lost to us
    now,

Ere life's early lustre had time to grow
    pale,
  And the garland of Love was yet fresh
    on her brow.
Oh, then was her moment, dear spirit,
    for flying
  From this gloomy world, while its
    gloom was unknown —
And the wild hymns she warbled so
    sweetly, in dying,
  Were echoed in Heaven by lips like
    her own.
Weep not for her — in her spring-time
    she flew
  To that land where the wings of the
    soul are unfurled;
And now, like a star beyond evening's
    cold dew,
  Looks radiantly down on the tears of
    this world.

THE TURF SHALL BE MY FRA-
GRANT SHRINE.

(AIR. — STEVENSON.)

THE turf shall be my fragrant shrine;
My temple, LORD! that Arch of thine;
My censer's breath the mountain airs,
And silent thoughts my only prayers.[2]

My choir shall be the moonlight waves,
When murmuring homeward to their
    caves,
Or when the stillness of the sea,
Even more than music, breathes of Thee!

I 'll seek, by day, some glade un-
    known,
All light and silence, like thy Throne;
And the pale stars shall be, at night,
The only eyes that watch my rite.

1 This second verse, which I wrote long after
the first, alludes to the fate of a very lovely and
amiable girl, the daughter of the late Colonel
Bainbrigge, who was married in Ashbourne
church, October 31, 1815, and died of a fever in
a few weeks after: the sound of her marriage-
bells seemed scarcely out of our ears when we
heard of her death. During her last delirium
she sung several hymns, in a voice even clearer
and sweeter than usual, and among them were
some from the present collection, (particularly,
"There 's nothing bright but Heaven,") which
this very interesting girl had often heard me sing
during the summer.

2 *pii orant tacite.*

Thy Heaven, on which 't is bliss to look,
Shall be my pure and shining book,
Where I shall read, in words of flame,
The glories of thy wondrous name.

I 'll read thy anger in the rack
That clouds awhile the day-beam's track;
Thy mercy in the azure hue
Of sunny brightness, breaking thro'.

There 's nothing bright, above, below,
From flowers that bloom to stars that
glow,
But in its light my soul can see
Some feature of thy Deity:

There 's nothing dark, below, above,
But in its gloom I trace thy Love,
And meekly wait that moment, when
Thy touch shall turn all bright again!

SOUND THE LOUD TIMBREL.

MIRIAM'S SONG.

(AIR. — AVISON.) [1]

"And Miriam, the Prophetess, the sister of
Aaron, took a timbrel in her hand; and all the
women went out after her with timbrels and with
dances." — *Exod.* xv. 20.

SOUND the loud Timbrel o'er Egypt's
dark sea!
JEHOVAH has triumphed — his people
are free.
Sing — for the pride of the Tyrant is
broken,
His chariots, his horsemen, all splen-
did and brave —
How vain was their boast, for the LORD
hath but spoken,
And chariots and horsemen are sunk
in the wave.
Sound the loud Timbrel o'er Egypt's
dark sea;
JEHOVAH has triumphed — his people are
free.
Praise to the Conqueror, praise to the
LORD!

1 I have so much altered the character of this
air, which is from the beginning of one of
Avison's old-fashioned concertos, that, without
this acknowledgment, it could hardly, I think, be
recognized.

His word was our arrow, his breath was
our sword. —
Who shall return to tell Egypt the story
Of those she sent forth in the hour of
her pride?
For the LORD hath looked out from his
pillar of glory,[2]
And all her brave thousands are dashed
in the tide.
Sound the loud Timbrel o'er Egypt's
dark sea,
JEHOVAH has triumphed — his people
are free!

GO, LET ME WEEP.

(AIR. — STEVENSON.)

Go, let me weep — there 's bliss in tears,
When he who sheds them inly feels
Some lingering stain of early years
Effaced by every drop that steals.
The fruitless showers of worldly woe
Fall dark to earth and never rise;
While tears that from repentance flow,
In bright exhalement reach the skies.
Go, let me weep.

Leave me to sigh o'er hours that flew
More idly than the summer's wind,
And, while they past, a fragrance threw,
But left no trace of sweets behind. —
The warmest sigh that pleasure heaves
Is cold, is faint to those that swell
The heart where pure repentance grieves
O'er hours of pleasure, loved too well.
Leave me to sigh.

COME NOT, OH LORD.

(AIR. — HAYDN.)

COME not, oh LORD, in the dread robe
of splendor
Thou worest on the Mount, in the day
of thine ire;
Come veiled in those shadows, deep,
awful, but tender,
Which Mercy flings over thy features
of fire!

2 "And it came to pass, that, in the morning
watch the LORD looked unto the host of the
Egyptians, through the pillar of fire and of the
cloud, and troubled the host of the Egyptians."
— *Exod.* xiv. 24.

LORD, thou rememberest the night, when
    thy Nation [1]
Stood fronting her Foe by the red-roll-
    ing stream;
O'er Egypt thy pillar shed dark desola-
    tion,
    While Israel basked all the night in its
      beam.

So, when the dread clouds of anger enfold
    Thee,
    From us, in thy mercy, the dark side
      remove;
While shrouded in terrors the guilty be-
    hold Thee,
    Oh, turn upon us the mild light of thy
      Love!

WERE NOT THE SINFUL MARY'S
TEARS.

(AIR. — STEVENSON.)

WERE not the sinful Mary's tears
An offering worthy Heaven,
When, o'er the faults of former years,
She wept — and was forgiven?

When, bringing every balmy sweet
    Her day of luxury stored,
She o'er her Saviour's hallowed feet
    The precious odors poured; —

And wiped them with that golden hair,
    Where once the diamond shone;
Tho' now those gems of grief were
    there
    Which shine for GOD alone!

Were not those sweets, so humbly shed —
    That hair — those weeping eyes —
And the sunk heart, that inly bled —
    Heaven's noblest sacrifice?

Thou that hast slept in error's sleep
    Oh, would'st thou wake in Heaven,
Like Mary kneel, like Mary weep,
    " Love much" [2] and be forgiven!

1 "And it came between the camp of the
Egyptians and the camp of Israel; and it was
a cloud and darkness to them, but it gave light
by night to these." — *Exod.* xiv. 20.
2 " Her sins, which are many, are forgiven;
for she loved much." — *St. Luke*, vii. 47.

AS DOWN IN THE SUNLESS RE-
TREATS.

(AIR. — HADYN.)

As down in the sunless retreats of the
    Ocean,
Sweet flowers are springing no mortal
    can see,
So, deep in my soul the still prayer of
    devotion,
    Unheard by the world, rises silent to
      Thee,
      My GOD! silent, to Thee —
      Pure, warm, silent, to Thee.

As still to the star of its worship, tho'
    clouded,
    The needle points faithfully o'er the
    dim sea,
So, dark as I roam, in this wintry world
    shrouded,
    The hope of my spirit turns trembling
    to Thee,
      My GOD! trembling, to Thee —
      True, fond, trembling, to Thee.

BUT WHO SHALL SEE.[6]

(AIR. — STEVENSON.)

BUT who shall see the glorious day
    When, throned on Zion's brow,
The LORD shall rend that veil away
    Which hides the nations now? [3]
When earth no more beneath the fear
Of his rebuke shall lie; [4]
When pain shall cease, and every tear
Be wiped from every eye. [5]

Then, Judah, thou no more shalt mourn
    Beneath the heathen's chain;
Thy days of splendor shall return,
    And all be new again. [6]

3 "And he will destroy, in this mountain, the
face of the covering cast over all people, and the
vail that is spread over all nations." — *Isaiah*,
xxv. 7.
4 "The rebuke of his people shall he take
away from off all the earth."—*Isaiah*, xxv. 8.
5 "And GOD shall wipe away all tears from
their eyes; neither shall there be any more pain."
— *Rev.* xxi. 4.
6 "And he that sat upon the throne said, Behold, I make all things new."— *Rev.* xxi. 5.

The Fount of Life shall then be quaft
In peace, by all who come ; [1]
And every wind that blows shall waft
Some long-lost exile home.

ALMIGHTY GOD!
CHORUS OF PRIESTS.
(AIR. — MOZART.)

ALMIGHTY GOD! when round thy shrine
The Palm-tree's heavenly branch we
twine,[2]
(Emblem of Life's eternal ray,
And Love that "fadeth not away,")
We bless the flowers, expanded all,[3]
We bless the leaves that never fall,
And trembling say, — " In Eden thus
"The Tree of Life may flower for us!"
When round thy Cherubs — smiling calm,
Without their flames [4] — we wreathe the
Palm,
Oh GOD! we feel the emblem true —
Thy Mercy is eternal too.
Those Cherubs, with their smiling eyes,
That crown of Palm which never dies,
Are but the types of Thee above —
Eternal Life, and Peace, and Love!

OH FAIR! OH PUREST!
SAINT AUGUSTINE TO HIS SISTER.[5]
(AIR. — MOORE.)

OH fair! oh purest! be thou the dove
That flies alone to some sunny grove,

And lives unseen, and bathes her wing,
All vestal white, in the limpid spring.
There, if the hovering hawk be near,
That limpid spring in its mirror clear
Reflects him ere he reach his prey
And warns the timorous bird away.
  Be thou this dove;
Fairest, purest, be thou this dove.

The sacred pages of GOD'S own book
Shall be the spring, the eternal brook,
In whose holy mirror, night and day,
Thou 'lt study Heaven's reflected ray; —
And should the foes of virtue dare,
With gloomy wing, to seek thee there,
Thou wilt see how dark their shadows
lie
Between Heaven and thee, and trembling
fly!
  Be thou that dove;
Fairest, purest, be thou that dove.

ANGEL OF CHARITY.
(AIR. — HANDEL.)

ANGEL of Charity, who, from above,
  Comest to dwell a pilgrim here,
Thy voice is music, thy smile is love,
  And Pity's soul is in thy tear.
When on the shrine of GOD were laid
  First-fruits of all most good and fair,
That ever bloomed in Eden's shade,
  Thine was the holiest offering there.

Hope and her sister, Faith, were given
  But as our guides to yonder sky;
Soon as they reach the verge of heaven,
  There, lost in perfect bliss, they die.
But, long as Love, Almighty Love,
  Shall on his throne of thrones abide,
Thou, Charity, shalt dwell above,
  Smiling for ever by His side!

---

1 " And whosoever will, let him take the water of life freely."— *Rev.* xxii. 17.

2 "The Scriptures having declared that the Temple of Jerusalem was a type of the Messiah, it is natural to conclude that the *Palms*, which made so conspicuous a figure in that structure, represented that *Life* and *Immortality* which were brought to light by the Gospel."— "*Observations on the Palm, as a sacred Emblem*," by W. Tighe.

3 "And he carved all the walls of the house round about with carved figures of cherubim, and palm-trees, and *open flowers*." — 1 *Kings*, vi. 29.

4 "When the passover of the tabernacles was revealed to the great lawgiver in the mount, then the cherubic images which appeared in that structure were no longer surrounded by flames; for the tabernacle was a type of the dispensation of mercy, by which JEHOVAH confirmed his gracious convenant to redeem mankind." — " *Observations on the Palm*."

5 In St. Augustine's Treatise upon the advan-

tages of a solitary life, addressed to his sister, there is the following fanciful passage, from which, the reader will perceive, the thought of this song was taken: — "*te, soror, nunquam nolo esse securam, sed timere semperque tuam fragilitatem habere suspectam, ad instar pavidæ columbæ frequentare rivos aquarum et quasi in speculo accipitris cernere supervolantis effigiem et cavere. rivi aquarum sententiæ sunt scripturarum, quæ de limpidissimo sapientiæ fonte profluentes,*" etc. —"*De Vit. Eremit. ad Sororem.*"

6 " Then Faith shall fail, and holy Hope shall die, One lost in certainty and one in joy." — *Prior.*

BEHOLD THE SUN.

(AIR. — LORD MORNINGTON.)

BEHOLD the Sun, how bright
From yonder East he springs,
As if the soul of life and light
Were breathing from his wings.

So bright the Gospel broke
Upon the souls of men;
So fresh the dreaming world awoke
In Truth's full radiance then.

Before yon Sun arose,
Stars clustered thro' the sky —
But oh how dim, how pale were those,
To His one burning eye!

So Truth lent many a ray,
To bless the Pagan's night —
But, LORD, how weak, how cold were they
To Thy One glorious Light!

LORD, WHO SHALL BEAR THAT DAY.

(AIR. — DR. BOYCE.)

LORD, who shall bear that day, so dread,
so splendid,
When we shall see thy Angel hovering
o'er
This sinful world with hand to heaven
extended,
And hear him swear by Thee that
Time 's no more? [1]
When Earth shall feel thy fast consuming
ray —
Who, Mighty GOD, oh who shall bear
that day?

When thro' the world thy awful call hath
sounded —
"Wake, all ye Dead, to judgment
wake, ye Dead!" [2]
And from the clouds, by seraph eyes surrounded,
The Saviour shall put forth his radiant
head; [3]

While Earth and Heaven before Him
pass away [4] —
Who, Mighty GOD, oh who shall bear
that day?

When, with a glance, the Eternal Judge
shall sever
Earth's evil spirits from the pure and
bright,
And say to *those*, "Depart from me for
ever!"
To *these*, "Come, dwell with me in
endless light!" [5]
When each and all in silence take their
way —
Who, Mighty GOD, oh who shall bear
that day?

OH, TEACH ME TO LOVE THEE.

(AIR. — HAYDN.)

OH, teach me to love Thee, to feel what
thou art,
Till, filled with the one sacred image, my
heart
Shall all other passions disown;
Like some pure temple that shines
apart,
Reserved for Thy worship alone.

In joy and in sorrow, thro' praise and
thro' blame,
Thus still let me, living and dying the
same,
In *Thy* service bloom and decay —
Like some lone altar whose votive
flame
In holiness wasteth away.

Tho' born in this desert, and doomed by
my birth
To pain and affliction, to darkness and
dearth,
On Thee let my spirit rely —
Like some rude dial, that, fixt on earth,
Still looks for its light from the sky.

[1] "And the angel which I saw stand upon the sea and upon the earth, lifted up his hand to heaven, and sware by Him that liveth for ever and ever, . . . that there should be time no longer." — *Rev.* x. 5, 6.

[2] "Awake, ye Dead, and come to judgment."

[3] "They shall see the Son of Man coming in the clouds of heaven — and all the angels with him." — *Matt.* xxiv. 30. and xxv. 30.

[4] "From whose face the earth and the heaven fled away." — *Rev.* xx. 11.

[5] "And before Him shall be gathered all nations, and He shall separate them one from another.

"Then shall the King say unto them on his

WEEP, CHILDREN OF ISRAEL.

(AIR. — STEVENSON.)

WEEP, weep for him, the Man of GOD —[1]
In yonder vale he sunk to rest;
But none of earth can point the sod [2]
  That flowers above his sacred breast.
    Weep, children of Israel, weep!

His doctrine fell like Heaven's rain,[3]
  His words refreshed like Heaven's
    dew —
Oh, ne'er shall Israel see again
  A Chief, to GOD and her so true.
    Weep, children of Israel, weep!

Remember ye his parting gaze,
  His farewell song by Jordan's tide,
When, full of glory and of days,
  He saw the promised land — and died.[4]
    Weep, children of Israel, weep!

Yet died he not as men who sink,
  Before our eyes, to soulless clay;
But, changed to spirit, like a wink
  Of summer lightning, past away.[5]
    Weep, children of Israel, weep!

LIKE MORNING, WHEN HER EARLY BREEZE.

(AIR. — BEETHOVEN.)

LIKE morning, when her early breeze
Breaks up the surface of the seas,
That, in those furrows, dark with night,
Her hand may sow the seeds of light —

right hand, Come, ye blessed of my Father, inherit the kingdom prepared for you, etc.
"Then shall He say also unto them on the left hand, Depart from me, ye cursed, etc.
"And these shall go away into everlasting punishment; but the righteous into life eternal."
— *Matt.* xxv. 32. *et seq.*

1 "And the children of Israel wept for Moses in the plains of Moab." — *Deut.* xxxiv. 8.

2 "And he buried him in a valley in the land of Moab: . . . but no man knoweth of his sepulchre unto this day." — *Ibid.* ver. 6.

3 "My doctrine shall drop as the rain, my speech shall distil as the dew." — *Moses' Song.*

4 "I have caused thee to see it with thine eyes, but thou shalt not go over thither." — *Deut.* xxxiv. 4.

5 "As he was going to embrace Eleazer and Joshua, and was still discoursing with them, a cloud stood over him on the sudden, and he disappeared in a certain valley, although he wrote

Thy Grace can send its breathings o'er
The Spirit, dark and lost before,
And, freshening all its depths, prepare
For Truth divine to enter there.

Till David touched his sacred lyre,
In silence lay the unbreathing wire;
But when he swept its chords along,
Even Angels stooped to hear that song.

So sleeps the soul, till Thou, oh LORD,
Shalt deign to touch its lifeless chord —
Till, waked by Thee, its breath shall rise
In music, worthy of the skies!

COME, YE DISCONSOLATE.

(AIR. — GERMAN.)

COME, ye disconsolate, where'er you
    languish,
  Come, at God's altar fervently kneel;
Here bring your wounded hearts, here
    tell your anguish —
  Earth has no sorrow that Heaven cannot heal.

Joy of the desolate, Light of the straying,
  Hope, when all others die, fadeless
    and pure,
Here speaks the Comforter, in GOD'S
    name saying—
  "Earth has no sorrow that Heaven
    cannot cure."

Go, ask the infidel, what boon he brings
    us
  What charm for aching hearts *he* can
    reveal,
Sweet as that heavenly promise Hope
    sings us —
  "Earth has no sorrow that GOD cannot heal."

AWAKE, ARISE, THY LIGHT IS COME.

(AIR. — STEVENSON.)

AWAKE, arise, thy light is come; [6]
  The nations, that before outshone thee,

in the Holy Books that he died, which was done out of fear, lest they should venture to say that, because of his extraordinary virtue, he went to GOD." — *Josephus*, book iv. chap. viii.

6 " Arise, shine ; for thy light is come, and the glory of the LORD is risen upon thee," — *Isaiah*, xl.

Now at thy feet lie dark and dumb —
The glory of the LORD is on thee!

Arise — the Gentiles to thy ray,
From every nook of earth shall cluster;
And kings and princes haste to pay
Their homage to thy rising lustre.[1]

Lift up thine eyes around, and see
O'er foreign fields, o'er farthest waters,
Thy exiled sons return to thee,
To thee return thy home-sick daughters.[2]

And camels rich, from Midian's tents,
Shall lay their treasures down before thee;
And Saba bring her gold and scents,
To fill thy air and sparkle o'er thee.[3]

See, who are these that, like a cloud,[4]
Are gathering from all earth's dominions,
Like doves, long absent, when allowed
Homeward to shoot their trembling pinions.

Surely the isles shall wait for me,[5]
The ships of Tarshish round will hover,
To bring thy sons across the sea,
And waft their gold and silver over.

And Lebanon thy pomp shall grace[6] —
The fir, the pine, the palm victorious
Shall beautify our Holy Place,
And make the ground I tread on glorious.

1 " And the Gentiles shall come to thy light, and kings to the brightness of thy rising." — *Isaiah*, xl.

2 " Lift up thine eyes round about, and see; all they gather themselves together, they come to thee: thy sons shall come from afar, and thy daughters shall be nursed at thy side." — *Isaiah*, lx.

3 " The multitude of camels shall cover thee; the dromedaries of Midian and Ephah; all they from Sheba shall come; they shall bring gold and incense." — *Ib.*

4 " Who are these that fly as a cloud, and as the doves to their windows?" — *Ib.*

5 " Surely the isles shall wait for me, and the ships of Tarshish first, to bring thy sons from far, their silver and their gold with them." — *Ib.*

6 " The glory of Lebanon shall come unto thee; the fir-tree, the pine-tree, and the box together, to beautify the place of my sanctuary; and I will make the place of my feet glorious." — *Ib.*

No more shall dischord haunts thy ways,[7]
Nor ruin waste thy cheerless nation;
But thou shalt call thy portals Praise,
And thou shalt name thy walls Salvation.

The sun no more shall make thee bright,[8]
Nor moon shall lend her lustre to thee;
But GOD, Himself, shall be thy Light,
And flash eternal glory thro' thee.

Thy sun shall never more go down;
A ray from heaven itself descended
Shall light thy everlasting crown —
Thy days of mourning all are ended.[9]

My own, elect, and righteous Land!
The Branch, for ever green and vernal,
Which I have planted with this hand —
Live thou shalt in Life Eternal.[10]

THERE IS A BLEAK DESERT.

(AIR. — CRESCENTINI.)

THERE is a bleak Desert, where daylight grows weary
Of wasting its smile on a region so dreary —
What may that Desert be?
'T is Life, cheerless Life, where the few joys that come
Are lost, like that daylight, for 't is not their home.

There is a lone Pilgrim, before whose faint eyes
The water he pants for but sparkles and flies —
Who may that Pilgrim be?

7 " Violence shall no more be heard in thy land, wasting nor destruction within thy borders; but thou shalt call thy walls, Salvation, and thy gates, Praise." — *Isaiah*, lx.

8 " Thy sun shall be no more thy light by day; neither for brightness shall the moon give light unto thee: but the LORD shall be unto thee an everlasting light, and thy GOD thy glory." — *Ib.*

9 " Thy sun shall no more go down; ... for the LORD shall be thine everlasting light, and the days of thy mourning shall be ended." — *Ib.*

10 " Thy people also shall be all righteous; they shall inherit the land for ever, the branch of my planting, the work of my hands." — *Ib.*

'T is Man, hapless Man, thro' this life
    tempted on
By fair shining hopes, that in shining
    are gone.

There is a bright Fountain, thro' that
    Desert stealing
To pure lips alone its refreshment re-
    vealing —
        What may that Fountain be?
'T is Truth, holy Truth, that, like springs
    under ground,
By the gifted of Heaven alone can be
    found.[1]

There is a fair Spirit whose wand hath
    the spell
To point where those waters in secrecy
    dwell —
        Who may that Spirit be?
'T is Faith, humble Faith, who hath
    learned that where'er
Her wand bends to worship the Truth
    must be there!

SINCE FIRST THY WORD.

(AIR. — NICHOLAS FREEMAN.)

SINCE first Thy Word awaked my heart,
    Like new life dawning o'er me,
Where'er I turn mine eyes, Thou art,
    All light and love before me.
Naught else I feel, or hear or see —
    All bonds of earth I sever —
Thee, O GOD, and only Thee
    I live for, now and ever.

Like him whose fetters dropt away
    When light shone o'er his prison,[2]
My spirit, touched by Mercy's ray,
    Hath from her chains arisen.
And shall a soul Thou bidst be free,
    Return to bondage? — never!
Thee, O GOD, and only Thee
    I live for, now and ever.

1 In singing, the following line had better be
adopted, —
    "Can but by the gifted of Heaven be found."

2 "And, behold, the angel of the LORD came
upon him, and a light shined in the prison, . . .
and his chains fell off from his hands." — *Acts,*
xii. 7.

HARK! 'T IS THE BREEZE.

(AIR. — ROUSSEAU.)

HARK! 't is the breeze of twilight call-
    ing
Earth's weary children to repose;
While, round the couch of Nature falling,
    Gently the night's soft curtains close.
Soon o'er a world, in sleep reclining,
    Numberless stars, thro' yonder dark,
Shall look, like eyes of Cherubs shin-
    ing
From out the veils that hid the Ark.

Guard us, oh Thou, who never sleepest,
    Thou who in silence throned above,
Throughout all time, unwearied, keepest
    Thy watch of Glory, Power, and Love.
Grant that, beneath thine eye, securely,
    Our souls awhile from life withdrawn
May in their darkness stilly, purely,
    Like "sealed fountains," rest till dawn.

WHERE IS YOUR DWELLING,
YE SAINTED?

(AIR. — HASSE.)

WHERE is your dwelling, ye Sainted?
    Thro' what Elysium more bright
Than fancy or hope ever painted,
    Walk ye in glory and light?
Who the same kingdom inherits?
    Breathes there a soul that may dare
Look to that world of Spirits,
    Or hope to dwell with you there?

Sages! who, even in exploring
    Nature thro' all her bright ways,
Went like the Seraphs adoring,
    And veiled your eyes in the blaze —
Martyrs! who left for our reaping
    Truths you had sown in your blood —
Sinners! whom long years of weeping
    Chastened from evil to good —

Maidens! who like the young Crescent,
    Turning away your pale brows
From earth and the light of the Present,
    Looked to your Heavenly Spouse —
Say, thro' what region enchanted
    Walk ye in Heaven's sweet air?
Say, to what spirits 't is granted,
    Bright souls, to dwell with you there?

HOW LIGHTLY MOUNTS THE MUSE'S WING.

(AIR. — ANONYMOUS.)

How lightly mounts the Muse's wing,
　Whose theme is in the skies —
Like morning larks that sweeter sing
　The nearer Heaven they rise.

Tho' Love his magic lyre may tune,
　Yet ah, the flowers he round it wreathes
Were plucked beneath pale Passion's
　moon,
　Whose madness in their odor breathes.

How purer far the sacred lute,
　Round which Devotion ties
Sweet flowers that turn to heavenly fruit,
　And palm that never dies.

Tho' War's high-sounding harp may be
　Most welcome to the hero's ears,
Alas, his chords of victory
　Are wet, all o'er, with human tears.

How far more sweet their numbers run,
　Who hymn like Saints above,
No victor but the Eternal One,
　No trophies but of Love !

GO FORTH TO THE MOUNT.

(AIR. — STEVENSON.)

Go forth to the Mount — bring the olive-
　branch home,[1]
And rejoice, for the day of our Freedom
　is come !
From that time,[2] when the moon upon
　Ajalon's vale,
　Looking motionless down,[3] saw the
　　kings of the earth,
In the presence of GOD's mighty Cham-
　pion grow pale —
　Oh, never had Judah an hour of such
　　mirth !

1 " And that they should publish and proclaim
in all their cities, and in Jerusalem, saying, Go
forth unto the mount, and fetch olive-branches,"
etc. — *Neh.* viii. 15.

2 " For since the days of Joshua the son of
Nun unto that day had not the children of Israel
done so : and there was very great gladness." —
Ib. 17.

3 " Sun, stand thou still upon Gibeon; and
thou, Moon, in the valley of Ajalon." — *Josh.* x. 12.

Go forth to the Mount — bring the olive-
　branch home,
And rejoice, for the day of our Freedom
　is come !

Bring myrtle and palm — bring the
　boughs of each tree
That 's worthy to wave o'er the tents of
　the Free.[4]
From that day when the footsteps of
　Israel shone
　With a light not their own, thro' the
　　Jordan's deep tide,
Whose waters shrunk back as the Ark
　glided on [5] —
　Oh, never had Judah an hour of such
　　pride !
Go forth to the Mount — bring the olive-
　branch home,
And rejoice, for the day of our Freedom
　is come !

IS IT NOT SWEET TO THINK, HEREAFTER.

(AIR. — HADYN.)

Is it not sweet to think, hereafter,
　When the Spirit leaves this sphere,
Love, with deathless wing, shall waft her
　To those she long hath mourned for
　　here ?

Hearts from which 't was death to sever,
　Eyes this world can ne'er restore,
There, as warm, as bright as ever,
　Shall meet us and be lost no more.

When wearily we wander, asking
　Of earth and heaven, where are they,
Beneath whose smile we once lay basking,
　Blest and thinking bliss would stay ?

Hope still lifts her radiant finger
　Pointing to the eternal Home,
Upon whose portal yet they linger,
　Looking back for us to come.

4 " Fetch olive-branches, and pine-branches,
and myrtle-branches, and palm-branches, and
branches of thick trees, to make booths." — *Neh.*
viii. 15.

5 " And the priests that bare the ark of the
covenant of the LORD stood firm on dry ground
in the midst of Jordan, and all the Israelites
passed over on dry ground." — *Josh.* iii. 17.

Alas, alas — doth Hope deceive us?
　Shall friendship — love — shall all
　　those ties
That bind a moment, and then leave us,
　Be found again where nothing dies?

Oh, if no other boon were given,
　To keep our hearts from wrong and
　　stain,
Who would not try to win a Heaven
　Where all we love shall live again?

WAR AGAINST BABYLON.

(AIR. — NOVELLO.)

" WAR against Babylon ! " shout we
　around,[1]
Be our banners through earth unfurled;
Rise up, ye nations, ye kings, at the
　sound [2] —
　" War against Babylon !" shout thro'
　　the world !

1 "Shout against her round about."—*Jer.* l. 15.
2 " Set ye up a standard in the land, blow the
trumpet among the nations, prepare the nations
against her, call together against her the kingdoms," etc. — *Ib.* li. 27.

Oh thou, that dwellest on many waters,[3]
　Thy day of pride is ended now;
And the dark curse of Israel's daughters
　Breaks like a thunder-cloud over thy
　　brow !
　　　War, war, war against Babylon !

Make bright the arrows, and gather the
　shields,[4]
Set the standard of God on high;
Swarm we, like locusts, o'er all her
　fields.
" Zion" our watchword, and " ven-
　geance " our cry !
Woe ! woe ! — the time of thy visitation[5]
　Is come, proud Land, thy doom is
　　cast —
And the black surge of desolation
　Sweeps o'er thy guilty head, at last !
　　　War, war, war against Babylon !

3 " Oh thou that dwellest upon many waters,
. . . thine end is come."—*Jer.* li. 13.
4 " Make bright the arrows ; gather the shields
. . . set up the standard upon the walls of Babylon."—*Jer.* li. 11, 12.
5 "Woe unto them ! for their day is come, the
time of their visitation !"—*Jer.* l. 27.

A MELOLOGUE

UPON

NATIONAL MUSIC.

ADVERTISEMENT.

THESE verses were written for a Benefit at the Dublin Theatre, and were spoken by Miss Smith, with a degree of success, which they owed solely to her admirable manner of reciting them. I wrote them in haste; and it very rarely happens that poetry which has cost but little labor to the writer is productive of any great pleasure to the reader. Under this impression, I certainly should not have published them if they had not found their way into some of the newspapers with such an addition of errors to their own original stock that I thought it but fair to limit their responsibility to those faults alone which really belong to them.

With respect to the title which I have invented for this Poem, I feel even more than the scruples of the Emperor Tiberius, when he humbly asked pardon of the Roman Senate for using "the outlandish term, *monopoly*." But the truth is, having written the Poem with the sole view of serving a Benefit, I thought that an unintelligible word of this kind would not be without its attraction for the multitude, with whom, "If 't is not sense, at least 't is Greek." To some of my readers, however, it may not be superfluous to say, that by "Melologue," I mean that mixture of recitation and music, which is frequently adopted in the performance of Collins's Ode on the Passions, and of which the most striking example I can remember is the prophetic speech of Joad in the Athalie of Racine.

T. M.

MELOLOGUE.

THERE breathes a language known
and felt
Far as the pure air spreads its living
zone;
Wherever rage can rouse, or pity melt,
That language of the soul is felt and
known.
From those meridian plains,
Where oft, of old, on some high
tower
The soft Peruvian poured his midnight
strains,
And called his distant love with such
sweet power,
That, when she heard the lonely lay,
Not worlds could keep her from his
arms away,[1]
To the bleak climes of polar night,
Where blithe, beneath a sunless sky,
The Lapland lover bids his reindeer
fly,
And sings along the lengthening waste
of snow,
Gayly as if the blessed light
Of vernal Phœbus burned upon his
brow;
Oh Music! thy celestial claim
Is still resistless, still the same;
And, faithful as the mighty sea
To the pale star that o'er its realm pre-
sides,
The spell-bound tides
Of human passion rise and fall for thee!

1 "A certain Spaniard, one night late, met an Indian woman in the streets of Cozco, and would have taken her to his home, but she cried out, ' For God's sake, Sir, let me go; for that pipe, which you hear in yonder tower, calls me with great passion, and I cannot refuse the summons; for love constrains me to go, that I may be his wife, and he my husband.'" — "*Garcilasso de la Vega*," in Sir Paul Rycaut's translation.

GREEK AIR.

List! 't is a Grecian maid that sings,
While, from Ilissus' silvery springs,
She draws the cool lymph in her grace-
ful urn;
And by her side, in Music's charm dis-
solving,
Some patriot youth, the glorious past
revolving,
Dreams of bright-days that never can
return;
When Athens nurst her olive bough
With hands by tyrant power un-
chained;
And braided for the muse's brow
A wreath by tyrant touch unstained.
When heroes trod each classic field
Where coward feet now faintly falter;
When every arm was Freedom's shield,
And every heart was Freedom's altar!

FLOURISH OF TRUMPETS.

Hark, 't is the sound that charms
The war-steed's wakening ears! —
Oh! many a mother folds her arms
Round her boy-soldier when that call she
hears;
And, tho' her fond heart sink with fears,
Is proud to feel his young pulse bound
With valor's fever at the sound.
See, from his native hills afar
The rude Helvetian flies to war;
Careless for what, for whom he fights,
For slave or despot, wrongs or rights;
A conqueror oft — a hero never —
Yet lavish of his life-blood still,
As if 't were like his mountain rill,
And gushed for ever!

Yes, Music, here, even here,
Amid this thoughtless, vague career,
Thy soul-felt charm asserts its wondrous
power. —

There 's a wild air which oft, among
    the rocks
Of his own loved land, at evening hour,
Is heard, when shepherds homeward
    pipe their flocks,
Whose every note hath power to thrill
    his mind
With tenderest thoughts; to bring around
    his knees
The rosy children whom he left behind,
    And fill each little angel eye
    With speaking tears, that ask him why
He wandered from his hut for scenes
    like these.
Vain, vain is then the trumpet's brazen
    roar;
Sweet notes of home, of love, are all
    he hears;
And the stern eyes that looked for blood
    before
Now melting, mournful, lose themselves
    in tears.

SWISS AIR. — "RANZ DES VACHES."

But wake the trumpet's blast again,
    And rouse the ranks of warrior-men!
Oh War, when Truth thy arm employs,
And Freedom's spirit guides the labor-
    ing storm,
'T is then thy vengeance takes a hallowed
    form,
    And like Heaven's lightning sacredly
    destroys.
Nor, Music, thro' thy breathing sphere,
Lives there a sound more grateful to
    the ear

Of Him who made all harmony,
Than the blest sound of fetters break-
    ing,
And the first hymn that man awaking
From Slavery's slumber breathes to
    Liberty.

SPANISH CHORUS.

Hark! from Spain, indignant Spain,
Bursts the bold, enthusiast strain,
Like morning's music on the air;
And seems in every note to swear
By Saragossa's ruined streets,
    By brave Gerona's deathful story,
That, while *one* Spaniard's life-blood
    beats,
    That blood shall stain the conqueror's
    glory.

SPANISH AIR. — "YA DESPERTO."

But ah! if vain the patriot's zeal,
If neither valor's force nor wisdom's
    light
Can break or melt that blood-cemented
    seal
Which shuts so close the book of
    Europe's right —
What song shall then in sadness tell
    Of broken pride, of prospects shaded,
    Of buried hopes, remembered well,
    Of ardor quenched, and honor faded?
What muse shall mourn the breathless
    brave,
    In sweetest dirge at Memory's shrine?
What harp shall sigh o'er Freedom's
    grave?
    Oh Erin, Thine!

SET OF GLEES,

MUSIC BY MOORE.

THE MEETING OF THE SHIPS.

WHEN o'er the silent seas alone,
For days and nights we 've cheerless
gone,
Oh they who 've felt it know how sweet,
Some sunny morn a sail to meet.

Sparkling at once is every eye,
" Ship ahoy ! " our joyful cry;
While answering back the sounds we
hear,
" Ship ahoy ! " what cheer? what cheer?

Then sails are backed, we nearer come,
Kind words are said of friends and
home;
And soon, too soon, we part with pain,
To sail o'er silent seas again.

HIP, HIP, HURRA !

COME, fill round a bumper, fill up to the
brim,
He who shrinks from a bumper I pledge
not to him;
Here 's the girl that each loves, be her
eye of what hue,
Or lustre, it may, so her heart is but true.
Charge ! (drinks) hip, hip, hurra,
hurra !

Come charge high, again, boy, nor let
the full wine
Leave a space in the brimmer, where
daylight may shine;
Here 's " the friends of our youth —
tho' of some we 're bereft.
May the links that are lost but endear
what are left ! "
Charge ! (drinks) hip, hip, hurra,
hurra !

Once more fill a bumper — ne'er talk of
the hour;
On hearts thus united old Time has no
power.
May our lives, tho', alas ! like the wine
of to-night,
They must soon have an end, to the last
flow as bright.
Charge ! (drinks) hip, hip, hurra,
hurra !

Quick, quick, now, I 'll give you, since
Time's glass will run
Even faster than ours doth, three bum-
pers in one;
Here 's the poet who sings — here 's the
warrior who fights —
Here 's the statesman who speaks, in the
cause of men's rights !
Charge ! (drinks) hip, hip, hurra,
hurra !

Come, once more, a bumper ! — then
drink as you please,
Tho', *who* could fill half-way to toast
such as these?
Here 's our next joyous meeting — and
oh when we meet,
May our wine be as bright and our union
as sweet !
Charge ! (drinks) hip, hip, hurra,
hurra !

HUSH, HUSH !

" HUSH, hush ! " — how well
That sweet word sounds,
When Love, the little sentinel,
Walks his night-rounds;
Then, if a foot but dare
One rose-leaf crush,
Myriads of voices in the air
Whisper, " Hush, hush ! "

"Hark, hark, 't is he!"
The night elves cry,
And hush their fairy harmony,
While he steals by;
But if his silvery feet
One dew-drop brush,
Voices are heard in chorus sweet,
Whispering, "Hush, hush!"

THE PARTING BEFORE THE BATTLE.

HE.

On to the field, our doom is sealed,
To conquer or be slaves:
This sun shall see our nation free,
Or set upon our graves.

SHE.

Farewell, oh farewell, my love,
May Heaven thy guardian be,
And send bright angels from above
To bring thee back to me.

HE.

On to the field, the battle-field,
Where freedom's standard waves,
This sun shall see our tyrant yield,
Or shine upon our graves.

THE WATCHMAN.

A TRIO.

WATCHMAN.

Past twelve o'clock — past twelve.

Good night, good night, my dearest —
How fast the moments fly!
'T is time to part, thou hearest
That hateful watchman's cry.

WATCHMAN.

Past one o'clock — past one.

Yet stay a moment longer —
Alas! why is it so,
The wish to stay grows stronger,
The more 't is time to go?

WATCHMAN.

Past two o'clock — past two.

Now wrap thy cloak about thee —
The hours must sure go wrong,
For when they 're past without thee,
They 're, oh, ten times as long.

WATCHMAN.

Past three o'clock — past three.

Again that dreadful warning!
Had ever time such flight?
And see the sky, 't is morning —
So now, *indeed*, good night.

WATCHMAN.

Past three o'clock — past three.

Good night, good night.

SAY, WHAT SHALL WE DANCE?

Say, what shall we dance?
Shall we bound along the moonlight plain,
To music of Italy, Greece, or Spain?
Say, what shall we dance?
Shall we, like those who rove
Thro' bright Grenada's grove,
To the light Bolero's measures move?
Or choose the Guaracia's languishing lay,
And thus to its sound die away?

Strike the gay chords,
Let us hear each strain from every shore
That music haunts, or young feet wander o'er.
Hark! 't is the light march, to whose measured time,
The Polish lady, by her lover led,
Delights thro' gay saloons with step untried to tread,
Or sweeter still, thro' moonlight walks
Whose shadows serve to hide
The blush that 's raised by him who talks
Of love the while by her side,
Then comes the smooth waltz, to whose floating sound
Like dreams we go gliding around,
Say, which shall we dance? which shall we dance?

THE EVENING GUN.

REMEMBER'ST thou that setting sun,
　The last I saw with thee,
When loud we heard the evening gun
　Peal o'er the twilight sea?
Boom!— the sounds appeared to sweep
　Far o'er the verge of day,
Till, into realms beyond the deep,
　They seemed to die away.

Oft, when the toils of day are done,
　In pensive dreams of thee,
I sit to hear that evening gun,
　Peal o'er the stormy sea.
Boom!—and while, o'er billows curled,
　The distant sounds decay,
I weep and wish, from this rough world
　Like them to die away.

LEGENDARY BALLADS.

TO

THE MISS FEILDINGS,

THIS VOLUME

IS INSCRIBED

BY

THEIR FAITHFUL FRIEND AND SERVANT,

THOMAS MOORE.

LEGENDARY BALLADS.

THE VOICE.

IT came o'er her sleep, like a voice of
    those days,
When love, only love, was the light of
    her ways;
And, soft as in moments of bliss long ago,
It whispered her name from the garden
    below.

" Alas," sighed the maiden, " how fancy
    can cheat!
" The world once had lips that could
    whisper thus sweet;
" But cold now they slumber in yon fatal
    deep,
" Where, oh that beside them this heart
    too could sleep! "

She sunk on her pillow — but no, 't was
    in vain
To chase the illusion, that Voice came
    again!
She flew to the casement — but, husht
    as the grave,
In moonlight lay slumbering woodland
    and wave.

" Oh sleep, come and shield me," in
    anguish she said,
" From that call of the buried, that cry
    of the Dead! "
And sleep came around her — but, start-
    ing, she woke,
For still from the garden that spirit Voice
    spoke!

" I come," she exclaimed, " be thy home
    where it may,
" On earth or in heaven, that call I
    obey; "
Then forth thro' the moonlight, with
    heart beating fast
And loud as a death-watch, the pale
    maiden past.

Still round her the scene all in loneliness
    shone;
And still, in the distance, that Voice led
    her on;
But whither she wandered, by wave or
    by shore,
None ever could tell, for she came back
    no more.

No, ne'er came she back, — but the
    watchman who stood,
That night, in the tower which o'er-
    shadows the flood,
Saw dimly, 't is said, o'er the moon-
    lighted spray,
A youth on a steed bear the maiden away.

CUPID AND PSYCHE.

THEY told her that he, to whose vows
    she had listened
    Thro' night's fleeting hours, was a
      Spirit unblest; —
Unholy the eyes, that beside her had
    glistened,
    And evil the lips she in darkness had
      prest.

" When next in thy chamber the bride-
    groom reclineth,
    " Bring near him thy lamp, when in
      slumber he lies;
" And there, as the light o'er his dark
    features shineth,
    " Thou 'lt see what a demon hath won
      all thy sighs! "

Too fond to believe them, yet doubting,
    yet fearing,
    When calm lay the sleeper she stole
      with her light;
And saw — such a vision! — no image,
    appearing
    To bards in their day-dreams, was ever
      so bright.

A youth, but just passing from childhood's
    sweet morning,
  While round him still lingered its in-
    nocent ray;
Tho' gleams, from beneath his shut eye-
    lids gave warning
  Of summer-noon lightnings that under
    them lay.

His brow had a grace more than mortal
    around it,
  While, glossy as gold from a fairy-land
    mine,
His sunny hair hung, and the flowers
    that crowned it
  Seemed fresh from the breeze of some
    garden divine.

Entranced stood the bride, on that mira-
    cle gazing,
  What late was but love is idolatry now;
But, ah — in her tremor the fatal lamp
    raising —
  A sparkle flew from it and dropt on his
    brow.

All 's lost — with a start from his rosy
    sleep waking,
  The Spirit flashed o'er her his glances
    of fire;
Then, slow from the clasp of her snowy
    arms breaking,
  Thus said, in a voice more of sorrow
    than ire:

" Farewell — what a dream thy suspicion
    hath broken !
" Thus ever Affection's fond vision is
    crost;
" Dissolved are her spells when a doubt
    is but spoken,
" And love, once distrusted, for ever
    is lost ! "

HERO AND LEANDER.

" THE night-wind is moaning with mourn-
    ful sigh,
" There gleameth no moon in the misty
    sky,
  " No star over Helle's sea;
" Yet, yet, there is shining one holy light,
" One love-kindled star thro' the deep
    of night,
  " To lead me, sweet Hero, to thee ! "

Thus saying, he plunged in the foamy
    stream,
Still fixing his gaze on that distant beam
    No eye but a lover's could see;
And still, as the surge swept over his
    head,
" To-night," he said tenderly, " living
    or dead,
  " Sweet Hero, I 'll rest with thee ! "

But fiercer around him the wild waves
    speed;
Oh, Love ! in that hour of thy votary's
    need,
  Where, where could thy Spirit be ?
He struggles — he sinks — while the hur-
    ricane's breath
Bears rudely away his last farewell in
    death —
  " Sweet Hero, I die for thee ! "

THE LEAF AND THE FOUNTAIN.

" TELL me, kind Seer, I pray thee,
" So may the stars obey thee,
    " So may each airy
    " Moon-elf and fairy
" Nightly their homage pay thee !
" Say, by what spell, above, below,
" In stars that wink or flowers that
    blow,
    " I may discover,
    " Ere night is over,
" Whether my love loves me, or no,
" Whether my love loves me."

" Maiden, the dark tree nigh thee
" Hath charms no gold could buy thee;
    " Its stem enchanted,
    " By moon-elves planted,
" Will all thou seek'st supply thee.
" Climb to yon boughs that highest grow,
" Bring thence their fairest leaf below;
    " And thou 'lt discover,
    " Ere night is over,
" Whether thy love loves thee or no,
" Whether thy love loves thee."

" See, up the dark tree going,
" With blossoms round me blowing,
    " From thence, oh Father,
    " This leaf I gather,
" Fairest that there is growing.

" Say, by what sign I now shall know
" If in this leaf lie bliss or woe
　　" And thus discover
　　" Ere night is over,
" Whether my love loves me or no,
" Whether my love loves me."

" Fly to yon fount that 's welling
" Where moonbeam ne'er had dwelling,
　　" Dip in its water
　　" That leaf, oh Daughter,
" And mark the tale 't is telling; [1]
" Watch thou if pale or bright it grow,
" List thou, the while, that fountain's
　　　　flow,
　　" And thou 'lt discover
　　" Whether thy lover,
" Loved as he is, loves thee or no,
" Loved as he is, loves thee."

Forth flew the nymph, delighted,
To seek that fount benighted;
　　But, scarce a minute
　　The leaf lay in it,
When, lo, its bloom was blighted!
And as she asked, with voice of woe —
Listening, the while, that fountain's
　　　　flow —
　　" Shall I recover
　　" My truant lover?"
The fountain seemed to answer, " No;"
The fountain answered, " No."

CEPHALUS AND PROCRIS.

A HUNTER once in that grove reclined,
　　To shun the noon's bright eye,
And oft he wooed the wandering wind,
　　To cool his brow with its sigh.
While mute lay even the wild bee's hum,
　　Nor breath could stir the aspen's hair,
His song was still " Sweet air, oh
　　　　come!"
　　While Echo answered, " Come, sweet
　　　　Air!"

But, hark, what sounds from the thicket
　　　　rise!
What meaneth that rustling spray?

1 The ancients had a mode of divination
somewhat similar to this; and we find the
Emperor Adrian, when he went to consult the
Fountain of Castalia, plucking a bay-leaf and
dipping it into the sacred water.

" 'T is the white-horned doe," the Hun-
　　　　ter cries,
　　" I have sought since break of day."
Quick o'er the sunny glade he springs,
　　The arrow flies from his sounding bow,
" Hilliho — hilliho!" he gayly sings,
　　While Echo sighs forth " Hilliho!"

Alas, 't was not the white-horned doe
He saw in the rustling grove,
But the bridal veil, as pure as snow,
Of his own young wedded love.
And, ah, too sure that arrow sped,
　　For pale at his feet he sees her lie;—
" I die, I die," was all she said,
　　While Echo murmured, " I die, I
　　　　die!"

YOUTH AND AGE. [2]

"TELL me, what 's Love?" said Youth,
　　　　one day,
To drooping Age, who crost his way. —
" It is a sunny hour of play,
" For which repentance dear doth pay;
　　" Repentance! Repentance!
" And this is Love, as wise men say."

" Tell me, what 's Love?" said Youth
　　　　once more,
Fearful, yet fond, of Age's lore. —
" Soft as a passing summer's wind,
" Wouldst know the blight it leaves
　　　　behind?
　　" Repentance! Repentance!
" And this is Love — when love is
　　　　o'er."

" Tell me, what 's Love?" said Youth
　　　　again,
Trusting the bliss, but not the pain.
" Sweet as a May tree's scented air —
" Mark ye what bitter fruit 't will bear,
　　" Repentance! Repentance!
" This, this is Love — sweet Youth,
　　　　beware."

Just then, young Love himself came by,
And cast on Youth a smiling eye;
Who could resist that glance's ray?
In vain did Age his warning say,
　　" Repentance! Repentance!"
Youth laughing went with Love away.

2 The air, to which I have adapted these
words, was composed by Mrs. Arkwright to

THE DYING WARRIOR.

A WOUNDED Chieftain, lying
　By the Danube's leafy side,
Thus faintly said, in dying,
　"Oh! bear, thou foaming tide,
　"This gift to my lady-bride."

'T was then, in life's last quiver,
　He flung the scarf he wore
Into the foaming river,
　Which, ah too quickly, bore
　That pledge of one no more!

With fond impatience burning,
　The Chieftain's lady stood,
To watch her love returning
　In triumph down the flood,
　From that day's field of blood.

But, field, alas, ill-fated!
　The lady saw, instead
Of the bark whose speed she waited,
　Her hero's scarf, all red
With the drops his heart had shed.

One shriek — and all was over —
　Her life-pulse ceased to beat;
The gloomy waves now cover
　That bridal-flower so sweet,
And the scarf is her winding sheet!

THE MAGIC MIRROR.

"COME, if thy magic Glass have power
　"To call up forms we sigh to see;
"Show me my love, in that rosy bower,
　"Where last she pledged her truth to
　me."

The Wizard showed him his Lady bright,
　Where lone and pale in her bower she
　lay;
"True-hearted maid," said the happy
　Knight,
　"She's thinking of one, who is far
　away."

But, lo! a page, with looks of joy,
　Brings tidings to the Lady's ear;

some old verses, "Tell me what's love, kind
shepherd, pray?" and it has been my object to
retain as much of the structure and phraseology
of the original words as possible.

"'T is," said the Knight, "the same
　bright boy,
　"Who used to guide me to my dear."
The Lady now, from her favorite tree,
　Hath, smiling, plucked a rosy flower;
"Such," he exclaimed, "was the gift
　that she
　"Each morning sent me from that
　bower!"

She gives her page the blooming rose,
　With looks that say, "Like lightning,
　fly!"
"Thus," thought the Knight, "she
　soothes her woes,
　"By fancying, still, her true-love
　nigh."

But the page returns, and — oh, what a
　sight,
　For trusting lover's eyes to see! —
Leads to that bower another Knight,
　As young and, alas, as loved as he!

"Such," quoth the Youth, "is Woman's
　love!"
Then, darting forth, with furious bound,
Dashed at the Mirror his iron glove,
　And strewed it all in fragments round.

MORAL.

Such ills would never have come to pass,
　Had he ne'er sought that fatal view;
The Wizard would still have kept his
　Glass,
　And the Knight still thought his Lady
　true.

THE PILGRIM.

STILL thus, when twilight gleamed,
Far off his Castle seemed,
　Traced on the sky;
And still, as fancy bore him
To those dim towers before him,
He gazed, with wishful eye,
　And thought his home was nigh.

"Hall of my Sires!" he said,
"How long, with weary tread,
　"Must I toil on?
"Each eve, as thus I wander,
"Thy towers seem rising yonder,
"But, scarce hath daylight shone,
　"When, like a dream, thou 'rt gone!"

So went the Pilgrim still,
Down dale and over hill,
　Day after day;
That glimpse of home, so cheering,
At twilight still appearing,
But still, with morning's ray,
　Melting, like mist, away!

Where rests the Pilgrim now?
Here, by this cypress bough,
　Closed his career;
That dream, of fancy's weaving,
No more his steps deceiving,
Alike past hope and fear,
　The Pilgrim's home is here.

THE HIGH-BORN LADYE.

In vain all the Knights of the Underwald
　wooed her,
　Tho' brightest of maidens, the proud-
　　est was she;
Brave chieftains they sought, and young
　minstrels they sued her,
　But worthy were none of the high-born
　　Ladye.

"Whomsoever I wed," said this maid,
　so excelling,
　"That Knight must the conqueror of
　　conquerors be;
"He must place me in halls fit for
　monarchs to dwell in; —
　"None else shall be Lord of the high-
　　born Ladye!"

Thus spoke the proud damsel, with scorn
　looking round her
　On Knights and on Nobles of highest
　　degree;
Who humbly and hopelessly left as they
　found her,
　And worshipt at distance the high-
　　born Ladye.

At length came a Knight, from a far land
　to woo her,
　With plumes on his helm like the
　　foam of the sea;
His visor was down — but, with voice
　that thrilled thro' her,
　He whispered his vows to the high-
　　born Ladye.

"Proud maiden! I come with high spou-
　sals to grace thee,
　"In me the great conqueror of con-
　　querors see;
"Enthroned in a hall fit for monarchs
　I'll place thee,
　"And mine thou 'rt for ever, thou
　　high-born Ladye!"

The maiden she smiled, and in jewels
　arrayed her,
Of thrones and tiaras already dreamt
　she;
And proud was the step, as her bride-
　groom conveyed her
　In pomp to his home, of that high-
　　born Ladye.

"But whither," she, starting, exclaims,
　"have you led me?
　"Here's naught but a tomb and a dark
　　cypress tree;
"Is *this* the bright palace in which thou
　wouldst wed me?"
With scorn in her glance said the high-
　born Ladye.

"'T is the home," he replied, "of earth's
　loftiest creatures" —
Then lifted his helm for the fair one to
　see;
But she sunk on the ground — 't was a
　skeleton's features,
　And Death was the Lord of the high-
　　born Ladye!

THE INDIAN BOAT.

'T was midnight dark,
　The seaman's bark,
Swift o'er the waters bore him,
　When, thro' the night,
　He spied a light
Shoot o'er the wave before him.
"A sail! a sail!" he cries;
　"She comes from the Indian shore,
"And to-night shall be our prize,
　"With her freight of golden ore:
　"Sail on! sail on!"
　　When morning shone
He saw the gold still clearer;
　But, though so fast
　The waves he past,
That boat seemed never the nearer.

Bright daylight came,
    And still the same
Rich bark before him floated;
    While on the prize
    His wishful eyes
Like any young lover's doted:
" More sail! more sail!'' he cries,
    While the waves o'ertop the mast;
And his bounding galley flies,
    Like an arrow before the blast.
        Thus on, and on,
        Till day was gone,
And the moon thro' heaven did hie
        her,
        He swept the main,
        But all in vain,
That boat seemed never the nigher.

    And many a day
    To night gave way,
And many a morn succeeded:
    While still his flight,
    Thro' day and night,
That restless mariner speeded.
Who knows — who knows what seas
    He is now careering o'er?
Behind, the eternal breeze,
    And that mocking bark, before!
    For, oh, till sky
    And earth shall die,
And their death leave none to rue it,
    That boat must flee
    O'er the boundless sea,
And that ship in vain pursue it.

THE STRANGER.

COME list, while I tell of the heart-
        wounded Stranger
    Who sleeps her last slumber in this
        haunted ground;
Where often, at midnight, the lonely
        wood-ranger
    Hears soft fairy music re-echo around.

None e'er knew the name of that heart-
        stricken lady,
    Her language, tho' sweet, none could
        e'er understand;
But her features so sunned, and her eye-
        lash so shady,
    Bespoke her a child of some far East-
        ern land.

'T was one summer night, when the vil-
        lage lay sleeping,
    A soft strain of melody came o'er our
        ears;
So sweet, but so mournful, half song and
        half weeping,
    Like music that Sorrow had steeped in
        her tears.

We thought 't was an anthem some an-
        gel had sung us; —
    But, soon as the day-beams had gushed
        from on high,
With wonder we saw this bright stranger
        among us,
    All lovely and lone, as if strayed from
        the sky.

Nor long did her life for this sphere seem
        intended,
    For pale was her cheek, with that
        spirit-like hue,
Which comes when the day of this world
        is nigh ended,
    And light from another already shines
        through.

Then her eyes, when she sung   oh, but
        once to have seen them —
    Left thoughts in the soul that can
        never depart;
While her looks and her voice made a
        language between them,
    That spoke more than holiest words to
        the heart.

But she past like a day-dream, no skill
        could restore her —
    Whate'er was her sorrow, its ruin came
        fast;
She died with the same spell of mystery
        o'er her,
    That song of past days on her lips to
        the last.

Nor even in the grave is her sad heart
        reposing —
    Still hovers the spirit of grief round
        her tomb;
For oft, when the shadows of midnight
        are closing,
    The same strain of music is heard
        thro' the gloom.

BALLADS, SONGS, ETC.

TO–DAY, DEAREST! IS OURS.

To-day, dearest! is ours;
  Why should Love carelessly lose it?
This life shines or lowers
  Just as we, weak mortals, use it.
'T is time enough, when its flowers
    decay,
  To think of the thorns of Sorrow;
And Joy, if left on the stem to-day,
  May wither before to-morrow.

Then why, dearest! so long
  Let the sweet moments fly over?
Tho' now, blooming and young,
  Thou hast me devoutly thy lover;
Yet Time from both, in his silent lapse,
  Some treasure may steal or borrow;
Thy charms may be less in bloom, per-
    haps,
  Or I less in love to-morrow.

WHEN ON THE LIP THE SIGH DELAYS.

When on the lip the sigh delays,
  As if 't would linger there for ever;
When eyes would give the world to gaze,
  Yet still look down and venture never;
When, tho' with fairest nymphs we rove,
  There 's one we dream of more than
    any —
If all this is not real love,
  'T is something wondrous like it,
    Fanny!

To think and ponder, when apart,
  On all we 've got to say at meeting;
And yet when near, with heart to heart,
  Sit mute and listen to their beating:
To see but one bright object move,
  The only moon, where stars are
    many —
If all this is not downright love,
  I prithee say what *is*, my Fanny!

When Hope foretells the brightest, best,
  Tho' Reason on the darkest reckons;
When Passion drives us to the west,
  Tho' Prudence to the eastward beck-
    ons;
When all turns round, below, above,
  And our own heads the most of any —
If this is not stark, staring love,
  Then you and I are sages, Fanny.

HERE, TAKE MY HEART.

Here, take my heart — 't will be safe in
    thy keeping,
  While I go wandering o'er land and
    o'er sea;
Smiling or sorrowing, waking or sleep-
    ing,
  What need I care, so my heart is with
    thee?

If in the race we are destined to run,
    love,
  They who have light hearts the happi-
    est be,
Then happier still must be they who have
    none, love,
  And that will be *my* case when mine
    is with thee.

It matters not where I may now be a
    rover,
  I care not how many bright eyes I may
    see;
Should Venus herself come and ask me
    to love her,
  I 'd tell her I could n't — my heart is
    with thee.

And there let it lie, growing fonder and
    fonder —
  For, even should Fortune turn truant
    to me,

266

Why, let her go — I 've a treasure beyond her,
 As long as my heart 's out at interest
 with thee !

OH, CALL IT BY SOME BETTER NAME.

OH, call it by some better name,
 For Friendship sounds too cold,
While Love is now a worldly flame,
 Whose shrine must be of gold;
And Passion, like the sun at noon,
 That burns o'er all he sees,
Awhile as warm, will set as soon —
 Then call it none of these.

Imagine something purer far,
 More free from stain of clay
Than Friendship, Love, or Passion are,
 Yet human still as they :
And if thy lip, for love like this,
 No mortal word can frame,
Go, ask of angels what it is,
 And call it by that name !

POOR WOUNDED HEART.

POOR wounded heart, farewell !
 Thy hour of rest is come;
 Thou soon wilt reach thy home,
Poor wounded heart, farewell !
The pain thou 'lt feel in breaking
 Less bitter far will be,
Than that long, deadly aching,
 This life has been to thee.

There — broken heart, farewell !
 The pang is o'er —
 The parting pang is o'er;
 Thou now wilt bleed no more,
Poor broken heart, farewell !
No rest for thee but dying —
Like waves, whose strife is past,
On death's cold shore thus lying,
 Thou sleepst in peace at last —
 Poor broken heart, farewell !

THE EAST INDIAN.

COME, May, with all thy flowers,
 Thy sweetly-scented thorn,
Thy cooling evening showers,
 Thy fragrant breath at morn :

When May-flies haunt the willow,
 When May-buds tempt the bee,
Then o'er the shining billow
 My love will come to me.

From Eastern Isles she 's winging
 Thro' watery wilds her way,
And on her cheek is bringing
 The bright sun's orient ray :
Oh, come and court her hither,
 Ye breezes mild and warm —
One winter's gale would wither
 So soft, so pure a form.

The fields where she was straying
 Are blest with endless light,
With zephyrs always playing
 Thro' gardens always bright.
Then now, sweet May ! be sweeter
 Than e'er thou 'st been before;
Let sighs from roses meet her
 When she comes near our shore.

POOR BROKEN FLOWER.

POOR broken flower ! what art can now
 recover thee ?
Torn from the stem that fed thy rosy
 breath —
  In vain the sunbeams seek
  To warm that faded cheek ;
The dews of heaven, that once like balm
 fell over thee,
Now are but tears, to weep thy early
 death.

So droops the maid whose lover hath for-
 saken her, —
Thrown from his arms, as lone and
 lost as thou ;
  In vain the smiles of all
  Like sun-beams round her fall ;
The only smile that could from death
 awaken her,
That smile, alas ! is gone to others now.

THE PRETTY ROSE–TREE.

BEING weary of love,
 I flew to the grove,
And chose me a tree of the fairest;
 Saying, " Pretty Rose-tree,
 " Thou my mistress shalt be,
" And I 'll worship each bud thou bearest.

" For the hearts of this world are hol-
    low,
" And fickle the smiles we follow;
    " And 't is sweet, when all
    " Their witcheries pall
" To have a pure love to fly to:
    " So, my pretty Rose-tree,
    " Thou my mistress shalt be,
" And the only one now I shall sigh to."

When the beautiful hue
    Of thy cheek thro' the dew
Of morning is bashfully peeping,
    " Sweet tears," I shall say
    (As I brush them away),
" At least there 's no art in this weeping."
Altho' thou shouldst die to-morrow,
'T will not be from pain or sorrow;
    And the thorns of thy stem
    Are not like them
With which men wound each other:
    So my pretty Rose-tree,
    Thou my mistress shalt be,
And I 'll ne'er again sigh to another.

SHINE OUT, STARS!

SHINE out, Stars! let Heaven assemble
    Round us every festal ray,
Lights that move not, lights that tremble,
    All to grace this Eve of May.
Let the flower-beds all lie waking,
    And the odors shut up there,
From their downy prisons breaking,
    Fly abroad thro' sea and air.

And would Love, too, bring his sweet-
    ness,
    With our other joys to weave,
Oh what glory, what completeness,
    Then would crown this bright May
        Eve !
Shine out, Stars! let night assemble
    Round us every festal ray,
Lights that move not, lights that tremble,
    To adorn this Eve of May.

THE YOUNG MULETEERS OF GRENADA.

OH, the joys of our evening posada,
    Where, resting at close of day,
We, young Muleteers of Grenada,
    Sit and sing the sunshine away;

So merry, that even the slumbers
    That round us hung seem gone;
Till the lute's soft drowsy numbers
    Again beguile them on.
        Oh the joys, etc.

Then as each to his loved sultana
    In sleep still breathes the sigh,
The name of some black-eyed Tirana
    Escapes our lips as we lie.
Till, with morning's rosy twinkle,
    Again we 're up and gone —
While the mule-bell's drowsy tinkle
    Beguiles the rough way on.
Oh the joys of our merry posada,
    Where, resting at close of day,
We, young Muleteers of Grenada,
    Thus sing the gay moments away.

TELL HER, OH, TELL HER.

TELL her, oh, tell her, the lute she left
        lying
    Beneath the green arbor is still lying
        there;
And breezes like lovers around it are
        sighing,
    But not a soft whisper replies to their
        prayer.

Tell her, oh, tell her, the tree that, in
        going,
    Beside the green arbor she playfully
        set,
As lovely as ever is blushing and blow-
        ing,
    And not a bright leaflet has fallen from
        it yet.

So while away from that arbor forsaken,
    The maiden is wandering, still let her be
As true as the lute that no sighing can
        waken
    And blooming for ever, unchanged as
        the tree !

NIGHTS OF MUSIC.

NIGHTS of music, nights of loving,
    Lost too soon, remembered long.
When we went by moonlight roving,
    Hearts all love and lips all song.
When this faithful lute recorded
    All my spirit felt to thee;
And that smile the song rewarded —
    Worth whole years of fame to me !

Nights of song, and nights of splendor,
    Filled with joys too sweet to last —
Joys that, like the star-light, tender,
    While they shone no shadow cast.
Tho' all other happy hours
    From my fading memory fly,
Of that starlight, of those bowers,
    Not a beam, a leaf shall die !

OUR FIRST YOUNG LOVE.

Our first young love resembles
    That short but brilliant ray,
Which smiles and weeps and trembles
    Thro' April's earliest day.
And not all life before us,
    Howe'er its lights may play,
Can shed a lustre o'er us
    Like that first April ray.

Our summer sun may squander
A blaze serener, grander;
    Our autumn beam
    May, like a dream
Of heaven, die calm away;
But no — let life before us
    Bring all the light it may,
'T will ne'er shed lustre o'er us
    Like that first youthful ray.

BLACK AND BLUE EYES.

The brilliant black eye
    May in triumph let fly
All its darts without caring who feels
    'em;
    But the soft eye of blue,
    Tho' it scatter wounds too,
Is much better pleased when it heals
    'em —
    Dear Fanny !
Is much better pleased when it heals 'em.

The black eye may say,
    " Come and worship my ray —
" By adoring, perhaps you may move
    me ! "
    But the blue eye, half hid,
    Says from under its lid,
" I love and am yours, if you love me ! "
    Yes, Fanny !
    The blue eye, half hid,
    Says, from under its lid,
" I love and am yours if you love me ! "

Come tell me, then, why
    In that lovely blue eye
Not a charm of its tint I discover;
    Oh why should you wear
    The only blue pair
That ever said " No " to a lover?
    Dear Fanny !
    Oh, why should you wear
    The only blue pair
That ever said " No " to a lover?

DEAR FANNY.

" She has beauty, but still you must
    keep your heart cool;
    " She has wit, but you must n't be
    caught so:"
Thus Reason advises, but Reason 's a
    fool,
    And 't is not the first time I have
    thought so,
        Dear Fanny.
'Tis not the first time I have thought
    so.

" She is lovely; then love her, nor let
    the bliss fly;
    " 'T is the charm of youth's vanishing
    season : "
Thus Love has advised me and who will
    deny
    That Love reasons much better than
    Reason,
        Dear Fanny?
    Love reasons much better than Reason.

FROM LIFE WITHOUT FREEDOM.

From life without freedom, say, who
    would not fly?
For one day of freedom, oh ! who would
    not die?
Hark ! — hark ! 't is the trumpet ! the
    call of the brave,
The death-song of tyrants, the dirge of
    the slave.
Our country lies bleeding — haste, haste
    to her aid;
One arm that defends is worth hosts that
    invade.

In death's kindly bosom our last hope
    remains —
The dead fear no tyrants, the grave has
    no chains.

On, on to the combat! the heroes that
    bleed
For virtue and mankind are heroes
    indeed.
And oh, even if Freedom from *this* world
    be driven,
Despair not — at least we shall find her
    in heaven.

HERE 'S THE BOWER.

HERE 's the bower she loved so much,
    And the tree she planted;
Here 's the harp she used to touch —
    Oh, how that touch enchanted!
Roses now unheeded sigh;
    Where 's the hand to wreathe them?
Songs around neglected lie;
    Where 's the lip to breathe them?
        Here 's the bower, etc.

Spring may bloom, but she we loved
    Ne'er shall feel its sweetness;
Time, that once so fleetly moved,
    Now hath lost its fleetness.
Years were days, when here she stray-
    ed,
    Days were moments near her;
Heaven ne'er formed a brighter maid,
    Nor Pity wept a dearer!
        Here 's the bower, etc.

I SAW THE MOON RISE CLEAR.

A FINLAND LOVE SONG.

I SAW the moon rise clear
    O'er hills and vales of snow,
Nor told my fleet rein-deer
    The track I wished to go.
Yet quick he bounded forth;
    For well my rein-deer knew
I 've but one path on earth —
    The path which leads to you.

The gloom that winter cast
    How soon the heart forgets,
When Summer brings, at last,
    Her sun that never sets!
So dawned my love for you;
    So, fixt thro' joy and pain,
Than summer sun more true,
    'T will never set again.

LOVE AND THE SUN–DIAL.

YOUNG Love found a Dial once in a dark
    shade
Where man ne'er had wandered nor sun-
    beam played;
" Why thus in darkness lie? " whispered
    young Love,
" Thou, whose gay hours in sunshine
    should move."
" I ne'er," said the Dial, " have seen
    the warm sun,
" So noonday and midnight to me, Love,
    are one."

Then Love took the Dial away from the
    shade,
And placed her where Heaven's beam
    warmly played.
There she reclined, beneath Love's gazing
    eye,
While, marked all with sunshine, her
    hours flew by.
" Oh, how," said the Dial, " can any
    fair maid
" That 's born to be shone upon rest in
    the shade? "

But night now comes on and the sun-
    beam 's o'er,
And Love stops to gaze on the Dial no
    more.
Alone and neglected, while bleak rain
    and winds
Are storming around her, with sorrow
    she finds
That Love had but numbered a few
    sunny hours, —
Then left the remainder to darkness and
    showers!

LOVE AND TIME.

'T IS said — but whether true or not
    Let bards declare who 've seen 'em —
That Love and Time have only got
    One pair of wings between 'em.
In courtship's first delicious hour,
    The boy full oft can spare 'em;
So, loitering in his lady's bower,
    He lets the grey-beard wear 'em.
        Then is Time's hour of play;
        Oh, how he flies, flies away!

But short the moments, short as bright,
    When he the wings can borrow;
If Time to-day has had his flight,
    Love takes his turn to-morrow.
Ah! Time and Love, your change is then
    The saddest and most trying,
When one begins to limp again,
    And t' other takes to flying.
        Then is Love's hour to stray;
        Oh, how he flies, flies away!

But there 's a nymph, whose chains I feel,
    And bless the silken fetter,
Who knows, the dear one, how to deal
    With Love and Time much better.
So well she checks their wanderings,
    So peacefully she pairs 'em,
That Love with her ne'er thinks of wings,
    And Time for ever wears 'em.
        This is Time's holiday;
        Oh, how he flies, flies away!

LOVE'S LIGHT SUMMER–CLOUD.

PAIN and sorrow shall vanish before us —
    Youth may wither, but feeling will last;
All the shadow that e'er shall fall o'er us
    Love's light summer-cloud only shall
        cast.
            Oh, if to love thee more
            Each hour I number o'er —
            If this a passion be
            Worthy of thee,
Then be happy, for thus I adore thee.
    Charms may wither, but feeling shall
        last:
All the shadow that e'er shall fall o'er
        thee,
    Love's light summer-cloud sweetly shall
        cast.

Rest, dear bosom, no sorrows shall pain
        thee,
    Sighs of pleasure alone shalt thou steal;
Beam, bright eyelid, no weeping shall
        stain thee,
    Tears of rapture alone shalt thou feel.
            Oh, if there be a charm
            In love, to banish harm —
            If pleasure's truest spell
            Be to love well,
Then be happy, for thus I adore thee.
    Charms may wither, but feeling shall
        last:

All the shadow that e'er shall fall o'er
        thee,
    Love's light summer-cloud sweetly shall
        cast.

LOVE, WANDERING THRO' THE GOLDEN MAZE.

LOVE, wandering thro' the golden maze
    Of my beloved's hair,
Traced every lock with fond delays,
    And, doting, lingered there.
And soon he found 't were vain to fly;
    His heart was close confined,
For, every ringlet was a tie —
    A chain by beauty twined.

MERRILY EVERY BOSOM BOUND–ETH.

(THE TYROLESE SONG OF LIBERTY.)

MERRILY every bosom boundeth,
            Merrily, oh!
Where the song of Freedom soundeth,
            Merrily, oh!
    There the warrior's arms
        Shed more splendor;
    There the maiden's charms
        Shine more tender;
Every joy the land surroundeth,
    Merrily, oh! merrily, oh!

Wearily every bosom pineth,
            Wearily, oh!
Where the bond of slavery twineth
            Wearily, oh!
    There the warrior's dart
        Hath no fleetness;
    There the maiden's heart
        Hath no sweetness —
Every flower of life declineth,
    Wearily, oh! wearily, oh!

Cheerily then from hill and valley,
            Cheerily, oh!
Like your native fountains sally,
            Cheerily, oh!
    If a glorious death,
        Won by bravery,
    Sweeter be than breath
        Sighed in slavery,
Round the flag of Freedom rally,
    Cheerily, oh! cheerily, oh!

REMEMBER THE TIME.

(THE CASTILIAN MAID.)

REMEMBER the time, in La Mancha's
  shades,
When our moments so blissfully flew;
When you called me the flower of Castil-
  ian maids,
And I blushed to be called so by you;
When I taught you to warble the gay
  seguadille,
  And to dance to the light castanet;
Oh, never, dear youth, let you roam
  where you will,
  The delight of those moments forget.

They tell me, you lovers from Erin's green
  isle,
  Every hour a new passion can feel;
And that soon, in the light of some love-
  lier smile,
  You 'll forget the poor maid of Castile.
But they know not how brave in the battle
  you are,
  Or they never could think you would
  rove;
For 't is always the spirit most gallant in
  war
  That is fondest and truest in love.

OH, SOON RETURN.

OUR white sail caught the evening ray,
  The wave beneath us seemed to burn,
When all the weeping maid could say
  Was, " Oh, soon return ! "
Thro' many a clime our ship was
  driven,
  O'er many a billow rudely thrown;
Now chilled beneath a northern heaven,
  Now sunned in summer's zone:
And still, where'er we bent our way,
  When evening bid the west wave burn,
I fancied still I heard her say,
  " Oh, soon return ! "

If ever yet my bosom found
  Its thoughts one moment turned from
  thee,
'T was when the combat raged around,
  And brave men looked to me.
But tho' the war-field's wild alarm
  For gentle Love was all unmeet,
He lent to Glory's brow the charm,
  Which made even danger sweet.

And still, when victory's calm came o'er
  The hearts where rage had ceased to
  burn,
Those parting words I heard once more,
  " Oh, soon return ! — Oh, soon re-
  turn ! "

LOVE THEE ?

LOVE thee? — so well, so tenderly
  Thou 'rt loved, adored by me,
Fame, fortune, wealth, and liberty,
  Were worthless without thee.
Tho' brimmed with blessings, pure and
  rare,
  Life's cup before me lay,
Unless thy love were mingled there,
  I'd spurn the draught away.
Love thee? — so well, so tenderly
  Thou 'rt loved, adored by me,
Fame, fortune, wealth, and liberty,
  Are worthless without thee.

Without thy smile, the monarch's lot
  To me were dark and lone,
While, *with* it, even the humblest cot
  Were brighter than his throne.
Those worlds for which the conqueror
  sighs
  For me would have no charms;
My only world thy gentle eyes —
  My throne thy circling arms !
Oh, yes, so well, so tenderly
  Thou 'rt loved, adored by me,
Whole realms of light and liberty
  Were worthless without thee.

ONE DEAR SMILE.

COULDST thou look as dear as when
  First I sighed for thee;
Couldst thou make me feel again
Every wish I breathed thee then,
  Oh, how blissful life would be !
Hopes that now beguiling leave me,
  Joys that lie in slumber cold —
All would wake, couldst thou but give me
  One dear smile like those of old.

No — there 's nothing left us now,
  But to mourn the past;
Vain was every ardent vow —
Never yet did Heaven allow
  Love so warm, so wild, to last.

Not even hope could now deceive me —
 Life itself looks dark and cold:
Oh, thou never more canst give me
 One dear smile like those of old.

YES, YES, WHEN THE BLOOM.

YES, yes, when the bloom of Love's boyhood is o'er,
 He 'll turn into friendship that feels no
 decay;
And, tho' Time may take from him the
 wings he once wore,
The charms that remain will be bright as
 before,
 And he 'll lose but his young trick of
 flying away.

Then let it console thee, if Love should
 not stay,
 That Friendship our last happy moments will crown:
Like the shadows of morning, Love les-
 sens away,
While Friendship, like those at the closing of day,
 Will linger and lengthen as life's sun
 goes down.

THE DAY OF LOVE.

THE beam of morning trembling
 Stole o'er the mountain brook,
With timid ray resembling
 Affection's early look.
Thus love begins — sweet morn of love!

The noon-tide ray ascended,
 And o'er the valley's stream
Diffused a glow as splendid
 As passion's riper dream.
Thus love expands — warm noon of love!

But evening came, o'ershading
 The glories of the sky,
Like faith and fondness fading
 From passion's altered eye.
Thus love declines — cold eve of love!

LUSITANIAN WAR–SONG.

THE song of war shall echo thro' our
 mountains,
 Till not one hateful link remains
 Of slavery's lingering chains;

Till not one tyrant tread our plains,
 Nor traitor lip pollute our fountains.
No! never till that glorious day
 Shall Lusitania's sons be gay,
Or hear, oh Peace, thy welcome lay
Resounding thro' her sunny mountains.

The song of war shall echo thro' our
 mountains,
 Till Victory's self shall, smiling, say,
 "Your cloud of foes hath past away,
 "And Freedom comes with new-born
 ray
"To gild your vines and light your foun-
 tains."
 Oh, never till that glorious day
 Shall Lusitania's sons be gay,
 Or hear, sweet Peace, thy welcome lay
Resounding thro' her sunny mountains.

THE YOUNG ROSE.

THE young rose I give thee, so dewy and
 bright,
Was the floweret most dear to the sweet
 bird of night,
Who oft, by the moon, o'er her blushes
 hath hung,
And thrilled every leaf with the wild lay
 he sung.

Oh, take thou this young rose, and let
 her life be
Prolonged by the breath she will borrow
 from thee;
For, while o'er her bosom thy soft notes
 shall thrill,
She 'll think the sweet night-bird is courting her still.

WHEN MIDST THE GAY I MEET.

WHEN midst the gay I meet
 That gentle smile of thine,
Tho' still on me it turns most sweet,
 I scarce can call it mine:
But when to me alone
 Your secret tears you show,
Oh, then I feel those tears my own,
 And claim them while they flow.
Then still with bright looks bless
 The gay, the cold, the free;
Give smiles to those who love you less,
 But keep your tears for me.

The snow on Jura's steep
　Can smile in many a beam,
Yet still in chains of coldness sleep,
　How bright soe'er it seem.
But, when some deep-felt ray
　Whose touch is fire appears,
Oh, then the smile is warmed away,
　And, melting, turns to tears.
Then still with bright looks bless
　The gay, the cold, the free;
Give smiles to those who love you
　less,
　But keep your tears for me.

WHEN TWILIGHT DEWS.

WHEN twilight dews are falling soft
　Upon the rosy sea, love,
I watch the star, whose beam so oft
　Has lighted me to thee, love.
And thou too, on that orb so dear,
　Dost often gaze at even,
And think, tho' lost for ever here,
　Thou 'lt yet be mine in heaven.

There 's not a garden walk I tread,
　There 's not a flower I see, love,
But brings to mind some hope that 's
　fled,
　Some joy that 's gone with thee, love.
And still I wish that hour was near,
　When, friends and foes forgiven,
The pains, the ills we 've wept thro'
　here,
　May turn to smiles in heaven.

YOUNG JESSICA.

YOUNG Jessica sat all the day,
　With heart o'er idle love-thoughts
　pining;
Her needle bright beside her lay,
　So active once! — now idly shining.
Ah, Jessy, 't is in idle hearts
　That love and mischief are most
　nimble;
The safest shield against the darts
　Of Cupid is Minerva's thimble.

The child who with a magnet plays
　Well knowing all its arts, so wily,
The tempter near a needle lays,
　And laughing says, " We 'll steal it
　slily."

The needle, having naught to do,
　Is pleased to let the magnet wheedle;
Till closer, closer come the two,
　And — off, at length, elopes the
　needle.

Now, had this needle turned its eye
　To some gay reticule's construction,
It ne'er had strayed from duty's tie,
　Nor felt the magnet's sly seduction.
Thus, girls, would you keep quiet hearts,
　Your snowy fingers must be nimble;
The safest shield against the darts
　Of Cupid is Minerva's thimble.

HOW HAPPY, ONCE.

How happy, once, tho' winged with
　sighs,
　My moments flew along,
While looking on those smiling eyes,
　And listening to thy magic song!
But vanished now, like summer dreams,
　Those moments smile no more;
For me that eye no longer beams,
　That song for me is o'er.
Mine the cold brow,
That speaks thy altered vow,
While others feel thy sunshine now.

Oh, could I change my love like thee,
　One hope might yet be mine —
Some other eyes as bright to see,
　And hear a voice as sweet as thine:
But never, never can this heart
　Be waked to life again;
With thee it lost its vital part,
　And withered then!
Cold its pulse lies,
And mute are even its sighs,
All other grief it now defies.

I LOVE BUT THEE.

IF, after all, you still will doubt and fear
　me,
　And think this heart to other loves will
　stray,
If I must swear, then, lovely doubter,
　hear me;
　By every dream I have when thou 'rt
　away,
By every throb I feel when thou art
　near me,
I love but thee — I love but thee!

By those dark eyes, where light is ever
    playing,
  Where Love in depth of shadow holds
    his throne,
And by those lips, which give whate'er
    thou 'rt saying,
  Or grave or gay, a music of its own,
A music far beyond all minstrel's playing,
  I love but thee — I love but thee!

By that fair brow, where Innocence re-
    poses,
  As pure as moonlight sleeping upon
    snow,
And by that cheek, whose fleeting blush
    discloses
  A hue too bright to bless this world
    below,
And only fit to dwell on Eden's roses,
  I love but thee — I love but thee!

LET JOY ALONE BE REMEM-
BERED NOW.

LET thy joys alone be remembered now,
  Let thy sorrows go sleep awhile;
Or if thought's dark cloud come o'er thy
    brow,
  Let Love light it up with his smile.
For thus to meet, and thus to find,
  That Time, whose touch can chill
Each flower of form, each grace of mind,
  Hath left thee blooming still, —
Oh, joy alone should be thought of now,
  Let our sorrows go sleep awhile;
Or, should thought's dark cloud come
    o'er thy brow,
  Let Love light it up with his smile.

When the flowers of life's sweet garden
    fade,
  If but *one* bright leaf remain,
Of the many that once its glory made,
  It is not for us to complain.
But thus to meet and thus to wake
  In all Love's early bliss;
Oh, Time all other gifts may take,
  So he but leaves us this!
Then let joy alone be remembered now,
  Let our sorrows go sleep awhile;
Or if thought's dark cloud come o'er the
    brow,
  Let Love light it up with his smile!

LOVE THEE, DEAREST? LOVE
THEE?

LOVE thee, dearest? love thee?
  Yes, by yonder star I swear,
Which thro' tears above thee
  Shines so sadly fair;
Tho' often dim,
With tears, like him,
Like him my truth will shine,
  And — love thee, dearest? love thee?
Yes, till death I 'm thine.

Leave thee, dearest? leave thee?
  No, that star is not more true;
When my vows deceive thee,
  He will wander too.
A cloud of night
May veil his light,
And death shall darken mine —
  But — leave thee, dearest? leave thee?
No, till death I 'm thine.

MY HEART AND LUTE.

I GIVE thee all — I can no more —
  Tho' poor the offering be;
My heart and lute are all the store
  That I can bring to thee.
A lute whose gentle song reveals
  The soul of love full well;
And, better far, a heart that feels
  Much more than lute could tell.

Tho' love and song may fail, alas!
  To keep life's clouds away,
At least 't will make them lighter pass,
  Or gild them if they stay.
And even if Care at moments flings
  A discord o'er life's happy strain,
Let Love but gently touch the strings,
  'T will all be sweet again!

PEACE, PEACE TO HIM THAT 'S
GONE!

  WHEN I am dead,
    Then lay my head
In some lone, distant dell,
    Where voices ne'er
    Shall stir the air,
Or break its silent spell.

    If any sound
    Be heard around,

Let the sweet bird alone,
 That weeps in song,
 Sing all night long,
"Peace, peace, to him that 's
 gone!"

Yet, oh, were mine
 One sigh of thine,
One pitying word from thee,
 Like gleams of heaven,
 To sinners given,
Would be that word to me.

Howe'er unblest,
 My shade would rest
While listening to that tone; —
 Enough 't would be
 To hear from thee,
"Peace, peace, to him that 's
 gone!"

ROSE OF THE DESERT.

ROSE of the Desert! thou, whose blush-
 ing ray,
Lonely and lovely, fleets unseen away;
No hand to cull thee, none to woo thy
 sigh, —
In vestal silence left to live and die, —
Rose of the Desert! thus should woman
 be,
Shining uncourted, lone and safe, like
 thee.

Rose of the Garden, how unlike thy
 doom!
Destined for others, not thyself, to
 bloom:
Culled ere thy beauty lives thro' half its
 day;
A moment cherished, and then cast away;
Rose of the Garden! such is woman's
 lot, —
Worshipt, while blooming — when she
 fades, forgot.

'T IS ALL FOR THEE.

IF life for me hath joy or light,
 'T is all from thee,
My thoughts by day, my dreams by night,
 Are but of thee, of only thee.
Whate'er of hope or peace I know,
My zest in joy, my balm in woe,
To those dear eyes of thine I owe,
 'T is all from thee.

My heart, even ere I saw those eyes,
 Seemed doomed to thee;
Kept pure till then from other ties,
 'T was all for thee, for only thee.
Like plants that sleep till sunny May
Calls forth their life my spirit lay,
Till, touched by Love's awakening ray,
 It lived for thee, it lived for thee.

When Fame would call me to her
 heights,
 She speaks by thee;
And dim would shine her proudest lights,
 Unshared by thee, unshared by thee.
Whene'er I seek the Muse's shrine,
Where Bards have hung their wreaths
 divine,
And wish those wreaths of glory mine,
 'T is all for thee, for only thee.

THE SONG OF THE OLDEN TIME.[1]

THERE 's a song of the olden time,
 Falling sad o'er the ear,
Like the dream of some village chime,
 Which in youth we loved to hear.
And even amidst the grand and gay,
 When Music tries her gentlest art,
I never hear so sweet a lay,
 Or one that hangs so round my heart,
As that song of the olden time,
 Falling sad o'er the ear,
Like the dream of some village chime,
 Which in youth we loved to hear.

And when all of this life is gone, —
 Even the hope, lingering now,
Like the last of the leaves left on
 Autumn's sere and faded bough, —
'T will seem as still those friends were
 near,
Who loved me in youth's early day,
If in that parting hour I hear
 The same sweet notes and die away, —
To that song of the olden time,
 Breathed, like Hope's farewell strain,
To say, in some brighter clime,
 Life and youth will shine again!

[1] In this song, which is one of the many set
to music by myself, the occasional lawlessness of
the metre arises, I need hardly say, from the
peculiar structure of the air.

WAKE THEE, MY DEAR.

WAKE thee, my dear — thy dreaming
  Till darker hours will keep;
While such a moon is beaming,
  'T is wrong towards Heaven to sleep.

Moments there are we number,
Moments of pain and care,
Which to oblivious slumber
  Gladly the wretch would spare.
But now, — who 'd think of dreaming
  When Love his watch should keep?
While such a moon is beaming,
  'T is wrong towards Heaven to sleep.

If e'er the fates should sever
  My life and hopes from thee, love,
The sleep that lasts for ever
  Would then be sweet to me, love;
But now, — away with dreaming!
  Till darker hours 't will keep;
While such a moon is beaming,
  'T is wrong towards Heaven to sleep.

THE BOY OF THE ALPS.[1]

LIGHTLY, Alpine rover,
Tread the mountains over;
Rude is the path thou 'st yet to go;
  Snow cliffs hanging o'er thee,
  Fields of ice before thee,
While the hid torrent moans below.
Hark, the deep thunder,
Thro' the vales yonder!
'T is the huge avalanche downward cast;
  From rock to rock
  Rebounds the shock.
But courage, boy! the danger 's past.
  Onward, youthful rover,
  Tread the glacier over,
Safe shalt thou reach thy home at last.
On, ere light forsake thee,
Soon will dusk o'ertake thee:
O'er yon ice-bridge lies thy way!
  Now, for the risk prepare thee;
  Safe it yet may bear thee,
Tho' 't will melt in morning's ray.

Hark, that dread howling!
'T is the wolf prowling, —
Scent of thy track the foe hath got;

1 This and the Songs that follow (as far as
page 287) have been published, with music, by
Messrs. Addison and Beale, Regent Street.

And cliff and shore
Resound his roar.
But courage, boy, — the danger 's past!
  Watching eyes have found thee,
  Loving arms are round thee,
Safe hast thou reached thy father's cot.

FOR THEE ALONE.

FOR thee alone I brave the boundless
    deep,
  Those eyes my light through every
    distant sea;
My waking thoughts, the dream that
    gilds my sleep,
  The noon-tide revery, all are given to
    thee,
    To thee alone, to thee alone.

Tho' future scenes present to Fancy's eye
  Fair forms of light that crowd the distant
    air,
When nearer viewed, the fairy phantoms
    fly,
  The crowds dissolve, and thou alone
    art there,
    Thou, thou alone.

To win thy smile, I speed from shore to
    shore,
  While Hope's sweet voice is heard in
    every blast,
Still whispering on that when some years
    are o'er,
  One bright reward shall crown my toil
    at last,
    Thy smile alone, thy smile alone.

Oh place beside the transport of that
    hour
  All earth can boast of fair, of rich, and
    bright,
Wealth's radiant mines, the lofty thrones
    of power, —
  Then ask where first thy lover's choice
    would light?
    On thee alone, on thee alone.

HER LAST WORDS, AT PARTING.

HER last words, at parting, how *can* I
    forget?
  Deep treasured thro' life, in my heart
    they shall stay;

Like music, whose charm in the soul lingers yet,
  When its sounds from the ear have long
   melted away.
Let Fortune assail me, her threatenings
   are vain;
  Those still-breathing words shall my
   talisman be, —
" Remember, in absence, in sorrow, and
   pain,
  " There 's one heart, unchanging, that
   beats but for thee."

From the desert's sweet well tho' the
   pilgrim must hie,
  Never more of that fresh-springing
   fountain to taste,
He hath still of its bright drops a treasured
   supply,
  Whose sweetness lends life to his lips
   thro' the waste.
So, dark as my fate is still doomed to remain,
  These words shall my well in the wilderness be, —
" Remember, in absence, in sorrow, and
   pain,
  " There 's one heart, unchanging, that
   beats but for thee."

LET 'S TAKE THIS WORLD AS SOME WIDE SCENE.

LET 's take this world as some wide
   scene,
Thro' which in frail but buoyant boat,
With skies now dark and now serene,
   Together thou and I must float;
Beholding oft on either shore
  Bright spots where we should love to
   stay;
But Time plies swift his flying oar,
  And away we speed, away, away.

Should chilling winds and rains come
   on,
  We 'll raise our awning 'gainst the
   shower;
Sit closer till the storm is gone,
  And, smiling, wait a sunnier hour.
And if that sunnier hour should shine,
  We 'll know its brightness can not stay,
But happy while 't is thine and mine,
  Complain not when it fades away.

So shall we reach at last that Fall
  Down which life's currents all must
   go, —
The dark, the brilliant, destined all
  To sink into the void below.
Nor even that hour shall want its charms,
  If, side by side, still fond we keep,
And calmly, in each other's arms
  Together linked, go down the steep.

LOVE'S VICTORY.

SING to Love — for, oh, 't was he
  Who won the glorious day;
Strew the wreaths of victory
  Along the conqueror's way.
Yoke the Muses to his car,
  Let them sing each trophy won;
While his mother's joyous star
  Shall light the triumph on.

Hail to Love, to mighty Love,
  Let spirits sing around;
While the hill, the dale, and grove,
  With " mighty Love " resound;
Or, should a sigh of sorrow steal
  Amid the sounds thus echoed o'er,
'T will but teach the god to feel
  His victories the more.

See his wings, like amethyst
  Of sunny Ind their hue;
Bright as when, by Psyche kist,
  They trembled thro' and thro'.
Flowers spring beneath his feet;
  Angel forms beside him run;
While unnumbered lips repeat
  " Love's victory is won ! "
    Hail to Love, to mighty Love, etc.

SONG OF HERCULES TO HIS DAUGHTER.[1]

" I 'VE been, oh, sweet daughter,
  " To fountain and sea,
" To seek in their water
  " Some bright gem for thee.
" Where diamonds were sleeping,
  " Their sparkle I sought,
" Where crystal was weeping,
  " Its tears I have caught.

[1] Founded on the fable reported by Arrian (in Indicis) of Hercules having searched the Indian Ocean, to find the pearl with which he adorned his daughter Pandæa.

" The sea-nymph I 've courted
" In rich coral halls;
" With Naiads have sported
" By bright waterfalls.
" But sportive or tender,
" Still sought I around
" That gem, with whose splendor
" Thou yet shalt be crowned.

" And see, while I 'm speaking,
" Yon soft light afar ; —
" The pearl I 've been secking
" There floats like a star !
" In the deep Indian Ocean
" I see the gem shine,
" And quick as light's motion
" Its wealth shall be thine."

Then eastward, like lightning,
The hero-god flew,
His sunny looks brightening
The air he went thro'.
And sweet was the duty,
And hallowed the hour,
Which saw thus young Beauty
Embellished by Power.

THE DREAM OF HOME.

Who has not felt how sadly sweet
The dream of home, the dream of
home,
Steals o'er the heart, too soon to fleet,
When far o'er sea or land we roam?
Sunlight more soft may o'er us fall,
To greener shores our bark may come;
But far more bright, more dear than
all,
That dream of home, that dream of
home.

Ask of the sailor youth when far
His light bark bounds o'er ocean's
foam,
What charms him most, when evening's
star
Smiles o'er the wave? to dream of
home.
Fond thoughts of absent friends and
loves
At that sweet hour around him come;
His heart's best joy where'er he roves,
That dream of home, that dream of
home.

THEY TELL ME THOU 'RT THE FAVORED GUEST.[1]

They tell me thou 'rt the favored guest
Of every fair and brilliant throng;
No wit like thine to wake the jest,
No voice like thine to breathe the song ;
And none could guess, so gay thou art,
That thou and I are far apart.

Alas ! alas ! how different flows
With thee and me the time away !
Not that I wish thee sad — heaven
knows —
Still if thou canst, be light and gay;
I only know, that without thee
The sun himself is dark to me.

Do I thus haste to hall and bower,
Among the proud and gay to shine?
Or deck my hair with gem and flower,
To flatter other eyes than thine?
Ah, no, with me love's smiles are past,
Thou hadst the first, thou hadst the
last.

THE YOUNG INDIAN MAID.

There came a nymph dancing
Gracefully, gracefully,
Her eye a light glancing
Like the blue sea;
And while all this gladness
Around her steps hung,
Such sweet notes of sadness
Her gentle lips sung,
That ne'er while I live from my memory
shall fade
The song or the look of that young
Indian maid.

Her zone of bells ringing
Cheerily, cheerily,
Chimed to her singing
Light echoes of glee;
But in vain did she borrow
Of mirth the gay tone,
Her voice spoke of sorrow,
And sorrow alone.

[1] Part of a translation of some Latin verses, supposed to have been addressed by Hippolyta Taurella to her husband, during his absence at the gay court of Leo the Tenth. The verses may be found in the Appendix to Roscoe's Work.

Nor e'er while I live from my memory
    shall fade
The song or the look of that young
    Indian maid.

THE HOMEWARD MARCH.

Be still my heart: I hear them come:
    Those sounds announce my lover near:
The march that brings our warriors home
    Proclaims he 'll soon be here.

Hark, the distant tread,
    O'er the mountain's head,
While hills and dales repeat the sound;
    And the forest deer
    Stand still to hear,
As those echoing steps ring round.

Be still my heart, I hear them come,
    Those sounds that speak my soldier
        near;
Those joyous steps seem winged for
    home, —
    Rest, rest, he 'll soon be here.

But hark, more faint the footsteps grow,
    And now they wind to distant glades;
Not here their home, — alas, they go
    To gladden happier maids!

Like sounds in a dream,
    The footsteps seem,
As down the hills they die away;
    And the march, whose song
    So pealed along,
Now fades like a funeral lay.

'T is past, 't is o'er, — hush, heart, thy
    pain!
And tho' not here, alas, they come,
Rejoice for those, to whom that strain
    Brings sons and lovers home.

WAKE UP, SWEET MELODY.

Wake up, sweet melody!
    Now is the hour
When young and loving hearts
    Feel most thy power.
One note of music, by moonlight's soft
    ray —
Oh, 't is worth thousands heard coldly
    by day.

Then wake up, sweet melody!
    Now is the hour
When young and loving hearts
    Feel most thy power.

Ask the fond nightingale,
    When his sweet flower
Loves most to hear his song,
    In her green bower?
Oh, he will tell thee, thro' summer-nights
    long,
Fondest she lends her whole soul to his
    song.
    Then wake up, sweet melody!
    Now is the hour
When young and loving hearts
    Feel most thy power.

CALM BE THY SLEEP.

Calm be thy sleep as infants' slumbers!
    Pure as angel thoughts thy dreams!
May every joy this bright world numbers
    Shed o'er thee their mingled beams!
Or if, where Pleasure's wing hath glided,
    There ever must some pang remain,
Still be thy lot with me divided, —
    Thine all the bliss and mine the pain!

Day and night my thoughts shall hover
    Round thy steps where'er they stray;
As, even when clouds his idol cover,
    Fondly the Persian tracks its ray.
If this be wrong, if Heaven offended
    By worship to its creature be,
Then let my vows to both be blended,
    Half breathed to Heaven and half to
        thee.

THE EXILE.

Night waneth fast, the morning star
    Saddens with light the glimmering sea,
Whose waves shall soon to realms afar
    Waft me from hope, from love, and
        thee.
Coldly the beam from yonder sky
    Looks o'er the waves that onward stray;
But colder still the stranger's eye
    To him whose home is far away.

Oh, not at hour so chill and bleak,
    Let thoughts of me come o'er thy
        breast;

But of the lost one think and speak,
  When summer suns sink calm to rest.
So, as I wander, Fancy's dream
  Shall bring me o'er the sunset seas,
Thy look in every melting beam,
  Thy whisper in each dying breeze.

THE FANCY FAIR.

COME, maids and youths, for here we sell
  All wondrous things of earth and air;
Whatever wild romancers tell,
  Or poets sing, or lovers swear,
  You 'll find at this our Fancy Fair.

Here eyes are made like stars to shine,
  And kept for years in such repair,
That even when turned of thirty-nine,
  They 'll hardly look the worse for wear,
  If bought at this our Fancy Fair.

We 've lots of tears for bards to shower,
  And hearts that such ill usage bear,
That, tho' they 're broken every hour,
  They 'll still in rhyme fresh breaking
    bear,
  If purchased at our Fancy Fair.

As fashions change in every thing,
  We 've goods to suit each season's
    air,
Eternal friendships for the spring,
  And endless loves for summer wear, —
  All sold at this our Fancy Fair.

We 've reputations white as snow,
  That long will last if used with care,
Nay, safe thro' all life's journey go,
  If packed and marked as "brittle
    ware," —
  Just purchased at the Fancy Fair.

IF THOU WOULDST HAVE ME SING AND PLAY.

IF thou wouldst have me sing and play,
  As once I played and sung,
First take this time-worn lute away,
  And bring one freshly strung.
Call back the time when pleasure's sigh
  First breathed among the strings;
And Time himself, in flitting by,
  Made music with his wings.

But how is this? tho' new the lute,
  And shining fresh the chords,
Beneath this hand they slumber mute,
  Or speak but dreamy words.
In vain I seek the soul that dwelt
  Within that once sweet shell,
Which told so warmly what it felt,
  And felt what naught could tell.

Oh, ask not then for passion's lay,
  From lyre so coldly strung;
With this I ne'er can sing or play,
  As once I played and sung.
No, bring that long-loved lute again, —
  Tho' chilled by years it be,
If *thou* wilt call the slumbering strain,
  T' will wake again for thee.

Tho' time have frozen the tuneful stream
  Of thoughts that gushed along,
One look from thee, like summer's beam,
  Will thaw them into song.
Then give, oh give, that wakening ray,
  And once more blithe and young,
Thy bard again will sing and play,
  As once he played and sung.

STILL WHEN DAYLIGHT.

STILL when daylight o'er the wave
Bright and soft its farewell gave,
I used to hear, while light was falling,
O'er the wave a sweet voice calling,
  Mournfully at distance calling.

Ah! once how blest that maid would
    come,
To meet her sea-boy hastening home;
And thro' the night those sounds repeat-
    ing,
Hail his bark with joyous greeting,
  Joyously his light bark greeting.

But, one sad night, when winds were high,
Nor earth, nor heaven could hear her cry,
She saw his boat come tossing over
Midnight's wave, — but not her lover!
  No, never more her lover.

And still that sad dream loath to leave,
She comes with wandering mind at eve,
And oft we hear, when night is falling,
Faint her voice thro' twilight calling,
  Mournfully at twilight calling.

THE SUMMER WEBS.

THE summer webs that float and shine,
　The summer dews that fall,
Tho' light they be, this heart of mine
　Is lighter still than all.
It tells me every cloud is past
　Which lately seemed to lour;
That Hope hath wed young Joy at last,
　And now 's their nuptial hour!

With light thus round, within, above,
　With naught to wake one sigh,
Except the wish that all we love
　Were at this moment nigh, —
It seems as if life's brilliant sun
　Had stopt in full career,
To make this hour its brightest one,
　And rest in radiance here.

MIND NOT THO' DAYLIGHT.

MIND not tho' daylight around us is
　breaking, —
Who 'd think now of sleeping when
　morn 's but just waking?
Sound the merry viol, and daylight or
　not,
Be all for one hour in the gay dance
　forgot.

See young Aurora up heaven's hill
　advancing,
Tho' fresh from her pillow, even she too
　is dancing:
While thus all creation, earth, heaven,
　and sea,
Are dancing around us, oh, why should
　not we?

Who 'll say that moments we use thus
　are wasted?
Such sweet drops of time only flow to be
　tasted;
While hearts are high beating and harps
　full in tune,
The fault is all morning's for coming so
　soon.

THEY MET BUT ONCE.

THEY met but once, in youth's sweet
　hour,
　And never since that day
Hath absence, time, or grief had power
　To chase that dream away.

They 've seen the suns of other skies,
　On other shores have sought delight;
But never more to bless their eyes
　Can come a dream so bright!
They met but once, — a day was all
　Of Love's young hopes they knew;
And still their hearts that day recall
　As fresh as then it flew.

Sweet dream of youth! oh, ne'er again
　Let either meet the brow
They left so smooth and smiling then,
　Or see what it is now.
For, Youth, the spell was only thine,
　From thee alone the enchantment
　　flows,
That makes the world around thee shine
　With light thyself bestows.
They met but once, — oh, ne'er again
　Let either meet the brow
They left so smooth and smiling then,
　Or see what it is now.

WITH MOONLIGHT BEAMING.

WITH moonlight beaming
　Thus o'er the deep,
Who 'd linger dreaming
　In idle sleep?
Leave joyless souls to live by day,—
Our life begins with yonder ray;
　And while thus brightly
　　The moments flee,
　Our barks skim lightly
　　The shining sea.

To halls of splendor
　Let great ones hie;
Thro' light more tender
　Our pathways lie.
While round, from banks of brook or
　lake,
Our company blithe echoes make;
　And as we lend 'em
　　Sweet word or strain,
　Still back they send 'em
　　More sweet again.

CHILD'S SONG. FROM A MASQUE.

I HAVE a garden of my own,
　Shining with flowers of every hue;
I loved it dearly while alone,
　But I shall love it more with you:

And there the golden bees shall come,
  In summer-time at break of morn,
And wake us with their busy hum
  Around the Siha's fragrant thorn.

I have a fawn from Aden's land,
  On leafy buds and berries nurst;
And you shall feed him from your
    hand,
  Though he may start with fear at
    first.
And I will lead you where he lies
  For shelter in the noon-tide heat;
And you may touch his sleeping eyes,
  And feel his little silvery feet.

THE HALCYON HANGS O'ER OCEAN.

THE halcyon hangs o'er ocean,
  The sea-lark skims the brine;
This bright world 's all in motion,
  No heart seems sad but mine.

To walk thro' sun-bright places,
  With heart all cold the while;
To look in smiling faces,
  When we no more can smile;

To feel, while earth and heaven
  Around thee shine with bliss,
To thee no light is given, —
  Oh, what a doom is this!

THE WORLD WAS HUSHT.

THE world was husht, the moon above
  Sailed thro' ether slowly,
When near the casement of my love,
  Thus I whispered lowly, —
" Awake, awake, how canst thou sleep?
  " The field I seek to-morrow
" Is one where man hath fame to reap,
  " And woman gleans but sorrow."

" Let battle's field be what it may,"
  Thus spoke a voice replying,
" Think not thy love, while thou 'rt away,
  " Will sit here idly sighing.
" No — woman's soul, if not for fame,
  " For love can brave all danger ! "
Then forth from out the casement came
  A plumed and armed stranger.

A stranger? No; 't was she, the maid,
  Herself before me beaming,
With casque arrayed and falchion blade
  Beneath her girdle gleaming !
Close side by side, in freedom's fight,
  That blessed morning found us;
In Victory's light we stood ere night,
  And Love the morrow crowned us !

THE TWO LOVES.

THERE are two Loves, the poet sings,
  Both born of Beauty at a birth:
The one, akin to heaven, hath wings,
  The other, earthly, walks on earth.
With *this* thro' bowers below we play,
  With *that* thro' clouds above we soar;
With both, perchance, may lose our
    way: —
      Then, tell me which,
    Tell me which shall we adore?

The one, when tempted down from air,
  At Pleasure's fount to lave his lip,
Nor lingers long, nor oft will dare
  His wing within the wave to dip.
While plunging deep and long beneath,
  The other bathes him o'er and o'er
In that sweet current, even to death: —
      Then, tell me which,
    Tell me which shall we adore?

The boy of heaven, even while he lies
  In Beauty's lap, recalls his home;
And when most happy, inly sighs
  For something happier still to come.
While he of earth, too fully blest
  With this bright world to dream of
    more,
Sees all his heaven on Beauty's breast: —
      Then, tell me which,
    Tell me which shall we adore?

The maid who heard the poet sing
  These twin-desires of earth and sky,
And saw while one inspired his string,
  The other glistened in his eye, —
To name the earthlier boy ashamed,
  To chose the other fondly loath,
At length all blushing she exclaimed, —
      " Ask not which,
    " Oh, ask not which — we 'll worship
      both.

"The extremes of each thus taught to
  shun,
  "With hearts and souls between them
    given,
"When weary of this earth with one,
  "We 'll with the other wing to
    heaven."
Thus pledged the maid her vow of
  bliss;
  And while *one* Love wrote down the
    oath,
The other sealed it with a kiss;
    And Heaven looked on,
Heaven looked on and hallowed both.

THE LEGEND OF PUCK THE FAIRY.

WOULDST know what tricks, by the pale
  moonlight,
Are played by me, the merry little Sprite,
Who wing thro' air from the camp to the
  court,
From king to clown, and of all make
  sport;
    Singing, I am the Sprite
    Of the merry midnight,
Who laugh at weak mortals and love the
  moonlight.

To a miser's bed, where he snoring
  slept
And dreamt of his cash, I slyly crept;
Chink, chink o'er his pillow like money
  I rang,
And he waked to catch — but away I
  sprang,
    Singing, I am the Sprite, etc.

I saw thro' the leaves, in a damsel's
  bower,
She was waiting her love at that starlight
  hour:
"Hist — hist!" quoth I, with an amorous
  sigh,
And she flew to the door, but away flew I,
    Singing, I am the Sprite, etc.

While a bard sat inditing an ode to his
  love,
Like a pair of blue meteors I stared from
  above,

And he swooned — for he thought 't was
  the ghost, poor man!
Of his lady's eyes, while away I ran,
  Singing, I am the Sprite, etc.

BEAUTY AND SONG.

DOWN in yon summer vale,
  Where the rill flows,
Thus said a Nightingale
  To his loved Rose: —
"Tho' rich the pleasures
"Of song's sweet measures,
"Vain were its melody,
"Rose, without thee."

Then from the green recess
  Of her night-bower,
Beaming with bashfulness,
  Spoke the bright flower: —
"Tho' morn should lend her
"Its sunniest splendor,
"What would the Rose be,
"Unsung by thee?"

Thus still let Song attend
  Woman's bright way;
Thus still let woman lend
  Light to the lay.
Like stars thro' heaven's sea
Floating in harmony
Beauty should glide along
Circled by Song.

WHEN THOU ART NIGHT.

WHEN thou art nigh, it seems
  A new creation round;
The sun hath fairer beams,
  The lute a softer sound.
Tho' thee alone I see,
  And hear alone thy sigh,
'T is light, 't is song to me,
  'T is all — when thou art nigh.

When thou art nigh, no thought
  Of grief comes o'er my heart;
I only think — could aught
  But joy be where thou art?
Life seems a waste of breath,
  When far from thee I sigh;
And death — ay, even death
  Were sweet, if thou wert nigh.

SONG OF A HYPERBOREAN.

I COME from a land in the sun-bright
deep,
Where golden gardens grow;
Where the winds of the north, becalmed
in sleep,
Their conch-shells never blow.[1]
Haste to that holy Isle with me,
Haste — haste!

So near the track of the stars are we,[2]
That oft on night's pale beams
The distant sounds of their harmony
Come to our ear, like dreams.
Then haste to that holy Isle with me,
etc.

The Moon too brings her world so
nigh,[3]
That when the night-seer looks
To that shadowless orb, in a vernal
sky,
He can number its hills and brooks.
Then, haste, etc.

To the Sun god all our hearts and lyres[4]
By day, by night, belong;
And the breath we draw from his living
fires,
We give him back in song.
Then, haste, etc.

From us descends the maid who brings
To Delos gifts divine;
And our wild bees lend their rainbow
wings
To glitter on Delphi's shrine.[5]
Then haste to that holy Isle with
me,
Haste — haste!

1 On the Tower of the Winds, at Athens, there
is a conch-shell placed in the hands of Boreas. —
See *Stuart's Antiquities.* "The north wind,"
says Herodotus, in speaking of the Hyperboreans, "never blows with them."

2 "*sub ipso siderum cardine jacent.*" —
POMPON. MELA.

3 "They can show the moon very near." —
DIODOR. SICUL.

4 Hecatæus tells us, that this Hyperborean
island was dedicated to Apollo; and most of the
inhabitants were either priests or songsters.

5 Pausan.

THOU BIDST ME SING.

THOU bidst me sing the lay I sung to thee
In other days ere joy had left this brow;
But think, tho' still unchanged the notes
may be,
How different feels the heart that
breathes them now!
The rose thou wearst to-night is still the
same
We saw this morning on its stem so
gay;
But, ah! that dew of dawn, that breath
which came
Like life o'er all its leaves, hath past
away.

Since first that music touched thy heart
and mine,
How many a joy and pain o'er both
have past, —
The joy, a light too precious long to
shine, —
The pain, a cloud whose shadows
always last.
And tho' that lay would like the voice
of home
Breathe o'er our ear, 't would waken
now a sigh —
Ah! not, as then, for fancied woes to
come,
But, sadder far, for real bliss gone by.

CUPID ARMED.

PLACE the helm on thy brow,
In thy hand take the spear; —
Thou art armed, Cupid, now,
And thy battle-hour is near.
March on! march on! thy shaft and bow
Were weak against such charms;
March on! march on! so proud a foe
Scorns all but martial arms.

See the darts in her eyes,
Tipt with scorn, how they shine!
Every shaft, as it flies,
Mocking proudly at thine.
March on! march on! thy feathered darts
Soft bosoms soon might move;
But ruder arms to ruder hearts
Must teach what 't is to love.
Place the helm on thy brow;
In thy hand take the spear, —
Thou art armed, Cupid, now,
And thy battle-hour is near.

ROUND THE WORLD GOES.

ROUND the world goes, by day and
night,
   While with it also round go we;
And in the flight of one day's light
   An image of all life's course we see.
Round, round, while thus we go round,
   The best thing a man can do,
Is to make it, at least, a *merry*-go-round,
   By — sending the wine round too.

Our first gay stage of life is when
   Youth in its dawn salutes the eye —
Season of bliss! Oh, who would n't then
   Wish to cry, " Stop! " to earth and
      sky?
But, round, round, both boy and girl
   Are whisked thro' that sky of blue;
And much would their hearts enjoy the
      whirl,
   If — their heads did n't whirl round
      too.

Next, we enjoy our glorious noon,
   Thinking all life a life of light;
But shadows come on, 't is evening soon,
   And ere we can say, " How short! "
      — 't is night.
Round, round, still all goes round,
   Even while I 'm thus singing to you;
And the best way to make it a *merry*-go-
   round,
   Is to — chorus my song round too.

OH, DO NOT LOOK SO BRIGHT
AND BLEST.

OH, do not look so bright and blest,
   For still there comes a fear,
When brow like thine looks happiest,
   That grief is then most near.
There lurks a dread in all delight,
   A shadow near each ray,
That warns us then to fear their flight,
   When most we wish their stay.
Then look not thou so bright and blest,
   For ah! there comes a fear,
When brow like thine looks happiest,
   That grief is then most near.

Why is it thus that fairest things
   The soonest fleet and die? —
That when most light is on their wings,
   They 're then but spread to fly!

And, sadder still, the pain will stay —
   The bliss no more appears;
As rainbows take their light away,
   And leave us but the tears!
Then look not thou so bright and blest,
   For ah! there comes a fear,
When brow like thine looks happiest,
   That grief is then most near.

THE MUSICAL BOX.

" LOOK here," said Rose, with laughing
      eyes,
   " Within this box, by magic hid,
" A tuneful Sprite imprisoned lies,
   " Who sings to me whene'er he 's bid.
" Tho' roving once his voice and wing,
   " He 'll now lie still the whole day
      long;
" Till thus I touch the magic spring —
   "Then hark, how sweet and blithe
      his song! "
                        (*A symphony.*)

" Ah, Rose," I cried, " the poet's lay
   " Must ne'er even Beauty's slave
      become;
" Thro' earth and air his song may stray,
   " If all the while his heart 's at home.
" And tho' in freedom's air he dwell,
   " Nor bond nor chain his spirit knows,
" Touch but the spring thou knowst so
      well,
   " And — hark, how sweet the love-
      song flows! "
                        (*A symphony.*)

Thus pleaded I for freedom's right;
   But when young Beauty takes the
      field,
And wise men seek defence in flight,
   The doom of poets is to yield.
No more my heart the enchantress
      braves,
   I 'm now in Beauty's prison hid;
The Sprite and I are fellow-slaves,
   And I, too, sing whene'er I 'm bid.

WHEN TO SAD MUSIC SILENT
YOU LISTEN.

WHEN to sad Music silent you listen,
   And tears on those eyelids tremble
      like dew,

Oh, then there dwells in those eyes as
    they glisten
    A sweet holy charm that mirth never
    knew.
But when some lively strain resounding
    Lights up the sunshine of joy on that
    brow,
Then the young reindeer o'er the hills
    bounding
    Was ne'er in its mirth so graceful as
    thou.

When on the skies at midnight thou
    gazest,
    A lustre so pure thy features then
    wear,
That, when to some star that bright eye
    thou raisest,
    We feel 't is thy home thou 'rt looking
    for there.
But when the word for the gay dance is
    given,
    So buoyant thy spirit, so heartfelt thy
    mirth,
Oh then we exclaim, " Ne'er leave earth
    for heaven,
    " But linger still here, to make heaven
    of earth."

THE LANGUAGE OF FLOWERS.

FLY swift, my light gazelle,
    To her who now lies waking,
To hear thy silver bell
    The midnight silence breaking.
And, when thou com'st, with gladsome
    feet,
    Beneath her lattice springing,
Ah, well she 'll know how sweet
    The words of love thou 'rt bringing.

Yet, no — not words, for they
    But half can tell love's feeling;
Sweet flowers alone can say
    What passion fears revealing.
A once bright rose's withered leaf,
    A towering lily broken, —
Oh these may paint a grief
    No words could e'er have spoken.

Not such, my gay gazelle,
    The wreath thou speedest over

Yon moonlight dale, to tell
    My lady how I love her.
And, what to her will sweeter be
    Than gems the richest, rarest, —
From Truth's immortal tree [1]
    One fadeless leaf thou bearest.

THE DAWN IS BREAKING
O'ER US.

THE dawn is breaking o'er us,
    See, heaven hath caught its hue!
We 've day's long light before us,
    What sport shall we pursue?
The hunt o'er hill and lea?
    The sail o'er summer sea?
Oh let not hour so sweet
    Unwinged by pleasure fleet.
The dawn is breaking o'er us,
    See, heaven hath caught its hue!
We 've day's long light before us,
    What sport shall we pursue?

But see, while we 're deciding,
    What morning sport to play,
The dial's hand is gliding,
    And morn hath past away!
Ah, who 'd have thought that noon
    Would o'er us steal so soon, —
That morn's sweet hour of prime
    Would last so short a time?
But come, we 've day before us,
    Still heaven looks bright and blue;
Quick, quick, ere eve comes o'er us,
    What sport shall we pursue?

Alas! why thus delaying?
    We 're now at evening's hour;
Its farewell beam is playing
    O'er hill and wave and bower.
That light we thought would last,
    Behold, even now 't is past;
And all our morning dreams
    Have vanisht with its beams
But come! 't were vain to borrow
    Sad lessons from this lay,
For man will be to-morrow —
    Just what he 's been to-day.

[1] The tree called in the East, Amrita, or the
Immortal.

UNPUBLISHED SONGS,

ETC.

ASK NOT IF STILL I LOVE.

Ask not if still I love,
  Too plain these eyes have told thee;
Too well their tears must prove
  How near and dear I hold thee.
If, where the brightest shine,
  To see no form but thine,
To feel that earth can show
  No bliss above thee, —
If this be love, then know
  That thus, that thus, I love thee.

'T is not in pleasure's idle hour
  That thou canst know affection's
    power.
No, try its strength in grief or pain;
  Attempt as now its bonds to sever,
Thou 'lt find true love 's a chain
  That binds for ever!

DEAR? YES.

Dear? yes, tho' mine no more,
  Even this but makes thee dearer;
And love, since hope is o'er,
  But draws thee nearer.

Change as thou wilt to me,
  The same thy charm must be;
New loves may come to weave
  Their witchery o'er thee,
Yet still, tho' false, believe
  That I adore thee, yes, still adore
    thee.
Think'st thou that aught but death could
    end
A tie not falsehood's self can rend?
No, when alone, far off I die,
  No more to see, no more caress thee,
Even then, my life's last sigh
  Shall be to bless thee, yes, still to bless
    thee.

UNBIND THEE, LOVE.

Unbind thee, love, unbind thee, love,
  From those dark ties unbind thee;
Tho' fairest hand the chain hath wove,
  Too long its links have twined thee.
Away from earth! — thy wings were made
  In yon mid-sky to hover,
With earth beneath their dove-like shade,
  And heaven all radiant over.

Awake thee, boy, awake thee, boy,
  Too long thy soul is sleeping;
And thou mayst from this minute's joy
  Wake to eternal weeping.
Oh, think, this world is not for thee;
  Tho' hard its links to sever;
Tho' sweet and bright and dear they be,
  Break or thou 'rt lost for ever.

THERE'S SOMETHING STRANGE.

A Buffalo Song.

There 's something strange, I know not
    what,
      Come o'er me,
Some phantom I 've for ever got
      Before me.
I look on high and in the sky
      'T is shining;
On earth, its light with all things bright
      Seems twining.
In vain I try this goblin's spells
      To sever;
Go where I will, it round me dwells
      For ever.

And then what tricks by day and night
      It plays me;
In every shape the wicked sprite
      Waylays me.
Sometimes like two bright eyes of blue
      'T is glancing;

288

Sometimes like feet, in slippers neat,
  Comes dancing.
By whispers round of every sort
  I 'm taunted.
Never was mortal man, in short,
  So haunted.

NOT FROM THEE.

NOT from thee the wound should come,
  No, not from thee.
I care not what or whence my doom,
  So not from thee!
Cold triumph! first to make
  This heart thy own;
And then the mirror break
  Where fixt thou shin'st alone.
Nor from thee the wound should come,
  Oh, not from thee.
I care not what, or whence, my doom,
  So not from thee.

Yet no — my lips that wish recall;
  From thee, from thee —
If ruin o'er this head must fall,
  'T will welcome be.
Here to the blade I bare
  This faithful heart;
Wound deep — thou 'lt find that there,
  In every pulse thou art.
Yes from thee I' ll bear it all:
  If ruin be
The doom that o'er this heart must fall,
  'T were sweet from thee.

GUESS, GUESS.

I LOVE a maid, a mystic maid,
  Whose form no eyes but mine can see;
She comes in light, she comes in shade,
  And beautiful in both is she.
Her shape in dreams I oft behold,
  And oft she whispers in my ear
Such words as when to others told,
  Awake the sigh, or wring the tear; —
Then guess, guess, who she,
The lady of my love, may be.

I find the lustre of her brow,
  Come o'er me in my darkest ways;
And feel as if her voice, even now,
  Were echoing far off my lays.
There is no scene of joy or woe
  But she doth gild with influence bright;

And shed o'er all so rich a glow
  As makes even tears seem full of
    light:
Then guess, guess, who she,
The lady of my love, may be.

WHEN LOVE, WHO RULED.

WHEN Love, who ruled as Admiral o'er
  His rosy mother's isles of light,
Was cruising off the Paphian shore,
  A sail at sunset hove in sight.
"A chase, a chase! my Cupids all,"
Said Love, the little Admiral.

Aloft the winged sailors sprung,
  And, swarming up the mast like bees,
The snow-white sails expanding flung,
  Like broad magnolias to the breeze.
"Yo ho, yo ho, my Cupids all!"
Said Love, the little Admiral.

The chase was o'er — the bark was
    caught,
  The winged crew her freight explored;
And found 't was just as Love had
    thought,
  For all was contraband aboard.
"A prize, a prize, my Cupids all!"
Said Love, the little Admiral.

Safe stowed in many a package there,
  And labelled slyly o'er, as "Glass,"
Were lots of all the illegal ware,
  Love's Custom-House forbids to pass.
"O'erhaul, o'erhaul, my Cupids all,"
Said Love, the little Admiral.

False curls they found, of every hue,
  With rosy blushes ready made;
And teeth of ivory, good as new,
  For veterans in the smiling trade.
"Ho ho, ho ho, my Cupids all,"
Said Love, the little Admiral.

Mock sighs, too, — kept in bags for use,
  Like breezes bought of Lapland
    seers, —
Lay ready here to be let loose,
  When wanted, in young spinsters' ears.
"Ha ha, ha ha, my Cupids all,"
Said Love, the little Admiral.

False papers next on board were found,
  Sham invoices of flames and darts,
Professedly for Paphos bound,
  But meant for Hymen's golden marts.
" For shame, for shame, my Cupids all !"
Said Love, the little Admiral.

Nay, still to every fraud awake,
  Those pirates all Love's signals knew,
And hoisted oft his flag, to make
  Rich wards and heiresses *bring-to*.[1]
" A foe, a foe, my Cupids all !"
Said Love, the little Admiral.

" This must not be," the boy exclaims,
  " In vain I rule the Paphian seas,
" If Love's and Beauty's sovereign names
  " Are lent to cover frauds like these.
" Prepare, prepare, my Cupids all ! "
Said Love, the little Admiral.

Each Cupid stood with lighted match —
  A broadside struck the smuggling foe,
And swept the whole unhallowed batch
  Of Falsehood to the depths below.
" Huzza, huzza ! my Cupids all ! "
Said Love, the little Admiral.

STILL THOU FLIEST.

STILL thou fliest, and still I woo thee,
  Lovely phantom, — all in vain;
Restless ever, my thoughts pursue thee,
  Fleeting ever, thou mock'st their pain.
Such doom, of old, that youth betided,
  Who wooed, he thought, some angel's
    charms,
But found a cloud that from him glided, —
  As thou dost from these out-stretched
    arms.

Scarce I 've said, " How fair thou shin-
    est,"
  Ere thy light hath vanished by;
And 't is when thou look'st divinest
  Thou art still most sure to fly.
Even as the lightning, that, dividing
  The clouds of night, saith, " Look on
    me,"
Then flits again, its splendor hiding, —
  Even such the glimpse I catch of thee.

[1] " *To Bring-to,* to check the course of a
ship." — *Falconer.*

THEN FIRST FROM LOVE.

THEN first from Love, in Nature's bowers,
  Did Painting learn her fairy skill,
And cull the hues of loveliest flowers,
  To picture woman lovelier still.
For vain was every radiant hue,
  Till Passion lent a soul to art,
And taught the painter, ere he drew,
  To fix the model in his heart.

Thus smooth his toil awhile went on,
  Till, lo, one touch his art defies;
The brow, the lip, the blushes shone,
  But who could dare to paint those eyes?
'T was all in vain the painter strove;
  So turning to that boy divine,
" Here take," he said, " the pencil, Love,
  " No hand should paint such eyes but
    thine."

HUSH, SWEET LUTE.

HUSH, sweet Lute, thy songs remind me
  Of past joys, now turned to pain;
Of ties that long have ceased to bind me,
  But whose burning marks remain.
In each tone, some echo falleth
  On my ear of joys gone by;
Every note some dream recalleth
  Of bright hopes but born to die.

Yet, sweet Lute, though pain it bring me,
  Once more let thy numbers thrill;
Tho' death were in the strain they sing
    me,
  I must woo its anguish still.
Since no time can e'er recover
  Love's sweet light when once 't is set,—
Better to weep such pleasures over,
  Than smile o'er any left us yet.

BRIGHT MOON.

BRIGHT moon, that high in heaven art
    shining,
  All smiles, as if within thy bower to-
    night
Thy own Endymion lay reclining,
  And thou wouldst wake him with a
    kiss of light ! —
By all the bliss thy beam discovers,
  By all those visions far too bright for
    day,

Which dreaming bards and waking lovers
    Behold, this night, beneath thy linger-
        ing ray, —

I pray thee, queen of that bright heaven,
    Quench not to-night thy love-lamp in
        the sea,
Till Anthe, in this bower, hath given
    Beneath thy beam, her long-vowed
        kiss to me.
Guide hither, guide her steps benighted,
    Ere thou, sweet moon, thy bashful
        crescent hide;
Let Love but in this bower be lighted,
    Then shroud in darkness all the world
        beside.

LONG YEARS HAVE PAST.

Long years have past, old friend, since
        we
    First met in life's young day;
And friends long loved by thee and me,
    Since then have dropt away; —
But enough remain to cheer us on,
    And sweeten, when thus we 're met,
The glass we fill to the many gone,
    And the few who 're left us yet.

Our locks, old friend, now thinly grow,
    And some hang white and chill;
While some, like flowers mid Autumn's
        snow,
    Retain youth's color still.
And so, in our hearts, tho' one by one,
    Youth's sunny hopes have set,
Thank heaven, not all their light is
        gone, —
    We 've some to cheer us yet.

Then here 's to thee, old friend, and
        long
    May thou and I thus meet,
To brighten still with wine and song
    This short life, ere it fleet.
And still as death comes stealing on,
    Let 's never, old friend, forget,
Even while we sigh o'er blessings gone,
    How many are left us yet.

DREAMING FOR EVER.

Dreaming for ever, vainly dreaming,
    Life to the last, pursues its flight;

Day hath its visions fairly beaming,
    But false as those of night.
The one illusion, the other real,
    But both the same brief dreams at last;
And when we grasp the bliss ideal,
    Soon as it shines, 't is past.

Here, then, by this dim lake reposing,
    Calmly I 'll watch, while light and
        gloom
Flit o'er its face till night is closing —
    Emblem of life's short doom!
But tho', by turns, thus dark and shining,
    'T is still unlike man's changeful day,
Whose light returns not, once declining,
    Whose cloud, once come, will stay.

THO' LIGHTLY SOUNDS THE SONG I SING.

A SONG OF THE ALPS.

Tho' lightly sounds the song I sing to
        thee,
Tho' like the lark's its soaring music be,
Thou 'lt find even here some mournful
        note that tells
How near such April joy to weeping
        dwells.
'T is 'mong the gayest scenes that often-
        est steal
Those saddening thoughts we fear, yet
        love to feel;
And music never half so sweet appears,
As when her mirth forgets itself in
        tears.

Then say not thou this Alpine song is
        gay —
It comes from hearts that, like their
        mountain-lay,
Mix joy with pain, and oft when pleas-
        ure's breath
Most warms the surface feel most sad
        beneath.
The very beam in which the snow-wreath
        wears
Its gayest smile is that which wins its
        tears, —
And passion's power can never lend the
        glow
Which wakens bliss, without some touch
        of woe.

THE RUSSIAN LOVER.

FLEETLY o'er the moonlight snows
  Speed we to my lady's bower;
Swift our sledge as lightning goes,
  Nor shall stop till morning's hour.
Bright, my steed, the northern star
  Lights us from yon jewelled skies;
But, to greet us, brighter far,
  Morn shall bring my lady's eyes.

Lovers, lulled in sunny bowers,
  Sleeping out their dream of time,
Know not half the bliss that 's ours,
  In this snowy, icy clime.

Like yon star that livelier gleams
  From the frosty heavens around,
Love himself the keener beams
  When with snows of coyness crowned.

Fleet then on, my merry steed,
  Bound, my sledge, o'er hill and
    dale;—
What can match a lover's speed?
  See, 't is daylight, breaking pale!
Brightly hath the northern star
  Lit us from yon radiant skies;
But, behold, how brighter far
  Yonder shine my lady's eyes!

M. P.; OR, THE BLUE-STOCKING:

A COMIC OPERA IN THREE ACTS.

1811.

BOAT GLEE.

THE song that lightens the languid way,
    When brows are glowing,
    And faint with rowing,
Is like the spell of Hope's airy lay,
To whose sound thro' life we stray;
The beams that flash on the oar awhile,
    As we row along thro' the waves so
        clear,
Illume its spray, like the fleeting smile
    That shines o'er sorrow's tear.

Nothing is lost on him who sees
    With an eye that feeling gave;—
For him there 's a story in every breeze,
    And a picture in every wave.
Then sing to lighten the languid way;
    When brows are glowing,
    And faint with rowing,
'T is like the spell of Hope's airy lay,
To whose sound thro' life we stray.

'T IS sweet to behold when the billows
    are sleeping,
    Some gay-colored bark moving grace-
        fully by;
No damp on her deck but the eventide's
    weeping,
    No breath in her sails but the summer
        wind's sigh.

Yet who would not turn with a fonder
    emotion,
    To gaze on the life-boat, tho' rugged
        and worn,

Which often hath wafted o'er hills of
    the ocean
    The lost light of hope to the seaman
        forlorn!

Oh! grant that of those who in life's
    sunny slumber
    Around us like summer-barks idly
        have played,
When storms are abroad we may find in
    the number
    One friend, like the life-boat, to fly to
        our aid.

WHEN Lelia touched the lute,
    Not *then* alone 't was felt,
But when the sounds were mute,
    In memory still they dwelt.
Sweet lute! in nightly slumbers
Still we heard thy morning numbers.

Ah, how could she who stole
    Such breath from simple wire,
Be led, in pride of soul,
    To string with gold her lyre?
Sweet lute! thy chords she breaketh;
Golden now the strings she waketh!

But where are all the tales
    Her lute so sweetly told?
In lofty themes she fails,
    And soft ones suit not gold.
Rich lute! we see thee glisten,
But, alas! no more we listen!

YOUNG Love lived once in a humble
    shed,.
    Where roses breathing
    And woodbines wreathing
Around the lattice their tendrils spread,
As wild and sweet as the life he led.
    His garden flourisht,
    For young Hope nourisht
The infant buds with beams and
    showers;
But lips, tho' blooming, must still be
    fed,
    And not even Love can live on
    flowers.

Alas! that Poverty's evil eye
    Should e'er come hither,
    Such sweets to wither!
The flowers laid down their heads to die,
And Hope fell sick as the witch drew
    nigh.
    She came one morning,
    Ere Love had warning,
And raised the latch, where the young
    god lay;
"Oh ho!" said Love — "is it you?
    good-by;"
    So he oped the window and flew
    away!

    ———

SPIRIT of Joy, thy altar lies
    In youthful hearts that hope like
    mine;
And 't is the light of laughing eyes
    That leads us to thy fairy shrine.
There if we find the sigh, the tear,
    They are not those to sorrow known;
But breathe so soft, and drop so clear,
    That bliss may claim them for her
    own.
Then give me, give me, while I weep,
    The sanguine hope that brightens
    woe,
And teaches even our tears to keep
    The tinge of pleasure as they flow.

The child who sees the dew of night
    Upon the spangled hedge at morn,
Attempts to catch the drops of light,
    But wounds his finger with the thorn.
Thus oft the brightest joys we seek,
    Are lost when touched, and turned to
    pain;

The flush they kindle leaves the cheek,
    The tears they waken long remain.
      But give me, give me, etc.

    ———

To sigh, yet feel no pain,
    To weep, yet scarce know why;
To sport an hour with Beauty's chain,
    Then throw it idly by;
To kneel at many a shrine,
    Yet lay the heart on none;
To think all other charms divine,
    But those we just have won;
This is love, careless love,
Such as kindleth hearts that rove.

To keep one sacred flame,
    Thro' life unchilled, unmoved,
To love in wintry age the same
    As first in youth we loved;
To feel that we adore
    To such refined excess,
That tho' the heart would break with
    more,
    We could not live with *less;*
This is love, faithful love,
Such as saints might feel above.

    ———

DEAR aunt, in the olden time of love,
    When women like slaves were spurned,
A maid gave her heart, as she would her
    glove,
    To be teased by a fop, and returned!
But women grow wiser as men improve,
And, tho' beaux, like monkeys, amuse us,
Oh! think not we 'd give such a delicate
    gem
As the heart to be played with or sullied
    by them;
    No, dearest aunt, excuse us.

We may know by the head on Cupid's seal
    What impression the heart will take;
If shallow the head, oh! soon we feel
    What a poor impression 't will make!
Tho' plagued, Heaven knows! by the
    foolish zeal
Of the fondling fop who pursues me,
Oh, think not I 'd follow their desperate
    rule,
Who get rid of the folly by wedding the
    fool;
    No, dearest aunt! excuse me.

WHEN Charles was deceived by the maid
he loved,
    We saw no cloud his brow o'er-casting,
But proudly he smiled as if gay and unmoved,
    Tho' the wound in his heart was deep
and lasting.
And oft at night when the tempest
rolled
    He sung as he paced the dark deck
over —
" Blow, wind, blow ! thou art not so cold
As the heart of a maid that deceives
her lover."

Yet he lived with the happy and seemed
to be gay,
    Tho' the wound but sunk more deep
for concealing;
And Fortune threw many a thorn in his
way,
    Which, true to one anguish, he trod
without feeling !
And still by the frowning of Fate unsubdued
    He sung as if sorrow had placed him
above her —
" Frown, Fate, frown ! thou art not so
rude
    As the heart of a maid that deceives
her lover."

At length his career found a close in
death,
    The close he long wished to his cheer-
less roving,
For Victory shone on his latest breath,
    And he died in a cause of his heart's
approving.
But still he remembered his sorrow, —
and still
    He sung till the vision of life was over—
" Come, death, come ! thou art not so
chill
    As the heart of a maid that deceiv s
her lover."

WHEN life looks lone and dreary,
    What light can dispel the gloom?
When Time's swift wing grows weary,
    What charm can refresh his plume?
'T is woman whose sweetness beameth
    O'er all that we feel or see;

And if man of heaven e'er dreameth,
    'T is when he thinks purely of thee,
        O woman !

Let conquerors fight for glory,
    Too dearly the meed they gain;
Let patriots live in story —
    Too often they die in vain;
Give kingdoms to those who choose 'em,
    This world can offer to me
No throne like Beauty's bosom,
    No freedom like serving thee,
        O woman !

CUPID'S LOTTERY.

A LOTTERY, a Lottery,
In Cupid's court there used to be;
        Two roguish eyes
        The highest prize
In Cupid's scheming Lottery;
        And kisses, too,
        As good as new,
Which were n't very hard to win,
        For he who won
        The eyes of fun
Was sure to have the kisses in
        A Lottery, a Lottery, etc.

This Lottery, this Lottery,
In Cupid's court went merrily,
        And Cupid played
        A Jewish trade
In this his scheming Lottery;
        For hearts, we 're told,
        In *shares* he sold
To many a fond believing drone,
        And cut the hearts
        In sixteen parts
So well, each thought the whole his
own.
        Chor. — A Lottery, a Lottery, etc.

THO' sacred the tie that our country en-
twineth,
    And dear to the heart her remembrance
remains,
Yet dark are the ties where no liberty
shineth,
    And sad the remembrance that slavery
stains.
O thou who wert born in the cot of the
peasant,
    But diest in languor in luxury's dome,

Our vision, when absent — our glory,
  when present —
Where thou art, O Liberty! there is
  my home.

Farewell to the land where in childhood
  I 've wandered!
In vain is she mighty, in vain is she
  brave!
Unblest is the blood that for tyrants is
  squandered,
And fame has no wreaths for the brow
  of the slave.
But hail to thee, Albion! who meet'st
  the commotion
Of Europe as calm as thy cliffs meet
  the foam!
With no bonds but the law, and no slave
  but the ocean,
Hail, Temple of Liberty! thou art my
  home.

———

OH think, when a hero is sighing,
  What danger in such an adorer!
What woman can dream of denying
  The hand that lays laurels before her?
No heart is so guarded around,
  But the smile of a victor will take it;
No bosom can slumber so sound,
  But the trumpet of glory will wake it.

Love sometimes is given to sleeping,
  And woe to the heart that allows him;
For oh, neither smiling nor weeping
  Has power at those moments to rouse
  him.
But tho' he was sleeping so fast,
  That the life almost seemed to forsake
  him,
Believe me, one soul-thrilling blast
  From the trumpet of glory would wake
  him.

MR. ORATOR PUFF had two tones in his
  voice,
The one squeaking thus, and the other
  down so!
In each sentence he uttered he gave you
  your choice,
For one was B alt, and the rest G below.
    Oh! oh, Orator Puff!
One voice for one orator's surely
  enough.

But he still talked away spite of coughs
  and of frowns,
So distracting all ears with his ups and
  his downs,
That a wag once on hearing the orator
  say,
" My voice is for war," asked him,
  . " Which of them, pray? "
    Oh! oh! etc.

Reeling homewards one evening, top-
  heavy with gin,
  And rehearsing his speech on the
  weight of the crown,
He tript near a sawpit, and tumbled
  right in,
  " Sinking Fund," the last words as his
  noddle came down.
    Oh! oh! etc.

" Help! help!" he exclaimed, in his he
  and she tones,
" Help me out! help me out — I have
  broken my bones! "
" Help you out? " said a Paddy who
  passed, " what a bother!
Why, there 's two of you there, can't
  you help one another? "
    Oh! oh! etc.

MISCELLANEOUS POEMS.

OCCASIONAL EPILOGUE.

SPOKEN BY MR. CORRY, IN THE CHARACTER OF
VAPID, AFTER THE PLAY OF THE DRAMATIST',
AT THE KILKENNY THEATRE.

(Entering as if to announce the Play.)

LADIES and Gentlemen, on Monday night,
For the ninth time — oh accents of delight
To the poor author's ear, when *three times
three*
With a full bumper crowns his Comedy!
When, long by money, and the muse,
forsaken,
He finds at length his jokes and boxes
taken,
And sees his play-bill circulate — alas,
The only bill on which his name will pass!
Thus, Vapid, thus shall Thespian scrolls
of fame
Thro' box and gallery waft your well-
known name,
While critic eyes the happy cast shall con,
And learned ladies spell your *Dram. Per-
son.*

'T is said our worthy Manager [1] intends
To help my night, and *he*, you know, has
friends.
Friends, did I say? for fixing friends, or
parts,
Engaging actors, or engaging hearts,
There 's nothing like him! wits, at his
request,
Are turned to fools, and dull dogs learn
to jest;
Soldiers, for him, good "trembling
cowards" make,
And beaus, turned clowns, look ugly for
his sake;
For him even lawyers talk without a fee,
For him (oh friendship!) *I* act tragedy!
In short, like Orpheus, his persuasive
tricks
Make *boars* amusing, and put life in *sticks*.

[1] The late Mr. Richard Power.

With *such* a manager we can't but
please,
Tho' London sent us all her loud
O. P.'s,[2]
Let them come on, like snakes, all hiss
and rattle,
Armed with a thousand fans, we 'd give
them battle;
You, on our side, R. P.[3] upon our banners,
Soon should we teach the saucy O. P.'s
manners:
And show that, here — howe'er John Bull
may doubt —
In all *our* plays, the Riot-Act 's cut
out;
And, while we skim the cream of many a
jest,
Your well-timed thunder never sours its
zest.

Oh gently thus, when three short weeks
are past,
At Shakspeare's altar,[4] shall we breathe
our last;
And, ere this long-loved dome to ruin
nods,
Die all, die nobly, die like demigods!

EXTRACT

FROM A PROLOGUE WRITTEN AND SPOKEN BY
THE AUTHOR, AT THE OPENING OF THE
KILKENNY THEATRE, OCTOBER, 1809.

. . . . . .

YET, even here, tho' Fiction rules the
hour,
There shine some genuine smiles, beyond
her power;

[2] The brief appellation by which those persons
were distinguished who, at the opening of the new
theatre of Covent Garden, clamored for the continuance of the old prices of admission.

[3] The initials of our manager's name.

[4] This alludes to a scenic representation then
preparing for the last night of the performances.

And there are tears, too — tears that
    Memory sheds
Even o'er the feast that mimic fancy
    spreads,
When her heart misses one lamented
    guest,[1]
Whose eye so long threw light o'er all
    the rest!
There, there, indeed, the Muse forgets
    her task,
And drooping weeps behind Thalia's
    mask.

Forgive this gloom — forgive this joyless
    strain,
Too sad to welcome pleasure's smiling
    train.
But, meeting thus, our hearts will part
    the lighter,
As mist at dawn but makes the setting
    brighter;
Gay Epilogue will shine where Prologue
    fails —
As glow-worms keep their splendor for
    their tails.

I know not why — but time, methinks,
    hath past
More fleet than usual since we parted last.
It seems but like a dream of yester-night,
Whose charm still hangs, with fond, de-
    laying light;
And, ere the memory lose one glowing
    hue
Of former joy, we come to kindle new.
Thus ever may the flying moments haste
With trackless foot along life's vulgar
    waste,
But deeply print and lingeringly move,
When thus they reach the sunny spots we
    love.
Oh yes, whatever be our gay career,
Let this be still the solstice of the year,
Where Pleasure's sun shall at its height
    remain,
And slowly sink to level life again.

THE SYLPH'S BALL.

A SYLPH, as bright as ever sported
    Her figure thro' the fields of air,

1 The late Mr. John Lyster, one of the oldest
members and best actors of the Kilkenny Theatrical Society.

By an old swarthy Gnome was courted,
    And, strange to say, he won the fair.

The annals of the oldest witch
    A pair só sorted could not show,
But how refuse? — the Gnome was rich,
    The Rothschild of the world below;

And Sylphs, like other pretty creatures,
    Are told, betimes, they must consider
Love as an auctioneer of features,
    Who knocks them down to the best
      bidder.

Home she was taken to his Mine —
    A Palace paved with diamonds all —
And, proud as Lady Gnome to shine,
    Sent out her tickets for a Ball.

The *lower* world of course was there,
    And all the best; but of the *upper*
The sprinkling was but shy and rare, —
    A few old Sylphids who loved supper.

As none yet knew the wondrous Lamp
    Of DAVY, that renowned Aladdin,
And the Gnome's Halls exhaled a damp
    Which accidents from fire were bad in;

The chambers were supplied with light
    By many strange but safe devices;
Large fire-flies, such as shine at night
    Among the Orient's flowers and
      spices; —

Musical flint-mills — swiftly played
    By elfin hands — that, flashing round,
Like certain fire-eyed minstrel maids,
    Gave out at once both light and sound.

Bologna stones that drink the sun;
    And water from that Indian sea,
Whose waves at night like wild-fire run —
    Corked up in crystal carefully.

Glow-worms that round the tiny dishes
    Like little light-houses, were set up;
And pretty phosphorescent fishes
    That by their own gay light were eat
      up.

'Mong the few guests from Ether came
    That wicked Sylph whom Love we
      call —

My Lady knew him but by name,
My Lord, her husband, not at all.

Some prudent Gnomes, 't is said, apprised
That he was coming, and, no doubt
Alarmed about his torch, advised
He should by all means be kept out.

But others disapproved this plan,
And, by his flame tho' somewhat
frighted,
Thought Love too much a gentleman
In such a dangerous place to light it.

However, *there* he was — and dancing
With the fair Sylph, light as a feather;
They looked like two fresh sunbeams
glancing
At daybreak down to earth together.

And all had gone off safe and well,
But for that plaguy torch whose light,
Though not *yet* kindled — who could tell
How soon, how devilishly, it *might?*

And so it chanced — which, in those dark
And fireless halls was quite amazing;
Did we not know how small a spark
Can set the torch of Love a-blazing.

Whether it came (when close entangled
In the gay waltz) from her bright eyes,
Or from the *lucciole*, that spangled
Her locks of jet — is all surmise;

But certain 't is the ethereal girl
Did drop a spark at some odd turning,
Which by the waltz's windy whirl
Was fanned up into actual burning

Oh for that Lamp's metallic gauze,
That curtain of protecting wire,
Which DAVY delicately draws
Around illicit, dangerous fire ! —

The wall he sets 'twixt Flame and Air,
(Like that which barred young This-
be's bliss,)
Thro' whose small holes this dangerous
pair
May see each other but not kiss.[1]

---

[1] —— *partique dedère
oscula quisque suæ, non pervenientia con à.*
                                        OVID.

At first the torch looked rather bluely, —
A sign, they say, that no good boded —
Then quick the gas became unruly,
And, crack ! the ball-room all ex-
ploded.

Sylphs, gnomes, and fiddlers mixt together,
With all their aunts, sons, cousins,
nieces,
Like butterflies in stormy weather,
Were blown — legs, wings, and tails
— to pieces !

While, mid these victims of the torch,
The Sylph, alas, too, bore her part —
Found lying with a livid scorch
As if from lightning o'er her heart !

. . . .

"Well done"—a laughing Goblin said —
Escaping from this gaseous strife —
" 'T is not the *first* time Love has made
" A *blow-up* in connubial life ! "

REMONSTRANCE.

*After a Conversation with Lord John Russell,
in which he had intimated some Idea of giving up all political Pursuits.*

WHAT ! *thou*, with thy genius, thy youth,
and thy name —
Thou, born of a Russell — whose instinct to run
The accustomed career of thy sires, is
the same
As the eaglet's, to soar with his eyes
on the sun !

Whose nobility comes to thee, stampt
with a seal,
Far, far more ennobling than monarch
e'er set;
With the blood of thy race, offered up
for the weal
Of a nation that swears by that martyrdom yet !

Shalt *thou* be faint-hearted and turn from
the strife,
From the mighty arena, where all that
is grand
And devoted and pure and adorning in
life,
'T is for high-thoughted spirits like
thine to command?

Oh no, never dream it — while good
          men despair
Between tyrants and traitors, and
          timid men bow,
Never think for an instant thy country
          can spare
Such a light from her darkening hori-
          zon as thou.

With a spirit, as meek as the gentlest of
          those
Who in life's sunny valley lie sheltered
          and warm;
Yet bold and heroic as ever yet rose
          To the top cliffs of Fortune and
          breasted her storm;

With an ardor for liberty fresh as in
          youth
          It first kindles the bard and gives life
          to his lyre;
Yet mellowed, even now, by that mild-
          ness of truth
          Which tempers but chills not the
          patriot fire;

With an eloquence — not like those rills
          from a height,
          Which sparkle and foam and in vapor
          are o'er;
But a current that works out its way
          into light
Thro' the filtering recesses of thought
          and of lore.

Thus gifted, thou never canst sleep in
          the shade;
          If the stirrings of Genius, the music
          of fame,
And the charms of thy cause have not
          power to persuade,
          Yet think how to Freedom thou 'rt
          pledged by thy Name.

Like the boughs of that laurel by Del-
          phi's decree
          Set apart for the Fane and its service
          divine,
So the branches that spring from the
          old Russell tree
          Are by Liberty *claimed* for the use of
          her Shrine.

MY BIRTH–DAY.

"MY birth-day" — what a different
          sound
That word had in my youthful ears!
And how, each time the day comes
          round,
          Less and less white its mark appears!

When first our scanty years are told,
It seems like pastime to grow old;
And as Youth counts the shining links
          That Time around him binds so fast,
Pleased with the task, he little thinks
          How hard that chain will press at
          last.
Vain was the man, and false as vain,
          Who said[1] — "were he ordained to
          run
" His long career of life again,
          " He would do all that he *had*
          done." —
Ah, 't is not thus the voice that dwells
          In sober birth-days speaks to me;
Far otherwise — of time it tells,
          Lavished unwisely, carelessly;
Of counsel mockt; of talents made
          Haply for high and pure designs,
But oft, like Israel's incense, laid
          Upon unholy, earthly shrines;
Of nursing many a wrong desire,
          Of wandering after Love too far,
And taking every meteor fire
          That crost my pathway, for his star. —
All this it tells, and, could I trace
          The imperfect picture o'er again,
With power to add, retouch, efface
          The lights and shades, the joy and
          pain,
How little of the past would stay!
How quickly all should melt away —
All — but that Freedom of the Mind
          Which hath been more than wealth to
          me;
Those friendships, in my boyhood twined,
          And kept till now unchangingly;
And that dear home, that saving ark,
          Where Love's true light at last I 've
          found,
Cheering within, when all grows dark
          And comfortless and stormy round!

1 FONTENELLE. — "*Si je recommençais ma
carrière, je ferais tout ce que j'ai fait.*"

FANCY.

THE more I 've viewed this world, the
    more I 've found,
    That filled as 't is with scenes and
        creatures rare,
Fancy commands within her own bright
    round
    A world of scenes and creatures far
        more fair.

Nor is it that her power can call up there
    A single charm, that 's not from Nature
        won, —
No more than rainbows in their pride can
    wear
    A single tint unborrowed from the sun;

But 't is the mental medium it shines
    thro',
    That lends to Beauty all its charm and
        hue;
As the same light that o'er the level lake
    One dull monotony of lustre flings,
Will, entering in the rounded rain-drop,
    make
    Colors as gay as those on angels'
        wings!

SONG.

FANNY, DEAREST!

YES! had I leisure to sigh and mourn,
    Fanny, dearest, for thee I 'd sigh;
And every smile on my cheek should
    turn
    To tears when thou art nigh.
But between love and wine and sleep,
    So busy a life I live,
That even the time it would take to
    weep
    Is more than my heart can give.
Then wish me not to despair and pine,
    Fanny, dearest of all the dears!
The Love that 's ordered to bathe in
    wine,
    Would be sure to take cold in tears.

Reflected bright in this heart of mine,
    Fanny, dearest, thy image lies;
But ah! the mirror would cease to shine,
    If dimmed too often with sighs.
They lose the half of beauty's light,
    Who view it thro' sorrow's tear;
And 't is but to see thee truly bright
    That I keep my eye-beams clear.

Then wait no longer till tears shall flow —
    Fanny, dearest! the hope is vain;
If sunshine cannot dissolve thy snow,
    I shall never attempt it with rain.

TRANSLATIONS FROM CATUL-LUS.

CARM. 70.

dicebas quondam, etc.

TO LESBIA.

THOU told'st me, in our days of love,
    That I had all that heart of thine;
That, even to share the couch of Jove,
    Thou wouldst not, Lesbia, part from
        mine.

How purely wert thou worshipt then!
    Not with the vague and vulgar fires
Which Beauty wakes in soulless men, —
    But loved, as children by their sires.

That flattering dream, alas, is o'er; —
    I know thee now — and tho' these eyes
Doat on thee wildly as before,
    Yet, even in doating, I despise.

Yes, sorceress — mad as it may seem —
    With all thy craft, such spells adorn
        thee,
That passion even outlives esteem,
    And I at once adore — and scorn thee.

CARM. 11.

pauca nunciate meæ puellæ.

. . . .

COMRADES and friends! with whom,
    where'er
    The fates have willed thro' life I 've
        roved,
Now speed ye home and with you bear
    These bitter words to her I 've loved.

Tell her from fool to fool to run,
    Where'er her vain caprice may call;
Of all her dupes not loving one,
    But ruining and maddening all.

Bid her forget — what now is past —
    Our once dear love, whose ruin lies
Like a fair flower, the meadow's last,
    Which feels the ploughshare's edge
        and dies!

CARM. 29.

peninsularum Sirmio, insularumque
ocelle.

SWEET Sirmio ! thou, the very eye
　　Of all peniusulas and isles,
That in our lakes of silver lie,
　　Or sleep enwreathed by Neptune's
　　　　smiles —

How gladly back to thee I fly !
　　Still doubting, asking — *can* it be
That I have left Bithynia's sky,
　　And gaze in safety upon thee?

Oh ! what is happier than to find
　　Our hearts at ease, our perils past;
When, anxious long, the lightened mind
　　Lays down its load of care at last:

When, tired with toil o'er land and deep,
　　Again we tread the welcome floor
Of our own home, and sink to sleep
　　On the long-wished-for bed once more.[1]

This, this it is that pays alone
　　The ills of all life's former track.—
Shine out, my beautiful, my own
　　Sweet Sirmio, greet thy master back.

And thou, fair Lake, whose water quaffs
　　The light of heaven like Lydia's sea,
Rejoice, rejoice — let all that laughs
　　Abroad, at home, laugh out for me !

TIBULLUS TO SULPICIA.

nulla tuum nobis subducet femina lectum, etc.
　　　　　　Lib. iv. *Carm.* 13.

" NEVER shall woman's smile have power
　　" To win me from those gentle
　　　　charms ! " —
Thus swore I, in that happy hour,
　　When Love first gave thee to my arms.

And still alone thou charm'st my sight —
　　Still, tho' our city proudly shine
With forms and faces, fair and bright,
　　I see none fair or bright but thine.

Would thou wert fair for only me,
　　And couldst no heart but mine allure !—
To all men else unpleasing be,
　　So shall I feel my prize secure.[2]

Oh, love like mine ne'er wants the zest
　　Of others' envy, others' praise;
But, in its silence safely blest,
　　Broods o'er a bliss it ne'er betrays.

Charm of my life ! by whose sweet power
　　All cares are husht, all ills subdued—
My light in even the darkest hour,
　　My crowd in deepest solitude ![3]

No, not tho' heaven itself sent down
　　Some maid of more than heavenly
　　　　charms,
With bliss undreamt thy bard to crown,
　　Would he for her forsake those arms !

IMITATION.

FROM THE FRENCH.

WITH women and apples both Paris and
　　　　Adam
　　Made mischief enough in their day : —
God be praised that the fate of mankind,
　　　　my dear Madam,
　　Depends not on *us*, the same way.
For, weak as I am with temptation to
　　　　grapple,
　　The world would have doubly to rue
　　　　thee;
Like Adam, I 'd gladly take *from* thee
　　　　the apple,
　　Like Paris, at once give it *to* thee

INVITATION TO DINNER.

ADDRESSED TO LORD LANSDOWNE.

　　　　　　　　　　September, 1818.

SOME think we bards have nothing real;
　　That poets live among the stars so,
Their very dinners are ideal, —
　　(And, heaven knows, too oft they *are*
　　　　so,) —
For instance, that we have, instead
　　Of vulgar chops and stews and hashes,

---

[1] *o quid solutis est beatius curis,*
　cum mens onus reponit, ac peregrino
　labore fessi venimus larem ad nostrum,
　desideratoque acquiescimus lecto.

[2] *displiceas aliis, sic ego tutus ero.*
[3] *tu mihi curarum requies, tu nocte vel atrâ*
　lumen, et in solis tu mihi turba locis.

First course — a Phœnix, at the head,
  Done in its own celestial ashes;
At foot, a cygnet which kept singing
All the time its neck was wringing.
Side dishes, thus — Minerva's owl,
Or any such like learned fowl:
Doves, such as heaven's poulterer gets,
When Cupid shoots his mother's pets.
Larks stewed in Morning's roseate
    breath,
  Or roasted by a sunbeam's splendor;
And nightingales, berhymed to death —
  Like young pigs whipt to make them
    tender.

Such fare may suit those bards, who 're
    able
To banquet at Duke Humphrey's table;
But as for me, who 've long been taught
  To eat and drink like other people;
And can put up with mutton, bought
    Where Bromham [1] rears its ancient
      steeple —
If Lansdowne will consent to share
My humble feast, tho' rude the fare,
Yet, seasoned by that salt he brings
From Attica's salinest springs,
'T will turn to dainties; — while the cup,
Beneath his influence brightening up,
Like that of Baucis, touched by Jove,
Will sparkle fit for gods above!

VERSES TO THE POET CRABBE'S INKSTAND.[2]

WRITTEN MAY, 1832.

ALL, as he left it! — even the pen,
  So lately at that mind's command,
Carelessly lying, as if then
  Just fallen from his gifted hand.

Have we then lost him? scarce an hour,
  A little hour, seems to have past,
Since Life and Inspiration's power
  Around that relic breathed their last.

Ah, powerless now — like talisman
  Found in some vanished wizard's halls,
Whose mighty charm with him began,
  Whose charm with him extinguisht
    falls.

Yet tho', alas! the gifts that shone
  Around that pen's exploring track,
Be now, with its great master, gone,
  Nor living hand can call them back;

Who does not feel, while thus his eyes
  Rest on the enchanter's broken wand,
Each earth-born spell it worked arise
  Before him in succession grand?

Grand, from the Truth that reigns o'er
    all;
  The unshrinking Truth that lets her
    light
Thro' Life's low, dark, interior fall,
  Opening the whole, severely bright:

Yet softening, as she frowns along,
  O'er scenes which angels weep to see —
Where Truth herself half veils the
    Wrong,
  In pity of the Misery.

True bard! — and simple, as the race
  Of true-born poets ever are,
When, stooping from their starry place,
  They 're children near, tho' gods afar.

How freshly doth my mind recall,
  'Mong the few days I 've known with
    thee,
One that, most buoyantly of all,
  Floats in the wake of memory; [3]

When he, the poet, doubly graced,
  In life, as in his perfect strain,
With that pure, mellowing power of
    Taste,
  Without which Fancy shines in vain;

Who in his page will leave behind,
  Pregnant with genius tho' it be,
But half the treasures of a mind,
  Where Sense o'er all holds mastery: —

---

1 A picturesque village in sight of my cottage, and from which it is separated but by a small verdant valley.

2 Soon after Mr. Crabbe's death, the sons of that gentleman did me the honor of presenting to me the inkstand, pencil, etc., which their distinguished father had long been in the habit of using.

3 The lines that follow allude to a day passed in company with Mr. Crabbe, many years since, when a party, consisting only of Mr. Rogers, Mr. Crabbe, and the author of these verses, had the pleasure of dining with Mr. Thomas Campbell, at his house at Sydenham.

Friend of long years! of friendship tried
  Thro' many a bright and dark event;
In doubts, my judge — in taste, my
    guide —
  In all, my stay and ornament!

He, too, was of our feast that day,
  And all were guests of one whose hand
Hath shed a new and deathless ray
  Around the lyre of this great land;

In whose sea-odes — as in those shells
  Where Ocean's voice of majesty
Seems still to sound — immortal dwells
  Old Albion's Spirit of the Sea.

Such was our host; and tho', since then,
  Slight clouds have risen 'twixt him and
    me,
Who would not grasp such hand again,
  Stretched forth again in amity?

Who can, in this short life, afford
  To let such mists a moment stay,
When thus one frank, atoning word,
  Like sunshine, melts them all away?

Bright was our board that day — tho' *one*
  Unworthy brother there had place;
As 'mong the horses of the Sun,
  One was, they say, of earthly race.

Yet, *next* to Genius is the power
  Of feeling where true Genius lies;
And there was light around that hour
  Such as, in memory, never dies;

Light which comes o'er me, as I gaze,
  Thou Relic of the Dead, on thee,
Like all such dreams of vanisht days,
  Brightly, indeed — but mournfully!

TO CAROLINE, VISCOUNTESS VALLETORT.

WRITTEN AT LACOCK ABBEY, JANUARY, 1832.

WHEN I would sing thy beauty's light,
Such various forms, and all so bright,
I 've seen thee, from thy childhood, wear,
I know not which to call most fair,
Nor 'mong the countless charms that
    spring
For ever round thee, *which* to sing.

When I would paint thee as thou *art*,
Then all thou *wert* comes o'er my heart —
The graceful child in Beauty's dawn
Within the nursery's shade withdrawn,
Or peeping out — like a young moon
Upon a world 't will brighten soon.
Then next in girlhood's blushing hour,
As from thy own loved Abbey-tower
I 've seen thee look, all radiant, down,
With smiles that to the hoary frown
Of centuries round thee lent a ray,
Chasing even Age's gloom away; —
Or in the world's resplendent throng,
As I have markt thee glide along,
Among the crowds of fair and great
A spirit, pure and separate,
To which even Admiration's eye
Was fearful to approach too nigh; —
A creature circled by a spell
Within which nothing wrong could dwell;
And fresh and clear as from the source,
Holding thro' life her limpid course,
Like Arethusa thro' the sea,
Stealing in fountain purity.

Now, too, another change of light!
As noble bride, still meekly bright,
Thou bring'st thy Lord a dower above
All earthly price, pure woman's love;
And show'st what lustre Rank receives,
When with his proud Corinthian leaves
Her rose thus high-bred Beauty weaves.

Wonder not if, where all 's so fair,
To choose were more than bard can dare;
Wonder not if, while every scene
I 've watched thee thro' so bright hath
    been,
The enamoured Muse should, in her quest
Of beauty, know not where to rest,
But, dazzled, at thy feet thus fall,
Hailing thee beautiful in all!

A SPECULATION.

OF all speculations the market holds
    forth,
  The best that I know for a lover of
    pelf,
Is to buy Marcus up, at the price he is
    worth,
  And then sell him at that which he sets
    on himself.

TO MY MOTHER.

WRITTEN IN A POCKET BOOK, 1822.

THEY tell us of an Indian tree,
　Which, howsoe'er the sun and sky
May tempt its boughs to wander free,
　And shoot and blossom wide and high,
Far better loves to bend its arms
　Downward again to that dear earth,
From which the life that fills and warms
　Its grateful being, first had birth.

'Tis thus, tho' wooed by flattering friends,
　And fed with fame (*if* fame it be)
This heart, my own dear mother, bends,
　With love's true instinct, back to thee !

LOVE AND HYMEN

LOVE had a fever — ne'er could close
　His little eyes till day was breaking;
And wild and strange enough, Heaven
　knows,
　The things he raved about while
　waking.

To let him pine so were a sin; —
　One to whom all the world's a
　debtor —
So Doctor Hymen was called in,
　And Love that night slept rather better.

Next day the case gave further hope yet,
　Tho' still some ugly fever latent; —
" Dose, as before " — a gentle opiate,
　For which old Hymen has a patent.

After a month of daily call,
　So fast the dose went on restoring,
That Love, who first ne'er slept at all,
　Now took, the rogue ! to downright
　snoring.

LINES

ON THE

ENTRY OF THE AUSTRIANS INTO NAPLES,

1821.

carbone notati.

AY — down to the dust with them, slaves
　as they are,
　From this hour let the blood in their
　dastardly veins,

That shrunk at the first touch of Liberty's
　war,
　Be wasted for tyrants, or stagnate in
　chains.

On, on like a cloud, thro' their beautiful
　vales,
　Ye locusts of tyranny, blasting them
　o'er —
Fill, fill up their wide sunny waters, ye
　sails
　From each slave-mart of Europe and
　shadow their shore !

Let their fate be a mock-word — let men
　of all lands
　Laugh out with a scorn that shall ring
　to the poles,
When each sword that the cowards let
　fall from their hands
　Shall be forged into fetters to enter
　their souls.

And deep, and more deep, as the iron is
　driven,
　Base slaves ! let the whet of their
　agony be,
To think — as the Doomed often think
　of that heaven
　They had once within reach — that
　they *might* have been free.

Oh shame ! when there was not a bosom
　whose heat
　Ever rose 'bove the *zero* of Castlereagh's
　heart,
That did not, like echo, your war-hymn
　repeat,
　And send all its prayers with your
　Liberty's start;

When the world stood in hope — when a
　spirit that breathed
　The fresh air of the olden time whis-
　pered about;
And the swords of all Italy, half-way
　unsheathed,
　But waited one conquering cry to
　flash out !

When around you the shades of your
　Mighty in fame,
　FILICAJAS and PETRARCHS, seemed
　bursting to view,

And their words and their warnings, like
    tongues of bright flame
  Over Freedom's apostles, fell kindling
    on you!

Oh shame! that in such a proud moment
    of life
  Worth the history of ages, when, had
    you but hurled
One bolt at your tyrant invader, that strife
  Between freemen and tyrants had
    spread thro' the world —

That then — oh! disgrace upon manhood
    — even then,
  You should falter, should cling to your
    pitiful breath;
Cower down into beasts, when you might
    have stood men,
  And prefer the slave's life of prostration
    to death.

It is strange, it is dreadful: — shout,
    Tyranny, shout
  Thro' your dungeons and palaces,
    "Freedom is o'er;" —
If there lingers one spark of her light,
    tread it out,
  And return to your empire of darkness
    once more.

For if *such* are the braggarts that claim
    to be free,
  Come, Despot of Russia, thy feet let
    me kiss;
Far nobler to live the brute bondman of
    thee,
  Than to sully even chains by a struggle
    like this!

SCEPTICISM.

ERE Psyche drank the cup that shed
    Immortal Life into her soul,
Some evil spirit poured, 't is said,
    One drop of Doubt into the bowl —

Which, mingling darkly with the stream,
    To Psyche's lips — she knew not why—
Made even that blessed nectar seem
    As tho' its sweetness soon would die.

Oft, in the very arms of Love,
    A chill came o'er her heart — a fear
That Death might, even yet, remove
    Her spirit from that happy sphere.

"Those sunny ringlets," she exclaimed,
    Twining them round her snowy fingers;
"That forehead, where a light unnamed,
    "Unknown on earth, for ever lingers;

"Those lips, thro' which I feel the breath
    "Of Heaven itself, whene'er they
        sever —
"Say, are they mine, beyond all death,
    "My own, hereafter, and for ever?

"Smile not — I know that starry brow,
    "Those ringlets, and bright lips of
        thine,
"Will always shine, as they do now —
    "But shall *I* live to *see* them shine?"

In vain did Love say, "Turn thine eyes
    "On all that sparkles round thee here—
"Thou 'rt now in heaven where nothing
        dies,
    "And in these arms — what *canst* thou
        fear?"

In vain — the fatal drop, that stole
    Into that cup's immortal treasure,
Had lodged its bitter near her soul,
    And gave a tinge to every pleasure

And, tho' there ne'er was transport given
    Like Psyche's with that radiant boy,
Hers is the only face in heaven,
    That wears a cloud amid its joy.

A JOKE VERSIFIED.

"COME, come," said Tom's father, "at
    your time of life,
    "There 's no longer excuse for thus
        playing the rake —
"It is time you should think, boy, of
    taking a wife" —
    "Why, so it is, father — whose wife
        shall I take?"

ON THE DEATH OF A FRIEND.

PURE as the mantle, which, o'er him
    who stood
  By Jordan's stream, descended from
    the sky,
Is that remembrance which the wise and
    good
  Leave in the hearts that love them,
    when they die.

So pure, so precious shall the memory be,
Bequeathed, in dying, to our souls by
   thee —
So shall the love we bore thee, cherisht
   warm
  Within our souls thro' grief and pain
    and strife,
Be, like Elisha's cruse, a holy charm,
  Wherewith to " heal the waters " of
    this life !

TO JAMES CORRY, ESQ.

ON HIS MAKING ME A PRESENT OF A WINE STRAINER.

BRIGHTON, June, 1825.

THIS life, dear Corry, who can doubt? —
  Resembles much friend Ewart's [1] wine,
When *first* the rosy drops come out,
  How beautiful, how clear they shine !

And thus awhile they keep their tint,
  So free from even a shade with some,
That they would smile, did you but hint,
  That darker drops would *ever* come.

But soon the ruby tide runs short,
  Each minute makes the sad truth
    plainer,
Till life, like old and crusty port,
  When near its close, requires a strainer.

This friendship can alone confer,
  Alone can teach the drops to pass,
If not as bright as *once* they were,
  At least unclouded, thro' the glass.

Nor, Corry, could a boon be mine,
  Of which this heart were fonder, vainer,
Than thus, if life grow like old wine,
  To have *thy* friendship for its strainer.

FRAGMENT OF A CHARACTER.

HERE lies Factotum Ned at last;
  Long as he breathed the vital air,
Nothing throughout all Europe past
  In which Ned had n't some small share.

Whoe'er was *in*, whoe'er was *out*,
  Whatever statesmen did or said,
If not exactly brought about,
  'T was all, at least, contrived by Ned.

1 A wine-merchant.

With Nap, if Russia went to war,
  'T was owing, under Providence,
To certain hints Ned gave the Tsar —
  (Vide his pamphlet — price, sixpence.)

If France was beat at Waterloo —
  As all but Frenchmen think she was —
To Ned, as Wellington well knew,
  Was owing half that day's applause.

Then for his news — no envoy's bag
  E'er past so many secrets thro' it;
Scarcely a telegraph could wag
  Its wooden finger, but Ned knew it.

Such tales he had of foreign plots,
  With foreign names, one's ear to buzz
    in !
From Russia, *shefs* and *ofs* in lots,
  From Poland, *owskis* by the dozen.

When George, alarmed for England's
    creed,
  Turned out the last Whig ministry,
And men asked — who advised the deed?
  Ned modestly confest 't was he.

For tho', by some unlucky miss,
  He had not downright *seen* the King,
He sent such hints thro' Viscount *This*,
  To Marquis *That*, as clenched the
    thing.

The same it was in science, arts,
  The Drama, Books, MS. and printed —
Kean learned from Ned his cleverest
    parts,
  And Scott's last work by him was
    hinted.

Childe Harold in the proofs he read,
  And, here and there, infused some
    soul in 't —
Nay, Davy's Lamp, till seen by Ned,
  Had — odd enough — an awkward
    hole in 't.

'T was thus, all-doing and all-knowing,
  Wit, statesman, boxer, chymist, singer,
Whatever was the best pie going,
  In *that* Ned — trust him — had his
    finger.

. . . . .

WHAT SHALL I SING THEE?

TO ———.

WHAT shall I sing thee?   Shall I tell
Of that bright hour, remembered well
As tho' it shone but yesterday,
When loitering idly in the ray
Of a spring sun I heard o'er-head,
My name as by some spirit said,
And, looking up, saw two bright eyes
　　Above me from a casement shine,
Dazzling my mind with such surprise
　　As they, who sail beyond the Line,
Feel when new stars above them rise; —
And it was thine, the voice that spoke,
　　Like Ariel's, in the mid-air then;
And thine the eye whose lustre broke —
　　Never to be forgot again!

What shall I sing thee?   Shall I weave
A song of that sweet summer-eve,
(Summer, of which the sunniest part
Was that we, each, had in the heart,)
When thou and I, and one like thee,
　　In life and beauty, to the sound
Of our own breathless minstrelsy,
　　Danced till the sunlight faded round,
Ourselves the whole ideal Ball,
Lights, music, company, and all!
Oh, 't is not in the languid strain
　　Of lute like mine, whose day is past,
To call up even a dream again
　　Of the fresh light those moments cast.

COUNTRY DANCE AND QUA-
DRILLE.

ONE night the nymph called country
　　dance —
(Whom folks, of late, have used so ill,
Preferring a coquette from France,
　　That mincing thing, *Mamselle* qua-
　　　drille —

Having been chased from London down
　　To that most humble haunt of all
She used to grace — a Country Town —
　　Went smiling to the New-Year's Ball.

"Here, here, at least," she cried, "tho'
　　　driven
　　"From London's gay and shining
　　　tracks —
"Tho', like a Peri cast from heaven,
　　"I 've lost, for ever lost, Almack's —

"Tho' not a London Miss alive
　　"Would now for her acquaintance
　　　own me;
"And spinsters, even, of forty-five,
　　"Upon their honors ne'er have known
　　　me;

"Here, here, at least, I triumph still,
　　"And — spite of some few dandy
　　　Lancers,
"Who vainly try to preach Quadrille —
　　"See naught but *true-blue* Country
　　　Dancers.

"Here still I reign, and, fresh in charms,
　　"My throne, like Magna Charta, raise
"'Mong sturdy, free-born legs and arms,
　　"That scorn the threaten'd *chaine
　　　anglaise.*"

'T was thus she said, as mid the din
Of footmen, and the town sedan,
She lighted at the King's Head Inn,
And up the stairs triumphant ran.

The Squires and their Squiresses all,
　　With young Squirinas, just *come out*,
And my Lord's daughters from the Hall,
　　(Quadrillers in their hearts no doubt,)—

All these, as light she tript up stairs,
　　Were in the cloak-room seen assem-
　　　bling —
When, hark! some new, outlandish airs,
　　From the First Fiddle, set her trem-
　　　bling.

She stops — she listens — *can* it be?
Alas, in vain her ears would 'scape it —
It *is* "*Di tanti palpiti*"
As plain as English bow can scrape it.

"Courage!" however — in she goes,
　　With her best, sweeping country grace;
When, ah too true, her worst of foes,
　　Quadrille, there meets her, face to
　　　face.

Oh for the lyre, or violin,
　　Or kit of that gay Muse, Terpsichore,
To sing the rage these nymphs were in,
　　Their looks and language, airs and
　　　trickery.

There stood Quadrille, with cat-like face
(The beau-ideal of French beauty),
A band-box thing, all art and lace
Down from her nose-tip to her shoe-
    tie.

Her flounces, fresh from *Victorine* —
From *Hippolyte*, her rouge and hair —
Her poetry, from *Lamartine* —
    Her morals, from — the Lord knows
    where.

And, when she danced — so slidingly,
So near the ground she plied her art,
You 'd swear her mother-earth and she
    Had made a compact ne'er to part.

Her face too, all the while, sedate,
No signs of life or motion showing,
Like a bright *pendule's* dial-plate —
    So still, you 'd hardly think 't was
    going.

Full fronting her stood Country Dance —
A fresh, frank nymph, whom you would
    know
For English, at a single glance —
    English all o'er, from top to toe.

A little *gauche*, 't is fair to own,
And rather given to skips and bounces;
Endangering thereby many a gown,
    And playing, oft, the devil with
    flounces.

Unlike *Mamselle* — who would pref
(As morally a lesser ill)
A thousand flaws of character,
    To one vile rumple of a frill.

No rouge did She of Albion wear;
Let her but run that two-heat race
She calls a *Set*, not Dian e'er
    Came rosier from the woodland chase.

Such was the nymph, whose soul had in 't
Such anger now — whose eyes of blue
(Eyes of that bright, victorious tint,
    Which English maids call " *Water-*
    loo ") —

Like summer lightnings, in the dusk
Of a warm evening, flashing broke,

While — to the tune of " Money Musk," [1]
Which struck up now — she proudly
    spoke —

" Heard you that strain — that joyous
    strain?
    " 'T was such as England loved to
    hear,
" Ere thou and all thy frippery train,
    " Corrupted both her foot and ear —

" Ere Waltz, that rake from foreign
    lands,
    " Presumed, in sight of all beholders,
" To lay his rude, licentious hands
    " On virtuous English backs and
    shoulders —

" Ere times and morals both grew bad,
    " And, yet unfleeced by funding block-
    heads,
" Happy John Bull not only *had*,
    " But danced to, ' Money in both
    pockets.'

" Alas, the change ! — Oh, Londonderry,
    " Where is the land could 'scape dis-
    asters,
" With *such* a Foreign Secretary,
    " Aided by Foreign Dancing Masters?

" Woe to ye, men of ships and shops !
    " Rulers of day-books and of waves !
" Quadrilled, on one side, into fops,
    " And drilled, on t' other, into slaves !

" Ye, too, ye lovely victims, seen,
    " Like pigeons, trussed for exhibition,
" With elbows, *à la crapaudine*,
    " And feet, in — God knows what
    position;

" Hemmed in by watchful chaperons,
    " Inspectors of your airs and graces,
" Who intercept all whispered tones,
    " And read your telegraphic faces;

" Unable with the youth adored,
    " In that grim *cordon* of Mammas,
" To interchange one tender word,
    " Tho' whispered but in *queue-de-chats*.

1 An old English country dance.

" Ah did you know how blest we ranged,
　" Ere vile Quadrille usurpt the fiddle —
" What looks in *setting* were exchanged,
　" What tender words in *down the
　　middle;*

" How many a couple, like the wind,
　" Which nothing in its course controls,
" Left time and chaperons far behind,
　" And gave a loose to legs and souls;

" How matrimony throve — ere stopt
　" By this cold, silent, foot-coquetting—
" How charmingly one's partner popt
　" The important question in *poussette-
　　ing.*

" While now, alas — no sly advances —
　" No marriage hints — all goes on
　　badly —
" 'Twixt Parson Malthus and French
　　Dances,
　" We, girls, are at a discount sadly.

" Sir William Scott (now Baron Stowell)
　" Declares not half so much is made
" By Licences — and he must know
　　well —
　" Since vile Quadrilling spoiled the
　　trade."

She ceased — tears fell from every Miss—
　She now had touched the true pa-
　　thetic : —
One such authentic fact as this,
　Is worth whole volumes theoretic.

Instant the cry was " Country Dance ! "
　And the maid saw, with brightening
　　face,
The Steward of the night advance,
　And lead her to her birthright place.

The fiddles, which awhile had ceased,
　Now tuned again their summons sweet,
And, for one happy night, at least,
　Old England's triumph was complete.

GAZEL.

HASTE, Maami, the spring is nigh;
　Already, in the unopened flowers
That sleep around us, Fancy's eye
　Can see the blush of future bowers;
And joy it brings to thee and me,
My own beloved Maami !

The streamlet frozen on its way,
　To feed the marble Founts of Kings,
Now, loosened by the vernal ray,
　Upon its path exulting springs —
As doth this bounding heart to thee,
My ever blissful Maami !

Such bright hours were not made to stay;
　Enough if they awhile remain,
Like Irem's bowers, that fade away,
　From time to time, and come again.
And life shall all one Irem be
For us, my gentle Maami.

O haste, for this impatient heart,
　Is like the rose in Yemen's vale,
That rends its inmost leaves apart
　With passion for the nightingale;
So languishes this soul for thee,
My bright and blushing Maami !

LINES

ON THE DEATH OF

JOSEPH ATKINSON, ESQ., OF
DUBLIN.

IF ever life was prosperously cast,
　If ever life was like the lengthened
　　flow
Of some sweet music, sweetness to the
　　last,
　'T was his who, mourned by many,
　　sleeps below.

The sunny temper, bright where all is
　　strife,
　The simple heart above all worldly
　　wiles;
Light wit that plays along the calm of
　　life,
　And stirs its languid surface into smiles ;

Pure charity that comes not in a shower,
　Sudden and loud, oppressing what it
　　feeds,
But, like the dew, with gradual silent
　　power,
　Felt in the bloom it leaves along the
　　meads;

The happy grateful spirit, that improves
　And brightens every gift by fortune
　　given;

That, wander where it will with those it
loves,
    Makes every place a home, and home
    a heaven:

All these were his. — Oh, thou who
read'st this stone,
    When for thyself, thy children, to the
    sky
Thou humbly prayest, ask this boon
alone,
    That ye like him may live, like him
    may die!

GENIUS AND CRITICISM.

scripsit quidem fata, sed sequitur.
                    SENECA.

OF old, the Sultan Genius reigned,
    As Nature meant, supreme, alone;
With mind uncheckt, and hands unchained,
    His views, his conquests were his
    own.

But power like his, that digs its grave
    With its own sceptre, could not last;
So Genius' self became the slave
    Of laws that Genius' self had past.

As Jove, who forged the chain of Fate,
    Was, ever after, doomed to wear it;
His nods, his struggles all too late —
    " *Qui semel jussit, semper paret.*"

To check young Genius' proud career,
    The slaves who now his throne in-
    vaded,
Made Criticism his prime Vizir,
    And from that hour his glories faded.

Tied down in Legislation's school,
    Afraid of even his own ambition,
His very victories were by rule,
    And he was great but by permission.

His most heroic deeds — the same,
    That dazzled, when spontaneous ac-
    tions —
Now, done by law, seemed cold and
tame,
    And shorn of all their first attractions.

If he but stirred to take the air,
    Instant, the Vizir's Council sat —
" Good Lord, your Highness can't go
there —
    " Bless me, your Highness can't do
    that."

If, loving pomp, he chose to buy
    Rich jewels for his diadem,
" The taste was bad, the price was high —
    " A flower were simpler than a gem."

To please them if he took to flowers —
    "What trifling, what unmeaning things!
" Fit for a woman's toilet hours,
    " But not at all the style for Kings."

If, fond of his domestic sphere,
    He played no more the rambling
    comet —
" A dull, good sort of man, 't was clear,
    " But, as for great or brave, far from
    it."

Did he then look o'er distant oceans,
    For realms more worthy to enthrone
    him? —
" Saint Aristotle, what wild notions!
    " Serve a ' *ne exeat regno* ' on him."

At length, their last and worst to do,
    They round him placed a guard of
    watchmen,
Reviewers, knaves in brown, or blue
    Turned up with yellow—chiefly Scotch-
    men;

To dog his footsteps all abo
    Like those in Longwood's prison
    grounds,
Who at Napoleon's heels rode out,
    For fear the Conqueror should break
    bounds.

Oh for some Champion of his power,
    Some *Ultra* spirit, to set free,
As erst in Shakspeare's sovereign hour,
    The thunders of his Royalty! —

To vindicate his ancient line,
    The first, the true, the only one,
Of Right eternal and divine,
    That rules beneath the blessed sun.

TO LADY JERSEY,

ON BEING ASKED TO WRITE SOMETHING IN HER
ALBUM.

Written at Middleton.

OH albums, albums, how I dread
   Your everlasting scrap and scrawl!
How often wish that from the dead
Old Omar would pop forth his head,
   And make a bonfire of you all!

So might I 'scape the spinster band,
   The blushless blues, who, day and
     night,
Like duns in doorways, take their stand,
To waylay bards, with book in hand,
   Crying for ever, " Write, sir, write! "

So might I shun the shame and pain,
   That o'er me at this instant come,
When Beauty, seeking Wit in vain,
Knocks at the portal of my brain,
   And gets, for answer, " Not at home! "

November, 1828.

TO THE SAME.

ON LOOKING THROUGH HER ALBUM.

No wonder bards, both high and low,
   From Byron down to * * * * * and
     me,
Should seek the fame which all bestow
   On him whose task is praising thee.

Let but the theme be Jersey's eyes,
   At once all errors are forgiven;
As even old Sternhold still we prize,
   Because, tho' dull, he sings of heaven.

AT NIGHT.[1]

AT night, when all is still around,
   How sweet to hear the distant sound
Of footstep, coming soft and light!
What pleasure in the anxious beat,
With which the bosom flies to meet
   That foot that comes so soft at night!

And then, at night, how sweet to say
" 'T is late, my love! " and chide delay,
   Tho' still the western clouds are bright;

1 These lines allude to a curious lamp, which
has for its device a Cupid, with the words "at
night " written over him.

Oh! happy, too, the silent press,
The eloquence of mute caress,
   With those we love exchanged at night!

TO LADY HOLLAND,

ON NAPOLEON'S LEGACY OF A SNUFF-BOX.

GIFT of the Hero, on his dying day,
   To her, whose pity watched, for ever
     nigh;
Oh! could he see the proud, the happy
     ray,
   This relic lights up on her generous eye,
Sighing, he 'd feel how easy 't is to pay
   A friendship all his kingdoms could
     not buy.

Paris, July, 1821.

EPILOGUE.

WRITTEN FOR LADY DACRE'S TRAGEDY OF INA.

LAST night, as lonely o'er my fire I sat,
Thinking of cues, starts, exits, and — all
   that,
And wondering much what little knavish
   sprite
Had put it first in women's heads to
   write: —
Sudden I saw — as in some witching
   dream —
A bright-blue glory round my book-case
   beam,
From whose quick-opening folds of azure
   light
Out flew a tiny form, as small and bright
As Puck the Fairy, when he pops his
   head,
Some sunny morning from a violet bed.
" Bless me! " I starting cried, " what
   imp are you? " —
" A small he-devil, Ma'am — my name
   BAS BLEU —
" A bookish sprite, much given to routs
   and reading;
" 'T is I who teach your spinsters of good
   breeding,
" The reigning taste in chemistry and
   caps,
" The last new bounds of tuckers and of
   maps,
" And when the waltz has twirled her
   giddy brain
" With metaphysics twirl it back again! "

I viewed him, as he spoke — his hose
 were blue,
His wings — the covers of the last Re-
 view —
Cerulean, bordered with a jaundice hue,
And tinselled gayly o'er, for evening
 wear,
Till the next quarter brings a new-fledged
 pair.
" Inspired by me — (pursued this waggish
 Fairy) —
" That best of wives and Sapphos, Lady
 Mary,
" Votary alike of Crispin and the Muse,
" Makes her own splay-foot epigrams
 and shoes.
" For me the eyes of young Camilla shine,
" And mingle Love's blue brilliances with
 mine;
" For me she sits apart, from coxcombs
 shrinking,
" Looks wise — the pretty soul! — and
 thinks she 's thinking.
" By my advice Miss Indigo attends
" Lectures on Memory, and assures her
 friends,
" ' 'Pon honor! — (*mimics*) — nothing
 can surpass the plan
" ' Of that professor — (*trying to recol-
 lect*) — psha! that memory-man —
" ' That — what 's his name? — him I
 attended lately —
" ' 'Pon honor, he improved *my* memory
 greatly.' "
Here curtsying low, I asked the blue-
 legged sprite,
What share he had in this our play to-
 night.
" Nay, there — (he cried) — there I am
 guiltless quite —
" What! choose a heroine from that
 Gothic time
" When no one waltzed and none but
 monks could rhyme;
" When lovely woman, all unschooled
 and wild,
" Blushed without art, and without cul-
 ture smiled —
" Simple as flowers, while yet unclassed
 they shone,
" Ere Science called their brilliant world
 her own,
" Ranged the wild, rosy things in learned
 orders,

" And filled with Greek the garden's
 blushing borders! —
" No, no — your gentle Inas will not
 do —
" To-morrow evening, when the lights
 burn blue,
" I 'll come — (*pointing downwards*) —
 you understand — till then adieu! "

And *has* the sprite been here? No —
 jests apart —
Howe'er man rules in science and in
 art,
The sphere of woman's glories is the
 heart.
And, if our Muse have sketched with
 pencil true
The wife — the mother — firm, yet gentle
 too —
Whose soul, wrapt up in ties itself hath
 spun,
Trembles, if touched in the remotest
 one;
Who loves — yet dares even Love himself
 disown,
When Honor's broken shaft supports his
 throne:
If such our Ina, she may scorn the evils,
Dire as they are, of Critics and — Blue
 Devils.

THE DAY-DREAM.[1]

THEY both were husht, the voice, the
 chords, —
I heard but once that witching lay;
And few the notes, and few the words,
 My spell-bound memory brought away;

Traces, remembered here and there,
 Like echoes of some broken strain; —
Links of a sweetness lost in air,
 That nothing now could join again.

Even these, too, ere the morning, fled;
 And, tho' the charm still lingered
 on,
That o'er each sense her song had shed,
 The song itself was faded, gone; —

1 In these stanzas I have done little more than
relate a fact in verse; and the lady, whose singing gave rise to this curious instance of the power
of memory in sleep, is Mrs. Robert Arkwright.

Gone, like the thoughts that once were
    ours,
  On summer days, ere youth had set;
Thoughts bright, we know, as summer
    flowers,
  Tho' *what* they were we now forget.

In vain with hints from other strains
  I wooed this truant air to come —
As birds are taught on eastern plains
  To lure their wilder kindred home.

In vain : — the song that Sappho gave,
  In dying, to the mournful sea,
Not muterslept beneath the wave
  Than this within my memory.

At length, one morning, as I lay
  In that half-waking mood when dreams
Unwillingly at last gave way
  To the full truth of daylight's beams,

A face — the very face, methought,
  From which had breathed, as from a
    shrine
Of song and soul, the notes I sought —
  Came with its music close to mine;

And sung the long-lost measure o'er, —
  Each note and word, with every tone
And look, that lent it life before, —
  All perfect, all again my own!

Like parted souls, when, mid the Blest
  They meet again, each widowed sound
Thro' memory's realm had winged in
    quest
  Of its sweet mate, till all were found.

Nor even in waking did the clew,
  Thus strangely caught, escape again ;
For never lark its matins knew
  So well as now I knew this strain.

And oft when memory's wondrous spell
  Is talked of in our tranquil bower,
I sing this lady's song, and tell
  The vision of that morning hour.

SONG.

WHERE is the heart that would not give
  Years of drowsy days and nights,
One little hour, like this, to live —
  Full, to the brim, of life's delights?

Look, look around,
  This fairy ground,
With love-lights glittering o'er;
  While cups that shine
  With freight divine
Go coasting round its shore.

Hope is the dupe of future hours,
  Memory lives in those gone by;
Neither can see the moment's flowers
  Springing up fresh beneath the eye,
    Wouldst thou, or thou,
    Forego what 's *now*,
For all that Hope may say?
    No — Joy's reply,
    From every eye,
Is, "Live we while we may."

SONG OF THE POCO–CURANTE SOCIETY.

haud curat Hippoclides.
ERASM. *Adag.*

To those we love we've drank to-night;
  But now attend and stare not,
While I the ampler list recite
  Of those for whom WE CARE NOT.

For royal men, howe'er they frown,
  If on their fronts they bear not
That noblest gem that decks a crown,
  The People's Love — WE CARE NOT.

For slavish men who bend beneath
  A despot yoke, yet dare not
Pronounce the will whose very breath
  Would rend its links — WE CARE NOT.

For priestly men who covet sway
  And wealth, tho' they declare not;
Who point, like finger-posts, the way
  They never go — WE CARE NOT.

For martial men who on their sword,
  Howe'er it conquers, wear not
The pledges of a soldier's word,
  Redeemed and pure — WE CARE NOT.

For legal men who plead for wrong,
  And, tho' to lies they swear not,
Are hardly better than the throng
  Of those who *do* — WE CARE NOT.

For courtly men who feed upon
   The land, like grubs, and spare not
The smallest leaf where they can sun
   Their crawling limbs — WE CARE NOT.

For wealthy men who keep their mines
   In darkness hid, and share not
The paltry ore with him who pines
   In honest want — WE CARE NOT.

For prudent men who hold the power
   Of Love aloof, and bare not
Their hearts in any guardless hour
   To Beauty's shaft — WE CARE NOT.

For all, in short, on land or sea,
   In camp or court, who *are* not,
Who never *were*, or e'er *will* be
   Good men and true — WE CARE NOT.

ANNE BOLEYN.

TRANSLATION FROM THE METRICAL
"*Histoire d'Anne Boleyn.*"

"*S'elle estoit belle et de taille élégante,*
Estoit des yeulx encor plus attirante,
Lesquelz sçavoit bien conduyre à propos
En les tenant quelquesfoys en repos ;
Aucune foys envoyant en message
Porter du cueur le secret tesmoignage."

MUCH as her form seduced the sight,
   Her eyes could even more surely woo;
And when and how to shoot their light
   Into men's hearts full well she knew.
For sometimes in repose she hid
   Their rays beneath a downcast lid;
And then again, with wakening air,
   Would send their sunny glances out,
Like heralds of delight, to bear
   Her heart's sweet messages about.

THE DREAM OF THE TWO SISTERS.

FROM DANTE.

Nell ora, credo, che dell' oriente
  Prima raggiò nel monte Citerea,
Che di fuoco d' amor par sempre ardente,
   Giovane e bella in sogno mi parea
   Donna vedere andar per una landa
  Cogliendo fiori ; e cantando dicea : —

Sappia qualunque 'l mio nome dimanda,
  Ch' io mi son Lia, e vo movendo 'ntorno
  Le belle mani a farmi una ghirlanda —
Per piacermi allo specchio qui m' adorno ;
  Ma mia suora Rachel mai non si smaga
  Dal suo ammiraglio, e siede tutto il giorno.

Ell' è de' suoi begli occhi veder vaga,
  Com' io dell' adornarmi con le mani ;
  Lei lo vedere e me l' ovrare appaga.
        DANTE, *Purg.* canto xxvii.

'T WAS eve's soft hour, and bright, above,
   The star of Beauty beamed,
While lulled by light so full of love,
   In slumber thus I dreamed —
Methought, at that sweet hour,
   A nymph came o'er the lea,
Who, gathering many a flower,
   Thus said and sung to me:
"Should any ask what Leila loves,
   " Say thou, To wreathe her hair
" With flowerets culled from glens and
     groves,
   " Is Leila's only care.

" While thus in quest of flowerets rare,
   " O'er hill and dale I roam,
" My sister, Rachel, far more fair,
   " Sits lone and mute at home.
" Before her glass untiring,
   " With thoughts that never stray,
" Her own bright eyes admiring,
   " She sits the live-long day;
" While I ! — oh, seldom even a look
   " Of self salutes my eye; —
" My only glass, the limpid brook,
   " That shines and passes by."

SOVEREIGN WOMAN.

A BALLAD.

THE dance was o'er, yet still in dreams
   That fairy scene went on;
Like clouds still flusht with daylight
     gleams
   Tho' day itself is gone.
And gracefully to music's sound,
   The same bright nymphs went gliding
     round;
While thou, the Queen of all, wert there—
The Fairest still, where all were fair.

The dream then changed — in halls of
     state,
   I saw thee high enthroned;
While, ranged around, the wise, the great
   In there their mistress owned:
And still the same, thy gentle sway
O'er willing subjects won its way —
Till all confest the Right Divine
To rule o'er man was only thine !

But, lo, the scene now changed again —
    And borne on plumed steed,
I saw thee o'er the battle-plain
    Our land's defenders lead:
And stronger in thy beauty's charms,
Than man, with countless hosts in arms,
Thy voice, like music, cheered the Free,
Thy very smile was victory!

Nor reign such queens on thrones alone —
    In cot and court the same,
Wherever woman's smile is known,
    Victoria 's still her name.
For tho' she almost blush to reign,
Tho' Love's own flowerets wreath the chain,
Disguise our bondage as we will,
'T is woman, woman, rules us still.

COME, PLAY ME THAT SIMPLE AIR AGAIN.

A BALLAD.

COME, play me that simple air again,
    I used so to love, in life's young day,
And bring, if thou canst, the dreams that then
    Were wakened by that sweet lay.
The tender gloom its strain
    Shed o'er the heart and brow,
Grief's shadow without its pain —
    Say where, where is it now?
But play me the well-known air once more,
    For thoughts of youth still haunt its strain,
Like dreams of some far, fairy shore
    We never shall see again.

Sweet air, how every note brings back
    Some sunny hope, some day-dream bright,
That, shining o'er life's early track,
    Filled even its tears with light.
The new-found life that came
    With love's first echoed vow;—
The fear, the bliss, the shame —
    Ah — where, where are they now?
But, still the same loved notes prolong,
    For sweet 't were thus, to that old lay,
In dreams of youth and love and song,
    To breathe life's hour away.

POEMS FROM THE EPICUREAN.

(1827.)

THE VALLEY OF THE NILE.

FAR as the sight can reach, beneath as
    clear
And blue a heaven as ever blest this
    sphere,
Gardens and pillared streets and por-
    phyry domes
And high-built temples, fit to be the
    homes
Of mighty gods, and pyramids whose
    hour
Outlasts all time, above the waters tower !

Then, too, the scenes of pomp and joy
    that make
One theatre of this vast peopled lake,
Where all that Love, Religion, Commerce
    gives
Of life and motion, ever moves and lives.
Here, up the steps of temples, from the
    wave
Ascending, in procession slow and grave,
Priests in white garments go, with sacred
    wands
And silver cymbals gleaming in their
    hands :
While there, rich barks — fresh from
    those sunny tracts
Far off, beyond the sounding cataracts —
Glide with their precious lading to the sea,
Plumes of bright birds, rhinoceros' ivory,
Gems from the isle of Meroë, and those
    grains
Of gold, washed down by Abyssinian
    rains.

Here, where the waters wind into a bay
Shadowy and cool, some pilgrims on
    their way
To Saïs or Bubastus, among beds
Of lotos flowers that close above their
    heads,

Push their light barks, and hid as in a
    bower
Sing, talk, or sleep away the sultry
    hour,
While haply, not far off, beneath a bank
Of blossoming acacias, many a prank
Is played in the cool current by a train
Of laughing nymphs, lovely as she whose
    chain
Around two conquerors of the world
    was cast ;
But, for a third too feeble, broke at last.

SONG OF THE TWO CUPBEARERS.

FIRST CUPBEARER.

DRINK of this cup — Osiris sips
    The same in his halls below ;
And the same he gives, to cool the
    lips
    Of the dead, who downward go.

Drink of this cup — the water within
    Is fresh from Lethe's stream ;
'T will make the past, with all its sin,
    And all its pain and sorrows, seem
    Like a long forgotten dream !

The pleasure, whose charms
    Are steeped in woe ;
The knowledge, that harms
    The soul to know ;

The hope, that bright
    As the lake of the waste,
Allures the sight
    And mocks the taste ;

The love, that binds
    Its innocent wreath,
Where the serpent winds
    In venom beneath ! —

All that of evil or false, by thee
　Hath ever been known or seen,
Shalt melt away in this cup, and be
　Forgot as it never had been!

SECOND CUPBEARER.

DRINK of this cup — when Isis led
　Her boy of old to the beaming sky,
She mingled a draught divine and said, —
　" Drink of this cup, thou 'lt never
　　die ! "

Thus do I say and sing to thee,
　Heir of that boundless heaven on high,
Though frail and fallen and lost thou be,
　" Drink of this cup, thou 'lt never
　　die ! "

And Memory, too, with her dreams shall
　　come,
　Dreams of a former, happier day,
When heaven was still the spirit's home,
　And her wings had not yet fallen away.

Glimpses of glory ne'er forgot,
　That tell, like gleams on a sunset sea,
What once hath been, what now is not,
　But oh ! what again shall brightly be ! "

SONG OF THE NUBIAN GIRL.

O ABYSSINIAN tree,
　We pray, we pray to thee;
By the glow of thy golden fruit
　And the violet hue of thy flower,
　And the greeting mute
　Of thy boughs' salute
To the stranger who seeks thy bow

O Abyssinian tree !
　How the traveller blesses thee
When the light no moon allows,
　And the sunset hour is near,
　And thou bend'st thy boughs
　To kiss his brows,
Saying, " Come, rest thee here."
　O Abyssinian tree !
Thus bow thy head to me !

THE SUMMER FÊTE.

TO THE HONORABLE MRS. NORTON.

For the groundwork of the following Poem I am indebted to a memorable Fête, given some years since, at Boyle Farm, the seat of the late Lord Henry Fitzgerald. In commemoration of that evening — of which the lady to whom these pages are inscribed was, I well recollect, one of the most distinguished ornaments — I was induced at the time to write some verses, which were afterwards, however, thrown aside unfinished, on my discovering that the same task had been undertaken by a noble poet,[1] whose playful and happy *jeu-d'esprit* on the subject has since been published. It was but lately, that, on finding the fragments of my own sketch among my papers, I thought of founding on them such a description of an imaginary Fête as might furnish me with situations for the introduction of music.

Such is the origin and object of the following Poem, and to Mrs. Norton it is, with every feeling of admiration and regard, inscribed by her father's warmly attached friend,

THOMAS MOORE.

Sloperton Cottage,
November 1831.

1 Lord Francis Egerton.

THE SUMMER FETE.

"Where are ye now, ye summer days,
"That once inspired the poet's lays?
"Blest time! ere England's nymphs and
    swains,
    "For lack of sunbeams, took to coals —
"Summers of light, undimmed by rains,
"Whose only mocking trace remains
    "In watering-pots and parasols."

Thus spoke a young Patrician maid,
    As, on the morning of that Fête
    Which bards unborn shall celebrate,
She backward drew her curtain's shade,
And, closing one half-dazzled eye,
Peeped with the other at the sky —
The important sky, whose light or gloom
Was to decide, this day, the doom
Of some few hundred beauties, wits,
Blues, Dandies, Swains, and Exquisites.

Faint were her hopes; for June had now
    Set in with all his usual rigor!
Young Zephyr yet scarce knowing how
To nurse a bud, or fan a bough,
    But Eurus in perpetual vigor;
And, such the biting summer air,
That she, the nymph now nestling there —
Snug as her own bright gems recline
At night within their cotton shrine —
Had more than once been caught of late
Kneeling before her blazing grate,
Like a young worshipper of fire,
    With hands uplifted to the flame,
Whose glow as if to woo them nigher,
    Thro' the white fingers flushing came.

But oh! the light, the unhoped-for light,
    That now illumed this morning's
        heaven!
Up sprung Iänthe at the sight,
    Tho' — hark! — the clocks but strike
        eleven,
And rarely did the nymph surprise
Mankind so early with her eyes.

Who now will say that England's sun
    (Like England's self, these spendthrift
        days)
His stock of wealth hath near outrun,
    And must retrench his golden rays —
Pay for the pride of sunbeams past,
And to mere moonshine come at last?

"Calumnious thought!" Iänthe cries,
    While coming mirth lit up each glance,
And, prescient of the ball, her eyes
    Already had begun to dance:
For brighter sun than that which now
    Sparkled o'er London's spires and
        towers,
Had never bent from heaven his brow
    To kiss Firenze's City of Flowers.

What must it be — if thus so fair
Mid the smoked groves of Grosvenor
    Square —
What must it be where Thames is seen
Gliding between his banks of green,
While rival villas, on each side,
Peep from their bowers to woo his tide,
And, like a Turk between two rows
Of Harem beauties, on he goes —
A lover, loved for even the grace
With which he slides from their embrace.

In one of those enchanted domes,
    One, the most flowery, cool, and bright
Of all by which that river roams,
    The Fête is to be held to-night —
That Fête already linked to fame,
    Whose cards, in many a fair one's sight
(When looked for long, at last they came,)
    Seemed circled with a fairy light; —
That Fête to which the cull, the flower
Of England's beauty, rank and power,
From the young spinster, just come *out*,
    To the old Premier, too long *in* —
From legs of far descended gout,
    To the last new-mustachioed chin —

320

All were convoked by Fashion's spells
To the small circle where she dwells,
Collecting nightly, to allure us,
  Live atoms, which, together hurled,
She, like another Epicurus,
  Sets dancing thus, and calls " the
    World."

Behold how busy in those bowers
(Like May-flies in and out of flowers,)
The countless menials swarming run,
To furnish forth ere set of sun
The banquet-table richly laid
Beneath yon awning's lengthened shade,
Where fruits shall tempt and wines entice,
  And Luxury's self, at Gunter's call,
Breathe from her summer-throne of ice
  A spirit of coolness over all.

And now the important hour drew nigh,
When, 'neath the flush of evening's sky,
The west-end " world " for mirth let
    loose,
And moved, as he of Syracuse [1]
Ne'er dreamt of moving worlds, by force
Of four-horse power, had all combined
Thro' Grosvenor Gate to speed their
    course,
  Leaving that portion of mankind,
Whom they call " Nobody," behind; —
No star for London's feasts to-day,
No moon of beauty, new this May,
To lend the night her crescent ray; —
Nothing, in short, for ear or eye,
But veteran belles and wits gone by,
The relics of a past beau-monde,
A world like Cuvier's, long dethroned!
Even Parliament this evening nods
Beneath the harangues of minor Gods,
  On half its usual opiate's share;
The great dispensers of repose,
The first-rate furnishers of prose
  Being all called to — prose elsewhere.

Soon as thro' Grosvenor's lordly square[2]—
  That last impregnable redoubt,
Where, guarded with Patrician care,
  Primeval Error still holds out —

Where never gleam of gas must dare
  'Gainst ancient Darkness to revolt,
Nor smooth Macadam hope to spare
  The dowagers one single jolt; —
Where, far too stately and sublime
To profit by the lights of time,
Let Intellect march how it will,
They stick to oil and watchmen still: —
Soon as thro' that illustrious square
  The first epistolary bell,
Sounding by fits upon the air,
  Of parting pennies rung the knell;
Warned by that tell-tale of the hours,
  And by the day-light's westering beam,
The young Iänthe, who, with flowers
  Half crowned, had sat in idle dream
Before her glass, scarce knowing where
Her fingers roved thro' that bright hair,
  While, all capriciously, she now
  Dislodged some curl from her white
    brow,
And now again replaced it there; —
As tho' her task was meant to b
One endless change of ministry —
A routing-up of Loves and Graces,
But to plant others in their places.

Meanwhile — what strain is that which
    floats
Thro' the small boudoir near — like notes
Of some young bird, its task repeating
For the next linnet music-meeting?
A voice it was, whose gentle sounds
Still kept a modest octave's bounds,
Nor yet had ventured to exalt
Its rash ambition to *B alt*,
That point towards which when ladies
    rise,
The wise man takes his hat and — flies.
Tones of a harp, too, gently played,
  Came with this youthful voice com-
    muning;
Tones true, for once, without the aid
  Of that inflictive process, tuning —
A process which must oft have given
  Poor Milton's ears a deadly wound;
So pleased, among the joys of Heaven,
He specifies " harps *ever* tuned." [3]
She who now sung this gentle strain
  Was our young nymph's still younger
    sister —

1 Archimedes.

2 I am not certain whether the Dowagers of
this Square have yet yielded to the innovations
of Gas and Police, but at the time when the above
lines were written they still obstinately persevered
in their old *régime*; and would not suffer themselves to be either well guarded or well lighted.

3 —— their golden harps they took —
  Harps ever tuned. *"Paradise Lost,"* book
iii.

Scarce ready yet for Fashion's train
  In their light legions to enlist her,
But counted on, as sure to bring
  Her force into the field next spring.

The song she thus, like Jubal's shell,
  Gave forth "so sweetly and so well,"
Was one in Morning Post much famed,
  From a *divine* collection, named,
  " Songs of the Toilet " — every Lay
Taking for subject of its Muse,
  Some branch of feminine array,
Some item, with full scope, to choose,
  From diamonds down to dancing shoes;
From the last hat that Herbault's hands
  Bequeathed to an admiring world,
Down to the latest flounce that stands
  Like Jacob's Ladder — or expands
  Far forth, tempestuously unfurled.

Speaking of one of these new Lays,
The Morning Post thus sweetly says:—
" Not all that breathes from Bishop's lyre,
  " That Barnett dreams, or Cooke con-
    ceives,
" Can match for sweetness, strength, or
    fire,
  " This fine Cantata upon Sleeves.
" The very notes themselves reveal
  " The cut of each new sleeve so well;
" A *flat* betrays the *Imbécilles*,[1]
  " Light fugues the flying lappets tell;
" While rich cathedral chords awake
" Our homage for the *Manches d'É-
    vêque.*"

'T was the first opening song — the Lay
Of all least deep in toilet-lore,
That the young nymph, to while away
The tiring-hour, thus warbled o'er:—

SONG.

ARRAY thee, love, array thee, love,
  In all thy best array thee;
The sun 's below — the moon 's above —
  And Night and Bliss obey thee.
Put on thee all that 's bright and rare,
  The zone, the wreath, the gem,
Not so much gracing charms so fair,
  As borrowing grace from them.

1 The name given to those large sleeves that
hang loosely.

Array thee, love, array thee, love,
  In all that 's bright array thee;
The sun 's below — the moon 's above —
  And Night and Bliss obey thee.

Put on the plumes thy lover gave,
  The plumes, that, proudly dancing,
Proclaim to all, where'er they wave,
  Victorious eyes advancing.
Bring forth the robe whose hue of heaven
  From thee derives such light,
That Iris would give all her seven
  To boast but *one* so bright.
Array thee, love, array thee, love, etc.

Now hie thee, love, now hie thee, love,
  Thro' Pleasure's circles hie thee,
And hearts, where'er thy footsteps move,
  Will beat when they come nigh thee.
Thy every word shall be a spell,
  Thy every look a ray,
And tracks of wondering eyes shall tell
  The glory of thy way!
Now hie thee, love, now hie thee, love,
  Thro' Pleasure's circles hie thee,
And hearts, where'er thy footsteps move,
  Shall beat when they come nigh thee.

───────

Now in his Palace of the West,
  Sinking to slumber, the bright Day,
Like a tired monarch fanned to rest,
  Mid the cool airs of Evening lay;
While round his couch's golden rim
  The gaudy clouds, like courtiers,
    crept —
Struggling each other's light to dim,
  And catch his last smile e'er he slept.
How gay, as o'er the gliding Thames
  The golden eve its lustre poured,
Shone out the high-born knights and
    dames
  Now grouped around that festal board;
A living mass of plumes and flowers,
  As tho' they 'd robbed both birds and
    bowers —
A peopled rainbow, swarming thro'
  With habitants of every hue;
While, as the sparkling juice of France
  High in the crystal brimmers flowed,
  Each sunset ray that mixt by chance
With the wine's sparkles, showed
  How sunbeams may be taught to dance.

If not in written form exprest,
'T was known at least to every guest,
That, tho' not bidden to parade
Their scenic powers in masquerade,
(A pastime little found to thrive
  In the bleak fog of England's skies,
Where wit 's the thing we best contrive,
  As masqueraders, to *disguise*,)
It yet was hoped — and well that hope
  Was answered by the young and gay —
That in the toilet's task to-day
Fancy should take her wildest scope; —
That the rapt milliner should be
Let loose thro' fields of poesy,
The tailor, in inventive trance,
  Up to the heights of Epic clamber,
And all the regions of Romance
  Be ransackt by the *femme de chambre*.

Accordingly, with gay Sultanas,
Rebeccas, Sapphos, Roxalanas —
Circassian slaves whom Love would pay
  Half his maternal realms to ransom; —
Young nuns, whose chief religion lay
  In looking most profanely handsome; —
Muses in muslin — pastoral maids
With hats from the *Arcade-ian* shades,
And fortune-tellers, rich, 't was plain,
As fortune-*hunters* formed their train.

With these and more such female groups,
Were mixt no less fantastic troops
Of male exhibiters — all willing
To look even more than usual killing; —
Beau tyrants, smock-faced braggadocios,
And brigands, charmingly ferocious; —
M. P.'s turned Turks, good Moslems then,
  Who, last night, voted for the Greeks;
And Friars, stanch No-Popery men,
  In close confab with Whig Caciques.

But where is she — the nymph whom late
  We left before her glass delaying,
Like Eve, when by the lake she sate,
  In the clear wave her charms surveying,
And saw in that first glassy mirror
The first fair face that lured to error.
"Where is she," ask'st thou? — watch
    all looks
As centring to one point they bear,
Like sun-flowers by the sides of brooks,
  Turned to the sun — and she is there.
Even in disguise, oh never doubt
By her own light you 'd track her out:

As when the moon, close shawled in fog,
Steals as she thinks, thro' heaven *incog.*,
Tho' hid herself, some sidelong ray,
At every step, detects her way.

But not in dark disguise to-night
Hath our young heroine veiled her
    light; —
For see, she walks the earth, Love's own,
  His wedded bride, by holiest vow
Pledged in Olympus, and made known
  To mortals by the type which now
Hangs glittering on her snowy brow,
That butterfly, mysterious trinket,
Which means the Soul (tho' few would
    think it),
And sparkling thus on brow so white,
Tells us we 've Psyche here to-night!

But hark! some song hath caught her
    ears —
  And, lo, how pleased, as tho' she 'd
    ne'er
Heard the Grand Opera of the Spheres,
  Her goddess-ship approves the air;
And to a mere terrestrial strain,
Inspired by naught but pink champagne,
  Her butterfly as gayly nods
As tho' she sate with all her train
  At some great Concert of the Gods,
With Phœbus, leader — Jove, director,
And half the audience drunk with nectar.

From the male group the carol came —
  A few gay youths whom round the
    board
The last-tried flask's superior fame
  Had lured to taste the tide it poured;
And one who from his youth and lyre
Seemed grandson to the Teian sire,
Thus gayly sung, while, to his song,
Replied in chorus the gay throng: —

SONG.

Some mortals there may be, so wise, or
    so fine,
  As in evenings like this no enjoyment
    to see;
But, as I 'm not particular — wit, love,
    and wine,
  Are for one night's amusement suffi-
    cient for me.

Nay — humble and strange as my tastes
    may appear —
  If driven to the worst, I could man-
    age, thank Heaven,
To put up with eyes such as beam round
    me here,
  And such wine as we 're sipping, six
    days out of seven.
So pledge me a bumper — your sages
    profound
  May be blest, if they will, on their
    own patent plan:
But as we are *not* sages, why — send the
    cup round —
  We must only be happy the best way
    we can.

A reward by some king was once offered,
    we 're told,
  To whoe'er could invent a new bliss
    for mankind;
But talk of *new* pleasures! — give me
    but the old,
  And I 'll leave your inventors all new
    ones they find.
Or should I, in quest of fresh realms of
    bliss,
  Set sail in the pinnace of Fancy some
    day,
Let the rich rosy sea I embark on be this,
  And such eyes as we 've here be the
    stars of my way!
In the mean time, a bumper — your An-
    gels, on high,
  May have pleasures unknown to life's
    limited span;
But, as we are *not* Angels, why — let
    the flask fly —
  We must only be happy *all* ways that
    we can.

Now nearly fled was sunset's light,
  Leaving but so much of its beam
As gave to objects, late so bright,
  The coloring of a shadowy dream;
And there was still where Day had set
  A flush that spoke him loath to die —
A last link of his glory yet,
  Binding together earth and sky.
Say, why is it that twilight best
Becomes even brows the loveliest?
That dimness with its softening Touch
  Can bring out grace unfelt before,

And charms we ne'er can see too much,
  When seen but half enchant the more?
Alas, it is that every joy
In fulness finds its worst alloy,
And half a bliss, but hoped or guessed,
Is sweeter than the whole possest; —
That Beauty, when least shone upon,
  A creature most ideal grows;
And there 's no light from moon or sun
  Like that Imagination throws; —
It is, alas, that Fancy shrinks
  Even from a bright reality,
And turning inly, feels and thinks
  Far heavenlier things than e'er will *be.*

Such was the effect of twilight's hour
  On the fair groups that, round and
    round,
From glade to grot, from bank to bower,
  Now wandered thro' this fairy ground;
And thus did Fancy — and champagne —
  Work on the sight their dazzling spells,
Till nymphs that looked at noon-day
    plain,
  Now brightened in the gloom to
    belles;
And the brief interval of time,
  'Twixt after dinner and before,
To dowagers brought back their prime,
  And shed a halo round two-score.

Meanwhile, new pastimes for the eye,
  The ear, the fancy, quick succeed;
And now along the waters fly
  Light gondoles, of Venetian breed,
With knights and dames who, calm re-
    clined,
  Lisp out love-sonnets as they glide —
Astonishing old Thames to find
  Such doings on his moral tide.

So bright was still that tranquil river,
With the last shaft from Daylight's quiver.
That many a group in turn were seen
Embarking on its wave serene;
And, 'mong the rest, in chorus gay,
  A band of mariners, from the isles
  Of sunny Greece, all song and smiles,
As smooth they floated, to the play
Of their oar's cadence, sung this lay: —

TRIO.

OUR home is on the sea, boy,
  Our home is on the sea;

When Nature gave
The ocean-wave,
She markt it for the Free.
Whatever storms befall, boy,
Whatever storms befall,
The island bark
Is Freedom's ark,
And floats her safe thro' all.

Behold yon sea of isles, boy,
Behold yon sea of isles,
Where every shore
Is sparkling o'er
With Beauty's richest smiles.
For us hath Freedom claimed, boy,
For us hath Freedom claimed
Those ocean-nests
Where Valor rests
His eagle wing untamed.

And shall the Moslem dare, boy,
And shall the Moslem dare,
While Grecian hand
Can wield a brand,
To plant his Crescent there?
No — by our fathers, no, boy,
No, by the Cross we show —
From Maina's rills
To Thracia's hills
All Greece re-echoes "No!"

Like pleasant thoughts that o'er the mind
A minute come and go again,
Even so by snatches in the wind,
Was caught and lost that choral strain,
Now full, now faint upon the ear,
As the bark floated far or near.
At length when, lost, the closing note
Had down the waters died along,
Forth from another fairy boat,
Freighted with music, came this song: —

SONG.

Smoothly flowing thro' verdant vales,
Gentle river, thy current runs,
Sheltered safe from winter gales,
Shaded cool from summer suns.
Thus our Youth's sweet moments glide,
Fenced with flowery shelter round;
No rude tempest wakes the tide,
All its path is fairy ground.

But, fair river, the day will come,
When, wooed by whispering groves in
vain,
Thou 'lt leave those banks, thy shaded
home,
To mingle with the stormy main.
And thou, sweet Youth, too soon wilt
pass
Into the world's unsheltered sea,
Where, once thy wave hath mixt, alas,
All hope of peace is lost for thee.

Next turn we to the gay saloon,
Resplendent as a summer noon,
Where, 'neath a pendent wreath of
lights,
A Zodiac of flowers and tapers —
(Such as in Russian ball-rooms sheds
Its glory o'er young dancers' heads) —
Quadrille performs her mazy rites,
And reigns supreme o'er slides and
capers; —
Working to death each opera strain,
As, with a foot that ne'er reposes,
She jigs thro' sacred and profane,
From "Maid and Magpie" up to
"Mosès;" [1] —
Wearing out tunes as fast as shoes,
Till fagged Rossini scarce respires;
Till Meyerbeer for mercy sues,
And Weber at her feet expires.

And now the set hath ceased — the
bows
Of fiddlers taste a brief repose,
While light along the painted floor,
Arm within arm, the couples stray,
Talking their stock of nothings o'er,
Till — nothing 's left at last to say.
When, lo! — most opportunely sent —
Two Exquisites, a he and she,
Just brought from Dandyland, and meant
For Fashion's grand Menagerie,
Entered the room — and scarce were
there
When all flocked round them, glad to
stare
At *any* monsters, *any* where.

[1] In England the *partition* of this opera of
Rossini was transferred to the story of Peter the
Hermit; by which means the indecorum of giving
such names as "Moÿse," "Pharaon," etc., to
the dancers selected from it (as was done in
Paris), has been avoided.

Some thought them perfect, to their
    tastes;
While others hinted that the waists
(That in particular of the *he* thing)
Left far too ample room for breathing:
Whereas, to meet these critics' wishes,
    The isthmus there should be so small,
That Exquisites, at last, like fishes,
    Must manage not to breathe at all.
The female (these same critics said),
    Tho' orthodox from toe to chin,
Yet lacked that spacious width of head
    To hat of toadstool much akin —
That build of bonnet, whose extent
Should, like a doctrine of dissent,
    Puzzle church-doors to let it in.

However — sad as 't was, no doubt,
That nymph so smart should go about,
With head unconscious of the place
It *ought* to fill in Infinite Space —
Yet all allowed that, of *her kind*,
A prettier show 't was hard to find;
While of that doubtful genus, " dressy
    men,"
The male was thought a first-rate speci-
    men.
Such *Savans*, too, as wisht to trace
The manners, habits, of this race —
To know what rank (if rank at all)
'Mong reasoning things to them should
    fall —
What sort of notions heaven imparts
To high-built heads and tight-laced
    hearts,
And how far Soul, which, Plato says,
Abhors restraint, can act in stays —
Might now, if gifted with discerning,
Find opportunities of learning:
As these two creatures — from their pout
And frown, 't was plain — had just fallen
    out;
And all their little thoughts, of course,
Were stirring in full fret and force; —
Like mites, thro' microscope espied,
A world of nothings magnified.

But mild the vent such beings seek,
The tempest of their souls to speak:
As Opera swains to fiddles sigh,
To fiddles fight, to fiddles die,
Even so this tender couple set
Their well-bred woes to a Duet.

WALTZ DUET.[1]

HE.

LONG as I waltzed with only thee,
    Each blissful Wednesday that went by,
Nor stylish Stultz, nor neat Nugee
    Adorned a youth so blest as I.
        Oh! ah! ah! oh!
        Those happy days are gone —
            heighho!

SHE.

Long as with thee I skimmed the ground,
    Nor yet was scorned for Lady Jane,
No blither nymph tetotumed round
    To Collinet's immortal strain.
        Oh! ah! etc.
        Those happy days are gone —
            heighho!

HE.

With Lady Jane now whirled about,
    I know no bounds of time or breath;
And, should the charmer's head hold
    out,
    My heart and heels are hers till death.
        Oh! ah! etc.
        Still round and round thro' life
            we 'll go.

SHE.

To Lord Fitznoodle's eldest son,
    A youth renowned for waistcoats
        smart,
I now have given (excuse the pun)
    A vested interest in my heart.
        Oh! ah! etc.
        Still round and round with him I 'll
            go.

HE.

What if, by fond remembrance led
    Again to wear our mutual chain,
For me thou cut'st Fitznoodle dead,
    And I *levant* from Lady Jane.
        Oh! ah! etc.
        Still round and round again we 'll
            go.

1 It is hardly necessary to remind the reader
that this Duet is a parody of the often-translated
and parodied ode of Horace, "*donec gratus eram
tibi*," etc.

SHE.

Tho' he the Noodle honors give,
  And thine, dear youth, are not so high,
With thee in endless waltz I 'd live,
  With thee, to Weber's Stop-Waltz,
    die!
    Oh! ah! etc.
    Thus round and round thro' life
  we 'll go.
                [*Exeunt waltzing.*

While thus, like motes that dance away
Existence in a summer ray,
These gay things, born but to quadrille,
The circle of their doom fulfil —
(That dancing doom whose law decrees
  That they should live on the alert
    toe
A life of ups-and-downs, like keys
  Of Broadwood's in a long con-
    certo: —)
While thus the fiddle's spell, *within*,
  Calls up its realm of restless sprites,
Without, as if some Mandarin
  Were holding there his Feast of
    Lights,
Lamps of all hues, from walks and
    bowers,
Broke on the eye, like kindling flowers,
Till, budding into light, each tree
Bore its full fruit of brilliancy.

Here shone a garden — lamps all o'er,
  As tho' the Spirits of the Air
Had taken it in their heads to pour
  A shower of summer meteors there; —
While here a lighted shrubbery led
To a small lake that sleeping lay,
Cradled in foliage, but, o'er-head,
  Open to heaven's sweet breath and
    ray;
While round its rim there burning stood
  Lamps, with young flowers beside them
    bedded,
That shrunk from such warm neighbor-
    hood,
And, looking bashful in the flood,
  Blushed to behold themselves so wed-
    ded.

Hither, to this embowered retreat,
Fit but for nights so still and sweet;

Nights, such as Eden's calm recall
In its first lonely hour, when all
  So silent is, below, on high,
  That if a star falls down the sky,
You almost think you hear it fall —
Hither, to this recess, a few,
  To shun the dancers' wildering noise,
And give an hour, ere night-time flew,
  To music's more ethereal joys,
Came with their voices — ready all
As Echo waiting for a call —
In hymn or ballad, dirge or glee,
To weave their mingling ministrelsy.
And first a dark-eyed nymph, arrayed—
Like her whom Art hath deathless made,
Bright Mona Lisa [1] — with that braid
Of hair across the brow, and one
Small gem that in the centre shone —
With face, too, in its form resembling
  Da Vinci's Beauties — the dark eyes,
Now lucid as thro' crystal trembling,
  Now soft as if suffused with sighs —
Her lute that hung beside her took,
And, bending o'er it with shy look,
More beautiful, in shadow thus,
Than when with life most luminous,
Past her light finger o'er the chords,
And sung to them these mournful
    words: —

SONG.

BRING hither, bring thy lute, while day
    is dying —
  Here will I lay me and list to thy song;
Should tones of other days mix with its
    sighing,
  Tones of a light heart, now banisht
    so long,
Chase them away — they bring but pain,
And let thy theme be woe again.

Sing on, thou mournful lute — day is fast
    going,
  Soon will its light from thy chords die
    away;
One little gleam in the west is still glow-
    ing,
  When that hath vanisht, farewell to
    thy lay.
Mark, how it fades! — see, it is fled!
Now, sweet lute, be thou, too, dead.

1 The celebrated portrait by Leonardo da
Vinci, which he is said to have occupied four
years in painting. — *Vasari*, vol. vii.

The group that late in garb of Greeks
　　Sung their light chorus o'er the tide —
Forms, such as up the wooded creeks
　　Of Helle's shore at noon-day glide,
Or nightly on her glistening sea,
Woo the bright waves with melody —
Now linked their triple league again
Of voices sweet, and sung a strain,
Such as, had Sappho's tuneful ear
　　But caught it, on the fatal steep,
She would have paused, entranced, to
　　hear,
　　And for that day deferred her leap.

SONG AND TRIO.

On one of those sweet nights that oft
　　Their lustre o'er the Ægean fling,
Beneath my casement, low and soft,
　　I heard a Lesbian lover sing;
And, listening both with ear and thought,
These sounds upon the night-breeze
　　caught —
　　" Oh, happy as the gods is he,
　　" Who gazes at this hour on thee ! "

The song was one by Sappho sung,
　　In the first love-dreams of her lyre,
When words of passion from her tongue
　　Fell like a shower of living fire.
And still, at close of every strain,
I heard these burning words again —
　　" Oh, happy as the gods is he,
　　" Who listens at this hour on thee ! "

Once more to Mona Lisa turned
　　Each asking eye — nor turned in vain;
Tho' the quick, transient blush that
　　burned
　　Bright o'er her cheek and died again,
Showed with what inly shame and fear
Was uttered what all loved to hear.
Yet not to sorrow's languid lay
　　Did she her lute-song now devote;
But thus, with voice that like a ray
　　Of southern sunshine seemed to float—
So rich with climate was each note —
Called up in every heart a dream
Of Italy with this soft theme: —

SONG.

Oh, where art thou dreaming,
　　On land, or on sea?
In my lattice is gleaming
　　The watch-light for thee;

And this fond heart is glowing
　　To welcome thee home,
And the night is fast going,
　　But thou art not come:
　　　　No, thou com'st not !

'T is the time when night-flowers
　　Should wake from their rest;
'T is the hour of all hours,
　　When the lute singeth best.
But the flowers are half sleeping
　　Till *thy* glance they see;
And the husht lute is keeping
　　Its music for thee.
　　　　Yet, thou com'st not !

Scarce had the last word left her lip,
When a light, boyish form, with trip
Fantastic, up the green walk came,
Prankt in gay vest to which the
　　flame
Of every lamp he past, or blue
Or green or crimson, lent its hue;
As tho' a live chameleon's skin
He had despoiled, to robe him in.
A zone he wore of clattering shells,
　　And from his lofty cap, where shone
A peacock's plume, there dangled bells
That rung as he came dancing on.
Close after him, a page — in dress
And shape, his miniature express —
An ample basket, filled with store
Of toys and trinkets, laughing bore;
Till, having reached this verdant seat,
He laid it at his master's feet,
Who, half in speech and half in song,
Chanted this invoice to the throng: —

SONG.

Who 'll buy? — 't is Folly's shop, who
　　'll buy? —
　　We 've toys to suit all ranks and ages;
Besides our usual fools' supply,
　　We 've lots of playthings, too, for
　　sages.
For reasoners here 's a juggler's cup
　　That fullest seems when nothing 's in
　　it;
And nine-pins set, like systems, up,
　　To be knocked down the following
　　minute.
　　　　Who 'll buy? — 't is Folly's shop,
　　　　who 'll buy?

Gay caps we here of foolscap make,
　For bards to wear in dog-day weather;
Or bards the bells alone may take,
　And leave to wits the cap and feather.
Tetotums we 've for patriots got,
　Who court the mob with antics humble;
Like theirs the patriot's dizzy lot,
　A glorious spin, and then — a tumble.
　　　　　　　Who 'll buy, etc.

Here, wealthy misers to inter,
　We 've shrouds of neat post-obit paper;
While, for their heirs, we 've *quick*silver,
　That, fast as they can wish, will caper.
For aldermen we 've dials true,
　That tell no hour but that of dinner;
For courtly parsons sermons new,
　That suit alike both saint and sinner.
　　　　　　　Who 'll buy, etc.

No time we 've now to name our terms,
　But, whatsoe'er the whims that seize
　　you,
This oldest of all mortal firms,
　Folly and Co., will try to please you.
Or, should you wish a darker hue
　Of goods than *we* can recommend you,
Why then (as we with lawyers do)
　To Knavery's shop next door we 'll send
　　you.
　　　　　　　Who 'll buy, etc.

While thus the blissful moments rolled,
　Moments of rare and fleeting light,
That show themselves, like grains of gold
　In the mine's refuse, few and bright;
Behold where, opening far away,
　The long Conservatory's range,
Stript of the flowers it wore all day,
　But gaining lovelier in exchange,
Presents, on Dresden's costliest ware,
A supper such as Gods might share.

Ah much-loved Supper! — blithe repast
Of other times, now dwindling fast,
Since Dinner far into the night
Advanced the march of appetite;
Deployed his never-ending forces
Of various vintage and three courses,
And, like those Goths who played the
　dickens
With Rome and all her sacred chickens,
Put Supper and her fowls so white,
Legs, wings, and drumsticks, all to flight.

Now waked once more by wine — whose
　tide
Is the true Hippocrene, where glide
The Muse's swans with happiest wing,
Dipping their bills before they sing —
The minstrels of the table greet
The listening ear with descant sweet: —

SONG AND TRIO.
THE LEVÉE AND COUCHÉE.

CALL the Loves around,
　Let the whispering sound
Of their wings be heard alone,
　Till soft to rest
　My Lady blest
At this bright hour hath gone.
　Let Fancy's beams
　Play o'er her dreams,
Till, touched with light all through,
　Her spirit be
　Like a summer sea,
Shining and slumbering too.
　And, while thus husht she lies,
　Let the whispered chorus rise —
" Good evening, good evening, to our
　　Lady's bright eyes."

　But the day-beam breaks,
　See, our Lady wakes!
Call the Loves around once more,
　Like stars that wait
　At Morning's gate,
Her first steps to adore.
　Let the veil of night
　From her dawning sight
All gently pass away,
　Like mists that flee
　From a summer sea,
Leaving it full of day.
　And, while her last dream flies,
　Let the whispered chorus rise —
" Good morning, good morning, to our
　　Lady's bright eyes."

SONG.

IF to see thee be to love thee,
　If to love thee be to prize
Naught of earth or heaven above thee,
　Nor to live but for those eyes:
If such love to mortal given,
Be wrong to earth, be wrong to heaven,
'T is not for thee the fault to blame,
For from those eyes the madness came.

Forgive but thou the crime of loving,
    In this heart more pride 't will raise
To be thus wrong with thee approving,
    Than right with all a world to praise!

But say, while light these songs resound,
What means that buzz of whispering
        round,
From lip to lip — as if the Power
    Of Mystery, in this gay hour,
Had thrown some secret (as we fling
Nuts among children) to that ring
Of rosy, restless lips, to be
Thus scrambled for so wantonly?
And, mark ye, still as each reveals
The mystic news, her hearer steals
A look towards yon enchanted chair,
    Where, like the Lady of the Masque,
A nymph, as exquisitely fair
    As Love himself for bride could ask,
Sits blushing deep, as if aware
Of the winged secret circling there.
Who is this nymph? and what, oh Muse,
    What, in the name of all odd things
That woman's restless brain pursues,
    What mean these mystic whisperings?

Thus runs the tale: — yon blushing maid,
Who sits in beauty's light arrayed,
While o'er her leans a tall young Dervise,
(Who from her eyes, as all observe, is
Learning by heart the Marriage Service,)
Is the bright heroine of our song, —
The Love-wed Psyche, whom so long
We 've missed among this mortal train,
We thought her winged to heaven again.

But no — earth still demands her smile;
Her friends, the Gods, must wait awhile.
And if, for maid of heavenly birth,
    A young Duke's proffered heart and
        hand
Be things worth waiting for on earth,
    Both are, this hour, at her command.
To-night, in yonder half-lit shade,
    For love concerns expressly meant,

The fond proposal first was made,
    And love and silence blusht consent.
Parents and friends (all here, as Jews,
Enchanters, house-maids, Turks, Hin-
        doos,)
Have heard, approved, and blest the tie;
And now, hadst thou a poet's eye,
Thou might'st behold, in the air, above
That brilliant brow, triumphant Love,
Holding, as if to drop it down
Gently upon her curls, a crown
Of Ducal shape — but, oh, such gems!
Pilfered from Peri diadems,
And set in gold like that which shines
To deck the Fairy of the Mines:
In short, a crown all glorious — such as
Love orders when he makes a Duchess.

But see, 't is morn in heaven; the Sun
Up in the bright orient hath begun
To canter his immortal team;
    And, tho' not yet arrived in sight,
His leaders' nostrils send a steam
    Of radiance forth, so rosy bright
As makes their onward path all light.
What 's to be done? if Sol will be
So deuced early, so must we;
And when the day thus shines outright,
Even dearest friends must bid good night.
So, farewell, scene of mirth and mask-
        ing,
    Now almost a by-gone tale;
Beauties, late in lamp-light basking,
    Now, by daylight, dim and pale;
Harpers, yawning o'er your harps,
Scarcely knowing flats from sharps;
Mothers who, while bored you keep
Time by nodding, nod to sleep;
Heads of hair, that stood last night
    Crêpé, crispy, and upright,
But have now, alas, one sees, a
Leaning like the tower of Pisa;
Fare ye well — thus sinks away
    All that 's mighty, all that 's bright;
Tyre and Sidon had their day,
    And even a Ball — has but its night!

EVENINGS IN GREECE.

In thus connecting together a series of Songs by a thread of poetical narrative, my chief object has been to combine Recitation with Music, so as to enable a greater number of persons to join in the performance, by enlisting as readers those who may not feel willing or competent to take a part as singers.

The Island of Zea where the scene is laid was called by the ancients Ceos, and was the birthplace of Simonides, Bacchylides, and other eminent persons. An account of its present state may be found in the Travels of Dr. Clarke, who says, that "it appeared to him to be the best cultivated of any of the Grecian Isles."— Vol. vi. p. 174.

T. M.

EVENINGS IN GREECE.

FIRST EVENING.

"THE sky is bright — the breeze is fair,
  "And the mainsail flowing, full and
  free —
"Our farewell word is woman's prayer,
  "And the hope before us — Liberty!
    "Farewell, farewell.
  "To Greece we give our shining
  blades,
  "And our hearts to you, young Zean
  Maids!

"The moon is in the heavens above,
  "And the wind is on the foaming
  sea —
"Thus shines the star of woman's love
  "On the glorious strife of Liberty!
    "Farewell, farewell.
  "To Greece we give our shining
  blades,
  "And our hearts to you, young Zean
  Maids!"

Thus sung they from the bark, that
  now
Turned to the sea its gallant prow,
Bearing within it hearts as brave,
As e'er sought Freedom o'er the wave;
And leaving on that islet's shore,
  Where still the farewell beacons burn,
Friends that shall many a day look o'er
The long, dim sea for their return.

Virgin of Heaven! speed their way —
  Oh, speed their way, — the chosen
  flower,
Of Zea's youth, the hope and stay
  Of parents in their wintry hour,
The love of maidens and the pride
Of the young, happy, blushing bride,
Whose nuptial wreath has not yet died —

All, all are in that precious bark,
  Which now, alas! no more is seen —
Tho' every eye still turns to mark
  The moonlight spot where it had been.

Vainly you look, ye maidens, sires,
  And mothers, your beloved are gone!—
Now may you quench those signal fires,
  Whose light they long looked back
  upon
From their dark deck — watching the
  flame
  As fast it faded from their view,
With thoughts, that, but for manly shame,
  Had made them droop and weep like
  you.
Home to your chambers! home, and pray
For the bright coming of that day,
When, blest by heaven, the Cross shall
  sweep
The Crescent from the Ægean deep,
And your brave warriors, hastening back,
  Will bring such glories in their track,
As shall, for many an age to come,
Shed light around their name and home.

There is a Fount on Zea's isle,
Round which, in soft luxuriance, smile
All the sweet flowers, of every kind,
  On which the sun of Greece looks
  down,
  Pleased as a lover on the crown
His mistress for her brow hath twined,
When he beholds each floweret there,
Himself had wisht her most to wear;
Here bloomed the laurel-rose,[1] whose
  wreath
  Hangs radiant round the Cypriot
  shrines,

1 "*Nerium Oleander*. In Cyprus it retains
its ancient name, Rhododaphne, and the Cypriots

332

And here those bramble-flowers, that
  breathe
  Their odor into Zante's wines: [1] —
The splendid woodbine that, at eve,
  To grace their floral diadems,
The lovely maids of Patmos weave: [2] —
  And that fair plant whose tangled
    stems
  Shine like a Nereid's hair,[3] when
    spread,
  Dishevelled, o'er her azure bed; —
All these bright children of the clime,
  (Each at its own most genial time,
  The summer, or the year's sweet prime,)
  Like beautiful earth-stars, adorn
  The Valley where that Fount is born:
While round, to grace its cradle green,
Groups of Velani oaks are seen
Towering on every verdant height —
Tall, shadowy, in the evening light,
Like Genii set to watch the birth
Of some enchanted child of earth —
Fair oaks that over Zea's vales,
  Stand with their leafy pride unfurled;
While Commerce from her thousand
    sails
  Scatters their fruit throughout the
    world ! [4]

'T was here — as soon as prayer and
    sleep
(Those truest friends to all who weep)
Had lightened every heart, and made
Even sorrow wear a softer shade —
'T was here, in this secluded spot,
  Amid whose breathings calm and sweet
Grief might be soothed if not forgot,
  The Zean nymphs resolved to meet
Each evening now, by the same light
That saw their farewell tears that
    night;

adorn their churches with the flowers on feast-
days." —*Journal of Dr. Sibthorpe, Walpole's
Turkey.*

1 *Id.*

2 *Lonicera caprifolium,* used by the girls of
Patmos for garlands.

3 *Cuscuta europæa.* " From the twisting and
twining of the stems, it is compared by the Greeks
to the dishevelled hair of the Nereids." — *Walpole's Turkey.*

4 " The produce of the island in these acorns
alone amounts annually to fifteen thousand quin-
tals." — *Clarke's Travels.*

And try if sound of lute and song,
  If wandering mid the moonlight
    flowers
In various talk, could charm along
  With lighter step, the lingering hours,
Till tidings of that Bark should come,
Or Victory waft their warriors home !

When first they met — the wonted
    smile
Of greeting having gleamed awhile —
'T would touch even Moslem heart to see
The sadness that came suddenly
O'er their young brows, when they looked
    round
Upon that bright, enchanted ground;
And thought how many a time with those
  Who now were gone to the rude wars
They there had met at evening's close,
  And danced till morn outshone the
    stars !

But seldom long doth hang the eclipse
  Of sorrow o'er such youthful breasts —
The breath from her own blushing lips,
  That on the maiden's mirror rests,
Not swifter, lighter from the glass,
Than sadness from her brow doth pass.

Soon did they now, as round the Well
  They sat, beneath the rising moon —
And some with voice of awe would tell
Of midnight fays and nymphs who
    dwell
  In holy founts — while some would
    tune
Their idle lutes that now had lain
For days without a single strain; —
And others, from the rest apart,
With laugh that told the lightened heart,
Sat whispering in each other's ear
Secrets that all in turn would hear; —
Soon did they find this thoughtless play
So swiftly steal their griefs away,
  That many a nymph tho' pleased
    the while,
  Reproached her own forgetful smile,
And sighed to think she *could* be gay.

Among these maidens there was one
  Who to Leucadia [5] late had been —

5 Now Santa Maura — the island, from whose
cliffs Sappho leaped into the sea.

Had stood beneath the evening sun
  On its white towering cliffs and seen
The very spot where Sappho sung
Her swan-like music, ere she sprung
(Still holding, in that fearful leap,
By her loved lyre,) into the deep,
And dying quenched the fatal fire,
At once, of both her heart and lyre.

  Mutely they listened all — and well
Did the young travelled maiden tell
Of the dread height to which that steep
Beetles above the eddying deep [1] —
Of the lone sea-birds, wheeling round
The dizzy edge with mournful sound —
And of those scented lilies [2] found
Still blooming on that fearful place —
As if called up by Love to grace
The immortal spot o'er which the last
Bright footsteps of his martyr past!

  While fresh to every listener's thought
These legends of Leucadia brought
All that of Sappho's hapless flame
Is kept alive, still watcht by Fame —
The maiden, tuning her soft lute,
While all the rest stood round her,
    mute,
Thus sketched the languishment of soul,
That o'er the tender Lesbian stole;
And in a voice whose thrilling tone
Fancy might deem the Lesbian's own,
One of those fervid fragments gave,
  Which still, — like sparkles of Greek
    Fire,
Undying, even beneath the wave, —
  Burn on thro' Time and ne'er expire.

SONG.

As o'er her loom the Lesbian Maid
In love-sick languor hung her head,
Unknowing where her fingers strayed,
  She weeping turned away, and said,
" Oh, my sweet Mother — 't is in vain —
  " I cannot weave, as once I wove —

" So wildered is my heart and brain
  " With thinking of that youth I
    love ! " [3]

Again the web she tried to trace,
  But tears fell o'er each tangled thread;
While looking in her mother's face,
  Who watchful o'er her leaned, she
    said,
" Oh, my sweet Mother — 't is in vain —
  " I can not weave, as once I wove —
" So wildered is my heart and brain
  " With thinking of that youth I
    love ! "

A silence followed this sweet air,
  As each in tender musing stood,
Thinking, with lips that moved in
    prayer,
  Of Sappho and that fearful flood :
While some who ne'er till now had
    known
  How much their hearts resembled
    hers,
Felt as they made her griefs their own,
  That *they* too were Love's wor-
    shippers.

At length a murmur, all but mute,
So faint it was, came from the lute
Of a young melancholy maid,
Whose fingers, all uncertain played
From chord to chord, as if in chase
  Of some lost melody, some strain
Of other times, whose faded trace
  She sought among those chords again.
Slowly the half-forgotten theme
  (Tho' born in feelings ne'er forgot)
Came to her memory — as a beam
  Falls broken o'er some shaded spot ; —
And while her lute's sad symphony
  Filled up each sighing pause between;
And Love himself might weep to see
  What ruin comes where he hath
    been —
As withered still the grass is found
Where fays have danced their merry
    round —
Thus simply to the listening throng
She breathed her melancholy song : —

---

1 " The precipice, which is fearfully dizzy, is
about one hundred and fourteen feet from the
water, which is of a profound depth, as appears
from the dark blue color and the eddy that plays
round the pointed and projecting rocks." —
Goodisson's Ionian Isles.

2 See Mr. Goodisson's very interesting description of all these circumstances.

3 I have attempted, in these four lines, to
give some idea of that beautiful fragment of

SONG.

WEEPING for thee, my love, thro' the
    long day,
Lonely and wearily life wears away.
Weeping for thee, my love, thro' the
    long night —
No rest in darkness, no joy in light!
Naught left but Memory whose dreary
    tread
Sounds thro' this ruined heart, where all
    lies dead —
Wakening the echoes of joy long fled!

Of many a stanza, this alone
Had 'scaped oblivion — like the one
Stray fragment of a wreck which thrown
With the lost vessel's name ashore
Tells who they were that live no more.

When thus the heart is in a vein
Of tender thought, the simplest strain
Can touch it with peculiar power —
    As when the air is warm, the scent
Of the most wild and rustic flower
Can fill the whole rich element —
And in such moods the homeliest tone
That 's linked with feelings, once our
    own —
With friends or joys gone by — will be
Worth choirs of loftiest harmony!

But some there were among the group
Of damsels there too light of heart
To let their spirits longer droop,
Even under music's melting art;
And one upspringing with a bound
From a low bank of flowers, looked
    round
With eyes that tho' so full of light
Had still a trembling tear within;
And, while her fingers in swift flight
    Flew o'er a fairy mandolin,
Thus sung the song her lover late
    Had sung to her — the eve before
That joyous night, when as of yore
All Zea met to celebrate
    The Feast of May on the sea-shore.

Sappho, beginning γλυκεῖα μᾶτερ, which represents so truly (as Warton remarks) " the languor
and listlessness of a person deeply in love."

SONG.

WHEN the Balaika [1]
    Is heard o'er the sea,
I 'll dance the Romaika
    By moonlight with thee.
If waves then advancing
    Should steal on our play,
Thy white feet in dancing
    Shall chase them away.[2]
When the Balaika
    Is heard o'er the sea,
Thou 'lt dance the Romaika
    My own love, with me.

Then at the closing
    Of each merry lay,
How sweet 't is, reposing
    Beneath the night ray!
Or if declining
    The moon leave the skies,
We 'll talk by the shining
    Of each other's eyes.

Oh then how featly
    The dance we 'll renew,
Treading so fleetly
    Its light mazes thro': [3]
Till stars, looking o'er us
    From heaven's high bowers,
Would change their bright chorus
    For one dance of ours!
When the Balaika
    Is heard o'er the sea,
Thou 'lt dance the Romaika,
    My own love, with me.

1 This word is defrauded here, I suspect, of a
syllable; Dr. Clarke, if I recollect right, makes
it " Balalaika."

2 " I saw above thirty parties engaged in dancing the Romaika upon the sand; in some of these
groups, the girl who led them chased the retreating wave." — *Douglas on the Modern Greeks.*

3 " In dancing the Romaika [says Mr. Doug
las] they begin in slow and solemn step till they
have gained the time, but by degrees the air becomes more sprightly; the conductress of the
dance sometimes setting to her partner, sometimes
darting before the rest, and leading them through
the most rapid revolutions; sometimes crossing
under the hands, which are held up to let her
pass, and giving as much liveliness and intricacy
as she can to the figures, into which she conducts
her companions, while their business is to follow
her in all her movements, without breaking the
chain, or losing the measure."

How changingly for ever veers
The heart of youth 'twixt smiles and
tears !
Even as in April the light vane
Now points to sunshine, now to rain.
Instant this lively lay dispelled
The shadow from each blooming brow,
And Dancing, joyous Dancing, held
Full empire o'er each fancy now.

But say — *what* shall the measure be?
" Shall we the old Romaika tread,"
(Some eager asked) " as anciently
" 'T was by the maids of Delos led,
" When slow at first, then circling fast,
" As the gay spirits rose — at last,
" With hand in hand like links enlocked,
"Thro' the light air they seemed to
flit
" In labyrinthine maze, that mocked
" The dazzled eye that followed it? "
Some called aloud " the Fountain
Dance ! " —
While one young, dark-eyed Amazon,
Whose step was air-like and whose
glance
Flashed, like a sabre in the sun,
Sportively said, " Shame on these soft
" And languid strains we hear so oft.
" Daughters of Freedom ! have not we
" Learned from our lovers and our sires
" The Dance of Greece, while Greece
was free —
" That Dance, where neither flutes nor
lyres,
" But sword and shield clash on the ear
" A music tyrants quake to hear ? [1]
" Heroines of Zea, arm with me
" And dance the dance of Victory ! "

Thus saying, she, with playful grace,
Loosed the wide hat, that o'er her face
(From Anatolia [2] came the maid)
Hung shadowing each sunny charm;
And with a fair young armorer's aid,
Fixing it on her rounded arm,
A mimic shield with pride displayed;

Then, springing towards a grove that
spread
Its canopy of foliage near,
Plucked off a lance-like twig, and said,
" To arms, to arms ! " while o'er her
head
She waved the light branch, as a
spear.

Promptly the laughing maidens all
Obeyed their Chief's heroic call; —
Round the shield-arm of each was tied
Hat, turban, shawl, as chance might
be;
The grove, their verdant armory,
Falchion and lance [3] alike supplied;
And as their glossy locks, let free,
Fell down their shoulders carelessly,
You might have dreamed you saw a
throng
Of youthful Thyads, by the beam
Of a May moon, bounding along
Peneus' silver-eddied [4] stream !

And now they stept, with measured
tread,
Martially o'er the shining field;
Now to the mimic combat led
(A heroine at each squadron's head),
Struck lance to lance and sword to
shield:
While still, thro' every varying feat,
Their voices heard in contrast sweet
With some of deep but softened sound
From lips of aged sires around,
Who smiling watched their children's
play —
Thus sung the ancient Pyrrhic lay: —

SONG.

" RAISE the buckler — poise the lance —
" Now here — now there — retreat —
advance ! "

Such were the sounds to which the war-
rior boy
Danced in those happy days when
Greece was free;

---

[1] For a description of the Pyrrhic Dance see De Guys, etc. — It appears from Apuleius (*lib.* x.) that this war-dance was, among the ancients, sometimes performed by females.

[2] See the *costume* of the Greek women of Natolia in *Castellan's " Mœurs des Othomans."*

[3] The sword was the weapon chiefly used in this dance.

[4] Homer, Il. 2. 753.

When Sparta's youth, even in the hour
  of joy,
  Thus trained their steps to war and
    victory.
" Raise the buckler — poise the lance —
" Now here — now there — retreat —
    advance ! "
Such was the Spartan warriors' dance.
  " Grasp the falchion—gird the shield—
" Attack — defend — do all but yield."

Thus did thy sons, oh Greece, one glori-
  ous night,
  Dance by a moon like this, till o'er
    the sea
That morning dawned by whose immortal
  light
  They nobly died for thee and liberty ! [1]
" Raise the buckler — poise the lance —
" Now here — now there — retreat —
    advance ! "
Such was the Spartan heroes' dance.

Scarce had they closed this martial lay
When, flinging their light spears away,
  The combatants, in broken ranks,
All breathless from the war-field fly;
And down upon the velvet banks
  And flowery slopes exhausted lie,
Like rosy huntresses of Thrace,
Resting at sunset from the chase.

" Fond girls ! " an aged Zean said —
One who himself had fought and bled,
And now with feelings half delight,
Half sadness, watched their mimic fight—
" Fond maids ! who thus with War can
  jest —
" Like Love in Mars's helmet drest,
" When, in his childish innocence,
  " Pleased with the shade that helmet
    flings,
" He thinks not of the blood that thence
  " Is dropping o'er his snowy wings.
" Ay — true it is, young patriot maids,
  " If Honor's arm still won the fray,
" If luck but shone on righteous blades,
  " War were a game for gods to play !

" But, no, alas ! — hear one, who well
  " Hath tracked the fortunes of the
    brave —
" Hear *me*, in mournful ditty, tell
  " What glory waits the patriot's
    grave : " —

SONG.

As by the shore, at break of day,
A vanquisht Chief expiring lay,
Upon the sands, with broken sword,
  He traced his farewell to the Free;
And, there, the last unfinished word
  He dying wrote was " Liberty ! "

At night a Sea-bird shrieked the knell
Of him who thus for Freedom fell;
  The words he wrote, ere evening came,
    Were covered by the sounding sea; —
So pass away the cause and name
Of him who dies for Liberty !

That tribute of subdued applause
  A charmed but timid audience pays,
That murmur which a minstrel draws
  From hearts that feel but fear to praise,
Followed this song, and left a pause
Of silence after it, that hung
Like a fixt spell on every tongue.

At length a low and tremulous sound
Was heard from midst a group that round
A bashful maiden stood to hide
Her blushes while the lute she tried —
Like roses gathering round to veil
The song of some young nightingale,
Whose trembling notes steal out between
The clustered leaves, herself unseen.
And while that voice in tones that more
  Thro' feeling than thro' weakness erred,
Came with a stronger sweetness o'er
  The attentive ear, this strain was
    heard : —

SONG.

I saw from yonder silent cave,[2]
  Two Fountains running side by side;

---

1 It is said that Leonidas and his companions
employed themselves, on the eve of the battle,
in music and the gymnastic exercises of their
country.

2 " This morning we paid our visit to the Cave
of Trophonius, and the Fountains of Memory
and Oblivion, just upon the water of Hercyna,
which flows through stupendous rocks." —
Williams's Travels in Greece.

The one was Memory's limpid wave,
　　The other cold Oblivion's tide.
"Oh Love!" said I, in thoughtless mood,
　As deep I drank of Lethe's stream,
"Be all my sorrows in this flood
　　"Forgotten like a vanisht dream!"

But who could bear that gloomy blank
　　Where joy was lost as well as pain?
Quickly of Memory's fount I drank,
　　And brought the past all back again;
And said, "Oh Love! whate'er my lot,
　　"Still let this soul to thee be true —
"Rather than have one bliss forgot,
　　"Be all my pains remembered too!"

The group that stood around to shade
The blushes of that bashful maid,
Had by degrees as came the lay
More strongly forth retired away,
Like a fair shell whose valves divide
To show the fairer pearl inside:
For such she was — a creature, bright
And delicate as those day-flowers,
Which while they last make up in light
And sweetness what they want in hours.

So rich upon the ear had grown
　Her voice's melody — its tone
Gathering new courage as it found
An echo in each bosom round —
That, ere the nymph with downcast eye
Still on the chords, her lute laid by,
"Another Song," all lips exclaimed,
And each some matchless favorite named;
While blushing as her fingers ran
O'er the sweet chords she thus began: —

SONG.

Oh, Memory, how coldly
　Thou paintest joy gone by:
Like rainbows, thy pictures
　But mournfully shine and die
Or if some tints thou keepest,
　　That former days recall,
As o'er each line thou weepest,
　　Thy tears efface them all.

But, Memory, too truly
　Thou paintest grief that's past;
Joy's colors are fleeting,
　But those of Sorrow last.

And, while thou bring'st before us
　Dark pictures of past ill,
Life's evening closing o'er us
　But makes them darker still.

So went the moonlight hours along,
In this sweet glade; and so with song
And witching sounds — not such as they,
　The cymbalists of Ossa, played,
To chase the moon's eclipse away,[1]
　But soft and holy — did each maid
Lighten her heart's eclipse awhile,
And win back Sorrow to a smile.

Not far from this secluded place,
On the sea-shore a ruin stood; —
A relic of the extinguisht race,
　Who once looked o'er that foamy flood,
When fair Ioulis [2] by the light
　Of golden sunset on the sight
Of mariners who sailed that sea,
　Rose like a city of chrysolite
　　Called from the wave by witchery.
This ruin — now by barbarous hands
　Debased into a motley shed,
Where the once splendid column stands
　Inverted on its leafy head —
Formed, as they tell in times of old
　The dwelling of that bard whose lay
Could melt to tears the stern and cold,
　And sadden mid their mirth the gay—
Simonides,[3] whose fame thro' years
And ages past still bright appears —
Like Hesperus, a star of tears!

'T was hither now — to catch a view
　Of the white waters as they played
Silently in the light — a few
　Of the more restless damsels strayed;
And some would linger mid the scent
　Of hanging foliage that perfumed
The ruined walls; while others went
　Culling whatever floweret bloomed

1 This superstitious custom of the Thessalians
exists also, as Pietro della Valle tells us, among
the Persians.

2 An ancient city of Zea, the walls of which
were of marble. Its remains (says Clarke) "extend from the shore, quite into a valley watered
by the streams of a fountain, whence Ioulis received its name."

3 Zea was the birthplace of this poet, whose
verses are by Catullus called "tears."

In the lone leafy space between,
Where gilded chambers once had been;
Or, turning sadly to the sea,
    Sent o'er the wave a sigh unblest
To some brave champion of the Free —
Thinking, alas, how cold might be
    At that still hour his place of rest!

Meanwhile there came a sound of song
    From the dark ruins — a faint strain,
As if some echo that among
    Those minstrel halls had slumbered long
Were murmuring into life again.

But, no — the nymphs knew well the
        tone —
A maiden of their train, who loved
Like the night bird to sing alone,
    Had deep into those ruins roved,
And there, all other thoughts forgot,
    Was warbling o'er, in lone delight,
A lay that, on that very spot,
    Her lover sung one moonlight
        night: —

SONG.

AH! where are they, who heard, in former
        hours,
The voice of Song in these neglected
        bowers?
        They are gone — all gone!

The youth who told his pain in such
        sweet tone
That all who heard him wisht his pain
        their own —
        He is gone — he is gone!

And she who while he sung sat listening by
And thought to strains like these 't were
        sweet to die —
        She is gone — she too is gone!

'T is thus in future hours some bard will
        say
Of her who hears and him who sings this
        lay —
        They are gone — they both are
        gone!

The moon was now, from heaven's steep,
    Bending to dip her silvery urn
Into the bright and silent deep —
    And the young nymphs, on their return

From those romantic ruins, found
Their other playmates ranged around
The sacred Spring, prepared to tune
Their parting hymn,[1] ere sunk the moon,
To that fair Fountain by whose stream
Their hearts had formed so many a
    dream.

Who has not read the tales that tell
Of old Eleusis' sacred Well,
Or heard what legend-songs recount
Of Syra and its holy Fount,[2]
Gushing at once from the hard rock
Into the laps of living flowers —
Where village maidens loved to flock,
    On summer-nights and like the Hours
Linked in harmonious dance and song,
Charmed the unconscious night along;
While holy pilgrims on their way
    To Delos' isle stood looking on,
Enchanted with a scene so gay,
    Nor sought their boats till morning
        shone.

Such was the scene this lovely glade
And its fair inmates now displayed,
As round the Fount in linked ring
They went in cadence slow and light
And thus to that enchanted Spring
Warbled their Farewell for the
    night: —

SONG.

HERE, while the moonlight dim
Falls on that mossy brim,
Sing we our Fountain Hymn,
    Maidens of Zea!
Nothing but Music's strain,
When Lovers part in pain,
Soothes till they meet again,
    Oh, Maids of Zea!

1 These "Songs of the Well," as they were
called among the ancients, still exist in Greece.
De Guys tells us that he has seen "the young
women in Prince's Island, assembled in the evening at a public well, suddenly strike up a dance,
while others sung in concert to them."

2 "The inhabitants of Syra, both ancient and
modern, may be considered as the worshippers
of water. The old fountain, at which the nymphs
of the island assembled in the earliest ages, exists
in its original state; the same rendezvous as it
was formerly, whether of love and gallantry, or
of gossiping and tale-telling. It is near to the
town, and the most limpid water gushes continually from the solid rock. It is regarded by the
inhabitants with a degree of religious venera-

Bright Fount so clear and cold
Round which the nymphs of old
Stood with their locks of gold,
 Fountain of Zea!
Not even Castaly,
Famed tho' its streamlet be,
Murmurs or shines like thee,
 Oh, Fount of Zea!

Thou, while our hymn we sing,
Thy silver voice shalt bring,
Answering, answering,
 Sweet Fount of Zea!
For of all rills that run
Sparkling by moon or sun
Thou art the fairest one,
 Bright Fount of Zea!

tion; and they preserve a tradition, that the pilgrims of old time, in their way to Delos, resorted
hither for purification." — *Clarke.*

Now, by those stars that glance
Over heaven's still expanse,
Weave we our mirthful dance,
 Daughters of Zea!
Such as in former days
Danced they by Dian's rays
Where the Eurotas strays,[1]
 Oh, Maids of Zea!

But when to merry feet
Hearts with no echo beat,
Say, can the dance be sweet?
 Maidens of Zea!
No, naught but Music's strain,
When lovers part in pain,
Soothes till they meet again,
 Oh, Maids of Zea!

[1] " *qualis in Eurotæ ripis, aut per juga Cynthi
exercet Diana choros.*" — *Vergil.*

SECOND EVENING.

SONG.

When evening shades are falling
 O'er Ocean's sunny sleep,
To pilgrims' hearts recalling
 Their home beyond the deep;
When rest o'er all descending
 The shores with gladness smile,
And lutes their echoes blending
 Are heard from isle to isle,
Then, Mary, Star of the Sea,[2]
 We pray, we pray, to thee!

The noon-day tempest over,
 Now Ocean toils no more,
And wings of halcyons hover
 Where all was strife before.
Oh thus may life in closing
 Its short tempestuous day
Beneath heaven's smile reposing
 Shine all its storms away.

[2] One of the titles of the Virgin: — " *Maria
illuminatrix, sive Stella Maris.*" — *Isidor.*

Thus, Mary, Star of the Sea,
 We pray, we pray, to thee!

On Helle's sea the light grew dim
As the last sounds of that sweet hymn
 Floated along its azure tide —
Floated in light as if the lay
Had mixt with sunset's fading ray
 And light and song together died.
So soft thro' evening's air had breathed
That choir of youthful voices wreathed
In many-linked harmony,
That boats then hurrying o'er the sea
Paused when they reached this fairy
 shore,
And lingered till the strain was o'er.

Of those young maids who 've met to
 fleet
 In song and dance this evening's
 hours,

Far happier now the bosoms beat
 Than when they last adorned these
 bowers;
For tidings of glad sound had come,
 At break of day from the far isles —
Tidings like breath of life to some —
That Zea's sons would soon wing home,
 Crowned with the light of Victory's
 smiles
To meet that brightest of all meeds
That wait on high, heroic deeds,
When gentle eyes that scarce for tears
 Could trace the warrior's parting
 track,
Shall like a misty morn that clears
When the long-absent sun appears
 Shine out all bliss to hail him back.

How fickle still the youthful breast ! —
 More fond of change than a young
 moon,
No joy so new was e'er possest
 But Youth would leave for newer
 soon.
These Zean nymphs tho' bright the spot
 Where first they held their evening
 play
As ever fell to fairy's lot
 To wanton o'er by midnight's ray,
Had now exchanged that sheltered scene
For a wide glade beside the sea —
 A lawn whose soft expanse of green
 Turned to the west sun smilingly
As tho' in conscious beauty bright
It joyed to give him light for light.

And ne'er did evening more serene
Look down from heaven on lovelier
 scene.
Calm lay the flood around while fleet
 O'er the blue shining element
Light barks as if with fairy feet
 That stirred not the husht waters
 went;
Some that ere rosy eve fell o'er
 The blushing wave, with mainsail free,
Had put forth from the Attic shore,
 Or the near Isle of Ebony; —
Some, Hydriot barks that deep in caves
 Beneath Colonna's pillared cliffs,
Had all day lurked and o'er the waves
 Now shot their long and dart-like
 skiffs.

Woe to the craft however fleet
These sea-hawks in their course shall
 meet,
Laden with juice of Lesbian vines,
Or rich from Naxos' emery mines;
For not more sure, when owlets flee
O'er the dark crags of Pendelee,
Doth the night-falcon mark his prey,
Or pounce on it more fleet than they.

And what a moon now lights the glade
 Where these young island nymphs are
 met !
Full-orbed yet pure as if no shade
 Had touched its virgin lustre yet;
And freshly bright as if just made
By Love's own hands of new-born light
Stolen from his mother's star to night.

On a bold rock that o'er the flood
Jutted from that soft glade there stood
A Chapel, fronting towards the sea, —
Built in some by-gone century, —
Where nightly as the seaman's mark
When waves rose high or clouds were
 dark,
A lamp bequeathed by some kind Saint
Shed o'er the wave its glimmer faint,
Waking in way-worn men a sigh
And prayer to heaven as they went by.
'T was there, around that rock-built shrine
 A group of maidens and their sires
Had stood to watch the day's decline,
 And as the light fell o'er their lyres
Sung to the Queen-Star of the Sea
That soft and holy melody.

But lighter thoughts and lighter song
Now woo the coming hours along.
For mark, where smooth the herbage lies,
Yon gay pavilion curtained deep
With silken folds thro' which bright eyes
 From time to time are seen to peep;
While twinkling lights that to and fro
Beneath those veils like meteors go,
 Tell of some spells at work and keep
Young fancies chained in mute suspense,
Watching what next may shine from
 thence,
Nor long the pause ere hands unseen
 That mystic curtain backward drew
And all that late but shone between
 In half-caught gleams now burst to
 view.

A picture 't was of the early days
Of glorious Greece ere yet those rays
Of rich, immortal Mind were hers
That made mankind her worshippers;
While yet unsung her landscapes shone
With glory lent by heaven alone;
Nor temples crowned her nameless hills,
Nor Muse immortalized her rills;
Nor aught but the mute poesy
Of sun and stars and shining sea
Illumed that land of bards to be.
While prescient of the gifted race
That yet would realm so blest adorn
Nature took pains to deck the place
Where glorious Art was to be born.

Such was the scene that mimic stage
Of Athens and her hills portrayed;
Athens in her first, youthful age,
Ere yet the simple violet braid,[1]
Which then adorned her had shone
down
The glory of earth's loftiest crown.
While yet undreamed, her seeds of Art
Lay sleeping in the marble mine —
Sleeping till Genius bade them start
To all but life in shapes divine;
Till deified the quarry shone
And all Olympus stood in stone!

There in the foreground of that scene,
On a soft bank of living green
Sate a young nymph with her lap full
Of newly gathered flowers, o'er which
She graceful leaned intent to cull
All that was there of hue most rich,
To form a wreath such as the eye
Of her young lover who stood by,
With pallet mingled fresh might choose
To fix by Painting's rainbow hues.

The wreath was formed; the maiden
raised
Her speaking eyes to his, while he —
Oh *not* upon the flowers now gazed,
But on that bright look's witchery.
While, quick as if but then the thought
Like light had reached his soul, he
caught
His pencil up and warm and true
As life itself that love-look drew:

1 "Violet-crowned Athens." — *Pindar*.

And, as his raptured task went on,
And forth each kindling feature shone,
Sweet voices thro' the moonlight air
From lips as moonlight fresh and pure
Thus hailed the bright dream passing
there,
And sung the Birth of Portraiture.[2]

SONG.

As once a Grecian maiden wove
    Her garland mid the summer bowers,
There stood a youth with eyes of love
    To watch her while she wreathed the
        flowers.
The youth was skilled in Painting's art,
    But ne'er had studied woman's brow,
Nor knew what magic hues the heart
    Can shed o'er Nature's charms till now.

CHORUS.

    Blest be Love to whom we owe
    All that 's fair and bright below.

His hand had pictured many a rose,
    And sketched the rays that light the
        brook;
But what were these or what were those
    To woman's blush, to woman's look?
" Oh, if such magic power there be,
" This, this," he cried, " is all my prayer,
" To paint that living light I see
    " And fix the soul that sparkles there."

His prayer as soon as breathed was
        heard;
    His pallet touched by Love grew warm,
And Painting saw her hues transferred
    From lifeless flowers to woman's form.
Still as from tint to tint he stole,
    The fair design shone out the more
And there was now a life, a soul,
    Where only colors glowed before.

Then first carnations learned to speak
    And lilies into life were brought;
While mantling on the maiden's cheek
    Young roses kindled into thought.
Then hyacinths their darkest dyes
    Upon the locks of Beauty threw;

2 The whole of this scene was suggested by
Pliny's account of the artist Pausias and his
mistress Glycera, *Lib.* 35. c. 40.

And violets transformed to eyes
Inshrined a soul within their blue.

CHORUS.

Blest be Love to whom we owe
All that 's fair and bright below.
Song was cold and Painting dim
Till song and Painting learned from
him.

Soon as the scene had closed, a cheer
Of gentle voices old and young
Rose from the groups that stood to hear
This tale of yore so aptly sung;
And while some nymphs in haste to
tell
The workers of that fairy spell
How crowned with praise their task had
been
Stole in behind the curtained scene,
The rest in happy converse strayed —
Talking that ancient love-tale o'er —
Some to the groves that skirt the glade,
Some to the chapel by the shore,
To look what lights were on the sea,
And think of the absent silently.

But soon that summons known so well
Thro' bower and hall in Eastern lands,
Whose sound more sure than gong or
bell
Lovers and slaves alike commands, —
The clapping of young female hands,
Calls back the groups from rock and
field
To see some new-formed scene re-
vealed; —
And fleet and eager down the slopes
Of the green glade like antelopes
When in their thirst they hear the sound
Of distant rills, the light nymphs bound.

Far different now the scene — a waste
Of Libyan sands, by moonlight's ray;
An ancient well, whereon were traced
The warning words, for such as stray
Unarmed there, " Drink and away ! " [1]

While near it from the night-ray screened,
And like his bells in husht repose,
A camel slept — young as if weaned
When last the star Canopus rose.[2]

Such was the back-ground's silent
scene; —
While nearer lay fast slumbering too
In a rude tent with brow serene
A youth whose cheeks of way-worn hue
And pilgrim-bonnet told the tale
That he had been to Mecca's Vale:
Haply in pleasant dreams, even now
Thinking the long wished hour is come
When o'er the well-known porch at
home
His hand shall hang the aloe bough —
Trophy of his accomplished vow.[3]

But brief his dream — for now the call
Of the camp-chiefs from rear to van,
" Bind on your burdens," [4] wakes up all
The widely slumbering caravan;
And thus meanwhile to greet the ear
Of the young pilgrim as he wakes,
The song of one who lingering near
Had watched his slumber, cheerly
breaks.

SONG.

Up and march ! the timbrel's sound
Wakes the slumbering camp around;
Fleet thy hour of rest hath gone,
Armed sleeper, up, and on !
Long and weary is our way
O'er the burning sands to day;
But to pilgrim's homeward feet
Even the desert's path is sweet.

---

1 The traveller Shaw mentions a beautiful rill
in Barbary, which is received into a large basin
called *Shrub wee krub,* " Drink and away " —
there being great danger of meeting with thieves
and assassins in such places.

2 The Arabian shepherd has a peculiar ceremony in weaning the young camel : when the
proper time arrives, he turns the camel towards
the rising star, Canopus, and says, " Do you see
Canopus ? from this moment you taste not another drop of milk." — *Richardson.*

3 " Whoever returns from a pilgrimage to
Mecca hangs this plant (the mitre-shaped Aloe)
over his street door, as a token of his having performed this holy journey." — *Hasselquist.*

4 This form of notice to the caravans to prepare for marching was applied by Hafiz to the
necessity of relinquishing the pleasures of this
world, and preparing for death : — " For me
what room is there for pleasure in the bower of
Beauty, when every moment the bell makes
proclamation, ' Bind on your burdens ' ? "

When we lie at dead of night,
Looking up to heaven's light,
Hearing but the watchman's tone
Faintly chanting " God is one," [1]
Oh what thoughts then o'er us come
Of our distant village home,
Where that chant when evening sets
Sounds from all the minarets.

Cheer thee! — soon shall signal lights,
Kindling o'er the Red-Sea heights,
Kindling quick from man to man,
Hail our coming caravan: [2]
Think what bliss that hour will be!
Looks of home again to see,
And our names again to hear
Murmured out by voices dear.

So past the desert dream away,
Fleeting as his who heard this lay.
Nor long the pause between, nor moved
    The spell-bound audience from that
        spot;
While still as usual Fancy roved
On to the joy that yet was not; —
Fancy who hath no present home,
But builds her bower in scenes to come,
Walking for ever in a light
That flows from regions out of sight.

But see by gradual dawn descried
    A mountain realm — rugged as e'er
    Upraised to heaven its summits bare,
Or told to earth with frown of pride
    That Freedom's falcon nest was there,
Too high for hand of lord or king
To hood her brow, or chain her wing.

'T is Maina's land — her ancient hills,
The abode of nymphs [3] — her countless
    rills
And torrents in their downward dash
    Shining like silver thro' the shade

Of the sea-pine and flowering ash —
    All with a truth so fresh portrayed
As wants but touch of life to be
A world of warm reality.

And now light bounding forth a band
    Of mountaineers, all smiles, ad-
        vance —
Nymphs with their lovers hand in hand
    Linked in the Ariadne dance; [4]
And while, apart from that gay throng,
A minstrel youth in varied song
Tells of the loves, the joys, the ills
Of these wild children of the hills,
The rest by turns or fierce or gay
As war or sport inspires the lay
Follow each change that wakes the
    strings
And act what thus the lyrist sings:—

SONG.

No life is like the mountaineer's,
    His home is near the sky,
Where throned above this world he hears
    Its strife at distance die.
Or should the sound of hostile drum
Proclaim below, " We come — we
    come,"
Each crag that towers in air
Gives answer, " Come who dare ! "
While like bees from dell and dingle,
Swift the swarming warriors mingle,
And their cry " Hurra ! " will be,
" Hurra, to victory ! "

Then when battle's hour is over
See the happy mountain lover
With the nymph who 'll soon be bride
Seated blushing by his side, —
Every shadow of his lot
In her sunny smile forgot.
Oh, no life is like the mountaineer's,
    His home is near the sky,
Where throned above this world he hears
    Its strife at distance die.
Nor only thus thro' summer suns
His blithe existence cheerly runs —
    Even winter bleak and dim
    Brings joyous hours to him;

---

1 The watchmen, in the camp of the caravans, go their rounds, crying one after another, "God is one," etc.

2 " It was customary," says Irwin, "to light up fires on the mountains, within view of Cosseir, to give notice of the approach of the caravans that came from the Nile."

3 —— *virginibus bacchata Laconis Taygeta.*   VERGIL.

4 See, for an account of this dance, De Guy's Travels.

When his rifle behind him flinging
He watches the roe-buck springing,
And away, o'er the hills away
Re-echoes his glad " hurra."

Then how blest when night is closing,
By the kindled hearth reposing,
To his rebeck's drowsy song,
He beguiles the hour along;
Or provoked by merry glances
To a brisker movement dances,
Till, weary at last, in slumber's chain,
He dreams o'er chase and dance again,
    Dreams, dreams them o'er again.

As slow that minstrel at the close
Sunk while he sung to feigned repose,
Aptly did they whose nimble art
    Followed the changes of his lay
Portray the lull, the nod, the start,
    Thro' which as faintly died away
His lute and voice, the minstrel past,
Till voice and lute lay husht at last.

But now far other song came o'er
    Their startled ears — song that at first
As solemnly the night-wind bore
    Across the wave its mournful burst,
Seemed to the fancy like a dirge
    Of some lone Spirit of the Sea,
Singing o'er Helle's ancient surge
    The requiem of her Brave and Free.

Sudden amid their pastime pause
    The wondering nymphs; and as the
        sound
Of that strange music nearer draws,
    With mute inquiring eye look round,
Asking each other what can be
The source of this sad minstrelsy?
Nor longer can they doubt, the song
    Comes from some island-bark which
        now
Courses the bright waves swift along
And soon perhaps beneath the brow
Of the Saint's Rock will shoot its prow.

Instantly all with hearts that sighed
    'Twixt fear's and fancy's influence,
    Flew to the rock and saw from thence
A red-sailed pinnace towards them glide,
Whose shadow as it swept the spray
Scattered the moonlight's smiles away.

Soon as the mariners saw that throng
    From the cliff gazing, young and old,
Sudden they slacked their sail and song,
    And while their pinnace idly rolled
    On the light surge, these tidings
        told:—

'T was from an isle of mournful name,
From Missolonghi, last they came —
Sad Missolonghi sorrowing yet
O'er him, the noblest Star of Fame
That e'er in life's young glory set! —
And now were on their mournful way,
    Wafting the news thro' Helle's
        isles;—
News that would cloud even Freedom's
        ray
And sadden Victory mid her smiles.

Their tale thus told and heard with pain,
Out spread the galliot's wings again;
And as she sped her swift career
Again that Hymn rose on the ear —
"Thou art not dead — thou art not
        dead! "
    As oft 't was sung in ages flown
Of him, the Athenian, who to shed
    A tyrant's blood poured out his own.

SONG.

THOU art not dead — thou art not
    dead! [1]
    No, dearest Harmodius, no.
Thy soul to realms above us fled
Tho' like a star it dwells o'er head
    Still lights this world below.
Thou art not dead — thou art not dead!
    No, dearest Harmodius, no.

Thro' isles of light where heroes tread
    And flowers ethereal blow,
Thy god-like Spirit now is led,
Thy lip with life ambrosial fed
    Forgets all taste of woe.
Thou art not dead — thou art not dead!
    No, dearest Harmodius, no.

The myrtle round that falchion spread
    Which struck the immortal blow,
Throughout all time with leaves un-
        shed —

---

1 φίλταθ' Ἀρμόδι' οὔπω τέθνηκας.

The patriot's hope, the tyrant's dread —
　Round Freedom's shrine shall grow.
Thou art not dead — thou art not dead!
　No, dearest Harmodius, no.

Where hearts like thine have broke or
　　bled,
　Tho' quenched the vital glow,
Their memory lights a flame instead,
Which even from out the narrow bed
　Of death its beams shall throw.
Thou art not dead — thou art not dead!
　No, dearest Harmodius, no.

Thy name, by myriads sung and said,
　From age to age shall go,
Long as the oak and ivy wed,
As bees shall haunt Hymettus' head,
　Or Helle's waters flow.
Thou art not dead — thou art not dead!
　No, dearest Harmodius, no.

'Mong those who lingered listening
　　there, —
　Listening with ear and eye as long
As breath of night could towards them
　　bear
A murmur of that mournful song, —
A few there were in whom the lay
Had called up feelings far too sad
To pass with the brief strain away,
　Or turn at once to theme more glad;
And who in mood untuned to meet
The light laugh of the happier train,
Wandered to seek some moonlight seat
Where they might rest, in converse
　　sweet,
　Till vanisht smiles should come
　　again.

And seldom e'er hath noon of night
To sadness lent more soothing light.
On one side in the dark blue sky
Lonely and radiant was the eye
Of Jove himself, while on the other
　'Mong tiny stars that round her
　　gleamed,
The young moon like the Roman mother
　Among her living "jewels" beamed.[1]

Touched by the lovely scenes around,
　A pensive maid — one who, tho' young,

1 See "Alciphron," p. 353.

Had known what 't was to see unwound
　The ties by which her heart had clung—
Wakened her soft tamboura's sound,
　And to its faint accords thus sung: —

SONG.

Calm as beneath its mother's eyes
In sleep the smiling infant lies,
So watched by all the stars of night
Yon landscape sleeps in light.
And while the night-breeze dies away,
　Like relics of some faded strain,
Loved voices, lost for many a day,
　Seem whispering round again.
Oh youth! oh love! ye dreams that shed
Such glory once — where are ye fled?

Pure ray of light that down the sky
　Art pointing like an angel's wand,
As if to guide to realms that lie
　In that bright sea beyond:
Who knows but in some brighter deep
　Than even that tranquil, moon-lit main,
Some land may lie where those who weep
　Shall wake to smile again!

With cheeks that had regained their
　　power
　And play of smiles, — and each bright
　　eye
Like violets after morning's shower
　The brighter for the tears gone by,
Back to the scene such smiles should grace
These wandering nymphs their path re-
　trace,
And reach the spot with rapture new
Just as the veils asunder flew
And a fresh vision burst to view.

There by her own bright Attic flood,
The blue-eyed Queen of Wisdom stood;—
Not as she haunts the sage's dreams,
　With brow unveiled, divine, severe;
But softened as on bards she beams
　When fresh from Poesy's high sphere
A music not her own she brings,
And thro' the veil which Fancy flings
O'er her stern features gently sings.

But who is he — that urchin nigh,
　With quiver on the rose-trees hung,
Who seems just dropt from yonder sky,

And stands to watch that maid with eye
  So full of thought for one so young? —
That child — but, silence ! lend thine ear,
And thus in song the tale thou 'lt hear:—

SONG.

As Love one summer eve was straying,
  Who should he see at that soft hour
But young Minerva gravely playing
  Her flute within an olive bower.
I need not say, 't is Love's opinion
  That grave or merry, good or ill,
The sex all bow to his dominion,
  As woman will be woman still.

Tho' seldom yet the boy hath given
  To learned dames his smiles or sighs,
So handsome Pallas looked that even
  Love quite forgot the maid was wise.
Besides, a youth of his discerning
  Knew well that by a shady rill
At sunset hour whate'er her learning
  A woman will be woman still.

Her flute he praised in terms extatic, —
  Wishing it dumb, nor cared how
    soon; —
For Wisdom's notes, howe'er chromatic,
  To Love seem always out of tune.
But long as he found face to flatter,
  The nymph found breath to shake and
    thrill;
As, weak or wise — it does n't matter —
  Woman at heart is woman still.

Love changed his plan, with warmth ex-
    claiming,
  " How rosy was her lips' soft dye !"
And much that flute the flatterer blaming,
  For twisting lips so sweet awry.
The nymph looked down, beheld her
    features
  Reflected in the passing rill,
And started, shocked — for, ah, ye
    creatures !
  Even when divine you 're women still.

Quick from the lips it made so odious,
  That graceless flute the Goddess took,
And while yet filled with breath melo-
    dious,
  Flung it into the glassy brook;

Where as its vocal life was fleeting
  Adown the current, faint and shrill,
'T was heard in plaintive tone repeating,
  " Woman, alas, vain woman still !"

An interval of dark repose —
Such as the summer lightning knows,
'Twixt flash and flash, as still more bright
  The quick revealment comes and goes,
Opening each time the veils of night,
To show within a world of light —
Such pause, so brief, now past between
This last gay vision and the scene
  Which now its depth of light disclosed.
A bower it seemed, an Indian bower,
  Within whose shade a nymph reposed,
Sleeping away noon's sunny hour —
Lovely as she, the Sprite, who weaves
Her mansion of sweet Durva leaves,
And there, as Indian legends say,
Dreams the long summer hours away.
And mark how charmed this sleeper seems
With some hid fancy — she, too, dreams !
Oh for a wizard's art to tell
  The wonders that now bless her sight !
'T is done — a truer, holier spell
Than e'er from wizard's lip yet fell
  Thus brings her vision all to light:—

SONG.

  " Who comes so gracefully
    " Gliding along
  " While the blue rivulet
    " Sleeps to her song;
  " Song richly vying
  " With the faint sighing
  " Which swans in dying
    " Sweetly prolong ? "

So sung the shepherd-boy
  By the stream's side,
Watching that fairy boat
  Down the flood glide,
Like a bird winging,
Thro' the waves bringing
That Syren, singing
  To the husht tide.

  " Stay," said the shepherd-boy,
    " Fairy-boat, stay,
  " Linger, sweet minstrelsy,
    " Linger a day."

But vain his pleading,
Past him, unheeding,
Song and boat, speeding,
Glided away.

So to our youthful eyes
Joy and hope shone;
So while we gazed on them
Fast they flew on; —
Like flowers declining
Even in the twining,
One moment shining,
And the next gone!

Soon as the imagined dream went by,
Uprose the nymph, with anxious eye
Turned to the clouds as tho' some boon
She waited from that sun-bright dome,
And marvelled that it came not soon
As her young thoughts would have it
come.

But joy is in her glance! — the wing
Of a white bird is seen above;
And oh, if round his neck he bring
The long-wished tidings from her love,
Not half so precious in her eyes
Even that high-omened bird[1] would
be,
Who dooms the brow o'er which he
flies
To wear a crown of royalty.

She had herself last evening sent
A winged messenger whose flight
Thro' the clear, roseate element,
She watched till lessening out of sight
Far to the golden West it went,
Wafting to him, her distant love,
A missive in that language wrought
Which flowers can speak when aptly
wove,
Each hue a word, each leaf a thought.

And now — oh speed of pinion, known
To Love's light messengers alone! —
Ere yet another evening takes
Its farewell of the golden lakes,
She sees another envoy fly,
With the wished answer, thro' the sky.

1 The Huma.

SONG.

WELCOME sweet bird, thro' the sunny air
winging,
  Swift hast thou come o'er the far-shin-
ing sea,
Like Seba's dove on thy snowy neck
bringing
  Love's written vows from my lover to
me.
Oh, in thy absence what hours did I
number! —
  Saying oft, "Idle bird, how could he
rest?"
But thou art come at last, take now thy
slumber,
  And lull thee in dreams of all thou
lov'st best.

Yet dost thou droop — even now while
I utter
  Love's happy welcome, thy pulse dies
away;
Cheer thee, my bird — were it life's
ebbing flutter,
  This fondling bosom should woo it to
stay.
But no — thou 'rt dying — thy last task
is over —
  Farewell, sweet martyr to Love and to
me!
The smiles thou hast wakened by news
from my lover,
  Will now all be turned into weeping
for thee.

While thus this scene of song (their last
For the sweet summer season) past,
A few presiding nymphs whose care
Watched over all invisibly,
As do those guardian sprites of air
  Whose watch we feel but cannot see,
Had from the circle — scarcely missed,
  Ere they were sparkling there again —
Glided like fairies to assist
  Their handmaids on the moonlight
plain,
Where, hid by intercepting shade
  From the stray glance of curious eyes,
A feast of fruits and wines was laid —
  Soon to shine out, a glad surprise!

And now the moon, her ark of light
  Steering thro' Heaven, as tho' she bore

In safety thro' that deep of night
Spirits of earth, the good, the bright,
  To some remote immortal shore,
Had half-way sped her glorious way,
  When round reclined on hillocks green
In groups beneath that tranquil ray,
  The Zeans at their feast were seen.
Gay was the picture — every maid
Whom late the lighted scene displayed,
Still in her fancy garb arrayed; —
The Arabian pilgrim, smiling here
  Beside the nymph of India's sky;
While there the Mainiote mountaineer
  Whispered in young Minerva's ear,
  And urchin Love stood laughing by.

Meantime the elders round the board,
  By mirth and wit themselves made young,
High cups of juice Zacynthian poured,
  And while the flask went round thus sung: —

SONG.

Up with the sparkling brimmer,
  Up to the crystal rim;
Let not a moon-beam glimmer
  'Twixt the flood and brim.
When hath the world set eyes on
  Aught to match this light,
Which o'er our cup's horizon
  Dawns in bumpers bright?

Truth in a deep well lieth —
  So the wise aver:
But Truth the fact denieth —
  Water suits not her.
No, her abode 's in brimmers,
  Like this mighty cup —
Waiting till we, good swimmers,
  Dive to bring her up.

Thus circled round the song of glee,
  And all was tuneful mirth the while,
Save on the cheeks of some whose smile
As fixt they gaze upon the sea,
Turns into paleness suddenly!
What see they there? a bright blue light
  That like a meteor gliding o'er
The distant wave grows on the sight,
  As tho' 't were winged to Zea's shore.

To some, 'mong those who came to gaze,
  It seemed the night-light far away
Of some lone fisher by the blaze
  Of pine torch luring on his prey;
While others, as 'twixt awe and mirth
  They breathed the blest Panaya's[1]
  name,
Vowed that such light was not of earth
  But of that drear, ill-omen'd flame
Which mariners see on sail or mast
When Death is coming in the blast.
While marvelling thus they stood, a maid
  Who sate apart with downcast eye,
Nor yet had like the rest surveyed
  That coming light which now was nigh,
Soon as it met her sight, with cry
  Of pain-like joy, "'T is he! 't is he!"
Loud she exclaimed, and hurrying by
  The assembled throng, rushed towards the sea.
At burst so wild, alarmed, amazed,
All stood like statues mute and gazed
Into each other's eyes to seek
What meant such mood in maid so meek?

Till now, the tale was known to few,
But now from lip to lip it flew: —
A youth, the flower of all the band,
  Who late had left this sunny shore,
When last he kist that maiden's hand,
  Lingering to kiss it o'er and o'er,
By his sad brow too plainly told
  The ill-omened thought which crost him then,
That once those hands should lose their hold,
  They ne'er would meet on earth again!
In vain his mistress sad as he,
But with a heart from Self as free
As generous woman's only is,
Veiled her own fears to banish his: —
With frank rebuke but still more vain,
  Did a rough warrior who stood by
Call to his mind this martial strain,
  His favorite once, ere Beauty's eye
Had taught his soldier-heart to sigh: —

SONG.

March! nor heed those arms that hold thee,
  Tho' so fondly close they come;

1 The name which the Greeks give to the Virgin Mary.

Closer still will they enfold thee
  . When thou bring'st fresh laurels home.
Dost thou dote on woman's brow?
  Dost thou live but in her breath?
March! — one hour of victory now
  Wins thee woman's smile till death.

Oh what bliss when war is over
  Beauty's long-missed smile to meet,
And when wreaths our temples cover
  Lay them shining at her feet.
Who would not that hour to reach
  Breathe out life's expiring sigh, —
Proud as waves that on the beach
  Lay their war-crests down and die.

There! I see thy soul is burning —
  She herself who clasps thee so
Paints, even now, thy glad returning,
  And while clasping bids thee go.
One deep sigh to passion given,
  One last glowing tear and then —
March! — nor rest thy sword till Heaven
  Brings thee to those arms again.

Even then ere loath their hands could part
  A promise the youth gave which bore
Some balm unto the maiden's heart,
  That, soon as the fierce fight was o'er,
To home he'd speed, if safe and free —
  Nay, even if dying, still would come,
So the blest word of "Victory!"
  Might be the last he'd breathe at home.
"By day," he cried, "thou'lt know my bark;
"But should I come thro' midnight dark,
" A blue light on the prow shall tell
"That Greece hath won and all is well!"

Fondly the maiden every night,
Had stolen to seek that promised light;
Nor long her eyes had now been turned
From watching when the signal burned.
Signal of joy — for her, for all —
  Fleetly the boat now nears the land,
While voices from the shore-edge call
  For tidings of the long-wished band.

Oh the blest hour when those who've been
  Thro' peril's paths by land or sea
Locked in our arms again are seen
  Smiling in glad security;

When heart to heart we fondly strain,
  Questioning quickly o'er and o'er —
Then hold them off to gaze again
  And ask, tho' answered oft before,
  If they *indeed* are ours once more?

Such is the scene so full of joy
Which welcomes now this warrior-boy,
As fathers, sisters, friends all run
Bounding to meet him — all but one,
Who, slowest on his neck to fall,
Is yet the happiest of them all.

And now behold him circled round
  With beaming faces at that board,
While cups with laurel foliage crowned,
  Are to the coming warriors poured —
Coming, as he, their herald, told,
With blades from victory scarce yet cold,
With hearts untouched by Moslem steel
And wounds that home's sweet breath
  . will heal.

"Ere morn," said he, — and while he spoke
  Turned to the east, where clear and pale
The star of dawn already broke —
  "We'll greet on yonder wave their sail!"
Then wherefore part? all, all agree
  To wait them here beneath this bower;
And thus, while even amidst their glee,
Each eye is turned to watch the sea,
  With song they cheer the anxious hour.

SONG.

"'T IS the Vine! 't is the Vine!" said
  the cup-loving boy
As he saw it spring bright from the earth,
And called the young Genii of Wit, Love, and Joy,
  To witness and hallow its birth.
The fruit was full grown, like a ruby it flamed
  Till the sun-beam that kist it looked pale:
"'T is the Vine! 't is the Vine!" every Spirit exclaimed
  "Hail, hail to the Wine-tree, all hail!"

First, fleet as a bird to the summons Wit
flew,
    While a light on the vine-leaves there
    broke
In flashes so quick and so brilliant all
knew
    'T was the light from his lips as he
    spoke.
" Bright tree ! let thy nectar but cheer
me," he cried,
    " And the fount of Wit never can fail : "
" 'T is the Vine ! 't is the Vine !" hills
and valleys reply,
    " Hail, hail to the Wine-tree, all hail ! "

Next Love as he leaned o'er the plant to
admire
    Each tendril and cluster it wore,
From his rosy mouth sent such a breath
of desire,
    As made the tree tremble all o'er.

Oh ! never did flower of the earth, sea, or
sky,
    Such a soul-giving odor inhale :
" 'T is the Vine ! 't is the Vine !" all re-
echo the cry,
    " Hail, hail to the Wine-tree, all hail ! "

Last, Joy, without whom even Love and
Wit die,
    Came to crown the bright hour with
    his ray;
And scarce had that mirth-waking tree
met his eye,
    When a laugh spoke what Joy could
    not say;—
A laugh of the heart which was echoed
around
    Till like music it swelled on the gale :
" 'T is the Vine ! 't is the Vine !" laugh-
ing myriads resound,
    " Hail, hail to the Wine-tree, all hail ! "

ALCIPHRON:

A FRAGMENT.

LETTER I.

FROM ALCIPHRON AT ALEXANDRIA TO CLEON
AT ATHENS.

WELL may you wonder at my flight
　From those fair Gardens in whose
　　bowers
Lingers whate'er of wise and bright,
Of Beauty's smile or Wisdom's light,
　Is left to grace this world of ours.
Well may my comrades as they roam
　On such sweet eves as this inquire
Why I have left that happy home
　Where all is found that all desire,
　　And Time hath wings that never tire;
Where bliss in all the countless shapes
　That Fancy's self to bliss hath given
Comes clustering round like road-side
　　grapes
　That woo the traveller's lip at even;
Where Wisdom flings not joy away —
　As Pallas in the stream they say
Once flung her flute — but smiling owns
That woman's lip can send forth tones
Worth all the music of those spheres
So many dream of but none hears;
　Where Virtue's self puts on so well
　　Her sister Pleasure's smile that, loath
From either nymph apart to dwell,
　We finish by embracing both.

Yes, such the place of bliss, I own,
From all whose charms I just have flown;
And even while thus to thee I write,
　And by the Nile's dark flood recline,
Fondly, in thought I wing my flight
Back to those groves and gardens bright,
And often think by this sweet light
　How lovelily they all must shine;
Can see that graceful temple throw
　Down the green slope its lengthened
　　shade,

While on the marble steps below
　There sits some fair Athenian maid,
Over some favorite volume bending;
　And by her side a youthful sage
Holds back the ringlets that descend-
　　ing
　Would else o'ershadow all the page.
But hence such thoughts ! — nor let me
　　grieve
O'er scenes of joy that I but leave,
　As the bird quits awhile its nest
To come again with livelier zest.

And now to tell thee — what I fear
Thou 'lt gravely smile at — why I 'm
　　here.
Tho' thro' my life's short, sunny dream,
　I 've floated without pain or care
Like a light leaf down pleasure's stream,
　Caught in each sparkling eddy there;
Tho' never Mirth awaked a strain
That my heart echoed not again;
Yet have I felt, when even most gay,
　Sad thoughts — I knew not whence or
　　why —
　Suddenly o'er my spirit fly,
Like clouds that ere we 've time to say
" How bright the sky is ! " shade the
　　sky.
Sometimes so vague, so undefined
　Were these strange darkenings of my
　　mind —
While naught but joy around me beamed
　So causelessly they 've come and flown,
That not of life or earth they seemed,
　But shadows from some world un-
　　known.
More oft, however, 't was the thought
　How soon that scene with all its
　　play
Of life and gladness must decay —
Those lips I prest, the hands I caught —

Myself — the crowd that mirth had
    brought
  Around me — swept like weeds away!

This thought it was that came to shed
  O'er rapture's hour its worst alloys;
And close as shade with sunshine wed
  Its sadness with my happiest joys.
Oh, but for this disheartening voice
  Stealing amid our mirth to say
That all in which we most rejoice
    Ere night may be the earth-worm's
      prey
But for this bitter — only this —
Full as the world is brimmed with bliss,
And capable as feels my soul
Of draining to its dregs the whole,
I should turn earth to heaven and be,
If bliss made Gods, a Deity!

Thou know'st that night — the very last
That 'mong my Garden friends I past —
When the School held its feast of mirth
To celebrate our founder's birth.
And all that He in dreams but saw
  When he set Pleasure on the throne
Of this bright world and wrote her law
  In human hearts was felt and known —
Not in unreal dreams but true,
Substantial joy as pulse e'er knew —
By hearts and bosoms, that each felt
Itself the realm where Pleasure dwelt.

That night when all our mirth was o'er,
  The minstrels silent, and the feet
Of the young maidens heard no more —
  So stilly was the time, so sweet,
And such a calm came o'er that scene,
Where life and revel late had been —
Lone as the quiet of some bay
From which the sea hath ebbed away —
That still I lingered, lost in thought,
  Gazing upon the stars of night,
Sad and intent as if I sought
  Some mournful secret in their light;
And asked them mid that silence why
Man, glorious man, alone must die,
While they, less wonderful than he,
Shine on thro' all eternity.

That night — thou haply may'st forget
  Its loveliness — but 't was a night
To make earth's meanest slave regret
  Leaving a world so soft and bright.

On one side in the dark blue sky
Lonely and radiant was the eye
Of Jove himself, while on the other,
  'Mong stars that came out one by one,
The young moon — like the Roman
    mother
  Among her living jewels — shone.[1]
" Oh that from yonder orbs," I thought,
  " Pure and eternal as they are,
" There could to earth some power be
    brought,
  " Some charm with their own essence
    fraught
    " To make man deathless as a star,
" And open to his vast desires
    " A course, as boundless and sublime
" As that which waits those comet-fires,
    " That burn and roam throughout all
      time! "

While thoughts like these absorbed my
    mind,
  That weariness which earthly bliss
However sweet still leaves behind,
  As if to show how earthly 't is,
Came lulling o'er me and I laid
  My limbs at that fair statue's base —
That miracle, which Art hath made
  Of all the choice of Nature's grace —
To which so oft I 've knelt and sworn,
  That could a living maid like her
Unto this wondering world be born,
  I would myself turn worshipper.

Sleep came then o'er me — and I seemed
  To be transported far away
To a bleak desert plain where gleamed
  One single, melancholy ray,
Throughout that darkness dimly shed
  From a small taper in the hand
Of one who pale as are the dead
  Before me took his spectral stand,
And said while awfully a smile
  Came o'er the wanness of his cheek —
" Go and beside the sacred Nile
  " You 'll find the Eternal Life you
    seek."

Soon as he spoke these words the hue
Of death o'er all his features grew
Like the pale morning when o'er night
She gains the victory full of light;

1 See " Evenings in Greece," p. 346.

While the small torch he held became
A glory in his hand whose flame
Brightened the desert suddenly,
   Even to the far horizon's line —
Along whose level I could see
   Gardens and groves that seemed to
      shine
As if then o'er them freshly played
A vernal rainbow's rich cascade;
And music floated every where,
Circling, as 't were itself the air,
And spirits on whose wings the hue
Of heaven still lingered round me flew,
Till from all sides such splendors broke,
That with the excess of light I woke!

Such was my dream; — and I confess
   Tho' none of all our creedless school
E'er conned, believed, or reverenced less
   The fables of the priest-led fool
Who tells us of a soul, a mind,
Separate and pure within us shrined,
Which is to live — ah, hope too
   bright! —
For ever in yon fields of light;
Who fondly thinks the guardian eyes
   Of Gods are on him — as if blest
And blooming in their own blue skies
The eternal Gods were not too wise
   To let weak man disturb their rest! —
Tho' thinking of such creeds as thou
   And all our Garden sages think,
Yet is there something, I allow,
   In dreams like this — a sort of link
With worlds unseen which from the
   hour
I first could lisp my thoughts till now
Hath mastered me with spell-like power.

And who can tell, as we 're combined
Of various atoms — some refined,
Like those that scintillate and play
In the fixt stars — some gross as they
That frown in clouds or sleep in clay —
Who can be sure but 't is the best
   And brightest atoms of our frame,
   Those most akin to stellar flame,
That shine out thus, when we 're at
   rest; —
Even as the stars themselves whose light
Comes out but in the silent night.
Or is it that there lurks indeed
Some truth in Man's prevailing creed

And that our Guardians from on high
   Come in that pause from toil and sin
To put the senses' curtain by
   And on the wakeful soul look in!

Vain thought! — but yet, howe'er it be,
Dreams more than once have proved to
   me
Oracles, truer far than Oak
Or Dove or Tripod ever spoke.
And 't was the words — thou 'lt hear and
   smile —
   The words that phantom seemed to
      speak —
" Go and beside the sacred Nile
   " You 'll find the Eternal Life you
      seek " —
That haunting me by night, by day,
   At length as with the unseen hand
Of Fate itself urged me away
   From Athens to this Holy Land;
Where 'mong the secrets still untaught,
   The mysteries that as yet nor sun
Nor eye hath reached — oh, blessed
   thought! —
   May sleep this everlasting one.

Farewell — when to our Garden friends
Thou talk'st of the wild dream that sends
The gayest of their school thus far,
Wandering beneath Canopus' star,
Tell them that wander where he will
   Or howsoe'er they now condemn
His vague and vain pursuit he still
   Is worthy of the School and them; —
Still all their own — nor e'er forgets
   Even while his heart and soul pursue
The Eternal Light which never sets,
   The many meteor joys that *do*,
But seeks them, hails them with delight
Where'er they meet his longing sight.
And if his life *must* wane away
Like other lives at least the day,
The hour it lasts shall like a fire
With incense fed in sweets expire.

LETTER II.

FROM THE SAME TO THE SAME.
   Memphis.

'T IS true, alas — the mysteries and the
   lore
I came to study on this wondrous shore,

Are all forgotten in the new delights,
The strange, wild joys that fill my days
　　and nights.
Instead of dark, dull oracles that speak
From subterranean temples, those *I* seek
Come from the breathing shrines where
　　Beauty lives,
And Love, her priest, the soft responses
　　gives.
Instead of honoring Isis in those rites
At Coptos held, I hail her when she lights
Her first young crescent on the holy
　　stream —
When wandering youths and maidens
　　watch her beam
And number o'er the nights she hath to
　　run,
Ere she again embrace her bridegroom
　　sun.
While o'er some mystic leaf that dimly
　　lends
A clew into past times the·student bends,
And by its glimmering guidance learns
　　to tread
Back thro' the shadowy knowledge of the
　　dead —
The only skill, alas, *I* yet can claim
Lies in deciphering some new loved-one's
　　name —
Some gentle missive hinting time and
　　place,
In language soft as Memphian reed can
　　trace.

And where — oh where's the heart that
　　could withstand
The unnumbered witcheries of this sun-
　　born land,
Where first young Pleasure's banner was
　　unfurled
And Love hath temples ancient as the
　　world!
Where mystery like the veil by Beauty
　　worn
Hides but to win and shades but to
　　adorn;
Where that luxurious melancholy born
Of passion and of genius sheds a gloom
Making joy holy; — where the bower and
　　tomb
Stand side by side and Pleasure learns
　　from Death
The instant value of each moment's
　　breath.

Couldst thou but see how like a poet's
　　dream
This lovely land now looks! — the glori-
　　ous stream
That late between its banks was seen to
　　glide
'Mong shrines and marble cities on each
　　side
Glittering like jewels strung along a
　　chain
Hath now sent forth its waters, and o'er
　　plain
And valley like a giant from his bed
Rising with outstretched limbs hath
　　grandly spread.
While far as sight can reach beneath as
　　clear
And blue a heaven as ever blest our
　　sphere,
Gardens and pillared streets and porphyry
　　domes
And high-built temples fit to be the
　　homes
Of mighty Gods, and pyramids whose
　　hour
Outlasts all time above the waters tower!

Then, too, the scenes of pomp and joy
　　that make
One theatre of this vast, peopled lake,
Where all that Love, Religion, Commerce
　　gives
Of life and motion ever moves and lives.
Here, up the steps of temples from the
　　wave
Ascending in procession slow and grave,
Priests in white garments go, with sacred
　　wands
And silver cymbals gleaming in their
　　hands;
While there, rich barks — fresh from
　　those sunny tracts
Far off beyond the sounding cataracts —
Glide with their precious lading to the
　　sea,
Plumes of bright birds, rhinoceros ivory,
Gems from the Isle of Meroe, and those
　　grains
Of gold washed down by Abyssinian
　　rains.
Here, where the waters wind into a
　　bay
Shadowy and cool some pilgrims on their
　　way

To Saïs or Bubastus among beds
Of lotus flowers that close above their
   heads
Push their light barks, and there as in a
   bower,
Sing, talk, or sleep away the sultry hour;
Oft dipping in the Nile, when faint with
   heat,
That leaf from which its waters drink
   most sweet. —
While haply not far off beneath a bank
Of blossoming acacias many a prank
Is played in the cool current by a train
Of laughing nymphs, lovely as she,[1] whose
   chain
Around two conquerors of the world was
   cast,
But, for a third too feeble, broke at last.

For oh! believe not them who dare to
   brand
As poor in charms the women of this
   land.
Tho' darkened by that sun whose spirit
   flows
Thro' every vein and tinges as it goes,
'T is but the embrowning of the fruit
   that tells
How rich within the soul of ripeness
   dwells —
The hue their own dark sanctuaries
   wear,
Announcing heaven in half-caught
   glimpses there.
And never yet did tell-tale looks set free
The secret of young hearts more tenderly.
Such eyes! — long, shadowy, with that
   languid fall
Of the fringed lids which may be seen in
   all
Who live beneath the sun's too ardent
   rays —
Lending such looks as on their marriage
   days
Young maids cast down before a bride-
   groom's gaze!
Then for their grace — mark but the
   nymph-like shapes
Of the young village girls, when carry-
   ing grapes
From green Anthylla or light urns of
   flowers —

Not our own Sculpture in her happiest
   hours
E'er imaged forth even at the touch of
   him [2]
Whose touch was life, more luxury of
   limb!
Then, canst thou wonder if mid scenes
   like these
I should forget all graver mysteries,
All lore but Love's, all secrets but that
   best
In heaven or earth, the art of being blest!
Yet are there times — tho' brief I own
   their stay,
Like summer-clouds that shine them-
   selves away —
Moments of gloom, when even these
   pleasures pall
Upon my saddening heart and I recall
That Garden dream — that promise of a
   power,
Oh, were there such! — to lengthen out
   life's hour,
On, on, as thro' a vista far away
Opening before us into endless day!
And chiefly o'er my spirit did this
   thought
Come on that evening — bright as ever
   brought
Light's golden farewell to the world —
   when first
The eternal pyramids of Memphis burst
Awfully on my sight — standing sublime
'Twixt earth and heaven, the watch-
   towers of Time,
From whose lone summit when his reign
   hath past
From earth for ever he will look his last!

There hung a calm and solemn sunshine
   round
Those mighty monuments, a hushing
   sound
In the still air that circled them which
   stole
Like music of past times into my soul.
I thought what myriads of the wise and
   brave
And beautiful had sunk into the grave,
Since earth first saw these wonders —
   and I said
"Are things eternal only for the Dead?

---

[1] Cleopatra.

[2] Apelles.

" Hath Man no loftier hope than this
which dooms
" His only lasting trophies to be tombs?
" But '*t is* not so — earth, heaven, all
nature shows
" He *may* become immortal — *may* unclose
" The wings within him wrapt, and
proudly rise
" Redeemed from earth, a creature of
the skies !

" And who can say, among the written
spells
" From Hermes' hand that in these
shrines and cells
" Have from the Flood lay hid there
may not be
" Some secret clew to immortality,
" Some amulet whose spell can keep
life's fire
" Awake within us never to expire !
" 'T is known that on the Emerald Table,[1]
hid
" For 'ages in yon loftiest pyramid,
" The Thrice-Great [2] did himself engrave
of old
" The chymic mystery that gives end-
less gold.
" And why may not this mightier secret
dwell
" Within the same dark chambers? who
can tell
" But that those kings who by the writ-
ten skill
" Of the Emerald Table called forth gold
at will
" And quarries upon quarries heapt and
hurled,
" To build them domes that might out-
stand the world —
" Who knows but that the heavenlier art
which shares
" The life of Gods with man was also
theirs —
" That they themselves, triumphant o'er
the power
" Of fate and death, are living at this
hour;
" And these, the giant homes they still
possess,

" Not tombs but everlasting palaces
" Within whose depths hid from the
world above
" Even now they wander with the few
they love,
" Thro' subterranean gardens, by a light
" Unknown on earth which hath nor
dawn nor night !
" Else, why those deathless structures?
why the grand
" And hidden halls that undermine this
land?
" Why else hath none of earth e'er dared
to go
" Thro' the dark windings of that realm
below,
" Nor aught from heaven itself except
the God
" Of Silence thro' those endless laby-
rinths trod ? "
Thus did I dream — wild, wandering
dreams, I own,
But such as haunt me ever, if alone,
Or in that pause 'twixt joy and joy I
be,
Like a ship husht between two waves at
sea,
Then do these spirit whisperings like the
sound
Of the Dark Future come appalling
round;
Nor can I break the trance that holds
me then,
Till high o'er Pleasure's surge I mount
again !

Even now for new adventure, new delight,
My heart is on the wing; — this very
night,
The Temple on that island half-way o'er
From Memphis' gardens to the eastern
shore
Sends up its annual rite [3] to her whose
beams
Bring the sweet time of night-flowers and
dreams;
The nymph who dips her urn in silent
lakes
And turns to silvery dew each drop it
takes; —

1 See Notes on the Epicurean.
2 The Hermes Trismegitus.

3 The great Festival of the Moon.

Oh! not our Dian of the North who
    chains
In vestal ice the current of young veins,
But she who haunts the gay Bubastian [1]
    grove
And owns she sees from her bright heaven
    above,
Nothing on earth to match that heaven
    but Love.
Think then what bliss will be abroad to-
    night! —
Besides those sparkling nymphs who
    meet the sight
Day after day, familiar as the sun,
Coy buds of beauty yet unbreathed upon
And all the hidden loveliness that lies, —
Shut up as are the beams of sleeping eyes
Within these twilight shrines — to-night
    shall be
Let loose like birds for this festivity!

And mark, 't is nigh; already the sun bids
His evening farewell to the Pyramids,
As he hath done age after age till they
Alone on earth seem ancient as his ray;
While their great shadows stretching
    from the light
Look like the first colossal steps of Night
Stretching across the valley to invade
The distant hills of porphyry with their
    shade.
Around, as signals of the setting beam,
Gay, gilded flags on every house-top
    gleam:
While, hark! — from all the temples a
    rich swell
Of music to the Moon — farewell — fare-
    well.

LETTER III.

Memphis.

THERE is some star — or may it be
    That moon we saw so near last night —
Which comes athwart my destiny
    For ever with misleading light.
If for a moment pure and wise
    And calm I feel there quick doth fall
A spark from some disturbing eyes,
That thro' my heart, soul, being flies,
    And makes a wildfire of it all.

1 Bubastis, or Isis, was the Diana of the
Egyptian mythology.

I 've seen — oh, Cleon, that this earth
Should e'er have given such beauty
    birth! —
That man — but, hold — hear all that
    past
Since yester-night from first to last.

The rising of the Moon, calm, slow,
    And beautiful, as if she came
Fresh from the Elysian bowers below,
    Was with a loud and sweet acclaim
Welcomed from every breezy height,
Where crowds stood waiting for her
    light.
And well might they who viewed the
    scene
    Then lit up all around them, say
That never yet had Nature been
    Caught sleeping in a lovelier ray
Or rivalled her own noon-tide face
With purer show of moonlight grace.

Memphis — still grand, tho' not the same
    Unrivalled Memphis that could seize
From ancient Thebes the crown of Fame,
    And wear it bright thro' centuries —
Now, in the moonshine, that came down
Like a last smile upon that crown,
Memphis, still grand, among her lakes,
    Her pyramids and shrines of fire,
Rose like a vision that half breaks
On one who dreaming still awakes
    To music from some midnight choir:
While to the west — where gradual sinks
    In the red sands from Libya rolled,
Some mighty column or fair sphynx
    That stood in kingly courts of old —
It seemed as, mid the pomps that shone
Thus gayly round him Time looked on,
Waiting till all now bright and blest,
Should sink beneath him like the rest

No sooner had the setting sun
Proclaimed the festal rite begun,
And mid their idol's fullest beams
    The Egyptian world was all afloat,
Than I who live upon these streams
    Like a young Nile-bird turned my boat
To the fair island on whose shores
Thro' leafy palms and sycamores
Already shone the moving lights
Of pilgrims hastening to the rites.
While, far around, like ruby sparks
Upon the water, lighted barks,

Of every form and kind — from those
  That down Syene's cataract shoots,
To the grand, gilded barge that rows
  To tambour's beat and breath of flutes,
And wears at night in words of flame
On the rich prow its master's name; —
All were alive and made this sea
  Of cities busy as a hill
Of summer ants caught suddenly
  In the overflowing of a rill.

Landed upon the isle, I soon
  Thro' marble alleys and small groves
Of that mysterious palm she loves,
Reached the fair Temple of the Moon;
  And there — as slowly thro' the last
Dim-lighted vestibule I past —
Between the porphyry pillars twined
  With palm and ivy, I could see
A band of youthful maidens wind
  In measured walk half dancingly,
Round a small shrine on which was placed
  That bird [1] whose plumes of black and
      white
Wear in their hue by Nature traced
A type of the moon's shadowed light.

In drapery like woven snow
These nymphs were clad; and each below
The rounded bosom loosely wore
  A dark blue zone or bandelet,
With little silver stars all o'er
  As are the skies at midnight set.
While in their tresses, braided thro',
  Sparkled that flower of Egypt's lakes,
The silvery lotus in whose hue
  As much delight the young Moon takes
As doth the Day-God to behold
The lofty bean-flower's buds of gold.
And, as they gracefully went round
  The worshipt bird, some to the beat
Of castanets, some to the sound
  Of the shrill sistrum timed their feet;
While others at each step they took
A tinkling chain of silver shook.

They seemed all fair — but there was one
On whom the light had not yet shone,
Or shone but partly — so downcast
She held her brow, as slow she past.
And yet to me there seemed to dwell
  A charm about that unseen face —

1 The Ibis.

A something in the shade that fell
  Over that brow's imagined grace
Which won me more than all the best
Outshining beauties of the rest.
And *her* alone my eyes could see,
Enchained by this sweet mystery;
And her alone I watched as round
She glided o'er that marble ground,
Stirring not more the unconscious air
Than if a Spirit were moving there.
Till suddenly, wide open flew
The Temple's folding gates and threw
A splendor from within, a flood
Of glory where these maidens stood.
While with that light — as if the same
Rich source gave birth to both — there
    came
A swell of harmony as grand
As e'er was born of voice and hand,
Filling the gorgeous aisles around
With luxury of light and sound.

Then was it, by the flash that blazed
  Full o'er her features — oh 't was
      then,
As startingly her eyes she raised,
  But quick let fall their lids again,
I saw — not Psyche's self when first
  Upon the threshold of the skies
She paused, while heaven's glory burst
  Newly upon her downcast eyes,
Could look more beautiful or blush
  With holier shame than did this maid,
Whom now I saw in all that gush
  Of splendor from the aisles, dis-
      played.
Never — tho' well thou know'st how
    much
  I've felt the sway of Beauty's star —
Never did her bright influence touch
  My soul into its depths so far;
And had that vision lingered there
One minute more I should have flown,
Forgetful *who* I was and where,
  And at her feet in worship thrown
Proffered my soul thro' life her own.

But scarcely had that burst of light
And music broke on ear and sight,
Than up the aisle the bird took wing
  As if on heavenly mission sent,
While after him with graceful spring
  Like some unearthly creatures, meant

To live in that mixt element
Of light and song the young maids
    went;
And she who in my heart had thrown
A spark to burn for life was flown.

In vain I tried to follow; — bands
Of reverend chanters filled the aisle:
Where'er I sought to pass, their wands
    Motioned me back, while many a file
Of sacred nymphs — but ah, not they
Whom my eyes looked for thronged the
    way.
Perplext, impatient, mid this crowd
Of faces, lights — the o'erwhelming cloud
Of incense round me, and my blood
Full of its new-born fire — I stood,
Nor moved, nor breathed, but when I
    caught
    A glimpse of some blue, spangled
    zone,
Or wreath of lotus, which I thought
    Like those she wore at distance shone.

But no, 't was vain — hour after hour,
    Till my heart's throbbing turned to
    pain,
And my strained eyesight lost its power,
    I sought her thus, but all in vain.
At length, hot — wildered — in despair,
I rushed into the cool night-air,
And hurrying (tho' with many a look
Back to the busy Temple) took
My way along the moonlight shore,
And sprung into my boat once more.

There is a Lake that to the north
Of Memphis stretches grandly forth,
Upon whose silent shore the Dead
    Have a proud City of their own,[1]
With shrines and pyramids o'erspread —
Where many an ancient kingly head
    Slumbers, immortalized in stone;
And where thro' marble grots beneath
    The lifeless, ranged like sacred things,
Nor wanting aught of life but breath,
    Lie in their painted coverings,
And on each new successive race
    That visit their dim haunts below
Look with the same unwithering face
    They wore three thousand years ago.

1 Necropolis, or the City of the Dead, to the
south of Memphis.

There, Silence, thoughtful God, who loves
The neighborhood of death in groves
Of asphodel lies hid and weaves
    His hushing spell among the leaves —
Nor ever noise disturbs the air
    Save the low, humming, mournful
    sound
Of priests within their shrines at prayer
    For the fresh Dead entombed around.

'T was toward this place of death — in
    mood
    Made up of thoughts, half bright, half
    dark —
I now across the shining flood
    Unconscious turned my light-winged
    bark.
The form of that young maid in all
    Its beauty was before me still;
And oft I thought, if thus to call
    Her image to my mind at will,
If but the memory of that one
Bright look of hers for ever gone,
Was to my heart worth all the rest
Of woman-kind, beheld, possest —
What would it be, if wholly mine,
Within these arms, as in a shrine,
Hallowed by Love, I saw her shine —
An idol, worship by the light
Of her own beauties, day and night —
If 't was a blessing but to see
And lose again, what would *this* be?

In thoughts like these — but often crost
By darker threads — my mind was lost,
Till near that City of the Dead,
Waked from my trance, I saw o'erhead —
As if by some enchanter bid
    Suddenly from the wave to rise —
Pyramid over pyramid
    Tower in succession to the skies;
While one, aspiring, as if soon
    'T would touch the heavens, rose over
    all;
And, on its summit, the white moon
    Rested as on a pedestal!

The silence of the lonely tombs
    And temples round where naught was
    heard
But the high palm-tree's tufted plumes,
    Shaken at times by breeze or bird,
Formed a deep contrast to the scene
Of revel where I late had been;

To those gay sounds that still came o'er,
Faintly from many a distant shore,
And the unnumbered lights that shone
Far o'er the flood from Memphis on
To the Moon's Isle and Babylon.

My oars were lifted and my boat
    Lay rocked upon the rippling stream;
While my vague thoughts alike afloat,
    Drifted thro' many an idle dream,
With all of which, wild and unfixt
As was their aim, that vision mixt,
That bright nymph of the Temple — now,
With the same innocence of brow
She wore within the lighted fane —
Now kindling, thro' each pulse and vein
With passion of such deep-felt fire
As Gods might glory to inspire; —
And now — oh Darkness of the tomb,
    That must eclipse even light like hers!
Cold, dead, and blackening mid the gloom
    Of those eternal sepulchres.

Scarce had I turned my eyes away
    From that dark death-place, at the
        thought,
When by the sound of dashing spray
    From a light oar her ear was caught,
While past me, thro' the moonlight, sailed
    A little gilded bark that bore
Two female figures closely veiled
    And mantled towards that funeral
        shore.
They landed — and the boat again
Put off across the watery plain.

Shall I confess — to *thee* I may —
    That never yet hath come the chance
Of a new music, a new ray
    From woman's voice, from woman's
        glance,
Which — let it find me how it might,
    In joy or grief — I did not bless,
And wander after as a light
    Leading to undreamt happiness.
And chiefly now when hopes so vain
Were stirring in my heart and brain,
When Fancy had allured my soul
Into a chase as vague and far
As would be his who fixt his goal
    In the horizon or some star —
Any bewilderment that brought
More near to earth my high-flown
    thought —

The faintest glimpse of joy, less pure,
Less high and heavenly, but more sure,
Came welcome — and was then to me
What the first flowery isle must be
To vagrant birds blown out to sea.

Quick to the shore I urged my bark,
    And by the bursts of moonlight shed
Between the lofty tombs could mark
    Those figures as with hasty tread
They glided on — till in the shade
    Of a small pyramid, which thro'
Some boughs of palm its peak displayed,
    They vanisht instant from my view.

I hurried to the spot — no trace
Of life was in that lonely place;
And had the creed I hold by taught
Of other worlds I might have thought
Some mocking spirits had from thence
Come in this guise to cheat my sense.

At length, exploring darkly round
The Pyramid's smooth sides, I found
An iron portal — opening high
    'Twixt peak and base — and, with a
        prayer
To the bliss-loving Moon whose eye
    Alone beheld me sprung in there.
Downward the narrow stairway led
Thro' many a duct obscure and dread,
    A labyrinth for mystery made,
With wanderings onward, backward,
        round,
And gathering still, where'er it wound,
    But deeper density of shade.

Scarce had I asked myself, " Can aught
    " That man delights in sojourn
        here? " —
When, suddenly, far off, I caught
    A glimpse of light, remote, but clear —
Whose welcome glimmer seemed to pour
    From some alcove or cell that ended
The long, steep, marble corridor,
    Thro'which I now, all hope, descended.
Never did Spartan to his bride
With warier foot at midnight glide.
It seemed as echo's self were dead
In this dark place, so mute my tread.
Reaching at length that light, I saw —
    Oh! listen to the scene now raised
Before my eyes — then guess the awe,
    The still, rapt awe with which I gazed.

'T was a small chapel, lined around
With the fair, spangling marble found
In many a ruined shrine that stands
Half seen above the Libyan sands.
The walls were richly sculptured o'er,
And charactered with that dark lore
Of times before the Flood, whose key
Was lost in the "Universal Sea." —
While on the roof was pictured bright
  The Theban beetle as he shines,
  When the Nile's mighty flow declines
And forth the creature springs to light,
With life regenerate in his wings: —
Emblem of vain imaginings!
Of a new world, when this is gone,
In which the spirit still lives on!

Direct beneath this type, reclined
  On a black granite altar, lay
A female form, in crystal shrined,
  And looking fresh as if the ray
  Of soul had fled but yesterday.
While in relief of silvery hue
  Graved on the altar's front were seen
A branch of lotus, broken in two,
  As that fair creature's life had been,
And a small bird that from its spray
Was winging like her soul away.

But brief the glimpse I now could spare
  To the wild, mystic wonders round;
For there was yet *one* wonder there
  That held me as by witchery bound.
The lamp that thro' the chamber shed
Its vivid beam was at the head
Of her who on that altar slept;
  And near it stood when first I came —
Bending her brow, as if she kept
Sad watch upon its silent flame —
A female form as yet so placed
  Between the lamp's strong glow and
    me,
That I but saw, in outline traced,
  The shadow of her symmetry.
Yet did my heart — I scarce knew why —
Even at that shadowed shape beat high.
Nor was it long ere full in sight
The figure turned; and by the light
That touched her features as she bent
Over the crystal monument,
I saw 't was she — the same — the same —
  That lately stood before me, brightening

The holy spot where she but came
  And went again like summer lightning!

Upon the crystal o'er the breast
Of her who took that silent rest,
There was a cross of silver lying —
  Another type of that blest home,
Which hope and pride and fear of dying
  Build for us in a world to come: —
This silver cross the maiden raised
To her pure lips: — then, having gazed
Some minutes on that tranquil face,
Sleeping in all death's mournful grace,
Upward she turned her brow serene,
  As if intent on heaven those eyes
Saw then nor roof nor cloud between
  Their own pure orbits and the skies,
And, tho' her lips no motion made,
  And that fixt look was all her speech,
I saw that the rapt spirit prayed
  Deeper within than words could reach.

Strange power of Innocence, to turn
  To its own hue whate'er comes near,
And make even vagrant Passion burn
  With purer warmth within its sphere!
She who but one short hour before
Had come like sudden wild-fire o'er
My heart and brain — whom gladly even
  From that bright Temple in the face
Of those proud ministers of heaven,
  I would have borne in wild embrace,
And risked all punishment, divine
And human, but to make her mine; —
She, she was now before me, thrown
  By fate itself into my arms —
There standing, beautiful, alone,
  With naught to guard her but her
    charms.
Yet did I, then — did even a breath
  From my parched lips, too parched to
    move,
Disturb a scene where thus, beneath
  Earth's silent covering, Youth and
    Death
  Held converse thro' undying love?
No — smile and taunt me as thou wilt —
  Tho' but to gaze thus was delight,
Yet seemed it like a wrong, a guilt,
  To win by stealth so pure a sight:
And rather than a look profane
  Should then have met those thoughtful
    eyes,

Or voice or whisper broke the chain
  That linked her spirit with the skies,
I would have gladly in that place
From which I watched her heavenward
    face,
Let my heart break, without one beat
That could disturb a prayer so sweet.
Gently, as if on every tread,
  My life, my more than life depended,
Back thro' the corridor that led
  To this blest scene I now ascended,
And with slow seeking and some pain
And many a winding tried in vain
Emerged to upper air again.

The sun had freshly risen, and down
  The marble hills of Araby,
Scattered as from a conqueror's crown
  His beams into that living sea.
There seemed a glory in his light,
  Newly put on — as if for pride
Of the high homage paid this night
  To his own Isis, his young bride,
Now fading feminine away
In her proud Lord's superior ray.

My mind's first impulse was to fly
  At once from this entangling net —
New scenes to range, new loves to try,
Or in mirth, wine, and luxury
  Of every sense that night forget.
But vain the effort — spell-bound still,
  I lingered, without power or will
To turn my eyes from that dark door,
Which now enclosed her 'mong the dead;
  Oft fancying, thro' the boughs that o'er
The sunny pile their flickering shed,
'T was her light form again I saw
  Starting to earth — still pure and bright,
But wakening, as I hoped, less awe,
  Thus seen by morning's natural light,
Than in that strange, dim cell at night.

But no, alas — she ne'er returned:
  Nor yet — tho' still I watch — nor yet,
Tho' the red sun for hours hath burned,
  And now in his mid course hath met
The peak of that eternal pile
He pauses still at noon to bless,
Standing beneath his downward smile,
  Like a great Spirit shadowless! —
Nor yet she comes — while here, alone,
  Sauntering thro' this death-peopled
    place,

Where no heart beats except my own,
Or 'neath a palm-tree's shelter thrown,
  By turns I watch and rest and trace
These lines that are to waft to thee
My last night's wondrous history.

Dost thou remember, in that Isle
  Of our own Sea where thou and I
Lingered so long, so happy a while,
  Till all the summer flowers went by —
How gay it was when sunset brought
  To the cool Well our favorite maids
Some we had won, and some we sought —
  To dance within the fragrant shades,
And till the stars went down attune
Their Fountain Hymns [1] to the young
    moon?

That time, too — oh, 't is like a dream —
  When from Scamander's holy tide
I sprung as Genius of the Stream,
  And bore away that blooming bride,
Who thither came, to yield her charms
  (As Phrygian maids are wont ere wed)
Into the cold Scamander's arms,
  But met and welcomed mine, instead —
Wondering as on my neck she fell,
How river-gods could love so well!
Who would have thought that he who
    roved
Like the first bees of summer then,
Rifling each sweet nor ever loved
  But the free hearts that loved again,
Readily as the reed replies
To the least breath that round it sighs —
Is the same dreamer who last night
Stood awed and breathless at the sight
Of one Egyptian girl; and now
Wanders among these tombs with brow
Pale, watchful, sad, as tho' he just,
Himself, had risen from out their dust!

Yet so it is — and the same thirst
  For something high and pure, above
This withering world, which from the
    first
  Made me drink deep of woman's
    love —
As the one joy, to heaven most near
Of all our hearts can meet with here —

1 These Songs of the Well, as they were called
by the ancients, are still common in the Greek
isles.

Still burns me up, still keeps awake
A fever naught but death can slake.

Farewell; whatever may befall —
Or bright, or dark — thou 'lt know it all.

LETTER IV.

FROM ORCUS, HIGH PRIEST OF MEMPHIS, TO
DECIUS, THE PRÆTORIAN PREFECT.

REJOICE, my friend, rejoice : — the youthful Chief
Of that light Sect which mocks at all belief,
And gay and godless makes the present
hour
Its only heaven, is now within our power.
Smooth, impious school ! — not all the
weapons aimed,
At priestly creeds, since first a creed was
framed,
E'er struck so deep as that sly dart they
wield,
The Bacchant's pointed spear in laugh-
ing flowers concealed.
And oh, 't were victory to this heart, as
sweet
As any *thou* canst boast — even when the
feet
Of thy proud war-steed wade thro' Chris-
tian blood,
To wrap this scoffer in Faith's blinding
hood,
And bring him tamed and prostrate to im-
plore
The vilest gods even Egypt's saints
adore.
What ! — do these sages think, to *them*
alone
The key of this world's happiness is
known?
That none but they who make such proud
parade
Of Pleasure's smiling favors win the maid,
Or that Religion keeps no secret place,
No niche in her dark fanes for Love to
grace?
Fools ! — did they know how keen the
zest that 's given
To earthly joy when seasoned well with
heaven;
How Piety's grave mask improves the hue
Of Pleasure's laughing features, half
seen thro',

And how the Priest set aptly within reach
Of two rich worlds, traffics for bliss with
each,
Would they not, Decius — thou, whom
the ancient tie
'Twixt Sword and Altar makes our best
ally —
Would they not change their creed, their
craft, for ours?
Leave the gross daylight joys that in their
bowers
Languish with too much sun, like o'er-
blown flowers,
For the veiled loves, the blisses undis-
played
That slyly lurk within the Temple's shade?
And, 'stead of haunting the trim Garden's
school —
Where cold Philosophy usurps a rule,
Like the pale moon's, o'er passion's
heaving tide,
Till Pleasure's self is chilled by Wisdom's
pride —
Be taught by *us*, quit shadows for the
true,
Substantial joys we sager Priests pursue,
Who far too wise to theorize on bliss
Or pleasure's substance for its shade to
miss,
Preach *other* worlds but live for only
this : —
Thanks to the well-paid Mystery round
us flung,
Which like its type the golden cloud that
hung
O'er Jupiter's love-couch its shade be-
nign,
Round human frailty wraps a veil divine.

Still less should they presume, weak wits,
that they
Alone despise the craft of us who pray; —
Still less their creedless vanity deceive
With the fond thought that we who pray
believe.
Believe ! — Apis forbid — forbid it, all
Ye monster Gods before whose shrines
we fall —
Deities framed in jest as if to try
How far gross Man can vulgarise the sky;
How far the same low fancy that com-
bines
Into a drove of brutes yon zodiac's signs,

And turns that Heaven itself into a place
Of sainted sin and deified disgrace,
Can bring Olympus even to shame more deep,
Stock it with things that earth itself holds cheap,
Fish, flesh, and fowl, the kitchen's sacred brood,
Which Egypt keeps for worship, not for food —
All, worthy idols of a Faith that sees
In dogs, cats, owls, and apes, divinities!

Believe! — oh, Decius, thou, who feel'st no care
For things divine beyond the soldier's share,
Who takes on trust the faith for which he bleeds,
A good, fierce God to swear by, all he needs —
Little canst thou, whose creed around thee hangs
Loose as thy summer war-cloak guess the pangs
Of loathing and self-scorn with which a heart
Stubborn as mine is acts the zealot's part —
The deep and dire disgust with which I wade
Thro' the foul juggling of this holy trade —
This mud profound of mystery where the feet
At every step sink deeper in deceit.
Oh! many a time, when, mid the Temple's blaze,
O'er prostrate fools the sacred cist I raise,
Did I not keep still proudly in my mind
The power this priestcraft gives me o'er mankind —
A lever, of more might, in skilful hand,
To move this world, than Archimede e'er planned —
I should in vengeance of the shame I feel
At my own mockery crush the slaves that kneel
Besotted round; and — like that kindred breed
Of reverend, well-drest crocodiles they feed,

At famed Arsinoë [1] — make my keepers bless,
With their last throb, my sharp-fanged Holiness.

Say, *is* it to be borne, that scoffers, vain
Of their own freedom from the altar's chain,
Should mock thus all that thou thy blood hast sold,
And I my truth, pride, freedom, to uphold?
It must not be: — think'st thou that Christian sect,
Whose followers quick as broken waves, erect
Their crests anew and swell into a tide,
That threats to sweep away our shrines of pride —
Think'st thou with all their wondrous spells even they
Would triumph thus, had not the constant play
Of Wit's resistless archery cleared their way? —
That mocking spirit, worst of all the foes,
Our solemn fraud, our mystic mummery knows,
Whose wounding flash thus ever 'mong the signs
Of a fast-falling creed, prelusive shines,
Threatening such change as do the awful freaks
Of summer lightning ere the tempest breaks.

But, to my point — a youth of this vain school,
But one, whom Doubt itself hath failed to cool
Down to that freezing point where Priests despair
Of any spark from the altar catching there —
Hath, some nights since — it was, methinks, the night
That followed the full Moon's great annual rite —

1 For the trinkets with which the sacred Crocodiles were ornamented, see the "Epicurean," chap. x.

Thro' the dark, winding ducts that downward stray
To these earth-hidden temples, tracked
his way,
Just at that hour when, round the Shrine,
and me,
The choir of blooming nymphs thou
long'st to see,
Sing their last night-hymn in the Sanctuary.
The clangor of the marvellous Gate that
stands
At the Well's lowest depth — which none
but hands
Of new, untaught adventurers, from
above,
Who know not the safe path, e'er dare
to move —
Gave signal that a foot profane was
nigh : —
'T was the Greek youth, who, by that
morning's sky,
Had been observed, curiously wandering
round
The mighty fanes of our sepulchral
ground.

Instant, the Initiate's Trials were pre-
pared, —
The Fire, Air, Water; all that Orpheus
dared,
That Plato, that the bright-haired Sa-
mian [1] past,
With trembling hope, to come to — *what*,
at last?
Go, ask the dupes of Priestcraft; ques-
tion him
Who mid terrific sounds and spectres
dim
Walks at Eleusis; ask of those who
brave
The dazzling miracles of Mithra's Cave
With its seven starry gates; ask all who
keep
Those terrible night-mysteries where they
weep
And howl sad dirges to the answering
breeze,
O'er their dead Gods, their mortal
Deities —
Amphibious, hybrid things that died as
men,

1 Pythagoras.

Drowned, hanged, empaled, to rise as
gods again; —
Ask *them*, what mighty secret lurks
below
This seven-fold mystery — can they tell
thee? No;
Gravely they keep that only secret, well
And fairly kept — that they have none
to tell;
And duped themselves console their
humbled pride
By duping thenceforth all mankind beside.

And such the advance in fraud since
Orpheus' time —
That earliest master of our craft sub-
lime —
So many minor Mysteries, imps of fraud,
From the great Orphic Egg have winged
abroad,
That, still to uphold our Temple's an-
cient boast,
And seem most holy, we must cheat the
most;
Work the best miracles, wrap nonsense
round
In pomp and darkness till it seems pro-
found;
Play on the hopes, the terrors of man-
kind,
With changeful skill; and make the hu-
man mind
Like our own Sanctuary, where no ray
But by the Priest's permission wins its
way —
Where thro' the gloom as wave our
wizard rods,
Monsters at will are conjured into Gods;
While Reason like a grave-faced mummy
stands
With her arms swathed in hieroglyphic
bands.
But chiefly in that skill with which we use
Man's wildest passions for Religion's
views,
Yoking them to her car like fiery steeds,
Lies the main art in which our craft
succeeds.
And oh be blest, ye men of yore, whose
toil
Hath, for our use, scooped out from
Egypt's soil

This hidden Paradise, this mine of fanes,
Gardens and palaces where Pleasure reigns
In a rich, sunless empire of her own,
With all earth's luxuries lighting up her throne; —
A realm for mystery made, which undermines
The Nile itself and, 'neath the Twelve Great Shrines
That keep Initiation's holy rite,
Spreads its long labyrinths of unearthly light,
A light that knows no change — its brooks that run
Too deep for day, its gardens without sun,
Where soul and sense, by turns, are charmed, surprised,
And all that bard or prophet e'er devised
For man's Elysium, priests have realized.

Here, at this moment — all his trials past,
And heart and nerve unshrinking to the last —
Our new Initiate roves — as yet left free
To wander thro' this realm of mystery;
Feeding on such illusions as prepare
The soul, like mist o'er waterfalls, to wear
All shapes and hues at Fancy's varying will,
Thro' every shifting aspect, vapor still; —
Vague glimpses of the Future, vistas shown,
By scenic skill, into that world unknown,
Which saints and sinners claim alike their own;
And all those other witching, wildering arts,
Illusions, terrors, that make human hearts,
Ay, even, the wisest and the hardiest quail
To *any* goblin throned behind a veil.

Yes — such the spells shall haunt his eye, his ear,
Mix with his night-dreams, form his atmosphere;
Till, if our Sage be not tamed down, at length,
His wit, his wisdom, shorn of all their strength,
Like Phrygian priests, in honor of the shrine —
If he become not absolutely mine,
Body and soul and like the tame decoy
Which wary hunters of wild doves employ
Draw converts also, lure his brother wits
To the dark cage where his own spirit flits,
And give us if not saints good hypocrites —
If I effect not this then be it said
The ancient spirit of our craft hath fled,
Gone with that serpent-god the Cross hath chased
To hiss its soul out in the Theban waste.

•   •   •   •   •   •

LALLA ROOKH.

TO

SAMUEL ROGERS, ESQ.

THIS EASTERN ROMANCE

IS INSCRIBED,

BY

HIS VERY GRATEFUL AND AFFECTIONATE FRIEND,

THOMAS MOORE.

May 19, 1817.

LALLA ROOKH.

In the eleventh year of the reign of Aurungzebe, Abdalla, King of the Lesser Bucharia, a lineal descendant from the Great Zingis, having abdicated the throne in favor of his son, set out on a pilgrimage to the Shrine of the Prophet; and, passing into India through the delightful valley of Cashmere, rested for a short time at Delhi on his way. He was entertained by Aurungzebe in a style of magnificent hospitality, worthy alike of the visitor and the host, and was afterwards escorted with the same splendor to Surat, where he embarked for Arabia.[1] During the stay of the Royal Pilgrim at Delhi, a marriage was agreed upon between the Prince, his son, and the youngest daughter of the Emperor, LALLA ROOKH; [2] — a Princess described by the poets of her time as more beautiful than Leila,[3] Shirine,[4] Dewildé,[5] or any of those heroines whose names and loves embellish the songs of Persia and Hindostan. It was intended that the nuptials should be celebrated at Cashmere; where the young King, as soon as the cares of empire would permit, was to meet, for the first time, his lovely bride, and, after a few months' repose in that enchanting valley, conduct her over the snowy hills into Bucharia.

The day of LALLA ROOKH'S departure from Delhi was as splendid as sunshine and pageantry could make it. The bazaars and baths were all covered with the richest tapestry; hundreds of gilded barges upon the Jumna floated with their banners shining in the water; while through the streets groups of beautiful children went strewing the most delicious flowers around, as in that Persian festival called the Scattering of the Roses; [6] till every part of the city was as fragrant as if a caravan of musk from Khoten had passed through it. The Princess, having taken leave of her kind father, who at parting hung a cornelian of Yemen round her neck, on which was inscribed a verse from the Koran, and having sent a considerable present to the Fakirs, who kept up the Perpetual Lamp in her sister's tomb, meekly ascended the palankeen prepared for her; and, while Aurungzebe stood to take a last look from his balcony, the procession moved slowly on the road to Lahore.

Seldom had the Eastern world seen a cavalcade so superb. From the gardens in the suburbs to the Imperial palace, it was one unbroken line of splendor. The gallant appearance of the Rajahs and Mogul lords, distinguished by those insignia

---

1 These particulars of the visit of the King of Bucharia to Aurungzebe are found in *Dow's "History of Hindostan,"* vol. iii. p. 392.

2 Tulip cheek.

3 The mistress of Mejnoun, upon whose story so many Romances in all the languages of the East are founded.

4 For the loves of this celebrated beauty with Khosrou and with Ferhad, see *D'Herbelot, Gibbon, Oriental Collections,* etc.

5 "The history of the loves of Dewildé and Chizer, the son of the Emperor Alla, is writen in an elegant poem, by the noble Chusero." — *Ferishta.*

6 Gul Reazee.

of the Emperor's favor,[1] the feathers of the egret of Cashmere in their turbans, and the small silver-rimm'd kettle-drums at the bows of their saddles; — the costly armor of their cavaliers, who vied, on this occasion, with the guards of the great Keder Khan,[2] in the brightness of their silver battle-axes and the massiness of their maces of gold; — the glittering of the gilt pine-apple [3] on the tops of the palankeens; — the embroidered trappings of the elephants, bearing on their backs small turrets, in the shape of little antique temples, within which the Ladies of LALLA ROOKH lay as it were enshrined; — the rose-colored veils of the Princess's own sumptuous litter,[4] at the front of which a fair young female slave sat fanning her through the curtains, with feathers of the Argus pheasant's wing;[5] — and the lovely troop of Tartarian and Cashmerian maids of honor, whom the young King had sent to accompany his bride, and who rode on each side of the litter, upon small Arabian horses; — all was brilliant, tasteful, and magnificent, and pleased even the critical and fastidious FADLADEEN, Great Nazir or Chamberlain of the Haram, who was borne in his palankeen immediately after the Princess, and considered himself not the least important personage of the pageant.

FADLADEEN was a judge of everything, — from the pencilling of a Circassian's eyelids to the deepest questions of science and literature; from the mixture of a conserve of rose-leaves to the composition of an epic poem : and such influence had his opinion upon the various tastes of the day, that all the cooks and poets of Delhi stood in awe of him. His political conduct and opinions were founded upon that line of Sadi, — "Should the Prince at noon-day say, It is night, declare that you behold the moon and stars." — And his zeal for religion, of which Aurungzebe was a munificent protector,[6] was about as disinterested as

---

[1] "One mark of honor or knighthood bestowed by the Emperor is the permission to wear a small kettle-drum at the bows of their saddles, which at first was invented for the training of hawks, and to call them to the lure, and is worn in the field by all sportsmen to that end." — *Fryer's Travels.*

"Those on whom the King has conferred the privilege must wear an ornament of jewels on the right side of the turban, surmounted by a high plume of the feathers of a kind of egret. This bird is found only in Cashmere, and the feathers are carefully collected for the King, who bestows them on his nobles." — *Elphinstone's* Account of Cabul.

[2] "Khedar Khan, the Khakan, or King of Turquestan beyond the Gihon (at the end of the eleventh century), whenever he appeared abroad was preceded by seven hundred horsemen with silver battle-axes, and was followed by an equal number bearing maces of gold. He was a great patron of poetry, and it was he who used to preside at public exercises of genius, with four basins of gold and silver by him to distribute among the poets who excelled." — *Richardson's* Dissertation prefixed to his Dictionary.

[3] "The kubdeh, a large golden knob, generally in the shape of a pine-apple, on the top of the canopy over the litter or palanquin." — *Scott's* Notes on the Bahardanush.

[4] In the Poem of Zohair, in the Moallakat, there is the following lively description of "a company of maidens seated on camels."

"They are mounted in carriages covered with costly awnings, and with rose-colored veils, the linings of which have the hue of crimson Andem-wood.

"When they ascend from the bosom of the vale, they sit forward on the saddle-cloth, with every mark of a voluptuous gayety.

"Now, when they have reached the brink of yon blue-gushing rivulet, they fix the poles of their tents like the Arab with a settled mansion."

[5] See *Bernier's* description of the attendants on Rauchanara-Begum, in her progress to Cashmere.

[6] This hypocritical Emperor would have made a worthy associate of certain Holy Leagues. — "He held the cloak of religion [says Dow] between his actions and the vulgar; and impicusly thanked the Divinity for a success which he owed to his own wickedness. When he was murdering and persecuting his brothers and their families, he was building a magnificent mosque at Delhi, as an offering to God for his assistance to him in the civil wars. He acted as high priest at the consecration of this temple ; and made a practice of attending divine service there, in the humble dress of a Fakeer. But when he lifted one hand to the Divinity, he, with the other, signed warrants for the assassination of his relations." — "*History of Hindostan,*" vol. iii. p. 335. See also the curious letter of Aurungzebe, given in the *Oriental Collections,* vol. i. p. 320.

that of the goldsmith who fell in love with the diamond eyes of the idol of Jaghernaut.[1]

During the first days of their journey, LALLA ROOKH, who had passed all her life within the shadow of the Royal Gardens of Delhi,[2] found enough in the beauty of the scenery through which they passed to interest her mind, and delight her imagination; and when at evening or in the heat of the day they turned off from the high road to those retired and romantic places which had been selected for her encampments, — sometimes on the banks of a small rivulet, as clear as the waters of the Lake of Pearl;[3] sometimes under the sacred shade of a Banyan tree, from which the view opened upon a glade covered with antelopes; and often in those hidden, embowered spots, described by one from the Isles of the West,[4] as "places of melancholy, delight, and safety, where all the company around was wild peacocks and turtle-doves;" — she felt a charm in these scenes, so lovely and so new to her, which, for a time, made her indifferent to every other amusement. But LALLA ROOKH was young, and the young love variety; nor could the conversation of her Ladies and the Great Chamberlain, FADLADEEN, (the only persons, of course, admitted to her pavilion,) sufficiently enliven those many vacant hours, which were devoted neither to the pillow nor the palankeen. There was a little Persian slave who sung sweetly to the Vina, and who, now and then, lulled the Princess to sleep with the ancient ditties of her country, about the loves of Wamak and Ezra,[5] the fair-haired Zal and his mistress Rodahver;[6] not forgetting the combat of Rustam with the terrible White Demon.[7] At other times she was amused by those graceful dancing-girls of Delhi, who had been permitted by the Bramins of the Great Pagoda to attend her, much to the horror of the good Mussulman FADLADEEN, who could see nothing graceful or agreeable in idolaters, and to whom the very tinkling of their golden anklets[8] was an abomination.

But these and many other diversions were repeated till they lost all their charm,

1 " The idol at Jaghernat has two fine diamonds for eyes. No goldsmith is suffered to enter the Pagoda, one having stole one of these eyes, being locked up all night with the Idol." — *Tavernier.*

2 See a description of these royal Gardens in "An Account of the present State of Delhi, by Lieut. W. Franklin." — *Asiat. Research.* vol. iv. p. 417.

3 "In the neighborhood is Notte Gill, or the Lake of Pearl, which receives this name from its pellucid water." — *Pennant's* "Hindostan."

"Nasir Jung encamped in the vicinity of the Lake of Tonoor, amused himself with sailing on that clear and beautiful water, and gave it the fanciful name of Motee Talah, 'the Lake of Pearls,' which it still retains." — *Wilks's* "South of India."

4 Sir Thomas Roe, Ambassador from James I. to Jehanguire.

5 "The romance Wemakweazra, written in Persian verse, which contains the loves of Wamak and Ezra, two celebrated lovers who lived before the time of Mahomet." — *Note on the Oriental Tales.*

6 Their amour is recounted in the Shah-Namêh of Ferdousi; and there is much beauty in the passage which describes the slaves of Rodahver sitting on the bank of the river and throwing flowers into the stream, in order to draw the attention of the young Hero who is encamped on the opposite side. — See *Champion's* translation.

7 Rustam is the Hercules of the Persians. For the particulars of his victory over the Sepeed Deeve, or White Demon, see *Oriental Collections,* vol. ii. p. 45. — Near the city of Shiraz is an immense quadrangular monument, in commemoration of this combat, called the Kelaat-i-Deev Sepeed, or castle of the White Giant, which Father Angelo, in his " *Gazophilacium Persicum,*" p. 127, declares to have been the most memorable monument of antiquity which he had seen in Persia. — See *Ouseley's* "Persian Miscellanies."

8 "The women of the Idol, or dancing girls of the Pagoda, have little golden bells, fastened to their feet, the soft harmonious tinkling of which vibrates in unison with the exquisite melody of their voices." — *Maurice's* "Indian Antiquities."

"The Arabian courtesans, like the Indian women, have little golden bells fastened round their legs, neck, and elbows, to the sound of which they dance before the King. The Arabian princesses wear golden rings on their fingers; to which little bells are suspended, as well as in the flowing tresses of their hair, that their superior rank may be known, and they themselves receive in passing the homage due to them." — See *Calmet's* Dictionary, art. "Bells."

and the nights and noon-days were beginning to move heavily, when, at length, it was recollected that, among the attendants sent by the bridegroom, was a young poet of Cashmere, much celebrated throughout the Valley for his manner of reciting the Stories of the East, on whom his Royal Master had conferred the privilege of being admitted to the pavilion of the Princess, that he might help to beguile the tediousness of the journey by some of his most agreeable recitals. At the mention of a poet, FADLADEEN elevated his critical eyebrows, and, having refreshed his faculties with a dose of that delicious opium [1] which is distilled from the black poppy of the Thebais, gave orders for the minstrel to be forthwith introduced into the presence.

The Princess, who had once in her life seen a poet from behind the screens of gauze in her Father's hall, and had conceived from that specimen no very favorable ideas of the Caste, expected but little in this new exhibition to interest her; — she felt inclined, however, to alter her opinion on the very first appearance of FERA-MORZ. He was a youth about LALLA ROOKH'S own age, and graceful as that idol of women, Crishna,[2] — such as he appears to their young imaginations, heroic, beautiful, breathing music from his very eyes, and exalting the religion of his worshippers into love. His dress was simple, yet not without some marks of costliness; and the Ladies of the Princess were not long in discovering that the cloth, which encircled his high Tartarian cap, was of the most delicate kind that the shawl-goats of Tibet supply.[3] Here and there, too, over his vest, which was confined by a flowered girdle of Kashan, hung strings of fine pearl, disposed with an air of studied negligence; — nor did the exquisite embroidery of his sandals escape the observation of these fair critics; who, however they might give way to FADLADEEN upon the unimportant topics of religion and government, had the spirit of martyrs in everything relating to such momentous matters as jewels and embroidery.

For the purpose of relieving the pauses of recitation by music, the young Cash-merian held in his hand a kitar; — such as, in old times, the Arab maids of the West used to listen to by moonlight in the gardens of the Alhambra — and, having premised, with much humility, that the story he was about to relate was founded on the adventures of that Veiled Prophet of Khorassan,[4] who, in the year of the Hegira 163, created such alarm throughout the Eastern Empire, made an obeisance to the Princess, and thus began: —

1 "*Abou-Tige, ville de la Thebaïde, où il croit beaucoup de pavot noir, dont se fait le meilleur opium.*" — *D'Herbelot.*

2 The Indian Apollo. — "He and the three Rámas are described as youths of perfect beauty · and the princesses of Hindustán were all passionately in love with Chrishna, who continues to this hour the darling God of the Indian women." — *Sir W. Jones,* on the Gods of Greece, Italy, and India.

3 See *Turner's* Embassy for a description of this animal, "the most beautiful among the whole tribe of goats." The material for the shawls (which is carried to Cashmere) is found next the skin.

4 For the real history of this Impostor, whose original name was Hakem ben Haschem, and who was called Mocanna from the veil of silver gauze (or, as others say, golden) which he always wore, see *D'Herbelot.*

THE VEILED PROPHET OF KHORASSAN.[1]

In that delightful Province of the Sun,
The first of Persian lands he shines
   upon,
Where all the loveliest children of his
   beam,
Flowerets and fruits, blush over every
   stream,[2]
And, fairest of all streams, the MURGA
   roves
Among MEROU'S[3] bright palaces and
   groves; —
There on that throne, to which the blind
   belief
Of millions raised him, sat the Prophet-
   Chief,
The Great MOKANNA. O'er his features
   hung
The Veil, the Silver Veil, which he had
   flung
In mercy there, to hide from mortal
   sight
His dazzling brow, till man could bear
   its light.
For, far less luminous, his votaries said,
Were even the gleams, miraculously shed
O'er MOUSSA'S[4] cheek,[5] when down the
   Mount he trod
All glowing from the presence of his
   God!

On either side, with ready hearts and
   hands,
His chosen guard of bold Believers
   stands;
Young fire-eyed disputants, who deem
   their swords,
On points of faith, more eloquent than
   words;

And such their zeal, there 's not a youth
   with brand
Uplifted there, but at the Chief's com-
   mand,
Would make his own devoted heart its
   sheath,
And bless the lips that doomed so dear
   a death!
In hatred to the Caliph's hue of night,[6]
Their vesture, helms and all, is snowy
   white;
Their weapons various — some equipt for
   speed,
With javelins of the light Kathaian
   reed; [7]
Or bows of buffalo horn and shining
   quivers
Filled with the stems[8] that bloom on
   IRAN'S rivers; [9]
While some, for war's more terrible at-
   tacks,
Wield the huge mace and ponderous
   battle-axe;
And as they wave aloft in morning's
   beam
The milk-white plumage of their helms,
   they seem
Like a chenar-tree grove[10] when winter
   throws
O'er all its tufted heads his feathery
   snows.

1 Khorassan signifies, in the old Persian language, Province or Region of the Sun. — *Sir W. Jones.*

2 "The fruits of Meru are finer than those of any other place; and one cannot see in any other city such palaces with groves, and streams, and gardens." — *Ebn Haukal's* Geography.

3 One of the royal cities of Khorassan.

4 Moses.

5 "*Ses disciples assuroient qu'il se couvroit le visage, pour ne pas éblouir ceux qui l'approchoient par l'éclat de son visage comme Moyse.*" — *D'Herbelot.*

6 Black was the color adopted by the Caliphs of the House of Abbas, in their garments, turbans, and standards. — "*Il faut remarquer ici touchant les habits blancs des disciples de Hakem, que la couleur des habits, des coiffures et des étendarts des Khalifes Abassides étant la noire, ce chef de Rebelles ne pouvoit pas choisir une qui lui fût plus opposée.*" — *D'Herbelot.*

7 "Our dark javelins, exquisitely wrought of Khathaian reeds, slender and delicate." — *Poem of Amru.*

8 Pichula, used anciently for arrows by the Persians.

9 The Persians call this plant Gaz. The celebrated shaft of Isfendiar, one of their ancient heroes, was made of it. — "Nothing can be more beautiful than the appearance of this plant in flower during the rains on the banks of rivers, where it is usually interwoven with a lovely twining asclepias." — *Sir W. Jones,* "Botanical Observations on Select Indian Plants."

10 The oriental plane. "The chenar is a de-

Between the porphyry pillars that up-
hold
The rich moresque-work of the roof of
gold,
Aloft the Haram's curtained galleries rise,
Where thro' the silken net-work, glan-
cing eyes,
From time to time, like sudden gleams
that glow
Thro' autumn clouds, shine o'er the
pomp below. —
What impious tongue, ye blushing saints,
would dare
To hint that aught but Heaven hath
placed you there?
Or that the loves of this light world
could bind,
In their gross chain, your Prophet's soar-
ing mind?
No — wrongful thought ! — commissioned
from above
To people Eden's bowers with shapes of
love,
(Creatures so bright, that the same lips
and eyes
They wear on earth will serve in Para-
dise,)
There to recline among Heaven's native
maids,
And crown the Elect with bliss that never
fades —
Well hath the Prophet-Chief his bidding
done;
And every beauteous race beneath the
sun,
From those who kneel at BRAHMA'S
burning fount,[1]
To the fresh nymphs bounding o'er YE-
MEN'S mounts;
From PERSIA'S eyes of full and fawn-
like ray,
To the small, half-shut glances of
KATHAY; [2]
And GEORGIA'S bloom, and AZAB'S
darker smiles,
And the gold ringlets of the Western
Isles;

All, all are there ; — each Land its flower
hath given,
To form that fair young Nursery for
Heaven !

But why this pageant now? this armed
array?
What triumph crowds the rich Divan to-
to-day
With turbaned heads of every hue and
race,
Bowing before that veiled and awful face,
Like tulip-beds,[3] of different shape and
dyes,
Bending beneath the invisible West-
wind's sighs !
What new-made mystery now for Faith
to sign
And blood to seal, as genuine and divine,
What dazzling mimicry of God's own
power
Hath the bold Prophet planned to grace
this hour?

Not such the pageant now, tho' not
less proud;
Yon warrior youth advancing from the
crowd
With silver bow, with belt of broidered
crape
And fur-bound bonnet of Bucharian
shape,[4]
So fiercely beautiful in form and eye,
Like war's wild planet in a summer
sky;
That youth to-day, — a proselyte, worth
hordes
Of cooler spirits and less practised
swords, —
Is come to join, all bravery and belief,
The creed and standard of the heaven-
sent Chief.

Tho' few his years, the West already
knows
Young AZIM'S fame; — beyond the
Olympian snows

lightful tree; its bole is of a fine white and smooth
bark; and its foliage, which grows in a tuft at
the summit, is of a bright green." — *Morier's*
Travels.

1 The burning fountains of Brahma near
Chittogong, esteemed as holy. — *Turner.*

2 China.

3 "The name of tulip is said to be of Turkish extraction, and given to the flower on account
of its resembling a turban." — *Beckmann's* History of Inventions.

4 "The inhabitants of Bucharia wear a round
cloth bonnet, shaped much after the Polish fashion, having a large fur border. They tie their

Ere manhood darkened o'er his downy
  cheek,
O'erwhelmed in fight and captive to the
  Greek,[1]
He lingered there, till peace dissolved
  his chains; —
Oh! who could even in bondage tread
  the plains
Of glorious GREECE nor feel his spirit rise
Kindling within him? who with heart
  and eyes
Could walk where Liberty had been nor
  see
The shining foot-prints of her Deity,
Nor feel those god-like breathings in the
  air
Which mutely told her spirit had been
  there?
Not he, that youthful warrior, — no, too
  well
For his soul's quiet worked the awaken-
  ing spell;
And now, returning to his own dear land,
Full of those dreams of good that, vainly
  grand,
Haunt the young heart, — proud views
  of human-kind,
Of men to Gods exalted and refined, —
False views like that horizon's fair deceit
Where earth and heaven but *seem*, alas,
  to meet! —
Soon as he heard an Arm Divine was
  raised
To right the nations, and beheld, em-
  blazed
On the white flag MOKANNA'S host un-
  furled,
Those words of sunshine, "Freedom to
  the World,"
At once his faith, his sword, his soul
  obeyed
The inspiring summons; every chosen
  blade
That fought beneath that banner's sacred
  text
Seemed doubly edged for this world and
  the next;

And ne'er did Faith with her smooth
  bandage bind
Eyes more devoutly willing to be blind,
In virtue's cause; — never was soul in-
  spired
With livelier trust in what it most desired,
Than his, the enthusiast there, who kneel-
  ing, pale
With pious awe before that Silver Veil,
Believes the form to which he bends his
  knee
Some pure, redeeming angel sent to free
This lettered world from every bond and
  stain,
And bring its primal glories back again!

Low as young AZIM knelt, that motley
  crowd
Of all earth's nations sunk the knee and
  bowed,
With shouts of "ALLA!" echoing long
  and loud;
While high in air, above the Prophet's
  head,
Hundreds of banners to the sunbeam
  spread
Waved, like the wings of the white birds
  that fan
The flying throne of star-taught SOLI-
  MAN.[2]
Then thus he spoke: — "Stranger, tho'
  new the frame
"Thy soul inhabits now, I 've trackt its
  flame
"For many an age,[3] in every chance and
  change
"Of that existence, thro' whose varied
  range, —

kaftans about the middle with a girdle of a kind
of silk crape, several times round the body." —
*Account of Independent Tartary, in Pinkerton's
Collection.*

1 In the war of the Caliph Mahadi against
the Empress Irene, for an account of which *vide*
Gibbon, vol. x.

2 This wonderful Throne was called The Star
of the Genii. For a full description of it, see the
Fragment, translated by Captain Franklin, from
a Persian MS. entitled "The History of Jerusalem," *Oriental Collections*, vol. i. p. 235. —
When Soliman travelled, the eastern writers say,
"He had a carpet of green silk on which his throne
was placed, being of a prodigious length and
breadth, and sufficient for all his forces to stand
upon, the men placing themselves on his right
hand, and the spirits on his left ; and that when
all were in order, the wind, at his command, took
up the carpet, and transported it, with all that
were upon it, wherever he pleased ; the army of
birds at the same time flying over their heads, and
forming a kind of canopy to shade them from the
sun." — *Sale's* Koran, vol. ii. p. 214. note.

3 The transmigration of souls was one of his
doctrines. — *Vide D'Herbelot.*

" As thro' a torch-race where from hand
　　to hand
" The flying youths transmit their shin-
　　ing brand,
" From frame to frame the unextinguisht
　　soul
" Rapidly passes till it reach the goal!

" Nor think 't is only the gross Spirits
　　warmed
" With duskier fire and for earth's me-
　　dium formed
" That run this course; — Beings the most
　　divine
" Thus deign thro' dark mortality to shine.
" Such was the Essence that in ADAM
　　dwelt,
" To which all Heaven except the Proud
　　One knelt: [1]
" Such the refined Intelligence that
　　glowed
" In MOUSSA'S [2] frame, — and thence
　　descending flowed
" Thro' many a Prophet's breast; [3] — in
　　ISSA [4] shone
" And in MOHAMMED burned; till hasten-
　　ing on,
" (As a bright river that from fall to fall
" In many a maze descending bright thro'
　　all,
" Finds some fair region where, each
　　labyrinth past,
" In one full lake of light it rests at
　　last)
" That Holy Spirit settling calm and
　　free
" From lapse or shadow centres all in
　　me!"

1 " And when we said unto the angels, Worship Adam, they all worshipped him except Eblis
(Lucifer), who refused." — *The Koran,* chap. ii.

2 Moses.

3 This is according to D'Herbelot's account
of the doctrines of Mokanna: — " *Sa doctrine
étoit, que Dieu avoit pris une forme et figure
humaine, depuis qu'il eut commandé aux Anges
d'adorer Adam, le premier des hommes. Qu'
après la mort d'Adam, Dieu étoit apparu sous la
figure de plusieurs Prophètes, et autres grands
hommes qu'il avoit choisis, jusqu'à ce qu'il prit
celle d'Abu Moslem, Prince de Khorassan, lequel
professoit l'erreur de la Tenassukhiah ou Me-
tempschychose ; et qu'après la mort de ce Prince,
la Divinité étoit passée, et descendue en sa per-
sonne.*"

4 Jesus.

Again throughout the assembly at these
　　words
Thousands of voices rung: the warriors'
　　swords
Were pointed up to heaven; a sudden
　　wind
In the open banners played, and from
　　behind
Those Persian hangings that but ill could
　　screen
The Haram's loveliness, white hands
　　were seen
Waving embroidered scarves whose mo-
　　tion gave
A perfume forth — like those the Houris
　　wave
When beckoning to their bowers the
　　immortal Brave.

" But these," pursued the Chief, " are
　　truths sublime,
" That claim a holier mood and calmer
　　time
" Than earth allows us now; — this sword
　　must first
" The darkling prison-house of Mankind
　　burst
" Ere Peace can visit them or Truth let in
" Her wakening daylight on a world of
　　sin.
" But then, — celestial warriors, then
　　when all
" Earth's shrines and thrones before our
　　banner fall,
" When the glad Slave shall at these feet
　　lay down
" His broken chain, the tyrant Lord his
　　crown,
" The Priest his book, the Conqueror his
　　wreath,
" And from the lips of Truth one mighty
　　breath
" Shall like a whirlwind scatter in its
　　breeze
" That whole dark pile of human mock-
　　eries: —
" Then shall the reign of mind commence
　　on earth,
" And starting fresh as from a second
　　birth,
" Man in the sunshine of the world's
　　new spring
" Shall walk transparent like some holy
　　thing!

" Then too your Prophet from his angel
brow
" Shall cast the Veil that hides its splendors now,
" And gladdened Earth shall thro' her
wide expanse
" Bask in the glories of this countenance !

" For thee, young warrior, welcome !
— thou hast yet
" Some tasks to learn, some frailties to
forget,
" Ere the white war-plume o'er thy brow
can wave; —
" But, once my own, mine all till in the
grave !''

The pomp is at an end — the crowds
are gone —
Each ear and heart still haunted by the
tone
Of that deep voice, which thrilled like
ALLA's own !
The Young all dazzled by the plumes and
lances,
The glittering throne and Haram's half-
caught glances,
The Old deep pondering on the promised
reign
Of peace and truth, and all the female
train
Ready to risk their eyes could they but
gaze
A moment on that brow's miraculous
blaze !

But there was one among the chosen
maids
Who blushed behind the gallery's silken
shades,
One, to whose soul the pageant of to-day
Has been like death : — you saw her pale
dismay,
Ye wondering sisterhood, and heard the
burst
Of exclamation from her lips when first
She saw that youth, too well, too dearly
known,
Silently kneeling at the Prophet's throne.

Ah ZELICA ! there *was* a time when
bliss
Shone o'er thy heart from every look of
his,

When but to see him, hear him, breathe
the air
In which he dwelt was thy soul's fondest
prayer;
When round him hung such a perpetual
spell,
Whate'er he did, none ever did so well.
Too happy days ! when, if he touched a
flower
Or gem of thine, 't was sacred from that
hour;
When thou didst study him till every tone
And gesture and dear look became thy
own, —
Thy voice like his, the changes of his face
In thine reflected with still lovelier grace,
Like echo, sending back sweet music,
fraught
With twice the aërial sweetness it had
brought !
Yet now he comes, — brighter than even
he
E'er beamed before, — but, ah ! not
bright for thee;
No — dread, unlookt for, like a visitant
From the other world he comes as if to
haunt
Thy guilty soul with dreams of lost delight,
Long lost to all but memory's aching
sight : —
Sad dreams ! as when the Spirit of our
Youth
Returns in sleep, sparkling with all the
truth
And innocence once ours and leads us
back,
In mournful mockery o'er the shining
track
Of our young life and points out every ray
Of hope and peace we' ve lost upon the
way !

Once happy pair ! — In proud Bo-
KHARA's groves,
Who had not heard of their first youth-
ful loves ?
Born by that ancient flood,[1] which from
its spring
In the dark Mountains swiftly wandering,

1 The Amu, which rises in the Belur Tag, or
Dark Mountains, and running nearly from east to
west, splits into two branches ; one of which falls
into the Caspian sea, and the other into Aral Nahr,
or the Lake of Eagles.

Enriched by every pilgrim brook that shines
With relics from BUCHARIA'S ruby mines,
And, lending to the CASPIAN half its strength,
In the cold Lake of Eagles sinks at length; —
There, on the banks of that bright river born,
The flowers that hung above its wave at morn
Blest not the waters as they murmured by
With holier scent and lustre than the sigh
And virgin-glance of first affection cast
Upon their youth's smooth current as it past!
But war disturbed this vision, — far away
From her fond eyes summoned to join the array
Of PERSIA'S warriors on the hills of THRACE,
The youth exchanged his sylvan dwelling-place
For the rude tent and war-field's deathful clash;
His ZELICA'S sweet glances for the flash
Of Grecian wild-fire, and Love's gentle chains
For bleeding bondage on BYZANTIUM'S plains.

Month after month in widowhood of soul
Drooping the maiden saw two summers roll
Their suns away — but, ah, how cold and dim
Even summer suns when not beheld with him!
From time to time ill-omened rumors came
Like spirit-tongues muttering the sick man's name
Just ere he dies: — at length those sounds of dread
Fell withering on her soul, " AZIM is dead!"
Oh Grief beyond all other griefs when fate
First leaves the young heart lone and desolate

In the wide world without that only tie
For which it loved to live or feared to die; —
Lorn as the hung-up lute, that ne'er hath spoken
Since the sad day its master-chord was broken!

Fond maid, the sorrow of her soul was such,
Even reason sunk, — blighted beneath its touch;
And tho' ere long her sanguine spirit rose
Above the first dead pressure of its woes,
Tho' health and bloom returned, the delicate chain
Of thought once tangled never cleared again.
Warm, lively, soft as in youth's happiest day,
The mind was still all there but turned astray, —
A wandering bark upon whose pathway shone
All stars of heaven except the guiding one!
Again she smiled, nay, much and brightly smiled,
But 't was a lustre, strange, unreal, wild;
And when she sung to her lute's touching strain,
'T was like the notes, half ecstasy, half pain,
The bulbul [1] utters ere her soul depart,
When, vanquisht by some minstrel's powerful art,
She dies upon the lute whose sweetness broke her heart!

Such was the mood in which that mission found
Young ZELICA, — that mission which around
The Eastern world in every region blest
With woman's smile sought out its loveliest
To grace that galaxy of lips and eyes
Which the Veiled Prophet destined for the skies: —

[1] The nightingale.

And such quick welcome as a spark
  receives
Dropt on a bed of Autumn's withered
  leaves,
Did every tale of these enthusiasts find
In the wild maiden's sorrow-blighted
  mind.
All fire at once the maddening zeal she
  caught;—
Elect of Paradise! blest, rapturous
  thought!
Predestined bride, in heaven's eternal
  dome,
Of some brave youth—ha! durst they
  say "of *some?*"
No—of the one, one only object traced
In her heart's core too deep to be ef-
  faced;
The one whose memory, fresh as life, is
  twined
With every broken link of her lost mind;
Whose image lives tho' Reason's self be
  wreckt
Safe mid the ruins of her intellect!

Alas, poor ZELICA! it needed all
The fantasy which held thy mind in
  thrall
To see in that gay Haram's glowing
  maids
A sainted colony for Eden's shades;
Or dream that he,—of whose unholy
  flame
Thou wert too soon the victim,—shining
  came
From Paradise to people its pure sphere
With souls like thine which he hath
  ruined here!
No—had not reason's light totally set,
And left thee dark thou hadst an amulet
In the loved image graven on thy heart
Which would have saved thee from the
  tempter's art,
And kept alive in all its bloom of
  breath
That purity whose fading is love's
  death!—
But lost, inflamed,—a restless zeal took
  place
Of the mild virgin's still and feminine
  grace;
First of the Prophet's favorites, proudly
  first

In zeal and charms,—too well the Im-
  postor nurst
Her soul's delirium in whose active
  flame,
Thus lighting up a young, luxuriant
  frame,
He saw more potent sorceries to bind
To his dark yoke the spirits of mankind,
More subtle chains than hell itself e'er
  twined.
No art was spared, no witchery;—all the
  skill
His demons taught him was employed to
  fill
Her mind with gloom and ecstasy by
  turns—
That gloom, thro' which Frenzy but
  fiercer burns,
That ecstasy which from the depth of
  sadness
Glares like the maniac's moon whose
  light is madness!

'T was from a brilliant banquet where
  the sound
Of poesy and music breathed around,
Together picturing to her mind and ear
The glories of that heaven, her destined
  sphere,
Where all was pure, where every stain
  that lay
Upon the spirit's light should pass away,
And realizing more than youthful love
E'er wisht or dreamed, she should for
  ever rove
Thro' fields of fragrance by her AZIM's
  side,
His own blest, purified, eternal bride!—
'T was from a scene, a witching trance
  like this,
He hurried her away, yet breathing bliss,
To the dim charnel-house;—thro' all its
  steams
Of damp and death led only by those
  gleams
Which foul Corruption lights, as with
  design
To show the gay and proud *she* too can
  shine—
And passing on thro' upright ranks of
  Dead
Which to the maiden, doubly crazed by
  dread,

Seemed, thro' the bluish death-light
  round them cast,
To move their lips in mutterings as she
  past —
There in that awful place, when each
  had quaft
And pledged in silence such a fearful
  draught,
Such — oh! the look and taste of that
  red bowl
Will haunt her till she dies — he bound
  her soul
By a dark oath, in hell's own language
  framed,
Never, while earth his mystic presence
  claimed,
While the blue arch of day hung o'er
  them both,
Never, by that all-imprecating oath,
In joy or sorrow from his side to
  sever. —
She swore and the wide charnel echoed,
  "Never, never!"

From that dread hour, entirely, wildly
  given
To him and — she believed, lost maid!
  — to heaven;
Her brain, her heart, her passions all
  inflamed,
How proud she stood, when in full
  Haram named
The Priestess of the Faith! — how flasht
  her eyes
With light, alas, that was not of the
  skies,
When round in trances only less than
  hers
She saw the Haram kneel, her prostrate
  worshippers.
Well might MOKANNA think that form
  alone
Had spells enough to make the world
  his own:—
Light, lovely limbs to which the spirit's
  play
Gave motion, airy as the dancing spray,
When from its stem the small bird wings
  away:
Lips in whose rosy labyrinth when she
  smiled
The soul was lost, and blushes, swift and
  wild

As are the momentary meteors sent
Across the uncalm but beauteous firma-
  ment.
And then her look — oh! where's the
  heart so wise
Could unbewildered meet those match-
  less eyes?
Quick, restless, strange, but exquisite
  withal,
Like those of angels just before their
  fall;
Now shadowed with the shames of earth
  — now crost
By glimpses of the Heaven her heart had
  lost;
In every glance there broke without
  control,
The flashes of a bright but troubled soul,
Where sensibility still wildly played
Like lightning round the ruins it had
  made!

And such was now young ZELICA — so
  changed
From her who some years since delighted
  ranged
The almond groves that shade Bo-
  KHARA'S tide
All life and bliss with AZIM by her
  side!
So altered was she now, this festal day,
When, mid the proud Divan's dazzling
  array,
The vision of that Youth whom she had
  loved,
Had wept as dead, before her breathed
  and moved;—
When — bright, she thought, as if from
  Eden's track
But half-way trodden, he had wandered
  back
Again to earth, glistening with Eden's
  light —
Her beauteous AZIM shone before her
  sight.

O Reason! who shall say what spells
  renew,
When least we look for it, thy broken
  clew!
Thro' what small vistas o'er the darkened brain
Thy intellectual day-beam bursts again;

And how like forts to which beleaguerers
  win
Unhoped-for entrance thro' some friend
  within,
One clear idea, wakened in the breast
By memory's magic, lets in all the rest.
Would it were thus, unhappy girl, with
  thee!
But tho' light came, it came but partially;
Enough to show the maze, in which thy
  sense
Wandered about, — but not to guide it
  thence;
Enough to glimmer o'er the yawning
  wave,
But not to point the harbor which might
  save.
Hours of delight and peace, long left
  behind,
With that dear form came rushing o'er
  her mind;
But, oh! to think how deep her soul had
  gone
In shame and falsehood since those mo-
  ments shone;
And then her oath — *there* madness lay
  again,
And shuddering, back she sunk into her
  chain
Of mental darkness, as if blest to flee
From light whose every glimpse was
  agony!
Yet *one* relief this glance of former years
Brought mingled with its pain, — tears,
  floods of tears,
Long frozen at her heart, but now like
  rills
Let loose in spring-time from the snowy
  hills,
And gushing warm after a sleep of frost,
Thro' valleys where their flow had long
  been lost.

Sad and subdued, for the first time her
  frame
Trembled with horror when the summons
  came
(A summons proud and rare, which all
  but she,
And she, till now, had heard with ecs-
  tasy,)
To meet MOKANNA at his place of prayer,
A garden oratory cool and fair

By the stream's side, where still at close
  of day
The Prophet of the Veil retired to
  pray,
Sometimes alone — but oftener far with
  one,
One chosen nymph to share his orison.

Of late none found such favor in his
  sight
As the young Priestess; and tho', since
  that night
When the death-caverns echoed every
  tone
Of the dire oath that made her all his
  own,
The Impostor sure of his infatuate prize
Had more than once thrown off his soul's
  disguise,
And uttered such unheavenly, monstrous
  things,
As even across the desperate wander-
  ings
Of a weak intellect, whose lamp was
  out,
Threw startling shadows of dismay and
  doubt; —
Yet zeal, ambition, her tremendous vow,
The thought, still haunting her, of that
  bright brow,
Whose blaze, as yet from mortal eye con-
  cealed,
Would soon, proud triumph! be to her
  revealed,
To her alone; — and then the hope, most
  dear,
Most wild of all, that her transgression
  here
Was but a passage thro' earth's grosser
  fire,
From which the spirit would at last as-
  pire,
Even purer than before, — as perfumes
  rise
Thro' flame and smoke, most welcome
  to the skies —
And that when AZIM's fond, divine em-
  brace
Should circle her in heaven, no darkening trace
Would on that bosom he once loved remain,
But all be bright, be pure, be *his* again!—

These were the wildering dreams, whose curst deceit
Had chained her soul beneath the tempter's feet,
And made her think even damning falsehood sweet.
But now that Shape, which had appalled her view,
That Semblance — oh how terrible, if true !
Which came across her frenzy's full career
With shock of consciousness, cold, deep, severe,
As when in northern seas at midnight dark
An isle of ice encounters some swift bark,
And startling all its wretches from their sleep
By one cold impulse hurls them to the deep; —
So came that shock not frenzy's self could bear,
And waking up each long-lulled image there,
But checkt her headlong soul to sink it in despair !

Wan and dejected, thro' the evening dusk,
She now went slowly to that small kiosk,
Where, pondering alone his impious schemes,
MOKANNA waited her — too wrapt in dreams
Of the fair-ripening future's rich success,
To heed the sorrow, pale and spiritless,
That sat upon his victim's downcast brow,
Or mark how slow her step, how altered now
From the quick, ardent Priestess, whose light bound
Came like a spirit's o'er the unechoing ground, —
From that wild ZELICA whose every glance
Was thrilling fire, whose every thought a trance !

Upon his couch the Veiled MOKANNA lay,
While lamps around — not such as lend their ray,
Glimmering and cold, to those who nightly pray
In holy KOOM,[1] or MECCA's dim arcades, —
But brilliant, soft, such lights as lovely maids
Look loveliest in, shed their luxurious glow
Upon his mystic Veil's white glittering flow.
Beside him, 'stead of beads and books of prayer,
Which the world fondly thought he mused on there,
Stood Vases, filled with KISHMEE'S[2] golden wine,
And the red weepings of the SHIRAZ vine;
Of which his curtained lips full many a draught
Took zealously, as if each drop they quaft
Like ZEMZEM's Spring of Holiness[3] had power
To freshen the soul's virtues into flower !
And still he drank and pondered — nor could see
The approaching maid, so deep his revery;
At length with fiendish laugh like that which broke
From EBLIS at the Fall of Man he spoke: —
" Yes, ye vile race, for hell's amusement given,
" Too mean for earth, yet claiming kin with heaven;
" God's images, forsooth ! — such gods as he
" Whom INDIA serves, the monkey deity;[4] —

1 The cities of Com (or Koom) and Cashan are full of mosques, mausoleums, and sepulchres of the descendants of Ali, the Saints of Persia. — *Chardin.*

2 An island in the Persian Gulf, celebrated for its white wine.

3 The miraculous well at Mecca; so called, says Sale, from the murmuring of its waters.

4 The god Hannaman. — " Apes are in many parts of India highly venerated, out of respect to the God Hannaman, a deity partaking of the form of that race." — *Pennant's* Hindoostan.

See a curious account, in *Stephen's Persia,* of a solemn embassy from some part of the Indies to Goa, when the Portuguese were there, offering vast treasures for the recovery of a monkey's

" Ye creatures of a breath, proud things
 of clay,
" To whom if LUCIFER, as grandams say,
" Refused tho' at the forfeit of heaven's
 light
" To bend in worship, LUCIFER was
 right ! [1] —
" Soon shall I plant this foot upon the
 neck
" Of your foul race and without fear or
 check,
" Luxuriating in hate, avenge my shame,
" My deep-felt, long-nurst loathing of
 man's name ! —
" Soon at the head of myriads, blind and
 . fierce
" As hooded falcons, thro' the universe
" I 'll sweep my darkening, desolating
 way,
" Weak man my instrument, curst man
 my prey !

 " Ye wise, ye learned, who grope your
  dull way on
" By the dim twinkling gleams of ages
 gone,
" Like superstitious thieves who think
 the light
" From dead men's marrow guides them
 best at night [2] —
" Ye shall have honors — wealth — yes,
 Sages, yes —
" I know, grave fools, your wisdom's
 nothingness;

tooth, which they held in great veneration, and
which had been taken away upon the conquest
of the kingdom of Jafanapatan.

1 This resolution of Eblis not to acknowledge
the new creature, man, was, according to Mahometan tradition, thus adopted : — " The earth
(which God had selected for the materials of his
work) was carried into Arabia to a place between
Mecca and Tayef, where, being first kneaded by
the angels, it was afterwards fashioned by God
himself into a human form, and left to dry for
the space of forty days, or, as others say, as
many years ; the angels, in the mean time, often
visiting it, and Eblis (then one of the angels nearest to God's presence, afterwards the devil) among
the rest ; but he, not contented with looking at
it, kicked it with his foot till it rung ; and knowing God designed that creature to be his superior,
took a secret resolution never to acknowledge
him as such." — *Sale* on the Koran.

2 A kind of lantern formerly used by robbers,
called the Hand of Glory, the candle for which
was made of the fat of a dead malefactor. This,
however, was rather a western than an eastern
superstition.

" Undazzled it can track yon starry
 sphere,
" But a gilt stick, a bauble blinds it here.
" How I shall laugh, when trumpeted
 along
" In lying speech and still more lying
 song,
" By these learned slaves, the meanest
 of the throng;
" Their wits bought up, their wisdom
 shrunk so small,
" A sceptre's puny point can wield it all !

 " Ye too, believers of incredible creeds,
" Whose faith enshrines the monsters
  which it breeds;
" Who, bolder even than NEMROD, think
 to rise
" By nonsense heapt on nonsense to the
 skies;
" Ye shall have miracles, ay, sound ones
 too,
" Seen, heard, attested, every thing —
 but true.
" Your preaching zealots too inspired to
 seek
" One grace of meaning for the things
 they speak;
" Your martyrs ready to shed out their
 blood,
" For truths too heavenly to be understood;
" And your State Priests, sole venders
 of the lore,
" That works salvation; — as, on AVA'S
 shore,
" Where none *but* priests are privileged
 to trade
" In that best marble of which Gods are
 made ; [3]
" They shall have mysteries — ay, precious stuff
" For knaves to thrive by — mysteries
 enough;
" Dark, tangled doctrines, dark as fraud
 can weave,
" Which simple votaries shall on trust
 receive,

3 The material of which images of Gaudma
(the Birman Deity) are made, is held sacred.
" Birmans may not purchase the marble in mass,
but are suffered, and indeed encouraged, to buy
figures of the Deity ready made." — *Symes's*
"Ava," vol. ii. p. 376.

" While craftier feign belief till they
  believe.
" A Heaven too ye must have, ye lords
  of dust, —
" A splendid Paradise, — pure souls, ye
  must:
" That Prophet ill sustains his holy call,
" Who finds not heavens to suit the
  tastes of all;
" Houris for boys, omniscience for sages,
" And wings and glories for all ranks
  and ages.
" Vain things! — as lust or vanity in-
  spires,
" The heaven of each is but what each
  desires,
" And, soul or sense, whate'er the object
  be,
" Man would be man to all eternity!
" So let him — EBLIS! grant this crown-
  ing curse,
" But keep him what he is, no Hell were
  worse."

" Oh my lost soul!" exclaimed the
  shuddering maid,
Whose ears had drunk like poison all he
said: —
MOKANNA started — not abasht, afraid, —
He knew no more of fear than one who
  dwells
Beneath the tropics knows of icicles!
But in those dismal words that reached
  his ear,
" Oh my lost soul!" there was a sound
  so drear,
So like that voice among the sinful dead
In which the legend o'er Hell's Gate is
  read,
That, new as 't was from her whom
  naught could dim
Or sink till now, it startled even him.

" Ha, my fair Priestess!" — thus,
  with ready wile,
The impostor turned to greet her —
  " thou whose smile
" Hath inspiration in its rosy beam
" Beyond the Enthusiast's hope or Prophet's dream,
" Light of the Faith! who twin'st religion's zeal
" So close with love's, men know not
  which they feel,

" Nor which to sigh for, in their trance
  of heart,
" The heaven thou preachest or the
  heaven thou art!
" What should I be without thee? with-
  out thee
" How dull were power, how joyless
  victory!
" Tho' borne by angels, if that smile of
  thine
" Blest not my banner 't were but half
  divine.
" But — why so mournful, child? those
  eyes that shone
" All life last night — what! — is their
  glory gone?
" Come, come — this morn's fatigue hath
  made them pale,
" They want rekindling — suns them-
  selves would fail
" Did not their comets bring, as I to thee,
" From light's own fount supplies of
  brilliancy.
" Thou seest this cup — no juice of earth
  is here,
" But the pure waters of that upper
  sphere,
" Whose rills o'er ruby beds and topaz
  flow,
" Catching the gem's bright color as they
  go.
" Nightly my Genii come and fill these
  urns —
" Nay, drink — in every drop life's es-
  sence burns;
" 'T will make that soul all fire, those
  eyes all light —
" Come, come, I want thy loveliest smiles
  to-night:
" There is a youth — why start? — thou
  saw'st him then;
" Lookt he not nobly? such the godlike
  men
" Thou 'lt have to woo thee in the bowers
  above; —
" Tho' *he*, I fear, hath thoughts too stern
  for love,
" Too ruled by that cold enemy of bliss
" The world calls virtue — we must con-
  quer this;
" Nay, shrink not, pretty sage! 't is not
  for thee
" To scan the mazes of Heaven's mystery:

" The steel must pass thro' fire, ere it can
yield
" Fit instruments for mighty hands to
wield.
" This very night I mean to try the art
" Of powerful beauty on that warrior's
heart.
" All that my Haram boasts of bloom
and wit,
" Of skill and charms, most rare and
exquisite,
" Shall tempt the boy; — young MIR-
ZALA'S blue eyes
" Whose sleepy lid like snow on violets
lies;
" AROUYA'S cheeks warm as a spring-day
sun
" And lips that like the seal of SOLOMON
" Have magic in their pressure; ZEBA'S
lute,
" And LILLA'S dancing feet that gleam
and shoot
" Rapid and white as sea-birds o'er the
deep —
" All shall combine their witching powers
to steep
" My convert's spirit in that softening
trance,
" From which to heaven is but the next
advance; —
" That glowing, yielding fusion of the
breast,
" On which Religion stamps her image
best.
" But hear me, Priestess! — tho' each
nymph of these
" Hath some peculiar, practised power
to please,
" Some glance or step which at the
mirror tried
" First charms herself, then all the world
beside;
" There still wants *one* to make the victory sure,
" One who in every look joins every
lure,
" Thro' whom all beauty's beams con-
centered pass,
" Dazzling and warm as thro' love's
burning glass;
" Whose gentle lips persuade without a
word,
" Whose words, even when unmeaning,
are adored,

" Like inarticulate breathings from a
shrine,
" Which our faith takes for granted are
divine !
" Such is the nymph we want, all warmth
and light,
" To crown the rich temptations of to-
night;
" Such the refined enchantress that must
be
" This hero's vanquisher, — and thou art
she ! "

With her hands claspt, her lips apart
and pale,
The maid had stood gazing upon the Veil
From which these words like south winds
thro' a fence
Of Kerzrah flowers, came filled with
pestilence;[1]
So boldly uttered too ! as if all dread
Of frowns from her, of virtuous frowns,
were fled,
And the wretch felt assured that, once
plunged in,
Her woman's soul would know no pause
in sin !

At first, tho' mute she listened, like a
dream
Seemed all he said: nor could her mind
whose beam
As yet was weak penetrate half his
scheme.
But when at length he uttered, "Thou
art she ! "
All flasht at once and shrieking piteously,
" Oh not for worlds ! " she cried —
" Great God ! to whom
" I once knelt innocent, is this my doom?
" Are all my dreams, my hopes of
heavenly bliss,
" My purity, my pride, then come to
this, —
" To live, the wanton of a fiend ! to be
" The pander of his guilt — oh infamy !
" And sunk myself as low as hell can
steep
" In its hot flood, drag others down as
deep !

1 " It is commonly said in Persia, that if a man
breathe in the hot south wind, which in June or
July passes over that flower (the Kerzereh), it
will kill him." — *Thevenot.*

" Others — ha! yes — that youth who
   came to-day —
" *Not* him I loved — not him — oh! do
   but say,
" But swear to me this moment 't is not
   he,
" And I will serve, dark fiend, will worship even thee!"

" Beware, young raving thing! — in
   time beware,
" Nor utter what I can not, must not
   bear,
" Even from *thy* lips. Go — try thy lute,
   thy voice,
" The boy must feel their magic; — I
   rejoice
" To see those fires, no matter whence
   they rise,
" Once more illuming my fair Priestess'
   eyes;
" And should the youth whom soon those
   eyes shall warm,
" *Indeed* resemble thy dead lover's form,
" So much the happier wilt thou find thy
   doom,
" As one warm lover full of life and
   bloom
" Excels ten thousand cold ones in the
   tomb.
" Nay, nay, no frowning, sweet! — those
   eyes were made
" For love, not anger — I must be
   obeyed."

" Obeyed! — 't is well — yes, I de-
   serve it all —
" On me, on me Heaven's vengeance
   can not fall
" Too heavily — but AZIM, brave and
   true
" And beautiful — must *he* be ruined too?
" Must *he* too, glorious as he is, be driven
" A renegade like me from Love and
   Heaven?
" Like me? — weak wretch, I wrong him
   — not like me;
" No — he 's all truth and strength and
   purity!
" Fill up your maddening hell-cup to the
   brim,
" Its witchery, fiends, will have no charm
   for him.

" Let loose your glowing wantons from
   their bowers,
" He loves, he loves, and can defy their
   powers!
" Wretch as I am, in *his* heart still I
   reign
" Pure as when first we met, without a
   stain!
" Tho' ruined — lost — my memory like
   a charm
" Left by the dead still keeps his soul
   from harm.
" Oh! never let him know how deep the
   brow
" He kist at parting is dishonored now; —
" Ne'er tell him how debased, how sunk
   is she,
" Whom once he loved — once! — *still*
   loves dotingly.
" Thou laugh'st, tormentor, — what! —
   thou 'lt brand my name?
" Do, do — in vain — he 'll not believe
   my shame —
" He thinks me true, that naught beneath
   God's sky
" Could tempt or change me, and — so
   once thought I.
" But this is past — tho' worse than
   death my lot,
" Than hell — 't is nothing while *he*
   knows it not.
" Far off to some benighted land I 'll
   fly,
" Where sunbeam ne'er shall enter till I
   die;
" Where none will ask the lost one
   whence she came,
" But I may fade and fall without a name.
" And thou — curst man or fiend, whate'er
   thou art,
" Who found'st this burning plague-spot
   in my heart,
" And spread'st it — oh, so quick! —
   thro' soul and frame,
" With more than demon's art, till I
   became
" A loathsome thing, all pestilence, all
   flame! —
" If, when I 'm gone "—
              " Hold, fearless maniac, hold,
" Nor tempt my rage — by Heaven, not
   half so bold
" The puny bird that dares with teasing
   hum

" Within the crocodile's stretched jaws
 to come ! [1]
" And so thou 'lt fly, forsooth? — what !
 — give up all
" Thy chaste dominion in the Haram
 Hall,
" Where now to Love and now to ALLA
 given,
" Half mistress and half saint, thou
 hang'st as even
" As doth MEDINA'S tomb, 'twixt hell
 and heaven !
" Thou 'lt fly? — as easily may reptiles
 run,
" The gaunt snake once hath fixt his eyes
 upon;
" As easily, when caught, the prey may
 be
" Pluckt from his loving folds, as thou
 from me.
" No, no, 't is fixt — let good or ill betide,
" Thou 'rt mine till death, till death
 MOKANNA'S bride !
" Hast thou forgot thy oath? " —
    At this dread word,
The Maid whose spirit his rude taunts
 had stirred
Thro' all its depths and roused an anger
 there,
That burst and lightened even thro' her
 despair —
Shrunk back as if a blight were in the
 breath
That spoke that word and staggered pale
 as death.

" Yes, my sworn pride, let others seek
 in bowers
" Their bridal place — the charnel vault
 was ours !
" Instead of scents and balms, for thee
 and me
" Rose the rich steams of sweet mortal-
 ity,
" Gay, flickering death-lights shone while
 we were wed,
" And for our guests a row of goodly
 Dead,

" (Immortal spirits in their time, no
 doubt,)
" From reeking shrouds upon the rite
 looked out !
" That oath thou heard'st more lips than
 thine repeat —
" That cup — thou shudderest, Lady, —
 was it sweet?
" That cup we pledged, the charnel's
 choicest wine,
" Hath bound thee — ay — body and
 soul all mine;
" Bound thee by chains that, whether
 blest or curst
" No matter now, not hell itself shall
 burst !
" Hence, woman, to the Haram, and
 look gay,
" Look wild, look — any thing but sad;
 yet stay —
" One moment more — from what this
 night hath past,
" I see thou know'st me, know'st me
 well at last.
" Ha ! ha ! and so, fond thing, thou
 thought'st all true,
" And that I love mankind? — I do, I
 do —
" As victims, love them; as the sea-dog
 dotes
" Upon the small, sweet fry that round
 him floats;
" Or, as the Nile-bird loves the slime
 that gives
" That rank and venomous food on which
 she lives ! [2] —

" And, now thou seest my *soul*'s angelic hue,
" 'T is time these *features* were uncur-
 tained too; —
" This brow, whose light — oh rare
 celestial light !
" Hath been reserved to bless thy favored sight;

---

[1] The humming bird is said to run this risk
for the purpose of picking the crocodile's teeth.
The same circumstance is related of the lapwing,
as a fact to which he was witness, by *Paul Lucas,*
"*Voyage fait en* 1714."

The ancient story concerning the Trochilus,
or humming-bird, entering with impunity into the
mouth of the crocodile, is firmly believed at Java.
— *Barrow's "Cochin-China."*

[2] *circum easdem ripas (Nili, viz.) ales est
Ibis. ea serpentium populatur ova, gratissi-
mamque ex his escam nidis suis refert. —
Solinus.*

"These dazzling eyes before whose
    shrouded might
"Thou'st seen immortal Man kneel
    down and quake —
"Would that they *were* heaven's light-
    nings for his sake!
"But turn and look — then wonder, if
    thou wilt,
"That I should hate, should take re-
    venge, by guilt,
"Upon the hand whose mischief or
    whose mirth
"Sent me thus maimed and monstrous
    upon earth;

"And on that race who, tho' more vile
    they be
"Than mowing apes, are demi-gods to
    me!
"Here — judge if hell, with all its
    power to damn,
"Can add one curse to the foul thing I
    am!" —

He raised his veil — the Maid turned
    slowly round,
Looked at him — shrieked — and sunk
    upon the ground!

ON their arrival next night at the place of encampment they were surprised and delighted to find the groves all around illuminated; some artists of Yamtcheou [1] having been sent on previously for the purpose. On each side of the green alley, which led to the Royal Pavilion, artificial sceneries of bamboo-work [2] were erected, representing arches, minarets, and towers, from which hung thousands of silken lanterns painted by the most delicate pencils of Canton. — Nothing could be more beautiful than the leaves of the mango-trees and acacias shining in the light of the bamboo-scenery which shed a lustre round as soft as that of the nights of Peristan.

LALLA ROOKH, however, who was too much occupied by the sad story of ZELICA and her lover to give a thought to any thing else, except perhaps him who related it, hurried on through this scene of splendor to her pavilion, — greatly to the mortification of the poor artists of Yamtcheou, — and was followed with equal rapidity by the Great Chamberlain, cursing, as he went, that ancient Mandarin, whose parental anxiety in lighting up the shores of the lake, where his beloved daughter had wandered and been lost, was the origin of these fantastic Chinese illuminations. [3]

Without a moment's delay, young FERAMORZ was introduced, and FADLADEEN, who could never make up his mind as to the merits of a poet till he knew the religious sect to which he belonged was about to ask him whether he was a Shia or a Sooni when LALLA ROOKH impatiently clapped her hands for silence, and the youth being seated upon the musnud near her proceeded: —

1 "The feast of Lanterns is celebrated at Yamtcheou with more magnificence than any where else : and the report goes, that the illuminations there are so splendid, that an Emperor once, not daring openly to leave his Court to go thither, committed himself with the Queen and several Princesses of his family into the hands of a magician, who promised to transport them thither in a trice. He made them in the night to ascend magnificent thrones that were borne up by swans, which in a moment arrived at Yamtcheou. The Emperor saw at his leisure all the solemnity, being carried upon a cloud that hovered over the city and descended by degrees; and came back again with the same speed and equipage, nobody at court perceiving his absence." — " *The Present State of China,*" p. 156.

2 See a description of the nuptials of Vizier Alee in the *Asiatic Annual Register of* 1804.

3 "The vulgar ascribe it to an accident that happened in the family of a famous mandarin, whose daughter, walking one evening upon the shore of a lake, fell in and was drowned; this afflicted father, with his family, ran thither, and, the better to find her, he caused a great company of lanterns to be lighted. All the inhabitants of the place thronged after him with torches. The year ensuing they made fires upon the shores the same day; they continued the ceremony every year, every one lighted his lantern, and by degrees it commenced into a custom." —"*The Present State of China.*"

PREPARE thy soul, young AZIM! — thou
  hast braved
The bands of GREECE, still mighty tho'
  enslaved;
Hast faced her phalanx armed with all
  its fame, —
Her Macedonian pikes and globes of
  fame,
All this hast fronted with firm heart and
  brow,
But a more perilous trial waits thee
  now, —
Woman's bright eyes, a dazzling host of
  eyes
From every land where woman smiles or
  sighs;
Of every hue, as Love may chance to raise
His black or azure banner in their blaze;
And each sweet mode of warfare, from
  the flash
That lightens boldly thro' the shadowy
  lash,
To the sly, stealing splendors almost hid
Like swords half-sheathed beneath the
  downcast lid; —
Such, AZIM, is the lovely, luminous host
Now led against thee; and let conquerors
  boast
Their fields of fame, he who in virtue
  arms
A young, warm spirit against beauty's
  charms,
Who feels her brightness, yet defies her
  thrall,
Is the best, bravest conqueror of them all.

Now, thro' the Haram chambers, moving lights
And busy shapes proclaim the toilet's
  rites; —
From room to room the ready handmaids
  hie,
Some skilled to wreath the turban taste-
  fully,
Or hang the veil in negligence of shade
O'er the warm blushes of the youthful
  maid,
Who, if between the folds but *one* eye
  shone,
Like SEBA's Queen could vanquish with
  that one: [1] —

While some bring leaves of Henna to
  imbue
The fingers' ends with a bright roseate
  hue, [2]
So bright that in the mirror's depth they
  seem
Like tips of coral branches in the stream:
And others mix the Kohol's jetty dye,
To give that long, dark languish to the
  eye, [3]
Which makes the maids whom kings are
  proud to cull
From fair Circassia's vales, so beautiful.
All is in motion; rings and plumes and
  pearls
Are shining everywhere: — some younger
  girls
Are gone by moonlight to the garden-
  beds,
To gather fresh, cool chaplets for their
  heads; —
Gay creatures! sweet, tho' mournful,
  't is to see
How each prefers a garland from that tree
Which brings to mind her childhood's
  innocent day
And the dear fields and friendships far
  away.
The maid of INDIA, blest again to hold
In her full lap the Champac's leaves of
  gold, [4]

[1] "Thou hast ravished my heart with one of
thine eyes." — *Sol. Song.*

[2] "They tinged the ends of her fingers scarlet
with Henna, so that they resembled branches of
coral." — *Story of Prince Futtun in Bahardanush.*

[3] "The women blacken the inside of their
eyelids with a powder named the black Kohol."
— *Russel.*

"None of these ladies," says *Shaw*, "take
themselves to be completely dressed, till they
have tinged the hair and edges of their eyelids
with the powder of lead ore. Now, as this oper-
tion is performed by dipping first into the powder
a small wooden bodkin of the thickness of a
quill, and then drawing it afterwards through the
eyelids over the ball of the eye, we shall have a
lively image of what the Prophet (Jer. iv. 30.)
may be supposed to mean by *rending the eyes
with painting*. This practice is no doubt of great
antiquity; for besides the instance already taken
notice of, we find that where Jezebel is said
(2 Kings ix. 30.) *to have painted her face*, the
original words are, *she adjusted her eyes with
the powder of lead-ore.*" — *Shaw's Travels.*

[4] "The appearance of the blossoms of the
gold-colored Campac on the black hair of the Indian women has supplied the Sanscrit Poets
with many elegant allusions." — See *Asiatic Researches,* vol. iv.

Thinks of the time when, by the GANGES'
flood,
Her little playmates scattered many a bud
Upon her long black hair with glossy
gleam
Just dripping from the consecrated
stream;
While the young Arab haunted by the
smell
Of her own mountain flowers as by a
spell,—
The sweet Elcaya [1] and that courteous
tree
Which bows to all who seek its canopy, [2]
Sees called up round her by these magic
scents
The well, the camels, and her father's
tents;
Sighs for the home she left with little
pain,
And wishes even its sorrows back again!

Meanwhile thro' vast illuminated halls,
Silent and bright, where nothing but the
falls
Of fragrant waters gushing with cool
sound
From many a jasper fount is heard around,
Young AZIM roams bewildered, — nor
can guess
What means this maze of light and lone-
liness.
Here the way leads o'er tesselated floors
Or mats of CAIRO thro' long corridors,
Where ranged in cassolets and silver urns
Sweet wood of aloe or of sandal burns,
And spicy rods such as illume at night
The bowers of TIBET [3] send forth odor-
ous light,
Like Peris' wands, when pointing out
the road
For some pure Spirit to its blest abode:—
And here at once the glittering saloon
Bursts on his sight, boundless and bright
as noon;

Where in the midst reflecting back the
rays
In broken rainbows a fresh fountain plays
High as the enamelled cupola which
towers
All rich with Arabesques of gold and
flowers:
And the mosaic floor beneath shines
thro'
The sprinkling of that fountain's silvery
dew,
Like the wet, glistening shells of every
dye
That on the margin of the Red Sea lie.

Here too he traces the kind visitings
Of woman's love in those fair, living
things
Of land and wave, whose fate — in bond-
age thrown
For their weak loveliness — is like her
own!
On one side gleaming with a sudden
grace
Thro' water brilliant as the crystal vase
In which it undulates, small fishes shine
Like golden ingots from a fairy mine; —
While, on the other, latticed lightly in
With odoriferous woods of COMORIN, [4]
Each brilliant bird that wings the air is
seen; —
Gay, sparkling loories such as gleam be-
tween
The crimson blossoms of the coral-
tree [5]
In the warm isles of India's sunny
sea:
Mecca's blue sacred pigeon, [6] and the
thrush
Of Hindostan [7] whose holy warblings
gush
At evening from the tall pagoda's top; —

---

1 A tree famous for its perfume, and common
on the hills of Yemen. — *Niebuhr.*

2 Of the genus mimosa, "which droops its
branches whenever any person approaches it,
seeming as if it saluted those who retire under
its shade." — *Niebuhr.*

3 "Cloves are a principal ingredient in the
composition of the perfumed rods, which men of
rank keep constantly burning in their presence."
— *Turner's* "Tibet."

4 "*C'est d'où vient le bois d'aloes, que les
Arabes appellent Oud Comari, et celui du sandal,
qui s'y trouve en grande quantité.*"—*D'Herbelot.*

5 "Thousands of variegated loories visit the
coral-trees." — *Barrow.*

6 "In Mecca there are quantities of blue
pigeons, which none will affright or abuse, much
less kill." — *Pitt's* Account of the Mahometans.

7 "The Pagoda Thrush is esteemed among
the first choristers of India. It sits perched on
the sacred pagodas, and from thence delivers its
melodious song." — *Pennant's* "Hindostan."

Those golden birds that in the spice-time
    drop
About the gardens, drunk with that sweet
    food [1]
Whose scent hath lured them o'er the
    summer flood; [2]
And those that under Araby's soft sun
Build their high nests of budding cinna-
    mon; [3]
In short, all rare and beauteous things
    that fly
Thro' the pure element here calmly lie
Sleeping in light, like the green birds [4]
    that dwell
In Eden's radiant fields of asphodel!

So on, thro' scenes past all imagining,
More like the luxuries of that impious
    King, [5]
Whom Death's dark Angel with his light-
    ning torch
Struck down and blasted even in Pleas-
    ure's porch,
Than the pure dwelling of a Prophet
    sent
Armed with Heaven's sword for man's
    enfranchisement —
Young AZIM wandered, looking sternly
    round,
His simple garb and war-boots' clanking
    sound
But ill according with the pomp and
    grace
And silent lull of that voluptuous place.

"Is this, then," thought the youth,
    "is this the way
"To free man's spirit from the deadening
    sway

"Of worldly sloth, — to teach him while
    he lives
"To know no bliss but that which virtue
    gives,
"And when he dies to leave his lofty
    name
"A light, a landmark on the cliffs of
    fame?
"It was not so, Land of the generous
    thought
"And daring deed, thy god-like sages
    taught;
"It was not thus in bowers of wanton ease
"Thy Freedom nurst her sacred energies;
"Oh! not beneath the enfeebling, wither-
    ing glow
"Of such dull luxury did those myrtles
    grow
"With which she wreathed her sword
    when she would dare
"Immortal deeds; but in the bracing air
"Of toil, — of temperance, — of that
    high, rare,
"Ethereal virtue, which alone can
    breathe
"Life, health, and lustre into Freedom's
    wreath.
"Who that surveys this span of earth we
    press, —
"This speck of life in time's great wilder-
    ness,
"This narrow isthmus 'twixt two bound-
    less seas,
"The past, the future, two eternities! —
"Would sully the bright spot, or leave
    it bare,
"When he might build him a proud
    temple there,
"A name that long shall hallow all its
    space,
"And be each purer soul's high resting-
    place.
"But no — it can not be, that one whom
    God
"Has sent to break the wizard False-
    hood's rod, —
"A Prophet of the Truth, whose mission
    draws
"Its rights from Heaven, should thus
    profane its cause

1 *Tavernier* adds, that while the Birds of
Paradise lie in this intoxicated state, the emmets
come and eat off their legs; and that hence it is
they are said to have no feet.

2 Birds of Paradise, which, at the nutmeg
season, come in flights from the southern isles to
India; and "the strength of the nutmeg," says
Tavernier, "so intoxicates them that they fall
dead drunk to the earth."

3 "That bird which liveth in Arabia, and
buildeth its nest with cinnamon." — *Brown's
Vulgar Errors.*

4 "The spirits of the martyrs will be lodged
in the crops of green birds." — *Gibbon*, vol. ix.
p. 421.

5 Shedad, who made the delicious gardens of

Irim, in imitation of Paradise, and was destroyed
by lightning the first time he attempted to enter
them.

" With the world's vulgar pomps ; — no,
no, — I see —
" He thinks me weak — this glare of
luxury
" Is but to tempt, to try the eaglet gaze
" Of my young soul — shine on, 't will
stand the blaze ! "

So thought the youth ; — but even
while he defied
This witching scene he felt its witchery
glide
Thro' every sense.   The perfume breath-
ing round,
Like a pervading spirit ; — the still sound
Of falling waters, lulling as the song
Of Indian bees at sunset when they
throng
Around the fragrant NILICA, and deep
In its blue blossoms hum themselves to
sleep ; [1]
And music, too — dear music ! that can
touch
Beyond all else the soul that loves it
much —
Now heard far off, so far as but to seem
Like the faint, exquisite music of a
dream ;
All was too much for him, too full of
bliss,
The heart could nothing feel, that felt
not this ;
Softened he sunk upon a couch and gave
His soul up to sweet thoughts, like wave
on wave
Succeeding in smooth seas when storms
are laid ;
He thought of ZELICA, his own dear
maid,
And of the time when full of blissful sighs
They sat and lookt into each other's
eyes,
Silent and happy — as if God had given
Naught else worth looking at on this side
heaven.

" Oh, my loved mistress, thou whose
spirit still
" Is with me, round me, wander where
I will —

" It is for thee, for thee alone I seek
" The paths of glory ; to light up thy
cheek
" With warm approval — in that gentle
look
" To read my praise as in an angel's
book,
" And think all toils rewarded when from
thee
" I gain a smile worth immortality !
" How shall I bear the moment, when
restored
" To that young heart where I alone am
Lord,
" Tho' of such bliss unworthy, — since
the best
" Alone deserve to be the happiest : —
" When from those lips unbreathed upon
for years
" I shall again kiss off the soul-felt tears,
" And find those tears warm as when
last they started,
" Those sacred kisses pure as when we
parted.
" O my own life ! — why should a single
day,
" A moment keep me from those arms
away ? "

While thus he thinks, still nearer on
the breeze
Come those delicious, dream-like har-
monies,
Each note of which but adds new, downy
links
To the soft chain in which his spirit sinks.
He turns him toward the sound, and far
away
Thro' a long vista sparkling with the play
Of countless lamps, — like the rich track
which Day
Leaves on the waters, when he sinks
from us,
So long the path, its light so tremulous ; —
He sees a group of female forms advance,
Some chained together in the mazy dance
By fetters forged in the green sunny
bowers,
As they were captives to the King of
Flowers ; [2]

---

1 " My Pandits assure me that the plant before us (the Nilica) is their Sephalica, thus named
because the bees are supposed to sleep on its
blossoms." — *Sir W. Jones.*

2 They deferred it till the King of Flowers
should ascend his throne of enamelled foliage."
— *The Bahardanush.*

And some disporting round, unlinkt and
free,
Who seemed to mock their sisters' slavery;
And round and round them still in wheel-
ing flight
Went like gay moths about a lamp at
night;
While others waked, as gracefully along
Their feet kept time, the very soul of song
From psaltery, pipe, and lutes of heavenly
thrill,
Or their own youthful voices heavenlier
still.
And now they come, now pass before his
eye,
Forms such as Nature moulds when she
would vie
With Fancy's pencil and give birth to
things
Lovely beyond its fairest picturings.
Awhile they dance before him, then
divide,
Breaking like rosy clouds at even-tide
Around the rich pavilion of the sun, —
Till silently dispersing, one by one,
Thro' many a path that from the cham-
ber leads
To gardens, terraces and moonlight
meads,
Their distant laughter comes upon the
wind,
And but one trembling nymph remains
behind, —
Beckoning them back in vain — for they
are gone
And she is left in all that light alone;
No veil to curtain o'er her beauteous brow,
In its young bashfulness more beauteous
now;
But a light golden chain-work round her
hair,[1]
Such as the maids of YEZD [2] and SHIRAS
wear,

From which on either side gracefully hung
A golden amulet in the Arab tongue,
Engraven o'er with some immortal line
From Holy Writ or bard scarce less di-
vine;
While her left hand, as shrinkingly she
stood,
Held a small lute of gold and sandal-
wood,
Which once or twice she touched with
hurried strain,
Then took her trembling fingers off again.
But when at length a timid glance she stole
At AZIM, the sweet gravity of soul
She saw thro' all his features calmed her
fear,
And like a half-tamed antelope more near,
Tho' shrinking still, she came; — then
sat her down
Upon a musnud's [3] edge, and, bolder
grown,
In the pathetic mode of ISFAHAN [4]
Touched a preluding strain and thus
began: —

There 's a bower of roses by BENDE-
MEER'S [5] stream,
And the nightingale sings round it all
the day long;
In the time of my childhood 't was like
a sweet dream,
To sit in the roses and hear the bird's
song.

That bower and its music I never forget,
But oft when alone in the bloom of the
year
I think — is the nightingale singing there
yet?
Are the roses still bright by the calm
BENDEMEER?

No, the roses soon withered that hung
o'er the wave,
But some blossoms were gathered while
freshly they shone,

1 " One of the head-dresses of the Persian
women is composed of a light golden chain-work,
set with small pearls, with a thin gold plate pendant, about the bigness of a crown-piece, on which
is impressed an Arabian prayer, and which hangs
upon the cheek below the ear." — *Hanway's*
Travels.

2 " Certainly the women of Yezd are the hand-
somest women in Persia. The proverb is, that
to live happy a man must have a wife of Yezd,
eat the bread of Yezdecas, and drink the wine of
Shiras." — *Tavernier.*

3 Musnuds are cushioned seats, usually reserved for persons of distinction.

4 The Persians, like the ancient Greeks, call
their musical modes or Perdas by the names of
different countries or cities, as the mode of Isfahan, the mode of Irak, etc.

5 A river which flows near the ruins of Chilminar.

And a dew was distilled from their flowers
that gave
 All the fragrance of summer when
summer was gone.

Thus memory draws from delight ere it
dies
 An essence that breathes of it many a
year;
Thus bright to my soul, as 't was then to
my eyes,
 Is that bower on the banks of the calm
 BENDEMEER!

" Poor maiden!" thought the youth,
 " if thou wert sent
" With thy soft lute and beauty's blan-
dishment
" To wake unholy wishes in this heart,
" Or tempt its truth, thou little know'st
the art.
" For tho' thy lips should sweetly counsel
wrong,
" Those vestal eyes would disavow its
song.
" But thou hast breathed such purity,
thy lay
" Returns so fondly to youth's virtuous
day,
" And leads thy soul — if e'er it wan-
dered thence —
" So gently back to its first innocence,
" That I would sooner stop the unchained
dove,
" When swift returning to its home of
love,
" And round its snowy wing new fetters
twine,
" Than turn from virtue one pure wish
of thine!"

Scarce had this feeling past, when
sparkling thro'
The gently open'd curtains of light blue
That veiled the breezy casement, count-
less eyes
Peeping like stars thro' the blue evening
skies,
Looked laughing in as if to mock the pair
That sat so still and melancholy there :—
And now the curtains fly apart and in
From the cool air mid showers of jessamine
Which those without fling after them in
play,

Two lightsome maidens spring, — light-
some as they
Who live in the air on odors, — and
around
The bright saloon, scarce conscious of
the ground,
Chase one another in a varying dance
Of mirth and languor, coyness and ad-
vance,
Too eloquently like love's warm pur-
suit :—
While she who sung so gently to the lute
Her dream of home steals timidly away,
Shrinking as violets do in summer's ray,—
But takes with her from AZIM'S heart
that sigh
We sometimes give to forms that pass us
by
In the world's crowd, too lovely to re-
main,
Creatures of light we never see again!

Around the white necks of the nymphs
who danced
Hung carcanets of orient gems that
glanced
More brilliant than the sea-glass glitter-
ing o'er
The hills of crystal on the Caspian shore;[1]
While from their long, dark tresses, in a
fall
Of curls descending, bells as musical
As those that on the golden-shafted trees
Of EDEN shake in the eternal breeze,[2]
Rung round their steps, at every bound
more sweet,
As 't were the ecstatic language of their
feet.
At length the chase was o'er, and they
stood wreathed
Within each other's arms; while soft
there breathed
Thro' the cool casement, mingled with
the sighs

1 "To the north of us (on the coast of the
Caspian, near Badku,) was a mountain, which
sparkled like diamonds, arising from the sea-glass
and crystals with which it abounds."—*Journey
of the Russian Ambassador to Persia,* 1746.

2 "To which will be added the sound of the
bells, hanging on the trees, which will be put in
motion by the wind proceeding from the throne
of God, as often as the blessed wish for music."
—*Sale.*

Of moonlight flowers, music that seemed
  to rise
From some still lake, so liquidly it rose;
And as it swelled again at each faint
  close
The ear could track thro' all that maze
  of chords
And young sweet voices these impassioned words:—

A SPIRIT there is whose fragrant sigh
  Is burning now thro' earth and air;
Where cheeks are blushing the Spirit is
  nigh,
  Where lips are meeting the Spirit is
  there!

His breath is the soul of flowers like
  these,
  And his floating eyes — oh! *they* resemble [1]
Blue water-lilies,[2] when the breeze
  Is making the stream around them
  tremble.

Hail to thee, hail to thee, kindling
  power!
  Spirit of Love, Spirit of Bliss!
Thy holiest time is the moonlight hour,
  And there never was moonlight so
  sweet as this.

  By the fair and brave
    Who blushing unite,
  Like the sun and wave,
    When they meet at night;

  By the tear that shows
    When passion is nigh,
  As the rain-drop flows
    From the heat of the sky;

  By the first love-beat
    Of the youthful heart,
  By the bliss to meet,
    And the pain to part;

  By all that thou hast
    To mortals given,
  Which — oh, could it last,
    This earth were heaven!

1 " Whose wanton eyes resemble blue water-
lilies, agitated by the breeze." —*Jayadeva.*
2 The blue lotos, which grows in Cashmere
and in Persia.

We call thee hither, entrancing Power!
  Spirit of Love! Spirit of Bliss!
Thy holiest time is the moonlight hour,
  And there never was moonlight so
  sweet as this.

Impatient of a scene whose luxuries
  stole,
Spite of himself, too deep into his soul,
And where, midst all that the young
  heart loves most,
Flowers, music, smiles, to yield was to
  be lost,
The youth had started up and turned
  away
From the light nymphs and their luxuri-
  ous lay
To muse upon the pictures that hung
  round,[3] —
Bright images, that spoke without a
  sound,
And views like vistas into fairy ground.
But here again new spells came o'er his
  sense:
All that the pencil's mute omnipotence
Could call up into life, of soft and fair,
Of fond and passionate, was glowing
  there;
Nor yet too warm, but touched with
  that fine art
Which paints of pleasure but the purer
  part;
Which knows even Beauty when half-
  veiled is best, —
Like her own radiant planet of the
  west,
Whose orb when half retired looks love-
  liest.[4]
There hung the history of the Genii-
  King,
Traced thro' each gay, voluptuous wan-
  dering

3 It has been generally supposed that the
Mahometans prohibit all pictures of animals; but
Toderini shows that, though the practice is forbidden by the Koran, they are not more averse
to painted figures and images than other people.
From Mr. Murphy's work, too, we find that the
Arabs of Spain had no objection to the introduction of figures into painting.
4 This is not quite astronomically true. "Dr.
Hadley [says Keil] has shown that Venus is
brightest when she is about forty degrees removed from the sun; and that then but *only a
fourth part* of her lucid disk is to be seen from
the earth."

With her from SABA's bowers, in whose
    bright eyes
He read that to be blest is to be
    wise;[1] —
Here fond ZULEIKA [2] woos with open
    arms
The Hebrew boy who flies from her
    young charms,
Yet flying turns to gaze and half undone
Wishes that Heaven and she could *both*
    be won;
And here MOHAMMED born for love and
    guile
Forgets the Koran in his MARY's
    smile; —
Then beckons some kind angel from
    above
With a new text to consecrate their
    love.[3]

With rapid step, yet pleased and lin-
    gering eye,
Did the youth pass these pictured stories
    by,
And hastened to a casement where the
    light
Of the calm moon came in and freshly
    bright

1 For the loves of King Solomon (who was
supposed to preside over the whole race of
Genii) with Balkis, the Queen of Sheba or Saba,
see *D'Herbelot*, and the *Notes on the Koran*,
chap. 2.
    " In the palace which Solomon ordered to be
built against the arrival of the Queen of Saba,
the floor or pavement was of transparent glass,
laid over running water, in which fish were
swimming." This led the Queen into a very
natural mistake, which the Koran has not thought
beneath its dignity to commemorate. "It was
said unto her, ' Enter the palace.' And when
she saw it she imagined it to be a great water;
and she discovered her legs, by lifting up her
robe to pass through it. Whereupon Solomon
said to her, ' Verily, this is the place evenly
floored with glass.' " — Chap. 27.
    2 The wife of Potiphar, thus named by the
Orientals.
    The passion which this frail beauty of antiq-
uity conceived for her young Hebrew slave has
given rise to a much esteemed poem in the Persian language, entitled *Yusef vau Zelikha*, by
Noureddin Jami; the manuscript copy of which,
in the Bodleian Library at Oxford, is supposed
to be the finest in the whole world." — *Note
upon Nott's Translation of Hafez.*
    3 The particulars of Mahomet's amour with
Mary, the Coptic girl, in justification of which
he added a new chapter to the Koran, may be
found in *Gagnier's Notes upon Abulfeda*, p. 151.

The fields without were seen, sleeping as
    still
As if no life remained in breeze or rill.
Here paused he while the music now
    less near
Breathed with a holier language on his
    ear,
As tho' the distance and that heavenly
    ray
Thro' which the sounds came floating
    took away
All that had been too earthly in the lay.

Oh! could he listen to such sounds
    unmoved,
And by that light — nor dream of her he
    loved?
Dream on, unconscious boy! while yet
    thou may'st;
'T is the last bliss thy soul shall ever
    taste.
Clasp yet awhile her image to thy heart,
Ere all the light that made it dear de-
    part.
Think of her smiles as when thou saw'st
    them last,
Clear, beautiful, by naught of earth
    o'ercast;
Recall her tears to thee at parting given,
Pure as they weep, *if* angels weep in
    Heaven.
Think in her own still bower she waits
    thee now
With the same glow of heart and bloom
    of brow,
Yet shrined in solitude — thine all, thine
    only,
Like the one star above thee, bright and
    lonely.
Oh! that a dream so sweet, so long
    enjoyed,
Should be so sadly, cruelly destroyed!

The song is husht, the laughing
    nymphs are flown,
And he is left musing of bliss, alone; —
Alone? — no, not alone — that heavy
    sigh,
That sob of grief which broke from some
    one nigh —
Whose could it be? — alas! is misery.
    found
Here, even here, on this enchanted
    ground?

He turns and sees a female form close
   veiled,
Leaning, as if both heart and strength
   had failed,
Against a pillar near; — not glittering
   o'er
With gems and wreaths such as the
   others wore,
But in that deep-blue, melancholy dress,[1]
BOKHARA'S maidens wear in mindful-
   ness
Of friends or kindred, dead or far
   away; —
And such as ZELICA had on that day
He left her — when with heart too full
   to speak
He took away her last warm tears upon
   his cheek.

A strange emotion stirs within him, —
   more
Than mere compassion ever waked be-
   fore;
Unconsciously he opes his arms while
   she
Springs forward as with life's last
   energy,
But, swooning in that one convulsive
   bound,
Sinks ere she reach his arms upon the
   ground; —
Her veil falls off — her faint hands clasp
   his knees —
'T is she herself! — 't is ZELICA he
   sees!
But, ah, so pale, so changed — none but
   a lover
Could in that wreck of beauty's shrine
   discover
The once adored divinity — even he
Stood for some moments mute, and
   doubtingly
Put back the ringlets from her brow, and
   gazed
Upon those lids where once such lustre
   blazed,
Ere he could think she was *indeed* his
   own,
Own darling maid whom he so long had
   known
In joy and sorrow, beautiful in both;

Who, even when grief was heaviest —
   when loath
He left her for the wars — in that worst
   hour
Sat in her sorrow like the sweet night-
   flower,[2]
When darkness brings its weeping glories
   out,
And spreads its sighs like frankincense
   about.

" Look up, my ZELICA — one moment
   show
" Those gentle eyes to me that I may
   know
" Thy life, thy loveliness is not all gone,
" But *there* at least shines as it ever
   shone.
" Come, look upon thy AZIM — one dear
   glance,
" Like those of old, were heaven ! what-
   ever chance
" Hath brought thee here, oh, 't was a
   blessed one !
" There — my loved lips — they move —
   that kiss hath run
" Like the first shoot of life thro' every
   vein,
" And now I clasp her, mine, all mine
   again.
" Oh the delight — now, in this very
   hour,
" When had the whole rich world been
   in my power,
" I should have singled out thee, only
   thee,
" From the whole world's collected
   treasury
" To have thee here — to hang thus
   fondly o'er
" My own, best, purest ZELICA once
   more ! "

It was indeed the touch of those fond
   lips
Upon her eyes that chased their short
   eclipse,
And gradual as the snow at Heaven's
   breath
Melts off and shows the azure flowers
   beneath,

---

1 " Deep blue is their mourning color." —
Hanway.

2 The sorrowful nyctanthes, which begins to
spread its rich odor after sunset.

Her lids unclosed and the bright eyes
    were seen —
Gazing on his — his, not, as they late had
    been,
Quick, restless, wild, but mournfully
    serene;
As if to lie even for that tranced minute
So near his heart had consolation in it;
And thus to wake in his beloved caress
Took from her soul one half its wretch-
    edness.
But, when she heard him call her good
    and pure,
Oh! 't was too much — too dreadful to
    endure!
Shuddering she broke away from his
    embrace,
And hiding with both hands her guilty
    face
Said in a tone whose anguish would have
    riven
A heart of very marble, "Pure! — oh
    Heaven!" —

That tone — those looks so changed —
    the withering blight,
That sin and sorrow leave where'er they
    light;
The dead despondency of those sunk
    eyes,
Where once, had he thus met her by
    surprise,
He would have seen himself, too happy
    boy,
Reflected in a thousand lights of joy;
And then the place, — that bright, un-
    holy place,
Where vice lay hid beneath each win-
    ning grace
And charm of luxury as the viper weaves
Its wily covering of sweet balsam
    leaves,[1] —
All struck upon his heart, sudden and
    cold
As death itself; — it needs not to be
    told —
No, no — he sees it all plain as the
    brand
Of burning shame can mark — whate'er
    the hand,

[1] "Concerning the vipers, which Pliny says
were frequent among the balsam-trees, I made
very particular inquiry; several were brought
me alive both to Yambo and Jidda." — *Bruce.*

That could from Heaven and him such
    brightness sever,
'T is done — to Heaven and him she 's
    lost for ever!
It was a dreadful moment; not the tears,
The lingering, lasting misery of years
Could match that minute's anguish — all
    the worst
Of sorrow's elements in that dark burst
Broke o'er his soul and with one crash
    of fate
Laid the whole hopes of his life deso-
    late.

"Oh! curse me not," she cried, as
    wild he tost
His desperate hand towards Heav'n —
    "tho' I am lost,
"Think not that guilt, that falsehood
    made me fall,
"No, no — 't was grief, 't was madness
    did it all!
"Nay, doubt me not — tho' all thy love
    hath ceased —
"I know it hath — yet, yet believe, at
    least,
"That every spark of reason's light
    must be
"Quenched in this brain ere I could
    stray from thee.
"They told me thou wert dead — why,
    AZIM, why
"Did we not, both of us, that instant
    die
"When we were parted? oh! couldst
    thou but know
"With what a deep devotedness of woe
"I wept thy absence — o'er and o'er
    again
"Thinking of thee, still thee, till
    thought grew pain,
"And memory like a drop that night
    and day
"Falls cold and ceaseless wore my heart
    away.
"Didst thou but know how pale I sat at
    home,
"My eyes still turned the way thou
    wert to come,
"And, all the long, long night of hope
    and fear,
"Thy voice and step still sounding in
    my ear —

" Oh God ! thou wouldst not wonder
      that at last,
" When every hope was all at once
      o'ercast,
" When I heard frightful voices round
      me say
" *Azim is dead !* — this wretched brain
      gave way,
" And I became a wreck, at random
      driven,
" Without one glimpse of reason or of
      Heaven —
" All wild — and even this quenchless
      love within
" Turned to foul fires to light me into
      sin ! —
" Thou pitiest me — I knew thou
      wouldst — that sky
" Hath naught beneath it half so lorn
      as I.
" The fiend, who lured me hither — hist !
      come near,
" Or thou too, *thou* art lost, if he should
      hear —
" Told me such things — oh ! with such
      devilish art,
" As would have ruined even a holier
      heart —
" Of thee, and of that ever-radiant sphere,
" Where blest at length, if I but served
      him here,
" I should for ever live in thy dear sight,
" And drink from those pure eyes eternal
      light.
" Think, think how lost, how maddened
      I must be,
" To hope that guilt could lead to God
      or thee !
" Thou weep'st for me — do weep — oh,
      that I durst
" Kiss off that tear ! but, no — these lips
      are curst,
" They must not touch thee; — one divine
      caress,
" One blessed moment of forgetfulness
" I 've had within those arms and *that*
      shall lie
" Shrined in my soul's deep memory till
      I die;
" The last of joy's last relics here below,
" The one sweet drop, in all this waste
      of woe,
" My heart has treasured from affection's
      spring,

" To soothe and cool its deadly wither-
      ing !
" But thou — yes, thou must go — for
      ever go;
" This place is not for thee — for thee !
      oh no,
" Did I but tell thee half, thy tortured
      brain
" Would burn like mine, and mine go
      wild again !
" Enough that Guilt reigns here — that
      hearts once good
" Now tainted, chilled and broken are
      his food. —
" Enough that we are parted — that
      there rolls
" A flood of headlong fate between our
      souls,
" Whose darkness severs me as wide from
      thee
" As hell from heaven to all eternity !"

" ZELICA, ZELICA !" the youth ex-
      claimed,
In all the tortures of a mind inflamed
Almost to madness — " by that sacred
      Heaven,
" Where yet, if prayers can move, thou 'lt
      be forgiven,
" As thou art here — here, in this writh-
      ing heart,
" All sinful, wild, and ruined as thou
      art !
" By the remembrance of our once pure
      love,
" Which like a church-yard light still
      burns above
" The grave of our lost souls — which
      guilt in thee
" Cannot extinguish nor despair in me !
" I do conjure, implore thee to fly hence —
" If thou hast yet one spark of innocence,
" Fly with me from this place " —
            " With thee ! oh bliss !
" ' T is worth whole years of torment to
      hear this.
" What ! take the lost one with thee ? —
      let her rove
" By thy dear side, as in those days of
      love,
" When we were both so happy, both so
      pure —
" Too heavenly dream ! if there 's on
      earth a cure

" For the sunk heart, 't is this — day
    after day
" To be the blest companion of thy way;
" To hear thy angel eloquence — to see
" Those virtuous eyes for ever turned on
    me;
" And in their light re-chastened silently,
" Like the stained web that whitens in
    the sun,
" Grow pure by being purely shone upon !
" And thou wilt pray for me — I know
    thou wilt —
" At the dim vesper hour when thoughts
    of guilt
" Come heaviest o'er the heart thou 'lt
    lift thine eyes
" Full of sweet tears unto the darkening
    skies
" And plead for me with Heaven till I
    can dare
" To fix my own weak, sinful glances
    there;
" Till the good angels when they see me
    cling
" For ever near thee, pale and sorrow-
    ing,
" Shall for thy sake pronounce my soul
    forgiven,
" And bid thee take thy weeping slave to
    Heaven !
" Oh yes, I 'll fly with thee " —
                Scarce had she said
These breathless words when a voice
    deep and dread
As that of MONKER waking up the dead
From their first sleep — so startling 't was
    to both —
Rung thro' the casement near, " Thy
    oath ! thy oath !"
Oh Heaven, the ghastliness of that Maid's
    look ! —
" 'T is he," faintly she cried, while terror
    shook
Her inmost core, nor durst she lift her
    eyes,
Tho' thro' the casement, now naught but
    the skies

And moonlight fields were seen, calm as
    before —
" 'T is he, and I am his — all, all is o'er —
" Go — fly this instant, or thou 'rt ruin'd
    too —
" My oath, my oath, oh God ! 't is all too
    true,
" True as the worm in this cold heart it
    is —
" I am MOKANNA'S bride — his, AZIM,
    his —
" The Dead stood round us while I spoke
    that vow,
" Their blue lips echoed it — I hear them
    now !
" Their eyes glared on me, while I pledged
    that bowl,
" 'T was burning blood — I feel it in my
    soul !
" And the Veiled Bridegroom — hist !
    I 've seen to-night
" What angels know not of — so foul a
    sight,
" So horrible — oh ! never may'st thou
    see
" What *there* lies hid from all but hell
    and me !
" But I must hence — off, off — I am
    not thine,
" Nor Heaven's, nor Love's, nor aught
    that is divine —
" Hold me not — ha ! think'st thou the
    fiends that sever
" Hearts cannot sunder hands? — thus,
    then — for ever !"

With all that strength which madness
    lends the weak
She flung away his arm; and with a shriek
Whose sound tho' he should linger out
    more years
Than wretch e'er told can never leave
    his ears —
Flew up thro' that long avenue of light,
Fleetly as some dark, ominous bird of
    night,
Across the sun, and soon was out of sight !

LALLA ROOKH could think of nothing all day but the misery of these two
young lovers. Her gayety was gone, and she looked pensively even upon FADLA-
DEEN. She felt, too, without knowing why, a sort of uneasy pleasure in imagining
that AZIM must have been just such a youth as FERAMORZ; just as worthy to
enjoy all the blessings, without any of the pangs, of that illusive passion, which

too often like the sunny apples of Istkahar [1] is all sweetness on one side and all bitterness on the other.

As they passed along a sequestered river after sunset they saw a young Hindoo girl upon the bank,[2] whose employment seemed to them so strange that they stopped their palankeens to observe her. She had lighted a small lamp filled with oil of cocoa, and placing it in an earthen dish adorned with a wreath of flowers, had committed it with a trembling hand to the stream; and was now anxiously watching its progress down the current, heedless of the gay cavalcade which had drawn up beside her. LALLA ROOKH was all curiosity; — when one of her attendants, who had lived upon the banks of the Ganges, (where this ceremony is so frequent that often in the dusk of the evening the river is seen glittering all over with lights, like the Otou-tala or Sea of Stars,[3]) informed the Princess that it was the usual way in which the friends of those who had gone on dangerous voyages offered up vows for their safe return. If the lamp sunk immediately the omen was disastrous; but if it went shining down the stream and continued to burn till entirely out of sight, the return of the beloved object was considered as certain.

LALLA ROOKH as they moved on more than once looked back to observe how the young Hindoo's lamp proceeded; and while she saw with pleasure that it was still unextinguished she could not help fearing that all the hopes of this life were no better than that feeble light upon the river. The remainder of the journey was passed in silence. She now for the first time felt that shade of melancholy which comes over the youthful maiden's heart as sweet and transient as her own breath upon a mirror; nor was it till she heard the lute of FERAMORZ, touched lightly at the door of her pavilion that she waked from the revery in which she had been wandering. Instantly her eyes were lighted up with pleasure; and after a few unheard remarks from FADLADEEN upon the indecorum of a poet seating himself in presence of a Princess every thing was arranged as on the preceding evening and all listened with eagerness while the story was thus continued: —

WHOSE are the gilded tents that crowd
    the way,
Where all was waste and silent yesterday?
This City of War which, in a few short
    hours,
Hath sprung up here,[4] as if the magic
    powers

Of Him who, in the twinkling of a star,
Built the high pillared halls of CHIL-
    MINAR,[5]
Had conjur'd up, far as the eye can see,
This world of tents and domes and sun-
    bright armory: —

1 "In the territory of Istkahar there is a kind of apple, half of which is sweet and half sour." — *Ebn Haukal.*

2 For an account of this ceremony, see *Grand-prés* "Voyage in the Indian Ocean."

3 "The place where the Whangho, a river of Tibet, rises, and where there are more than a hundred springs, which sparkle like stars; whence it is called Hotun-nor, that is, the Sea of Stars." — *Description of Tibet in Pinkerton.*

4 "The Lescar or Imperial Camp is divided, like a regular town, into squares, alleys, and streets, and from a rising ground furnishes one of the most agreeable prospects in the world. Starting up in a few hours in an uninhabited plain, it raises the idea of a city built by enchantment. Even those who leave their houses in cities to follow the prince in his progress are fre-

5 The edifices of Chilminar and Balbec are supposed to have been built by the Genii, acting under the orders of Jan ben Jan, who governed the world long before the time of Adam.

quently so charmed with the Lescar, when situated in a beautiful and convenient place, that they cannot prevail with themselves to remove. To prevent this inconvenience to the court, the Emperor, after sufficient time is allowed to the tradesmen to follow, orders them to be burnt out of their tents." — *Dow's* Hindostan.

Colonel Wilks gives a lively picture of an Eastern encampment: — "His camp, like that of most Indian armies, exhibited a motley collection of covers from the scorching sun and dews of the night, variegated according to the taste or means of each individual, by extensive inclosures of colored calico surrounding superb suites of tents; by ragged cloths or blankets stretched

Princely pavilions screened by many a
　　fold
Of crimson cloth and topt with balls of
　　gold : —
Steeds with their housings of rich silver
　　spun,
Their chains and poitrels glittering in the
　　sun;
And camels tufted o'er with Yemen's
　　shells [1]
Shaking in every breeze their light-toned
　　bells !

But yester-eve, so motionless around,
So mute was this wide plain that not a
　　sound
But the far torrent or the locust bird [2]
Hunting among the thickets could be
　　heard; —
Yet hark ! what discords now of every
　　kind,
Shouts, laughs, and screams are revelling
　　in the wind;
The neigh of cavalry; — the tinkling
　　throngs
Of laden camels and their drivers'
　　songs; [3] —

Ringing of arms, and flapping in the
　　breeze
Of streamers from ten thousand cano-
　　pies; —
War-music bursting out from time to time
With gong and tymbalon's tremendous
　　chime; —
Or in the pause when harsher sounds are
　　mute,
The mellow breathings of some horn or
　　flute,
That far off, broken by the eagle note
Of the Abyssinian trumpet,[4] swell and
　　float.

Who leads this mighty army? — ask
　　ye "who?"
And mark ye not those banners of dark
　　hue,
The Night and Shadow,[5] over yonder
　　tent? —
It is the CALIPH'S glorious armament.
Roused in his Palace by the dread alarms,
That hourly came, of the false Prophet's
　　arms,
And of his host of infidels who hurled
Defiance fierce at Islam [6] and the world,
Tho' worn with Grecian warfare, and
　　behind
The veils of his bright Palace calm re-
　　clined,
Yet brooked he not such blasphemy
　　should stain,
Thus unrevenged, the evening of his
　　reign ;
But having sworn upon the Holy Grave [7]
To conquer or to perish, once more
　　gave
His shadowy banners proudly to the
　　breeze,
And with an army nurst in victories,

1 "A superb camel, ornamented with strings
and tufts of small shells." — *Ali Bey*.

2 A native of Khorassan, and allured south-
ward by means of the water of a fountain between Shiraz and Ispahan, called the Fountain of
Birds, of which it is so fond that it will follow
wherever that water is carried.

3 "Some of the camels have bells about their
necks, and some about their legs, like those which
our carriers put about their fore-horses' necks,
which together with the servants (who belong to
the camels, and travel on foot,) singing all night,
make a pleasant noise, and the journey passes
away delightfully." — *Pitt's* Account of the Mahometans.

"The camel-driver follows the camels singing,
and sometimes playing upon his pipe ; the louder
he sings and pipes, the faster the camels go.
Nay, they will stand still when he gives over his
music." — *Tavernier.*

over sticks or branches ; palm leaves hastily
spread over similar supports; handsome tents
and splendid canopies ; horses, oxen, elephants,
and camels ; all intermixed without any exterior
mark of order or design, except the flags of the
chiefs, which usually mark the centres of a con-
geries of these masses ; the only regular part of
the encampment being the streets of shops, each
of which is constructed nearly in the manner of a
booth at an English fair. " — *Historical Sketches
of the South of India.*

4 " This trumpet is often called, in Abyssinia,
nesser cano, which signifies the Note of the
Eagle." — *Note of Bruce's Editor.*

5 The two black standards borne before the
Caliphs of the House of Abbas were called,
allegorically, The Night and The Shadow. — See
Gibbon.

6 The Mahometan religion.

7 "The Persians swear by the Tomb of Shah
Besade, who is buried at Casbin ; and when one
desires another to asseverate a matter, he will
ask him, if he dare swear by the Holy Grave."
— *Struy.*

Here stands to crush the rebels that o'er-
    run
His blest and beauteous Province of the
    Sun.

Ne'er did the march of MAHADI display
Such pomp before; — not even when on
    his way
To MECCA'S Temple, when both land
    and sea
Were spoiled to feed the Pilgrim's lux-
    ury; [1]
When round him mid the burning sands
    he saw
Fruits of the North in icy freshness thaw,
And cooled his thirsty lip beneath the
    glow
Of MECCA'S sun with urns of Persian
    snow: [2] —
Nor e'er did armament more grand than
    that
Pour from the kingdoms of the Caliphat.
First, in the van, the People of the Rock [3]
On their light mountain steeds of royal
    stock: [4]
Then chieftains of DAMASCUS proud to see
The flashing of their swords' rich mar-
    quetry; [5] —
Men from the regions near the VOLGA'S
    mouth
Mixt with the rude, black archers of the
    South;
And Indian lancers in white-turbaned
    ranks
From the far SINDE or ATTOCK'S sacred
    banks,
With dusky legions from the Land of
    Myrrh, [6]
And many a mace-armed Moor and Mid-
    sea islander.

Nor less in number tho' more new and
    rude
In warfare's school was the vast multi-
    tude
That, fired by zeal or by oppression
    wronged,
Round the white standard of the impos-
    tor thronged.
Beside his thousands of Believers — blind,
Burning and headlong as the Samiel
    wind —
Many who felt and more who feared to
    feel
The bloody Islamite's converting steel,
Flockt to his banner; — Chiefs of the
    UZBEK race,
Waving their heron crests with martial
    grace; [7]
TURKOMANS, countless as their flocks,
    led forth
From the aromatic pastures of the North;
Wild warriors of the turquoise hills, [8] —
    and those
Who dwell beyond the everlasting snows
Of HINDOO KOSH, [9] in stormy freedom
    bred,
Their fort the rock, their camp the tor-
    rent's bed.
But none of all who owned the Chief's
    command
Rushed to that battle-field with bolder
    hand
Or sterner hate than IRAN'S outlawed
    men,
Her Worshippers of Fire [10] — all panting
    then
For vengeance on the accursed Saracen;
Vengeance at last for their dear country
    spurned,
Her throne usurpt, and her bright
    shrines o'erturned.

1 Mahadi, in a single pilgrimage to Mecca,
expended six millions of dinars of gold.

2 *nivem Meccam apportavit, rem ibi aut
nunquam aut raro visam.* — *Abulfeda.*

3 The inhabitants of Hejaz or Arabia Petræa,
called by an Eastern writer "The People of the
Rock." — *Ebn Haukal.*

4 "Those horses, called by the Arabians Koch-
lani, of whom a written genealogy has been kept
for 2000 years. They are said to derive their
origin from King Solomon's steeds." — *Niebuhr.*

5 "Many of the figures on the blades of their
swords are wrought in gold or silver, or in mar-
quetry with small gems." — *Asiat. Misc.* v. i.

6 Azab or Saba.

7 "The chiefs of the Uzbek Tartars wear a
plume of white heron's feathers in their turbans."
— *Account of Independent Tartary.*

8 In the mountains of Nishapour and Tous
in Khorassan) they find turquoises. — *Ebn
Haukal.*

9 For a description of these stupendous ranges
of mountains, see *Elphinstone's Caubul.*

10 The Ghebers or Guebres, those original natives of Persia, who adhered to their ancient
faith, the religion of Zoroaster, and who, after
the conquest of their country by the Arabs, were
either persecuted at home, or forced to become
wanderers abroad.

From YEZD'S [1] eternal Mansion of the Fire
Where aged saints in dreams of Heaven expire:
From BADKU and those fountains of blue flame
That burn into the CASPIAN,[2] fierce they came,
Careless for what or whom the blow was sped,
So vengeance triumpht and their tyrants bled.

Such was the wild and miscellaneous host
That high in air their motley banners tost
Around the Prophet-Chief — all eyes still bent
Upon that glittering Veil, where'er it went,
That beacon thro' the battle's stormy flood,
That rainbow of the field whose showers were blood!

Twice hath the sun upon their conflict set
And risen again and found them grappling yet;
While streams of carnage in his noontide blaze,
Smoke up to Heaven — hot as that crimson haze
By which the prostrate Caravan is awed [3]
In the red Desert when the wind 's abroad.

"On, Swords of God!" the panting CALIPH calls, —
"Thrones for the living — Heaven for him who falls!" —
"On, brave avengers, on," MOKANNA cries,
" And EBLIS blast the recreant slave that flies! "
Now comes the brunt, the crisis of the day —
They clash — they strive — the CALIPH'S troops give way!
MOKANNA'S self plucks the black Banner down,
And now the Orient World's Imperial crown
Is just within his grasp — when, hark, that shout!
Some hand hath checkt the flying Moslem's rout;
And now they turn, they rally — at their head
A warrior, (like those angel youths who led,
In glorious panoply of Heaven's own mail,
The Champions of the Faith thro' BEDER'S vale,[4])
Bold as if gifted with ten thousand lives,
Turns on the fierce pursuers' blades, and drives
At once the multitudinous torrent back —
While hope and courage kindle in his track;
And at each step his bloody falchion makes
Terrible vistas thro' which victory breaks!
In vain MOKANNA, midst the general flight,
Stands like the red moon on some stormy night
Among the fugitive clouds that hurrying by
Leave only her unshaken in the sky —
In vain he yells his desperate curses out,
Deals death promiscuously to all about,

1 " Yezd, the chief residence of those ancient natives who worship the Sun and the Fire, which latter they have carefully kept lighted, without being once extinguished for a moment, about 3000 years, on a mountain near Yezd, called Ater Quedah, signifying the House or Mansion of the Fire. He is reckoned very unfortunate who dies off that mountain. — *Stephen's Persia.*

2 " When the weather is hazy, the springs of Naphtha (on an island near Baku) boil up the higher, and the Naphtha often takes fire on the surface of the earth, and runs in a flame into the sea to a distance almost incredible." — *Hanway on the Everlasting Fire at Baku.*

3 *Savary* says of the south wind, which blows in Egypt from February to May, " Sometimes it appears only in the shape of an impetuous whirlwind, which passes rapidly, and is fatal to the traveller, surprised in the middle of the deserts. Torrents of burning sand roll before it, the firma-

ment is enveloped in a thick veil, and the sun appears of the color of blood. Sometimes whole caravans are buried in it."

4 In the great victory gained by Mahomed at Beder, he was assisted, say the Mussulmans, by three thousand angels led by Gabriel mounted on his horse Hiazum. — See *The Koran and its Commentators.*

To foes that charge and coward friends
    that fly,
And seems of *all* the Great Arch-enemy.
The panic spreads — "A miracle!"
    throughout
The Moslem ranks, "a miracle!" they
    shout,
All gazing on that youth whose coming
    seems
A light, a glory, such as breaks in dreams;
And every sword, true as o'er billows
    dim
The needle tracks the load-star, follow-
    ing him!

Right towards MOKANNA now he
    cleaves his path,
Impatient cleaves as tho' the bolt of
    wrath
He bears from Heaven withheld its
    awful burst
From weaker heads and souls but half
    way curst,
To break o'er Him, the mightiest and
    the worst!
But vain his speed — tho', in that hour
    of blood,
Had all God's seraphs round MOKANNA
    stood
With swords of fire ready like fate to
    fall,
MOKANNA'S soul would have defied them
    all;
Yet now, the rush of fugitives, too
    strong
For human force, hurries even *him* along;
In vain he struggles mid the wedged
    array
Of flying thousands — he is borne away;
And the sole joy his baffled spirit knows,
In this forced flight, is — murdering as
    he goes!
As a grim tiger whom the torrent's
    might
Surprises in some parched ravine at
    night,
Turns even in drowning on the wretched
    flocks
Swept with him in that snow-flood from
    the rocks,
And, to the last, devouring on his way,
Bloodies the stream he hath not power
    to stay.

"Alla illa Alla!" — the glad shout
    renew —
"Alla Akbar!" [1] — the Caliph's in
    MEROU.
Hang out your gilded tapestry in the
    streets,
And light your shrines and chant your
    ziraleets.[2]
The Swords of God have triumpht — on
    his throne
Your Caliph sits and the veiled Chief
    hath flown.
Who does not envy that young warrior
    now,
To whom the Lord of Islam bends his
    brow,
In all the graceful gratitude of power,
For his throne's safety in that perilous
    hour?
Who doth not wonder, when, amidst the
    acclaim
Of thousands heralding to heaven his
    name —
Mid all those holier harmonies of fame
Which sound along the path of virtuous
    souls,
Like music round a planet as it rolls, —
He turns away — coldly, as if some
    gloom
Hung o'er his heart no triumphs can il-
    lume; —
Some sightless grief upon whose blasted
    gaze
Tho' glory's light may play, in vain it
    plays.
Yes, wretched AZIM! thine is such a
    grief,
Beyond all hope, all terror, all relief;
A dark, cold calm, which nothing now
    can break,
Or warm or brighten, — like that Syrian
    Lake [3]
Upon whose surface morn and summer
    shed
Their smiles in vain, for all beneath is
    dead! —

1 The Tecbir, or cry of the Arabs. "Alla
Acbar!" says Ockley, means, "God is most
mighty."

2 The ziraleet is a kind of chorus, which the
women of the East sing upon joyful occasions. —
Russel.

3 The Dead Sea, which contains neither animal nor vegetable life.

Hearts there have been o'er which this
　　weight of woe
Came by long use of suffering, tame and
　　slow;
But thine, lost youth! was sudden — over
　　thee
It broke at once, when all seemed
　　ecstasy;
When Hope lookt up and saw the
　　gloomy Past
Melt into splendor and Bliss dawn at
　　last —
'T was then, even then, o'er joys so
　　freshly blown
This mortal blight of misery came down;
Even then, the full, warm gushings of
　　thy heart
Were checkt — like fount-drops, frozen
　　as they start —
And there like them cold, sunless relics
　　hang,
Each fixt and chilled into a lasting pang.

One sole desire, one passion now re-
　　mains
To keep life's fever still within his veins,
Vengeance! — dire vengeance on the
　　wretch who cast
O'er him and all he loved that ruinous
　　blast.
For this, when rumors reached him in
　　his flight
Far, far away, after that fatal night, —
Rumors of armies thronging to the attack
Of the Veiled Chief, — for this he winged
　　him back,
Fleet as the vulture speeds to flags un-
　　furled,
And when all hope seemed desperate,
　　wildly hurled
Himself into the scale and saved a world.
For this he still lives on, careless of all
The wreaths that Glory on his path lets
　　fall;
For this alone exists — like lightning-fire,
To speed one bolt of vengeance and ex-
　　pire!

But safe as yet that Spirit of Evil lives;
With a small band of desperate fugitives,
The last sole stubborn fragment left un-
　　riven
Of the proud host that late stood fronting
　　Heaven,

He gained MEROU — breathed a short
　　curse of blood
O'er his lost throne — then past the
　　JIHON'S flood,[1]
And gathering all whose madness of be-
　　lief
Still saw a Saviour in their down-fallen
　　Chief,
Raised the white banner within NEK-
　　SHEB'S gates,[2]
And there, untamed, the approaching
　　conqueror waits.

Of all his Haram, all that busy hive,
With music and with sweets sparkling
　　alive,
He took but one, the partner of his
　　flight,
One — not for love — not for her beauty's
　　light —
No, ZELICA stood withering midst the
　　gay,
Wan as the blossom that fell yesterday
From the Alma tree and dies, while over-
　　head
To-day's young flower is springing in its
　　stead.[3]
Oh, not for love — the deepest Damned
　　must be
Touched with Heaven's glory ere such
　　fiends as he
Can feel one glimpse of Love's divinity.
But no, she is his victim; — *there* lie all
Her charms for him — charms that can
　　never pall,
As long as hell within his heart can stir,
Or one faint trace of Heaven is left in
　　her.
To work an angel's ruin, — to behold
As white a page as Virtue e'er unrolled
Blacken beneath his touch into a scroll
Of damning sins, sealed with a burning
　　soul —
This is his triumph; this the joy accurst,
That ranks him among demons all but
　　first:

1 The ancient Oxus.
2 A city of Transoxiana.
3 " You never can cast your eyes on this tree,
but you meet there either blossoms or fruit; and
as the blossom drops underneath on the ground
(which is frequently covered with these purple-
colored flowers), others come forth in their
stead," etc. — *Nieuhoff.*

This gives the victim that before him lies
Blighted and lost, a glory in his eyes,
A light like that with which hell-fire il-
    lumes
The ghastly, writhing wretch whom it
    consumes!

But other tasks now wait him — tasks
    that need
All the deep daringness of thought and
    deed
With which the Divs [1] have gifted him —
    for mark,
Over yon plains which night had else
    made dark,
Those lanterns countless as the winged
    lights
That spangle INDIA's fields on showery
    nights,[2] —
Far as their formidable gleams they shed,
The mighty tents of the beleaguerer
    spread,
Glimmering along the horizon's dusky
    line
And thence in nearer circles till they
    shine
Among the founts and groves o'er which
    the town
In all its armed magnificence looks down.
Yet, fearless, from his lofty battlements
MOKANNA views that multitude of tents;
Nay, smiles to think that, tho' entoiled,
    beset,
Not less than myriads dare to front him
    yet; —
That friendless, throneless, he thus stands
    at bay,
Even thus a match for myriads such as
    they.
"Oh, for a sweep of that dark Angel's
    wing,
"Who brushed the thousands of the
    Assyrian King [3]
"To darkness in a moment that I might
"People Hell's chambers with yon host
    to-night!
"But come what may, let who will grasp
    the throne,

"Caliph or Prophet, Man alike shall
    groan;
"Let who will torture him, Priest —
    Caliph — King —
"Alike this loathsome world of his shall
    ring
"With victims' shrieks and howlings of
    the slave, —
"Sounds that shall glad me even within
    my grave!"
Thus, to himself — but to the scanty
    train
Still left around him, a far different
    strain: —
"Glorious Defenders of the sacred Crown
"I bear from Heaven whose light nor
    blood shall drown
"Nor shadow of earth eclipse; — before
    whose gems
"The paly pomp of this world's diadems,
"The crown of GERASHID, the pillared
    throne
"Of PARVIZ [4] and the heron crest that
    shone [5]
"Magnificent o'er ALI's beauteous
    eyes,[6]
"Fade like the stars when morn is in
    the skies:
"Warriors, rejoice — the port to which
    we 've past
"O'er Destiny's dark wave beams out
    at last!
"Victory 's our own — 't is written in
    that Book
"Upon whose leaves none but the
    angels look,
"That ISLAM's sceptre shall beneath the
    power

4 Chosroes. For the description of his
Throne or Palace, see *Gibbon* and *D'Herbelot.*
  There were said to be under this Throne or
Palace of Khosrou Parviz a hundred vaults filled
with "treasures so immense that some Mahometan writers tell us, their Prophet to encourage
his disciples carried them to a rock which at his
command opened and gave them a prospect
through it of the treasures of Khosrou." — *Universal History.*

5 "The crown of Gerashid is cloudy and tar-
nished before the heron tuft of thy turban."—
From one of the elegies or songs in praise of Ali,
written in characters of gold round the gallery of
Abbas's tomb. — See *Chardin.*

6 The beauty of Ali's eyes was so remarkable,
that whenever the Persians would describe any
thing as very lovely, they say it is Ayn Hali, or
the Eyes of Ali. — *Chardin.*

---

1 The Demons of the Persian mythology.
2 Carreri mentions the fire-flies in India during the rainy season. — See his Travels.
3 Sennacherib, called by the Orientals King
of Moussal. — *D'Herbelot.*

" Of her great foe fall broken in that
 hour
" When the moon's mighty orb before
 all eyes
" From NEKSHEB'S Holy Well porten-
 tously shall rise !
" Now turn and see ! " —
   They turned, and, as he spoke,
A sudden splendor all around them
 broke,
And they beheld an orb, ample and
 bright,
Rise from the Holy Well [1] and cast its
 light
Round the rich city and the plain for
 miles,[2] —
Flinging such radiance o'er the gilded
 tiles
Of many a dome and fair-roofed imaret
As autumn suns shed round them when
 they set.
Instant from all who saw the illusive
 sign
A murmur broke — " Miraculous ! di-
 vine ! "
The Gheber bowed, thinking his idol
 star
Had waked, and burst impatient thro'
 the bar
Of midnight to inflame him to the
 war ;
While he of MOUSSA'S creed saw in that
 ray
The glorious Light which in his freedom's day
Had rested on the Ark,[3] and now
 again
Shone out to bless the breaking of his
 chain.

" To victory ! " is at once the cry of
 all —
Nor stands MOKANNA loitering at that
 call ;
But instant the huge gates are flung
 aside,
And forth like a diminutive mountain-
 tide
Into the boundless sea they speed their
 course
Right on into the MOSLEM'S mighty
 force.
The watchmen of the camp, — who in
 their rounds
Had paused and even forgot the punc-
 tual sounds
Of the small drum with which they count
 the night,[4]
To gaze upon that supernatural light, —
Now sink beneath an unexpected arm,
And in a death-groan give their last
 alarm.
" On for the lamps that light yon lofty
 screen [5]
" Nor blunt your blades with massacre
 so mean ;
" *There* rests the CALIPH — speed —
 one lucky lance
" May now achieve mankind's deliver-
 ance."
Desperate the die — such as they only cast
Who venture for a world and stake their
 last.
But Fate 's no longer with him — blade
 for blade
Springs up to meet them thro' the glim-
 mering shade,
And as the clash is heard new legions soon
Pour to the spot, like bees of KAUZ-
 EROON [6]

1 We are not told more of this trick of the
Impostor, than that it was " *une machine, qu'il
disoit être la Lune.*" According to Richardson,
the miracle is perpetuated in Nekscheb. —
" Nakshab, the name of a city in Transoxiania,
where they say there is a well, in which the
appearance of the moon is to be seen night and
day."

2 " *Il amusa pendant deux mois le peuple de
la ville de Nekhscheb, en faisant sortir toutes les
nuits du fond d'un puits un corps lumineux sem-
blable à la Lune, qui portoit sa lumière jusqu'à
la distance de plusieurs milles.*" — *D'Herbelot.*
Hence he was called Sazendéhmah, or the
Moon-maker.

3 The Shechinah, called Sakînat in the Koran.
— See *Sale's Note*, chap. ii.

4 The parts of the night are made known as
well by instruments of music, as by the rounds
of the watchmen with cries and small drums. —
See *Burder's Oriental Customs*, vol. i. p. 119.

5 The Serrapurda, high screens of red cloth,
stiffened with cane, used to enclose a considerable space round the royal tents. — *Notes on the
Bahardanush.*
The tents of Princes were generally illuminated. Norden tells us that the tent of the Bey
of Girge was distinguished from the other tents
by forty lanterns being suspended before it. —
See *Harmer's* Observations on Job.

6 " From the groves of orange trees at Kauz-
eroon the bees cull a celebrated honey." —
Morier's Travels.

To the shrill timbrel's summons, — till
    at length
The mighty camp swarms out in all its
    strength,
And back to NEKSHEB'S gates covering
    the plain
With random slaughter drives the adven-
    turous train;
Among the last of whom the Silver Veil
Is seen glittering at times, like the white
    sail
Of some lost vessel on a stormy night
Catching the tempest's momentary light!

And hath not *this* brought the proud
    spirit low?
Nor dashed his brow nor checkt his
    daring? No
Tho' half the wretches whom at night
    he led
To thrones and victory lie disgraced and
    dead,
Yet morning hears him with unshrinking
    crest,
Still vaunt of thrones and victory to the
    rest; —
And they believe him! — oh, the lover may
Distrust that look which steals his soul
    away; —
The babe may cease to think that it can
    play
With Heaven's rainbow; — alchymists
    may doubt
The shining gold their crucible gives out;
But Faith, fanatic Faith, once wedded fast
To some dear falsehood hugs it to the last.

And well the Impostor knew all lures
    and arts,
That LUCIFER e'er taught to tangle hearts;
Nor, mid these last bold workings of his
    plot
Against men's souls, is ZELICA forgot.
Ill-fated ZELICA! had reason been
Awake, thro' half the horrors thou hast
    seen,
Thou never couldst have borne it—Death
    had come
At once and taken thy wrung spirit home.
But 't was not so — a torpor, a suspense
Of thought, almost of life, came o'er the
    intense
And passionate struggles of that fearful
    night,

When her last hope of peace and heaven
    took flight:
And tho' at times a gleam of frenzy
    broke, —
As thro' some dull volcano's veil of smoke
Ominous flashings now and then will start,
Which show the fire's still busy at its
    heart;
Yet was she mostly wrapt in solemn
    gloom, —
Not such as AZIM'S, brooding o'er its
    doom
And calm without as is the brow of death
While busy worms are gnawing under-
    neath —
But in a blank and pulseless torpor free
From thought or pain, a sealed-up apathy
Which left her oft with scarce one living
    thrill
The cold, pale victim of her torturer's
    will.

Again, as in MEROU, he had her deckt
Gorgeously out, the Priestess of the
    sect;
And led her glittering forth before the eyes
Of his rude train as to a sacrifice, —
Pallid as she, the young, devoted Bride
Of the fierce NILE, when, deckt in all
    the pride
Of nuptial pomp, she sinks into his tide.[1]
And while the wretched maid hung down
    her head,
And stood as one just risen from the dead
Amid that gazing crowd, the fiend would
    tell
His credulous slaves it was some charm
    or spell
Possest her now, — and from that dark-
    ened trance
Should dawn ere long their Faith's deliv-
    erance.
Or if at times goaded by guilty shame,
Her soul was roused and words of wild-
    ness came,
Instant the bold blasphemer would
    translate
Her ravings into oracles of fate,

---

1 " A custom still subsisting at this day, seems
to me to prove that the Egyptians formerly sacrificed a young virgin to the God of the Nile ; for
they now make a statue of earth in shape of a girl,
to which they give the name of the Betrothed
Bride, and throw it into the river."— *Savary*.

Would hail Heaven's signals in her flash-
    ing eyes
And call her shrieks the language of the
    skies !

But vain at length his arts — despair is
    seen
Gathering around ; and famine comes to
    glean
All that the sword had left unreaped : —
    in vain
At morn and eve across the northern
    plain
He looks impatient for the promised
    spears
Of the wild Hordes and TARTAR moun-
    taineers;
They come not — while his fierce be-
    leaguerers pour
Engines of havoc in, unknown before,[1]

1 That they knew the secret of the Greek fire
among the Mussulmans early in the eleventh
century, appears from *Dow's* Account of Mamood
I. "When he arrived at Moultan, finding that
the country of the Jits was defended by great
rivers, he ordered fifteen hundred boats to be
built, each of which he armed with six iron spikes,
projecting from their prows and sides, to prevent
their being boarded by the enemy, who were very
expert in that kind of war. When he had launched
this fleet, he ordered twenty archers into each
boat, and five others with fire-balls, to burn the
craft of the Jits, and naphtha to set the whole
river on fire."
    The *agnee aster*, too, in Indian poems the
Instrument of Fire, whose flame cannot be extinguished, is supposed to signify the Greek Fire.
— See *Wilks's* South of India, vol. i. p. 471. —
And in the curious Javan poem, the *Brata Yudha*
given by *Sir Stamford Raffles* in his History of
Java, we find, "He aimed at the heart of Soéta
with the sharp-pointed Weapon of Fire."
    The mention of gunpowder as in use among
the Arabians, long before its supposed discovery
in Europe, is introduced by *Ebn Fadhl*, the
Egyptian geographer, who lived in the thirteenth
century. "Bodies," he says, "in the form of
scorpions, bound round and filled with nitrous
powder, glide along, making a gentle noise; then,
exploding, they lighten, as it were, and burn.
But there are others which, cast into the air,
stretch along like a cloud, roaring horribly, as
thunder roars, and on all sides vomiting out
flames, burst, burn, and reduce to cinders whatever comes in their way." The historian *Ben
Abdalla*, in speaking of the sieges of Abulualid
in the year of the Hegira 712, says, "A fiery
globe, by means of combustible matter, with a
mighty noise suddenly emitted, strikes with the
force of lightning, and shakes the citadel."— See
the extracts from *Casiri's* Biblioth. Arab. Hispan.
in the Appendix to *Berington's* Literary History
of the Middle Ages.

And horrible as new;[2] — javelins, that fly
Enwreathed with smoky flames thro' the
    dark sky,
And red-hot globes that opening as they
    mount
Discharge as from a kindled Naphtha
    fount [3]
Showers of consuming fire o'er all below;
Looking as thro' the illumined night they
    go
Like those wild birds [4] that by the Ma-
    gians oft
At festivals of fire were sent aloft
Into the air with blazing fagots tied
To their huge wings, scattering com-
    bustion wide.
All night the groans of wretches who
    expire
In agony beneath these darts of fire
Ring thro' the city—while descending o'er
Its shrines and domes and streets of
    sycamore, —
Its lone bazars, with their bright cloths
    of gold,
Since the last peaceful pageant left un-
    rolled, —
Its beauteous marble baths whose idle
    jets

2 The Greek fire, which was occasionally lent
by the emperors to their allies. "It was," says
Gibbon, "either launched in red-hot balls of stone
and iron, or darted in arrows and javelins, twisted
round with flax and tow, which had deeply imbibed the inflammable oil."

3 See *Hanway's* Account of the Springs of
Naphtha at Baku (which is called by *Lieutenant
Pottinger* Joala Mookee, or, the Flaming Mouth,)
taking fire and running into the sea. *Dr. Cooke*,
in his Journal, mentions some wells in Circassia,
strongly impregnated with this inflammable oil,
from which issues boiling water. "Though the
weather," he adds, "was now very cold, the
warmth of these wells of hot water produced near
them the verdure and flowers of spring."
    Major Scott Waring says, that naphtha is
used by the Persians, as we are told it was in
hell, for lamps.

    . . . . many a row
    Of starry lamps and blazing cressets, fed
    With naphtha and asphaltus, yielding light
    As from a sky.

4 "At the great festival of fire, called the Sheb
Sezê, they used to set fire to large bunches of dry
combustibles, fastened round wild beasts and
birds, which being then let loose, the air and
earth appeared one great illumination ; and as
these terrified creatures naturally fled to the woods
for shelter, it is easy to conceive the conflagrations they produced." — *Richardson's* Dissertation.

Now gush with blood, — and its tall
  minarets
That late have stood up in the evening
  glare
Of the red sun, unhallowed by a prayer; —
O'er each in turn the dreadful flame-bolts
  fall,
And death and conflagration throughout
  all
The desolate city hold high festival!

MOKANNA sees the world is his no
  more; —
One sting at parting and his grasp is o'er.
" What! drooping now? " — thus, with
  unblushing cheek,
He hails the few who yet can hear him
  speak,
Of all those famished slaves around him
  lying,
And by the light of blazing temples
  dying; —
" What! — drooping now? — now, when
  at length we press
" Home o'er the very threshold of suc-
  cess;
" When ALLA from our ranks hath
  thinned away
" Those grosser branches that kept out
  his ray
" Of favor from us and we stand at
  length
" Heirs of his light and children of his
  strength,
" The chosen few who shall survive the
  fall
" Of Kings and Thrones, triumphant
  over all!
" Have you then lost, weak murmurers
  as you are,
" All faith in him who was your Light,
  your Star?
" Have you forgot the eye of glory hid
" Beneath this Veil, the flashing of whose
  lid
" Could like a sun-stroke of the desert
  wither
" Millions of such as yonder Chief brings
  hither?
" Long have its lightnings slept — too
  long — but now
" All earth shall feel the unveiling of
  this brow!

" To-night — yes, sainted men! this very
  night,
" I bid you all to a fair festal rite,
" Where — having deep refreshed each
  weary limb
" With viands such as feast Heaven's
  cherubim
" And kindled up your souls now sunk
  and dim
" With that pure wine the Dark-eyed
  Maids above
" Keep, sealed with precious musk, for
  those they love,[1] —
" I will myself uncurtain in your sight
" The wonders of this brow's ineffable
  light;
" Then lead you forth and with a wink
  disperse
" Yon myriads howling thro' the uni-
  verse! "

Eager they listen — while each accent
  darts
New life into their chilled and hope-sick
  hearts;
Such treacherous life as the cool draught
  supplies
To him upon the stake who drinks and
  dies!
Wildly they point their lances to the
  light
Of the fast sinking sun, and shout " To-
  night! " —
" To-night," their Chief re-echoes in a
  voice
Of fiend-like mockery that bids hell rejoice.
Deluded victims! — never hath this earth
Seen mourning half so mournful as their
  mirth.
Here, to the few whose iron frames had
  stood
This racking waste of famine and of
  blood,
Faint, dying wretches clung, from whom
  the shout
Of triumph like a maniac's laugh broke
  out: —
There, others, lighted by the smouldering
  fire,

1 " The righteous shall be given to drink of
pure wine, sealed; the seal whereof shall be
musk." — *Koran*, chap. lxxxiii.

Danced like wan ghosts about a funeral
    pyre
Among the dead and dying strewed
    around; —
While some pale wretch lookt on and
    from his wound
Plucking the fiery dart by which he bled,
In ghastly transport waved it o'er his
    head!

'T was more than midnight now — a
    fearful pause
Had followed the long shouts, the wild
    applause,
That lately from those Royal Gardens
    burst,
Where the Veiled demon held his feast
    accurst,
When ZELICA — alas, poor ruined heart,
In every horror doomed to bear its
    part! —
Was bidden to the banquet by a slave,
Who, while his quivering lip the sum-
    mons gave,
Grew black, as tho' the shadows of the
    grave
Compast him round and ere he could re-
    peat
His message thro', fell lifeless at her
    feet!
Shuddering she went — a soul-felt pang
    of fear,
A presage that her own dark doom was
    near,
Roused every feeling and brought Reason
    back
Once more to writhe her last upon the
    rack.
All round seemed tranquil — even the foe
    had ceased
As if aware of that demoniac feast
His fiery bolts; and tho' the heavens
    looked red,
'T was but some distant conflagration's
    spread.
But hark — she stops — she listens —
    dreadful tone!
'T is her Tormentor's laugh — and now,
    a groan,
A long death-groan comes with it: — can
    this be
The place of mirth, the bower of revelry?
She enters — Holy ALLA, what a sight

Was there before her! By the glimmer-
    ing light
Of the pale dawn, mixt with the flare of
    brands
That round lay burning dropt from life-
    less hands,
She saw the board in splendid mockery
    spread,
Rich censers breathing — garlands over-
    head —
The urns, the cups, from which they late
    had quaft
All gold and gems, but — what had been
    the draught?
Oh! who need ask that saw those livid
    guests,
With their swollen heads sunk blackening
    on their breasts,
Or looking pale to Heaven with glassy
    glare,
As if they sought but saw no mercy there;
As if they felt, tho' poison racked them
    thro',
Remorse the deadlier torment of the two!
While some, the bravest, hardiest in the
    train
Of their false Chief, who on the battle-
    plain
Would have met death with transport by
    his side,
Here mute and helpless gasped; — but
    as they died
Lookt horrible vengeance with their
    eyes' last strain,
And clenched the slackening hand at
    him in vain.

Dreadful it was to see the ghastly stare,
The stony look of horror and despair,
Which some of these expiring victims
    cast
Upon their souls' tormentor to the
    last; —
Upon that mocking Fiend whose Veil
    now raised,
Showed them as in death's agony they
    gazed,
Not the long promised light, the brow
    whose beaming
Was to come forth, all conquering, all
    redeeming,
But features horribler than Hell e'er
    traced

On its own brood; — no Demon of the
Waste,[1]
No church-yard Ghoul caught lingering
in the light
Of the blest sun, e'er blasted human
sight
With lineaments so foul, so fierce as
those
The Impostor now in grinning mockery
shows: —
"There, ye wise Saints, behold your
Light, your Star —
"Ye *would* be dupes and victims and ye
are.
"Is it enough? or must I, while a
thrill
"Lives in your sapient bosoms, cheat
you still?
"Swear that the burning death ye feel
within
"Is but the trance with which Heaven's
joys begin;
"That this foul visage, foul as e'er dis-
graced
"Even monstrous man, is — after God's
own taste;
"And that — but see! — ere I have half-
way said
"My greetings thro', the uncourteous
souls are fled.
"Farewell, sweet spirits! not in vain ye
die,
"If EBLIS loves you half so well as I. —
"Ha, my young bride! — 't is well —
take thou thy seat;
"Nay come — no shuddering — didst
thou never meet
"The Dead before? — they graced our
wedding, sweet;
"And these, my guests to-night, have
brimmed so true
"Their parting cups, that *thou* shalt
pledge one too.
"But — how is this? — all empty? all
drunk up?
"Hot lips have been before thee in the
cup,

"Young bride — yet stay — one precious drop remains,
"Enough to warm a gentle Priestess'
veins; —
"Here, drink — and should thy lover's
conquering arms
"Speed hither ere thy lip lose all its
charms,
"Give him but half this venom in thy kiss,
"And I 'll forgive my haughty rival's
bliss!

"For, *me* — I too must die — but not
like these
"Vile rankling things to fester in the
breeze;
"To have this brow in ruffian triumph
shown,
"With all death's grimness added to its
own,
"And rot to dust beneath the taunting eyes
"Of slaves, exclaiming, 'There his God-
ship lies!'
"No — cursed race — since first my soul
drew breath,
"They 've been my dupes and *shall* be
even in death.
"Thou seest yon cistern in the shade —
't is filled
"With burning drugs for this last hour
distilled : [2] —
"There will I plunge me, in that liquid
flame —
"Fit bath to lave a dying Prophet's
frame! —
"There perish, all — ere pulse of thine
shall fail —
"Nor leave one limb to tell mankind
the tale.
"So shall my votaries, wheresoe'er they
rave,
"Proclaim that Heaven took back the
Saint it gave; —
"That I 've but vanish from this earth
awhile,
"To come again with bright, unshrouded
smile!

---

1 "The Afghauns believe each of the numerous solitudes and deserts of their country to be
inhabited by a lonely demon, whom they call the
Ghoolee Beeabau, or Spirit of the Waste. They
often illustrate the wildness of any sequestered
tribe, by saying, they are wild as the Demon of
the Waste." — *Elphinstone's Caubul.*

2 " *Il donna du poison dans le vin à tous ses
gens, et se jetta lui-même ensuite dans une cuve
pleine de drogues brûlantes et consumantes, afin
qu'il ne restât rien de tous les membres de son
corps, et que ceux qui restoient de sa secte puis-
sent croire qu'il étoit monté au ciel, ce qui ne
manqua pas d arriver.*" — *D'Herbelot.*

" So shall they build me altars in their
zeal,
" Where knaves shall minister and fools
shall kneel;
" Where Faith may mutter o'er her
mystic spell,
" Written in blood — and Bigotry may
swell
" The sail he spreads for Heaven with
blasts from hell!
" So shall my banner thro' long ages be
" The rallying sign of fraud and an-
archy; —
" Kings yet unborn shall rue MOKANNA'S
name,
" And tho' I die my spirit still the same
" Shall walk abroad in all the stormy
strife,
" And guilt and blood that were its bliss
in life.
" But hark! their battering engine shakes
the wall —
" Why, *let* it shake — thus I can brave
them all.
" No trace of me shall greet them when
they come,
" And I can trust thy faith, for — thou
'lt be dumb.
" Now mark how readily a wretch like me
" In one bold plunge commences Deity!"

He sprung and sunk as the last words
were said —
Quick closed the burning waters o'er his
head,
And ZELICA was left — within the ring
Of those wide walls the only living thing;
The only wretched one still curst with
breath
In all that frightful wilderness of death!
More like some bloodless ghost — such
as, they tell,
In the Lone Cities of the Silent [1] dwell,
And there unseen of all but ALLA sit
Each by its own pale carcass watching it.

But morn is up and a fresh warfare
stirs
Throughout the camp of the beleaguerers.

1 " They have all a great reverence for burial-
grounds, which they sometimes call by the poetical name of Cities of the Silent, and which they
people with the ghosts of the departed, who sit
each at the head of his own grave, invisible to
mortal eyes." — *Elphinstone.*

Their globes of fire (the dread artillery
lent
By GREECE to conquering MAHADI) are
spent;
And now the scorpion's shaft, the quarry
sent
From high balistas and the shielded throng
Of soldiers swinging the huge ram along,
All speak the impatient Islamite's in-
tent
To try, at length, if tower and battlement
And bastioned wall be not less hard to
win,
Less tough to break down than the hearts
within.
First in impatience and in toil is he,
The burning AZIM — oh! could he but
see
The Impostor once alive within his grasp,
Not the gaunt lion's hug nor boa's clasp
Could match that gripe of vengeance or
keep pace
With the fell heartiness of Hate's em-
brace!

Loud rings the ponderous ram against
the walls;
Now shake the ramparts, now a buttress
falls,
But still no breach — " Once more, one
mighty swing
" Of all your beams, together thunder-
ing!"
There — the wall shakes — the shouting
troops exult,
" Quick, quick discharge your weightiest
catapult
" Right on that spot and NEKSHEB is our
own!"
'T is done — the battlements come crashing down,
And the huge wall by that stroke riven in
two
Yawning like some old crater rent anew,
Shows the dim, desolate city smoking
thro'.
But strange! no sign of life — naught
living seen
Above, below — what can this stillness
mean?
A minute's pause suspends all hearts and
eyes —
" In thro' the breach," impetuous AZIM
cries;

But the cool CALIPH fearful of some wile
In this blank stillness checks the troops
    awhile. —
Just then a figure with slow step advanced
Forth from the ruined walls and as there
    glanced
A sunbeam over it all eyes could see
The well-known Silver Veil! — "'T is
    He, 't is He,
" MOKANNA and alone!" they shout
    around;
Young AZIM from his steed springs to the
    ground —
" Mine, Holy Caliph! mine," he cries,
    " the task
" To crush yon daring wretch — 't is all
    I ask."
Eager he darts to meet the demon foe
Who still across wide heaps of ruin slow
And falteringly comes, till they are near;
Then with a bound rushes on AZIM's
    spear,
And casting off the Veil in falling shows —
Oh! — 't is his ZELICA's life-blood that
    flows!

" I meant not, AZIM," soothingly
    she said,
As on his trembling arm she leaned her
    head,
And looking in his face saw anguish
    there
Beyond all wounds the quivering flesh
    can bear —
" I meant not *thou* shouldst have the pain
    of this: —
" Tho' death with thee thus tasted is a
    bliss
" Thou wouldst not rob me of, didst thou
    but know
" How oft I 've prayed to God I might
    die so!
" But the Fiend's venom was too scant
    and slow; —
" To linger on were maddening — and I
    thought
" If once that Veil — nay, look not on it
    — caught
" The eyes of your fierce soldiery, I
    should be
" Struck by a thousand death-darts in-
    stantly.
" But this is sweeter — oh! believe me,
    yes —

" I would not change this sad, but dear
    caress,
" This death within thy arms I would
    not give
" For the most smiling life the happiest
    live!
" All that stood dark and drear before
    the eye
" Of my strayed soul is passing swiftly
    by ;
" A light comes o'er me from those looks
    of love,
" Like the first dawn of mercy from
    above ;
" And if thy lips but tell me I 'm for-
    given,
" Angels will echo the blest words in
    Heaven !
" But live, my AZIM; — oh! to call thee
    mine
" Thus once again! *my* AZIM — dream
    divine !
" Live, if thou ever lovedst me, if to
    meet
" Thy ZELICA hereafter would be sweet,
" Oh, live to pray for her — to bend the
    knee
" Morning and night before that Deity
" To whom pure lips and hearts without
    a stain,
" As thine are, AZIM, never breathed in
    vain, —
" And pray that He may pardon her, —
    may take
" Compassion on her soul for thy dear
    sake,
" And naught remembering but her love
    to thee,
" Make her all thine, all His, eternally !
" Go to those happy fields where first
    we twined
" Our youthful hearts together — every
    wind
" That meets thee there fresh from the
    well-known flowers
" Will bring the sweetness of those in-
    nocent hours
" Back to thy soul and thou mayst feel
    again
" For thy poor ZELICA as thou didst
    then.
" So shall thy orisons like dew that flies
" To Heaven upon the morning's sun-
    shine rise

"With all love's earliest ardor to the
    skies !
" And should they — but, alas, my senses
    fail —
" Oh for one minute ! — should thy
    prayers prevail —
" If pardoned souls may from that World
    of Bliss
" Reveal their joy to those they love in
    this —
" I'll come to thee — in some sweet
    dream — and tell —
" Oh Heaven — I die — dear love ! fare-
    well, farewell."

Time fleeted — years on years had past
    away,
And few of those who on that mournful
    day
Had stood with pity in their eyes to see
The maiden's death and the youth's
    agony,
Were living still — when, by a rustic
    grave,
Beside the swift Amoo's transparent
    wave,

An aged man who had grown aged there
By that lone grave, morning and night in
    prayer,
For the last time knelt down — and tho'
    the shade
Of death hung darkening over him there
    played
A gleam of rapture on his eye and
    cheek,
That brightened even Death — like the
    last streak
Of intense glory on the horizon's brim,
When night o'er all the rest hangs chill
    and dim.
His soul had seen a Vision while he
    slept;
She for whose spirit he had prayed and
    wept
So many years had come to him all drest
In angel smiles and told him she was
    blest !
For this the old man breathed his thanks
    and died. —
And there upon the banks of that loved
    tide,
He and his ZELICA sleep side by side.

THE story of the Veiled Prophet of Khorassan being ended, they were now
doomed to hear FADLADEEN'S criticisms upon it. A series of disappointments and
accidents had occurred to this learned Chamberlain during the journey. In the
first place, those couriers stationed, as in the reign of Shah Jehan, between Delhi
and the Western coast of India, to secure a constant supply of mangoes for the
Royal Table, had by some cruel irregularity failed in their duty; and to eat any
mangoes but those of Mazagong was of course impossible.[1] In the next place, the
elephant laden with his fine antique porcelain,[2] had, in an unusual fit of liveliness,
shattered the whole set to pieces: — an irreparable loss, as many of the vessels
were so exquisitely old, as to have been used under the Emperors Yan and Chun,
who reigned many ages before the dynasty of Tang. His Koran too, supposed to
be the identical copy between the leaves of which Mahomet's favorite pigeon
used to nestle, had been mislaid by his Koran-bearer three whole days; not without much spiritual alarm to FADLADEEN who though professing to hold with other
loyal and orthodox Mussulmans that salvation could only be found in the Koran
was strongly suspected of believing in his heart that it could only be found in his

1 The celebrity of Mazagong is owing to its mangoes, which are certainly the best fruit I ever
tasted.   The parent-tree, from which all those of this species have been grafted, is honored during
the fruit-season by a guard of sepoys ; and, in the reign of Shah Jehan, couriers were stationed between Delhi and the Mahratta coast, to secure an abundant and fresh supply of mangoes for the
royal table." — *Mrs. Graham's* Journal of a Residence in India.

2 This old porcelain is found in digging, and " if it is esteemed, it is not because it has acquired any new degree of beauty in the earth, but because is has retained its ancient beauty; and
this alone is of great importance in China, where they give large sums for the smallest vessels
which were used under the Emperors Yan and Chun, who reigned many ages before the dynasty of
Tang, at which time porcelain began to be used by the Emperors" (about the year 442). — *Dunn's*
Collection of curious Observations, etc. ; — a bad translation of some parts of the " *Lettres Édifiantes et Curieuses* " of the Missionary Jesuits.

own particular copy of it. When to all these grievances is added the obstinacy of the cooks in putting the pepper of Canara into his dishes instead of the cinnamon of Serendib, we may easily suppose that he came to the task of criticism with at least a sufficient degree of irritability for the purpose.

"In order," said he, importantly swinging about his chaplet of pearls, "to convey with clearness my opinion of the story this young man has related, it is necessary to take a review of all the stories that have ever " — — "My good FADLADEEN!" exclaimed the Princess, interrupting him, "we really do not deserve that you should give yourself so much trouble. Your opinion of the poem we have just heard, will I have no doubt be abundantly edifying without any further waste of your valuable erudition." — "If that be all," replied the critic, — evidently mortified at not being allowed to show how much he knew about every thing but the subject immediately before him — "if that be all that is required the matter is easily despatched." He then proceeded to analyze the poem, in that strain (so well known to the unfortunate bards of Delhi), whose censures were an infliction from which few recovered and whose very praises were like the honey extracted from the bitter flowers of the aloe. The chief personages of the story were, if he rightly understood them, an ill-favored gentleman with a veil over his face; — a young lady whose reason went and came according as it suited the poet's convenience to be sensible or otherwise; — and a youth in one of those hideous Bokharian bonnets, who took the aforesaid gentleman in a veil for a Divinity. "From such materials," said he, "what can be expected?— after rivalling each other in long speeches and absurdities through some thousands of lines as indigestible as the filberts of Berdaa, our friend in the veil jumps into a tub of aquafortis; the young lady dies in a set speech whose only recommendation is that it is her last; and the lover lives on to a good old age for the laudable purpose of seeing her ghost which he at last happily accomplishes, and expires. This you will allow is a fair summary of the story; and if Nasser, the Arabian merchant, told no better, our Holy Prophet (to whom be all honor and glory!) had no need to be jealous of his abilities for story-telling." [1]

With respect to the style, it was worthy of the matter; — it had not even those politic contrivances of structure which make up for the commonness of the thoughts by the peculiarity of the manner nor that stately poetical phraseology by which sentiments mean in themselves, like the blacksmith's [2] apron converted into a banner, are so easily gilt and embroidered into consequence. Then as to the versification it was, to say no worse of it, execrable: it had neither the copious flow of Ferdosi, the sweetness of Hafez, nor the sententious march of Sadi; but appeared to him in the uneasy heaviness of its movements to have been modelled upon the gait of a very tired dromedary. The licenses too in which it indulged were unpardonable; — for instance this line, and the poem abounded with such; —

> Like the faint, exquisite music of a dream.

"What critic that can count," said FADLADEEN, "and has his full complement of fingers to count withal, would tolerate for an instant such syllabic superfluities?" — He here looked round, and discovered that most of his audience were asleep;

---

1 "*La lecture de ces Fables plaisoit si fort aux Arabes, que, quand Mahomet les entretenoit de l'Histoire de l'Ancien Testament, ils les méprisoient, lui disant que celles que Nasser leur racontoient étoient beaucoup plus belles. Cette préférence attira à Nasser la malediction de Mahomet et de tous ses disciples.*" — *D'Herbelot.*

2 The blacksmith Gao, who successfully resisted the tyrant Zohak, and whose apron became the Royal Standard of Persia.

while the glimmering lamps seemed inclined to follow their example. It became necessary therefore, however painful to himself, to put an end to his valuable animadversions for the present and he accordingly concluded with an air of dignified candor, thus:— "Notwithstanding the observations which I have thought it my duty to make, it is by no means my wish to discourage the young man:— so far from it indeed that if he will but totally alter his style of writing and thinking I have very little doubt that I shall be vastly pleased with him."

Some days elapsed after this harangue of the Great Chamberlain before LALLA ROOKH could venture to ask for another story. The youth was still a welcome guest in the pavilion — to *one* heart perhaps too dangerously welcome;— but all mention of poetry was as if by common consent avoided. Though none of the party had much respect for FADLADEEN, yet his censures thus magisterially delivered evidently made an impression on them all. The Poet himself to whom criticism was quite a new operation, (being wholly unknown in that Paradise of the Indies, Cashmere,) felt the shock as it is generally felt at first, till use has made it more tolerable to the patient;— the Ladies began to suspect that they ought not to be pleased and seemed to conclude that there must have been much good sense in what FADLADEEN said from its having set them all so soundly to sleep;— while the self-complacent Chamberlain was left to triumph in the idea of having for the hundred and fiftieth time in his life extinguished a Poet. LALLA ROOKH alone — and Love knew why — persisted in being delighted with all she had heard and in resolving to hear more as speedily as possible. Her manner however of first returning to the subject was unlucky. It was while they rested during the heat of noon near a fountain on which some hand had rudely traced those well-known words from the Garden of Sadi, — "Many like me have viewed this fountain, but they are gone and their eyes are closed for ever!" — that she took occasion from the melancholy beauty of this passage to dwell upon the charms of poetry in general. "It is true," she said, "few poets can imitate that sublime bird which flies always in the air and never touches the earth: [1] — it is only once in many ages a Genius appears whose words, like those on the Written Mountain last for ever: [2] — but still there are some as delightful perhaps, though not so wonderful, who if not stars over our head are at least flowers along our path and whose sweetness of the moment we ought gratefully to inhale without calling upon them for a brightness and a durability beyond their nature. In short," continued she, blushing as if conscious of being caught in an oration, "it is quite cruel that a poet cannot wander through his regions of enchantment without having a critic for ever, like the old Man of the Sea, upon his back!" [3] — FADLADEEN, it was plain, took this

---

[1] "The Huma, a bird peculiar to the East. It is supposed to fly constantly in the air, and never touch the ground; it is looked upon as a bird of happy omen; and that every head it overshades will in time wear a crown." — *Richardson.*

In the terms of alliance made by Fuzzel Oola Khan with Hyder in 1760, one of the stipulations was, "that he should have the distinction of two honorary attendants standing behind him, holding fans composed of the feathers of the humma, according to the practice of his family." — *Wilks's South of India.* He adds in a note; — "The Humma is a fabulous bird. The head over which its shadow once passes will assuredly be circled with a crown. The splendid little bird suspended over the throne of Tippoo Sultaun, found at Seringapatam in 1799, was intended to represent this poetical fancy."

[2] "To the pilgrims to Mount Sinai we must attribute the inscriptions, figures, etc. on those rocks, which have from thence acquired the name of the Written Mountain." — *Volney.*

M. Gebelin and others have been at much pains to attach some mysterious and important meaning to these inscriptions; but Niebuhr, as well as Volney, thinks that they must have been executed at idle hours by the travellers to Mount Sinai, "who were satisfied with cutting the unpolished rock with any pointed instrument; adding to their names and the date of their journeys some rude figures, which bespeak the hand of a people but little skilled in the arts." — *Niebuhr.*

[3] The Story of Sinbad.

last luckless allusion to himself and would treasure it up in his mind as a whet-stone for his next criticism. A sudden silence ensued; and the Princess, glancing a look at FERAMORZ, saw plainly she must wait for a more courageous moment.

But the glories of Nature and her wild, fragrant airs playing freshly over the current of youthful spirits will soon heal even deeper wounds than the dull Fadla-deens of this world can inflict. In an evening or two after, they came to the small Valley of Gardens which had been planted by order of the Emperor for his favorite sister Rochinara during their progress to Cashmere some years before; and never was there a more sparkling assemblage of sweets since the Gulzar-e-Irem or Rose-bower of Irem. Every precious flower was there to be found that poetry or love or religion has ever consecrated; from the dark hyacinth to which Hafez compares his mistress's hair[1] to the *Cámalatá* by whose rosy blossoms the heaven of Indra is scented.[2] As they sat in the cool fragrance of this delicious spot and LALLA ROOKH remarked that she could fancy it the abode of that Flower-loving Nymph whom they worship in the temples of Kathay,[3] or of one of those Peris, those beautiful creatures of the air who live upon perfumes and to whom a place like this might make some amends for the Paradise they have lost, — the young Poet in whose eyes she appeared while she spoke to be one of the bright spiritual creatures she was describing said hesitatingly that he remembered a Story of a Peri, which if the Princess had no objection he would venture to relate. "It is," said he, with an appealing look to FADLADEEN, "in a lighter and humbler strain than the other:" then, striking a few careless but melancholy chords on his kitar, he thus began: —

PARADISE AND THE PERI.

ONE morn a Peri at the gate
Of Eden stood disconsolate;
And as she listened to the Springs
Of Life within like music flowing
And caught the light upon her wings
Thro' the half-open portal glowing,
She wept to think her recreant race
Should e'er have lost that glorious place!

"How happy," exclaimed this child of air,
"Are the holy Spirits who wander there
"Mid flowers that never shall fade or fall;

"Tho' mine are the gardens of earth and sea
"And the stars themselves have flowers for me,
"One blossom of Heaven out-blooms them all!

"Tho' sunny the Lake of cool CASHMERE
"With its plane-tree Isle reflected clear,[4]
"And sweetly the founts of that Valley fall;
"Tho' bright are the waters of SING-SU-HAY

---

1 See *Nott's* Hafez, Ode v.

2 "The Cámalatá (called by Linnæus, Ipomæa) is the most beautiful of its order, both in the color and form of its leaves and flowers; its elegant blossoms are 'celestial rosy red, Love's proper hue,' and have justly procured it the name of Cámalatá, or Love's creeper." — *Sir W. Jones.*

"Cámalatá may also mean a mythological plant, by which all desires are granted to such as inhabit the heaven of Indra; and if ever flower was worthy of paradise, it is our charming Ipo-mæa." — *Ib.*

3 "According to Father Premare, in his tract on Chinese Mythology, the mother of Fo-hi was the daughter of heaven, surnamed Flower-loving; and as the nymph was walking alone on the bank of a river, she found herself encircled by a rainbow, after which she became pregnant, and, at the end of twelve years, was delivered of a son radiant as herself." — *Asiat. Res.*

4 "Numerous small islands emerge from the Lake of Cashmere. One is called Char Chenaur, from the plane trees upon it. — *Foster.*

" And the golden floods that thitherward
    stray,[1]
" Yet — oh, 't is only the Blest can say
    " How the waters of Heaven outshine
      them all !

" Go, wing thy flight from star to star,
" From world to luminous world as far
    " As the universe spreads its flaming
      wall :
" Take all the pleasures of all the spheres
" And   multiply   each thro' endless
    years
    " One minute of Heaven is worth them
      all ! "

The glorious Angel who was keeping
The gates of Light beheld her weeping,
And as he nearer drew and listened
To her sad song, a tear-drop glistened
Within his eyelids, like the spray
    From Eden's fountain when it lies
On the blue flower which — Bramins
    say —
Blooms nowhere but in Paradise.[2]

" Nymph of a fair but erring line ! "
Gently he said — " One hope is thine.
" 'T is written in the Book of Fate,
    " *The Peri yet may be forgiven*
" *Who brings to this Eternal gate*
    " *The Gift that is most dear to Heaven !*
" Go seek it and redeem thy sin —
    " 'T is sweet to let the Pardoned in."

Rapidly as comets run
To the embraces of the Sun ; —
Fleeter than the starry brands
Flung at night from angel hands [3]

---

1 " The Altan Kol or Golden River of Tibet,
which runs into the Lakes of Sing-su-hay, has
abundance of gold in its sands, which employs
the inhabitants all the summer in gathering it."
— *Description of Tibet in Pinkerton.*

2 " The Brahmins of this province insist that
the blue campac flowers only in Paradise." —
Sir W. Jones. It appears, however, from a curious letter of the Sultan of Menangcabow, given
by Marsden, that one place on earth may lay
claim to the possession of it. " This is the Sultan, who keeps the flower champaka that is blue,
and to be found in no other country but his, being
yellow elsewhere." — *Marsden's* Sumatra.

3 " The Mahometans suppose that falling stars
are the firebrands wherewith the good angels
drive away the bad, when they approach too near
the empyrean or verge of the heavens." —*Fryer.*

At those dark and daring sprites
Who would climb the empyreal heights,
Down the blue vault the PERI flies,
    And lighted earthward by a glance
That just then broke from morning's eyes,
    Hung hovering o'er our world's ex-
      panse.

But whither shall the Spirit go
To find this gift for Heaven ? — " I know
" The wealth," she cries, " of every urn
" In which unnumbered rubies burn
" Beneath the pillars of CHILMINAR ; [4]
" I know where the Isles of Perfume are [5]
" Many a fathom down in the sea,
" To the south of sun-bright ARABY ; [6]
" I know too where the Genii hid
" The jewelled cup of their King JAM-
    SHID,[7]
" With Life's elixir sparkling high —
" But gifts like these are not for the sky.
" Where was there ever a gem that shone
" Like the steps of ALLA'S wonderful
    Throne ?
" And the Drops of Life — oh ! what
    would they be
" In the boundless Deep of Eternity ? "

While thus she mused her pinions fanned
The air of that sweet Indian land
Whose air is balm, whose ocean spreads
O'er coral rocks and amber beds,[8]

---

4 The Forty Pillars ; so the Persians call the
ruins of Persepolis. It is imagined by them
that this palace and the edifices at Balbec were
built by Genii, for the purpose of hiding in their
subterraneous caverns immense treasures, which
still remain there. — *D'Herbelot, Volney.*

5 *Diodorus* mentions the Isle of Panchaia, to
the south of Arabia Felix, where there was a
temple of Jupiter. This island, or rather cluster
of isles, has disappeared, " sunk [says *Grandpré*]
in the abyss made by the fire beneath their foundations." — *Voyage to the Indian Ocean.*

6 The Isles of Panchaia.

7 " The cup of Jamshid, discovered, they say,
when digging for the foundations of Persepolis."
— *Richardson.*

8 " It is not like the Sea of India, whose bottom is rich with pearls and ambergris, whose
mountains of the coast are stored with gold and
precious stones, whose gulfs breed creatures that
yield ivory, and among the plants of whose shores
are ebony, red wood, and the wood of Hairzan,
aloes, camphor, cloves, sandal-wood, and all
other spices and aromatics ; where parrots and
peacocks are birds of the forests, and musk and
civit are collected upon the lands." — *Travels of
Two Mohammedans.*

Whose mountains pregnant by the beam
Of the warm sun with diamonds teem,
Whose rivulets are like rich brides,
Lovely, with gold beneath their tides,
Whose sandal groves and bowers of spice
Might be a Peri's Paradise!
But crimson now her rivers ran
  With human blood — the smell of death
Came reeking from those spicy bowers,
And man the sacrifice of man
  Mingled his taint with every breath
Upwafted from the innocent flowers.
Land of the Sun! what foot invades
Thy Pagods and thy pillared shades [1] —
Thy cavern shrines and Idol stones,
Thy Monarchs and their thousand Thrones? [2]

'T is He of GAZNA [3] — fierce in wrath
  He comes and INDIA'S diadems
Lie scattered in his ruinous path. —
  His bloodhounds he adorns with gems,
Torn from the violated necks
  Of many a young and loved Sultana; [4]
Maidens within their pure Zenana,
  Priests in the very fane he slaughters,
And chokes up with the glittering wrecks
  Of golden shrines the sacred waters!

1 . . . . in the ground
The bended twigs take root and daughters grow
About the mother-tree, *a pillared shade*,
High over-arched and echoing walks between.
                                    MILTON.

For a particular description and plate of the Banyan-tree, see *Cordiner's* Ceylon.

2 "With this immense treasure Mamood returned to Ghizni, and in the year 400 prepared a magnificent festival, where he displayed to the people his wealth in golden thrones and in other ornaments, in a great plain without the city of Ghizni." — *Ferishta.*

3 "Mahmood of Gazna, or Chizni, who conquered India in the beginning of the 11th century." — See his History in *Dow* and Sir *J. Malcolm.*

4 "It is reported that the hunting equipage of the Sultan Mahmood was so magnificent, that he kept 400 greyhounds and bloodhounds each of which wore a collar set with jewels and a covering edged with gold and pearls." — *Universal History*, vol. iii.

Downward the PERI turns her gaze,
And thro' the war-field's bloody haze
Beholds a youthful warrior stand
  Alone beside his native river, —
The red blade broken in his hand
  And the last arrow in his quiver.
"Live," said the Conqueror, "live to share
"The trophies and the crowns I bear!"
Silent that youthful warrior stood —
Silent he pointed to the flood
All crimson with his country's blood,
Then sent his last remaining dart,
For answer, to the Invader's heart.

False flew the shaft tho' pointed well;
The Tyrant lived, the Hero fell! —
Yet marked the PERI where he lay,
  And when the rush of war was past
Swiftly descending on a ray
  Of morning light she caught the last —
Last glorious drop his heart had shed
Before its free-born spirit fled!

" Be this," she cried, as she winged her flight,
" My welcome gift at the Gates of Light.
" Tho' foul are the drops that oft distil
  " On the field of warfare, blood like this
  " For Liberty shed so holy is, [5]
" It would not stain the purest rill
  " That sparkles among the Bowers of Bliss!
" Oh, if there be on this earthly sphere
" A boon, an offering Heaven holds dear,
" 'T is the last libation Liberty draws
" From the heart that bleeds and breaks in her cause!"

5 Objections may be made to my use of the word Liberty in this, and more especially in the story that follows it, as totally inapplicable to any state of things that has ever existed in the East; but though I cannot, of course, mean to employ it in that enlarged and noble sense which is so well understood at the present day, and, I grieve to say, so little acted upon, yet it is no disparagement to the word to apply it to that national independence, that freedom from the interference and dictation of foreigners, without which, indeed, no liberty of any kind can exist; and for which both Hindoos and Persians fought against their Mussulman invaders with, in many cases, a bravery that deserved much better success.

"Sweet," said the Angel, as she gave
  The gift into his radiant hand,
"Sweet is our welcome of the Brave
  "Who die thus for their native
    Land. —
"But see — alas ! — the crystal bar
"Of Eden moves not — holier far
"Than even this drop the boon must be
"That opes the Gates of Heaven for
    thee ! "

Her first fond hope of Eden blighted,
  Now among AFRIC'S lunar Mountains [1]
Far to the South the PERI lighted
  And sleeked her plumage at the foun-
    tains
Of that Egyptian tide whose birth
Is hidden from the sons of earth
Deep in those solitary woods
Where oft the Genii of the Floods
Dance round the cradle of their Nile
And hail the new-born Giant's smile.[2]
Thence over EGYPT'S palmy groves,
  Her grots, and sepulchres of Kings,[3]
The exiled Spirit sighing roves
And now hangs listening to the doves
In warm ROSETTA'S vale; [4] now loves
  To watch the moonlight on the
    wings
Of the white pelicans that break
The azure calm of MŒRIS' Lake.[5]
'T was a fair scene: a Land more
    bright
  Never did mortal eye behold !
Who could have thought that saw this
    night
  Those valleys and their fruits of gold

---

1 "The Mountains of the Moon, or the
Montes Lunæ of antiquity, at the foot of which
the Nile is supposed to arise." — *Bruce.*
  "Sometimes called," says *Jackson*, "Jibbel
Kumrie, or the white or lunar colored mountains; so a white horse is called by the Arabians
a moon-colored horse."

2 "The Nile, which the Abyssinians know by
the names of Abey and Alawy, or the Giant." —
Asiat. Research. vol. i. p. 387.

3 See Perry's View of the Levant for an account of the sepulchres in Upper Thebes, and
the numberless grots, covered all over with
hieroglyphics in the mountains of Upper Egypt.

4 "The orchards of Rosetta are filled with
turtle-doves." — *Sonnini.*

5 Savary mentions the pelicans upon Lake
Mœris.

Basking in Heaven's serenest light,
Those groups of lovely date-trees bend-
    ing
  Languidly their leaf-crowned heads,
Like youthful maids, when sleep de-
    scending
  Warns them to their silken beds,[6]
Those virgin lilies all the night
  Bathing their beauties in the lake
That they may rise more fresh and
    bright,
  When their beloved Sun 's awake,
Those ruined shrines and towers that
    seem
The relics of a splendid dream,
  Amid whose fairy loneliness
Naught but the lapwing's cry is heard,
Naught seen but (when the shadows
    flitting.
Fast from the moon unsheath its gleam,)
Some purple-winged Sultana [7] sitting
  Upon a column motionless
And glittering like an Idol bird ! —
Who could have thought that there, even
    there,
  Amid those scenes so still and fair,
The Demon of the Plague hath cast
From his hot wing a deadlier blast,
More mortal far than ever came
From the red Desert's sands of flame !
So quick that every living thing
Of human shape touched by his wing,
Like plants where the Simoom hath
    past
At once falls black and withering !
The sun went down on many a brow
  Which, full of bloom and freshness
    then,
Is rankling in the pest-house now
  And ne'er will feel that sun again.
And, oh ! to see the unburied heaps
On which the lonely moonlight sleeps —
The very vultures turn away,
And sicken at so foul a prey !

---

6 "The superb date-tree, whose head languidly reclines, like that of a handsome woman
overcome with sleep." — *Dafard el Hadad.*

7 "That beautiful bird, with plumage of the
finest shining blue, with purple beak and legs,
the natural and living ornament of the temples
and palaces of the Greeks and Romans, which,
from the stateliness of its port, as well as the
brilliancy of its colors, has obtained the title of
Sultana." — *Sonnini.*

Only the fierce hyæna stalks [1]
Throughout the city's desolate walks [2]
At midnight and his carnage plies: —
  Woe to the half-dead wretch who
    meets
The glaring of those large blue eyes [3]
  Amid the darkness of the streets!

" Poor race of men! " said the pitying
    Spirit,
  " Dearly ye pay for your primal
    Fall
" Some flowerets of Eden ye still inherit,
  " But the trail of the Serpent is over
    them all ! "
She wept — the air grew pure and clear
Around her as the bright drops ran,
For there 's a magic in each tear
  Such kindly Spirits weep for man !

Just then beneath some orange trees
Whose fruit and blossoms in the breeze
Were wantoning together, free,
Like age at play with infancy —
Beneath that fresh and springing bower
  Close by the Lake she heard the
    moan
Of one who at this silent hour,
  Had thither stolen to die alone.
One who in life where'er he moved,
  Drew after him the hearts of many;
Yet now, as tho' he ne'er were loved,
  Dies here unseen, unwept by any!
None to watch near him — none to slake
  The fire that in his bosom lies,
With even a sprinkle from that lake
  Which shines so cool before his eyes.
No voice well known thro' many a day
  To speak the last, the parting word
Which when all other sounds decay
  Is still like distant music heard; —

1 Jackson, speaking of the plague that occurred in West Barbary, when he was there,
says, " The birds of the air fled away from the
abodes of men. The hyænas, on the contrary,
visited the cemeteries," etc.

2 " Gondar was full of hyænas from the time
it turned dark, till the dawn of day, seeking the
different pieces of slaughtered carcasses, which
this cruel and unclean people expose in the
streets without burial, and who firmly believe
that these animals are Falashta from the neighboring mountains, transformed by magic, and
come down to eat human flesh in the dark in
safety." — *Bruce*.

3 *Bruce*.

That tender farewell on the shore
Of this rude world when all is o'er,
Which cheers the spirit ere its bark
Puts off into the unknown Dark.

Deserted youth ! one thought alone
  Shed joy around his soul in death —
That she whom he for years had known,
And loved and might have called his
    own
  Was safe from this foul midnight's
    breath, —
Safe in her father's princely halls
Where the cool airs from fountain falls,
Freshly perfumed by many a brand
Of the sweet wood from India's land,
  Were pure as she whose brow they
    fanned.

But see — who yonder comes by stealth, [4]
  This melancholy bower to seek,
Like a young envoy sent by Health
  With rosy gifts upon her cheek?
'T is she — far off, thro' moonlight dim
  He knew his own betrothed bride,
She who would rather die with him
  Than live to gain the world beside ! —
Her arms are round her lover now,
  His livid cheek to hers she presses
And dips to bind his burning brow
  In the cool lake her loosened tresses.
Ah ! once, how little did he think
An hour would come when he should
    shrink
With horror from that dear embrace,
  Those gentle arms that were to him
Holy as is the cradling place
  Of Eden's infant cherubim !
And now he yields — now turns away,
Shuddering as if the venom lay
All in those proffered lips alone —
Those lips that then so fearless grown
Never until that instant came
Near his unasked or without shame.
" Oh ! let me only breathe the air,
  " The blessed air, that 's breathed by
    thee,
" And whether on its wings it bear
  " Healing or death 't is sweet to me !

4 This circumstance has been often introduced
into poetry ; — by Vincentius Fabricius, by Dar-
win, and lately, with very powerful effect, by
Mr. Wilson.

" There — drink my tears while yet they
    fall —
" Would that my bosom's blood were
    balm,
" And, well thou knowst, I 'd shed it all
    " To give thy brow one minute's calm.
" Nay, turn not from me that dear face —
    " Am I not thine — thy own loved
    bride —
" The one, the chosen one, whose place
    " In life or death is by thy side?
" Thinkst thou that she whose only light,
    " In this dim world from thee hath
    shone
" Could bear the long, the cheerless
    night
    " That must be hers when thou art
    gone?
" That I can live and let thee go,
" Who art my life itself? — No, no —
" When the stem dies the leaf that grew
" Out of its heart must perish too!
" Then turn to me, my own love, turn,
" Before, like thee, I fade and burn;
" Cling to these yet cool lips and share
" The last pure life that lingers there ! "
She fails — she sinks — as dies the lamp
In charnel airs or cavern-damp,
So quickly do his baleful sighs
Quench all the sweet light of her eyes.
One struggle — and his pain is past —
    Her lover is no longer living !
One kiss the maiden gives, one last,
    Long kiss, which she expires in giving !

" Sleep," said the PERI, as softly she
    stole
The farewell sigh of that vanishing soul,
As true as e'er warmed a woman's breast—
    " Sleep on, in visions of odor rest
    " In balmier airs than ever yet stirred
    " The enchanted pile of that lonely bird
    " Who sings at the last his own death-lay[1]
    " And in music and perfume dies away ! "
Thus saying, from her lips she spread
    Unearthly breathings thro' the place

And shook her sparkling wreath and shed
    Such lustre o'er each paly face
That like two lovely saints they seemed,
    Upon the eve of doomsday taken
From their dim graves in odor sleeping;
    While that benevolent PERI beamed
Like their good angel calmly keeping
    Watch o'er them till their souls would
    waken.

But morn is blushing in the sky;
    Again the PERI soars above,
Bearing to Heaven that precious sigh
    Of pure, self-sacrificing love.
High throbbed her heart with hope elate
    The Elysian palm she soon shall win,
For the bright Spirit at the gate
    Smiled as she gave that offering in ;
And she already hears the trees
    Of Eden with their crystal bells
Ringing in that ambrosial breeze
    That from the throne of ALLA swells;
And she can see the starry bowls
    That lie around that lucid lake
Upon whose banks admitted Souls
    Their first sweet draught of glory take ![2]

But, ah ! even PERIS' hopes are vain —
Again the Fates forbade, again
The immortal barrier closed—" Not yet,"
The Angel said as with regret
He shut from her that glimpse of glory —
    " True was the maiden, and her story
    " Written in light o'er ALLA's head
    " By seraph eyes shall long be read.
    " But, PERI, see — the crystal bar
    " Of Eden moves not — holier far
    " Than even this sigh the boon must be
    " That opes the Gates of Heaven for
    thee."

Now upon SYRIA's land of roses [3]
Softly the light of Eve reposes,
And like a glory the broad sun
Hangs over sainted LEBANON,

---

1 " In the East, they suppose the Phœnix to
have fifty orifices in his bill, which are continued
to his tail ; and that, after living one thousand
years, he builds himself a funeral pile, sings a
melodious air of different harmonies through his
fifty organ pipes, flaps his wings with a velocity
which sets fire to the wood and consumes himself."— *Richardson.*

2 " On the shores of a quadrangular lake stand
a thousand goblets, made of stars, out of which
souls predestined to enjoy felicity drink the crystal wave."— From *Chateaubriand's* Description
of the Mahometan Paradise, in his "*Beauties of
Christianity.*"

3 Richardson thinks that Syria had its name
from Suri, a beautiful and delicate species of rose,
for which that country has always been famous ;
— hence, Suristan, the Land of Roses.

Whose head in wintry grandeur towers
  And whitens with eternal sleet,
While summer in a vale of flowers
  Is sleeping rosy at his feet.

To one who looked from upper air
O'er all the enchanted regions there,
How beauteous must have been the glow,
The life, the sparkling from below!
Fair gardens, shining streams, with ranks
Of golden melons on their banks,
More golden where the sun-light falls;—
Gay lizards, glittering on the walls [1]
Of ruined shrines, busy and bright
As they were all alive with light;
And yet more splendid numerous flocks
Of pigeons settling on the rocks
With their rich restless wings that gleam
Variously in the crimson beam
Of the warm West, —as if inlaid
With brilliants from the mine or made
Of tearless rainbows such as span
The unclouded skies of PERISTAN.
And then the mingling sounds that come,
Of shepherd's ancient reed,[2] with hum
Of the wild bees of PALESTINE,[3]
  Banqueting thro' the flowery vales;
And, JORDAN, those sweet banks of thine
  And woods so full of nightingales.[4]
But naught can charm the luckless PERI;
Her soul is sad—her wings are weary—
Joyless she sees the Sun look down
On that great Temple once his own,[5]
Whose lonely columns stand sublime,
  Flinging their shadows from on high
Like dials which the wizard Time
  Had raised to count his ages by!

Yet haply there may lie concealed
  Beneath those Chambers of the Sun

Some amulet of gems, annealed
In upper fires, some tablet sealed
  With the great name of SOLOMON,
  Which spelled by her illumined eyes,
May teach her where beneath the moon,
In earth or ocean, lies the boon,
The charm, that can restore so soon
  An erring Spirit to the skies.

Cheered by this hope she bends her thither;—
  Still laughs the radiant eye of Heaven,
  Nor have the golden bowers of Even
In the rich West begun to wither;—
When o'er the vale of BALBEC winging
  Slowly she sees a child at play,
Among the rosy wild flowers singing,
  As rosy and as wild as they;
Chasing with eager hands and eyes
The beautiful blue damsel-flies,[6]
That fluttered round the jasmine stems
Like winged flowers or flying gems: —
And near the boy, who tired with play
Now nestling mid the roses lay,
She saw a wearied man dismount
  From his hot steed and on the brink
Of a small imaret's rustic fount [7]
  Impatient fling him down to drink.
Then swift his haggard brow he turned
To the fair child who fearless sat,
Tho' never yet hath day-beam burned
  Upon a brow more fierce than that, —
Sullenly fierce — a mixture dire
Like thunder-clouds of gloom and fire;
In which the PERI's eye could read
Dark tales of many a ruthless deed;
The ruined maid — the shrine profaned —
Oaths broken — and the threshold stained
With blood of guests! — *there* written, all,
Black as the damning drops that fall
From the denouncing Angel's pen,
Ere Mercy weeps them out again.

---

1 "The number of lizards I saw one day in the great court of the Temple of the Sun at Balbec amounted to many thousands; the ground, the walls, and stones of the ruined buildings, were covered with them."—*Bruce.*

2 "The Syrinx or Pan's pipe is still a pastoral instrument in Syria."—*Russel.*

3 "Wild bees, frequent in Palestine, in hollow trunks or branches of trees, and the clefts of rocks. Thus it is said (Psalm lxxxi.), '*honey out of the stony rock.*'"—*Burder's* Oriental Customs.

4 "The river Jordan is on both sides beset with little, thick, and pleasant woods, among which thousands of nightingales warble all together."—*Thevenot.*

5 The Temple of the Sun at Balbec.

6 "You behold there a considerable number of a remarkable species of beautiful insects, the elegance of whose appearance and their attire procured for them the name of Damsels."—*Sonnini.*

7 Imaret, "*hospice où on loge et nourrit, gratis, les pèlerins pendant trois jours.*"—*Toderini, translated by the Abbé de Cournand.*—See also *Castellan's "Mœurs des Othomans," tom.* v. p. 145.

Yet tranquil now that man of crime
(As if the balmy evening time
Softened his spirit) looked and lay,
Watching the rosy infant's play: —
Tho' still whene'er his eye by chance
Fell on the boy's, its lurid glance
 Met that unclouded, joyous gaze,
As torches that have burnt all night
Thro' some impure and godless rite,
 Encounter morning's glorious rays.

But, hark! the vesper call to prayer,
 As slow the orb of daylight sets,
Is rising sweetly on the air,
 From SYRIA'S thousand minarets!
The boy has started from the bed
Of flowers where he had laid his head,
And down upon the fragrant sod
 Kneels [1] with his forehead to the south
Lisping the eternal name of God
From Purity's own cherub mouth,
And looking while his hands and eyes
Are lifted to the glowing skies
Like a stray babe of Paradise
Just lighted on that flowery plain
And seeking for its home again.
Oh! 't was a sight — that Heaven —
 that child —
A scene, which might have well beguiled
Even haughty EBLIS of a sigh
For glories lost and peace gone by!

And how felt *he*, the wretched Man
Reclining there — while memory ran
O'er many a year of guilt and strife,
Flew o'er the dark flood of his life

1 "Such Turks as at the common hours of prayer are on the road, or so employed as not to find convenience to attend the mosques, are still obliged to execute that duty; nor are they ever known to fail, whatever business they are then about, but pray immediately when the hour alarms them, whatever they are about, in that very place they chance to stand on; insomuch that when a janissary, whom you have to guard you up and down the city, hears the notice which is given him from the steeples, he will turn about, stand still, and beckon with his hand, to tell his charge he must have patience for awhile; when, taking out his handkerchief, he spreads it on the ground, sits cross-legged thereupon, and says his prayers, though in the open market, which, having ended, he leaps briskly up, salutes the person whom he undertook to convey, and renews his journey with the mild expression of *Ghell gohnnum ghell,* or Come, dear, follow me." — *Aaron Hill's* Travels.

Nor found one sunny resting-place,
Nor brought him back one branch of
 grace.
"There *was* a time," he said, in mild,
Heart-humbled tones — "thou blessed
 child!
"When young and haply pure as thou
"I looked and prayed like thee — but
 now" —
He hung his head — each nobler aim
And hope and feeling which had slept
From boyhood's hour that instant came
Fresh o'er him and he wept — he wept!

Blest tears of soul-felt penitence!
 In whose benign, redeeming flow
Is felt the first, the only sense
 Of guiltless joy that guilt can know.
"There 's a drop," said the PERI, "that
 down from the moon
"Falls thro' the withering airs of June
"Upon EGYPT'S land,[2] of so healing a
 power,
"So balmy a virtue, that even in the hour
"That drop descends contagion dies
"And health reanimates earth and
 skies! —
"Oh, is it not thus, thou man of sin,
 "The precious tears of repentance
 fall?
"Tho' foul thy fiery plagues within
 "One heavenly drop hath dispelled
 them all!"

And now — behold him kneeling there
By the child's side, in humble prayer,
While the same sunbeam shines upon
The guilty and the guiltless one,
And hymns of joy proclaim thro' Heaven
The triumph of a Soul Forgiven!

'T was when the golden orb had set,
While on their knees they lingered yet,
There fell a light more lovely far
Than ever came from sun or star,
Upon the tear that, warm and meek,
Dewed that repentant sinner's cheek.
To mortal eye this light might seem
A northern flash or meteor beam —

2 The Nucta, or Miraculous Drop, which falls in Egypt precisely on St. John's day in June and is supposed to have the effect of stopping the plague.

But well the enraptured PERI knew
'T was a bright smile the Angel threw
From Heaven's gate to hail that tear
Her harbinger of glory near!

" Joy, joy for ever ! my task is done —
" The Gates are past and Heaven is won !
" Oh ! am I not happy? I am, I am —
" To thee, sweet Eden ! how dark and
sad
" Are the diamond turrets of SHADU-
KIAM,[1]
" And the fragrant bowers of AMBER-
ABAD !

" Farewell ye odors of Earth that die
" Passing away like a lover's sigh; —

" My feast is now of the Tooba Tree[2]
" Whose scent is the breath of Eternity !

" Farewell, ye vanishing flowers that
shone
" In my fairy wreath so bright an⁊
brief; —
" Oh ! what are the brightest that e'er
have blown
" To the lote-tree springing by ALLA'S
throne[3]
" Whose flowers have a soul in every
leaf.
" Joy, joy for ever. — my task is
done —
" The Gates are past and Heaven is
won ! "

" AND this," said the Great Chamberlain, " is poetry ! this flimsy manufacture of the brain, which in comparison with the lofty and durable monuments of genius is as the gold filigree-work of Zamara beside the eternal architecture of Egypt ! " After this gorgeous sentence, which, with a few more of the same kind, FADLA-DEEN kept by him for rare and important occasions, he proceeded to the anatomy of the short poem just recited. The lax and easy kind of metre in which it was written ought to be denounced, he said, as one of the leading causes of the alarming growth of poetry in our times. If some check were not given to this lawless facility we should soon be overrun by a race of bards as numerous and as shallow as the hundred and twenty thousand Streams of Basra.[4] They who succeeded in this style deserved chastisement for their very success; — as warriors have been punished even after gaining a victory because they had taken the liberty of gaining it in an irregular or unestablished manner. What then was to be said to those who failed? to those who presumed as in the present lamentable instance to imitate the license and ease of the bolder sons of song without any of that grace or vigor which gave a dignity even to negligence; who like them flung the jereed[5] carelessly, but not, like them, to the mark; — " and who," said he, raising his voice to excite a proper degree of wakefulness in his hearers, " contrive to appear heavy and constrained in the midst of all the latitude they allow themselves, like one of those young pagans that dance before the Princess, who is ingenious enough to move as if her limbs were fettered, in a pair of the lightest and loosest drawers of Masulipatam ! "

1 The Country of Delight — the name of a province in the kingdom of Jinnistan, or Fairy Land, the capital of which is called the City of Jewels. Amberabad is another of the cities of Jinnistan.

2 The tree Tooba, that stands in Paradise, in the palace of Mahomet. See *Sale's Prelim. Disc.* — Tooba, says *D'Herbelot*, signifies beatitude, or eternal happiness.

3 Mahomet is described, in the 53d chapter of the Koran, as having seen the angel Gabriel "by the lote-tree, beyond which there is no passing: near it is the Garden of Eternal Abode." This tree, say the commentators, stands in the seventh Heaven, on the right hand of the Throne of God.

4 " It is said that the rivers or streams of Basra were reckoned in the time of Pelal ben Abi Bordeh, and amounted to the number of one hundred and twenty thousand streams." — *Ebn Haukal.*

5 The name of the javelin with which the Easterns exercise. See *Castellan*, "*Mœurs des Othomans*," *tom.* iii. p. 161.

It was but little suitable, he continued, to the grave march of criticism to follow this fantastical Peri of whom they had just heard, through all her flights and adventures between earth and heaven, but he could not help adverting to the puerile conceitedness of the Three Gifts which she is supposed to carry to the skies, — a drop of blood, forsooth, a sigh, and a tear ! How the first of these articles was delivered into the Angel's " radiant hand " he professed himself at a loss to discover; and as to the safe carriage of the sigh and the tear, such Peris and such poets were beings by far too incomprehensible for him even to guess how they managed such matters. "But, in short," said he, "it is a waste of time and patience to dwell longer upon a thing so incurably frivolous, — puny even among its own puny race, and such as only the Banyan Hospital [1] for Sick Insects should undertake."

In vain did LALLA ROOKH try to soften this inexorable critic; in vain did she resort to her most eloquent commonplaces, reminding him that poets were a timid and sensitive race whose sweetness was not to be drawn forth like that of the fragrant grass near the Ganges by crushing and trampling upon them,[2] that severity often extinguished every chance of the perfection which it demanded, and that after all perfection was like the Mountain of the Talisman, — no one had ever yet reached its summit.[3] Neither these gentle axioms nor the still gentler looks with which they were inculcated could lower for one instant the elevation of FADLADEEN'S eyebrows or charm him into any thing like encouragement or even toleration of her poet. Toleration, indeed, was not among the weaknesses of FADLADEEN: — he carried the same spirit into matters of poetry and of religion, and though little versed in the beauties or sublimities of either was a perfect master of the art of persecution in both. His zeal was the same too in either pursuit, whether the game before him was pagans or poetasters, worshippers of cows, or writers of epics.

They had now arrived at the splendid city of Lahore whose mausoleums and shrines, magnificent and numberless where Death appeared to share equal honors with Heaven would have powerfully affected the heart and imagination of LALLA ROOKH, if feelings more of this earth had not taken entire possession of her already. She was here met by messengers despatched from Cashmere who informed her that the King had arrived in the Valley and was himself superintending the sumptuous preparations that were then making in the Saloons of the Shalimar for her reception. The chill she felt on receiving this intelligence, — which to a bride whose heart was free and light would have brought only images of affection and pleasure, — convinced her that her peace was gone for ever and that she was in love, irretrievably in love, with young FERAMORZ. The veil had fallen off in which this passion at first disguises itself, and to know that she loved was now as painful as to love *without* knowing it had been delicious. FERAMORZ, too, — what

---

1 "This account excited a desire of visiting the Banyan Hospital, as I had heard much of their benevolence to all kinds of animals that were either sick, lame, or infirm, through age or accident. On my arrival, there were presented to my view many horses, cows, and oxen, in one apartment; in another, dogs, sheep, goats, and monkeys, with clean straw for them to repose on. Above stairs were depositories for seeds of many sorts, and flat, broad dishes for water, for the use of birds and insects." — *Parsons's* Travels.
It is said that all animals know the Banyans, that the most timid approach them, and that birds will fly nearer to them than to other people. — See *Grandpré.*

2 "A very fragrant grass from the banks of the Ganges, near Heridwar, which in some places covers whole acres, and diffuses, when crushed, a strong odor." — *Sir W. Jones* on the Spikenard of the Ancients.

3 " Near this is a curious hill, called Koh Talism, the Mountain of the Talisman, because, according to the traditions of the country, no person ever succeeded in gaining its summit." — *Kinneir.*

misery would be his, if the sweet hours of intercourse so imprudently allowed them should have stolen into his heart the same fatal fascination as into hers; — if, notwithstanding her rank and the modest homage he always paid to it, even *he* should have yielded to the influence of those long and happy interviews where music, poetry, the delightful scenes of nature, — all had tended to bring their hearts close together and to waken by every means that too ready passion which often like the young of the desert-bird is warmed into life by the eyes alone![1] She saw but one way to preserve herself from being culpable as well as unhappy, and this however painful she was resolved to adopt. FERAMORZ must no more be admitted to her presence. To have strayed so far into the dangerous labyrinth was wrong, but to linger in it while the clew was yet in her hand would be criminal. Though the heart she had to offer to the King of Bucharia might be cold and broken, it should at least be pure, and she must only endeavor to forget the short dream of happiness she had enjoyed, — like that Arabian shepherd who in wandering into the wilderness caught a glimpse of the Gardens of Irim and then lost them again for ever![2]

The arrival of the young Bride at Lahore was celebrated in the most enthusiastic manner. The Rajas and Omras in her train, who had kept at a certain distance during the journey and never encamped nearer to the Princess than was strictly necessary for her safeguard here rode in splendid cavalcade through the city and distributed the most costly presents to the crowd. Engines were erected in all the squares which cast forth showers of confectionery among the people, while the artisans in chariots[3] adorned with tinsel and flying streamers exhibited the badges of their respective trades through the streets. Such brilliant displays of life and pageantry among the palaces and domes and gilded minarets of Lahore made the city altogether like a place of enchantment; — particularly on the day when LALLA ROOKH set out again upon her journey, when she was accompanied to the gate by all the fairest and richest of the nobility and rode along between ranks of beautiful boys and girls who kept waving over their heads plates of gold and silver flowers,[4] and then threw them around to be gathered by the populace.

For many days after their departure from Lahore a considerable degree of gloom hung over the whole party. LALLA ROOKH who had intended to make illness her excuse for not admitting the young minstrel, as usual, to the pavilion, soon found that to feign indisposition was unnecessary; — FADLADEEN felt the loss of the good road they had hitherto travelled and was very near cursing Jehan-Guire (of blessed memory!) for not having continued his delectable alley of trees[5] at least as far as the mountains of Cashmere; — while the Ladies who had nothing now to do all day but to be fanned by peacocks' feathers and listen to FADLADEEN seemed heartily weary of the life they led and in spite of all the Great Chamberlain's criticisms were so tasteless as to wish for the poet again. One evening as they were proceeding to their place of rest for the night the Princess who for the freer enjoyment of the air had mounted her favorite Arabian palfrey, in passing by

---

1 "The Arabians believe that the ostriches hatch their young by only looking at them." — *P. Vanslebe, "Relat. d'Egypte."*

2 See *Sale's Koran*, note, vol. ii. p. 484.

3 Oriental Tales.

4 Ferishta. "Or rather," says *Scott*, upon the passage of Ferishta, from which this is taken, "small coins, stamped with the figure of a flower. They are still used in India to distribute in charity and on occasion thrown by the purse-bearers of the great among the populace."

5 The fine road made by the Emperor Jehan-Guire from Agra to Lahore, planted with trees on each side. This road is 250 leagues in length. It has "little pyramids or turrets," says *Bernier*, "erected every half league, to mark the ways, and frequent wells to afford drink to passengers, and to water the young trees."

a small grove heard the notes of a lute from within its leaves and a voice which she but too well knew singing the following words: —

> Tell me not of joys above,
> If that world can give no bliss,
> Truer, happier than the Love
> Which enslaves our souls in this.
>
> Tell me not of Houris' eyes; —
> Far from me their dangerous glow,
> If those looks that light the skies
> Wound like some that burn below.
>
> Who that feels what Love is here,
> All its falsehood — all its pain —
> Would, for even Elysium's sphere,
> Risk the fatal dream again?
>
> Who that midst a desert's heat
> Sees the waters fade away
> Would not rather die than meet
> Streams again as false as they?

The tone of melancholy defiance in which these words were uttered went to LALLA ROOKH'S heart; — and as she reluctantly rode on she could not help feeling it to be a sad but still sweet certainty that FERAMORZ was to the full as enamoured and miserable as herself.

The place where they encamped that evening was the first delightful spot they had come to since they left Lahore. On one side of them was a grove full of small Hindoo temples and planted with the most graceful trees of the East, where the tamarind, the cassia, and the silken plantains of Ceylon were mingled in rich contrast with the high fan-like foliage of the Palmyra, — that favorite tree of the luxurious bird that lights up the chambers of its nest with fire-flies.[1] In the middle of the lawn where the pavilion stood there was a tank surrounded by small mango-trees on the clear cold waters of which floated multitudes of the beautiful red lotus,[2] while at a distance stood the ruins of a strange and awful-looking tower which seemed old enough to have been the temple of some religion no longer known and which spoke the voice of desolation in the midst of all that bloom and loveliness. This singular ruin excited the wonder and conjectures of all. LALLA ROOKH guessed in vain, and the all-pretending FADLADEEN who had never till this journey been beyond the precincts of Delhi was proceeding most learnedly to show that he knew nothing whatever about the matter, when one of the Ladies suggested that perhaps FERAMORZ could satisfy their curiosity. They were now approaching his native mountains and this tower might perhaps be a relic of some of those dark superstitions which had prevailed in that country before the light of Islam dawned upon it. The Chamberlain who usually preferred his own ignorance to the best knowledge that any one else could give him was by no means pleased with this officious reference, and the Princess too was about to interpose a faint word of objection, but before either of them could speak a slave was despatched for FERAMORZ, who in a very few minutes made his appearance before them — looking so pale and unhappy in LALLA ROOKH'S eyes that she repented already of her cruelty in having so long excluded him.

1 The Baya, or Indian Grosbeak. — *Sir W. Jones.*

2 "Here is a large pagoda by a tank, on the water of which float multitudes of the beautiful red lotus: the flower is larger than that of the white water-lily, and is the most lovely of the nymphæas I have seen." — *Mrs. Graham's* Journal of a Residence in India.

That venerable tower he told them was the remains of an ancient Fire-Temple, built by those Ghebers or Persians of the old religion, who many hundred years since had fled hither from their Arab conquerors,[1] preferring liberty and their altars in a foreign land to the alternative of apostasy or persecution in their own. It was impossible, he added, not to feel interested in the many glorious but unsuccessful struggles which had been made by these original natives of Persia to cast off the yoke of their bigoted conquerors. Like their own Fire in the Burning Field at Bakou[2] when suppressed in one place they had but broken out with fresh flame in another; and as a native of Cashmere, of that fair and Holy Valley which had in the same manner become the prey of strangers[3] and seen her ancient shrines and native princes swept away before the march of her intolerant invaders he felt a sympathy, he owned, with the sufferings of the persecuted Ghebers which every monument like this before them but tended more powerfully to awaken.

It was the first time that FERAMORZ had ever ventured upon so much *prose* before FADLADEEN and it may easily be conceived what effect such prose as this must have produced upon that most orthodox and most pagan-hating personage. He sat for some minutes aghast, ejaculating only at intervals, " Bigoted conquerors ! — sympathy with Fire-worshippers ! "[4] — while FERAMORZ happy to take advantage of this almost speechless horror of the Chamberlain proceeded to say that he knew a melancholy story connected with the events of one of those struggles of the brave Fire-worshippers against their Arab masters, which if the evening was not too far advanced he should have much pleasure in being allowed to relate to the Princess. It was impossible for LALLA ROOKH to refuse; — he had never before looked half so animated, and when he spoke of the Holy Valley his eyes had sparkled she thought like the talismanic characters on the scimitar of Solomon. Her consent was therefore most readily granted; and while FADLADEEN sat in unspeakable dismay, expecting treason and abomination in every line, the poet thus began his story of the Fire-worshippers: —

THE FIRE-WORSHIPPERS.

'T is moonlight over OMAN's SEA;[5]
  Her banks of pearl and palmy isles
Bask in the night-beam beauteously
  And her blue waters sleep in smiles.
'T is moonlight in HARMOZIA's[6] walls,
And thro' her EMIR's porphyry halls
Where some hours since was heard the swell
Of trumpet and the clash of zel[7]
Bidding the bright-eyed sun farewell; —
The peaceful sun whom better suits
  The music of the bulbul's nest
Or the light touch of lovers' lutes
  To sing him to his golden rest.
All husht — there 's not a breeze in motion;

---

1 " *On les voit persécutés par les Khalifes se retirer dans les montagnes du Kerman : plusieurs choisirent pour retraite la Tartarie et la Chine ; d'autres s'arrêtèrent sur les bords du Gange, à l'est de Delhi.*" — *M. Anquetil,* "*Mémoires de l'Académie, tom.* xxxi. p. 346.

2 The "*ager ardens*" described by *Kempfer,* "*Amœnitat. Exot.*"

3 " Cashmere (says its historians) had its own princes 4000 years before its conquest by Akbar in 1585. Akbar would have found some difficulty to reduce this paradise of the Indies, situated as it is within such a fortress of mountains, but its monarch, Yusef-Khan, was basely betrayed by his Omrahs." — *Pennant.*

4 Voltaire tells us that in his Tragedy, " *Les Guèbres,*" he was generally supposed to have alluded to the Jansenists. I should not be surprised if this story of the Fire-worshippers were found capable of a similar doubleness of application.

5 The Persian Gulf, sometimes so called, which separates the shores of Persia and Arabia.

6 The present Gombaroon, a town on the Persian side of the Gulf.

7 A Moorish instrument of music.

The shore is silent as the ocean.
If zephyrs come, so light they come,
  Nor leaf is stirred nor wave is
    driven; —
The wind-tower on the EMIR'S dome [1]
  Can hardly win a breath from heaven.

Even he, that tyrant Arab, sleeps
Calm while a nation round him weeps,
While curses load the air he breathes
And falchions from unnumbered sheaths
Are starting to avenge the shame
His race hath brought on IRAN'S [2] name.
Hard, heartless Chief, unmoved alike
Mid eyes that weep and swords that
  strike; —
One of that saintly, murderous brood,
  To carnage and the Koran given,
Who think thro' unbelievers' blood
  Lies their directest path to heaven,—
One who will pause and kneel unshod
  In the warm blood his hand hath
    poured,
To mutter o'er some text of God
  Engraven on his reeking sword; [3] —
Nay, who can coolly note the line,
The letter of those words divine,
To which his blade with searching art
Had sunk into its victim's heart!

Just ALLA! what must be thy look
When such a wretch before thee stands
Unblushing, with thy Sacred Book, —
  Turning the leaves with blood-stained
    hands,
And wresting from its page sublime
His creed of lust and hate and crime;—
Even as those bees of TREBIZOND,
  Which from the sunniest flowers that
    glad
With their pure smile the gardens round,
  Draw venom forth that drives men
    mad. [4]

1 "At Gombaroon and other places in Persia,
they have towers for the purpose of catching the
wind and cooling the houses." — *Le Bruyn.*

2 "Iran is the true general name for the empire of Persia." — *Asiat. Res. Disc.* 5.

3 "On the blades of their scimitars some
verse from the Koran is usually inscribed." —
Russel.

4 "There is a kind of Rhododendros about
Trebizond, whose flowers the bee feeds upon,
and the honey thence drives people mad." —
Tournefort.

Never did fierce ARABIA send
  A satrap forth more direly great;
Never was IRAN doomed to bend
  Beneath a yoke of deadlier weight.
Her throne had fallen — her pride was
  crusht —
Her sons were willing slaves, nor
  blusht,
In their own land, — no more their
  own, —
To crouch beneath a stranger's throne.
Her towers where MITHRA once had
  burned,
To Moslem shrines — oh shame! — were
  turned,
Where slaves converted by the sword,
Their mean, apostate worship poured,
And curst the faith their sires adored.
Yet has she hearts, mid all this ill,
O'er all this wreck high buoyant still
With hope and vengeance; — hearts
  that yet —
  Like gems, in darkness, issuing rays
They 've treasured from the sun that 's
  set,—
  Beam all the light of long-lost days!
And swords she hath, nor weak nor
  slow
To second all such hearts can dare;
As he shall know, well, dearly know,
  Who sleeps in moonlight luxury there,
Tranquil as if his spirit lay
Becalmed in Heaven's approving ray.
Sleep on — for purer eyes than thine
Those waves are husht, those planets
  shine;
Sleep on and be thy rest unmoved
  By the white moonbeam's dazzling
    power; —
None but the loving and the loved
  Should be awake at this sweet hour.

And see — where high above those rocks
  That o'er the deep their shadows
    fling,
Yon turret stands; — where ebon locks,
  As glossy as a heron's wing
  Upon the turban of a king, [5]
Hang from the lattice, long and wild, —
'T is she, that EMIR'S blooming child,

5 "Their kings wear plumes of black herons'
feathers upon the right side, as a badge of sover-
eignty." — *Hanway.*

All truth and tenderness and grace,
Tho' born of such ungentle race; —
An image of Youth's radiant Fountain
Springing in a desolate mountain ! [1]

Oh what a pure and sacred thing
Is Beauty curtained from the sight
Of the gross world, illumining
One only mansion with her light !
Unseen by man's disturbing eye, —
The flower that blooms beneath the sea,
Too deep for sunbeams, doth not lie
Hid in more chaste obscurity.
So, HINDA, have thy face and mind,
Like holy mysteries, lain enshrined.
And oh ! what transport for a lover
To lift the veil that shades them
o'er ! —
Like those who all at once discover
In the lone deep some fairy shore
Where mortal never trod before,
And sleep and wake in scented airs
No lip had ever breathed but theirs.

Beautiful are the maids that glide
On summer-eves thro' YEMEN'S [2]
dales,
And bright the glancing looks they hide
Behind their litters' roseate veils; —
And brides as delicate and fair
As the white jasmine flowers they wear,
Hath YEMEN in her blissful clime,
Who lulled in cool kiosk or bower,[3]
Before their mirrors count the time [4]
And grow still lovelier every hour.

But never yet hath bride or maid
In ARABY'S gay Haram smiled,
Whose boasted brightness would not fade
Before AL HASSAN'S blooming child.

Light as the angel shapes that bless
An infant's dream, yet not the less
Rich in all woman's loveliness; —
With eyes so pure that from their ray
Dark Vice would turn abasht away,
Blinded like serpents when they gaze
Upon the emerald's virgin blaze;[5] —
Yet filled with all youth's sweet desires,
Mingling the meek and vestal fires
Of other worlds with all the bliss,
The fond, weak tenderness of this:
A soul too more than half divine,
Where, thro' some shades of earthly
feeling,
Religion's softened glories shine,
Like light thro' summer foliage stealing,
Shedding a glow of such mild hue,
So warm and yet so shadowy too,
As makes the very darkness there
More beautiful than light elsewhere.

Such is the maid who at this hour
Hath risen from her restless sleep
And sits alone in that high bower,
Watching the still and shining deep.
Ah ! 't was not thus, — with tearful eyes
And beating heart, — she used to gaze
On the magnificent earth and skies,
In her own land, in happier days.
Why looks she now so anxious down
Among those rocks whose rugged frown
Blackens the mirror of the deep?
Whom waits she all this lonely night?
Too rough the rocks, too bold the steep,
For man to scale that turret's height ! —

So deemed at least her thoughtful sire,
When high, to catch the cool night-air

1 "The Fountain of Youth, by a Mahometan tradition, is situated in some dark region of the East." — *Richardson.*

2 Arabia Felix.

3 "In the midst of the garden is the chiosk, that is, a large room, commonly beautified with a fine fountain in the midst of it. It is raised nine or ten steps, and enclosed with gilded lattices, round which vines, jessamines, and honeysuckles, make a sort of green wall ; large trees are planted round this place, which is the scene of their greatest pleasures." — *Lady M. W. Montagu.*

4 The women of the East are never without their looking-glasses. " In Barbary," says *Shaw,* " they are so fond of their looking-glasses, which they hang upon their breasts, that they will not lay them aside, even when after the drudgery of the day they are obliged to go two or three miles with a pitcher or a goat's skin to fetch water." — *Travels.*

In other parts of Asia they wear little looking-glasses on their thumbs. " Hence (and from the

lotus being considered the emblem of beauty) is the meaning of the following mute intercourse of two lovers before their parents : —

" 'He with salute of deference due
    A lotus to his forehead prest;
  She raised her mirror to his view,
    Then turned it inward to her breast.' "
                        Asiatic Miscellany, vol. ii.

5 " They say that if a snake or serpent fix his eyes on the lustre of those stones (emeralds), he immediately becomes blind." — *Ahmed ben Abdalaziz,* Treatise on Jewels.

After the day-beam's withering fire,[1]
　He built her bower of freshness there,
And had it deckt with costliest skill
　And fondly thought it safe as fair:—
Think, reverend dreamer! think so still,
　Nor wake to learn what Love can
　　dare;—
Love, all-defying Love, who sees
No charm in trophies won with ease;—
Whose rarest, dearest fruits of bliss
Are plucked on Danger's precipice!
Bolder than they who dare not dive
For pearls but when the sea's at rest,
Love, in the tempest most alive,
　Hath ever held that pearl the best
He finds beneath the stormiest water.
Yes — ARABY's unrivalled daughter,
Tho' high that tower, that rock-way rude,
　There's one who but to kiss thy cheek
Would climb the untrodden solitude
　Of ARARAT's tremendous peak,[2]
And think its steeps, tho' dark and dread,
Heaven's pathways, if to thee they led!
Even now thou seest the flashing spray,
That lights his oar's impatient way;—
Even now thou hearest the sudden shock
Of his swift bark against the rock,
And stretchest down thy arms of snow
As if to lift him from below!
Like her to whom at dead of night
The bridegroom with his locks of light[3]
Came in the flush of love and pride

And scaled the terrace of his bride;—
When as she saw him rashly spring,
And midway up in danger cling,
She flung him down her long black hair,
Exclaiming breathless, "There, love,
　there!"
And scarce did manlier nerve uphold
　The hero ZAL in that fond hour,
Than wings the youth who, fleet and bold,
　Now climbs the rocks to HINDA's
　　bower.
See — light as up their granite steeps
　The rock-goats of ARABIA clamber,[4]
Fearless from crag to crag he leaps,
　And now is in the maiden's chamber.
She loves — but knows not whom she
　loves,
　Nor what his race, nor whence he
　　came;—
Like one who meets in Indian groves
　Some beauteous bird without a name,
Brought by the last ambrosial breeze
From isles in the undiscovered seas,
To show his plumage for a day
To wondering eyes and wing away!
Will *he* thus fly — her nameless lover?
　ALLA forbid! 't was by a moon
As fair as this, while singing over
　Some ditty to her soft Kanoon,[5]
Alone, at this same witching hour,
　She first beheld his radiant eyes
Gleam thro' the lattice of the bower,
　Where nightly now they mix their
　　sighs;
And thought some spirit of the air
(For what could waft a mortal there?)
Was pausing on his moonlight way
To listen to her lonely lay!
This fancy ne'er hath left her mind:
　And — tho', when terror's swoon had
　　past,
She saw a youth of mortal kind
　Before her in obeisance cast, —
Yet often since, when he hath spoken
Strange, awful words, — and gleams have
　broken
From his dark eyes, too bright to bear,
Oh! she hath feared her soul was given

---

1 "At Gombaroon and the Isle of Ormus it is sometimes so hot, that the people are obliged to lie all day in the water." — *Marco Polo.*

2 This mountain is generally supposed to be inaccessible. *Struy* says, "I can well assure the reader that their opinion is not true, who suppose this mount to be inaccessible." He adds, that "the lower part of the mountain is cloudy, misty, and dark, the middlemost part very cold, and like clouds of snow, but the upper regions perfectly calm." — It was on this mountain that the Ark was supposed to have rested after the Deluge, and part of it, they say, exists there still, which Struy thus gravely accounts for: — "Whereas none can remember that the air on the top of the hill did ever change or was subject either to wind or rain, which is presumed to be the reason that the Ark has endured so long without being rotten." — See *Carreri's* Travels, where the Doctor laughs at this whole account of Mount Ararat.

3 In one of the books of the Shâh Nâmeh, when Zal (a celebrated hero of Persia, remarkable for his white hair,) comes to the terrace of his mistress Rodahver at night, she lets down her long tresses to assist him in his ascent; — he, however, manages it in a less romantic way by fixing his crook in a projecting beam. — See *Champion's Ferdosi.*

4 "On the lofty hills of Arabia Petræa are rock-goats." — *Niebuhr.*

5 "*Canun, espèce de psalterion, avec des cordes de boyaux; les dames en touchent dans le serrail, avec des décailles armées de pointes de cooc.*" — *Toderini, translated by De Cournand.*

To some unhallowed child of air,
  Some erring Spirit cast from heaven,
Like those angelic youths of old
Who burned for maids of mortal mould,
Bewildered left the glorious skies
And lost their heaven for woman's eyes.
Fond girl! nor fiend nor angel he
Who wooes thy young simplicity;
But one of earth's impassioned sons,
  As warm in love, as fierce in ire
As the best heart whose current runs
  Full of the Day-God's living fire.

But quenched to-night that ardor seems,
  And pale his cheek and sunk his
    brow; —
Never before but in her dreams
Had she beheld him pale as now:
And those were dreams of troubled sleep
From which 't was joy to wake and weep;
Visions that will not be forgot,
  But sadden every waking scene
Like warning ghosts that leave the spot
  All withered where they once have
    been.

  "How sweetly," said the trembling
    maid,
Of her own gentle voice afraid,
So long had they in silence stood
Looking upon that tranquil flood —
  "How sweetly does the moon-beam
    smile
  "To-night upon yon leafy isle!
  "Oft, in my fancy's wanderings,
  "I 've wisht that little isle had wings,
  "And we within its fairy bowers
    "Were wafted off to seas unknown,
  "Where not a pulse should beat but ours,
    "And we might live, love, die alone!
  "Far from the cruel and the cold, —
    "Where the bright eyes of angels only
  "Should come around us to behold
    "A paradise so pure and lonely.
  "Would this be world enough for
    thee?" —
Playful she turned that he might see
  The passing smile her cheek put on;
But when she markt how mournfully
  His eyes met hers, that smile was gone;
And bursting into heart-felt tears,
"Yes, yes," she cried, "my hourly fears,
"My dreams have boded all too right —

"We part — for ever part — to-night!
"I knew, I knew it *could* not last —
"'T was bright, 't was heavenly, but
  't is past!
"Oh! ever thus from childhood's hour
"I 've seen my fondest hopes decay;
"I never loved a tree or flower,
  "But 't was the first to fade away.
"I never nurst a dear gazelle
  "To glad me with its soft black eye
"But when it came to know me well
  "And love me it was sure to die!
"Now too — the joy most like divine
  "Of all I ever dreamt or knew,
"To see thee, hear thee, call thee mine,—
  "Oh misery! must I lose *that* too?
"Yet go — on peril's brink we meet; —
  "Those frightful rocks — that treacher-
    ous sea —
"No, never come again — tho' sweet,
  "Tho' heaven, it may be death to
    thee.
"Farewell — and blessings on thy way,
  "Where'er thou goest, beloved
    stranger!
"Better to sit and watch that ray
"And think thee safe, tho' far away,
  "Than have thee near me and in
    danger!"

"Danger! — oh, tempt me not to
  boast" —
The youth exclaimed — "thou little
  know'st
"What he can brave, who, born and
  nurst
"In Danger's paths, has dared her worst;
"Upon whose ear the signal-word
  "Of strife and death is hourly break-
    ing;
"Who sleeps with head upon the sword
  "His fevered hand must grasp in wak-
    ing.
"Danger!" —
    "Say on — thou fearest not then,
"And we may meet — oft meet again?"

"Oh! look not so — beneath the skies
"I now fear nothing but those eyes.
"If aught on earth could charm or force
"My spirit from its destined course, —
"If aught could make this soul forget
"The bond to which its seal is set,

" 'T would be those eyes; — they, only
they,
" Could melt that sacred seal away !
" But no — 'tis fixt — *my* awful doom
" Is fixt — on this side of the tomb
" We meet no more; — why, why did
Heaven
" Mingle two souls that earth has riven,
" Has rent asunder wide as ours?
" Oh, Arab maid, as soon the Powers
" Of Light and Darkness may combine,
" As I be linkt with thee or thine !
" Thy Father " —
　　　" Holy ALLA save
　" His gray head from that lightning
glance !
" Thou knowest him not — he loves the
brave;
　" Nor lives there under heaven's ex-
panse
" One who would prize, would worship
thee
" And thy bold spirit more than he.
" Oft when in childhood I have played
　" With the bright falchion by his
side,
" I 've heard him swear his lisping
maid
　" In time should be a warrior's bride.
" And still whene'er at Haram hours
" I take him cool sherbets and flowers,
" He tells me when in playful mood
　" A hero shall my bridegroom be,
" Since maids are best in battle wooed,
　" And won with shouts of victory !
" Nay, turn not from me — thou alone
" Art formed to make both hearts thy
own.
" Go — join his sacred ranks — thou
knowest
　" The unholy strife these Persians
wage : —
" Good Heaven, that frown ! — even
now thou glowest
　" With more than mortal warrior's
rage.
" Haste to the camp by morning's light,
" And when that sword is raised in fight,
" Oh still remember, Love and I
" Beneath its shadow trembling lie !
" One victory o'er those Slaves of Fire,
" Those impious Ghebers whom my sire
" Abhors " —

" Hold, hold — thy words are
death " —
The stranger cried as wild he flung
His mantle back and showed beneath
The Gheber belt that round him
clung.[1] —
" Here, maiden, look — weep — blush
to see
" All that thy sire abhors in me !
" Yes — *I* am of that impious race,
　" Those Slaves of Fire who, morn and
even,
" Hail their Creator's dwelling-place
　" Among the living lights of heaven : [2]
" Yes — *I* am of that outcast few,
" To IRAN and to vengeance true,
" Who curse the hour your Arabs came
" To desolate our shrines of flame,
" And swear before God's burning eye
" To break our country's chains or die !
" Thy bigot sire, — nay, tremble not, —
　" He who gave birth to those dear
eyes
" With me is sacred as the spot
　" From which our fires of worship rise !

1 " They (the Ghebers) lay so much stress on
their cushee or girdle, as not to dare to be an
instant without it." — *Grose's* Voyage. — " *Le
jeune homme nia d'abord la chose ; mais, ayant
été dépouillé de sa robe, et la large ceinture qu'il
portoit comme Ghébr,*" etc. — *D'Herbelot,* art.
" *Agduani.*" " *Pour se distinguer des Idolatres
de l'Inde, les Guèbres se ceignent tous d'un cordon de laine, ou de poil de chameau.*" — " *Encyclopédie Françoise.*"
　D'Herbelot says this belt was generally of
leather.

2 " They suppose the Throne of the Almighty
is seated in the sun, and hence their worship of
that luminary." — *Hanway.* " As to fire the
Ghebers place the spring-head of it in that globe
of fire, the Sun, by them called Mythras, or
Mihir, to which they pay the highest reverence,
in gratitude for the manifold benefits flowing from
its ministerial omniscience. But they are so far
from confounding the subordination of the Servant with the majesty of its Creator, that they
not only attribute no sort of sense or reasoning
to the sun or fire, in any of its operations, but
consider it as a purely passive blind instrument,
directed and governed by the immediate impression on it of the will of God ; but they do not
even give that luminary, all-glorious as it is,
more than the second rank amongst his works,
reserving the first for that stupendous production
of divine power, the mind of man." — *Grose.*
The false charges brought against the religion of
these people by their Mussulman tyrants is but
one proof among many of the truth of this writer's
remark, that " calumny is often added to oppression, if but for the sake of justifying it."

" But know — 't was he I sought that
    night,
  " When from my watch-boat on the
    sea
" I caught this turret's glimmering light,
  " And up the rude rocks desperately
" Rusht to my prey — thou knowest the
    rest —
" I climbed the gory vulture's nest,
  " And found a trembling dove within; —
" Thine, thine the victory — thine the
    sin —
" If Love hath made one thought his
    own,
" That Vengeance claims first — last —
    alone !
" Oh ! had we never, never met,
" Or could this heart even now forget
" How linkt, how blest we might have
    been,
" Had fate not frowned so dark between !
" Hadst thou been born a Persian maid,
  " In neighboring valleys had we dwelt,
" Thro' the same fields in childhood
    played,
  " At the same kindling altar knelt, —
" Then, then, while all those nameless
    ties
" In which the charm of Country lies
" Had round our hearts been hourly spun,
" Till IRAN's cause and thine were one;
" While in thy lute's awakening sigh
" I heard the voice of days gone by,
" And saw in every smile of thine
" Returning hours of glory shine; —
" While the wronged Spirit of our Land
  " Lived, lookt, and spoke her wrongs
    thro' thee, —
" God ! who could then this sword with-
    stand?
  " Its very flash were victory !
" But now — estranged, divorced for ever,
" Far as the grasp of Fate can sever ;
" Our only ties what love has wove, —
  " In faith, friends, country, sundered
    wide;
" And then, then only, true to love,
  " When false to all that 's dear beside !
" Thy father IRAN's deadliest foe —
" Thyself, perhaps, even now — but
    no —
" Hate never looked so lovely yet !
  " No — sacred to thy soul will be

" The land of him who could forget
  " All but that bleeding land for thee.
" When other eyes shall see, unmoved,
  " Her widows mourn, her warriors fall,
" Thou 'lt think how well one Gheber
    loved,
  "And for *his* sake thou 'lt weep for all !
" But look " —
          With sudden start he turned
And pointed to the distant wave
Where lights like charnel meteors burned
Bluely as o'er some seaman's grave;
And fiery darts at intervals [1]
Flew up all sparkling from the main
As if each star that nightly falls
Were shooting back to heaven again.

" My signal lights ! — I must away —
" Both, both are ruined, if I stay.
" Farewell — sweet life ! thou clingest in
    vain —
" Now, Vengeance, I am thine again ! "
Fiercely he broke away, nor stopt,
Nor lookt — but from the lattice dropt
Down mid the pointed crags beneath
As if he fled from love to death.
While pale and mute young HINDA stood,
Nor moved till in the silent flood
A momentary plunge below
Startled her from her trance of woe; —
Shrieking she to the lattice flew,
  " I come — I come — if in that tide
" Thou sleepest to-night, I 'll sleep there
    too
  " In death's cold wedlock by thy side.
"Oh ! I would ask no happier bed
  " Than the chill wave my love lies
    under : —
" Sweeter to rest together dead,
  " Far sweeter than to live asunder ! "
But no — their hour is not yet come —
  Again she sees his pinnace fly,
Wafting him fleetly to his home,
  Where'er that ill-starred home may lie;
And calm and smooth it seemed to win
Its moonlight way before the wind
As if it bore all peace within
Nor left one breaking heart behind !

---

1 " The Mameluks that were in the other
boat, when it was dark used to shoot up a sort of
fiery arrows into the air which in some measure
resembled lightning or falling stars." — *Baum-
garten.*

THE Princess whose heart was sad enough already could have wished that FERAMORZ had chosen a less melancholy story; as it is only to the happy that tears are a luxury. Her Ladies however were by no means sorry that love was once more the Poet's theme; for, whenever he spoke of love, they said, his voice was as sweet as if he had chewed the leaves of that enchanted tree, which grows over the tomb of the musician, Tan-Sein.[1]

Their road all the morning had lain through a very dreary country; — through valleys, covered with a low bushy jungle, where in more than one place the awful signal of the bamboo staff[2] with the white flag at its top reminded the traveller that in that very spot the tiger had made some human creature his victim. It was therefore with much pleasure that they arrived at sunset in a safe and lovely glen and encamped under one of those holy trees whose smooth columns and spreading roofs seem to destine them for natural temples of religion. Beneath this spacious shade some pious hands had erected a row of pillars ornamented with the most beautiful porcelain[3] which now supplied the use of mirrors to the young maidens as they adjusted their hair in descending from the palankeens. Here while as usual the Princess sat listening anxiously with FADLADEEN in one of his loftiest moods of criticism by her side the young Poet leaning against a branch of the tree thus continued his story: —

THE morn hath risen clear and calm
    And o'er the Green Sea[4] palely shines,
Revealing BAHREIN'S[5] groves of palm
    And lighting KISHMA'S[5] amber vines.
Fresh smell the shores of ARABY,
While breezes from the Indian sea
Blow round SELAMA'S[6] sainted cape
    And curl the shining flood beneath, —
Whose waves are rich with many a
        grape
And cocoa-nut and flowery wreath
Which pious seamen as they past
Had toward that holy headland cast —
Oblations to the Genii there
For gentle skies and breezes fair !
The nightingale now bends her flight[7]
From the high trees where all the night
    She sung so sweet with none to listen;
And hides her from the morning star
    Where thickets of pomegranate glisten
In the clear dawn, — bespangled o'er
    With dew whose night-drops would not
        stain
The best and brightest scimitar[8]

1 " Within the enclosure which surrounds this monument (at Gualior) is a small tomb to the memory of Tan-Sein, a musician of incomparable skill, who flourished at the court of Akbar. The tomb is overshadowed by a tree, concerning which a superstitious notion prevails, that the chewing of its leaves will give an extraordinary melody to the voice." — *Narrative of a Journey from Agra to Ouzein, by W. Hunter, Esq.*

2 " It is usual to place a small white triangular flag, fixed to a bamboo staff of ten or twelve feet long, at the place where a tiger has destroyed a man. It is common for the passengers also to throw each a stone or brick near the spot, so that in the course of a little time a pile equal to a good wagon-load is collected. The sight of these flags and piles of stones imparts a certain melancholy, not perhaps altogether void of apprehension." — *Oriental Field Sports,* vol. ii.

3 " The Ficus Indica is called the Pagod Tree and Tree of Councils; the first, from the idols placed under its shade ; the second, because meetings were held under its cool branches. In some places it is believed to be the haunt of spectres, as the ancient spreading oaks of Wales have been of fairies ; in others are erected beneath the shade pillars of stone, or posts, elegantly carved, and ornamented with the most beautiful porcelain to supply the use of mirrors." — *Pennant.*

4 The Persian Gulf. — " To dive for pearls in the Green Sea, or Persian Gulf."— *Sir. W Jones.*

5 Islands in the Gulf.

6 Or Selemeh, the genuine name of the headland at the entrance of the Gulf, commonly called Cape Musseldom. " The Indians when they pass the promontory throw cocoa-nuts, fruits, or flowers into the sea to secure a propitious voyage." — *Morier.*

7 " The nightingale sings from the pomegranate-groves in the day-time and from the loftiest trees at night." — *Russel's* "Aleppo."

8 In speaking of the climate of Shiraz, Francklin says, " The dew is of such a pure nature, that if the brightest scimitar should be exposed to it all night, it would not receive the least rust."

That ever youthful Sultan wore
  On the first morning of his reign.

And see — the Sun himself ! — on wings
Of glory up the East he springs.
Angel of Light ! who from the time
Those heavens began their march sublime,
Hath first of all the starry choir
Trod in his Maker's steps of fire !
  Where are the days, thou wondrous
    sphere,
When IRAN, like a sun-flower, turned
To meet that eye where'er it burned ? —
  When from the banks of BENDEMEER
To the nut-groves of SAMARCAND
Thy temples flamed o'er all the land ?
Where are they ? ask the shades of them
  Who, on CADESSIA'S [1] bloody plains,
Saw fierce invaders pluck the gem
From IRAN'S broken diadem,
  And bind her ancient faith in chains : —
Ask the poor exile cast alone
On foreign shores, unloved, unknown,
Beyond the Caspian's Iron Gates,[2]
Or on the snowy Mossian mountains,
Far from his beauteous land of dates,
  Her jasmine bowers and sunny foun-
    tains:
Yet happier so than if he trod
His own beloved but blighted sod
Beneath a despot stranger's nod ! —
Oh, he would rather houseless roam
  Where Freedom and his God may
    lead,
Than be the sleekest slave at home
  That crouches to the conqueror's creed !

Is IRAN'S pride then gone for ever,
  Quenched with the flame in MITHRA'S
    caves ? —
No — she has sons that never — never —
  Will stoop to be the Moslem's slaves
While heaven has light or earth has
    graves ; —
Spirits of fire that brood not long
But flash resentment back for wrong ;
And hearts where, slow but deep, the
    seeds

Of vengeance ripen into deeds,
Till in some treacherous hour of calm
They burst like ZEILAN'S giant palm [3]
Whose buds fly open with a sound
That shakes the pigmy forests round !
Yes, EMIR ! he, who scaled that tower,
  And had he reached thy slumbering
    breast
Had taught thee in a Gheber's power
  How safe even tyrant heads may rest —
Is one of many, brave as he,
Who loathe thy haughty race and thee ;
Who tho' they knew the strife is vain,
Who tho' they know the riven chain
Snaps but to enter in the heart
Of him who rends its links apart,
Yet dare the issue, — blest to be
Even for one bleeding moment free
And die in pangs of liberty !
Thou knowest them well — 't is some
    moons since
  Thy turbaned troops and blood-red
    flags,
Thou satrap of a bigot Prince,
  Have swarmed among these Green Sea
    crags ;
Yet here, even here, a sacred band
Ay, in the portal of that land
Thou, Arab, darest to call thy own,
Their spears across thy path have thrown ;
Here — ere the winds half winged thee
    o'er —
Rebellion braved thee from the shore.

Rebellion ! foul, dishonoring word,
  Whose wrongful blight so oft has
    stained
The holiest cause that tongue or sword
  Of mortal ever lost or gained.
How many a spirit born to bless
  Hath sunk beneath that withering
    name,
Whom but a day's, an hour's success
  Had wafted to eternal fame !
As exhalations when they burst
From the warm earth if chilled at first,

---

1 The place where the Persians were finally
defeated by the Arabs, and their ancient monarchy destroyed.

2 Derbend. — *" Les Turcs appellent cette
ville Demir Capi, Porte de Fer ; ce sont les
Caspiæ Portæ des anciens."* — *D'Herbelot.*

3 The Talpot or Talipot tree. *" This beautiful palm-tree, which grows in the heart of the
forests, may be classed among the loftiest trees,
and becomes still higher when on the point of
bursting forth from its leafy summit. The sheath
which then envelopes the flower is very large,
and, when it bursts, makes an explosion like the
report of a cannon."* — *Thunberg.*

If checkt in soaring from the plain
Darken to fogs and sink again; —
But if they once triumphant spread
Their wings above the mountain-head,
Become enthroned in upper air,
And turn to sun-bright glories there !

And who is he that wields the might
　Of Freedom on the Green Sea brink,
Before whose sabre's dazzling light [1]
　The eyes of YEMEN's warriors wink?
Who comes embowered in the spears
Of KERMAN's hardy mountaineers? —
Those mountaineers that truest, last,
　Cling to their country's ancient rites,
As if that God whose eyelids cast
　Their closing gleam on IRAN's heights,
Among her snowy mountains threw
The last light of his worship too !

'T is HAFED — name of fear, whose
　　sound
　Chills like the muttering of a charm !—
Shout but that awful name around,
　And palsy shakes the manliest arm.
'T is HAFED, most accurst and dire
(So rankt by Moslem hate and ire)
Of all the rebel Sons of Fire;
Of whose malign, tremendous power
The Arabs at their mid-watch hour
Such tales of fearful wonder tell
That each affrighted sentinel
Pulls down his cowl upon his eyes,
Lest HAFED in the midst should rise !
A man, they say, of monstrous birth,
A mingled race of flame and earth,
Sprung from those old, enchanted kings [2]
　Who in their fairy helms of yore
A feather from the mystic wings
　Of the Simoorgh resistless wore;
And gifted by the Fiends of Fire,
Who groaned to see their shrines expire
With charms that all in vain withstood
Would drown the Koran's light in blood !

Such were the tales that won belief,
　And such the coloring Fancy gave
To a young, warm, and dauntless Chief,—
　One who, no more than mortal brave,
Fought for the land his soul adored,
　For happy homes and altars free, —
His only talisman, the sword,
　His only spell-word, Liberty !
One of that ancient hero line,
Along whose glorious current shine
Names that have sanctified their blood;
As LEBANON's small mountain-flood
Is rendered holy by the ranks
Of sainted cedars on its banks.[3]
'T was not for him to crouch the knee
Tamely to Moslem tyranny;
'T was not for him whose soul was
　　cast
In the bright mould of ages past,
Whose melancholy spirit fed
With all the glories of the dead
Tho' framed for IRAN's happiest years,
Was born among her chains and tears !—
'T was not for him to swell the crowd
Of slavish heads, that shrinking bowed
Before the Moslem as he past
Like shrubs beneath the poison-blast —
No — far he fled — indignant fled
　The pageant of his country's shame;
While every tear her children shed
　Fell on his soul like drops of flame;
And as a lover hails the dawn
　Of a first smile, so welcomed he
The sparkle of the first sword drawn
　For vengeance and for liberty !

But vain was valor — vain the flower
Of KERMAN, in that deathful hour,
Against AL HASSAN's whelming power.—
In vain they met him helm to helm
Upon the threshold of that realm
He came in bigot pomp to sway,

---

1 "When the bright scimitars make the eyes of our heroes wink." — *The Moallakat, Poem of Amru.*

2 Tahmuras, and other ancient Kings of Persia; whose adventures in Fairy-land among the Peris and Divs may be found in Richardson's curious Dissertation. The griffin Simoorgh, they say, took some feathers from her breast for Tahmuras, with which he adorned his helmet, and transmitted them afterwards to his descendants.

3 This rivulet, says Dandini, is called the Holy River from the "cedar-saints" among which it rises.
　In the "*Lettres Édifiantes,*" there is a different cause assigned for its name of Holy. "In these are deep caverns, which formerly served as so many cells for a great number of recluses, who had chosen these retreats as the only witnesses upon earth of the severity of their penance. The tears of these pious penitents gave the river of which we have just treated the name of the Holy River." — See *Chateaubriand's* "Beauties of Christianity."

And with their corpses blockt his way —
In vain — for every lance they raised
Thousands around the conqueror blazed;
For every arm that lined their shore
Myriads of slaves were wafted o'er, —
A bloody, bold, and countless crowd,
Before whose swarm as fast they bowed
As dates beneath the locust cloud.

There stood — but one short league away
From old HARMOZIA'S sultry bay —
A rocky mountain o'er the Sea
Of OMAN beetling awfully;[1]
A last and solitary link
Of those stupendous chains that reach
From the broad Caspian's reedy brink
Down winding to the Green Sea beach.
Around its base the bare rocks stood
Like naked giants, in the flood
As if to guard the Gulf across;
While on its peak that braved the sky
A ruined Temple towered so high
That oft the sleeping albatross[2]
Struck the wild ruins with her wing,
And from her cloud-rockt slumbering
Started — to find man's dwelling there
In her own silent fields of air!
Beneath, terrific caverns gave
Dark welcome to each stormy wave
That dasht like midnight revellers in;
And such the strange, mysterious din
At times throughout those caverns
  rolled, —
And such the fearful wonders told
Of restless sprites imprisoned there,
That bold were Moslem who would dare
At twilight hour to steer his skiff
Beneath the Gheber's lonely cliff.[3]

On the land side those towers sublime,
That seemed above the grasp of Time,
Were severed from the haunts of men
By a wide, deep, and wizard glen,
So fathomless, so full of gloom,
  No eye could pierce the void between:
It seemed a place where Ghouls might
  come
With their foul banquets from the tomb
  And in its caverns feed unseen.
Like distant thunder, from below
  The sound of many torrents came,
Too deep for eye or ear to know
If 't were the sea's imprisoned flow,
  Or floods of ever-restless flame.
For each ravine, each rocky spire
Of that vast mountain stood on fire;[4]
And tho' for ever past the days
When God was worship in the blaze
That from its lofty altar shone, —
Tho' fled the priests, the votaries gone,
Still did the mighty flame burn on,[5]
Thro' chance and change, thro' good and
  ill,
Like its own God's eternal will,
Deep, constant, bright, unquenchable!

Thither the vanquisht HAFED led
  His little army's last remains; —
" Welcome, terrific glen ! " he said,
" Thy gloom, that Eblis' self might dread,
  " Is Heaven to him who flies from
    chains ! "
O'er a dark, narrow bridge-way known
To him and to his Chiefs alone
They crost the chasm and gained the
  towers; —

---

1 This mountain is my own creation, as the
"stupendous chain," of which I suppose it a
link, does not extend quite so far as the shores of
the Persian Gulf. "This long and lofty range of
mountains formerly divided Media from Assyria,
and now forms the boundary of the Persian and
Turkish empires. It runs parallel with the river
Tigris and Persian Gulf, and almost disappearing
in the vicinity of Gomberoon (Harmozia) seems
once more to rise in the southern districts of Kerman, and following an easterly course through
the centre of Meckraun and Balouchistan, is entirely lost in the deserts of Sinde." — *Kinnier's*
" Persian Empire."

2 These birds sleep in the air. They are most
common about the Cape of Good Hope.

3 " There is an extraordinary hill in this neighborhood, called Kohé Gubr, or the Guebre's
mountain. It rises in the form of a lofty cupola,

and on the summit of it, they say, are the remains
of an Atush Kudu or Fire Temple. It is super-
stitiously held to be the residence of Deeves
or Sprites, and many marvellous stories are recounted of the injury and witchcraft suffered by
those who essayed in former days to ascend or
explore it." — *Pottinger's* " Beloochistan."
4 The Ghebers generally built their temples
over subterraneous fires.

5 " At the city of Yezd, in Persia, which is
distinguished by the appellation of the Darub
Abadut, or Seat of Religion, the Guebres are
permitted to have an Atush Kudu or Fire Temple (which, they assert, has had the sacred fire in
it since the days of Zoroaster) in their own com-
partment of the city; but for this indulgence
they are indebted to the avarice, not the tolerance
of the Persian government, which taxes them
at twenty-five rupees each man." — *Pottinger's*
" Beloochistan."

" This home," he cried, " at least is
 ours ; —
" Here we may bleed, unmockt by hymns
 " Of Moslem triumph o'er our head;
" Here we may fall nor leave our limbs
 " To quiver to the Moslem's tread.
" Stretched on this rock while vultures'
 beaks
" Are whetted on our yet warm cheeks,
" Here — happy that no tyrant's eye
" Gloats on our torments — we may
 die ! " —

'T was night when to those towers they
 came,
And gloomily the fitful flame
That from the ruined altar broke
Glared on his features as he spoke : —
" 'T is o'er — what men could do, we 've
 done —
" If IRAN *will* look tamely on
" And see her priests, her warriors driven
 " Before a sensual bigot's nod,
" A wretch who shrines his lusts in heaven
 " And makes a pander of his God;
" If her proud sons, her high-born souls,
 " Men in whose veins — oh last dis-
 grace !
" The blood of ZAL and RUSTAM [1] rolls, —
 " If they *will* court this upstart race
" And turn from MITHRA's ancient ray
" To kneel at shrines of yesterday;
" If they *will* crouch to IRAN's foes,
 " Why, let them — till the land's de-
 spair
" Cries out to Heaven, and bondage
 grows
 " Too vile for even the vile to bear !
" Till shame at last, long hidden, burns
" Their inmost core, and conscience turns
" Each coward tear the slave lets fall
" Back on his heart in drops of gall.
" But *here* at least are arms unchained
" And souls that thraldom never
 stained; —
 " This spot at least no foot of slave
" Or satrap ever yet profaned,
" And tho' but few — tho' fast the
 wave
" Of life is ebbing from our veins,

" Enough for vengeance still remains.
" As panthers after set of sun
" Rush from the roots of LEBANON
" Across the dark-sea robber's way,[2]
" We 'll bound upon our startled prey.
" And when some hearts that proudest
 swell
" Have felt our falchion's last farewell,
" When Hope's expiring throb is o'er
" And even Despair can prompt no more,
" This spot shall be the sacred grave
" Of the last few who vainly brave
" Die for the land they cannot save ! "

His Chiefs stood round — each shining
 blade
Upon the broken altar laid —
And tho' so wild and desolate
Those courts where once the Mighty sate ;
Nor longer on those mouldering towers
Was seen the feast of fruits and flowers
With which of old the Magi fed
The wandering Spirits of their Dead ; [3]
Tho' neither priest nor rites were there,
 Nor charmed leaf of pure pomegran-
 ate,[4]
Nor hymn, nor censer's fragrant air,
Nor symbol of their worship planet;[5]
Yet the same God that heard their sires
Heard *them* while on that altar's fires
They swore [6] the latest, holiest deed
Of the few hearts, still left to bleed,

---

1 Ancient heroes of Persia. " Among the
Guebres there are some who boast their descent
from Rustam." — *Stephen's Persia.*

2 See Russel's account of the panther's at-
tacking travellers in the night on the sea-shore
about the roots of Lebanon.

3 " Among other ceremonies the Magi used to
place upon the tops of high towers various kinds
of rich viands, upon which it was supposed the
Peris and the spirits of their departed heroes re-
galed themselves." — *Richardson.*

4 In the ceremonies of the Ghebers round
their Fire, as described by Lord, " the Daroo,"
he says, " giveth them water to drink, and a
pomegranate leaf to chew in the mouth, to cleanse
them from inward uncleanness."

5 " Early in the morning, they (the Parsees
or Ghebers at Oulam) go in crowds to pay their
devotions to the Sun, to whom upon all the
altars there are spheres consecrated, made by
magic, resembling the circles of the sun, and
when the sun rises, these orbs seem to be inflamed, and to turn round with a great noise.
They have every one a censer in their hands, and
offer incense to the sun." — *Rabbi Benjamin.*

6 " *Nul d'entre eux oseroit se perjurer,
quand il a pris à témoin cet élément terrible et
vengeur.*" — "*Encyclopédie Françoise.*"

Should be in IRAN's injured name
To die upon that Mount of Flame —
The last of all her patriot line,
Before her last untrampled Shrine!

Brave, suffering souls! they little knew
How many a tear their injuries drew
From one meek maid, one gentle foe,
Whom love first touched with others'
    woe —
Whose life, as free from thought as sin,
Slept like a lake till Love threw in
His talisman and woke the tide
And spread its trembling circles wide.
Once, EMIR! thy unheeding child
Mid all this havoc bloomed and smiled, —
Tranquil as on some battle plain
The Persian lily shines and towers [1]
Before the combat's reddening stain
    Hath fallen upon her golden flowers.
Light-hearted maid, unawed, unmoved,
While Heaven but spared the sire she
    loved,
Once at thy evening tales of blood
Unlistening and aloof she stood —
And oft when thou hast paced along
    Thy Haram halls with furious heat,
Hast thou not curst her cheerful song,
    That came across thee, calm and
    sweet,
Like lutes of angels touched so near
Hell's confines that the damned can
    hear!

Far other feelings Love hath brought —
    Her soul all flame, her brow all sad-
    ness,
She now has but the one dear thought,
    And thinks that o'er, almost to mad-
    ness!
Oft doth her sinking heart recall
His words — "for *my* sake weep for
    all;"
And bitterly as day on day
    Of rebel carnage fast succeeds,
She weeps a lover snatched away
    In every Gheber wretch that bleeds.
There 's not a sabre meets her eye
    But with his life-blood seems to swim;

1 "A vivid verdure succeeds the autumnal
rains, and the ploughed fields are covered with
the Persian lily, of a resplendent yellow color."
— *Russel's* "Aleppo."

There 's not an arrow wings the sky
    But fancy turns its point to him.
No more she brings with footstep light
AL HASSAN's falchion for the fight;
And — had he lookt with clearer sight,
Had not the mists that ever rise
From a foul spirit dimmed his eyes —
He would have markt her shuddering
    frame,
When from the field of blood he came,
The faltering speech — the look es-
    tranged —
Voice, step and life and beauty
    changed —
He would have markt all this, and
    known
Such change is wrought by Love alone!

Ah! not the Love that should have
    blest
So young, so innocent a breast;
Not the pure, open, prosperous Love,
That, pledged on earth and sealed
    above,
Grows in the world's approving eyes,
    In friendship's smile and home's ca-
    ress,
Collecting all the heart's sweet ties
    Into one knot of happiness!
No, HINDA, no, — thy fatal flame
Is nurst in silence, sorrow, shame; —
    A passion without hope or pleasure,
In thy soul's darkness buried deep,
    It lies like some ill-gotten treasure, —
Some idol without shrine or name,
O'er which its pale-eyed votaries keep
Unholy watch, while others sleep.

Seven nights have darkened OMAN's sea,
    Since last beneath the moonlight ray
She saw his light oar rapidly
    Hurry her Gheber's bark away, —
And still she goes at midnight hour
To weep alone, in that high bower
And watch and look along the deep
For him whose smiles first made her
    weep; —
But watching, weeping, all was vain,
She never saw his bark again.
The owlet's solitary cry,
The night-hawk flitting darkly by,
    And oft the hateful carrion bird,
Heavily flapping his clogged wing,

Which reeked with that day's banqueting —
Was all she saw, was all she heard.

'T is the eighth morn — AL HASSAN'S
   brow
Is brightened with unusual joy —
What mighty mischief glads him now,
  Who never smiles but to destroy?
The sparkle upon HERKEND'S Sea,
When tost at midnight furiously,[1]
Tells not of wreck and ruin nigh,
More surely than that smiling eye!
" Up, daughter, up — the KERNA'S [2]
   breath
" Has blown a blast would waken
   death,
" And yet thou sleepest — up, child, and
   see
" This blessed day for Heaven and me,
" A day more rich in Pagan blood
" Than ever flasht o'er OMAN'S flood.
" Before another dawn shall shine,
" His head — heart — limbs — will all
   be mine;
" This very night his blood shall steep
" These hands all over ere I sleep!" —

" *His* blood!" she faintly screamed —
   her mind
Still singling *one* from all mankind —
" Yes — spite of his ravines and towers,
" HAFED, my child, this night is ours.
" Thanks to all-conquering treachery,
  " Without whose aid the links accurst,
" That bind these impious slaves, would
   be
  " Too strong for ALLA'S self to burst!
" That rebel fiend whose blade has
   spread
" My path with piles of Moslem dead,
" Whose baffling spells had almost
   driven
" Back from their course the Swords of
   Heaven,

" This night with all his band shall know
" How deep an Arab's steel can go,
" When God and Vengeance speed the
   blow.
" And — Prophet! by that holy wreath
" Thou worest on OHOD'S field of death,[3]
" I swear, for every sob that parts
" In anguish from these heathen hearts,
" A gem from PERSIA'S plundered mines
" Shall glitter on thy Shrine of Shrines.
" But, ha! — she sinks — that look so
   wild —
" Those livid lips — my child, my child,
" This life of blood befits not thee,
" And thou must back to ARABY.
 " Ne'er had I riskt thy timid sex
" In scenes that man himself might dread,
" Had I not hoped our every tread
  " Would be on prostrate Persian
   necks —
" Curst race, they offer swords instead!
" But cheer thee, maid, — the wind that
   now
" Is blowing o'er thy feverish brow
" To-day shall waft thee from the shore;
" And ere a drop of this night's gore
" Have time to chill in yonder towers,
" Thou 'lt see thy own sweet Arab
   bowers!"

His bloody boast was all too true;
There lurkt one wretch among the few
Whom HAFED'S eagle eye could count
Around him on that Fiery Mount, —
One miscreant who for gold betrayed
The pathway thro' the valley's shade
To those high towers where Freedom
   stood
In her last hold of flame and blood.
Left on the field last dreadful night,
When sallying from their sacred height
The Ghebers fought hope's farewell fight,
He lay — but died not with the brave;
That sun which should have gilt his grave
Saw him a traitor and a slave; —
And while the few who thence returned
To their high rocky fortress mourned
For him among the matchless dead
They left behind on glory's bed,

1 " It is observed, with respect to the Sea of
Herkend, that when it is tossed by tempestuous
winds it sparkles like fire." — *Travels of Two
Mohammedans.*

2 A kind of trumpet; — it " was that used by
Tamerlane, the sound of which is described as
uncommonly dreadful, and so loud as to be
heard at the distance of several miles." — *Richardson.*

3 " Mohammed had two helmets, an interior
and exterior one; the latter of which, called Al
Mawashah, the fillet, wreath, or wreathed gar
land, he wore at the battle of Ohod." — *Universal History.*

He lived, and in the face of morn
Laught them and Faith and Heaven to
   scorn.

Oh for a tongue to curse the slave
  Whose treason like a deadly blight
Comes o'er the councils of the brave
  And blasts them in their hour of
    might!
May Life's unblessed cup for him
Be drugged with treacheries to the brim,—
  With hopes that but allure to fly,
    With joys that vanish while he sips,

Like Dead-Sea fruits that tempt the eye,
  But turn to ashes on the lips![1]
His country's curse, his children's shame,
Outcast of virtue, peace and fame,
May he at last with lips of flame
On the parched desert thirsting die, —
While lakes that shone in mockery nigh,[2]
Are fading off, untouched, untasted,
Like the once glorious hopes he blasted!
And when from earth his spirit flies,
  Just Prophet, let the damned-one dwell
Full in the sight of Paradise
Beholding heaven and feeling hell!

LALLA ROOKH had the night before been visited by a dream which in spite of the impending fate of poor HAFED made her heart more than usually cheerful during the morning and gave her cheeks all the freshened animation of a flower that the Bidmusk had just passed over.[3] She fancied that she was sailing on that Eastern Ocean where the sea-gypsies who live for ever on the water[4] enjoy a perpetual summer in wandering from isle to isle when she saw a small gilded bark approaching her. It was like one of those boats which the Maldivian islanders send adrift, at the mercy of winds and waves, loaded with perfumes, flowers, and odoriferous wood, as an offering to the Spirit whom they call King of the Sea. At first, this little bark appeared to be empty but on coming nearer —

She had proceeded thus far in relating the dream to her Ladies, when FERAMORZ appeared at the door of the pavilion. In his presence of course every thing else

1 "They say that there are apple-trees upon the sides of this sea, which bear very lovely fruit, but within are all full of ashes." — *Thevenot.* The same is asserted of the oranges there; v. *Witman's* Travels in Asiatic Turkey. ·

"The Asphalt Lake, known by the name of the Dead Sea, is very remarkable on account of the considerable proportion of salt which it contains. In this respect it surpasses every other known water on the surface of the earth. This great proportion of bitter tasted salts is the reason why neither animal nor plant can live in this water." — *Klaproth's* Chemical Analysis of the Water of the Dead Sea, Annals of Philosophy, January, 1813. *Hasselquist,* however, doubts the truth of this last assertion, as there are shell-fish to be found in the lake.

Lord Byron has a similar allusion to the fruits of the Dead Sea, in that wonderful display of genius, his third Canto of "Childe Harold," — magnificent beyond anything, perhaps, that even *he* has ever written.

2 "The Suhrab or Water of the Desert is said to be caused by the rarefaction of the atmosphere from extreme heat; and, which augments the delusion, it is most frequent in hollows, where water might be expected to lodge. I have seen bushes and trees reflected in it, with as much accuracy as though it had been the face of a clear and still lake." — *Pottinger.*

"As to the unbelievers, their works are like a vapor in a plain, which the thirsty traveller thinketh to be water, until when he cometh thereto he findeth it to be nothing." — *Koran,* chap. 24.

3 "A wind which prevails in February, called Bidmusk, from a small and odoriferous flower of that name." —"The wind which blows these flowers commonly lasts till the end of the month." — *Le Bruyn.*

4 "The Biajús are of two races: the one is settled on Borneo, and are a rude but warlike and industrious nation, who reckon themselves the original possessors of the island of Borneo. The other is a species of sea-gypsies or itinerant fishermen, who live in small covered boats, and enjoy a perpetual summer on the eastern ocean, shifting to leeward from island to island, with the variations of the monsoon. In some of their customs this singular race resemble the natives of the Maldivia islands. The Maldivians annually launch a small bark, loaded with perfumes, gums, flowers, and odoriferous wood, and turn it adrift at the mercy of winds and waves, as an offering to the *Spirit of the Winds;* and sometimes similar offerings are made to the spirit whom they term *the King of the Sea.* In like manner the Biajús perform their offering to the god of evil, launching a small bark, loaded with all the sins and misfortunes of the nation, which are imagined to fall on the unhappy crew that may be so unlucky as first to meet with it." — *Dr. Leyden* on the Languages and Literature of the Indo-Chinese Nations.

was forgotten and the continuance of the story was instantly requested by all. Fresh wood of aloes was set to burn in the cassolets; — the violet sherbets [1] were hastily handed round, and after a short prelude on his lute in the pathetic measure of Nava,[2] which is always used to express the lamentations of absent lovers, the Poet thus continued: —

THE day is lowering — stilly black
Sleeps the grim wave, while heaven's rack,
Disperst and wild, 'twixt earth and sky
Hangs like a shattered canopy.
There 's not a cloud in that blue plain
But tells of storm to come or past; —
Here flying loosely as the mane
Of a young war-horse in the blast; —
There rolled in masses dark and swelling,
As proud to be the thunder's dwelling!
While some already burst and riven
Seen melting down the verge of heaven;
As tho' the infant storm had rent
The mighty womb that gave him birth,
And having swept the firmament
Was now in fierce career for earth.

On earth 't was yet all calm around,
A pulseless silence, dread, profound,
More awful than the tempest's sound.
The diver steered for ORMUS' bowers,
And moored his skiff till calmer hours;
The sea-birds with portentous screech
Flew fast to land; — upon the beach
The pilot oft had paused, with glance
Turned upward to that wild expanse; —
And all was boding, drear and dark
As her own soul when HINDA's bark
Went slowly from the Persian shore. —
No music timed her parting oar,[3]
Nor friends upon the lessening strand

Lingered to wave the unseen hand
Or speak the farewell, heard no more; —
But lone, unheeded, from the bay
The vessel takes its mournful way,
Like some ill-destined bark that steers
In silence thro' the Gate of Tears.[4]
And where was stern AL HASSAN then?
Could not that saintly scourge of men
From bloodshed and devotion spare
One minute for a farewell there?
No — close within in changeful fits
Of cursing and of prayer he sits
In savage loneliness to brood
Upon the coming night of blood, —
With that keen, second-scent of death,
By which the vulture snuffs his food
In the still warm and living breath! [5]
While o'er the wave his weeping daughter
Is wafted from these scenes of slaughter, —
As a young bird of BABYLON,[6]
Let loose to tell of victory won,
Flies home, with wing, ah! not unstained
By the red hands that held her chained.

And does the long-left home she seeks
Light up no gladness on her cheeks?
The flowers she nurst — the well-known groves,
Where oft in dreams her spirit roves —

1 "The sweet-scented violet is one of the plants most esteemed, particularly for its great use in Sorbet, which they make of violet sugar." — *Hasselquist.*
"The sherbet they most esteem, and which is drank by the Grand Signor himself, is made of violets and sugar." — *Tavernier.*

2 "Last of all she took a guitar, and sung a pathetic air in the measure called Nava, which is always used to express the lamentations of absent lovers." — *Persian Tales.*

3 "The Easterns used to set out on their longer voyages with music." — *Harmer.*

4 "The Gate of Tears, the straits or passage into the Red Sea, commonly called Babelmandel. It received this name from the old Arabians, on account of the danger of the navigation and the number of shipwrecks by which it was distinguished; which induced them to consider as dead, and to wear mourning for all who had the boldness to hazard the passage through it into the Ethiopic ocean." — *Richardson.*

5 "I have been told that whensoever an animal falls down dead, one or more vultures, unseen before, instantly appear." — *Pennant.*

6 "They fasten some writing to the wings of a Bagdat, or Babylonian pigeon." — *Travels of certain Englishmen.*

Once more to see her dear gazelles
Come bounding with their silver bells;
Her birds' new plumage to behold
  And the gay, gleaming fishes count,
She left all filleted with gold
  Shooting around their jasper fount; [1]
Her little garden mosque to see,
  And once again, at evening hour,
To tell her ruby rosary [2]
  In her own sweet acacia bower. —
Can these delights that wait her now
Call up no sunshine on her brow?
No, — silent, from her train apart, —
As if even now she felt at heart
The chill of her approaching doom, —
She sits, all lovely in her gloom
As a pale Angel of the Grave;
And o'er the wide, tempestuous wave
Looks with a shudder to those towers
Where in a few short awful hours
Blood, blood, in streaming tides shall
    run,
Foul incense for to-morrow's sun!
"Where art thou, glorious stranger!
    thou,
"So loved, so lost, where art thou now?
"Foe — Gheber — infidel — whate'er
"The unhallowed name thou 'rt doomed
    to bear,
"Still glorious — still to this fond heart
"Dear as its blood, whate'er thou art!
"Yes — ALLA, dreadful ALLA! yes —
"If there be wrong, be crime in this,
"Let the black waves that round us roll,
"Whelm me this instant ere my soul
"Forgetting faith — home — father —
    all —
"Before its earthly idol fall,
"Nor worship even Thyself above him —
"For, oh, so wildly do I love him,
"Thy Paradise itself were dim
"And joyless, if not shared with him!"
Her hands were claspt — her eyes up-
    turned,

1 "The Empress of Jehan-Guire used to divert herself with feeding tame fish in her canals,
some of which were many years afterwards known
by fillets of gold, which she caused to be put
round them." — *Harris.*

2 "*Le Tespih, qui est un chapelet, composé de
99 petites boules d'agathe, de jaspe, d'ambre, de
corail, ou d'autre matière precieuse. J'en ai vu
un superbe au Seigneur Jerpos; il étoit de belles
et grosses perles parfaites et égales, estimé trente
mille piastres.*" — *Toderini.*

Dropping their tears like moonlight
    rain;
And, tho' her lip, fond raver! burned
  With words of passion, bold, profane,
Yet was there light around her brow,
  A holiness in those dark eyes,
Which showed, — tho' wandering earth-
    ward now, —
  Her spirit's home was in the skies.
Yes — for a spirit pure as hers
Is always pure, even while it errs;
As sunshine broken in the rill
Tho' turned astray is sunshine still!

So wholly had her mind forgot
All thoughts but one she heeded not
The rising storm — the wave that cast
A moment's midnight as it past —
Nor heard the frequent shout, the tread
Of gathering tumult o'er her head —
Clasht swords and tongues that seemed
    to vie
With the rude riot of the sky. —
But, hark! — that war-whoop on the
    deck —
  That crash as if each engine there,
Mast, sails and all, were gone to
    wreck,
  Mid yells and stampings of despair!
Merciful Heaven! what *can* it be?
'T is not the storm, tho' fearfully
The ship has shuddered as she rode
O'er mountain-waves — "Forgive me,
    God!
"Forgive me" — shrieked the maid and
    knelt,
Trembling all over — for she felt
As if her judgment-hour was near;
While crouching round half dead with
    fear,
Her handmaids clung, nor breathed nor
    stirred —
When, hark! — a second crash — a
    third —
And now as if a bolt of thunder
Had riven the laboring planks asunder,
The deck falls in — what horrors then!
Blood, waves and tackle, swords and
    men
Come mixt together thro' the chasm, —
Some wretches in their dying spasm
Still fighting on — and some that call
"For GOD and IRAN!" as they fall!

Whose was the hand that turned away
The perils of the infuriate fray,
And snatcht her breathless from beneath
This wilderment of wreck and death?
She knew not — for a faintness came
Chill o'er her and her sinking frame
Amid the ruins of that hour
Lay like a pale and scorched flower
Beneath the red volcano's shower.
But, oh! the sights and sounds of dread
That shockt her ere her senses fled!
The yawning deck — the crowd that strove
Upon the tottering planks above —
The sail whose fragments, shivering o'er
The strugglers' heads all dasht with gore
Fluttered like bloody flags — the clash
Of sabres and the lightning's flash
Upon their blades, high tost about
Like meteor brands [1] — as if throughout
The elements one fury ran,
One general rage that left a doubt
    Which was the fiercer, Heaven or
    Man!

Once too — but no — it could not be —
    'T was fancy all — yet once she thought,
While yet her fading eyes could see,
    High on the ruined deck she caught
A glimpse of that unearthly form,
    That glory of her soul — even then,
Amid the whirl of wreck and storm,
    Shining above his fellow-men,
As on some black and troublous night
The Star of Egypt,[2] whose proud light
Never hath beamed on those who rest
In the White Islands of the West,[3]
Burns thro' the storm with looks of flame
That put Heaven's cloudier eyes to shame.
But no — 't was but the minute's dream —
A fantasy — and ere the scream
Had half-way past her pallid lips,
A death-like swoon, a chill eclipse
Of soul and sense its darkness spread
Around her and she sunk as dead.

How calm, how beautiful comes on
The stilly hour when storms are gone,
When warring winds have died away,
And clouds beneath the glancing ray
Melt off and leave the land and sea
Sleeping in bright tranquillity, —
Fresh as if Day again were born,
Again upon the lap of Morn! —
When the light blossoms rudely torn
And scattered at the whirlwind's will,
Hang floating in the pure air still,
Filling it all with precious balm,
In gratitude for this sweet calm; —
And every drop the thunder-showers
Have left upon the grass and flowers
Sparkles, as 't were that lightening-gem [4]
Whose liquid flame is born of them!
When, 'stead of one unchanging breeze,
    There blow a thousand gentle airs
    And each a different perfume bears, —
As if the loveliest plants and trees
Had vassal breezes of their own
To watch and wait on them alone,
And waft no other breath than theirs:
When the blue waters rise and fall,
In sleepy sunshine mantling all;
And even that swell the tempest leaves
Is like the full and silent heaves
Of lovers' hearts when newly blest,
Too newly to be quite at rest.

Such was the golden hour that broke
Upon the world when Hinda woke
From her long trance and heard around
No motion but the water's sound
Rippling against the vessel's side,
As slow it mounted o'er the tide. —
But where is she? — her eyes are dark,
Are wildered still — is this the bark,
The same, that from Harmozia's bay
Bore her at morn — whose bloody way
The sea-dog trackt? — no — strange and new
Is all that meets her wondering view.
Upon a galliot's deck she lies,
    Beneath no rich pavilion's shade, —

---

1 The meteors that Pliny calls "*faces.*"

. 2 "The brilliant Canopus, unseen in European climates." — *Brown.*

3 See Wilford's learned Essays on the Sacred Isles in the West.

4 A precious stone of the Indies, called by the ancients, Ceraunium, because it was supposed to be found in places where thunder had fallen. Tertullian says it has a glittering appearance, as if there had been fire in it; and the author of the Dissertation in Harris's Voyages, supposes it to be the opal.

No plumes to fan her sleeping eyes,
　Nor jasmine on her pillow laid.
But the rude litter roughly spread
With war-cloaks is her homely bed,
And shawl and sash on javelins hung
For awning o'er her head are flung.
Shuddering she lookt around — there lay
　A group of warriors in the sun,
Resting their limbs, as for that day
　Their ministry of death were done.
Some gazing on the drowsy sea
Lost in unconscious revery;
And some who seemed but ill to brook
That sluggish calm with many a look
To the slack sail impatient cast,
As loose it flagged around the mast.

Blest ALLA! who shall save her now?
　There 's not in all that warrior band
One Arab sword, one turbaned brow
From her own Faithful Moslem land.
Their garb — the leathern belt [1] that
　　wraps
　Each yellow vest [2] — that rebel hue —
The Tartar fleece upon their caps [3] —
　Yes — yes — her fears are all too true,
And Heaven hath in this dreadful hour
Abandoned her to HAFED'S power; —
HAFED, the Gheber! — at the thought
　Her very heart's blood chills within;
He whom her soul was hourly taught
　To loathe as some foul fiend of sin,
Some minister whom Hell had sent
To spread its blast where'er he went
And fling as o'er our earth he trod
His shadow betwixt man and God!
And she is now his captive, — thrown
In his fierce hands, alive, alone;
His the infuriate band she sees,
All infidels — all enemies!
What was the daring hope that then
Crost her like lightning, as again
With boldness that despair had lent
　She darted thro' that armed crowd
A look so searching, so intent,
　That even the sternest warrior bowed
Abasht, when he her glances caught,

As if he guessed whose form they sought.
But no — she sees him not — 't is gone,
The vision that before her shone
Thro' all the maze of blood and storm,
Is fled — 't was but a phantom form —
One of those passing, rainbow dreams,
Half light, half shade, which Fancy's
　beams
Paint on the fleeting mists that roll
In trance or slumber round the soul.

But now the bark with livelier bound
　　Scales the blue wave — the crew 's in
　　　motion,
The oars are out and with light sound
　Break the bright mirror of the ocean,
Scattering its brilliant fragments round.
And now she sees — with horror sees,
　　Their course is toward that mountain-
　　　hold, —
Those towers that make her life-blood
　　freeze,
Where MECCA'S godless enemies
　Lie beleaguered scorpions rolled
In their last deadly, venomous fold!
Amid the illumined land and flood
Sunless that mighty mountain stood;
Save where above its awful head,
There shone a flaming cloud, blood-red,
As 't were the flag of destiny
Hung out to mark where death would be!

Had her bewildered mind the power
Of thought in this terrific hour,
She well might marvel where or how
Man's foot could scale that mountain's
　brow,
Since ne'er had Arab heard or known
Of path but thro' the glen alone. —
But every thought was lost in fear,
When, as their bounding bark drew near
The craggy base, she felt the waves
Hurry them toward those dismal caves
That from the Deep in windings pass
Beneath that Mount's volcanic mass ; —
And loud a voice on deck commands
To lower the mast and light the brands !—
Instantly o'er the dashing tide
Within a cavern's mouth they glide,
Gloomy as that eternal Porch
　Thro' which departed spirits go: —
Not even the flare of brand and torch
　Its flickering light could further throw
　Than the thick flood that boiled below.

1 *D'Herbelot*, art. "Agduani."

2 " The Guebres are known by a dark yellow
color, which the men affect in their clothes." —
Thevenot.

3 " The Kolah, or cap, worn by the Persians,
is made of the skin of the sheep of Tartary." —
Waring.

Silent they floated — as if each
Sat breathless, and too awed for speech
In that dark chasm where even sound
Seemed dark, — so sullenly around
The goblin echoes of the cave
Muttered it o'er the long black wave
As 't were some secret of the grave!

But soft — they pause — the current turns
  Beneath them from its onward track; —
Some mighty, unseen barrier spurns
  The vexed tide all foaming back
And scarce the oars' redoubled force
Can stem the eddy's whirling course;
When, hark! — some desperate foot has
  sprung
Among the rocks — the chain is flung —
The oars are up — the grapple clings,
And the tost bark in moorings swings.
Just then, a day-beam thro' the shade
Broke tremulous — but ere the maid
Can see from whence the brightness
  steals,
Upon her brow she shuddering feels
A viewless hand that promptly ties
A bandage round her burning eyes;
While the rude litter where she lies,
Uplifted by the warrior throng,
O'er the steep rocks is borne along.

Blest power of sunshine! — genial Day,
What balm, what life is in thy ray!
To feel thee is such real bliss,
That had the world no joy but this,
To sit in sunshine calm and sweet, —
It were a world too exquisite
For man to leave it for the gloom,
The deep, cold shadow of the tomb.
Even HINDA, tho' she saw not where
  Or whither wound the perilous road,
Yet knew by that awakening air,
  Which suddenly around her glowed,
That they had risen from the darkness
  there,
And breathed the sunny world again!

But soon this balmy freshness fled —
For now the steepy labyrinth led
Thro' damp and gloom — mid crash of
  boughs,
And fall of loosened crags that rouse
The leopard from his hungry sleep,
  Who starting thinks each crag a prey,

And long is heard from steep to steep
  Chasing them down their thundering
  way!
The jackal's cry — the distant moan
Of the hyena, fierce and lone —
And that eternal saddening sound
Of torrents in the glen beneath,
As 't were the ever-dark Profound
  That rolls beneath the Bridge of Death!
All, all is fearful — even to see,
  To gaze on those terrific things
She now but blindly hears, would be
  Relief to her imaginings;
Since never yet was shape so dread,
  But Fancy thus in darkness thrown
And by such sounds of horror fed
  Could frame more dreadful of her own.

But does she dream? has Fear again
Perplext the workings of her brain,
Or did a voice, all music, then
Come from the gloom, low whispering
  near —
"Tremble not, love, thy Gheber's
  here"?
She *does* not dream — all sense, all ear,
She drinks the words, "Thy Gheber's
  here."
'T was his own voice — she could not
  err —
  Throughout the breathing world's ex
  tent
There was but *one* such voice for her,
  So kind, so soft, so eloquent!
Oh, sooner shall the rose of May
  Mistake her own sweet nightingale,
And to some meaner minstrel's lay
  Open her bosom's glowing veil,[1]
Than Love shall ever doubt a tone,
A breath of the beloved one!

Though blest mid all her ills to think
  She has that one beloved near,
Whose smile tho' met on ruin's brink
  Hath power to make even ruin dear, —
Yet soon this gleam of rapture crost
By fears for him is chilled and lost.
How shall the ruthless HAFED brook
That one of Gheber blood should look,

[1] A frequent image among the oriental poet
"The nightingales warbled their enchantir
notes, and rent the thin veils of the rose-bu
and the rose." — *Jami.*

With aught but curses in his eye,
On her — a maid of ARABY —
A Moslem maid — the child of him,
Whose bloody banner's dire success
Hath left their altars cold and dim,
    And their fair land a wilderness!
And worse than all that night of blood
    Which comes so fast — Oh! who shall
        stay
The sword, that once hath tasted food
    Of Persian hearts or turn its way?
What arm shall then the victim cover,
Or from her father shield her lover?

" Save him, my God! " she inly cries —
" Save him this night — and if thine eyes
    " Have ever welcomed with delight
" The sinner's tears, the sacrifice
    " Of sinners' hearts — guard him this
        night,
" And here before thy throne I swear
" From my heart's inmost core to tear
    " Love, hope, remembrance, tho' they
        be
" Linkt with each quivering life-string
    there,

" And give it bleeding all to Thee!
" Let him but live, — the burning tear,
" The sighs, so sinful, yet so dear,
" Which have been all too much his
    own,
" Shall from this hour be Heaven's
    alone.
" Youth past in penitence and age
" In long and painful pilgrimage
" Shall leave no traces of the flame
" That wastes me now — nor shall his
    name
" E'er bless my lips but when I pray
" For his dear spirit, that away
" Casting from its angelic ray
" The eclipse of earth, he too may
    shine
" Redeemed, all glorious and all Thine!
" Think — think what victory to win
" One radiant soul like his from sin, —
" One wandering star of virtue back
" To its own native, heavenward track!
" Let him but live, and both are Thine,
    " Together thine — for blest or crost,
" Living or dead, his doom is mine,
    " And if *he* perish, both are lost! "

THE next evening LALLA ROOKH was entreated by her Ladies to continue the
relation of her wonderful dream; but the fearful interest that hung round the fate
of HINDA and her lover had completely removed every trace of it from her mind;
— much to the disappointment of a fair seer or two in her train, who prided themselves on their skill in interpreting visions, and who had already remarked, as an
unlucky omen, that the Princess, on the very morning after the dream, had worn a
silk dyed with the blossoms of the sorrowful tree, Nilica.[1]

FADLADEEN, whose indignation had more than once broken out during the
recital of some parts of this heterodox poem, seemed at length to have made up
his mind to the infliction; and took his seat this evening with all the patience of a
martyr, while the Poet resumed his profane and seditious story as follows: —

To tearless eyes and hearts at ease
The leafy shores and sun-bright seas
That lay beneath that mountain's height,
Had been a fair enchanting sight.
'T was one of those ambrosial eves
A day of storm so often leaves
At its calm setting — when the West
Opens her golden bowers of rest,
And a moist radiance from the skies
Shoots trembling down, as from the eyes

Of some meek penitent whose last
Bright hours atone for dark ones past,
And whose sweet tears o'er wrong for-
    given
Shine as they fall with light from
    heaven!

'T was stillness all — the winds that late
    Had rusht thro' KERMAN'S almond
    groves,

1 " Blossoms of the sorrowful Nyctanthes give a durable color to silk."— *Remarks on the
Husbandry of Bengal*, p. 200. Nilica is one of the Indian names of this flower. — *Sir W. Jones.*
The Persians call it Gul. — *Carreri.*

And shaken from her bowers of date
  That cooling feast the traveller loves,[1]
Now lulled to languor scarcely curl
  The Green Sea wave whose waters
    gleam
Limpid as if her mines of pearl
  Were melted all to form the stream:
And her fair islets small and bright
  With their green shores reflected there·
Look like those PERI isles of light
  That hang by spell-work in the air.

But vainly did those glories burst
On HINDA'S dazzled eyes, when first
The bandage from her brow was taken,
And, pale and awed as those who waken
In their dark tombs — when, scowling
    near,
The Searchers of the Grave[2] appear, —
She shuddering turned to read her fate
  In the fierce eyes that flasht around;
And saw those towers all desolate,
  That o'er her head terrific frowned,
As if defying even the smile
Of that soft heaven to gild their pile.
In vain with mingled hope and fear,
She looks for him whose voice so dear
Had come, like music, to her ear —
Strange, mocking dream! again 't is fled.
And oh, the shoots, the pangs of dread
That thro' her inmost bosom run,
  When voices from without proclaim
" HAFED, the Chief " — and, one by one,
  The warriors shout that fearful name!
He comes — the rock resounds his tread —
How shall she dare to lift her head
Or meet those eyes whose scorching
    glare
Not YEMEN'S boldest sons can bear?
In whose red beam, the Moslem tells,
Such rank and deadly lustre dwells
As in those hellish fires that light
The mandrake's charnel leaves at night.[3]

How shall she bear that voice's tone,
At whose loud battle-cry alone
Whole squadrons oft in panic ran,
Scattered like some vast caravan,
When stretched at evening round the
    well
They hear the thirsting tiger's yell.

Breathless she stands with eyes cast down
Shrinking beneath the fiery frown
Which, fancy tells her, from that brow
Is flashing o'er her fiercely now:
And shuddering as she hears the tread
  Of his retiring warrior band. —
Never was pause so full of dread;
  Till HAFED with a trembling hand
Took hers, and leaning o'er her said,
" HINDA; " — that word was all he spoke,
And 't was enough — the shriek that broke
  From her full bosom told the rest. —
Panting with terror, joy, surprise,
The maid but lifts her wondering eyes,
  To hide them on her Gheber's breast!
'T is he, 't is he — the man of blood,
The fellest of the Fire-fiend's brood,
HAFED, the demon of the fight,
Whose voice unnerves, whose glances
    blight, —
Is her own loved Gheber, mild
And glorious as when first he smiled
In her lone tower and left such beams
Of his pure eye to light her dreams,
That she believed her bower had given
Rest to some wanderer from heaven!

Moments there are, and this was one,
Snatched like a minute's gleam of sun
Amid the black Simoom's eclipse —
  Or like those verdant spots that bloom
Around the crater's burning lips,
  Sweetening the very edge of doom!
The past — the future — all that Fate
Can bring of dark or desperate
Around such hours but makes them cast
Intenser radiance while they last!

Even he, this youth — tho' dimmed and
    gone
Each star of Hope that cheered him on —
His glories lost — his cause betrayed —
IRAN, his dear-loved country, made
A land of carcasses and slaves,
One dreary waste of chains and graves! —

---

1 " In parts of Kerman, whatever dates are
shaken from the trees by the wind they do not
touch, but leave them for those who have not
any, or for travellers." — *Ebn Haukal.*

2 The two terrible angels, Monkir and Nakir,
who are called " the Searchers of the Grave " in
the " Creed of the orthodox Mahometans " given
by Ockley, vol. ii.

3 " The Arabians call the mandrake 'the
Devil's candle,' on account of its shining appearance in the night." — *Richardson.*

Himself but lingering, dead at heart,
    To see the last, long struggling breath
Of Liberty's great soul depart,
    Then lay him down and share her
        death —
Even he so sunk in wretchedness
    With doom still darker gathering o'er
        him,
Yet, in this moment's pure caress,
    In the mild eyes that shone before him,
Beaming that blest assurance worth
All other transports known on earth,
That he was loved — well, warmly
        loved —
Oh! in this precious hour he proved
How deep, how thorough-felt the glow
Of rapture kindling out of woe; —
How exquisite one single drop
Of bliss thus sparkling to the top
Of misery's cup — how keenly quaft,
Tho' death must follow on the draught!

She too while gazing on those eyes
    That sink into her soul so deep,
Forgets all fears, all miseries,
    Or feels them like the wretch in sleep,
Whom fancy cheats into a smile,
Who dreams of joy and sobs the while!
The mighty Ruins where they stood
    Upon the mount's high, rocky verge
Lay open towards the ocean flood,
    Where lightly o'er the illumined surge
Many a fair bark that, all the day,
Had lurkt in sheltering creek or bay
Now bounded on and gave their sails,
Yet dripping to the evening gales;
Like eagles when the storm is done,
Spreading their wet wings in the sun.
The beauteous clouds, tho' daylight's Star
Had sunk behind the hills of LAR,
Were still with lingering glories bright, —
As if to grace the gorgeous West
The Spirit of departing Light
    That eve had left his sunny vest
Behind him ere he winged his flight.
Never was scene so formed for love!
Beneath them waves of crystal move
In silent swell — Heaven glows above
And their pure hearts, to transport given,
Swell like the wave and glow like heaven.

But ah! too soon that dream is past —
    Again, again her fear returns; —

Night, dreadful night, is gathering fast,
    More faintly the horizon burns,
And every rosy tint that lay
On the smooth sea hath died away.
Hastily to the darkening skies
A glance she casts — then wildly cries
"*At night*, he said—and, look, 't is near—
    " Fly, fly— if yet thou lovest me, fly —
" Soon will his murderous band be here,
    " And I shall see thee bleed and die.—
" Hush! heardest thou not the tramp of
        men
" Sounding from yonder fearful glen? —
" Perhaps, even now they climb the
        wood —
    " Fly, fly— tho' still the West is bright,
" He 'll come — oh! yes — he wants
        thy blood —
    " I know him — he 'll not wait for
        night! "

In terrors even to agony
    She clings around the wondering
        Chief; —
" Alas, poor wildered maid! to me
    " Thou owest this raving trance of
        grief.
" Lost as I am, naught ever grew
" Beneath my shade but perisht too —
" My doom is like the Dead Sea air,
" And nothing lives that enters there!
" Why were our barks together driven
" Beneath this morning's furious heaven?
" Why when I saw the prize that chance
    " Had thrown into my desperate
        arms, —
" When casting but a single glance
    " Upon thy pale and prostrate charms,
"I vowed (tho' watching viewless o'er
    " Thy safety thro' that hour's alarms)
" To meet the unmanning sight no more—
" Why have I broke that heart-wrung
        vow?
" Why weakly, madly met thee now? —
" Start not — that noise is but the shock
    " Of torrents thro' yon valley
        hurled —
" Dread nothing here — upon this rock
    " We stand above the jarring world,
" Alike beyond its hope — its dread —
" In gloomy safety, like the Dead!
" Or could even earth and hell unite
" In league to storm this Sacred Height,

" Fear nothing thou — myself, to-night,
" And each o'erlooking star that dwells
" Near God will be thy sentinels; —
" And ere to-morrow's dawn shall glow,
" Back to thy sire " —
　　　　　　　　　" To-morrow! — no " —
The maiden screamed — "Thou 'lt never
　　　see
" To-morrow's sun — death, death will
　　　be
" The night-cry thro' each reeking tower,
" Unless we fly, ay, fly this hour!
" Thou art betrayed — some wretch who
　　　knew
" That dreadful glen's mysterious clew —
" Nay, doubt not — by yon stars, 't is
　　　true —
" Hath sold thee to my vengeful sire;
" This morning, with that smile so dire
" He wears in joy he told me all
" And stampt in triumph thro' our hall,
" As tho' thy heart already beat
" Its last life-throb beneath his feet!
" Good Heaven, how little dreamed I
　　　then
　　" His victim was my own loved
　　　youth! —
　　" Fly — send — let some one watch the
　　　glen —
　　" By all my hopes of heaven 't is
　　　truth! "

Oh! colder than the wind that freezes
　　Founts that but now in sunshine
　　　played,
Is that congealing pang which seizes
　　The trusting bosom, when betrayed.
He felt it — deeply felt — and stood,
As if the tale had frozen his blood,
　　So mazed and motionless was he; —
Like one whom sudden spells enchant,
Or some mute, marble habitant
　　Of the still Halls of ISHMONIE! [1]
But soon the painful chill was o'er,
And his great soul herself once more
Lookt from his brow in all the rays
Of her best, happiest, grandest days.
Never in moment most elate
　　Did that high spirit loftier rise; —

While bright, serene, determinate,
　　His looks are lifted to the skies,
As if the signal lights of Fate
　　Were shining in those awful eyes!
'T is come — his hour of martyrdom
In IRAN'S sacred cause is come;
And tho' his life hath past away
Like lightning on a stormy day,
Yet shall his death-hour leave a track
　　Of glory permanent and bright
To which the brave of after-times,
The suffering brave, shall long look
　　back
　　With proud regret, — and by its light
　　Watch thro' the hours of slavery's
　　　night
For vengeance on the oppressor's crimes.
This rock, his monument aloft,
　　Shall speak the tale to many an age;
And hither bards and heroes oft
　　Shall come in secret pilgrimage,
And bring their warrior sons and tell
The wondering boys where HAFED fell;
And swear them on those lone remains
Of their lost country's ancient fanes,
Never — while breath of life shall live
Within them — never to forgive
The accursed race whose ruthless chain
Hath left on IRAN'S neck a stain
Blood, blood alone can cleanse again!

Such are the swelling thoughts that now
Enthrone themselves on HAFED'S brow;
And ne'er did Saint of ISSA [2] gaze
On the red wreath for martyrs twined,
More proudly than the youth surveys
　　That pile which thro' the gloom be-
　　　hind,
Half lighted by the altar's fire,
Glimmers — his destined funeral pyre!
Heaped by his own, his comrades' hands,
　　Of every wood of odorous breath,
There, by the Fire-God's shrine it stands,
　　Ready to fold in radiant death
The few still left of those who swore
To perish there when hope was o'er —
The few to whom that couch of flame,
Which rescues them from bonds and
　　shame,
Is sweet and welcome as the bed
For their own infant Prophet spread,

---

1 For an account of Ishmonie, the petrified
city in Upper Egypt, where it is said there are
many statues of men, women, etc , to be seen to
this day, see *Perry's* " *View of the Levant.*"

2 Jesus.

When pitying Heaven to roses turned
The death-flames that beneath him
burned ! [1]

With watchfulness the maid attends
His rapid glance where'er it bends —
Why shoot his eyes such awful beams?
What plans he now? what thinks or
dreams?
Alas ! why stands he musing here,
When every moment teems with fear?
" HAFED, my own beloved Lord,"
She kneeling cries — " first, last adored !
" If in that soul thou 'st ever felt
    " Half what thy lips impassioned
    swore,
" Here on my knees that never knelt
    " To any but their God before,
" I pray thee, as thou lovest me, fly —
" Now, now — ere yet their blades are
nigh.
" Oh haste — the bark that bore me
hither
    " Can waft us o'er yon darkening sea
" East — west — alas, I care not whither,
    " So thou art safe, and I with thee !
" Go where we will, this hand in thine,
    " Those eyes before me smiling thus,
" Thro' good and ill, thro' storm and
    shine,
    " The world 's a world of love for
    us !
" On some calm, blessed shore we 'll
    dwell,
" Where 't is no crime to love too well; —
" Where thus to worship tenderly
" An erring child of light like thee
" Will not be sin — or if it be
" Where we may weep our faults away,
" Together kneeling, night and day,
" Thou, for *my* sake, at ALLA's shrine,
" And I — at *any* God's, for thine !"

1 The Ghebers say that when Abraham, their
great Prophet, was thrown into the fire by order
of Nimrod, the flame turned instantly into "a
bed of roses, where the child sweetly reposed."
— *Tavernier*.
    Of their other Prophet, Zoroaster, there is a
story told in *Dion Prusæus*, Orat. 36., that the
love of wisdom and virtue leading him to a solitary life upon a mountain, he found it one day
all in a flame, shining with celestial fire, out of
which he came without any harm, and instituted
certain sacrifices to God, who, he declared, then
appeared to him. — v. *Patrick* on Exodus, iii. 2.

Wildly these passionate words she
spoke —
Then hung her head and wept for
shame;
Sobbing as if a heart-string broke
With every deep-heaved sob that came.
While he, young, warm — oh ! wonder
not
If, for a moment, pride and fame,
His oath — his cause — that shrine of
flame,
And IRAN's self are all forgot
For her, whom at his feet he sees
Kneeling in speechless agonies.
No, blame him not if Hope awhile
Dawned in his soul and threw her smile
O'er hours to come — o'er days and
nights,
Winged with those precious, pure de-
lights
Which she who bends all beauteous there
Was born to kindle and to share.
A tear or two which as he bowed
    To raise the suppliant, trembling stole,
First warned him of this dangerous cloud
    Of softness passing o'er his soul.
Starting he brusht the drops away
Unworthy o'er that cheek to stray; —
Like one who on the morn of fight
Shakes from his sword the dews of
    night,
That had but dimmed not stained its light.

Yet tho' subdued the unnerving thrill,
Its warmth, its weakness lingered still
So touching in each look and tone,
That the fond, fearing, hoping maid
Half counted on the flight she prayed,
    Half thought the hero's soul was
    grown
As soft, as yielding as her own,
And smiled and blest him while he
    said, —
" Yes — if there be some happier sphere
" Where fadeless truth like ours is
    dear, —
" If there be any land of rest
    " For those who love and ne'er forget,
" Oh ! comfort thee — for safe and blest
    " We 'll meet in that calm region yet !"

Scarce had she time to ask her heart
If good or ill these words impart,

When the roused youth impatient flew
To the tower-wall, where high in view
A ponderous sea-horn [1] hung, and blew
A signal deep and dread as those
The storm-fiend at his rising blows. —
Full well his Chieftains, sworn and true
Thro' life and death, that signal knew;
For 't was the appointed warning-blast,
The alarm to tell when hope was past
And the tremendous death-die cast!
And there upon the mouldering tower
Hath hung this sea-horn many an hour,
Ready to sound o'er land and sea
That dirge-note of the brave and free.

They came — his Chieftains at the call
Came slowly round and with them all —
Alas, how few! — the worn remains
Of those who late o'er KERMAN'S plains
Went gayly prancing to the clash
Of Moorish zel and tymbalon
Catching new hope from every flash
Of their long lances in the sun,
And as their coursers charged the wind
And the white ox-tails streamed behind,[2]
Looking as if the steeds they rode
Were winged and every Chief a God!
How fallen, how altered now! how wan
Each scarred and faded visage shone,
As round the burning shrine they
    came; —
How deadly was the glare it cast,
As mute they paused before the flame
To light their torches as they past!
'T was silence all — the youth hath
    planned
The duties of his soldier-band;
And each determined brow declares
His faithful Chieftains well know theirs.

But minutes speed — night gems the
    skies —
And oh, how soon, ye blessed eyes
That look from heaven ye may behold
Sights that will turn your star-fires cold!

1 "The shell called Siiankos, common to
India, Africa, and the Mediterranean, and still
used in many parts as a trumpet for blowing
alarms or giving signals: it sends forth a deep
and hollow sound." — *Pennant.*

2 "The finest ornament for the horses is
made of six large flying tassels of long white
hair, taken out of the tails of wild oxen, that are
to be found in some places of the Indies." —
Thevenot.

Breathless with awe, impatience, hope,
The maiden sees the veteran group
Her litter silently prepare,
    And lay it at her trembling feet; —
And now the youth with gentle care,
    Hath placed her in the sheltered seat
And prest her hand — that lingering
    press
Of hands that for the last time sever;
Of hearts whose pulse of happiness
    When that hold breaks is dead for
    ever.
And yet to *her* this sad caress
    Gives hope — so fondly hope can err!
'T was joy, she thought, joy's mute
    excess —
    Their happy flight's dear harbinger;
'T was warmth — assurance — tender-
    ness —
    'T was any thing but leaving her.

"Haste, haste!" she cried, "the clouds
    grow dark,
"But still, ere night, we 'll reach the
    bark;
"And by to-morrow's dawn — oh bliss!
    "With thee upon the sun-bright deep,
"Far off, I 'll but remember this,
    "As some dark vanisht dream of sleep;
"And thou" — but ah! — he answers
    not —
    Good Heaven! — and does she go
    alone?
She now has reached that dismal spot,
    Where some hours since his voice's
    tone
Had come to soothe her fears and ills,
Sweet as the angel ISRAFIL'S,[3]
When every leaf on Eden's tree
Is trembling to his minstrelsy —
Yet now — oh, now, he is not nigh. —
    "HAFED! my HAFED! — if it be
"Thy will, thy doom this night to die
    "Let me but stay to die with thee
"And I will bless thy loved name,
"Till the last life-breath leave this
    frame.
"Oh! let our lips, our cheeks be laid
"But near each other while they fade;
"Let us but mix our parting breaths,
"And I can die ten thousand deaths!

3 "The angel Israfil, who has the most melodious voice of all God's creatures." — *Sale.*

"You too, who hurry me away
"So cruelly, one moment stay —
    "Oh! stay — one moment is not
    much —
"He yet may come — for *him* I pray —
"HAFED! dear HAFED!"—all the way
In wild lamentings that would touch
A heart of stone she shrieked his name
To the dark woods — no HAFED came: —
No — hapless pair — you 've lookt your
    last: —
    Your hearts should both have broken
    then:
The dream is o'er — your doom is cast —
You 'll never meet on earth again!

Alas for him who hears her cries!
    Still half-way down the steep he
    stands,
Watching with fixt and feverish eyes
    The glimmer of those burning brands
That down the rocks with mournful ray,
Light all he loves on earth away!
Hopeless as they who far at sea
By the cold moon have just consigned
The corse of one loved tenderly
    To the bleak flood they leave behind,
And on the deck still lingering stay,
And long look back with sad delay
To watch the moonlight on the wave
That ripples o'er that cheerless grave.

But see — he starts — what heard he
    then?
That dreadful shout! — across the glen
From the land-side it comes and loud
Rings thro' the chasm, as if the crowd
Of fearful things that haunt that dell,
Its Ghouls and Divs and shapes of hell,
Had all in one dread howl broke out,
So loud, so terrible that shout!
"They come — the Moslems come!" —
    he cries,
His proud soul mounting to his eyes, —
"Now, Spirits of the Brave, who roam
"Enfranchised thro' yon starry dome,
"Rejoice — for souls of kindred fire
"Are on the wing to join your choir!"
He said — and, light as bridegrooms
    bound
    To their young loves, reclimbed the
    steep
And gained the Shrine — his Chiefs stood
round —

    Their swords, as with instinctive leap,
Together at that cry accurst
Had from their sheaths like sunbeams
    burst.
And hark! — again — again it rings;
Near and more near its echoings
Peal thro' the chasm — oh! who that
    then
Had seen those listening warrior-men,
With their swords graspt, their eyes of
    flame
Turned on their Chief — could doubt the
    shame,
The indignant shame with which they
    thrill
To hear those shouts and yet stand still?

He read their thoughts — they were his
    own —
    "What! while our arms can wield these
    blades,
"Shall we die tamely? die alone?
    "Without one victim to our shades,
"One Moslem heart, where buried deep
"The sabre from its toil may sleep?
"No — God of IRAN's burning skies!
"Thou scornest the inglorious sacrifice.
"No — tho' of all earth's hope bereft,
"Life, swords, and vengeance still are
    left.
"We 'll make yon valley's reeking caves
    "Live in the awe-struck minds of
    men
"Till tyrants shudder, when their slaves
    "Tell of the Gheber's bloody glen.
"Follow, brave hearts! — this pile re-
    mains
"Our refuge still from life and chains;
"But his the best, the holiest bed,
"Who sinks entombed in Moslem
    dead!"

Down the precipitous rocks they
    sprung,
While vigor more than human strung
Each arm and heart. — The exulting foe
Still thro' the dark defiles below,
Trackt by his torches' lurid fire,
    Wound slow, as thro' GOLCONDA'S
    vale[1]
The mighty serpent in his ire
    Glides on with glittering, deadly trail.

1 See Hoole upon the Story of Sinbad.

No torch the Ghebers need — so well
They know each mystery of the dell,
So oft have in their wanderings
Crost the wild race that round them
    dwell,
The very tigers from their delves
Look out and let them pass as things
    Untamed and fearless like themselves!

There was a deep ravine that lay
Yet darkling in the Moslem's way;
Fit spot to make invaders rue
The many fallen before the few.
The torrents from that morning's sky
Had filled the narrow chasm breast-high,
And on each side aloft and wild
Huge cliffs and toppling crags were
    piled, —
The guards with which young Freedom
    lines
The pathways to her mountain-shrines.
Here at this pass the scanty band
Of IRAN's last avengers stand;
Here wait in silence like the dead
And listen for the Moslem's tread
So anxiously the carrion-bird
Above them flaps his wing unheard!

They come — that plunge into the
    water
Gives signal for the work of slaughter.
Now, Ghebers, now — if e'er your blades
    Had point or prowess prove them
    now —
Woe to the file that foremost wades!
    They come — a falchion greets each
    brow,
And as they tumble trunk on trunk
Beneath the gory waters sunk
Still o'er their drowning bodies press
New victims quick and numberless;
Till scarce an arm in HAFED's band,
    So fierce their toil, hath power to stir,
But listless from each crimson hand
    The sword hangs clogged with mas-
    sacre.
Never was horde of tyrants met
With bloodier welcome — never yet
To patriot vengeance hath the sword
More terrible libations poured!

All up the dreary, long ravine,
By the red, murky glimmer seen

Of half-quenched brands, that o'er the
    flood
Lie scattered round and burn in blood,
What ruin glares! what carnage swims!
Heads, blazing turbans, quivering limbs,
Lost swords that dropt from many a
    hand,
In that thick pool of slaughter stand; —
Wretches who wading, half on fire
    From the tost brands that round them
    fly,
'Twixt flood and flame in shrieks ex-
    pire; —
    And some who graspt by those that
    die
Sink woundless with them, smothered
    o'er
In their dead brethren's gushing gore!

But vainly hundreds, thousands bleed,
Still hundreds, thousands more succeed;
Countless as toward some flame at
    night
The North's dark insects wing their flight
And quench or perish in its light,
To this terrific spot they pour —
Till, bridged with Moslem bodies o'er,
It bears aloft their slippery tread,
And o'er the dying and the dead,
Tremendous causeway! on they pass.
Then, hapless Ghebers, then, alas,
What hope was left for you? for you,
Whose yet warm pile of sacrifice
Is smoking in their vengeful eyes; —
Whose swords how keen, how fierce they
    knew,
And burned with shame to find how few.

Crusht down by that vast multitude
Some found their graves where first they
    stood;
While some with hardier struggle died,
And still fought on by HAFED's side,
Who fronting to the foe trod back
Towards the high towers his gory track;
And as a lion swept away
    By sudden swell of JORDAN's pride
From the wild covert where he lay, [1]
    Long battles with the o'erwhelming
    tide,

1 " In this thicket upon the banks of the Jordan several sorts of wild beasts are wont to harbor
themselves, whose being washed out of the cov-

So fought he back with fierce delay
And kept both foes and fate at bay.

But whither now? their track is lost,
  Their prey escaped — guide, torches
    gone —
By torrent-beds and labyrinths crost,
  The scattered crowd rush blindly on —
" Curse on those tardy lights that wind,"
They panting cry, " so far behind;
" Oh, for a bloodhound's precious scent,
" To track the way the Ghebers went ! "
Vain wish — confusedly along
They rush more desperate as more
    wrong :
Till wildered by the far-off lights,
Yet glittering up those gloomy heights,
Their footing mazed and lost they miss,
And down the darkling precipice
Are dasht into the deep abyss ;
Or midway hang impaled on rocks,
A banquet yet alive for flocks
Of ravening vultures, — while the dell
Re-echoes with each horrible yell.

Those sounds — the last, to vengeance
    dear,
That e'er shall ring in HAFED'S ear, —
Now reached him as aloft alone
Upon the steep way breathless thrown,
He lay beside his reeking blade,
  Resigned, as if life's task were o'er,
Its last blood-offering amply paid,
  And IRAN'S self could claim no
    more.
One only thought, one lingering beam
Now broke across his dizzy dream
Of pain and weariness — 't was she,
  His heart's pure planet shining-yet
Above the waste of memory
  When all life's other lights were set.
And never to his mind before
Her image such enchantment wore.
It seemed as if each thought that
    stained,
  Each fear that chilled their loves was
    past,
And not one cloud of earth remained
  Between him and her radiance cast ; —

As if to charms, before so bright,
  New grace from other worlds was
    given,
And his soul saw her by the light
  Now breaking o'er itself from heaven !

A voice spoke near him — 't was the tone
Of a loved friend, the only one
Of all his warriors left with life
From that short night's tremendous
    strife. —
" And must we then, my chief, die here?
" Foes round us and the Shrine so near ! "
These words have roused the last remains
  Of life within him : — "What ! not yet
" Beyond the reach of Moslem chains !"
  The thought could make even Death
    forget
His icy bondage : — with a bound
He springs all bleeding from the ground
And grasps his comrade's arm now grown
Even feebler, heavier than his own,
And up the painful pathway leads,
Death gaining on each step he treads.
Speed them, thou God, who heardest their
    vow !
They mount — they bleed — oh save
    them now —
The crags are red they 've clambered
    o'er,
The rock-weed 's dripping with their
    gore ; —
Thy blade too, HAFED, false at length,
Now breaks beneath thy tottering
    strength !
Haste, haste — the voices of the Foe
Come near and nearer from below —
One effort more — thank Heaven ! 't is
    past,
They 've gained the topmost steep at last.
And now they touch the temple's walls,
  Now HAFED sees the Fire divine —
When, lo ! — his weak, worn comrade
    falls
  Dead on the threshold of the shrine.
" Alas, brave soul, too quickly fled !
  " And must I leave thee withering
    here,
" The sport of every ruffian's tread,
  " The mark for every coward's spear?
" No, by yon altar's sacred beams ! "
He cries and with a strength that seems
Not of this world uplifts the frame

ert by the overflowings of the river, gave occasion to that allusion of Jeremiah, *he shall come
up like a lion from the swelling of Jordan.*" —
Maundrell's " *Aleppo.*"

Of the fallen Chief and toward the flame
Bears him along;— with death-damp
hand
  The corpse upon the pyre he lays,
Then lights the consecrated brand
  And fires the pile whose sudden blaze
Like lightning bursts o'er OMAN'S Sea.—
" Now, Freedom's God ! I come to
Thee,"
The youth exclaims and with a smile
Of triumph vaulting on the pile,
In that last effort ere the fires
Have harmed one glorious limb expires !

What shriek was that on OMAN'S tide?
  It came from yonder drifting bark,
That just hath caught upon her side
  The death-light — and again is dark.
It is the boat — ah ! why delayed? —
That bears the wretched Moslem maid;
Confided to the watchful care
  Of a small veteran band with whom
Their generous Chieftain would not share
  The secret of his final doom,
But hoped when HINDA safe and free
  Was rendered to her father's eyes,
Their pardon full and prompt would be
  The ransom of so dear a prize. —
Unconscious thus of HAFED'S fate,
And proud to guard their beauteous
freight,
Scarce had they cleared the surfy waves
That foam around those frightful caves
When the curst war-whoops known so
well
Came echoing from the distant dell —
Sudden each oar, upheld and still,
  Hung dripping o'er the vessel's side,
And driving at the current's will,
  They rockt along the whispering tide;
While every eye in mute dismay
  Was toward that fatal mountain turned,
Where the dim altar's quivering ray
  As yet all lone and tranquil burned.

Oh ! 't is not, HINDA, in the power
  Of Fancy's most terrific touch
To paint thy pangs in that dread hour —
  Thy silent agony — 't was such
As those who feel could paint too well,
But none e'er felt and lived to tell !
'T was not alone the dreary state
Of a lorn spirit crusht by fate,

When tho' no more remains to dread
  The panic chill will not depart;—
When tho' the inmate Hope be dead,
  Her ghost still haunts the mouldering
heart;
No — pleasures, hopes, affections gone,
The wretch may bear and yet live on
Like things within the cold rock found
Alive when all 's congealed around.
But there 's a blank repose in this,
A calm stagnation, that were bliss
To the keen, burning, harrowing pain,
Now felt thro' all thy breast and brain;—
That spasm of terror, mute, intense,
That breathless, agonized suspense
From whose hot throb whose deadly
aching,
The heart hath no relief but breaking !

Calm is the wave — heaven's brilliant
lights
  Reflected dance beneath the prow;—
Time was when on such lovely nights
  She who is there so desolate now
Could sit all cheerful tho' alone
  And ask no happier joy than seeing
That star-light o'er the waters thrown —
No joy but that to make her blest,
  And the fresh, buoyant sense of Being
Which bounds in youth's yet careless
breast, —
Itself a star not borrowing light
But in its own glad essence bright.
How different now !— but, hark ! again
The yell of havoc rings — brave men !
In vain with beating hearts ye stand
On the bark's edge — in vain each hand
Half draws the falchion from its sheath;
  All 's o'er — in rust your blades may
lie :—
He at whose word they 've scattered
death
  Even now this night himself must
die !
Well may ye look to yon dim tower,
  And ask and wondering guess what
means
The battle-cry at this dead hour —
  Ah ! she could tell you — she who leans
Unheeded there, pale, sunk, aghast,
With brow against the dew-cold mast;—
  Too well she knows — her more than
life,

Her soul's first idol and its last
   Lies bleeding in that murderous strife.
But see — what moves upon the height?
Some signal! — 't is a torch's light.
   What bodes its solitary glare?
In gasping silence toward the Shrine
All eyes are turned — thine, HINDA,
   thine
   Fix their last fading life-beams there.
'T was but a moment — fierce and high
The death-pile blazed into the sky
And far away o'er rock and flood
   Its melancholy radiance sent;
While HAFED like a vision stood
Revealed before the burning pyre,
Tall, shadowy, like a Spirit of Fire
   Shrined in its own grand element!
" 'T is he!" — the shuddering maid ex-
   claims, —
   But while she speaks he's seen no
   more;
High burst in air the funeral flames,
   And IRAN's hopes and hers are o'er!

One wild, heart-broken shriek she gave;
   Then sprung as if to reach that blaze
Where still she fixt her dying gaze,
And gazing sunk into the wave, —
   Deep, deep, — where never care or
   pain
Shall reach her innocent heart again!

Farewell — farewell to thee, ARABY's
   daughter!
(Thus warbled a PERI beneath the dark
   sea,)
No pearl ever lay under OMAN's green
   water
   More pure in its shell than thy Spirit
   in thee.

Oh! fair as the sea-flower close to thee
   growing,
   How light was thy heart till Love's
   witchery came,
Like the wind of the south [1] o'er a summer
   lute blowing,
   And husht all its music and withered
   its frame!

But long upon ARABY's green sunny
   highlands
Shall maids and their lovers remember
   the doom
Of her who lies sleeping among the Pearl
   Islands
   With naught but the sea-star [2] to light
   up her tomb.

And still when the merry date-season is
   burning [3]
And calls to the palm-groves the young
   and the old,
The happiest there from their pastime
   returning
   At sunset will weep when thy story is
   told.

The young village-maid when with flowers
   she dresses
Her dark flowing hair for some festival
   day
Will think of thy fate till neglecting her
   tresses
   She mournfully turns from the mirror
   away.

Nor shall IRAN, beloved of her Hero!
   forget thee —
Tho' tyrants watch over her tears as
   they start,
Close, close by the side of that Hero
   she 'll set thee,
   Embalmed in the innermost shrine of
   her heart.

Farewell — be it ours to embellish thy
   pillow
With every thing beauteous that grows
   in the deep;
Each flower of the rock and each gem of
   the billow
   Shall sweeten thy bed and illumine thy
   sleep.

---

1 "This wind (the Samoor) so softens the strings of lutes, that they can never be tuned while it lasts." — *Stephen's Persia.*

2 "One of the greatest curiosities found in the Persian Gulf is a fish which the English call Star-fish. It is circular, and at night very luminous, resembling the full moon surrounded by rays." — *Mirza Abu Taleb.*

3 For a description of the merriment of the date-time, of their work, their dances, and their return home from the palm-groves at the end of autumn with the fruits, see *Kempfer*, "*Amœnitat. Exot.*"

Around thee shall glisten the loveliest
amber
That ever the sorrowing sea-bird has
wept;[1]
With many a shell in whose hollow-
wreathed chamber
We Peris of Ocean by moonlight have
slept.

We 'll dive where the gardens of coral
lie darkling
And plant all the rosiest stems at thy
head;

We 'll seek where the sands of the Caspian [2] are sparkling
And gather their gold to strew over
thy bed.

Farewell — farewell !— Until Pity's sweet
fountain
Is lost in the hearts of the fair and the
brave,
They 'll weep for the Chieftain who died
on that mountain,
They 'll weep for the Maiden who
sleeps in this wave.

THE singular placidity with which FADLADEEN had listened during the latter part of this obnoxious story surprised the Princess and FERAMORZ exceedingly; and even inclined towards him the hearts of these unsuspicious young persons who little knew the source of a complacency so marvellous. The truth was he had been organizing for the last few days a most notable plan of persecution against the poet in consequence of some passages that had fallen from him on the second evening of recital, — which appeared to this worthy Chamberlain to contain language and principles for which nothing short of the summary criticism of the Chabuk [3] would be advisable. It was his intention therefore immediately on their arrival at Cash-mere to give information to the King of Bucharia of the very dangerous sentiments of his minstrel; and if unfortunately that monarch did not act with suitable vigor on the occasion, (that is, if he did not give the Chabuk to FERAMORZ and a place to FADLADEEN,) there would be an end, he feared, of all legitimate government in Bucharia. He could not help however auguring better both for himself and the cause of potentates in general; and it was the pleasure arising from these mingled anticipations that diffused such unusual satisfaction through his features and made his eyes shine out like poppies of the desert over the wide and lifeless wilderness of that countenance.

Having decided upon the Poet's chastisement in this manner he thought it but humanity to spare him the minor tortures of criticism. Accordingly when they assembled the following evening in the pavilion and LALLA ROOKH was expecting to see all the beauties of her bard melt away one by one in the acidity of criticism, like pearls in the cup of the Egyptian queen, — he agreeably disappointed her by merely saying with an ironical smile that the merits of such a poem deserved to be tried at a much higher tribunal; and then suddenly passed off into a panegyric upon all Mussulman sovereigns, more particularly his august and Imperial master, Au-rungzebe, — the wisest and best of the descendants of Timur, — who among other great things he had done for mankind had given to him, FADLADEEN, the very profitable posts of Betel-carrier and Taster of Sherbets to the Emperor, Chief Holder of the Girdle of Beautiful Forms,[4] and Grand Nazir or Chamberlain of the Haram.

1 Some naturalists have imagined that amber is a concretion of the tears of birds. — See *Trevoux, Chambers.*

2 "The bay Kieselarke, which is otherwise called the Golden Bay, the sand whereof shines as fire." — *Struy.*

3 " The application of whips or rods." — *Dubios.*

4 Kempfer mentions such an officer among the attendants of the King of Persia, and calls him "*formæ corporis estimator.*" His business was, at stated periods, to measure the ladies of the

They were now not far from that Forbidden River [1] beyond which no pure Hindoo can pass, and were reposing for a time in the rich valley of Hussun Abdaul, which had always been a favorite resting-place of the Emperors in their annual migrations to Cashmere. Here often had the Light of the Faith, Jehan-Guire, been known to wander with his beloved and beautiful Nourmahal, and here would LALLA ROOKH have been happy to remain for ever, giving up the throne of Bucharia and the world for FERAMORZ and love in this sweet, lonely valley. But the time was now fast approaching when she must see him no longer, — or, what was still worse, behold him with eyes whose every look belonged to another, and there was a melancholy preciousness in these last moments, which made her heart cling to them as it would to life. During the latter part of the journey, indeed, she had sunk into a deep sadness from which nothing but the presence of the young minstrel could awake her. Like those lamps in tombs which only light up when the air is admitted, it was only at his approach that her eyes became smiling and animated. But here in this dear valley every moment appeared an age of pleasure; she saw him all day and was therefore all day happy, — resembling, she often thought, that people of Zinge [2] who attribute the unfading cheerfulness they enjoy to one genial star that rises nightly over their heads. [3]

The whole party indeed seemed in their liveliest mood during the few days they passed in this delightful solitude. The young attendants of the Princess who were here allowed a much freer range than they could safely be indulged with in a less sequestered place ran wild among the gardens and bounded through the meadows lightly as young roes over the aromatic plains of Tibet. While FADLADEEN, in addition to the spiritual comfort derived by him from a pilgrimage to the tomb of the Saint from whom the valley is named, had also opportunities of indulging in a small way his taste for victims by putting to death some hundreds of those unfortunate little lizards,[4] which all pious Mussulmans make it a point to kill;—taking for granted that the manner in which the creature hangs its head is meant as a mimicry of the attitude in which the Faithful say their prayers.

About two miles from Hussun Abdaul were those Royal Gardens [5] which had grown beautiful under the care of so many lovely eyes, and were beautiful still though those eyes could see them no longer. This place, with its flowers and its holy silence interrupted only by the dipping of the wings of birds in its marble basins filled with the pure water of those hills, was to LALLA ROOKH all that her heart could fancy of fragrance, coolness, and almost heavenly tranquillity. As the

Haram by a sort of regulation-girdle whose limits it was not thought graceful to exceed. If any of them outgrew this standard of shape, they were reduced by abstinence till they came within proper bounds.

1 The Attock.
"Akbar on his way ordered a fort to be built upon the Nilab, which he called Attock, which means in the Indian language Forbidden ; for, by the superstition of the Hindoos, it was held unlawful to cross that river." — *Dow's* Hindostan.

2 "The inhabitants of this country (Zinge) are never afflicted with sadness or melancholy ; on this subject the Sheikh *Abu-al-Kheir-Azhari* has the following distich :—

"'Who is the man without care or sorrow, (tell) that I may rub my hand to him.

"'(Behold) the Zingians, without care and sorrow, frolicsome with tipsiness and mirth.'

"The philosophers have discovered that the cause of this cheerfulness proceeds from the influence of the star Soheil, or Canopus, which rises over them every night." — *Extract from a Geographical Persian Manuscript called "Heft Aklim," or the Seven Climates, translated by W. Ouseley, Esq.*

3 The star Soheil, or Canopus.

4 "The lizard Stellio. The Arabs call it Hardun. The Turks kill it, for they imagine that by declining the head it mimics them when they say their prayers." — *Hasselquist.*

5 For these particulars respecting Hussun Abdaul I am indebted to the very interesting Introduction of Mr. Elphinstone's work upon Caubul.

Prophet said of Damascus, "it was too delicious;"[1] — and here in listening to the sweet voice of FERAMORZ or reading in his eyes what yet he never dared to tell her, the most exquisite moments of her whole life were passed. One evening when they had been talking of the Sultana Nourmahal, the Light of the Haram,[2] who had so often wandered among these flowers, and fed with her own hands in those marble basins the small shining fishes of which she was so fond,[3] — the youth in order to delay the moment of separation proposed to recite a short story or rather rhapsody of which this adored Sultana was the heroine. It related, he said, to the reconcilement of a sort of lovers' quarrel which took place between her and the Emperor during a Feast of Roses at Cashmere; and would remind the Princess of that difference between Haroun-al-Raschid and his fair mistress Marida,[4] which was so happily made up by the soft strains of the musician Moussali. As the story was chiefly to be told in song and FERAMORZ had unluckily forgotten his own lute in the valley, he borrowed the vina of LALLA ROOKH's little Persian slave, and thus began : —

THE LIGHT OF THE HARAM.

WHO has not heard of the Vale of CASH-
　　MERE,
　　With its roses the brightest that earth
　　ever gave,[5]
Its temples and grottos and fountains as
　　clear
　　As the love-lighted eyes that hang over
　　their wave?

Oh! to see it at sunset, — when warm
　　o'er the Lake
Its splendor at parting a summer eve
　　throws,
Like a bride full of blushes when linger-
　　ing to take
A last look of her mirror at night ere
　　she goes ! —

When the shrines thro' the foliage are
　　gleaming half shown,
And each hallows the hour by some rites
　　of its own.
Here the music of prayer from a minaret
　　swells,
　　Here the Magian his urn full of per-
　　fume is swinging,
And here at the altar a zone of sweet bells
　　Round the waist of some fair Indian
　　dancer is ringing.[6]
Or to see it by moonlight when mellowly
　　shines
The light o'er its palaces, gardens, and
　　shrines,
When the water-falls gleam like a quick
　　fall of stars

1　"As you enter at that Bazar, without the gate of Damascus, you see the Green Mosque, so called because it hath a steeple faced with green glazed bricks, which render it very resplendent; it is covered at top with a pavilion of the same stuff. The Turks say this mosque was made in that place, because Mahomet being come so far, would not enter the town, saying it was too delicious." — *Thevenot.* This reminds one of the following pretty passage in Isaac Walton : — "When I sat last on this primrose bank, and looked down these meadows, I thought of them as Charles the Emperor did of the city of Florence, 'that they were too pleasant to be looked on, but only on holidays.'"

2　Nourmahal signifies Light of the Haram. She was afterwards called Nourjehan, or the Light of the World.

3　See note, p. 447.

4　"*Haroun Al Raschid, cinquième Khalife des Abassides, s'étant un jour brouillé avec une de ses maîtresses nommée Maridah, qu'il aimoit cependant jusqu'à l'excès, et cette mésintelligence ayant déjà duré quelque tems commença à s'ennuyer. Giafar Barmaki, son favori, qui s'en apperçût, commanda à Abbas ben Ahnaf, excellent poëte de ce tems là, de composer quelques vers sur le sujet de cette brouillerie. Ce poëte exécuta l'ordre de Giafar, qui fit chanter ces vers par Moussali en présence du Khalife, et ce prince fut tellement touché de la tendresse des vers du poëte et de la douceur de la voix du musicien qu'il alla aussi-tôt trouver Maridah, et fit sa paix avec elle.*" — *D'Herbelot.*

5　"The rose of Kashmire for its brilliancy and delicacy of odor has long been proverbial in the East." — *Forster.*

6　"Tied round her waist the zone of bells, that sounded with ravishing melody." — *Song of Jayadeva.*

And the nightingale's hymn from the Isle
  of Chenars
Is broken by laughs and light echoes of
  feet
From the cool, shining walks where the
  young people meet. —
Or at morn when the magic of daylight
  awakes
A new wonder each minute as slowly it
  breaks,
Hills, cupolas, fountains, called forth
  every one
Out of darkness as if but just born of
  the Sun.
When the Spirit of Fragrance is up with
  the day
From his Haram of night-flowers steal-
  ing away,
And the wind full of wantonness wooes
  like a lover
The young aspen-trees,[1] till they tremble
  all over.
When the East is as warm as the light of
  first hopes,
  And Day with his banner of radiance
    unfurled
Shines in thro' the mountainous portal[2]
  that opes,
  Sublime, from that Valley of bliss to
    the world!

But never yet by night or day,
In dew of spring or summer's ray,
Did the sweet Valley shine so gay
As now it shines — all love and light,
Visions by day and feasts by night!
A happier smile illumes each brow,
  With quicker spread each heart un-
    closes,
And all is ecstasy — for now
  The Valley holds its Feast of Roses;[3]
The joyous Time when pleasures pour
Profusely round and in their shower
Hearts open like the Season's Rose, —
  The Floweret of a hundred leaves[4]

Expanding while the dew-fall flows
And every leaf its balm receives.

'T was when the hour of evening came
  Upon the Lake, serene and cool,
When Day had hid his sultry flame
  Behind the palms of BARAMOULE,[5]
When maids began to lift their heads,
Refresht from their embroidered beds
Where they had slept the sun away,
And waked to moonlight and to play.
All were abroad : — the busiest hive
On BELA'S[6] hills is less alive
When saffron-beds are full in flower,
Than lookt the Valley in that hour.
A thousand restless torches played
Thro' every grove and island shade;
A thousand sparkling lamps were set
On every dome and minaret;
And fields and pathways far and near
Were lighted by a blaze so clear
That you could see in wandering round
The smallest rose-leaf on the ground.
Yet did the maids and matrons leave
Their veils at home, that brilliant eve;
And there were glancing eyes about
And cheeks that would not dare shine
  out
In open day but thought they might
Look lovely then, because 't was night.
And all were free and wandering
  And all exclaimed to all they met,
That never did the summer bring
  So gay a Feast of Roses yet;—
The moon had never shed a light
  So clear as that which blest them there;
The roses ne'er shone half so bright,
  Nor they themselves lookt half so fair.

And what a wilderness of flowers !
It seemed as tho' from all the bowers
And fairest fields of all the year,
The mingled spoil were scattered here.
The Lake too like a garden breathes
  With the rich buds that o'er it lie, —
As if a shower of fairy wreaths
  Had fallen upon it from the sky !

---

1 "The little isles in the Lake of Cachemire
are set with arbours and large-leaved aspen-trees,
slender and tall. — *Bernier.*

2 "The Tuckt Suliman, the name bestowed
by the Mahommetans on this hill, forms one side
of a grand portal to the Lake." — *Forster.*

3 "The Feast of Roses continues the whole
time of their remaining in bloom." — See *Pietro
de la Valle.*

4 "Gul sad berk, the Rose of a hundred

leaves. I believe a particular species." — *Ouseley.*

5 *Bernier.*

6 A place mentioned in the Toozek Jehangeery, or Memoirs of Jehan-Guire, where there is
an account of the beds of saffron-flowers about
Cashmere.

And then the sounds of joy, — the beat
Of tabors and of dancing feet; —
The minaret-crier's chant of glee
Sung from his lighted gallery,[1]
And answered by a ziraleet
From neighboring Haram, wild and
sweet; —
The merry laughter echoing
From gardens where the silken swing[2]
Wafts some delighted girl above
The top leaves of the orange-grove;
Or from those infant groups at play
Among the tents[3] that line the way,
Flinging, unawed by slave or mother,
Handfuls of roses at each other. —
Then the sounds from the Lake, — the
low whispering in boats,
As they shoot thro' the moonlight, —
the dipping of oars
And the wild, airy warbling that every
where floats
Thro' the groves, round the islands, as
if all the shores
Like those of KATHAY uttered music
and gave
An answer in song to the kiss of each
wave.[4]
But the gentlest of all are those sounds
full of feeling
That soft from the lute of some lover
are stealing, —
Some lover who knows all the heart-
touching power
Of a lute and a sigh in this magical hour.

Oh! best of delights as it every where
is
To be near the loved *One*, — what a rap-
ture is his
Who in moonlight and music thus sweetly
may glide
O'er the Lake of CASHMERE with that
One by his side!

If woman can make the worst wilderness
dear,
Think, think what a Heaven she must
make of CASHMERE!

So felt the magnificent Son of ACBAR,[5]
When from power and pomp and the
trophies of war
He flew to that Valley forgetting them all
With the Light of the HARAM, his young
NOURMAHAL.
When free and uncrowned as the Con-
queror roved
By the banks of that Lake with his only
beloved
He saw in the wreaths she would play-
fully snatch
From the hedges a glory his crown could
not match,
And preferred in his heart the least ring-
let that curled
Down her exquisite neck to the throne
of the world.

There 's a beauty for ever unchangingly
bright,
Like the long, sunny lapse of a summer-
day's light,
Shining on, shining on, by no shadow
made tender
Till Love falls asleep in its sameness of
splendor.
This *was* not the beauty — oh, nothing
like this
That to young NOURMAHAL gave such
magic of bliss!

1 " It is the custom among the women to employ the Maazeen to chant from the gallery of
the nearest minaret, which on that occasion is
illuminated, and the women assembled at the
house respond at intervals with a ziraleet or joyous chorus." — *Russel.*

2 "The swing is a favorite pastime in the
East, as promoting a circulation of air, extremely
refreshing in those sultry climates." — *Richardson.*

"The swings are adorned with festoons. This
pastime is accompanied with music of voices
and of instruments, hired by the masters of the
swings." — *Thevenot.*

3 At the keeping of the Feast of Roses we
beheld an infinite number of tents pitched, with
such a crowd of men, women, boys, and girls,
with music, dances, etc." — *Herbert.*

4 " An old commentator of the Chou-King
says, the ancients having remarked that a current
of water made some of the stones near its banks
send forth a sound, they detached some of them,
and being charmed with the delightful sound they

emitted, constructed King or musical instruments
of them." — *Grosier.*

This miraculous quality has been attributed
also to the shore of Attica. " *hujus littus, ai.
Capella, concentum musicum illisis terræ undi.
reddere, quod propter tantam eruditionis vin
puto dictum.*" — *Ludov. Vives in Augustin.
" de Civitat. Dei." lib.* xviii. c. 8.

5 Jehan-Guire was the son of the Great Acbar

But that loveliness ever in motion which
  plays
Like the light upon autumn's soft shadowy days,
Now here and now there, giving warmth
  as it flies
From the lip to the cheek, from the
  cheek to the eyes;
Now melting in mist and now breaking
  in gleams,
Like the glimpses a saint hath of Heaven
  in his dreams.
When pensive it seemed as it that very
  grace,
That charm of all others, was born with
  her face!
And when angry, — for even in the tran-
  quillest climes
Light breezes will ruffle the blossoms
  sometimes —
The short, passing anger but seemed to
  awaken
New beauty like flowers that are sweetest
  when shaken.
If tenderness touched her, the dark of
  her eye
At once took a darker, a heavenlier dye,
From the depth of whose shadow like
  holy revealings
From innermost shrines came the light
  of her feelings.
Then her mirth — oh! 't was sportive as
  ever took wing
From the heart with a burst like the
  wild-bird in spring;
Illumed by a wit that would fascinate
  sages,
Yet playful as Peris just loosed from their
  cages.[1]
While her laugh full of life, without any
  control
But the sweet one of gracefulness, rung
  from her soul;
And where it most sparkled no glance
  could discover,
In lip, cheek, or eyes, for she brightened
  all over, —
Like any fair lake that the breeze is upon

When it breaks into dimples and laughs
  in the sun.
Such, such were the peerless enchant-
  ments that gave
NOURMAHAL the proud Lord of the East
  for her slave:
And tho' bright was his Haram, — a
  living parterre
Of the flowers [2] of this planet — tho'
  treasures were there,
For which SOLIMAN's self might have
  given all the store
That the navy from OPHIR e'er winged
  to his shore,
Yet dim before *her* were the smiles of
  them all
And the Light of his Haram was young
  NOURMAHAL!

But where is she now, this night of
  joy,
When bliss is every heart's employ? —
When all around her is so bright,
So like the visions of a trance,
That one might think, who came by
  chance
Into the vale this happy night,
He saw that City of Delight [3]
In Fairy-land, whose streets and towers
Are made of gems and light and flowers!
Where is the loved Sultana? where,
When mirth brings out the young and
  fair,
Does she, the fairest, hide her brow
In melancholy stillness now?

Alas! — how light a cause may move
Dissension between hearts that love!
Hearts that the world in vain had tried
And sorrow but more closely tied;
That stood the storm when waves were
  rough
Yet in a sunny hour fall off,
Like ships that have gone down at sea
When heaven was all tranquillity!
A something light as air — a look,
  A word unkind or wrongly taken —
Oh! love that tempests never shook,
  A breath, a touch like this hath shaken.

---

1 In the wars of the Divs with the Peris,
whenever the former took the latter prisoners,
"they shut them up in iron cages, and hung them
on the highest trees. Here they were visited by
their companions, who brought them the choicest
odors." — *Richardson.*

2 In the Malay language the same word signifies women and flowers.

3 The capital of Shadukiam. See note p. 427.

And ruder words will soon rush in
To spread the breach that words begin;
And eyes forget the gentle ray
They wore in courtship's smiling day;
And voices lose the tone that shed
A tenderness round all they said;
Till fast declining one by one
The sweetnesses of love are gone,
And hearts so lately mingled seem
Like broken clouds, — or like the stream
That smiling left the mountain's brow
As tho' its waters ne'er could sever,
Yet ere it reach the plain below,
    Breaks into floods that part for ever.

Oh, you that have the charge of Love,
    Keep him in rosy bondage bound,
As in the Fields of Bliss above
    He sits with flowerets fettered
        round;[1] —
Loose not a tie that round him clings,
Nor ever let him use his wings;
For even an hour, a minute's flight
Will rob the plumes of half their light.
Like that celestial bird whose nest
    Is found beneath far Eastern skies,
Whose wings tho' radiant when at rest
    Lose all their glory when he flies![2]

Some difference of this dangerous kind, —
By which, tho' light, the links that bind
The fondest hearts may soon be riven;
Some shadow in Love's summer heaven,
Which, tho' a fleecy speck at first
May yet in awful thunder burst; —
Such cloud it is that now hangs over
The heart of the Imperial Lover,
And far hath banisht from his sight
His NOURMAHAL, his Haram's Light!
Hence is it on this happy night
When Pleasure thro' the fields and
        groves
Has let loose all her world of loves
And every heart has found its own,
He wanders joyless and alone

And weary as that bird of Thrace
Whose pinion knows no resting-place.[3]

In vain the loveliest cheeks and eyes
This Eden of the Earth supplies
    Come crowding round — the cheeks
        are pale,
The eyes are dim: — tho' rich the spot
With every flower this earth has got
    What is it to the nightingale
If there his darling rose is not?[4]
In vain the Valley's smiling throng
Worship him as he moves along;
He heeds them not — one smile of hers
Is worth a world of worshippers.
They but the Star's adorers are,
She is the Heaven that lights the Star!

Hence is it too that NOURMAHAL,
    Amid the luxuries of this hour,
Far from the joyous festival
    Sits in her own sequestered bower,
With no one near to soothe or aid,
But that inspired and wondrous maid,
NAMOUNA, the Enchantress; — one
O'er whom his race the golden sun
For unremembered years has run,
Yet never saw her blooming brow
Younger or fairer than 't is now.
Nay, rather, — as the west wind's sigh
Freshens the flower it passes by, —
Time's wing but seemed in stealing
        o'er
To leave her lovelier than before.
Yet on her smiles a sadness hung,
And when as oft she spoke or sung
Of other worlds there came a light
From her dark eyes so strangely bright
That all believed nor man nor earth
Were conscious of NAMOUNA's birth!
All spells and talismans she knew,
    From the great Mantra,[5] which around

---

1 See the representation of the Eastern Cupid,
pinioned closely round with wreaths of flowers,
in *Picart's "Cérémonies Religieuses."*

2 "Among the birds of Tonquin is a species
of goldfinch, which sings so melodiously that it
is called the Celestial Bird. Its wings, when it is
perched, appear variegated with beautiful colors,
but when it flies they lose all their splendor." —
Grosier.

3 "As these birds on the Bosphorus are never
known to rest, they are called by the French '*les
âmes damnées.*'" — *Dalloway.*

4 "You may place a hundred handfuls of
fragrant herbs and flowers before the nightingale, yet he wishes not in his constant heart for
more than the sweet breath of his beloved rose."
—*Jami.*

5 "He is said to have found the great *Man-
tra*, spell or talisman, through which he ruled
over the elements and spirits of all denominations." — *Wilford.*

The Air's sublimer Spirits drew,
  To the gold gems[1] of AFRIC, bound
Upon the wandering Arab's arm
To keep him from the Siltim's[2] harm.
And she had pledged her powerful art, —
Pledged it with all the zeal and heart
Of one who knew tho' high her sphere,
What 't was to lose a love so dear, —
To find some spell that should recall
Her Selim's[3] smile to NOURMAHAL!

'T was midnight — thro' the lattice
  wreathed
With woodbine many a perfume breathed
From plants that wake when others
  sleep,
From timid jasmine buds that keep
Their odor to themselves all day
But when the sunlight dies away
Let the delicious secret out
To every breeze that roams about; —
When thus NAMOUNA: — "'T is the
  hour
"That scatters spells on herb and flower,
"And garlands might be gathered now,
"That twined around the sleeper's brow
"Would make him dream of such de-
  lights,
"Such miracles and dazzling sights
"As Genii of the Sun behold
"At evening from their tents of gold
"Upon the horizon — where they play
"Till twilight comes and ray by ray
"Their sunny mansions melt away.
"Now too a chaplet might be wreathed
"Of buds o'er which the moon has
  breathed,
"Which worn by her whose love has
  strayed
  "Might bring some Peri from the
    skies,
"Some sprite, whose very soul is made
  "Of flowerets' breaths and lovers'
    sighs,
"And who might tell" —
              "For me, for me,"
Cried NOURMAHAL impatiently, —

1 "The gold jewels of Jinnie, which are
called by the Arabs El Herrez, from the supposed charm they contain." — *Jackson.*

2 "A demon, supposed to haunt woods, etc.,
in a human shape." — *Richardson.*

3 The name of Jehan-Guire before his accession
to the throne.

"Oh! twine that wreath for me to
  night."
Then rapidly with foot as light
As the young musk-roe's out she flew
To cull each shining leaf that grew
Beneath the moonlight's hallowing beams
For this enchanted Wreath of Dreams.
Anemones and Seas of Gold,[4]
And new-blown lilies of the river,
And those sweet flowerets that unfold
  Their buds on CAMADEVA's quiver; [5] —
The tuberose, with her silvery light,
  That in the Gardens of Malay
Is called the Mistress of the Night,[6]
So like a bride, scented and bright,
  She comes out when the sun 's away; —
Amaranths such as crown the maids
That wander thro' ZAMARA's shades;[7]
And the white moon-flower as it shows,
On SERENDIB's high crags to those
Who near the isle at evening sail,
Scenting her clove-trees in the gale;
In short all flowerets and all plants,
  From the divine Amrita tree[8]
That blesses heaven's habitants
  With fruits of immortality,
Down to the basil tuft[9] that waves
Its fragrant blossom over graves,
  And to the humble rosemary

4 "Hemasagara, or the Sea of Gold, with
flowers of the brightest gold color." — *Sir W.
Jones.*

5 "This tree (the Nagacesara) is one of the
most delightful on earth, and the delicious odor
of its blossoms justly gives them a place in the
quiver of Camadeva, or the God of Love." — *Id.*

6 "The Malayans style the tuberose (*poli-
anthes tuberosa*) Sandal Malam, or the Mistress
of the Night." — *Pennant.*

7 The people of the Batta country in Sumatra
(of which Zamara is one of the ancient names),
"when not engaged in war, lead an idle, inactive
life, passing the day in playing on a kind of flute,
crowned with garlands of flowers, among which
the globe-amaranthus, a native of the country,
mostly prevails." — *Marsden.*

8 "The largest and richest sort (of the Jambu
or rose-apple) is called Amrita, or immortal, and
the mythologists of Tibet apply the same word
to a celestial tree, bearing ambrosial fruit." —
Sir W. Jones.

9 Sweet basil, called Rayhan in Persia, and
generally found in churchyards.
  "The women in Egypt go, at least two days
in the week, to pray and weep at the sepulchres
of the dead; and the custom then is to throw
upon the tombs a sort of herb, which the Arabs
call *rihan*, and which is our sweet basil." —
Maillet, Lett. 10.

Whose sweets so thanklessly are shed
To scent the desert [1] and the dead: —
All in that garden bloom and all
Are gathered by young NOURMAHAL,
Who heaps her baskets with the flowers
  And leaves till they can hold no more;
Then to NAMOUNA flies and showers
  Upon her lap the shining store.
With what delight the Enchantress views
So many buds bathed with the dews
And beams of that blest hour! — her
    glance
  Spoke something past all mortal pleas-
    ures,
As in a kind of holy trance
  She hung above those fragrant treas-
    ures,
Bending to drink their balmy airs,
As if she mixt her soul with theirs.
And 't was indeed the perfume shed
From flowers and scented flame that fed
Her charmed life — for none had e'er
Beheld her taste of mortal fare,
Nor ever in aught earthly dip,
But the morn's dew, her roseate lip.
Filled with the cool, inspiring smell,
The Enchantress now begins her spell,
Thus singing as she winds and weaves
In mystic form the glittering leaves: —

I know where the winged visions dwell
  That around the night-bed play;
I know each herb and floweret's bell,
  Where they hide their wings by day.
      Then hasten we, maid,
      To twine our braid,
To-morrow the dreams and flowers will
    fade.

The image of love that nightly flies
  To visit the bashful maid,
Steals from the jasmine flower that sighs
  Its soul like her in the shade.
The dream of a future, happier hour
  That alights on misery's brow,
Springs out of the silvery almond-flower
  That blooms on a leafless bough.[2]
      Then hasten we, maid,

1 "In the Great Desert are found many stalks
of lavender and rosemary." — *Asiat. Res.*

2 "The almond-tree, with white flowers,
blossoms on the bare branches." — *Hasselquist.*

      To twine our braid,
To-morrow the dreams and flowers will
    fade.

The visions that oft to worldly eyes
  The glitter of mines unfold
Inhabit the mountain-herb [3] that dyes
  The tooth of the fawn like gold.
The phantom shapes — oh touch not
    them —
  That appal the murderer's sight,
Lurk in the fleshly mandrake's stem,
  That shrieks when pluckt at night!
      Then hasten we, maid,
      To twine our braid,
To-morrow the dreams and flowers will
    fade.

The dream of the injured, patient mind
  That smiles at the wrongs of men
Is found in the bruised and wounded rind
  Of the cinnamon, sweetest then.
      Then hasten we, maid,
      To twine our braid,
To-morrow the dreams and flowers will
    fade.

No sooner was the flowery crown
Placed on her head than sleep came down,
Gently as nights of summer fall,
Upon the lids of NOURMAHAL; —
And suddenly a tuneful breeze
As full of small, rich harmonies
As ever wind that o'er the tents
Of AZAB [4] blew was full of scents,

3 An herb on Mount Libanus, which is said
to communicate a yellow golden hue to the teeth
of the goats and other animals that graze upon it.
  Niebuhr thinks this may be the herb which
the Eastern alchymists look to as a means of
making gold. "Most of those alchymical enthusiasts think themselves sure of success, if
they could but find out the herb which gilds the
teeth and gives a yellow color to the flesh of the
sheep that eat it. Even the oil of this plant
must be of a golden color. It is called *Haschi-
schat ed dab.*"
  Father Jerom Dandini, however, asserts that
the teeth of the goats of Mount Libanus are of a
silver color; and adds, "this confirms me that
which I observed in Candia: to wit, that the
animals that live on Mount Ida eat a certain
herb which renders their teeth of a golden color;
which, according to my judgment, can not otherwise proceed than from the mines which are
under ground." — *Dandini,* "Voyage to Mount
Libanus."

4 The myrrh country.

Steals on her ear and floats and swells
  Like the first air of morning creeping
Into those wreathy, Red-Sea shells
  Where Love himself of old lay sleep-
    ing; [1]
And now a Spirit formed, 't would seem,
  Of music and of light, — so fair,
So brilliantly his features beam,
  And such a sound is in the air
Of sweetness when he waves his wings, —
Hovers around her and thus sings:

From CHINDARA'S [2] warbling fount I
    come,
  Called by that moonlight garland's
    spell;
From CHINDARA'S fount, my fairy home,
  Where in music, morn and night, I
    dwell.
Where lutes in the air are heard about
  And voices are singing the whole day
    long,
And every sigh the heart breathes out
  Is turned, as it leaves the lips, to
    song!
      Hither I come
      From my fairy home,
  And if there 's a magic in Music's
    strain
      I swear by the breath
      Of that moonlight wreath
  Thy Lover shall sigh at thy feet again.

For mine is the lay that lightly floats
And mine are the murmuring, dying notes
That fall as soft as snow on the sea
And melt in the heart as instantly: —
And the passionate strain that, deeply
    going,
  Refines the bosom it trembles thro'
As the musk-wind over the water blowing
  Ruffles the wave but sweetens it too.

Mine is the charm whose mystic sway
The Spirits of past Delight obey; —
Let but the tuneful talisman sound,
And they come like Genii hovering round.

And mine is the gentle song that bears
  From soul to soul the wishes of love,
As a bird that wafts thro' genial airs
  The cinnamon-seed from grove to
    grove. [3]

'T is I that mingle in one sweet measure
The past, the present and future of pleas-
    ure; [4]
When Memory links the tone that is
    gone
  With the blissful tone that 's still in the
    ear;
And Hope from a heavenly note flies on
  To a note more heavenly still that is
    near.

The warrior's heart when touched by
    me,
Can be as downy soft and as yielding be
As his own white plume that high amid
    death
Thro' the field has shone — yet moves
    with a breath!
And oh, how the eyes of Beauty glisten,
  When Music has reached her inward
    soul,
Like the silent stars that wink and listen
  While Heaven's eternal melodies roll.
      So hither I come
      From my fairy home,

1 "This idea (of deities living in shells) was
not unknown to the Greeks, who represent the
young Nerites, one of the Cupids, as living in
shells on the shores of the Red Sea." — *Wilford.*

2 "A fabulous fountain, where instruments
are said to be constantly playing." — *Richardson.*

3 "The Pompadour pigeon is the species,
which, by carrying the fruit of the cinnamon to
different places, is a great disseminator of this
valuable tree." — See *Brown's Illustr.* Tab. 19.

4 "Whenever our pleasure arises from a succession of sounds, it is a perception of a compli-
cated nature, made up of a *sensation* of the present
sound or note, and an *idea* or remembrance of the
foregoing, while their mixture and concurrence
produce such a mysterious delight, as neither
could have produced alone. And it is often
heightened by an anticipation of the succeeding
notes. Thus Sense, Memory, and Imagination,
are conjunctively employed." — *Gerrard* on
Taste.
This is exactly the Epicurean theory of Pleasure, as explained by Cicero : — "*quocirca corpus
gaudere tamdiu, dum præsentem sentiret volup-
tatem : animum et præsentem percipere pariter
cum corpore et prospicere venientem, nec præteri-
tam præterfluere sinere.*"
Madame de Staël accounts upon the same principle for the gratification we derive from *rhyme* :
—"*Elle est l'image de l'espérance et du souvenir.
Un son nous fait désirer celui qui doit lui répon-
dre, et quand le second retentit il nous rappelle
celui qui vient de nous échapper.*"

And if there's a magic in Music's strain,
  I swear by the breath
  Of that moonlight wreath
Thy Lover shall sigh at thy feet again.

'T is dawn — at least that earlier dawn
Whose glimpses are again withdrawn,[1]
As if the morn had waked, and then
Shut close her lids of light again.
And NOURMAHAL is up and trying
The wonders of her lute whose
    strings —
Oh, bliss!— now murmur like the sighing
From that ambrosial Spirit's wings.
And then her voice — 't is more than
    human —
Never till now had it been given
To lips of any mortal woman
To utter notes so fresh from heaven;
Sweet as the breath of angel sighs
  When angel sighs are most divine. —
"Oh! let it last till night," she cries,
  "And he is more than ever mine."

And hourly she renews the lay,
  So fearful lest its heavenly sweetness
Should ere the evening fade away, —
  For things so heavenly have such fleet-
    ness!
But far from fading it but grows
Richer, diviner as it flows;
Till rapt she dwells on every string
  And pours again each sound along,
Like echo, lost and languishing,
  In love with her own wondrous song.

That evening, (trusting that his soul
  Might be from haunting love released

By mirth, by music and the bowl,)
  The Imperial SELIM held a feast
In his magnificent Shalimar:[2] —
In whose Saloons, when the first star
Of evening o'er the waters trembled,
The Valley's loveliest all assembled;
All the bright creatures that like dreams
Glide thro' its foliage and drink beams
Of beauty from its founts and streams;[3]
And all those wandering minstrel-maids,
Who leave — how *can* they leave?— the
    shades
Of that dear Valley and are found
  Singing in gardens of the South [4]
Those songs that ne'er so sweetly sound
  As from a young Cashmerian's mouth.

There too the Haram's inmates smile;—
  Maids from the West, with sun-bright
    hair,
And from the Garden of the NILE,
  Delicate as the roses there;[5] —

[1] " The Persians have two mornings, the Soobhi Kazim and the Soobhi Sadig, the false and the real daybreak. They account for this phenomenon in a most whimsical manner. They say that as the sun rises from behind the Kohi Qaf (Mount Caucasus), it passes a hole perforated through that mountain, and that darting its rays through it, it is the cause of the Soobhi Kazim, or this temporary appearance of day-break. As it ascends, the earth is again veiled in darkness, until the sun rises above the mountain, and brings with it the Soobhi Sadig, or real morning." — *Scott Waring*. He thinks Milton may allude to this, when he says, —

  " Ere the blabbing Eastern scout,
   The nice morn on the Indian steep
   From her cabined loop-hole peep."

[2] " In the centre of the plain, as it approaches the Lake, one of the Delhi Emperors, I believe Shan Jehan, constructed a spacious garden called the Shalimar, which is abundantly stored with fruit-trees and flowering shrubs. Some of the rivulets which intersect the plain are led into a canal at the back of the garden, and flowing through its centre, or occasionally thrown into a variety of water-works, compose the chief beauty of the Shalimar. To decorate this spot the Mogul Princes of India have displayed an equal magnificence and taste; especially Jehan Gheer, who, with the enchanting Noor Mahl, made Kashmire his usual residence during the summer months. On arches thrown over the canal are erected, at equal distances, four or five suites of apartments, each consisting of a saloon, with four rooms at the angles, where the followers of the court attend, and the servants prepare sherbets, coffee, and the hookah. The frame of the doors of the principal saloon is composed of pieces of a stone of a black color, streaked with yellow lines, and of a closer grain and higher polish than porphyry. They were taken, it is said, from a Hindoo temple, by one of the Mogul princes, and are esteemed of great value." — *Forster*.

[3] "The waters of Cachemir are the more renowned from its being supposed that the Cachemirians are indebted for their beauty to them."— *Ali Yezdi*.

[4] " From him I received the following little Gazzel, or Love Song, the notes of which he committed to paper from the voice of one of those singing girls of Cashmere, who wander from that delightful valley over the various parts of India." — *Persian Miscellanies*.

[5] "The roses of the Jinan Nile, or Garden of the Nile (attached to the Emperor of Marocco's palace), are unequalled, and mattresses are made

Daughters of Love from CYPRUS' rocks,
With Paphian diamonds in their locks;[1]—
Light PERI forms such as there are
On the gold Meads of CANDAHAR;[2]
And they before whose sleepy eyes
    In their own bright Kathaian bowers
Sparkle such rainbow butterflies
    That they might fancy the rich flowers
That round them in the sun lay sighing
Had been by magic all set flying.[3]

Every thing young, every thing fair
From East and West is blushing there,
Except — except — oh, NOURMAHAL!
Thou loveliest, dearest of them all,
The one whose smile shone out alone,
Amidst a world the only one;
Whose light among so many lights
Was like that star on starry nights,
The seaman singles from the sky,
To steer his bark for ever by!
Thou wert not there — so SELIM thought,
    And every thing seemed drear without
        thee;
But, ah! thou wert, thou wert, — and
        brought
    Thy charm of song all fresh about thee.
Mingling unnoticed with a band
Of lutanists from many a land,
And veiled by such a mask as shades
The features of young Arab maids,[4] —
A mask that leaves but one eye free,
To do its best in witchery, —
She roved with beating heart around
    And waited trembling for the minute

When she might try if still the sound
    Of her loved lute had magic in it.

The board was spread with fruits and
    wine,
With grapes of gold, like those that
    shine
On CASBIN'S hills;[5] — pomegranates full
    Of melting sweetness, and the pears,
And sunniest apples[6] that CAUBUL
    In all its thousand gardens[7] bears;—
Plantains, the golden and the green,
MALAYA'S nectared mangusteen;[8]
Prunes of BOKHARA, and sweet nuts
    From the far groves of SAMARCAND,
And BASRA dates, and apricots,
    Seed of the Sun,[9] from IRAN'S land;—
With rich conserve of Visna cherries,[10]
Of orange flowers, and of those berries
That, wild and fresh, the young gazelles
Feed on in ERAC'S rocky dells.[11]
All these in richest vases smile,
    In baskets of pure santal-wood,
And urns of porcelain from that isle[12]
Sunk underneath the Indian flood,
Whence oft the lucky diver brings
Vases to grace the halls of kings.
Wines too of every clime and hue
Around their liquid lustre threw;
Amber Rosolli,[13] — the bright dew

of their leaves for the men of rank to recline
upon." — *Jackson.*

1 "On the side of a mountain near Paphos
there is a cavern which produces the most beautiful rock-crystal. On account of its brilliancy
it has been called the Paphian diamond." —
Mariti.

2 "There is a part of Candahar, called Peria,
or Fairy Land." — *Thevenot.* In some of those
countries to the north of India vegetable gold is
supposed to be produced.

3 "These are the butterflies which are called
in the Chinese language Flying Leaves. Some
of them have such shining colors, and are so
variegated, that they may be called flying flowers;
and indeed they are always produced in the finest
flower-gardens." — *Dunn.*

4 "The Arabian women wear black masks
with little clasps prettily ordered." — *Carreri.*
Niebuhr mentions their showing but one eye in
conversation.

5 "The golden grapes of Casbin." — *Description of Persia.*

6 "The fruits exported from Caubul are apples, pears, pomegranates," etc. — *Elphinstone.*

7 "We sat down under a tree, listened to the
birds, and talked with the son of our Mehmaun-
dar about our country and Caubul, of which he
gave an enchanting account: that city and its
100,000 gardens," etc. — *Id.*

8 "The mangusteen, the most delicate fruit
in the world; the pride of the Malay islands." —
Marsden.

9 "A delicious kind of apricot, called by the
Persians tokmek-shems, signifying sun's seed."
— *Description of Persia.*

10 "Sweetmeats, in a crystal cup, consisting
of rose-leaves in conserve, with lemon of Visna
cherry, orange flowers," etc. — *Russel.*

11 "Antelopes cropping the fresh berries of
Erac." — The *Moallakat,* Poem of Tarafa.

12 "Mauri-ga-Sima, an island near Formosa,
supposed to have been sunk in the sea for the
crimes of its inhabitants. The vessels which the
fishermen and divers bring up from it are sold
at an immense price in China and Japan."—See
Kempfer.

13 Persian Tales.

From vineyards of the Green-Sea gush-
　　　ing; [1]
And SHIRAZ wine that richly ran
　As if that jewel large and rare,
The ruby for which KUBLAI–KHAN
Offered a city's wealth,[2] was blushing
　Melted within the goblets there!

And amply SELIM quaffs of each,
And seems resolved the flood shall reach
His inward heart, — shedding around
A genial deluge, as they run,
That soon shall leave no spot undrowned
For Love to rest his wings upon.
He little knew how well the boy
　Can float upon a goblet's streams,
Lighting them with his smile of joy;—
　As bards have seen him in their dreams,
Down the blue GANGES laughing glide
　Upon a rosy lotus wreath,[3]
Catching new lustre from the tide
　That with his image shone beneath.

But what are cups without the aid
Of song to speed them as they flow?
And see — a lovely Georgian maid
　With all the bloom, the freshened
　　glow
Of her own country maidens' looks,
When warm they rise from TEFLIS'
　brooks; [4]
And with an eye whose restless ray,
　Full, floating, dark — oh, he, who
　　knows
His heart is weak, of Heaven should
　pray
　To guard him from such eyes as
　　those! —
With a voluptuous wildness flings
Her snowy hand across the strings
Of a syrinda [5] and thus sings:—

Come hither, come hither — by night and
　　by day,
　We linger in pleasures that never are
　　gone;
Like the waves of the summer as one dies
　　away
　Another as sweet and as shining comes
　　on.
And the love that is o'er, in expiring gives
　　birth
　To a new one as warm, as unequalled
　　in bliss;
And, oh! if there be an Elysium on
　　earth,
　　　It is this, it is this.[6]

Here maidens are sighing, and fragrant
　　their sigh
　As the flower of the Amra just oped by
　　a bee; [7]
And precious their tears as that rain from
　　the sky,[8]
　Which turns into pearls as it falls in
　　the sea.
Oh! think what the kiss and the smile
　　must be worth
　When the sigh and the tear are so per-
　　fect in bliss,
And own if there be an Elysium on
　　earth,
　　　It is this, it is this.

Here sparkles the nectar that hallowed
　　by love
　Could draw down those angels of old
　　from their sphere,
Who for wine of this earth [9] left the
　　fountains above,
　And forgot heaven's stars for the eyes
　　we have here.

1 The white wine of Kishma.

2 "The King of Zeilan is said to have the
very finest ruby that was ever seen. Kublai-
Khan sent and offered the value of a city for it,
but the king answered he would not give it for
the treasure of the world." — *Marco Polo.*

3 The Indians feign that Cupid was first
seen floating down the Ganges on the Nym-
phæa Nelumbo. — See *Pennant.*

4 Teflis is celebrated for its natural warm
baths. — See *Ebn Haukal.*

5 " The Indian Syrinda, or guitar."— *Symez.*

6 " Around the exterior of the Dewan Khafs
(a building of Shah Allum's) in the cornice are
the following lines in letters of gold upon a ground
of white marble — ' *If there be a paradise upon
earth, it is this, it is this.*' " — *Franklin.*

7 " Delightful are the flowers of the Amra
trees on the mountain-tops while the murmuring
bees pursue their voluptuous toil." — *Song of
Jayadeva.*

8 " The Nison or drops of spring rain, which
they believe to produce pearls if they fall into
shells." — *Richardson.*

9 For an account of the share which wine had
in the fall of the angels, see *Mariti.*

And, blest with the odor our goblet gives forth,
  What Spirit the sweets of his Eden would miss?
For, oh! if there be an Elysium on earth,
  It is this, it is this.

The Georgian's song was scarcely mute,
  When the same measure, sound for sound,
Was caught up by another lute
  And so divinely breathed around
That all stood husht and wondering,
  And turned and lookt into the air,
As if they thought to see the wing
  Of ISRAFIL [1] the Angel there; —
So powerfully on every soul
That new, enchanted measure stole,
While now a voice sweet as the note
Of the charmed lute was heard to float
Along its chords and so entwine
  Its sounds with theirs that none knew whether
The voice or lute was most divine,
  So wondrously they went together: —

There's a bliss beyond all that the minstrel has told,
  When two that are linkt in one heavenly tie,
With heart never changing and brow never cold,
  Love on thro' all ills and love on till they die!
One hour of a passion so sacred is worth
  Whole ages of heartless and wandering bliss;
And, oh! if there be an Elysium on earth,
  It is this, it is this.

'T was not the air, 't was not the words,
But that deep magic in the chords
And in the lips that gave such power
As Music knew not till that hour.
At once a hundred voices said,
" It is the maskt Arabian maid! "
While SELIM who had felt the strain
Deepest of any and had lain
Some minutes rapt as in a trance
  After the fairy sounds were o'er,
Too inly touched for utterance,
  Now motioned with his hand for more: —

1 The Angel of Music. — See note, p. 456.

Fly to the desert, fly with me,
Our Arab tents are rude for thee;
But oh! the choice what heart can doubt,
Of tents with love or thrones without?

Our rocks are rough, but smiling there
The acacia waves her yellow hair,
Lonely and sweet nor loved the less
For flowering in a wilderness.

Our sands are bare, but down their slope
The silvery-footed antelope
As gracefully and gayly springs
As o'er the marble courts of kings.

Then come — thy Arab maid will be
The loved and lone acacia-tree,
The antelope whose feet shall bless
With their light sound thy loneliness.

Oh! there are looks and tones that dart
An instant sunshine thro' the heart, —
As if the soul that minute caught
Some treasure it thro' life had sought;

As if the very lips and eyes,
Predestined to have all our sighs
And never be forgot again,
Sparkled and spoke before us then!

So came thy every glance and tone,
When first on me they breathed and shone,
New as if brought from other spheres
Yet welcome as if loved for years.

Then fly with me, — if thou hast known
No other flame nor falsely thrown
A gem away, that thou hadst sworn
Should ever in thy heart be worn.

Come if the love thou hast for me
Is pure and fresh as mine for thee, —
Fresh as the fountain under ground,
When first 't is by the lapwing found. [2]

But if for me thou dost forsake
Some other maid and rudely break
Her worship image from its base,
To give to me the ruined place; —

2 The Hudhud, or Lapwing, is supposed to have the power of discovering water under ground.

Then fare thee well — I 'd rather make
My bower upon some icy lake
When thawing suns begin to shine
Than trust to love so false as thine

There was a pathos in this lay,
　　That, even without enchantment's art,
Would instantly have found its way
　　Deep into SELIM'S burning heart;
But breathing as it did a tone
To earthly lutes and lips unknown;
With every chord fresh from the touch
Of Music's Spirit, — 't was too much !
Starting he dasht away the cup, —
　　Which all the time of this sweet air
His hand had held, untasted, up,
　　As if 't were fixt by magic there, —
And naming her, so long unnamed,
So long unseen, wildly exclaimed,

"Oh NOURMAHAL! oh NOURMAHAL!
　　"Hadst thou but sung this witching strain,
"I could forget — forgive thee all
　　"And never leave those eyes again."

The mask is off — the charm is wrought —
And SELIM to his heart has caught,
In blushes, more than ever bright,
His NOURMAHAL, his Haram's Light !
And well do vanisht frowns enhance
The charm of every brightened glance;
And dearer seems each dawning smile
For having lost its light awhile:
And happier now for all her sighs
As on his arm her head reposes
She whispers him, with laughing eyes,
　　"Remember, love, the Feast of Roses!"

FADLADEEN, at the conclusion of this light rhapsody, took occasion to sum up his opinion of the young Cashmerian's poetry, — of which, he trusted, they had that evening heard the last. Having recapitulated the epithets, "frivolous" — "inharmonious" — "nonsensical," he proceeded to say that, viewed in the most favorable light it resembled one of those Maldivian boats, to which the Princess had alluded in the relation of her dream,[1] — a slight, gilded thing, sent adrift without rudder or ballast, and with nothing but vapid sweets and faded flowers on board. The profusion, indeed, of flowers and birds, which this poet had ready on all occasions, — not to mention dews, gems, etc. — was a most oppressive kind of opulence to his hearers; and had the unlucky effect of giving to his style all the glitter of the flower-garden without its method, and all the flutter of the aviary without its song. In addition to this, he chose his subjects badly, and was always most inspired by the worst parts of them. The charms of paganism, the merits of rebellion, — these were the themes honored with his particular enthusiasm; and, in the poem just recited, one of his most palatable passages was in praise of that beverage of the Unfaithful, wine; — "being, perhaps," said he, relaxing into a smile, as conscious of his own character in the Haram on this point, "one of those bards, whose fancy owes all its illumination to the grape, like that painted porcelain,[2] so curious and so rare, whose images are only visible when liquor is poured into it." Upon the whole, it was his opinion, from the specimens which they had heard, and which, he begged to say, were the most tiresome part of the journey, that — whatever other merits this well-dressed young gentleman might possess — poetry was by no means his proper avocation: "and indeed," concluded the critic, "from his fondness for flowers and for birds, I would venture to suggest that a florist or a bird-catcher is a much more suitable calling for him than a poet."

1 See p. 445.

2 "The Chinese had formerly the art of painting on the sides of porcelain vessels fish and other animals, which were only perceptible when the vessel was full of some liquor. They call this species Kia-tsin, that is, *azure is put in press*, on account of the manner in which the azure is laid on." — "They are every now and then trying to discover the art of this magical painting, but to no purpose." — *Dunn.*

They had now begun to ascend those barren mountains, which separate Cashmere from the rest of India; and, as the heats were intolerable, and the time of their encampments limited to the few hours necessary for refreshment and repose, there was an end to all their delightful evenings, and LALLA ROOKH saw no more of FERAMORZ. She now felt that her short dream of happiness was over, and that she had nothing but the recollection of its few blissful hours, like the one draught of sweet water that serves the camel across the wilderness, to be her heart's refreshment during the dreary waste of life that was before her. The blight that had fallen upon her spirits soon found its way to her cheek, and her ladies saw with regret — though not without some suspicion of the cause — that the beauty of their mistress, of which they were almost as proud as of their own, was fast vanishing away at the very moment of all when she had most need of it. What must the King of Bucharia feel, when, instead of the lively and beautiful LALLA ROOKH, whom the poets of Delhi had described as more perfect than the divinest images in the house of AZOR,[1] he should receive a pale and inanimate victim, upon whose cheek neither health nor pleasure bloomed, and from whose eyes Love had fled, — to hide himself in her heart?

If any thing could have charmed away the melancholy of her spirits, it would have been the fresh airs and enchanting scenery of that Valley, which the Persians so justly called the Unequalled.[2] But neither the coolness of its atmosphere, so luxurious after toiling up those bare and burning mountains, — neither the splendor of the minarets and pagodas, that shone out from the depth of its woods, nor the grottoes, hermitages, and miraculous fountains,[3] which make every spot of that region holy ground, — neither the countless waterfalls, that rush into the Valley from all those high and romantic mountains that encircle it, nor the fair city on the Lake, whose houses, roofed with flowers,[4] appeared at a distance like one vast and variegated parterre; — not all these wonders and glories of the most lovely country under the sun could steal her heart for a minute from those sad thoughts which but darkened and grew bitterer every step she advanced.

The gay pomps and processions that met her upon her entrance into the Valley, and the magnificence with which the roads all along were decorated, did honor to the taste and gallantry of the young King. It was night when they approached the city, and, for the last two miles, they had passed under arches, thrown from hedge to hedge, festooned with only those rarest roses from which the Attar Gul, more precious than gold, is distilled, and illuminated in rich and

---

1 An eminent carver of idols, said in the Koran to be father to Abraham. "I have such a lovely idol as is not to be met with in the house of Azor." — *Hafiz.*

2 Kachmire be Nazeer. — *Forster.*

3 "The pardonable superstition of the sequestered inhabitants has multiplied the places of worship of Mahadeo, of Beschan, and of Brama. All Cashmere is holy land, and miraculous fountains abound." — *Major Rennel's* Memoirs of a Map of Hindostan.

Jehan-Guire mentions "a fountain in Cashmere called Tirnagh, which signifies a snake; probably because some large snake had formerly been seen there." — "During the lifetime of my father, I went twice to this fountain, which is about twenty coss from the city of Cashmere. The vestiges of places of worship and sanctity are to be traced without number amongst the ruins and the caves, which are interspersed in its neighborhood." — *Toozek Jehangeery.* — v. *Asiat. Misc.* vol. ii.

There is another account of Caahmere by Abul-Fazil, the author of the Ayin-Acbaree, "who," says *Major Rennel,* "appears to have caught some of the enthusiasm of the valley, by his description of the holy places in it."

4 "On a standing roof of wood is laid a covering of fine earth, which shelters the building from the great quantity of snow that falls in the winter season. This fence communicates an equal warmth in winter, as a refreshing coolness in the summer season, when the tops of the houses, which are planted with a variety of flowers, exhibit at a distance the spacious view of a beautifully checkered parterre." — *Forster.*

fanciful forms with lanterns of the triple-colored tortoise-shell of Pegu.[1] Sometimes, from a dark wood by the side of the road, a display of fireworks would break out, so sudden and so brilliant, that a Brahmin might fancy he beheld that grove, in whose purple shade the God of Battles was born, bursting into a flame at the moment of his birth; — while, at other times, a quick and playful irradiation continued to brighten all the fields and gardens by which they passed, forming a line of dancing lights along the horizon; like the meteors of the north as they are seen by those hunters [2] who pursue the white and blue foxes on the confines of the Icy Sea.

These arches and fireworks delighted the Ladies of the Princess exceedingly; and, with their usual good logic, they deduced from his taste for illuminations, that the King of Bucharia would make the most exemplary husband imaginable. Nor, indeed, could LALLA ROOKH herself help feeling the kindness and splendor with which the young bridegroom welcomed her; — but she also felt how painful is the gratitude which kindness from those we cannot love excites; and that their best blandishments come over the heart with all that chilling and deadly sweetness which we can fancy in the cold, odoriferous wind [3] that is to blow over this earth in the last days.

The marriage was fixed for the morning after her arrival, when she was, for the first time, to be presented to the monarch in that Imperial Palace beyond the lake, called the Shalimar. Though never before had a night of more wakeful and anxious thought been passed in the Happy Valley, yet, when she rose in the morning, and her Ladies came around her, to assist in the adjustment of the bridal ornaments, they thought they had never seen her look half so beautiful. What she had lost of the bloom and radiancy of her charms was more than made up by that intellectual expression, that soul beaming forth from the eyes, which is worth all the rest of loveliness. When they had tinged her fingers with the Henna leaf, and placed upon her brow a small coronet of jewels, of the shape worn by the ancient Queens of Bucharia, they flung over her head the rose-colored bridal veil, and she proceeded to the barge that was to convey her across the lake; — first kissing, with a mournful look, the little amulet of cornelian, which her father at parting had hung about her neck.

The morning was as fresh and fair as the maid on whose nuptials it rose, and the shining lake, all covered with boats, the minstrels playing upon the shores of the islands, and the crowded summer-houses on the green hills around, with shawls and banners waving from their roofs, presented such a picture of animated rejoicing, as only she, who was the object of it all, did not feel with transport. To LALLA ROOKH alone it was a melancholy pageant; nor could she have even borne to look upon the scene, were it not for a hope that, among the crowds around, she might once more perhaps catch a glimpse of FERAMORZ. So much was her imagination haunted by this thought that there was scarcely an islet or boat she passed on the way at which her heart did not flutter with the momentary fancy that he was there. Happy, in her eyes, the humblest slave upon whom the light of his dear

---

1 " Two hundred slaves there are, who have no other office than to hunt the woods and marshes for triple-colored tortoises for the King's Vivary. Of the shells of these also lanterns are made." — *Vincent le Blanc's* Travels.

2 For a description of the Aurora Borealis as it appears to these hunters, v. *Encyclopædia.*

3 This wind, which is to blow from Syria Damascena, is, according to the Mahometans, one of the signs of the Last Day's approach.
Another of the signs is, " Great distress in the world, so that a man when he passes by another's grave shall say, Would to God I were in his place!" — *Sale's* Preliminary Discourse.

looks fell! — In the barge immediately after the Princess sat FADLADEEN, with his silken curtains thrown widely apart, that all might have the benefit of his august presence, and with his head full of the speech he was to deliver to the King, "concerning FERAMORZ and literature and the Chabuk as connected therewith."

They now had entered the canal which leads from the Lake to the splendid domes and saloons of the Shalimar and went gliding on through the gardens that ascended from each bank, full of flowering shrubs that made the air all perfume; while from the middle of the canal rose jets of water, smooth and unbroken, to such a dazzling height that they stood like tall pillars of diamond in the sunshine. After sailing under the arches of various saloons they at length arrived at the last and most magnificent, where the monarch awaited the coming of his bride; and such was the agitation of her heart and frame that it was with difficulty she could walk up the marble steps which were covered with cloth of gold for her ascent from the barge. At the end of the hall stood two thrones, as precious as the Cerulean Throne of Koolburga,[1] on one of which sat ALIRIS, the youthful King of Bucharia, and on the other was in a few minutes to be placed the most beautiful Princess in the world. Immediately upon the entrance of LALLA ROOKH into the saloon the monarch descended from his throne to meet her; but scarcely had he time to take her hand in his when she screamed with surprise and fainted at his feet. It was FERAMORZ himself that stood before her! — FERAMORZ was, himself, the Sovereign of Bucharia, who in this disguise had accompanied his young bride from Delhi, and having won her love as an humble minstrel now amply deserved to enjoy it as a King.

The consternation of FADLADEEN at this discovery was, for the moment, almost pitiable. But change of opinion is a resource too convenient in courts for this experienced courtier not to have learned to avail himself of it. His criticisms were all, of course, recanted instantly: he was seized with an admiration of the King's verses, as unbounded as, he begged him to believe, it was disinterested; and the following week saw him in possession of an additional place, swearing by all the Saints of Islam that never had there existed so great a poet as the Monarch ALIRIS, and moreover ready to prescribe his favorite regimen of the Chabuk for every man, woman and child that dared to think otherwise.

Of the happiness of the King and Queen of Bucharia, after such a beginning, there can be but little doubt; and among the lesser symptoms it is recorded of LALLA ROOKH that to the day of her death in memory of their delightful journey she never called the King by any other name than FERAMORZ.

---

1 "On Mahommed Shaw's return to Koolburga (the capital of Dekkan), he made a great festival, and mounted this throne with much pomp and magnificence, calling it Firozeh or Cerulean. I have heard some old persons, who saw the throne Firozeh in the reign of Sultan Mamood Bhamenee, describe it. They say that it was in length nine feet, and three in breadth; made of ebony covered with plates of pure gold, and set with precious stones of immense value. Every prince of the house of Bhamenee, who possessed this throne, made a point of adding to it some rich stones; so that when in the reign of Sultan Mamood it was taken to pieces to remove some of the jewels to be set in vases and cups, the jewellers valued it at one corore of oons (nearly four millions sterling). I learned also that it was called Firozeh from being partly enamelled of a sky-blue color which was in time totally concealed by the number of jewels." — *Ferishta.*

THE LOVES OF THE ANGELS.

PREFACE.

THE Eastern story of the angels Harut and Marut [1] and the Rabbinical fictions of the loves of Uzziel and Shámchazai [2] are the only sources to which I need refer for the origin of the notion on which this Romance is founded. In addition to the fitness of the subject for poetry, it struck me also as capable of affording an allegorical medium through which might be shadowed out (as I have endeavored to do in the following stories) the fall of the Soul from its original purity [3] — the loss of light and happiness which it suffers, in the pursuit of this world's perishable pleasures — and the punishments both from conscience and Divine justice with which impurity, pride, and presumptuous inquiry into the awful secrets of Heaven are sure to be visited. The beautiful story of Cupid and Psyche owes its chief charm to this sort of "veiled meaning," and it has been my wish (however I may have failed in the attempt) to communicate to the following pages the same *moral* interest.

Among the doctrines or notions derived by Plato from the East, one of the most natural and sublime is that which inculcates the pre-existence of the soul and its gradual descent into this dark material world from that region of spirit and light which it is supposed to have once inhabited and to which after a long lapse of purification and trial it will return. This belief under various symbolical forms may be traced through almost all the Oriental theologies. The Chaldeans represent the Soul as originally endowed with wings which fall away when it sinks from its native element and must be re-produced before it can hope to return. Some disciples of Zoroaster once inquired of him, "How the wings of the Soul might be made to grow again?"

"By sprinkling them," he replied, "with the Waters of Life."

"But where are those Waters to be found?" they asked.

"In the Garden of God," replied Zoroaster.

---

1 See note on page 485.

2 Hyde, "*de Relig. Vet. Persarum*," p. 272.

3 The account which Macrobius gives * of the downward journey of the Soul, through that gate of the zodiac which opens into the lower spheres, is a curious specimen of the wild fancies that passed for philosophy in ancient times.

In the system of Manes, the luminous or spiritual principle owes its corruption not to any evil tendency of its own, but to a violent inroad of the spirits of darkness, who, finding themselves in the neighborhood of this pure light, and becoming passionately enamoured of its beauty, break the boundaries between them, and take forcible possession of it.†

   * In "*Somn. Scipionis*," *cap.* 12.

   † See a Treatise "*De la Religion des Perses*," by the Abbé Foucher, *Mémoires de l'Académie*, *tom.* xxxi. p. 456.

The mythology of the Persians has allegorized the same doctrine, in the history of those genii of light who strayed from their dwellings in the stars and obscured their original nature by mixture with this material sphere; while the Egyptians connecting it with the descent and ascent of the sun in the zodiac considered Autumn as emblematic of the Soul's decline toward darkness and the re-appearance of Spring as its return to life and light.

Besides the chief spirits of the Mahometan heaven, such as Gabriel the angel of Revelation, Israfil by whom the last trumpet is to be sounded, and Azrael the angel of death, there were also a number of subaltern intelligences of which tradition has preserved the names, appointed to preside over the different stages or ascents into which the celestial world was supposed to be divided.[1] Thus Kelail governs the fifth heaven; while Sadiel, the presiding spirit of the third, is also employed in steadying the motions of the earth which would be in a constant state of agitation if this angel did not keep his foot planted upon its orb.[2]

Among other miraculous interpositions in favor of Mahomet we find commemorated in the pages of the Koran the appearance of five thousand angels on his side at the battle of Bedr.

The ancient Persians supposed that Ormuzd appointed thirty angels to preside successively over the days of the month and twelve greater ones to assume the government of the months themselves; among whom Bahman (to whom Ormuzd committed the custody of all animals, except man,) was the greatest. Mihr, the angel of the 7th month, was also the spirit that watched over the affairs of friendship and love; — Chûr had the care of the disk of the sun; — Mah was agent for the concerns of the moon; — Isphandârmaz (whom Cazvin calls the Spirit of the Earth) was the tutelar genius of good and virtuous women, etc. For all this the reader may consult the 19th and 20th chapters of Hyde, " *de Religione Veterum Persarum,*" where the names and attributes of these daily and monthly angels are with much minuteness and erudition explained. It appears from the Zend-avesta that the Persians had a certain office or prayer for every day of the month (addressed to the particular angel who presided over it), which they called the Sirouzé.

The Celestial Hierarchy of the Syrians, as described by Kircher, appears to be the most regularly graduated of any of these systems. In the sphere of the Moon they placed the angels, in that of Mercury the archangels, Venus and the Sun contained the Principalities and the Powers; and so on to the summit of the planetary system, where, in the sphere of Saturn, the Thrones had their station. Above this was the habitation of the Cherubim in the sphere of the fixed stars; and still higher, in the region of those stars which are so distant as to be imperceptible, the Seraphim, we are told, the most perfect of all celestial creatures, dwelt.

The Sabeans also (as D'Herbelot tells us) had their classes of angels, to whom they prayed as mediators, or intercessors; and the Arabians worshipped *female* angels, whom they called Benab Hasche, or, Daughters of God.

---

1 " We adorned the lower heaven with lights, and placed therein a guard of angels." — *Koran,* chap. xli.

2 See D'Herbelot, *passim.*

THE LOVES OF THE ANGELS.

'T was when the world was in its prime,
  When the fresh stars had just begun
Their race of glory and young Time
  Told his first birth-days by the sun;
When in the light of Nature's dawn
  Rejoicing, men and angels met [1]
On the high hill and sunny lawn,—
Ere sorrow came or Sin had drawn
  'Twixt man and heaven her curtain
    yet!
When earth lay nearer to the skies
  Than in these days of crime and
    woe,
And mortals saw without surprise
In the mid-air angelic eyes
  Gazing upon this world below.

Alas! that Passion should profane
  Even then the morning of the earth!
That, sadder still, the fatal stain
  Should fall on hearts of heavenly
    birth —
And that from Woman's love should
    fall
So dark a stain, most sad of all!

One evening, in that primal hour,
  On a hill's side where hung the ray
Of sunset brightening rill and bower,
  Three noble youths conversing lay;
And, as they lookt from time to time
  To the far sky where Daylight furled
His radiant wing, their brows sublime
  Bespoke them of that distant world —
Spirits who once in brotherhood
Of faith and bliss near ALLA stood,
And o'er whose cheeks full oft had
    blown

The wind that breathes from ALLA's
    throne,[2]
Creatures of light such as *still* play,
  Like motes in sunshine, round the
    Lord,
And thro' their infinite array
Transmit each moment, night and day,
  The echo of His luminous word!

Of Heaven they spoke and, still more
    oft,
  Of the bright eyes that charmed them
    thence;
Till yielding gradual to the soft
  And balmy evening's influence —
The silent breathing of the flowers —
  The melting light that beamed above,
As on their first, fond, erring hours, —
  Each told the story of his love,
The history of that hour unblest,
  When like a bird from its high nest
Won down by fascinating eyes,
  For Woman's smile he lost the skies.

The First who spoke was one, with look
  The least celestial of the three —
A Spirit of light mould that took
  The prints of earth most yieldingly;
Who even in heaven was not of those
  Nearest the Throne [3] but held a place

---

1 The Mahometans believe, says D'Herbelot, that in that early period of the world, "*les hommes n'eurent qu'une seule religion, et furent souvent visités des Anges, qui leur donnoient la main.*"

2 "To which will be joined the sound of the bells hanging on the trees, which will be put in motion by the wind proceeding from the Throne, so often as the Blessed wish for music." — See *Sale's Koran, Prelim. Dissert.*

3 The ancient Persians supposed that this Throne was placed in the Sun, and that through the stars were distributed the various classes of Angels that encircled it.
The Basilidians supposed that there were three hundred and sixty-five orders of angels, "*dont la perfection alloit en décroissant à mesure qu'ils s'éloignoient de la première classe d'esprits placés dans le premier ciel.*" See *Dupuis, "Orig. des Cultes," tom. ii. p. 112.*

Far off among those shining rows
   That circle out thro' endless space,
And o'er whose wings the light from
   Him
In Heaven's centre falls most dim.

Still fair and glorious, he but shone
Among those youths the unheavenliest
   one —
A creature to whom light remained
From Eden still, but altered, stained,
And o'er whose brow not Love alone
   A blight had in his transit cast,
But other, earthlier joys had gone,
   And left their foot-prints as they past.
Sighing, as back thro' ages flown,
   Like a tomb-searcher, Memory ran,
Lifting each shroud that Time had
   thrown
   O'er buried hopes, he thus began: —

FIRST ANGEL'S STORY.

'T was in a land that far away
   Into the golden orient lies,
Where Nature knows not night's delay,
But springs to meet her bridegroom,
   Day,
   Upon the threshold of the skies,
One morn, on earthly mission sent,[1]
   And mid-way choosing where to light,
I saw from the blue element —
   Oh beautiful, but fatal sight! —
One of earth's fairest womankind,
Half veiled from view, or rather shrined
In the clear crystal of a brook;
   Which while it hid no single gleam
Of her young beauties made them look
   More spirit-like, as they might seem
   Thro' the dim shadowing of a dream.
Pausing in wonder I lookt on,
   While playfully around her breaking
The waters that like diamonds shone
   She moved in light of her own making.
At length as from that airy height
I gently lowered my breathless flight,
The tremble of my wings all o'er
   (For thro' each plume I felt the thrill)

1 It appears that, in most languages, the term employed for an angel means also a messenger. Firischteh, the Persian word for angel, is derived (says D'Herbelot) from the verb Firischtin, to send. The Hebrew term, too, Melak, has the same signification.

Startled her as she reached the shore
Of that small lake — her mirror still —
Above whose brink she stood, like snow
When rosy with a sunset glow,
Never shall I forget those eyes! —
The shame, the innocent surprise
Of that bright face when in the air
Uplooking she beheld me there.
It seemed as if each thought and look
   And motion were that minute chained
Fast to the spot, such root she took,
And — like a sunflower by a brook,
   With face upturned — so still re-
   mained!

In pity to the wondering maid,
   Tho' loath from such a vision turning,
Downward I bent, beneath the shade
   Of my spread wings to hide the burn-
   ing
Of glances, which — I well could feel —
   For me, for her, too warmly shone;
But ere I could again unseal
   My restless eyes or even steal
   One sidelong look the maid was
   gone —
Hid from me in the forest leaves,
   Sudden as when in all her charms
Of full-blown light some cloud receives
   The Moon into his dusky arms.

'T is not in words to tell the power,
The despotism that from that hour
Passion held o'er me. Day and night
   I sought around each neighboring
   spot;
And in the chase of this sweet light,
   My task and heaven and all forgot; —
All but the one, sole, haunting dream
Of her I saw in that bright stream.

Nor was it long ere by her side
   I found myself whole happy days
Listening to words whose music vied
   With our own Eden's seraph lays,
When seraph lays are warmed by love,
But wanting *that*, far, far above! —
And looking into eyes where, blue
And beautiful, like skies seen thro'
The sleeping wave, for me there shone
A heaven, more worship than my own.
Oh what, while I could hear and see
Such words and looks, was heaven to
   me?

Tho' gross the air on earth I drew,
'T was blessed, while she breathed it
    too;
Tho' dark the flowers, tho' dim the sky,
Love lent them light while she was nigh.
Throughout creation I but knew
Two separate worlds — the *one*, that
    small,
Beloved and consecrated spot
Where LEA *was* — the other, all
    The dull, wide waste where she was
    not!

But vain my suit, my madness vain;
Tho' gladly, from her eyes to gain
    One earthly look, one stray desire,
I would have torn the wings that hung
    Furled at my back and o'er the Fire
In GEHIM'S[1] pit their fragments flung; —
'T was hopeless all — pure and unmoved
She stood as lilies in the light
    Of the hot noon but look more
    white; —
And tho' she loved me, deeply loved,
'T was not as man, as mortal — no,
Nothing of earth was in that glow —
She loved me but as one, of race
Angelic, from that radiant place
She saw so oft in dreams — that Heaven
    To which her prayers at morn were
    sent
And on whose light she gazed at even,
Wishing for wings that she might go
Out of this shadowy world below
    To that free, glorious element!

Well I remember by her side
Sitting at rosy even-tide,
When, — turning to the star whose head
Lookt out as from a bridal bed,

1 The name given by the Mahometans to the
infernal regions, over which, they say, the angel
Tabhek presides.
    By the seven gates of hell, mentioned in the
Koran, the commentators understand seven different departments or wards, in which seven different sorts of sinners are to be punished. The
first, called Gehennem, is for sinful Mussulmans;
the second, Ladha, for Christian offenders; the
third, Hothama, is appointed for Jews; and the
fourth and fifth, called Sair and Sacar, are destined to receive the Sabæans and the worshippers
of fire: in the sixth, named Gehim, those pagans
and idolaters who admit a plurality of gods are
placed; while into the abyss of the seventh,
called Derk Asfal, or the Deepest, the hypocritical canters of *all* religions are thrown.

At that mute, blushing hour, — she said,
"Oh! that it were my doom to be
    "The Spirit of yon beauteous star,
"Dwelling up there in purity,
    "Alone as all such bright things are; —
"My sole employ to pray and shine,
    "To light my censer at the sun,
"And cast its fire towards the shrine
    "Of Him in heaven, the Eternal
    One!"

So innocent the maid, so free
    From mortal taint in soul and frame,
Whom 't was my crime — my destiny —
    To love, ay, burn for, with a flame
To which earth's wildest fires are tame.
Had you but seen her look when first
From my mad lips the avowal burst;
Not angered — no! — the feeling came
From depths beyond mere anger's
    flame —
It was a sorrow calm as deep,
A mournfulness that could not weep,
So filled her heart was to the brink,
So fixt and frozen with grief to think
That angel natures — that even I
Whose love she clung to, as the tie
Between her spirit and the sky —
Should fall thus headlong from the height
Of all that heaven hath pure and
    bright!

That very night — my heart had grown
    Impatient of its inward burning;
The term, too, of my stay was flown,
And the bright Watchers near the throne,
Already, if a meteor shone
Between them and this nether zone,
    Thought 't was their herald's wing re-
    turning.
Oft did the potent spell-word, given
    To Envoys hither from the skies,
To be pronounced when back to heaven
    It is their time or wish to rise,
Come to my lips that fatal day;
    And once too was so nearly spoken,
That my spread plumage in the ray
And breeze of heaven began to play; —
    When my heart failed — the spell was
    broken —
The word unfinisht died away,
And my checkt plumes ready to soar,
Fell slack and lifeless as before.

How could I leave a world which she,
Or lost or won, made all to me?
No matter where my wanderings were,
  So there she lookt, breathed, moved
    about —
Woe, ruin, death, more sweet with her,
  Than Paradise itself, without!

But to return — that very day
  A feast was held, where, full of
    mirth,
Came — crowding thick as flowers that
    play
In summer winds — the young and gay
  And beautiful of this bright earth.
And she was there and mid the young
  And beautiful stood first, alone;
Tho' on her gentle brow still hung
  The shadow I that morn had thrown —
The first that ever shame or woe
Had cast upon its vernal snow.
My heart was maddened; — in the flush
  Of the wild revel I gave way
To all that frantic mirth — that rush
  Of desperate gayety which they,
Who never felt how pain's excess
Can break out thus, think happiness!
Sad mimicry of mirth and life
Whose flashes come but from the strife
Of inward passions — like the light
Struck out by clashing swords in fight

Then too that juice of earth, the bane
And blessing of man's heart and brain—
That draught of sorcery which brings
Phantoms of fair, forbidden things —
Whose drops like those of rainbows smile
Upon the mists that circle man,
Brightening not only Earth the while,
  But grasping Heaven too in their
    span!—
Then first the fatal wine-cup rained
  Its dews of darkness thro' my lips,[1]

1 I have already mentioned that some of the
circumstances of this story were suggested to me
by the eastern legend of the two angels, Harut
and Marut, as given by Mariti, who says that the
author of the Taalim founds upon it the Mahometan prohibition of wine.* I have since found
that Mariti's version of the tale (which differs
also from that of Dr. Prideaux, in his Life of Mahomet,) is taken from the French Encyclopédie,
in which work, under the head *"Arot et Marot,"*
the reader will find it.

* The Bahardanush tells the fable differently.

Casting whate'er of light remained
  To my lost soul into eclipse;
And filling it with such wild dreams,
  Such fantasies and wrong desires,
As in the absence of heaven's beams
  Haunt us for ever — like wild-fires
That walk this earth when day retires.

Now hear the rest; — our banquet done,
  I sought her in the accustomed bower,
Where late we oft, when day was gone
And the world husht, had met alone,
  At the same silent, moonlight hour.
Her eyes as usual were upturned
  To her loved star whose lustre burned
  Purer than ever on that night;
While she in looking grew more bright
  As tho' she borrowed of its light.

There was a virtue in that scene,
  A spell of holiness around,
Which had my burning brain not been
  Thus maddened would have held me
    bound,
  As tho' I trod celestial ground.
Even as it was, with soul all flame
  And lips that burned in their own sighs,
I stood to gaze with awe and shame—
The memory of Eden came
  Full o'er me when I saw those eyes;
And tho' too well each glance of mine
To the pale, shrinking maiden proved
How far, alas! from aught divine,
Aught worthy of so pure a shrine,
  Was the wild love with which I
    loved,
Yet must she, too, have seen — oh yes,
  'T is soothing but to *think* she saw
The deep, true, soul-felt tenderness,
  The homage of an Angel's awe
To her, a mortal, whom pure love
Then placed above him — far above—
And all that struggle to repress
A sinful spirit's mad excess,
Which workt within me at that hour,
  When with a voice where Passion
    shed
All the deep sadness of her power,
  Her melancholy power — I said,
"Then be it so; if back to heaven
  "I must unloved, unpitied fly,
"Without one blest memorial given
  "To soothe me in that lonely sky;

" One look like those the young and fond
  " Give when they 're parting — which
    would be,
" Even in remembrance far beyond
  " All heaven hath left of bliss for me!

" Oh, but to see that head recline
  " A minute on this trembling arm,
" And those mild eyes look up to mine,
  " Without a dread, a thought of harm!
" To meet but once the thrilling touch
  " Of lips too purely fond to fear me —
" Or if that boon be all too much,
  " Even thus to bring their fragrance
    near me!
" Nay, shrink not so — a look — a
  word —
  " Give them but kindly and I fly;
" Already, see, my plumes have stirred
  " And tremble for their home on high.
"Thus be our parting —cheek to cheek—
  " One minute's lapse will be forgiven,
" And thou, the next, shalt hear me speak
  " The spell that plumes my wing for
    heaven! "

While thus I spoke, the fearful maid,
Of me and of herself afraid,
Had shrinking stood like flowers beneath
The scorching of the south-wind's breath:
But when I named — alas, too well,
  I now recall, tho' wildered then, —
Instantly, when I named the spell
  Her brow, her eyes uprose again;
And with an eagerness that spoke
The sudden light that o'er her broke,
" The spell, the spell!— oh, speak it now,
  " And I will bless thee!" she ex-
    claimed —
Unknowing what I did, inflamed,
And lost already, on her brow
I stampt one burning kiss, and named
The mystic word till then ne'er told
To living creature of earth's mould!
Scarce was it said when quick as thought,
Her lips from mine like echo caught
The holy sound — her hands and eyes
Were instant lifted to the skies,
And thrice to heaven she spoke it out
  With that triumphant look Faith wears,
When not a cloud of fear or doubt,
  A vapor from this vale of tears,
  Between her and her God appears!

That very moment her whole frame
All bright and glorified became,
And at her back I saw unclose
Two wings magnificent as those
  That sparkle around ALLA'S Throne,
Whose plumes, as buoyantly she rose
  Above me, in the moon-beam shone
With a pure light, which — from its
  hue,
Unknown upon this earth — I knew
Was light from Eden, glistening thro'!
Most holy vision! ne'er before
Did aught so radiant — since the day
When EBLIS in his downfall, bore
  The third of the bright stars away —
Rise in earth's beauty to repair
That loss of light and glory there!

But did I tamely view her flight?
  Did not I too proclaim out thrice
The powerful words that were that
  night,—
Oh even for heaven too much delight!—
  Again to bring us, eyes to eyes
And soul to soul, in Paradise?
I did — I spoke it o'er and o'er —
  I prayed, I wept, but all in vain;
For me the spell had power no more.
  There seemed around me some dark
    chain
Which still as I essayed to soar
  Baffled, alas, each wild endeavor;
Dead lay my wings as they have lain
Since that sad hour and will remain —
  So wills the offended God — for ever!

It was to yonder star I traced
Her journey up the illumined waste —
That isle in the blue firmament
To which so oft her fancy went
  In wishes and in dreams before,
And which was now — such, Purity,
Thy blest reward — ordained to be
  Her home of light for evermore!
Once — or did I but fancy so?—
  Even in her flight to that fair sphere,
Mid all her spirit's new-felt glow,
  A pitying look she turned below
On him who stood in darkness here;
Him whom perhaps if vain regret
Can dwell in heaven she pities yet;
And oft when looking to this dim
And distant world remembers him.

But soon that passing dream was gone;
Farther and farther off she shone,
Till lessened to a point as small
As are those specks that yonder burn,—
Those vivid drops of light that fall
The last from Day's exhausted urn.
And when at length she merged, afar,
Into her own immortal star,
And when at length my straining sight
Had caught her wing's last fading ray,
That minute from my soul the light
Of heaven and love both past away;
And I forgot my home, my birth,
Profaned my spirit, sunk my brow,
And revelled in gross joys of earth
Till I became — what I am now!

The Spirit bowed his head in shame,
A shame that of itself would tell —
Were there not even those breaks of
flame,
Celestial, thro' his clouded frame —
How grand the height from which he
fell!
That holy Shame which ne'er forgets
The unblenched renown it used to
wear;
Whose blush remains when Virtue sets
To show her sunshine *has* been there.

Once only while the tale he told
Were his eyes lifted to behold
That happy stainless star where she
Dwelt in her bower of purity!
One minute did he look and then —
As tho' he felt some deadly pain
From its sweet light thro' heart and
brain —
Shrunk back and never lookt again.

Who was the Second Spirit? he
With the proud front and piercing
glance —
Who seemed when viewing heaven's
expanse
As tho' his far-sent eye could see
On, on into the Immensity
Behind the veils of that blue sky
Where ALLA'S grandest secrets lie? —
His wings, the while, tho' day was gone,
Flashing with many a various hue
Of light they from themselves alone,
Instinct with Eden's brightness drew.

'T was RUBI — once among the prime
And flower of those bright creatures,
named
Spirits of Knowledge,[1] who o'er Time
And Space and Thought an empire
claimed,
Second alone to Him whose light
Was even to theirs as day to night;
'Twixt whom and them was distance far
And wide as would the journey be
To reach from any island star
The vague shores of Infinity!

'T was RUBI in whose mournful eye
Slept the dim light of days gone by;
Whose voice tho' sweet fell on the ear
Like echoes in some silent place
When first awaked for many a year;
And when he smiled, if o'er his face
Smile ever shone, 't was like the grace
Of moonlight rainbows, fair, but wan,
The sunny life, the glory gone.
Even o'er his pride tho' still the same,
A softening shade from sorrow came;
And tho' at times his spirit knew
The kindlings of disdain and ire,
Short was the fitful glare they threw —
Like the last flashes, fierce but few,
Seen thro' some noble pile on fire!

Such was the Angel who now broke
The silence that had come o'er all,
When he the Spirit that last spoke
Closed the sad history of his fall;
And while a sacred lustre flown
For many a day relumed his cheek —
Beautiful as in days of old;
And not those eloquent lips alone
But every feature seemed to speak —
Thus his eventful story told: —

SECOND ANGEL'S STORY.

YOU both remember well the day
When unto Eden's new-made bowers
ALLA convoked the bright array
Of his supreme angelic powers
To witness the one wonder yet,
Beyond man, angel, star, or sun,

1 The Kerubiim, as the Mussulmans call
them, are often joined indiscriminately with the
Asrafil or Seraphim, under one common name of
Azazil, by which all spirits who approach near
the throne of Alla are designated.

He must achieve, ere he could set
    His seal upon the world as done —
To see that last perfection rise,
    That crowning of creation's birth,
When mid the worship and surprise
Of circling angels Woman's eyes
    First opened upon heaven and earth;
And from their lids a thrill was sent,
That thro' each living spirit went
Like first light thro' the firmament!

Can you forget how gradual stole
The fresh-awakened breath of soul
Throughout her perfect form — which
        seemed
To grow transparent as there beamed
That dawn of Mind within and caught
New loveliness from each new thought?
Slow as o'er summer seas we trace
    The progress of the noontide air,
Dimpling its bright and silent face
Each minute into some new grace,
        And varying heaven's reflections
            there —
Or like the light of evening stealing
    O'er some fair temple which all day
Hath slept in shadow, slow revealing
    Its several beauties ray by ray,
Till it shines out, a thing to bless,
All full of light and loveliness.

Can you forget her blush when round
Thro' Eden's lone, enchanted ground
She lookt, and saw the sea — the
        skies —
    And heard the rush of many a wing,
    On high behests then vanishing;
And saw the last few angel eyes,
    Still lingering — mine among the rest,—
Reluctant leaving scenes so blest?
From that miraculous hour the fate
    Of this new, glorious Being dwelt
For ever with a spell-like weight
Upon my spirit — early, late,
    Whate'er I did or dreamed or felt,
The thought of what might yet befall
That matchless creature mixt with all. —
Nor she alone but her whole race
    Thro' ages yet to come — whate'er
    Of feminine and fond and fair
Should spring from that pure mind and
        face,
    All waked my soul's intensest care;

Their forms, souls, feelings, still to me
Creation's strangest mystery!

It was my doom — even from the first,
When witnessing the primal burst
Of Nature's wonders, I saw rise
Those bright creations in the skies, —
Those worlds instinct with life and light,
Which Man, remote, but sees by
        night, —
It was my doom still to be haunted
    By some new wonder, some sublime
    And matchless work, that for the time
Held all my soul enchained, enchanted,
And left me not a thought, a dream,
A word but on that only theme!

The wish to know — that endless thirst,
    Which even by quenching is awaked,
And which becomes or blest or curst
    As is the fount whereat 't is slaked —
Still urged me onward with desire
Insatiate, to explore, inquire —
Whate'er the wondrous things might be
That waked each new idolatry —
    Their cause, aim, source, whencever
        sprung —
Their inmost powers, as tho' for me
    Existence on that knowledge hung.

Oh what a vision were the stars
When first I saw them burn on high,
Rolling along like living cars
    Of light for gods to journey by! [1]
They were my heart's first passion —
        days
And nights unwearied, in their rays
Have I hung floating till each sense
Seemed full of their bright influence.
Innocent joy! alas, how much
    Of misery had I shunned below,

---

[1] " C'est un fait indubitable que la plupart
des anciens philosophes, soit Chaldéens, soit
Grecs, nous ont donné les astres comme animés,
et ont soutenu que les astres, qui nous éclairent
n'étoient que, ou les chars, ou même les navires
des Intelligences qui les conduisoient. Pour les
Chars, cela se lit partout; on n'a qu'ouvrir
Pline, St. Clément," etc. — " Mémoire Historique, sur le Sabiisme," par M. FOURMONT.

A belief that the stars are either spirits or the
vehicles of spirits, was common to all the religions and heresies of the East. Kircher has
given the names and stations of the seven archangels, who were by the Cabala of the Jews distributed through the planets.

Could I have still lived blest with such;
   Nor, proud and restless, burned to
     know
The knowledge that brings guilt and
   woe.
Often — so much I loved to trace
The secrets of this starry race —
Have I at morn and evening run
Along the lines of radiance spun
Like webs between them and the sun,
Untwisting all the tangled ties
Of light into their different dyes
Then fleetly winged I off in quest
Of those, the farthest, loneliest,
That watch like winking sentinels,[1]
The void, beyond which Chaos dwells;
And there with noiseless plume pursued
Their track thro' that grand solitude,
Asking intently all and each
   What soul within their radiance dwelt,
And wishing their sweet light were
   speech,
     That they might tell me all they felt.

Nay, oft, so passionate my chase
Of these resplendent heirs of space,
Oft did I follow — lest a ray
   Should 'scape me in the farthest
     night —
Some pilgrim Comet on his way
   To visit distant shrines of light,
And well remember how I sung
   Exultingly when on my sight
New worlds of stars all fresh and young
As if just born of darkness sprung!

Such was my pure ambition then,
   My sinless transport night and morn
Ere yet this newer world of men,
   And that most fair of stars was born
Which I in fatal hour saw rise
Among the flowers of Paradise!
Thenceforth my nature all was changed,
   My heart, soul, senses turned below;
And he who but so lately ranged
   Yon wonderful expanse where glow

---

1 According to the cosmogony of the ancient
Persians, there were four stars set as sentinels in
the four quarters of the heavens, to watch over
the other fixed stars, and superintend the planets
in their course.   The names of these four Sentinel
stars are, according to the Boundesh, Taschter,
for the east ; Satevis, for the west; Venand, for
the south ; and Haftorang, for the north.

Worlds upon worlds, — yet found his
   mind
Even in that luminous range confined,—
Now blest the humblest, meanest sod
Of the dark earth where Woman trod!
In vain my former idols glistened
   From their far thrones; in vain these
     ears
To the once-thrilling music listened,
   That hymned around my favorite
     spheres —
To earth, to earth each thought was
   given,
That in this half-lost soul had birth;
Like some high mount, whose head's in
   heaven
While its whole shadow rests on earth!

Nor was it Love, even yet, that thralled
   My spirit in his burning ties;
And less, still less could it be called
   That grosser flame, round which Love
     flies
Nearer and nearer till he dies —
No, it was wonder, such as thrilled
   At all God's works my dazzled sense;
The same rapt wonder, only filled
   With passion, more profound, in-
     tense, —
A vehement, but wandering fire,
Which, tho' nor love, nor yet desire, —
Tho' thro' all womankind it took
   Its range, as lawless lightnings run,
Yet wanted but a touch, a look,
     To fix it burning upon *One.*

Then too the ever-restless zeal,
   The insatiate curiosity
To know how shapes so fair must feel —
To look but once beneath the seal
   Of so much loveliness and see
What souls belonged to such bright
   eyes —
Whether as sun-beams find their way
Into the gem that hidden lies,
   Those looks could inward turn their
     ray
And make the soul as bright as they:
All this impelled my anxious chase,
   And still the more I saw and knew
Of Woman's fond, weak, conquering
   race,
     The intenser still my wonder grew.

I had beheld their First, their EVE,
  Born in that splendid Paradise,
Which sprung there solely to receive
  The first light of her waking eyes.
I had seen purest angels lean
  In worship o'er her from above;
And man — oh yes, had envying seen
  Proud man possest of all her love.

I saw their happiness, so brief,
  So exquisite, — her error, too,
That easy trust, that prompt belief
  In what the warm heart wishes true;
That faith in words, when kindly said,
  By which the whole fond sex is led —
Mingled with — what I durst not blame,
  For 't is my own — that zeal to *know*,
Sad, fatal zeal, so sure of woe;
Which, tho' from heaven all pure it
    came,
  Yet stained, misused, brought sin and
    shame
    On her, on me, on all below !

I had seen this; had seen Man, armed
  As his soul is with strength and sense,
By her first words to ruin charmed;
  His vaunted reason's cold defence,
Like an ice-barrier in the ray
Of melting summer, smiled away.
Nay, stranger yet, spite of all this —
  Tho' by her counsels taught to err,
  Tho' driven from Paradise for her,
(And *with* her — *that* at least was bliss,)
Had I not heard him ere he crost
  The threshold of that earthly heaven,
Which by her bewildering smile he
    lost —
  So quickly was the wrong forgiven ! —
Had I not heard him, as he prest
  The frail, fond trembler to a breast
Which she had doomed to sin and strife,
  Call her — even then — his Life ! his
    Life ! [1]
Yes, such the love-taught name, the first,
  That ruined Man to Woman gave,
Even in his outcast hour, when curst
  By her fond witchery, with that worst
  And earliest boon of love, the grave !

[1] Chavah, or, as it is in Arabic, Havah (the
name by which Adam called the woman after
their transgression), means " Life."

She who brought death into the world
  There stood before him, with the light
  Of their lost Paradise still bright
Upon those sunny locks that curled
Down her white shoulders to her feet —
So beautiful in form, so sweet
In heart and voice, as to redeem
  The loss, the death of all things dear,
Except herself — and make it seem
  Life, endless Life, while she was near !
Could I help wondering at a creature,
  Thus circled round with spells so
    strong —
One to whose every thought, word, fea-
    ture,
  In joy and woe, thro' right and wrong,
Such sweet omnipotence heaven gave,
To bless or ruin, curse or save?

Nor did the marvel cease with her —
  New Eves in all her daughters came,
As strong to charm, as weak to err,
  As sure of man thro' praise and
    blame,
  Whate'er they brought him, pride or
    shame,
He still the unreasoning worshipper,
  And they, throughout all time, the same
  Enchantresses of soul and frame,
Into whose hands from first to last
  This world with all its destinies,
Devotedly by heaven seems cast,
  To save or ruin as they please !
Oh ! 't is not to be told how long,
  How restlessly I sighed to find
Some *one* from out that witching throng,
  Some abstract of the form and mind
Of the whole matchless sex, from which,
  In my own arms beheld, possest,
I might learn all the powers to witch,
  To warm, and (if my fate unblest
  Would have it) ruin, of the rest !
Into whose inward soul and sense,
  I might descend, as doth the bee
Into the flower's deep heart, and thence
  Rifle in all its purity
The prime, the quintessence, the whole
Of wondrous Woman's frame and soul !

At length, my burning wish, my
    prayer —
(For such — oh ! what will tongues not
    dare,

When hearts go wrong? — this lip pre-
  ferred) —
At length my ominous prayer was
  heard —
But whether heard in heaven or hell,
Listen — and thou wilt know *too* well.

There was a maid, of all who move
  Like visions o'er this orb most fit
To be a bright young angel's love —
  Herself so bright, so exquisite!
The pride too of her step, as light
  Along the unconscious earth she
    went,
Seemed that of one born with a right
  To walk some heavenlier element,
And tread in places where her feet
A star at every step should meet.
'T was not alone that loveliness
  By which the wildered sense is
    caught —
Of lips whose very breath could bless;
  Of playful blushes that seemed naught
But luminous escapes of thought;
Of eyes that, when by anger stirred,
  Were fire itself, but at a word
Of tenderness, all soft became
  As tho' they could, like the sun's bird,
  Dissolve away in their own flame —
Of form, as pliant as the shoots
  Of a young tree, in vernal flower;
Yet round and glowing as the fruits,
  That drop from it in summer's
    hour; —
'T was not alone this loveliness
  That falls to loveliest women's share,
Tho' even here her form could spare
From its own beauty's rich excess
  Enough to make even *them* more
    fair —
But 't was the Mind outshining clear
Thro' her whole frame — the soul, still
  near,
To light each charm, yet independent
  Of what it lighted, as the sun
That shines on flowers would be re-
  splendent
  Were there no flowers to shine
    upon —
'T was this, all this, in one combined —
  The unnumbered looks and arts that
    form
The glory of young womankind,

Taken, in their perfection, warm,
Ere time had chilled a single charm,
And stampt with such a seal of Mind,
  As gave to beauties that might be
Too sensual else, too unrefined,
  The impress of Divinity!

'T was this — a union, which the hand
  Of Nature kept for her alone,
Of every thing most playful, bland,
  Voluptuous, spiritual, grand,
  In angel-natures and her own
Oh! this it was that drew me nigh
One, who seemed kin to heaven as I,
A bright twin-sister from on high —
  One in whose love, I felt, were given
  The mixt delights of either sphere,
All that the spirit seeks in heaven,
  And all the senses burn for here.

Had we — but hold! — hear every part
  Of our sad tale — spite of the pain
Remembrance gives, when the fixt dart
  Is stirred thus in the wound again —
Hear every step, so full of bliss,
  And yet so ruinous, that led
Down to the last, dark precipice,
  Where perish both — the fallen, the
    dead!

From the first hour she caught my sight,
I never left her — day and night
Hovering unseen around her way,
  And mid her loneliest musings near,
I soon could track each thought that lay,
  Gleaming within her heart, as clear
  As pebbles within brooks appear;
And there among the countless things
  That keep young hearts for ever glow-
    ing —
Vague wishes, fond imaginings,
  Love-dreams, as yet no object know-
    ing —
Light, winged hopes that come when bid,
  And rainbow joys that end in weeping;
And passions among pure thoughts hid,
  Like serpents under flowerets sleep-
    ing: —
'Mong all these feelings — felt where'er
Young hearts are beating — I saw there
Proud thoughts, aspirings high — beyond
Whate'er yet dwelt in soul so fond —
Glimpses of glory, far away
  Into the bright, vague future given;

And fancies, free and grand, whose play,
　Like that of eaglets, is near heaven!
With this, too — what a soul and heart
To fall beneath the tempter's art! —
A zeal for knowledge, such as ne'er
Enshrined itself in form so fair,
Since that first, fatal hour, when Eve,
　With every fruit of Eden blest,
Save one alone — rather than leave
　That *one* unreached, lost all the rest.

It was in dreams that first I stole
　With gentle mastery o'er her mind —
In that rich twilight of the soul,
　When reason's beam, half hid behind
The clouds of sleep, obscurely gilds
Each shadowy shape that Fancy builds —
'T was then by that soft light I brought
　Vague, glimmering visions to her
　　view, —
Catches of radiance lost when caught,
Bright labyrinths that led to naught,
　And vistas with no pathway thro'; —
Dwellings of bliss that opening shone,
　Then closed, dissolved, and left no
　　trace —
All that, in short, could tempt Hope on,
But give her wing no resting-place;
Myself the while with brow as yet
Pure as the young moon's coronet,
Thro' every dream *still* in her sight,
　The enchanter of each mocking scene,
Who gave the hope, then brought the
　　blight,
Who said, " Behold yon world of light,"
　Then sudden dropt a veil between!

At length when I perceived each thought,
Waking or sleeping, fixt on naught
　But these illusive scenes and me —
The phantom who thus came and went,
In half revealments, only meant
　To madden curiosity —
When by such various arts I found
Her fancy to its utmost wound,
One night — 't was in a holy spot
Which she for prayer had chosen — a grot
Of purest marble built below
Her garden beds, thro' which a glow
From lamps invisible then stole,
　Brightly pervading all the place —
Like that mysterious light the soul,
　Itself unseen, sheds thro' the face.

There at her altar while she knelt,
And all that woman ever felt,
　When God and man both claimed ¹.er
　　sighs —
Every warm thought, that ever dwelt,
　Like summer clouds, 'twixt earth and
　　skies,
　Too pure to fall, too gross to rise,
　Spoke in her gestures, tones, and eyes—
Then, as the mystic light's soft ray
Grew softer still, as tho' its ray
Was breathed from her, I heard her
　say : —

" O idol of my dreams! whate'er
　" Thy nature be — human, divine,
" Or but half heavenly — still too fair,
　" Too heavenly to be ever mine!

" Wonderful Spirit who dost make
　" Slumber so lovely that it seems
" No longer life to live awake,
　" Since heaven itself descends in
　　dreams,

" Why do I ever lose thee? why
　" When on thy realms and thee I gaze
" Still drops that veil, which I could die,
　" Oh! gladly, but one hour to raise?

" Long ere such miracles as thou
　" And thine came o'er my thoughts,
　　a thirst
" For light was in this soul which now
　" Thy looks have into passion nurst.

" There 's nothing bright above, below,
　" In sky — earth — ocean, that this
　　breast
" Doth not intensely burn to know,
　" And thee, thee, thee, o'er all the
　　rest!

" Then come, oh Spirit, from behind
　" The curtains of thy radiant home,
" If thou wouldst be as angel shrined,
　" Or loved and claspt as mortal, come!

" Bring all thy dazzling wonders here,
　" That I may, waking, know and see;
" Or waft me hence to thy own sphere,
　" Thy heaven or — ay, even *that* with
　　thee!

"Demon or God, who hold'st the book
  "Of knowledge spread beneath thine
    eye,
"Give me, with thee, but one bright look
  "Into its leaves and let me die!

"By those ethereal wings whose way
  "Lies thro' an element so fraught
"With living Mind that as they play
  "Their every movement is a thought!

"By that bright, wreathed hair, between
  "Whose sunny clusters the sweet wind
"Of Paradise so late hath been
  "And left its fragrant soul behind!

"By those Impassioned eyes that melt
  "Their light into the inmost heart,
"Like sunset in the waters, felt
  "As molten fire thro' every part —

"I do implore thee, oh most bright
  "And worshipt Spirit, shine but o'er
"My waking, wondering eyes this night,
  "This one blest night — I ask no
    more!"

Exhausted, breathless, as she said
These burning words, her languid head
Upon the altar's steps she cast,
As if that brain-throb were its last —

Till, startled by the breathing, nigh,
Of lips that echoed back her sigh,
Sudden her brow again she raised;
  And there, just lighted on the shrine,
Beheld me — not as I had blazed
  Around her, full of light divine,
In her late dreams, but softened down
  Into more mortal grace; — my crown
Of flowers, too radiant for this world,
  Left hanging on yon starry steep;
My wings shut up, like banners furled,
  When Peace hath put their pomp to
    sleep;
Or like autumnal clouds that keep
Their lightnings sheathed rather than mar
The dawning hour of some young star;
And nothing left but what beseemed
  The accessible, tho' glorious mate
Of mortal woman — whose eyes beamed
  Back upon hers, as passionate;

Whose ready heart brought flame for
  flame,
Whose sin, whose madness was the same;
And whose soul lost in that one hour
  For her and for her love — oh more
Of heaven's light than even the power
  Of heaven itself could now restore!

And yet, that hour! —

            The Spirit here
Stopt in his utterance as if words
Gave way beneath the wild career
  Of his then rushing thoughts — like
    chords,
Midway in some enthusiast's song,
Breaking beneath a touch too strong;
While the clenched hand upon the brow
Told how remembrance throbbed there
    now!
But soon 't was o'er — that casual blaze
From the sunk fire of other days —
That relic of a flame whose burning
  Had been too fierce to be relumed,
Soon past away, and the youth turning
  To his bright listeners thus re-
    sumed: —

Days, months elapsed, and, tho' what
  most
  On earth I sighed for was mine, all —
Yet — was I happy? God, thou know'st,
  Howe'er they smile and feign and boast,
    What happiness is theirs, who fall!
'T was bitterest anguish — made more
    keen
Even by the love, the bliss, between
Whose throbs it came, like gleams of
    hell
  In agonizing cross-light given
Athwart the glimpses, they who dwell
  In purgatory [1] catch of heaven!

---

1 Called by the Mussulmans Al Araf — a sort
of wall or partition which, according to the 7th
chapter of the Koran, separates hell from paradise, and where they, who have not merits sufficient to gain them immediate admittance into
heaven, are supposed to stand for a certain
period, alternately tantalized and tormented by
the sights that are on either side presented to
them.

Manes, who borrowed in many instances from
the Platonists, placed his purgatories, or places
of purification, in the Sun and Moon. — *Beau-
sobre, liv.* iii. *chap.* 8.

The only feeling that to me
    Seemed joy — or rather my sole rest
From aching misery — was to see
    My young, proud, blooming LILIS
    blest.
She, the fair fountain of all ill
    To my lost soul — whom yet its thirst
Fervidly panted after still,
    And found the charm fresh as at first —
To see *her* happy — to reflect
    Whatever beams still round me played
Of former pride, of glory wreckt,
    On her, my Moon, whose light I
    made,
    And whose soul worshipt even my
    shade —
This was, I own, enjoyment — this
My sole, last lingering glimpse of bliss.
And proud she was, fair creature! —
    proud,
    Beyond what even most queenly stirs
In woman's heart, nor would have bowed
    That beautiful young brow of hers
To aught beneath the First above,
So high she deemed her Cherub's love!

Then too that passion hourly growing
    Stronger and stronger — to which even
Her love at times gave way — of knowing
    Every thing strange in earth and
    heaven;
Not only all that, full revealed,
    The eternal ALLA loves to show,
But all that He hath wisely sealed
    In darkness for man *not* to know —
Even this desire, alas! ill-starred
    And fatal as it was, I sought
To feed each minute, and unbarred
    Such realms of wonder on her thought
As ne'er till then had let their light
Escape on any mortal's sight!
In the deep earth — beneath the sea —
    Thro' caves of fire — thro' wilds of
    air —
Wherever sleeping Mystery
    Had spread her curtain, we were
    there —
Love still beside us as we went,
At home in each new element
    And sure of worship everywhere!

Then first was Nature taught to lay
    The wealth of all her kingdoms down

At woman's worshipt feet and say,
    "Bright creature, this is all thine
    own!"
Then first were diamonds from the
    night,[1]
Of earth's deep centre brought to light
And made to grace the conquering way
Of proud young beauty with their ray.

Then too the pearl from out its shell
    Unsightly, in the sunless sea,
(As 't were a spirit, forced to dwell
    In form unlovely) was set free,
And round the neck of woman threw
A light it lent and borrowed too.
For never did this maid — whate'er
    The ambition of the hour — forget
Her sex's pride in being fair;
Nor that adornment, tasteful, rare,
Which makes the mighty magnet, set
In Woman's form, more mighty yet.
Nor was there aught within the range
    Of my swift wing in sea or air,
Of beautiful or grand or strange,
    That, quickly as her wish could change,
    I did not seek, with such fond care,
That when I 've seen her look above
    At some bright star admiringly,
I 've said, "Nay, look not there, my
    love,[2]
    "Alas, I *can not* give it thee!"

But not alone the wonders found
    Thro' Nature's realm — the unveiled,
    material,
Visible glories, that abound
Thro' all her vast, enchanted ground —

---

1 *"Quelques gnomes désireux de devenir
immortels, avoient voulu gagner les bonnes
graces des nos filles, et leur avoient apporté des
pierreries dont ils sont gardiens naturels : et ces
auteurs ont crû, s'appuyans sur le livre d'Enoch
mal-entendu, que c'étoient des piéges que les
anges amoureux,"* etc. — Comte de Gabalis.
    As the fiction of the loves of angels with
women gave birth to the fanciful world of sylphs
and gnomes, so we owe to it also the invention
of those beautiful Genii and Peris, which embellish so much the mythology of the East; for in
the fabulous histories of Caïoumarath, of Tha-
murath, etc., these spiritual creatures are always
represented as the descendants of Seth, and
called the Bani Algiann, or children of Giann.

  2 I am aware that this happy saying of Lord
Albemarle's loses much of its grace and playfulness, by being put into the mouth of any but a
human lover.

But whatsoe'er unseen, ethereal,
Dwells far away from human sense,
Wrapt in its own intelligence —
The mystery of that Fountain-head,
From which all vital spirit runs,
All breath of Life, where'er 't is spread
Thro' men or angels, flowers or suns —
The workings of the Almighty Mind,
When first o'er Chaos he designed
The outlines of this world, and thro'
That depth of darkness — like the bow,
Called out of rain-clouds hue by hue [1] —
Saw the grand, gradual picture
grow; —
The covenant with human kind
By ALLA made [2] — the chains of Fate
He round himself and them hath twined,
Till his high task he consummate; —
Till good from evil, love from hate,
Shall be workt out thro' sin and pain,
And Fate shall loose her iron chain
And all be free, be bright again!

Such were the deep-drawn mysteries,
And some, even more obscure, pro-
found,
And wildering to the mind than these,
Which — far as woman's thought
could sound,
Or a fallen, outlawed spirit reach —
She dared to learn and I to teach.
Till — filled with such unearthly lore,
And mingling the pure light it brings
With much that fancy had before
Shed in false, tinted glimmerings —
The enthusiast girl spoke out, as one
Inspired, among her own dark race,
Who from their ancient shrines would
run,
Leaving their holy rites undone,
To gaze upon her holier face.
And tho' but wild the things she spoke,
Yet mid that play of error's smoke
Into fair shapes by fancy curled,

Some gleams of pure religion broke —
Glimpses that have not yet awoke,
But startled the still dreaming world!
Oh! many a truth, remote, sublime,
Which Heaven would from the minds
of men
Have kept concealed till its own time,
Stole out in these revealments then —
Revealments dim that have forerun,
By ages, the great, Sealing One! [3]
Like that imperfect dawn or light [4]
Escaping from the Zodiac's signs,
Which makes the doubtful east half
bright,
Before the real morning shines!

Thus did some moons of bliss go by —
Of bliss to her who saw but love
And knowledge throughout earth and
sky;
To whose enamoured soul and eye,
I seemed — as is the sun on high —
The light of all below, above,
The spirit of sea and land and air,
Whose influence, felt every where,
Spread from its centre, her own heart,
Even to the world's extremest part;
While thro' that world her reinless mind
Had now careered so fast and far,
That earth itself seemed left behind
And her proud fancy unconfined
Already saw Heaven's gates ajar!

Happy enthusiast! still, oh! still
Spite of my own heart's mortal chill,
Spite of that double-fronted sorrow
Which looks at once before and back,
Beholds the yesterday, the morrow,
And sees both comfortless, both
black —
Spite of all this, I could have still
In her delight forgot all ill;
Or if pain *would* not be forgot,
At least have borne and murmured not.
When thoughts of an offended heaven,
Of sinfulness, which I — even I,
While down its steep most headlong
driven —

1 According to Whitehurst's theory, the mention of rainbows by an antediluvian angel is an
anachronism; as he says, "There was no rain
before the flood, and consequently no rainbow,
which accounts for the novelty of this sight after
the Deluge."

2 For the terms of this compact, of which the
angels were supposed to be witnesses, see the
chapter of the Koran, entitled Al Araf, and
the article "Adam" in D'Herbelot.

3 In acknowledging the authority of the great
Prophets who had preceded him, Mahomet represented his own mission as the final "*Seal,*" or
consummation of them all.

4 The Zodiacal Light.

Well knew could never be forgiven,
　　Came o'er me with an agony
Beyond all reach of mortal woe —
A torture kept for those who know,
Know *every* thing, and — worst of all —
Know and love Virtue while they fall!
Even then her presence had the power
　　To soothe, to warm — nay, even to
　　　　bless —
If ever bliss could graft its flower
　　On stem so full of bitterness —
Even then her glorious smile to me
　　Brought warmth and radiance if not
　　　　balm;
Like moonlight o'er a troubled sea,
　　Brightening the storm it cannot calm.

Oft too when that disheartening fear,
　　Which all who love, beneath yon sky,
Feel when they gaze on what is dear —
　　The dreadful thought that it must die!
That desolating thought which comes
Into men's happiest hours and homes;
Whose melancholy boding flings
Death's shadow o'er the brightest things,
Sicklies the infant's bloom and spreads
The grave beneath young lovers' heads!
This fear, so sad to all — to me
　　Most full of sadness from the thought
That I must still live on,[1] when she
Would, like the snow that on the sea
　　Fell yesterday, in vain be sought;
That heaven to me this final seal
　　Of all earth's sorrow would deny,
And I eternally must feel
　　The death-pang without power to die!
Even this, her fond endearments — fond
As ever cherisht the sweet bond
'Twixt heart and heart — could charm
　　　　away;
Before her looks no clouds would stay,
Or if they did their gloom was gone,
Their darkness put a glory on!
But 't is not, 't is not for the wrong,
The guilty, to be happy long;
And she too now had sunk within
The shadow of her tempter's sin,
Too deep for even Omnipotence
To snatch the fated victim thence!

1 Pococke, however, gives it as the opinion of
the Mahometan doctors, that all souls, not only
of men and of animals, living either on land or in
the sea, but of the angels also, must necessarily
taste of death.

Listen and if a tear there be
Left in your hearts weep it for me.

'T was on the evening of a day,
Which we in love had dreamt away;
In that same garden, where — the pride
Of seraph splendor laid aside,
And those wings furled, whose open
　　　　light
For mortal gaze were else too bright —
I first had stood before her sight,
And found myself — oh, ecstasy,
　　Which even in pain I ne'er forget —
Worship as only God should be,
　　And loved as never man was yet!
In that same garden where we now,
　　Thoughtfully side by side reclining,
Her eyes turned upward and her brow
　　With its own silent fancies shining.

It was an evening bright and still
　　As ever blusht on wave or bower,
Smiling from heaven as if naught ill
　　Could happen in so sweet an hour.
Yet I remember both grew sad
　　In looking at that light — even she,
Of heart so fresh and brow so glad,
　　Felt the still hour's solemnity,
And thought she saw in that repose
　　The death-hour not alone of light,
But of this whole fair world — the close
　　Of all things beautiful and bright —
The last, grand sunset, in whose ray
Nature herself died calm away!

At length, as tho' some livelier thought
Had suddenly her fancy caught,
She turned upon me her dark eyes,
Dilated into that full shape
They took in joy, reproach, surprise,
　　As 't were to let more soul escape,
And, playfully as on my head
Her white hand rested, smiled and
　　　　said: —

" I had last night a dream of thee,
　　" Resembling those divine ones, given,
" Like preludes to sweet minstrelsy,
　　" Before thou camest thyself from
　　　　heaven.

" The same rich wreath was on thy brow,
　　" Dazzling as if of starlight made;

" And these wings, lying darkly now,
 " Like meteors round thee flasht and
  played.

" Thou stoodest, all bright, as in those
  dreams,
 " As if just wafted from above,
" Mingling earth's warmth with heaven's
  beams,
 " A creature to adore and love.

" Sudden I felt thee draw me near
 " To thy pure heart, where, fondly
  placed,
" I seemed within the atmosphere
 " Of that exhaling light embraced;

" And felt methought the ethereal flame
 " Pass from thy purer soul to mine;
" Till — oh, too blissful — I became,
 " Like thee, all spirit, all divine !

" Say, why did dream so blest come o'er
  me,
 " If, now I wake, 't is faded, gone?
" When will my Cherub shine before me
 " Thus radiant, as in heaven he
  shone?

" When shall I, waking, be allowed
 " To gaze upon those perfect charms,
" And clasp thee once without a cloud,
 " A chill of earth, within these arms?

" Oh what a pride to say, this, this
 " Is my own Angel — all divine,
" And pure and dazzling as he is
 " And fresh from heaven — he 's mine,
  he 's mine !

" Thinkest thou, were LILIS in thy
  place,
 " A creature of yon lofty skies,
" She would have hid one single grace,
 " One glory from her lover's eyes?

" No, no — then, if thou lovest like me,
 " Shine out, young Spirit in the blaze
" Of thy most proud divinity,
 " Nor think thou 'lt wound this mor-
  tal gaze.

" Too long and oft I 've looked upon
 " Those ardent eyes, intense even
  thus —
" Too near the stars themselves have
  gone,
 " To fear aught grand or luminous.

" Then doubt me not — oh! who can
  say
 " But that this dream may yet come
  true
" And my blest spirit drink thy ray,
 " Till it becomes all heavenly too?

" Let me this once but feel the flame
 " Of those spread wings, the very
  pride
" Will change my nature, and this frame
 " By the mere touch be deified ! ''

Thus spoke the maid, as one not used
To be by earth or heaven refused —
As one who knew her influence o'er
 All creatures, whatsoe'er they were,
And tho' to heaven she could not soar,
 At least would bring down heaven to
  her.

Little did she, alas ! or I —
 Even I, whose soul, but half-way yet
Immerged in sin's obscurity
Was as the earth whereon we lie,
 O'er half whose disk the sun is set —
Little did we foresee the fate,
 The dreadful — how can it be told?
Such pain, such anguish to relate
 Is o'er again to feel, behold !
But, charged as 'tis, my heart must
  speak
Its sorrow out or it will break !
Some dark misgivings *had*, I own,
 Past for a moment thro' my breast —
Fears of some danger, vague, unknown,
 To one, or both — something unblest
 To happen from this proud request.
But soon these boding fancies fled;
 Nor saw I aught that could forbid
My full revealment save the dread
 Of that first dazzle, when, unhid,
 Such light should burst upon a lid
Ne'er tried in heaven; — and even this
  glare
She might, by love's own nursing care,
Be, like young eagles, taught to bear.

For well I knew, the lustre shed
From cherub wings, when proudliest
    spread,
Was in its nature lambent, pure,
  And innocent as is the light
The glow-worm hangs out to allure
  Her mate to her green bower at night.
Oft had I in the mid-air swept
Thro' clouds in which the lightning
    slept,
  As in its lair, ready to spring,
Yet waked it not — tho' from my wing
  A thousand sparks fell glittering!
Oft too when round me from above
  The feathered snow in all its white-
    ness,
Fell like the moultings of heaven's
    Dove[1] —
  So harmless, tho' so full of brightness,
Was my brow's wreath that it would
    shake
From off its flowers each downy flake
  As delicate, unmelted, fair,
And cool as they had lighted there.

Nay even with LILIS — had I not
  Around her sleep all radiant beamed,
Hung o'er her slumbers nor forgot
  To kiss her eyelids as she dreamed?
And yet at morn from that repose,
  Had she not waked, unscathed and
    bright,
As doth the pure, unconscious rose,
  Tho' by the fire-fly kist all night?

Thus having — as, alas! deceived
By my sin's blindness, I believed —
No cause for dread and those dark eyes
  Now fixt upon me eagerly

As tho' the unlocking of the skies
  Then waited but a sign from me —
How could I pause? how even let fall
  A word, a whisper that could stir
In her proud heart a doubt that all
  I brought from heaven belonged to
    her?
Slow from her side I rose, while she
Arose too, mutely, tremblingly,
But not with fear — all hope, and pride,
  She waited for the awful boon,
Like priestesses at eventide
  Watching the rise of the full moon
Whose light, when once its orb hath
    shone,
'T will madden them to look upon!

Of all my glories, the bright crown
Which when I last from heaven came
    down
Was left behind me in yon star
That shines from out those clouds afar, —
Where, relic sad, 't is treasured yet,
The downfallen angel's coronet! —
Of all my glories, this alone
Was wanting : — but the illumined brow,
The sun-bright locks, the eyes that now
Had love's spell added to their own,
And poured a light till then unknown; —
  The unfolded wings that in their play
Shed sparkles bright as ALLA'S throne;
  All I could bring of heaven's array,
  Of that rich panoply of charms
A Cherub moves in, on the day
Of his best pomp, I now put on;
And, proud that in her eyes I shone
  Thus glorious, glided to her arms;
Which still (tho', at a sight so splendid,
  Her dazzled brow had instantly
Sunk on her breast,) were wide extended
  To clasp the form she durst not see![2]
Great Heaven! how *could* thy vengeance
    light
So bitterly on one so bright?
How could the hand that gave such
    charms,
Blast them again in love's own arms?
Scarce had I touched her shrinking frame,
  When — oh most horrible! — I felt

[1] The Dove, or pigeon which attended Mahomet as his Familiar, and was frequently seen
to whisper into his ear, was, if I recollect right,
one of that select number of animals (including
also the ant of Solomon, the dog of the Seven
Sleepers, etc.) which were thought by the
Prophet worthy of admission into Paradise.
  "The Moslems have a tradition that Mahomet
was saved (when he hid himself in a cave in
Mount Shur) by his pursuers finding the mouth
of the cave covered by a spider's web, and a
nest built by two pigeons at the entrance, with
two eggs unbroken in it, which made them
think no one could have entered it. In consequence of this, they say, Mahomet enjoined his
followers to look upon pigeons as sacred, and
never to kill a spider." — *Modern Universal
History,* vol. i.

[2] "Mohammed [says Sale], though a prophet,
was not able to bear the sight of Gabriel, when
he appeared in his proper form, much less would
others be able to support it."

That every spark of that pure flame,—
 Pure, while among the stars I dwelt —
Was now by my transgression turned
Into gross, earthly fire, which burned,
Burned all it touched as fast as eye
 Could follow the fierce, ravening
  flashes;
Till there — oh God, I still ask why
Such doom was hers? — I saw her lie
 Blackening within my arms to ashes!
That brow, a glory but to see —
 Those lips whose touch was what the
  first
Fresh cup of immortality
 Is to a new-made angel's thirst!
Those clasping arms, within whose
  round —
My heart's horizon — the whole bound
Of its hope, prospect, heaven was found!
Which, even in this dread moment, fond
 As when they first were round me cast,
Loosed not in death the fatal bond,
 But, burning, held me to the last!
All, all, that, but that morn, had seemed
As if Love's self there breathed and
  beamed,
Now parched and black before me lay,
Withering in agony away;
And mine, oh misery! mine the flame
From which this desolation came; —
I, the curst spirit whose caress
Had blasted all that loveliness!

'T was maddening! — but now hear even
  worse —
Had death, death only, been the curse
I brought upon her — had the doom
But ended here, when her young bloom
Lay in the dust — and did the spirit
No part of that fell curse inherit,
'T were not so dreadful — but, come
  near —
Too shocking 't is for earth to hear —
Just when her eyes in fading took
Their last, keen, agonized farewell,
And looked in mine with — oh, that look!
 Great vengeful Power, whate'er the
  hell
Thou mayst to human souls assign,
The memory of that look is mine! —

In her last struggle, on my brow
 Her ashy lips a kiss imprest,

So withering! — I feel it now —
 'T was fire—but fire, even more unblest
Than was my own, and like that flame,
The angels shudder but to name,
Hell's everlasting element!
 Deep, deep it pierced into my brain,
Maddening and torturing as it went;
 And here, mark here, the brand, the
  stain
It left upon my front — burnt in
By that last kiss of love and sin —
A brand which all the pomp and pride
Of a fallen Spirit cannot hide!

But is it thus, dread Providence —
 Can it indeed be thus, that she
Who, (but for *one* proud, fond offence,)
 Had honored heaven itself, should be
Now doomed — I cannot speak it — no,
Merciful ALLA! *'t is* not so —
Never could lips divine have said
The fiat of a fate so dread.
And yet, that look — so deeply fraught
 With more than anguish, with despair—
That new, fierce fire, resembling naught
 In heaven or earth — this scorch I
  bear! —
Oh — for the first time that these knees
 Have bent before thee since my fall,
Great Power, if ever thy decrees
 Thou couldst for prayer like mine recall,
Pardon that spirit, and on me,
 On me, who taught her pride to err,
Shed out each drop of agony
 Thy burning phial keeps for her!
See too where low beside me kneel
 Two other outcasts who, tho' gone
And lost themselves, yet dare to feel
 And pray for that poor mortal one.
Alas, too well, too well they know
The pain, the penitence, the woe
That Passion brings upon the best,
The wisest, and the loveliest. —
Oh! who is to be saved, if such
 Bright, erring souls are not forgiven;
So loath they wander, and so much
 Their very wanderings lean towards
  heaven!
Again, I cry, Just Power, transfer
 That creature's suffering's all to me —
 Mine, mine the guilt, the torment be,
To save one minute's pain to her,
 Let mine last all eternity!

He paused and to the earth bent down
　His throbbing head; while they who felt
That agony as 't were their own,
　Those angel youths, beside him knelt,
And in the night's still silence there,
While mournfully each wandering air
Played in those plumes that never more
To their lost home in heaven must soar,
Breathed inwardly the voiceless prayer,
Unheard by all but Mercy's ear —
And which if Mercy *did not* hear,
Oh, God would *not* be what this bright
　And glorious universe of His,
This world of beauty, goodness, light
　And endless love proclaims He *is !*

Not long they knelt, when from a wood
That crowned that airy solitude,
They heard a low, uncertain sound,
As from a lute, that just had found
Some happy theme and murmured round
The new-born fancy, with fond tone,
Scarce thinking aught so sweet its own !
Till soon a voice, that matched as well
　That gentle instrument, as suits
The sea-air to an ocean-shell,
　(So kin its spirit to the lute's),
Tremblingly followed the soft strain,
Interpreting its joy, its pain,
And lending the light wings of words
To many a thought that else had lain
　Unfledged and mute among the chords.

All started at the sound — but chief
　The third young Angel in whose face,
Tho' faded like the others, grief
　Had left a gentler, holier trace;
As if, even yet, thro' pain and ill,
Hope had not fled him — as if still
Her precious pearl in sorrow's cup
Unmelted at the bottom lay,
To shine again, when, all drunk up,
The bitterness should pass away.
Chiefly did he, tho' in his eyes
There shone more pleasure than surprise,
Turn to the wood from whence that sound
　Of solitary sweetness broke;
Then, listening, look delighted round
　To his bright peers, while thus it spoke : —

" Come, pray with me, my seraph love,
　" My angel-lord, come pray with me;
" In vain to-night my lip hath strove
　" To send one holy prayer above —
" The knee may bend, the lip may move,
　" But pray I can not, without thee !
" I 've fed the altar in my bower
　" With droppings from ţhe incense tree;
" I 've sheltered it from wind and shower,
" But dim it burns the livelong hour,
" As if, like me, it had no power
　" Of life or lustre without thee !

" A boat at midnight sent alone
　" To drift upon the moonless sea,
" A lute, whose leading chord is gone.
" A wounded bird that hath but one
" Imperfect wing to soar upon,
　" Are like what I am without thee !

" Then ne'er, my spirit-love, divide,
　" In life or death, thyself from me;
" But when again in sunny pride
" Thou walk'st thro' Eden, let me glide,
" A prostrate shadow, by thy side —
　" Oh happier thus than without thee !"

The song had ceased when from the wood
　Which sweeping down that airy height,
Reached the lone spot whereon they stood —
There suddenly shone out a light
From a clear lamp, which, as it blazed
Across the brow of one, who raised
Its flame aloft (as if to throw
The light upon that group below),
Displayed two eyes sparkling between
The dusky leaves, such as are seen
By fancy only, in those faces,
　That haunt a poet's walk at even,
Looking from out their leafy places
　Upon his dreams of love and heaven.
'T was but a moment — the blush brought
O'er all her features at the thought
　Of being seen thus, late, alone,
By any but the eyes she sought,
　Had scarcely for an instant shone
Thro' the dark leaves when she was gone —
Gone, like a meteor that o'erhead
Suddenly shines, and, ere we've said,
" Behold, how beautiful !" — 't is fled.

Yet ere she went the words, " I come,
  " I come, my NAMA," reached her ear,
  In that kind voice, familiar, dear,
Which tells of confidence, of home, —
  Of habit, that hath drawn hearts near,
Till they grow *one*, — of faith sincere,
And all that Love most loves to hear;
  A music breathing of the past,
The present and the time to be,
Where Hope and Memory to the last
  Lengthen out life's true harmony !

Nor long did he whom call so kind
Summoned away remain behind;
Nor did there need much time to tell
  What they — alas ! more fallen than he
From happiness and heaven — knew well,
  His gentler love's short history !

Thus did it run — *not* as he told
  The tale himself, but as 't is graved
Upon the tablets that, of old,
  By SETH [1] were from the deluge saved,
All written over with sublime
And saddening legends of the unblest
But glorious Spirits of that time,
  And this young Angel's 'mong the rest.

THIRD ANGEL'S STORY.

AMONG the Spirits, of pure flame,
  That in the eternal heavens abide —
Circles of light that from the same
  Unclouded centre sweeping wide,
  Carry its beams on every side —
Like spheres of air that waft around
The undulations of rich sound —

Till the far-circling radiance be
Diffused into infinity !
First and immediate near the Throne
Of ALLA,[2] as if most his own,
The Seraphs stand [3] this burning sign
Traced on their banner, " Love Divine !"
Their rank, their honors, far above
  . Even those to high-browed Cherubs
    given,
Tho' knowing all; — so much doth Love
  Transcend all Knowledge, even in
    heaven !

'Mong these was ZARAPH once — and
    none
  E'er felt affection's holy fire,
Or yearned towards the Eternal One,
  With half such longing, deep desire.
Love was to his impassioned soul
  Not as with others a mere part
Of its existence, but the whole —
  The very life-breath of his heart !

Oft, when from ALLA'S lifted brow
A lustre came, too bright to bear,
And all the seraph ranks would bow,
  To shade their dazzled sight nor dare
To look upon the effulgence there —
This Spirit's eyes would court the blaze
(Such pride he in adoring took),

2 The Mussulmans, says D'Herbelot, apply
the general name, Mocarreboun, to all those
Spirits " *qui approchent le plus près le Trône.*"
Of this number are Mikail and Gebrail.

3 The Seraphim, or Spirits of Divine Love.
  There appears to be, among writers on the
East, as well as among the Orientals themselves,
considerable indecision with regard to the respective claims of Seraphim and Cherubim to the
highest rank in the celestial hierarchy. The
derivation which Hyde assigns to the word
Cherub seems to determine the precedence in
favor of that order of spirits : — " Cherubim, i.e.
*Propinqui Angeli, qui sc. Deo proprius quam alii
accedunt ; nam Charab est* i. q. Karab, *appro-
pinquare.*" (P. 263.) Al Beidawi, too, one of
the commentators of the Koran, on that passage,
" the angels, who bear the throne, and those who
stand about it," (chap. xl.) says, " These are the
Cherubim, the highest order of angels." On the
other hand, we have seen, in a preceding note,
that the Syrians place the sphere in which the
Seraphs dwell at the very summit of all the
celestial systems ; and even, among Mahometans,
the word Azazil and Mocarreboun (which mean
the spirits that stand nearest to the throne of
Alla) are indiscriminately applied to both Seraphim and Cherubim.

1 Seth is a favorite personage among the
Orientals, and acts a conspicuous part in many
of their most extravagant romances. The Syrians pretended to have a Testament of this Patriarch in their possession, in which was explained
the whole theology of angels, their different
orders, etc. The Curds, too (as Hyde mentions
in his Appendix), have a book, which contains
all the rites of their religion, and which they call
Sohuph Sheit, or the Book of Seth.
  In the same manner that Seth and Cham are
supposed to have preserved these memorials of
antediluvian knowledge, Xixuthrus is said in
Chaldæan fable to have deposited in Siparis, the
city of the Sun, those monuments of science
which he had saved out of the waters of a deluge.
— See Jablonski's learned remarks upon these
columns or tablets of Seth, which he supposes to
be the same with the pillars of Mercury, or the
Egyptian Thoth. — " *Pantheon. Egypt.*" lib. v.
cap. 5.

And rather lose in that one gaze
  The power of looking than *not* look!
Then too when angel voices sung
The mercy of their God and strung
Their harps to hail with welcome sweet
  That moment, watched for by all eyes,
When some repentant sinner's feet
  First touched the threshold of the
    skies,
Oh! then how clearly did the voice
Of ZARAPH above all rejoice!
Love was in every buoyant tone —
  Such love as only could belong
To the blest angels and alone
  Could, even from angels, bring such
    song!

Alas! that it should e'er have been
  In heaven as 't is too often here,
Where nothing fond or bright is seen,
  But it hath pain and peril near; —
Where right and wrong so close re-
    semble,
  That what we take for virtue's thrill
Is often the first downward tremble
  Of the heart's balance unto ill;
Where Love hath not a shrine so pure,
  So holy, but the serpent, Sin,
In moments, even the most secure,
  Beneath his altar may glide in!

So was it with that Angel — such
  The charm, that sloped his fall along,
From good to ill, from loving much,
  Too easy lapse, to loving wrong. —
Even so that amorous Spirit, bound
By beauty's spell where'er 't was found,
From the bright things above the moon
  Down to earth's beaming eyes de-
    scended,
Till love for the Creator soon
  In passion for the creature ended.

'T was first at twilight, on the shore
  Of the smooth sea, he heard the lute
And voice of her he loved steal o'er
  The silver waters that lay mute,
As loath, by even a breath, to stay
The pilgrimage of that sweet lay;
Whose echoes still went on and on,
Till lost among the light that shone
Far off beyond the ocean's brim —
  There where the rich cascade of day

Had o'er the horizon's golden rim,
  Into Elysium rolled away!
Of God she sung and of the mild
  Attendant Mercy that beside
His awful throne for ever smiled,
  Ready with her white hand to guide
His bolts of vengeance to their prey —
That she might quench them on the
    way!
Of Peace — of that Atoning Love,
  Upon whose star, shining above
This twilight world of hope and fear,
  The weeping eyes of Faith are fixt
So fond that with her every tear
  The light of that love-star is mixt! —
All this she sung, and such a soul
  Of piety was in that song
That the charmed Angel as it stole
  Tenderly to his ear, along
Those lulling waters where he lay,
Watching the daylight's dying ray,
Thought 't was a voice from out the
    wave,
An echo, that some sea-nymph gave
To Eden's distant harmony,
Heard faint and sweet beneath the sea!

Quickly, however, to its source,
Tracking that music's melting course,
He saw upon the golden sand
Of the sea-shore a maiden stand,
Before whose feet the expiring waves
  Flung their last offering with a sigh —
As, in the East, exhausted slaves
  Lay down the far-brought gift and
    die —
And while her lute hung by her hushed
  As if unequal to the tide
Of song that from her lips still gushed,
  She raised, like one beatified,
Those eyes whose light seemed rather
    given
  To be adored than to adore —
Such eyes as may have lookt *from*
    heaven
  But ne'er were raised to it before!

Oh Love, Religion, Music [1] — all
  That's left of Eden upon earth —

---

[1] "*Les Egyptiens disent que la Musique est
Sœur de la Religion.*" — "*Voyages de Pytha-
gore,*" *tom.* i. p. 422.

The only blessings, since the fall
Of our weak souls, that still recall
A trace of their high, glorious birth —
How kindred are the dreams you bring !
    How Love tho' unto earth so prone,
Delights to take Religion's wing,
    When time or grief hath stained his
        own !
How near to Love's beguiling brink
    Too oft entranced Religion lies !
While Music, Music is the link
    They *both* still hold by to the skies,
The language of their native sphere
Which they had else forgotten here.

How then could ZARAPH fail to feel
    That moment's witcheries? — one, so
    fair,
Breathing out music, that might steal
    Heaven from itself, and rapt in prayer
    That seraphs might be proud to share !
Oh, he *did* feel it, all too well —
    With warmth, that far too dearly
        cost —
Nor knew he, when at last he fell,
To which attraction, to which spell,
Love, Music, or Devotion, most
His soul in that sweet hour was lost.

Sweet was the hour, tho' dearly won,
    And pure, as aught of earth could be,
For then first did the glorious sun
    Before religion's altar see
Two hearts in wedlock's golden tie
Self-pledged, in love to live and die.
Blest union ! by that Angel wove,
    And worthy from such hands to
        come;
Safe, sole asylum, in which Love,
When fallen or exiled from above,
    In this dark world can find a home.

And, tho' the Spirit had transgrest,
Had, from his station 'mong the blest
Won down by woman's smile, allow'd
    Terrestrial passion to breathe o'er
The mirror of his heart, and cloud
    God's image there so bright before —
Yet never did that Power look down
    On error with a brow so mild;
Never did Justice wear a frown,
    Thro' which so gently Mercy smiled.

For humble was their love — with awe
    And trembling like some treasure
        kept,
That was not theirs by holy law —
Whose beauty with remorse they saw,
    And o'er whose preciousness they
        wept.
Humility, that low, sweet root,
From which all heavenly virtues shoot,
Was in the hearts of both — but most
In NAMA'S heart, by whom alone
Those charms, for which a heaven was
        lost,
    Seemed all unvalued and unknown;
And when her Seraph's eyes she caught,
    And hid hers glowing on his breast,
Even bliss was humbled by the
        thought —
"What claim have I to be so blest "?
Still less could maid, so meek, have
        nurst
Desire of knowledge — that vain thirst,
With which the sex hath all been curst
From luckless EVE to her who near
The Tabernacle stole to hear
The secrets of the Angels: [1] no —
    To love as her own Seraph loved,
With Faith, the same thro' bliss and
        woe —
Faith that were even its light removed,
Could like the dial fixt remain
And wait till it shone out again; —
With Patience that tho' often bowed
    By the rude storm can rise anew;
And Hope that even from Evil's cloud
    Sees sunny Good half breaking thro' !
This deep, relying Love, worth more
In heaven than all a Cherub's lore —
This Faith more sure than aught beside
Was the sole joy, ambition, pride
Of her fond heart — the unreasoning
        scope
Of all its views, above, below —
So true she felt it that to *hope*,
    To *trust*, is happier than to *know*.
And thus in humbleness they trod,
Abasht but pure before their God;
Nor e'er did earth behold a sight
    So meekly beautiful as they,
When with the altar's holy light
    Full on their brows they knelt to pray,
Hand within hand and side by side,

1 Sara.

Two links of love awhile untied
From the great chain above, but fast
Holding together to the last ! —
Two fallen Splendors [1] from that tree
Which buds with such eternally , [2]
Shaken to earth yet keeping all
Their light and freshness in the fall.

Their only punishment, (as wrong,
  However sweet, must bear its brand,)
Their only doom was this — that, long
  As the green earth and ocean stand,
They both shall wander here — the same,
Throughout all time, in heart and
  frame —
Still looking to that goal sublime,
  Whose light remote but sure they see;
Pilgrims of Love whose way is Time,
  Whose home is in Eternity !
Subject the while to all the strife
True Love encounters in this life —
The wishes, hopes, he breathes in vain;
  The chill that turns his warmest sighs
  To earthly vapor ere they rise;
The doubt he feeds on and the pain
  That in his very sweetness lies : —
Still worse, the illusions that betray
  His footsteps to their shining brink;
That tempt him on his desert way
  Thro' the bleak world, to bend and
    drink,
Where nothing meets his lips, alas ! —
But he again must sighing pass
On to that far-off home of peace,
In which alone his thirst will cease.

All this they bear but not the less
Have moments rich in happiness —
Blest meetings, after many a day
Of widowhood past far away,
When the loved face again is seen
Close, close, with not a tear between —
Confidings frank, without control,
Poured mutually from soul to soul ;

As free from any fear or doubt
  As is that light from chill or strain
The sun into the stars sheds out
  To be by them shed back again ! —
That happy minglement of hearts,
  Where, changed as chymic compounds
    are,
Each with its own existence parts
  To find a new one, happier far !
Such are their joys — and crowning all
That blessed hope of the bright hour,
When, happy and no more to fall,
  Their spirits shall with freshened power
Rise up rewarded for their trust
  In Him from whom all goodness
    springs,
And shaking off earth's soiling dust
  From their emancipated wings,
Wander for ever thro' those skies
Of radiance where Love never dies !

In what lone region of the earth
  These Pilgrims now may roam or
    dwell,
God and the Angels who look forth
  To watch their steps, alone can tell.
But should we in our wanderings
  Meet a young pair whose beauty
    wants
But the adornment of bright wings
  To look like heaven's inhabitants —
Who shine where'er they tread and yet
  Are humble in their earthly lot,
As is the way-side violet,
  That shines unseen, and were it not
For its sweet breath would be forgot —
Whose hearts in every thought are one,
  Whose voices utter the same wills —
Answering, as Echo doth some tone
  Of fairy music 'mong the hills,
So like itself we seek in vain
Which is the echo, which the strain —

1 An allusion to the Sephiroths or Splendors
of the Jewish Cabbala, represented as a tree, of
which God is the crown or summit.
  The Sephiroths are the higher orders of eman-
ative beings in the strange and incomprehensible
system of the Jewish Cabbala.   They are called
by various names, Pity, Beauty, etc. ; and their
influences are supposed to act through certain
canals which communicate with each other.
  2 The reader may judge of the rationality of
this Jewish system by the following explanation

of part of the machinery : — "*Les canaux qui
sortent de la Miséricorde et de la Force, et qui
vont aboutir à la Beauté, sont chargés d'un
grand nombre d'Anges.   Il y en a trente-cinq
sur le canal de la Miséricorde, qui recompen-
sent et qui couronnent la vertu des Saints,*" etc.
— For a concise account of the Cabalistic Philosophy, see Enfield's very useful compendium
of Brucker.
  "*On les représente qnelquefois sous la figure
d'un arbre . . . l'Ensoph qu'on met au-dessus
de l'arbre Séphirotique ou des Splendeurs divins,
est l'Infini.*" — L'Histoire des Juifs, liv. ix. 11.

Whose piety is love, whose love
  Tho' close as 't were their souls' embrace,
Is not of earth but from above —
  Like two fair mirrors face to face,
Whose light from one to the other thrown, ·
Is heaven's reflection, not their own —
Should we e'er meet with aught so pure,
So perfect here, we may be sure
  'T is ZARAPH and his bride we see ;
And call young lovers round to view
The pilgrim pair as they pursue
  Their pathway towards eternity.

RHYMES ON THE ROAD,

EXTRACTED FROM THE JOURNAL OF

A TRAVELLING MEMBER OF

THE POCO-CURANTE SOCIETY,

1819.

———

THE greater part of the following Rhymes were written or composed in an old *calêche*, for the purpose of beguiling the *ennui* of solitary travelling; and as verses, made by a gentleman in his sleep, have been lately called "a *psychological* curiosity," it is to be hoped that verses, composed by a gentleman to keep himself awake, may be honored with some appellation equally Greek.

RHYMES ON THE ROAD.

INTRODUCTORY RHYMES.

*Different Attitudes in which Authors compose.
—Bayes, Henry Stevens, Herodotus, etc.
Writing in Bed — in the Fields. — Plato and
Sir Richard Blackmore. — Fiddling with
Gloves and Twigs. — Madame de Staël. —
Rhyming on the Road, in an old Calèche.*

WHAT various attitudes and ways
And tricks we authors have in writing!
While some write sitting, some like
    BAYES
  Usually stand while they 're inditing.
Poets there are who wear the floor out,
  Measuring a line at every stride;
While some like HENRY STEPHENS pour
  out
  Rhymes by the dozen while they
    ride.[1]
HERODOTUS wrote most in bed;
  And RICHERAND, a French physician,
Declares the clock-work of the head
  Goes best in that reclined position.
If you consult MONTAIGNE[2] and PLINY
  on
The subject, 't is their joint opinion
That Thought its richest harvest yields
  Abroad among the woods and fields,
That bards who deal in small retail
  At home may at their counters stop;
But that the grove, the hill, the vale,
  Are Poesy's true wholesale shop.
And verily I think they 're right —
  For many a time on summer eves,
Just at that closing hour of light,
  When, like an Eastern Prince, who
    leaves
For distant war his Haram bowers,
The Sun bids farewell to the flowers,

Whose heads are sunk, whose tears are
  flowing
Mid all the glory of his going ! —
Even *I* have felt, beneath those beams,
  When wandering thro' the fields
    alone,
Thoughts, fancies, intellectual gleams,
  Which, far too bright to be my own,
Seemed lent me by the Sunny Power
That was abroad at that still hour.

If thus I 've felt, how must *they* feel,
  The few whom genuine Genius warms,
Upon whose soul he stamps his seal,
  Graven with Beauty's countless
    forms; —
The few upon this earth, who seem
Born to give truth to PLATO's dream,
Since in their thoughts, as in a glass,
  Shadows of heavenly things appear,
Reflections of bright shapes that pass
  Thro' other worlds, above our sphere !

But this reminds me I digress; —
  For PLATO, too, produced, 't is said,
(As one indeed might almost guess,)
  His glorious visions all in bed.[3]
'T was in his carriage the sublime
Sir RICHARD BLACKMORE used to
  rhyme;
  And (if the wits don't do him
    wrong)
'Twixt death[4] and epics past his time,
  Scribbling and killing all day long —
Like Phœbus in his car, at ease,
Now warbling forth a lofty song,
Now murdering the young Niobes.

---

1 *pleraque sua carmina equitans composuit.* —
PARAVICIN. *Singular.*

2 *" Mes pensées dorment, si je les assis."* —
MONTAIGNE.
  *animus eorum qui in aperto aere ambulant
attollitur.* .   PLINY.

3 The only authority I know for imputing this
practice to Plato and Herodotus, is a Latin poem
by M. de Valois on his Bed, in which he says : —
*Lucifer Herodotum vidit Vesperque cubantem,
  desedit totos heic Plato sæpe dies.*

4 Sir Richard Blackmore was a physician, as
well as a bad poet.

507

There was a hero 'mong the Danes,
Who wrote, we 're told, mid all the
    pains
And horrors of exenteration,
Nine charming odes, which, if you 'll
    look,
You 'll find preserved with a transla-
    tion
By BARTHOLINUS in his book.[1]
In short 't were endless to recite
The various modes in which men write.
Some wits are only in the mind,
    When beaus and belles are round them
      prating;
Some when they dress for dinner find
    Their muse and valet both in waiting
And manage at the self-same time
To adjust a neckcloth and a rhyme.

Some bards there are who cannot
    scribble
Without a glove to tear or nibble
Or a small twig to whisk about —
    As if the hidden founts of Fancy,
Like wells of old, were thus found out
    By mystic tricks of rhabdomancy.
Such was the little feathery wand,[2]
That, held for ever in the hand
Of her[3] who won and wore the crown
    Of female genius in this age,
Seemed the conductor that drew down
    Those words of lightning to her
      page.

As for myself — to come, at last,
    To the odd way in which *I* write —
Having employed these few months past
    Chiefly in travelling, day and night,
I 've got into the easy mode
Of rhyming thus along the road —
Making a way-bill of my pages,
Counting my stanzas by my stages —
'Twixt lays and *re*-lays no time lost —
In short, in two words, *writing post.*

1 *eâdem curâ nec minores inter cruciatus
animam infelicem agenti fuit Asbiorno Prudæ
Danico heroi, cum Bruso ipsum, intestina extra-
hens, immaniter torqueret, tunc enim novem carmina cecinit, etc.* — BARTHOLIN. *" de Causis
Contempt. Mort."*

2 Made of paper, twisted up like a fan or
feather.

3 Madame de Staël.

EXTRACT I.

Geneva.

View of the Lake of Geneva from the Jura.[4] —
  Anxious to reach it before the Sun went down.
  — *Obliged to proceed on Foot.* — *Alps.* — *Mont
  Blanc.* — *Effect of the Scene.*

'T WAS late — the sun had almost shone
His last and best when I ran on
Anxious to reach that splendid view
Before the day-beams quite withdrew
And feeling as all feel on first
    Approaching scenes where, they are
      told,
Such glories on their eyes will burst
    As youthful bards in dreams behold.

'T was distant yet and as I ran
    Full often was my wistful gaze
Turned to the sun who now began
    To call in all his out-posts rays,
And form a denser march of light,
Such as beseems a hero's flight.
Oh, how I wisht for JOSHUA's power,
To stay the brightness of that hour !
But no — the sun still less became,
    Diminisht to a speck as splendid
And small as were those tongues of flame,
    That on the Apostles' heads de-
      scended !

'T was at this instant — while there
    glowed
This last, intensest gleam of light —
Suddenly thro' the opening road
The valley burst upon my sight !
That glorious valley with its Lake
    And Alps on Alps in clusters swelling,
Mighty and pure and fit to make
    The ramparts of a Godhead's dwelling.

I stood entranced — as Rabbins say
    This whole assembled, gazing world
Will stand, upon that awful day,
    When the Ark's Light aloft unfurled
Among the opening clouds shall shine,
Divinity's own radiant sign !

Mighty MONT BLANC, thou wert to me
    That minute, with thy brow in heaven,
As sure a sign of Deity
    As e'er to mortal gaze was given.

4 Between Vattay and Gex.

Nor ever, were I destined yet
　To live my life twice o'er again,
Can I the deep-felt awe forget,
　The dream, the trance that rapt me
　　then!

'T was all that consciousness of power
And life, beyond this mortal hour; —
Those mountings of the soul within
At thoughts of Heaven — as birds begin
By instinct in the cage to rise,
When near their time for change of
　　skies; —
That proud assurance of our claim
　To rank among the Sons of Light,
Mingled with shame—oh bitter shame!—
　At having riskt that splendid right,
For aught that earth thro' all its range
Of glories offers in exchange!
'T was all this, at that instant brought
Like breaking sunshine o'er my thought—
'T was all this, kindled to a glow
　Of sacred zeal which could it shine
Thus purely ever man might grow,
　Even upon earth a thing divine,
And be once more the creature made
To walk unstained the Elysian shade!

No, never shall I lose the trace
Of what I 've felt in this bright place.
And should my spirit's hope grow weak,
　Should I, oh God! e'er doubt thy
　　power,
This mighty scene again I 'll seek,
　At the same calm and glowing hour,
And here at the sublimest shrine
　That Nature ever reared to Thee
Rekindle all that hope divine
And *feel* my immortality!

EXTRACT II.

Geneva.

FATE OF GENEVA IN THE YEAR 1782.

A FRAGMENT.

YES — if there yet live some of those,
Who, when this small Republic rose,
Quick as a startled hive of bees,
Against her leaguering enemies [1] —

When, as the Royal Satrap shook
　His well-known fetters at her gates,
Even wives and mothers armed and took
　Their stations by their sons and mates;
And on these walls there stood — yet, no,
　Shame to the traitors — *would* have
　　stood
As firm a band as e'er let flow
　At Freedom's base their sacred blood;
If those yet live, who on that night
When all were watching, girt for fight,
Stole like the creeping of a pest
From rank to rank, from breast to breast,
Filling the weak, the old with fears,
Turning the heroine's zeal to tears, —
Betraying Honor to that brink,
Where, one step more, and he must
　　slink —
And quenching hopes which tho' the last,
Like meteors on a drowning mast,
Would yet have led to death more
　　bright,
Than life e'er lookt, in all its light!
Till soon, too soon, distrust, alarms
　Throughout the embattled thousands
　　ran,
And the high spirit, late in arms,
The zeal that might have workt such
　　charms,
　Fell like a broken talisman —
Their gates, that they had sworn should
　　be
The gates of Death, that very dawn,
Gave passage widely, bloodlessly,
　To the proud foe — nor sword was
　　drawn,
Nor even one martyred body cast
To stain their footsteps, as they past;
But of the many sworn at night
To do or die, some fled the sight,
Some stood to look with sullen frown,
　While some in impotent despair
Broke their bright armor and lay down,
　Weeping, upon the fragments there!—
If those, I say, who brought that shame,
That blast upon GENEVA'S name,
Be living still — tho' crime so dark
　Shall hang up, fixt and unforgiven,

1 In the year 1782, when the forces of Berne,
Sardinia, and France laid siege to Geneva, and
when, after a demonstration of heroism and self-
devotion, which promised to rival the feats of
their ancestors in 1602 against Savoy, the Gene-
vans, either panic-struck or betrayed, to the surprise of all Europe, opened their gates to the
besiegers, and submitted without a struggle to
the extinction of their liberties. — See an account
of this Revolution in Coxe's Switzerland.

In History's page, the eternal mark
  For Scorn to pierce — so help me,
    Heaven,
I wish the traitorous slaves no worse,
  No deeper, deadlier disaster,
From all earth's ills no fouler curse
  Than to have * * * * * * * * * * * their
    master!

EXTRACT III.

Geneva.

Fancy and Truth. — Hippomenes and Atalanta.
  Mont Blanc. — Clouds.

EVEN here in this region of wonders I
    find
That light-footed Fancy leaves Truth far
    behind;
Or at least like Hippomenes turns her
    astray
By the golden illusions he flings in her
    way.[1]

What a glory it seemed the first evening
    I gazed!
MONT BLANC like a vision then suddenly
    raised
On the wreck of the sunset — and all his
    array
  Of high-towering Alps, touched still
    with a light
Far holier, purer than that of the Day,
  As if nearness to Heaven had made
    them so bright!
Then the dying at last of these splendors
    away
From peak after peak, till they left but a
    ray,
One roseate ray, that, too precious to
    fly,
  O'er the Mighty of Mountains still
    glowingly hung,
Like the last sunny step of ASTRÆA, when
    high
  From the summit of earth to Elysium
    she sprung!
And those infinite Alps stretching out
    from the sight
Till they mingled with Heaven, now
    shorn of their light,

1 ——*nitidique cupidine pomi*
    declinat cursus, aurumque volubile tollit.
                                  OVID.

Stood lofty and lifeless and pale in the sky,
Like the ghosts of a Giant Creation
    gone by!

That scene — I have viewed it this even-
    ing again,
By the same brilliant light that hung over
    it then —
The valley, the lake in their tenderest
    charms —
  MONT BLANC in his awfullest pomp —
    and the whole
A bright picture of Beauty, reclined in
    the arms
  Of Sublimity, bridegroom elect of her
    soul!
But where are the mountains that round
    me at first
One dazzling horizon of miracles burst?
Those Alps beyond Alps, without end
    swelling on
Like the waves of eternity — where are
    they gone?
Clouds — clouds — they were nothing
    but clouds, after all![2]
  That chain of MONT BLANCS, which
    my fancy flew o'er,
With a wonder that naught on this earth
    can recall,
  Were but clouds of the evening and
    now are no more.

What a picture of Life's young illusions!
    Oh, Night,
Drop thy curtain at once and hide *all*
    from my sight.

EXTRACT IV.

Milan.

The Picture Gallery. — Albano's Rape of Pros-
  erpine. — Reflections. — Universal Salvation.
  — Abraham sending away Agar, by Guer-
  cino. — Genius.

WENT to the *Brera* — saw a Dance of
    Loves
  By smooth ALBANO;[3] him whose pencil
    teems

2 It is often very difficult to distinguish between clouds and Alps; and on the evening when
I first saw this magnificent scene, the clouds were
so disposed along the whole horizon, as to deceive
me into an idea of the stupendous extent of these
mountains, which my subsequent observation was
very far, of course, from confirming.

3 This picture, the Agar of Guercino, and the

With Cupids numerous as in summer
    groves
The leaflets are or motes in summer
    beams.

'T is for the theft of Enna's flower [1] from
    earth,
These urchins celebrate their dance of
    mirth
Round the green tree, like fays upon a
    heath —
    Those that are nearest linkt in order
      bright,
Cheek after cheek, like rose-buds in a
    wreath;
And those more distant showing from
    beneath
    The others' wings their little eyes of
      light.
While see! among the clouds, their eldest
    brother
    But just flown up tells with a smile of
      bliss
This prank of Pluto to his charmed
    mother
    Who turns to greet the tidings with a
      kiss!

Well might the Loves rejoice — and well
    did they
    Who wove these fables picture in their
      weaving
That blessed truth, (which in a darker
    day
    ORIGEN lost his saintship for believ-
      ing, [2]) —
That Love, eternal Love, whose fadeless
    ray
    Nor time nor death nor sin can over-
      cast,
Even to the depths of hell will find his
    way,
    And soothe and heal and triumph there
      at last!

Apostles of Guido (the two latter of which are
now the chief ornaments of the Brera), were
formerly in the Palazzo Zampieri at Bologna.

1 —— that fair field
Of Enna, where Proserpine, gathering flowers,
Herself a fairer flower, by gloomy Dis was
gathered.

2 The extension of the Divine Love ultimately even to the regions of the damned.

GUERCINO'S Agar — where the bond-
    maid hears
    From Abram's lips that he and she
      must part,
And looks at him with eyes all full of
    tears
    That seem the very last drops from her
      heart.
Exquisite picture! — let me not be told
Of minor faults, of coloring tame and
    cold —
If thus to conjure up a face so fair, [3]
So full of sorrow; with the story
    there
Of all that woman suffers when the stay
    Her trusting heart hath leaned on falls
      away —
If thus to touch the bosom's tenderest
    spring,
By calling into life such eyes as bring
Back to our sad remembrance some of
    those
We 've smiled and wept with in their
    joys and woes,
Thus filling them with tears, like tears
    we 've known,
Till all the pictured grief becomes our
    own —
If *this* be deemed the victory of Art —
    If thus by pen or pencil to lay bare
The deep, fresh, living fountains of the
    heart
Before all eyes be Genius — it is *there!*

EXTRACT V.

Padua.

*Fancy and Reality. — Rain-drops and Lakes. —
Plan of a Story. — Where to place the Scene
of it. — In some unknown Region. — Psalm-
anazar's Imposture with respect to the Island
of Formosa.*

THE more I 've viewed this world the
    more I 've found,
    That, filled as 't is with scenes and
      creatures rare,
Fancy commands within her own bright
    round
    A world of scenes and creatures far
      more fair.

3 It is probable that this fine head is a portrait, as we find it repeated in a picture by Guercino, which is in the possession of Signor Ca-
muccini, the brother of the celebrated painter at
Rome.

Nor is it that her power can call up there
  A single charm, that 's not from Na-
    ture won,
No more than rainbows in their pride can
    wear
  A single hue unborrowed from the
    sun —
But 't is the mental medium it shines
    thro'
That lends to Beauty all its charm and
    hue;
As the same light that o'er the level lake
  One dull monotony of lustre flings,
Will, entering in the rounded rain-drop,
    make
  Colors as gay as those on Peris' wings!

  And such, I deem, the difference be-
    tween real,
Existing Beauty and that form ideal
Which she assumes when seen by poets'
    eyes,
Like sunshine in the drop — with all
    those dyes
Which Fancy's variegating prism sup-
    plies.

I have a story of two lovers, filled
  With all the pure romance, the blissful
    sadness,
And the sad, doubtful bliss that ever
    thrilled
  Two young and longing hearts in that
    sweet madness.
But where to choose the region of my
    vision
  In this wide, vulgar world — what real
    spot
Can be found out sufficiently Elysian
  For two such perfect lovers I know
    not.
Oh for some fair FORMOSA, such as he,
The young Jew fabled of, in the Indian
    Sea,
By nothing but its name of Beauty known,
And which Queen Fancy might make all
    her own,
Her fairy kingdom — take its people,
    lands,
And tenements into her own bright
    hands,
And make at least one earthly corner fit
For Love to live in, pure and exquisite!

EXTRACT VI.

Venice.

The Fall of Venice not to be lamented. —
Former Glory. — Expedition against Con-
stantinople. — Giustinianis. — Republic. —
Characteristics of the old Government.—
Golden Book. — Brazen Mouths. — Spies. —
Dungeons. — Present Desolation.

MOURN not for VENICE — let her rest
In ruin, 'mong those States unblest,
Beneath whose gilded hoofs of pride,
Where'er they trampled, Freedom died.
No — let us keep our tears for them,
  Where'er they pine, whose fall hath
    been
Not from a blood-stained diadem,
  Like that which deckt this ocean-
    queen,
But from high daring in the cause
  Of human Rights — the only good
And blessed strife, in which man draws
  His mighty sword on land or flood.

Mourn not for VENICE; tho' her fall
  Be awful, as if Ocean's wave
Swept o'er her, she deserves it all,
  And Justice triumphs o'er her grave.
Thus perish every King and State
  That run the guilty race she ran,
Strong but in ill and only great
  By outrage against God and man!

True, her high spirit is at rest,
  And all those days of glory gone,
When the world's waters, east and west,
  Beneath her white-winged commerce
    shone;
When with her countless barks she went
  To meet the Orient Empire's might,[1]
And her Giustinianis sent
  Their hundred heroes to that fight.[2]

Vanisht are all her pomps, 't is true,
But mourn them not — for vanisht too
  (Thanks to that Power, who, soon or
    late,
  Hurls to the dust the guilty Great,)

1 Under the Doge Michaeli, in 1171.

2 "*La famille entière des Justiniani, l'une*
des plus illustres de Venise, voulut marcher
toute entière dans cette expédition; elle fournit
cent combattans; c'était renouveler l'exemple
d'une illustre famille de Rome; le même mal-
heur les attendait." — "*Histoire de Venise,*"
par DARU.

Are all the outrage, falsehood, fraud,
　The chains, the rapine, and the blood,
That filled each spot, at home, abroad,
　Where the Republic's standard stood.
Desolate VENICE! when I track
Thy haughty course thro' centuries back;
Thy ruthless power, obeyed but curst —
　The stern machinery of thy State,
Which hatred would, like steam, have
　　burst,
　　Had stronger fear not chilled even
　　　hate; —
Thy perfidy, still worse than aught
Thy own unblushing SARPI [1] taught; —
Thy friendship which, o'er all beneath
　Its shadow, rained down dews of
　　death; [2] —
Thy Oligarchy's Book of Gold,
　Closed against humble Virtue's name, [3]

But opened wide for slaves who sold
　Their native land to thee and shame; [4] —
Thy all-pervading host of spies
　Watching o'er every glance and breath,
Till men lookt in each others' eyes,
　To read their chance of life or death; —
Thy laws that made a mart of blood,
　And legalized the assassin's knife; [5] —

[4] Among those admitted to the honor of being inscribed in the *Libro d'oro* were some families of Brescia, Treviso, and other places, whose only claim to that distinction was the zeal with which they prostrated themselves and their country at the feet of the republic.

[5] By the infamous statutes of the State Inquisition,* not only was assassination recognized as a regular mode of punishment, but this secret power over life was delegated to their minions at a distance, with nearly as much facility as a license is given under the game laws of England. The only restriction seems to have been the necessity of applying for a new certificate, after every individual exercise of the power.

[1] The celebrated Fra Paolo. The collections of Maxims which this bold monk drew up at the request of the Venetian Government, for the guidance of the Secret Inquisition of State, are so atrocious as to seem rather an over-charged satire upon despotism, than a system of policy, seriously inculcated, and but too readily and constantly pursued.
　The spirit, in which these maxims of Father Paul are conceived, may be judged from the instructions which he gives for the management of the Venetian colonies and provinces. Of the former he says: — "*Il faut les traitor comme des animaux féroces, les rogner les dents, et les griffes, les humilier souvent, surtout leur ôter les occasions de s'aguerrir. Du pain et le bâton, voilà ce qu'il leur faut; gardons l'humanité pour une meilleure occasion.*"
　For the treatment of the provinces he advises thus: —
　"*Tendre à dépouiller les villes de leurs privilèges, faire que les habitans s'appauvrissent, et que leurs biens soient achetés par les Vénitiens. Ceux qui, dans les conseils municipaux, se montreront ou plus audacieux ou plus dévoués aux intérêts de la population, il faut les perdre ou les gagner à quelque prix que ce soit: enfin, s'il se trouve dans les provinces quelques chefs de parti, il faut les exterminer sous un prétexte quelconque, mais en évitant de recourir à la justice ordinaire. Que le poison fasse l'office de bourreau, cela est moins odieux et beaucoup plus profitable.*"

[2] Conduct of Venice towards her allies and dependencies, particularly to unfortunate Padua. — Fate of Francesco Carrara, for which see *Daru*, vol. ii. p. 141.

[3] "*A l'exception des trente citadins admis au grand conseil pendant la guerre de Chiozzi, il n'est pas arrivé une seule fois que les talens ou les services aient paru à cette noblesse orgueilleuse des titres suffisans pour s'asseoir avec elle.*" — DARU.

* M. Daru has given an abstract of these Statutes, from a manuscript in the *Bibliothèque du Roi*, and it is hardly credible that such a system of treachery and cruelty should ever have been established by any government, or submitted to, for an instant, by any people. Among various precautions against the intrigues of their own Nobles, we find the following: — "*Pour persuader aux étrangers qu'il était difficile et dangereux d'entretenir quelqu' intrigue secrète avec les nobles Vénitiens, on imagina de faire avertir mystérieusement le Nonce du Pape (afin que les autres ministres en fussent informés) que l'Inquisition avait autorisé les patriciens à poignarder quiconque essaierait de tenter leur fidélité. Mais craignant que les ambassadeurs ne prêtassent foi difficilement à une délibération, qui en effet n'e xistait pas, l'Inquisition voulait prouver qu'elle en était capable. Elle ordonna des recherches pour découvrir s'il n'y avait pas dans Venise quelque exilé au-dessus du commun, qui eût rompu son ban; ensuite un des patriciens qui étaient aux gages du tribunal, reçut la mission d'assassiner ce malheureux, et l'ordre de s'en vanter, en disant qu'il s'était porté à cet acte, parce que ce banni était l'agent d'un ministre étranger, et avait cherché à le corrompre.*"
　— "*Remarquons,*" adds M. Daru, "*que ceci n'est pas une simple anecdote; c'est une mission projetée, délibérée, écrite d'avance; une règle de conduite tracée par des hommes graves à leurs successeurs, et consignée dans des statuts.*"
　The cases, in which assassination is ordered by these Statutes, are as follow: —
　"*Un ouvrier de l'arsenal, un chef de ce qu'on appelle parmi les marins le menstrance, passait-il au service d'une puissance étrangère: il fallait le faire assassiner, surtout si c'était un homme réputé brave et habile dans sa profession.*" (Art. 3. des Statuts.)
　"*Avait-il commis quelque action qu'on ne jugeait pas à propos de punir juridiquement, on devait le faire empoisonner.*" (Art. 14.)

Thy sunless cells beneath the flood,
  And racks and Leads[1] that burnt out
    life; —

When I review all this and see
The doom that now hath fallen on thee;
Thy nobles, towering once so proud,
Themselves beneath the yoke now
    bowed, —
A yoke by no one grace redeemed,
Such as of old around thee beamed,
But mean and base as e'er yet galled
Earth's tyrants when themselves en-
    thralled, —
I feel the moral vengeance sweet,
And smiling o'er the wreck repeat: —
"Thus perish every King and State
  "That tread the steps which VENICE
    trod,
  "Strong but in ill and only great,
    "By outrage against man and God!"

EXTRACT VII.

Venice.

*Lord Byron's Memoirs, written by himself. —
Reflections, when about to read them.*

LET me a moment — ere with fear and
    hope
Of gloomy, glorious things, these leaves
    I ope —
As one in fairy tale to whom the key
  Of some enchanter's secret halls is
    given,
Doubts while he enters slowly, trem-
    blingly,
  If he shall meet with shapes from hell
    or heaven —
Let me a moment think what thousands
    live

---

1 "*Les prisons des plombs; c'est-à-dire ces
fournaises ardentes qu'on avait distribuées en
petites cellule sous les terrasses qui couvrent le
palais.*"

"*Un artisan passait-il à l'étranger en y ex-
portant quelque procédé de l'industrie nationale:
c'était encore un crime capital, que la loi incon-
nue ordonnait de punir par un assassinat.*"
(*Art.* 26.)
  The facility with which they got rid of their
Duke of Bedfords, Lord Fitzwilliams, etc., was
admirable: it was thus: —
"*Le patricien qui se permettait le moindre
propos contre le gouvernement, était admonété
deux fois, et à la troisième* noyé *comme incorri-
gible.*" (*Art.* 39.)

O'er the wide earth this instant who
    would give,
Gladly, whole sleepless nights to bend
    the brow
Over these precious leaves as I do now.
How all who know — and where is he
    unknown?
To what far region have his songs not
    flown,
Like PSAPHON'S birds[2] speaking their
    master's name,
In every language syllabled by Fame? —
How all who 've felt the various spells
    combined
Within the circle of that master-mind, —
Like spells derived from many a star and
    met
Together in some wondrous amulet, —
Would burn to know when first the
    Light awoke
In his young soul, — and if the gleams
    that broke
From that Aurora of his genius, raised
Most pain or bliss in those on whom they
    blazed;
Would love to trace the unfolding of
    that power,
Which hath grown ampler, grander,
    every hour;
And feel in watching o'er his first ad-
    vance
  As did the Egyptian traveller[3] when
    he stood
By the young Nile and fathomed with
    his lance
  The first small fountains of that mighty
    flood.

They too who mid the scornful thoughts
    that dwell
  In his rich fancy, tingeing all its
    streams, —
As if the Star of Bitterness which fell
  On earth of old,[4] had touched them
    with its beams, —

---

2 Psaphon, in order to attract the attention of
the world, taught multitudes of birds to speak
his name, and then let them fly away in various
directions; whence the proverb, "*Psaphoni
aves.*"

3 Bruce.

5 "And the name of the star is called Wormwood, and the third part of the waters became
wormwood." — *Rev.* viii.

Can track a spirit which tho' driven to
hate,
From Nature's hands came kind, affec-
tionate;
And which even now, struck as it is with
blight,
Comes out at times in love's own native
light; —
How gladly all who 've watched these
struggling rays
Of a bright, ruined spirit thro' his lays,
Would here inquire, as from his own
frank lips,
What desolating grief, what wrongs
had driven
That noble nature into cold eclipse;
Like some fair orb that, once a sun in
heaven,
And born not only to surprise but cheer
With warmth and lustre all within its
sphere,
Is now so quenched that of its grandeur
lasts
Naught but the wide, cold shadow which
it casts !

Eventful volume ! whatsoe'er the change
Of scene and clime — the adventures
bold and strange —
The griefs — the frailties but too frankly
told —
The loves, the feuds thy pages may unfold,
If Truth with half so prompt a hand unlocks
His virtues as his failings, we shall
find
The record there of friendships held like
rocks,
And enmities like sun-touched snow
resigned;
Of fealty, cherisht without change or
chill,
In those who served him, young, and
serve him still;
Of generous aid given, with that noiseless art
Which wakes not pride, to many a
wounded heart;
Of acts — but, no — *not* from himself
must aught
Of the bright features of his life be
sought.

While they who court the world, like
MILTON'S cloud,[1]
"Turn forth their silver lining" on the
crowd,
This gifted Being wraps himself in night;
And keeping all that softens and adorns
And gilds his social nature hid from
sight,
Turns but its darkness on a world he
scorns.

EXTRACT VIII.

Venice.

*Female Beauty at Venice. — No longer what it
was in the Time of Titian. — His mistress.
— Various Forms in which he has painted
her. — Venus. — Divine and profane Love. —
Lu Fragilità d' Amore. — Paul Veronese. —
His Women. — Marriage of Cana. — Charac-
ter of Italian Beauty. — Raphael's Fornarina.
— Modesty.*

THY brave, thy learned have past away:
Thy beautiful ! — ah, where are they?
The forms, the faces that once shone,
    Models of grace, in Titian's eye,
Where are they now? while flowers live
        on
    In ruined places, why, oh ! why
    Must Beauty thus with Glory die?
That maid whose lips would still have
        moved,
    Could art have breathed a spirit thro'
        them;
Whose varying charms her artist loved
    More fondly every time he drew them,
(So oft beneath his touch they past,
Each semblance fairer than the last);
Wearing each shape that Fancy's range
Offers to Love — yet still the one
Fair idol seen thro' every change,
    Like facets of some orient stone, —
    In each the same bright image shown.
Sometimes a Venus, unarrayed
    But in her beauty [2] — sometimes deckt
In costly raiment, as a maid
    That kings might for a throne select.[3]
Now high and proud, like one who
        thought
The world should at her feet be brought;

---

1   "Did a sable cloud
Turn forth her silver lining on the night?"
                                    Comus.

2 In the Tribune at Florence.
3 In the Palazzo Pitti.

Now with a look reproachful, sad,[1] —
Unwonted look from brow so glad; —
And telling of a pain too deep
For tongue to speak or eyes to weep.
Sometimes thro' allegory's veil,
   In double semblance seen to shine,
Telling a strange and mystic tale
   Of Love Profane and Love Divine [2] —
Akin in features, but in heart
As far as earth and heaven apart.
Or else (by quaint device to prove
The frailty of all worldly love)
Holding a globe of glass as thin
   As air-blown bubbles in her hand,
With a young Love confined therein,
   Whose wings seem waiting to ex-
      pand —
And telling by her anxious eyes
That if that frail orb breaks he flies![3]

Thou too with touch magnificent,
   PAUL of VERONA! — where are they,
The oriental forms[4] that lent
   Thy canvas such a bright array?
Noble and gorgeous dames whose dress
Seems each of their own loveliness;
Like the sun's drapery which at eve
The floating clouds around him weave
Of light they from himself receive!
Where is there now the living face
   Like those that in thy nuptial throng [5]
By their superb, voluptuous grace,
Make us forget the time, the place,
 • The holy guests they smile among, —
Till in that feast of heaven-sent wine
We see no miracles but thine.

1 Alludes particularly to the portrait of her in the Sciarra collection at Rome, where the look of mournful reproach in those full, shadowy eyes, as if she had been unjustly accused of something wrong, is exquisite.

2 The fine picture in the Palazzo Borghese, called (it is not easy to say why) "Sacred and Profane Love," in which the two figures, sitting on the edge of the fountain, are evidently portraits of the same person.

3 This fanciful allegory is the subject of a picture by Titian in the possession of the Marquis Cambian at Turin, whose collection, though small, contains some beautiful specimens of all the great masters.

4 As Paul Veronese gave but little into the *beau idéal*, his women may be regarded as pretty close imitations of the living models which Venice afforded in his time.

5 The Marriage of Cana.

If e'er, except in Painting's dream,
   There bloomed such beauty here, t 'is
      gone,—
Gone like the face that in the stream
   Of Ocean for an instant shone,
When Venus at that mirror gave
A last look ere she left the wave.
And tho,' among the crowded ways,
We oft are startled by the blaze
Of eyes that pass with fitful light,
Like fire-flies on the wing at night [6]
'T is not that nobler beauty given
To show how angels look in heaven.
Even in its shape most pure and fair,
   'T is Beauty with but half her zone, —
All that can warm the Sense is there,
   But the Soul's deeper charm is flown:—
'T is RAPHAEL'S Fornarina, — warm,
   Luxuriant, arch, but unrefined;
A flower round which the noontide
      swarm
Of young Desires may buzz and wind,
But where true Love no treasure meets
Worth hoarding in his hive of sweets.

Ah no, — for this and for the hue
   Upon the rounded cheek, which tells
How fresh within the heart this dew
   Of Love's unrifled sweetness dwells,
We must go back to our own Isles,
   Where Modesty, which here but gives
A rare and transient grace to smiles,
   In the heart's holy centre lives;
And thence as from her throne diffuses
   O'er thoughts and looks so bland a
      reign,
That not a thought or feeling loses
   Its freshness in that gentle chain.

EXTRACT IX.
Venice.

The English to be met with every where. — Alps and Threadneedle Street. — The Simplon and the Stocks. — Rage for travelling. — Blue Stockings among the Wahabees. — Parasols and Pyramids. — Mrs. Hopkins and the Wall of China.

AND is there then no earthly place,
   Where we can rest in dream Elysian,
Without some curst, round English face,
Popping up near to break the vision?

6 "Certain it is [as Arthur Young truly and feelingly says] one now and then meets with terrible eyes in Italy."

Mid northern lakes, mid southern
  vines,
Unholy cits we 're doomed to meet;
Nor highest Alps nor Apennines
  Are sacred from Threadneedle Street!

If up the Simplon's path we wind,
Fancying we leave this world behind,
Such pleasant sounds salute one's ear
As — " Baddish news from 'Change, my
  dear —
" The Funds — (phew! curse this ugly
  hill) —
" Are lowering fast — (what, higher
  still?) —
" And — (zooks, we 're mounting up to
  heaven!) —
" Will soon be down to sixty seven."

Go where we may — rest where we
  will,
Eternal London haunts us still.
The trash of Almack's or Fleet Ditch —
And scarce a pin's head difference
  which —
Mixes, tho' even to Greece we run,
With every rill from Helicon!
And if this rage for travelling lasts,
If Cockneys of all sects and castes,
Old maidens, aldermen, and squires,
Will leave their puddings and coal
  fires,
To gape at things in foreign lands
No soul among them understands;
If Blues desert their coteries,
To show off 'mong the Wahabees;
If neither sex nor age controls,
  Nor fear of Mamelukes forbids
Young ladies with pink parasols
  To glide among the Pyramids [1] —

Why, then, farewell all hope to find
A spot that 's free from London-kind!
Who knows, if to the West we roam,
But we may find some *Blue* " at home "
  Among the *Blacks* of Carolina —
Or flying to the Eastward see
Some Mrs. HOPKINS taking tea
  And toast upon the Wall of China!

[1] It was pink *spencers*, I believe, that the
imagination of the French traveller conjured up.

EXTRACT X.

Mantua.

Verses of Hippolyta to her Husband.

THEY tell me thou 'rt the favored guest [2]
  Of every fair and brilliant throng;
No wit like thine to wake the jest,
  No voice like thine to breathe the song.
And none could guess, so gay thou art,
That thou and I are far apart.
Alas, alas! how different flows,
  With thee and me the time away!
Not that I wish thee sad, heaven
  knows —
  Still if thou canst, be light and gay;
I only know that without thee
The sun himself is dark for me.

Do I put on the jewels rare
Thou 'st always loved to see me wear?
Do I perfume the locks that thou
So oft hast braided o'er my brow,
Thus deckt thro' festive crowds to run,
  And all the assembled world to see, —
All but the one, the absent one,
  Worth more than present worlds to
  me!
No, nothing cheers this widowed heart —
My only joy from thee apart,
From thee thyself, is sitting hours
  And days before thy pictured form —
That dream of thee, which Raphael's
  powers
  Have made with all but life-breath
  warm!
And as I smile to it, and say
The words I speak to thee in play,

2 *utque ferunt lætus convivia læta*
  et celebras lentis otia mista jocis;
  aut cithara æstivum attenuas cantuque calo-
  rem.
  hei mihi, quam dispar nunc mea vita tuæ!
  nec mihi displiceant quæ sunt tibi grata; sed
  ipsa est,
  te sine, lux oculis pene inimica meis.
non auro aut gemmâ caput exornare nitenti
  me juvat, aut Arabo spargere odore comas:
  non celebres ludos fastis spectare diebus.

  sola tuos vultus referens Raphaelis imago
  picta manu, curas allevat usque meas.
huic ego delicias facio, arrideoque jocorque,
  alloquor et tanquam reddere verba queat.
assensu nutuque mihi sæpe illa videtur
  dicere velle aliquid et tua verba loqui.
agnoscit balboque patrem puer ore salutat.
  hoc solor longas decipioque dies.

I fancy from their silent frame,
Those eyes and lips give back the same;
And still I gaze, and still they keep
Smiling thus on me — till I weep!
Our little boy too knows it well,
    For there I lead him every day
And teach his lisping lips to tell
    The name of one that 's far away.
Forgive me, love, but thus alone
My time is cheered while thou art gone.

EXTRACT XI.

Florence.

No — 't is not the region where Love's
    to be found —
    They have bosoms that sigh, they have
        glances that rove,
They have language a Sappho's own lip
        might resound,
    When she warbled her best — but
        they 've nothing like Love.

Nor is 't that pure *sentiment* only they
        want,
    Which Heaven for the mild and the
        tranquil hath made —
Calm, wedded affection, that home-
        rooted plant
    Which sweetens seclusion and smiles
        in the shade;

That feeling which, after long years
        have gone by,
    Remains like a portrait we 've sat for
        in youth,
Where, even tho' the flush of the colors
        may fly,
    The features still live in their first
        smiling truth;

That union where all that in Woman is
        kind,
    With all that in Man most ennoblingly
        towers,
Grow wreathed into one — like the col-
        umn, combined
    Of the *strength* of the shaft and the
        capital's *flowers*.

Of this — bear ye witness, ye wives,
        every where,
    By the ARNO, the PO, by all ITALY'S
        streams —

Of this heart-wedded love, so delicious
    to share,
    Not a husband hath even one glimpse
        in his dreams.

But it *is* not this only; — born full of
        the light
    Of a sun from whose fount the luxuri-
        ant festoons
Of these beautiful valleys drink lustre so
        bright
    That beside him our suns of the north
        are but moons, —

We might fancy at least, like their cli-
        mate they burned;
    And that Love tho' unused in this
        region of spring
To be thus to a tame Household Deity
        turned,
    Would yet be all soul when abroad on
        the wing.

And there *may* be, there *are* those ex-
        plosions of heart
    Which burst when the senses have first
        caught the flame;
Such fits of the blood as those climates
        impart,
    Where Love is a sun-stroke that mad-
        dens the frame.

But that Passion which springs in the
        depth of the soul;
    Whose beginnings are virginly pure as
        the source
Of some small mountain rivulet destined
        to roll
    As a torrent ere long, losing peace in
        its course —

A course to which Modesty's struggle
        but lends
    A more headlong descent without
        chance of recall;
But which Modesty even to the last edge
        attends,
    And then throws a halo of tears round
        its fall!

This exquisite Passion — ay, exquisite,
        even
    Mid the ruin its madness too **often**
        hath made,

As it keeps even then a bright trace of
    the heaven,
      That heaven of Virtue from which it
      has strayed —

This entireness of love which can only
    be found,
      Where Woman like something that's
      holy, watched over,
And fenced from her childhood with
    purity round,
      Comes body and soul fresh as Spring
      to a lover!

Where not an eye answers, where not a
    hand presses,
      Till spirit with spirit in sympathy
      move;
And the Senses asleep in their sacred
    recesses
      Can only be reached thro' the temple
      of Love! —

This perfection of Passion — how *can* it
    be found,
      Where the mystery Nature hath hung
      round the tie
By which souls are together attracted
    and bound,
      Is laid open for ever to heart, ear and
      eye; —

Where naught of that innocent doubt
    can exist,
      That ignorance even than knowledge
      more bright,
Which circles the young like the morn's
    sunny mist,
      And curtains them round in their own
      native light; —

Where Experience leaves nothing for
    Love to reveal,
      Or for Fancy in visions to gleam o'er
      the thought;
But the truths which alone we would die
    to conceal
      From the maiden's young heart are
      the *only* ones taught.

No, no, 't is not here, howsoever we
    sigh,
      Whether purely to Hymen's *one*
      planet we pray,

Or adore, like Sabæans, each light of
    Love's sky,
      Here *is* not the region to fix or to
      stray.

For faithless in wedlock, in gallantry
    gross,
      Without honor to guard, or reserve to
      restrain,
What have they a husband can mourn
    as a loss?
      What have they a lover can prize as a
      gain?

EXTRACT XII.

                          Florence.

*Music in Italy. — Disappointed by it. — Recol-
lections of other Times and Friends. — Dalton. — Sir John Stevenson. — His Daughter.
— Musical Evenings together.*

      .   .   .   .

IF it *be* true that Music reigns,
    Supreme, in ITALY's soft shades,
'T is like that Harmony so famous,
Among the spheres, which He of Samos
Declared had such transcendent merit
That not a soul on earth could hear it;
For, far as I have come — from Lakes,
Whose sleep the Tramontana breaks,
Thro' MILAN and that land which gave
The Hero of the rainbow vest [1] —
By MINCIO's banks, and by that wave,[2]
    Which made VERONA's bard so blest —
Places that (like the Attic shore,
    Which rung back music when the sea
Struck on its marge) should be all o'er
    Thrilling alive with melody —
I 've heard no music — not a note
Of such sweet native airs as float
In my own land among the throng
And speak our nation's soul for song.

Nay, even in higher walks, where Art
Performs, as 't were, the gardener's part,
And richer if not sweeter makes
The flowers she from the wild-hedge
    takes —
Even there, no voice hath charmed my
    ear,

1 Bermago — the birth-place, it is said, of
Harlequin.
2 The Lago di Garda.

No taste hath won my perfect praise,
Like thine, dear friend[1] — long, truly
    dear —
Thine, and thy loved OLIVIA's lays.
She, always beautiful, and growing
    Still more so every note she sings —
Like an inspired young Sibyl,[2] glowing
    With her own bright imaginings!
And thou, most worthy to be tied
    In music to her, as in love,
Breathing that language by her side,
    All other language far above,
Eloquent Song — whose tones and words
In every heart find answering chords!

How happy once the hours we past,
    Singing or listening all day long,
Till Time itself seemed changed at last
    To music, and we lived in song!
Turning the leaves of HAYDN o'er,
    As quick beneath her master hand
They opened all their brilliant store,
    Like chambers, touched by fairy wand;
Or o'er the page of MOZART bending,
    Now by his airy warblings cheered,
Now in his mournful *Requiem* blending
Voices thro' which the heart was heard.

And still, to lead our evening choir,
    Was He invoked, thy loved-one's Sire[3] —
He who if aught of grace there be
    In the wild notes I write or sing,
First smoothed their links of harmony,
    And lent them charms they did not
        bring; —
He, of the gentlest, simplest heart,
With whom, employed in his sweet art,
(That art which gives this world of ours
    A notion how they speak in heaven,)
I 've past more bright and charmed hours
    Than all earth's wisdom could have
        given.
Oh happy days, oh early friends,
    How Life since then hath lost its
        flowers!
But yet — tho' Time *some* foliage rends,
    The stem, the Friendship, still is ours;

And long may it endure, as green
And fresh as it hath always been!

How I have wandered from my theme!
    But where is he, that could return
To such cold subjects from a dream,
    Thro' which these best of feelings
        burn? —
Not all the works of Science, Art,
    Or Genius in this world are worth
One genuine sigh that from the heart
    Friendship or Love draws freshly forth.

EXTRACT XIII.

Rome.

*Reflections on reading Du Cerceau's Account of
    the Conspiracy of Rienzi, in 1347.[4] — The
    Meeting of the Conspirators on the Night of
    the 19th of May. — Their Procession in the
    Morning to the Capitol. — Rienzi's Speech.*

'T WAS a proud moment — even to hear
        the words
    Of Truth and Freedom mid these tem-
        ples breathed,
And see once more the Forum shine with
        swords
    In the Republic's sacred name un-
        sheathed —
That glimpse, that vision of a brighter
        day
    For his dear ROME, must to a Roman
        be,
Short as it was, worth ages past away
    In the dull lapse of hopeless slavery.

'T was on a night of May, beneath that
        moon
Which had thro' many an age seen Time
        untune
The strings of this Great Empire, till it
        fell
From his rude hands, a broken, silent
        shell —
The sound of the church clock[5] near
        ADRIAN'S Tomb
Summoned the warriors who had risen
        for ROME,

1 Edward Tuite Dalton, the first husband of
Sir John Stevenson's daughter, the late Marchioness of Headfort.

2 Such as those of Domenichino in the Palazzo Borghese, at the Capitol, etc.

3 Sir John Stevenson.

4 The "*Conjuration de Nicolas Gabrini, dit
de Rienzi,*" by the Jesuit Du Cerceau, is chiefly
taken from the much more authentic work of
Fortifiocca on the same subject. Rienzi was the
son of a laundress.

5 It is not easy to discover what church is
meant by Du Cerceau here : — "*Il fit crier dans
les rues de Rome, à son de trompe, que chacun*

To meet unarmed, — with none to watch
 them there,
But God's own eye, — and pass the
 night in prayer.
Holy beginning of a holy cause,
When heroes girt for Freedom's combat
 pause
Before high Heaven, and humble in their
 might
Call down its blessing on that coming
 fight.

At dawn, in arms went forth the patriot
 band;
And as the breeze, fresh from the TIBER,
 fanned
Their gilded gonfalons, all eyes could see
The palm-tree there, the sword, the
 keys of Heaven [1] —
Types of the justice, peace and liberty,
 That were to bless them when their
 chains were riven.
On to the Capitol the pageant moved,
 While many a Shade of other times,
 that still
Around that grave of grandeur sighing
 roved,
 Hung o'er their footsteps up the Sacred
 Hill
And heard its mournful echoes as the last
High-minded heirs of the Republic past.
'T was then that thou, their Tribune,[2]
 (name which brought
Dreams of lost glory to each patriot's
 thought,)

eût à se trouver, sans armes, la nuit du lende-
main, dix neuvième, dans l'église du château de
Saint-Ange, au son de la cloche, afin de pourvoir
au Bon Etat."

1 "*Les gentilshommes conjurés portaient devant lui trois étendarts. Nicolas Guallato, sur-
nommé le bon diseur, portait le premier, qui était
de couleur rouge, et plus grand que les autres.
On y voyait des caractères d'or avec une femme
assise sur deux lions, tenant d'une main le globe
du monde, et de l'autre une Palme pour repré-
senter la ville de Rome. C'était le Gonfalon de
la Liberté. Le second, à fonds blanc, avec un
St. Paul tenant de la droite une Epée nue et de
la gauche la couronne de Justice, était porté par
Étienne Magnacuccia, notaire apostolique. Dans
le troisième, St. Pierre avait en main les clefs de
la Concorde et de la Paix. Tout cela insinuait
le dessein de Rienzi, qui était de rétablir la liberté, la justice et la paix.*" — DU CERCEAU,
iv. ii.

2 Rienzi.

Didst, with a spirit Rome in vain shall
 seek
To wake up in her sons again, thus
 speak : —
"ROMANS, look round you — on this
 sacred place
 "There once stood shrines and gods
 and godlike men.
"What see you now? what solitary trace
 "Is left of all that made ROME's glory
 then?
"The shrines are sunk, the Sacred Mount
 bereft
 "Even of its name — and nothing now
 remains
"But the deep memory of that glory, left
 "To whet our pangs and aggravate
 our chains!
"But *shall* this be? — our sun and sky
 the same, —
 "Treading the very soil our fathers
 trod, —
"What withering curse hath fallen on
 soul and frame,
 "What visitation hath there come from
 God
"To blast our strength and rot us into
 slaves,
"*Here* on our great forefathers' glorious
 graves?
"It cannot be — rise up, ye Mighty
 Dead, —
 "If we, the living, are too weak to
 crush
"These tyrant priests that o'er your
 empire tread,
 "Till all but Romans at Rome's tame-
 ness blush !

"Happy, PALMYRA, in thy desert domes
 "Where only date-trees sigh and ser-
 pents hiss ;
"And thou whose pillars are but silent
 homes
 "For the stork's brood, superb PER-
 SEPOLIS !
"Thrice happy both, that your ex-
 tinguisht race
"Have left no embers — no half-living
 trace —
"No slaves to crawl around the once
 proud spot,
"Till past renown in present shame 's
 forgót.

" While ROME, the Queen of all, whose
very wrecks,
" If lone and lifeless thro' a desert
hurled,
" Would wear more true magnificence
than decks
" The assembled thrones of all the
existing world —
" ROME, ROME alone, is haunted, stained
and curst,
" Thro' every spot her princely TIBER
laves,
" By living human things — the deadliest,
worst,
" This earth engenders — tyrants and
their slaves !
" And we — oh shame ! — we who have
pondered o'er
" The patriot's lesson and the poet's
lay;[1]
" Have mounted up the streams of an-
cient lore,
" Tracking our country's glories all
the way —
" Even *we* have tamely, basely kist the
ground
" Before that Papal Power, — that
Ghost of Her,
" The World's Imperial Mistress — sit-
ting crowned
" And ghastly on her mouldering
sepulchre ![2]

" But this is past : — too long have lordly
priests
" And priestly lords led us, with all our
pride
" Withering about us — like devoted
beasts,
" Dragged to the shrine, with faded
garlands tied.

1 The fine Canzone of Petrarch, beginning
" *Spirto gentil*," is supposed, by Voltaire and
others, to have been addressed to Rienzi : but
there is much more evidence of its having been
written, as Ginguené asserts, to the young Stephen Colonna, on his being created a Senator of
Rome. That Petrarch, however, was filled with
high and patriotic hopes by the first measures of
this extraordinary man, appears from one of his
letters, quoted by Du Cerceau, where he says, —
" *Pour tout dire, en un mot, j'atteste, non comme
lecteur, mais comme témoin oculaire, qu'il nous
a ramené le justice, la paix, la bonne foi, la
sécurité, et tous les autres vestiges de l'âge d'or.*"

2 This image is borrowed from Hobbes, whose
words are, as near as I can recollect : — " For

" 'T is o'er — the dawn of our deliver-
ance breaks !
" Up from his sleep of centuries awakes
" The Genius of the Old Republic, free
" As first he stood, in chainless majesty,
" And sends his voice thro' ages yet to
come,
" Proclaiming ROME, ROME, ROME,
Eternal ROME ! ' "

EXTRACT XIV.

Rome.

*Fragment of a Dream. — The great Painters
supposed to be Magicians. — The Beginnings
of the Art. — Gildings on the Glories and
Draperies. — Improvements under Giotto, etc.
— The first Dawn of the true Style in Masaccio. — Studied by all the great Artists who
followed him. — Leonardo da Vinci, with
whom commenced the Golden Age of Painting.
— His Knowledge of Mathematics and of Music. — His female Heads all like each other. —
Triangular Faces. — Portraits of Mona Lisa,
etc. — Picture of Vanity and Modesty. — His
chef-d'œuvre, the Last Supper. — Faded and
almost effaced.*

FILLED with the wonders I had seen
In Rome's stupendous shrines and
halls,
I felt the veil of sleep serene
Come o'er the memory of each scene,
As twilight o'er the landscape falls.
Nor was it slumber, sound and deep,
But such as suits a poet's rest —
That sort of thin, transparent sleep,
Thro' which his day-dreams shine the
best.
Methought upon a plain I stood,
Where certain wondrous men, 't wa[s]
said,
With strange, miraculous power endued
Were coming each in turn to shed
His art's illusions o'er the sight
And call up miracles of light.
The sky above this lonely place,
Was of that cold, uncertain hue,
The canvas wears ere, warmed apace,
Its bright creation dawns to view.

But soon a glimmer from the east
Proclaimed the first enchantment
nigh;[3]

what is the Papacy, but the Ghost of the ol[d]
Roman Empire, sitting crowned on the grav[e]
thereof ? "

3 The paintings of those artists who were i[n]
troduced into Venice and Florence from Greec[e]

And as the feeble light increased,
  Strange figures moved across the sky,
With golden glories deckt and streaks
  Of gold among their garments' dyes;[1]
And life's resemblance tinged their
    cheeks,
  But naught of life was in their eyes;—
Like the fresh-painted Dead one meets,
  Borne slow along Rome's mournful
    streets.

But soon these figures past away;
  And forms succeeded to their place
With less of gold in their array,
  But shining with more natural grace,
And all could see the charming wands
Had past into more gifted hands.[2]
Among these visions there was one,[3]
Surpassing fair, on which the sun,
That instant risen, a beam let fall,
  Which thro' the duskytwilighttrembled,
And reached at length the spot where
    all
  Those great magicians stood assembled.
And as they turned their heads to view
  The shining lustre, I could trace
The bright varieties it threw
  On each uplifted studying face;[4]
While many a voice with loud acclaim,
Called forth, " Masaccio " as the name
Of him, the Enchanter who had raised
This miracle on which all gazed.

'T was daylight now — the sun had risen
  From out the dungeon of old Night, —
Like the Apostle from his prison
  Led by the Angel's hand of light;

And — as the fetters, when that ray
  Of glory reached them, dropt away,[5]
So fled the clouds at touch of day !
Just then a bearded sage [6] came forth,
  Who oft in thoughtful dream would
    stand,
To trace upon the dusky earth
  Strange learned figures with his wand;[7]
And oft he took the silver lute [8]
  His little page behind him bore, .
And waked such music as, when mute,
  Left in the soul a thirst for more !

Meanwhile his potent spells went on,
  And forms and faces that from out
A depth of shadow mildly shone
  Were in the soft air seen about.
Tho' thick as midnight stars they beamed,
Yet all like living sisters seemed,
So close in every point resembling
  Each other's beauties — from the eyes
Lucid as if thro' crystal trembling,
  Yet soft as if suffused with sighs,
To the long, fawn-like mouth, and chin,
  Lovelily tapering, less and less,
  Till by this very charm's excess,
Like virtue on the verge of sin,
  It touched the bounds of ugliness.
Here lookt as when they lived the
    shades
Of some of Arno's dark-eyed maids —
Such maids as should alone live on
In dreams thus when their charms are
    gone:
Some Mona Lisa on whose eyes
  A painter for whole years might gaze,[9]
Nor find in all his pallet's dyes
  One that could even approach their
    blaze !

---

1 Margaritone of Orezzo, who was a pupil and imitator of the Greeks, is said to have invented this art of gilding the ornaments of pictures, a practice which, though it gave way to a purer taste at the beginning of the 16th century, was still occasionally used by many of the great masters: as by Raphael in the ornaments of the Fornarina, and by Rubens not unfrequently in glories and flames.

2 Cimabue, Giotto, etc.

3 The works of Masaccio. — For the character of this powerful and original genius, see Sir Joshua Reynolds's twelfth discourse. His celebrated frescoes are in the church of St. Pietro del Carmine, at Florence.

4 All the great artists studied, and many of them borrowed from Masaccio. Several figures in the Cartoons of Raphael are taken, with but little alteration, from his frescoes.

5 " And a light shined in the prison . . . and his chains fell off from his hands." — *Acts.*

6 Leonardo da Vinci.

7 His treatise on Mechanics, Optics, etc., preserved in the Ambrosian library at Milan.

8 *On dit que Léonard parut pour la première fois à la cour de Milan, dans un espèce de concours ouvert entre les meilleurs joueurs de lyre d'Italie. Il se présenta avec une lyre de sa façon, construit en argent.* — " *Histoire de la Peinture en Italie.*"

9 He is said to have been four years employed upon the portrait of this fair Florentine, without being able, after all, to come up to his idea of her beauty.

Here float two spirit shapes,[1] the one,
With her white fingers to the sun
Outspread as if to ask his ray
Whether it e'er had chanced to play
On lilies half so fair as they !
This self-pleased nymph was Vanity —
And by her side another smiled,
  In form as beautiful as she,
But with that air subdued and mild,
  That still reserve of purity,
Which is to beauty like the haze
  Of evening to some sunny view,
Softening such charms as it displays
  And veiling others in that hue,
  Which fancy only can see thro' !
This phantom nymph, who could she be,
But the bright Spirit, Modesty?

Long did the learned enchanter stay
  To weave his spells and still there
    past,
As in the lantern's shifting play
Group after group in close array,
  Each fairer, grander, than the last.
But the great triumph of his power
  Was yet to come : — gradual and slow,
(As all that is ordained to tower
  Among the works of man must grow,)
The sacred vision stole to view,
  In that half light, half shadow shown,
Which gives to even the gayest hue
  A sobered, melancholy tone.
It was a vision of that last,[2]
Sorrowful night which Jesus past
With his disciples when he said
  Mournfully to them — " I shall be
" Betrayed by one who here hath fed
  " This night at the same board with
    me."
And tho' the Saviour in the dream

Spoke not these words, we saw them
  beam
Legibly in his eyes (so well
The great magician workt his spell),
And read in every thoughtful line
Imprinted on that brow divine,
The meek, the tender nature, grieved,
Not angered to be thus deceived —
Celestial love requited ill
For all its care, yet loving still —
Deep, deep regret that there should fall
  From man's deceit so foul a blight
Upon that parting hour — and all
His Spirit must have felt that night,
Who, soon to die for human-kind,
  Thought only, mid his mortal pain,
How many a soul was left behind
  For whom he died that death in vain !

Such was the heavenly scene — alas !
That scene so bright so soon should pass !
But pictured on the humid air,
Its tints, ere long, grew languid there;[3]
And storms came on, that, cold ·and
  rough,
  Scattered its gentlest glories all —
As when the baffling winds blow off
  The hues that hang o'er Terni's fall, —
Till one by one the vision's beams
  Faded away and soon it fled,
To join those other vanisht dreams
  That now flit palely 'mong the dead, —
The shadows of those shades that go,
Around Oblivion's lake below !

EXTRACT XV.

Rome.

Mary Magdalen. — Her Story. — Numerous Pic-
tures of her. — Correggio. — Guido. — Ra-
phael, etc. — Canova's two exquisite Statues. —
The Somariva Magdalen. — Chantrey's Ad-
miration of Canova's Works.

No wonder, MARY, that thy story
  Touches all hearts — for there we see
The soul's corruption and its glory,
  Its death and life combined in thee.

From the first moment when we find
  Thy spirit haunted by a swarm

---

1 Vanity and Modesty in the collection of
Cardinal Fesch, at Rome. The composition of
the four hands here is rather awkward, but the
picture, altogether, is very delightful. There is
a repetition of the subject in the possession of
Lucien Bonaparte.

2 The Last Supper of Leonardo da Vinci,
which is in the Refectory of the Convent delle
Grazie at Milan. See " *L'Histoire de la Pein-*
ture in Italie," *liv.* iii. *chap.* 45. The writer of
that interesting work (to whom I take this opportunity of offering my acknowledgments, for
the copy he sent me a year since from Rome,)
will see I have profited by some of his observations on this celebrated picture.

3 Leonardo appears to have used a mixture
of oil and varnish for this picture, which alone,
without the various other causes of its ruin,
would have prevented any long duration of its
beauties. It is now almost entirely effaced.

Of dark desires, — like demons shrined
  Unholily in that fair form, —
Till when by touch of Heaven set free,
  Thou camest, with those bright locks
      of gold
(So oft the gaze of BETHANY),
  And covering in their precious fold
Thy Saviour's feet didst shed such tears
As paid, each drop, the sins of years! —
Thence on thro' all thy course of love
  To Him, thy Heavenly Master, — Him
Whose bitter death-cup from above
  Had yet this cordial round the brim,
That woman's faith and love stood fast
And fearless by Him to the last: —
Till, oh! blest boon for truth like thine!
  Thou wert of all the chosen one,
Before whose eyes that Face Divine
  When risen from the dead first shone;
That thou might'st see how, like a cloud,
  Had past away its mortal shroud,
And make that bright revealment known
To hearts less trusting than thy own.
All is affecting, cheering, grand;
  The kindliest record ever given,
Even under God's own kindly hand,
  Of what Repentance wins from
      Heaven!

No wonder, MARY, that thy face,
  In all its touching light of tears,
Should meet us in each holy place,
  Where Man before his God appears,
Hopeless — were he not taught to see
All hope in Him who pardoned thee!
No wonder that the painter's skill
  Should oft have triumpht in the power
Of keeping thee all lovely still
  Even in thy sorrow's bitterest hour;
That soft CORREGGIO should diffuse
  His melting shadows round thy form;
That GUIDO's pale, unearthly hues
  Should in portraying thee grow
      warm;
That all — from the ideal, grand,
Inimitable Roman hand,
Down to the small, enameling touch
  Of smooth CARLINO — should delight
In picturing her, who "who loved so
      much,"
And was, in spite of sin, so bright!

But MARY, 'mong these bold essays
Of Genius and of Art to raise

A semblance of those weeping eyes —
  A vision worthy of the sphere
Thy faith has earned thee in the skies,
  And in the hearts of all men here, —
None e'er hath matched, in grief or grace,
CANOVA's day-dream of thy face,
In those bright sculptured forms, more
      bright
With true expression's breathing light,
Than ever yet beneath the stroke
Of chisel into life awoke.
The one,[1] portraying what thou wert
  In thy first grief, — while yet the flower
Of those young beauties was unhurt
  By sorrow's slow, consuming power;
And mingling earth's seductive grace
  With heaven's subliming thoughts so
      well,
We doubt, while gazing, in *which* place
  Such beauty was most formed to
      dwell! —
The other, as thou look'dst, when years
Of fasting, penitence and tears
Had worn thy frame; — and ne'er did
      Art
With half such speaking power ex-
      press
The ruin which a breaking heart
  Spreads by degrees o'er loveliness.
Those wasting arms, that keep the trace,
Even still, of all their youthful grace,
That loosened hair of which thy brow
Was once so proud, — neglected now! —
Those features even in fading worth
  The freshest bloom to others given,
And those sunk eyes now lost to earth
  But to the last still full of heaven!

Wonderful artist! praise, like mine —
  Tho' springing from a soul that feels
Deep worship of those works divine
  Where Genius all his light reveals —
How weak 't is to the words that came
From him, thy peer in art and fame,[2]
Whom I have known, by day, by night,
Hang o'er thy marble with delight;

1 This statute is one of the last works of Canova, and was not yet in marble when I left Rome.
The other, which seems to prove, in contradiction
to very high authority, that expression of the intensest kind is fully within the sphere of sculpture, was executed many years ago, and is in the
possession of the Count Somariva at Paris.

2 Chantrey.

And while his lingering hand would
    steal
O'er every grace the taper's rays [1]
Give thee with all the generous zeal
Such master spirits only feel,
    That best of fame, a rival's praise!

EXTRACT XVI.
Les Charmettes.

A Visit to the house where Rousseau lived with
* Madame de Warrens. — Their Ménage. —*
* Its Grossness. — Claude Anet. — Reverence*
* with which the Spot is now visited.—Absurdity*
* of this blind Devotion to Fame.— Feelings ex-*
* cited by the Beauty and Seclusion of the Scene.*
* — Disturbed by its Associations with Rous-*
* seau's History. — Impostures of Men of Ge-*
* nius. — Their Power of mimicking all the best*
* Feelings, Love, Independence, etc.*

STRANGE power of Genius, that can
    throw
Round all that 's vicious, weak, and low,
Such magic lights, such rainbow dyes
As dazzle even the steadiest eyes.

  .   .   .   .   .

'T is worse than weak — 't is wrong, 't is
    shame,
This mean prostration before Fame;
This casting down beneath the car
Of Idols, whatsoe'er they are,
Life's purest, holiest decencies,
To be careered o'er as they please.
No — give triumphant Genius all
For which his loftiest wish can call:
If he be worship, let it be
    For attributes, his noblest, first;
Not with that base idolatry
    Which sanctifies his last and worst.

I may be cold; — may want that glow
Of high romance which bards should
    know;
That holy homage which is felt
In treading where the great have dwelt;
This reverence, whatsoe'er it be,
    I fear, I feel, I have it *not* : —
For here at this still hour, to me
    The charms of this delightful spot,
Its calm seclusion from the throng,
    From all the heart would fain forget,

---

1 Canova always shows his fine statue, the
Venere Vincitrice, by the light of a small candle.

This narrow valley and the song
  Of its small murmuring rivulet,
The flitting to and fro of birds,
  Tranquil and tame as they were once
In Eden ere the startling words
  Of Man disturbed their orisons,
Those little, shadowy paths that wind
Up the hill-side, with fruit-trees lined
And lighted only by the breaks
The gay wind in the foliage makes,
Or vistas here and there that ope
  Thro' weeping willows, like the
    snatches
Of far-off scenes of light, which Hope
  Even thro' the shade of sadness
    catches ! —
All this, which — could I once but lose
  The memory of those vulgar ties
Whose grossness all the heavenliest hues
  Of Genius can no more disguise
Than the sun's beams can do away
The filth of fens o'er which they play —
This scene which would have filled my
    heart
  With thoughts of all that happiest is; —
Of Love where self hath only part,
  As echoing back another's bliss;
Of solitude secure and sweet,
Beneath whose shade the Virtues meet.
Which while it shelters never chills
  Our sympathies with human woe,
But keeps them like sequestered rills
  Purer and fresher in their flow;
Of happy days that share their beams
  'Twixt quiet mirth and wise employ;
Of tranquil nights that give in dreams
  The moonlight of the morning's joy ! —
All this my heart could dwell on here,
But for those gross mementoes near;
Those sullying truths that cross the track
Of each sweet thought and drive them
    back
Full into all the mire and strife
And vanities of that man's life,
Who more than all that e'er have
    glowed
  With Fancy's flame (and it was *his*,
In fullest warmth and radiance) showed
  What an impostor Genius is;
How with that strong, mimetic art
  Which forms its life and soul, it takes
All shapes of thought, all hues of heart,
  Nor feels itself one throb it wakes;

How like a gem its light may smile
   O'er the dark path by mortals trod,
Itself as mean a worm the while
   As crawls at midnight o'er the sod;
What gentle words and thoughts may
      fall
   From its false lip, what zeal to bless,
While home, friends, kindred, country,
      all,
   Lie waste beneath its selfishness ;
How with the pencil hardly dry
   From coloring up such scenes of love
And beauty as make young hearts sigh
   And dream and think thro' heaven
      they rove,
They who can thus describe and move,
   The very workers of these charms,
Nor seek nor know a joy above
   Some Maman's or Theresa's arms !

How all in short that makes the boast
Of their false tongues they want the
      most;
And while with freedom on their lips,
   Sounding their timbrels, to set free
This bright world, laboring in the eclipse
   Of priestcraft and of slavery, —
They may themselves be slaves as low
   As ever Lord or Patron made
To blossom in his smile or grow
   Like stunted brushwood in his shade.
Out on the craft ! — I 'd rather be
   One of those hinds that round me tread,
With just enough of sense to see
   The noonday sun that 's o'er his head,
Than thus with high-built genius curst,
   That hath no heart for its foundation,
Be all at once that 's brightest, worst,
   Sublimest, meanest in creation !

CORRUPTION,

AND

INTOLERANCE.

TWO POEMS.

ADDRESSED TO AN ENGLISHMAN BY AN IRISHMAN.

PREFACE.

THE practice which has been lately introduced into literature, of writing very long notes upon very indifferent verses, appears to me a rather happy invention, as it supplies us with a mode of turning dull poetry to account; and as horses too heavy for the saddle may yet serve well enough to draw lumber, so Poems of this kind make excellent beasts of burden and will bear notes though they may not bear reading. Besides, the comments in such cases are so little under the necessity of paying any servile deference to the text, that they may even adopt that Socratic dogma, " *quod supra nos nihil ad nos.*"

In the first of the two following Poems, I have ventured to speak of the Revolution of 1688, in language which has sometimes been employed by Tory writers and which is therefore neither very new nor popular. But however an Englishman might be reproached with ingratitude for depreciating the merits and results of a measure which he is taught to regard as the source of his liberties — however ungrateful it might appear in Alderman Birch to question for a moment the purity of that glorious era to which he is indebted for the seasoning of so many orations — yet an Irishman who has none of these obligations to acknowledge, to whose country the Revolution brought nothing but injury and insult, and who recollects that the book of Molyneux was burned by order of William's Whig Parliament for daring to extend to unfortunate Ireland those principles on which the Revolution was professedly founded — an Irishman *may* be allowed to criticise freely the measures of that period without exposing himself either to the imputation of ingratitude or to the suspicion of being influenced by any Popish remains of Jacobitism. No nation, it is true, was ever blessed with a more golden opportunity of establishing and securing its liberties for ever than the conjuncture of Eighty-eight presented to the people of Great Britain. But the disgraceful reigns of Charles and James had weakened and degraded the national character. The

528

bold notions of popular right which had arisen out of the struggles between Charles the First and his Parliament were gradually supplanted by those slavish doctrines for which Lord Hawkesbury eulogizes the churchmen of that period, and as the Reformation had happened too soon for the purity of religion, so the Revolution came too late for the spirit of liberty. Its advantages accordingly were for the most part specious and transitory, while the evils which it entailed are still felt and still increasing. By rendering unnecessary the frequent exercise of Prerogative, — that unwieldy power which cannot move a step without alarm, — it diminished the only interference of the Crown, which is singly and independently exposed before the people, and whose abuses therefore are obvious to their senses and capacities. Like the myrtle over a celebrated statue in Minerva's temple at Athens, it skilfully veiled from the public eye the only obtrusive feature of royalty. At the same time, however, that the Revolution abridged this unpopular attribute, it amply compensated by the substitution of a new power, as much more potent in its effect as it is more secret in its operations. In the disposal of an immense revenue and the extensive patronage annexed to it, the first foundations of this power of the Crown were laid; the innovation of a standing army at once increased and strengthened it, and the few slight barriers which the Act of Settlement opposed to its progress have all been gradually removed during the Whiggish reigns that succeeded; till at length this spirit of influence has become the vital principle of the state, — an agency, subtle and unseen, which pervades every part of the Constitution, lurks under all its forms and regulates all its movements, and, like the invisible sylph or grace which presides over the motions of beauty,

> " *illam, quicquid agit, quoquo vestigia flectit,*
> *componit furtim subsequiturque.*"

The cause of Liberty and the Revolution are so habitually associated in the minds of Englishmen that probably in objecting to the latter I may be thought hostile or indifferent to the former. But assuredly nothing could be more unjust than such a suspicion. The very object indeed which my humble animadversions would attain is that in the crisis to which I think England is now hastening, and between which and foreign subjugation she may soon be compelled to choose, the errors and omissions of 1688 should be remedied; and, as it was then her fate to experience a Revolution without Reform, so she may now endeavor to accomplish a Reform without Revolution.

In speaking of the parties which have so long agitated England, it will be observed that I lean as little to the Whigs as to their adversaries. Both factions have been equally cruel to Ireland and perhaps equally insincere in their efforts for the liberties of England. There is one name indeed connected with Whiggism, of which I can never think but with veneration and tenderness. As justly, however, might the light of the sun be claimed by any particular nation as the sanction of that name be monopolized by any party whatsoever. Mr. Fox belonged to mankind and they have lost in him their ablest friend.

With respect to the few lines upon Intolerance, which I have subjoined, they are but the imperfect beginning of a long series of Essays with which I here menace my readers upon the same important subject. I shall look to no higher merit in the task than that of giving a new form to claims and remonstrances which have often been much more eloquently urged and which would long ere now have produced their effect, but that the minds of some of our statesmen, like the pupil of the human eye, contract themselves the more, the stronger light there is shed upon them.

CORRUPTION,

AN EPISTLE.

νῦν δ᾽ ἅπανθ᾽ ὥσπερ ἐξ ἀγορᾶς ἐκπέπραται ταῦτα· ἀντείσηκται δὲ ἀντὶ τούτων, ὑφ᾽ ὧν
ἀπόλωλε καὶ νενόσηκεν ἡ Ἑλλάς. ταῦτα δ᾽ ἐστὶ τί; ζῆλος, εἴ τις εἴληφέ τι· γέλως ἂν ὁμολογῇ·
συγγνώμη τοῖς ἐλεγχομένοις· μῖσος, ἂν τούτοις, τις ἐπιτιμᾷ· τἄλλα πάνθ, ὅσα ἐκ τοῦ δωροδοκεῖν
ἤρτηται.   DEMOSTH. *Philipp.* iii.

Boast on, my friend — tho' stript of all
  beside,
Thy struggling nation still retains her
  pride:[1]
That pride which once in genuine glory
  woke
When Marlborough fought and brilliant
  St. John spoke;
That pride which still, by time and shame
  unstung,
Outlives even Whitelocke's sword and
  Hawkesbury's tongue!
Boast on, my friend, while in this hum-
  bled isle [2]
Where Honor mourns and Freedom fears
  to smile,
Where the bright light of England's
  fame is known
But by the shadow o'er our fortunes
  thrown;
Where, doomed ourselves to naught but
  wrongs and slights,[3]

We hear you boast of Britain's glorious
  rights,
As wretched slaves that under hatches
  lie
Hear those on deck extol the sun and
  sky!
Boast on, while wandering thro' my native haunts,
I coldly listen to thy patriot vaunts;
And feel, tho' close our wedded countries twine,
More sorrow for my own than pride from
  thine.

Yet pause a moment — and if truths
  severe
Can find an inlet to that courtly ear,
Which hears no news but Ward's gazetted
  lies,
And loves no politics in rhyme but
  Pye's, —
If aught can please thee but the good
  old saws
Of "Church and State," and "William's
  matchless laws,"
And "Acts and Rights of glorious Eighty-
  eight," —
Things which tho' now a century out of
  date
Still serve to ballast with convenient
  words

1 *Angli suos ac sua omnia impense mirantur;
cæteras nationes despectui habent.*—*Barclay* (as
quoted in one of Dryden's prefaces).

2 England began very early to feel the effects
of cruelty towards her dependencies. "The
severity of her government [says Macpherson]
contributed more to deprive her of the continental
dominions of the family of the Plantagenet than
the arms of France." — See his *History*, vol. i.

3 "By the total reduction of the kingdom of
Ireland in 1691 [says Burke], the ruin of the
native Irish, and in a great measure, too, of the
first races of the English, was completely accomplished. The new English interest was settled with as solid a stability as any thing in
human affairs can look for. All the penal laws
of that unparalleled code of oppression, which
were made after the last event, were manifestly

the effects of national hatred and scorn towards
a conquered people, whom the victors delighted
to trample upon, and were not at all afraid to
provoke." Yet this is the era to which the wise
Common Council of Dublin refer us for "invaluable blessings," etc.

A few crank arguments for speeching
  lords,[1] —
Turn while I tell how England's freedom
  found,
Where most she lookt for life, her deadliest wound;
How brave she struggled while her foe
  was seen,
How faint since Influence lent that foe a
  screen;
How strong o'er James and Popery she
  prevailed,
How weakly fell when Whigs and gold
  assailed.[2]

While kings were poor and all those
  schemes unknown
Which drain the people to enrich the
  throne;

[1] It never seems to occur to those orators
and addressers who round off so many sentences
and paragraphs with the Bill of Rights, the Act
of Settlement, etc., that most of the provisions
which these Acts contained for the preservation
of parliamentary independence have been long
laid aside as romantic and troublesome. I never
meet, I confess, with a politician who quotes seriously the Declaration of Rights, etc., to prove
the actual existence of English liberty, that I do
not think of that marquis whom Montesquieu
mentions,* who set about looking for mines in
the Pyrenees, on the strength of authorities
which he had read in some ancient authors. The
poor marquis toiled and searched in vain. He
quoted his authorities to the last, but found no
mines after all.

[2] The chief, perhaps the only advantage which
has resulted from the system of influence, is that
tranquil course of uninterrupted action which it
has given to the administration of government.
If kings *must* be paramount in the state (and
their ministers for the time being always think
so), the country is indebted to the Revolution
for enabling them to become so quietly, and for
removing skilfully the danger of those shocks
and collisions which the alarming efforts of prerogative never failed to produce.

Instead of vain and disturbing efforts to establish that speculative balance of the constitution,
which, perhaps, has never existed but in the
pages of Montesquieu and De Lolme, a preponderance is now silently yielded to one of the
three estates, which carries the other two almost
insensibly, but still effectually, along with it;
and even though the path may lead eventually to
destruction, yet its specious and gilded smooth-
ness almost atones for the danger; and, like
Milton's bridge over Chaos, it may be said to
lead,

"Smooth, easy, inoffensive, down to —— "

* *Liv.* xxi. *chap.* 2.

Ere yet a yielding Commons had sup-
  plied
Those chains of gold by which them-
  selves are tied,
Then proud Prerogative, untaught to
  creep
With bribery's silent foot on Freedom's
  sleep,
Frankly avowed his bold enslaving plan
And claimed a right from God to trample
  man !
But Luther's schism had too much roused
  mankind
For Hampden's truths to linger long
  behind;
Nor then, when king-like popes had
  fallen so low,
Could pope-like kings [3] escape the level-
  ling blow.
That ponderous sceptre (in whose place
  we bow
To the light talisman of influence now),
Too gross, too visible to work the spell
Which modern power performs, in frag-
  ments fell:
In fragments lay, till, patched and
  painted o'er
With fleurs-de-lis, it shone and scourged
  once more.

'T was then, my friend, thy kneeling
  nation quaft
Long, long and deep, the churchman's
  opiate draught
Of passive, prone obedience — then took
  flight
All sense of man's true dignity and right;
And Britons slept so sluggish in their
  chain
That Freedom's watch-voice called al-
  most in vain.
Oh England ! England ! what a chance
  was thine,
When the last tyrant of that ill-starred
  line
Fled from his sullied crown and left thee
  free
To found thy own eternal liberty !

[3] The drivelling correspondence between
James I. and his "dog Steenie" (the Duke of
Buckingham), which we find among the Hard-
wicke Papers, sufficiently shows, if we wanted
any such illustration, into what doting, idiotic
brains the plan of arbitrary power may enter.

How nobly high in that propitious hour
Might patriot hands have raised the triple
    tower.[1]
Of British freedom on a rock divine
Which neither force could storm nor
    treachery mine!
But no — the luminous, the lofty plan,
Like mighty Babel, seemed too bold for
    man;
The curse of jarring tongues again was
    given
To thwart a work which raised men
    nearer heaven.
While Tories marred what Whigs had
    scarce begun,
While Whigs undid what Whigs them-
    selves had done.[2]

The hour was lost and William with a
    smile
Saw Freedom weeping o'er the unfinisht
    pile!

Hence all the ills you suffer, — hence
    remain
Such galling fragments of that feudal
    chain[3]

effect till after the decease of the latter sovereign, and she very considerately repealed it altogether. So that, as representation has continued ever since, if the king were simple enough to send to foreign courts ambassadors who were most of them in the pay of those courts, he would be just as honestly and faithfully represented as are his people. It would be endless to enumerate all the favors which were conferred upon William by those "apostate Whigs." They complimented him with the first suspension of the Habeas Corpus Act which had been hazarded since the confirmation of that privilege; and this example of our Deliverer's reign has not been lost upon any of his successors. They promoted the establishment of a standing army, and circulated in its defence the celebrated "Balancing Letter," in which it is insinuated that England, even then, in her boasted hour of regeneration, was arrived at such a pitch of faction and corruption that nothing could keep her in order but a Whig ministry and a standing army. They refused as long as they could to shorten the duration of parliaments; and though, in the Declaration of Rights, the necessity of such a reform was acknowledged, they were able, by arts not unknown to modern ministers, to brand those as traitors and republicans who urged it.* But the grand and distinguishing trait of their measures was the power they bestowed on the Crown of almost annihilating the freedom of elections, — of turning from its course, and for ever defiling that great stream of Representation, which had, even in the most agitated periods, reflected some features of the people, but which from thenceforth became the Pactolus, the "aurifer amnis," of the court and served as a mirror of the national will and popular feeling no longer. We need but consult the writings of that time to understand the astonishment then excited by measures which the practice of a century has rendered not only familiar but necessary. See a pamphlet called "The Danger of mercenary Parliaments," 1698; State Tracts, Will. III. vol. ii.; see also "Some Paradoxes presented as a New Year's Gift" ("State Poems," vol. iii.).

1 Tacitus has expressed his opinion, in a passage very frequently quoted, that such a distribution of power as the theory of the British constitution exhibits is merely a subject of bright speculation, "a system more easily praised than practised, and which, even could it happen to exist, would certainly not prove permanent;" and, in truth, a review of England's annals would dispose us to agree with the great historian's remark. For we find that at no period whatever has this balance of the three estates existed; that the nobles predominated till the policy of Henry VII., and his successor reduced their weight by breaking up the feudal system of property; that the power of the Crown became then supreme and absolute, till the bold encroachments of the Commons subverted the fabric altogether; that the alternate ascendency of prerogative and privilege distracted the period which followed the Restoration; and that, lastly, the Acts of 1688, by laying the foundation of an unbounded court-influence, have secured a preponderance to the Throne, which every succeeding year increases. So that the vaunted British constitution has never perhaps existed but in mere theory.

2 The monarchs of Great Britain can never be sufficiently grateful for that accommodating spirit which led the Revolutionary Whigs to give away the crown, without imposing any of those restraints or stipulations which other men might have taken advantage of so favorable a moment to enforce, and in the framing of which they had so good a model to follow as the limitations proposed by the Lords Essex and Halifax, in the debate upon the Exclusion Bill. They not only condescended, however, to accept of places, but took care that these dignities should be no impediment to their "voice potential" in affairs of legislation; and although an Act was after many years suffered to pass, which by one of its articles disqualified placemen from serving as members of the House of Commons, it was yet no allowed to interfere with the influence of the reigning monarch, nor with that of his successor Anne. The purifying clause, indeed, was not to take

3 The last great wound given to the feudal system was the Act of the 12th of Charles II., which abolished the tenure of knight's service in capite, and which Blackstone compares, for its

* See a pamphlet published in 1693, upon the King's refusing to sign the Triennial Bill, called "A Discourse between a Yeoman of Kent and a Knight of a Shire." — "Hereupon [says the Yeoman] the gentleman grew angry, and said that I talked like a base commons-wealth man."

Whose links, around you by the Norman
  flung,
Tho' loosed and broke so often, still have
  clung.
Hence sly Prerogative like Jove of old
Has turned his thunder into showers of
  gold,
Whose silent courtship wins securer joys,[1]

salutary influence upon property, to the boasted
provisions of Magna Charta itself. Yet even in
this Act we see the effects of that counteracting
spirit which has contrived to weaken every effort
of the English nation towards liberty. The exclusion of copyholders from their share of elec-
tive rights was permitted to remain as a brand of
feudal servitude, and as an obstacle to the rise of
that strong counterbalance which an equal representation of property would oppose to the weight
of the Crown. If the managers of the Revolution had been sincere in their wishes for reform
they would not only have taken this fetter off the
rights of election but would have renewed the
mode adopted in Cromwell's time of increasing
the number of knights of the shire, to the exclusion of those rotten insignificant boroughs,
which have tainted the whole mass of the constitution. Lord Clarendon calls this measure of
Cromwell's "an alteration fit to be more war-
rantable made, and in a better time." It formed
part of Mr. Pitt's plan in 1783; but Pitt's plan
of reform was a kind of announced dramatic
piece, about as likely to be ever acted as Mr.
Sheridan's "Foresters."

  1 —— *fore enim tutum iter et patens*
      converso in pretium Deo.
  aurum per medios ire satellites, etc.
              Horat.

  It would be a task not uninstructive to trace
the history of Prerogative from the date of its
strength under the Tudor princes, when Henry
VII. and his successors "taught the people [as
Nathaniel Bacon says] * to dance to the tune of
Allegiance," to the period of the Revolution,
when the Throne, in its attacks upon liberty,
began to exchange the noisy explosions of Prerogative for the silent and effectual air-gun of
Influence. In following its course, too, since
that memorable era, we shall find that, while the
royal power has been abridged in branches where
it might be made conducive to the interests of the
people, it has been left in full and unshackled
vigor against almost every point where the integrity of the constitution is vulnerable. For instance, the power of chartering boroughs, to
whose capricious abuse in the hands of the
Stuarts we are indebted for most of the present
anomalies of representation, might, if suffered
to remain, have in some degree atoned for its mischief, by restoring the old unchartered boroughs
to their rights, and widening more equally the
basis of the legislature. But by the Act of
Union with Scotland this part of the prerogative
was removed, lest Freedom should have a chance
of being healed even by the rust of the spear

  * *"Historic. and Politic. Discourse,"* etc.,
part ii. p. 114.

Taints by degrees, and ruins without
  noise.
While parliaments, no more those sacred
  things
Which make and rule the destiny of
  kings,
Like loaded dice by ministers are thrown,
And each new set of sharpers cog their
  own.
Hence the rich oil that from the Treas-
  ury steals
Drips smooth o'er all the Constitution's
  wheels,
Giving the old machine such pliant play [2]

which had formerly wounded her. The dangerous power however of creating peers, which has
been so often exercised *for* the government
against the constitution, is still left in free and
unqualified activity; notwithstanding the example of that celebrated Bill for the limitation of
this ever-budding branch of prerogative, which
was proposed in the reign of George I. under the
peculiar sanction and recommendation of the
Crown, but which the Whigs thought right to
reject, with all that characteristic delicacy, which,
in general, prevents them when enjoying the
sweets of office themselves, from taking any un-
courtly advantage of the Throne. It will be
recollected however that the creation of the
twelve peers by the Tories in Anne's reign (a
measure which Swift, like a true party man,
defends) gave these upright Whigs all possible
alarm for their liberties.

  With regard to the generous fit about his prerogative which seized so unroyally the good king
George I., historians have hinted that the par-
oxysm originated far more in hatred to his son
than in love to the constitution." * This, of
course, however, is a calumny: no loyal person,
acquainted with the annals of the three Georges,
could possibly suspect any *one* of those gracious
monarchs either of ill-will to his heir or indifference for the constitution.

  2 "They drove so fast [says Wellwood of the
ministers of Charles I.], that it was no wonder
that the wheels and chariot broke." (*Memoirs,*
p. 35.) — But this fatal accident, if we may judge
from experience, is to be imputed far less to the
folly and impetuosity of the drivers, than to the
want of that suppling oil from the Treasury which
has been found so necessary to make a government like that of England run smoothly.
Had Charles been as well provided with this
article as his successors have been since the
happy Revolution, his Commons would never
have merited from him the harsh appellation of
"seditious vipers," but would have been (as they
now are, and I trust always will be) "dutiful
Commons," "loyal Commons," etc., and would
have given him ship-money, or any other sort of
money he might have fancied.

  * Coxe says that this Bill was projected by
Sunderland.

That Court and Commons jog one joltless
way,
While Wisdom trembles for the crazy car,
So gilt, so rotten, carrying fools so far;
And the duped people, hourly doomed
to pay
The sums that bribe their liberties
away,[1] —
Like a young eagle who has lent his
plume
To fledge the shaft by which he meets
his doom, —
See their own feathers pluckt, to wing
the dart
Which rank corruption destines for their
heart!
But soft! methinks I hear thee proudly
say,
"What! shall I listen to the impious
lay
"That dares with Tory license to profane
"The bright bequests of William's glori-
ous reign?

1 Among those auxiliaries which the Revolution of 1688 marshalled on the side of the Throne,
the bugbear of Popery has not been the least
convenient and serviceable. Those unskilful
tyrants, Charles and James, instead of profiting
by that useful subserviency which has always distinguished the ministers of our religious establishment, were so infatuated as to plan the ruin of
this best bulwark of their power and moreover
connected their designs upon the Church so un-
disguisedly with their attacks upon the Constitution that they identified in the minds of the
people the interests of their religion and their
liberties. During those times therefore " No
Popery " was the watchword of freedom and
served to keep the public spirit awake against
the invasions of bigotry and prerogative. The
Revolution however by removing this object of
jealousy has produced a reliance on the orthodoxy of the Throne, of which the Throne has not
failed to take advantage; and the cry of " No
Popery " having thus lost its power of alarming
the people against the inroads of the Crown, has
served ever since the very different purpose of
strengthening the Crown against the pretensions
and struggles of the people. The danger of the
Church from Papists and Pretenders was the
chief pretext for the repeal of the Triennial Bill,
for the adoption of a standing army, for the
numerous suspensions of the Habeas Corpus
Act, and, in short, for all those spirited infrac-
tions of the constitution by which the reigns of
the last century were so eminently distinguished.
We have seen very lately too how the Throne has
been enabled by the same scarecrow sort of alarm
to select its ministers from among men whose
servility is their only claim to elevation and who
are pledged (if such an alternative *could* arise) to
take part with the scruples of the King against
the salvation of the empire.

" Shall the great wisdom of our patriot
sires,
" Whom Hawkesbury quotes and savory
Birch admires,
" Be slandered thus? shall honest Steele
agree
" With virtuous Rose to call us pure and
free,
" Yet fail to prove it? Shall our patent
pair
" Of wise state-poets waste their words
in air,
" And Pye unheeded breathe his pros-
perous strain,
" And Canning *take the people's sense* in
vain? "[2]

The people! — ah! that Freedom's
form should stay
Where Freedom's spirit long hath past
away!
That a false smile should play around the
dead
And flush the features when the soul
hath fled![3]
When Rome had lost her virtue with her
rights,
When her foul tyrant sat on Capreæ's
heights,[4]

Somebody has said, *"Quand tous les poètes
seraient noyés, ce ne serait pas grand dommage;"*
but I am aware that this is not fit language to be
held at a time when our birth-day odes and state-
papers are written by such pretty poets as Mr.
Pye and Mr. Canning. All I wish is, that the
latter gentleman would change places with his
brother Pye, by which means we should have
somewhat less prose in our odes, and certainly
less poetry in our politics.

3 " It is a scandal [said Sir Charles Sedley in
William's reign] that a government so sick at
heart as ours is should look so well in the face;"
and Edmund Burke has said, in the present reign,
" When the people conceive that laws and tri-
bunals, and even popular assemblies, are perverted from the ends of their institution, they
find in these names of degenerated establishments
only new motives to discontent Those bodies
which, when full of life and beauty, lay in their
arms and were their joy and comfort, when dead
and putrid become more loathsome from remembrance of former endearments." — " *Thoughts
on the present Discontents,*" 1770.

4 —— *tutor haberi
principis, Augastâ Caprearum in rupe sedentis
cum grege Chaldæo.* Juvenal. *Sat* x. v 92
The senate still continued, during the reign of
Tiberius, to manage all the business of the public; the money was then and long after coined

Amid his ruffian spies and doomed to
death
Each noble name they blasted with
their breath, —
Even then, (in mockery of that golden
time,
When the Republic rose revered, sublime,
And her proud sons, diffused from zone
to zone,
Gave kings to every nation but their
own,)
Even then the senate and the tribunes
stood,
Insulting marks, to show how high the
flood
Of Freedom flowed, in glory's by-gone
day,
And how it ebbed, — for ever ebbed
away ! [1]

Look but around — tho' yet a tyrant's
sword
Nor haunts our sleep nor glitters o'er our
board,
Tho' blood be better drawn, by modern
quacks,
With Treasury leeches than with sword
or axe;
Yet say, could even a prostrate tribune's
power
Or a mock senate in Rome's servile hour
Insult so much the claims, the rights of
man,
As doth that fettered mob, that free divan,
Of noble tools and honorable knaves,
Of pensioned patriots and privileged
slaves; —

That party-colored mass which naught
can warm
But rank corruption's heat — whose
quickened swarm
Spread their light wings in Bribery's
golden sky,
Buzz for a period, lay their eggs and
die;—
That greedy vampire which from Free-
dom's tomb
Comes forth with all the mimicry of bloom
Upon its lifeless cheek and sucks and
drains
A people's blood to feed its putrid veins !

Thou start'st, my friend, at picture
drawn so dark —
" Is there no light? " thou ask'st — " no
lingering spark
" Of ancient fire to warm us? Lives
there none,
"To act a Marvell's part?" [2] — alas!
not one.
To place and power all public spirit tends,
In place and power all public spirit ends; [3]
Like hardy plants that love the air and
sky,
When *out*, 't will thrive — but taken *in*,
't will die '

Not bolder truths of sacred Freedom
hung
From Sidney's pen or burned on Fox's
tongue,
Than upstart Whigs produce each market-
night,

by their authority, and every other public affair
received their sanction.

We are told by Tacitus of a certain race of
men, who made themselves particularly useful to
the Roman emperors, and were therefore called
" *instrumenta regni*," or " court tools." From
this it appears, that my Lords M——, C——, etc.,
are by no means things of modern invention.

[1] There is something very touching in what
Tacitus tells us of the hopes that revived in a few
patriot bosoms, when the death of Augustus was
near approaching, and the fond expectation with
which they already began " *bona libertatis incas-
sum disserere.*"

According to Ferguson, Cæsar's interference
with the rights of election "made the subversion
of the republic more felt than any of the former
acts of his power." — "*Roman Republic*," book
v. chap. i.

[2] Andrew Marvell, the honest opposer of the
court during the reign of Charles the Second,
and the last member of parliament who, according to the ancient mode, took wages from his
constituents. The Commons have, since then,
much changed their pay-masters. — See the *State
Poems* for some rude but spirited effusions of
Andrew Marvell.

[3] The following artless speech of Sir Francis
Winnington, in the reign of Charles the Second,
will amuse those who are fully aware of the perfection we have since attained in that system of
government whose humble beginnings so much
astonished the worthy baronet. " I did observe
[says he] that all those who had pensions, and
most of those who had offices, voted all of a side,
as they were directed by some great officer, exactly as if their business in this House had been
to preserve their pensions and offices, and not to
make laws for the good of them who sent them
here." — He alludes to that parliament which
was called, *par excellence*, the Pensionary Parliament.

While yet their conscience, as their purse,
is light;
While debts at home excite their care for
those
Which, dire to tell, their much-loved
country owes,
And loud and upright, till their prize be
known,
They thwart the King's supplies to raise
their own.
But bees on flowers alighting cease their
hum —
So, settling upon places, Whigs grow
dumb.
And, tho' most base is he who, 'neath
the shade
Of Freedom's ensign plies corruption's
trade,
And makes the sacred flag he dares to show
His passport to the market of her foe,
Yet, yet, I own, so venerably dear
Are Freedom's grave old anthems to my
ear,
That I enjoy them, tho' by traitors sung,
And reverence Scripture even from
Satan's tongue.
Nay, when the constitution has expired,
I 'll have such men, like Irish wakers,
hired
To chant old "*Habeas Corpus*" by its side,
And ask in purchased ditties why it died?

See yon smooth lord whom nature's
plastic pains
Would seem to 've fashioned for those
Eastern reigns
When eunuchs flourisht, and such nerve-
less things
As men rejected were the chosen of
kings;[1] —
Even *he*, forsooth, (oh fraud, of all the
worst!)

1 According to Xenophon, the chief circumstance which recommended these creatures to the
service of Eastern princes was the ignominious
station they held in society, and the probability
of their being, upon this account, more devoted
to the will and caprice of a master, from whose
notice alone they derived consideration, and in
whose favor they might seek refuge from the
general contempt of mankind. — ἄδοξοι ὄντες οἱ
εὐνοῦχοι παρὰ τοῖς ἄλλοις ἀνθρώποις καὶ διὰ
τοῦτο δεσπότου ἐπικούρου προσδέονται. — But I
doubt whether even an Eastern prince would
have chosen an entire administration upon this
principle.

Dared to assume the patriot's name at
first —
Thus Pitt began, and thus begin his
apes;
Thus devils when *first* raised take pleas-
ing shapes.
But oh, poor Ireland! if revenge be
sweet
For centuries of wrong, for dark deceit
And withering insult — for the Union
thrown
Into thy bitter cup,[2] when that alone
Of slavery's draught was wanting [3] — if
for this
Revenge be sweet, thou *hast* that dæ-
mon's bliss;

2 "And in the cup an *Union* shall be thrown."
    Hamlet.

3 Among the many measures, which, since the
Revolution, have contributed to increase the
influence of the Throne, and to feed up this
"Aaron's serpent" of the constitution to its
present healthy and respectable magnitude, there
have been few more nutritive than the Scotch
and Irish Unions. Sir John Packer said, in a
debate upon the former question, that "he would
submit it to the House, whether men who had
basely betrayed their trust, by giving up their
independent constitution, were fit to be admitted
into the English House of Commons." But Sir
John would have known, if he had not been out
of place at the time, that the pliancy of such
materials was not among the least of their rec-
ommendations. Indeed, the promoters of the
Scotch Union were by no means disappointed in
the leading object of their measure, for the triumphant majorities of the court-party in parliament may be dated from the admission of the 45
and the 16. Once or twice, upon the alteration
of their law of treason and the imposition of the
malt-tax (measures which were in direct violation
of the Act of Union), these worthy North Britons
arrayed themselves in opposition to the court;
but finding this effort for their country unavailing, they prudently determined to think thence-
forward of themselves, and few men have ever
kept to a laudable resolution more firmly. The
effect of Irish representation on the liberties of
England will be no less perceptible and permanent.

——ονδ' ὄγε Ταύρον
Λείπεται αντέλλουτος.*

The infusion of such cheap and useful ingredients as my Lord L., Mr. D. B., etc., into the legislature, cannot but act as a powerful alterative
on the constitution, and clear it by degrees of all
troublesome humors of honesty.

* From Aratus (v. 715.) a poet who wrote upon
astronomy, though, as Cicero assures us, he knew
nothing whatever about the subject : just as the
great Harvey wrote "*De Generatione*," though
he had as little to do with the matter as my Lord
Viscount C.

For sure 't is more than hell's revenge
to see
That England trusts the men who 've
ruined thee; —
That in these awful days when every hour
Creates some new or blasts some ancient
power,
When proud Napoleon like the en-
chanted shield [1]
Whose light compelled each wondering
foe to yield,
With baleful lustre blinds the brave and
free
And dazzles Europe into slavery, —
That in this hour when patriot zeal
should guide,
When Mind should rule and — Fox
should *not* have died,
All that devoted England can oppose
To enemies made fiends and friends made
foes,
Is the rank refuse, the despised remains
Of that unpitying power, whose whips
and chains

Drove Ireland first to turn with harlot
glance
Towards other shores and woo the em-
brace of France; —
Those hacked and tainted tools, so foully
fit
For the grand artisan of mischief, Pitt,
So useless ever but in vile employ,
So weak to save, so vigorous to de-
stroy —
Such are the men that guard thy threat-
ened shore,
Oh England! sinking England! [2] boast
no more.

1 The magician's shield in Ariosto: —

E tolto per vertù dello splendore
La libertate a loro. Cant. 2.

We are told that Cæsar's code of morality was
contained in the following lines of Euripides,
which that great man frequently repeated:

εἴπερ γὰρ ἀδικεῖν χρῆ τυραννίδος περὶ
κάλλιστον ἀδικεῖν τ᾽ ἄλλα δ᾽ εὐσεβεῖν χρεών.

This is also, as it appears, the moral code of
Napoleon.

2 The following prophetic remarks occur in a
letter written by Sir Robert Talbot, who attended the Duke of Bedford to Paris in 1762.
Talking of states which have grown powerful in
commerce, he says, "According to the nature
and common course of things, there is a confed-
eracy against them, and consequently in the same
proportion as they increase in riches, they approach to destruction. The address of our King
William, in making all Europe take the alarm at
France, has brought that country before us near
that inevitable period. We must necessarily
have our turn, and Great Britain will attain it
as soon as France shall have a declaimer with
organs as proper for that political purpose as
were those of our William the Third. . . . . .
Without doubt, my Lord, Great Britain must
lower her flight. Europe will remind us of the
balance of commerce, as she has reminded France
of the balance of power. The address of our
statesmen will immortalize them by contriving
for us a descent which shall not be a fall, by
making us rather resemble Holland than Car-
thage and Venice." — *Letters on the French*
Nation.

INTOLERANCE,

A SATIRE.

"This clamor which pretends to be raised for the safety of religion has almost worn out the very appearance of it, and rendered us not only the most divided but the most immoral people upon the face of the earth."

ADDISON, *Freeholder*, No. 37.

START not, my friend, nor think the Muse will stain
Her classic fingers with the dust profane
Of Bulls, Decrees and all those thundering scrolls
Which took such freedom once with royal souls,[1]

When heaven was yet the pope's exclusive trade,
And kings were *damned* as fast as now they 're *made*.
No, no — let Duigenan search the papal chair [2]
For fragrant treasures long forgotten there;

1 The king-deposing doctrine, notwithstanding its many mischievous absurdities, was of no little service to the cause of political liberty, by inculcating the right of resistance to tyrants and asserting the will of the people to be the only true fountain of power. Bellarmine, the most violent of the advocates for papal authority, was one of the first to maintain ("*De Pontif.*" *lib.* i. *cap.* 7), "that kings have not their authority or office immediately from God nor his law, but only from the law of nations;" and in King James's "Defence of the Rights of Kings against Cardinal Perron," we find his Majesty expressing strong indignation against the Cardinal for having asserted "that to the deposing of a king the consent of the people must be obtained"—"for by these words [says James] the people are exalted above the king, and made the judges of the king's deposing," p. 424. — Even in Mariana's celebrated book, where the nonsense of bigotry does not interfere, there may be found many liberal and enlightened views of the principles of government, of the restraints which should be imposed upon royal power, of the subordination of the Throne to the interests of the people, etc. ("*De Rege et Regis Intitutione.*" See particularly *lib.* i. *cap.* 6. 8. and 9.) — It is rather remarkable, too, that England should be indebted to another Jesuit for the earliest defence of that principle upon which the Revolution was founded, namely, the right of the people to change the succession. — (See Doleman's "Conferences," written in support of the title of the Infanta of Spain against that of James I.) — When Englishmen, therefore, say that Popery is the religion of slavery, they should not only recollect that their own boasted constitution is the work

and bequest of popish ancestors; they should not only remember the laws of Edward III., "under whom [says Bolingbroke] the constitution of our parliaments, and the whole form of our government, became reduced into better form;" but they should know that even the errors charged on Popery have leaned to the cause of liberty, and that Papists were the first promulgators of the doctrines which led to the Revolution. — In general, however, the political principles of the Roman Catholics have been described as happened to suit the temporary convenience of their oppressors, and have been represented alternately as slavish or refractory, according as a pretext for tormenting them was wanting. The same inconsistency has marked every other imputation against them. They are charged with laxity in the observance of oaths, though an oath has been found sufficient to shut them out from all worldly advantages. If they reject certain decisions of their church, they are said to be sceptics and bad Christians; if they admit those very decisions, they are branded as bigots and bad subjects. We are told that confidence and kindness will make them enemies to the government, though we know that exclusion and injuries have hardly prevented them from being its friends. In short, nothing can better illustrate the misery of those shifts and evasions by which a long course of cowardly injustice must be supported, than the whole history of Great Britain's conduct towards the Catholic part of her empire.

2 The "Sella *Stercoraria*" of the popes. — The Right Honorable and learned Doctor will

And, as the witch of sunless Lapland
  thinks
That little swarthy gnomes delight in
  stinks,
Let sallow Perceval snuff up the gale
Which wizard Duigenan's gathered
  sweets exhale.
Enough for me whose heart has learned
  to scorn
Bigots alike in Rome or England born,
Who loathe the venom whencesoe'er it
  springs,
From popes or lawyers,[1] pastry-cooks or
  kings, —
Enough for me to laugh and weep by
  turns,
As mirth provokes or indignation burns,
As Canning vapors or as France suc-
  ceeds,
As Hawkesbury proses, or as Ireland
  bleeds!

And thou, my friend, if, in these head-
  long days,
When bigot Zeal her drunken antics
  plays
So near a precipice, that men the while
Look breathless on and shudder while
  they smile —
If in such fearful days thou 'lt dare to
  look
To hapless Ireland, to this rankling nook
Which Heaven hath freed from poison-
  ous things in vain,
While Gifford's tongue and Musgrave's
  pen remain —
If thou hast yet no golden blinkers got
To shade thine eyes from this devoted
  spot,
Whose wrongs tho' blazoned o'er the
  world they be,
Placemen alone are privileged *not* to
  see —

Oh! turn awhile, and tho' the shamrock
  wreathes
My homely harp, yet shall the song it
  breathes
Of Ireland's slavery and of Ireland's
  woes
Live when the memory of her tyrant foes
Shall but exist, all future knaves to
  warn,
Embalmed in hate and canonized by
  scorn.
When Castlereagh in sleep still more
  profound
Than his own opiate tongue now deals
  around,
Shall wait the impeachment of that
  awful day
Which even *his* practised hand can't
  bribe away.

Yes, my dear friend, wert thou but
  near me now,
To see how Spring lights up on Erin's
  brow
Smiles that shine out unconquerably fair
Even thro' the blood-marks left by
  Camden [2] there,
Couldst thou but see what verdure paints
  the sod
Which none but tyrants and their slaves
  have trod,
And didst thou know the spirit, kind and
  brave,
That warms the soul of each insulted
  slave,
Who tired with struggling sinks beneath
  his lot
And seems by all but watchful France
  forgot [3] —

find an engraving of this chair in Spanheim's
"*Disquisitio Historica de Papâ Fœminâ*,"
(p. 118); and I recommended it as a model for
the fashion of that seat which the Doctor is
about to take in the privy-council of Ireland.

1 When Innocent X. was entreated to decide
the controversy between the Jesuits and the Jansenists, he answered, that "he had been bred a
lawyer, and had therefore nothing to do with
divinity." — It were to be wished that some of
our English pettifoggers knew their own fit element as well as Pope Innocent X.

2 Not the Camden who speaks thus of Ireland : —
  "To wind up all, whether we regard the fruit-
fulness of the soil, the advantage of the sea, with
so many commodious havens, or the natives themselves, who are warlike, ingenious, handsome, and
well-complexioned, soft-skinned and very nimble,
by reason of the pliantness of their muscles, this
Island is in many respects so happy, that Giraldus
might very well say, 'Nature had regarded with
more favorable eyes than ordinary this Kingdom
of Zephyr.'"

3 The example of toleration, which Bonaparte has held forth, will, I fear, produce no
other effect than that of determining the British
government to persist, from the very spirit of

Thy heart would burn — yes, even thy
    Pittite heart
Would burn to think that such a bloom-
    ing part
Of the world's garden, rich in nature's
    charms
And filled with social souls and vigorous
    arms,
Should be the victim of that canting
    crew,
So smooth, so godly, — yet so devilish
    too;
Who, armed at once with prayer-books
    and with whips,[1]

Blood on their hands and Scripture on
    their lips,
Tyrants by creed and torturers by text,
Make *this* life hell in honor of the *next!*
Your Redesdales, Percevals, — great, glo-
    rious Heaven,
If I 'm presumptuous, be my tongue for-
    given,
When here I swear by my soul's hope
    of rest,
I 'd rather have been born ere man was
    blest
With the pure dawn of Revelation's
    light,
Yes, — rather plunge me back in Pagan
    night,
And take my chance with Socrates for
    bliss,[2]

opposition, in their own old system of intolerance and injustice; just as the Siamese blacken
their teeth, "because," as they say, "the devil
has white ones."*

1 One of the unhappy results of the controversy between Protestants and Catholics, is the
mutual exposure which their criminations and
recriminations have produced. In vain do the
Protestants charge the Papists with closing the
door of salvation upon others, while many of
their own writings and articles breathe the same
uncharitable spirit. No canon of Constance or
Lateran ever damned heretics more effectually
than the eighth of the Thirty-nine Articles consigns to perdition every single member of the
Greek Church; and I doubt whether a more
sweeping clause of damnation was ever proposed
in the most bigoted council, than that which the
Calvinistic theory of predestination in the seven-
teenth of these Articles exhibits. It is true that
no liberal Protestant avows such exclusive opinions; that every honest clergyman must feel a
pang while he subscribes to them; that some
even assert the Athanasian Creed to be the forgery of one Vigilius Tapsensis, in the beginning
of the 6th century, and that eminent divines,
like Jortin, have not hesitated to say, "There
are propositions contained in our Liturgy and Articles, which no man of common sense amongst
us believes." † But while all this is freely conceded to Protestants; while nobody doubts their
sincerity, when they declare that their articles are
not essentials of faith, but a collection of opinions which have been promulgated by fallible
men, and from many of which they feel themselves justified in dissenting, — while so much
liberty of retractation is allowed to Protestants
upon their own declared and subscribed Articles
of religion, is it not strange that a similar indulgence should be so obstinately refused to the
Catholics, upon tenets which their church has
uniformly resisted and condemned, in every
country where it has independently flourished?
When the Catholics say, "The Decree of the
Council of Lateran, which you object to us, has
no claim whatever upon either our faith or our

reason; it did not even profess to contain any
doctrinal decision, but was merely a judicial proceeding of that assembly; and it would be as fair
for us to impute a *wife-killing* doctrine to the
Protestants, because their first pope, Henry
VIII., was sanctioned in an indulgence of that
propensity, as for you to conclude that we have
inherited a king-deposing taste from the *acts* of
the Council of Lateran, or the secular pretensions of our popes. With respect, too, to the
Decree of the Council of Constance, upon the
strength of which you accuse us of breaking faith
with heretics, we do not hesitate to pronounce
that Decree a calumnious forgery, a forgery, too,
so obvious and ill-fabricated, that none but our
enemies have ever ventured to give it the slightest credit for authenticity." — When the Catholics make these declarations (and they are almost
weary with making them), when they show, too,
by their conduct, that these declarations are sincere, and that their faith and morals are no more
regulated by the absurd decrees of old councils
and popes, than their science is influenced by the
papal anathema against that Irishman ‡ who first
found out the Antipodes, — is it not strange that so
many still wilfully distrust what every good man is
so much interested in believing? That so many
should prefer the dark-lantern of the 13th century to the sunshine of intellect which has since
overspread the world, and that every dabbler in
theology, from Mr. Le Mesurier down to the
Chancellor of the Exchequer, should dare to oppose the rubbish of Constance and Lateran to
the bright and triumphant progress of justice,
generosity, and truth?

2 In a singular work, written by one Franciscus Collius, "upon the Souls of the Pagans," the
author discusses, with much coolness and erudition, all the probable chances of salvation upon

* See "*l'Histoire Naturelle et Polit. du Roy-
aume de Siam*," etc.

† Strictures on the Articles, Subscriptions, etc.

‡ Virgilius, surnamed Solivagus, a native of
Ireland, who maintained, in the 8th century, the
doctrine of the Antipodes, and was anathema-
tized accordingly by the Pope. John Scotus
Erigena, another Irishman, was the first that
ever wrote against transubstantiation.

Than be the Christian of a faith like this,
Which builds on heavenly cant its earthly
   sway
And in a convert mourns to lose a prey;
Which, grasping human hearts with
   double hold, —
Like Danäe's lover mixing god and
   gold,[1] —
Corrupts both state and church and
   makes an oath
The knave and atheist's passport into
   both;

Which, while it dooms dissenting souls
   to know
Nor bliss above nor liberty below,
Adds the slave's suffering to the sinner's
   fear,
And lest he 'scape hereafter racks him
   here![2]

[2] There has been, after all, quite as much intolerance among Protestants as among Papists. According to the hackneyed quotation —

Iliacos intra muros peccatur et extra.

Even the great champion of the Reformation, Melanchthon, whom Jortin calls "a divine of much mildness and *good-nature*," thus expresses his approbation of the burning of Servetus: "*legi* [he says to Bullinger] *quæ de Serveti blasphemiis respondistis, et pietatem ac judicia vestra probo. Iudicia etiam senatum Genevensem rectè fecisse, quod hominem pertinacem et non omissurum blasphemias sustulit; ac miratus sum esse qui severitatem illam improbent.*" — I have great pleasure in contrasting with these "mild and good-natured" sentiments the following words of the Papist Baluze, in addressing his friend Conringius: "*interim amemus, mi Conringi, et tametsi diversas opiniones tuemur in causà religionis, moribus tamen diversi non simus, qui eadem literarum studia sectamur.*" — *Herman. Conring. Epistol. par. secund.* p. 56.

Hume tells us that the Commons, in the beginning of Charles the First's reign, "attacked Montague, one of the King's chaplains, on account of a moderate book which he had lately composed, and which, to their great disgust, saved virtuous Catholics, as well as other Christians, from eternal torments." — In the same manner a complaint was lodged before the Lords of the Council against that excellent writer Hooker, for having, in a Sermon against Popery, attempted to save many of his Popish ancestors for *ignorance*. — To these examples of Protestant toleration I shall beg leave to oppose the following extract from a letter of old Roger Ascham (the tutor of Queen Elizabeth), which is preserved among the Harrington Papers, and was written in 1566, to the Earl of Leicester, complaining of the Archbishop Young, who had taken away his prebend in the church of York: "Master Bourne[*] did never grieve me half so moche in offering me wrong, as Mr. Dudley and the Byshopp of York doe, in taking away my right. No byshopp in Q. Mary's time would have so dealt with me; not Mr. Bourne hymself, when Winchester lived, durst have so dealt with me. For suche good estimation in those dayes even the learnedst and wysest men, as Gardener and Cardinal Poole, made of my poore service, that although they knewe perfectly that in religion, both by open wrytinge and pryvie talke, I was contrarye unto them; yea, when Sir Francis Englefield by name did note me speciallye at the councill-board, Gardener would not suffer me to be called thither, nor touched ellswheare, saiinge suche words of me in a lettre, as though lettres

[*] Sir John Bourne, Principal Secretary of State to Queen Mary.

which a heathen philosopher might calculate. Consigning to perdition without much difficulty Plato, Socrates, etc., the only sage at whose fate he seems to hesitate is Pythagoras, in consideration of his golden thigh, and the many miracles which he performed. But having balanced a little his claims and finding reason to father all these miracles on the devil, he at length, in the twenty-fifth chapter, decides upon damning him also. ("*De Animabus Paganorum,*" *lib.* iv. *cap.* 20 and 25.) — The poet Dante compromises the matter with the Pagans, and gives them a neutral territory or limbo of their own, where their employment, it must be owned, is not very enviable — "*Senza speme vivemo in desio.*" — Cant. iv. — Among the numerous errors imputed to Origen, he is accused of having denied the eternity of future punishment; and, if he never advanced a more irrational doctrine, we may venture, I think, to forgive him. He went so far, however, as to include the devil himself in the general hell-delivery which he supposed would one day or other take place, and in this St. Augustin thinks him rather too merciful — *miserecordior profecto fuit Origenes, qui et ipsum diabolum,*" etc. ("*De Civitat. Dei, lib.* xxi. *cap.* 17.) — According to St. Jerome, it was Origen's opinion, that "the devil himself, after a certain time, will be as well off as the angel Gabriel" — "*id ipsum fore Gabrielem quod diabolum.*" (See his "*Epistle to Pammachius.*") But Halloix, in his Defence of Origen, denies strongly that this learned father had any such misplaced tenderness for the devil.

[1] Mr. Fox, in his Speech on the Repeal of the Test Act (1790), thus condemns the intermixture of religion with the political constitution of a state: — "What purpose [he asks] can it serve, except the baleful purpose of communicating and receiving contamination? Under such an alliance corruption must alight upon the one, and slavery overwhelm the other."

Locke, too, says of the connection between church and state, "The boundaries on both sides are fixed and immovable. He jumbles heaven and earth together, the things most remote and opposite, who mixes these two societies, which are in their original, end, business, and in every thing, perfectly distinct and infinitely different from each other." — *First Letter on Toleration.*

The corruptions introduced into Christianity may be dated from the period of its establishment under Constantine, nor could all the splendor which it then acquired atone for the peace and purity which it lost.

But no — far other faith, far milder
  beams
Of heavenly justice warm the Christian's
  dreams;
His creed is writ on Mercy's page above,
By the pure hands of all-atoning Love;
He weeps to see abused Religion twine
Round Tyranny's coarse brow her wreath
  divine;
And *he*, while round him sects and nations
  raise
To the one God their varying notes of
  praise,

cannot, I blushe to write them to your lordshipp.
Winchester's good-will stoode not in speaking
faire and wishing well, but he did in deede that
for me,* whereby my wife and children shall live
the better when I am gone." (See *"Nugæ An-
tiquæ,"* vol. i. pp. 98, 99.) — if men who acted
thus were bigots, what shall we call Mr. Perceval?

In Sutcliffe's " Survey of Popery " there
occurs the following assertion : — " Papists that
positively hold the heretical and false doctrines
of the modern church of Rome cannot possibly
be saved." — As a contrast to this and other
specimens of Protestant liberality, which it would
be much more easy than pleasant to collect, I
refer my readers to the Declaration of Le Père
Courayer ; — doubting not that, while he reads
the sentiments of this pious man upon toleration,
he will feel inclined to exclaim with Belsham,
" Blush, ye Protestant bigots ! and be confounded
at the comparison of your own wretched and
malignant prejudices with the generous and enlarged ideas, the noble and animated language of
this Popish priest." — *Essays,* xxvii. p. 86.

* By Gardener's favor Ascham long held his
fellowship, though not resident.

Blesses each voice, whate'er its tone
  may be,
That serves to swell the general harmony.[1]

Such was the spirit, gently, grandly
  bright,
That filled, oh Fox! thy peaceful soul
  with light;
While free and spacious as that ambient
  air
Which folds our planet in its circling
  care,
The mighty sphere of thy transparent
  mind
Embraced the world, and breathed for
  all mankind.
Last of the great, farewell ! — yet *not*
  the last —
Tho' Britain's sunshine hour with thee
  be past,
Ierne still one ray of glory gives
And feels but half thy loss while Grattan
  lives.

1 " *La tolérance est la chose du monde la plus
propre à ramener le siècle d'or, et à faire un
concert et une harmonie de plusieurs voix et instruments de différents tons et notes, aussi agréable pour le moins que l'uniformité d'une seule
voix.*" Bayle, " *Commentaire Philosophique,*"
etc. *part* ii. *chap.* vi. — Both Bayle and Locke
would have treated the subject of Toleration in a
manner much more worthy of themselves and of
the cause if they had written in an age less distracted by religious prejudices.

APPENDIX.

To the foregoing Poem, as first published, were subjoined, in the shape of a Note, or Appendix, the following remarks on the History and Music of Ireland. This fragment was originally intended to form part of a Preface to the Irish Melodies; but afterwards, for some reason which I do not now recollect, was thrown aside.

. . . .

Our history, for many centuries past, is creditable neither to our neighbors nor to ourselves and ought not to be read by any Irishman who wishes either to love England or to feel proud of Ireland. The loss of independence very early debased our character; and our feuds and rebellions, though frequent and ferocious, but seldom displayed that generous spirit of enterprise with which the pride of an independent monarchy so long dignified the struggles of Scotland. It is true this island has given birth to heroes who under more favorable circumstances might have left in the hearts of their countrymen recollections as dear as those of a Bruce or a Wallace; but success was wanting to consecrate resistance, their cause was branded with the disheartening name of treason and their oppressed country was such a blank among nations, that like the adventures of those woods which Rinaldo wished to explore, the fame of their actions was lost in the obscurity of the place where they achieved them.

> —— *Errando in quelli boschi*
> *Trovar potria strane avventure e molte,*
> *Ma come i luoghi i fatti ancor son foschi,*
> *Che non se'n ha notizia le più volte.*[1]

Hence is it that the annals of Ireland through a lapse of six hundred years exhibit not one of those shining names, not one of those themes of national pride, from which poetry borrows her noblest inspiration; and that history which ought to be the richest garden of the Muse yields no growth to her in this hapless island but cypress and weeds. In truth, the poet who would embellish his song with allusions to Irish names and events must be contented to seek them in those early periods when our character was yet unalloyed and original, before the impolitic craft of our conquerors had divided, weakened and disgraced us. The sole traits of heroism indeed which he can venture at this day to commemorate either with safety to himself or honor to his country are to be looked for in those ancient times when the native monarchs of Ireland displayed and fostered virtues worthy of a better age; when our Malachies wore around their necks collars of gold which they had won in single combat from the invader,[2] and our Briens deserved and won the warm affections of a people by exhibiting all the most estimable qualities of a king. It may be said that the magic of tradition has shed a charm over this remote period to which it is in reality but little entitled and that most of the pictures which we dwell on so fondly, of days when this island was distinguished

---

1 Ariosto, *canto* iv.
2 See Warner's " History of Ireland," vol. i. book ix.

543

amidst the gloom of Europe, by the sanctity of her morals, the spirit of her knighthood and the polish of her schools, are little more than the inventions of national partiality, — that bright but spurious offspring which vanity engenders upon ignorance and with which the first records of every people abound. But the sceptic is scarcely to be envied who would pause for stronger proofs than we already possess of the early glories of Ireland; and were even the veracity of all these proofs surrendered, yet who would not fly to such flattering fictions from the sad degrading truths which the history of later times presents to us?

The language of sorrow however is in general best suited to our Music, and with themes of this nature the poet may be amply supplied. There is scarcely a page of our annals that will not furnish him a subject, and while the national Muse of other countries adorns her temple proudly with trophies of the past, in Ireland her melancholy altar, like the shrine of Pity at Athens, is to be known only by the tears that are shed upon it; *"lacrymis altaria sudant."* [1]

There is a well-known story, related of the Antiochians under the reign of Theodosius, which is not only honorable to the powers of music in general, but which applies so peculiarly to the mournful melodies of Ireland, that I cannot resist the temptation of introducing it here. — The piety of Theodosius would have been admirable had it not been stained with intolerance; but under his reign was, I believe, first set the example of a disqualifying penal code enacted by Christians against Christians. [2] Whether his interference with the religion of the Antiochians had any share in the alienation of their loyalty is not expressly ascertained by historians; but severe edicts, heavy taxation, and the rapacity and insolence of the men whom he sent to govern them, sufficiently account for the discontents of a warm and susceptible people. Repentance soon followed the crimes into which their impatience had hurried them; but the vengeance of the Emperor was implacable, and punishments of the most dreadful nature hung over the city of Antioch, whose devoted inhabitants, totally resigned to despondence, wandered through the streets and public assemblies, giving utterance to their grief in dirges of the most touching lamentation. [3] At length, Flavianus, their bishop, whom they had sent to intercede with Theodosius, finding all his entreaties coldly rejected, adopted the expedient of teaching these songs of sorrow which he had heard from the lips of his unfortunate countrymen to the minstrels who performed for the Emperor at table. The heart of Theodosius could not resist this appeal; tears fell fast into his cup while he listened, and the Antiochians were forgiven. — Surely, if music ever spoke the misfortunes of a people, or could ever conciliate forgiveness for their errors, the music of Ireland ought to possess those powers.

---

1 Statius, "Thebaid." *lib.* xii.

2 " A sort of civil excommunication [says Gibbon], which separated them from their fellow-citizens by a peculiar brand of infamy; and this declaration of the supreme magistrate tended to justify, or at least to excuse, the insults of a fanatic populace. The sectaries were gradually disqualified for the possession of honorable or lucrative employments, and Theodosius was satisfied with his own justice when he decreed, that, as the Eunomians distinguished the nature of the Son from that of the Father, they should be incapable of making their wills or of receiving any advantage from testamentary donations."

3 μέλη τινὰ ὀλοφυρμοῦ πλήρη καὶ συμπαθείας συνθέμενοι, ταῖς μελῳδίαις ἐπῆδον.—*Nicephor. lib.* xii. *cap.* 43. This story is told also in Sozomen, *lib.* vii. *cap.* 23; but unfortunately Chrysostom says nothing whatever about it, and he not only had the best opportunities of information but was too fond of music, as appears by his praises of psalmody (" *Exposit. in Psalm* xli."), to omit such a flattering illustration of its powers. He imputes their reconciliation to the interference of the Antiochian solitaries, while Zozimus attributes it to the remonstrances of the sophist Libanius. — Gibbon, I think, does not even allude to this story of the musicians.

THE SCEPTIC,

A PHILOSOPHICAL SATIRE.

νόμον πάντων βασιλέα.
PINDAR. *ap. Herodot. lib.* iii.

PREFACE.

THE Sceptical Philosophy of the Ancients has been no less misrepresented than the Epicurean. Pyrrho may perhaps have carried it to rather an irrational excess; — but we must not believe with Beattie all the absurdities imputed to this philosopher; and it appears to me that the doctrines of the school, as explained by Sextus Empiricus,[1] are far more suited to the wants and infirmities of human reason as well as more conducive to the mild virtues of humility and patience, than any of those systems of philosophy which preceded the introduction of Christianity. The Sceptics may be said to have held a middle path between the Dogmatists and Academicians; the former of whom boasted that they had attained the truth while the latter denied that any attainable truth existed. The Sceptics however, without either asserting or denying its existence, professed to be modestly and anxiously in search of it; or, as St. Augustine expresses it, in his liberal tract against the Manichæans, "*nemo nostrum dicat jam se invenisse veritatem; sic eam quæramus quasi ab utrisque nesciatur.*"[2] From this habit of impartial investigation and the necessity which it imposed upon them of studying not only every system of philosophy but every art and science which professed to lay its basis in truth, they necessarily took a wider range of erudition and were far more travelled in the regions of philosophy than those whom conviction or bigotry had domesticated in any particular system. It required all the learning of dogmatism to overthrow the dogmatism of learning; and the Sceptics may be said to resemble in this respect that ancient incendiary who stole from the altar the fire with which he destroyed the temple. This advantage over all the other sects is allowed to them even by Lipsius, whose treatise on the miracles of the Virgo Hallensis will sufficiently save him from all suspicion of scepticism. "*labore, ingenio, memoria,*" he says, "*supra omnes pene philosophos fuisse. — quid nonne omnia aliorum secta tenere debuerunt et inquirere, si poterunt refellere? res dicit. nonne orationes varias, raras, subtiles inveniri ad tam receptas, claras, certas (ut videbatur) sententias evertendas?*" etc.[3] — "*Manuduct. ad Philosoph. Stoic.*" *Dissert.* 4.

---

1 Pyrrh. Hypoth. — The reader may find a tolerably clear abstract of this work of Sextus Empiricus in "*La Vérité des Sciences,*" by Mersenne, *liv.* i. *chap.* ii. etc.

2 "*Lib. contra Epist. Manichæi quam vocant Fundamenti,*" *Op. Paris. tom.* vi.

3 See Martin. Schoockius "*de Scepticismo,*" who endeavors, — weakly, I think, — to refute this opinion of Lipsius.

Between the scepticism of the ancients and the moderns the great difference is that the former doubted for the purpose of investigating, as may be exemplified by the third book of Aristotle's Metaphysics,[1] while the latter investigate for the purpose of doubting, as may be seen through most of the philosophical works of Hume.[2] Indeed the Pyrrhonism of latter days is not only more subtle than that of antiquity, but, it must be confessed, more dangerous in its tendency. The happiness of a Christian depends so essentially upon his belief, that it is but natural he should feel alarm at the progress of doubt, lest it should steal by degrees into that region from which he is most interested in excluding it, and poison at last the very spring of his consolation and hope. Still however the abuses of doubting ought not to deter a philosophical mind from indulging mildly and rationally in its use; and there is nothing surely more consistent with the meek spirit of Christianity than that humble scepticism which professes not to extend its distrust beyond the circle of human pursuits and the pretensions of human knowledge. A follower of this school may be among the readiest to admit the claims of a superintending Intelligence upon his faith and adoration: it is only to the wisdom of this weak world that he refuses or at least delays his assent;—it is only in passing through the shadow of earth that his mind undergoes the eclipse of scepticism. No follower of Pyrrho has ever spoken more strongly against the dogmatists than St. Paul himself, in the First Epistle to the Corinthians; and there are passages in Ecclesiastes and other parts of Scripture, which justify our utmost diffidence in all that human reason originates. Even the Sceptics of antiquity refrained carefully from the mysteries of theology, and in entering the temples of religion laid aside their philosophy at the porch. Sextus Empiricus thus declares the acquiescence of his sect in the general belief of a divine and fore-knowing Power: — τῷ μὲν βίῳ κατακολουθοῦντες ἀδοξάστως φαμὲν εἶναι θεοὺς καὶ σεβομεν θεοὺς καὶ προνόειν αὐτοὺς φαμεν.[3] In short it appears to me that this rational and well-regulated scepticism is the only daughter of the Schools that can safely be selected as a handmaid for Piety. He who distrusts the light of reason will be the first to follow a more luminous guide; and if with an ardent love for truth he has sought her in vain through the ways of this life, he will but turn with the more hope to that better world where all is simple, true and everlasting: for there is no parallax at the zenith; — it is only near our troubled horizon that objects deceive us into vague and erroneous calculations.

1 ἐστι δὲ τοῖσε ὑπορῆσαι βουλομένοις προῦργου τὸ διαπορῆσαι καλῶς.—*Metaphys. lib.* iii. *cap.* 1.

2 Neither Hume however nor Berkeley are to be judged by the misrepresentations of Beattie, whose book, however amiably intended, puts forth a most unphilosophical appeal to popular feelings and prejudices and is a continued *petitio principii* throughout.

3 *Lib.* iii. *cap.* 1.

THE SCEPTIC.

As the gay tint that decks the vernal
   rose [1]
Not in the flower but in our vision glows;
As the ripe flavor of Falernian tides
Not in the wine but in our taste resides;
So when with heartfelt tribute we declare
That Marco 's honest and that Susan 's
   fair,
T is in our minds and not in Susan's eyes
Or Marco's life the worth or beauty lies:
'or she in flat-nosed China would appear
As plain a thing as Lady Anne is here;
And one light joke at rich Loretto's dome
Would rank good Marco with the damned
   at Rome.

There 's no deformity so vile, so base,
That 't is not somewhere thought a charm,
   a grace;
No foul reproach that may not steal a
   beam
'rom other suns to bleach it to esteem. [2]

Ask who is wise? — you 'll find the self-
   same man
A sage in France, a madman in Japan;
And *here* some head beneath a mitre
   swells,
Which *there* had tingled to a cap and
   bells:
Nay, there may yet some monstrous region
   be,
Unknown to Cook and from Napoleon
   free,
Where Castlereagh would for a patriot
   pass
And mouthing Musgrave scarce be
   deemed an ass!

" List not to reason (Epicurus cries),
" But trust the senses, *there* conviction
   lies: " [3] —

1 "The particular bulk, number, figure, and
notion of the parts of fire or snow are really in
them, whether any one perceives them or not,
and therefore they may be called real qualities
because they really exist in those bodies; but
light, heat, whiteness or coldness are no more
really in them than sickness or pain is in manna.
Take away the sensation of them; let not the
eye see light or colors, nor the ears hear sounds;
let the palate not taste nor the nose smell, and all
colors, tastes, odors and sounds, as they are such
particular ideas, vanish and cease." — *Locke*,
book ii. chap. 8.

Bishop Berkeley, it is well known, extended
his doctrine even to primary qualities, and supposed that matter itself has but an ideal existence.
But, how are we to apply his theory to that
period which preceded the formation of man,
when our system of sensible things was produced, and the sun shone and the waters flowed
without any sentient being to witness them?
The spectator whom Whiston supplies will
scarcely solve the difficulty : "To speak my mind
freely," says he, "I believe that the Messias was
were actually present." — See *Whiston*, "*of the
Mosaic Creation.*"

2 Boethius employs this argument of the Scep-

tics among his consolatory reflections upon the
emptiness of fame. "*quid quod diversarum gen-
tium mores inter se atque instituta discordant,
ut quod apud alios laude, apud alios supplicio
dignum judicetur?*" — *Lib.* ii. *prosa 7.* Many
amusing instances of diversity, in the tastes,
manners, and morals of different nations, may
be found throughout the works of that amusing
Sceptic, Le Mothe le Vayer. — See his "*Opus-
cule Sceptique,*" his Treatise "*De la Secte Sceptique,*" and, above all, those Dialogues, not to be
found in his works, which he published under the
name of Horatius Tubero. — The chief objection
to these writings of Le Vayer (and it is a blemish
which may be felt also in the *Esprit des Loix*),
is the suspicious obscurity of the sources from
whence he frequently draws his instances and the
indiscriminate use made by him of the lowest
populace of the library, — those lying travellers
and wonder-mongers, of whom Shaftesbury, in his
"Advice to an Author," complains, as having
tended in his own time to the diffusion of a very
shallow and vicious sort of scepticism. — Vol.
i. p. 352. The Pyrrhonism of Le Vayer, however, is of the most innocent and playful kind;
and Villemandy, the author of "Scepticismus
Debellatus," exempts him specially in the declaration of war which he denounces against the
other armed neutrals of the sect, in consideration
of the othodox limits within which he confines
his incredulity.

3 This was the creed also of those modern

Alas! *they* judge not by a purer light,
Nor keep their fountains more untinged
and bright:
Habit so mars them that the Russian
swain
Will sigh for train-oil while he sips
Champagne;
And health so rules them, that a fever's
heat
Would make even Sheridan think water
sweet.

Just as the mind the erring sense [1]
believes,
The erring mind in turn the sense deceives;

Epicureans, whom Ninon de l'Enclos collected
around her in the Rue des Tournelles, and whose
object seems to have been to decry the faculty
of reason, as tending only to embarrass our
wholesome use of pleasures, without enabling us,
in any degree, to avoid their abuse. Madame
des Houlières, the fair pupil of Des Barreaux
in the arts of poetry and gallantry, has devoted
most of her verses to this laudable purpose, and
is even such a determined foe to reason, that,
in one of her pastorals, she congratulates her
sheep on the want of it. St. Évremont speaks
thus upon the subject: —

" *Un mélange incertain d'esprit et de matière*
Nous fait vivre avec trop ou trop peu de lumière.

· · · · · · · · · · · ·

Nature, élève-nous à la clarté des anges,
Ou nous abaise au sens des simples animaux."
Which may be thus paraphrased: —

     Had man been made at nature's birth
       Of only flame or only earth,
     Had he been formed a perfect whole
       Of purely *that* or grossly *this,*
     Then sense would ne'er have clouded soul,
       Nor soul restrained the sense's bliss.
     Oh happy had his light been strong,
       Or had he never shared a light
     Which shines enough to show he 's wrong,
       But *not* enough to lead him right.

   1 See, among the fragments of Petronius, those
verses beginning "*fallunt nos oculi,*" etc. The
most sceptical of the ancient poets was Euripides; and it would, I think, puzzle the whole
school of Pyrrho to produce a doubt more
startling than the following: —

     τίς δ᾽ οἶδεν εἰ ζῆν τοῦθ᾽ ὁ κέκληται θανεῖν,
     τὸ ζῆν δὲ θνῄσκειν ἐστί.
See Laert. "*in Pyrrh.*"

   Socrates and Plato were the grand sources of
ancient scepticism. According to Cicero ("*de
Orator.*" *lib.* iii.), they supplied Arcesilas with
the doctrines of the Middle Academy; and how
closely these resembled the tenets of the Sceptics, may be seen even in Sextus Empiricus (*lib.*
i. cap. 33), who with all his distinctions can
scarcely prove any difference. It appears strange

And cold disgust can find but wrinkles
there,
Where passion fancies all that 's smooth
and fair.
P * * * *, who sees, upon his pillow laid,
A face for which ten thousand pounds
were paid,
Can tell how quick before a jury flies
The spell that mockt the warm seducer's
eyes.

Self is the medium thro' which Judgment's ray
Can seldom pass without being turned
astray.
The smith of Ephesus [2] thought Dian's
shrine,
By which his craft most throve, the most
divine;
And even the *true* faith seems not half
so true,
When linkt with *one* good living as with
two.
Had Wolcot first been pensioned by the
throne,
Kings would have suffered by his praise
alone;
And Paine perhaps, for something snug
per ann.,
Had laught like Wellesley at all Rights
of Man.

But 't is not only individual minds, —
Whole nations too the same delusion
blinds.

that Epicurus should have been a dogmatist
and his natural temper would most probably
have led him to the repose of scepticism had not
the Stoics by their violent opposition to his
doctrines compelled him to be as obstinate as
themselves. Plutarch, indeed, in reporting some
of his opinions, represents him as having delivered them with considerable hesitation. —
Ἐπίκουρος οὐδὲν ἀπογινώσκει τούτων, ἐχόμενος
τοῦ ἐνδεχομένου. — "*De Placit. Philosoph.*"
lib. ii. *cap.* 13. See also the 21st and 22d chapters. But that the leading characteristics of the
sect were self-sufficiency and dogmatism, appears from what Cicero says of Velleius, "*De
Natur. Deor.*" — "*tum Velleius, fidenter sane
ut solent isti, nihil tam verens quam ne dubitar
aliquâ de re videretur.*"

   2 *Acts,* chap. xix. "For a certain man named
Demetrius, a silversmith, which made silver
shrines for Diana, brought no small gain unto
the craftsmen."

Thus England, hot from Denmark's smoking meads,
Turns up her eyes at Gallia's guilty
   deeds;
Thus, self-pleased still, the same dishonoring chain
She binds in Ireland she would break
   in Spain;
While praised at distance, but at home
   forbid,
Rebels in Cork are patriots at Madrid.

If Grotius be thy guide, shut, shut the
   book, —
In force alone for Laws of Nations look.
Let shipless Danes and whining Yankees
   dwell
On naval rights, with Grotius and Vattel,
While Cobbet's pirate code alone appears
Sound moral sense to England and
   Algiers.

Woe to the Sceptic in these party days
Who wafts to neither shrine his puffs of
   praise !
For him no pension pours its annual
   fruits,
No fertile sinecure spontaneous shoots;
Not *his* the meed that crowned Don
   Hookham's rhyme,
Nor sees he e'er in dreams of future
   time
Those shadowy forms of sleek reversions
   rise,
So dear to Scotchmen's second-sighted
   eyes.
Yet who that looks to History's damning
   leaf,
Where Whig and Tory, thief opposed
   to thief,
On either side in lofty shame are seen,[1]
While Freedom's form lies crucified
   between —
Who, Burdett, who such rival rogues can
   see,
But flies from *both* to Honesty and thee?

If weary of the world's bewildering
   maze,[2]
Hopeless of finding thro' its weedy ways

One flower of truth, the busy crowd we
   shun,
And to the shades of tranquil learning
   run,
How many a doubt pursues![3] how oft
   we sigh
When histories charm to think that his-
   tories lie !
That all are grave romances, at the best,
And Musgrave's [4] but more clumsy than
   the rest.
By Tory Hume's seductive page beguiled,
We fancy Charles was just and Strafford
   mild; [5]
And Fox himself with party pencil draws
Monmouth a hero, "for the good old
   cause!" [6]

difficulties which impede the discovery of the
longitude at sea; and the tumult and hurry of
life are equally unfavorable to that calm level
of mind which is necessary to an inquirer after
truth.

In the meantime, our modest Sceptic, in the
absence of truth, contents himself with probabili-
ties, resembling in this respect those suitors of
Penelope who on finding that they could not possess the mistress herself very wisely resolved to
put up with her maids; τῇ Πηνελόπῃ πλησιάζειν
μὴ δυνάμενοι, ταῖς ταύτης ἐμίγνυντο θεραπαίναις.
— *Plutarch,* Περὶ Παίδων Ἀγωγῆς.

3 See a curious work, entitled "Reflections
upon Learning," written on the plan of Agrippa's "*De Vanitate Scientiarum,*" but much
more honestly and skilfully executed.

4 This historian of the Irish rebellions has
outrun even his predecessor in the same task,
Sir John Temple, for whose character with
respect to veracity the reader may consult Carte's
Collection of Ormond's Original Papers, p. 207.
See also Dr. Nalson's account of him, in the
introduction to the second volume of his Historic.
Collect.

5 He defends Strafford's conduct as "innocent and even laudable." In the same spirit,
speaking of the arbitrary sentences of the Star
Chamber, he says, — "The severity of the Star
Chamber, which was generally ascribed to Laud's
passionate disposition, was perhaps in itself
somewhat blamable."

6 That flexibility of temper and opinion which
the habits of scepticism are so calculated to produce are thus pleaded for by Mr. Fox, in the very
sketch of Monmouth to which I allude; and this
part of the picture the historian may be thought
to have drawn from himself. "One of the most
conspicuous features in his character seems to
have been a remarkable, and, as some think,
a culpable degree of flexibility. That such a
disposition is preferable to its opposite extreme
will be admitted by all who think that modesty
even in excess is more nearly allied to wisdom
than conceit and self-sufficiency. He who has
attentively considered the political, or indeed

1 "Those two thieves," says Ralph, "be-
ween whom the nation is crucified." — "*Use
and Abuse of Parliaments.*"

2 The agitation of the ship is one of the chief

Then rights are wrongs and victories
　　are defeats,
As French or English pride the tale
　　repeats ;
And when they tell Corunna's story o'er,
They 'll disagree in all but honoring
　　Moore :
Nay, future pens to flatter future courts
May cite perhaps the Park-guns' gay
　　reports,
To prove that England triumpht on the
　　morn
Which found her Junot's jest and
　　Europe's scorn.

In science too — how many a system,
　　raised
Like Neva's icy domes, awhile hath
　　blazed
With lights of fancy and with forms of
　　pride,
Then, melting, mingled with the obliv-
　　ious tide !
Now Earth usurps the centre of the sky,
Now Newton puts the paltry planet by ;
Now whims revive beneath Descartes's[1]
　　pen,
Which *now*, assailed by Locke's, expire
　　again.

And when perhaps in pride of chemic
　　powers,
We think the keys of Nature's kingdom
　　ours,
Some Davy's magic touch the dream
　　unsettles,
And turns at once our alkalis to metals.
Or should we roam in metaphysic maze
Thro' fair-built theories of former days,
Some Drummond [2] from the north, more
　　ably skilled,
Like other Goths, to ruin than to build,
Tramples triumphant thro' our fanes
　　o'erthrown,
Nor leaves one grace, one glory of its
　　own.

Oh ! Learning, whatsoe'er thy pomp
　　and boast,
*Un*lettered minds have taught and
　　charmed men most.
The rude, unread Columbus was our
　　guide
To worlds, which learned Lactantius had
　　denied ;
And one wild Shakespeare following
　　Nature's lights
Is worth whole planets filled with
　　Stagyrites.

See grave Theology, when once she
　　strays
From Revelation's path, what tricks she
　　plays ;
What various heavens, — all fit for bard
　　to sing, —
Have churchmen dreamed, from Papias,
　　down to King ! [4]

the general concerns of life, may possibly go still further, and may rank a willingness to be convinced, or, in some cases, even without conviction, to concede our own opinion to that of other men, among the principal ingredients in the composition of practical wisdom." — It is right to observe, however, that the Sceptic's readiness of concession arises rather from uncertainty than conviction, more from a suspicion that his own opinion may be wrong, than from any persuasion that the opinion of his adversary is right. " It may be so," was the courteous and sceptical formula, with which the Dutch were accustomed to reply to the statements of ambassadors. See *Lloyd's* " *State Worthies,*" art, Sir Thomas Wyat.

1 Descartes, who is considered as the parent of modern scepticism, says, that there is nothing in the whole range of philosophy which does not admit of two opposite opinions, and which is not involved in doubt and uncertainty. " *in Philosophia nihil adhuc reperiri, de quo non in utramque partem disputatur, hoc est, quod non sit incertum et dubium.*" Gassendi is likewise to be added to the list of modern Sceptics, and Wedderkopff, in his Dissertation " *De Scepticismo profano et sacro*" (*Argentorat.* 1666), has denounced Erasmus also as a follower of Pyrrho, for his opinions upon the Trinity, and some other subjects. To these if we add the names of Bayle, Malebranche,

Dryden, Locke, etc., I think there is no one who need be ashamed of doubting in such company.

2 See this gentleman's " Academic Questions."

3 Papias lived about the time of the apostles and is supposed to have given birth to the heresy of the Chiliastæ, whose heaven was by no means of a spiritual nature, but rather an anticipation of the Prophet of Hera's elysium. See Eusebius " *Hist. Ecclesiast.*" *lib.* iii. *cap.* 33, and Hieronym. " *de Scriptor. Ecclesiast.*" — From all can find in these authors concerning Papias, seems hardly fair to impute to him those gross imaginations in which the believers of the sensual millennium indulged.

4 King, in his " Morsels of Criticism," vol. i supposes the sun to be the receptacle of blessed spirits.

While hell itself, in India naught but
  smoke,[1]
In Spain 's a furnace and in France — a
  joke.

Hail! modest Ignorance, thou goal
  and prize,
Thou last, best knowledge of the simply
  wise!
Hail! humble Doubt, when error's waves
  are past,
How sweet to reach thy sheltered port [2]
  at last,
And there by changing skies nor lured
  nor awed,
Smile at the battling winds that roar
  abroad.

1 The Indians call hell "the House of
Smoke." See Picart upon the Religion of the
Banians. The reader who is curious about infernal matters, may be edified by consulting
Rusca "de Inferno," particularly *lib.* ii. *cap.* 7, 8,
where he will find the precise sort of fire ascertained in which wicked spirits are to be burned
hereafter.

2 "*Chère Sceptique, douce pâture de mon
âme, et l'unique port de salut à un esprit qui
aime le repos!*" — *La Mothe le Vayer.*

There gentle Charity who knows how
  frail
The bark of Virtue, even in summer's
  gale,
Sits by the nightly fire whose beacon
  glows
For all who wander, whether friends or
  foes.
There Faith retires and keeps her white
  sail furled,
Till called to spread it for a better
  world;
While Patience watching on the weedy
  shore,
And mutely waiting till the storm be
  o'er,
Oft turns to Hope who still directs her
  eye
To some blue spot just breaking in the
  sky!

Such are the mild, the blest associates
  given
To him who doubts, — and trusts in
  naught but Heaven!

TWOPENNY POST-BAG,

BY

THOMAS BROWN,
THE YOUNGER

elapsæ manibus secidère tabellæ. — OVID.

DEDICATION.

TO

STEPHEN WOOLRICHE, ESQ.

MY DEAR WOOLRICHE, —

IT is now about seven years since I promised (and I grieve to think it is almost as long since we met) to dedicate to you the very first Book, of whatever size or kind, I should publish. Who could have thought that so many years would elapse, without my giving the least signs of life upon the subject of this important promise? Who could have imagined that a volume of doggerel, after all, would be the first offering that Gratitude would lay upon the shrine of Friendship?

If you continue, however, to be as much interested about me and my pursuits as formerly, you will be happy to hear that doggerel is not my *only* occupation; but that I am preparing to throw my name to the Swans of the Temple of Immortality,[1] leaving it of course to the said Swans to determine whether they ever will take the trouble of picking it from the stream.

In the meantime, my dear Woolriche, like an orthodox Lutheran, you must judge of me rather by my *faith* than my *works;* and however trifling the tribute which I here offer, never doubt the fidelity with which I am and always shall be

> Your sincere and attached friend,

> THE AUTHOR.

March 4, 1813.

1 Ariosto, *canto* 35.

PREFACE.

THE Bag, from which the following Letters are selected, was dropped by a Twopenny Postman about two months since, and picked up by an emissary of the Society for the Suppression of Vice, who supposing it might materially assist the private researches of that Institution, immediately took it to his employers and was rewarded handsomely for his trouble. Such a treasury of secrets was worth a whole host of informers; and, accordingly, like the Cupids of the poet (if I may use so profane a simile) who "fell at odds about the sweet-bag of a bee," [1] those venerable Suppressors almost fought with each other for the honor and delight of first ransacking the Post-Bag. Unluckily, however, it turned out upon examination that the discoveries of profligacy which it enabled them to make, lay chiefly in those upper regions of society, which their well-bred regulations forbid them to molest or meddle with. — In consequence they gained but very few victims by their prize, and after lying for a week or two under Mr. Hatchard's counter the Bag with its violated contents was sold for a trifle to a friend of mine.

It happened that I had been just then seized with an ambition (having never tried the strength of my wing but in a Newspaper) to publish something or other in the shape of a Book; and it occurred to me that, the present being such a letter-writing era, a few of these Twopenny-Post Epistles turned into easy verse would be as light and popular a task as I could possibly select for a commencement. I did not, however, think it prudent to give too many Letters at first and accordingly have been obliged (in order to eke out a sufficient number of pages) to reprint some of those trifles, which had already appeared in the public journals. As in the battles of ancient times, the shades of the departed were sometimes seen among the combatants, so I thought I might manage to remedy the thinness of my ranks, by conjuring up a few dead and forgotten ephemerons to fill them.

Such are the motives and accidents that led to the present publication; and as this is the first time my Muse has ever ventured out of the go-cart of a Newspaper, though I feel all a parent's delight at seeing little Miss go alone, I am also not without a parent's anxiety lest an unlucky fall should be the consequence of the experiment; and I need not point out how many living instances might be found of Muses that have suffered very severely in their heads from taking rather too early and rashly to their feet. Besides, a Book is so very different a thing from a Newspaper! — in the former, your doggerel without either company or shelter must stand shivering in the middle of a bleak page by itself; whereas in the latter it is comfortably backed by advertisements and has sometimes even a Speech of Mr. Stephen's, or something equally warm, for a *chauffe-pieds* — so that, in general, the very reverse of "*laudatur et alget*" is its destiny.

Ambition, however, must run some risks and I shall be very well satisfied if the reception of these few Letters should have the effect of sending me to the Post-Bag for more.

1 Herrick.

PREFACE TO THE FOURTEENTH EDITION.

BY A FRIEND OF THE AUTHOR.

In the absence of Mr. Brown, who is at present on a tour through ———, I feel myself called upon, as his friend, to notice certain misconceptions and misrepresentations, to which this little volume of Trifles has given rise.

In the first place, it is not true that Mr. Brown has had any accomplices in the work. A note indeed which has hitherto accompanied his Preface may very naturally have been the origin of such a supposition; but that note, which was merely the coquetry of an author, I have in the present edition taken upon myself to remove, and Mr. Brown must therefore be considered (like the mother of that unique production, the Centaur, μόνα καὶ μόνον [1]) as alone responsible for the whole contents of the volume.

In the next place it has been said that in consequence of this graceless little book a certain distinguished Personage prevailed upon another distinguished Personage to withdraw from the author that notice and kindness with which he had so long and so liberally honored him. In this story there is not one syllable of truth. For the magnanimity of the *former* of these persons I would indeed in no case answer too rashly: but of the conduct of the *latter* towards my friend I have a proud gratification in declaring that it has never ceased to be such as he must remember with indelible gratitude;—a gratitude the more cheerfully and warmly paid, from its not being a debt incurred solely on his own account but for kindness shared with those nearest and dearest to him.

To the charge of being an Irishman, poor Mr. Brown pleads guilty; and I believe it must also be acknowledged that he comes of a Roman Catholic family: an avowal which I am aware is decisive of his utter reprobation in the eyes of those exclusive patentees of Christianity, so worthy to have been the followers of a certain enlightened Bishop, Donatus,[2] who held " that God is in Africa *and not elsewhere*." But from all this it does not necessarily follow that Mr. Brown is a Papist; and indeed I have the strongest reasons for suspecting that they who say so are somewhat mistaken. Not that I presume to have ascertained his opinions upon such subjects. All I profess to know of his orthodoxy is that he has a Protestant wife and two or three little Protestant children and that he has been seen at church every Sunday, for a whole year together, listening to the sermons of his truly reverend and amiable friend, Dr. ———, and behaving there as well and as orderly as most people.

There are yet a few other mistakes and falsehoods about Mr. Brown, to which I had intended with all becoming gravity to advert; but I begin to think the task is quite as useless as it is tiresome. Misrepresentations and calumnies of this sort are like the arguments and statements of Dr. Duigenan, — not at all the less vivacious or less serviceable to their fabricators for having been refuted and disproved a thousand times over. They are brought forward again as good as new whenever malice or stupidity may be in want of them; and are quite as useful as the old broken lantern, in Fielding's Amelia, which the watchman always keeps ready by him to produce in proof of riotous conduct against his victims. I shall therefore

---

1 Pindar, Pyth. 2. — My friend certainly cannot add οὔτ' ἐν ἀνδράσι γερασφόρον.
2 Bishop of Casæ Nigræ, in the fourth century.

give up the fruitless toil of vindication, and would even draw my pen over what I have already written, had I not promised to furnish my publisher with a Preface, and know not how else I could contrive to eke it out.

I have added two or three more trifles to this edition, which I found in the Morning Chronicle, and knew to be from the pen of my friend. The rest of the volume remains [1] in its original state.

April 20, 1814.

1 A new reading has been suggested in the original of the Ode of Horace, freely translated by Lord Eldon, page 189. In the line, " *sive per Syrteis iter æstuosas,*" it is proposed, by a very trifling alteration, to read " *Surtees,*" instead of " Syrteis," which brings the Ode, it is said, more home to the noble translator, and gives a peculiar force and aptness to the epithet " *æstuosas.*" I merely throw out this emendation for the learned, being unable myself to decide upon its merits.

INTERCEPTED LETTERS,

ETC.

LETTER I.

FROM THE PRINCESS CHARLOTTE OF WALES TO THE LADY BARBARA ASHLEY.[1]

My dear Lady Bab, you 'll be shockt
    I 'm afraid,
When you hear the sad rumpus your
    Ponies have made ;
Since the time of horse-consuls (now
    long out of date),
No nags ever made such a stir in the
    state.
Lord Eldon first heard — and as instantly
    prayed he
To "God and his King" — that a Popish
    young Lady
(For tho' you 've bright eyes and twelve
    thousand a year,
It is still but too true you 're a Papist,
    my dear,)
Had insidiously sent, by a tall Irish
    groom,
Two priest-ridden Ponies just landed from
    Rome,
And so full, little rogues, of pontifical
    tricks
That the dome of St. Paul's was scarce
    safe from their kicks.

Off at once to Papa in a flurry he
    flies —
For Papa always does what these states-
    men advise
On condition that they 'll be in turn so
    polite
As in no case whate'er to advise him *too*
    right —

"Pretty doings are here, Sir (he angrily
    cries,
While by dint of dark eyebrows he strives
    to look wise) —
"'T is a scheme of the Romanists, so
    help me God!
"To ride over your *most* Royal Highness
    roughshod —
"Excuse, Sir, my tears — they 're from
    loyalty's source —
"Bad enough 't was for Troy to be sackt
    by a *Horse*,
"But for us to be ruined by *Ponies* still
    worse ! "
Quick a Council is called — the whole
    Cabinet sits —
The Archbishops declare, frightened out
    of their wits,
That if once Popish Ponies should eat at
    my manger,
From that awful moment the Church is in
    danger !
As, give them but stabling and shortly no
    stalls
Will suit their proud stomachs but those
    at St. Paul's.

The Doctor,[2] and he, the devout man
    of Leather,[3]
Vansittart, now laying their Saint-heads
    together,
Declare that these skittish young *a*-bom-
    inations
Are clearly foretold in Chap. vi. Revela-
    tions —
Nay, they verily think they could point
    out the one
Which the Doctor's friend Death was to
    canter upon.

---

1 This young Lady, who is a Roman Catholic, had lately made a present of some beautiful
Ponies to the Princess.

2 Mr. Addington, so nicknamed.
3 Alluding to a tax lately laid upon leather.

Lord Harrowby hoping that no one imputes
To the Court any fancy to persecute brutes,
Protests on the word of himself and his cronies
That had these said creatures been Asses, not Ponies,
The Court would have started no sort of objection,
As Asses were, *there*, always sure of protection.

"If the Princess *will* keep them (says Lord Castlereagh),
"To make them quite harmless, the only true way
"Is (as certain Chief Justices do with their wives)
"To flog them within half an inch of their lives,
"If they 've any bad Irish blood lurking about,
"This (he knew by experience) would soon draw it out."
Should this be thought cruel his Lordship proposes
"The new *Veto* snaffle[1] to bind down their noses —
"A pretty contrivance made out of old chains,
"Which appears to indulge while it doubly restrains;
"Which, however high-mettled, their gamesomeness checks
"(Adds his Lordship humanely), or else breaks their necks!"

This proposal received pretty general applause
From the Statesmen around — and the neck-breaking clause
Had a vigor about it, which soon reconciled
Even Eldon himself to a measure so mild.
So the snaffles, my dear, were agreed to *nem. con.,*

And my Lord Castlereagh, having so often shone
In the *fettering* line, is to buckle them on.

I shall drive to your door in these *Vetoes* some day,
But, at present, adieu! — I must hurry away
To go see my Mamma, as I 'm suffered to meet her
For just half an hour by the Queen's best repeater.

CHARLOTTE.

LETTER II.

FROM COLONEL M'MAHON TO GOULD FRANCIS LECKIE, ESQ.

DEAR SIR —
    I 've just had time to look
Into your very learned Book,[2]
Wherein — as plain as man can speak,
Whose English is half modern Greek —
You prove that we can ne'er intrench
Our happy isles against the French,
Till Royalty in England 's made
A much more independent trade; —
In short until the House of Guelph
Lays Lords and Commons on the shelf,
And boldly sets up for itself.

All that can well be understood
In this said Book is vastly good;
And as to what 's incomprehensible,
I dare be sworn 't is full as sensible.

But to your work's immortal credit
The Prince, good Sir, the Prince has read it
(The only Book, himself remarks,
Which he has read since Mrs. Clarke's).
Last levee-morn he lookt it thro',
During that awful hour or two
Of grave tonsorial preparation,
Which to a fond, admiring nation
Sends forth, announced by trump and drum,
The best-wigged Prince in Christendom.

---

1 The question whether a Veto was to be allowed to the Crown in the appointment of Irish Catholic Bishops was, at this time, very generally and actively agitated.

2 For an account of this extraordinary work of Mr. Leckie, see *The Edinburgh Review,* vol. xx.

He thinks with you, the imagination
Of *partnership* in legislation
Could only enter in the noddles
Of dull and ledger-keeping twaddles,
Whose heads on *firms* are running so,
They even must have a King and Co.,
And hence most eloquently show forth
On *checks* and *balances* and so forth.

But now, he trusts, we 're coming
    near a
Far more royal, loyal era;
When England's monarch need but say,
"Whip me those scoundrels, Castle-
    reagh!"
Or, "Hang me up those Papists, Eldon,"
And 't will be done—ay, faith, and well
    done.

With view to which I 've his com-
    mand
To beg, Sir, from your travelled hand,
(Round which the foreign graces swarm)[1]
A Plan of radical Reform;
Compiled and chosen as best you can,
In Turkey or at Ispahan,
And quite upturning, branch and root,
Lords, Commons, and Burdétt to boot.

But, pray, whate'er you may impart,
    write
Somewhat more brief than Major Cart-
    wright:
Else, tho' the Prince be long in rigging,
'T would take at least a fortnight's wig-
    ging,—
Two wigs to every paragraph—
Before he well could get thro' half.

You 'll send it also speedily—
As truth to say 'twixt you and me,
His Highness, heated by your work,
Already thinks himself Grand Turk!
And you 'd have laught, had you seen how
He scared the Chancellor just now,
When (on his Lordship's entering puft)
    he
Slapt his back and called him "Mufti!"

The tailors too have got commands
To put directly into hands
All sorts of Dulimans and Pouches,
With Sashes, Turbans and Paboutches,
(While Yarmouth 's sketching out a
    plan
Of new *Moustaches à l' Ottomane*)
And all things fitting and expedient
To *turkify* our gracious Regent!

You therefore have no time to waste—
So, send your System. —
                Yours in haste.

POSTSCRIPT.

BEFORE I send this scrawl away,
I seize a moment just to say
There 's some parts of the Turkish sys-
    tem
So vulgar 't were as well you missed 'em.
For instance—in *Seraglio* matters—
Your Turk whom girlish fondness flatters,
Would fill his Haram (tasteless fool!)
With tittering, red-cheekt things from
    school.
But *here* (as in that fairy land,
Where Love and Age went hand in
    hand;[2]
Where lips, till sixty, shed no honey,
And Grandams were worth any money,)
Our Sultan has much riper notions—
So, let your list of *she*-promotions
Include those only, plump and sage,
Who 've reached the *regulation*-age;
That is, (as near as one can fix
From Peerage dates) full fifty-six.

This rule 's for *favorites*—nothing
    more—
For, as to *wives*, a Grand Signor,
Tho' not decidedly *without* them,
Need never care one curse about them.

---

[1] "The truth indeed seems to be, that having
lived so long abroad as evidently to have lost, in
a great degree, the use of his native language,
Mr. Leckie has gradually come not only to speak,
but to feel, like a foreigner." — *Edinburgh Review.*

[2] The learned Colonel must allude here to a
description of the Mysterious Isle, in the History
of Abdalla, Son of Hanif, where such inversions
of the order of nature are said to have taken
place. — "A score of old women and the same
number of old men played here and there in the
court, some at chuck-farthing, others at tip-cat or
at cockles." — And again, "There is nothing
believe me, more engaging than those lovely
wrinkles," etc. — See "*Tales of the East,*" vol
iii. pp. 607, 608.

LETTER III.

FROM GEORGE PRINCE REGENT TO THE EARL OF YARMOUTH.[1]

WE missed you last night at the " hoary
    old sinner's,"
Who gave us as usual the cream of good
    dinners;
His soups scientific, his fishes quite
    prime —
His *pâtés* superb, and his cutlets sub-
    lime !
In short, 't was the snug sort of dinner
    to stir a
Stomachic orgasm in my Lord Ellen-
    borough,
Who *set to*, to be sure, with miraculous
    force,
And exclaimed between mouthfuls, " a
    He-Cook, of course ! —
" While you live — (what 's there under
    that cover ? pray, look) —
" While you live — (I 'll just taste it)—
    ne'er keep a She-Cook.
" 'T is a sound Salic Law — (a small bit
    of that toast) —
" Which ordains that a female shall
    ne'er rule the roast;
" For Cookery 's a secret — (this turtle 's
    uncommon) —
" Like Masonry, never found out by a
    woman ! "

The dinner you know was in gay
    celebration
Of *my* brilliant triumph and Hunt's con-
    demnation;
A compliment too to his Lordship the
    Judge
For his Speech to the Jury — and zounds !
    who would grudge
Turtle soup tho' it came to five guineas
    a bowl,
To reward such a loyal and complaisant
    soul?
We were all in high gig — Roman Punch
    and Tokay
Travelled round till our heads travelled
    just the same way;

1 This letter, as the reader will perceive, was
written the day after a dinner given by the Marquis of Headfort.

And we cared not for Juries or Libels —
    no — damme ! nor
Even for the threats of last Sunday's
    Examiner !

More good things were eaten than said
    — but Tom Tyrrhitt
In quoting Joe Miller you know has
    some merit;
And hearing the sturdy Justiciary Chief
Say — sated with turtle — " I 'll now try
    the beef " —
Tommy whispered him (giving his Lord-
    ship a sly hit)
" I fear 't will be *hung*-beef, my Lord, if
    YOU *try* it ! "

And Camden was there, who that
    morning had gone
To fit his new Marquis's coronet on;
And the dish set before him — oh ! dish
    well-devised ! —
Was what old Mother Glasse calls, " a
    calf's head surprised ! "
The *brains* were near Sherry and *once*
    had been fine,
But of late they had lain so long soaking
    in wine,
That tho' we from courtesy still chose to
    call
These brains very fine they were no
    brains at all.

When the dinner was over, we drank,
    every one
In a bumper, " the venial delights of
    Crim. Con.;"
At which Headfort with warm reminis-
    cences gloated,
And Ellenb'rough chuckled to hear him-
    self quoted.

Our next round of toasts was a fancy
    quite new,
For we drank — and you 'll own 't was
    benevolent too —
To those well-meaning husbands, cits,
    parsons or peers,
Whom we 've any time honored by
    courting their dears:
This museum of wittols was comical
    rather;

Old Headfort gave Massey, and *I* gave
 your father.
In short, not a soul till this morning
 would budge —
We were all fun and frolic, and even the
 Judge
Laid aside for the time his juridical
 fashion,
And thro' the whole night was n't *once*
 in a passion!

I write this in bed while my whiskers
 are airing,
And Mac [1] has a sly dose of jalap pre-
 paring
For poor Tommy Tyrrhitt at breakfast to
 quaff —
As I feel I want something to give me a
 laugh,
And there's nothing so good as old
 Tommy kept close
To his Cornwall accounts after taking a
 dose.

LETTER IV.

FROM

THE RIGHT HON. PATRICK DUIGENAN TO
THE RIGHT HON. SIR JOHN NICHOL.

Dublin. [2]

LAST week, dear Nichol, making merry
At dinner with our Secretary,
When all were drunk or pretty near
(The time for doing business here),
Says he to me, " Sweet Bully Bottom!
" These Papist dogs — hiccup —'od rot
 'em! —
" Deserve to be bespattered — hiccup —
" With all the dirt even *you* can pick
 up.
" But, as the Prince (here 's to him —
 fill —
" Hip, hip, hurra!) — is trying still
" To humbug them with kind profes-
 sions,
" And as *you* deal in *strong* expres-
 sions —

1 Colonel M'Mahon.

2 This letter, which contained some very heavy
enclosures, seems to have been sent to London
by a private hand, and then put into the Twopenny Post-Office, to save trouble. See the
Appendix.

" *Rogue* " — " *traitor* " — hiccup — and
 all that —
" You must be muzzled, Doctor Pat! —
" You must indeed — hiccup — that 's
 flat." —

Yes — " muzzled " was the word, Sir
 John —
These fools have clapt a muzzle on
The boldest mouth that e'er ran o'er
With slaver of the times of yore! [3] —
Was it for this that back I went
As far as Lateran and Trent,
To prove that they who damned us then
Ought now in turn be damned again? —
The silent victim still to sit
Of Grattan's fire and Canning's wit,
To hear even noisy Mathew gabble
 on,
Nor mention once the Whore of Baby-
 lon!
Oh! 't is too much — who now will be
The Nightman of No-Popery?
What Courtier, Saint or even Bishop
Such learned filth will ever fish up?
If there among our ranks be one
To take my place, 't is *thou*, Sir John;
Thou who like me art dubbed Right
 Hon.
Like me too art a Lawyer Civil
That wishes Papists at the devil.

To whom then but to thee, my friend,
Should Patrick [4] his Port-folio send?
Take it — 't is thine — his learned Port-
 folio,
With all its theologic olio
Of Bulls, half Irish and half Roman —
Of Doctrines now believed by no man —
Of Councils held for men's salvation,
Yet always ending in damnation —
(Which shows that since the world's
 creation
Your Priests, whate'er their gentle
 shamming,
Have always had a taste for damning,)

3 In sending this sheet to the Press, however,
I learn that the " muzzle," has been taken off,
and the Right Hon. Doctor again let loose!

4 A bad name for poetry; but Duigenan is
still worse. — As Prudentius says upon a very
different subject —

torquetur Apollo
nomine percussus.

And many more such pious scraps,
To prove (what *we 've* long proved,
    perhaps,)
That mad as Christians used to be
About the Thirteenth Century,
There still are Christians to be had
In this, the Nineteenth, just as mad!

. . . . . .

Farewell — I send with this, dear
    Nichol,
A rod or two I 've had in pickle
Wherewith to trim old Grattan's
    jacket. —
The rest shall go by Monday's packet.

P. D.

*Among the Enclosures in the foregoing Letter
was the following " Unanswerable Argument
against the Papists."*

. . . . . .

WE 'RE told the ancient Roman nation
Made use of spittle in lustration;[1]
(*Vide* "*Lactantium ap. Gallæum*"[2] —
i.e. you need not *read* but *see* 'em;)
Now Irish Papists — fact surprising —
Make use of spittle in baptizing;
Which proves them all, O'Finns, O'Fa-
    gans,
Connors and Tooles all downright Pa-
    gans.
This fact 's enough; — let no one tell us
To free such sad, *salivous* fellows. —
No, no — the man, baptized with spittle,
Hath no truth in him — not a tittle!

. . . . . .

LETTER V.

FROM THE COUNTESS DOWAGER OF CORK TO LADY ———.

MY dear Lady ———! I 've been just
    sending out
About five hundred cards for a snug little
    Rout —

(By the by, you 've seen " Rokeby "?—
    this moment got mine —
The " Mail-Coach Edition "[3] — prodi-
    giously fine!)
But I can't conceive how in this very
    cold weather
I 'm ever to bring my five hundred to-
    gether;
As, unless the thermometer 's near boil-
    ing heat,
One can never get half of one's hundreds
    to meet.
(Apropos — you 'd have laught to see
    Townsend last night,
Escort to their chairs, with his staff, so
    polite,
The " three maiden Miseries," all in a
    fright,
Poor Townsend, like Mercury, filling two
    posts,
Supervisor of *thieves* and chief-usher of
    ghosts!)

But, my dear Lady ———, can't you hit
    on some notion,
At least for one night to set London in
    motion? —
As to having the Regent, *that* show is
    gone by —
Besides, I 've remarkt that (between you
    and I)
The Marchesa and he, inconvenient in
    more ways,
Have taken much lately to whispering in
    doorways;
Which — considering, you know, dear,
    the *size* of the two —
Makes a block that one's company *can
    not* get thro';
And a house such as mine is, with door-
    ways so small,
Has no room for such cumbersome love-
    work at all. —
(Apropos, tho', of love-work — you 've
    heard it, I hope,
That Napoleon's old mother 's to marry
    the Pope,
What a comical pair!) — but, to stick to
    my Rout,
'T will be hard if some novelty can't be
    struck out.

---

1 ———*lustralibus antè salivis
    expiat.*   PERS. *sat.* 2.

2 I have taken the trouble of examining the
Doctor's reference here, and find him for once
correct. The following are the words of his indignant referee Gallæus — " *asserere non vere-
mur sacrum baptismum a Papistis profanari, et
sputi usum in peccatorum expiatione a Paganis
non a Christianis* manâsse."

3 See Mr. Murray's Advertisement about the
Mail-Coach copies of " Rokeby."

Is there no Algerine, no Kamchatkan arrived?
No Plenipo Pacha, three-tailed and ten-
wived?
No Russian whose dissonant consonant
name
Almost rattles to fragments the trumpet
of fame?

I remember the time three or four win-
ters back,
When — provided their wigs were but
decently black —
A few Patriot monsters from Spain were
a sight
That would people one's house for one,
night after night.
But — whether the Ministers _pawed_ them
too much —
(And you know how they spoil whatsoever they touch)
Or, whether Lord George (the young
man about town)
Has by dint of bad poetry written them
down,
One has certainly lost one's _peninsular_
rage;
And the only stray Patriot seen for an
age
Has been at such places (think, how the
fit cools!)
As old Mrs. Vaughan's or Lord Liverpool's.

But, in short, my dear, names like
Wintztschitstopschinzoudhoff
Are the only things now make an even-
ing go smooth off:
So, get me a Russian — till death I 'm
your debtor —
If he brings the whole Alphabet, so much
the better.
And — Lord! if he would but, _in char-
acter_, sup
Off his fish-oil and candles, he 'd quite
set me up!

Au revoir, my sweet girl — I must
leave you in haste —
Little Gunter has brought me the Li-
queurs to taste.

POSTSCRIPT.

By the by, have you found any friend
that can conster
That Latin account, t' other day, of a
Monster? [1]
If we can't get a Russian, and _that thing_
in Latin
Be not _too_ improper, I think I 'll bring
that in.

LETTER VI.

FROM ABDALLAH,[2] IN LONDON, TO MO-
HASSAN, IN ISPAHAN.

WHILST thou, Mohassan, (happy thou!)
Dost daily bend thy loyal brow
Before our King — our Asia's treasure!
Nutmeg of Comfort; Rose of Pleasure!—
And bearest as many kicks and bruises
As the said Rose and Nutmeg chooses;
Thy head still near the bowstring's bor-
ders,
And but left on till further orders —
Thro' London streets with turban fair,
And caftan floating to the air,
I saunter on, the admiration
Of this short-coated population —
This sewed up race — this buttoned na-
tion —
Who while they boast their laws so free
Leave not one limb at liberty,
But live with all their lordly speeches
The slaves of buttons and tight breeches.

Yet tho' they thus their knee-pans fet-
ter
(They 're Christians and they know no
better) [3]
In _some_ things they 're a thinking nation;
And on Religious Toleration

1 Alluding, I suppose, to the Latin Advertisement of a _lusus Naturæ_ in the Newspapers lately.

2 I have made many inquiries about this Persian gentleman, but can not satisfactorily ascer-
tain who he is. From his notions of Religious
Liberty, however, I conclude that he is an im-
portation of Ministers; and he has arrived just
in time to assist the Prince and Mr. Leckie in
their new Oriental Plan of Reform. — See the
second of these letters. — How Abdallah's epistle to Ispahan found its way into the Twopenny
Post-Bag is more than I can pretend to account
for.

3 " _C'est un honnête homme_," said a Turkish
governor of De Ruyter; " _c'est grand dommage
qu'il soit Chrétien._"

I own I like their notions *quite*,
They are so Persian and so right!
You know our Sunnites,[1] — hateful dogs!
Whom every pious Shiite flogs
Or longs to flog[2] — 't is true, they pray
To God, but in an ill-bred way;
With neither arms nor legs nor faces
Stuck in their right, canonic places.[3]
'T is true, they worship Ali's name[4] —
Their heaven and *ours* are just the same—
(A Persian's Heaven is easily made,
'T is but black eyes and lemonade.)
Yet tho' we 've tried for centuries back —
We can't persuade this stubborn pack,
By bastinadoes, screws or nippers,
To wear the establisht pea-green slippers.[5]
Then, only think, the libertines!
They wash their toes — they comb their
   chins,[6]
With many more such deadly sins;
And what 's the worst, (tho' last I rank
   it)
Believe the Chapter of the Blanket!

Yet spite of tenets so flagitious,
(Which *must* at bottom be seditious;
Since no man living would refuse
Green slippers but from treasonous views;
Nor wash his toes but with intent
To overturn the government,) —

1 *Sunnites* and *Shiites* are the two leading sects into which the Mahometan world is divided; and they have gone on cursing and persecuting each other, without any intermission, for about eleven hundred years. The *Sunni* is the established sect in Turkey, and the *Shia* in Persia; and the differences between them turn chiefly upon those important points, which our pious friend Abdallah, in the true spirit of Shiite Ascendency, reprobates in this Letter.

2 "*Les Sunnites, qui étoient comme les Catholiques de Musulmanisme.*" — *D'Herbelot.*

3 "In contradistinction to the Sounis, who in their prayers cross their hands on the lower part of the breast, the Schiahs drop their arms in straight lines; and as the Sounis, at certain periods of the prayer, press their foreheads on the ground or carpet, the Schiahs," etc. — *Forster's Voyage.*

4 "*Les Turcs ne détestent pas Ali réciproquement; au contraire, ils le reconnoissent,*" etc. — *Chardin.*

5 "The Shiites wear green slippers, which the Sunnites consider as a great abomination." — *Mariti.*

6 For these points of difference, as well as for the Chapter of the Blanket, I must refer the reader (not having the book by me) to Picart's "Account of the Mahometan Sects."

Such is our mild and tolerant way,
We only curse them twice a day
(According to a Form that 's set),
And, far from torturing, only let
All orthodox believers beat 'em,
And twitch their beards where'er they
   meet 'em.

As to the rest, they 're free to do
Whate'er their fancy prompts them to,
Provided they make nothing of it
Towards rank or honor, power or profit;
Which things we naturally expect,
Belong to us, the Establisht sect,
Who disbelieve (the Lord be thanked!)
The aforesaid Chapter of the Blanket.
The same mild views of Toleration
Inspire, I find, this buttoned nation,
Whose Papists (full as given to rogue,
And only Sunnites with a brogue)
Fare just as well, with all their fuss,
As rascal Sunnites do with us.

The tender Gazel I enclose
Is for my love, my Syrian Rose —
Take it when night begins to fall,
And throw it o'er her mother's wall.

GAZEL.

REMEMBEREST thou the hour we past,—
That hour the happiest and the last?
Oh! not so sweet the Siha thorn
To summer bees at break of morn,
Not half so sweet, thro' dale and dell,
To Camels' ears the tinkling bell,
As is the soothing memory
Of that one precious hour to me.

How can we live, so far apart?
Oh! why not rather, heart to heart,
   United live and die —
Like those sweet birds, that fly together,
With feather always touching feather,
   Linkt by a hook and eye![7]

7 This will appear strange to an English reader, but it is literally translated from Abdallah's Persian, and the curious bird to which he alludes is the *Juftak*, of which I find the following account in Richardson: — "A sort of bird, that is said to have but one wing; on the opposite side to which the male has a hook and the female a ring, so that, when they fly, they are fastened together."

LETTER VII.

FROM MESSRS. LACKINGTON AND CO.
TO THOMAS MOORE, ESQ. [1]

PER POST, Sir, we send your MS. —
lookt it thro' —
Very *sorry* — but — can't undertake —
't would n't do.
Clever work, Sir! — would *get up* prodigiously well —
Its only defect is — it never would sell.
And tho' *Statesmen* may glory in being
unbought,
In an *Author* 't is not so desirable
thought.

Hard times, Sir, — most books are too
dear to be read —
Tho' the *gold* of Good-sense and Wit's
small-change are fled,
Yet the *paper* we Publishers pass, in
their stead,
Rises higher each day, and ('t is frightful
to think it)
Not even such names as Fitzgerald's can
sink it!

However, Sir — if you 're for trying
again,
And at somewhat that 's vendible — we
are your men.

Since the Chevalier Carr [2] took to
marrying lately,
The Trade is in want of a *Traveller*
greatly —
No job, Sir, more easy — your *Country*
once planned,
A month aboard ship and a fortnight on
land
Puts your Quarto of Travels, Sir, clean
out of hand.

An East-India pamphlet 's a thing that
would tell —
And a lick at the Papists is *sure* to sell
well.
Or — supposing you 've nothing *original*
in you —

Write Parodies, Sir, and such fame it
will win you,
You 'll get to the Blue-stocking Routs of
Albinia! [3]
(Mind — *not* to her *dinners* — a *second-
hand* Muse
Must n't think of aspiring to *mess* with
the *Blues.*)
Or — in case nothing else in this world
you can do —
The deuce is in 't, Sir, if you can not
review!

Should you feel any touch of *poetical*
glow,
We 've a Scheme to suggest — Mr.
Scott, you must know,
(Who, we 're sorry to say it, now works
for *the Row,* [4])
Having quitted the Borders to seek new
renown,
Is coming by long Quarto stages to
Town;
And beginning with "Rokeby" (the
job 's sure to pay)
Means to *do* all the Gentlemen's Seats
on the way.
Now, the Scheme is (tho' none of our
hackneys can beat him)
To start a fresh Poet thro' Highgate to
meet him;
Who by means of quick proofs — no re-
vises — long coaches —
May do a few Villas, before Scott ap-
proaches.
Indeed if our Pegasus be not curst
shabby,
He 'll reach, without foundering, at least
Woburn-Abbey.
Such, Sir, is our plan — if you 're up to
the freak,
'T is a match! and we 'll put you *in
training* next week.
At present, no more — in reply to this
Letter, a
Line will oblige very much
　　　　　　Yours, *et cetera.*
Temple of the Muses.

1 From motives of delicacy, and, indeed, of
fellow-feeling, I suppress the name of the Author, whose rejected manuscript was inclosed
in this letter. — See the Appendix.
2 Sir John Carr, the author of "Tours in Ireland, Holland, Sweden," etc.

3 This alludes, I believe, to a curious correspondence, which is said to have passed lately
between Albina, Countess of Buckinghamshire,
and a certain ingenious Parodist.
4 Paternoster Row.

LETTER VIII.

FROM COLONEL THOMAS TO —— SKEF-FINGTON, ESQ.

COME to our Fête [1] and bring with thee
Thy newest, best embroidery.
Come to our Fête and show again
That pea-green coat, thou pink of men,
Which charmed all eyes that last sur-
    veyed it;
When Brummel's self inquired " who
    made it? " —
When Cits came wondering from the
    East
And thought thee Poet Pye *at least* !

Oh ! come, (if haply 't is thy week
For looking pale,) with paly cheek;
Tho' more we love thy roseate days,
When the rich rouge-pot pours its
    blaze
Full o'er thy face and amply spread,
Tips even thy whisker-tops with red —
Like the last tints of dying Day
That o'er some darkling grove delay.

Bring thy best lace, thou gay Philander,
(That lace, like Harry Alexander,
Too precious to be washt,) — thy rings,
Thy seals — in short, thy prettiest things !
Put all thy wardrobe's glories on,
And yield in frogs and fringe to none
But the great Regent's self alone;
Who — by particular desire —
For that night only, means to hire
A dress from Romeo Coates, Esquire.[2]
Hail, first of Actors ! [3] best of Regents !
Born for each other's fond allegiance !
Both gay Lotharios — both good dress-
    ers —
Of serious Farce *both* learned Profes-
    sors —

Both circled round, for use or show,
With cock's combs, wheresoe'er they
    go ! [4]

Thou knowest the time, thou man of
    lore !
It takes to chalk a ball-room floor —
Thou knowest the time, too, well-a-day !
It takes to dance that chalk away.[5]
The Ball-room opens — far and nigh
Comets and suns beneath us lie ;
O'er snow-white moons and stars we
    walk,
And the floor seems one sky of chalk !
But soon shall fade that bright deceit,
When many a maid, with busy feet
That sparkle in the lustre's ray,
O'er the white path shall bound and play
Like Nymphs along the Milky Way : —
With every step a star hath fled,
And suns grow dim beneath their tread !
So passeth life — (thus Scott would
    write,
And spinsters read him with delight,) —
Hours are not feet, yet hours trip on,
Time is not chalk, yet time 's soon gone ! [6]

But, hang this long digressive flight ! —
I meant to say, thou 'lt see that night
What falsehood rankles in their hearts,
Who say the Prince neglects the arts —
Neglects the arts? — no, Strahlweg,[7] no;
Thy Cupids answer " 't is not so; "
And every floor that night shall tell
How quick thou daubest and how well.
Shine as thou mayst in French vermilion,
Thou 'rt *best* beneath a French cotillion;
And still comest off, whate'er thy faults,
With *flying colors* in a Waltz.

---

1 This Letter enclosed a Card for the Grand
Fête on the 5th of February.

2 An amateur actor of much risible renown.

3 *quem tu Melpomene semel*
nascentem placido lumine, *videris*, etc.
                                    HORAT.

The Man upon whom thou hast deigned to look
funny,
Oh Tragedy's Muse ! at the hour of his birth —
Let them say what they will, that 's the Man for
my money,
Give others thy tears, but let *me* have thy mirth !

4 The crest of Mr. Coates, the very amusing
amateur tragedian here alluded to, was a cock ;
and most profusely were his liveries, harness, etc.
covered with this ornament.

5 To those who neither go to balls nor read
The Morning Post, it may be necessary to mention, that the floors of Ball-rooms, in general, are
chalked for safety and for ornament with various
fanciful devices.

6 Hearts are not flint, yet flints are rent,
    Hearts are not steel, yet steel is bent.

After all, however, Mr. Scott may well say to
the Colonel, (and, indeed, to much better wags
than the Colonel,) ῥᾷον μωμεῖσθαι ἢ μιμεῖσθαι.

7 A foreign artist much patronized by the
Prince Regent.

Nor needest thou mourn the transient
   date
To thy best works assigned by fate.
While *some chef-d'œuvres* live to weary
   one,
Thine boast a short life and a merry one;
Their hour of glory past and gone
With " Molly put the kettle on ! " [1]

But, bless my soul ! I 've scarce a leaf
Of paper left — so must be brief.

This festive Fête, in fact, will be
The former Fête's *fac-simile ;* [2]
The same long Masquerade of Rooms,
All trickt up in such odd costumes,
(These, Porter,[3] are thy glorious works !)
You 'd swear Egyptians, Moors and
   Turks,

1 The name of a popular country-dance.

2 " Carleton House will exhibit a complete
fac-simile, in respect to interior ornament, to
what it did at the last Fête. The same splendid
draperies," etc. — *Morning Post.*

3 Mr. Walsh Porter, to whose taste was left
the furnishing of the rooms of Carleton House.

Bearing Good-Taste some deadly malice,
Had clubbed to raise a Pic-Nic Palace;
And each to make the olio pleasant
Had sent a State-Room as a present.
The same *fauteuils* and girondoles —
The same gold Asses,[4] pretty souls !
That in this rich and classic dome
Appear so perfectly at home.
The same bright river 'mong the dishes,
But *not* — ah ! not the same dear fishes —
Late hours and claret killed the old
   ones —
So 'stead of silver and of gold ones,
(It being rather hard to raise
Fish of that *specie* now-a-days)
Some sprats have been by Yarmouth's
   wish,
Promoted into *Silver* Fish,
And Gudgeons (so Vansittart told
The Regent) are as good as *Gold !*

So, prithee, come — our Fête will be
But half a Fête if wanting thee.

4 The salt-cellars on the Prince's *own* table
were in the form of an Ass with panniers.

APPENDIX.

LETTER IV.   PAGE 560.

AMONG the papers, enclosed in Dr.
Duigenan's Letter, was found an Heroic
Epistle in Latin verse, from Pope Joan
to her Lover, of which, as it is rather a
curious document, I shall venture to give
some account. This female Pontiff was
a native of England, (or, according to
others, of Germany,) who at an early
age disguised herself in male attire and
followed her lover, a young ecclesiastic,
to Athens where she studied with such
effect that upon her arrival at Rome she
was thought worthy of being raised to
the Pontificate. This Epistle is addressed
to her Lover (whom she had elevated to
the dignity of Cardinal), soon after the

fatal *accouchement*, by which her Falli-
bility was betrayed.

She begins by reminding him tenderly
of the time, when they were together at
Athens — when, as she says,

        —— " by Ilissus' stream
" We whispering walkt along, and
    learned to speak
" The tenderest feelings in the purest
    Greek ;—
" Ah ! then how little did we think or
    hope,
" Dearest of men, that I should e'er be
    Pope ! [1]

1 Spanheim attributes the unanimity with
which Joan was elected to that innate and irre-

" That I, the humble Joan, whose house-
wife art
" Seemed just enough to keep thy house
and heart,
" (And those, alas! at sixes and at
sevens,)
" Should soon keep all the keys of all
the heavens!"

Still less (she continues to say) could
they have foreseen, that such a catastrophe as had happened in Council would
befall them — that she

" Should thus surprise the Conclave's
grave decorum,
" And let a *little Pope* pop out before
'em —
" Pope *Innocent!* alas, the only one
" That name could e'er be justly fixt
upon."

She then very pathetically laments the
downfall of her greatness, and enumerates the various treasures to which she
is doomed to bid farewell forever : —

" But oh, more dear, more precious ten
times over —
" Farewell my Lord, my Cardinal, my
Lover!
" I made *thee* Cardinal — thou madest
me — ah!
" Thou madest the Papa of the world
Mamma!"

I have not time at present to translate
any more of this Epistle; but I presume
the argument which the Right Hon.
Doctor and his friends mean to deduce
from it, is (in their usual convincing
strain) that Romanists must be unworthy
of Emancipation *now*, because they had
a Petticoat Pope in the Ninth Century.
Nothing can be more logically clear, and
I find that Horace had exactly the same
views upon the subject.

Romanus (*eheu posteri negabitis!*)
emancipatus FŒMINÆ
fert vallum!

sistible charm by which her sex, though latent,
operated upon the instinct of the Cardinals —
"*non vi aliquâ, sed concorditer, omnium in se
converso desiderio, quæ sunt blandientis sexus
artes, latentes in hâc quanquam!*"

LETTER VII. PAGE 564.

THE Manuscript, found enclosed in
the Bookseller's Letter, turns out to be
a Melo-Drama, in two Acts, entitled
" The Book," [1] of which the Theatres,
of course, had had the refusal, before
it was presented to Messrs. Lackington
and Co. This rejected Drama however
possesses considerable merit and I shall
take the liberty of laying a sketch of it
before my Readers.

The first Act opens in a very awful
manner — *Time*, three o'clock in the
morning — *Scene*, the Bourbon Chamber [2] in Carleton House — Enter the
Prince Regent *solus* — After a few broken
sentences, he thus exclaims : —

Away — Away —
Thou haunt'st my fancy so, thou devilish
Book,
I meet thee — trace thee, wheresoe'er I
look.
I see thy damned *ink* in Eldon's
brows —
I see thy *foolscap* on my Hertford's
Spouse —
Vansittart's head recalls thy *leathern*
case,
And all thy *blank leaves* stare from
R — d — r's face!
While, turning here (*laying his hand on
his heart,*)
I find, ah wretched elf,
Thy *List* of dire *Errata* in myself.
(*Walks the stage in considerable
agitation.*)

1 There was, in like manner, a mysterious
Book, in the 16th Century, which employed all
the anxious curiosity of the Learned of that time.
Every one spoke of it; many wrote against it;
though it does not appear that anybody had ever
seen it; and Grotius is of opinion that no such
Book ever existed. It was entitled, " *Liber de
tribus impostoribus.*" (See Morhof. Cap. " *de
Libris damnatis.*") — Our more modern mystery
of " the Book" resembles this in many particulars; and, if the number of Lawyers employed
in drawing it up be stated correctly, a slight
alteration of the title into " *à tribus impostoribus*" would produce a coincidence altogether
very remarkable.

2 The same Chamber, doubtless, that was
prepared for the reception of the Bourbons at
the first Grand Fête, and which was ornamented
(all " for the Deliverance of Europe") with
fleurs-de-lys.

Oh Roman Punch! oh potent Curaçoa!
Oh Mareschino! Mareschino oh!
Delicious drams! why have you not the
　　art
To kill this gnawing *Book-worm* in my
　　heart?

He is here interrupted in his Soliloquy
by perceiving on the ground some scribbled fragments of paper, which he instantly collects, and "by the light of
two magnificent candelabras" discovers
the following unconnected words, "*Wife
neglected*" — "*the Book*" — "*Wrong
Measures*" — "*the Queen*" — "*Mr.
Lambert*" — "*the* Regent.*"

Ha! treason in my house! — Curst
　　words, that wither
My princely soul, (*shaking the papers
　　violently*) what Demon brought you
　　hither?
"My Wife;" — "the Book" too! —
　　stay — a nearer look —
(*holding the fragments closer to the
　　Candelabras*)
Alas! too plain, B, double O, K,
　　Book —
Death and destruction!

He here rings all the bells, and a whole
legion of valets enter. A scene of cursing and swearing (very much in the German style) ensues, in the course of
which messengers are despatched, in
different directions, for the Lord Chancellor, the Duke of Cumberland, etc.
The intermediate time is filled up by
another Soliloquy, at the conclusion of
which the aforesaid Personages rush on
alarmed; the Duke with his stays only
half-laced, and the Chancellor with his
wig thrown hastily over an old red
night-cap, "to maintain the becoming
splendor of his office." [1] The Regent
produces the appalling fragments, upon
which the Chancellor breaks out into
exclamations of loyalty and tenderness,
and relates the following portentous
dream:

1 "To enable the individual who holds the
office of Chancellor to maintain it in becoming
splendor." (*A loud laugh.*) — Lord CASTLE-
REAGH's *Speech upon the Vice-Chancellor's Bill.*

'T is scarcely two hours since
I had a fearful dream of thee, my
　　Prince! —
Methought I heard thee midst a courtly
　　crowd
Say from thy throne of gold, in mandate
　　loud,
"Worship my whiskers!" — (*weeps*)
　　not a knee was there
But bent and worshipt the Illustrious
　　Pair,
Which curled in conscious majesty!
　　(*pulls out his handkerchief*) — while
　　cries
Of "Whiskers, whiskers!" shook the
　　echoing skies. —
Just in that glorious hour, methought,
　　there came,
With looks of injured pride, a Princely
　　Dame
And a young maiden, clinging by her
　　side,
As if she feared some tyrant would di-
　　vide
Two hearts that nature and affection
　　tied!
The Matron came — within her *right*
　　hand glowed
A radiant torch; while from her *left* a load
Of Papers hung — (*wipes his eyes*) col-
　　lected in her veil —
The venal evidence, the slanderous tale,
The wounding hint, the current lies that
　　pass
From *Post* to *Courier*, formed the mot-
　　ley mass;
Which with disdain before the Throne
　　she throws,
And lights the Pile beneath thy princely
　　nose.
　　　　　　　　　　(*Weeps.*)
Heavens, how it blazed! — I 'd ask no
　　livelier fire,
(*With animation*) To roast a Papist by,
　　my gracious Sire! —
But ah! the Evidence — (*weeps again*)
　　I mourned to see —
Cast as it burned, a deadly light on
　　thee:
And Tales and Hints their random
　　sparkles flung,
And hissed and crackled, like an old
　　maid's tongue;

While *Post* and *Courier*, faithful to their
    fame,
Made up in stink for what they lackt in
    flame.
When, lo, ye Gods! the fire ascending
    brisker,
Now singes *one*, now lights the *other*
    whisker.
Ah! where was then the Sylphid that
    unfurls
Her fairy standard in defence of curls ?
Throne, Whiskers, Wig soon vanisht into
    smoke,
The watchman cried "Past One," and
    — I awoke.

Here his Lordship weeps more profusely
than ever, and the Regent (who has
been very much agitated during the recital of the Dream) by a movement as
characteristic as that of Charles XII.
when he was shot, claps his hands to his
whiskers to feel if all be really safe. A
Privy Council is held — all the Servants,
etc. are examined, and it appears that a
Tailor, who had come to measure the
Regent for a Dress (which takes three
whole pages of the best superfine *clin-
quant* in describing) was the only person
who had been in the Bourbon Chamber
during the day. It is, accordingly, determined to seize the Tailor, and the
Council breaks up with a unanimous
resolution to be vigorous.

The commencement of the Second Act
turns chiefly upon the Trial and Impris-
onment of two Brothers [1] — but as this
forms the *under* plot of the Drama, I shall
content myself with extracting from it
the following speech, which is addressed
to the two Brothers, as they "*exeunt*
severally*" to Prison: —

Go to your prisons — tho' the air of
    Spring
No mountain coolness to your cheeks
    shall bring;
Tho' Summer flowers shall pass unseen
    away,
And all your portion of the glorious day

1 Mr. Leigh Hunt and his brother.

May be some solitary beam that falls
At morn or eve upon your dreary
    walls —
Some beam that enters, trembling as if
    awed,
To tell how gay the young world laughs
    abroad !
Yet go — for thoughts as blessed as the
    air
Of Spring or Summer flowers await you
    there;
Thoughts such as He who feasts his
    courtly crew
In rich conservatories *never* knew;
Pure self-esteem — the smiles that light
    within —
The Zeal, whose circling charities begin
With the few loved-ones Heaven has
    placed it near,
And spread till all Mankind are in its
    sphere;
The Pride that suffers without vaunt or
    plea,
And the fresh Spirit that can warble
    free
Thro' prison-bars its hymn to Liberty !

The Scene next changes to a Tailor's
Workshop, and a fancifully-arranged
group of these Artists is discovered upon
the Shop-board — Their task evidently
of a *royal* nature, from the profusion
of gold-lace, frogs, etc. that lie about —
They all rise and come forward, while
one of them sings the following Stanzas
to the tune of "Derry Down."

My brave brother Tailors, come,
    straighten your knees,
For a moment, like gentlemen, stand up
    at ease,
While I sing of our Prince (and a fig for
    his railers),
The Shop-board's delight ! the Mæcenas
    of Tailors !
        Derry down, down, down derry
        down.

Some monarchs take roundabout ways
    into note,
While *His* short cut to fame is — the cut
    of his coat;

Philip's Son thought the World was too
  small for his Soul,
But our Regent's finds room in a laced
  button-hole.

> Derry down, etc.

Look thro' all Europe's Kings — those,
  at least, who go loose —
Not a King of them all 's such a friend
  to the Goose.
So, God keep him increasing in size and
  renown,
Still the fattest and best fitted Prince
  about town!

> Derry down, etc.

During the "Derry down" of this last
verse, a messenger from the Secretary of
State's Office rushes on, and the singer
(who, luckily for the effect of the scene,
is the very Tailor suspected of the mysterious fragments) is interrupted in the
midst of his laudatory exertions and hurried away, to the no small surprise and
consternation of his comrades. The
Plot now hastens rapidly in its development — the management of the Tailor's
examination is highly skilful, and the
alarm which he is made to betray is
natural without being ludicrous. The

explanation too which he finally gives
is not more simple than satisfactory. It
appears that the said fragments formed
part of a self-exculpatory note, which
he had intended to send to Colonel
M'Mahon upon subjects purely professional, and the corresponding bits
(which still lie luckily in his pocket)
being produced and skilfully laid beside
the others, the following *billet-doux* is
the satisfactory result of their juxta-
position.

Honored Colonel — my Wife, who 's the
  Queen of all slatterns,
Neglected to put up the Book of new
  Patterns.
She sent the wrong Measures too —
  shamefully wrong —
They 're the same used for poor Mr.
  Lambert, when young;
But, bless you! they would n't go half
  round the Regent —
So, hope you 'll excuse yours till death,
  most obedient.

This fully explains the whole mystery —
the Regent resumes his wonted smiles,
and the Drama terminates as usual to the
satisfaction of all parties.

SATIRICAL AND HUMOROUS POEMS.

ΣΧΟΛΛΑΖΟΝΤΟΣ ΛΗΝΟΛΙΑ.

THE INSURRECTION OF THE PAPERS.

A DREAM.

"It would be impossible for his Royal Highness to disengage his person from the accumulating pile of papers that encompassed it." — Lord CASTLEREAGH's *Speech upon Colonel M'Mahon's Appointment, April* 14, 1812.

LAST night I tost and turned in bed,
But could not sleep — at length I said,
"I 'll think of Viscount Castlereagh,
"And of his speeches — that 's the way."
And so it was, for instantly
I slept as sound as sound could be.
And then I dreamt — so dread a dream!
Fuseli has no such theme;
Lewis never wrote or borrowed
Any horror half so horrid!

Methought the Prince in whiskered state
Before me at his breakfast sate;
On one side lay unread Petitions,
On t'other, Hints from five Physicians;
Here tradesmen's bills, — official papers,
Notes from my Lady, drams for vapors —
There plans of Saddles, tea and toast,
Death-warrants and *The Morning Post.*

When lo! the Papers, one and all,
As if at some magician's call,
Began to flutter of themselves
From desk and table, floor and shelves,
And, cutting each some different capers,
Advanced, oh jacobinic papers!
As tho' they said, "Our sole design is
"To suffocate his Royal Highness!"
The Leader of this vile sedition

Was a huge Catholic Petition,
With grievances so full and heavy,
It threatened worst of all the bevy.
Then Common-Hall Addresses came
In swaggering sheets and took their aim
Right at the Regent's well-drest head,
As if *determined* to be read.
Next Tradesmen's Bills began to fly,
And Tradesmen's Bills, we know, mount high;
Nay even Death-warrants thought they 'd best
Be lively too and join the rest.

But, oh the basest of defections!
His Letter about "predilections" —
His own dear Letter, void of grace,
Now flew up in its parent's face!
Shockt with this breach of filial duty,
He just could murmur "*et* Tu *Brute?*"
Then sunk, subdued upon the floor
At Fox's bust, to rise no more!

I waked — and prayed, with lifted hand,
"Oh! never may this Dream prove true;
"Tho' paper overwhelms the land,
"Let it not crush the Sovereign too!"

PARODY

OF A CELEBRATED LETTER.[1]

AT length, dearest Freddy, the moment is nigh,
When, with Perceval's leave, I may throw my chains by;

[1] Letter from his Royal Highness the Prince Regent to the Duke of York, Feb. 13, 1812.

And as time now is precious the first
    thing I do
Is to sit down and write a wise letter to
    you.

     *   *   *   *
     *   *   *   *
     *   *   *   *
     *   *   *   *
     *   *   *   *

I meant before now to have sent you this
    Letter,
But Yarmouth and I thought perhaps
    't would be better
To wait till the Irish affairs were de-
    cided —
(That is, till both Houses had prosed and
    divided,
With all due appearance of thought and
    digestion) —
For, tho' Hertford House had long
    settled the question,
I thought it but decent, between me and
    you,
That the two *other* Houses should settle it
    too.

    I need not remind you how cursedly
    bad
Our affairs were all looking, when Father
    went mad;[1]
A strait waistcoat on him and restric-
    tions on me,
A more *limited* Monarchy could not well
    be.
I was called upon then, in that moment
    of puzzle,
To choose my own Minister — just as
    they muzzle
A playful young bear, and then mock his
    disaster
By bidding him choose out his own dan-
    cing-master.

    I thought the best way, as a dutiful
    son,
Was to do as Old Royalty's self would
    have done.[2]

So I sent word to say, I would keep the
    whole batch in,
The same chest of tools, without cleans-
    ing or patching;
For tools of this kind, like Martinus's
    sconce,[3]
Would loose all their beauty if purified
    once;
And think — only think — if our Father
    should find,
Upon graciously coming again to his
    mind,[4]
That improvement had spoiled any favor-
    ite adviser —
That Rose was grown honest, or West-
    moreland wiser —
That R — d — r was, ev'n by one twin-
    kle, the brighter —
Or Liverpool's speeches but half a
    pound lighter —
What a shock to his old royal heart it
    would be !
No ! — far were such dreams of improve-
    ment from me :
And it pleased me to find, at the House,
    where, you know,[5]
There 's such good mutton cutlets, and
    strong curaçoa,[6]
That the Marchioness called me a du-
    teous old boy,
And my Yarmouth's red whiskers grew
    redder for joy.

    You know, my dear Freddy, how oft,
    if I *would*,
By the law of last Sessions I *might* have
    done good.
I *might* have withheld these political
    noodles
From knocking their heads against hot
    Yankee Doodles;
I *might* have told Ireland I pitied her lot,
Might have soothed her with hope — but
    you know I did not.

---

1 " I think it hardly necessary to call your
recollection to the recent circumstances under
which I assumed the authority delegated to me
by Parliament." — *Prince's Letter.*

2 " My sense of duty to our Royal father
solely decided that choice." — *Ibid.*

3 The antique shield of Martinus Scriblerus,
which, upon scouring, turned out to be only an
old sconce.

4 " I waived any personal gratification, in
order that his Majesty might resume, on his
restoration to health, every power and prerogative," etc. — *Prince's Letter.*

5 " And I have the satisfaction of knowing
that such was the opinion of persons for whose
judgment," etc. — *Ibid.*

6 The letter-writer's favorite luncheon.

And my wish is, in truth, that the best
    of old fellows
Should not, on recovering, have cause
    to be jealous,
But find that while he has been laid on
    the shelf
We 've been all of us nearly as mad as
    himself.
You smile at my hopes — but the Doctors
    and I
Are the last that can think the King *ever*
    will die.[1]

A new era 's arrived [2] — tho' you 'd
    hardly believe it —
And all things of course must be new to
    receive it.
New villas, new fêtes (which even Waith
    man attends)
New saddles, new helmets, and — why
    not *new friends ?*

  .   .   .   .   .   .
  .   .   .   .   .   .

I repeat it, "New Friends" — for I
    cannot describe
The delight I am in with this Perceval
    tribe.
Such capering! — Such vaporing! —
    Such rigor ! — Such vigor !
North, South, East, and West, they have
    cut such a figure,
That soon they will bring the whole
    world round our ears,
And leave us no friends — but Old Nick
    and Algiers.

When I think of the glory they 've
    beamed on my chains,
'T is enough quite to turn my illustrious
    brains.
It is true we are bankrupts in commerce
    and riches,
But think how we find our Allies in new
    breeches !
We 've lost the warm hearts of the Irish,
    't is granted,
But then we 've got Java, an island much
    wanted,

To put the last lingering few who re-
    main,
Of the Walcheren warriors, out of their
    pain.
Then how Wellington fights ! and how
    squabbles his brother !
For Papists the one and *with* Papists the
    other;
One crushing Napoleon by taking a
    City,
While t' other lays waste a whole Catholic
    Committee.
Oh deeds of renown ! shall I boggle
    or flinch,
With such prospects before me ? by Jove,
    not an inch.
No — let *England's* affairs go to rack, if
    they will,
We 'll look after the affairs of the *Con-
    tinent* still;
And with nothing at home but starvation
    and riot,
Find Lisbon in bread and keep Sicily
    quiet.

I am proud to declare I have no pred-
    ilections,[3]
My heart is a sieve where some scattered
    affections
Are just danced about for a moment or
    two,
And the *finer* they are, the more sure to
    run thro' :
Neither feel I resentments, nor wish there
    should come ill
To mortal — except (now I think on 't)
    Beau Brummel,
Who threatened last year, in a superfine
    passion,
To cut *me* and bring the old King into
    fashion.
This is all I can lay to my conscience at
    present;
When such is my temper, so neutral, so
    pleasant,
So royally free from all troublesome
    feelings,
So little encumbered by faith in my deal-
    ings
(And that I 'm consistent the world will
    allow,

---

1 " I certainly am the last person in the kingdom to whom it can be permitted to despair of
our royal father's recovery." — *Prince's Letter.*

2 " A new era is now arrived, and I cannot
but reflect with satisfaction," etc. — *Ibid.*

3 " I have no predilections to indulge, — no
resentments to gratify." — *Prince's Letter.*

What I was at Newmarket the same I
    am now).
When such are my merits (you know I
    hate cracking),
I hope, like the Vender of Best Patent
    Blacking,
" To meet with the generous and kind
    approbation
" Of a candid, enlightened, and liberal
    nation."

    By the by, ere I close this magnificent
    Letter,
(No man, except Pole, could have writ
    you a better,)
'T would please me if those, whom I 've
    humbugged so long [1]
With the notion (good men!) that I
    knew right from wrong,
Would a few of them join me — mind,
    only a few —
To let *too* much light in on me never
    would do;
But even Grey's brightness shan't make
    me afraid,
While I 've Camden and Eldon to fly to
    for shade;
Nor will Holland's clear intellect do us
    much harm,
While there 's Westmoreland near him to
    weaken the charm.
As for Moira's high spirit, if aught can
    subdue it,
Sure joining with Hertford and Yarmouth
    will do it!
Between R — d — r and Wharton let
    Sheridan sit,
And the fogs will soon quench even
    Sheridan's wit:
And against all the pure public feeling
    that glows
Even in Whitbread himself we 've a
    Host in George Rose!
So in short if they wish to have Places,
    they may,
And I 'll thank you to tell all these
    matters to Grey.[2]

Who, I doubt not, will write (as there 's
    no time to lose)
By the twopenny post to tell Grenville
    the news;
And now, dearest Fred (tho' I 've no
    predilection),
Believe me yours always with truest af-
    fection.

    P.S. A copy of this is to Perceval
    going [3] —
Good Lord, how St. Stephen's will ring
    with his crowing!

ANACREONTIC

TO A PLUMASSIER.

FINE and feathery artisan,
Best of Plumists (if you can
With your art so far presume)
Make for me a Prince's Plume —
Feathers soft and feathers rare,
Such as suits a Prince to wear.

First thou downiest of men,
Seek me out a fine Pea-hen;
Such a Hen, so tall and grand,
As by Juno's side might stand,
If there were no cocks at hand.
Seek her feathers, soft as down,
Fit to shine on Prince's crown;
If thou canst not find them, stupid!
Ask the way of Prior's Cupid.[4]

Ranging these in order due,
Pluck me next an old Cuckoo;
Emblem of the happy fates
Of easy, kind, cornuted mates.
Pluck him well — be sure you do —
Who would n't be an old Cuckoo,
Thus to have his plumage blest,
Beaming on a Royal crest?

Bravo, Plumist! — now what bird
Shall we find for Plume the third?
You must get a learned Owl,
Bleakest of black-letter fowl —

---

1 " I cannot conclude without expressing the
gratification I should feel if some of those persons with whom the early habits of my public
life were formed would strengthen my hands,
and constitute a part of my government." —
Prince's Letter.

2 " You are authorized to communicate these
sentiments to Lord Grey, who, I have no doubt,
will make them known to Lord Grenville." —
Prince's Letter.

3 " I shall send a copy of this letter immediately to Mr. Perceval." — *Prince's Letter.*

4 See Prior's poem, entitled " The Dove."

Bigot bird that hates the light,[1]
Foe to all that 's fair and bright.
Seize his quills, (so formed to pen
Books [2] that shun the search of men;
Books that, far from every eye,
In "sweltered venom sleeping" lie,)
Stick them in between the two,
Proud Pea-hen and Old Cuckoo.
Now you have the triple feather,
Bind the kindred stems together
With a silken tie whose hue
Once was brilliant Buff and Blue;
Sullied now — alas, how much!
Only fit for Yarmouth's touch.

There — enough — thy task is done;
Present, worthy George's Son;
Now, beneath, in letters neat,
Write "I SERVE," and all 's complete.

EXTRACTS

FROM THE DIARY OF A POLITICIAN.

Wednesday.

THRO' Manchester Square took a canter
just now —
Met the *old yellow chariot* [3] and made a
low bow.
This I did, of course, thinking 't was
loyal and civil,
But got such a look — oh! 't was black
as the devil!
How unlucky! — *incog.* he was travelling
about,
And I like a noodle, must go find him
out.

Mem. — when next by the old yellow
chariot I ride,
To remember there *is* nothing princely
inside.

Thursday.

At Levee to-day made another sad blunder —
What *can* be come over me lately, I
wonder?
The Prince was as cheerful as if all his
life
He had never been troubled with Friends
or a Wife —

1 Perceval.

2 In allusion to "the Book" which created
such a sensation at that period.

3 The *incog.* vehicle of the Prince.

"Fine weather," says he — to which I,
who *must* prate,
Answered, "Yes, Sir, but *changeable*
rather, of late."
He took it, I fear, for he lookt somewhat
gruff,
And handled his new pair of whiskers so
rough,
That before all the courtiers I feared
they 'd come off,
And then, Lord, how Geramb[4] would
triumphantly scoff!

Mem. — to buy for son Dicky some unguent or lotion
To nourish his whiskers — sure road to
promotion! [5]

Saturday.

Last night a Concert — vastly gay —
Given by Lady Castlereagh.
My Lord loves music, and we know
Has "two strings always to his bow." [6]
In choosing songs, the Regent named
"*Had I a heart for falsehood framed.*"
While gentle Hertford begged and prayed
For "*Young I am and sore afraid.*"

EPIGRAM.

WHAT news to-day? — "Oh! worse and
worse —
"Mac [7] is the Prince's Privy Purse!" —
The Prince's *Purse!* no, no, you fool,
You mean the Prince's *Ridicule.*

KING CRACK [8] AND HIS IDOLS.

WRITTEN AFTER THE LATE NEGOTIA-
TION FOR A NEW MINISTRY.

KING CRACK was the best of all possible
Kings,
(At least, so his Courtiers would swear
to you gladly,)

4 Baron Geramb, the rival of his R. H. in
whiskers.

5 England is not the only country where merit
of this kind is noticed and rewarded. "I remember," says Tavernier, "to have seen one of
the King of Persia's porters, whose mustaches
were so long that he could tie them behind his
neck, for which reason he had a double pension."

6 A rhetorical figure used by Lord Castlereagh, in one of his speeches.

7 Colonel M'Mahon.

8 One of these antediluvian Princes, with

But Crack now and then would do heterodox things,
And at last took to worshipping *Images*
sadly.

Some broken-down Idols, that long had
been placed
In his father's old *Cabinet*, pleased
him so much,
That he knelt down and worshipt, tho'
— such was his taste ! —
They were monstrous to look at and
rotten to touch.

And these were the beautiful Gods of
King Crack ! —
But his People disdaining to worship
such things
Cried aloud, one and all, " Come, your
Godships must pack —
" You 'll not do for *us*, tho' you *may*
do for *Kings*."

Then trampling these images under their
feet,
They sent Crack a petition, beginning
" Great Cæsar !
" We 're willing to worship ; but only
entreat
"That you 'll find us some *decenter*
godheads than these are."

" I 'll try," says King Crack — so they
furnisht him models
Of better shaped Gods but he sent
them all back ;
Some were chiselled too fine, some had
heads stead of noddles,
In short they were all *much* too god-
like for Crack.

So he took to his darling old Idols again,
And just mending their legs and new
bronzing their faces,
In open defiance of Gods and of man,
Set the monsters up grinning once
more in their places.

whom Manetho and Whiston seem so intimately
acquainted. If we had the Memoirs of Thoth,
from which Manetho compiled his History, we
should find, I dare say, that Crack was only a
Regent, and that he, perhaps, succeeded Typhon,
who (as Whiston says) was the last King of the
Antediluvian Dynasty.

WHAT 'S MY THOUGHT LIKE?

Quest. WHY is a Pump like Viscount
Castlereagh?
Answ. Because it is a slender thing o₁
wood,
That up and down its awkward arm
⁻ doth sway,
And coolly spout and spout and spout
away,
In one weak, washy, everlasting flood !

EPIGRAM.

DIALOGUE BETWEEN A CATHOLIC DELE-GATE AND HIS ROYAL HIGHNESS THE DUKE OF CUMBERLAND.

SAID his Highness to Ned,[1] with that
grim face of his,
" Why refuse us the *Veto*, dear Catholic Neddy? "
" Because, Sir," said Ned, looking full
in his phiz,
" You 're *forbidding* enough, in all
conscience, already ! "

WREATHS FOR THE MINISTERS.

AN ANACREONTIC.

HITHER, Flora, Queen of Flowers !
Haste thee from old Brompton's bowers—
Or, (if sweeter that abode)
From the King's well-odored Road,
Where each little nursery bud
Breathes the dust and quaffs the mud.
Hither come and gayly twine
Brightest herbs and flowers of thine
Into wreaths for those who rule us,
Those who rule and (some say) fool us —
Flora, sure, will love to please
England's Household Deities ! [2]

First you must then, willy-nilly,
Fetch me many an orange lily —
Orange of the darkest dye
Irish Gifford can supply ; —

1 Edward Byrne, the head of the Delegates
of the Irish Catholics.

2 The ancients, in like manner, crowned their
Lares, or Household Gods. See Juvenal, Sat.
9. v. 138 — Plutarch, too, tells us that Household Gods were then, as they are now, " much
given to War and penal Statutes." — ἐρινννώδεις
καὶ ποινίμους δαίμονας.

Choose me out the longest sprig,
And stick it in old Eldon's wig.

Find me next a Poppy posy,
Type of his harangues so dozy,
Garland gaudy, dull and cool,
To crown the head of Liverpool.
'T will console his brilliant brows
For that loss of laurel boughs,
Which they suffered (what a pity!)
On the road to Paris City.

Next, our Castlereagh to crown,
Bring me from the County Down,
Withered Shamrocks which have been
Gilded o'er to hide the green —
(Such as Headfort brought away
From Pall-Mall last Patrick's Day)[1] —
Stitch the garland thro' and thro'
With shabby threads *of every hue;* —
And as, Goddess! — *entre nous* —
His Lordship loves (tho' best of men)·
A little *torture* now and then,
Crimp the leaves, thou first of Syrens,
Crimp them with thy curling-irons.

That's enough — away, away —
Had I leisure, I could say
How the *oldest rose* that grows
Must be pluckt to deck Old Rose —
How the Doctor's [2] brow should smile
Crowned with wreaths of camomile.
But time presses — to thy taste
I leave the rest, so, prithee, haste!

EPIGRAM.

DIALOGUE BETWEEN A DOWAGER AND HER MAID ON THE NIGHT OF LORD YARMOUTH'S FÊTE.

"I WANT the Court Guide," said my
    lady, "to look
"If the House, Seymour Place, be at
    30. or 20." —
"We 've lost the *Court Guide*, Ma'am,
    but here's *the Red Book*,
"Where you 'll find, I dare say, Sey-
    mour *Places* in plenty!"

1 Certain tinsel imitations of the Shamrock which are distributed by the Servants of Carleton House every Patrick's Day.

2 The *sobriquet* given to Lord Sidmouth.

HORACE, ODE XI. LIB. II.

FREELY TRANSLATED BY THE PRINCE REGENT.[3]

[4] COME, Yarmouth, my boy, never
        trouble your brains,
    About what your old crony,
    The Emperor Boney,
    Is doing or brewing on Muscovy's
        plains;

[5] Nor tremble, my lad, at the state of
        our granaries:
    Should there come famine,
    Still plenty to cram in
    You always shall have, my dear Lord
        of the Stannaries.

Brisk let us revel, while revel we may;
[6] For the gay bloom of fifty soon passes
        away,
    And then people get fat,
    And infirm, and — all that,
[7] And a wig (I confess it) so clumsily sits,
    That it frightens the little Loves out
        of their wits;

[8] Thy whiskers, too, Yarmouth! — alas,
        even they,
    Tho' so rosy they burn,
    Too quickly must turn
    (What a heart-breaking change for
        thy whiskers!) to Grey.

[9] Then why, my Lord Warden, oh! why
        should you fidget
    Your mind about matters you don't
        understand?

3 This and the following are extracted from a Work, which may, some time or other, meet the eye of the Public — entitled "Odes of Horace, done into English by several Persons of Fashion."

4   *quid bellicosus Cantaber, et Scythes,
      Hirpine Quincti, cogitet, Hadria
          divisus objecto, remittas
              quærere.*

5   *nec trepides in usum
      poscentis ævi pauca.*

6   *fugit retro
      levis juventas et decor.*

7   *pellente lascivos amores
              Canitie.*

8   *neque uno Luna* rubens *nitet*
      Vultu.

9   *quid æternis minorem
          consiliis animum fatigas?*

Or why should you write yourself down
    for an idiot,
Because "*you*," forsooth, "*have the
    pen in your hand !*"

Think, think how much better
Than scribbling a letter,
  (Which both you and I
  Should avoid by the by,)
[1] How much pleasanter 't is to sit under
    the bust
Of old Charley,[2] my friend here, and
    drink like a new one;
While Charley looks sulky and frowns
    at me, just
  As the Ghost in the Pantomime
    frowns at Don Juan.
To Crown us, Lord Warden,
In Cumberland's garden
Grows plenty of *monk's hood* in ven-
    omous sprigs:
  While Otto of Roses
  Refreshing all noses
Shall sweetly exhale from our whiskers
    and wigs.

[4] What youth of the Household will cool
    our Noyau
  In that streamlet delicious,
  That down midst the dishes,
  All full of gold fishes,
  Romantic doth flow? —
[5] Or who will repair
  Unto Manchester Square,
And see if the gentle *Marchesa* be
    there?

Go — bid her haste hither,
[6] And let her bring with her

---

1 *cur non sub alta vel platano, vel hac
  pinu jacentes sic temere.*

2 Charles Fox.

3   *rosâ
  canos odorati capillos,
    dum licet, Assyriaque nardo
  potamus uncti.*

4   *quis puer ocius
  restinguet ardentis Falerni
    pocula prætereunte lympha ?*

5 *quis . . . . eliciet domo
  Lyden ?*

6 *eburna, dic age, cum lyra* (*qu.* liar-a)
  maturet.

The newest No-Popery Sermon that 's
    going —
[7] Oh! let her come, with her dark
    tresses flowing,
All gentle and juvenile, curly and gay,
In the manner of — Ackermann's
    Dresses for May!

HORACE, ODE XXII. LIB. I.

FREELY TRANSLATED BY LORD ELDON.

[8] THE man who keeps a conscience pure,
  (If not his own, at least his Prince's,)
Thro' toil and danger walks secure,
  Looks big and black and never
    winces.

[9] No want has he of sword or dagger,
  Cockt hat or ringlets of Geramb;
Tho' Peers may laugh and Papists
    swagger,
  He does n't care one single damn.

[10] Whether midst Irish chairmen going,
  Or thro' St. Giles's alleys dim,
Mid drunken Sheelahs, blasting, blow-
    ing,
  No matter, 't is all one to him.

[11] For instance, I, one evening late,
  Upon a gay vacation sally,
Singing the praise of Church and State,
  Got (God knows how) to Cran-
    bourne Alley.

---

7   *incomtam Lacænæ
  more comam religata nodo.*

8   *integer vitæ scelerisque purus.*

9   *non eget Mauri jaculis, neque arcu,
  nec venantis gravida sagittis,
    Fusce, pharetra.*

10 *sive per Syrtes iter æstuosas,
  sive facturus per inhospitalem
  Caucasum, vel quæ loca fabulosus
    lambit Hydaspes*

The Noble Translator had, at first, laid the
scene of these imagined dangers of his Man of
Conscience among the Papists of Spain, and had
translated the words "*quæ loca* fabulosus lambit
Hydaspes" thus — " The *fabling* Spaniard *licks*
the French ; " but, recollecting that it is our interest just now to be respectful to *Spanish* Catholics (though there is certainly no earthly reason
for our being even commonly civil to *Irish* ones),
he altered the passage as it stands at present.

11 *namque me silvâ lupus in Sabinâ,
  dum meam canto Lalagen, et ultra
  terminum curis vagor expeditis,
    fugit inermem.*

When lo! an Irish Papist darted
  Across my path, gaunt, grim, and
      big —
I did but frown and off he started,
  Scared at me even without my wig.

1 Yet a more fierce and raw-boned dog
     Goes not to Mass in Dublin City,
   Nor shakes his brogue o'er Allen's Bog,
     Nor spouts in Catholic Committee.

2 Oh! place me midst O'Rourkes,
       O'Tooles,
     The ragged royal-blood of Tara;
   Or place me where Dick Martin rules
     The houseless wilds of Connemara;

3 Of Church and State I 'll warble still,
     Though even Dick Martin's self
       should grumble;
   Sweet Church and State, like Jack and
       Jill,
4 So lovingly upon a hill —
     Ah! ne'er like Jack and Jill to
       tumble!

I cannot help calling the reader's attention to
the peculiar ingenuity with which these lines are
paraphrased. Not to mention the happy conversion of the Wolf into a Papist, (seeing that
Romulus was suckled by a wolf, that Rome was
founded by Romulus, and that the Pope has always reigned at Rome,) there is something particularly neat in supposing "*ultra ter*mi*num*" to
mean vacation-time; and then the modest consciousness with which the Noble and Learned
Translator has avoided touching upon the words
"*curis expeditis*," (or, as it has been otherwise
read, "*causis expeditis*,") and the felicitous idea
of his being "*inermis*" when "without his wig,"
are altogether the most delectable specimens of
paraphrase in our language.

1   *quale portentum neque militaris*
       Daunias latis alit æsculetis,
     nec Jubæ tellus generat leonum
         arida nutrix.

2   *pone me pigris ubi nulla campis*
       arbor æstiva recreatur aura :
     quod latus mundi, nebulæ, malusque
         Jupiter urget.

I must here remark, that the said Dick Martin
being a very good fellow, it was not at all fair to
make a "*malus Jupiter*" of him.

3   *dulce ridentem Lalagen amabo,*
         dulce loquentem.

4 There cannot be imagined a more happy
illustration of the inseparability of Church and
State, and their (what is called) "standing and
falling together," than this ancient apologue of

THE NEW COSTUME OF THE
MINISTERS.

—— nova monstra creavit.
   OVID. "*Metamorph.*" l. i. v. 437.

HAVING sent off the troops of brave
    Major Camac,
With a swinging horse-tail at each valor-
    ous back,
And such helmets, God bless us! as never
    deckt any
Male creature before, except Signor
    Giovanni —
"Let 's see," said the Regent (like
    Titus, perplext
With the duties of empire,) "whom
    shall I dress next?"

He looks in the glass — but perfection
    is there,
Wig, whiskers, and chin-tufts all right to
    a hair; [5]
Not a single *ex*-curl on his forehead he
    traces —
For curls are like Ministers, strange as
    the case is,
The *falser* they are, the more firm in
    their places.
His coat he next views — but the coat
    who could doubt?
For his Yarmouth's own Frenchified hand
    cut it out;
Every pucker and seam were made mat-
    ters of state,
And a Grand Household Council was
    held on each plait.

Then whom shall he dress? shall he
    new-rig his brother,
Great Cumberland's Duke, with some
    kickshaw or other?

Jack and Jill. Jack, of course, represents the
State in this ingenious little Allegory.

      Jack fell down,
      And broke his *Crown*,
    And Jill came tumbling after.

5 That model of Princes, the Emperor Com-
modus, was particularly luxurious in the dressing
and ornamenting of his hair. His conscience,
however, would not suffer him to trust himself
with a barber, and he used, accordingly, to burn
off his beard — "*timore tonsoris*," says Lam-
pridius. ("*Hist. August. Scriptor*") The dissolute Ælius Verus too was equally attentive to
the decoration of his wig. (See Jul. Capitolin.)
— Indeed, this was not the *only* princely trait in

And kindly invent him more Christian-
like shapes
For his feather-bed neckcloths and pillory
capes.
Ah! no — here his ardor would meet
with delays,
For the Duke had been lately packt up
in new Stays,
So complete for the winter, he saw very
plain
'T would be devilish hard work to *un*-
pack him again.

So what 's to be done? — there 's
the Ministers, bless 'em! —
As he *made* the puppets, why should n't
he *dress* 'em?
" An excellent thought! — call the tailors — be nimble —
" Let Cum bring his spy-glass, and Hertford her thimble;
" While Yarmouth shall give us, in spite
of all quizzers,
" The last Paris cut with his true Gallic
scissors."

So saying, he calls Castlereagh, and
the rest
Of his heaven-born statesmen, to come
and be drest.
While Yarmouth, with snip-like and
brisk expedition,
Cuts up all at once a large Catholic
Petition
In long tailors' measures, (the Prince
crying " Well-done! ")
And first *puts in hand* my Lord Chan-
cellor Eldon.

. . . .

CORRESPONDENCE

BETWEEN A LADY AND GENTLEMAN,

UPON THE ADVANTAGE OF (WHAT IS CALLED)
" HAVING LAW [1] ON ONE'S SIDE."

The Gentleman's Proposal.

" *Legge aurea,*
S'ei piace, ei lice."

COME fly to these arms nor let beauties
so bloomy
To one frigid owner be tied;

the character of Verus, as he had likewise a
most hearty and dignified contempt for his Wife.
— See his insulting answer to her in Spartianus.

[1] In allusion to Lord Ellenborough.

Your prudes may revile and your old
ones look gloomy,
But, dearest, we 've *Law* on our side.

Oh! think the delight of two lovers congenial,
Whom no dull decorums divide;
Their error how sweet and their raptures
how *venial*,
When once they 've got Law on their
side.

'T is a thing that in every King's reign
has been done too:
Then why should it now be decried?
If the Father has done it why should n't
the Son too?
For so argues Law on our side.

And even should our sweet violation of
duty
By cold-blooded jurors be tried,
They can *but* bring it in " a misfortune,"
my beauty,
As long as we 've Law on our side.

The Lady's Answer.

HOLD, hold, my good Sir, go a little
more slowly;
For grant me so faithless a bride,
Such sinners as we, are a little too *lowly*,
To hope to have Law on our side.

Had you been a great Prince, to whose
star shining o'er 'em
The People should look for their guide,
Then your Highness (and welcome!)
might kick down decorum —
You 'd always have Law on your side.

Were you even an old Marquis, in mis-
chief grown hoary,
Whose heart tho' it long ago died
To the *pleasures* of vice, is alive to its
glory —
You still would have Law on your side.

But for *you*, Sir, Crim. Con. is a path
full of troubles;
By *my* advice therefore abide,
And leave the pursuit to those Princes
and Nobles
Who have *such* a *Law* on their side.

OCCASIONAL ADDRESS

FOR THE OPENING OF THE NEW THEATRE OF ST. STEPHEN,

INTENDED TO HAVE BEEN SPOKEN BY THE PROPRIETOR IN FULL COSTUME, ON THE 24TH OF NOVEMBER, 1812.

THIS day a New House for your edification
We open, most thinking and right-
    headed nation !
Excuse the materials — tho' rotten and
    bad,
They 're the best that for money just
    now could be had;
And if *echo* the charm of such houses
    should be,
You will find it shall echo my speech to
    a T.

As for actors, we've got the old Com-
    pany yet,
The same motley, odd, tragi-comical set;
And considering they all were but clerks
    t' other day,
It is truly surprising how well they can
    play.
Our Manager,[1] (he who in Ulster was
    nurst,
And sung *Erin go Bragh* for the gal-
    leries first,
But on finding *Pitt*-interest a much better
    thing,
Changed his note of a sudden to *God
    save the King*,)
Still wise as he 's blooming and fat as
    he 's clever,
Himself and his speeches as *lengthy* as
    ever,
Here offers you still the full use of his
    breath,
Your devoted and long-winded proser
    till death.

You remember last season, when things
    went perverse on,
We had to engage (as a block to rehearse
    on)
One Mr. Vansittart, a good sort of person,
Who 's also employed for this season to
    play,
In " Raising the Wind," and " the Devil
    to Pay."[2]

1 Lord Castlereagh.
2 He had recently been appointed Chancellor of the Exchequer.

We expect too — at least we 've been
    plotting and planning —
To get that great actor from Liverpool,
    Canning ;
And, as at the Circus there 's nothing
    attracts
Like a good *single combat* brought in
    'twixt the acts,
If the Manager should, with the help
    of Sir Popham,
Get up new *diversions* and Canning
    should stop 'em,
Who knows but we 'll have to announce
    in the papers,
" Grand fight — second time — with ad-
    ditional capers."

Be your taste for the ludicrous, hum-
    drum, or sad,
There is plenty of each in this House
    to be had.
Where our Manager ruleth, there weep-
    ing will be,
For a *dead hand at tragedy* always was
    he ;
And there never was dealer in dagger
    and cup,
Who so *smilingly* got all his tragedies
    up.
His powers poor Ireland will never for-
    get,
And the widows of Walcheren weep o'er
    them yet.

So much for the actors ; — for secret
    machinery,
Traps, and deceptions, and shifting of
    scenery,
Yarmouth and Cum are the best we can
    find,
To transact all that trickery business be-
    hind.
The former 's employed too to teach us
    French jigs,
Keep the whiskers in curl and look after
    the wigs.

In taking my leave now, I 've only
    to say,
A few *Seats in the House*, not as yet
    sold away,
May be had of the Manager, Pat Castle-
    reagh.

THE SALE OF THE TOOLS.

Instrumenta regni. — TACITUS.

HERE 's a choice set of Tools for you,
   Ge'mmen and Ladies,
They 'll fit you quite handy, whatever
   your trade is ;
(Except it be *Cabinet-making ;* — no
   doubt,
In that delicate service they 're rather
   worn out ;
Tho' their owner, bright youth ! if he 'd
   had his own will,
Would have bungled away with them
   joyously still.)
You see they 've been pretty well *hackt*
   — and alack !
What tool is there job after job will
   not hack?
Their edge is but dullish it must be
   confest,
And their temper, like Ellenborough's,
   none of the best ;
But you 'll find them good hard-working
   Tools, upon trying,
Were 't but for their *brass* they are well
   worth the buying;
They 're famous for making *blinds*,
   sliders, and *screens*,
And are some of them excellent *turning*
   machines.

The first Tool I 'll put up (they call
   it a *Chancellor*),
Heavy concern to both purchaser *and*
   seller.
Tho' made of pig iron yet worthy of
   note 't is,
'T is ready to *melt* at a half minute's
   notice.[1]
Who bids? Gentle buyer ! 't will turn
   as thou shapest ;
'T will make a good thumb-screw to
   torture a Papist ;
Or else a cramp-iron to stick in the wall
Of some church that old women are
   fearful will fall ;
Or better, perhaps, (for I 'm guessing
   at random,)
A heavy *drag-chain* for some Lawyer's
   old *Tandem.*

[1] An allusion to Lord Eldon's lachrymose tendencies.

Will nobody bid? It is cheap, I am sure,
   Sir —
Once, twice, — going, going, — thrice,
   gone ! — it is yours, Sir.
To pay ready money you sha'n't be
   distrest,
As a *bill* at *long date* suits the Chancellor
   best.

Come, where 's the next Tool? — Oh !
   't is here in a trice —
This implement, Ge'mmen, at first was
   a *Vice ;*
(A tenacious and close sort of tool that
   will let
Nothing out of its grasp it once happens
   to get ;)
But it since has received a new coating
   of *Tin,*
Bright enough for a Prince to behold
   himself in.
Come, what shall we say for it? briskly !
   bid on,
We 'll the sooner get rid of it — going —
   quite gone.
God be with it, such tools, if not quickly
   knockt down,
Might at last cost their owner — how
   much? why, a *Crown !*

The next Tool I 'll set up has hardly
   had handsel or
Trial as yet and is *also* a Chancellor —
Such dull things as these should be sold
   by the gross;
Yet, dull as it is, 't will be found to *shave
   close,*
And like *other* close shavers, some courage
   to gather,
This *blade* first began by a flourish on
   leather.[2]
You shall have it for nothing — then,
   marvel with me
At the terrible *tinkering* work there
   must be,
Where a Tool such as this is (I 'll leave
   you to judge it)
Is placed by ill luck at the top of *the
   Budget !*

[2] " Of the taxes proposed by Mr. Vansittart, that principally opposed in Parliament was the additional duty on leather." — *Ann. Register.*

LITTLE MAN AND LITTLE SOUL.

A BALLAD.

To the tune of "There was a little man, and he wooed a little maid."

DEDICATED TO THE RT. HON. CHARLES ABBOT.

arcades ambo
et cant-*are pares.*

1813.

THERE was a little Man and he had a
　　little Soul,
And he said, "Little Soul, let us try,
　　try, try,
　" Whether it 's within our reach
　" To make up a little Speech,
" Just between little you and little I, I, I,
　" Just between little you and little I ! "

　　Then said his little Soul,
　　Peeping from her little hole,
" I protest, little Man, you are stout,
　　stout, stout,
　　" But, if it 's not uncivil,
　　" Pray tell me what the devil,
" Must our little, little speech be about,
　　bout, bout,
" Must our little, little speech be about ? "

　　The little Man lookt big,
　　With the assistance of his wig,
And he called his little Soul to order,
　　order, order,
　Till she feared he 'd make her jog in
　To jail, like Thomas Croggan,
(As she was n't Duke or Earl) to re-
　　ward her, ward her, ward her,
　As she was n't Duke or Earl, to re-
　　ward her.

　　The little Man then spoke,
　　" Little soul, it is no joke,
" For as sure as Jacky Fuller loves a
　　sup, sup, sup,
　　" I will tell the Prince and People
　　" What I think of Church and Stee-
　　ple,
" And my little patent plan to prop them
　　up, up, up,
　" And my little patent plan to prop
　　them up."

　　Away then, cheek by jowl,
　　Little Man and little Soul
Went and spoke their little speech to
　　a tittle, tittle, tittle,
　And the world all declare
　That this priggish little pair

Never yet in all their lives lookt so little,
　　little, little,
　Never yet in all their lives lookt so
　　little !

REINFORCEMENTS FOR LORD WELLINGTON.

suosque tibi commendat Troja Penates
hos cape fatorum comites.　　VERGIL.

1813.

As recruits in these times are not easily
　　got,
And the Marshal *must* have them — pray,
　　why should we not,
As the last and, I grant it, the worst of
　　our loans to him,
Ship off the Ministry, body and bones to
　　him?
There 's not in all England, I 'd venture
　　to swear,
Any men we could half so conveniently
　　spare;
And tho' they 've been helping the
　　French for years past,
We may thus make them useful to Eng-
　　land at last.
Castlereagh in our sieges might save
　　some disgraces,
Being used to the *taking* and *keeping* of
　　places ;
And Volunteer Canning, still ready for
　　joining,
Might show off his talent for sly *under-
　　mining.*
Could the Household but spare us its
　　glory and pride,
Old Headfort at *horn-works* again might
　　be tried,
And the Chief Justice make a *bold charge*
　　at his side :
While Vansittart could victual the troops
　　upon tick,
And the Doctor look after the baggage
　　and sick.

　　Nay, I do not see why the great Regent
　　himself
Should in times such as these stay at
　　home on the shelf :
Tho' thro' narrow defiles he 's not fitted
　　to pass,
Yet who could resist, if he bore down
　　en masse ?

And tho' oft of an evening perhaps he
    might prove,
Like our Spanish confederates, "unable
    to move," [1]
Yet there 's *one* thing in war of advantage
    unbounded,
Which is, that he could not with ease be
    surrounded.

In my next I shall sing of their arms
    and equipment;
At present no more, but — good luck to
    the shipment!

HORACE, ODE I. LIB. III.

A FRAGMENT.

odi profanum vulgus et arceo :
favete linguis : carmina non prius
audita Musarum sacerdos
virginibus puerisque canto.
regum timendorum in proprios greges,
reges in ipsos imperium est-Jovis.

1813.

I HATE thee, oh, Mob, as my Lady hates
    delf;
    To Sir Francis I 'll give up thy claps
        and thy hisses,
Leave old Magna Charta to shift for it-
    self,
    And, like Godwin, write books for
        young masters and misses.
Oh! it *is* not high rank that can make
    the heart merry,
    Even monarchs themselves are not free
        from mishap:
Tho' the Lords of Westphalia must
    quake before Jerry,
    Poor Jerry himself has to quake before
        Nap.

. . . .

HORACE, ODE XXXVIII. LIB. I.

A FRAGMENT.

persicos odi, puer, adparatus ;
displicent nexæ philyra coronæ ;
mitte sectari, Rosa quo locorum
        sera moretur.

TRANSLATED BY A TREASURY CLERK, WHILE
WAITING DINNER FOR THE RIGHT HON.
GEORGE ROSE.

Boy, tell the Cook that I hate all nick-
    nackeries,
Fricassees, vol-au-vents, puffs, and gim-
    crackeries —

1 The character given to the Spanish soldier,
in Sir John Murray's memorable despatch.

Six by the Horse-Guards! — old Georgy
    is late —
But come — lay the table-cloth — zounds!
    do not wait,
Nor stop to inquire, while the dinner is
    staying,
At which of his places Old Rose is de-
    laying! [2]

. . . .

IMPROMPTU.

UPON BEING OBLIGED TO LEAVE A PLEASANT
PARTY, FROM THE WANT OF A PAIR OF
BREECHES TO DRESS FOR DINNER IN.

1810.

BETWEEN Adam and me the great dif-
    ference is,
    Tho' a paradise each has been forced
    to resign,
That he never wore breeches, till turned
    out of his,
    While for want of my breeches, I 'm
    banisht from mine.

LORD WELLINGTON AND THE MINISTERS.

1813.

So gently in peace Alcibiades smiled,
    While in battle he shone forth so ter-
    ribly grand,
That the emblem they graved on his
    seal, was a child
    With a thunderbolt placed in its in-
    nocent hand.

2 The literal closeness of the version here
cannot but be admired. The Translator has
added a long, erudite, and flowery note upon
Roses, of which I can merely give a specimen
at present. In the first place, he ransacks the
Rosarium Politicum of the Persian poet Sadi,
with the hope of finding some *Political* Roses,
to match the gentleman in the text — but in vain :
he then tells us that Cicero accused Verres of
reposing upon a cushion "Melitensi rosâ far-
tum," which, from the odd mixture of words, he
supposes to be a kind of *Irish* Bed of Roses, like
Lord Castlereagh's. The learned Clerk next
favors us with some remarks upon a well-
know punning epitaph on fair Rosamond, and
expresses a most loyal hope, that, if "*Rosa
munda*" mean "a Rose with clean hands" it
may be found applicable to the Right Honorable Rose in question. He then dwells at some
length upon the "Rosa *aurea*," which, though
descriptive in one sense of the old Treasury
Statesman, yet as being consecrated and worn

Oh Wellington, long as such Ministers
 wield
 Your magnificent arm, the same emblem will do;

For while *they* 're in the Council and *you*
 in the Field,
 We 've the *babies* in *them*, and the
 thunder in *you*!

by the Pope, must of course not be brought into
the same atmosphere with him. Lastly, in reference to the words "*old* Rose," he winds up

with the pathetic lamentation of the Poet "*con-
senuisse Rosas.*" The whole note indeed shows
a knowledge of Roses, that is quite edifying.

THE following trifles, having enjoyed in their circulation through the newspapers all the celebrity and length of life to which they were entitled, would have
been suffered to pass quietly into oblivion without pretending to any further distinction, had they not already been published, in a collective form, both in London
and Paris, and, in each case, been mixed up with a number of other productions,
to which, whatever may be their merit, the author of the following pages has no
claim. A natural desire to separate his own property, worthless as it is, from that
of others, is, he begs to say, the chief motive of the publication of this volume.

TO SIR HUDSON LOWE.

effare causam nominis,
utrumne mores hoc tui
nomen dedere, an nomen hoc
secuta morum regula. AUSONIUS.

1816.

SIR HUDSON LOWE, Sir Hudson *Low*,
 (By name, and ah! by nature so)
As thou art fond of persecutions,
Perhaps thou 'st read, or heard repeated,
How Captain Gulliver was treated,
 When thrown among the Lilliputians.

They tied him down — these little men
 did —
And having valiantly ascended
 Upon the Mighty Man's protuberance,
They did so strut! — upon my soul,
It must have been extremely droll
 To see their pigmy pride's exuberance!

And how the doughty mannikins
Amused themselves with sticking pins
 And needles in the great man's
 breeches:
And how some *very* little things,
That past for Lords, on scaffoldings
 Got up and worried him with speeches.

Alas, alas! that it should happen
To mighty men to be caught napping! —
 Tho' different too these persecutions;
For Gulliver, *there*, took the nap,
While, *here*, the *Nap*, oh sad mishap,
 Is taken by the Lilliputians!

AMATORY COLLOQUY BETWEEN BANK AND GOVERNMENT.

1826.

BANK.

Is all then forgotten? those amorous
 pranks
 You and I in our youth, my dear Government, played;
When you called me the fondest, the
 truest of Banks,
 And enjoyed the endearing *advances* I
 made!

When left to ourselves, unmolested and
 free,
 To do all that a dashing young couple
 should do,
A law against *paying* was laid upon me,
 But none against *owing*, dear help-
 mate, on you.

And is it then vanisht? — that "hour (as
 Othello
 So happily calls it) of Love and *Di-
 rection*?"[1]
And must we, like other fond doves, my
 dear fellow,
 Grow good in our old age and cut the
 connection?

1 ———— "An hour
Of love, of worldly matter and direction."

GOVERNMENT.

Even so, my beloved Mrs. Bank, it must
be;
 This paying in cash plays the devil
  with wooing: [1]
We 've both had our swing, but I plainly
  foresee
There must soon be a stop to our *bill-*
  ing and cooing.

Propagation in reason — a small child or
  two —
 Even Reverend Malthus himself is a
  friend to;
The issue of some folks is moderate and
  few —
 But *ours,* my dear corporate Bank,
  there 's no end to !

So — hard tho' it be on a pair, who 've
  already
 Disposed of so many pounds, shillings
  and pence ;
And in spite of that pink of prosperity,
  Freddy,[2]
 So lavish of cash and so sparing of
  sense —

The day is at hand, my Papyria [3] Venus,
 When — high as we once used to carry
  our capers —
Those soft *billet-doux* we 're now passing
  between us,
 Will serve but to keep Mrs. Coutts in
  curl-papers :

And when — if we *still* must continue our
  love,
 (After all that has past) — our amour,
  it is clear,
Like that which Miss Danäe managed
  with Jove,
 Must all be transacted in *bullion,* my
  dear !

February, 1826.

---

1 It appears, however, that Ovid was a friend
to the resumption of payment in specie : —

—— "*finem,* specie *cœleste* resumptâ,
luctibus imposuit, venitque salutifer urbi."
     Met. l. 15. v. 743.

2 Honorable Frederick Robinson.

3 So called, to distinguish her from the
"*Aurea*" or *Golden* Venus.

DIALOGUE BETWEEN A SOVER-EIGN AND A ONE POUND NOTE.

"*o ego non felix, quam tu fugis, ut pavet acres
agna lupos, capreæque leones.*" Hor.

Said a Sovereign to a Note,
 In the pocket of my coat,
Where they met in a neat purse of leather,
 " How happens it, I prithee,
 " That, tho' I 'm wedded *with* thee,
" Fair Pound, we can never live together ?

 " Like your sex, fond of *change,*
 " With Silver you can range,
" And of lots of young sixpences be
  mother;
 " While with *me* — upon my word,
 " Not my Lady and my Lord
" Of Westmouth see so little of each
  other ! "

The indignant Note replied
 (Lying crumpled by his side),
" Shame, shame, it is *yourself* that roam,
  Sir —
 " One cannot look askance,
 " But, whip ! you 're off to France,
" Leaving nothing but old rags at home,
  Sir.

 " Your scampering began
 " From the moment Parson Van,
" Poor man, made us *one* in Love's fet-
  ter;
 " ' For better or for worse '
 " Is the usual marriage curse,
" But ours is all ' worse ' and no ' better.'

 " In vain are laws past,
 " There 's nothing holds you fast,
" Tho' you know, sweet Sovereign, I
  adore you —
 " At the smallest hint in life,
 " You forsake your lawful wife,
" As *other* Sovereigns did before you.

 " I flirt with Silver, true —
 " But what can ladies do,
" When disowned by their natural pro-
  tectors?
 " And as to falsehood, stuff !
 " I shall soon be *false* enough,
" When I get among those wicked Bank
  Directors."

The Sovereign, smiling on her,
Now swore upon his honor,
To be henceforth domestic and loyal;
But, within an hour or two,
Why — I sold him to a Jew,
And he 's now at No. 10, Palais Royal.

AN EXPOSTULATION TO LORD KING.

" quem das finem, rex magne, laborum ?"
VERGIL.
1826.

HOW *can* you, my Lord, thus delight to torment all
  The Peers of the realm about cheapening their corn,[1]
When you know, if one has n't a very high rental,
  'T is hardly worth while being very high born?

Why bore them so rudely, each night of your life,
  On a question, my Lord, there 's so much to abhor in?
A question — like asking one, "How is your wife?" —
  At once so confounded *domestic* and *foreign.*

As to weavers, no matter how poorly they feast;
  But Peers and such animals, fed up for show,
(Like the well-physickt elephant, lately deceased,)
  Take a wonderful quantum of cramming, you know.

You might see, my dear Baron, how bored and distrest
  Were their high noble hearts by your merciless tale,
When the force of the agony wrung even a jest
  From the frugal Scotch wit of my Lord Lauderdale![2]

Bright Peer! to whom Nature and Berwickshire gave
  A humor endowed with effects so provoking,
That when the whole House looks unusually grave
  You may always conclude that Lord Lauderdale 's joking!

And then, those unfortunate weavers of Perth —
  Not to know the vast difference Providence dooms
Between weavers of Perth and Peers of high birth,
  'Twixt those who have *heir*-looms, and those who 've but looms!

"To talk *now* of starving!" — as great Athol said [3]
  (And the nobles all cheered and the bishops all wondered,)
"When some years ago he and others had fed
  "Of these same hungry devils about fifteen hundred!"

It follows from hence — and the Duke's very words
  Should be publisht wherever poor rogues of this craft are —
That weavers, *once* rescued from starving by Lords,
  Are bound to be starved by said Lords ever after.

When Rome was uproarious, her knowing patricians
  Made "Bread and the Circus" a cure for each *row ;*
But not so the plan of *our* noble physicians,
  "No Bread and the Tread-mill," 's the regimen now.

---

1 See the proceedings of the Lords, Wednesday, March 1, 1826, when Lord King was severely reproved by several of the noble Peers, for making so many speeches against the Corn Laws.

2 This noble Earl said, that "when he heard the petition came from ladies' boot and shoemakers, he thought it must be against the 'corns' which they inflicted on the fair sex."

3 The Duke of Athol said, that "at a former period, when these weavers were in great distress, the landed interest of Perth had supported 1500 of them. It was a poor return for these very men now to petition against the persons who had fed them."

So cease, my dear Baron of Ockham,
    your prose,
As I shall my poetry — *neither* con-
    vinces;
And all we have spoken and written but
    shows,
    When you tread on a nobleman's
    corn,[1] how he winces.

THE SINKING FUND CRIED.

" Now what, we ask, is become of this Sinking
Fund — these eight millions of surplus above
expenditure, which were to reduce the interest of
the national debt by the amount of four hundred
thousand pounds annually ? Where, indeed, is
the Sinking Fund itself?" — *The Times.*

TAKE your bell, take your bell,
    Good Crier, and tell
To the Bulls and the Bears, till their ears
    are stunned,
    That, lost or stolen,
    Or fallen thro' a hole in
The Treasury floor, is the Sinking Fund !

O yes ! O yes !
    Can anybody guess
What the deuce has become of this Treas-
    ury wonder ?
    It has Pitt's name on 't,
    All brass, in the front,
And Robinson's scrawled with a goose-
    quill under.

Folks well knew what
    Would soon be its lot,
When Frederick and Jenky set hob-
    nobbing,[2]
    And said to each other,
" Suppose, dear brother,
" We make this funny old Fund worth
    robbing."

We are come, alas !
    To a very pretty pass —
Eight Hundred Millions of score, to pay,
    With but Five in the till,
    To discharge the bill,
And even that Five, too, whipt away !

1 An improvement, we flatter ourselves, on
Lord L.'s joke.

2 In 1824, when the Sinking Fund was raised
by the imposition of new taxes to the sum of five
millions.

Stop thief ! stop thief ! —
    From the Sub to the Chief,
These *Gemmen* of Finance are plunder-
    ing cattle —
    Call the watch — call Brougham,
    Tell Joseph Hume,
That best of Charleys, to spring his
    rattle.

    Whoever will bring
    This aforesaid thing
To the well-known House of Bobinson
    and Jenkin,
    Shall be paid, with thanks,
    In the notes of banks,
Whose Funds have all learned " the Art
    of Sinking."

    O yes ! O yes !
    Can anybody guess
What the devil has become of this Treas-
    ury wonder ?
    It has Pitt's name on 't,
    All brass, in the front,
And Robinson's, scrawled with a goose-
    quill under.

ODE TO THE GODDESS CERES.

BY SIR THOMAS LETHBRIDGE.

" legiferæ Cereri Phœboque." — VERGIL.

DEAR Goddess of Corn whom the an-
    cients, we know,
    (Among other odd whims of those
    comical bodies,)
Adorned with somniferous poppies to
    show
    Thou wert always a true Country-gen-
    tleman's Goddess.

Behold in his best shooting-jacket be-
    fore thee
    An eloquent 'Squire, who most hum-
    bly beseeches,
Great Queen of Mark-lane (if the thing
    does n't bore thee),
    Thou 'lt read o 'er the last of his —
    never-last speeches.

Ah ! Ceres, thou knowest not the slander
    and scorn
    Now heapt upon England's 'Squire-
    archy, so boasted ;

Improving on Hunt,[1] 't is no longer the
 Corn,
 'T is the *growers* of Corn that are now,
  alas! roasted.

In speeches, in books, in all shapes they
 attack us —
 Reviewers, economists — fellows no
  doubt
That you, my dear Ceres and Venus and
 Bacchus
 And Gods of high fashion, know little
  about.

There 's Bentham, whose English is all
 his own making, —
 Who thinks just as little of settling a
  nation
As he would of smoking his pipe or of
 taking
 (What he himself calls) his "post-
  prandial vibration."[2]

There are two Mr. Mills too whom those
 that love reading
 Thro' all that 's unreadable call very
  clever; —
And whereas Mill Senior makes war on
 good breeding,
 Mill Junior makes war on all *breeding*
  whatever!

in short, my dear Goddess, Old England 's divided
 Between *ultra* blockheads and superfine sages; —
With *which* of these classes we landlords
 have sided
 Thou 'lt find in my Speech if thou 'lt
  read a few pages.

For therein I 've proved to my own satisfaction
 And that of all 'Squires I 've the honor
  of meeting
That 't is the most senseless and foul-
 mouthed detraction
 To say that poor people are fond of
  cheap eating.

1 A sort of "breakfast-powder," composed
of roasted corn, was about this time introduced
by Mr. Hunt, as a substitute for coffee.

2 The venerable Jeremy's phrase for his
after-dinner walk.

On the contrary, such the "*chaste* notions"[3] of food
 That dwell in each pale manufacturer's
  heart,
They would scorn any law, be it ever so
 good,
 That would make thee, dear Goddess,
  less dear than thou art!

And, oh! for Monopoly what a blest day,
 When the Land and the Silk[4] shall in
  fond combination
(Like *Sulky* and *Silky*, that pair in the
 play,)[5]
 Cry out with one voice for High Rents
  and Starvation!

Long life to the Minister! no matter
 who,
 Or how dull he may be, if with digni-
  fied spirit he
Keeps the ports shut — and the people's
 mouths too —
 We shall all have a long run of
  Freddy's prosperity.

And, as for myself, who 've, like Hanni-
 bal, sworn
 To hate the whole crew who would
  take our rents from us,
Had England but *One* to stand by thee,
 Dear Corn,
 That last, honest Uni-Corn[6] would be
  Sir Thomas!

A HYMN OF WELCOME AFTER THE RECESS.

"*animas sapientiores fieri quiescendo.*"

AND now — cross-buns and pancakes
 o'er —
Hail, Lords and Gentlemen, once more!
 Thrice hail and welcome, Houses
  Twain!

3 A phrase in one of Sir Thomas's last
speeches.

4 Great efforts were, at that time, making for
the exclusion of foreign silk.

5 "Road to Ruin."

6 This is meant not so much for a pun, as
in allusion to the natural history of the Unicorn,
which is supposed to be something between the
Bos and the *Asinus*, and, as Rees's Cyclopædia
assures us, has a particular liking for everything
"chaste."

The short eclipse of April-Day
Having (God grant it!) past away,
　Collective Wisdom, shine again!

Come, Ayes and Noes, thro' thick and
　　thin, —
With Paddy Holmes for whipper-in, —
　Whate'er the job, prepared to back it;
Come, voters of Supplies — bestowers
Of jackets upon trumpet-blowers,
　At eighty mortal pounds the jacket![1]

Come — free, at length, from Joint-Stock
　　cares —
Ye Senators of many Shares,
　Whose dreams of premium knew no
　　boundary;
So fond of aught like *Company*,
That you would even have taken *tea*
　(Had you been askt) with Mr. Goun-
　　dry.[2]

Come, matchless country-gentlemen;
Come, wise Sir Thomas — wisest then
　When creeds and corn-laws are de-
　　bated;
Come, rival even the Harlot Red,
And show how wholly into *bread*
　A 'Squire is *transubstantiated*.

Come, Lauderdale, and tell the world,
That — surely as thy scratch is curled,
　As never scratch was curled before —
Cheap eating does more harm than good,
And working-people spoiled by food,
　The less they eat, will work the more.

Come, Goulburn, with thy glib defence
(Which thou 'dst have made for Peter's
　　Pence)
　Of Church-Rates, worthy of a halter;
Two pipes of port (*old* port, 't was said
By honest *New*port)[3] bought and paid
　By Papists for the Orange Altar![4]

Come, Horton, with thy plan so merry
For peopling Canada from Kerry —
　Not so much rendering Ireland quiet,
As grafting on the dull Canadians
That liveliest of earth's contagions,
　The *bull*-pock of Hibernian riot!

Come all, in short, ye wondrous men
Of wit and wisdom, come again;
　Tho' short your absence, all deplore
　　it —
Oh, come and show, whate'er men say,
That you can *after* April-Day,
　Be just as — sapient as *before* it.

MEMORABILIA OF LAST WEEK.

MONDAY, MARCH 13, 1826.

THE Budget — quite charming and witty
　　— no hearing,
　For plaudits and laughs, the good
　　things that were in it; —
Great comfort to find, tho' the Speech
　　is n't *cheering*,
　That all its gay auditors *were* every
　　minute.

What, *still* more prosperity! — mercy
　　upon us,
　"This boy 'll be the death of me" —
　　oft as, already,
Such smooth Budgeteers have genteelly
　　undone us,
　For *Ruin made easy* there 's no one
　　like Freddy.

TUESDAY.

Much grave apprehension exprest by
　　the Peers,
　Lest — calling to life the old Peachums
　　and Lockitts —
The large stock of gold we 're to have
　　in three years,
　Should all find its way into highway-
　　men's pockets![5]

·　　·　　·　　·　　·

of rates levied upon their Catholic fellow-parish-
ioners by the Irish Protestants.

　"The thirst that from the soul doth rise
　　Doth ask a drink divine."

5 "Another objection to a metallic currency
was, that it produced a greater number of high-
way robberies." — *Debate in the Lords.*

---

1 An item of expense which Mr. Hume in
vain endeavored to get rid of: — trumpeters, it
appears like the men of All-Souls, must be "*bene
vestiti.*"

3 The gentleman, lately before the public,
who kept his *Joint*-Stock Tea Company all to
himself, singing "Te *solo adoro*."

3 Sir John Newport.

4 This charge of two pipes of port for the sacramental wine is a precious specimen of the sort

WEDNESDAY.

Little doing — for sacred, oh Wednesday,
  thou art
To the seven-o'-clock joys of full many
  a table —
When *the Members* all meet, to make
  much of that part,
With which they so rashly fell out in
  the Fable.

It appeared, tho', to-night, that — as
  church-wardens yearly,
Eat up a small baby — those cormo-
  rant sinners,
The Bankrupt-Commissioners, *bolt* very
  nearly
A moderate-sized bankrupt, *tout chaud,*
  for their dinners! [1]

Nota bene — a rumor to-day, in the City,
"Mr. Robinson just has resigned " —
  what a pity!
The Bulls and the Bears all fell a sob-
  bing,
When they heard of the fate of poor
  Cock *Robin ;*
While thus, to the nursery tune, so
  pretty,
A murmuring *Stock*-dove breathed her
  ditty: —

Alas, poor *Robin,* he crowed as long
And as sweet as a prosperous Cock
  could crow;
But his *note* was *small* and the *gold*-finch's
  song
Was a pitch too high for Robin to go.
              Who 'll make his shroud?

"I," said the Bank, "tho' he played
  me a prank,
  "While I have a rag, poor *Rob* shall
    be rolled in 't,
  "With many a pound I 'll paper him
    round,
  "Like a plump rouleau — *without* the
    gold in it."

    .   .   .   .

1 Mr. Abercromby's statement of the enormous tavern bills of the Commissioners of Bankrupts.

ALL IN THE FAMILY WAY.

A NEW PASTORAL BALLAD.

(SUNG IN THE CHARACTER OF BRITANNIA.)

"The Public Debt is due from ourselves to
ourselves, and resolves itself into a Family Account." — *Sir Robert Peel's Letter*.

Tune — *My banks are all furnisht with bees.*

My banks are all furnisht with rags,
  So thick, even Freddy can't thin 'em;
I 've torn up my old money-bags,
  Having little or naught to put in 'em.
My tradesmen are smashing by dozens,
  But this is all nothing, they say;
For bankrupts since Adam are cousins, —
  So, it 's all in the family way.

My Debt not a penny takes from me,
  As sages the matter explain; —
Bob owes it to Tom, and then Tommy
  Just owes it to Bob back again.
Since all have thus taken to *owing,*
  There 's nobody left that can *pay ;*
And this is the way to keep going, —
  All quite in the family way.

My senators vote away millions,
  To put in Prosperity's budget;
And tho 'it were billions or trillions,
  The generous rogues would n't grudge
    it.
'T is all but a family *hop,*
  'T was Pitt began dancing the hay;
Hands round! — why the deuce should
  we stop?
  'T is all in the family way.

My laborers used to eat mutton,
  As any great man of the State does;
And now the poor devils are put on
  Small rations of tea and potatoes.
But cheer up, John, Sawney, and Paddy,
  The King is your father, they say;
So even if you starve for your Daddy,
  'T is all in the family way.

My rich manufacturers tumble,
  My poor ones have nothing to chew;
And even if themselves do not grumble
  Their stomachs undoubtedly do.
But coolly to fast *en famille,*
  Is as good for the soul as to pray;
And famine itself is genteel,
  When one starves in a family way.

I have found out a secret for Freddy,
　　A secret for next Budget day;
Tho' perhaps he may know it already,
　　As *he* too 's a sage in his way.
When next for the Treasury scene he
　　Announces " the Devil to pay,"
Let him write on the bills, " *nota bene*,
　　" 'T is all in the family way."

BALLAD FOR THE CAMBRIDGE ELECTION.

" I authorized my Committee to take the step
which they did, of proposing a fair comparison
of strength, upon the understanding that *whichever of the two should prove to be the weakest*,
should give way to the other." — *Extract from
Mr. W. J. Bankes's Letter to Mr. Goulbourn.*

BANKES is weak, and Goulbourn too,
　　No one e'er the fact denied; —
Which is " *weakest* " of the two,
　　Cambridge can alone decide.
Choose between them, Cambridge, pray,
Which is weakest, Cambridge, say.

Goulbourn of the Pope afraid is,
　　Bankes, as much afraid as he;
Never yet did two old ladies
　　On this point so well agree.
Choose between them, Cambridge, pray,
Which is weakest, Cambridge, say.

Each a different mode pursues,
　　Each the same conclusion reaches;
Bankes is foolish in Reviews,
　　Goulbourn foolish in his speeches.
Choose between them, Cambridge, pray,
Which is weakest, Cambridge, say.

Each a different foe doth damn,
　　When his own affairs have gone ill;
Bankes he damneth Buckingham,
　　Goulbourn damneth Dan O'Connell.
Choose between them, Cambridge, pray,
Which is weakest, Cambridge, say.

Once we know a horse's neigh
　　Fixt the election to a throne,
So whichever first shall *bray*,
　　Choose him, Cambridge, for thy own.
Choose him, choose him by his bray,
Thus elect him, Cambridge, pray.

June, 1826.

MR. ROGER DODSWORTH.

To the Editor of the Times. 1826.

Sir, — Having just heard of the wonderful
resurrection of Mr. Roger Dodsworth from
under an *avalanche*, where he had remained,
bien frappé, it seems, for the last 166 years, I
hasten to impart to you a few reflections on the
subject. — Yours, etc.

Laudator Temporis Acti.

WHAT a lucky turn-up ! — just as El-
　　don 's withdrawing,
To find thus a gentleman, frozen in the
　　year
Sixteen hundred and sixty, who only
　　wants thawing
To serve for *our* times quite as well as
　　the Peer; —

To bring thus to light, not the Wisdom
　　alone
Of our Ancestors, such as 't is found
　　on our shelves,
But in perfect condition, full-wigged and
　　full-grown,
To shovel up one of those wise bucks
　　themselves !

Oh thaw Mr. Dodsworth and send him
　　safe home —
Let him learn nothing useful or new
　　on the way;
With his wisdom kept snug from the
　　light let him come,
And our Tories will hail him with
　　" Hear ! " and " Hurra ! "

What a God-send to *them!* — a good,
　　obsolete man,
Who has never of Locke or Voltaire
　　been a reader; —
Oh thaw Mr. Dodsworth as fast as you
　　can,
And the Lonsdales and Hertfords shall
　　choose him for leader.

Yes, Sleeper of Ages, thou *shalt* be their
　　chosen;
And deeply with thee will they sorrow,
　　good men,
To think that all Europe has, since thou
　　wert frozen,
So altered thou hardly wilt know it
　　again.

And Eldon will weep o'er each sad innovation
Such oceans of tears, thou wilt fancy
that he
Has been also laid up in a long congela-
tion,
And is only now thawing, dear Roger,
like thee.

COPY OF AN INTERCEPTED DESPATCH.

FROM HIS EXCELLENCY DON STREPITOSO DIA-
BOLO, ENVOY EXTRAORDINARY TO HIS SA-
TANIC MAJESTY.

St. James's Street, July 1, 1826.

GREAT Sir, having just had the good
luck to catch
An official young Demon, preparing to
go,
Ready booted and spurred, with a black-
leg despatch
From the Hell here at Crockford's, to
our Hell below —

I write these few lines to your Highness
Satanic,
To say that first having obeyed your
directions
And done all the mischief I could in
"the Panic,"
My next special care was to help the
Elections.

Well knowing how dear were those times
to thy soul,
When every good Christian tormented
his brother,
And caused, in thy realm, such a saving
of coal,
From all coming down, ready grilled
by each other;

Remembering besides how it pained thee
to part
With the Old Penal Code — that *chef-
d'œuvre* of Law,
In which (tho' to own it too modest
thou art)
We could plainly perceive the fine
touch of thy claw;

I thought, as we ne'er can those good
times revive,
(Tho' Eldon, with help from your
Highness would try,)
'T would still keep a taste for Hell's
music alive,
Could we get up a thundering No-
Popery cry; —

That yell which when chorused by laics
and clerics,
So like is to *ours*, in its spirit and tone,
That I often nigh laugh myself into hysterics,
To think that Religion should make it
her own.

So, having sent down for the original
notes
Of the chorus as sung by your Majesty's
choir
With a few pints of lava to gargle the
throats
Of myself and some others who sing it
" with fire," [1]

Thought I, " if the Marseillais Hymn
could command
" Such audience, tho' yelled by a *Sans-
culotte* crew,
" What wonders shall *we* do, who 've
men in our band,
" That not only wear breeches but
petticoats too."

Such *then* were my hopes; but with
sorrow, your Highness,
I 'm forced to confess — be the cause
what it will,
Whether fewness of voices or hoarseness
or shyness, —
Our Beelzebub Chorus has gone off but
ill.

The truth is no placeman now knows his
right key,
The Treasury pitch-pipe of late is so
various;
And certain *base* voices, that lookt for a
fee
At the *York* music-meeting now think
it precarious.

1 *Con fuoco* — a music-book direction.

Even some of our Reverends *might* have
   been warmer, —
Tho' one or two capital roarers we 've
   had;
Doctor Wise [1] is for instance a charming
   performer,
And *Huntingdon* Maberley's yell was
   not bad !

Altogether however the thing was not
   hearty; —
Even Eldon allows we got on but so so;
And when next we attempt a No-Popery
   party,
We *must*, please your Highness, recruit
   from below.

But hark ! the young Black-leg is crack-
   ing his whip —
Excuse me, Great Sir — there 's no
   time to be civil; —
The next opportunity shan't be let slip,
But, till then,
    I 'm, in haste, your most dutiful
July, 1826.   Devil.

THE MILLENNIUM.

SUGGESTED BY THE LATE WORK OF THE REVER-
END MR. IRVING "ON PROPHECY."
1826.

A Millennium at hand ! — I 'm delighted
   to hear it —
As matters both public and private
   now go,
With multitudes round us all starving or
   near it,
A good, rich Millennium will come
   à-propos.

Only think, Master Fred, what delight to
   behold,
Instead of thy bankrupt old City of
   Rags,
A bran-new Jerusalem built all of gold,
Sound bullion throughout from the
   roof to the flags —

A City where wine and cheap corn [2] shall
   abound —
A celestial *Cocaigne* on whose buttery
   shelves

1 This reverend gentleman distinguished himself at the Reading election.

2 "A measure of wheat for a penny, and three
measures of barley for a penny." — *Rev.* vi.

We may swear the best things of this
   world will be found,
As your Saints seldom fail to take care
   of themselves !

Thanks, reverend expounder of raptures
   Elysian, [3]
Divine Squintifobus who, placed within
   reach
Of two opposite worlds, by a twist of
   your vision
Can cast at the same time a sly look at
   each; —

Thanks, thanks for the hope thou afford-
   est, that we
May even in our own times a Jubilee
   share,
Which so long has been promist by prophets like thee,
And so often postponed, we began to
   despair.

There was Whiston [4] who learnedly took
   Prince Eugene
For the man who must bring the Mil-
   lennium about;
There 's Faber whose pious productions
   have been
All belied ere his book's first edition
   was out; —

There was Counsellor Dobbs, too, an
   Irish M. P.,
Who discoursed on the subject with
   signal *éclât*,
And, each day of his life sat expecting to
   see
A Millennium break out in the town
   of Armagh ! [5]

3 See the oration of this reverend gentleman,
where he describes the connubial joys of Paradise, and paints the angels hovering round "each
happy fair."

4 When Whiston presented to Prince Eugene
the Essay in which he attempted to connect his
victories over the Turks with Revelation, the
Prince is said to have replied, that "he was not
aware he had ever had the honor of being known
to St. John."

5 Mr. Dobbs was a member of the Irish
Parliament, and, on all other subjects but the
Millennium, a very sensible person : he chose
Armagh as the scene of his Millennium, on ac-
count of the name Armageddon mentioned in
Revelation.

There was also — but why should I burden my lay
  With your Brotherses, Southcotes, and names less deserving,
When all past Millenniums henceforth must give way
  To the last new Millennium of Orator Irving.

Go on, mighty man, — doom them all to the shelf, —
  And when next thou with Prophecy troublest thy sconce,
Oh forget not, I pray thee, to prove that thyself
  Art the Beast (Chapter iv.) that sees nine ways at once.

THE THREE DOCTORS.

doctoribus lætamur tribus.

1826.

Tho' many great Doctors there be,
  There are three that all Doctors outtop,
Doctor Eady, that famous M.D.,
  Doctor Southey, and dear Doctor Slop.[1]

The purger, the proser, the bard —
  All quacks in a different style;
Doctor Southey writes books by the yard,
  Doctor Eady writes puffs by the mile![2]

Doctor Slop, in no merit outdone
  By his scribbling or physicking brother,
Can dose us with stuff like the one,
  Ay and *doze* us with stuff like the other.

Doctor Eady good company keeps
  With "No Popery" scribes, on the walls;
Doctor Southey as gloriously sleeps
  With "No Popery" scribes on the stalls.

Doctor Slop, upon subjects divine,
  Such bedlamite slaver lets drop,

That if Eady should take the *mad* line,
  He 'll be sure of a patient in Slop.

Seven millions of Papists, no less,
  Doctor Southey attacks, like a Turk;[3]
Doctor Eady, less bold, I confess,
  Attacks but his maid-of-all-work[4]

Doctor Southey, for *his* grand attack,
  Both a laureate and pensioner is;
While poor Doctor Eady, alack,
  Has been *had up* to Bow-street for his!

And truly, the law does so blunder,
  That tho' little blood has been spilt, he
May probably suffer as, under
  The *Chalking* Act, *known* to be guilty.

So much for the merits sublime
  (With whose catalogue ne'er should I stop)
Of the three greatest lights of our time,
  Doctor Eady and Southey and Slop!

Should you ask me, to *which* of the three
  Great Doctors the preference should fall,
As a matter of course I agree
  Doctor Eady must go to *the wall.*

But as Southey with laurels is crowned,
  And Slop with a wig and a tail is,
Let Eady's bright temples be bound
  With a swingeing "Corona *Muralis!*"[5]

3 This seraphic doctor, in the preface to his last work (" *Vindiciæ Ecclesiæ Anglicanæ* "), is pleased to anathematize not only all Catholics, but all advocates of Catholics : — "They have for their immediate allies [he says] every faction that is banded against the State, every demagogue, every irreligious and seditious journalist, every open and every insidious enemy to Monarchy and to Christianity."

4 See the late accounts in the newspapers of the appearance of this gentleman at one of the Police-offices, in consequence of an alleged assault on his "maid-of-all-work."

5 A crown granted as a reward among the Romans to persons who performed any extraordinary exploits upon *walls*, such as scaling them, battering them, etc. — No doubt, writing upon them, to the extent Dr. Eady does, would equally establish a claim to the honor.

1 The editor of the *Morning Herald,* so nicknamed.

2 Alluding to the display of this doctor's name, in chalk, on all the walls round the metropolis.

EPITAPH ON A TUFT-HUNTER.

LAMENT, lament, Sir Isaac Heard,
    Put mourning round thy page, Debrett,
For here lies one who ne'er preferred
    A Viscount to a Marquis yet.

Beside him place the God of Wit,
    Before him Beauty's rosiest girls,
Apollo for a *star* he 'd quit,
    And Love's own sister for an Earl's.

Did niggard fate no peers afford,
    He took of course to peers' relations;
And rather than not sport a Lord
    Put up with even the last creations.

Even Irish names could he but tag 'em
    With "Lord" and "Duke," were
        sweet to call;
And at a pinch Lord Ballyraggum
    Was better than no Lord at all.

Heaven grant him now some noble nook,
    For rest his soul! he 'd rather be
Genteelly damned beside a Duke,
    Than saved in vulgar company.

ODE TO A HAT.

—— "*altum*
        ædificat caput."   JUVENAL.
                                1826.

HAIL, reverent Hat! — sublime mid all
    The minor felts that round thee
        grovel; —
Thou that the Gods "a Delta" call
    While meaner mortals call thee
        "shovel."

When on thy shape (like pyramid,
    Cut horizontally in two) [1]
I raptured gaze, what dreams unbid
    Of stalls and mitres bless my view!

That brim of brims so sleekly good —
    Not flapt, like dull Wesleyans', down,
But looking (as all churchmen's should)
    Devoutly upward — towards the *crown.*

[1] So described by a Reverend Historian of
the Church: — "A Delta hat like the horizontal
section of a pyramid." — GRANT's "*History of
the English Church.*"

Gods! when I gaze upon that brim,
    So redolent of Church all over,
What swarms of Tithes in vision dim, —
Some pig-tailed, some like cherubim,
    With ducklings' wings — around it
        hover!
Tenths of all dead and living things,
That Nature into being brings,
From calves and corn to chitterlings.

Say, holy Hat, that hast, of cocks,
The very cock most orthodox,
To *which* of all the well-fed throng
Of Zion,[2] joy'st thou to belong?
Thou 'rt *not* Sir Harcourt Lees's — no —
For hats grow like the heads that wear
    'em;
And hats, on heads like his, would grow
    Particularly *harum-scarum.*

Who knows but thou mayst deck the pate
Of that famed Doctor Ad—mth—te,
(The reverend rat, whom we saw stand
On his hind-legs in Westmoreland,)
Who changed so quick from *blue* to *yel-
    low,*
    And would from *yellow* back to *blue,*
And back again, convenient fellow,
    If 't were his interest so to do.

Or haply smartest of triangles,
    Thou art the hat of Doctor Owen;
The hat that, to his vestry wrangles,
    That venerable priest doth go in, —
And then and there amid the stare
Of all St. Olave's, takes the chair
And quotes with phiz right orthodox
The example of his reverend brothers,
To prove that priests all fleece their flocks
    And *he* must fleece as well as others.

Blest Hat! (whoe'er thy lord may be)
Thus low I take off mine to thee,
The homage of a layman's *castor,*
To the spruce *delta* of his pastor.
Oh mayst thou be, as thou proceedest,
    Still smarter cockt, still brusht the
        brighter,
Till, bowing all the way, thou leadest
    Thy sleek possessor to a mitre!

[2] Archbishop Magee affectionately calls the
Church Establishment of Ireland "the little
Zion."

NEWS FOR COUNTRY COUSINS.

DEAR Coz, as I know neither you nor
Miss Draper,
When Parliament 's up, ever take in a
paper,
But trust for your news to such stray
odds and ends
As you chance to pick up from political
friends —
Being one of this well-informed class, I
sit down
To transmit you the last newest news
that 's in town.

As to Greece and Lord Cochrane, things
could n't look better —
His Lordship (who promises now to
fight faster)
Has just taken Rhodes and despatched
off a letter
To Daniel O'Connell, to make him
Grand Master;
Engaging to change the old name, if he
can,
From the Knights of St. John to the
Knights of St. Dan; —
Or if Dan should prefer (as a still better
whim)
Being made the Colossus, 't is all one to
him.

From Russia the last accounts are that
the Tsar —
Most generous and kind as all sovereigns
are,
And whose first princely act (as you
know, I suppose)
Was to give away all his late brother's
old clothes [1] —
Is now busy collecting with brotherly care
The late Emperor's nightcaps, and thinks
of bestowing
One nightcap apiece (if he has them to
spare)
On all the distinguisht old ladies now
going.
(While I write, an arrival from Riga —
the " Brothers " —
Having nightcaps on board for Lord
Eldon and others.)

Last advices from India — Sir Archy,
't is thought,
Was near catching a Tartar (the first
ever caught
In N. Lat. 21.) — and his Highness
Burmese,
Being very hard prest to shell out the
rupees,
And not having rhino sufficient, they
say, meant
To pawn his august Golden Foot [2] for
the payment.
(How lucky for monarchs, that thus
when they choose
Can establish a *running* account with
the Jews!)
The security being what Rothschild calls
"good,"
A loan will be shortly, of course, set *on
foot;*
The parties are Rothschild, A. Baring
and Co.
With three other great pawnbrokers :
each takes a toe,
And engages (lest Gold-foot should give
us *leg*-bail,
As he did once before) to pay down *on
the nail.*

This is all for the present — what vile
pens and paper!
Yours truly, dear Cousin — best love to
Miss Draper.

September, 1826.

A VISION.

BY THE AUTHOR OF " CHRISTABEL."

" UP! " said the Spirit and ere I could
pray
One hasty orison, whirled me away
To a Limbo, lying — I wist not where —
Above or below, in earth or air;
For it glimmered o'er with a *doubtful*
light,
One could n't say whether 't was day or
night;
And 't was crost by many a mazy track,
One did n't know how to get on or
back;

---

1 A distribution was made of the Emperor
Alexander's military wardrobe by his successor.

2 This potentate styles himself the Monarch
of the Golden Foot.

And I felt like a needle that 's going
  astray
(With its *one* eye out) thro' a bundle of
  hay;
When the Spirit he grinned, and whispered me,
"Thou 'rt now in the Court of Chancery!"

Around me flitted unnumbered swarms
Of shapeless, bodiless, tailless forms;
(Like bottled-up babes that grace the
  room
Of that worthy knight, Sir Everard
  Home) —
All of them, things half-killed in rear-
  ing;
Some were lame — some wanted *hear-
  ing*;
Some had thro' half a century run,
Tho' they had n't a leg to stand upon.
Others, more merry, as just beginning,
Around on a *point of law* were spinning;
Or balanced aloft, 'twixt *Bill* and *An-
  swer*,
Lead at each end, like a tight-rope
  dancer.
Some were so *cross* that nothing could
  please 'em; —
Some gulpt down *affidavits* to ease
  'em; —
All were in motion, yet never a one,
Let it *move* as it might, could ever move
  on.
"These," said the Spirit, "you plainly
  see,
"Are what they call suits in Chancery!"

I heard a loud screaming of old and
  young,
Like a chorus by fifty Vellutis sung;
Or an Irish Dump ("the words by
  Moore")
At an amateur concert screamed in
  score; —
So harsh on my ear that wailing fell
Of the wretches who in this Limbo
  dwell!
It seemed like the dismal symphony
Of the shapes Æneas in hell did see;
Or those frogs whose legs a barbarous
  cook
Cut off and left the frogs in the brook,

To cry all night, till life's last dregs,
"Give us our legs! — give us our legs!"
Touched with the sad and sorrowful
  scene,
I askt what all this yell might mean,
When the Spirit replied, with a grin of
  glee,
"'T is the cry of the Suitors in Chan-
  cery!"

I lookt and I saw a wizard rise,[3]
With a wig like a cloud before men's
  eyes.
In his aged hand he held a wand,
Wherewith he beckoned his embryo
  band,
And they moved and moved as he waved
  it o'er,
But they never got on one inch the more.
And still they kept limping to and fro,
Like Ariels round old Prospero —
Saying, "Dear Master, let us go,"
But still old Prospero answered "No."
And I heard the while that wizard elf
Muttering, muttering spells to himself,
While o'er as many old papers he turned,
As Hume e'er moved for or Omar burned.
He talkt of his virtue — "tho' some,
  less nice,
(He owned with a sigh) preferred his
  Vice" —
And he said, "I think" — "I doubt"
  — "I hope,"
Called God to witness, and damned the
  Pope;
With many more sleights of tongue and
  hand
I could n't for the soul of me under-
  stand.
Amazed and posed, I was just about
To ask his name, when the screams with-
  out,
The merciless clack of the imps within,
And that conjuror's mutterings, made
  such a din,
That, startled, I woke — leapt up in my
  bed —
Found the Spirit, the imps, and the con-
  juror fled,
And blest my stars, right pleased to see,
That I was n't as yet in Chancery.

1 The Lord Chancellor Eldon.

THE PETITION OF THE ORANGE-MEN OF IRELAND.

1826.

To the people of England, the humble Petition
  Of Ireland's disconsolate Orangemen, showing —
That sad, very sad, is our present condition; —
  Our jobbing all gone and our noble selves going; —

That forming one seventh, within a few fractions,
  Of Ireland's seven millions of hot heads and hearts,
We hold it the basest of all base transactions
  To keep us from murdering the other six parts; —

That as to laws made for the good of the many,
  We humbly suggest there is nothing less true;
As all human laws (and our own, more than any)
  Are made *by* and *for* a particular few; —

That much it delights every true Orange brother
  To see you in England such ardor evince,
In discussing *which* sect most tormented the other,
  And burned with most *gusto* some hundred years since; —

That we love to behold, while old England grows faint,
  Messrs. Southey and Butler nigh coming to blows,
To decide whether Dunstan, that strong-bodied Saint,
  Ever truly and really pulled the De'il's nose;

Whether t' other Saint, Dominic, burnt the De'il's paw —
  Whether Edwy intrigued with Elgiva's old mother[1] —

And many such points, from which Southey can draw
  Conclusions most apt for our hating each other.

That 't is very well known this devout Irish nation
  Has now for some ages, gone happily on
Believing in two kinds of Substantiation,
  One party in *Trans* and the other in *Con* ;[2]

That we, your petitioning *Cons*, have in right
  Of the said monosyllable ravaged the lands
And embezzled the goods and annoyed, day and night,
  Both the bodies and souls of the sticklers for *Trans* ; —

That we trust to Peel, Eldon, and other such sages,
  For keeping us still in the same state of mind;
Pretty much as the world used to be in those ages,
  When still smaller syllables maddened mankind; —

When the words *ex* and *per*[3] served as well to annoy
  One's neighbors and friends with, as *con* and *trans* now;
And Christians, like Southey, who stickled for *oi*,
  Cut the throats of all Christians who stickled for *ou*.[4]

That relying on England whose kindness already
  So often has helpt us to play this game o'er,

1 To such important discussions as these the greater part of Dr. Southey's *Vindiciæ Ecclesiæ Anglicanæ* is devoted.

2 Consubstantiation — the true Reformed belief; at least, the belief of Luther, and, as Mosheim asserts, of Melancthon also.

3 When John of Ragusa went to Constantinople (at the time this dispute between "*ex*" and "*per*" was going on), he found the Turks, we are told, "laughing at the Christians for being divided by two such insignificant particles."

4 The Arian controversy. — Before that time, says Hooker, "in order to be a sound believing

We have got our red coats and our cara-
    bines ready,
And wait but the word to show sport
    as before.

That as to the expense — the few millions
    or so,
Which for all such diversions John
    Bull has to pay —
'T is at least a great comfort to John
    Bull to know
That to Orangemen's pockets 't will
    all find its way.
For which your petitioners ever will
    pray,
          Etc., etc., etc., etc., etc.

COTTON AND CORN.

A DIALOGUE.

SAID Cotton to Corn, t' other day,
    As they met and exchanged a salute —
(Squire Corn in his carriage so gay,
    Poor Cotton half famished on foot):

" Great Squire, if it is n't uncivil
  " To hint at starvation before you,
" Look down on a poor hungry devil,
  " And give him some bread, I implore
    you ! "

Quoth Corn then in answer to Cotton,
    Perceiving he meant to make *free* —
" Low fellow, you 've surely forgotten
  " The distance between you and me !

" To expect that we Peers of high birth
  " Should waste our illustrious acres,
" For no other purpose on earth
  " Than to fatten curst calico-ma-
    kers ! —

" That Bishops to bobbins should bend —
  " Should stoop from their Bench's
    sublimity !
" Great dealers in *lawn*, to befriend
  " Such contemptible dealers in dimity !

" No — vile Manufacture ! ne'er harbor
  " A hope to be fed at our boards ; —

Christian, men were not curious what syllables
or particles of speech they used."

" Base offspring of Arkwright the barber,
  " What claim canst *thou* have upon
    Lords ?

" No — thanks to the taxes and debt,
  " And the triumph of paper o'er
    guineas,
" Our race of Lord Jemmys, as yet,
  " May defy your whole rabble of
    Jennys ! "

So saying — whip, crack, and away
    Went Corn in his chaise thro' the
    throng,
So headlong, I heard them all say,
  " Squire Corn will be *down* before
    long."

THE CANONIZATION OF SAINT BUTTERWORTH.

" A Christian of the best edition." — RABELAIS.

CANONIZE him ! — yea, verily, we 'll
    canonize him,
    Tho' Cant is his hobby and meddling
    his bliss,
Tho' sages may pity and wits may despise
    him,
    He 'll ne'er make a bit the worse Saint
    for all this.

Descend, all ye Spirits, that ever yet
    spread
    The dominion of Humbug o'er land
    and o'er sea,
Descend on our Butterworth's biblical
    head,
    Thrice-Great, Bibliopolist, Saint, and
    M. P.

Come, shade of Joanna, come down
    from thy sphere,
    And bring little Shiloh — if 't is n't
    too far —
Such a sight will to Butterworth's bosom
    be dear,
    His conceptions and *thine* being much
    on a par.

Nor blush, Saint Joanna, once more to
    behold
    A world thou hast honored by cheat-
    ing so many;

Thou 'lt find still among us one Person-
    age old,
Who also by tricks and the *Seals*[1]
    makes a penny.

Thou, too, of the Shakers, divine Mother
    Lee![2]
    Thy smiles to beatified Butterworth
    deign;
Two "lights of the Gentiles" are thou,
    Anne, and he,
One hallowing Fleet Street, and *t'other*
    Toad Lane![3]

The heathen, we know, made their Gods
    out of wood,
And Saints may be framed of as handy
    materials; —
Old women and Butterworths make just
    as good
    As any the Pope ever *bookt* as Ethe-
    reals.

Stand forth, Man of Bibles! — not Ma-
    homet's pigeon,
When perched on the Koran, he
    dropt there, they say,
Strong marks of his faith, ever shed o'er
    religion
Such glory as Butterworth sheds every
    day.

Great Galen of souls, with what vigor
    he crams
Down Erin's idolatrous throats, till
    they crack again,
Bolus on bolus, good man! — and then
    damns
    Both their stomachs and souls, if they
    dare cast them back again.

1 A great part of the income of Joanna South-
cott arose from the Seals of the Lord's protection
which she sold to her followers.

2 Mrs. Anne Lee, the "chosen vessel" of
the Shakers, and "Mother of all the children
of regeneration."

3 Toad Lane, in Manchester, where Mother
Lee was born. In her "Address to Young Believers," she says, that "it is a matter of no importance with them from whence the means of
their deliverance come, whether from a stable in
Bethlehem, or from Toad Lane, Manchester."

How well might his shop — as a type
    representing
The creed of himself and his sanctified
    clan —
On its counter exhibit "the Art of Tor-
    menting,"
    Bound neatly, and lettered "Whole
    Duty of Man!"

Canonize him! — by Judas, we *will* can-
    onize him;
For Cant is his hobby and twaddling
    his bliss;
And tho' wise men may pity and wits
    may despise him,
He'll make but the better *shop*-saint
    for all this.

Call quickly together the whole tribe of
    Canters,
    Convoke all the *serious* Tag-rag of the
    nation;
Bring Shakers and Snufflers and Jumpers
    and Ranters
    To witness their Butterworth's Canon-
    ization!

Yea, humbly I 've ventured his merits to
    paint,
    Yea, feebly have tried all his gifts to
    portray,
And they form a sum-total for making a
    Saint,
    That the Devil's own advocate could
    not gainsay.

Jump high, all ye Jumpers, ye Ranters
    all roar,
    While Butterworth's spirit, upraised
    from your eyes,
Like a kite made of foolscap, in glory
    shall soar,
    With a long tail of rubbish behind, to
    the skies!

AN INCANTATION.

SUNG BY THE BUBBLE SPIRIT.

Air. — *Come with me, and we will go*
      Where the rocks of coral grow.

COME with me and we will blow
Lots of bubbles as we go;
Bubbles bright as ever Hope
Drew from fancy — or from soap;

Bright as e'er the South Sea sent
From its frothy element !
Come with me and we will blow
Lots of bubbles as we go.
Mix the lather, Johnny Wilks,
Thou, who rhym'st so well to bilks;[1]
Mix the lather — who can be
Fitter for such tasks than thee,
Great M. P. for *Suds*bury !

Now the frothy charm is ripe,
Puffing Peter,[2] bring thy pipe, —
Thou whom ancient Coventry
Once so dearly loved that she
Knew not which to her was sweeter,
Peeping Tom or Puffing Peter; —
Puff the bubbles high in air,
Puff thy best to keep them there.

Bravo, bravo, Peter More !
Now the rainbow humbugs[3] soar,
Glittering all with golden hues
Such as haunt the dreams of Jews; —
Some reflecting mines that lie
Under Chili's glowing sky,
Some, those virgin pearls that sleep
Cloistered in the southern deep;
Others, as if lent a ray
From the streaming Milky Way,
Glistening o'er with curds and whey
From the cows of Alderney.

Now 's the moment — who shall first
Catch the bubbles ere they burst ?
Run, ye Squires, ye Viscounts, run,
Brogden, Teynham, Palmerston; —
John Wilks junior runs beside ye !
Take the good the knaves provide ye ![4]
See, with upturned eyes and hands,
Where the *Share*man,[5] Brogden,
　　stands,

1 Strong indications of character may be
sometimes traced in the rhymes to names. Marvell thought so when he wrote
　　　　　" Sir Edward Sutton,
The foolish Knight who rhymes to mutton."

2 The Member, during a long period, for
Coventry.

3 An humble imitation of one of our modern
poets, who, in a poem against War, after describing the splendid habiliments of the soldier, thus
apostrophizes him — " thou rainbow ruffian ! "

4 " Lovely Thais sits beside thee :
　　Take the good the Gods provide thee."

5 So called by a sort of Tuscan dulcification
of the *ch*, in the word " Chairman."

Gaping for the froth to fall
Down his gullet — *lye* and all.
See ! —
　　　　But, hark, my time is out —
Now, like some great water-spout,
Scattered by the cannon's thunder,
Burst, ye bubbles, all asunder !

[*Here the stage darkens — a discordant crash
is heard from the orchestra — the broken bubbles
descend in a saponaceous but uncleanly mist over
the heads of the* Dramatis Personæ, *and the scene
drops, leaving the bubble-hunters — all in the
suds.*]

A DREAM OF TURTLE.

BY SIR W. CURTIS.

1826.

'T WAS evening time, in the twilight
　　sweet
I sailed along, when — whom should I
　　meet
But a Turtle journeying o'er the sea,
" On the service of his Majesty."[6]

When spying him first thro' twilight dim,
I didn't know what to make of him;
But said to myself, as slow he plied
His fins and rolled from side to side
Conceitedly o'er the watery path —
" 'T is my Lord of Stowell taking a bath,
" And I hear him now, among the fishes,
" Quoting Vatel and Burgersdicius ! "
But, no — 't was, indeed, a Turtle wide
And plump as ever these eyes descried;
A Turtle juicy as ever yet
Glued up the lips of a Baronet !
And much did it grieve my soul to see
That an animal of such dignity,
Like an absentee abroad should roam,
When he *ought* to stay and be ate at
　　home.

But now " a change came o'er my
　　dream,"
　　Like the magic lantern's shifting
　　slider; —
I lookt and saw by the evening beam
　　On the back of that Turtle sat a rider —

6 We are told that the passport of this grand
diplomatic Turtle (sent by the Secretary for Foreign Affairs to a certain noble envoy) described
him as " on his majesty's service."
　　—— *dapibus supremi*
　　　　grata testudo Jovis.

A goodly man with an eye so merry,
I knew 't was our Foreign Secretary,[1]
Who there at his ease did sit and smile,
Like Waterton on his crocodile;[2]
Cracking such jokes, at every motion,
  As made the Turtle squeak with glee,
And own they gave him a lively notion
  Of what his *forced*-meat balls would be.

So, on the Sec. in his glory went,
Over that briny element,
Waving his hand as he took farewell
With graceful air, and bidding me tell
Inquiring friends that the Turtle and he
Were gone on a foreign embassy —
To soften the heart of a *Diplomat*,
Who is known to dote upon verdant fat,
And to let admiring Europe see,
That *calipash* and *calipee*
Are the English forms of Diplomacy.

THE DONKEY AND HIS PANNIERS.

A FABLE.

—— *"fessus jam sudat asellus,*
"parce illi; vestrum delicium est asinus."
                              VERGIL. *Copa.*

A DONKEY whose talent for burdens was
    wondrous,
  So much that you 'd swear he rejoiced
    in a load,
One day had to jog under panniers so
    ponderous,
  That — down the poor Donkey fell
    smack on the road!

His owners and drivers stood round in
    amaze —
  What! Neddy, the patient, the pros-
    perous Neddy,
So easy to drive thro' the dirtiest ways
  For every description of job-work so
    ready!

One driver (whom Ned might have
    "hailed" as a "brother")[3]
  Had just been proclaiming his Don-
    key's renown

1 Mr. Canning.

2 *Wanderings in South America.* "It was
the first and last time [says Mr. Waterton] I was
ever on a crocodile's back."

3 Alluding to an early poem of Mr. Cole-
ridge's, addressed to an Ass, and beginning, "I
hail thee, brother!"

For vigor, for spirit, for one thing or
    other —
  When, lo! mid his praises the Donkey
    came down!

But how to upraise him? — *one* shouts,
    t' other whistles,
  While Jenky, the Conjuror, wisest of
    all,
Declared that an "over-production of
    thistles[4]
  (Here Ned gave a stare) — was the
    cause of his fall."

Another wise Solomon cries as he passes —
  "There, let him alone and the fit will
    soon cease;
"The beast has been fighting with other
    jack-asses,
  "And this is his mode of '*transition
    to peace.*'"

Some lookt at his hoofs, and with learned
    grimaces
  Pronounced that too long without shoes
    he had gone —
"Let the blacksmith provide him a *sound
    metal basis*
  (The wise-acres said), "and he 's sure
    to jog on."

Meanwhile, the poor Neddy in torture
    and fear
  Lay under his panniers, scarce able
    to groan;
And — what was still dolefuller —lend-
    ing an ear
  To advisers whose ears were a match
    for his own.

At length a plain rustic whose wit went
    so far
  As to see others' folly, roared out,
    as he past —
"Quick — off with the panniers, all dolts
    as ye are,
  "Or your prosperous Neddy will soon
    kick his last!"

October, 1826.

4 A certain country gentleman having said in
the House, "that we must return at last to the
food of our ancestors," somebody asked Mr. T.
"what food the gentleman meant?" — "This-
tles, I suppose," answered Mr. T.

ODE TO THE SUBLIME PORTE.
1826.

GREAT Sultan, how wise are thy state
    compositions!
  And oh! above all I admire that De-
    cree,
In which thou command'st, that all *she*
    politicians
  Shall forthwith be strangled and cast
    in the sea.

'T is my fortune to know a lean Bentha-
    mite spinster —
  A maid who her faith in old Jeremy
    puts,
Who talks with a lisp of "the last new
    West*minster*,"
  And hopes you 're delighted with
    "Mill upon Gluts;"

Who tells you how clever one Mr. Fun-
    blank is,
  How charming his Articles 'gainst the
    Nobility; —
And assures you that even a gentleman's
    rank is,
  In Jeremy's school, of no sort of
    utility.

To see her, ye Gods, a new Number
    perusing —
  ART. 1. — "On the *Needle's* varia-
    tions," by Pl — ce; [1]
ART. 2. — By her favorite Fun-blank [2]
    — "so amusing!
  "Dear man! he makes Poetry quite
    a *Law* case."

ART. 3. — "Upon Fallacies," Jeremy's
    own —
  (Chief Fallacy being his hope to find
    readers); —
ART. 4. — "Upon Honesty," author un-
    known; —
  ART. 5. — (by the young Mr. Mill)
    "Hints to Breeders."

---

[1] A celebrated political tailor.

[2] This pains-taking gentleman has been at the
trouble of counting, with the assistance of Cocker,
the number of metaphors in Moore's "Life of
Sheridan," and has found them to amount, as
nearly as possible, to 2235 — and some *fractions*.

Oh, Sultan, oh, Sultan, tho' oft for the
    bag
  And the bowstring, like thee, I am
    tempted to call —
Tho' drowning 's too good for each
    blue-stocking hag,
  I would bag this *she* Benthamite first
    of them all!

And lest she should ever again lift her
    head
  From the watery bottom, her clack
    to renew —
As a clog, as a sinker, far better than
    lead,
  I would hang round her neck her own
    darling Review.

CORN AND CATHOLICS.

utrum horum
dirius borum? *Incerti Auctoris.*

WHAT! *still* those two infernal questions,
  That with our meals our slumbers
    mix —
That spoil our tempers and digestions —
  Eternal Corn and Catholics!

Gods! were there ever two such bores?
  Nothing else talkt of night or morn —
Nothing *in* doors or *out* of doors,
  But endless Catholics and Corn!

Never was such a brace of pests —
  While Ministers, still worse than
    either,
Skilled but in feathering their nests,
  Plague us with both and settle neither.

So addled in my cranium meet
  Popery and Corn that oft I doubt,
Whether, this year, 't was bonded Wheat,
  Or bonded Papists, they let out.

Here, landlords, *here* polemics nail you,
  Armed with all rubbish they can rake
    up;
Prices and *Texts* at once assail you —
  From Daniel *these*, and *those* from
    Jacob. [3]

And when you sleep, with head still torn
  Between the two, their shapes you mix,

---

[3] Author of the late report on Foreign Corn.

Till sometimes Catholics seem Corn —
Then Corn again seems Catholics.

Now Dantsic wheat before you floats —
Now Jesuits from California —
Now Ceres linkt with Titus *Oats*,
    Comes dancing thro' the "Porta
    Corn*e*a."[1]

Oft too the Corn grows animate,
    And a whole crop of heads appears,
Like Papists, *bearding* Church and
    State —
    Themselves, together *by the ears!*

In short these torments never cease,
    And oft I wish myself transferred off
To some far, lonely land of peace
    Where Corn or Papists ne'er were
        heard of.

Yes, waft me, Parry, to the Pole ;
    For — if my fate is to be chosen
'Twixt bores and icebergs — on my soul,
    I 'd rather, of the two, be frozen !

A CASE OF LIBEL.

"The greater the truth, the worse the libel."

A CERTAIN Sprite, who dwells below,
    ('T were a libel perhaps to mention
    where,)
Came up *incog.* some years ago
    To try for a change the London air.

So well he lookt and drest and talkt,
    And hid his tail and horns so handy,
You 'd hardly have known him as he
    walkt
    From C——e, or any other Dandy.

(His horns, it seems, are made to un-
    screw;
So he has but to take them out of the
    socket,
And — just as some fine husbands do —
    Conveniently clap them into his
    pocket.)

In short, he lookt extremely natty,
    And even contrived — to his own great
        wonder —

1 The Horn Gate, through which the ancients
supposed all true dreams (such as those of the
Popish Plot, etc.) to pass.

By dint of sundry scents from Gattie,
    To keep the sulphurous *hogo* under.

And so my gentleman hoofed about,
    Unknown to all but a chosen few
At White's and Crockford's, where no
    doubt
    He had many *post-obits* falling due.

Alike a gamester and a wit,
    At night he was seen with Crockford's
    crew,
At morn with learned dames would sit —
    So past his time 'twixt *black* and *blue.*

Some wisht to make him an M. P.,
    But, finding Wilks was also one, he
Swore, in a rage, "he 'd be damned,
    if he
    "Would ever sit in one house with
    Johnny."

At length as secrets travel fast,
    And devils, whether he or she,
Are sure to be found out at last,
    The affair got wind most rapidly.

The Press, the impartial Press, that snubs
    Alike a fiend's or an angel's capers —
Miss Paton's soon as Beelzebub's —
    Fired off a squib in the morning
    papers :

"We warn good men to keep aloof
    "From a grim old Dandy seen about
"With a fire-proof wig and a cloven
    hoof
    "Thro' a neat-cut Hoby smoking out."

Now, — the Devil being a gentleman,
    Who piques himself on well-bred deal-
    ings, —
You may guess, when o'er these lines he
    ran,
    How much they hurt and shockt his
    feelings.

Away he posts to a Man of Law,
    And 't would make you laugh could
    you have seen 'em,
As paw shook hand, and hand shook
    paw,
    And 't was "hail, good fellow, well
    met," between 'em.

Straight an indictment was preferred —
And much the Devil enjoyed the jest,
When, asking about the Bench, he heard
That, of all the Judges, his own was
        Best.[1]

In vain Defendant proffered proof
        That Plaintiff's self was the Father of
                Evil —
Brought Hoby forth to swear to the hoof
        And Stultz to speak to the tail of the
                Devil.

The Jury (saints, all snug and rich,
        And readers of virtuous Sunday pa-
                pers)
Found for the Plaintiff — on hearing
        which
        The Devil gave one of his loftiest
                capers.

For oh, 't was nuts to the Father of Lies
        (As this wily fiend is named in the
                Bible)
To find it settled by laws so wise,
        That the greater the truth, the worse
                the libel!

LITERARY ADVERTISEMENT.

Wanted — Authors of all-work to job
        for the season,
        No matter which party, so faithful to
                neither;
Good hacks who, if posed for a rhyme
        or a reason,
        Can manage, like ******, to do with-
                out either.

If in jail, all the better for out-o'-door
        topics;
        Your jail is for Travellers a charming
                retreat;
They can take a day's rule for a trip to
        the Tropics,
        And sail round the world at their ease
                in the Fleet.

For a Dramatist too the most useful of
        schools —
        He can study high life in the King's
                Bench community;

1 A celebrated Judge, so named.

Aristotle could scarce keep him more
        within rules,
        And of *place* he at least must adhere
                to the *unity.*

Any lady or gentleman, come to an age
        To have good "Reminiscences"
                (three-score or higher),
Will meet with encouragement — so
        much, *per* page,
        And the spelling and grammar both
                found by the buyer.

No matter with *what* their remembrance
        is stockt,
        So they'll only remember the *quan-
                tum* desired; —
Enough to fill handsomely Two Vol-
        umes, *oct.,*
        Price twenty-four shillings, is all
                that 's required.

They may treat us, like Kelly, with old
        jeu-d'esprits,
        Like Dibdin, may tell of each farcical
                frolic;
Or kindly inform us, like Madame Genlis,[2]
        That gingerbread-cakes always give
                them the colic.

Wanted also a new stock of Pamphlets
        on Corn
        By "Farmers" and "Landholders"
                — (worthies whose lands
Enclosed all in bow-pots, their attics
        adorn,
        Or whose share of the soil may be
                seen on their hands).

No-Popery Sermons, in ever so dull a vein,
        Sure of a market; — should they too
                who pen 'em
Be renegade Papists, like Murtagh O'Sul-
        livan,[3]
        Something *extra* allowed for the addi-
                tional venom.

2 This lady also favors us, in her Memoirs,
with the address of those apothecaries, who have,
from time to time, given her pills that agreed
with her; always desiring that the pills should
be ordered "*comme pour elle.*"

3 A gentleman, who distinguished himself by
his evidence before the Irish Committees.

Funds, Physic, Corn, Poetry, Boxing,
Romance,
   All excellent subjects for turning a
   penny; —
To write upon *all* is an author's sole
chance
   For attaining, at last, the least knowl-
   edge of *any*.

Nine times out of ten, if his *title* is good,
   The material *within* of small consequence is; —
Let him only write fine, and, if not
understood,
   Why — that 's the concern of the
   reader, not his.

Nota Bene — an Essay, now printing, to
show,
   That Horace (as clearly as words
   could express it)
Was for taxing the Fund-holders, ages
ago,
   When he wrote thus — " *Quodcunque
in Fund is, assess it.*" [1]

THE IRISH SLAVE. [2]
1827.

I HEARD as I lay, a wailing sound,
   " He is dead — he is dead," the ru-
   mor flew;
And I raised my chain and turned me
round,
   And askt, thro' the dungeon-window,
   " Who ? "

I saw my livid tormentors pass;
   Their grief 't was bliss to hear and see !
For never came joy to them alas !
   That did n't bring deadly bane to me.

Eager I lookt thro' the mist of night,
   And askt, " What foe of my race hath
   died?
" Is it he — that Doubter of law and
right,
   " Whom nothing but wrong could
   e'er decide —

" Who, long as he sees but wealth to win,
   " Hath never yet felt a qualm or doubt
" What suitors for justice he 'd keep in,
   " Or what suitors for freedom he' d
   shut out —

" Who, a clog for ever on Truth's advance,
   " Hangs round her (like the Old Man
   of the Sea
" Round Sinbad's neck [3]), nor leaves a
chance
   " Of shaking him off — is 't he? is 't
   he? "

Ghastly my grim tormentors smiled,
   And thrusting me back to my den of
   woe,
With a laughter even more fierce and
wild
   Than their funeral howling, answered
   " No."

But the cry still pierced my prison-gate,
   And again I askt, " What scourge is
   gone?
" Is it he — that Chief, so coldly great,
   " Whom Fame unwillingly shines
   upon —

" Whose name is one of the ill-omened
words
   " They link with hate on his native
   plains;
" And why? — they lent him hearts and
swords,
   " And he in return gave scoffs and
   chains !

" Is it he? is it he? " I loud inquired,
   When, hark ! — there sounded a Royal
   knell;
And I knew what spirit had just expired,
   And slave as I was my triumph fell.

He had pledged a hate unto me and mine,
   He had left to the future nor hope nor
   choice,
But sealed that hate with a Name Divine,
   And he now was dead and — I *could n't*
   rejoice !

1 According to the common reading, " *quodcunque infundis, acescit.*"
2 Written on the death of the Duke of York.

3 " You fell, said they, into the hands of the
Old Man of the Sea, and are the first who ever
escaped strangling by his malicious tricks." —
Story of Sinbad.

He had fanned afresh the burning brands
  Of a bigotry waxing cold and dim;
He had armed anew my torturers' hands,
  And *them* did I curse — but sighed for
    him.

For, *his* was the error of head not heart;
  And — oh! how beyond the ambushed
    foe,
Who to enmity adds the traitor's part,
  And carries a smile with a curse below!

If ever a heart made bright amends
  For the fatal fault of an erring head —
Go, learn *his* fame from the lips of
    friends,
  In the orphan's tear be his glory read.

A Prince without pride, a man without
    guile,
  To the last unchanging, warm, sincere,
For Worth he had ever a hand and
    smile,
  And for Misery ever his purse and
    tear.

Touched to the heart by that solemn
    toll,
  I calmly sunk in my chains again;
While, still as I said "Heaven rest his
    soul!"
  My mates of the dungeon sighed
    "Amen!"

January, 1827.

ODE TO FERDINAND.

1827.

Quit the sword, thou King of men,
Grasp the needle once again;
Making petticoats is far
Safer sport than making war;
Trimming is a better thing,
Than the *being* trimmed, oh King!
Grasp the needle bright with which
Thou didst for the Virgin stitch
Garment, such as ne'er before
Monarch stitched or Virgin wore.
Not for her, oh semster nimble!
Do I now invoke thy thimble;
Not for her thy wanted aid is,
But for certain grave old ladies,
Who now sit in England's cabinet,
Waiting to be clothed in tabinet,
Or whatever choice *étoffe* is
Fit for Dowagers in office.
First, thy care, oh King, devote
To Dame Eldon's petticoat.
Make it of that silk whose dye
Shifts for ever to the eye,
Just as if it hardly knew
Whether to be pink or blue.
Or — material fitter yet —
If thou couldst a remnant get
Of that stuff with which, of old,
Sage Penelope, we 're told,
Still by doing and undoing,
Kept her *suitors* always wooing —
That 's the stuff which I pronounce, is
Fittest for Dame Eldon's flounces.

After this, we 'll try thy hand,
Mantua-making Ferdinand,
For old Goody Westmoreland;
One who loves, like Mother Cole,
Church and State with all her soul;
And has past her life in frolics
Worthy of your Apostolics.
Choose, in dressing this old flirt,
Something that won't show the dirt,
As, from habit, every minute
Goody Westmoreland is in it.

This is all I now shall ask,
Hie thee, monarch, to thy task;
Finish Eldon's frills and borders,
Then return for further orders.
Oh what progress for our sake,
Kings in millinery make!
Ribands, garters, and such things,
Are supplied by *other* Kings —
Ferdinand his rank denotes
By providing petticoats.

HAT *VERSUS* WIG.

1827.

"At the interment of the Duke of York, Lord
Eldon, in order to guard against the effects of
the damp, stood upon his hat during the whole
of the ceremony."

—— *metus omnes et inexorabile fatum
subjecit pedibus, strepitumque Acherontis avari.*

'Twixt Eldon's Hat and Eldon's Wig
  There lately rose an altercation, —
Each with its own importance big,
  Disputing *which* most serves the na-
    tion.

Quoth Wig, with consequential. air,
   " Pooh ! pooh ! you surely can't de-
     sign,
" My worthy beaver, to compare
   " Your station in the state with mine.

" Who meets the learned legal crew ?
   " Who fronts the lordly Senate's pride ?
" The Wig, the Wig, my friend — while
     you
   " Hang dangling on some peg outside.

" Oh ! 't is the Wig, that rules, like
     Love,
   " Senate and Court, with like *éclat* —
" And wards below and lords above,
   " For Law is Wig and Wig is Law ! [1]

" Who tried the long, *Long* WELLESLEY
     suit,
   " Which tried one's patience, in re-
     turn ?
" Not thou, oh Hat ! — tho' *couldst*
     thou do 't,
   " Of other *brims* [2] than thine thou 'dst
     learn.

" 'Twas mine our master's toil to share;
   " When, like ' Truepenny,' in the
     play, [3]
" He, every minute, cried out ' Swear,'
   " And merrily to swear went they ; [4] —

" When, loath poor WELLESLEY to con-
     demn, he
   " With nice discrimination weighed,
" Whether 't was only ' Hell and
     Jemmy,'
   " Or ' Hell and Tommy ' that he
     played.

" No, no, my worthy beaver, no —
   " Tho' cheapened at the cheapest
     hatter's,

1 " Love rules the court, the camp, the grove,
    And men below and gods above,
    For Love is Heaven, and Heaven is
    Love."
                    SCOTT.
2 " *Brim* — a naughty woman." — GROSE.
3 " *Ghost* [beneath]. — Swear !
   " *Hamlet.* — Ha, ha ! say'st thou so ? Art
thou there, Truepenny ? Come on."
4 His Lordship's demand for fresh affidavits
was incessant.

" And smart enough as beavers go
   " Thou ne'er wert made for public
     matters."

Here Wig concluded his oration,
   Looking, as wigs do, wondrous wise;
While thus, full cockt for declamation,
   The veteran Hat enraged replies : —

" Ha ! dost thou then so soon forget
   " What thou, what England owes to
     me ?
" Ungrateful Wig ! — when will a debt,
   " So deep, so vast, be owed to thee ?

" Think of that night, that fearful night,
   " When, thro' the steaming vault be-
     low,
" Our master dared, in gout's despite,
   " To venture his podagric toe !

" Who was it then, thou boaster, say,
   " When thou hadst to thy box sneaked
     off,
" Beneath his feet protecting lay,
   " And saved him from a mortal
     cough ?

" Think, if Catarrh had quenched that
     sun,
   " How blank this world had been to
     thee !
" Without that head to shine upon,
   " Oh Wig, where would thy glory be ?

" You, too, ye Britons, — had this hope
   " Of Church and state been ravisht
     from ye,
" Oh think, how Canning and the Pope
   " Would then have played up ' Hell
     and Tommy ' !

" At sea, there 's but a plank, they say,
   " 'Twixt seamen and annihilation;
" A Hat, that awful moment, lay
   " 'Twixt England and Emancipation !

" Oh ! ! ! — "

At this " Oh ! ! ! " *The Times* Reporter
   Was taken poorly, and retired;
Which made him cut Hat's rhetoric
     shorter,
   Than justice to the case required.

On his return, he found these shocks
  Of eloquence all ended quite;
And Wig lay snoring in his box,
  And Hat was — hung up for the night.

THE PERIWINKLES AND THE LOCUSTS.

A SALMAGUNDIAN HYMN.

"To Panurge was assigned the Lairdship of Salmagundi, which was yearly worth 6,789,106,-789 ryals, besides the revenue of the *Locusts* and *Periwinkles*, amounting one year with another to the value of 2,435,768," etc. — RABELAIS.

"HURRA! hurra!" I heard them say,
And they cheered and shouted all the
    way,
As the Laird of Salmagundi went,
To open in state his Parliament.

The Salmagundians once were rich,
  Or *thought* they were — no matter
    which —
For, every year, the Revenue [1]
  From their Periwinkles larger grew;
And their rulers, skilled in all the trick
  And legerdemain of arithmetic,
Knew how to place 1, 2, 3, 4,
  5, 6, 7, 8, and 9 and 10,
Such various ways, behind, before,
That they made a unit seem a score,
  And proved themselves most wealthy
    men!
So, on they went, a prosperous crew,
  The people wise, the rulers clever —
And God help those, like me and you,
  Who dared to doubt (as some now do)
That the Periwinkle Revenue
  Would thus go flourishing on for ever.

"Hurra! hurra!" I heard them say,
And they cheered and shouted all the
    way,
As the Great Panurge in glory went
To open his own dear Parliament.

But folks at length began to doubt
What all this conjuring was about;
For, every day, more deep in debt
They saw their wealthy rulers get: —
"Let 's look (said they) the items thro'

[1] Accented as in Swift's line —
  "Not so a nation's revenues are paid."

"And see if what we 're told be true
"Of our Periwinkle Revenue."

But, lord! they found there was n't a
    tittle
Of truth in aught they heard before;
For they gained by Periwinkles little
  And lost by Locusts ten times more!
These Locusts are a lordly breed
Some Salmagundians love to feed.
Of all the beasts that ever were born,
Your Locust most delights in *corn ;*
And tho' his body be but small,
To fatten him takes the devil and all!
"Oh fie! oh fie!" was now the cry,
As they saw the gaudy show go by,
And the Laird of Salmagundi went
To open his Locust Parliament!

NEW CREATION OF PEERS.

BATCH THE FIRST.

"His 'prentice han'
  He tried on man,
And then he made the lasses."
                                1827.

"AND now," quoth the Minister, (eased
    of his panics,
  And ripe for each pastime the summer
    affords,)
"Having had our full swing at destroy-
    ing mechanics,
  "By way of *set-off*, let us make a few
    Lords.

"'T is pleasant — while nothing but
    mercantile fractures,
  "Some simple, some *compound*, is
    dinned in our ears —
"To think that, tho' robbed of all coarse
    manufactures,
  "We still have our fine manufacture
    of Peers; —

"Those *Gobelin* productions which
    Kings take a pride
  "In engrossing the whole fabrication
    and trade of;
"Choice tapestry things very grand on
    one side,
  "But showing, on t' other, what rags
    they are made of."

The plan being fixt, raw material was
  sought, —
  No matter how middling, if Tory the
    creed be;
And first, to begin with, Squire W——,
  't was thought,
  For a Lord was as raw a material as
    need be.

Next came with his *penchant* for painting
  and pelf
  The tasteful Sir Charles,[1] so renowned
    tar and near
For purchasing pictures and selling him-
  self —
  And *both* (as the public well knows)
    very dear.

Beside him Sir John comes, with equal
  éclat, in; —
  Stand forth, chosen pair, while for
    titles we measure ye;
Both connoisseur baronets, both fond of
  drawing,
  Sir John, after nature, Sir Charles, on
    the Treasury.

But, bless us ! — behold a new candidate
  come —
  In his hand he upholds a prescription,
    new written;
He poiseth a pill-box 'twixt finger and
  thumb,
  And he asketh a seat 'mong the Peers
    of Great Britain !-!

" Forbid it," cried Jenky, "ye Vis-
  counts, ye Earls ! —
  " Oh Rank, how thy glories would
    fall disenchanted,
" If coronets glistened with pills 'stead
  of pearls,
  " And the strawberry-leaves were by
    rhubarb supplanted !

" No — ask it not, ask it not, dear Doc-
  tor Holford —
  " If naught but a Peerage can gladden
    thy life,
" And young Master Holford as yet is
  too small for 't,
  " Sweet Doctor, we 'll make a *she*
    Peer of thy wife.

1 Created Lord Farnborough.

" Next to bearing a coronet on our *own*
  brows
  " Is to bask in its light from the brows
    of another;
" And grandeur o'er thee shall reflect
  from thy spouse,
  " As o'er Vesey Fitzgerald 't will
    shine thro' his mother." [2]

Thus ended the *First* Batch — and
  Jenky, much tired
  (It being no joke to make Lords by
    the heap),
Took a large dram of ether — the same
  that inspired
  His speech 'gainst the Papists — and
    prosed off to sleep.

SPEECH ON THE UMBRELLA[3] QUESTION.

BY LORD ELDON.

1827.
" *vos* inumbrelles *video.*"[4] — *Ex Juvenil.*
GEORGII CANNINGII.

MY Lords, I 'm accused of a trick that
  God knows is
  The last into which at my age I could
    fall —
Of leading this grave House of Peers by
  their noses,
  Wherever I choose, princes, bishops
    and all.

My Lords, on the question before us at
  present,
  No doubt I shall hear, " 'T is that
    cursed old fellow,
" That bugbear of all that is liberal and
  pleasant,
  " Who won't let the Lords give the
    man his umbrella ! "

2 Among the persons mentioned as likely to
be raised to the Peerage are the mother of Mr.
Vesey Fitzgerald, etc.

3 A case which interested the public very much
at this period. A gentleman, of the name of
Bell, having left his umbrella behind him in the
House of Lords, the doorkeepers (standing, no
doubt, on the privileges of that noble body) refused to restore it to him; and the above speech,
which may be considered as a *pendant* to that of
the Learned Earl on the Catholic Question,
arose out of the transaction.

4 From Mr. Canning's translation of Jekyl's —
  " I say, my good fellows,
    As you 've no umbrellas."

God forbid that your Lordships should
  knuckle to me;
I am ancient — but were I as old as
  King Priam,
Not much, I confess, to your credit
  't would be,
To mind such a twaddling old Trojan
  as I am.

I own, of our Protestant laws I am jeal-
  ous,
  And long as God spares me will al-
    ways mount,
That *once* having taken men's rights, or
  umbrellas,
  We ne'er should consent to restore
    them again.

What security have you, ye Bishops and
  Peers,
  If thus you give back Mr. Bell's *para-
    pluie,*
That he may n't with its stick, come
  about all your ears,
  And then — *where* would your Prot-
    estant periwigs be?

No! heaven be my judge, were I dying
  to-day,
  Ere I dropt in the grave, like a med-
    lar that 's mellow,
" For God's sake " — at that awful mo-
  ment I 'd say —
  " For God's sake, *don't* give Mr. Bell
    his umbrella."

[" This address," says a ministerial journal,
" delivered with amazing emphasis and earnest-
ness, occasioned an extraordinary sensation in
the House. Nothing since the memorable address of the Duke of York has produced so remarkable an impression."]

A PASTORAL BALLAD.

BY JOHN BULL.

Dublin, March 12, 1827. — Friday, after the
arrival of the packet bringing the account of the
defeat of the Catholic Question, in the House of
Commons, orders were sent to the Pigeon House
to forward 5,000,000 rounds of musket-ball cart-
ridge to the different garrisons round the country.
— *Freeman's Journal.*

I HAVE found out a gift for my Erin,
  A gift that will surely content her; —
Sweet pledge of a love so endearing!
  Five millions of bullets I 've sent her.

She askt me for Freedom and Right,
  But ill she her wants understood; —
Ball cartridges, morning and night,
  Is a dose that will do her more good.

There is hardly a day of our lives
  But we read, in some amiable trials,
How husbands make love to their wives
  Thro' the medium of hemp and of
    vials.

One thinks, with his mistress or mate
  A good halter is sure to agree —
That love-knot which, early and late,
  I have tried, my dear Erin, on thee.

While *another,* whom Hymen has blest
  With a wife that is not over placid,
Consigns the dear charmer to rest,
  With a dose of the best Prussic acid.

Thus, Erin! my love do I show —
  Thus quiet thee, mate of my bed!
And, as poison and hemp are too slow,
  Do thy business with bullets instead.

Should thy faith in my medicine be
  shaken,
  Ask Roden, that mildest of saints;
He 'll tell thee, lead, inwardly taken,
  Alone can remove thy complaints; —

That, blest as thou art in thy lot,
  Nothing 's wanted to make it more
    pleasant
But being hanged, tortured and shot,
  Much oftener than thou art at present.

Even Wellington's self hath averred
  Thou art yet but half sabred and hung,
And I loved him the more when I
  heard
  Such tenderness fall from his tongue.

So take the five millions of pills,
  Dear partner, I herewith inclose;
'T is the cure that all quacks for thy ills,
  From Cromwell to Eldon, propose.

And you, ye brave bullets that go,
  How I wish that, before you set out,
The *Devil* of the Freischütz could know
  The good work you are going about.

For he 'd charm ye, in spite of your lead,
  Into such supernatural wit,
That you 'd all of you know, as you
    sped,
  Where a bullet of sense *ought* to hit.

A LATE SCENE AT SWANAGE.[1]

regni EX-*sul ademptis.* — VERG.

1827.

To Swanage — that neat little town in
    whose bay
  Fair Thetis shows off in her best silver
    slippers —
Lord Bags[2] took his annual trip t' other
    day,
  To taste the sea breezes and chat with
    the dippers.

There — learned as he is in conundrums
    and laws —
  Quoth he to his dame (whom he oft
    plays the wag on),
"Why are chancery suitors like bath-
    ers?" — "Because
  Their *suits* are *put off*, till they
    have n't a rag on."

Thus on he went chatting — but, lo!
    while he chats,
  With a face full of wonder around
    him he looks;
For he misses his parsons, his dear
    shovel hats,
  Who used to flock round him at Swan-
    age like rooks.

"How is this, Lady Bags? — to this
    region aquatic
  "Last year they came swarming to
    make me their bow,
"As thick as Burke's cloud o'er the
    vales of Carnatic,
  "Deans, Rectors, D.D.'s — where the
    devil are they now?"

"My dearest Lord Bags!" saith his
    dame, "*can* you doubt?
  "I am loath to remind you of things
    so unpleasant;

1 A small bathing-place on the coast of Dor-
setshire, long a favorite summer resort of the ex-
nobleman in question and, *till this season*, much
frequented also by gentlemen of the church.

2 The Lord Chancellor Eldon.

"But *don't* you perceive, dear, the
    Church have found out
  "That you 're one of the people
    called *Ex's*, at present?"

"Ah, true — you have hit it — I *am*,
    indeed, one
  "Of those ill-fated *Ex's* (his Lord-
    ship replies),
"And with tears, I confess — God for-
    give me the pun!—
  "We X's have proved ourselves *not*
    to be Y's."

WO! WO![2]

Wo, wo unto him who would check or
    disturb it —
  That beautiful Light which is now on
    its way;
Which, beaming, at first, o'er the bogs of
    Belturbet,
  Now brightens sweet Ballinafad with
    its ray!

Oh Farnham, Saint Farnham, how much
    do we owe thee!
  How formed to all tastes are thy
    various employs.
The old, as a catcher of Catholics, know
    thee;
  The young, as an amateur scourger of
    boys.

Wo, wo to the man who such doings
    would smother!—
  On, Luther of Cavan! On, Saint of
    Kilgroggy!
With whip in one hand and with Bible
    in t 'other,
  Like Mungo's tormentor, both "preach-
    ee and floggee."

Come, Saints from all quarters, and mar-
    shal his way;
  Come, Lorton, who, scorning profane
    erudition,

2 Suggested by a speech of the Bishop of
Chester on the subject of the New Reformation
in Ireland, in which his Lordship denounced
"Wo! Wo! Wo!" pretty abundantly on all
those who dared to interfere with its progress.

Popt Shakespeare, they say, in the river
    one day,
Tho' 't was only old Bowdler's *Velluti*
    edition.

Come, Roden, who doubtest — so mild
    are thy views —
Whether Bibles or bullets are best for
    the nation;
Who leav'st to poor Paddy no medium to
    choose
'Twixt good *old* Rebellion and *new*
    Reformation.

What more from her Saints can Hiber-
    nia require?
St. Bridget of yore like a dutiful
    daughter
Supplied her, 't is said, with perpetual
    fire,[1]
And Saints keep her *now* in eternal
    hot water.

Wo, wo to the man who would check
    their career,
    Or stop the Millennium that 's sure to
    await us,
When blest with an orthodox crop every
    year,
    We shall learn to raise Protestants fast
    as potatoes.

In kidnapping Papists, our rulers, we
    know,
    Had been trying their talent for many
    a day;
Till Farnham, when all had been tried,
    came to show,
    Like the German flea-catcher, " anoder
    goot way."

And nothing 's more simple than Farn-
    ham's receipt;—
    " Catch your Catholic, first — soak him
    well in *poteen*,[2]
" Add *salary* sauce,[3] and the thing is
    complete.
    " You may serve up your Protestant
    smoking and clean."

1 The inextinguishable fire of St. Bridget, at
Kildare.

2 Whiskey.

3 " We understand that several applications
have lately been made to the Protestant clergy-

" Wo, wo to the wag, who would laugh
    at such cookery ! "
Thus, from his perch, did I hear a
    black crow[4]
Caw angrily out, while the rest of the
    rookery
    Opened their bills and re-echoed
    " Wo! wo ! "

TOUT POUR LA TRIPE.

" If in China or among the natives of India,
we claimed civil advantages which were connected with religious usages, little as we might
value those forms in our hearts, we should think
common decency required us to abstain from
treating them with offensive contumely; and,
though unable to consider them sacred, we
would not sneer at the name of *Fot*, or laugh
at the imputed divinity of *Visthnou*." — *Courier, Tuesday, Jan.* 16.

1827.

Come take my advice, never trouble your
    cranium,
    When " civil advantages " are to be
    gained,
What god or what goddess may help to
    obtain you 'em,
    Hindoo or Chinese, so they 're only ob-
    tained.

In this world (let me hint in your organ
    auricular)
    All the good things to good hypocrites
    fall;
And he who in swallowing creeds is par-
    ticular,
    Soon will have nothing to swallow at all.

Oh place me where *Fo* (or, as some call
    him, *Fot*)
    Is the god from whom " civil advan-
    tages " flow,
And you 'll find, if there 's any thing
    snug to be got,
    I shall soon be on excellent terms with
    old *Fo*.

Or were I where *Vishnu*, that four-
    handed god,
    Is the quadruple giver of pensions and
    places,

men of this town by fellows, inquiring ' What
are they giving a head for converts?' " — *Wex-
ford Post.*

4 Of the rook species — *Corvus frugilegus*,
i.e. a great consumer of corn.

I own I should feel it unchristian and odd
    Not to find myself also in *Vishnu's*
        good graces.

For among all the gods that humanely
        attend
    To our wants in this planet, the gods
        to *my* wishes
Are those that, like *Vishnu* and others,
        descend
    In the form so attractive, of loaves and
        of fishes! [1]

So take my advice — for if even the devil
    Should tempt men again as an idol to
        try him,
'T were best for us Tories even then to
        be civil,
    As nobody doubts we should get some-
        thing by him.

ENIGMA.

monstrum nulla virtute redemptum.

COME, riddle-me-ree, come, riddle-me-
        ree,
    And tell me what my name may be.
I am nearly one hundred and thirty years
        old,
    And therefore no chicken, as you may
        suppose; —
Tho' a dwarf in my youth (as my nurses
        have told),
    I have, every year since, been out-
        growing my clothes;
Till at last such a corpulent giant I stand,
    That if folks were to furnish me now
        with a suit,
It would take every morsel of *scrip* in
    the land
    But to measure my bulk from the head
        to the foot.
Hence they who maintain me, grown sick
        of my stature,
    To cover me nothing but *rags* will
        supply;
And the doctors declare that in due
        course of nature
    About the year 30 in rags I shall die.
Meanwhile, I stalk hungry and bloated
        around,
    An object of *interest* most painful to all;

---

[1] Vishnu was (as Sir W. Jones calls him) "a
pisciform god," — his first Avatar being in the
shape of a fish.

In the warehouse, the cottage, the palace
    I 'm found,
    Holding citizen, peasant, and king in
        my thrall.
    Then riddle-me-ree, oh riddle-me-
        ree,
    Come tell me what my name may
        be.

When the lord of the counting-house
        bends o'er his book,
    Bright pictures of profit delighting to
        draw,
O'er his shoulders with large cipher eye-
        balls I look,
    And down drops the pen from his
        paralyzed paw!
When the Premier lies dreaming of dear
        Waterloo,
    And expects thro' *another* to caper and
        prank it,
You 'd laugh did you see, when I bellow
        out "Boo!"
    How he hides his brave Waterloo head
        in the blanket.
When mighty Belshazzar brims high in
        the hall
    His cup, full of gout, to the Gaul's
        overthrow,
Lo, "*Eight Hundred Millions*" I write
        on the wall,
    And the cup falls to earth and — the
        gout to his toe!
But the joy of my heart is when largely
        I cram
    My maw with the fruits of the Squire-
        archy's acres,
And knowing who made me the thing
        that I am,
    Like the monster of Frankenstein,
        worry my makers.
Then riddle-me-ree, come, riddle-
        me-ree,
    And tell, if thou know'st, who *I*
        may be.

DOG-DAY REFLECTIONS.

BY A DANDY KEPT IN TOWN.

"*vox clamantis in deserto.*"

1827.

SAID Malthus one day to a clown
    Lying stretched on the beach in the
        sun, —

" What 's the number of souls in this
　　town? " " —
" The number ! Lord bless you, there 's
　　none.

" We have nothing but *dabs* in this place,
　" Of *them* a great plenty there are; —
" But the *soles*, please your reverence and
　　grace,
　" Are all t' other side of the bar."

And so 't is in London just now,
　　Not a soul to be seen up or down; —
Of *dabs* a great glut, I allow,
　　But your *soles*, every one, out of town.

East or west nothing wondrous or new,
　　No courtship or scandal worth know-
　　　ing;
Mrs. B——, and a Mermaid [1] or two,
　　Are the only loose fish that are going.

Ah, where is that dear house of Peers
　　That some weeks ago kept us merry?
Where, Eldon, art thou with thy tears?
　　And thou with thy sense, Londonderry?

Wise Marquis, how much the Lord
　　Mayor,
　　In the dog-days, with *thee* must be
　　　puzzled ! —
It being his task to take care
　　That such animals shan't go unmuz-
　　　zled.

Thou too whose political toils
　　Are so worthy a captain of horse —
Whose amendments [2] (like honest Sir
　　Boyle's)
　　Are " *amendments*, that make matters
　　　worse ; " [3]

Great Chieftain, who takest such pains
　　To prove — what is granted, *nem.
　　con.* —
With how moderate a portion of brains
　　Some heroes contrive to get on.

And thou too my Redesdale, ah ! where
　　Is the peer with a star at his button,
Whose *quarters* could ever compare
　　With Redesdale's five quarters of
　　　mutton? [4]

Why, why have ye taken your flight,
　　Ye diverting and dignified crew?
How ill do three farces a night,
　　At the Haymarket, pay us for you !

For what is Bombastes to thee,
　　My Ellenbro', when thou look'st big?
Or where 's the burletta can be
　　Like Lauderdale's wit and his wig?

I doubt if even Griffinhoof [5] could
　　(Tho' Griffin 's a comical lad)
Invent any joke half so good
　　As that precious one, " This is too
　　　bad ! "

Then come again, come again, Spring !
　　Oh haste thee, with Fun in thy train;
And — of all things the funniest — bring
　　These exalted Grimaldis again !

THE " LIVING DOG " AND " THE DEAD LION."

1828.

NEXT week will be publisht (as " Lives "
　　are the rage)
　　The whole Reminiscences, wondrous
　　　and strange,
Of a small puppy-dog that lived once in
　　the cage
　　Of the late noble Lion at Exeter
　　　'Change.

Tho' the dog is a dog of the kind they
　　call " sad,"
　　'T is a puppy that much to good breed-
　　　ing pretends;
And few dogs have such opportunities
　　had
　　Of knowing how Lions behave —
　　　among friends;

1 One of the shows of London.

2 More particularly his Grace's celebrated
amendment to the Corn Bill; for which, and the
circumstances connected with it, see Annual
Register for A.D. 1827.

3 From a speech of Sir Boyle Roche's, in the
Irish House of Commons

4 The learning his Lordship displayed on the
subject of the butcher's " fifth quarter " of mutton will not speedily be forgotten.

5 The *nom de guerre* under which Colman has
written some of his best farces.

How that animal eats, how he snores,
how he drinks,
　Is all noted down by this Boswell so
　small;
And 't is plain from each sentence, the
puppy-dog thinks
　That the Lion was no such great
　things after all.

Tho' he roared pretty well — this the
puppy allows —
　It was all, he says, borrowed — all
　second-hand roar;
And he vastly prefers his own little bow-
wows
　To the loftiest war-note the Lion
　could pour.

'T is indeed as good fun as a *Cynic*
could ask,
　To see how this cockney-bred setter of
　rabbits
Takes gravely the Lord of the Forest to
task,
　And judges of lions by puppy-dog
　habits.

Nay, fed as he was (and this makes it a
dark case)
　With sops every day from the Lion's
　own pan,
He lifts up his leg at the noble beast's
carcass,
　And — does all a dog so diminutive can.

However, the book 's a good book, being rich in
　Examples and warnings to lions high-
　bred,
How they suffer small mongrelly curs in
their kitchen,
　Who 'll feed on them living and foul
　them when dead.　T. PIDCOCK.
Exeter 'Change.

ODE TO DON MIGUEL.

Et tu, *Brute !*

1828.[1]

WHAT! Miguel, *not* patriotic? oh, fy!
　After so much good teaching 't is quite
　a *take-in*, Sir; —

First schooled as you were under Metternich's eye,
　And then (as young misses say)
　"finisht" at Windsor! [2]

I ne'er in my life knew a case that was
harder; —
　Such feasts as you had when you
　made us a call!
Three courses each day from his Majesty's larder, —
　And now to turn absolute Don after
　all! !

Some authors, like Bayes, to the style
and the matter
　Of each thing they *write* suit the way
　that they *dine*,
Roast sirloin for Epic, broiled devils for
Satire,
　And hotchpotch and *trifle* for rhymes
　such as mine.

That Rulers should feed the same way,
I 've no doubt; —
　Great Despots on *bouilli* served up *à
　la Russe*,[3]
Your small German Princes on frogs and
sour crout,
　And your Viceroy of Hanover always
　on *goose*.

Some Dons too have fancied (tho' this
may be fable)
　A dish rather dear, if in cooking they
　blunder it; —
Not content with the common *hot* meat
on a table,
　They 're partial (eh, Mig?) to a dish
　of *cold under* it! [4]

1 At the commencement of this year, the designs of Don Miguel and his partisans against
the constitution established by his brother had
begun more openly to declare themselves.

2 Don Miguel had paid a visit to the English
court at the close of the year 1827.

3 Dressed with a pint of the strongest spirits
— a favorite dish of the Great Frederick of Prussia, and which he persevered in eating even on
his death-bed, much to the horror of his physician Zimmerman.

4 This quiet case of murder, with all its particulars — the hiding the body under the dinner-
table, etc. — is, no doubt, well known to the
reader.

No wonder a Don of such appetites found
   Even Windsor's collations plebeianly
     plain;
Where the dishes most *high* that my Lady
   sends round
   Are her *Maintenon* cutlets and soup
     à la Reine.

Alas! that a youth with such charming
   beginnings,
   Should sink all at once to so sad a con-
     clusion,
And what is still worse, throw the losings
   and winnings
   Of worthies on 'Change into so much
     confusion!

The Bulls, in hysterics — the Bears just
   as bad —
   The few men who *have*, and the many
     who 've *not* tick,
All shockt to find out that that promising
   lad,
   Prince Metternich's pupil, is — *not* pa-
     triotic!

THOUGHTS ON THE PRESENT GOVERNMENT OF IRELAND.

1828.

OFT have I seen, in gay, equestrian pride,
Some well-rouged youth round Astley's
   Circus ride
Two stately steeds—standing, with grace-
   ful straddle,
Like him of Rhodes, with foot on either
   saddle,
While to soft tunes — some jigs and some
   andantes —
He steers around his light-paced Rosi-
   nantes.

So rides along, with canter smooth and
   pleasant,
That horseman bold, Lord Anglesea, at
   present; —
Papist and *Protestant* the coursers twain,
That lend their necks to his impartial
   rein,
And round the ring — each honored, as
   they go,
With equal pressure from his gracious
   toe —

To the old medley tune, half "Patrick's
   Day"
And half "Boyne Water," take their
   cantering way,
While Peel, the showman in the middle,
   cracks
His long-lasht whip to cheer the doubt-
   ful hacks.
Ah, ticklish trial of equestrian art!
How blest, if neither steed would bolt
   or start; —
If *Protestant's* old restive tricks were
   gone,
And *Papist's* winkers could be still kept
   on!
But no, false hopes — not even the great
   Ducrow
'Twixt two such steeds could 'scape an
   overthrow:
If *solar* hacks played Phaëton a trick,
What hope, alas, from hackneys *lunatic?*

If once my Lord his graceful balance
   loses,
Or fails to keep each foot where each
   horse chooses;
If Peel but gives one *extra* touch of whip
To *Papist's* tail or *Protestant's* ear-tip —
That instant ends their glorious horse-
   manship!
Off bolt the severed steeds, for mischief
   free,
And down between them plumps Lord
   Anglesea!

THE LIMBO OF LOST REPU-TATIONS.

A DREAM.

"Cio che si perde qui, là si raguna."
                    ARIOSTO.

"—— a valley, where he sees
Things that on earth were lost."   MILTON.

1828.

KNOWEST thou not him [1] the poet sings,
   Who flew to the moon's serene do-
     main,
And saw that valley where all the things,
   That vanish on earth are found again —
The hopes of youth, the resolves of age,
The vow of the lover, the dream of the
   sage,

       1 Astolpho.

The golden visions of mining cits,
  The promises great men strew about
    them;
And, packt in compass small, the wits
  Of monarchs who rule as well without
    them! —
Like him, but diving with wing profound,
I have been to a Limbo underground,
Where characters lost on earth, (and
    cried,
In vain, like Harris's, far and wide,)
In heaps, like yesterday's nuts, are thrown
And there, so worthless and fly-blown
That even the imps would not purloin
    them,
Lie till their worthy owners join them.

Curious it was to see this mass
  Of lost and torn-up reputations; —
Some of them female wares, alas!
  Mislaid at *innocent* assignations;
Some, that had sighed their last amen
  From the canting lips of saints that
    would be;
And some once owned by " the best of
    men,"
  Who had proved — no better than they
    should be.
'Mong others, a poet's fame I spied,
  Once shining fair, now soakt and
    black —
" No wonder " (an imp at my elbow
    cried),
  " For I pickt it out of a butt of sack! "

Just then a yell was heard o'er head,
  Like a chimney-sweeper's lofty sum-
    mons;
And lo! a devil right downward sped,
Bringing within his claws so red
Two statesmen's characters, found, he
    said,
  Last night, on the floor of the House
    of Commons;
The which, with black official grin,
He now to the Chief Imp handed in; —
Both these articles much the worse
  For their journey down, as you may
    suppose;
But *one* so devilish rank — " Odd's
    curse! "
  Said the Lord Chief Imp, and held his
    nose.

" Ho, ho! " quoth he, " I know full well
" From whom these two stray matters
    fell; " —
Then, casting away, with loathful shrug,
The uncleaner waif (as he would a drug
The Invisible's own dark hand had mixt),
His gaze on the other[1] firm he fixt,
And trying, tho' mischief laught in his
    eye,
To be moral because of the *young* imps
    by,
" What a pity! " he cried — " so fresh
    its gloss,
" So long preserved — 't is a public loss!
" This comes of a man, the careless block-
    head,
" Keeping his character in his pocket;
" And there — without considering
    whether
" There 's room for that and his gains
    together —
" Cramming and cramming and cram-
    ming away,
" Till — out slips character some fine
    day!

" However " — and here he viewed it
    round —
" This article still may pass for sound.
" Some flaws, soon patched, some stains
    are all
" The harm it has had in its luckless fall.
" Here, Puck! " — and he called to one
    of his train —
" The owner may have this back again.
" Tho' damaged for ever, if used with
    skill,
" It may serve perhaps to *trade on* still;
" Tho' the gem can never as once be set,
" It will do for a Tory Cabinet."

HOW TO WRITE BY PROXY.
qui facit per alium facit per se.

'MONG our neighbors, the French, in the
    good olden time
  When Nobility flourisht, great Barons
    and Dukes
Often set up for authors in prose and in
    rhyme,
  But ne'er took the trouble to write
    their own books.

---

[1] Huskisson.

Poor devils were found to do this for
    their betters; —
And one day a Bishop, addressing a
    Blue,
Said, " Ma'am, have you read my new
    Pastoral Letters? "
To which the *Blue* answered — " No,
    Bishop, have *you?* "

The same is now done by *our* privileged
    class;
And to show you how simple the pro-
    cess it needs,
If a great Major-General[1] wishes to pass
For an author of History, thus he pro-
    ceeds : —

First, scribbling his own stock of notions
    as well
As he can, with a *goose*-quill that claims
    him as *kin;*
He settles his neckcloth — takes snuff —
    rings the bell,
And yawningly orders a Subaltern in.

The Subaltern comes — sees his General
    seated,
In all the self-glory of authorship
    swelling; —
"There look," saith his Lordship, "my
    work is completed, —
" It wants nothing now but the gram-
    mar and spelling."

Well used to a *breach*, the brave Subal-
    tern dreads
    Awkward breaches of syntax a hun-
    dred times more;
And tho' often condemned to see break-
    ing of heads,
    He had ne'er seen such breaking of
    Priscian's before.

However, the job 's sure to *pay* — that 's
    enough —
So, to it he sets with his tinkering
    hammer,
Convinced that there never was job half
    so tough
    As the mending a great Major-Gener-
    al's grammar.

[1] Or Lieutenant-General, as it may happen
to be.

But lo! a fresh puzzlement starts up to
    view —
New toil for the Sub. — for the Lord
    new expense:
'T is discovered that mending his *gram-
    mar* won't do,
    As the Subaltern also must find him in
    sense!

At last — even this is achieved by his
    aid;
Friend Subaltern pockets the cash and
    — the story;
Drums beat — the new Grand March of
    Intellect 's played —
    And off struts my Lord, the Historian,
    in glory!

IMITATION OF THE INFERNO OF DANTE.

" *Così quel fiato gli spiriti mali
Di quà, di là, di giù, di su gli mena.*"
              Inferno, canto 5.

I TURNED my steps and lo! a shadowy
    throng
Of ghosts came fluttering towards me —
    blown along,
Like cockchafers in high autumnal storms,
By many a fitful gust that thro' their
    forms
Whistled, as on they came, with wheezy
    puff,
And puft as — tho' they 'd never puff
    enough.

" Whence and what are ye? " pitying I
    inquired
Of these poor ghosts, who, tattered, tost,
    and tired
With such eternal puffing, scarce could
    stand
On their lean legs while answering my
    demand.
" We once were authors " — thus the
    Sprite, who led
This tag-rag regiment of spectres, said —
" Authors of every sex, male, female,
    neuter,
" Who, early smit with love of praise
    and — *pewter*,[2]

[2] The *classical* term for money.

"On C—lb—n's[1] shelves first saw the
light of day,
"In ——'s puffs exhaled our lives
away—
"Like summer windmills, doomed to
dusty peace,
"When the brisk gales that lent them
motion, cease.
"Ah! little knew we then what ills
await
"Much-lauded scribblers in their after-
state;
"Bepuft on earth—how loudly Str—t
can tell—
"And, dire reward, now doubly puft in
hell!"

Touched with compassion for this
ghastly crew,
Whose ribs even now the hollow wind
sung thro'
In mournful prose,—such prose as Rosa's[2]
ghost
Still, at the accustomed hour of eggs and
toast,
Sighs thro' the columns of the *Morning
Post,*—
Pensive I turned to weep, when he who
stood
Foremost of all that flatulential brood,
Singling a *she*-ghost from the party, said,
"Allow me to present Miss X. Y. Z.,[3]
"One of our *lettered* nymphs—excuse
the pun—
"Who gained a name on earth by—
having none;
"And whose initials would immortal be,
"Had she but learned those plain ones,
A. B. C.

"Yon smirking ghost, like mummy dry
and neat,
"Wrapt in his own dead rhymes—fit
winding-sheet—

"Still marvels much that not a soul
should care
"One single pin to know who wrote
'May Fair;'—
"While this young gentleman," (here
forth he drew
A dandy spectre, puft quite thro' and
thro',
As tho' his ribs were an Æolian lyre
For the whole Row's soft *trade*-winds to
inspire,)
"This modest genius breathed one wish
alone,
"To have his volume read, himself un-
known;
"But different far the course his glory
took,
"All knew the author, and—none read
the book.

"Behold, in yonder ancient figure of fun,
"Who rides the blast, Sir Jonah Bar-
rington;—
"In tricks to raise the wind his life was
spent,
"And now the wind returns the compli-
ment.
"This lady here, the Earl of ——'s sis-
ter,
"Is a dead novelist; and this is Mister—
"Beg pardon—*Honorable* Mister Lister,
"A gentleman who some weeks since
came over
"In a smart puff (wind S. S. E.) to
Dover.
"Yonder behind us limps young Vivian
Grey,
"Whose life, poor youth, was long since
blown away—
"Like a torn paper-kite on which the
wind
"No further purchase for a puff can
find."

"And thou, thyself"—here, anxious, I
exclaimed—
"Tell us, good ghost, how thou, thyself,
art named."
"Me, Sir!" he blushing cried—"Ah!
there's the rub—
"Know, then—a waiter once at Brooks's
Club,
"A waiter still I might have long re-
mained,

---

1 The reader may fill up this gap with any one
of the *dissyllabic* publishers of London that occurs to him.

2 Rosa Matilda, who was for many years the
writer of the political articles in the journal alluded to, and whose spirit still seems to preside
—"*regnat Rosa*"—over its pages.

3 *Not* the charming L. E. L., and still less,
Mrs. F. H., whose poetry is among the most
beautiful of the present day.

" And long the club-room's jokes and
    glasses drained;
" But ah! in luckless hour, this last De-
    cember,
" I wrote a book,[1] and Colburn dubbed
    me ' Member ' —
" ' Member of Brooks's! ' — oh Prome-
    thean puff,
" To what wilt thou exalt even kitchen-
    stuff!
" With crumbs of gossip, caught from
    dining wits,
" And half-heard jokes, bequeathed, like
    half-chewed bits,
" To be, each night, the waiter's per-
    quisites; —
" With such ingredients served up oft
    before,
" But with fresh fudge and fiction gar-
    nisht o'er,
" I managed for some weeks to dose the
    town,
" Till fresh reserves of nonsense ran me
    down;
" And ready still even waiters' souls to
    damn,
" The Devil but rang his bell, and —
    here I am; —
" Yes — ' Coming up, Sir,' once my
    favorite cry,
" Exchanged for ' Coming down, Sir,'
    here am I! "

Scarce had the Spectre's lips these words
    let drop,
When, lo! a breeze — such as from ——— 's
    shop
Blows in the vernal hour when puffs pre-
    vail,
And speeds the sheets and swells the
    lagging sale —
Took the poor waiter rudely in the poop,
And whirling him and all his grisly group
Of literary ghosts — Miss X. Y. Z. —
The nameless author, better known than
    read —
Sir Jo. — the Honorable Mr. Lister,
And last, not least, Lord Nobody's twin-
    sister —
Blew them, ye gods, with all their prose
    and rhymes

1 " History of the Clubs of London," announced as by " a Member of Brooks's."

And sins about them, far into those climes
" Where Peter pitched his waistcoat "[2]
    in old times,
Leaving me much in doubt as on I prest,
With my great master, thro' this realm
    unblest,
Whether Old Nick or Colburn puffs the
    best.

LAMENT FOR THE LOSS OF LORD BATHURST'S TAIL.[3]

ALL in again — unlookt for bliss!
Yet, ah! one adjunct still we miss; —
One tender tie, attached so long
To the same head, thro' right and wrong.
Why, Bathurst, why didst thou cut off
    That memorable tail of thine?
Why — as if one was not enough —
    Thy pig-tie with thy place resign,
And thus at once both cut and run?
Alas! my Lord, 't was not well done,
'T was not, indeed, — tho' sad at heart,
From office and its sweets to part,
Yet hopes of coming in again,
Sweet Tory hopes! beguiled our pain;
But thus to miss that tail of thine,
Thro' long, long years our rallying
    sign —
As if the State and all its powers
By tenancy in tail were ours —
To see it thus by scissors fall,
This was " the unkindest cut of all! "
It seemed as tho' the ascendant day
Of Toryism had past away,
And proving Samson's story true,
She lost her vigor with her queue.

Parties are much like fish, 't is said —
The tail directs them, not the head;
Then how could any party fail,
That steered its course by Bathurst's
    tail?
Not Murat's plume thro' Wagram's fight
    E'er shed such guiding glories from it,
As erst in all true Tories' sight
    Blazed from our old Colonial comet!

2 A Dantesque allusion to the old saying,
" Nine miles beyond Hell, where Peter pitched
his waistcoat."

3 The noble Lord, as is well known, cut off
this much-respected appendage on his retirement
from office some months since.

If you, my Lord, a Bashaw were,
  (As Wellington will be anon)
Thou mightst have had a tail to spare;
  But no! alas! thou hadst but one,
  And *that* — like Troy, or Babylon,
  A tale of other times — is gone!
Yet — weep ye not, ye Tories true —
  Fate has not yet of all bereft us;
Though thus deprived of Bathurst's
  queue,
  We 've Ellenborough's *curls* still left
  us; —
Sweet curls, from which young Love, so
  vicious,
  His shots, as from nine-pounders, issues;
Grand, glorious curls, which in debate
Surcharged with all a nation's fate,
  His Lordship shakes, as Homer's God
  did,[1]
  And oft in thundering talk comes near
  him; —
Except that there the *speaker* nodded,
  And here 't is only those who hear
  him.
Long, long, ye ringlets, on the soil
  Of that fat cranium may ye flourish,
With plenty of Macassar oil
  Thro' many a year your growth to
  nourish!
And ah! should Time too soon un-
  sheath
  His barbarous shears such locks to
  sever,
Still dear to Tories even in death,
  Their last, loved relics we 'll bequeath,
A *hair*-loom to our sons for ever.

THE CHERRIES.

A PARABLE.[2]
1828.

SEE those cherries, how they cover
  Yonder sunny garden wall; —
Had they not that network over,
  Thieving birds would eat them all.

So to guard our posts and pensions,
  Ancient sages wove a net,
Thro' whose holes of small dimensions
  Only *certain* knaves can get.

1 " Shakes his ambrosial curls, and gives the
nod." — POPE'S *Homer*.
2 Written during the late discussion on the
Test and Corporation Acts.

Shall we then this network widen?
  Shall we stretch these sacred holes,
Thro' which even already slide in
  Lots of small dissenting souls?

" God forbid! " old *Testy* crieth;
  " God forbid! " so echo I;
Every ravenous bird that flieth
  Then would at our cherries fly.

Ope but half an inch or so,
  And, behold! what bevies break
  in; —
Here some curst old Popish crow
  Pops his long and lickerish beak in;

Here sly Arians flock unnumbered,
  And Socinians, slim and spare,
Who with small belief encumbered
  Slip in easy any where; —

Methodists, of birds the aptest,
  Where there 's *pecking* going on;
And that water-fowl, the Baptist —
  All would share our fruits anon;

Every bird of every city,
  That for years with ceaseless din,
Hath reverst the starling's ditty,
  Singing out " I can't get *in*."

" God forbid! " old *Testy* snivels;
  " God forbid! " I echo too;
Rather may ten thousand devils
  Seize the whole voracious crew!

If less costly fruit won't suit 'em,
  Hips and haws and such like berries,
Curse the cormorants! stone 'em,
  shoot 'em,
  Any thing — to save our cherries.

STANZAS WRITTEN IN ANTICI-
PATION OF DEFEAT.[3]
1828.

GO seek for some abler defenders of
  wrong,
  If we *must* run the gantlet thro' blood
  and expense;

3 During the discussion of the Catholic question in the House of Commons last session.

Or, Goths as ye are, in your multitude
    strong,
Be content with success and pretend
    not to sense.

If the words of the wise and the gener-
    ous are vain,
If Truth by the bowstring *must* yield
    up her breath,
Let Mutes do the office — and spare her
    the pain
Of an Inglis or Tyndal to talk her
    to death.

Chain, persecute, plunder — do all that
    you will —
But save us, at least, the old womanly
    lore
Of a Foster, who, dully prophetic of ill,
Is at once the *two* instruments, AUGUR [1]
    and BORE.

Bring legions of Squires — if they 'll
    only be mute —
And array their thick heads against
    reason and right,
Like the Roman of old, of historic re-
    pute,[2]
Who with droves of dumb animals
    carried the fight;

Pour out from each corner and hole of
    the Court
Your Bedchamber lordlings, your
    salaried slaves,
Who, ripe for all job-work, no matter
    what sort,
Have their consciences tackt to their
    patents and staves.

Catch all the small fry who, as Juvenal
    sings,
Are the Treasury's creatures, wherever
    they swim ; [3]
With all the base, time-serving *toadies*
    of Kings,
Who, if Punch were the monarch,
    would worship even him;

1 This rhyme is more for the ear than the eye,
as the carpenter's tool is spelt *auger.*

2 Fabius, who sent droves of bullocks against
the enemy.

3 *res Fisci est, ubicumque natat.* — JUVENAL.

And while on the *one* side each name of
    renown
That illumines and blesses our age is
    combined;
While the Foxes, the Pitts, and the Can-
    nings look down,
And drop o'er the cause their rich
    mantles of Mind;

Let bold Paddy Holmes show his troops
    on the other,
And, counting of noses the quantum
    desired,
Let Paddy but say, like the Gracchi's
    famed mother,
"Come forward, my *jewels* " — 't is
    all that 's required.

And thus let your farce be enacted here-
    after —
Thus honestly persecute, outlaw and
    chain;
But spare even your victims the torture
    of laughter,
And never, oh never, try *reasoning*
    again !

ODE TO THE WOODS AND FORESTS.

BY ONE OF THE BOARD.

1828.

LET other bards to groves repair,
    Where linnets strain their tuneful
      throats;
Mine be the Woods and Forests where
    The Treasury pours its sweeter *notes.*

No whispering winds have charms for me,
    Nor zephyr's balmy sighs I ask;
To raise the wind for Royalty
    Be all our Sylvan zephyr's task !

And 'stead of crystal brooks and floods,
    And all such vulgar irrigation,
Let Gallic rhino thro' our Woods
    Divert its " course of liquid-ation."

Ah, surely, Vergil knew full well
    What Woods and Forests *ought* to be,
When sly, he introduced in hell
    His guinea-plant, his bullion-tree : [4]

4 Called by Vergil, botanically, " species *auri
frondentis.*"

Nor see I why, some future day,
  When short of cash, we should not
    send
Our Herries down — he knows the
    way —
  To see if Woods in hell will *lend*.

Long may ye flourish, sylvan haunts,
  Beneath whose *" branches* of expense"
Our gracious King gets all he wants, —
  Except a little taste and sense.

Long, in your golden shade reclined,
  Like him of fair Armida's bowers,
May Wellington some *wood*-nymph find,
  To cheer his dozenth lustrum's hours;

To rest from toil the Great Untaught,
  And soothe the pangs his warlike brain
Must suffer, when, unused to thought,
  It tries to think and — tries in vain.

Oh long may Woods and Forests be
  Preserved in all their teeming graces,
To shelter Tory bards like me
  Who take delight in Sylvan *places!* [1]

STANZAS FROM THE BANKS OF THE SHANNON. [2]

1828

" Take back the virgin page."
  MOORE's *Irish Melodies.*

No longer dear Vesey, feel hurt and un-
    easy
  At hearing it said by the Treasury
    brother,
That thou art a sheet of blank paper,
    my Vesey,
  And he, the dear, innocent placeman,
    another.[3]

For lo! what a service we Irish have
    done thee; —
  Thou now art a sheet of blank paper
    no more;

1 *tu facis, ut* silvas, *ut amem* loca ——
  OVID.

2 These verses were suggested by the result
of the Clare election, in the year 1828, when the
Right Honorable W. Vesey Fitzgerald was rejected, and Mr. O'Connell returned.

3 Some expressions to this purport, in a published letter of one of these gentlemen, had then
produced a good deal of amusement.

By St. Patrick, we 've scrawled such a
    lesson upon thee
  As never was scrawled upon foolscap
    before.

Come — on with your spectacles, noble
    Lord Duke,
  (Or O'Connell has *green* ones he
    haply would lend you,)
Read Vesey all o'er (as you *can't* read a
    book)
  And improve by the lesson we bog-
    trotters send you;

A lesson, in large *Roman* characters
    traced,
  Whose awful impressions from you
    and your kin
Of blank-sheeted statesmen will ne'er
    be effaced —
  Unless, 'stead of *paper*, you 're mere
    asses' skin.

Shall I help you to construe it? ay, by
    the Gods,
  Could I risk a translation, you *should*
    have a rare one;
But pen against sabre is desperate odds,
  And you, my Lord Duke (as you
    hinted once), wear one.

Again and again I say, read Vesey
    o'er; —
  You will find him worth all the old
    scrolls of papyrus
That Egypt e'er filled with nonsensical
    lore,
  Or the learned Champollion e'er wrote
    of, to tire us.

All blank as he was, we 've returned
    him on hand,
  Scribbled o'er with a warning to
    Princes and Dukes,
Whose plain, simple drift if they *won't*
    understand,
  Tho' carest at St. James's, they 're fit
    for St. Luke's.

Talk of leaves of the Sibyls! — more
    meaning conveyed is
  In one single leaf such as now we
    have spelled on,

Than e'er hath been uttered by all the
    old ladies
That ever yet spoke, from the Sibyls
    to Eldon.

THE ANNUAL PILL.

Supposed to be sung by OLD PROSY, the Jew, in
the character of Major CARTWRIGHT.

VILL nobodies try my nice *Annual Pill*,
    Dat's to purify every ting nashty avay?
Pless ma heart, pless ma heart, let ma
    say vat I vill,
    Not a Chrishtian or Shentleman minds
    vat I say!
'T is so pretty a bolus! — just down let
    it go,
    And, at vonce, such a *radical* shange
    you vill see,
Dat I'd not be surprised, ike de horse
    in de show,
    If your heads all vere found, vere
    your tailsh ought to be!
        Vill nobodies try my nice *Annual
        Pill,* etc.

'T will cure all Electors and purge away
    clear
    Dat mighty bad itching dey've got in
    deir hands —
'T will cure too all Statesmen of dulness,
    ma tear,
    Tho' the case vas as desperate as poor
    Mister VAN'S.
Dere is noting at all vat dis Pill vill not
    reach —
    Give the Sinecure Ghentleman von
    little grain,
Pless ma heart, it vill act, like de salt on
    de leech,
    And he'll throw de pounds, shillings,
    and pence, up again!
        Vill nobodies try my nice *Annual
        Pill,* etc.

'T would be tedious, ma tear, all its
    peauties to paint —
    But, among oder tings *fundamentally*
    wrong,
It vill cure de *Proad Pottom* [1] — a com-
    mon complaint
    Among M. P.'s and weavers — from
    sitting too long.

[1] Meaning, I presume, *Coalition* Administrations.

Should symptoms of *speeching* preak out
    on a dunce
    (Vat is often de case), it vill stop de
    disease,
And pring avay all de long speeches at
    vonce,
    Dat else vould, like tape-worms, come
    by degrees!

Vill nobodies try my nice *Annual Pill*,
    Dat's to purify every ting nashty
    avay?
Pless ma heart, pless ma heart, let me
    say vat I vill,
    Not a Chrishtian or Shentleman minds
    vat I say!

"IF" AND "PERHAPS." [2]

OH tidings of freedom! oh accents of
    hope!
Waft, waft them, ye zephyrs, to Erin's
    blue sea,
And refresh with their sounds every son
    of the Pope,
    From Dingle-a-cooch to far Donagha-
    dee.

" *If* mutely the slave will endure and
    and obey,
    " Nor clanking his fetters nor breath-
    ing his pains,
" His masters *perhaps* at some far dis-
    tant day
    " May *think* (tender tyrants!) of
    loosening his chains."

Wise " if " and " perhaps ! " — precious
    salve for our wounds,
    If he who would rule thus o'er man-
    acled mutes,
Could check the free spring-tide of Mind
    that resounds,
    Even now at his feet, like the sea at
    Canute's.

But, no, 't is in vain — the grand im-
    pulse is given —
    Man knows his high Charter, and
    knowing will claim;

[2] Written after hearing a celebrated speech in
the House of Lords, June 10, 1828, when the
motion in favor of Catholic Emancipation,
brought forward by the Marquis of Lansdowne,
was rejected by the House of Lords.

And if ruin *must* follow where fetters
are riven,
Be theirs who have forged them the
guilt and the shame.

" *If* the slave will be silent ! " — vain
Soldier, beware —
There *is* a dead silence the wronged
may assume,
When the feeling, sent back from the
lips in despair,
But clings round the heart with a
deadlier gloom; —

When the blush that long burned on the
suppliant's cheek,
Gives place to the avenger's pale, re-
solute hue;
And the tongue that once threatened,
disdaining to *speak*,
Consigns to the arm the high office —
to *do*.

If men in that silence should think of
the hour
When proudly their fathers in panoply
stood,
Presenting alike a bold front-work of
power
To the despot on land and the foe on
the flood: —

That hour when a Voice had come forth
from the west,
To the slave bringing hopes, to the
tyrant alarms;
And a lesson long lookt for was taught
the opprest,
That kings are as dust before freemen
in arms !

If, awfuller still, the mute slave should
recall
That dream of his boyhood, when
Freedom's sweet day
At length seemed to break thro' a long
night of thrall,
And Union and Hope went abroad in
its ray; —

If Fancy should tell him, that Day-
spring of Good,
Tho' swiftly its light died away from
his chain,

Tho' darkly it set in a nation's best
blood,
Now wants but invoking to shine out
again;

If — *if*, I say — breathings like these
should come o'er
The chords of remembrance, and thrill
as they come,
Then, *perhaps* — ay, *perhaps* — but I
dare not say more;
Thou hast willed that thy slaves should
be mute   I am dumb.

WRITE ON, WRITE ON.

A BALLAD.

Air. — " *Sleep on, sleep on, my Kathleen dear.*"

salvete, fratres Asini.   St. Francis.

WRITE on, write on, ye Barons dear,
Ye Dukes, write hard and fast;
The good we 've sought for many a year
Your quills will bring at last.
One letter more, Newcastle, pen,
To match Lord Kenyon's *two*,
And more than Ireland's host of men,
One brace of Peers will do.
          Write on, write on, etc.

Sure never since the precious use
Of pen and ink began,
Did letters writ by fools produce
Such signal good to man.
While intellect, 'mong high and low,
Is marching *on*, they say,
Give *me* the Dukes and Lords who go
Like crabs, the *other* way.
          Write on, write on, etc.

Even now I feel the coming light —
Even now, could Folly lure
My Lord Mountcashel too to write,
Emancipation 's sure.
By geese (we read in history),
Old Rome was saved from ill;
And now to *quills* of geese we see
Old Rome indebted still.
          Write on, write on, etc.

Write, write, ye Peers, nor stoop to
style,
Nor beat for sense about —
Things little worth a Noble's while
You 're better far without.

Oh ne'er, since asses spoke of yore,
   Such miracles were done;
For, write but four such letters more,
   And Freedom's cause is won!

SONG OF THE DEPARTING SPIRIT OF TITHE.

"The parting Genius is with sighing sent."
MILTON.

IT is o'er, it is o'er, my reign is o'er;
I hear a Voice, from shore to shore,
From Dunfanaghy to Baltimore,
And it saith, in sad, parsonic tone,
"Great Tithe and Small are dead and
   gone!"

Even now I behold your vanishing
   wings,
Ye Tenths of all conceivable things,
Which Adam first, as Doctors deem,
Saw, in a sort of night-mare dream,[1]
After the feast of fruit abhorred —
First indigestion on record! —
Ye decimate ducks, ye chosen chicks,
Ye pigs which, tho' ye be Catholics,
Or of Calvin's most select depraved,
In the Church must have your bacon
   saved; —
Ye fields, where Labor counts his
   sheaves,
And, whatsoever *himself* believes,
Must bow to the Establisht *Church* be-
   lief,
That the tenth is always a *Protestant*
   sheaf; —
Ye calves of which the man of Heaven
Takes *Irish* tithe, one calf in seven;[2]
Ye tenths of rape, hemp, barley, flax,
Eggs,[3] timber, milk, fish and bees' wax;
All things in short since earth's creation,

1 A reverend prebendary of Hereford, in an Essay on the Revenues of the Church of England, has assigned the origin of Tithes to "some unrecorded revelation made to Adam."

2 "The tenth calf is due to the parson of common right; and if there are seven he shall have one." — REES's *Cyclopædia*, art. "*Tithes*."

3 Chaucer's Plowman complains of the parish rectors, that

"For the tithing of a duck,
  Or an apple, or an aye (egg),
They make him swear upon a boke;
  Thus they foulen Christ's fay."

Doomed, by the Church's dispensation,
To suffer eternal decimation —
Leaving the whole *lay*-world, since then,
Reduced to nine parts out of ten;
Or — as we calculate thefts and arsons —
Just *ten per cent.* the worse for Parsons!

Alas! and is all this wise device
For the saving of souls thus gone in a
   trice? —
The whole put down, in the simplest
   way,
By the souls resolving *not* to pay!
And even the Papists, thankless race,
Who have had so much the easiest
   case —
To *pay for* our sermons doomed, 't is
   true,
But not condemned to *hear them*, too —
(Our holy business being, 't is known,
With the ears of their barley, not their
   own,)
Even *they* object to let us pillage
By right divine their tenth of tillage,
And, horror of horrors, even decline
To find us in sacramental wine![4]

It is o'er, it is o'er, my reign is o'er,
Ah! never shall rosy Rector more,
Like the shepherds of Israel, idly eat,
And make of his flock "a prey and
   meat."[5]

No more shall be his the pastoral sport
Of suing his flock in the Bishop's Court,
Thro' various steps, Citation, Libel —
Scriptures all, but *not* the Bible;
Working the Law's whole apparatus,
To get at a few predoomed potatoes,
And summoning all the powers of wig,
To settle the fraction of a pig! —
Till, parson and all committed deep
In the case of "Shepherds *versus*
   Sheep,"
The Law usurps the Gospel's place,
And on Sundays meeting face to face,

4 Among the specimens laid before Parliament of the sort of Church rates levied upon Catholics in Ireland, was a charge of two pipes of port for sacramental wine.

5 Ezekiel, xxxiv., 10. — "Neither shall the shepherds feed themselves any more; for I will deliver my flock from their mouth, that they may not be meat for them."

While Plaintiff fills the preacher's
    station,
Defendants form the congregation.

So lives he, Mammon's priest, not
    Heaven's,
For *tenths* thus all at *sixes* and *sevens*, ·
Seeking what parsons love no less
Than tragic poets — a good *distress.*
Instead of studying St. Augustin,
Gregory Nyss., or old St. Justin
(Books fit only to hoard dust in),
His reverence stints his evening readings
To learned Reports of Tithe Proceed-
    ings,
Sipping the while that port so ruddy,
Which forms his only *ancient* study; —
Port so old, you 'd swear its tartar
Was of the age of Justin Martyr,
And, had he sipt of such, no doubt
His martyrdom would have been — to
    gout.

Is all then lost? — alas, too true —
Ye Tenths beloved, adieu, adieu !
My reign is o'er, my reign is o'er —
Like old Thumb's ghost, "I can no
    more."

THE EUTHANASIA OF VAN.

"We are told that the bigots are growing old
and fast wearing out. If it be so, why not let
us die in peace?" — LORD BEXLEY's *Letter to
the Freeholders of Kent.*

STOP, Intellect, in mercy stop,
    Ye curst improvements, cease;
And let poor Nick Vansittart drop
    Into his grave in peace.

Hide, Knowledge, hide thy rising sun,
    Young Freedom, veil thy head;
Let nothing good be thought or done,
    Till Nick Vansittart 's dead !

Take pity on a dotard's fears,
    Who much doth light detest;
And let his last few drivelling years
    Be dark as were the rest.

You too, ye fleeting one-pound notes,
    Speed not so fast away —
Ye rags on which old Nicky gloats,
    A few months longer stay.[1]

----

[1] *perituræ parcere chartæ.*

Together soon, or much I err,
    You *both* from life may go —
The notes unto the scavenger, ·
    And Nick — to Nick below.

Ye Liberals, whate'er your plan,
    Be all reforms suspended;
In compliment to dear old Van,
    Let nothing bad be mended.

Ye Papists, whom oppression wrings,
    Your cry politely cease,
And fret your hearts to fiddle-strings
    That Van may die in peace.

So shall he win a fame sublime
    By few old rag-men gained;
Since all shall own, in Nicky's time,
    Nor sense nor justice reigned.

So shall his name thro' ages past,
    And dolts ungotten yet,
Date from "the days of Nicholas,"
    With fond and sad regret; —

And sighing say, "Alas, had he
    "Been spared from Pluto's bowers,
"The blessed reign of Bigotry
    "And Rags might still be ours ! "

TO THE REVEREND ——.

ONE OF THE SIXTEEN REQUISITIONISTS
OF NOTINGHAM.

1828.

WHAT, *you*, too, my ******, in hashes
        so knowing,
    Of sauces and soups Aristarchus pro-
        fest !
Are *you*, too, my savory Brunswicker,
        going
    To make an old fool of yourself with
        the rest?

Far better to stick to your kitchen re-
        ceipts;
    And — if you want *something* to tease
        — for variety,
Go study how Ude, in his "Cookery,"
        treats
    Live eels when he fits them for polisht
        society.

Just snuggling them in, 'twixt the bars
    of the fire,
  He leaves them to wriggle and writhe
    on the coals,[1]
In a manner that Horner himself would
    admire,
  And wish, 'stead of *eels*, they were
    Catholic souls.

Ude tells us the fish little suffering feels;
  While Papists of late have more sensi-
    tive grown;
So take my advice, try your hand at live
    eels,
  And for *once* let the other poor devils
    alone.

I have even a still better receipt for your
    cook —
  How to make a goose die of confirmed
    hepatitis ; [2]
And if you 'll, for once, *fellow*-feelings
    o'erlook,
  A well-tortured goose a most capital
    sight is.

First, catch him, alive — make a good
    steady fire —
  Set your victim before it, both legs
    being tied,
(As if left to himself he *might* wish to
    retire,)
  And place a large bowl of rich cream
    by his side.

There roasting by inches, dry, fevered,
    and faint,
  Having drunk all the cream you so
    civilly laid, off,
He dies of as charming a liver complaint
  As ever sleek person could wish a pie
    made of.

Besides, only think, my dear one of Six-
    teen,
  What an emblem this bird, for the
    epicure's use meant,

Presents of the mode in which Ireland
    has been
  Made a tid-bit for yours and your
    brethren's amusement:

Tied down to the stake, while her limbs,
    as they quiver,
  A slow fire of tyranny wastes by de-
    grees —
No wonder disease should have swelled
    up her liver,
  No wonder you, Gourmands, should
    love her disease.

IRISH ANTIQUITIES.

ACCORDING to some learned opinions
The Irish once were Carthaginians;
But trusting to more late descriptions
I 'd rather say they were Egyptians.
My reason 's this : — the Priests of Isis,
  When forth they marched in long
    array,
Employed, 'mong other grave devices,
  A Sacred Ass to lead the way; [3]
And still the antiquarian traces
  'Mong Irish Lords this Pagan plan,
For still in all religious cases
  They put Lord Roden in the van.

A CURIOUS FACT.

THE present Lord Kenyon (the Peer
    who writes letters,
For which the waste-paper folks much
    are his debtors)
Hath one little oddity well worth reciting,
Which puzzleth observers even more
    than his writing.
Whenever Lord Kenyon doth chance to
    behold
A cold Apple-pie — mind, the pie *must*
    be cold —
His Lordship looks solemn (few people
    know why),
And he makes a low bow to the said
    apple-pie.
This idolatrous act, in so " vital " a Peer,
Is by most serious Protestants thought
    rather queer —
Pie-worship, they hold, coming under
    the head

---

1 The only way, Monsieur Ude assures us, to
get rid of the oil so objectionable in this fish.

2 A liver complaint. The process by which
the livers of geese are enlarged for the famous
Patés de foie d'oie.

3 To this practice the ancient adage alludes,
" *asinus portans mysteria.*"

(Vide *Crustium*, chap. iv.) of the Worship of Bread.

Some think 't is a tribute, as author, he owes
For the service that pie-crust hath done to his prose; —
The only good things in his pages, they swear,
Being those that the pastry-cook sometimes puts there.
Others say, 't is a homage, thro' pie-crust conveyed,
To our Glorious Deliverer's much-honored shade;
As that Protestant Hero (or Saint, if you please)
Was as fond of cold pie as he was of green peas,[1]
And 't is solely in loyal remembrance of that,
My Lord Kenyon to apple-pie takes off his hat.
While others account for this kind salutation
By what Tony Lumpkin calls " concatenation; " —
A certain good will that, from sympathy's ties,
'Twixt old *Apple*-women and *Orange*-men lies.

But 't is needless to add, these are all vague surmises,
For thus, we 're assured, the whole matter arises :
Lord Kenyon's respected old father (like many
Respected old fathers) was fond of a penny;
And loved so to save,[2] that — there 's not the least question —

[1] See the anecdote, which the Duchess of Marlborough relates in her Memoirs, of this polite hero appropriating to himself one day, at dinner, a whole dish of green peas — the first of the season — while the poor Princess Anne, who was then in a longing condition, sat by vainly entreating with her eyes for a share.

[2] The same prudent propensity characterizes his descendant, who (as is well known) would not even go to the expense of a diphthong on his father's monument, but had the inscription spelled, economically, thus : — " *mors janua vita* "

His death was brought on by a bad indigestion,
From cold apple-pie-crust his Lordship *would* stuff in
At breakfast to save the expense of hot muffin.
Hence it is, and hence only, that cold apple-pies
Are beheld by his Heir with such reverent eyes —
Just as honest King Stephen his beaver might doff
To the fishes that carried his kind uncle off —
And while *filial* piety urges so many on,
'T is pure *apple*-pie-ety moves my Lord Kenyon.

NEW-FASHIONED ECHOES.

Sir, —

Most of your readers are no doubt acquainted with the anecdote told of a certain not over-wise judge who, when in the act of delivering a charge in some country court-house, was interrupted by the braying of an ass at the door. "What noise is that ? " asked the angry judge. "Only an extraordinary *echo* there is in court, my Lord," answered one of the counsel.

As there are a number of such "extraordinary echoes" abroad just now, you will not, perhaps, be unwilling, Mr. Editor, to receive the following few lines suggested by them.

Yours, etc. S.

huc coeamus,[3] *ait ; nullique libentius unquam responsura sono, coeamus, retulit echo.*
OVID.

THERE are echoes, we know, of all sorts,
From the echo that " dies in the dale,"
To the " airy-tongued babbler" that sports
Up the tide of the torrent her " tale."

There are echoes that bore us, like Blues,
With the latest smart *mot* they have heard;
There are echoes extremely like shrews
Letting nobody have the last word.

In the bogs of old Paddy-land, too,
Certain " talented " echoes[4] there dwell,
Who on being askt, " How do you do ? "
Politely reply, " Pretty well."

[3] " Let us form Clubs."

[4] Commonly called " Paddy Blake's Echoes."

But why should I talk any more
　　Of such old-fashioned echoes as these,
When Britain has new ones in store,
　　That transcend them by many degrees?

For of all repercussions of sound
　　Concerning which bards make a
　　　　pother,
There 's none like that happy rebound
　　When one blockhead echoes an-
　　　　other;—

When Kenyon commences the bray,
　　And the Borough-Duke follows his
　　　　track;
And loudly from Dublin's sweet bay
　　Rathdowne brays, with interest,
　　　　back;—

And while, of *most* echoes the sound
　　On our ear by reflection doth fall,
These Brunswickers[1] pass the bray
　　round,
　　Without any reflection at all.

Oh Scott, were I gifted like you,
　　Who can name all the echoes there are
From Benvoirlich to bold Ben-venue,
　　From Benledi to wild Uamvar;

I might track thro' each hard Irish name
　　The rebounds of this asinine strain,
Till from Neddy to Neddy, it came
　　To the *chief* Neddy, Kenyon, again;

Might tell how it roared in Rathdowne,
　　How from Dawson it died off gen-
　　　　teelly—
How hollow it hung from the crown
　　Of the fat-pated Marquis of Ely;

How on hearing my Lord of Glandine,
　　Thistle-eaters the stoutest gave way,
Outdone in their own special line
　　By the forty-ass power of his bray!

But, no — for so humble a bard
　　'T is a subject too trying to touch on;
Such noblemen's names are too hard,
　　And their noddles too soft to dwell
　　　　much on.

1 Anti-Catholic associations, under the title
of Brunswick Clubs, were at this time becoming
numerous both in England and Ireland.

Oh Echo, sweet nymph of the hill,
　　Of the dell and the deep-sounding
　　　　shelves;
If in spite of Narcissus you still
　　Take to fools who are charmed with
　　　　themselves,

Who knows but, some morning retiring,
　　To walk by the Trent's wooded side,
You may meet with Newcastle, admiring
　　His own lengthened ears in the tide!

Or, on into Cambria straying,
　　Find Kenyon, that double tongued elf,
In his love of *ass*-cendency, braying
　　A Brunswick duet with himself!

INCANTATION.

FROM THE NEW TRADGEY OF " THE
　　　BRUNSWICKERS."
　　　　　　　　　　　　　1828.

SCENE.— *Penenden Plain. In the middle, a
caldron boiling. Thunder. = Enter three
Brunswickers.*

　　1*st Bruns.*— THRICE hath scribbling
　　　　Kenyon scrawled,
　　2*d Bruns.*— Once hath fool New-
　　　　castle bawled,
　　3*d Bruns.*— Bexley snores: — 't is
　　　　time, ' tis time,
　　1*st Bruns.*— Round about the caldron
　　　　go;
In the poisonous nonsense throw.
Bigot spite that long hath grown
Like a toad within a stone,
Sweltering in the heart of Scott,
Boil we in the Brunswick pot.
　　All.— Dribble, dribble, nonsense
　　　　dribble,
Eldon, talk, and Kenyon, scribble.
　　2*d Bruns.*— Slaver from Newcastle's
　　　　quill
In the noisome mess distil,
Brimming high our Brunswick broth
Both with venom and with froth.
Mix the brains (tho' apt to hash ill,
Being scant) of Lord Mountcashel,
With that malty stuff which Chandos
Drivels as no other man does.
Catch (*i. e.* if catch you can)
One idea, spick and span,
From my Lord of Salisbury, —
One idea, tho' it be
Smaller than the " happy flea "

Which his sire in sonnet terse
Wedded to immortal verse.[1]
Tho' to rob the son is sin,
Put his *one* idea in;
And, to keep it company,
Let that conjuror Winchelsea
Drop but *half* another there,
If he hath so much to spare.
Dreams of murders and of arsons,
Hatched in heads of Irish parsons,
Bring from every hole and corner,
Where ferocious priests like Horner
Purely for religious good
Cry aloud for Papist's blood,
Blood for Wells, and such old women,
At their ease to wade and swim in.
    All. — Dribble, dribble, nonsense
        dribble.
Bexley, talk, and Kenyon, scribble.
    3d Bruns. — Now the charm begin to
        brew;
Sisters, sisters, add thereto
Scraps of Lethbridge's old speeches,
Mixt with leather from his breeches.
Rinsings of old Bexley's brains,
Thickened (if you 'll take the pains)
With that pulp which rags create,
In their middle, *nympha* state,
Ere, like insects frail and sunny,
Forth they wing abroad as money.
There — the Hell-broth we 've en-
        chanted —
Now but *one* thing more is wanted.
Squeeze o'er all that Orange juice,
Castlereagh keeps corkt for use,
Which, to work the better spell, is
Colored deep with blood of ——,
Blood, of powers far more various,
Even than that of Januarius,
Since so great a charm hangs o'er it,
England's parsons bow before it !
    All. — Dribble, dribble, nonsense
        dribble,

1 Alluding to a well-known lyric composition
of the late Marquis, which, with a slight alteration, might be addressed either to a flea or a fly.
For instance : —
        " Oh, happy, happy, happy fly,
            If I were you, or you were I."
Or,
    " Oh, happy, happy, happy flea
        If I were you or you were *me* ;
        But since, alas ! that cannot be,
        I must remain Lord Salisbury."

Bexley, talk, and Kenyon, scribble.
    2d Bruns. — Cool it now with ——'s
        blood,
So the charm is firm and good. [*exeunt.*

HOW TO MAKE A GOOD POLI-
TICIAN.

WHENE'ER you 're in doubt, said a Sage
        I once knew,
'Twixt two lines of conduct *which* course
        to pursue,
Ask a woman's advice, and, whate'er
        she advise,
Do the very reverse and you 're sure to
        be wise.

Of the same use as guides are the Bruns-
wicker throng;
In their thoughts, words and deeds, so
        instinctively wrong,
That whatever they counsel act, talk or
        indite,
Take the opposite course and you 're
        sure to be right.

So golden this rule, that, had nature de-
        nied you
The use of that finger-post, Reason, to
        guide you —
Were you even more doltish than any
        given man is,
More soft than Newcastle, more twad-
        dling than Van is,
I 'd stake my repute, on the following
        conditions,
To make you the soundest of sound pol-
        iticians.

Place yourself near the skirts of some
        high-flying Tory —
Some Brunswicker parson, of port-drink-
        ing glory, —
Watch well how he dines, during any
        great Question —
What makes him feel gayly, what spoils
        his digestion —
And always feel sure that *his* joy o'er a
        stew
Portends a clear case of dyspepsia to *you.*
Read him backwards, like Hebrew —
        whatever he wishes
Or praises, note down as absurd or per-
        nicious.

Like the folks of a weather-house, shifting about,
When he 's *out* be an *In* — when he 's *in* be an *Out*.
Keep him always reversed in your thoughts, night and day,
Like an Irish barometer turned the wrong way : —
If he 's *up* you may swear that oul weather is nigh;
If he 's *down* you may look for a bit of blue sky.
Never mind what debaters or journalists say,
Only ask what *he* thinks and then think t' other way.
Does he hate the Small-note Bill? then firmly rely
The Small-note Bill 's a blessing, tho' *you* don't know why.
Is Brougham his aversion? then Harry 's your man.
Does he quake at O'Connell? take doubly to Dan.
Is he all for the Turks? then at once take the whole
Russian Empire (Tsar, Cossacks and all) to your soul.
In short, whatsoever he talks, thinks or is,
Be your thoughts, words and essence the constrast of his.
Nay, as Siamese ladies — at least, the polite ones —
All paint their teeth black, 'cause the devil has white ones —
If even by the chances of time or of tide
Your Tory for once should have sense on his side,
Even *then* stand aloof — for be sure that Old Nick
When a Tory talks sensibly, means you some trick.

Such my recipe is — and, in one single verse,
I shall now, in conclusion, its substance rehearse.
Be all that a Brunswicker *is* not nor *could* be,
And then — you 'll be all that an honest man should be.

EPISTLE OF CONDOLENCE,

FROM A SLAVE-LORD, TO A COTTON-LORD.

ALAS ! my dear friend, what a state of affairs !
How unjustly we both are despoiled of our rights !
Not a pound of black flesh shall I leave to my heirs,
Nor must *you* any more work to death little whites.

Both forced to submit to that general controller
Of King, Lords and cotton mills, Public Opinion,
No more shall *you* beat with a big billy-roller,
Nor *I* with the cart-whip assert my dominion.

Whereas, were we suffered to do as we please
With our Blacks and our Whites, as of yore we were let,
We might range them alternate, like harpsichord keys,
And between us thump out a good piebald duet.

But this fun is all over; — farewell to the zest
Which Slavery now lends to each tea-cup we sip;
Which makes still the cruellest coffee the best,
And that sugar the sweetest which smacks of the whip.

Farewell too the Factory's white picka-ninnies —
Small, living machines which if flogged to their tasks
Mix so well with their namesakes, the " Billies " and " Jennies,"
That *which* have got souls in 'em nobody asks ; —

Little Maids of the Mill, who themselves but ill-fed,
Are obliged, 'mong their other benevolent cares,

To "keep feeding the scribblers,"[1] —
and better, 't is said,
Than old Blackwood or Fraser have
ever fed theirs.

All this is now o'er and so dismal *my* loss
is,
So hard 't is to part from the smack of
the thong,
That I mean (from pure love for the old
whipping process),
To take to whipt syllabub all my life
long.

THE GHOST OF MILTIADES.

ah quoties dubius Scriptis e rarsit amator!
OVID.

THE Ghost of Miltiades came at night,
And he stood by the bed of the Ben-
thamite,
And he said, in a voice that thrilled the
frame,
"If ever the sound of Marathon's name
"Hath fired thy blood or flusht thy
brow,
"Lover of Liberty, rouse thee now!"

The Benthamite yawning left his bed —
Away to the Stock Exchange he sped,
And he found the Scrip of Greece so
high,
That it fired his blood, it flusht his eye,
And oh! 't was a sight for the Ghost to
see,
For never was Greek more Greek than
he!
And still as the premium higher went,
His ecstasy rose — so much *per cent.*
(As we see in a glass that tells the
weather
The heat and the *silver* rise together,)
And Liberty sung from the patriot's lip,
While a voice from his pocket whispered
"Scrip!"
The Ghost of Miltiades came again; —
He smiled, as the pale moon smiles thro'
rain,
For his soul was glad at that patriot
strain;

(And poor, dear ghost — how little he
knew
The jobs and the tricks of the Philhel-
lene crew!)
"Blessings and thanks!" was all he
said,
Then melting away like a night-dream
fled!

The Benthamite hears — amazed that
ghosts
Could be such fools — and away he
posts,
A patriot still? Ah no, ah no —
Goddess of Freedom, thy Scrip is low,
And warm and fond as thy lovers are,
Thou triest their passion, when under
par.
The Benthamite's ardor fast decays,
By turns he weeps and swears and
prays,
And wishes the devil had Crescent and
Cross,
Ere *he* had been forced to sell at a
loss.
They quote him the Stock of various na-
tions,
But, spite of his classic associations,
Lord! how he loathes the Greek *quota-
tions!*

"Who 'll buy my Scrip? Who 'll buy
my Scrip?"
Is now the theme of the patriot's lip,
As he runs to tell how hard his lot is
To Messrs. Orlando and Luriottis,
And says, "Oh Greece, for Liberty's
sake,
"Do buy my Scrip, and I vow to
break
"Those dark, unholy *bonds* of thine —
"If you 'll only consent to buy up
mine!"
The Ghost of Miltiades came once
more; —
His brow like the night was lowering
o'er,
And he said, with a look that flasht dis-
may,
"Of Liberty's foes the worst are they,
"Who turn to a trade her cause divine,
"And gamble for gold on Freedom's
shrine!"

1 One of the operations in cotton mills usually
performed by children.

Thus saying, the Ghost, as he took his
flight,
Gave a Parthian kick to the Benthamite,
Which sent him, whimpering, off to
Jerry —
And vanisht away to the Stygian ferry!

ALARMING INTELLIGENCE!

REVOLUTION IN THE DICTIONARY
— ONE *GALT* AT THE HEAD OF
IT.

GOD preserve us! — there 's nothing now
safe from assault; —
    Thrones toppling around, churches
    brought to the hammer;
And accounts have just reached us that
one Mr. *Galt*
    Has declared open war against Eng-
    lish and Grammar!

He had long been suspected of some
such design,
    And, the better his wicked intents to
    arrive at,
Had lately 'mong Colburn's troops of
the line
    (The penny-a-line men) enlisted as
    private.

There schooled, with a rabble of words
at command,
    Scotch, English and slang in promis-
    cuous alliance,
He at length against Syntax has taken
his stand,
    And sets all the Nine Parts of Speech
    at defiance.

Next advices, no doubt, further facts
will afford;
    In the mean time the danger most im-
    minent grows,
He has taken the Life of one eminent
Lord,
    And whom he 'll *next* murder the
    Lord only knows.

              Wednesday evening.
Since our last, matters, luckily, look
more serene;
    Tho' the rebel, 't is stated, to aid his
    defection,

Has seized a great Powder — no, Puff
Magazine,
    And the explosions are dreadful in
    every direction.

What his meaning exactly is, nobody
knows,
    As he talks (in a strain of intense
    botheration)
Of lyrical "ichor," [1] "gelatinous"
prose,[2]
    And a mixture called amber immortal-
    ization.[3]

Now, he raves of a bard he once happened to meet,
    Seated high "among rattlings" and
    churning a sonnet;[4]
Now, talks of a mystery, wrapt in a
sheet,
    With a halo (by way of a nightcap)
    upon it![5]

We shudder in tracing these terrible
lines;
    Something bad they must mean, tho'
    we can't make it out;
For whate'er may be guessed of Galt's
secret designs,
    That they 're all *Anti*-English no
    Christian can doubt.

RESOLUTIONS

PASSED AT A LATE MEETING OF REV-
ERENDS AND RIGHT REVERENDS.

RESOLVED — to stick to every particle
Of every Creed and every Article;
Reforming naught, or great or little,
We 'll stanchly stand by every tittle,[6]

1 "That dark diseased ichor which colored
his effusions." — GALT's *Life of Byron.*

2 "The gelatinous character of their effusions." — *Ibid.*

3 "The poetical embalmment or rather amber immortalization." — *Ibid.*

4 "Sitting amidst the shrouds and rattlings,
churning an inarticulate melody." — *Ibid.*

5 "He was a mystery in a winding sheet,
crowned with a halo."— *Ibid.*

6 One of the questions propounded to the
Puritans in 1573 was — "Whether the Book of
Service was good and godly, every tittle grounded
on the Holy Scripture?" On which an honest

And scorn the swallow of that soul
Which cannot boldly bolt the whole.

Resolved that tho' St. Athanasius
In damning souls is rather spacious —
Tho' wide and far his curses fall,
Our Church " hath stomach for them
all; "
And those who 're not content with such,
May e'en be damned ten times as much.

Resolved — such liberal souls are we —
Tho' hating Nonconformity,
We yet believe the cash no worse is
That comes from Nonconformist purses.
Indifferent *whence* the money reaches
The pockets of our reverend breeches,
To us the Jumper's jingling penny
Chinks with a tone as sweet as any;
And even our old friends Yea and Nay
May thro' the nose for ever pray,
If *also* thro' the nose they 'll pay.

Resolved that Hooper,[1] Latimer,[2]
And Crammer,[3] all extremely err,
In taking such a low-bred view
Of what Lords Spiritual ought to do: —
All owing to the fact, poor men,
That Mother Church was modest then,
Nor knew what golden eggs her goose,
The Public, would in time produce.
One Pisgah peep at modern Durham
To far more lordly thoughts would stir
'em.

Resolved that when we Spiritual Lords
Whose income just enough affords
To keep our Spiritual Lordships cosey,
Are told by Antiquarians prosy

Dissenter remarks — " Surely they had a wonderful opinion of their Service Book that there
was not a *tittle* amiss in it."

1 " They," the Bishops, " know that the primitive Church had no such Bishops. If the fourth
part of the bishopric remained unto the Bishop,
it were sufficient." — *On the Commandments,*
p. 72.

2 " Since the Prelates were made Lords and
Nobles, the plough standeth, there is no work
done, the people starve." — *Lat. Serm.*

3 " Of whom have come all these glorious
titles, styles, and pomps into the Church. But
I would that I, and all my brethren, the Bishops,
would leave all our styles, and write the styles
of our offices," etc. — *Life of Cranmer, by
Strype, Appendix.*

How ancient Bishops cut up theirs,
Giving the poor the largest shares —
Our answer is, in one short word,
We think it pious but absurd.
Those good men made the world their
debtor,
But we, the Church reformed, know
better;
And taking all that all can pay,
Balance the account the other way.

Resolved our thanks profoundly due are
To last month's Quarterly Reviewer,
Who proves (by arguments so clear
One sees how much he holds *per* year)
That England's Church, tho' out of date,
Must still be left to lie in state,
As dead, as rotten and as grand as
The mummy of King Osymandyas,
All pickled snug — the brains drawn
out[4] —
With costly cerements swathed about, —
And "Touch me not," those words ter-
rific,
Scrawled o'er her in good hieroglyphic.

SIR ANDREW'S DREAM.

*" nec tu sperne piis venientia somnia portis:
cum pia venerunt somnia, pondus habent."*
PROPERT. *lib.* iv. *eleg.* 7.

As snug, on a Sunday eve, of late,
In his easy chair Sir Andrew sate,
Being much too pious, as every one
knows,
To do aught, of a Sunday eve, but doze,
He dreamt a dream, dear, holy man,
And I 'll tell you his dream as well as I
can.
He found himself, to his great amaze,
In Charles the First's high Tory days,
And just at the time that gravest of
Courts
Had publisht its Book of Sunday
Sports.[5] —

4 Part of the process of embalment.

5 *The Book of Sports* drawn up by Bishop
Moreton was first put forth in the reign of James
I., 1618, and afterwards republished, at the advice
of Laud, by Charles I., 1633, with an injunction
that it should be "made public by order from the
Bishops." We find it therein declared, that
"for his good people's recreation, his Majesty's
pleasure was, that after the end of divine service
they should not be disturbed, letted, or discour-
aged from any lawful recreations, such as dan-

Sunday Sports! what a thing for the ear
Of Andrew even in sleep to hear! —
It chanced to be too a Sabbath day
When the people from church were coming away;
And Andrew with horror heard this song,
As the smiling sinners flockt along: —
" Long life to the Bishops, hurrah! hurrah!
" For a week of work and a Sunday of play
" Make the poor man's life run merry away."

" The Bishops! " quoth Andrew, " Popish, I guess,"
And he grinned with conscious holiness.
But the song went on, and, to brim the cup
Of poor Andy's grief, the fiddles struck up!

" Come, take out the lasses — let 's have a dance —
" For the Bishops allow us to skip our fill,
" Well knowing that no one's the more in advance
" On the road to heaven for standing still."
" Oh! it never was meant that grim grimaces
" Should sour the cream of a creed of love;
" Or that fellows with long, disastrous faces,
" Alone should sit among cherubs above.
" Then hurrah for the Bishops, etc.

" For Sunday fun we never can fail,
" When the Church herself each sport points out; —
" There 's May-games, archery, Whitsun-ale,
" And a May-pole high to dance about.

cing, either of men or women, archery for men, leaping, vaulting, or any such harmless recreations, nor having of May-games, Whitsun-ales, or Morris-dances, or setting up of May-poles, or other sports therewith used," etc.

" Or should we be for a pole hard driven,
" Some lengthy saint of aspect fell,
" With his pockets on earth and his nose in heaven,
" Will do for a May-pole just as well.
" Then hurrah for the Bishops, hurrah! hurrah!
" A week of work and a Sabbath of play
" Make the poor man's life run merry away."

To Andy, who does n't much deal in history,
This Sunday scene was a downright mystery;
And God knows where might have ended the joke,
But, in trying to stop the fiddles, he woke.
And the odd thing is (as the rumor goes)
That since that dream — which, one would suppose,
Should have made his godly stomach rise,
Even more than ever, 'gainst Sunday pies —
He has viewed things quite with different eyes;
Is beginning to take, on matters divine,
Like Charles and his Bishops, the *sporting* line —
Is all for Christians jigging in pairs,
As an interlude 'twixt Sunday prayers: —
Nay, talks of getting Archbishop Howley
To bring in a Bill enacting duly
That all good Protestants from this date
May freely and lawfully recreate,
Of a Sunday eve, their spirits moody,
With Jack in the Straw or Punch and Judy.

A BLUE LOVE-SONG.

TO MISS ———.

Air — " *Come live with me and be my love.*"

COME wed with me and we will write,
My Blue of Blues, from morn till night.
Chased from our classic souls shall be
All thoughts of vulgar progeny;
And thou shalt walk through smiling rows
Of chubby duodecimos,
While I, to match thy products nearly,
Shall lie-in of a quarto yearly.
'T is true, even books entail some trouble;
But *live* productions give one double.

Correcting children is *such* bother, —
While printers' devils correct the other.
Just think, my own Malthusian dear,
How much more decent 't is to hear
From male or female — as it may be —
" How is your book? " than " How 's
   your baby? "
And whereas physic and wet nurses
Do much exhaust paternal purses,
Our books if rickety may go
And be well dry-nurst in *the Row ;*
And when God wills to take them
   hence,
Are buried at *the Row's* expense.

Besides, (as 't is well proved by thee,
In thy own Works, vol. 93.)
The march, just now, of population
So much outstrips all moderation,
That even prolific herring-shoals
Keep pace not with our erring souls.[1]
Oh far more proper and well-bred
To stick to writing books instead;
And show the world how two Blue lovers
Can coalesce, like two book-covers,
(Sheep-skin, or calf, or such wise
   leather,)
Lettered at back and stitched together
Fondly as first the binder fixt 'em,
With naught but — literature betwixt
   'em.

SUNDAY ETHICS.

A SCOTCH ODE.

PUIR, profligate Londoners, having heard
   tell
  That the De'il's got amang ye, and
    fearing 't is true,
We ha' sent ye a mon wha 's a match for
   his spell,
A chiel o' our ain, that the De'il himsel
  Will be glad to keep clear of, one An-
    drew Agnew.

So at least ye may reckon for ane day
   entire
  In ilka lang week ye 'll be tranquil
    eneugh,

As Auld Nick, do him justice, abhors a
   Scotch squire,
An' would sooner gae roast by his ain
   kitchen fire
  Than pass a hale Sunday wi' Andrew
    Agnew.

For, bless the gude mon, gin he had his
   ain way,
  He 'd na let a cat on the Sabbath say
    " mew; "
Nae birdie maun whistle, nae lambie maun
   play,
An' Phœbus himsel could na travel that
   day,
  As he 'd find a new Joshua in Andie
    Agnew.

Only hear, in your Senate, how awfu' he
   cries,
  " Wae, wae to a' sinners who boil an'
    who stew !
" Wae, wae to a' eaters o' Sabbath-baked
   pies,
" For as surely again shall the crust
   thereof rise
  "In judgment against ye," saith An-
    drew Agnew !

Ye may think, from a' this, that our
   Andie 's the lad
  To ca' o'er the coals your nobeelity
    too;
That their drives, o' a Sunday, wi' flun-
   kies,[2] a' clad
Like Shawmen, behind 'em, would mak
   the mon mad —
  But he 's nae sic a noodle, our Andie
    Agnew.

If Lairds an' fine Ladies, on Sunday,
   think right
  To gang to the deevil — as maist o'
    'em do —
To stop them our Andie would think na
   polite;
And 't is odds (if the chiel could get ony
   thing by 't)
  But he 'd follow 'em, booing,[3] would
    Andrew Agnew.

---

1 See " Ella of Garveloch." — Garveloch being a place where there was a large herring-fish-
ery, but where, as we are told by the author,
" the people increased much faster than the
produce."

2 Servants in livery.

3 For the " gude effects and uteelity of booing," see the *Man of the World.*

AWFUL EVENT.

YES, Winchelsea (I tremble while I pen it),
Winchelsea's Earl hath *cut* the British Senate —
Hath said to England's Peers, in accent gruff,
" *That* for ye all " [snapping his fingers] and exit in a huff !

Disastrous news ! —like that of old which spread
From shore to shore, " our mighty Pan is dead,"
O'er the cross benches (cross from *being* crost)
Sounds the loud wail, " Our Winchelsea is lost ! "

Which of ye, Lords, that heard him can forget
The deep impression of that awful threat,
" I quit your house ! ! " — midst all that histories tell,
I know but *one* event that 's parallel : —

It chanced at Drury Lane, one Easter night,
When the gay gods too blest to be polite
Gods at their ease, like those of learned Lucretius,
Laught, whistled, groaned, uproariously facetious —
A well-drest member of the middle gallery,
Whose " ears polite " disdained such low canaillerie,
Rose in his place — so grand, you 'd almost swear
Lord Winchelsea himself stood towering there —
And like that Lord of dignity and *nous,*
Said, " Silence, fellows, or — I 'll leave the house ! ! "

How brookt the gods this speech ? Ah well-a-day,
That speech so fine should be so thrown away !
In vain did this mid-gallery grandee
Assert his own two-shilling dignity —
In vain he menaced to withdraw the ray

Of his own full-price countenance away —
Fun against Dignity is fearful odds,
And as the Lords laugh *now,* so giggled *then* the gods !

THE NUMBERING OF THE CLERGY.

PARODY ON SIR CHARLES HAN. WILLIAMS'S FAMOUS ODE,

" COME, CLOE, AND GIVE ME SWEET KISSES."
" We want more Churches and more Clergymen."
Bishop of London's late Charge.
" *rectorum numerum, terris pereuntibus, augent.*"
Claudian in Eutrop.

COME, give us more Livings and Rectors,
For, richer no realm ever gave;
But why, ye unchristian objectors,
Do ye ask us how many we crave ? [1]

Oh there can't be too many rich Livings
For souls of the Pluralist kind,
Who, despising old Crocker's misgivings,
To numbers can ne'er be confined. [2]

Count the cormorants hovering about, [3]
At the time their fish season sets in,
When these models of keen diners-out
Are preparing their beaks to begin.

Count the rooks that, in clerical dresses,
Flock round when the harvest 's in play,
And not minding the farmer's distresses,
Like devils in grain peck away.

Go, number the locusts in heaven, [4]
On the way to some titheable shore;
And when *so* many Parsons you 've given,
We still shall be craving for more.

1 Come, Cloe, and give me sweet kisses,
   For sweeter sure never girl gave ;
   But why, in the midst of my blisses,
   Do you ask me how many I 'd have?
2 For whilst I love thee above measure,
   To numbers I 'll ne'er be confined.
3 Count the bees that on Hybla are playing,
   Count the flowers that enamel its fields,
   Count the flocks, etc.
4 Go number the stars in the heaven,
   Count how many sands on the shore,
   When so many kisses you 've given,
   I still shall be craving for more.

Then, unless ye the Church would sub-
merge, ye
Must leave us in peace to augment,
For the wretch who could number the
Clergy,
With few will be ever content.[1]

A SAD CASE.

" If it be the undergraduate season at which
this *rabies religiosa* is to be so fearful, what security has Mr. Goulburn against it at this moment, when his son is actually exposed to the
full venom of an association with Dissenters? "
— *The Times*, March 25.

How sad a case ! — just think of it —
If Goulburn junior should be bit
By some insane Dissenter, roaming
Thro' Granta's halls, at large and foam-
ing,
And with that aspect *ultra* crabbed
Which marks Dissenters when they 're
rabid !
God only knows what mischiefs might
Result from this one single bite,
Or how the venom, once suckt in,
Might spread and rage thro' kith and kin.
Mad folks of all denominations
First turn upon their own relations.
So that *one* Goulburn, fairly bit,
Might end in maddening the whole kit,
Till ah ! ye gods ! we 'd have to rue
Our Goulburn senior bitten too;
The Hychurchphobia in those veins,
Where Tory blood now redly reigns; —
And that dear man who now perceives
Salvation only in lawn sleeves,
Might, tainted by such coarse infection,
Run mad in the opposite direction,
And think, poor man, 't is only given
To linsey-woolsey to reach Heaven !

Just fancy what a shock 't would be
Our Goulburn in his fits to see,
Tearing into a thousand particles
His once-loved Nine and Thirty Articles;
(Those Articles his friend, the Duke,[2]
For Gospel, t' other night, mistook;)
Cursing cathedrals, deans and singers —
Wishing the ropes might hang the ring-
ers —

Pelting the church with blasphemies,
Even worse than Parson Beverley's; —
And ripe for severing Church and State,
Like any creedless reprobate,
Or like that class of Methodists
Prince Waterloo styles " Atheists ! "

But 't is too much — the Muse turns pale,
And o'er the picture drops a veil,
Praying, God save the Goulburns all
From mad Dissenters great and small !

A DREAM OF HINDOSTAN.

—— risum *teneatis, amici.*

"THE longer one lives, the more one
learns,"
Said I, as off to sleep I went,
Bemused with thinking of Tithe con-
cerns,
And reading a book by the Bishop of
FERNS,[3]
On the Irish Church Establishment.
But lo ! in sleep not long I lay,
When Fancy her usual tricks began,
And I found myself bewitched away
To a goodly city in Hindostan —
A city where he who dares to dine
On aught but rice is deemed a sinner;
Where sheep and kine are held divine,
And accordingly — never drest for
dinner.

" But how is this? " I wondering cried —
As I walkt that city fair and wide,
And saw, in every marble street,
A row of beautiful butchers' shops —
" What means, for men who don't eat
meat,
"This grand display of loins and
chops? "
In vain I askt — 't was plain to see
That nobody dared to answer me.

So on from street to street I strode;
And you can't conceive how vastly odd
The butchers lookt — a roseate crew,
Inshrined in *stalls* with naught to do;
While some on a *bench*, half dozing, sat,
And the Sacred Cows were not more fat.
Still posed to think what all this scene

1 But the wretch who can number his kisses,
    With few will be ever content.

2 The Duke of Wellington, who styled them
" the Articles of Christianity."

3 An indefatigable scribbler of anti-Catholic
pamphlets.

Of sinecure trade was *meant* to mean,
" And, pray," askt I — " by whom is
    paid
The expense of this strange masque-
    rade ? " —
" The expense ! — oh ! that 's of course
    defrayed
(Said one of these well-fed Hecatombers)
" By yonder rascally rice-consumers."
" What ! *they* who must n't eat meat ! " —
                            No matter —
(And while he spoke his cheeks grew
    fatter,)
" The rogues may munch their *Paddy*
    crop,
" But the rogues must still support *our*
    shop.
" And depend upon it, the way to treat
    " Heretical stomachs that thus dissent,
" Is to burden all that won't eat meat,
    " With a costly MEAT ESTABLISH-
    MENT."

On hearing these words so gravely said,
    With a volley of laughter loud I shook,
And my slumber fled and my dream was
    sped,
And I found I was lying snug in bed,
    With my nose in the Bishop of FERNS's
    book.

THE BRUNSWICK CLUB.

A letter having been addressed to a very distinguished personage, requesting him to become
the Patron of this Orange Club, a polite answer
was forthwith returned, of which we have been
fortunate enough to obtain a copy.

Brimstone-hall, September 1, 1828.

Private. — LORD BELZEBUB presents
To the Brunswick Club his compliments,
And much regrets to say that he
Can not at present their Patron be.
In stating this, Lord Belzebub
Assures on his honor the Brunswick
    Club,
That 't is n't from any lukewarm lack
Of zeal or fire he thus holds back —
As even Lord *Coal*[1] himself is not
For the Orange party more red-hot :
But the truth is, till their Club affords
A somewhat decenter show of Lords,

---

[1] Usually written "Cole."

And on its list of members gets
A few less rubbishy Baronets,
Lord Belzebub must beg to be
Excused from keeping such company.

Who the devil, he humbly begs to
    know,
Are Lord Glandine, and Lord Dunlo ?
Or who, with a grain of sense, would
    go
To sit and be bored by Lord Mayo ?
What living creature — *except his nurse* —
For Lord Mountcashel cares a curse,
Or thinks 't would matter if Lord Mus-
    kerry
Were t' other side of the Stygian
    ferry ?
Breathes there a man in Dublin town,
Who-'d give but half of half-a-crown
To save from drowning my Lord Rath-
    downe,
Or who would n't also gladly hustle in
Lords Roden, Bandon, Cole, and Joce-
    lyn ?
In short, tho' from his tenderest years,
Accustomed to all sorts of Peers,
Lord Belzebub much questions whether
He ever yet saw mixt together
As 't were in one capacious tub,
Such a mess of noble silly-bub
As the twenty Peers of the Brunswick
    Club.
'T is therefore impossible that Lord B.
Could stoop to such society,
Thinking, he owns (tho' no great prig),
For one in his station 't were *infra dig.*
But he begs to propose, in the interim
(Till they find some properer Peers for
    him),
His Highness of Cumberland, as *Sub*,
To take his place at the Brunswick
    Club —
Begging, meanwhile, himself to dub
Their obedient servant,
                            BELZEBUB.

It luckily happens, the Royal Duke
Resembles so much, in air and look,
The head of the Belzebub family,
That few can any difference see ;
Which makes him of course the better
    suit
To serve as Lord B.'s substitute.

PROPOSALS FOR A GYNÆCOC-RACY.

ADDRESSED TO

A LATE RADICAL MEETING.

—— *" quas ipsa decus sibi dia Camilla*
delegit pacisque bonas bellique ministras."
VERGIL.

As Whig Reform has had its range,
  And none of us are yet content,
Suppose, my friends, by way of change,
  We try a *Female Parliament ;*
And since of late with *he* M.P.'s
We 've fared so badly, take to she's —
Petticoat patriots, flounced John Rus-
  sells,
Burdetts in *blonde* and Broughams in
  bustles.
The plan is startling, I confess —
But 't is but an affair of dress;
Nor see I much there is to choose
  'Twixt Ladies (so they 're thorough-
  bred ones)
In ribands of all sorts of hues,
  Or Lords in only blue or red ones.

At least the fiddlers will be winners,
  Whatever other trade advances;
As then, instead of Cabinet dinners,
  We 'll have, at Almack's, Cabinet
  dances;
Nor let this world's important questions
Depend on Ministers' digestions.

If Ude's receipts have done things ill,
  To Weippert's band they may go
  better;
There 's Lady * * , in one quadrille,
  Would settle Europe, if you 'd let her :
And who the deuce or asks or cares
  When Whigs or Tories have undone
  'em,
Whether they 've *danced* thro' State
  affairs,
  Or simply, dully, *dined* upon 'em?

Hurrah then for the Petticoats !
To them we pledge our free-born votes;
We 'll have all *she*, and only *she* —
  Pert blues shall act as " best de-
  baters,"
Old dowagers our Bishops be,
  And termagants our agitators.

If Vestris to oblige the nation
  Her own Olympus will abandon
And help to prop the Administration,
  It *can 't* have better legs to stand on.
The famed Macaulay (Miss) shall show
  Each evening, forth in learned ora-
  tion ;
Shall move (midst general cries of
  " Oh ! ")
  For full returns of population :
And finally to crown the whole,
  The Princess Olive,[1] Royal soul,
Shall from her bower in Banco Regis,
Descend to bless her faithful lieges,
And mid our Union's loyal chorus
Reign jollily for ever o'er us.

TO THE EDITOR OF THE * * *.

Sir,
  Having heard some rumors respecting the
strange and awful visitation under which Lord
Henley has for some time past been suffering,
in consequence of his declared hostility to " anthems, solos, duets," [2] etc., I took the liberty of
making inquiries at his Lordship's house this
morning, and lose no time in transmitting to you
such particulars as I could collect. It is said
that the screams of his Lordship, under the
operation of this nightly concert, (which is no
doubt some trick of the Radicals), may be
heard all over the neighborhood. The female
who personates St. Cecilia is supposed to be the
same that last year appeared in the character of
Isis at the Rotunda. How the cherubs are managed, I have not yet ascertained.
  Yours, etc.
  P. P.

LORD HENLEY AND ST. CECILIA.

—— *in Metii descendat Judicis aures.*
HORAT.

As snug in his bed Lord Henley lay,
  Revolving much his own renown,
And hoping to add thereto a ray
  By putting duets and anthems down,

Sudden a strain of choral sounds
  Mellifluous o'er his senses stole;
Whereat the Reformer muttered
  " Zounds ! "
  For he loathed sweet music with all
  his soul.

1 A personage, so styling herself, who attained considerable notoriety at that period.

2 In a work, on Church Reform, published by
his Lordship in 1832.

Then starting up he saw a sight
   That well might shock so learned a
      snorer —
Saint Cecilia robed in light
   With a portable organ slung before
      her.

And round were Cherubs on rainbow
      wings,
   Who, his Lordship feared, might tire
      of flitting,
So begged they 'd sit — but ah! poor
      things,
   They 'd, none of them, got the means
      of sitting. [1]

" Having heard," said the Saint, "you 're
      fond of hymns,
   " And indeed that musical snore be-
      trayed you,
" Myself and my choir of cherubims
   " Are come for a while to serenade
      you."

In vain did the horrified Henley say
   " 'T was all a mistake — she was mis-
      directed; "
And point to a concert over the way
   Where fiddlers and angels were ex-
      pected.

In vain — the Saint could see in his looks
   (She civilly said) much tuneful lore;
So at once all opened their music-books,
   And herself and her Cherubs set off at
      score.

All night duets, terzets, quartets,
   Nay, long quintets most dire to hear;
Ay, and old motets and canzonets
   And glees in sets kept boring his ear.

He tried to sleep — but it would n't do;
   So loud they squalled, he *must* attend
      to 'em;
Tho' Cherubs' songs to his cost he knew
   Were like themselves and had no end
      to 'em.

Oh judgment dire on judges bold,
   Who meddle with music's sacred
      strains!

1 " *Asseyez-vous, mes enfans.*" — " *Il n'y a
pas de quoi, mon Seigneur.*"

Judge Midas tried the same of old
   And was punisht like Henley for his
      pains.

But worse on the modern judge, alas!
   Is the sentence launched from Apollo's
      throne;
For Midas was given the ears of an ass,
   While Henley is doomed to keep his
      own!

ADVERTISEMENT. [2]

1830.

MISSING or lost, last Sunday night,
   A Waterloo coin whereon was traced
The inscription, "Courage!" in letters
      bright,
   Tho' a little by rust of years defaced.

The metal thereof is rough and hard,
   And ('t is thought of late) mixt up
      with brass;
But it bears the stamp of Fame's award,
   And thro' all Posterity's hands will
      pass.

How it was lost God only knows,
   But certain *City* thieves, they say,
Broke in on the owner's evening doze,
   And filched this "gift of gods" away!

One ne'er could, of course, the Cits sus-
      pect,
   If we had n't that evening chanced to
      see,
At the robbed man's door a *Mare* elect
   With an ass to keep her company.

Whoso'er of this lost treasure knows,
   Is begged to state all facts about it,
As the owner can't well face his foes,
   Nor even his friends just now without
      it.

And if Sir Clod will bring it back,
   Like a trusty Baronet, wise and able,

2 Written at that memorable crisis when a distinguished Duke, then Prime Minister, acting
under the inspirations of Sir Claudius Hunter,
and other City worthies, advised his Majesty to
give up his announced intention of dining with
the Lord Mayor.

He shall have a ride on the whitest hack[1]
That's left in old King George's stable.

MISSING.

Carlton Terrace, 1832.

WHEREAS, Lord ****** de *******
Left his home last Saturday,
And, tho' inquired for round and round
Thro' certain purlieus, can't be found ;
And whereas, none can solve our queries
As to where this virtuous Peer is,
Notice is hereby given that all
May forthwith to inquiring fall,
As, once the thing's well set about,
No doubt but we shall hunt him out.

His Lordship's mind, of late, they say,
Hath been in an uneasy way.
Himself and colleagues not being let
To climb into the Cabinet,
To settle England's state affairs,
Hath much, it seems, *un*settled theirs;
And chief to this stray Plenipo
Hath been a most distressing blow.
Already, — certain to receive a
Well-paid mission to the Neva,
And be the bearer of kind words
To tyrant Nick from Tory Lords, —
To fit himself for free discussion,
His Lordship had been learning Russian;
And all so natural to him were
The accents of the Northern bear,
That while his tones were in your ear, you
Might swear you were in sweet Siberia.
And still, poor Peer, to old and young,
He goes on raving in that tongue;
Tells you how much you would enjoy a
Trip to Dalnodubrovskoya;[2]
Talks of such places by the score on
As Oulisflirmchinagoboron,[3]
And swears (for he at nothing sticks)
That Russia swarms with Raskol-niks,[4]

---

1 Among other remarkable attributes by which Sir Claudius distinguished himself, the dazzling whiteness of his favorite steed was not the least conspicuous.

2 In the Government of Perm.

3 Territory belonging to the mines of Ko-livano-Kosskressense.

4 The Russian name of religious dissenters or heretics. " *Il existe en Russie plusieurs sectes ; la plus nombreuse est celle des Raskolniks, ou vrai-croyants.*" — GAMBA, " *Voyage dans la Russie Méridionale.*"

Tho' *one* such Nick, God knows, must be
A more than ample quantity.

Such are the marks by which to know
This strayed or stolen Plenipo;
And whosoever brings or sends
The unhappy statesman to his friends
On Carlton Terrace, shall have thanks,
And — any paper but the Bank's.

P.S. — Some think the disappearance
Of this our diplomatic Peer hence
Is for the purpose of reviewing,
In person, what dear Mig is doing,
So as to'scape all tell-tale letters
'Bout Beresford, and such abettors, —
The only " wretches " for whose aid[5]
Letters seem *not* to have been made.

THE DANCE OF BISHOPS;

OR, THE EPISCOPAL QUADRILLE.[6]

A DREAM.

1833.

" Solemn dances were, on great festivals and celebrations, admitted among the primitive Christians, in which even the Bishops and dignified Clergy were performers. Scaliger says, that the first Bishops were called *præsules*[7] for no other reason than that they led off these dances." — " *Cyclopædia*," art. *Dances*.

I 'VE had such a dream — a frightful
    dream —
Tho' funny mayhap to wags 't will seem,
By all who regard the Church, like us,
'T will be thought exceedingly ominous !

As reading in bed I lay last night —
Which (being insured) is my delight —
I happened to doze off just as I got to
The singular fact which forms my motto.
Only think, thought I, as I dozed
    away,
Of a party of Churchmen dancing the
    hay !
Clerks, curates and rectors capering all
With a neat-legged Bishop to open the
    ball !

---

5 " Heaven first taught letters for some wretch's aid." POPE.

6 Written on the passing of the memorable Bill, in the year 1833, for the abolition of ten Irish Bishoprics.

7 Literally, First Dancers.

Scarce had my eyelids time to close,
When the scene I had fancied before me
　　rose —
An Episcopal Hop on a scale so grand
As my dazzled eyes could hardly stand.
For Britain and Erin clubbed their Sees
To make it a Dance of Dignities,
And I saw — oh brightest of Church
　　events !
A quadrille of the two Establishments,
Bishop to Bishop *vis-à-vis*,
Footing away prodigiously.

There was Bristol capering up to Derry,
And Cork with London making merry;
While huge Llandaff, with a See, so so,
Was to dear old Dublin pointing his toe.
There was Chester, hatched by woman's
　　smile,
Performing a *chaine des Dames* in style;
While he who, whene'er the Lords'
　　House dozes,
Can waken them up by citing Moses,[1]
The portly Tuam, was all in a hurry
To set, *en avant*, to Canterbury.

Meantime, while pamphlets stuft his
　　pockets,
(All out of date like spent sky-rockets,)
Our Exeter stood forth to caper,
As high on the floor as he doth on
　　paper —
Much like a dapper Dancing Dervise,
Who pirouettes his whole church-ser-
　　vice —
Performing, midst those reverend souls,
Such *entrechats*, such *cabrioles*,
Such *balonnés*,[2] such — rigmaroles,
Now high, now low, now this, now that,
That none could guess what the devil
　　he 'd be at;
Tho', watching his various steps, some
　　thought
That a step in the Church was all he
　　sought.

1 "And what does Moses say?"— One of
the ejaculations with which this eminent prelate
enlivened his famous speech on the Catholic
question.

2 A description of the method of executing
this step may be useful to future performers in
the same line : — "*Ce pas est composé de deux
mouvemens différens, savoir, plier, et sauter
sur un pied, et se rejeter sur l'autre.*" —
"*Dictionnaire de Danse.*" art. *Contre-temps.*

But alas, alas ! while thus so gay,
These reverend dancers friskt away,
Nor Paul himself (not the saint, but he
Of the Opera-house) could brisker be,
There gathered a gloom around their
　　glee —
A shadow which came and went so fast,
That ere one could say " 'T is there,"
　　't was past —
And, lo! when the scene again was
　　cleared,
Ten of the dancers had disappeared !
Ten able-bodied quadrillers swept
From the hallowed floor where late they
　　stept,
While twelve was all that footed it still,
On the Irish side of that grand Qua-
　　drille !

Nor this the worst:— still danced they
　　on,
But the pomp was saddened, the smile
　　was gone ;
And again from time to time the same
Ill-omened darkness round them came —
While still as the light broke out anew,
Their ranks lookt less by a dozen or
　　two;
Till ah ! at last there were only found
Just Bishops enough for a four-hands-
　　round;
And when I awoke, impatient getting,
I left the last holy pair *poussetting !*

N. B. — As ladies in years, it seems,
Have the happiest knack at solving
　　dreams,
I shall leave to my ancient feminine
　　friends
Of the *Standard* to say what *this* por-
　　tends.

DICK * * * *.

A CHARACTER.

OF various scraps and fragments built,
　　Borrowed alike from fools and wits,
Dick's mind was like a patchwork quilt,
　　Made up of new, old, motley bits —
Where, if the *Co.* called in their shares,
　　If petticoats their quota got
And gowns were all refunded theirs,
　　The quilt would look but shy, God
　　　　wot.

And thus he still, new plagiaries seeking,
Reversed ventriloquism's trick,
For, 'stead of Dick thro' others speaking,
'T was others we heard speak thro' Dick.

A Tory now, all bounds exceeding,
Now best of Whigs, now worst of rats;
One day with Malthus, foe to breeding,
The next with Sadler, all for brats.

Poor Dick! — and how else could it be?
With notions all at random caught,
A sort of mental fricassee,
Made up of legs and wings of thought —
The leavings of the last Debate, or
A dinner, yesterday, of wits,
Where Dick sate by and, like a waiter,
Had the scraps for perquisites.

A CORRECTED REPORT OF SOME LATE SPEECHES.

1834.

"Then I heard one saint speaking, and another saint said unto that saint."

St. SINCLAIR rose and declared in sooth,
That he would n't give sixpence to Maynooth.
He had hated priests the whole of his life,
For a priest was a man who had no wife,[1]
And, having no wife, the Church was his mother,
The Church was his father, sister and brother.
This being the case, he was sorry to say
That a gulf 'twixt Papist and Protestant lay,[2]
So deep and wide, scarce possible was it
To say even "how d' ye do?" across it:

And tho' your Liberals, nimble as fleas,
Could clear such gulfs with perfect ease,
'T was a jump that naught on earth could make
Your proper, heavy-built Christian take.
No, no, — if a Dance of Sects *must* be,
He would set to the Baptist willingly,[3]
At the Independent deign to smirk,
And rigadoon with old Mother Kirk;
Nay even, for once, if needs must be,
He 'd take hands round with all the three;
But as to a jig with Popery, no, —
To the Harlot ne'er would he point his toe.

St. Mandeville was the next that rose, —
A saint who round as pedler goes
With his pack of piety and prose,
Heavy and hot enough, God knows, —
And he said that Papists were much inclined
To extirpate all of Protestant kind,
Which he could n't in truth so much condemn;
Having rather a wish to extirpate *them ;*
That is, — to guard against mistake, —
To extirpate them for their doctrine's sake;
A distinction Churchmen always make, —
Insomuch that when they 've prime control,
Tho' sometimes roasting heretics whole,
They but cook the body for sake of the soul.

Next jumpt St. Johnston jollily forth,
The spiritual Dogberry of the North,[4]
A right "wise fellow, and what 's more,
An officer,"[5] like his type of yore;
And he asked if we grant such toleration,

---

1 "He objected to the maintenance and education of a clergy *bound by the particular vows of celibacy, which as it were gave them the Church as their only family, making it fill the places of father and mother and brother.*" — Debate on the Grant to Maynooth College, *The Times,* April 19.

2 "It had always appeared to him that *between the Catholic and Protestant a great gulf* intervened, which rendered it impossible," etc.

3 The Baptist might acceptably extend the offices of religion to the Presbyterian and the Independent, or the member of the Church of England to any of the other three; but the Catholic," etc.

4 "Could he then, holding as he did a spiritual office in the Church of Scotland, (cries of hear, and laughter,) with any consistency give his consent to a grant of money?" etc.

5 "I am a wise fellow, and which is more, an officer." — *Much Ado About Nothing.*

Pray, what's the use of our Reforma-
     tion ?[1]
What is the use of our Church and
     State?
Our Bishops, Articles, Tithe and Rate?
And still as he yelled out " what's the
     use?"
Old Echoes, from their cells recluse
Where they'd for centuries slept, broke
     loose,
Yelling responsive, " *What's the use ?*"

MORAL POSITIONS.

A DREAM.

" His Lordship said that it took a long time
for a moral position to find its way across the
Atlantic. He was very sorry that its voyage
had been so long," etc. — Speech of Lord Dudley and Ward on Colonial Slavery, March 8.

T 'OTHER night, after hearing Lord
     Dudley's oration
     (A treat that comes once a-year as
          May-day does),
I dreamt that I saw — what a strange
     operation!
A " moral position " shipt off for Bar-
     badoes.

The whole Bench of Bishops stood by in
     grave attitudes,
     Packing the article tidy and neat; —
As their Reverences know that in south-
     erly latitudes
     " Moral positions " don't keep very
          sweet.

There was Bathurst arranging the cus-
     tom-house pass;
     And to guard the frail package from
          tousing and routing,
There stood my Lord Eldon, endorsing
     it " Glass,"
     Tho' as to which side should lie up-
          permost, doubting.

The freight was however stowed safe in
     the hold;
     The winds were polite and the moon
          lookt romantic,

While off in the good ship " The Truth "
     we were rolled,
With our ethical cargo, across the
     Atlantic.
Long, dolefully long, seemed the voyage
     we made;
     For " The Truth," at all times but a
          very slow sailer,
By friends, near as much as by foes, is
     delayed,
     And few come aboard her tho' so
          many hail her.

At length, safe arrived, I went thro'
     " tare and tret,"
     Delivered my goods in the primest
          condition,
And next morning read in the *Bridge-
          town Gazette*,
     " Just arrived by ' The Truth,' a new
          moral position.

" The Captain " — here, startled to find
     myself named
     As " the Captain " — (a thing which,
          I own it with pain,
I thro' life have avoided,) I woke —
     lookt ashamed,
     Found I *was n't* a captain and dozed
          off again.

THE MAD TORY AND THE COMET.

FOUNDED ON A LATE DISTRESSING
          INCIDENT.

1832-3.

" *mutantem regna cometem*." LUCAN.[2]

" THO' all the pet mischiefs we count
     upon fail,
     " Tho' Cholera, hurricanes, Welling-
          ton leave us,
" We 've still in reserve, mighty Comet,
     thy tail; —
     " Last hope of the Tories, wilt thou
          too deceive us?

1 " What, he asked, was the use of the Reformation? What was the use of the Articles of
the Church of England, or of the Church of
Scotland ?" etc.

2 Eclipses and comets have been always
looked to as great changers of administrations.
Thus Milton, speaking of the former : —

          " With fear of change
          Perplexing monarchs."

And in Statius we find,

          " *mutant quæ sceptra cometæ*."

"No — 't is coming, 't is coming, the
  avenger is nigh;
  "Heed, heed not, ye placemen, how
  Herapath flatters;
"One whisk from that tail as it passes
  us by
  "Will settle at once all political mat-
  ters; —

"The East-India Question, the Bank,
  the Five Powers,
  "(Now turned into two) with their
  rigmarole Protocols; [1] —
"Ha! ha! ye gods, how this new friend
  of ours
  "Will knock, right and left, all diplomacy's what-d' ye-calls!

"Yes, rather than Whigs at our downfall
  should mock,
  "Meet planets and suns in one general
  hustle!
"While happy in vengeance we welcome
  the shock
  "That shall jerk from their places,
  Grey, Althorp, and Russell."

Thus spoke a mad Lord, as, with tele-
  scope raised,
  His wild Tory eye on the heavens he
  set;
And tho' nothing destructive appeared
  as he gazed,
  Much hoped that there *would* before
  Parliament met.

And still, as odd shapes seemed to flit
  thro' his glass,
  "Ha! there it is now," the poor maniac cries;
While his fancy with forms but too monstrous, alas!
  From his own Tory zodiac peoples the
  skies : —

"Now I spy a big body, good heavens,
  how big!
  "Whether Bucky [2] or Taurus I cannot well say : —

"And yonder there's Eldon's old Chan-
  cery-wig,
  "In its dusty aphelion fast fading
  away.

"I see, 'mong those fatuous meteors behind,
  "Londonderry, *in vacuo,* flaring
  about; —
"While that dim double star, of the
  nebulous kind,
  "Is the Gemini, Roden and Lorton,
  no doubt.

"Ah, Ellenborough! 'faith, I first
  thought 't was the Comet;
  "So like that in Milton, it made me
  quite pale;
"The head with the same 'horrid hair' [3]
  coming from it,
  "And plenty of vapor, but — where
  is the tail?"

Just then, up aloft jumpt the gazer
  elated —
For lo! his bright glass a phenomenon
  showed,
Which he took to be Cumberland, *upwards* translated,
Instead of his natural course, *t'other*
  road!

But too awful that sight for a spirit so
  shaken, —
Down dropt the poor Tory in fits and
  grimaces,
Then off to the Bedlam in Charles Street
  was taken,
And is now one of Halford's most
  favorite cases.

FROM THE HON. HENRY ——, TO LADY EMMA ——.

Paris, March 30, 1832.

You bid me explain, my dear angry
  Ma'amselle,
How I came thus to bolt without saying
  farewell;

1 See, for some of these Protocols, the Annual Register, for the year 1832.
2 The Duke of Buckingham.

3 "And from his horrid hair
  Shakes pestilence and war."

And the truth is, — as truth you *will*
   have, my sweet railer, —
   There are two worthy persons I always
      feel loath
To take leave of at starting, — my mis-
   tress and tailor, —
   As somehow one always has *scenes*
      with them both;
The Snip in ill-humor, the Syren in
   tears,
   She calling on Heaven, and he on the
      attorney, —
Till sometimes, in short, 'twixt his duns
   and his dears,
   A young gentleman risks being stopt
      in his journey.

But to come to the point, tho' you think,
   I dare say,
That 't is debt or the Cholera drives me
   away,
'Pon honor you 're wrong; — such a
   mere bagatelle
As a pestilence, nobody now-a-days
   fears;
And the fact is, my love, I 'm thus bolt-
   ing, pell-mell,
   To get out of the way of these horrid
      new Peers;[1]
This deluge of coronets frightful to think
   of,
Which England is now for her sins on
   the brink of;
This coinage of *nobles*, — coined all of
   'em, badly,
And sure to bring Counts to a *dis*count
   most sadly.

Only think! to have Lords overrunning
   the nation,
As plenty as frogs in a Dutch inunda-
   tion;
No shelter from Barons, from Earls no
   protection,
And tadpole young Lords too in every
   direction, —
Things created in haste just to make a
   Court list of,
Two legs and a coronet all they consist of !

1 A new creation of Peers was generally expected at this time.

The prospect 's quite frightful, and what
   Sir George Rose
   (My particular friend) says is perfectly
      true,
That, so dire the alternative, nobody
   knows,
   'Twixt the Peers and the Pestilence,
      what he 's to do;
And Sir George even doubts, — could he
   choose his disorder, —
   'Twixt coffin and coronet, *which* he
      would order.
This being the case, why, I thought, my
   dear Emma,
   'T were best to fight shy of so curst a di-
      lemma;
And tho' I confess myself somewhat a
   villain,
   To 've left *idol mio* without an *addio*,
Console your sweet heart, and a week
   hence from Milan
   I 'll send you — some news of Bellini's
      last trio.

N.B. — Have just packt up my travelling
   set-out,
Things a tourist in Italy *can't* go with-
   out —
Viz., a pair of *gants gras*, from old Hou-
   bigant's shop,
Good for hands that the air of Mont
   Cenis might chap.
Small presents for ladies, — and nothing
   so wheedles
The creatures abroad as your golden-
   eyed needles.
A neat pocket Horace by which folks
   are cozened
To think one knows Latin, when — one,
   perhaps, does n't;
With some little book about heathen my-
   thology,
Just large enough to refresh one's theol-
   ogy;
Nothing on earth being half such a
   bore as
Not knowing the difference 'twixt Virgins
   and Floras.
Once more, love, farewell, best regards
   to the girls,
And mind you beware of damp feet and
   new Earls.

                                    HENRY.

TRIUMPH OF BIGOTRY.

"COLLEGE. — We announced, in our last, that Lefroy and Shaw were returned. They were chaired yesterday; the Students of the College determined, it would seem, to imitate the mob in all things, harnessing themselves to the car, and the Masters of Arts bearing Orange flags and bludgeons before, beside, and behind the car."
Dublin Evening Post, Dec. 20, 1832.

AY, yoke ye to the bigots' car,
  Ye chosen of Alma Mater's scions; —
Fleet chargers drew the God of War,
  Great Cybele was drawn by lions,
And Sylvan Pan, as Poets dream,
Drove four young panthers in his team.
Thus classical Lefroy, for once, is,
  Thus, studious of a like turn-out,
He harnesses young sucking dunces,
  To draw him as their Chief about,
And let the world a picture see
Of Dulness yoked to Bigotry:
Showing us how young College hacks
Can pace with bigots at their backs,
As tho' the cubs were *born* to draw
Such luggage as Lefroy and Shaw.
Oh! shade of Goldsmith, shade of Swift,
  Bright spirits whom, in days of yore,
This Queen of Dulness sent adrift,
  As aliens to her foggy shore; [1] —
Shade of our glorious Grattan, too,
  Whose very name her shame recalls;
Whose effigy her bigot crew
  Reversed upon their monkish walls, [2] —
Bear witness (lest the world should doubt)
  To your mute Mother's dull renown,
Then famous but for Wit turned *out*,
  And Eloquence *turned upside down ;*
But now ordained new wreaths to win,
  Beyond all fame of former days,
By breaking thus young donkies in
  To draw M.P.s amid the brays
Alike of donkies and M.A.s; —
Defying Oxford to surpass 'em
In this new " *Gradus ad Parnassum.*"

1 See the lives of these two poets for the circumstances under which they left Dublin College.

2 In the year 1799, the Board of Trinity College, Dublin, thought proper, as a mode of expressing their disapprobation of Mr. Grattan's public conduct, to order his portrait, in the Great Hall of the University, to be turned upside down, and in this position it remained for some time.

TRANSLATION FROM THE GULL LANGUAGE.

Scripta manet.

1833.

'T WAS graved on the Stone of Destiny, [3]
In letters four and letters three;
And ne'er did the King of the Gulls go by
But those awful letters scared his eye;
For he knew that a Prophet Voice had said,
" As long as those words by man were read,
" The ancient race of the Gulls should ne'er
" One hour of peace or plenty share."
But years on years successive flew,
And the letters still more legible grew, —
At top, a T, an H, an E,
And underneath, D. E. B. T.

Some thought them Hebrew, — such as Jews
More skilled in Scrip than Scripture use;
While some surmised 't was an ancient way
Of keeping accounts, (well known in the day
Of the famed Didlerius Jeremias,
Who had thereto a wonderful bias,)
And proved in books most learnedly boring,
'T was called the Pon*tick* way of scoring.

Howe'er this be there never were yet
Seven letters of the alphabet,
That 'twixt them formed so grim a spell,
Or scared a Land of Gulls so well,
As did this awful riddle-me-ree
Of T. H. E. D. E. B. T.

  .   .   .   .   .   .

Hark ! — it is struggling Freedom's cry;
" Help, help, ye nations, or I die;
" 'T is Freedom's fight and on the field
" Where I expire *your* doom is sealed."
The Gull-King hears the awakening call,
He hath summoned his Peers and Patriots all,

3 Liafail, or the Stone of Destiny, — for which see Westminster Abbey.

And he asks, "Ye noble Gulls, shall
    we
"Stand basely by at the fall of the Free,
"Nor utter a curse nor deal a blow?"
And they answer with voice of thunder,
    "No."

Out fly their flashing swords in the air!—
But,—why do they rest suspended there?
What sudden blight, what baleful charm,
Hath chilled each eye and checkt each
    arm?
Alas! some withering hand hath thrown
The veil from off that fatal stone,
And pointing now with sapless finger,
Showeth where dark those letters lin-
    ger,—
Letters four and letters three,
T. H. E. D. E. B. T.

At sight thereof, each lifted brand
Powerless falls from every hand;
In vain the Patriot knits his brow,—
Even talk, his staple, fails him now.
In vain the King like a hero treads,
His Lords of the Treasury shake their
    heads;
And to all his talk of "brave and free,"
No answer getteth His Majesty
But "T. H. E. D. E. B. T."

In short, the whole Gull nation feels
They're fairly spell-bound, neck and
    heels;
And so, in the face of the laughing
    world,
Must e'en sit down with banners furled,
Adjourning all their dreams sublime
Of glory and war to—some other time.

NOTIONS ON REFORM.

BY A MODERN REFORMER.

Of all the misfortunes as yet brought to
    pass
    By this comet-like Bill, with its long
    tail of speeches,
The saddest and worst is the schism
    which alas!
    It has caused between Wetherel's
    waistcoat and breeches.

Some symptoms of this Anti-Union pro-
    pensity
    Had oft broken out in that quarter
    before;
But the breach, since the Bill, has at-
    tained such immensity,
    Daniel himself could have scarce wisht
    it more.

Oh! haste to repair it, ye friends of good
    order,
    Ye Atwoods and Wynns, ere the mo-
    ment is past;
Who can doubt that we tread upon An-
    archy's border,
    When the ties that should hold men
    are loosening so fast?

Make Wetherel yield to "some sort of
    Reform"
    (As we all must, God help us! with
    very wry faces;)
And loud as he likes let him bluster and
    storm
    About Corporate Rights, so he'll only
    wear braces.

Should those he now sports have been
    long in possession,
    And, like his own borough, the worse
    for the wear,
Advise him at least as a prudent conces-
    sion
    To Intellect's progress, to buy a new
    pair.

Oh! who that e'er saw him when vocal
    he stands,
    With a look something midway 'twixt
    Filch's and Lockit's,
While still, to inspire him, his deeply-
    thrust hands
    Keep jingling the rhino in both
    breeches-pockets—

Who that ever has listened thro' groan
    and thro' cough,
    To the speeches inspired by this mu-
    sic of pence,—
But must grieve that there's any thing
    like *falling off*
    In that great nether source of his wit
    and his sense?

Who that knows how he lookt when,
  with grace debonair,
  He began first to court — rather late
  in the season —
Or when, less fastidious, he sat in the
  chair
  Of his old friend, the Nottingham
  Goddess of Reason; [1]

That Goddess whose borough-like virtue
  attracted
  All mongers in *both* wares to proffer
  their love;
Whose chair like the stool of the Py-
  thoness acted,
  As Wetherel's rants ever since go to
  prove; [2]

Who in short would not grieve if a man
  of his graces
  Should go on rejecting, unwarned by
  the past,
The "moderate Reform" of a pair of
  new braces,
  Till, some day, — he 'll all fall to
  pieces at last.

TORY PLEDGES.

I PLEDGE myself thro' thick and thin,
  To labor still with zeal devout
To get the Outs, poor devils, in,
  And turn the Ins, the wretches, out.

I pledge myself, tho' much bereft
  Of ways and means of ruling ill,
To make the most of what are left,
  And stick to all that 's rotten still.

Tho' gone the days of place and pelf,
  And drones no more take all the
  honey,
I pledge myself to cram myself
  With all I can of public money.

<hr/>

1 It will be recollected that the learned gentleman himself boasted, one night, in the House
of Commons, of having sat in the very chair
which this allegorical lady had occupied.

2 Lucan's description of the effects of the
tripod on the appearance and voice of the sitter,
shows that the symptoms are, at least, very similar :

spumea tunc primum rabies vesana per ora
effluit . . . .
  tunc mœstus vastis ululatus in antris.

To quarter on that social purse
  My nephews, nieces, sisters, brothers,
Nor, so *we* prosper, care a curse
  How much 't is at the expense of
  others.

I pledge myself, whenever Right
  And Might on any point divide,
Not to ask which is black or white,
  But take at once the strongest side.

For instance, in all Tithe discussions,
  I 'm *for* the Reverend encroachers : —
I loathe the Poles, applaud the Rus-
  sians, —
  Am *for* the Squires, *against* the Poach-
  ers.

Betwixt the Corn-Lords and the Poor
  I 've not the slightest hesitation, —
The People *must* be starved, to insure
  The Land its due remuneration.

I pledge myself to be no more
  With Ireland's wrongs beprosed or
  shammed, —
I vote her grievances a *bore*,
  So she may suffer and be damned.

Or if she kick, let it console us,
  We still have plenty of red coats,
To cram the Church, that general bolus,
  Down any given amount of throats.

I dearly love the Frankfort Diet, —
  Think newspapers the worst of crimes;
And would, to give some chance of quiet,
  Hang all the writers of " *The Times ;*"

Break all their correspondents' bones,
  All authors of " Reply," " Rejoinder,"
From the Anti-Tory, Colonel Jones,
  To the Anti-Suttee, Mr. Poynder.

Such are the Pledges I propose;
  And tho' I can't now offer gold,
There 's many a way of buying those
  Who 've but the taste for being sold.

So here 's, with three times three hurrahs,
  A toast, of which you 'll not com-
  plain, —
" Long life to jobbing; may the days
" Of Peculation shine again ! "

ST. JEROME ON EARTH.

FIRST VISIT.

1832.

As St. Jerome who died some ages ago,
Was sitting one day in the shades below,
" I 've heard much of English bishops,"
　quoth he,
" And shall now take a trip to earth to see
" How far they agree in their lives and
　ways
" With our good old bishops of ancient
　days."

He had learned — but learned without
　misgivings —
Their love for good living and eke good
　livings;
Not knowing (as ne'er having taken degrees)
That good *living* means claret and fricassees,
While its plural means simply — pluralities.

" From all I hear," said the innocent
　man,
" They are quite on the good old primitive plan.
" For wealth and pomp they little can
　care,
" As they all say ' *No* ' to the Episcopal
　chair;
" And their vestal virtue it well denotes
" That they all, good men, wear petticoats."

Thus saying, post-haste to earth he
　hurries,
And knocks at the Archbishop of Canterbury's.
The door was oped by a lackey in lace,
Saying, " What 's your business with his
　Grace? "
" His Grace ! " quoth Jerome — for posed
　was he,
Not knowing what *sort* this Grace could
　be;
Whether Grace *preventing*, Grace *particular*,
Grace of that breed called *Quinquarticular* [1] —

In short he rummaged his holy mind
The exact description of Grace to find,
Which thus could represented be
By a footman in full livery.
At last, out loud in a laugh he broke,
(For dearly the good saint loved his
　joke) [2]
And said — surveying, as sly he spoke,
The costly palace from roof to base —
" Well, it is n't, at least, a *saving* Grace !"
" Umph ! " said the lackey, a man of few
　words,
" The Archbishop is gone to the House
　of Lords."
" To the House of the Lord, you mean,
　my son,
" For in *my* time at least there was but
　one;
" Unless such many-*fold* priests as these
" Seek, even in their LORD, pluralities ! " [3]
" No time for gab," quoth the man in
　lace:
Then slamming the door in St. Jerome's
　face
With a curse to the single knockers all
Went to finish his port in the servants'
　hall,
And propose a toast (humanely meant
To include even Curates in its extent)
" To all as *serves* the Establishment."

ST. JEROME ON EARTH.

SECOND VISIT.

"This much I dare say, that, since *lording*
and loitering hath come up, preaching hath come
down, contrary to the Apostles' times. For they
preached and *lorded* not : and now they *lord* and
preach not . . . . . Ever since the Prelates were
made Lords and Nobles, the plough standeth;
there is no work done, the people starve." —
Latimer, "*Sermon of the Plough.*"

" ONCE more," said Jerome, " I 'll run
up and see
How the Church goes on," — and off set
he.
Just then the packet-boat which trades
Betwixt our planet and the shades

1 So called from the proceedings of the Synod
of Dort.

2 Witness his well known pun on the name of
his adversary Vigilantius, whom he calls facetiously Dormitantius.

3 The suspicion attached to some of the early
Fathers of being Arians in their doctrine would
appear to derive some confirmation from this
passage.

Had arrived below with a freight so
    queer,
"My eyes!" said Jerome, "what have
    we here?" —
For he saw, when nearer he explored,
They 'd a cargo of Bishops' wigs
    aboard.
"They are ghosts of wigs," said Charon,
    "all,
"Once worn by nobs Episcopal.[1]
"For folks on earth, who 've got a store
"Of cast off things they 'll want no
    more,
"Oft send them down, as gifts, you
    know,
"To a certain Gentleman here below.

"A sign of the times, I plainly see,"
Said the Saint to himself as, pondering,
    he
Sailed off in the death-boat gallantly.

Arrived on earth, quoth he, "No more
"I 'll affect a body as before;
"For I think I 'd best, in the company
"Of Spiritual Lords, a spirit be,
"And glide unseen from See to See."
But oh! to tell what scenes he saw, —
It was more than Rabelais's pen could
    draw.
For instance, he found Exeter,
Soul, body, inkstand, all in a stir, —
For love of God? for sake of King?
For good of people? — no such thing;
But to get for himself, by some new
    trick,
A shove to a better bishoprick.

He found that pious soul, Van Mildert,
Much with his money-bags bewildered;
Snubbing the Clerks of the Diocess,[2]
Because the rogues showed restlessness
At having too little cash to touch,
While he so Christianly bears too much.
He found old Sarum's wits as gone
As his own beloved text in John,[3] —

Text he hath prosed so long upon,
That 't is thought when askt, at the gate
    of heaven,
His name, he 'll answer, "John, v. 7."

"But enough of Bishops I 've had to-
    day,"
Said the weary Saint, — "I must away.
"Tho' I own I should like before I go
"To see for once (as I 'm askt below
"If really such odd sights exist)
"A regular six-fold Pluralist."
Just then he heard a general cry —
"There 's Doctor Hodgson galloping
    by!"
"Ay, that 's the man," says the Saint,
    "to follow,"
And off he sets with a loud view hollo,
At Hodgson's heels, to catch if he can
A glimpse of this singular plural man.
But, — talk of Sir Boyle Roche's bird![4]
To compare him with Hodgson is
    absurd.
"Which way, sir, pray, is the doctor
    gone?" —
"He is now at his living at Hilling
    don." —
"No, no, — you 're out, by many a mile,
"He 's away at his Deanery in Car-
    lisle." —
"Pardon me, sir; but I understand
"He 's gone to his living in Cumber-
    land." —
"God bless me, no, — he can't be there;
"You must try St. George's, Hanover
    Square."

Thus all in vain the Saint inquired,
From living to living, mockt and tired; —
'T was Hodgson here, 't was Hodgson
    there,
'T was Hodgson nowhere, everywhere;
Till fairly beat the Saint gave o'er
And flitted away to the Stygian shore,
To astonish the natives underground
With the comical things he on earth had
    found.

---

1 The wig, which had so long formed an essential part of the dress of an English bishop,
was at this time beginning to be dispensed with.

2 See the Bishop's Letter to Clergy of his
Diocese.

3 1 John v. 7. A text which, though long

given up by all the rest of the orthodox world, is
still pertinaciously adhered to by this Right Reverend scholar.

4 It was a saying of the well-known Sir Boyle,
that "a man could not be in two places at once,
unless he was a bird."

THOUGHTS ON TAR BARRELS.

(VIDE DESCRIPTION OF A LATE FÊTE.) [1]

1832.

WHAT a pleasing contrivance ! how aptly
    devised
'Twixt tar and magnolias to puzzle
    one's noses !
And how the tar-barrels must all be sur-
    prised
To find themselves seated like " Love
    among roses ! "

What a pity we can't, by precautions like
    these,
    Clear the air of that other still viler
        infection;
That radical pest, that old whiggish dis-
    ease,
    Of which cases, true-blue, are in every
        direction.

Stead of barrels, let 's light up an *Auto
    da Fè*
    Of a few good combustible Lords of
        " the Club;"
They would fume in a trice, the Whig
    cholera away,
    And there 's Bucky would burn like a
        barrel of bub.

How Roden would blaze ! and what rub-
    bish throw out !
    A volcano of nonsense in active dis-
        play;
While Vane, as a butt, amidst laughter,
    would spout
    The hot nothings he 's full of, all
        night and all day.

And then, for a finish, there 's Cumber-
    land's Duke, —
    Good Lord, how his chin-tuft would
        crackle in air !
Unless (as is shrewdly surmised from
    his look)
    He 's already bespoke for combustion
        elsewhere.

1 The Marquis of Hertford's Fête. — From
dread of cholera his Lordship had ordered tar-
barrels to be burned in every direction.

THE CONSULTATION.[2]

"When they *do* agree, their unanimity is won-
    derful."   *The Critic.*

1833.

*Scene discovers Dr. Whig and Dr. Tory in con-
sultation. Patient on the floor between them.*

Dr. Whig. — THIS wild Irish patient
    does pester me so,
That what to do with him, I 'm curst if I
    know.
I 've *promist* him anodynes —
    Dr. Tory.   Anodynes ! — Stuff.
Tie him down — gag him well — he 'll
    be tranquil enough.
That 's *my* mode of practice.
    Dr. Whig.   True, quite in *your* line,
But unluckily not much, till lately, in
    mine.
'T is so painful —
    Dr. Tory. — Pooh, nonsense — ask
        Ude how he feels,
When, for Epicure feasts, he prepares
    his live eels,
By flinging them in, 'twixt the bars of
    the fire,
And letting them wriggle on there till
    they tire.
He, too, says "'t is painful " — "quite
    makes his heart bleed " —
But " your eels are a vile, oleaginous
    breed." —
He would fain use them gently, but
    Cookery says " No,"
And — in short — eels were *born* to be
    treated just so.[3]
'T is the same with these Irish, — who 're
    odder fish still, —
Your tender Whig heart shrinks from
    using them ill;
I myself in my youth, ere I came to get
    wise,
Used at some operations to blush to the
    eyes; —
But, in fact, my dear brother, — if I
    may make bold
To style you, as Peachum did Lockit, of
    old, —

2 These verses, as well as some others that
follow, (p. 660) were extorted from me by that
lamentable measure of the Whig ministry, the
Irish Coercion Act.

3 This eminent artist, in the second edition
of the work wherein he propounds this mode

We, Doctors, *must* act with the firmness
of Ude,
And, indifferent like him, — so the fish
is *but* stewed, —
Must torture live Pats for the general
good.
 [*Here patient groans and kicks a
little.*
 Dr. Whig. — But what, if one's patient 's so devilish perverse,
That he *won't* be thus tortured?
 Dr. Tory. Coerce, sir, coerce.
You 're a juvenile performer, but once
you begin,
You can't think how fast you may train
your hand in :
And (*smiling*) who knows but old Tory
may take to the shelf,
With the comforting thought that, in
place and in pelf,
He 's succeeded by one just as — bad as
himself?
 Dr. Whig (*looking flattered*). — Why,
to tell you the truth, I 've a small
matter here,
Which you helped me to make for my
patient last year, —
 [*Goes to a cupboard and brings out
a strait-waistcoat and gag.*
And such rest I 've enjoyed from his
raving since then
That I 've made up my mind he shall
wear it again.
 Dr. Tory (*embracing him*). — Oh,
charming ! — My dear Doctor Whig,
you 're a treasure,
Next to torturing, *myself*, to help *you* is a
pleasure.
 [*Assisting Dr. Whig.*
Give me leave — I 've some practice in
these mad machines;
There — tighter — the gag in the mouth,
by all means.
Delightful ! — all 's snug — not a squeak
need you fear, —
You may now put your anodynes off till
next year.
 [*Scene closes.*

of purifying his eels, professes himself much concerned at the charge of inhumanity brought
against his practice, but still begs leave respectfully to repeat that it *is* the only proper mode of
preparing eels for the table.

TO
THE REV. CHARLES OVERTON,
CURATE OF ROMALDKIRK.

AUTHOR OF THE POETICAL PORTRAITURE OF
THE CHURCH.[1]

1833.

SWEET singer of Romaldkirk, thou who
art reckoned,
By critics Episcopal, David the Second,[2]
If thus, as a Curate, so lofty your
flight,
Only think, in a Rectory, how you *would*
write !
Once fairly inspired by the " Tithe-
crowned Apollo,"
(Who beats, I confess it, our *lay* Phœbus
hollow,
Having gotten, besides the old *Nine's*
inspiration,
The *Tenth* of all eatable things in creation,)
There 's nothing in fact that a poet like
you,
So be-*nined* and be-*tenthed*, could n't
easily do.

Round the lips of the sweet-tongued
Athenian [3] they say,
While yet but a babe in his cradle he
lay,
Wild honey-bees swarmed as a presage
to tell
Of the sweet-flowing words that thence
afterwards fell.
Just so round our Overton's cradle, no
doubt,
Tenth ducklings and chicks were seen
flitting about;
Goose embryos, waiting their doomed
decimation,
Came, shadowing forth his adult destina-
tion,
And small, sucking tithe-pigs, in musical
droves,
Announced the Church poet whom
Chester approves.

1 See *Edinburgh Review*, No. 117.

2 " Your Lordship," says Mr. Overton, in
the Dedication of his Poem to the Bishop of
Chester, " has kindly expressed your persuasion
that my ' Muse will always be a Muse of sacred
song and that *it will be tuned as David's was.*' "

3 Sophocles.

O Horace! when thou, in thy vision of
yore,
Didst dream that a snowy-white plumage
came o'er
Thy etherealized limbs, stealing downily
on,
Till, by Fancy's strong spell, thou wert
turned to a swan,[1]
Little thought'st thou such fate could a
poet befall,
Without any effort of fancy, at all;
Little thought'st thou the world would in
Overton find
A bird, ready-made, somewhat different
in kind,
But as perfect as Michaelmas' self could
produce,
By gods yclept *anser*, by mortals a *goose*.

SCENE

FROM A PLAY, ACTED AT OXFORD, CALLED

"MATRICULATION."[2]

1834.

[Boy discovered at a table, with the Thirty-Nine
Articles before him. — Enter the Rt. Rev.
Doctor Phillpots.]

Doctor P. — THERE, my lad, lie the Arti-
cles — (*Boy begins to count them*)
just thirty-nine —
No occasion to count — you 've now only
to sign.
At Cambridge where folks are less High-
church than we,
The whole Nine-and-Thirty are lumped
into Three.
Let 's run o'er the items; — there 's
Justification,
Predestination, and Supererogation, —
Not forgetting Salvation and Creed
Athanasian,
Till we reach, at last, Queen Bess's
Ratification.

1 —— *album mutor in alitem*
supernè : nascunturque læves
per digitos, humerosque plumæ.

2 "It appears that when a youth of fifteen
goes to be matriculated at Oxford, and is required first to subscribe Thirty-Nine Articles
of Religious Belief, this only means that he
engages himself afterwards to understand what
is now above his comprehension ; that he expresses no assent at all to what he signs; and

That 's sufficient — now, sign — having
read quite enough,
You " believe in the full and true meaning thereof "?
(*Boy stares.*)
Oh! a mere form of words, to make
things smooth and brief, —
A commodious and short make-believe
of belief,
Which our Church has drawn up in a
form thus articular
To keep out in general all who 're particular.
But what 's the boy doing? what! reading all thro',
And my luncheon fast cooling! — this
never will do.
Boy (*poring over the Articles*). —
Here are points which — pray, Doc-
tor, what 's "Grace of Congru-
ity"?
Doctor P. (*sharply*). — You 'll find
out, young sir, when you 've more
ingenuity.
At present, by signing, you pledge your-
self merely,
Whate'er it may be, to believe it sin-
cerely.
Both in *dining* and *signing* we take the
same plan, —
First, swallow all down, then digest —
as we can.
Boy (*still reading*). — I 've to gulp,
I see, St. Athanasius's Creed,
Which, I 'm told, is a very tough morsel
indeed ;
As he damns —
Doctor P. (*aside*). — Ay, and so would
I, willingly, too,
All confounded particular young boobies,
like you.
This comes of Reforming! — all 's o'er
with our land,
When people won't stand what they
can't *under*stand;
Nor perceive that our ever-revered Thirty-
Nine
Were made not for men to *believe* but to
sign.
(*Exit Dr. P. in a passion.*)

that he is (or, *ought* to be) at full liberty, when
he has studied the subject, to withdraw his pro-
visional assent." — *Edinburgh Review*, No. 120.

LATE TITHE CASE.

" sic vos non vobis."

1833.

" The Vicar of Birmingham desires me to state that, in consequence of the passing of a recent Act of Parliament, he is compelled to adopt measures which may by some be considered harsh or precipitate; but, *in duty to what he owes to his successors,* he feels bound to preserve the rights of the vicarage." — *Letter from Mr. S. Powell,* August 6.

No, *not* for yourselves, ye reverend men,
Do you take one pig in every ten,
But for Holy Church's future heirs,
Who 've an abstract right to that pig, as
    theirs; —
The law supposing that such heirs male
Are already seized of the pig, in tail.
No, *not* for himself hath Birmingham's
    priest
His " well-beloved " of their pennies
    fleeced:
But it is that, before his prescient eyes,
All future Vicars of Birmingham rise,
With their embryo daughters, nephews,
    nieces,
And 't is for *them* the poor he fleeces.
He heareth their voices, ages hence,
Saying, " Take the pig " — " oh take
    the pence; "
The cries of little Vicarial dears,
The unborn Birminghamites, reach his
    ears;
And, did he resist that soft appeal,
He would *not* like a true-born Vicar feel.

Thou, too, Lundy of Lackington !
A Rector true, if e'er there was one,
Who, for sake of the Lundies of coming
    ages,
Gripest the tenths of laborers' wages.[1]
'T is true, in the pockets of *thy* small-
    clothes
The claimed " obvention "[2] of four-
    pence goes;

1 Fourteen agricultural laborers (one of whom received so little as six guineas for yearly wages, one eight, one nine, another ten guineas, and the best paid of the whole not more than 18*l.* annually) were all, in the course of the autumn of 1832, served with demands of tithe at the rate of 4*d.* in the 1*l.* sterling, on behalf of the Rev. F. Lundy, Rector of Lackington, etc. — *The Times,* August, 1833.

2 One of the various general terms under which oblations, tithes, etc., are comprised.

But its abstract spirit, unconfined,
Spreads to all future Rector-kind,
Warning them all to their rights to wake,
And rather to face the block, the stake,
Than give up their darling right *to take.*

One grain of musk, it is said, perfumes
(So subtle its spirit) a thousand rooms,
And a single four-pence, pocketed well,
Thro' a thousand rectors' lives will tell.
Then still continue, ye reverend souls,
And still as your rich Pactolus rolls,
Grasp every penny on every side,
From every wretch, to swell its tide:
Remembering still what the Law lays
    down,
In that pure poetic style of its own,
" If the parson *in esse* submits to loss, he
" Inflicts the same on the parson *in
    posse.*"

FOOLS' PARADISE.

DREAM THE FIRST.

I HAVE been, like Puck, I have been, in
    a trice,
To a realm they call Fools' Paradise,
Lying N.N.E. of the Land of Sense,
And seldom blest with a glimmer thence.
But they want it not in this happy place,
Where a light of its own gilds every face;
Or if some wear a shadowy brow,
'T is the *wish* to look wise, — not know-
    ing *how.*
Self glory glistens o'er all that 's there,
The trees, the flowers have a jaunty air;
The well-bred wind in a whisper blows,
The snow, if it snows, is *couleur de rose,*
The falling founts in a titter fall,
And the sun looks simpering down on all.

Oh, 't is n't in tongue or pen to trace
The scenes I saw in that joyous place.
There were Lords and Ladies sitting to-
    gether,
In converse sweet, " What charming
    weather ! —
" You 'll all rejoice to hear, I 'm sure,
" Lord Charles has got a good sinecure;
" And the Premier says, my youngest
    brother
" (Him in the Guards) shall have an-
    other.

" Is n't this very, *very* gallant ! —
" As for my poor old virgin aunt,
" Who has lost her all, poor thing, at
    whist,
" We must quarter *her* on the Pension
    List."
Thus smoothly time in that Eden rolled;
It seemed like an Age of *real* gold,
Where all who liked might have a slice,
So rich was that Fools' Paradise.

But the sport at which most time they
    spent,
Was a puppet-show, called Parliament
Performed by wooden Ciceros,
As large as life, who rose to prose,
While, hid behind them, lords and
    squires,
Who owned the puppets, pulled the
    wires;
And thought it the very best device
Of that most prosperous Paradise,
To make the vulgar pay thro' the nose
For them and their wooden Ciceros.

And many more such things I saw
In this Eden of Church and State and
    Law ;
Nor e'er were known such pleasant folk
As those who had the *best* of the joke.
There were Irish Rectors, such as resort
To Cheltenham yearly, to drink — port,
And bumper, "Long may the Church
    endure,
" May her cure of souls be a sinecure,
" And a score of Parsons to every soul
" A moderate allowance on the whole."
There were Heads of Colleges lying
    about,
From which the sense had all run out,
Even to the lowest classic lees,
Till nothing was left but *quantities ;*
Which made them heads most fit to be
Stuck up on a University,
Which yearly hatches, in its schools,
Such flights of young Elysian fools.

Thus all went on, so snug and nice,
In this happiest possible Paradise.
But plain it was to see, alas !
That a downfall soon must come to pass.
For grief is a lot the good and wise
Don't quite so much monopolize,

But that ("lapt in Elysium " as they
    are)
Even blessed fools must have their share.
And so it happened : — but what befell,
In Dream the Second I mean to tell.

THE RECTOR AND HIS CURATE;

OR, ONE POUND TWO.

" I trust we shall part as we met, in peace and
charity. My last payment to you paid your salary up to the 1st of this month. Since that, I
owe you for one month, which, being a long
month, of thirty-one days, amounts, as near as I
can calculate, to six pounds eight shillings. My
steward returns you as a debtor to the amount of
SEVEN POUNDS TEN SHILLINGS FOR CON-ACRE-
GROUND, which leaves some trifling balance in
my favor." — *Letter of Dismissal from the Rev.
Marcus Beresford to his Curate, the Rev. T. A.
Lyons.*

THE account is balanced — the bill
    drawn out, —
The debit and credit all right, no
    doubt —
The Rector rolling in wealth and state,
Owes to his Curate six pound eight;
The Curate, that *least* well-fed of men,
Owes to his Rector seven pound ten,
Which maketh the balance clearly due
From Curate to Rector, one pound
    two.

Ah balance, on earth unfair, uneven !
But sure to be all set right in heaven,
Where bills like these will be checkt,
    some day,
And the balance settled the other way :
Where Lyons the curate's hard-wrung
    sum
Will back to his shade with interest
    come;
And Marcus, the rector, deep may rue
This tot, in his favor, of one pound two.

PADDY'S METAMORPHOSIS.[1]

1833.

ABOUT fifty years since, in the days of
    our daddies,
    That plan was commenced which the
        wise now applaud,

1 I have already, on p. 656 referred to this
squib, as being one of those wrung from me by
the Irish Coercion Act of my friends, the Whigs.

Of shipping off Ireland's most turbulent
Paddies,
    As good raw material for *settlers*,
    abroad.
Some West-India island, whose name
I forget,
    Was the region then chosen for this
    scheme so romantic;
And such the success the first colony met,
    That a second, soon after, set sail o'er
    the Atlantic.

Behold them now safe at the long-lookt-
for shore,
    Sailing in between banks that the Shan-
    non might greet,
And thinking of friends whom, but two
years before,
    They had sorrowed to lose, but would
    soon again meet.

And, hark! from the shore a glad welcome there came —
    " Arrah, Paddy from Cork, is it you,
    my sweet boy?"
While Pat stood astounded, to hear his
own name
    Thus hailed by black devils, who ca-
    pered for joy!

Can it possibly be? — half amazement —
half doubt,
    Pat listens again — rubs his eyes and
    looks steady;
Then heaves a deep sigh, and in horror
yells out,
    " Good Lord! only think, — black
    and curly already!"

Deceived by that well-mimickt brogue in
his ears,
    Pat read his own doom in these wool-
    headed figures,
And thought, what a climate, in less than
two years,
    To turn a whole cargo of Pats into
    niggers!

MORAL.

'T is thus, — but alas! by a marvel more
true
    Than is told in this rival of Ovid's best
    stories, —

Your Whigs, when in office a short year
or two,
    By a *lusus naturæ*, all turn into Tories.

And thus, when I hear them " strong
measures" advise,
    Ere the seats that they sit on have
    time to get steady,
I say, while I listen, with tears in my
eyes,
    " Good Lord! only think, — black
    and curly already!"

COCKER, ON CHURCH REFORM.

FOUNDED UPON SOME LATE CALCU-
LATIONS. 1833.

FINE figures of speech let your orators
follow,
Old Cocker has figures that beat them all
hollow.
Tho' famed for his rules Aris*totle* may be,
In but *half* of this Sage any merit I see,
For, as honest Joe Hume says, the "*tot-
tle*"[1] for me!

For instance, while others discuss and
debate,
It is thus about Bishops *I* ratiocinate.

In England, where, spite of the infidel's
laughter,
'T is certain our souls are lookt *very* well
after,
Two Bishops can well (if judiciously sundered)
Of parishes manage two thousand two
hundred, —
Said number of parishes, under said
teachers,
Containing three millions of Protestant
creatures, —
So that each of said Bishops full ably
controls
One million and five hundred thousands
of souls.

And now comes old Cocker. In Ireland
we're told,
Half a million includes the whole Protestant fold;

1 The *total*, — so pronounced by this industrious senator.

If, therefore, for *three* million souls, 't is
  conceded
Two proper-sized Bishops are all that is
  needed,
'T is plain, for the Irish *half* million who
  want 'em,
One third of *one* Bishop is just the right
  quantum.
And thus, by old Cocker's sublime Rule
  of Three,
The Irish Church question 's resolved to
  a T;
Keeping always that excellent maxim in
  view,
That, in saving men's souls, we must
  save money too.

Nay, if — as St. Roden complains is the
  case —
The half million of *soul* is decreasing
  apace,
The demand, too, for *bishop* will also fall
  off,
Till the *tithe* of one, taken in kind, be
  enough.
But, as fractions imply that we 'd have
  to dissect,
And to cutting up Bishops I strongly ob-
  ject,
We 've a small, fractious prelate whom
  well we could spare,
Who has just the same decimal worth, to
  a hair;
And, not to leave Ireland too much in
  the lurch,
We 'll let her have Exeter, *sole*,[1] as her
  Church.

LES HOMMES AUTOMATES.

1834.

"We are persuaded that this our artificial man
will not only walk and speak and perform most
of the outward functions of animal life, but (being
wound up once a week) will perhaps reason as
well as most of your country parsons."—"*Memoirs of Martinus Scriblerus,*" chap. xii.

It being an object now to meet
With Parsons that don't want to eat,
Fit men to fill those Irish rectories,
Which soon will have but scant refec-
  tories,

1 Corporation sole.

It has been suggested, — lest that Church
Should all at once be left in the lurch
For want of reverend men endued
With this gift of never requiring food, —
To try, by way of experiment, whether
There could n't be made of wood and
  leather,[2]
(Howe'er the notion may sound chimer-
  ical,)
Jointed figures, not *lay*,[3] but clerical,
Which, wound up carefully once a week,
Might just like parsons look and speak,
Nay even, if requisite, reason too,
As well as most Irish parsons do.

The experiment having succeeded quite,
(Whereat those Lords must much delight,
Who 've shown, by stopping the Church's
  food,
They think it is n't for her spiritual good
To be served by parsons of flesh and
  blood,)
The Patentees of this new invention
Beg leave respectfully to mention,
They now are enabled to produce
An ample supply, for present use,
Of these reverend pieces of machinery,
Ready for vicarage, rectory, deanery,
Or any such-like post of skill
That wood and leather are fit to fill.

N.B. — In places addicted to arson,
We can't recommend a wooden parson:
But if the Church any such appoints,
They 'd better at least have iron joints.
In parts, not much by Protestants
  haunted,
A figure to *look at*'s all that's wanted —
A block in black, to eat and sleep,
Which (now that the eating 's o'er)
  comes cheap.

P.S. — Should the Lords, by way of a
  treat,
Permit the clergy again to eat,
The Church will of course no longer
  need
Imitation-parsons that never feed;

2 The materials of which those Nuremberg
Savans, mentioned by Scriblerus, constructed
their artificial man.

3 The wooden models used by painters are,
it is well known, called "lay figures."

And these *wood* creatures of ours will
    sell
For secular purposes just as well —
Our Beresfords, turned to bludgeons
    stout,
May, 'stead of beating their own
    about,
Be knocking the brains of Papists out;
While our smooth O'Sullivans, by all
    means,
Should transmigrate into *turning* ma-
    chines.

HOW TO MAKE ONE'S SELF A PEER.

ACCORDING TO THE NEWEST RECEIPT,
AS DISCLOSED IN A LATE HERALDIC
WORK.[1]

1834.

CHOOSE some title that 's dormant — the
    Peerage hath many —
Lord Baron of Shamdos sounds nobly as
    any.
Next, catch a dead cousin of said de-
    funct Peer,
And marry him, off hand, in some given
    year,
To the daughter of somebody, — no mat-
    ter who, —
Fig, the grocer himself, if you 're hard
    run, will do;
For, the Medici *pills* still in heraldry
    tell,
And why should n't *lollypops* quarter as
    well ?
Thus, having your couple, and one a
    lord's cousin,
Young materials for peers may be had
    by the dozen;
And 't is hard if, inventing each small
    mother's son of 'em,
You can't somehow manage to prove
    yourself one of 'em.

Should registers, deeds and such matters
    refractory,
Stand in the way of this lord-manufac-
    tory,

I' ve merely to hint, as a secret auric-
    ular,
One *grand* rule of enterprise, — *don't*
    be particular.
A man who once takes such a jump at
    nobility,
Must *not* mince the matter, like folks of
    nihility,[2]
But clear thick and thin with true lordly
    agility.

'T is true, to a would-be descendant
    from Kings,
Parish-registers sometimes are trouble-
    some things;
As oft, when the vision is near brought
    about,
Some goblin, in shape of a grocer, grins
    out;
Or some barber, perhaps, with my Lord
    mingles bloods,
And one's patent of peerage is left in
    the suds.

But there *are* ways — when folks are re-
    solved to be lords —
Of expurging even troublesome parish
    records.
What think ye of scissors? depend on 't
    no heir
Of a Shamdos should go unsupplied
    with a pair,
As whate'er *else* the learned in such lore
    may invent,
Your scissors does wonders in proving
    descent.
Yes, poets may sing of those terrible
    shears
With which Atropos snips off both
    bumpkins and peers,
But they 're naught to that weapon
    which shines in the hands
Of some would-be Patrician, when
    proudly he stands
O'er the careless churchwarden's baptis-
    mal array,
And sweeps at each cut generations
    away.
By some babe of old times is his peerage
    resisted?

---

1 The claim to the barony of Chandos (if I
recollect right) advanced by the late Sir Egerin-
ton Brydges.

2 "This we call pure nihility, or mere nothing." — *Watts's Logic.*

One snip, — and the urchin hath *never*
existed!
Does some marriage, in days near the
Flood, interfere
With his one sublime object of being a
Peer?
Quick the shears at once nullify bride-
groom and bride, —
No such people have ever lived, married
or died!

Such the newest receipt for those high-
minded elves,
Who 've a fancy for making great lords
of themselves.
Follow this, young aspirer who pant'st
for a peerage,
Take S—m for thy model and B—z for
thy steerage,
Do all and much worse than old Nicho-
las Flam does,
And — *who* knows but you 'll be Lord
Baron of Shamdos?

THE DUKE IS THE LAD.

Air. —" A master I have, and I am his man,
Galloping dreary dun."
" Castle of Andalusia."

THE Duke is the lad to frighten a lass,
Galloping, dreary duke;
The Duke is the lad to frighten a
lass,
He 's an ogre to meet, and the devil
to pass,
With his charger prancing,
Grim eye glancing,
Chin, like a Mufti,
Grizzled and tufty,
Galloping, dreary Duke.

Ye misses, beware of the neighbor-
hood
Of this galloping dreary Duke;
Avoid him, all who see no good
In being run o'er by a Prince of the
Blood.
For, surely, no nymph is
Fond of a grim phiz,
And of the married,
Whole crowds have miscarried
At sight of this dreary Duke.

EPISTLE

FROM ERASMUS ON EARTH TO CICERO IN THE SHADES.

Southampton.

As 't is now, my dear Tully, some weeks
since I started
By rail-road for earth, having vowed ere
we parted
To drop you a line by the Dead-Letter
post,
Just to say how I thrive in my new line
of ghost,
And how deucedly odd this live world
all appears,
To a man who 's been dead now for three
hundred years,
I take up my pen, and with news of this
earth
Hope to waken by turns both your
spleen and your mirth.

In my way to these shores, taking Italy
first,
Lest the change from Elysium too sudden should burst,
I forgot not to visit those haunts where
of yore
You took lessons from Pætus in cookery's
lore.[1]
Turned aside from the calls of the ros-
trum and Muse,
To discuss the rich merits of *rôtis* and
stews,
And preferred to all honors of triumph
or trophy,
A supper on prawns with that rogue,
little Sophy.[2]

Having dwelt on such classical musings
awhile,
I set off by a steam-boat for this happy
isle,
(A conveyance *you* ne'er, I think, sailed
by, my Tully,
And therefore, *per* next, I 'll describe it
more fully,)
Having heard on the way what distresses
me greatly,

1 See his Letters to Friends, *lib.* ix. *epist.* 19,
20, etc.
2 *ingentium squillarum cum Sophia Septi-
mæ.* — *Lib.* ix. *epist.* 10.

That England 's o'errun by *idolaters*
    lately,
Stark, staring adorers of wood and of
    stone,
Who will let neither stick, stock or
    statue alone.
Such the sad news I heard from a tall
    man in black,
Who from sports continental was hurry-
    ing back,
To look after his tithes; — seeing, doubt-
    less, 't would follow,
That just as of old your great idol,
    Apollo,
Devoured all the Tenths,[1] so the idols in
    question,
These wood and stone gods, may have
    equal digestion,
And the idolatrous crew whom this Rec-
    tor despises,
May eat up the tithe-pig which *he* idol-
    izes.

London.

'T is all but too true — grim Idolatry
    reigns
In full pomp over England's lost cities
    and plains!
On arriving just now, as my first thought
    and care
Was as usual to seek out some near
    House of Prayer,
Some calm holy spot, fit for Christians
    to pray on,
I was shown to — what think you? — a
    downright Pantheon!
A grand, pillared temple with niches and
    halls,[2]
Full of idols and gods, which they nick-
    name St. Paul's; —
Tho' 't is clearly the place where the
    idolatrous crew
Whom the Rector complained of, their
    dark rites pursue;
And, 'mong all the " strange gods "
    Abr'ham's father carved out,[3]
That he ever carv'd *stranger* than these
    I much doubt.

Were it even, my dear TULLY, your
    Hebes and Graces,
And such pretty things, that usurpt the
    Saints' places,
I should n't much mind, — for in this
    classic dome
Such folks from Olympus would feel
    quite at home.
But the gods they 've got here! — such
    a queer omnium gatherum
Of misbegot things that no poet would
    father 'em; —
Britannias in light summer-wear for the
    skies, —
Old Thames turned to stone, to his no
    small surprise, —
Father Nile, too, — a portrait, (in spite
    of what 's said,
That no mortal e'er yet got a glimpse of
    his *head*,)[4]
And a Ganges which India would think
    somewhat fat for 't,
Unless 't was some full-grown Director
    had sat for 't; —
Not to mention the *et cæteras* of Genii
    and Sphinxes,
Fame, Victory, and other such semi-clad
    minxes; —
Sea Captains,[5] — the idols here most
    idolized;
And of whom some, alas! might too
    well be comprized
Among ready-made Saints, as they died
    *cannon*ized; —
With a multitude more of odd cockney-
    fied deities,
Shrined in such pomp that quite shock-
    ing to see it 't is;
Nor know I what better the Rector
    could do
Than to shrine there his own beloved
    quadruped too;
As most surely a tithe-pig, whate'er the
    world thinks, is
A much fitter beast for a church than a
    Sphinx is.

But I 'm called off to dinner — grace
    just has been said,
And my host waits for nobody, living or
    dead.

---

1 Tithes were paid to the Pythian Apollo.
2 See Dr. Wiseman's learned and able letter
to Mr. Poynder.
3 Joshua xxiv. 2.

4   — " *nec contigit ulli*
    hoc vidisse caput."   CLAUDIAN.
5 Captains Mosse, Riou, etc.

LINES.[1]

ON THE DEPARTURE OF LORDS CAS-
TLEREAGH AND STEWART FOR THE
CONTINENT.

*at Paris [2] et Fratres, et qui rapuère sub illis
vix tenuère manus (scis hoc, Menelaë) nefandas.*
OVID. *Metam. lib.* xiii. v. 202.

Go, Brothers in wisdom — go, bright
    pair of Peers,
    And may Cupid and Fame fan you
        both with their pinions!
The *one*, the best lover we have — *of his
    years*,
    And the *other* Prime Statesman of
        Britain's dominions.

Go, Hero of Chancery, blest with the
    smile
    Of the Misses that love and the mon-
        archs that prize thee;
Forget Mrs. Angelo Taylor awhile,
    And all tailors but him who so well
        dandifies thee.

Never mind how thy juniors in gallantry
    scoff,
    Never heed how perverse affidavits may
        thwart thee,
But show the young Misses thou 'rt scholar
    enough
    To translate " *Amor Fortis* " a love,
        about forty!

And sure 't is no wonder, when, fresh as
    young Mars,
    From the battle you came, with the
        Orders you 'd earned in 't,
That sweet Lady Fanny should cry out
    " My *stars!* "
    And forget that the *Moon*, too, was
        some way concerned in 't.

For not the great Regent himself has
    endured
    (Tho' I 've seen him with badges and
        orders all shine,

1 This and the following squib, which must
have been written about the year 1815-16, have
been by some oversight misplaced.

2 Ovid is mistaken in saying that it was "at
Paris" these rapacious transactions took place —
we should read "at Vienna."

Till he lookt like a house that was *over*
    insured)
    A much heavier burden of glories than
        thine.

And 't is plain, when a wealthy young
    lady so mad is,
    Or *any* young ladies can so go astray,
As to marry old Dandies that might be
    their daddies,
    The *stars* [3] are in fault, my Lord
        Stewart, not they!

Thou, too, t'other brother, thou Tully of
    Tories,
    Thou *Malaprop* Cicero, over whose
        lips
Such a smooth rigmarole about " mon-
    archs," and " glories,"
    And " *nullidge*," [4] and " features,"
        like syllabub slips.

Go, haste, at the Congress pursue thy
    vocation
    Of adding fresh sums to this National
        Debt of ours,
Leaguing with Kings, who for mere
    recreation
    Break promises, fast as your Lordship
        breaks metaphors.

Fare ye well, fare ye well, bright Pair of
    Peers,
    And may Cupid and Fame fan you
        both with their pinions!
The one, the best lover we have — *of his
    years*,
    And the other, Prime Statesman of
        Britain's dominions.

TO THE SHIP

IN WHICH LORD CASTLEREAGH SAILED
FOR THE CONTINENT.

Imitated from Horace, lib. 1, *ode* 3.

So may my Lady's prayers prevail,[5]
    And Canning's too, and *lucid* Bragge's,

3 " When weak women go astray,
    The stars are more in fault than they."

4 It is thus the noble lord pronounces the
word " knowledge " — deriving it, as far as his
own share is concerned, from the Latin, " *nullus.*"

5 *sic te Diva potens Cypri,
    sic fratres Helenæ, lucida sidera,
    ventorumque regat pater.*

And Eldon beg a favoring gale
 From Eolus, that *older* Bags,[1]
To speed thee on thy destined way,
Oh ship, that bearest our Castlereagh,[2]
Our gracious Regent's better half [3]
And *therefore* quarter of a King —
(As Van or any other calf
 May find without much figuring).
Waft him, oh ye kindly breezes,
 Waft this Lord of place and pelf,
Any where his Lordship pleases,
 Tho' 't were to Old Nick himself!

Oh, what a face of brass was his,[4]
Who first at Congress showed his phiz —
To sign away the Rights of Man
To Russian threats and Austrian juggle;
And leave the sinking African [5]
 To fall without one saving struggle —
'Mong ministers from North and South,
 To show his lack of shame and sense,
And hoist the sign of " Bull and Mouth "
 For blunders and for eloquence!

In vain we wish our *Secs.* at home [6]
 To mind their papers, desks, and shelves,
If silly *Secs.* abroad *will* roam
 And make such noodles of themselves.

But such hath always been the case —
For matchless impudence of face,
There 's nothing like your Tory race![7]
First, Pitt,[8] the chosen of England, taught her

---

1 See a description of the ἀσκοί, or *Bags* of Eolus, in the Odyssey, *lib.* 10.

2 *navis, quæ tibi creditum*
  debes Virgilium.

3 ——*animæ dimidium meum.*

4 *illi robur et æs triplex.*
  circa pectus erat, qui, etc.

5 ——— *præcipitem Africum*
  decertantem Aquilonibus.

6 *nequicquam Deus abscidit*
  prudens oceano dissociabili
 terras, si tamen impiæ
 non tangenda Rates transiliunt vada.

This last line we may suppose, alludes to some distinguished *Rats* that attended the voyager.

7 *audax omnia perpeti*
  gens ruit per vetitum nefas.

8 *audax Japeti genus*
  ignem fraude malâ gentibus intulit.

A taste for famine, fire and slaughter.
Then came the Doctor,[9] for our ease,
With Eldons, Chathams, Hawksburies,
And other deadly maladies.
When each in turn had run their rigs,
Necessity brought in the Whigs:[10]

And oh! I blush, I blush to say,
 When these, in turn, were put to flight, too,
Illustrious TEMPLE flew away
 With *lots of pens he had no right to!*[11]
In short, what *will* not mortal man do?[12]
And now, that — strife and bloodshed past —
We 've done on earth what harm we can do,
 We gravely take to heaven at last [13]
And think its favoring smile to purchase
(Oh Lord, good Lord!) by — building churches!

SKETCH OF THE FIRST ACT OF A NEW ROMANTIC DRAMA.

" AND now," quoth the goddess, in accents jocose,
" Having got good materials, I 'll brew such a dose
" Of Double X mischief as, mortals shall say,
" They 've not known its equal for many a long day."
Here she winkt to her subaltern imps to be steady,
And all wagged their fire-tipt tails and stood ready.

" So, now for the ingredients: — first, hand me that bishop;"
Whereon, a whole bevy of imps run to fish up

---

9 *Post* ———
  ——— *macies, et nova febrium*
 terris incubit cohors.

10 ———————*tarda necessitas*
  Lethi corripuit gradum.

11 *expertus* vacuum *Dædalus aëra*
  pennis non homini datis.

This alludes to the 1200*l.* worth of stationery, which his Lordship is said to have ordered, when on the point of *vacating* his place.

12 *nil mortalibus arduum est.*

13 *cœlum ipsum petimus stultitiâ*

From out a large reservoir wherein they
    pen 'em
The blackest of all its black dabblers in
    venom;
And wrapping him up (lest the virus
    should ooze,
And one " drop of the immortal "[1]
    Right Rev.[2] they might lose)
In the sheets of his own speeches,
    charges, reviews,
Pop him into the caldron, while loudly a
    burst
From the by-standers welcomes ingredi-
    ent the first !

" Now fetch the Ex-Chancellor," mut-
    tered the dame —
" He who 's called after Harry the
    Older, by name."
" The Ex-Chancellor ! " echoed her
    imps, the whole crew of 'em —
" Why talk of *one* Ex, when your Mis-
    chief has *two* of 'em? "
" True, true," said the hag, looking arch
    at her elves,
" And a double-*Ex* dose they compose,
    in themselves."
This joke, the sly meaning of which was
    seen lucidly,
Set all the devils a laughing most
    deucedly.
So, in went the pair, and (what none
    thought surprising)
Showed talents for sinking as great as for
    rising ;
While not a grim phiz in that realm but
    was lighted
With joy to see spirits so twin-like
    united —
Or (plainly to speak) two such birds of
    a feather,
In one mess of venom thus spitted to-
    gether.
Here a flashy imp rose — some connec-
    tion, no doubt,
Of the young lord in question — and,
    scowling about,
" Hoped his fiery friend, Stanley, would
    not be left out ;

[1] " To lose no drop of the immortal man.
[2] The present Bishop of Exeter.

" As no schoolboy unwhipt, the whole
    world must agree,
" Loved mischief, *pure* mischief, more
    dearly than he."

But, no — the wise hag would n't hear
    of the whipster;
Not merely because, as a shrew, he
    eclipst her,
And nature had given him, to keep him
    still young,
Much tongue in his head and no head in
    his tongue;
But because she well knew that, for
    change ever ready,
He 'd not even to mischief keep properly
    steady;
That soon even the *wrong* side would
    cease to delight,
And, for want of a change, he must
    swerve to the *right ;*
While, on *each*, so at random his missiles
    he threw,
That the side he attackt was most safe,
    of the two. —
This ingredient was therefore put by on
    the shelf,
There to bubble, a bitter, hot mess, by
    itself.
" And now," quoth the hag, as her
    caldron she eyed,
And the tidbits so friendlily rankling
    inside,
" There wants but some seasoning; — so,
    come, ere I stew 'em,
" By way of a relish, we 'll throw in ' +
    John Tuam.'
" In cooking up mischief, there 's no
    flesh or fish
" Like your meddling High Priest, to
    add zest to the dish."
Thus saying, she pops in the Irish Grand
    Lama —
Which great event ends the First Act of
    the Drama.

ANIMAL MAGNETISM.

Tho' famed was Mesmer, in his day,
Nor less so, in ours, is Dupotet,
To say nothing of all the wonders
    done
By that wizard, Dr. Elliotson,

When, standing as if the gods to invoke, he
Up waves his arm, and — down drops Okey![1]

Tho' strange these things, to mind and sense,
If you wish still stranger things to see —
If you wish to know the power immense
Of the true magnetic influence,
Just go to her Majesty's Treasury,
And learn the wonders working there —
And I 'll be hanged if you don't stare!
Talk of your animal magnetists,
And that wave of the hand no soul resists,
Not all its witcheries can compete
With the friendly beckon towards Downing Street,
Which a Premier gives to one who wishes
To taste of the Treasury loaves and fishes.
It actually lifts the lucky elf,
Thus acted upon, *above* himself; —
He jumps to a state of *clairvoyance*,
And is placeman, statesman, all, at once!

These effects, observe (with which I begin),
Take place when the patient's motioned *in ;*
Far different of course the mode of affection,
When the wave of the hand 's in the *out* direction;
The effects being then extremely unpleasant,
As is seen in the case of Lord Brougham, at present;
In whom this sort of manipulation
Has lately produced such inflammation,
Attended with constant irritation,
That, in short — not to mince his situation —
It has workt in the man a transformation
That puzzles all human calculation!

Ever since the fatal day which saw
That "pass"[2] performed on this Lord of Law —
A pass potential, none can doubt,
As it sent Harry Brougham to the right about —
The condition in which the patient has been
Is a thing quite awful to be seen.
Not that a casual eye could scan
This wondrous change by outward survey;
It being, in fact, the *interior* man
That 's turned completely topsy-turvy: —
Like a case that lately, in reading o'er 'em,
I found in the *Acta Eruditorum*,
Of a man in whose inside, when disclosed,
The whole order of things was found transposed;[3]
By a *lusus naturæ*, strange to see,
The liver placed where the heart should be,
And the *spleen* (like Brougham's, since laid on the shelf)
As diseased and as much *out of place* as himself.

In short, 't is a case for consultation,
If e'er there was one, in this thinking nation;
And therefore I humbly beg to propose,
That those *savans* who mean, as the rumor goes,
To sit on Miss Okey's wonderful case,
Should also Lord Parry's case embrace;
And inform us, in *both* these patients' states,
Which *ism* it is that predominates,
Whether magnetism and somnambulism,
Or, simply and solely, mountebankism.

THE SONG OF THE BOX.

LET History boast of her Romans and Spartans,
    And tell how they stood against tyranny's shocks;

---

[1] The name of the heroine of the performances at the North London Hospital.

[2] The technical term for the movements of the magnetizer's hand.

[3] *omnes feré internas corporis partes inverso ordine sitas.* — "*Act. Erudit.*" 1690.

They were all, I confess, in *my* eye,
  Betty Martins
    Compared to George Grote and his
      wonderful Box.

Ask, where Liberty now has her seat? —
  Oh, it is n't
By Delaware's banks or on Switzer-
  land's rocks; —
Like an imp in some conjuror's bottle
  imprisoned,
  She 's slyly shut up in Grote's won-
    derful Box.

How snug! — 'stead of floating thro'
  ether's dominions,
Blown *this* way and *that*, by the "*populi vox*,"
To fold thus in silence her sinecure pinions,
  And go fast asleep in Grote's wonder-
    ful Box.

Time was, when free speech was the
  life-breath of freedom —
So thought once the Seldens, the
  Hampdens, the Lockes;
But mute be *our* troops, when to am-
  bush we lead 'em,
  "For Mum" is the word with us
    Knights of the Box.

Pure, exquisite Box! no corruption can
  soil it;
There 's Otto of Rose in each breath
  it unlocks;
While Grote is the "Betty," that serves
  at the toilet,
  And breathes all Arabia around from
    his Box.[1]

'T is a singular fact, that the famed
  Hugo Grotius [2]
(A namesake of Grote's — being both
  of Dutch stocks),
Like Grote, too, a genius profound as
  precocious,
  Was also, like him, much renowned
    for a Box; —

An immortal old clothes-box, in which
  the great Grotius
When suffering in prison for views
  heterodox,
Was packt up incog. spite of jailers ferocious,[3]
  And sent to his wife,[4] carriage free, in
    a Box!

But the fame of old Hugo now rests on
  the shelf,
Since a rival hath risen that all parallel mocks; —
That Grotius ingloriously saved but himself,
  While *ours* saves the whole British
    realm by a Box!

And oh! when, at last, even this greatest of Grotes
Must bend to the Power that at every
  door knocks,[5]
May he drop in the urn like his own
  "silent votes,"
  And the tomb of his rest be a large
    Ballot-Box.

While long at his shrine, both from
  county and city,
Shall pilgrims triennially gather in
  flocks,
And sing, while they whimper, the appropriate ditty,
  "Oh breathe not his *name*, let it sleep
    — in the Box."

ANNOUNCEMENT OF A NEW THALABA.

ADDRESSED TO ROBERT SOUTHEY, ESQ.

WHEN erst, my Southey, thy tuneful
  tongue
The terrible tale of Thalaba sung —

---

[1] And all Arabia breathes from yonder box.
    POPE's "*Rape of the Lock.*"

[2] *Groot*, or *Grote*, latinized into Grotius.

[3] For the particulars of this escape of Grotius
from the Castle of Louvenstein, by means of a
box (only three feet and a half long, it is said) in
which books used to be occasionally sent to him
and foul linen returned, see any of the Biographical Dictionaries.

[4] This is not quite according to the facts of
the case; his wife having been the contriver of
the stratagem, and remained in the prison herself
to give him time for escape.

[5] *pallida Mors æquo pulsat pede, etc.* —
HORAT.

Of him, the Destroyer, doomed to rout
That grim divan of conjurors out,
Whose dwelling dark, as legends say,
Beneath the roots of the ocean lay,
(Fit place for deep ones, such as they,)
How little thou knewest, dear Dr.
    Southey,
Altho' bright genius all allow thee,
That, some years thence, thy wondering
    eyes
Should see a second Thalaba rise —
As ripe for ruinous rigs as thine,
Tho' his havoc lie in a different line,
And should find this new, improved De-
    stroyer
Beneath the wig of a Yankee lawyer;
A sort of an " alien," *alias* man,
Whose country or party guess who can,
Being Cockney half, half Jonathan;
And his life, to make the thing completer,
Being all in the genuine Thalaba metre,
Loose and irregular as thy feet are; —
First, into Whig Pindarics rambling,
Then in low Tory doggrel scrambling;
Now *love* his theme, now *Church* his glory
(At once both Tory and ama-tory),
Now in the Old Bailey-*lay* meandering,
Now in soft *couplet* style philandering;
And, lastly, in lame Alexandrine,
Dragging his wounded length along,[1]
When scourged by Holland's silken
    thong.

In short, dear Bob, Destroyer the Second
May fairly a match for the First be reck-
    oned;
Save that *your* Thalaba's talent lay
In sweeping old conjurors clean away,
While ours at aldermen deals his blows,
(Who no great conjurors are, God
    knows,)
Lays Corporations, by wholesale, level,
Sends Acts of Parliament to the devil,
Bullies the whole Milesian race —
Seven millions of Paddies, face to face;
And, seizing that magic wand, himself,
Which erst thy conjurors left on the shelf,
Transforms the boys of the Boyne and
    Liffey
All into *foreigners*, in a jiffy —

Aliens, outcasts, every soul of 'em,
Born but for whips and chains, the whole
    of 'em !

Never in short did parallel
Betwixt two heroes *gee* so well ;
And among the points in which they fit,
There 's one, dear Bob, I can't omit.
That hacking, hectoring blade of thine
Dealt much in the *Domdaniel* line;[2]
And 't is but rendering justice due,
To say that ours and his Tory crew
Damn Daniel most devoutly too.

RIVAL TOPICS.[3]

AN EXTRAVAGANZA.

OH Wellington and Stephenson,
    Oh morn and evening papers,
Times, Herald, Courier, Globe, and *Sun,*
When will ye cease our ears to stun
    With these two heroes' capers?
Still " Stephenson " and " Wellington,"
    The everlasting two ! —
Still doomed, from rise to set of sun,
To hear what mischief one has done,
    And t' other means to do : —
What bills the banker past to friends,
    But never meant to pay ;
What Bills the other wight intends,
    As honest, in their way ; —
Bills, payable at distant sight,
    Beyond the Grecian kalends,
When all good deeds will come to light,
When Wellington will do what 's right,
    And Rowland pay his balance.

To catch the banker all have sought,
    But still the rogue unhurt is;
While t' other juggler — who 'd have
    thought?
Tho' slippery long, has just been caught
    By old Archbishop Curtis ; —
And, such the power of papal crook,
    The crosier scarce had quivered
About his ears, when, lo ! the Duke
    Was of a Bull delivered !

---

1 " A needless Alexandrine ends the song,
    That, *like a wounded snake,* drags its slow
        length along,"

2 " Vain are the spells, the Destroyer
        Treads the Domdaniel floor."
        " *Thalaba,*" a Metrical Romance.

3 The date of this squib must have been, I
think, about 1828-9.

Sir Richard Birnie doth decide
  That Rowland " must be mad,"
In private coach, with crest, to ride,
  When chaises could be had.
And t' other hero, all agree,
  St Luke's will soon arrive at,
If thus he shows off publicly,
  When he might pass in private.
Oh Wellington, oh Stephenson,
  Ye ever-boring pair,
Where'er I sit, or stand, or run,
  Ye haunt me every where.
Tho' Job had patience tough enough,
  Such duplicates would try it;
Till one 's turned out and t' other off,
  We shan't have peace or quiet.
But small 's the chance that Law af-
  fords —
Such folks are daily let off;
And, 'twixt the old Bailey and the Lords,
  They both, I fear, will get off.

THE BOY STATESMAN.

BY A TORY.

" That boy will be the death of me."
                Matthews at Home.

AH, Tories dear, our ruin is near,
  With Stanley to help us, we can't but
    fall;
Already a warning voice I hear,
Like the late Charles Matthews' croak
    in my ear,
  " That boy — that boy 'll be the death
    of you all."

He will, God help us! — not even Scri-
    blerius
  In the " Art of Sinking " his match
    could be;
And our case is growing exceeding seri-
    ous,
  For, all being in the same boat as he,
If down my Lord goes, down go we,
Lord Baron Stanley and Company,
As deep in Oblivion's swamp below
As such " Masters Shallow " well could
    go;
And where we shall all both low and
    high,
Embalmed in mud, as forgotten lie
As already doth Graham of Netherby !

But that boy, that boy ! — there 's a tale
    I know,
Which in talking of him comes *à-propos*.
Sir Thomas More had an only son,
And a foolish lad was that only one,
  And Sir Thomas said one day to his
    wife,
" My dear, I can't but wish you joy,
" For you prayed for a boy, and you now
    have a boy,
  " Who 'll continue a boy to the end
    of his life."

Even such is our own distressing lot,
With the ever-young statesman we have
    got ; —
Nay even still worse ; for Master More
Was n't more a youth than he 'd been
    before,
While *ours* such power of boyhood
    shows,
That the older he gets the more juvenile
    he grows,
And at what extreme old age he 'll close
His schoolboy course, heaven only
    knows ; —
Some century hence, should he reach so
    far,
  And ourselves to witness it heaven
    condemn,
We shall find him a sort of *cub* Old
    Parr,
  A whipper-snapper Methusalem ;
Nay, even should he make still longer
    stay of it,
The boy 'll want *judgment*, even to the
    day of it !
Meanwhile, 't is a serious, sad inflic-
    tion ;
  And day and night with awe I recall
The late Mr. Matthews' solemn predic-
    tion,
  " That boy 'll be the death, the death of
    you all."

LETTER

FROM LARRY O'BRANIGAN TO THE REV.
MURTAGH O'MULLIGAN.

ARRAH, where were *you*, Murthagh, that
    beautiful day ? —
  Or how came it your riverence was
    laid on the shelf,

When that poor craythur, Bobby — as
  you were away —
Had to make *twice* as big a Tom-fool
  of *himself.*

Troth, it was n't at all civil to lave in the
  lurch
  A boy so desarving your tindh'rest
    affection; —
Too such iligant Siamase twins of the
  Church,
  As Bob and yourself, ne'er should cut
    the connection.

If thus in two different directions you
  pull,
  'Faith, they 'll swear that yourself and
    your riverend brother
Are like those quare foxes, in Gregory's
  Bull,
  Whose tails were joined *one* way, while
    they lookt *another !* [1]

Och blest be he, whosomdever he be,
  That helpt soft Magee to that Bull of
    a Letther !
Not even my own self, tho' I sometimes
  make free
  At such bull-manufacture, could make
    him a betther.

To be sure, when a lad takes to *forgin'*,
  this way,
  'Tis a thrick he 's much timpted to
    carry on gayly;
Till, at last, his "injanious devices," [2]
  Show him up, not at Exether Hall,
    but the Ould Bailey.

That parsons should forge thus appears
  mighty odd,
  And (as if somethin' "odd" in their
    names, too, must be,)
One forger, of ould, was a riverend Dod,
  While a riverend Todd 's now his
    match, to a T. [3]

But, no matther *who* did it all blessins
  betide him,
  For dishin' up Bob, in a manner so
    nate;
And there wanted but *you*, Murthagh
  'vourneen, beside him,
  To make the whole grand dish of *bull*-
    calf complate.

MUSINGS OF AN UNREFORMED PEER.

Of all the odd plans of this monstrously
  queer age,
The oddest is that of reforming the peerage; —
Just as if we, great dons, with a title and
  star,
Did not get on exceedingly well as we
  are,
And perform all the functions of noodles
  by birth
As completely as any born noodles on
  earth.

How *acres* descend, is in law-books displayed,
But we as *wise*acres descend, ready
  made;
And by right of our rank in Debrett's
  nomenclature,
Are all of us born legislators by nature; —
Like ducklings to water instinctively
  taking,
So we with like quackery take to law-
  making;
And God forbid any reform should come
  o'er us,
To make us more wise than our sires
  were before us.

The Egyptians of old the same policy
  knew —
If your sire was a cook, you must be a
  cook too:

---

1 "You will increase the enmity with which
they are regarded by their associates in heresy,
thus tying these foxes by the tails, that their faces
may tend in opposite directions." — Bob's *Bull*,
read at Exeter Hall, July 14.

2 "An ingenious device of my learned friend."
—Bob's *Letter to Standard.*

3 Had I consulted only my own wishes, I
should not have allowed this hasty attack on Dr.

Todd to have made its appearance in this Collection ; being now fully convinced that the charge
brought against that reverend gentleman of intending to pass off as genuine his famous mock
Papal Letter was altogether unfounded. Finding
it to be the wish, however, of my reverend friend
—as I am now glad to be permitted to call him —
that both the wrong and the reparation, the Ode
and the Palinode, should be thus placed in juxta-
position, I have thought it but due to him to
comply with his request.

Thus making, from father to son, a good
   trade of it,
Poisoners *by right* (so no more could be
   said of it),
The cooks like our lordships a pretty
   mess made of it;
While, famed for *conservative* stomachs,
   the Egyptians
Without a wry face bolted all the pre-
   scriptions.

It is true, we 've among us some peers of
   the past,
Who keep pace with the present most
   awfully fast —
Fruits that ripen beneath the new light
   now arising
With speed that to *us*, old conserves, is
   surprising,
Conserves, in whom — potted, for grand-
   mamma uses —
'T would puzzle a sunbeam to find any
   juices.
'T is true too, I fear, midst the general
   movement,
Even *our* House, God help it, is doomed
   to improvement,
And all its live furniture, nobly descended
But sadly worn out, must be sent to be
   mended.
With *movables* 'mong us, like Brougham
   and like Durham,
No wonder even *fixtures* should learn to
   bestir 'em;
And distant, ye gods, be that terrible
   day,
When — as playful Old Nick, for his
   pastime, they say,
Flies off with old houses, sometimes, in
   a storm —
So *ours* may be whipt off, some night,
   by Reform;
And as up, like Loretto's famed house,[1]
   thro' the air,
Not angels, but devils, our lordships
   shall bear,
Grim, radical phizzes, unused to the sky,
Shall flit round, like cherubs, to wish us
   "good-by,"

1 The *Casa Santa*, supposed to have been
carried by angels through the air from Galilee to
Italy.

While perched up on clouds little imps of
   plebeians,
Small Grotes and O'Connells, shall sing
   Io Pæans.

THE
REVEREND PAMPHLETEER.
A ROMANTIC BALLAD.

OH, have you heard what hapt of late?
   If not, come lend an ear,
While sad I state the piteous fate
   Of the Reverend Pamphleteer.

All praised his skilful jockeyship,
   Loud rung the Tory cheer,
While away, away, with spur and whip,
   Went the Reverend Pamphleteer.

The nag he rode — how *could* it err?
   'T was the same that took, last year,
That wonderful jump to Exeter
   With the Reverend Pamphleteer.

Set a beggar on horseback, wise men say,
   The course he will take is clear;
And in *that* direction lay the way
   Of the Reverend Pamphleteer.

" Stop, stop," said Truth, but vain her
   cry —
   Left far away in the rear,
She heard but the usual gay "Good-by"
   From her faithless Pamphleteer.

You may talk of the jumps of Homer's
   gods,
   When cantering o'er our sphere —
I 'd back for a *bounce*, 'gainst any odds,
   This Reverend Pamphleteer.

But ah! what tumbles a jockey hath!
   In the midst of his career,
A file of the *Times* lay right in the path
   Of the headlong Pamphleteer.

Whether he tript or shyed thereat,
   Doth not so clear appear:
But down he came, as his sermons flat —
   This Reverend Pamphleteer!

Lord King himself could scarce desire
   To see a spiritual Peer

Fall much more dead, in the dirt and
    mire,
  Than did this Pamphleteer.

Yet pitying parsons many a day
  Shall visit his silent bier,
And, thinking the while of Stanhope, say
  " Poor dear old Pamphleteer !

" He has finisht at last his busy span,
  " And now *lies coolly* here —
" As often he did in life, good man,
  " Good, Reverend Pamphleteer ! "

A RECENT DIALOGUE.

1825.

A BISHOP and a bold dragoon,
  Both heroes in their way,
Did thus, of late, one afternoon,
  Unto each other say : —
" Dear bishop," quote the brave huzzar,
  " As nobody denies
" That you a wise logician are,
  " And I am — otherwise,
" 'T is fit that in this question, we
  " Stick each to his own art —
" That *yours* should be the sophistry,
  " And *mine* the *fighting* part.
" My creed, I need not tell you, is
  " Like that of Wellington,
" To whom no harlot comes amiss,
  " Save her of Babylon; [1]
" And when we 're at a loss for words,
  " If laughing reasoners flout us,
" For lack of sense we 'll draw our
    swords —
  " The sole thing sharp about us." —

" Dear bold dragoon," the bishop said,
  " 'T is true for war thou art meant;
" And reasoning — bless that dandy
    head !
  " Is not in thy department.
" So leave the argument to me —
  " And, when my holy labor
" Hath lit the fires of bigotry,
  " Thou 'lt poke them with thy sabre.
" From pulpit and from sentry-box,
  " We 'll make our joint attacks,

[1] *cui nulla meretrix displicuit præter Baby-
lonicam.*

" I at the head of my *Cassocks,*
  " And you, of your *Cossacks.*
" So here 's your health, my brave
    huzzar,
  " My exquisite old fighter —
" Success to bigotry and war,
  " The musket and the mitre ! "
Thus prayed the minister of heaven —
  While York, just entering then,
Snored out (as if some *Clerk* had given
  His nose the cue) " Amen."

THE WELLINGTON SPA.

" And drink *oblivion* to our woes."
             ANNA MATILDA.

1829.

TALK no more of your Cheltenham and
    Harrowgate springs,
  'T is from *Lethe* we now our potations
    must draw;
Your *Lethe* 's a cure for — all possible
    things,
  And the doctors have named it the
    Wellington Spa.

Other physical waters but cure you in
    part;
  One cobbles your gout — *t'other* mends
    your digestion
Some settle your stomach, but *this* —
    bless your heart ! —
  It will settle for ever your Catholic
    Question.

Unlike too the potions in fashion at
    present,
  This Wellington nostrum, restoring by
    stealth,
So purges the memory of all that 's un-
    pleasant,
  That patients *forget* themselves into
    rude health.

For instance, the inventor — his having
    once said
  " He should think himself mad if at
    any one's call,
" He became what he is " — is so purged
    from his head
  That he now does n't think he 's a
    madman at all.

Of course, for your memories of very
    long standing —
  Old chronic diseases that date back
    undaunted
To Brian Boroo and Fitz-Stephens' first
    landing —
  A devil of a dose of the *Lethe* is wanted.

But even Irish patients can hardly regret
  An oblivion so much in their own
    native style,
So conveniently planned that, whate'er
    they forget,
  They may go on remembering it still
    all the while ! [1]

A CHARACTER.

1834.

HALF Whig, half Tory, like those mid-
    way things,
'Twixt bird and beast, that by mistake
    have wings;
A mongrel Statesman, 'twixt two factions
    nurst,
Who, of the faults of each, combines
    the worst —
The Tory's loftiness, the Whigling's
    sneer,
The leveller's rashness, and the bigot's
    fear :
The thirst for meddling, restless still to
    show
How Freedom's clock, repaired by
    Whigs, will go;
The alarm when others, more sincere
    than they,
Advance the hands to the true time of
    day.

By Mother Church, high-fed and haughty
    dame,
The boy was dandled, in his dawn of
    fame;
Listening, she smiled, and blest the
    flippant tongue
On which the fate of unborn tithe-pigs
    hung.
Ah ! who shall paint the grandam's grim
    dismay,

When loose Reform enticed her boy
    away;
When shockt she heard him ape the
    rabble's tone,
And in Old Sarum's fate foredoom her
    own !
Groaning she cried, while tears rolled
    down her cheeks,
" Poor, glib-tongued youth, he means
    not what he speaks.
" Like oil at top, these Whig professions
    flow,
" But, pure as lymph, runs Toryism
    below.
" Alas ! that tongue should start thus,
    in the race,
" Ere mind can reach and regulate its
    pace ! —
" For, once outstript by tongue, poor,
    lagging mind,
" At every step, still further limps be-
    hind.
" But, bless the boy ! — whate'er his
    wandering be,
" Still turns his heart to Toryism and me.
" Like those odd shapes, portrayed in
    Dante's lay, [2]
" With heads fixt on, the wrong and
    backward way,
" His feet and eyes pursue a diverse
    track,
" While *those* march onward, *these* look
    fondly back."
And well she knew him — well foresaw
    the day,
Which now hath come, when snatched
    from Whigs away,
The self-same changeling drops the mask
    he wore,
And rests, restored, in granny's arms
    once more.

But whither now, mixt brood of modern
    light
And ancient darkness, canst thou bend
    thy flight?
Tried by both factions and to neither
    true,
Feared by the *old* school, laught at by
    the *new* ;

---

[1] The only parallel I know to this sort of
oblivion is to be found in a line of the late Mr.
R. P. Knight —

    " The pleasing memory of things forgot."

[2] " *Che dalle reni era tornato 'l volto,*
    E indietro venir li convenia,
    Perchè 'l veder dinanzi era lor tolto."

For *this* too feeble and for *that* too rash,
This wanting more of fire, *that* less of
flash,
Lone shalt thou stand, in isolation cold,
Betwixt two worlds, the new one and
the old,
A small and " vext Bermoothes," which
the eye
Of venturous seaman sees — and passes
by.

A GHOST STORY.

TO THE AIR OF " UNFORTUNATE MISS BAILEY."
1835.

NOT long in bed had Lyndhurst lain,
When, as his lamp burned dimly,
The ghosts of corporate bodies slain,[1]
Stood by his bedside grimly.
Dead aldermen who once could feast,
But now, themselves, are fed on,
And skeletons of mayors deceased,
This doleful chorus led on : —
" Oh Lord Lyndhurst,
" Unmerciful Lord Lyndhurst,
" Corpses we,
" All burkt by thee,
" Unmerciful Lord Lyndhurst ! "

" Avaunt, ye frights ! " his Lordship
cried,
" Ye look most glum and whitely."
" Ah, Lyndhurst dear ! " the frights re-
plied,
" You 've used us unpolitely.
" And now, ungrateful man ! to drive
" Dead bodies from your door so,
" Who quite corrupt enough, alive,
" You 've made by death still more so.
" Oh, Ex-Chancellor,
" Destructive Ex-Chancellor,
" See thy work,
" Thou second Burke,
" Destructive Ex-Chancellor ! "

Bold Lyndhurst then, whom naught could
keep
Awake or surely *that* would,
Cried " Curse you all " — fell fast
asleep —

And dreamt of " Small *v.* Attwood."
While, shockt, the bodies flew down
stairs,
But courteous in their panic
Precedence gave to ghosts of mayors,
And corpses aldermanic,
Crying, " Oh, Lord Lyndhurst,
" That terrible Lord Lyndhurst,
" Not Old Scratch
" Himself could match
" That terrible Lord Lyndhurst."

THOUGHTS ON THE LATE DE-
STRUCTIVE PROPOSITIONS
OF THE TORIES.[2]

BY A COMMON-COUNCILMAN.
1835.

I SAT me down in my easy chair,
To read, as usual, the morning papers;
But — who shall describe my look of
despair,
When I came to Lefroy's " destruc-
tive " capers !
That *he* — that, of all live men, Lefroy
Should join in the cry " Destroy, de-
stroy ! "
Who, even when a babe, as I 've heard
said,
On Orange conserve was chiefly fed,
And never, till now, a movement made
That was n't most manfully retrograde !
Only think — to sweep from the light of
day
Mayors, maces, criers and wigs away;
To annihilate — never to rise again —
A whole generation of aldermen,
Nor leave them even the accustomed
tolls,
To keep together their bodies and
souls !
At a time too when snug posts and places
Are falling away from us one by one,
Crash — crash — like the mummy-cases
Belzoni, in Egypt, sat upon,
Wherein lay pickled, in state sublime,
Conservatives of the ancient time; —
To choose such a moment to overset
The few snug nuisances left us yet;

---

1 Referring to the line taken by Lord Lyndhurst, on the question of Municipal Reform.

2 These verses were written in reference to
the Bill brought in at this time, for the reform of
Corporations, and the sweeping amendments
proposed by Lord Lyndhurst and other Tory
Peers, in order to obstruct the measure.

To add to the ruin that round us
  reigns,
By knocking out mayors' and town-clerks'
  brains;
By dooming all corporate bodies to fall,
Till they leave at last no bodies at all —
Naught but the ghosts of by-gone glory,
Wrecks of a world that once was Tory ! —
Where pensive criers, like owls un-
  blest,
  Robbed of their roosts, shall still hoot
    o'er them;
Nor *mayors* shall know where to seek a
  nest,
  Till Gally Knight shall *find* one for
    them;—
Till mayors and kings, with none to rue
  'em,
  Shall perish all in one common plague ;
And the *sovereigns* of Belfast and
  Tuam
  Must join their brother, Charles Dix,
    at Prague.

Thus mused I, in my chair, alone,
(As above described) till dozy grown,
And nodding assent to my own opinions,
I found myself borne to sleep's domin-
  ions,
Where, lo ! before my dreaming eyes,
A new House of Commons appeared to
  rise,
Whose living contents, to fancy's survey,
Seemed to me all turned topsy-turvy —
A jumble of polypi — nobody knew
Which was the head or which the
  queue.
Here, Inglis, turned to a sans-culotte,
Was dancing the hays with Hume and
  Grote;
There, ripe for riot, Recorder Shaw
Was learning from Roebuck " Ça-ira;"
While Stanley and Graham, as *poissarde*
  wenches,
Screamed " *à-bas !* " from the Tory
  benches;
And Peel and O'Connell, cheek by
  jowl,
Were dancing an Irish carmagnole.

The Lord preserve us ! — if dreams come
  true,
What *is* this hapless realm to do?

ANTICIPATED MEETING OF THE BRITISH ASSOCIATION IN THE YEAR 1836.

1836.

AFTER some observations from Dr.
  M'Grig
On that fossile reliquium called Petrified
  Wig,
Or *Perruquolithus* — a specimen rare
Of those wigs made for antediluvian
  wear,
Which, it seems, stood the Flood without
  turning a hair —
Mr. Tomkins rose up, and requested
  attention
To facts no less wondrous which *he* had
  to mention.

Some large fossil creatures had lately
  been found,
Of a species no longer now seen above
  ground,
But the same (as to Tomkins most clearly
  appears)
With those animals, lost now for hundreds of years,
Which our ancestors used to call " Bishops " and " Peers,"
But which Tomkins more erudite names
  has bestowed on,
Having called the Peer fossil the *Aris-
  tocratodon*,[1]
And, finding much food under t' other
  one's thorax,
Has christened that creature the Episcopus Vorax.

Lest the *savantes* and dandies should
  think this all fable,
Mr. Tomkins most kindly produced, on
  the table,
A sample of each of these species of
  creatures,
Both tolerably human, in structure and
  features,
Except that the Episcopus seems, Lord
  deliver us !
To 've been carnivorous as well as gra-
  nivorous;

1 A term formed on the model of the Masto-
don, etc.

And Tomkins, on searching its stomach,
found there
Large lumps, such as no modern stomach
could bear,
Of a substance called Tithe, upon which,
as 't is said,
The whole *Genus Clericum* formerly
fed;
And which having lately himself decom-
pounded,
Just to see what 't was made of, he actually found it
Composed of all possible cookable things
That e'er tript upon trotters or soared
upon wings —
All products of earth, both gramineous,
herbaceous,
Hordeaceous, tabaceous and eke farina-
ceous,
All clubbing their quotas, to glut the
œsophagus
Of this ever greedy and grasping Ti-
thophagus.[1]
"Admire," exclaimed Tomkins, "the
kind dispensation
"By Providence shed on this much-fa-
vored nation,
"In sweeping so ravenous a race from
the earth,
"That might else have occasioned a
general dearth —
"And thus burying 'em, deep as even
Joe Hume would sink 'em,
"With the Ichthyosaurus and Palœo-
rynchum,
"And other queer *ci-devant* things,
under ground —
"Not forgetting that fossilized youth,[2]
so renowned,
"Who lived just to witness the Deluge
— was gratified
"Much by the sight, and has since been
found *stratified!*"

This picturesque touch — quite in Tomkins's way —
Called forth from the *savantes* a general
hurrah;

While inquiries among them went rapidly round,
As to where this young stratified man
could be found.
The "learned Theban's" discourse next
as livelily flowed on,
To sketch t' other wonder, the A*ris*tocratodon —
An animal, differing from most human
creatures
Not *so* much in speech, inward structure
or features,
As in having a certain excrescence, T.
said,
Which in form of a coronet grew from
its head,
And devolved to its heirs, when the
creature was dead;
Nor mattered it, while this heir-loom
was transmitted,
How unfit were the *heads*, so the *coronet*
fitted.

He then mentioned a strange zoölogical
fact,
Whose announcement appeared much applause to attract.
In France, said the learned professor,
this race
Had so noxious become, in some centuries' space,
From their numbers and strength, that
the land was o'errun with 'em,
Every one's question being, "What 's
to be done with 'em?"
When, lo! certain knowing ones —
savans, mayhap,
Who, like Buckland's deep followers,
understood *trap*,[3]
Slyly hinted that naught upon earth was
so good
For A*ris*tocratodons, when rampant and
rude,
As to stop or curtail their allowance of
food.
This expedient was tried and a proof it
affords
Of the effect that short commons will
have upon lords;
For this whole race of bipeds, one fine
summer's morn,

---

1 The zoölogical term for a tithe-eater.

2 The man found by Scheuchzer, and supposed by him to have witnessed the Deluge
("*homo diluvii testis*"), but who turned out, I
am sorry to say, to be merely a great lizard.

3 Particularly the formation called *Transition* Trap.

Shed their coronets, just as a deer sheds
　　his horn,
And the moment these gewgaws fell off,
　　they became
Quite a new sort of creature — so harm-
　　less and tame,
That zoölogists might, for the first time,
　　maintain 'em
To be near akin to the *genius humanum,*
And the experiment, tried so successfully
　　then,
Should be kept in remembrance when
　　wanted again.

．　．　．　．　．　．

SONGS OF THE CHURCH.
No. 1.
LEAVE ME ALONE.
A PASTORAL BALLAD.

"We are ever standing on the defensive. All
that we say to them is, '*leave us alone.*' The
Established Church is part and parcel of the
constitution of this country. You are bound to
conform to this constitution. We ask of you
nothing more; — *let us alone.*" — Letter in *The
Times,* Nov. 1838.

1838.

COME, list to my pastoral tones,
　　In clover my shepherds I keep;
My stalls are well furnisht with drones,
　　Whose preaching invites one to sleep.
At my *spirit* let infidels scoff,
　　So they leave but the *substance* my
　　　　own;
For in sooth I 'm extremely well off
　　If the world will but let me alone.

Dissenters are grumblers, we know; —
　　Tho' excellent men in their way,
They never like things to be *so,*
　　Let things be however they may.
But dissenting 's a trick I detest;
　　And besides 't is an axiom well known,
The creed that 's best paid is the best,
　　If the *un*paid would let it alone.

To me, I own, very surprising
　　Your Newmans and Puseys all seem,
Who start first with rationalizing,
　　Then jump to the other extreme.
Far better, 'twixt nonsense and sense,
　　A nice *half*-way concern, like our own,
Where piety 's mixt up with pence,
　　And the latter are *ne'er* left alone.

Of all our tormentors, the Press is
　　The one that most tears us to bits;
And now, Mrs. Woolfrey's "excesses"
　　Have thrown all its imps into fits.
The devils have been at us, for weeks,
　　And there 's no saying when they 'll
　　　　have done ; —
Oh dear! how I wish Mr. Breeks
　　Had left Mrs. Woolfrey alone!

If any need pray for the dead,
　　'T is those to whom post-obits fall;
Since wisely hath Solomon said,
　　'T is "money that answereth all."
But ours be the patrons who *live ;* —
　　For, once in their glebe they are
　　　　thrown,
The dead have no living to give,
　　And therefore we leave them alone.

Tho' in morals we may not excel,
　　Such perfection is rare to be had;
A good life is, of course, very well,
　　But good living is also — not bad.
And when, to feed earth-worms, I go,
　　Let this epitaph stare from my stone,
"Here lies the Right Rev. so and so;
　　"Pass, stranger, and — leave him
　　　　alone."

EPISTLE FROM HENRY OF EX-
ETER TO JOHN OF TUAM.

DEAR John, as I know, like our brother
　　of London,
You 've sipt of all knowledge, both
　　sacred and mundane,
No doubt, in some ancient Joe Miller,
　　you 've read
What Cato, that cunning old Roman,
　　once said —
That he ne'er saw two reverend sooth-
　　sayers meet,
Let it be where it might, in the shrine
　　or the street,
Without wondering the rogues, mid
　　their solemn grimaces,
Did n't burst out a laughing in each
　　other's faces.[1]
What Cato then meant, tho' 't is so long
　　ago,

1 *mirari se, si augur augurem aspiciens sibi
temperaret a risu.*

Even we in the present times pretty well
   know;
Having soothsayers also, who — sooth to
   say, John —
Are no better in some points than those
   of days gone,
And a pair of whom, meeting (between
   you and me),
Might laugh in their sleeves, too — all
   lawn tho' they be.

But this, by the way — my intention
   being chiefly
In this, my first letter, to hint to you
   briefly,
That, seeing how fond you of *Tuum* [1]
   must be,
While *Meum* 's at all times the main
   point with me,
We scarce could do better than form an
   alliance,
To set these sad Anti-Church times at
   defiance:
You, John, recollect, being still to em-
   bark,
With no share in the firm but your title [2]
   and *mark;*
Or even should you feel in your grandeur
   inclined
To call yourself Pope, why, I should n't
   much mind;
While *my* church as usual holds fast by
   your Tuum,
And every one else's, to make it all
   Suum.

Thus allied, I 've no doubt we shall
   nicely agree,
As no twins can be liker, in most points,
   than we;
Both, specimens choice of that mixt sort
   of beast,
(See Rev. xiii. 1.) a political priest;

1 So spelled in those ancient versicles which
John, we understand, frequently chants : —

   " Had every one *Suum,*
    You wouldn't have *Tuum,*
   But I should have *Meum,*
    And sing *Te Deum.*"

2 For his keeping the title he may quote classical authority, as Horace expressly says, " *po-
teris servare Tuam.*" — " *De Art. Poet.*" v. 329.
— *Chronicle.*

Both mettlesome *chargers*, both brisk
   pamphleteers,
Ripe and ready for all that sets men by
   the ears;
And I, at least one, who would scorn to
   stick longer
By any given cause than I found it the
   stronger,
And who, smooth in my turnings, as if
   on a swivel,
When the tone ecclesiastic won't do, try
   the *civil.*

In short (not to bore you, even *jure
   divino*)
We 've the same cause in common, John
   — all but the rhino;
And that vulgar surplus, whate'er it may
   be,
As you 're not used to cash, John, you 'd
   best leave to me.
And so, without form — as the postman
   won't tarry —
I 'm, dear Jack of Tuam,
      Yours,
          EXETER HARRY.

SONG OF OLD PUCK.

   " And those things do best please me,
    That befall preposterously."
   PUCK Junior, *Midsummer Night's Dream.*

WHO wants old Puck? for here am I,
A mongrel imp, 'twixt earth and sky,
Ready alike to crawl or fly;
Now in the mud, now in the air,
And, so 't is for mischief, reckless where.

As to my knowledge, there's no end
   to 't,
For, where I have n't it, I pretend to 't;
And, 'stead of taking a learned degree
At some dull university,
Puck found it handier to commence
With a certain share of impudence,
Which passes one off as learned and
   clever,
Beyond all other degrees whatever;
And enables a man of lively sconce
To be Master of *all* the Arts at once.
No matter what the science may be —
Ethics, Physics, Theology,
Mathematics, Hydrostatics,
Aerostatics or Pneumatics —

Whatever it be, I take my luck,
'T is all the same to ancient Puck;
Whose head 's so full of all sorts of
    wares,
That a brother imp, old Smugden, swears
If I had but of *law* a little smattering,
I 'd then be *perfect* [1] — which is flattering.

My skill as a linguist all must know
Who met me abroad some months ago;
(And heard me *abroad* exceedingly, too,
In the moods and tenses of *parlez vous*)
When, as old Chambaud's shade stood
    mute,
I spoke such French to the Institute
As puzzled those learned Thebans much,
To know if 't was Sanscrit or High
    Dutch,
And *might* have past with the unobserving
As one of the unknown tongues of Irving.
As to my talent for ubiquity,
There 's nothing like it in all antiquity.
Like Mungo (my peculiar care)
" I 'm here, I 'm dere, I 'm ebery
    where." [2]

If any one 's wanted to take the chair
Upon any subject, any where,
Just look around, and — Puck is there !
When slaughter 's at hand, your bird of
    prey
Is never known to be out of the way;
And wherever mischief 's to be got,
There 's Puck *instanter*, on the spot.

Only find me in negus and applause,
And I 'm your man for *any* cause.
If *wrong* the cause, the more my delight;
But I don't object to it, even when *right*,
If I only can vex some old friend by 't;
There 's Durham, for instance; — to
    worry *him*
Fills up my cup of bliss to the brim !

(NOTE BY THE EDITOR.)

Those who are anxious to run a muck
Can't do better than join with Puck.
They 'll find him *bon diable* — spite of
    his phiz —

1 Verbatim, as said. This tribute is only
equalled by that of Talleyrand to his medical
friend, Dr. ——: " *Il se connoît en tout ; et
même un peu en médecine.*"

2 Song in " The Padlock."

And, in fact, his great ambition is,
While playing old Puck in first-rate style,
To be *thought* Robin Good-fellow all the
    while.

POLICE REPORTS.

CASE OF IMPOSTURE.

AMONG other stray flashmen disposed of,
    this week,
    Was a youngster named Stanley, gen-
        teelly connected,
Who has lately been passing off coins as
    antique,
    Which have proved to be *sham* ones,
        tho' long unsuspected.

The ancients, our readers need hardly be
    told,
    Had a coin they called "Talents,"
        for wholesale demands; [3]
And 't was some of said coinage this
    youth was so bold
    As to fancy he 'd got, God knows
        how, in his hands.

People took him, however, like fools, at
    his word;
    And these talents (all prized at his
        own valuation,)
Were bid for, with eagerness even more
    absurd
    Than has often distinguisht this great
        thinking nation.

Talk of wonders one now and then sees
    advertised,
    " Black swans " — " Queen Anne
        farthings " — or even " a child's
        caul " —
Much and justly as all these rare objects
    are prized,
    " Stanley's talents " outdid them —
        swans, farthings and all !

At length some mistrust of this coin got
    abroad;
    Even quondam believers began much
        to doubt of it;

3 For an account of the coin called Talents by
the ancients, see Budæus *de Asse*, and the other
writers *de Re Nummariâ.*

Some rung it, some rubbed it, suspecting
    a fraud —
    And the hard rubs it got rather took
    the shine out of it.

Others, wishing to break the poor prodi-
    gy's fall,
    Said 't was known well to all who had
    studied the matter,
That the Greeks had not only *great* tal-
    ents but *small*,[1]
    And those found on the youngster
    were clearly *the latter*.

While others who viewed the grave farce
    with a grin —
    Seeing counterfeits pass thus for coin-
    age so massy,
By way of a hint to the dolts taken in,
    Appropriately quoted Budæus "*de
    Asse.*"

In short, the whole sham by degrees was
    found out,
    And this coin which they chose by
    such fine names to call,
Proved a mere lackered article — showy,
    no doubt,
    But, ye gods! not the true Attic Tal-
    ent at all.

As the impostor was still young enough
    to repent,
    And, besides, had some claims to a
    grandee connection,
Their Worships — considerate for once
    — only sent
    The young Thimblerig off to the
    House of Correction.

REFLECTIONS.

ADDRESSED TO THE AUTHOR OF THE ARTICLE
OF THE CHURCH IN THE LAST NUMBER OF
The Quarterly Review.

I 'M quite of your mind; — tho' these
    Pats cry aloud
    That they 've got "too much Church,"
    'T is all nonsense and stuff;

For Church is like Love, of which Fi-
    garo vowed
    That even *too much* of it 's not quite
    enough.[2]

Ay! dose them with parsons, 't will cure
    all their ills; —
    Copy Morison's mode when from pill-
    box undaunted he
Pours thro' the patient his black-coated
    pills,
    Nor cares what their quality, so
    there 's but quantity.

I verily think 't would be worth Eng-
    land's while
    To consider, for Paddy's own benefit,
    whether
'T would not be as well to give up the
    green isle
    To the care, wear and tear of the
    Church altogether.

The Irish are well used to treatment so
    pleasant;
    The harlot Church gave them to
    Henry Plantagenet,[3]
And now if King William would make
    them a present
    To t' other chaste lady — ye Saints,
    just imagine it!

Chief Secs., Lord-Lieutenants, Com-
    manders-in-chief,
    Might then all be culled from the
    episcopal benches;
While colonels in black would afford
    some relief
    From the hue that reminds one of the
    old scarlet wench's.

Think how fierce at a *charge* (being
    practised therein)
    The Right Reverend Brigadier Phill-
    potts would slash on!
How General Blomfield, thro' thick and
    thro' thin,
    To the end of the chapter (or chap-
    ters) would dash on!

---

1 The *talentum magnum* and the *talentum
atticum* appear to have been the same coin.

2 *En fait d'amour, trop même n'est pas assez.*
— "*Barbier de Séville.*"

3 Grant of Ireland to Henry II. by Pope
Adrian.

For in one point alone do the amply fed
race
    Of bishops to beggars similitude bear —
That, set them on horseback, in full steeple chase,
    And they 'll ride, if not pulled up in
time — you know where.

But, bless you! in Ireland, that matters
not much,
    Where affairs have for centuries gone
the same way;
And a good stanch Conservative's system is such
    That he 'd back even Beelzebub's
long-founded sway.

I am therefore, dear *Quarterly*, quite
of your mind; —
    Church, Church, in all shapes, into
Erin let 's pour;
And the more she rejecteth our medicine
so kind,
    The more let 's repeat it — " Black
dose, as before.''

Let Coercion, that peace-maker, go hand
in hand
    With demure-eyed Conversion, fit sis-
ter and brother;
And, covering with prisons and churches
the land,
    All that won't *go* to *one*, we 'll put *into*
the other.

For the sole, leading maxim of us who 're
inclined
    To rule over Ireland, not well but re-
ligiously,
Is to treat her like ladies who 've just
been confined
    (Or who *ought* to be so), and to *church*
her prodigiously.

NEW GRAND EXHIBITION OF
MODELS
OF THE
TWO HOUSES OF PARLIAMENT.

COME, step in, gentlefolks, here ye may
view
    An exact and natural representation

    (Like Siburn's Model of Waterloo [1])
    Of the Lords and Commons of this
here nation.

There they are — all cut out in cork —
    The " Collective Wisdom '' wondrous
to see;
My eyes! when all them heads are at
work,
    What a vastly weighty consarn it must
be.

As for the " wisdom,'' — *that* may come
anon;
    Tho', to say truth, we sometimes see
(And I find the phenomenon no uncommon 'un)
    A man who 's M.P. with a head that 's
M.T.

Our Lords are *rather* too small, 't is true;
    But they do well enough for Cabinet
shelves;
And, besides, — *what 's* a man with cree-
turs to do
    That make such *werry* small figures
themselves?

There — don't touch those lords, my
pretty dears — (*Aside.*)
    Curse the children! — this comes of
reforming a nation:
Those meddling young brats have so
damaged my peers,
    I must lay in more cork for a new
creation.

Them yonder 's our bishops — " to whom
much is given,''
    And who 're ready to take as much
more as you please:
The seers of old time saw visions of
heaven,
    But these holy seers see nothing but
Sees.

Like old Atlas [2] (the chap, in Cheapside,
there below,)
    'T is for so much *per cent*. they take
heaven on their shoulders;

---

1 One of the most interesting and curious of
all the exhibitions of the day.

2 The sign of the Insurance Office in Cheapside.

And joy 't is to know that old High
Church and Co.,
  Tho' not capital priests, are such capi-
tal-holders.

There 's one on 'em, Phillpotts, who now
is away,
  As we 're having him filled with bum-
bustible stuff,
Small crackers and squibs, for a great
gala-day,
  When we annually fire his Right Reverence off.

'T would do your heart good, ma'am,
then to be by,
  When, bursting with gunpowder, 'stead
of with bile,
Crack, crack, goes the bishop, while
dowagers cry,
  " How like the dear man, both in
matter and style ! "

Should you want a few Peers and M.P.s,
to bestow,
  As presents to friends, we can recommend these : [1] —
Our nobles are come down to nine-pence,
you know,
  And we charge but a penny a piece
for M.P.s.

Those of *bottle*-corks made take most
with the trade,
  (At least, 'mong such as my *Irish* writ
summons,)
Of old *whiskey* corks our O'Connells are
made,
  But those we make Shaws and Lefroys
of, are *rum* 'uns.

    So, step in, gentlefolks, etc.
               Da Capo.

ANNOUNCEMENT
OF A
NEW GRAND ACCELERATION COMPANY
FOR THE PROMOTION OF THE
SPEED OF LITERATURE.

LOUD complaints being made in these
quick-reading times,
Of too slack a supply both of prose
works and rhymes,

A new Company, formed on the keep-
moving plan,
First proposed by the great firm of
Catch-'em-who-can,
Beg to say they 've now ready, in full
wind and speed,
Some fast-going authors, of quite a new
breed —
Such as not he who *runs* but who *gallops*
may read —
And who, if well curried and fed, they 've
no doubt,
Will beat even Bentley' s swift stud out
and out.

It is true in these days such a drug is
renown,
We 've " Immortals " as rife as M. P.s
about town;
And not a Blue's rout but can off-hand
supply
Some invalid bard who 's insured " not
to die."
Still let England but once try *our* authors, she 'll find
How fast they 'll leave even these Immortals behind;
And how truly the toils of Alcides were
light,
Compared with *his* toil who can read all
they write.

In fact, there 's no saying, so gainful the
trade,
How fast immortalities now may be
made;
Since Helicon never will want an " Un-
dying One,"
As long as the public continues a Buying
One;
And the company hope yet to witness
the hour,
When, by strongly applying the mare-
motive [2] power,
A three-decker novel, midst oceans of
praise,
May be written, launched, read and —
forgot, in three days !

In addition to all this stupendous celerity,
Which — to the no small relief of posterity —

---

[1] Producing a bag full of lords and gentlemen.

[2] " T is money makes the mare to go."

Pays off at sight the whole debit of fame,
Nor troubles futurity even with a name
(A project that won't as much tickle
    Tom Tegg as *us*,
Since 't will rob *him* of his second-
    priced Pegasus);
We, the Company — still more to show
    how immense
Is the power o'er the mind of pounds,
    shillings, and pence;
And that not even Phœbus himself, in
    our day,
Could get up a *lay* without first an *out*-
    lay —
Beg to add, as our literature soon may
    compare,
In its quick make and vent, with our
    Birmingham ware,
And it does n't at all matter in either of
    these lines,
How *sham* is the article, so it but
    shines, —
We keep authors ready, all perched, pen
    in hand,
To write off, in any given style, at com-
    mand.
No matter what bard, be he living or
    dead,[1]
Ask a work from his pen, and 't is done
    soon as said:
There being on the establishment six
    Walter Scotts,
One capital Wordsworth and Southeys
    in lots; —
Three choice Mrs. Nortons, all singing
    like syrens,
While most of our pallid young clerks
    are Lord Byrons.
Then we 've * * *s and * * *s (for
    whom there 's small call),
And * * * s and * * * s (for whom no
    call at all).

In short, whosoe'er the last "Lion"
    may be;
We 've a Bottom who 'll copy his roar[2]
    to a T,

And so well, that not one of the buyers
    who 've got 'em
Can tell which is lion, and which only
    Bottom.

N.B. — The company, since they set up
    in this line,
Have moved their concern and are now
    at the sign
Of the Muse's Velocipede, *Fleet* Street,
    where all
Who wish well to the scheme are invited
    to call.

SOME ACCOUNT OF THE LATE DINNER TO DAN.

FROM tongue to tongue the rumor flew;
All askt, aghast, " Is 't true? is 't true? "
    But none knew whether 't was fact or
        fable:
And still the unholy rumor ran,
From Tory woman to Tory man,
    Tho' none to come at the truth was
        able —
Till, lo ! at last, the fact came out,
The horrible fact, beyond all doubt,
    That Dan had dined at the Viceroy's
        table;
Had flesht his Popish knife and fork
In the heart of the Establisht mutton
    and pork !

Who can forget the deep sensation
That news produced in this orthodox
    nation?
Deans, rectors, curates, all agreed,
If Dan was allowed at the Castle to feed,
'T was clearly *all up* with the Protestant
    creed !
There had n't indeed such an apparition
    Been heard of in Dublin since that
        day
When, during the first grand exhibition
    Of Don Giovanni, that naughty play,
There appeared, as if raised by necro-
    mancers,
An *extra* devil among the dancers !
Yes — every one saw with fearful thrill
That a devil too much had joined the
    quadrille;[3]

---

1 We have lodgings apart, for our posthumous
    people,
    As we find that, if left with the live ones,
        they *keep* ill.
2 " Bottom: Let me play the lion; I will
roar you as 't were any nightingale."

3 History of the Irish Stage.

And sulphur was smelt and the lamps
    let fall
A grim, green light o'er the ghastly ball,
And the poor *sham* devils did n't like it
    at all;
For they knew from whence the intruder
    had come,
Tho' he left, *that* night, his tail at home.

This fact, we see, is a parallel case
To the dinner that some weeks since
    took place.
With the difference slight of fiend and
    man,
    It shows what a nest of Popish sinners
That city must be, where the devil and
    Dan
    May thus drop in at quadrilles and
    dinners!

But mark the end of these foul proceed-
    ings,
These demon hops and Popish feedings.
Some comfort 't will be — to those, at
    least,
    Who 've studied this awful dinner
    question —
To know that Dan, on the night of that
    feast,
    Was seized with a dreadful indiges-
    tion;
That envoys were sent post-haste to his
    priest
To come and absolve the suffering sin-
    ner,
For eating so much at a heretic dinner;
And some good people were even afraid
That Peel's old confectioner — still at
    the trade —
Had poisoned the Papist with *orangeade*.

NEW HOSPITAL FOR SICK
LITERATI.

WITH all humility we beg
To inform the public, that Tom Tegg —
Known for his spunky speculations
In buying up dead reputations,
And by a mode of galvanizing
Which, all must own, is quite surprising,
Making dead authors move again,
As tho' they still were living men; —
All this too managed, in a trice,
By those two magic words, " Half Price,"

Which brings the charm so quick about,
That worn-out poets, left without
A second *foot* whereon to stand,
Are made to go at second *hand ;* —
'T will please the public, we repeat,
To learn that Tegg who works this feat,
And therefore knows what care it needs
To keep alive Fame's invalids,
Has oped an Hospital in town,
For cases of knockt-up renown —
Falls, fractures, dangerous Epic *fits*
(By some called *Cantoes*), stabs from
    wits;
And of all wounds for which they 're
    nurst,
Dead cuts from publishers, the worst; —
All these, and other such fatalities,
That happen to frail immortalities,
By Tegg are so expertly treated,
That oft-times, when the cure 's com-
    pleted,
The patient 's made robust enough
To stand a few more rounds of *puff*,
Till like the ghosts of Dante's lay
He 's puft into thin air away!

As titled poets (being phenomenons)
Don't like to mix with low and common
    'uns,
Tegg's Hospital has separate wards,
Express for literary lords,
Where *prose*-peers, of immoderate length,
Are nurst, when they 've outgrown their
    strength,
And poets, whom their friends despair of,
Are — put to bed and taken care of.

Tegg beggs to contradict a story
Now current both with Whig and Tory,
That Doctor Warburton, M.P.,
Well known for his antipathy,
His deadly hate, good man, to all
The race of poets great and small —
So much, that he 's been heard to own,
He would most willingly cut down
The holiest groves on Pindus' mount,
To turn the timber to account! —
The story actually goes, that he
Prescribes at Tegg's Infirmary;
And oft not only stints for spite
The patients in their copy-right,
But that on being called in lately
To two sick poets suffering greatly,

This vaticidal Doctor sent them
So strong a dose of Jeremy Bentham,
That one of the poor bards but cried,
"Oh, Jerry, Jerry!" and then died;
While t' other, tho' less stuff was
     given,
Is on his road, 't is feared, to heaven!

Of this event, howe'er unpleasant,
Tegg means to say no more at present,—
Intending shortly to prepare
A statement of the whole affair,
With full accounts, at the same time,
Of some late cases (prose and rhyme),
Subscribed with every author's name,
That 's now on the Sick List of Fame.

RELIGION AND TRADE.

"Sir Robert Peel believed it was necessary
to originate all respecting religion and trade in a
Committee of the House." — *Church Extension,*
May 22, 1830.

SAY, who was the wag, indecorously
     witty,
     Who first in a statute this libel con-
          veyed;
And thus slyly referred to the self-same
     commitee,
     As matters congenial, Religion and
          Trade?

Oh surely, my Phillpotts, 't was thou
     didst the deed;
     For none but thyself or some pluralist
          brother,
Accustomed to mix up the craft with the
     creed,
     Could bring such a pair thus to twin
          with each other.

And yet, when one thinks of times pres-
     ent and gone,
     One is forced to confess on maturer
          reflection
That 't is n't in the eyes of committees
     alone
     That the shrine and the shop seem to
          have some connection.

Not to mention those monarchs of Asia's
     fair land,
     Whose civil list all is in " god-money "
          paid;

And where the whole people, by royal
     command,
     Buy their gods at the government
          mart, ready made;[1] —

There was also (as mentioned, in rhyme
     and in prose, is)
     Gold heaped throughout Egypt on
          every shrine,
To make rings for right reverend croco-
     diles' noses —
     Just such as, my Phillpotts, would look
          well in thine.

But one need n't fly off in this erudite
     mood;
     And 't is clear without going to regions
          so sunny
That priests love to do the *least* possible
     good
For the largest *most* possible quantum of
     money.

"Of him," saith the text, "unto whom
     much is given,
     "Of him much, in turn, will be also
          required : " —
" By *me*," quoth the sleek and obese
     man of heaven —
     "Give as much as you will — more
          will still be desired."

More money ! more churches ! — oh Nim-
     rod, hadst thou
     'Stead of *Tower*-extension, some
          shorter way gone —
Hadst thou known by what methods we
     mount to heaven *now*,
     And tried *Church*-extension, the feat
          had been done !

MUSINGS,

SUGGESTED BY THE LATE PROMOTION
OF MRS. NETHERCOAT.

" The widow Nethercoat is appointed jailer of
Loughrea, in the room of her deceased husband "
— *Limerick Chronicle.*

WHETHER as queens or subjects, in these
     days,
     Women seem formed to grace alike
          each station; —

1 The Birmans may not buy the sacred marble
in mass but must purchase figures of the deity
already made. — SYMES.

As Captain Flaherty gallantly says,
" You, ladies, are the lords of the creation ! "

Thus o'er my mind did prescient visions
float
Of all that matchless woman yet may
be;
When hark ! in rumors less and less remote,
Came the glad news o'er Erin's ambient sea,
The important news — that Mrs. Nethercoat
Had been appointed jailer of Loughrea;
Yea, mark it, History — Nethercoat is
dead,
And Mrs. N. now rules his realm instead;
Hers the high task to wield the uplocking
keys,
To rivet rogues and reign o'er Rap-
parees !

Thus, while your blusterers of the Tory
school
Find Ireland's sanest sons so hard to
rule,
One meek-eyed matron in Whig doctrines nurst
Is all that 's askt to curb the maddest,
worst !

Show me the man that dares with blush-
less brow
Prate about Erin's rage and riot now; —
Now, when her temperance forms her
sole excess;
When long-loved whiskey, fading from
her sight,
" Small by degrees and beautifully less,"
Will soon like other *spirits* vanish
quite;
When of red coats the number 's grown
so small,
That soon, to cheer the warlike par-
son's eyes,
No glimpse of scarlet will be seen at
all,
Save that which she of Babylon sup-
plies; —

Or, at the most, a corporal's guard
will be,
Of Ireland's *red* defence the sole remains;
While of its jails bright woman keeps
the key,
And captive Paddies languish in her
chains !

Long may such lot be Erin's, long be
mine !
Oh yes — if even this world, tho' bright
it shine,
In Wisdom's eyes a prison-house must
be,
At least let woman's hand our fetters
twine,
And blithe I 'll sing, more joyous than
if free,
The Nethercoats, the Nethercoats for
me !

INTENDED TRIBUTE

TO THE

AUTHOR OF AN ARTICLE IN THE LAST NUMBER OF *The Quarterly Review*, ENTITLED

"ROMANISM IN IRELAND."

IT glads us much to be able to say,
That a meeting is fixt for some early
day,
Of all such dowagers — *he* or *she* —
(No matter the sex, so they dowagers
be,)
Whose opinions concerning Church and
State
From about the time of the Curfew
date —
Stanch sticklers still for days by-
gone,
And admiring *them* for their rust
alone —
To whom if we would a leader give,
Worthy their tastes conservative,
We need but some mummy-statesman
raise,
Who was pickled and potted in Ptolemy's
days;
For *that* 's the man, if waked from his
shelf,
To conserve and swaddle this world like
himself.

Such, we 're happy to state, are the old
he-dames
Who 've met in committee and given
their names
(In good hieroglyphics), with kind in-
tent
To pay some handsome compliment
To their sister author, the nameless he,
Who wrote, in the last new *Quarterly*,
That charming assault upon Popery;
An article justly prized by them,
As a perfect antediluvian gem —
The work, as Sir Sampson Legend would
say,
Of some "fellow the Flood could n't
wash away." [1]

The fund being raised, there remained
but to see
What the dowager-author's gift was to
be.
And here, I must say, the Sisters Blue
Showed delicate taste and judgment too.
For finding the poor man suffering greatly
From the awful stuff he has thrown up
lately —
So much so indeed to the alarm of all,
As to bring on a fit of what doctors call
The Antipapistico-monomania
(I 'm sorry with such a long word to de-
tain ye),
They 've acted the part of a kind physi-
cian,
By suiting their gift to the patient's con-
dition;
And as soon as 't is ready for presentation,
We shall publish the facts for the gratifi-
cation
Of this highly-favored and Protestant na-
tion.

Meanwhile, to the great alarm of his
neighbors,
He still continues his *Quarterly* labors;
And often has strong No-Popery fits,
Which frighten his old nurse out of her
wits.
Sometimes he screams, like Scrub in the
play,[2]
"Thieves! Jesuits! Popery!" night and
day;

Takes the Printer's Devil for Doctor
Dens,[3]
And shies at him heaps of High-church
pens;[4]
Which the Devil (himself a touchy Dis-
senter)
Feels all in his hide, like arrows, enter.
'Stead of swallowing wholesome stuff
from the druggist's,
He *will* keep raving of "Irish Thug-
gists;"[5]
Tells us they all go murdering for fun
From rise of morn till set of sun,
Pop, pop, as fast as a minute-gun![6]
If askt, how comes it the gown and cas-
sock are
Safe and fat, mid this general massacre —
How haps it that Pat's own population
But swarms the more for this trucida-
tion —
He refers you, for all such memoranda,
To the "*archives of the Propaganda!*"[7]

This is all we 've got, for the present, to
say —
But shall take up the subject some future
day.

GRAND DINNER OF TYPE AND CO.

A POOR POET'S DREAM.[8]

As I sate in my study, lone and still,
Thinking of Sergeant Talfourd's Bill,
And the speech by Lawyer Sugden made,
In spirit congenial, for "the Trade,"

---

1 See Congreve's "Love for Love."

2 "Beaux' Stratagem."

3 The writer of the article has groped about
with much success, in what he calls " the dark
recesses of Dr. Dens's disquisitions." — *Quarterly Review.*

4 "Pray, may we ask, has there been any rebellious movement of Popery in Ireland, since
the planting of the Ulster colonies, in which
something of the kind was not visible among the
Presbyterians of the North." — *Ibid.*

5 "Lord Lorton, for instance, who, for clearing his estate of a village of Irish Thuggists,"
etc. — *Quarterly Review.*

6 "Observe how murder after murder is committed like minute-guns." — *Ibid.*

7 "Might not the archives of the Propaganda
possibly supply the key?"

8 Written during the late agitation of the
question of Copyright.

Sudden I sunk to sleep and lo!
  Upon Fancy's reinless night-mare flit-
    ting,
I found myself, in a second or so,
  At the table of Messrs. Type and Co.
  With a goodly group of diners sitting; —
All in the printing and publishing line,
Drest, I thought, extremely fine,
And sipping like lords their rosy wine;
While I in a state near inanition
  With coat that had n't much nap to
    spare
(Having just gone into its second edition),
  Was the only wretch of an author there.
But think, how great was my surprise,
When I saw, in casting round my eyes,
That the dishes, sent up by Type's she-
    cooks,
Bore all, in appearance, the shape of
  books;
Large folios — God knows where they
  got 'em,
In these *small* times — at top and bottom;
And quartos (such as the Press provides
For no one to read them) down the
  sides.
Then flasht a horrible thought on my
  brain,
And I said to myself, "'T is all too plain,
"Like those well known in school quo-
    tations,
"Who ate up for dinner their own rela-
    tions,
"I see now, before me, smoking here,
"The bodies and bones of my brethren
    dear; —
"Bright sons of the lyric and epic
    Muse,
"All cut up in cutlets, or hasht in stews;
"Their *works*, a light thro' ages to go, —
"*Themselves*, eaten up by Type and
    Co. !"

While thus I moralized, on they went,
Finding the fare most excellent;
And all so kindly, brother to brother,
Helping the tidbits to each other:
"A slice of Southey let me send you " —
"This cut of Campbell I recommend
    you " —
"And here, my friends, is a treat indeed,
"The immortal Wordsworth fricas-
    seed !"

Thus having, the cormorants, fed some
    time,
Upon joints of poetry — all of the prime —
With also (as Type in a whisper averred
    it)
"Cold prose on the sideboard, for such
    as preferred it " —
They rested awhile, to recruit their force,
Then pounced, like kites, on the second
    course,
Which was singing-birds merely — Moore
    and others —
Who all went the way of their larger
    brothers;
And, numerous now tho' such songsters
    be,
'T was really quite distressing to see
A whole dishful of Toms — Moore, Dib-
    din, Bayly, —
Bolted by Type and Co. so gayly!

Nor was this the worst — I shudder to
    think
What a scene was disclosed when they
    came to drink.
The warriors of Odin, as every one knows,
Used to drink out of skulls of slaughtered
    foes:
And Type's old port, to my horror I
    found,
Was in skulls of bards sent merrily round.
And still as each well-filled cranium came,
A health was pledged to its owner's
    name;
While Type said slyly, midst general
    laughter,
"We eat them up first, then drink to them
    after."

There was *no* standing this — incensed I
    broke
From my bonds of sleep, and indignant
    woke,
Exclaiming, "Oh shades of other times,
"Whose voices still sound, like death-
    less chimes,
"Could you e'er have foretold a day
    would be,
"When a dreamer of dreams should live
    to see
"A party of sleek and honest John Bulls
"Hobnobbing each other in poets'
    skulls !"

CHURCH EXTENSION.

TO THE EDITOR OF THE MORNING CHRONICLE.

Sir — A well-known classical traveller, while employed in exploring, some time since, the supposed site of the Temple of Diana of Ephesus, was so fortunate, in the course of his researches, as to light upon a very ancient bark manuscript, which has turned out, on examination, to be part of an old Ephesian newspaper ; — a newspaper published, as you will see, so far back as the time when Demetrius, the great Shrine-Extender,[1] flourished.

I am, Sir, yours, etc.

EPHESIAN GAZETTE.

Second edition.

IMPORTANT event for the rich and religious !
Great Meeting of Silversmiths held in
    Queen Square ; —
Church Extension, their object, — the
    excitement prodigious ; —
Demetrius, head man of the craft,
    takes the chair !

Third edition.

The Chairman still up, when our devil
    came away ;
Having prefaced his speech with the
    usual state prayer,
That the Three-headed Dian [2] would
    kindly, this day,
Take the Silversmiths' Company under
    her care.

Being askt by some low, unestablisht
    divines,
" When your churches are up, where
    are flocks to be got ? "
He manfully answered, " Let *us* build
    the shrines,[2]
" And we care not if flocks are found
    for them or not."

He then added — to show that the Silver-
    smiths' Guild
Were above all confined and intolerant
    views —

---

1 " For a certain man named Demetrius, a silversmith, which made shrines for Diana, brought no small gain unto the craftsmen ; whom he called together with the workmen of like occupation, and said, Sirs, ye know that by this craft we have our wealth." — *Acts* xix.

2 *tria virginis ora Dianæ.*

3 The " shrines " are supposed to have been small churches, or chapels, adjoining to the great

---

" Only *pay* thro' the nose to the altars
    we build,
" You may *pray* thro' the nose to
    what altars you choose."

This tolerance, rare from a shrine-
    dealer's lip
(Tho' a tolerance mixt with due taste
    for the till) —
So much charmed all the holders of scrip-
    tural scrip,
That their shouts of " Hear ! "
    " Hear ! " are re-echoing still.

Fourth edition.

Great stir in the Shrine Market ! altars
    to Phœbus
Are going dog-cheap — may be had
    for a rebus.
Old Dian's, as usual, outsell all the
    rest ; —
But Venus's also are much in request.

LATEST ACCOUNTS FROM OLYMPUS.

As news from Olympus has grown rather
    rare,
Since bards, in their cruises, have ceased
    to *touch* there,
We extract for our readers the intelli-
    gence given,
In our latest accounts from that *ci-devant*
    Heaven —
That realm of the By-gones, where still
    sit in state
Old god-heads and nod-heads now long
    out of date.

Jove himself, it appears, since his love-
    days are o'er,
Seems to find immortality rather a
    bore ;
Tho' he still asks for news of earth's
    capers and crimes,
And reads daily his old fellow-Thun-
    derer, *the Times*.
He and Vulcan, it seems, by their wives
    still hen-*peckt* are,
And kept on a stinted allowance of
    nectar.

---

temples ; — " *ædiculæ, in quibus statuæ repone-bantur.*" — ERASM.

Old Phœbus, poor lad, has given up
inspiration,
And packt off to earth on a *puff*-specula-
tion.
The fact is, he found his old shrines had
grown dim,
Since bards lookt to Bentley and Colburn, not him.
So he sold off his stud of ambrosia-fed
nags,
Came incog. down to earth, and now
writes for the *Mags;*
Taking care that his work not a gleam
hath to linger in 't,
From which men could guess that the
god had a finger in 't.

There are other small facts, well deserv-
ing attention,
Of which our Olympic despatches make
mention.
Poor Bacchus is still very ill, they allege,
Having never recovered the Temperance
Pledge.
"What, the Irish!" he cried — "those
I lookt to the most!
"If they give up the *spirit*, I give up
the ghost:"
While Momus, who used of the gods to
make fun,
Is turned Socialist now and declares
there are none!

But these changes, tho' curious, are all a
mere farce
Compared to the new " *casus belli* " of
Mars,
Who, for years, has been suffering the
horrors of quiet,
Uncheered by one glimmer of bloodshed
or riot!
In vain from the clouds his belligerent
brow
Did he pop forth, in hopes that some-
where or somehow,
Like Pat at a fair, he might " coax up a
row:"
But the joke would n't take — the whole
world had got wiser;
Men liked not to take a Great Gun for
adviser;
And, still less, to march in fine clothes
to be shot,

Without very well knowing for whom or
for what.
The French, who of slaughter had had
their full swing,
Were content with a shot, now and then,
at their King;
While, in England, good fighting 's a
pastime so hard to gain,
Nobody 's left to fight *with*, but Lord
Cardigan.

'T is needless to say then how mon-
strously happy
Old Mars has been made by what 's now
on the *tapis;*
How much it delights him to see the
French rally,
In Liberty's name, around Mehemet
Ali;
Well knowing that Satan himself could
not find
A confection of mischief much more to
his mind
Than the old *Bonnet Rouge* and the Ba-
shaw combined.
Right well, too, he knows, that there
ne'er were attackers,
Whatever their cause, that they did n't
find backers;
While any slight care for Humanity's
woes
May be soothed by that " *Art Diploma-
tique,*" which shows
How to come in the most approved
method to blows.

This is all for to-day — whether Mars is
much vext
At his friend Thiers's exit, we 'll know by
our next.

THE TRIUMPHS OF FARCE.

OUR earth, as it rolls thro' the regions of
space,
Wears always two faces, the dark and
the sunny;
And poor human life runs the same sort
of race,
Being sad on one side — on the other
side, funny.

Thus oft we, at eve, to the Haymarket hie,
  To weep o'er the woes of Macready;
      — but scarce
Hath the tear-drop of Tragedy past from
    the eye,
  When lo! we're all laughing in fits at
      the Farce.

And still let us laugh — preach the world
    as it may —
  Where the cream of the joke is, the
      swarm will soon follow;
Heroics are very grand things in their way,
  But the laugh at the long run will carry
      it hollow.

For instance, what sermon on human af-
    fairs
  Could equal the scene that took place
      t'other day
'Twixt Romeo and Louis Philippe, on the
    stairs —
  The Sublime and Ridiculous meeting
      half-way!

Yes, Jocus! gay god, whom the Gentiles
    supplied,
  And whose worship not even among
      Christians declines,
In our senate thou'st languisht since
    Sheridan died,
  But Sydney still keeps thee alive in our
      shrines.

Rare Sydney! thrice honored the stall
    where he sits,
  And be his every honor he deigneth to
      climb at!
Had England a hierarchy formed all of
    wits,
  Who but Sydney would England pro-
      claim as its primate?

And long may he flourish, frank, merry
    and brave —
  A Horace to hear and a Paschal to
      read;[1]
While he *laughs*, all is safe, but, when
    Sydney grows grave,
  We shall then think the Church is in
      danger *indeed*.

Meanwhile it much glads us to find he's
    preparing
  To teach *other* bishops to "seek the
      right way;[2]"
And means shortly to treat the whole
    Bench to an airing,
  Just such as he gave to Charles James
      t'other day.

For our parts, tho' gravity's good for the
    soul,
  Such a fancy have we for the side that
      there's fun on,
We'd rather with Sydney south-west take
    a "stroll,"
  Than *coach* it north-east with his Lord-
      ship of Lunnun.

THOUGHTS ON PATRONS,
PUFFS, AND OTHER MATTERS.

IN AN EPISTLE FROM THOMAS MOORE
    TO SAMUEL ROGERS.

WHAT, *thou*, my friend! a man of rhymes,
    And, better still, a man of guineas,
To talk of "patrons," in these times,
    When authors thrive like spinning-
        jennies,
And Arkwright's twist and Bulwer's page
Alike may laugh at patronage!

No, no — those times are past away,
  When, doomed in upper floors to star
      it,
The bard inscribed to lords his lay, —
  Himself, the while, my Lord Mount-
      garret,
No more he begs with air dependent,
His "little bark may sail attendant"
    Under some lordly skipper's steerage;
But launched triumphant in the Row,
Or taken by Murray's self in tow,
  Cuts both *Star Chamber* and the peer-
      age.

Patrons, indeed! when scarce a sail
Is whiskt from England by the gale,
But bears on board some authors, shipt
For foreign shores, all well equipt

---

1 Some parts of the "*Provinciales*" may be
said to be of the highest order of *jeux d'esprit*,
or squibs.

2 "This stroll in the metropolis is extremely
well contrived for your Lordship's speech; but
suppose, my dear Lord, that instead of going E
and N. E. you had turned about," etc. — SYDNEY
SMITH's *Last Letter to the Bishop of London*.

With proper book-making machinery,
To sketch the morals, manners, scenery,
Of all such lands as they shall see,
Or *not* see, as the case may be : —
It being enjoined on all who go
To study first Miss Martineau,
And learn from her the method true,
To *do* one's books — and readers, too.
For so this nymph of *nous* and nerve
Teaches mankind " How to Observe ; "
And, lest mankind at all should swerve,
Teaches them also " *What* to Observe."

No, no, my friend — it can't be blinkt —
The Patron is a race extinct;
As dead as any Megatherion
That ever Buckland built a theory on.
Instead of bartering in this age
Our praise for pence and patronage,
We authors now more prosperous elves,
Have learned to patronize ourselves;
And since all-potent Puffing 's made
The life of song, the soul of trade,
More frugal of our praises grown,
We puff no merits but our own.

Unlike those feeble gales of praise
Which critics blew in former days,
Our modern puffs are of a kind
That truly, really *raise the wind ;*
And since they 've fairly set in blowing,
We find them the best *trade*-winds going.
'Stead of frequenting paths so slippy
As her old haunts near Aganippe,
The Muse now taking to the till
Has opened shop on Ludgate Hill
(Far handier than the Hill of Pindus,
As seen from bard's back attic windows);
And swallowing there without cessation
Large draughts (*at sight*) of inspiration,
Touches the *notes* for each new theme,
While still fresh " *change* comes o'er her
     dream."

What Steam is on the deep — and more —
Is the vast power of Puff on shore;
Which jumps to glory's future tenses
Before the present even commences;
And makes " immortal " and " divine "
     of us
Before the world has read one line of us.
In old times, when the God of Song

Drove his own two-horse team along,
Carrying inside a bard or two,
Bookt for posterity " all thro'; " —
Their luggage, a few close-packt rhymes,
(Like yours, my friend,) for after-times —
So slow the pull to Fame's abode,
That folks oft slept upon the road; —
And Homer's self, sometimes, they say,
Took to his nightcap on the way.[1]
Ye Gods ! how different is the story
With our new galloping sons of glory,
Who, scorning all such slack and slow
     time,
Dash to posterity in *no* time !
Raise but one general blast of Puff
To start your author — that 's enough.
In vain the critics set to watch him
Try at the starting post to catch him :
He 's off — the puffers carry it hollow —
The critics, if they please, may follow.
Ere *they* 've laid down their first posi-
     tions,
He 's fairly blown thro' six editions !
In vain doth Edinburgh dispense
Her blue and yellow pestilence
(That plague so awful in my time
To young and touchy sons of rhyme) —
The *Quarterly*, at three months' date,
To catch the Unread One, comes too late ;
And nonsense, littered in a hurry,
Becomes " immortal," spite of Murray.

But, bless me ! — while I thus keep fool-
     ing,
I hear a voice cry, " Dinner 's cooling."
That postman too (who, truth to tell,
'Mong men of letters bears the bell,)
Keeps ringing, ringing, so infernally
That I *must* stop —
               Yours sempiternally.

THOUGHTS ON MISCHIEF.

BY LORD STANLEY.

(HIS FIRST ATTEMPT IN VERSE.)

" Evil, be thou my good." — MILTON.

How various are the inspirations
Of different men in different nations !
As genius prompts to good or evil,
Some call the Muse, some raise the
     devil.

[1] *quandoque bonus dormitat Homerus.* —
HORAT.

Old Socrates, that pink of sages,
Kept a pet demon on board wages
To go about with him incog.,
And sometimes give his wits a jog.
So Lyndhurst, in *our* day, we know,
Keeps fresh relays of imps below,
To forward from that nameless spot
His inspirations, hot and hot.

But, neat as are old Lyndhurst's do-
　　ings —
Beyond even Hecate's "hell-broth"
　　brewings —
Had I, Lord Stanley, but my will,
I 'd show you mischief prettier still;
Mischief, combining boyhoods' tricks
With age's sourest politics;
The urchin's freaks, the veteran's gall,
Both duly mixt, and matchless all;
A compound naught in history reaches
But Machiavel, when first in breeches!

Yes, Mischief, Goddess multiform,
Whene'er thou, witch-like, ridest the
　　storm,
Let Stanley ride cockhorse behind thee —
No livelier lackey could they find thee.
And, Goddess, as I 'm well aware,
So mischief 's *done*, you care not
　　where,
I own, 't will most *my* fancy tickle
In Paddyland to play the Pickle;
Having got credit for inventing
A new, brisk method of tormenting —
A way they call the Stanley fashion,
Which puts all Ireland in a passion;
So neat it hits the mixture due
Of injury and insult too;
So legibly it bears upon 't
The stamp of Stanley's brazen front.

Ireland, we 're told, means the land of
　　of *Ire;*
And *why* she 's so, none need inquire,
Who sees her millions, martial, manly,
Spat upon thus by me, Lord Stanley.
Already in the breeze I scent
The whiff of coming devilment;
Of strife, to me more stirring far
Than the Opium or the Sulphur war,
Or any such drug ferments are.
Yes — sweeter to this Tory soul
Than all such pests, from pole to pole,

Is the rich, "sweltered venom" got
By stirring Ireland's "charmed pot;"[1]
And thanks to practice on that land
I stir it with a master-hand.

Again thou 'lt see, when forth hath gone
The War-Church-cry, "On, Stanley,
　　on!"
How Caravats and Shanavests
Shall swarm from out their mountain
　　nests,
With all their merry moonlight brothers,
To whom the Church (*step*-dame to
　　others)
Hath been the best of nursing mothers.
Again o'er Erin's rich domain
Shall Rockites and right reverends reign;
And both, exempt from vulgar toil,
Between them share that titheful soil;
Puzzling ambition *which* to climb at,
The post of Captain, or of Primate.

And so, long life to Church and Co. —
Hurrah for mischief! — here we go.

EPISTLE FROM CAPTAIN ROCK
TO LORD LYNDHURST.

DEAR Lyndhurst, — you 'll pardon my
　　making thus free, —
But form is all fudge 'twixt such "com-
　　rogues" as we,
Who, whate'er the smooth views we, in
　　public, may drive at,
Have both the same praiseworthy object,
　　in private —
Namely, never to let the old regions of
　　riot,
Where Rock hath long reigned, have
　　one instant of quiet,
But keep Ireland still in that liquid we 've
　　taught her
To love more than meat, drink, or cloth-
　　ing — *hot water*.

All the difference betwixt you and me,
　　as I take it,
Is simply, that *you* make the law and *I*
　　break it;

1 " Sweltered venom, sleeping got,
　　Boil thou first i' the charmed pot."

And never, of big-wigs and small, were there two
Played so well into each other's hands as we do;
Insomuch, that the laws you and yours manufacture,
Seem all made express for the Rock-boys to fracture.
Not Birmingham's self — to her shame be it spoken —
E'er made things more neatly contrived to be broken;
And hence, I confess, in this island religious,
The breakage of laws — and of heads *is* prodigious.

And long may it thrive, my Ex-Bigwig, say I, —
Tho', of late, much I feared all our fun was gone by;
As, except when some tithe-hunting parson showed sport,
Some rector — a cool hand at pistols and port,
Who "keeps dry" his *powder*, but never *himself* —
One who, leaving his Bible to rust on the shelf,
Sends his pious texts home, in the shape of ball-cartridges,
Shooting his "dearly beloved," like partridges; —
Except when some hero of this sort turned out,
Or, the Exchequer sent, flaming, its tithe-writs [1] about —
A contrivance more neat, I may say, without flattery,
Than e'er yet was thought of for bloodshed and battery;
So neat, that even *I* might be proud, I allow,
To have hit off so rich a receipt for a *row ;* —
Except for such rigs turning up, now and then,
I was actually growing the dullest of men ;
And, had this blank fit been allowed to increase,

---

1 Exchequer tithe processes, served under a commission of rebellion. — *Chronicle.*

Might have snored myself down to a Justice of Peace.
Like you, Reformation in Church and in State
Is the thing of all things I most cordially hate.
If once these curst Ministers do as they like,
All 's o'er, my good Lord, with your wig and my pike,
And one may be hung up on t' other, henceforth,
Just to show what *such* Captains and Chancellors were worth.

But we must not despair — even already Hope sees
You 're about, my bold Baron, to kick up a breeze
Of the true baffling sort, such as suits me and you,
Who have boxt the whole compass of party right thro',
And care not one farthing, as all the world knows,
So we *but* raise the wind, from what quarter it blows.
Forgive me, dear Lord, that thus rudely I dare
My own small resources with thine to compare :
Not even Jerry Diddler, in "raising the wind," durst
Compete, for one instant, with thee, my dear Lyndhurst.

But, hark, there 's a shot ! — some parsonic practitioner?
No — merely a bran-new Rebellion Commissioner ;
The Courts having now, with true law erudition,
Put even Rebellion itself "in commission."
As seldom, in *this* way, I 'm any man's debtor,
I 'll just *pay my shot* and then fold up this letter.
In the mean time, hurrah for the Tories and Rocks !
Hurrah for the parsons who fleece well their flocks !

Hurrah for all mischief in all ranks and
spheres,
And, above all, hurrah for that dear
House of Peers!

CAPTAIN ROCK IN LONDON.

LETTER FROM THE CAPTAIN TO TERRY ALT, ESQ.[1]

HERE I am, at head-quarters, dear Terry,
once more,
Deep in Tory designs, as I 've oft been
before: —
For, bless them! if 't was n't for this
wrong-headed crew,
You and I, Terry Alt, would scarce
know what to do;
So ready they 're always, when dull we
are growing,
To set our old concert of discord a-going,
While Lyndhurst 's the lad, with his
Tory-Whig face,
To play in such concert the true *double-
base*.
I had feared this old prop of my realm
was beginning
To tire of his course of political sinning,
And, like Mother Cole, when her heyday
was past,
Meant by way of a change to try virtue
at last.
But I wronged the old boy, who as
stanchly derides
All reform in himself as in most things
besides;
And, by using *two* faces thro' life, all allow,
Has acquired face sufficient for *any* thing
now.

In short, he 's all right; and, if mankind's old foe,
My " Lord Harry " himself — who 's
the leader, we know,
Of another red-hot Opposition, below —
If that " Lord," in his well-known dis-
cernment, but spares
Me and Lyndhurst, to look after Ireland's affairs,
We shall soon such a region of devilment make it,
That Old Nick himself for his own may
mistake it.

1 The subordinate officer or lieutenant of
Captain Rock.

Even already — long life to such Big-
wigs, say I,
For, as long as they flourish, we Rocks
cannot die —
He has served our right riotous cause by
a speech
Whose perfection of mischief he only
could reach;
As it shows off both *his* and *my* merits
alike,
Both the swell of the wig and the point
of the pike;
Mixes up, with a skill which one can't
but admire,
The lawyer's cool craft with the incendiary's fire,
And enlists, in the gravest, most plausi-
ble manner,
Seven millions of souls under Rockery's
banner!

Oh Terry, my man, let this speech *never*
die;
Thro' the regions of Rockland, like
flame, let it fly;
Let each syllable dark the Law-Oracle
uttered
By all Tipperary's wild echoes be mut-
tered,
Till naught shall be heard, over hill, dale
or flood,
But " *You're aliens in language, in
creed and in blood;* "
While voices, from sweet Connemara
afar,
Shall answer, like true *Irish* echoes,
" We are! "
And, tho' false be the cry, and tho'
sense must abhor it,
Still the echoes may quote *Law* authority
for it,
And naught Lyndhurst cares for my
spread of dominion
So he, in the end, touches cash " for
the *opinion*."

But I 've no time for more, my dear
Terry, just now,
Being busy in helping these Lords thro'
their *row*.
They 're bad hands at mob-work, but,
once they begin,
They 'll have plenty of practice to break
them well in.

POLITICAL AND SATIRICAL POEMS.

LINES ON THE DEATH OF MR. PERCEVAL.

IN the dirge we sung o'er him no censure was heard,
    Unembittered and free did the tear-
drop descend;
We forgot, in that hour, how the statesman had erred,
    And wept for the husband, the father
and friend.

Oh! proud was the meed his integrity
won,
    And generous indeed were the tears
that we shed,
When in grief we forgot all the ill he
had done,
    And tho' wronged by him living, be-
wailed him, when dead.

Even now if one harsher emotion intrude,
    'T is to wish he had chosen some low-
lier state,
Had known what he was — and, content to be *good*,
    Had ne'er for our ruin aspired to be
great.

So, left thro' their own little orbit to
move,
    His years might have rolled inoffensive
away;
His children might still have been blest
with his love,
    And England would ne'er have been
curst with his sway.

TO THE EDITOR OF "THE MORNING
CHRONICLE."

Sir, — In order to explain the following Fragment, it is necessary to refer
your readers to a late florid description
of the Pavillion at Brighton, in the apartments of which, we are told, "FUM, *The
Chinese Bird of Royalty*," is a principal
ornament.

        I am, Sir, yours, etc.
                    MUM.

FUM AND HUM, THE TWO BIRDS OF ROYALTY.

ONE day the Chinese Bird of Royalty,
FUM,
Thus accosted our own Bird of Royalty,
HUM,
In that Palace or China-shop (Brighton,
which is it?)
Where FUM had just come to pay HUM
a short visit. —
Near akin are these Birds, tho' they dif-
fer in nation
(The breed of the HUMS is as old as
creation);
Both, full-crawed Legitimates — both,
birds of prey,
Both, cackling and ravenous creatures,
half way
'Twixt the goose and the vulture, like
Lord CASTLEREAGH.
While FUM deals in Mandarins, Bonzes,
Bohea,
Peers, Bishops and Punch, HUM, are
sacred to thee!
So congenial their tastes, that, when
FUM first did light on
The floor of that grand China-warehouse
at Brighton,
The lanterns and dragons and things
round the dome
Were so like what he left, "Gad," says
FUM, "I'm at home." —

And when, turning, he saw Bishop
L——GE, "Zooks, it is,"
Quoth the Bird, "Yes — I know him —
a Bonze, by his phiz —
"And that jolly old idol he kneels to so
low
"Can be none but our round-about god-
head, fat Fo!"
It chanced at this moment, the Episcopal
Prig
Was imploring the Prince to dispense
with his wig,[1]
Which the Bird, overhearing, flew high
o'er his head,
And some ToBIT-like marks of his pa-
tronage shed,
Which so dimmed the poor Dandy's
idolatrous eye,
That, while FUM cried "Oh Fo!" all
the court cried "Oh fie!"

But a truce to digression; — these Birds
of a feather
Thus talkt, t'other night, on State matters
together;
(The PRINCE just in bed, or about to de-
part for 't,
His legs full of gout, and his arms full of
HARTFORD,)
"I say, HUM," says FUM — FUM, of
course, spoke Chinese,
But, bless you! that 's nothing — at
Brighton one sees
Foreign lingoes and Bishops *translated*
with ease —
"I say, HUM, how fares it with Royalty
now?
"Is it *up?* is it *prime?* is it *spooney* —
or how?"
(The Bird had just taken a flash-man's
degree
Under BARRYMORE, YARMOUTH, and
young Master L——E)
"As for us in Pekin" — here, a devil
of a din
From the bed-chamber came, where that
long Mandarin,
Castlereagh (whom FUM calls the *Confu-
sius* of Prose),

[1] In consequence of an old promise, that he
should be allowed to wear his own hair, whenever
he might be elevated to a Bishopric by his Royal
Highness.

Was rehearsing a speech upon Eur̊ope's
repose
To the deep, double bass of the fat Idol's
nose.

(*Nota bene* — his Lordship and LIVER-
POOL come,
In collateral lines, from the old Mother
HUM,
CASTLEREAGH a HUM-bug — LIVERPOOL
a HUM-drum.)
The Speech being finisht, out rusht
CASTLEREAGH,
Saddled HUM in a hurry, and, whip,
spur, away!
Thro' the regions of air, like a Snip on
his hobby,
Ne'er paused till he lighted in St.
Stephen's lobby.

.   .   .   .

LINES ON THE DEATH OF
SHERIDAN.

principibus placuisse viris! — HORAT.

YES, grief will have way — but the fast
falling tear
Shall be mingled with deep execrations
on those
Who could bask in that Spirit's meridian
career,
And yet leave it thus lonely and dark
at its close : —➝

Whose vanity flew round him, only while
fed
By the odor his fame in its summer-
time gave; —
Whose vanity now, with quick scent for
the dead,
Like the Ghoul of the East, comes to
feed at his grave.

Oh! it sickens the heart to see bosoms
so hollow,
And spirits so mean in the great and
high-born;
To think what a long line of titles may
follow
The relics of him who died — friendless and lorn!

How proud they can press to the funeral
 array
Of one whom they shunned in his sickness and sorrow :—
How bailiffs may seize his last blanket
 to-day,
Whose pall shall be held up by nobles
 to-morrow !

And Thou too whose life, a sick epicure's
 dream,
Incoherent and gross, even grosser had
 past,
Were it not for that cordial and soul-
 giving beam
Which his friendship and wit o'er thy
 nothingness cast :—

No ! not for the wealth of the land that
 supplies thee
With millions to heap upon Foppery's
 shrine ;—
No ! not for the riches of all who despise
 thee,
Tho' this would make Europe's whole
 opulence mine ;—

Would I suffer what — even in the heart
 that thou hast —
All mean as it is — must have con-
 sciously burned,
When the pittance, which shame had
 wrung from thee at last,
And which found all his wants at an
 end, was returned ! [1]

"Was *this* then the fate," — future ages
 will say,
When *some* names shall live but in
 history's curse ;
When Truth will be heard, and these
 Lords of a day
Be forgotten as fools or remembered
 as worse ;—

"Was this then the fate of that high-
 gifted man,
 "The pride of the palace, the bower
 and the hall,

"The orator,— dramatist, — minstrel, —
 who ran
 "Thro' each mode of the lyre and
 was master of all ;—

"Whose mind was an essence com-
 pounded with art
 "From the finest and best of all other
 men's powers ;—
"Who ruled, like a wizard, the world
 of the heart,
 "And could call up its sunshine or bring
 down its showers ;—

"Whose humor, as gay as the fire-fly's
 light,
 "Played round every subject and
 shone as it played ;—
"Whose wit in the combat, as gentle as
 bright,
 "Ne'er carried a heart-stain away on
 its blade ;

"Whose eloquence — brightening whatever it tried,
 "Whether reason or fancy, the gay or
 the grave,—
"Was as rapid, as deep and as brilliant
 a tide,
 "As ever bore Freedom aloft on its
 wave ! "

Yes — such was the man and so wretched
 his fate ;—
And thus, sooner or later, shall all have
 to grieve,
Who waste their morn's dew in the beams
 of the Great,
And expect 't will return to refresh
 them at eve.

In the woods of the North there are insects that prey
On the brain of the elk till his very
 last sigh ; [2]
Oh, Genius ! thy patrons, more cruel
 than they,
First feed on thy brains and then leave
 thee to die !

---

1 The sum was two hundred pounds — *offered*
when Sheridan could no longer take any sustenance, and declined, for him, by his friends.

2 Naturalists have observed that, upon dis-
secting an elk, there was found in its head some
large flies, with its brain almost eaten away by
them. — *History of Poland.*

EPISTLE

FROM

TOM CRIB TO BIG BEN.[1]

CONCERNING SOME FOUL PLAY IN A LATE
TRANSACTION.[2]

"Ahi, mio Ben!" — METASTASIO.[3]

WHAT! BEN, my old hero, is this your
 renown?
Is *this* the new *go?* — kick a man when
 he 's down!
When the foe has knockt under, to tread
 on him then —
By the fist of my father, I blush for thee,
 BEN!
"Foul! foul!" all the lads of the
 Fancy exclaim —
CHARLEY SHOCK is electrified — BEL-
 CHER spits flame —
And MOLYNEUX — ay, even BLACKY[4]
 cries "shame!"

Time was, when JOHN BULL little difference spied
'Twixt the foe at his feet and the friend
 at his side:
When he found (such his humor in fighting and eating)
His foe, like his beef-steak, the sweeter
 for beating.
But this comes, Master BEN, of your
 curst foreign notions,
Your trinkets, wigs, thingumbobs, gold
 lace and lotions;
Your Noyaus, Curaçoas, and the devil
 knows what —
(One swig of *Blue Ruin*[5] is worth the
 whole lot!)

1 A nickname given, at this time, to the Prince
Regent.

2 Written soon after Bonaparte's transporta-
tion to St. Helena.

3 Tom, I suppose, was "assisted" to this
Motto by Mr. Jackson, who, it is well known,
keeps the most learned company going.

4 Names and nicknames of celebrated pugi-
lists at that time.

5 Gin.

Your great and small *crosses* — (my eyes,
 what a brood!
A *cross*-buttock from *me* would do some
 of them good!)
Which have spoilt you, till hardly a drop,
 my old porpoise,
Of pure English *claret* is left in your
 corpus;
And (as JIM says) the only one trick,
 good or bad,
Of the Fancy you 're up to, is *fibbing*,
 my lad.
Hence it comes, — BOXIANA, disgrace to
 thy page! —
Having floored, by good luck, the first
 swell of the age,
Having conquered the *prime one*, that
 milled us all round,
You kickt him, old BEN, as he gaspt
 on the ground!
Ay — just at the time to show spunk, if
 you 'd got any —
Kickt him and jawed him and *lagged*[6]
 him to Botany!
Oh, shade of the *Cheesemonger!*[7] you,
 who, alas!
Doubled up by the dozen those Moun-
 seers in brass,
On that great day of *milling*, when
 blood lay in lakes,
When Kings held the bottle, and Europe
 the stakes,
Look down upon BEN — see him, *dung-
 hill* all o'er,
Insult the fallen foe that can harm him
 no more!
Out, cowardly *spooney!* — again and
 again,
By the fist of my father, I blush for thee,
 BEN.
To *show the white feather* is many men's
 doom,
But, what of *one* feather? — BEN shows
 a *whole Plume*.

6 Transported.

7 A Life Guardsman, one of *the Fancy* who
distinguished himself and was killed in the memorable *set-to* at Waterloo.

FABLES

FOR

THE HOLY ALLIANCE.

tu Regibus alas
eripe
Vergil, *Georg. lib.* iv.

————— Clip the wings
Of these high-flying arbitrary Kings.
Dryden's *Translation.*

DEDICATION.

TO LORD BYRON.

Dear Lord Byron, — Though this Volume should possess no other merit in your eyes, than that of reminding you of the short time we passed together at Venice, when some of the trifles which it contains were written, you will, I am sure, receive the dedication of it with pleasure, and believe that I am,

My dear Lord,
Ever faithfully yours,

T. B.

PREFACE.

Though it was the wish of the Members of the Poco-curante Society (who have lately done me the honor of electing me their Secretary) that I should prefix my name to the following Miscellany, it is but fair to them and to myself to state, that, except in the " painful pre-eminence " of being employed to transcribe their lucubrations, my claim to such a distinction in the title-page is not greater than that of any other gentleman, who has contributed his share to the contents of the volume.

I had originally intended to take this opportunity of giving some account of the origin and objects of our Institution, the names and characters of the different members, etc. — but as I am at present preparing for the press the First Volume of the "Transactions of the Poco-curante Society," I shall reserve for that occasion all further details upon the subject, and content myself here with referring, for a general insight into our tenets, to a Song which will be found at the end of this work and which is sung to us on the first day of every month, by one of our oldest members, to the tune of (as far as I can recollect, being no musician,) either "Nancy Dawson" or "He stole away the Bacon."

It may be as well also to state for the information of those critics who attack with the hope of being answered, and of being thereby brought into notice, that it is the rule of this Society to return no other answer to such assailants, than is contained in the three words " *non curat Hippoclides*," (meaning, in English, " Hippoclides does not care a fig,") which were spoken two thousand years ago by the first founder of Poco-curantism, and have ever since been adopted as the leading *dictum* of the sect.

THOMAS BROWN.

FABLES FOR THE HOLY ALLIANCE.

FABLE I.

THE DISSOLUTION OF THE HOLY ALLI-
ANCE.

A DREAM.

I 'VE had a dream that bodes no good
Unto the Holy Brotherhood.
I may be wrong, but I confess —
  As far as it is right or lawful
For one, no conjurer, to guess —
  It seems to me extremely awful.

Methought, upon the Neva's flood
A beautiful Ice Palace stood,
A dome of frost-work, on the plan
Of that once built by Empress Anne,[1]
Which shone by moonlight — as the tale
  is —
Like an Aurora Borealis.

In this said Palace, furnisht all
  And lighted as the best on land are,
I dreamt there was a splendid Ball,
  Given by the Emperor Alexander,
To entertain with all due zeal,
  Those holy gentlemen, who 've shown a
Regard so kind for Europe's weal,
  At Troppau, Laybach and Verona.

The thought was happy — and designed
To hint how thus the human Mind
May, like the stream imprisoned there,
Be checkt and chilled, till it can bear
The heaviest Kings, that ode or sonnet
E'er yet be-praised, to dance upon it.

And all were pleased and cold and
  stately,
  Shivering in grand illumination —

<hr>

1 "It is well known that the Empress Anne
built a palace of ice on the Neva, in 1740, which
was fifty-two feet in length, and when illuminated
had a surprising effect." — PINKERTON.

Admired the superstructure greatly,
  Nor gave one thought to the founda-
    tion.
Much too the Tsar himself exulted,
  To all plebeian fears a stranger,
For, Madame Krüdener, when consulted,
  Had pledged her word there was no
    danger.
So, on he capered, fearless quite,
  Thinking himself extremely clever,
And waltzed away with all his might,
  As if the Frost would last for ever.

Just fancy how a bard like me,
  Who reverence monarchs, must have
    trembled
To see that goodly company,
  At such a ticklish sport assembled.

Nor were the fears, that thus astounded
My loyal soul, at all unfounded —
For, lo! ere long, those walls so massy
  Were seized with an ill-omened drip-
    ping,
And o'er the floors, now growing glassy,
  Their Holinesses took to slipping.
The Tsar, half thro' a Polonaise,
  Could scarce get on for downright
    stumbling;
And Prussia, tho' to slippery ways
  Well used, was cursedly near tum-
    bling.

Yet still 't was, *who* could stamp the
  floor most,
Russia and Austria 'mong the fore-
  most. —
And now, to an Italian air,
  This precious brace would, hand in
    hand, go;
Now — while old Louis, from his chair,
Intreated them his toes to spare —
  Called loudly out for a Fandango.

And a Fandango, 'faith, they had,
At which they all set to, like mad!
Never were Kings (tho' small the expense is
Of wit among their Excellencies)
So out of all their princely senses.
But ah! that dance — that Spanish dance —
Scarce was the luckless strain begun,
When, glaring red, as 't were a glance
Shot from an angry Southern sun,
A light thro' all the chambers flamed,
Astonishing old Father Frost,
Who, bursting into tears, exclaimed,
"A thaw, by Jove — we 're lost, we 're lost!
"Run, France — a second *Water*loo
"Is come to drown you — *sauve qui peut!*"

Why, why will monarchs caper so
In palaces without foundations? —
Instantly all was in a flow,
Crowns, fiddles, sceptres, decorations —
Those Royal Arms, that lookt so nice,
Cut out in the resplendent ice —
Those Eagles, handsomely provided
With double heads for double dealings —
How fast the globes and sceptres glided
Out of their claws on all the ceilings!
Proud Prussia's double bird of prey
Tame as a spatch cock, slunk away;
While — just like France herself, when she
Proclaims how great her naval skill is—
Poor Louis's drowning fleurs-de-lys
Imagined themselves *water*-lilies.

And not alone rooms, ceilings, shelves,
But — still more fatal execution —
The Great Legitimates themselves
Seemed in a state of dissolution.
The indignant Tsar — when just about
To issue a sublime Ukase,
"Whereas all light must be kept out " —
Dissolved to nothing in its blaze.
Next Prussia took his turn to melt,
And, while his lips illustrious felt
The influence of this southern air,
Some word, like " Constitution " — long

Congealed in frosty silence there —
Came slowly thawing from his tongue.
While Louis, lapsing by degrees,
And sighing out a faint adieu
To truffles, salmis, toasted cheese
And smoking *fondus*, quickly grew,
Himself, into a *fondu* too; —
Or like that goodly King they make
Of sugar for a Twelfth-night cake,
When, in some urchin's mouth, alas!
It melts into a shapeless mass!

In short, I scarce could count a minute,
Ere the bright dome and all within it,
Kings, Fiddlers, Emperors, all were gone —
And nothing now was seen or heard
But the bright river, rushing on,
Happy as an enfranchised bird,
And prouder of that natural ray,
Shining along its chainless way —
More proudly happy thus to glide
In simple grandeur to the sea,
Than when, in sparkling fetters tied,
'T was deckt with all that kingly pride
Could bring to light its slavery!

Such is my dream — and, I confess,
I tremble at its awfulness.
That Spanish Dance — that southern beam —
But I say nothing — there 's my dream —
And Madame Krüdener, the she-prophet,
May make just what she pleases of it.

FABLE II.
THE LOOKING-GLASSES.
PROEM.

WHERE Kings have been by mob-elections
Raised to the throne, 't is strange to see
What different and what odd perfections
Men have required in Royalty.
Some, liking monarchs large and plumpy,
Have chosen their Sovereigns by the weight; —
Some wisht them tall, some thought your dumpy,
Dutch-built, the true Legitimate.[1]

1 The Goths had a law to choose always a short, thick man for their King. — MUNSTER, " Cosmog." *lib*. iii. p. 164.

The Easterns in a Prince, 't is said,
Prefer what 's called a jolter-head: [1]
The Egyptians were n't at all partic'lar,
  So that their Kings had *not* red hair —
This fault not even the greatest stickler
  For the blood-royal well could bear.

A thousand more such illustrations
Might be adduced from various nations.
But, 'mong the many tales they tell us,
  Touching the acquired or natural right
Which some men have to rule their fel-
  lows,
There 's one which I shall here re-
  cite: —

FABLE.

There was a land — to *name* the place
  Is neither now my wish nor duty —
Where reigned a certain Royal race,
  By right of their superior beauty.

What was the cut legitimate
  Of these great persons' chins and noses,
By right of which they ruled the state,
  No history I have seen discloses.

But so it was — a settled case —
  Some Act of Parliament, past snugly,
Had voted *them* a beauteous race,
  And all their faithful subjects ugly.

As rank indeed stood high or low,
  Some change it made in visual organs;
Your Peers were decent — Knights, so
  so —
But all your *common* people, gorgons!

Of course, if any knave but hinted
  That the King's nose was turned awry,
Or that the Queen (God bless her!)
  squinted —
The judges doomed that knave to die.

But rarely things like this occurred,
  The people to their King were duteous,
And took it, on his Royal word,
  That they were frights and He was
  beauteous.

The cause whereof, among all classes,
  Was simply this — these island elves
Had never yet seen looking-glasses,
  And therefore did not *know themselves.*

Sometimes indeed their neighbors' faces
  Might strike them as more full of
  reason,
More fresh than those in certain places —
  But, Lord, the very thought was
  treason!

Besides, howe'er we love our neighbor,
  And take his face's part, 't is known
We ne'er so much in earnest labor,
  As when the face attackt 's our own.

So on they went — the crowd believing —
  (As crowds well governed always do)
Their rulers, too, themselves deceiving —
  So old the joke, they thought 't was
  true.

But jokes, we know, if they too far go,
  Must have an end — and so, one day,
Upon that coast there was a cargo
  Of looking-glasses cast away.

'T was said, some Radicals, somewhere,
  Had laid their wicked heads together,
And forced that ship to founder there, —
  While some believe it was the weather.

However this might be, the freight
  Was landed without fees or duties;
And from that hour historians date
  The downfall of the Race of Beauties.

The looking-glasses got about,
  And grew so common thro' the land,
That scarce a tinker could walk out,
  Without a mirror in his hand.

Comparing faces, morning, noon,
  And night, their constant occupation —
By dint of looking-glasses, soon,
  They grew a most reflecting nation.

In vain the Court, aware of errors
  In all the old, establisht mazards,
Prohibited the use of mirrors
  And tried to break them at all haz-
  ards: —

In vain — their laws might just as well
  Have been waste paper on the shelves;
That fatal freight had broke the spell;
  People had lookt — and knew them-
    selves.

If chance a Duke, of birth sublime,
  Presumed upon his ancient face,
(Some calf-head, ugly from all time,)
  They popt a mirror to his Grace: —

Just hinting, by that gentle sign,
  How little Nature holds it true,
That what is called an ancient line,
  Must be the line of Beauty too.

From Dukes' they past to regal phizzes,
  Compared them proudly with their own,
And cried, " How *could* such monstrous
    quizzes
  " In   Beauty's   name   usurp   the
    throne ! " —

They then wrote essays, pamphlets,
    books,
Upon Cosmetical Œconomy,
Which made the King try various looks,
  But none improved his physiognomy.

And satires at the Court were levelled,
  And small lampoons, so full of sly-
    nesses,
That soon, in short, they quite be-deviled
  Their Majesties and Royal Highnesses.

At length — but here I drop the veil,
  To spare some royal folks' sensa-
    tions; —
Besides, what followed is the tale
  Of all such late-enlightened nations;

Of all to whom old Time discloses
  A truth they should have sooner
    known —
That Kings have neither rights nor noses
  A whit diviner than their own.

FABLE III.

THE TORCH OF LIBERTY.

I SAW it all in Fancy's glass —
  Herself, the fair, the wild magician,
Who bade this splendid day-dream pass,
  And named each gliding apparition.

'T was like a torch-race — such as they
  Of Greece performed, in ages gone,
When the fleet youths, in long array,
  Past the bright torch triumphant on.

I saw the expectant nations stand,
  To catch the coming flame in turn; —
I saw, from ready hand to hand,
  The clear tho' struggling glory burn.

And oh ! their joy, as it came near,
  'T was in itself a joy to see; —
While Fancy whispered in my ear,
  " That torch they pass is Liberty ! "

And each, as she received the flame,
  Lighted her altar with its ray;
Then, smiling, to the next who came,
  Speeded it on its sparkling way.

From ALBION first, whose ancient shrine
  Was furnish'd with the fire already,
COLUMBIA caught the boon divine,
  And lit a flame, like ALBION'S, steady.

The splendid gift then GALLIA took,
  And, like a wild Bacchante, raising
The brand aloft, its sparkles shook,
  As she would set the world a-blazing !

Thus kindling wild, so fierce and high
  Her altar blazed into the air,
That ALBION, to that fire too nigh,
  Shrunk back and shuddered at its
    glare !

Next, SPAIN, so new was light to her,
  Leapt at the torch — but, ere the spark
That fell upon her shrine could stir,
  'T was quenched — and all again was
    dark.

Yet, no — *not* quenched — a treasure
    worth
  So much to mortals rarely dies:
Again her living light lookt forth,
  And shone, a beacon, in all eyes.

Who next received the flame? alas !
  Unworthy NAPLES — shame of shames,
That ever thro' such hands should pass
  That brightest of all earthly flames !

Scarce had her fingers touched the torch,
  When, frighted by the sparks it shed,
Nor waiting even to feel the scorch,
  She dropt it to the earth — and fled.

And fallen it might have long remained;
  But GREECE, who saw her moment
    now,
Caught up the prize, tho' prostrate,
    stained,
  And waved it round her beauteous
    brow.

And Fancy bade me mark where, o'er
  Her altar, as its flame ascended,
Fair, laurelled spirits seemed to soar,
  Who thus in song their voices
    blended: —

" Shine, shine for ever, glorious Flame,
  " Divinest gift of Gods to men !
" From GREECE thy earliest splendor
    came,
  " To GREECE thy ray returns again.

"Take, Freedom, take thy radiant round,
  " When dimmed, revive, when lost, re-
    turn,
" Till not a shrine thro' earth be found,
  " On which thy glories shall not
    burn ' "

FABLE IV.

THE FLY AND THE BULLOCK.

PROEM.

OF all that, to the sage's survey,
This world presents of topsy-turvy,
There 's naught so much disturbs one's
    patience,
As little minds in lofty stations.
'T is like that sort of painful wonder,
Which slender columns, laboring under
  Enormous arches, give beholders; —
Or those poor Caryatides,
Condemned to smile and stand at ease,
  With a whole house upon their shoul-
    ders.

If as in some few royal cases,
Small minds are *born* into such places —
If they are there by Right Divine
  Or any such sufficient reason,

Why — Heaven forbid we should re-
    pine ! —
  To wish it otherwise were treason;
Nay, even to see it in a vision,
Would be what lawyers call *misprision*.

Sir ROBERT FILMER saith — and he,
  Of course, knew all about the matter —
" Both men and beasts love Monarchy;"
  Which proves how rational — the *lat-
    ter*.
SIDNEY, we know, or wrong or right,
Entirely differed from the Knight:
Nay, hints a King may lose his head,
  By slipping awkwardly his bridle: —
But this is treasonous, ill-bred,
And (now a days, when Kings are led
  In patent snaffles) downright idle.

No, no — it is n't right-line Kings,
(Those sovereign lords in leading-strings
Who, from their birth, are Faith-Defend-
    ers,)
That move my wrath — 't is your pre-
    tenders,
Your mushroom rulers, sons of earth,
Who — not, like t' others, bores by birth,
Establish *gratiâ Dei* blockheads,
Born with three kingdoms in their
    pockets —
Yet, with a brass that nothing stops,
  Push up into the loftiest stations,
And, tho' too dull to manage shops,
  Presume, the dolts, to manage nations !

This class it is, that moves my gall,
And stirs up bile, and spleen and all.
While other senseless things appear
To know the limits of their sphere —
While not a cow on earth romances
So much as to conceit she dances —
While the most jumping frog we know of,
Would scarce at Astley's hope to show
    off —
Your * * * s, your * * * s dare,
  Untrained as are their minds, to set
    them
To *any* business, *any* where,
  At *any* time that fools will let them.

But leave we here these upstart things —
My business is just now with Kings ;
To whom and to their right-line glory,
I dedicate the following story.

FABLE.

The wise men of Egypt were secret as
    dummies ;
    And even when they most conde-
        scended to teach,
They packt up their meaning, as they
    did their mummies,
    In so many wrappers, 't was out of
        one's reach.

They were also, good people, much
    given to Kings —
    Fond of craft and of crocodiles, mon-
        keys and mystery ;
But blue-bottle flies were their best be-
    loved things —
    As will partly appear in this very short
        history.

A Scythian philosopher (nephew, they
    say,
    To that other great traveller, young
        Anacharsis,)
Stept into a temple at Memphis one day,
    To have a short peep at their mystical
        farces.

He saw [1] a brisk blue-bottle Fly on an
    altar,
    Made much of, and worshipt, as some-
        thing divine ;
While a large, handsome Bullock, led
    there in a halter,
    Before it lay stabbed at the foot of the
        shrine.

Surprised at such doings, he whispered
    his teacher —
    " If 't is n't impertinent, may I ask
        why
" Should a Bullock, that useful and pow-
    erful creature,
    " Be thus offered up to a blue-bottle
        Fly ? "

" No wonder " — said t' other — " you
    stare at the sight,
    " But we as a Symbol of Monarchy
        view it —

" That Fly on the shrine is Legitimate
    Right,
    " And that Bullock, the People that 's
        sacrificed to it."

FABLE V.

CHURCH AND STATE.

PROEM.

"The moment any religion becomes national,
or established, its purity must certainly be lost,
because it is then impossible to keep it unconnected with men's interests; and, if connected,
it must inevitably be perverted by them." —
SOAME JENYNS.

THUS did SOAME JENYNS — tho' a Tory,
    A Lord of Trade and the Plantations ;
Feel how Religion's simple glory
    Is stained by State associations.

When CATHARINE, ere she crusht the
        Poles,
    Appealed to the benign Divinity ;
Then cut them up in protocols,
Made fractions of their very souls [2] —
    All in the name of the blest Trinity ;
Or when her grandson, ALEXANDER,
That mighty Northern salamander,[3]
    Whose icy touch, felt all about,
    Puts every fire of Freedom out —
When he, too, winds up his Ukases
With God and the Panagia's praises —
When he, of royal Saints the type,
    In holy water dips the sponge,
With which, at one imperial wipe,
    He would all human rights expunge ;
When LOUIS (whom as King, and eater,
Some name Dix-huit, and some Des-
        huitres,)
Calls down " St. Louis's God " to wit-
        ness
The right, humanity, and fitness
Of sending eighty thousand Solons,
    Sages with muskets and laced coats,
To cram instruction, nolens volens,
    Down the poor struggling Spaniards'
        throats —
I can't help thinking, (tho' to Kings
    I must, of course, like other men,
        bow,)

---

1 According to Ælian, it was in the island of
Leucadia they practised this ceremony — θύειν
βοῦν ταῖς μυίαις — " De Animal." lib. ii. cap. 8.

2 Âmes, demi-âmes, etc.

3 The salamander is supposed to have the
power of extinguishing fire by its natural coldness
and moisture.

That when a Christian monarch brings
Religion's name to gloss these things —
Such blasphemy out-Benbows Ben-
bow![1]

Or — not so far for facts to roam,
Having a few much nearer home —
When we see Churchmen, who, if askt,
" Must Ireland's slaves be tithed, and
taskt,
" And driven, like Negroes or Croäts,
" That *you* may roll in wealth and
bliss ? "
Look from beneath their shovel hats
With all due pomp and answer
" Yes ! "
But then, if questioned, " Shall the
brand
" Intolerance flings throughout that
land, —
" Shall the fierce strife now taught to
grow
" Betwixt her palaces and hovels,
" Be ever quenched ? " — from the same
shovels
Look grandly forth and answer " No." —
Alas, alas ! have *these* a claim
To merciful Religion's name ?
If more you seek, go see a bevy
Of bowing parsons at a levee —
(Choosing your time, when straw 's be-
fore
Some apoplectic bishop's door,)
Then if thou canst with life escape
That rush of lawn, that press of crape,
Just watch their reverences and graces,
As on each smirking suitor frisks,
And say, if those round shining faces
To heaven or earth most turn their
disks?

This, this it is — Religion, made,
'Twixt Church and State, a truck, a
trade —
This most ill-matched, unholy *Co.*,
From whence the ills we witness flow;
The war of many creeds with one —
The extremes of *too* much faith and
none —
Till, betwixt ancient trash and new,
'Twixt Cant and Blasphemy — the two
Rank ills with which this age is curst —

1 A well-known publisher of irreligious books.

We can no more tell *which* is worst,
Than erst could Egypt, when so rich
In various plagues, determine which
She thought most pestilent and vile,
Her frogs, like Benbow and Carlisle,
Croaking their native mud-notes loud,
Or her fat locusts, like a cloud
Of pluralists, obesely lowering,
At once benighting and devouring !—

This — this it is — and here I pray
Those sapient wits of the Reviews,
Who make us poor, dull authors say,
Not what we mean, but what they
choose;
Who to our most abundant shares
Of nonsense add still more of theirs,
And are to poets just such evils
As caterpillars find those flies,[2]
Which, not content to sting like devils,
Lay eggs upon their backs likewise —
To guard against such foul deposits
Of other's meaning in my rhymes,
(A thing more needful here, because
it 's
A subject, ticklish in these times) —
I, here, to all such wits make known,
Monthly and Weekly, Whig and Tory,
'T is *this* Religion — this alone —
I aim at in the following story : —

FABLE.

When Royalty was young and bold,
Ere, touched by Time, he had be
come —
If 't is n't civil to say *old*,
At least, a *ci-devant jeune homme ;*

One evening, on some wild pursuit,
Driving along, he chanced to see
Religion, passing by on foot,
And took him in his vis-à-vis.

This said Religion was a Friar,
The humblest and the best of men,
Who ne'er had notion or desire
Of riding in a coach till then.

2 " The greatest number of the ichneumon tribe
are seen settling upon the back of the caterpillar,
and darting at different intervals their stings into
its body — at every dart they depose an egg." —
GOLDSMITH.

"I say" — quoth Royalty, who rather
   Enjoyed a masquerading joke —
"I say, suppose, my good old father,
   "You lend me for a while your cloak."

The Friar consented — little knew
   What tricks the youth had in his head;
Besides, was rather tempted too
   By a laced coat he got instead.

Away ran Royalty, slap-dash,
   Scampering like mad about the town;
Broke windows, shivered lamps to smash,
   And knockt whole scores of watchmen
     down.

While naught could they, whose heads
     were broke,
   Learn of the "why" or the "where-
     fore,"
Except that 't was Religion's cloak
   The gentleman, who crackt them,
     wore.

Meanwhile, the Friar, whose head was
     turned
By the laced coat, grew frisky too;
Lookt big — his former habits spurned —
   And stormed about, as great men do:

Dealt much in pompous oaths and
     curses —
   Said "damn you" often, or as bad —
Laid claim to other people's purses —
   In short, grew either knave or mad.

As work like this was unbefitting,
   And flesh and blood no longer bore it,
The Court of Common Sense, then sit-
     ting,
   Summoned the culprits both before it.

Where, after hours in wrangling spent
   (As Courts must wrangle to decide
     well),
Religion to St. Luke's was sent,
   And Royalty packt off to Bridewell.

With this proviso — should they be
   Restored, in due time, to their senses,
They both must give security,
   In future, against such offences —

Religion ne'er to *lend his cloak*,
   Seeing what dreadful work it leads to;

And Royalty to crack his joke, —
   But *not* to crack poor people's heads
     too.

FABLE VI.

THE LITTLE GRAND LAMA.

PROEM.

NOVELLA, a young Bolognese,
   The daughter of a learned Law Doc-
     tor,[1]
Who had with all the subtleties
   Of old and modern jurists stockt her,
Was so exceeding fair, 't is said,
   And over hearts held such dominion,
That when her father, sick in bed,
   Or busy, sent her, in his stead,
     To lecture on the Code Justinian,
She had a curtain drawn before her,
   Lest, if her charms were seen, the
     students
Should let their young eyes wander o'er
     her,
   And quite forget their jurisprudence.[2]
Just so it is with Truth, when *seen*,
   Too dazzling far, — 't is from behind
A light, thin allegoric screen,
   She thus can safest teach mankind.

FABLE.

In Thibet once there reigned, we 're told,
A little Lama, one year old —
Raised to the throne, that realm to bless,
Just when his little Holiness
Had cut — as near as can be reckoned —
Some say his *first* tooth, some his
     second.
Chronologers and Nurses vary,
Which proves historians should be wary.
We only know the important truth,
His Majesty *had* cut a tooth.[3]

1 Andreas.

2 *Quand il étoit occupé d'aucune essoine, il
envoyoit Novelle, sa fille, en son lieu lire aux
escholes en charge, et, afin que la biaüté d'elle
n'empêchât la pensée des oyants, elle avoit une
petite courtine devant elle.* — Christ. de Pise,
Cité des Dames, p. 11. *cap.* 36.

3 See Turner's Embassy to Thibet for an
account of his interview with the Lama. — "Tes-
hoo Lama [he says] was at this time eighteen
months old. Though he was unable to speak
a word, he made the most expressive signs, and
conducted himself with astonishing *dignity* and
decorum."

And much his subjects were enchanted, —
  As well all Lamas' subjects *may* be,
And would have given their heads, if
    wanted,
  To make tee-totums for the baby.
Throned as he was by Right Divine —
  (What Lawyers call *Jure Divino*,
Meaning a right to yours and mine
  And everybody's goods and rhino,)
Of course, his faithful subjects' purses
  Were ready with their aids and succors;
Nothing was seen but pensioned Nurses,
  And the land groaned with bibs and
    tuckers.

Oh! had there been a Hume or Bennet,
  Then sitting in the Thibet Senate,
Ye Gods! what room for long debates
  Upon the Nursery Estimates!
What cutting down of swaddling-clothes
  And pinafores, in nightly battles!
What calls for papers to expose
  The waste of sugar-plums and rattles!
But no — if Thibet *had* M.P.s,
  They were far better bred than these;
Nor gave the slightest opposition,
  During the Monarch's whole dentition.

But short this calm; — for, just when he
  Had reached the alarming age of three,
When Royal natures and no doubt
  Those of *all* noble beasts break out —
The Lama, who till then was quiet,
  Showed symptoms of a taste for riot;
And, ripe for mischief, early, late,
  Without regard for Church or State,
Made free with whosoe'er came nigh;
  Tweakt the Lord Chancellor by the
    nose,
  Turned all the Judges' wigs awry,
  And trod on the old Generals' toes;
Pelted the Bishops with hot buns,
  Rode cock-horse on the City maces,
And shot from little devilish guns,
  Hard peas into his subjects' faces.
In short, such wicked pranks he played,
  And grew so mischievous, God bless
    him!
That his Chief Nurse — with even the
    aid
Of an Archbishop — was afraid,
  When in these moods, to comb or
    dress him.

Nay, even the persons most inclined
  Thro' thick and thin, for Kings to
    stickle,
Thought him (if they 'd but speak their
    mind,
  Which they did *not*) an odious pickle.

At length some patriot lords — a breed
  Of animals they 've got in Thibet,
Extremely rare and fit indeed
  For folks like Pidcock, to exhibit —
Some patriot lords, who saw the length
  To which things went, combined their
    strength,
And penned a manly, plain and free
  Remonstrance to the Nursery;
Protesting warmly that they yielded
  To none that ever went before 'em,
In loyalty to him who wielded
  The hereditary pap-spoon o'er 'em;
That, as for treason, 't was a thing
  That made them almost sick to think
    of —
That they and theirs stood by the King,
  Throughout his measles and his chin-
    cough,
When others, thinking him consump-
    tive,
Had ratted to the Heir Presumptive! —
But, still — tho' much admiring Kings
  (And chiefly those in leading-strings),
They saw, with shame and grief of soul,
  There was no longer now the wise
And constitutional control
  Of *birch* before their ruler's eyes;
But that of late such pranks and tricks
  And freaks occurred the whole day
    long,
As all but men with bishoprics
  Allowed, in even a King, were wrong.
Wherefore it was they humbly prayed
  That Honorable Nursery,
That such reforms be henceforth made,
  As all good men desired to see; —
In other words (lest they might seem
  Too tedious), as the gentlest scheme
For putting all such pranks to rest,
  And in its bud the mischief nipping —
They ventured humbly to suggest
  His Majesty should have a whipping!

When this was read, no Congreve rocket,
  Discharged into the Gallic trenches,

E'er equalled the tremendous shock it
  Produced upon the Nursery benches.
The Bishops, who of course had votes,
By right of age and petticoats,
Were first and foremost in the fuss —
  "What, whip a Lama! suffer birch
" To touch his sacred — infamous!
" Deistical! — assailing thus
  " The fundamentals of the Church! —
" No — no— such patriot plans as these,
" (So help them Heaven — and their
    Sees!)
" They held to be rank blasphemies."

The alarm thus given, by these and other
  Grave ladies of the Nursery side,
Spread thro' the land, till, such a
    pother,
  Such party squabbles, far and wide,
Never in history's page had been
Recorded, as were then between
The Whippers and Non-whippers seen.
Till, things arriving at a state,
  Which gave some fears of revolution,
The patriot lords' advice, tho' late,
  Was put at last in execution.
The Parliament of Thibet met —
  The little Lama, called before it,
Did, then and there, his whipping get,
And (as the *Nursery Gazette*
  Assures us) like a hero bore it.

And tho', 'mong Thibet Tories, some
Lament that Royal Martyr*d*om
(Please to observe, the letter D
In this last word 's pronounced like B),
Yet to the example of that Prince
  So much is Thibet's land a debtor,
That her long line of Lamas, since,
  Have all behaved themselves *much*
    better.

FABLE VII.

THE EXTINGUISHERS.

PROEM.

Tho' soldiers are the true supports,
The natural allies of Courts,
Woe to the Monarch, who depends
Too *much* on his red-coated friends;
For even soldiers sometimes *think* —
  Nay, Colonels have been known to
  reason, —

And reasoners, whether clad in pink
Or red or blue, are on the brink
  (Nine cases out of ten) of treason.

Not many soldiers, I believe, are
  As fond of liberty as Mina;
Else — woe to Kings! when Freedom's
    fever
Once turns into a *Scarletina!*
For then — but hold — 't is best to veil
My meaning in the following tale:—

FABLE.

A Lord of Persia, rich and great,
Just come into a large estate,
Was shockt to find he had, for neigh-
    bors,
Close to his gate, some rascal Ghebers,
Whose fires, beneath his very nose,
In heretic combustion rose.
But Lords of Persia can, no doubt,
  Do what they will — so, one fine
    morning,
He turned the rascal Ghebers out,
  First giving a few kicks for warning.
Then, thanking Heaven most piously,
  He knockt their Temple to the
    ground,
Blessing himself for joy to see
  Such Pagan ruins strewed around.
But much it vext my Lord to find,
  That, while all else obeyed his will,
The Fire these Ghebers left behind,
  Do what he would, kept burning still.
Fiercely he stormed, as if his frown
Could scare the bright insurgent down;
But, no — such fires are headstrong
    things,
And care not much for Lords or Kings.
Scarce could his Lordship well contrive
  The flashes in *one* place to smother,
Before — hey presto! — all alive,
  They sprung up freshly in another.

At length when, spite of prayers and
    damns,
  'T was found the sturdy flame defied
    him,
His stewards came, with low *salams*,
  Offering, by *contract*, to provide him
Some large Extinguishers, (a plan,
Much used, they said, at Ispahan,
Vienna, Petersburg — in short,

Wherever Light's forbid at court),
Machines no Lord should be without,
Which would at once put promptly out
All kinds of fires, — from staring, stark
Volcanoes to the tiniest spark;
Till all things slept as dull and dark,
As in a great Lord's neighborhood
'T was right and fitting all things
    should.

Accordingly, some large supplies
  Of these Extinguishers were furnisht
(All of the true Imperial size),
  And there, in rows, stood black and
    burnisht,
Ready, where'er a gleam but shone
Of light or fire, to be clapt on.

But ah! how lordly wisdom errs,
  In trusting to extinguishers!
One day, when he had left all sure,
  (At least, so thought he) dark, se-
    cure —
The flame, at all its exits, entries,
  Obstructed to his heart's content,
And black extinguishers, like sentries,
  Placed over every dangerous vent —
Ye Gods, imagine his amaze,
  His wrath, his rage, when, on return-
    ing,
He found not only the old blaze,
  Brisk as before, crackling and burn-
    ing, —
Not only new, young conflagrations,
Popping up round in various stations —
But still more awful, strange and dire,
The Extinguishers themselves on fire !! [1]
They, they — those trusty, blind ma-
    chines
  His Lordship had so long been prais-
    ing,
As, under Providence, the means
  Of keeping down all lawless blazing,
Were now, themselves — alas, too true
The shameful fact — turned blazers too,
And by a change as odd as cruel
Instead of dampers, served for fuel!

Thus, of his only hope bereft,
  "What," said the great man, "must
    be done?" —
All that, in scrapes like this, is left
  To great men is — to cut and run.
So run he did; while to their grounds,
  The banisht Ghebers blest returned;
And, tho' their Fire had broke its
    bounds,
  And all abroad now wildly burned,
Yet well could they, who loved the
    flame,
Its wandering, its excess reclaim;
And soon another, fairer Dome
Arose to be its sacred home,
Where, cherisht, guarded, not confined,
The living glory dwelt inshrined,
And, sheddling lustre strong, but even,
Tho' born of earth, grew worthy heaven.

MORAL.

The moral hence my Muse infers
  Is, that such Lords are simple elves,
    In trusting to Extinguishers,
    That are combustible themselves.

FABLE VIII.
LOUIS FOURTEENTH'S WIG.

THE money raised — the army ready —
Drums beating, and the Royal Neddy
Valiantly braying in the van,
To the old tune "*Eh, eh, Sire Âne !*" [2] —
Naught wanting, but some *coup* dramatic,
  To make French *sentiment* explode,
Bring in, at once, the *goût* fanatic,
  And make the war "*la dernière
    mode*" —
Instantly, at the *Pavillon Marsan*,
  Is held an Ultra consultation —
What 's to be done, to help the farce on?
  What stage-effect, what decoration,
To make this beauteous France forget,
  In one, grand, glorious *pirouette*,
All she had sworn to but last week,
And, with a cry of "*Magnifique !*"
Rush forth to this, or *any* war,
Without inquiring once — "What for?"

1 The idea of this Fable was caught from one
of those brilliant *mots*, which abound in the conversation of my friend, the author of the "Letters
to Julia," — a production which contains some
of the happiest specimens of playful poetry that
have appeared in this or any age.

2 They celebrated in the dark ages, at many
churches, particularly at Rouen, what was called
the Feast of the Ass. On this occasion the ass,
finely drest, was brought before the altar, and
they sung before him this elegant anthem, "*Eh,
eh, eh, Sire Âne, eh, eh, eh, Sire Âne.*" —
WARTON'S *Essay on Pope*.

After some plans proposed by each,
Lord Chateaubriand made a speech,
(Quoting, to show what men's rights
are,
Or rather what men's rights *should be*,
From Hobbes, Lord Castlereagh, the
Tsar,
And other friends to Liberty,)
Wherein he — having first protested
'Gainst humoring the mob — suggested
(As the most high-bred plan he saw
For giving the new War *éclat*)
A grand, Baptismal Melo-drame,
To be got up at Notre Dame,
In which the Duke (who, bless his High-
ness!
Had by his *hilt* acquired such fame,
'T was hoped that he as little shyness
Would show, when to *the point* he
came,)
Should, for his deeds so lion-hearted,
Be christened *Hero*, ere he started;
With power, by Royal Ordonnance,
To bear that name — at least in France.
Himself — the Viscount Chateaubriand —
(To help the affair with more *esprit* on)
Offering, for this baptismal rite,
Some of his own famed Jordan
water [1] —
(Marie Louise not having quite
Used all that, for young Nap, he
brought her,)
The baptism, in *this* case, to be
Applied to that extremity,
Which Bourbon heroes most expose;
And which (as well all Europe knows)
Happens to be, in this Defender
Of the true Faith, extremely tender. [2]

Or if (the Viscount said) this scheme
Too rash and premature should seem —
If thus discounting heroes, *on* tick —
This glory, by anticipation,
Was too much in the *genre romantique*
For such a highly classic nation,
He begged to say, the Abyssinians
A practice had in their dominions,

Which, if at Paris got up well,
In full *costume*, was sure to tell.
At all great epochs, good or ill,
They have, says BRUCE (and BRUCE
ne'er budges
From the strict truth), a Grand Quadrille
In public danced by the Twelve
Judges [3] —
And, he assures us, the grimaces,
The *entre-chats*, the airs and graces
Of dancers, so profound and stately,
Divert the Abyssinians greatly.

" Now (said the Viscount), there 's but
few
" Great Empires where this plan would
do :
" For instance, England; — let them take
" What pains they would — 't were
vain to strive —
" The twelve stiff Judges there would
make
" The worst Quadrille-set now alive.
" One must have seen them, ere one
could
" Imagine properly JUDGE WOOD,
" Performing, in his wig, so gayly,
" A *queue-de-chat* with JUSTICE BAILLY !
" *French* Judges, tho', are, by no means,
" This sort of stiff, be-wigged machines;
" And we, who 've seen them at *Saumur*
" And *Poitiers* lately, may be sure
" They 'd dance quadrilles or any thing,
" That would be pleasing to the King—
" Nay, stand upon their heads, and more
do,
" To please the little Duc de Bordeaux ! "

After these several schemes there came
Some others — needless now to name,
Since that, which Monsieur planned,
himself,
Soon doomed all others to the shelf,
And was received *par acclamation*,
As truly worthy the *Grande Nation*.

It seems (as Monsieur told the story)
That LOUIS the Fourteenth, — that glory,
That *Coryphée* of all crowned pates, —
That pink of the Legitimates —

---

1 Brought from the river Jordan by M. Chateaubriand, and presented to the French Empress for the christening of young Napoleon.

2 See the Duke's celebrated letter to madame,
written during his campaign in 1815, in which
he says, *"J'ai le postérieur légèrement endom-
magé."*

3 " On certain great occasions, the twelve
Judges (who are generally between sixty and
seventy years of age) sing the song and dance
the figure-dance," etc. — Book v.

Had, when, with many a pious prayer, he
Bequeathed unto the Virgin Mary
His marriage deeds, and *cordon bleu*,[1]
Bequeathed to her his State Wig too —
(An offering which, at Court, 't is
   thought,
The Virgin values as she ought) —
That Wig, the wonder of all eyes,
The Cynosure of Gallia's skies,
To watch and tend whose curls adored,
  Re-build its towering roof, when flat,
And round its rumpled base, a Board
Of sixty barbers daily sat,[2]
With Subs, on State-Days, to assist,
Well pensioned from the Civil List: —
That wondrous Wig, arrayed in which,
And formed alike to awe or witch,
He beat all other heirs of crowns,
In taking mistresses and towns,
Requiring but a shot at *one*,
A smile at *t'other*, and 't was done ! —

  "That Wig (said Monsieur, while his
   brow
Rose proudly,) "is existing now; —
"That Grand Perruque, amid the fall
  "Of every other Royal glory,
"With curls erect survives them all,
  "And tells in every hair their story.
"Think, think, how welcome at this
  time
"A relic, so beloved, sublime !
"What worthier standard of the Cause
  "Of Kingly Right can France demand?

"Or who among our ranks can pause
  "To guard it, while a curl shall stand?
"Behold, my friends" — (while thus he
  cried,
A curtain, which concealed this pride
Of Princely Wigs was drawn aside)
"Behold that grand Perruque — how big
  "With recollections for the world —
"For France — for us — Great LOUIS's
  Wig,
   "By HIPPOLYTE[3] new frizzed and
   curled—
"*New frizzed !* alas, 't is but too true,
"Well may you start at that word *new* —
"But such the sacrifice, my friends,
"The Imperial Cossack recommends;
"Thinking such small concessions sage,
"To meet the spirit of the age,
"And do what best that spirit flatters,
"In Wigs — if not in weightier matters.
"Wherefore to please the Tsar, and show
"That *we* too, much-wronged Bourbons,
  know
"What liberalism in Monarchs is,
"We have conceded the New Friz !
"Thus armed, ye gallant Ultras, say,
"Can men, can Frenchmen, fear the
  fray?
"With this proud relic in our van,
  "And D'ANGOULÊME our worthy
  leader,
"Let rebel Spain do all she can,
  "Let recreant England arm and feed
  her, —
"Urged by that pupil of HUNT's school,
"That Radical, Lord LIVERPOOL —
"France can have naught to fear — far
  from it —
  "When once astounded Europe sees
"The Wig of LOUIS, like a Comet,
  "Streaming above the Pyrenées,
"All 's o'er with Spain — then on, my
  sons,
  "On, my incomparable Duke,
"And, shouting for the Holy Ones,
  "Cry *Vive la Guerre — et la Per-
  ruque !*"

---

1 "*Louis XIV. fit présent à la Vierge de son cordon bleu, que l'on conserve soigneusement, et lui envoya ensuite, son Contrat de Mariage et le Traité des Pyrenées, magnifiquement relié.*" — *Mémoires, Anecdotes pour servir, etc.*

2 The learned author of *Recherches Historiques sur les Perruques* says that the Board consisted but of Forty — the same number as the Academy. "*Le plus beau tems des perruques fut celui où Louis XIV. commença à porter, lui-même, perruque ; . . . On ignore l'époque où se fit cette révolution ; mais on sait qu'elle engagea Louis le Grand à y donner ses soins paternels, en créant, en* 1656, *quarante charges de perruquiers, suivant la cour ; et en* 1673, *il forma un corps de deux cents perruquiers pour la Ville de Paris.*" — P. III.

3 A celebrated *Coiffeur* of the present day.

THE FUDGE FAMILY
IN PARIS.

Le Leggi della Maschera richiedono che una persona mascherata non sia salutata per nome da uno che la conosce malgrado il suo travestimento.   CASTIGLIONE.

PREFACE.

IN what manner the following Epistles came into my hands, it is not necessary for the public to know. It will be seen by Mr. FUDGE's Second Letter, that he is one of those gentlemen whose *Secret Services* in Ireland, under the mild ministry of my Lord CASTLEREAGH, have been so amply and gratefully remunerated. Like his friend and associate, THOMAS REYNOLDS, Esq., he had retired upon the reward of his honest industry; but has lately been induced to appear again in active life, and superintend the training of that *Delatorian Cohort*, which Lord SIDMOUTH, in his wisdom and benevolence, has organized.

Whether Mr. FUDGE, himself, has yet made any discoveries, does not appear from the following pages. But much may be expected from a person of his zeal and sagacity, and, indeed, to *him*, Lord SIDMOUTH, and the Greenland-bound ships, the eyes of all lovers of *discoveries* are now most anxiously directed.

I regret much that I have been obliged to omit Mr. BOB FUDGE's Third Letter, concluding the adventures of his Day with the Dinner, Opera, etc.; — but, in consequence of some remarks upon Marinette's thin drapery, which, it was thought, might give offence to certain well-meaning persons, the manuscript was sent back to Paris for his revision and had not returned when the last sheet was put to press.

It will not, I hope, be thought presumptuous, if I take this opportunity of complaining of a very serious injustice I have suffered from the public. Dr. KING wrote a treatise to prove that BENTLEY " was not the author of his own book," and a similar absurdity has been asserted of *me*, in almost all the best-informed literary circles. With the name of the real author staring them in the face, they have yet persisted in attributing my works to other people; and the fame of the " Twopenny Post-Bag " — such as it is — having hovered doubtfully over various persons, has at last settled upon the head of a certain little gentleman, who wears it, I understand, as complacently as if it actually belonged to him; without even the honesty of avowing, with his own favorite author, (he will excuse the pun)

ἐγὼ δ' Ὁ ΜΩΡΟΣ ἀρὰς
ἐθησάμην μετώπῳ.

I can only add, that if any lady or gentleman, curious in such matters, will take the trouble of calling at my lodgings, 245 Piccadilly, I shall have the honor of assuring them, *in propriâ personâ*, that I am — his, or her,
Very obedient and very humble Servant,

April 17, 1818.   THOMAS BROWN, THE YOUNGER.

718

THE FUDGE FAMILY IN PARIS.

LETTER I.

FROM

MISS BIDDY FUDGE TO MISS DOROTHY
——, OF CLONKILTY, IN IRELAND.

Amiens.

DEAR DOLL, while the tails of our horses
are plaiting,
  The trunks tying on, and Papa, at the
door,
Into very bad French Is as usual translating
  His English resolve not to give a *sou*
more,
I sit down to write you a line — only
think ! —
A letter from France, with French pens
and French ink,
How delightful ! tho,' would you be-
lieve it, my dear?
I have seen nothing yet *very* wonderful
here ;
No adventure, no sentiment, far as
we 've come,
But the corn-fields and trees quite as
   dull as at home ;
And *but* for the post-boy, his boots and
his queue,
I might *just* as well be at Clonkilty with
you !
In vain, at DESSEIN'S, did I take from
my trunk
That divine fellow, STERNE, and fall
reading "The Monk;"
In vain did I think of his charming Dead
Ass,
And remember the crust and the wallet
— alas !
No monks can be had now for love or
for money,
(All owing, Pa says, to that infidel
BONEY;)
And, tho' *one* little Neddy we saw in
our drive
Out of classical Nampont, the beast was
alive !

By the by, tho' at Calais, Papa *had* a
touch
Of romance on the pier, which affected
me much.
At the sight of that spot, where our dar-
ling DIXHUIT
Set the first of his own dear legitimate
feet,[1]
(Modelled out so exactly, and — God
bless the mark !
'T is a foot, DOLLY, worthy so *Grand* a
Monarque),
He exclaimed, "*Oh, mon Roi !*" and,
with tear-dropping eye,
Stood to gaze on the spot — while some
Jacobin, nigh,
Muttered out with a shrug (what an in-
solent thing !)
"*Ma foi*, he be right— 't is de English-
man's King;
And dat *gros pied de cochon* — begar, me
vil say
Dat de foot look mosh better, if turned
toder way."
There 's the pillar, too — Lord ! I had
nearly forgot —
What a charming idea ! — raised close
to the spot;
The mode being now, (as you 've heard,
I suppose,)
To build tombs over legs [2] and raise pil-
lars to toes.

This is all that 's occurred sentimental
as yet;
Except indeed some little flower-nymphs
we 've met,
Who disturb one's romance with pecu-
niary views,

1 To commemorate the landing of Louis le
Désiré from England, the impression of his foot
is marked out on the pier at Calais, and a pillar
with an inscription raised opposite to the spot.

2 *Ci-gît la jambe de, etc.*

719

Flinging flowers in your path, and then
— bawling for *sous!*
And some picturesque beggars, whose
multitudes seem
To recall the good days of the *ancien
régime,*
All as ragged and brisk, you 'll be
happy to learn,
And as thin as they were in the time of
dear STERNE.

Our party consists (in a neat Calais job)
Of Papa and myself, Mr. CONNOR and
BOB.
You remember how sheepish BOB lookt
at Kilrandy,
But, Lord! he 's quite altered —
they 've made him a Dandy;
A thing, you know, whiskered, great-
coated, and laced,
Like an hour-glass, exceedingly small in
the waist:
Quite a new sort of creatures, unknown
yet to scholars,
With heads so immovably stuck in shirt-
collars,
That seats, like our music-stools, soon
must be found them,
To twirl, when the creatures may wish to
look round them.
In short, dear, "a Dandy" describes
what I mean,
And BOB 's far the best of the *genus*
I 've seen:
An improving young man, fond of learn-
ing, ambitious,
And goes now to Paris to study French
dishes,
Whose names — think, how quick! he
already knows pat,
À la braise, petits pâtés, and — what
d' ye call that
They inflict on potatoes? — oh! *maître
d'hôtel* —
I assure you, dear DOLLY, he knows them
as well
As if nothing else all his life he had eat,
Tho' a bit of them BOBBY has never
touched yet;
But just knows the names of French
dishes and cooks,
As dear Pa knows the titles of authors
and books.

As to Pa, what d 'ye think? — mind,
it 's all *entre nous,*
But you know, love, I never keep se-
crets from you —
Why, he 's writing a book — what! a
tale? a romance?
No, ye Gods, would it were! — but his
Travels in France;
At the special desire (he let out t 'other
day)
Of his great friend and patron, my Lord
CASTLEREAGH,
Who said, " My dear FUDGE " — I for-
get the exact words,
And, it 's strange, no one ever remem-
bers my Lord's;
But 't was something to say that, as all
must allow
A good orthodox work is much wanting
just now,
To expound to the world the new —thing-
ummie — science,
Found out by the — what's-its-name —
Holy Alliance,
And prove to mankind that their rights
are but folly,
Their freedom a joke (which it *is*, you
know, DOLLY),
" There 's none," said his Lordship, " if
I may be judge,
Half so fit for this great undertaking as
FUDGE! "

The matter 's soon settled — Pa flies to
the Row
(The *first* stage your tourists now usually go),
Settles all for his quarto — advertisements, praises —
Starts post from the door, with his tablets — French phrases —
" SCOTT's Visit," of course — in short,
every thing *he* has
An author can want, except words and
ideas : —
And, lo! the first thing, in the spring of
the year,
Is PHIL. FUDGE at the front of a Quarto,
my dear!

But, bless me, my paper 's near out, so
I 'd better
Draw fast to a close: — this exceeding
long letter

You owe to a *déjeûner à la fourchette*,
Which BOBBY *would* have, and is hard
  at it yet. —
What 's next? oh! the tutor, the last of
  the party,
Young CONNOR : — they say he 's so like
  BONAPARTE,
His nose and his chin — which Papa
  rather dreads,
As the Bourbons, you know, are suppress-
  ing all heads
That resemble old NAP'S, and who knows
  but their honors
May think, in their fright, of suppressing
  poor CONNOR'S?
Au reste (as we say), the young lad 's
  well enough,
Only talks much of Athens, Rome, virtue
  and stuff;
A third cousin of ours, by the way —
  poor as Job
(Tho' of royal descent by the side of
  Mamma),
And for charity made private tutor to BOB;
Entre nous, too, a Papist — how lib-
  eral of Pa!

This is all, dear, — forgive me for break-
  ing off thus,
But BOB's *déjeûner* 's done, and Papa 's
  in a fuss.   B. F.
        P. S.
How provoking of Pa! he will not let
  me stop
Just to run in and rummage some mil-
  liner's shop;
And my *début* in Paris, I blush to think
  on it,
Must now, DOLL, be made in a hideous
  low bonnet.
But Paris, dear Paris! — oh, *there* will
  be joy,
And romance, and high bonnets, and
  Madame Le ROI![1]

LETTER II.

**FROM PHIL. FUDGE, ESQ., TO THE LORD
VISCOUNT CASTLEREAGH.**
                      Paris.

AT length, my Lord, I have the bliss
To date to you a line from this

" Demoralized" metropolis;
Where, by plebeians low and scurvy,
The throne was turned quite topsy-turvy,
And Kingship, tumbled from its seat,
" Stood prostrate " at the people's feet;
Where (still to use your Lordship's
  tropes)
The *level* of obedience *slopes*
Upward and downward, as the *stream*
Of *hydra* faction *kicks the beam !* [2]
Where the poor Palace changes masters
  Quicker than a snake its skin,
And LOUIS is rolled out on castors,
  While BONEY 's borne on shoulders
  in : —
But where, in every change, no doubt,
  One special good your Lordship
  traces, —
That 't is the *Kings* alone turn out,
  The *Ministers* still keep their places.

How oft, dear Viscount CASTLEREAGH,
I 've thought of thee upon the way,
As in my *job* (what place could be
More apt to wake a thought of thee?) —
Or, oftener far, when gravely sitting
Upon my dicky, (as is fitting
For him who writes a Tour, that he
May more of men and manners see,)
I 've thought of thee and of thy glories,
Thou guest of Kings and King of Tories!
Reflecting how thy fame has grown
  And spread, beyond man's usual share,
At home, abroad, till thou art known,
  Like Major SEMPLE, every where!
And marvelling with what powers of
  breath
Your Lordship, having speeched to death
Some hundreds of your fellow-men,
Next speeched to Sovereign's ears, — and
  when
All Sovereigns else were dozed, at last
Speeched down the Sovereign [3] of Bel-
  fast.

---

1 A celebrated mantua-maker in Paris.

2 This excellent imitation of the noble Lord's
style shows how deeply Mr. Fudge must have
studied his great original. Irish oratory, indeed,
abounds with such startling peculiarities. Thus
the eloquent Counsellor B——, in describing
some hypocritical pretender to charity, said,
" He put his hand in his breeches-pocket, like
a crocodile, and," etc.

3 The title of the chief magistrate of Belfast,
before whom his Lordship (with the "*studium
immane loquendi*" attributed by Ovid to that

Oh! mid the praises and the trophies
Thou gain'st from Morosophs and So-
  phis;
Mid all the tributes to thy fame,
  There's one thou shouldst be chiefly
    pleased at —
That Ireland gives her snuff thy name,
  And CASTLEREAGH's the thing now
    sneezed at!

But hold, my pen! — a truce to praising —
  Tho' even your Lordship will allow
The theme's temptations are amazing;
  But time and ink run short, and now,
(As *thou* wouldst say, my guide and
    teacher
  In these gay metaphoric fringes,
I must *embark* into the *feature*
  On which this letter chiefly *hinges;*)[1]
My Book, the Book that is to prove —
  And *will*, (so help ye Sprites above,
That sit on clouds, as grave as judges,
  Watching the labors of the FUDGES!)
Will prove that all the world, at
    present,
Is in a state extremely pleasant;
That Europe — thanks to royal swords
  And bayonets, and the Duke com-
    manding —
Enjoys a peace which, like the Lord's,
  Passeth all human understanding:
That France prefers her go-cart King
  To such a coward scamp as BONEY;
Tho' round, with each a leading-string,
  There standeth many a Royal crony,
For fear the chubby, tottering thing
  Should fall, if left there *loney-poney;* —
That England, too, the more her debts,
  The more she spends, the richer gets;
And that the Irish, grateful nation!
  Remember when by *thee* reigned over,
And bless thee for their flagellation,
  As HELOISA did her lover![2] —

chattering and rapacious class of birds, the pies)
delivered sundry long and self-congratulatory
orations, on his return from the Continent. It
was at one of these Irish dinners that his gallant
brother, Lord S., proposed the health of "The
best cavalry officer in Europe — the Regent!"

1 Verbatim from one of the noble Viscount's
Speeches — "And now, Sir, I must embark into
the feature on which this question chiefly
hinges."

2 See her Letters.

That Poland, left for Russia's lunch
  Upon the side-board, snug reposes:
While Saxony's as pleased as Punch,
  And Norway "on a bed of roses!"
That, as for some few million souls,
  Transferred by contract, bless the
    clods!
If half were strangled — Spaniards, Poles,
  And Frenchmen — 't would n't make
    much odds,
So Europe's goodly Royal ones
Sit easy on their sacred thrones;
So FERDINAND embroiders gayly,[3]
And Louis eats his *salmi*,[4] daily;
So time is left to Emperor SANDY
To be *half* Cæsar and *half* Dandy;
And GEORGE the REGENT (who'd forget
That doughtiest chieftain of the set?)
Hath wherewithal for trinkets new,
  For dragons, after Chinese models,
And chambers where Duke Ho and Soo
  Might come and nine times knock their
    noddles! —
All this my Quarto 'll prove — much
    more
Than Quarto ever proved before: —
In reasoning with the *Post* I 'll vie,
My facts the *Courier* shall supply,
My jokes VANSITTART, PEELE my sense,
And thou, sweet Lord, my eloquence!

My Journal, penned by fits and starts,
  On BIDDY's back or BOBBY's shoulder,
(My son, my Lord, a youth of parts,
  Who longs to be a small place-holder,)
Is — tho' *I* say 't, that should n't say —
Extremely good; and, by the way,
One extract from it — *only* one —
To show its spirit, and I 've done.
"*Jul. thirty-first.* — Went, after snack,
  "To the Cathedral of St. Denny;
"Sighed o'er the Kings of ages back,
  "And — gave the old Concierge a
    penny.

3 It would be an edifying thing to write a history of the private amusements of sovereigns,
tracing them down from the fly-sticking of Domi-
tian, the mole-catching of Artabanus, the hog-
mimicking of Parmenides, the horse-currying of
Aretas, to the petticoat-embroidering of Ferdinand, and the patience-playing of the Prince
Regent!

4 ὀψά τε, οἷα ἔδουσι διοτρεφέες βασιλῆες.
             HOMER, *Odyss.* 3.

" (*Mem.* — Must see *Rheims*, much
    famed, 't is said,
" For making Kings and gingerbread.)
" Was shown the tomb where lay, so
    stately,
" A little Bourbon, buried lately,
" Thrice high and puissant, we were
    told,
" Tho' only twenty-four hours old ! [1]
" Hear this, thought I, ye Jacobins:
" Ye Burdetts, tremble in your skins !
" If Royalty, but aged a day,
" Can boast such high and puissant
    sway,
" What impious hand its power would
    fix,
" Full fledged and wigged [2] at fifty-six ! "

The argument 's quite new, you see,
And proves exactly Q. E. D.
So now, with duty to the REGENT,
I am, dear Lord,
             Your most obedient,
                    P. F.

Hôtel Breteuil, Rue Rivoli.
Neat lodgings — rather dear for me;
But BIDDY said she thought 't would look
Genteeler thus to date my Book;
And BIDDY 's right — besides, it curries
Some favor with our friends at MURRAY'S,
Who scorn what any man can say,
That dates from Rue St. Honoré ! [3]

LETTER III.

FROM MR. BOB FUDGE TO RICHARD —, ESQ.

OH Dick ! you may talk of your writing
    and reading,
Your Logic and Greek, but there 's
    nothing like feeding;
And *this* is the place for it, DICKY, you
    dog,
Of all places on earth — the head-quar-
    ters of Prog !

---

[1] So described on the coffin: " *très-haute et puissante Princesse, agée d'un jour.*"

[2] There is a fulness and breadth in this portrait of Royalty, which reminds us of what Pliny says, in speaking of Trajan's great qualities: — " *nonne longè lateque Principem ostentant ?* "

[3] See the *Quarterly Review* for May, 1816, where Mr. Hobhouse is accused of having written his book " in a back street of the French capital."

Talk of England — her famed *Magna Charta*, I swear, is
A humbug, a flam, to the Carte [4] at old VÉRY'S;
And as for your Juries — *who* would not set o'er 'em
A Jury of Tasters,[5] with woodcocks be-
    fore 'em?
Give CARTWRIGHT his Parliaments, fresh
    every year;
But those friends of *short Commons*
    would never do here;
And, let ROMILLY speak as he will on
    the question,
No Digest of Law 's like the laws of
    digestion !

By the by, DICK, *I* fatten — but *n'importe* for that,
'T is the mode — your Legitimates al-
    ways get fat.
There 's the REGENT, there 's LOUIS
    and BONEY tried too,
But, tho' somewhat imperial in paunch,
    't would n't do: —
He improved indeed much in this point
    when he wed,
But he ne'er grew right royally fat *in the head.*

DICK, DICK, what a place is this Paris !
    — but stay —
As my raptures may bore you, I 'll just
    sketch a Day,
As we pass it, myself and some comrades
    I 've got,
All thorough-bred *Gnostics*, who know
    what is what.

After dreaming some hours of the land
    of Cocaigne,[6]
That Elysium of all that is *friand* and
    nice,

---

[4] The Bill of Fare. — Véry, a well-known Restaurateur.

[5] Mr. Bob alludes particularly, I presume, to the famous Jury Dégustateur, which used to assemble at the Hôtel of M. Grimod de la Reynière, and of which this modern Archestratus has given an account in his " *Almanach des Gourmands,*" *cinquième année,* p. 78.

[6] The fairy-land of cookery and *gourmandise ;* " *Pais, où le ciel offre les viandes toutes cuites, et où, comme on parle, les alouettes tombent toutes roties. Du Latin, coquere.*" — Duchat.

Where for hail they have *bon-bons*, and
　　claret for rain,
　And the skaters in winter show off on
　　cream-ice;
Where so ready all nature its cookery
　　yields,
Macaroni au parmesan grows in the
　　fields;
Little birds fly about with the true pheas-
　　ant taint,
And the geese are all born with a liver
　　complaint ! [1]
I rise — put on neck-cloth — stiff, tight,
　　as can be —
For a lad who *goes into the world*, DICK,
　　like me,
Should have his neck tied up, you know
　　— there 's no doubt of it —
Almost as tight as *some* lads who *go out
　　of it.*
With whiskers well oiled, and with boots
　　that " hold up
" The mirror to nature " — so bright you
　　could sup
Off the leather like china; with coat, too,
　　that draws
On the tailor, who suffers, a martyr's
　　applause ! —
With head bridled up, like a four-in-
　　hand leader,
And stays — devil 's in them — too tight
　　for a feeder,
I strut to the old Café Hardy, which yet
Beats the field at a *déjeûner à la four-
　　chette.*
There, DICK, what a breakfast ! — oh !
　　not like your ghost
Of a breakfast in England, your curst tea
　　and toast; [2]

But a side-board, you dog, where one's
　　eye roves about,
Like a turk's in the Haram, and thence
　　singles out
One's *pâté* of larks, just to tune up the
　　throat,
One's small limbs of chickens, done *en
　　papillote*,
One's erudite cutlets, drest all ways but
　　plain,
Or one's kidneys — imagine, DICK —
　　done with champagne !
Then, some glasses of *Beaune*, to dilute
　　— or, mayhap,
Chambertin,[3] which you know 's the pet
　　tipple of NAP,
And which Dad, by the by, that legiti-
　　mate stickler,
Much scruples to taste, but I 'm not so
　　partic'lar. —
Your coffee comes next, by prescription:
　　and then, DICK, 's
The coffee's ne'er-failing and glorious
　　appendix,
(If books had but such, my old Grecian,
　　depend on 't,
I 'd swallow e'en Watkins', for sake of
　　the end on 't,)
A neat glass of *parfait-amour*, which
　　one sips

this beverage of scholars, if he had read *Peter
Petit's* Poem in praise of Tea, addressed to the
learned *Huet* — or the Epigraphe which *Pechli-
nus* wrote for an altar he meant to dedicate to
this herb — or the Anacreontics of *Peter Fran-
cius*, in which he calls Tea

$$\theta\epsilon\grave{\alpha}\nu, \theta\epsilon\grave{\eta}\nu, \theta\acute{\epsilon}\alpha\iota\nu\alpha\nu.$$

The following passage from one of these Anacreontics will, I have no doubt, be gratifying to
all true Theists.

$$\theta\epsilon o\hat{\iota}\varsigma, \theta\epsilon\hat{\omega}\nu \tau\epsilon \pi\alpha\tau\rho\acute{\iota},$$
$$\grave{\epsilon}\nu \chi\rho\upsilon\sigma\acute{\epsilon}o\iota\varsigma \sigma\kappa\acute{\upsilon}\phi o\iota\sigma\iota$$
$$\delta\acute{\iota}\delta o\iota \tau\grave{o} \nu\acute{\epsilon}\kappa\tau\alpha\rho\,^{"}H\beta\eta.$$
$$\sigma\acute{\epsilon} \mu o\iota \delta\iota\alpha\kappa o\nu o\acute{\iota}\nu\tau o$$
$$\sigma\kappa\acute{\upsilon}\phi o\iota\varsigma \grave{\epsilon}\nu \mu\upsilon\rho\rho\acute{\iota}\nu o\iota\sigma\iota,$$
$$\tau\hat{\omega} \kappa\acute{\alpha}\lambda\lambda\epsilon\grave{\iota} \pi\rho\acute{\epsilon}\pi o\upsilon\sigma\alpha\iota$$
$$\kappa\alpha\lambda\alpha\hat{\iota}\varsigma \chi\epsilon\rho\acute{\epsilon}\sigma\sigma\iota \kappa o\acute{\upsilon}\rho\alpha\iota.$$

Which may be thus translated : —

　Yes, let Hebe, ever young,
　　High in heaven her nectar hold,
　And to Jove's immortal throng
　　Pour the tide in cups of gold —
　I 'll not envy heaven's Princes,
　　While, with snowy hands, for me,
　KATE the china tea-cup rinses,
　　And pours out her best Bohea !

1 The process by which the liver of the unfortunate goose is enlarged, in order to produce that
richest of all dainties, the *foie gras*, of which such
renowned *pâtés* are made at Strasbourg and Tou-
louse, is thus described in the *Cours Gastrono-
mique* : — " *On déplume l'estomac des oies ; on
attache ensuite ces animaux aux chenets d'une
cheminée, et on les nourrit devant le feu. La
captivité et la chaleur donnent à ces volatiles, une
maladie hépatique, qui fait gonfler leur foie*,"
etc., p 206.

2 Is Mr. Bob aware that his contempt for *tea*
renders him liable to a charge of *atheism ?* Such,
at least, is the opinion cited in *Christian. Fal-
ster. Amænitat. Philolog.* — "*atheum interpre-
tabatur hominem ad herbâ The aversum.*" He
would not, I think, have been so irreverent to

3 The favorite wine of Napoleon.

Just as if bottled velvet [1] tipt over one's
  lips.
This repast being ended, and *paid for* —
  (how odd!
Till a man 's used to paying, there 's
  something so queer in 't!) —
The sun now well out, and the girls all
  abroad,
  And the world enough aired for us
    Nobs to appear in 't,
We lounge up the boulevards, where —
  oh! DICK, the phizzes,
The turn-outs, we meet — what a nation
  of quizzes!
Here toddles along some old figure of fun,
With a coat you might date Anno Dom-
  ini 1.;
A laced hat, worsted stockings, and
  noble old soul!
A fine ribbon and cross in his best but-
  ton-hole;
Just such as our PRINCE, who nor reason
  nor fun dreads,
Inflicts, without even a court-martial on
  hundreds.[2]
Here trips a *grisette*, with a fond, roguish
  eye,
(Rather eatable things these *grisettes* by
  the by);
And there an old *demoiselle*, almost as
  fond,
In a silk that has stood since the time of
  the Fronde.
There goes a French Dandy — ah, DICK!
  unlike some ones
We 've seen about WHITE'S — the Moun-
  seers are but rum ones;
Such hats! — fit for monkies — I 'd back
  Mrs. DRAPER
To cut neater weather-boards out of
  brown paper:
And coats — how I wish, if it would n't
  distress 'em,
They 'd club for old BRUMMEL, from
  Calais, to dress 'em!
The collar sticks out from the neck such
  a space,
  That you 'd swear 't was the plan of
    this head-lopping nation,

To leave there behind them a snug little
  place
  For the head to drop into, on decapi-
    tation.
In short, what with mountebanks, counts
  and friseurs,
Some mummers by trade and the rest
  amateurs —
What with captains in new jockey-boots
  and silk breeches,
  Old dustmen with swinging great
    opera-hats,
And shoeblacks reclining by statues in
  niches,
  There never was seen such a race of
    Jack Sprats!

From the Boulevards but hearken! —
  yes — as I 'm a sinner,
The clock is just striking the half-hour to
  dinner:
So *no* more at present — short time for
  adorning —
My Day must be finisht some other fine
  morning.
Now, hey for old BEAUVILLIERS'S [3] lar-
  der, my boy!
And, once *there*, if the Goddess of Beauty
  and Joy
Were to write "Come and kiss me, dear
  BOB!" I 'd not budge —
Not a step, DICK, as sure as my name is
             R. FUDGE.

LETTER IV.

FROM PHELIM CONNOR TO ——.

"RETURN!" — no, never, while the
  withering hand
Of bigot power is on that hapless land;
While, for the faith my fathers held to
  God,
Even in the fields where free those
  fathers trod,
I am proscribed, and — like the spot left
  bare
In Israel's halls, to tell the proud and fair
Amidst their mirth, that Slavery had been
  there [4] —

---

1 *Velours en bouteille.*

2 It was said by Wicquefort, more than a hundred years ago, "*Le Roi d'Angleterre fait seul
plus de chevaliers que tous les autres Rois de la
Chrétienté ensemble.*"—What would he say now?

3 A celebrated restaurateur.

4 "They used to leave a square yard of the
wall of the house unplastered, on which they
write, in large letters, either the fore-mentioned

On all I love, home, parents, friends, I
  trace
The mournful mark of bondage and disgrace !
No ! — let *them* stay, who in their country's pangs
See naught but food for factions and
  harangues;
Who yearly kneel before their masters'
  doors,
And hawk their wrongs, as beggars do
  their sores :
Still let your [1] . . . . .

. . . .

Still hope and suffer, all who can ! —
  but I,
Who durst not hope, and cannot bear,
  must fly.

But whither ? — every where the scourge
  pursues —
Turn where he will, the wretched wanderer views,
In the bright, broken hopes of all his
  race,
Countless reflections of the Oppressor's
  face.
Every where gallant hearts and spirits
  true,
Are served up victims to the vile and few;
While England, every where — the general foe
Of Truth and Freedom, wheresoe'er they
  glow —
Is first, when tyrants strike, to aid the
  blow.

Oh, England ! could such poor revenge
  atone
For wrongs, that well might claim the
  deadliest one ;
Were it a vengeance, sweet enough to
  sate
The wretch who flies from thy intolerant
  hate,

To hear his curses on such barbarous
  sway
Echoed, where'er he bends his cheerless
  way; —
Could *this* content him, every lip he
  meets
Teems for his vengeance with such poi-
  sonous sweets;
Were *this* his luxury, never is thy name
Pronounced, but he doth banquet on thy
  shame;
Hears maledictions ring from every side
Upon that grasping power, that selfish
  pride,
Which vaunts its own and scorns all
  rights beside;
That low and desperate envy which to
  blast
A neighbor's blessings risks the few thou
  hast ; —
That monster, Self, too gross to be con-
  cealed,
Which ever lurks behind thy proffered
  shield; —
That faithless craft, which, in thy hour
  of need,
Can court the slave, can swear he shall
  be freed,
Yet basely spurns him, when thy point
  is gained,
Back to his masters, ready gagged and
  chained !
Worthy associate of that band of Kings,
That royal, ravening flock, whose vam-
  pire wings
O'er sleeping Europe treacherously brood,
And fan her into dreams of promist good,
Of hope, of freedom — but to drain her
  blood !
If *thus* to hear thee branded be a bliss
That Vengeance loves, there 's yet more
  sweet than this,
That 't was an Irish head, an Irish heart,
Made thee the fallen and tarnisht thing
  thou art;
That, as the centaur [2] gave the infected
  vest
In which he died, to rack his conqueror's
  breast,

---

verse of the Psalmist (' If I forget thee, O Jerusalem,' etc.) or the words — ' The memory of the
desolation.' " — *Leo of Modena.*

[1] I have thought it prudent to omit some parts
of Mr. Phelim Connor's letter. He is evidently
an intemperate young man, and has associated
with his cousins, the Fudges, to very little
purpose.

[2] *membra et Herculeos toros
urit lues Nessea. . . . .
ille, ille victor vincitur.*
      Senec. " *Hercul. Œt.*"

We sent thee CASTLEREAGH: — as heaps
of dead
Have slain their slayers by the pest they
spread,
So hath our land breathed out, thy fame
to dim,
Thy strength to waste and rot thee soul
and limb,
Her worst infections all condensed in
him!

. . . .

When will the world shake off such
yokes? oh, when
Will that redeeming day shine out on
men,
That shall behold them rise, erect and
free
As Heaven and Nature meant mankind
should be!
When Reason shall no longer blindly
bow
To the vile pagod things, that o'er her
brow,
Like him of Jaghernaut, drive trampling
now;
Nor Conquest dare to desolate God's
earth;
Nor drunken Victory, with a NERO's
mirth,
Strike her lewd harp amidst a people's
groans; —
But, built on love, the world's exalted
thrones
Shall to the virtuous and the wise be
given —
Those bright, those sole Legitimates of
Heaven!

When will this be? — or, oh! is it, in
truth,
But one of those sweet, day-break dreams
of youth,
In which the Soul, as round her morning
springs,
'Twixt sleep and waking, sees such dazzling things!
And must the hope, as vain as it is bright,
Be all resigned? — and are *they* only
right,
Who say this world of thinking souls
was made
To be by Kings partitioned, truckt and
weighed

In scales that, ever since the world be-
gun,
Have counted millions but as dust to one?
Are *they* the only wise, who laugh to
scorn
The rights, the freedom to which man
was born?
Who . . . .
Who, proud to kiss each separate rod of
power,
Bless, while he reigns, the minion of the
hour;
Worship each would-be god, that o'er
them moves,
And take the thundering of his brass for
JOVE's!
If *this* be wisdom, then farewell, my
books,
Farewell, ye shrines of old, ye classic
brooks,
Which fed my soul with currents, pure
and fair,
Of living Truth that now must stagnate
there! —
Instead of themes that touch the lyre
with light,
Instead of Greece and her immortal fight
For Liberty which once awaked my
strings,
Welcome the Grand Conspiracy of Kings,
The High Legitimates, the Holy Band,
Who, bolder even than He of Sparta's
land,
Against whole millions, panting to be free,
Would guard the pass of right line tyr-
anny.
Instead of him, the Athenian bard whose
blade
Had stood the onset which his pen por-
trayed,
Welcome . . . . . .

And, 'stead of ARISTIDES — woe the day
Such names should mingle! — welcome
Castlereagh!

Here break we off, at this unhallowed
name,[1]
Like priests of old, when words ill-
omened came.

1 The late Lord C. of Ireland had a curious
theory about names; — he held that every man

My next shall tell thee, bitterly shall tell,
Thoughts that   .   .   .   .

Thoughts that — could patience hold —
    't were wiser far
To leave still hid and burning where they
    are.

LETTER V.

FROM MISS BIDDY FUDGE TO MISS DOROTHY ——.

WHAT a time since I wrote! — I 'm a
    sad, naughty girl —
For, tho', like a tee-totum, I 'm all in a
    twirl ; —
Yet even (as you wittily say) a tee-totum
Between all its twirls gives a *letter* to
    note 'em.
But, Lord, such a place! and then,
    DOLLY, my dresses,
My gowns, so divine! — there 's no lan-
    guage expresses,
Except just the *two* words " *superbe*,"
    " *magnifique*,"
The trimmings of that which I had home
    last week!
It is called — I forget — *à la* — some-
    thing which sounded
Like *alicampane* — but in truth I 'm con-
    founded
And bothered, my dear, 'twixt that trou-
    blesome boy's
(BOB'S) cookery language, and Madame
    LE ROI'S :
What with fillets of roses, and fillets of
    veal,
Things *garni* with lace, and things *garni*
    with eel,
One's hair and one's cutlets both *en
    papillote*,

with *three* names was a jacobin. His instances
in Ireland were numerous : — viz. Archibald Hamilton Rowan, Theobald Wolfe Tone, James Nap-
per Tandy, John Philpot Curran, etc., and, in
England, he produced as examples Charles James
Fox, Richard Brinsley Sheridan, John Horne
Tooke, Francis Burdett Jones, etc.
    The Romans call a thief " *homo trium lite-
rarum*."
            *tun' trium literarum homo
            me vituperas ? Fur.**
        PLAUTUS, " *Aulular*." Act ii. Scene 4.

* *Dissaldeus* supposes this word to be a *glos-
sema :* — that is, he thinks " *fur* " has made his
escape from the margin into the text.

And a thousand more things I shall ne'er
    have by rote,
I can scarce tell the difference, at least
    as to phrase,
Between beef *à la Psyche* and curls *à la
    braise*. —
But in short, dear, I 'm trickt out quite
    à la Française,
With my bonnet — so beautiful! — high
    up and poking,
Like things that are put to keep chim-
    neys from smoking.

Where *shall* I begin with the endless de-
    lights
Of this Eden of milliners, monkeys and
    sights —
This dear busy place, where there 's
    nothing transacting
But dressing and dinnering, dancing and
    acting ?
Imprimis, the Opera — mercy, my ears !
    Brother BOBBY'S remark, t'other night,
        was a true one ; —
" This *must* be the music," said he, " of
    the *spears*,
    " For I 'm curst if each note of it does
        n't run thro' one ! "
Pa says (and you know, love, his Book 's
    to make out
'T was the Jacobins brought every mis-
    chief about)
That this passion for roaring has come in
    of late,
Since the rabble all tried for a *voice* in
    the State. —
What a frightful idea, one's mind to
    o'erwhelm !
    What a chorus, dear DOLLY, would
        soon be let loose of it,
If, when of age, every man in the realm
    Had a voice like old Laïs,[1] and chose
        to make use of it !
No — never was known in this riotous
    sphere
Such a breach of the peace as their sing-
    ing, my dear.
So bad too, you 'd swear that the God
    of both arts,
    Of Music and Physic, had taken a
        frolic

[1] The oldest, most celebrated, and most noisy
of the singers at the French Opera.

For setting a loud fit of asthma in parts,
And composing a fine rumbling bass
    to a cholic!

But, the dancing — *ah parlez-moi*,
    DOLLY, *de ça* —
There, *indeed*, is a treat that charms all
    but Papa.
Such beauty — such grace — oh ye sylphs
    of romance!
  Fly, fly to TITANIA, and ask her if *she*
    has
One light-footed nymph in her train, that
    can dance
    Like divine BIGOTTINI and sweet
    FANNY BIAS!
FANNY BIAS in FLORA — dear creature!
    — you 'd swear,
  When her delicate feet in the dance
    twinkle round,
That her steps are of light, that her home
    is the air,
  And she only *par complaisance* touches
    the ground.
And when BIGOTTINI in PSYCHE di-
    shevels
  Her black flowing hair, and by
    dæmons is driven,
Oh! who does not envy those rude little
    devils,
  That hold her and hug her, and keep
    her from heaven?
Then, the music — so softly its cadences
    die,
So divinely — oh, DOLLY! between you
    and I,
It 's as well for my peace that there 's
    nobody nigh
To make love to me then — *you 've* a
    soul, and can judge
What a crisis 't would be for your friend
    BIDDY FUDGE!
The next place (which BOBBY has near
    lost his heart in)
They call it the Play-house — I think —
    of St. Martin;[1]

Quite charming — and *very* religious —
    what folly
To say that the French are not pious,
    dear DOLLY,
Where here one beholds, so correctly
    and rightly,
The Testament turned into melo-drames
    nightly; [2]
And doubtless so fond they 're of scrip-
    tural facts;
They will soon get the Pentateuch up in
    five acts.
Here DANIEL, in pantomime,[3] bids bold
    defiance
To NEBUCHADNEZZAR and all his stuft
    lions,
While pretty young Israelites dance
    round the Prophet,
In very thin clothing, and *but* little of
    it; —
Here BÉGRAND,[4] who shines in this
    scriptural path,
  As the lovely SUSANNA, without even
    a relic
Of drapery round her, comes out of the
    bath
  In a manner that, BOB says, is quite
    Eve-angelic!
But in short, dear, 't would take me a
    month to recite
All the exquisite places we 're at, day
    and night;
And, besides, ere I finish, I think you 'll
    be glad
Just to hear one delightful adventure
    I 've had.

---

2 "The Old Testament," says the theatrical Critic in the *Gazette de France*, "is a mine of gold for the managers of our small play-houses. A multitude crowd round the Théâtre de la Gaieté every evening to see the Passage of the Red Sea."

In the play-bill of one of these sacred melo-drames at Vienna, we find "The Voice of God, by M. Schwartz."

3 A piece very popular last year, called "*Daniel, ou La Fosse aux Lions.*" The follow-ing scene will give an idea of the daring sublimity of these scriptural pantomimes. "*Scene* 20. — *La fournaise devient un berceau de nuages azurés, au fond duquel est un grouppe de nuages plus lumineux, et au milieu 'Jehovah' au centre d'un cercle de rayons brillans, qui annonce là présence de l'Éternel.*"

4 Madame Bégrand, a finely formed woman, who acts in "Susanna and the Elders," — "*L'Amour et la Folie,*" etc.

---

1 The Théâtre de la Porte St. Martin, which was built when the Opera House in the Palais Royal was burned down, in 1781. — A few days after this dreadful fire, which lasted more than a week, and in which several persons perished, the Parisian *élégantes* displayed flame-colored dresses, "*couléur de feu d'Opéra!*" — *Dulaure, Curiosités de Paris.*

Last night, at the Beaujon,[1] a place where
  — I doubt
If its charms I can paint — there are
  cars, that set out
From a lighted pavilion, high up in the
  air,
And rattle you down, DOLL — you hardly
  know where.
These vehicles, mind me, in which you
  go thro'
This delightfully dangerous journey, hold
  two.
Some cavalier asks, with humility,
  whether
  You 'll venture down *with* him — you
    smile — 't is a match ;
In an instant you 're seated, and down
  both together
  Go thundering, as if you went post to
    old scratch ! [2]
Well, it was but last night, as I stood
  and remarkt
On the looks and odd ways of the girls
  who embarkt,
The impatience of some for the perilous
  flight,
The forced giggle of others, 'twixt pleas-
  ure and fright, —
That there came up — imagine, dear
  DOLL, if you can —
A fine sallow, sublime, sort of Werter-
  faced man,
With mustachios that gave (what we
  read of so oft)
The dear Corsair expression, half savage,
  half soft,
As Hyenas in love may be fancied to
  look, or
A something between ABELARD and old
  BLUCHER !
Up he came, DOLL, to me, and uncover-
  ing his head,
(Rather bald, but so warlike !) in bad
  English said,
" Ah ! my dear — if Ma'mselle vil be so
  very good —

Just for von littel course " — tho' I scarce
  understood
What he wisht me to do, I said, thank
  him, I would.
Off we set — and, tho' 'faith, dear, I
  hardly knew whether
  My head or my heels were the upper-
    most then,
For 't was like heaven and earth, DOLLY,
  coming together, —
  Yet, spite of the danger, we dared it
    again.
And oh ! as I gazed on the features and
  air
  Of the man, who for me all this peril
    defied,
I could fancy almost he and I were a pair
  Of unhappy young lovers, who thus,
    side by side,
Were taking, instead of rope, pistol, or
  dagger, a
Desperate dash down the falls of Niagara !

This achieved, thro' the gardens [3] we
  sauntered about,
  Saw the fire-works, exclaimed " *mag-
    nifique !* " at each cracker,
And, when 't was all ɔ'er, the dear man
  saw us out
  With the air I *will* say, of a Prince,
    to our *fiacre*.

Now, hear me — this Stranger — it may
  be mere folly —
But *who* do you think we all think it is,
  DOLLY?
Why, bless you, no less than the great
  King of Prussia,
Who 's here now incog.[4] — he, who made
  so much fuss, you
Remember, in London, with BLUCHER
  and PLATOF,
When SAL was near kissing old BLU-
  CHER'S cravat off !

---

1 The *Promenades Aëriennes*, or French
Mountains. — See a description of this singular
and fantastic place of amusement in a pamphlet,
truly worthy of it, by " F. F. Cotterel, Médecin,
Docteur de la Faculté de Paris," etc.

2 According to Dr. Cotterel the cars go at the
rate of forty-eight miles an hour.

3 In the Café attached to these gardens there
are to be (as Doctor Cotterel informs us) " *douze
nègres, très alertes, qui contrasteront par l'ébène
de leur peau avec le teint de lis et de roses de nos
belles. Les glaces et les sorbets, servis par une
main bien noire, fera davantage ressortir l'al-
bâtre des bras arrondis de celles-ci.*" —P. 22.

4 His Majesty, who was at Paris under the
travelling name of Count Ruppin, is known to
have gone down the Beaujon very frequently.

Pa says he 's come here to look after his
    money,
(Not taking things now as he used under
    BONEY,)
Which suits with our friend, for BOB saw
    him, he swore,
Looking sharp to the silver received at
    the door.
Besides, too, they say that his grief for
    his Queen
(Which was plain in this sweet fellow's
    face to be seen)
Requires such a stimulant dose as this
    car is,
Used three times a day with young ladies
    in Paris.
Some Doctor, indeed, has declared that
    such grief
    Should — unless 't would to utter de-
        spairing its folly push —
Fly to the Beaujon, and there seek relief
    By rattling, as BOB says, "like shot
    thro' a holly-bush."

I must now bid adieu; — only think,
    DOLLY, think
If this *should* be the King — I have
    scarce slept a wink
With imagining how it will sound in the
    papers,
    And how all the Misses my good luck
        will grudge,
When they read that Count RUPPIN, to
    drive away vapors,
    Has gone down the Beaujon with Miss
        BIDDY FUDGE.

Nota Bene. — Papa 's almost certain 't is
    he —
For he knows the Legitimate cut and
    could see,
In the way he went poising and managed
    to tower
So erect in the car, the true *Balance of
    Power*.

LETTER VI.

FROM

PHIL. FUDGE, ESQ., TO HIS BROTHER
TIM FUDGE, ESQ., BARRISTER AT LAW.

YOURS of the 12th received just now —
    Thanks for the hint, my trusty
    brother!

'T is truly pleasing to see how
    We, FUDGES, stand by one another.
But never fear — I know my chap,
And he knows *me* too — *verbum sap.*
My Lord and I are kindred spirits,
Like in our ways as two young ferrets;
Both fashioned, as that supple race is,
To twist into all sorts of places; —
Creatures lengthy, lean and hungering,
Fond of blood and *burrow*-mongering.

As to my Book in '91,
    Called "Down with Kings, or, Who 'd
        have thought it?"
Bless you! the Book 's long dead and
        gone, —
    Not even the Attorney-General bought
        it.
And tho' some few seditious tricks
I played in '95 and '6,
As you remind me in your letter,
His Lordship likes me all the better; —
We proselytes, that come with news
        full,
Are, as he says, so vastly useful!

REYNOLDS and I — (you know TOM
        REYNOLDS —
    Drinks his claret, keeps his chaise —
Lucky the dog that first unkennels
    Traitors and Luddites now-a-days;
Or who can help to *bag* a few,
When SIDMOUTH wants a death or
        two;)
REYNOLDS and I and some few more,
    All men like us of *information*,
Friends whom his Lordship keeps in
        store,
    As *under*-saviors of the nation [1] —
Have formed a Club this season, where
His Lordship sometimes takes the chair,
And gives us many a bright oration
In praise of our sublime vocation;
Tracing it up to great King MIDAS,
Who, tho' in fable typified as
A royal Ass, by grace divine
And right of ears, most asinine,
Was yet no more, in fact historical,
    Than an exceeding well-bred tyrant;

1 Lord C.'s tribute to the character of his
friend, Mr. Reynolds, will long be remembered
with equal credit to both.

And these, his *ears*, but allegorical,
  Meaning Informers, kept at high
    rent [1] —
Gem'men, who touched the Treasury
    glisteners,
Like us, for being trusty listeners;
And picking up each tale and frag-
    ment,
For royal MIDAS's Green Bag meant.
"And wherefore," said this best of
    Peers,
"Should not the REGENT too have
    ears,[2]
"To reach as far, as long and wide as
"Those of his model, good King
    MIDAS?"
This speech was thought extremely good,
And (rare for him) was understood —
Instant we drank "The REGENT's
    Ears,"
With three times three illustrious cheers,
  Which made the room resound like
    thunder —
"The REGENT's Ears, and may he
    ne'er
"From foolish shame, like MIDAS, wear
  "Old paltry *wigs* to keep them [3] un-
    der!"
This touch at our old friends, the Whigs,
Made us as merry all as grigs.
In short (I 'll thank you not to men-
    tion
  These things again), we get on gayly;
And thanks to pension and Suspension,
  Our little Club increases daily.

1 This interpretation of the fable of Midas's
ears seems the most probable of any, and is thus
stated in Hoffmann : — " *hâc allegoriâ significa-
tum, Midam, utpote tyrannum, subanscultatores
dimittere solitum, per quos, quæcunque per om-
nem regionem vel fierent, vel dicerentur, cognos-
ceret, nimirum illis utens aurium vice.*"

2 Brossette, in a note on this line of Boileau,
" *Midas, le Roi Midas, a des oreilles d' Âne,*"
tells us, that " *M. Perrault le Médecin voulut
faire à notre auteur un crime d'état de ce vers,
comme d'une maligne allusion au Roi.*" I
trust, however, that no one will suspect the line
in the text of any such indecorous allusion.

3 It was not under wigs, but tiaras, that King
Midas endeavored to conceal these appendages :

    tempora purpureis tentat velare tiaris.
                   OVID.
The Noble Giver of the toast, however, had
evidently, with his usual clearness, confounded
King Midas, Mr. Liston, and the Prince Regent
together.

CASTLES, and OLIVER, and such,
Who don't as yet full salary touch,
Nor keep their chaise and pair, nor buy
Houses and lands, like TOM and I,
Of course don't rank with us, *salvators,*[4]
But merely serve the Club as waiters.
Like Knights, too, we 've our *collar*
    days,
(For *us*, I own, an awkward phrase,)
When, in our new costume adorned,—
The REGENT's buff-and-blue coats
    turned —
We have the honor to give dinners
  To the chief Rats in upper stations;[5]
Your WEMYS, VAUGHANS, — half-
    fledged sinners,
Who shame us by their imitations;
Who turn, 't is true — but what of that?
Give me the useful *peaching* Rat;
Not things as mute as Punch, when
    bought,
Whose wooden heads are all they 've
    brought;
Who, false enough to shirk their friends,
  But too faint-hearted to betray,
Are, after all their twists and bends,
  But souls in Limbo, damned half
    way.
No, no, we nobler vermin are
A *genus* useful as we 're rare;
Midst all the things miraculous
  Of which your natural histories brag,
The rarest must be Rats like us,
  Who *let the cat out of the bag.*
Yet still these Tyros in the cause
Deserve, I own, no small applause;
And they 're by us received and treated
With all due honors — only seated
In the inverse scale of their reward,
The merely *promised* next my Lord;
Small pensions then, and so on, down,
Rat after rat, they graduate
Thro' job, red ribbon and silk gown,
  To Chancellorship and Marquisate.
This serves to nurse the ratting spirit;
The less the bribe the more the merit.

4 Mr. Fudge and his friends ought to go by
this name — as the man who, some years since,
saved the late Right Hon. George Rose from
drowning, was ever after called *Salvator Rosa.*

5 This intimacy between the Rats and Informers is just as it should be — " *verè dulce
sodalitium.*"

Our music 's good, you may be sure;
My Lord, you know, 's an amateur [1] —
Takes every part with perfect ease,
  Tho' to the Base by nature suited;
And, formed for all, as best may please,
For whips and bolts, or chords and keys,
Turns from his victims to his glees,
  And has them both well *executed*.[2]
HERTFORD, who, tho' no Rat himself,
  Delights in all such liberal arts,
Drinks largely to the House of Guelph,
  And superintends the *Corni* parts.
While CANNING,[3] who 'd be *first* by
  choice,
Consents to take an *under* voice ;
And GRAVES,[4] who well that signal
  knows,
Watches the *Volti Subitos*.[5]

In short, as I 've already hinted,
  We take of late prodigiously;
But as our Club is somewhat stinted
  For *Gentlemen*, like TOM and me,
We 'll take it kind if you 'll provide
A few *Squireens*[6] from t 'other side ; —
Some of those loyal, cunning elves
  (We often tell the tale with laughter),
Who used to hide the pikes themselves,
  Then hang the fools who found them
    after.
I doubt not you could find us, too,
Some Orange Parsons that might do ;

---

1 His Lordship, during one of the busiest
periods of his Ministerial career, took lessons
three times a week from a celebrated music-mas-
ter, in glee-singing.

2 How amply these two propensities of the
Noble Lord would have been gratified among
that ancient people of Etruria, who, as Aristotle
tells us, used to whip their slaves once a year to
the sound of flutes!

3 This Right Hon. Gentleman ought to give
up his present alliance with Lord C., if upon no
other principle than that which is inculcated in
the following arrangement between two Ladies
of Fashion : —

  Says Clarinda, " tho' tears it may cost,
    It is time we should part, my dear Sue ;
  For *your* character 's totally lost,
    And *I* have not sufficient fo r*two* !"

4 The rapidity of this Noble Lord's trans-
formation, at the same instant, into a Lord of the
Bed-chamber and an opponent of the Catholic
Claims, was truly miraculous.

5 *Turn instantly* — a frequent direction in
music-books.

6 The Irish diminutive of *Squire*.

Among the rest, we 've heard of one,
The Reverend — something — HAMIL-
  TON,
Who stuft a figure of himself
  (Delicious thought !) and had it shot
    at,
To bring some Papists to the shelf,
  That could n't otherwise be got at —
If *he* 'll but join the Association,
We 'll vote him in by acclamation.

And now, my brother, guide and friend,
This somewhat tedious scrawl must end.
I 've gone into this long detail,
  Because I saw your nerves were shaken
With anxious fears lest I should fail
  In this new, *loyal*, course I 've taken.
But, bless your heart ! you need not
  doubt —
We FUDGES know what we 're about.
Look round and say if you can see
A much more thriving family.
There 's JACK, the Doctor — night and
  day
  Hundreds of patients so besiege him,
You 'd swear that all the rich and gay
  Fell sick on purpose to oblige him.
And while they think, the precious
  ninnies,
  He 's counting o'er their pulse so
    steady,
The rogue but counts how many guineas
  He 's fobbed for that day's work al-
    ready.
I 'll ne'er forget the old maid's alarm,
  When, feeling thus Miss Sukey Flirt,
    he
Said, as he dropt her shrivelled arm,
  " Damned bad this morning — only
    thirty !"

Your dowagers, too, every one,
  So generous are, when they call *him*
    in,
That he might now retire upon
  The rheumatisms of three old women.
Then whatsoe'er your ailments are,
  He can so learnedly explain ye 'em —
Your cold of course is a *catarrh*,
  Your headache is a *hemi-cranium* : —
His skill too in young ladies' lungs,
  The grace with which, most mild of
    men,

He begs them to put out their tongues,
　Then bids them — put them in again:
In short, there 's nothing now like
　　JACK ! —
Take all your doctors great and small,
Of present times and ages back,
　Dear Doctor FUDGE is worth them all.

So much for physic — then, in law too,
　Counsellor TIM, to thee we bow;
Not one of us gives more éclat to
　The immortal name of FUDGE than
　　thou.
Not to expatiate on the art
With which you played the patriot's part,
Till something good and snug should
　　offer; —
　Like one, who, by the way he acts
The *enlightening* part of candle-snuffer,
　The manager's keen eye attracts,
And is promoted thence by him
To strut in robes, like thee, my TIM ! —
Who shall describe thy powers of face,
Thy well-feed zeal in every case,
Or wrong or right — but ten times warmer
(As suits thy calling) in the former —
Thy glorious, lawyer-like delight
In puzzling all that 's clear and right,
Which, tho' conspicuous in thy youth,
　Improves so with a wig and band on,
That all thy pride 's to waylay Truth,
　And leave her not a leg to stand on.
Thy patent prime morality, —
　Thy cases cited from the Bible —
Thy candor when it falls to thee
　To help in trouncing for a libel ; —
" God knows, I, from my soul, profess
　" To hate all bigots and benighters !
" God knows, I love, to even excess,
　" The sacred Freedom of the Press,
　　" My only aim 's to — crush the
　　　writers."
These are the virtues, TIM, that draw
　The briefs into thy bag so fast;
And these, oh TIM — if Law be Law—
　Will raise thee to the Bench at last.

I blush to see this letter's length —
　But 't was my wish to prove to thee
How full of hope, and wealth, and
　　strength,
　Are all our precious family.
And, should affairs go on as pleasant

As, thank the Fates, they do at present —
Should we but still enjoy the sway
Of SIDMOUTH and of CASTLEREAGH,
I hope, ere long, to see the day
When England's wisest statesmen, judges,
Lawyers, peers, will all be — FUDGES !

Good-by — my paper 's out so nearly,
I 've room only for
　　　　　　Yours sincerely.

LETTER VII.

FROM PHELIM CONNOR TO ——.

BEFORE we sketch the Present — let us
　　cast
A few, short, rapid glances to the Past.

When he, who had defied all Europe's
　　strength,
Beneath his own weak rashness sunk at
　　length; —
When, loosed as if by magic from a
　　chain
That seemed like Fate's the world was
　　free again,
And Europe saw, rejoicing in the sight,
The cause of Kings, *for once*, the cause
　　of Right; —
Then was, indeed, an hour of joy to
　　those
Who sighed for justice — liberty — re-
　　pose,
And hoped the fall of *one* great vulture's
　　nest
Would ring its warning round, and scare
　　the rest.
All then was bright with promise; —
　　Kings began
To own a sympathy with suffering Man,
And man was grateful; Patriots of the
　　South
Caught wisdom from a Cossack Em-
　　peror's mouth,
And heard, like accents thawed in
　　Northern air,
Unwonted words of freedom burst forth
　　there !

Who did not hope, in that triumphant
　· time,
When monarchs, after years of spoil and
　　crime,

Met round the shrine of Peace, and
    Heaven lookt on; —
Who did not hope the lust of spoil was
    gone ;
That that rapacious spirit, which had
    played
The game of Pilnitz o'er so oft, was laid;
And Europe's Rulers, conscious of the
    past,
Would blush and deviate into right at
    last ?
But no — the hearts, that nurst a hope so
    fair,
Had yet to learn what men on thrones
    can dare;
Had yet to know, of all earth's ravening
    things,
The only *quite* untameable are Kings !
Scarce had they met when, to its nature
    true,
The instinct of their race broke out anew;
Promises, treaties, charters, all were
    vain,
And " Rapine ! rapine ! " was the cry
    again.
How quick they carved their victims,
    and how well,
Let Saxony, let injured Genoa tell; —
Let all the human stock that, day by day,
Was, at that Royal slave-mart, truckt
    away, —
The million souls that, in the face of
    heaven,
Were split to fractions,[1] bartered, sold or
    given
To swell some despot Power, too huge
    before,
And weigh down Europe with one Mam-
    moth more.
How safe the faith of Kings let France
    decide; —
Her charter broken, ere its ink had
    dried; —
Her Press enthralled — her Reason
    mockt again

With all the monkery it had spurned in
    vain;
Her crown disgraced by one, who dared
    to own
He thankt not France but England for
    his throne;
Her triumphs cast into the shade by
    those,
Who had grown old among her bitterest
    foes,
And now returned, beneath her con-
    queror's shields,
Unblushing slaves ! to claim her heroes'
    fields;
To tread down every trophy of her fame,
And curse that glory which to them was
    shame ! —
Let these — let all the damning deeds,
    that then
Were dared thro' Europe, cry aloud to
    men,
With voice like that of crashing ice that
    rings
Round Alpine huts, the perfidy of
    Kings;
And tell the world, when hawks shall
    harmless bear
The shrinking dove, when wolves shall
    learn to spare
The helpless victim for whose blood they
    lusted,
Then and then only monarchs may be
    trusted.

It could not last — these horrors *could*
    not last —
France would herself have risen in might
    to cast
The insulters off — and oh ! that then as
    now,
Chained to some distant islet's rocky
    brow,
NAPOLEON ne'er had come to force, to
    blight,
Ere half matured, a cause so proudly
    bright; —
To palsy patriot arts with doubt and
    shame,
And write on Freedom's flag a despot's
    name ; —
To rush into the list, unaskt, alone,
And make the stake of *all* the game of
    one !

---

1 " Whilst the Congress was re-constructing
Europe — not according to rights, natural affi-
ances, language, habits, or laws; but by tables
of finance, which divided and subdivided her
population into *souls, demi-souls,* and even *fractions,* according to a scale of the direct duties or
taxes, which could be levied by the acquiring
state," etc. — *Sketch of the Military and Political Power of Russia.* The words on the pro-
tocol are *âmes, demi-âmes,* etc.

Then would the world have seen again
    what power
A people can put forth in Freedom's
    hour;
Then would the fire of France once more
    have blazed; —
For every single sword, reluctant raised
In the stale cause of an oppressive throne,
Millions would then have leaped forth
    in her own;
And never, never had the unholy stain
Of Bourbon feet disgraced her shores
    again.

But fate decreed not so — the Imperial
    Bird,
That, in his neighboring cage, unfeared,
    unstirred,
Had seemed to sleep with head beneath
    his wing,
Yet watched the moment for a daring
    spring; —
Well might he watch, when deeds were
    done, that made
His own transgressions whiten in their
    shade;
Well might he hope a world thus trampled
    o'er
By clumsy tyrants would be his once
    more : —
Forth from his cage the eagle burst to
    light,
From steeple on to steeple [1] winged his
    flight,
With calm and easy grandeur, to that
    throne
From which a Royal craven just had
    flown;
And resting there, as in his eyry, furled
Those wings, whose very rustling shook
    the world!

What was your fury then, ye crowned
    array,
Whose feast of spoil, whose plundering
    holiday
Was thus broke up, in all its greedy
    mirth,
By one bold chieftain's stamp on Gallic
    earth!

Fierce was the cry, and fulminant the
    ban, —
" Assassinate, who will — enchain, who
    can,
" The vile, the faithless, outlawed, low-
    born man ! "
" Faithless !" — and this from *you* —
    from *you*, forsooth,
Ye pious Kings, pure paragons of truth,
Whose honesty all knew, for all had
    tried;
Whose true Swiss zeal had served on
    every side;
Whose fame for breaking faith so long
    was known,
Well might ye claim the craft as all your
    own,
And lash your lordly tails and fume to
    see
Such low-born apes of Royal perfidy !
Yes — yes — to you alone did it belong
To sin for ever, and yet ne'er do wrong,—
The frauds, the lies of Lords legitimate
Are but fine policy, deep strokes of
    state;
But let some upstart dare to soar so
    high
In Kingly craft, and " outlaw " is the
    cry !
What, tho' long years of mutual treachery
Had peopled full your diplomatic shelves
With ghosts of treaties, murdered 'mong
    yourselves;
Tho' each by turns was knave and dupe
    — what then?
A Holy League would set all straight
    again;
Like JUNO'S virtue, which a dip or two
In some blest fountain made as good
    as new ! [2]
Most faithful Russia — faithful to who-
    e'er
Could plunder best and give him amplest
    share;
Who, even when vanquisht, sure to gain
    his ends,
For want of *foes* to rob, made free with
    friends,[3]

---

[1] " *L'aigle volera de clocher en clocher, jusqu'aux tours de Notre-Dame.*" — Napoleon's
Proclamation on landing from Elba.

[2] *singulis annis in quodam Atticæ fonte lota
virginitatem recuperàsse fingitur.*

[3] At the Peace of Tilsit, where he abandoned
his ally, Prussia, to France, and received a portion of her territory.

And, deepening still by amiable grada-
tions,
When foes were stript of all, then fleeced
relations ! [1]
Most mild and saintly Prussia — steeped
to the ears
In persecuted Poland's blood and tears,
And now, with all her harpy wings out-
spread
O'er severed Saxony's devoted head !
Pure Austria too — whose history naught
repeats
But broken leagues and subsidized de-
feats;
Whose faith, as Prince, extinguisht Ven-
ice shows,
Whose faith, as man, a widowed daugh-
ter knows !
And thou, oh England — who, tho'
once as shy
As cloistered maids, of shame or perfidy,
Art now *broke in*, and, thanks to CAS-
TLEREAGH,
In all that 's worst and falsest lead'st
the way !

Such was the pure divan, whose pens
and wits
The escape from Elba frightened into
fits; —
Such were the saints, who doomed NA-
POLEON'S life,
In virtuous frenzy, to the assassin's knife.
Disgusting crew ! — *who* would not gladly
fly
To open, downright, bold-faced tyranny,
To honest guilt, that dares do all but lie,
From the false, juggling craft of men
like these,
Their canting crimes and varnisht vil-
lanies; —
These Holy Leaguers, who then loudest
boast
Of faith and honor, when they 've
stained them most;
From whose affection men should shrink
as loath
As from their hate, for they 'll be fleeced
by both;
Who, even while plundering, forge Reli-
gion's name

To frank their spoil, and without fear or
shame
Call down the Holy Trinity [2] to bless
Partition leagues and deeds of devilish-
ness !
But hold — enough — soon would this
swell of rage
O'erflow the boundaries of my scanty
page ; —
So, here I pause — farewell — another
day,
Return we to those Lords of prayer and
prey,
Whose loathsome cant, whose frauds by
right divine,
Deserve a lash — oh ! weightier far than
mine !

LETTER VIII.

FROM MR BOB FUDGE TO RICHARD
————, ESQ.

DEAR DICK, while old DONALDSON'S [3]
mending my stays, —
Which I *knew* would go smash with me
one of these days,
And, at yesterday's dinner, when, full
to the throttle,
We lads had begun our dessert with a
bottle
Of neat old Constantia, on *my* leaning
back
Just to order another, by Jove, I went
crack ! —
Or, as honest TOM said, in his nautical
phrase,
" Damn my eyes, BOB, in *doubling* the
Cape you 've *missed stays*." [4]
So, of course, as no gentleman 's seen
out without them,
They 're now at the *Schneider's* [5] — and,
while he 's about them,

[1] The seizure of Finland from his relative of
Sweden.

[2] The usual preamble of these flagitious com-
pacts. In the same spirit, Catherine, after the
dreadful massacre of Warsaw, ordered a solemn
" thanksgiving to God in all the churches, for the
blessings conferred upon the Poles ; " and commanded that each of them should " swear fidelity
and loyalty to her, and to shed in her defence the
last drop of their blood, as they should answer
for it to God, and his terrible judgment, kissing
the holy word and cross of their Saviour ! "

[3] An English tailor at Paris.

[4] A ship is said to miss stays, when she does
not obey the helm in tacking.

[5] The dandy term for a tailor.

Here goes for a letter, post-haste, neck
    and crop.
Let us see — in my last I was — where
    did I stop?
Oh! I know — at the Boulevards, as
    motley a road as
    Man ever would wish a day's lounging
        upon;
With its cafés and gardens, hotels and
    pagodas,
    Its founts and old Counts sipping beer
        in the sun:
With its houses of all architectures you
    please,
From the Grecian and Gothic, DICK,
    down by degrees
To the pure Hottentot or the Brighton
    Chinese;
Where in temples antique you may
    breakfast or dinner it,
Lunch at a mosque and see Punch from
    a minaret.
Then, DICK, the mixture of bonnets and
    bowers,
Of foliage and frippery, *fiacres* and
    flowers,
Green-grocers, green gardens — one
    hardly knows whether
'T is country or town, they 're so messed
    up together !
And there, if one loves the romantic, one
    sees
Jew clothes-men, like shepherds, re-
    clined under trees;
Or Quidnuncs, on Sunday, just fresh
    from the barber's,
Enjoying their news and *groseille* [1] in
    those arbors;
While gayly their wigs, like the tendrils,
    are curling,
And founts of red currant-juice [2] round
    them are purling.

Here, DICK, arm in arm as we chattering
    stray,
And receive a few civil " God-dems "
    by the way, —

For, 't is odd, these mounseers, — tho'
    we 've wasted our wealth
And our strength, till we 've thrown
    ourselves into a phthisic,
To cram down their throats an old King
    for their health,
    As we whip little children to make
        them take physic; —
Yet, spite of our good-natured money
    and slaughter,
They hate us, as Beelzebub hates holy-
    water !
But who the deuce cares, DICK, as long
    as they nourish us
Neatly as now, and good cookery flour-
    ishes —
Long as, by bayonets protected, we
    Natties
May have our full fling at their *salmis*
    and *pâtés ?*
And, truly, I always declared 't would
    be pity
To burn to the ground such a choice-
    feeding city.
Had *Dad* but his way, he 'd have long
    ago blown
The whole batch to old Nick — and the
    people, I own,
If for no other cause than their curst
    monkey looks,
Well deserve a blow-up — but then,
    damn it, their Cooks !
As to Marshals, and Statesmen, and all
    their whole lineage,
For aught that *I* care, you may knock
    them to spinage; ·
But think, DICK, their Cooks — what a
    loss to mankind !
What a void in the world would their
    art leave behind !
Their chronometer spits — their intense
    salamanders —
Their ovens — their pots, that can soften
    old ganders,
All vanish for ever — their miracles o'er,
And the *Marmite Perpétuelle* [3] bubbling
    no more !

---

1 " Lemonade and *eau-de-groseille* are measured out at every corner of every street, from
fantastic vessels, jingling with bells, to thirsty
tradesmen or wearied messengers." — See Lady
Morgan's lively description of the streets of Paris,
in her very amusing work upon France, book vi.

2 These gay, portable fountains, from which

the groseille water is administered, are among
the most characteristic ornaments of the streets
of Paris.

3 " *Cette merveilleuse Marmite Perpétuelle,
sur le feu depuis près d'un siècle ; qui a donné le
jour à plus de* 300,000 *chapons.*" — " *Alman. de
Gourmands,*" *Quatrième Année,* p. 152.

Forbid it, forbid it, ye Holy Allies!
　Take whatever ye fancy — take stat-
　　ues, take money —
But leave them, oh leave them, their
　Perigueux pies,
　Their glorious goose-livers and high
　　pickled tunny![1]
Tho' many, I own, are the evils they 've
　brought us,
　Tho' Royalty 's here on her very last
　　legs,
Yet who can help loving the land that
　has taught us
　Six hundred and eighty-five ways to
　　dress eggs?[2]

You see, DICK, in spite of their cries of
　" God-dam,"
　" *Coquin Anglais*," *et cætera* — how
　　generous I am!
And now (to return, once again, to my
　" Day,"
　Which will take us all night to get thro'
　　in this way,)
From the Boulevards we saunter thro'
　many a street,
　Crack jokes on the natives — mine, all
　　very neat —
Leave the Signs of the Times to political
　fops,
　And find *twice* as much fun in the Signs
　　of the Shops; —
Here, a Louis Dix-huit — *there*, a Mar-
　tinmas goose,
　(Much in vogue since your eagles are
　　gone out of use) —
Henri Quatres in shoals, and of Gods a
　great many,
　But Saints are the most on hard duty of
　　any: —
St. TONY, who used all temptations to
　spurn,
　Here hangs o'er a beer-shop, and tempts
　　in his turn;

While *there* St. VENECIA[3] sits hemming
　and frilling her
Holy *mouchoir* o'er the door of some
　milliner; —
Saint AUSTIN 's the " outward and visible
　sign
" Of an inward " cheap dinner, and pint
　of small wine;
While St. DENYS hangs out o'er some
　hatter of *ton*,
And possessing, good bishop, no head of
　his own,[4]
Takes an interest in Dandies, who 've
　got — next to none!
Then we stare into shops — read the
　evening's *affiches* —
Or, if some, who 're Lotharios in feed-
　ing, should wish
Just to flirt with a luncheon, (a devilish
　bad trick,
As it takes off the bloom of one's appe-
　tite, DICK,)
To the *Passage des* — what d 'ye call 't
　— *des Panoramas*[5]
We quicken our pace, and there heartily
　cram as
Seducing young *pâtés*, as ever could
　cozen
One out of one's appetite, down by the
　dozen.
We vary, of course — *petits pâtés* do *one*
　day,
The *next* we 've our lunch with the Gauf-
　frier Hollandais,[6]
That popular artist, who brings out, like
　SCOTT,
His delightful productions so quick, hot
　and hot;
Not the worse for the exquisite comment
　that follows, —
Divine *maresquino*, which — Lord, how
　one swallows!

---

1 *Le thon mariné*, one of the most favourite
and indigestible *hors-d'œuvres*. This fish is
taken chiefly in the Golfe de Lyon. "*La tête et
le dessous du ventre sont les parties les plus re-
cherchées des gourmets.*" — "*Cours Gastrono-
mique*," p. 252.

2 The exact number mentioned by M. de la
Reynière — "*On connoit en France 685 manières
différentes d'accommoder les œufs ; sans compter
celles que nos savans imaginent chaque jour.*"

3 Veronica, the Saint of the Holy Handkerchief, is also, under the name of Venisse or
Venecia, the tutelary saint of milliners.

4 St. Denys walked three miles after his head
was cut off. The *mot* of a woman of wit upon
this legend is well known: — "*Je le crois bien;
en pareil cas, il n'y a que le premier pas qui
coute.*"

5 Off the Boulevards Italiens.

6 In the Palais Royal; successor, I believe,
to the Flamand, so long celebrated for the *moël-
leux* of his Gaufres.

Once more, then, we saunter forth after
  our snack, or
Subscribe a few francs for the price of a
  fiacre,
And drive far away to the old *Montagnes
  Russes,*
Where we find a few twirls in the car of
  much use
To regenerate the hunger and thirst of
  us sinners,
Who 've lapst into snacks — the perdi-
  tion of dinners.
And here, DICK — in answer to one of
  your queries,
    About which we Gourmands have
    had much discussion —
I 've tried all these mountains, Swiss,
  French, and Ruggieri's,
    And think, for *digestion,*[1] there 's none
    like the Russian;
So equal the motion — so gentle, tho'
  fleet —
It in short such a light and salubrious
  scamper is,
That take whom you please — take old
  LOUIS DIX–HUIT,
And stuff him — ay, up to the neck —
  with stewed lampreys,[2]
So wholesome these Mounts, such a
  solvent I 've found them,
That, let me but rattle the Monarch well
  down them,
The fiend, Indigestion, would fly far away,
And the regicide lampreys[3] be foiled of
  their prey!

1 Doctor Cotterel recommends, for this purpose, the Beaujon or French Mountains, and
calls them "*une médecine aérienne, couleur de
rose ;*" but I own I prefer the authority of Mr.
Bob, who seems, from the following note found
in his own hand-writing, to have studied all these
mountains very carefully : —

Memoranda — The Swiss little notice deserves,
While the fall at Ruggieri's is death to weak
    nerves ;
And (whate'er Doctor Cott'rel may write on the
    question)
The turn at the Beaujon's too sharp for digestion.
I doubt whether Mr. Bob is quite correct in ac-
centing the second syllable of Ruggieri.

2 A dish so indigestible, that a late novelist,
at the end of his book, could imagine no more
summary mode of getting rid of all his heroes
and heroines than by a hearty supper of stewed
lampreys.

3 They killed Henry I. of England : — "a

Such, DICK, are the classical sports that
  content us,
Till five o'clock brings on that hour so
  momentous,[4]
That epoch — but whoa! my lad — here
  comes the *Schneider,*
And, curse him, has made the stays three
  inches wider —
Too wide by an inch and a half — what
  a Guy!
But, no matter — 't will all be set right
  by-and-by.
As we 've MASSINOT'S[5] eloquent *carte*
  to eat still up,
An inch and a half 's but a trifle to fill up.
So — not to lose time, DICK — here goes
  for the task;
Au revoir, my old boy — of the Gods I
  but ask,
That my life, like "the Leap of the
  German," [6] may be,
"*Du lit à la table, d' la table au lit !*"
                                    R. F.

LETTER IX.

FROM PHIL. FUDGE, ESQ., TO THE
  LORD VISCOUNT CASTLEREAGH.

MY Lord, the Instructions, brought to-
  day,
"I shall in all my best obey."

food [says Hume, gravely], which always agreed
better with his palate than his constitution."
   Lampreys, indeed, seem to have been always
a favorite dish with kings — whether from some
congeniality between them and that fish, I know
not ; but *Dio Cassius* tells us that Pollio fattened
his lampreys with human blood. St. Louis of
France was particularly fond of them. — See the
anecdote of Thomas Aquinas eating up his majesty's lamprey, in a note upon *Rabelais,* liv. iii.
chap. 2.

4 Had Mr. Bob's *Dinner* Epistle been inserted, I was prepared with an abundance of
learned matter to illustrate it, for which, as,
indeed, for all my "*scientia popinæ,*" * I am
indebted to a friend in the Dublin University,
— whose reading formerly lay in the *magic* line ;
but, in consequence of the Provost's enlightened
alarm at such studies, he has taken to the authors, "*de re cibariâ*" instead ; and has left
Bodin, Remigius, Agrippa and his little dog
Filiolus, for *Apicius, Nonius,* and that most
learned and savory Jesuit, *Bulengerus.*

5 A famous Restaurateur — now Dupont.

6 An old French saying ; — "*Faire le saut de
l'Allemand, du lit à la table et de la table au
lit.*"

* Seneca.

Your Lordship talks and writes so sensi-
bly!
And — whatsoe'er some wags may say —
Oh! not at *all* incomprehensibly.

I feel the inquiries in your letter
About my health and French most
flattering;
Thank ye, my French, tho' somewhat
better,
Is, on the whole, but weak and smat-
tering: —
Nothing, of course, that can compare
With his who made the Congress stare
(A certain Lord we need not name),
Who even in French, would have his
trope,
And talk of "*batir* un systême
"Sur *l'équilibre* de l'Europe!"
Sweet metaphor! — and then the Epistle,
Which bid the Saxon King go whistle, —
That tender letter to "*Mon Prince*," [1]
Which showed alike thy French and
sense; —
Oh no, my Lord — there's none can do
Or say *un-English* things like you;
And, if the schemes that fill thy breast
Could but a vent congenial seek,
And use the tongue that suits them best,
What charming Turkish wouldst thou
speak!
But as for *me*, a Frenchless grub,
At Congress never born to stammer,
Nor learn like thee, my Lord, to snub
Fallen Monarchs, out of CHAMBAUD'S
grammar —
Bless you, you do not, *can not* know
How far a little French will go;
For all one's stock, one need but draw
On some half-dozen words like these —
Comme ça — par-là — là-bas — ah ha!
They'll take you all thro' France with
ease.

Your Lordship's praises of the scraps
I sent you from my Journal lately,
(Enveloping a few laced caps
For Lady C.), delight me greatly.
Her flattering speech — "What pretty
things
"One finds in Mr. FUDGE's pages!"
Is praise which (as some poet sings)
Would pay one for the toils of ages.

Thus flattered, I presume to send
A few more extracts by a friend;
And I should hope they'll be no less
Approved of than my last MS. —
The former ones, I fear, were creased,
As BIDDY round the caps *would* pin
them;
But these will come to hand, at least
Unrumpled, for there's — nothing in
them.

Extracts from Mr. Fudge's Journal,
addressed to Lord C.

August 10.

Went to the Mad-house — saw the man,[2]
Who thinks, poor wretch, that, while
the Fiend
Of Discord here full riot ran,
He, like the rest, was guillotined; —
But that when, under BONEY'S reign,
(A more discreet, tho' quite as strong
one,)
The heads were all restored again,
He, in the scramble, got a *wrong one*.
Accordingly, he still cries out
This strange head fits him most un-
pleasantly;
And always runs, poor devil, about,
Inquiring for his own incessantly!

While to his case a tear I dropt,
And sauntered home, thought I — ye
Gods!
How many heads might thus be swopt,
And, after all, not make much odds!
For instance, there's VANSITTART'S
head —
("Tam *carum*" [3] it may well be said)

---

1 The celebrated letter to Prince Hardenburgh
(written, however, I believe, originally in English,) in which his Lordship, professing to see
"no moral or political objection" to the dismem-
berment of Saxony, denounced the unfortunate
King as "not only the most devoted, but the most
favored of Bonaparte's vassals."

2 This extraordinary madman is, I believe, in
the Bicêtre. He imagines, exactly as Mr. Fudge
states it, that when the heads of those who had
been guillotined were restored, he by mistake got
some other person's instead of his own.

3 *tam cari capitis.* — HORAT.

If by some curious chance it came
    To settle on BILL SOAMES's [1] shoul-
      ders,
The effect would turn out much the
    same
On all respectable cash-holders:
Except that while, in its *new* socket,
    The head was planning schemes to
      win
A *zig-zag* way into one's pocket,
    The hands would plunge *directly* in.

Good Viscount SIDMOUTH, too, instead
Of his own grave, respected head,
Might wear (for aught I see that bars)
    Old Lady WILHELMINA FRUMP's —
So while the hand signed *Circulars,*
    The head might lisp out " What is
      trumps? "—
The REGENT's brains could we transfer
To some robust man-milliner,
The shop, the shears, the lace, and ribbon
Would go, I doubt not, quite as glib on;
And, *vice versâ,* take the pains
    To give the PRINCE the shopman's
      brains,
One only change from thence would
    flow,
Ribbons would not be wasted so.

'T was thus I pondered on, my Lord;
    And, even at night, when laid in bed,
I found myself, before I snored,
    Thus chopping, swopping head for
      head.
At length I thought, fantastic elf !
How such a change would suit *myself.*
'Twixt sleep and waking, one by one,
    With various pericraniums saddled,
At last I tried your Lordship's on,
    And then I grew completely addled —
Forgot all other heads, od rot 'em !
And slept, and dreamt that I was — BOT-
    TOM.

                 August 21.
Walked out with daughter BID — was
    shown
The House of Commons and the Throne,
Whose velvet cushion 's just the same [2]
NAPOLEON sat on — what a shame !

1 A celebrated pickpocket.
2 The only change, if I recollect right, is the
substitution of lilies for bees. This war upon the

Oh ! can we wonder, best of speechers,
    When LOUIS seated thus we see,
That France's " fundamental features "
    Are much the same they used to be?
However, — God preserve the Throne,
    And *cushion* too — and keep them
      free
From accidents, which *have* been known
    To happen even to Royalty ! [3]

                 August 28.
Read, at a stall (for oft one pops
On something at these stalls and shops,
That does to *quote* and gives one's Book
A classical and knowing look. —
Indeed, I 've found, in Latin, lately,
A course of stalls improves me greatly) —
'T was thus I read that in the East
    A monarch's *fat* 's a serious matter;
And once in every year, at least,
    He 's weighed — to see if he gets fat-
      ter : [4]
Then, if a pound or two he be
Increased, there 's quite a jubilee ! [5]
Suppose, my Lord — and far from me
To treat such things with levity —
But just suppose the Regent's weight
Were made thus an affair of state;
And, every sessions, at the close, —
    'Stead of a speech, which, all can
      see, is
Heavy and dull enough, God knows —
We were to try how heavy *he* is.
Much would it glad all hearts to hear
    That, while the Nation's Revenue

bees is, of course, universal; "*exitium misère
apibus,*" like the angry nymphs in Vergil : — but
may not *new swarms* arise out of the *victims* of
Legitimacy yet?

3 I am afraid that Mr. Fudge alludes here to
a very awkward accident, which is well known
to have happened to poor Louis le Désiré, some
years since, at one of the Regent's Fêtes. He
was sitting next our gracious Queen at the time.

4 " The third day of the Feast the King caus-
eth himself to be weighed with great care." —
F. *Bernier's " Voyage to Surat,"* etc.

5 " I remember," says Bernier, " that all the
Omrahs expressed great joy that the King weighed
two pounds more now than the year preceding."
— Another author tells us that " Fatness, as
well as a very large head, is considered, throughout India, as one of the most precious gifts of
heaven. An enormous skull is absolutely revered, and the happy owner is looked up to as a
superior being. To a *Prince* a joulter head is
invaluable." — *Oriental Field Sports.*

Loses so many pounds a year,
   The PRINCE, God bless him! *gains* a
   few.

With bales of muslin, chintzes, spices,
   I see the Easterns weigh their Kings;—
But, for the REGENT, my advice is,
   We should throw in much *heavier*
   things:
For instance ———'s quarto volumes,
   Which, tho' not spices, serve to wrap
   them;
Dominie STODDART'S Daily columns,
   "Prodigious!"—in, of course, we'd
   clap them—
Letters, that CARTWRIGHT'S[1] pen in-
   dites,
   In which, with logical confusion,
The *Major* like a *Minor* writes,
   And never comes to a *Conclusion:*—
Lord SOMERS'S pamphlet—or his
   head—
(Ah! *that* were worth its weight in
   lead!)
Along with which we *in* may whip, sly,
   The Speeches of Sir JOHN COX HIPPISLY;
That Baronet of many words,
   Who loves so, in the House of Lords,
To whisper Bishops—and so nigh
   Unto their wigs in whispering goes,
That you may always know him by
   A patch of powder on his nose!—
If this won't do, we in must cram
   The "Reasons" of Lord BUCKINGHAM;
(A Book his Lordship means to write,
   Entitled "Reasons for my Ratting:")
Or, should these prove too small and
   light,
   His rump's a host—we'll bundle
   that in!
And, *still* should all these masses fail
   To stir the REGENT'S pondrous scale,
Why, then, my Lord, in heaven's name,
   Pitch in, without reserve or stint,
The whole of RAGLEY'S beauteous
   IfDame—
   that won't raise him, devil's in it!

August 31.

Consulted MURPHY'S TACITUS
   About those famous spies at Rome,[2]

1 Major Cartwright.
2 The name of the first worthy who set up the
trade of informer at Rome (to whom our Olivers

Whom certain Whigs—to make a
   fuss—
Describe as much resembling us,[3]
   Informing gentlemen, at home.
But, bless the fools, they *can't* be serious,
   To say Lord SIDMOUTH's like TIBERIUS!
What! *he,* the Peer, that injures no
   man,
Like that severe, blood-thirsty Roman!—
'T is true, the Tyrant lent an ear to
All sorts of spies—so doth the Peer,
   too.
'T is true, my Lord's elect tell fibs,
   And deal in perjury—*ditto* TIB's.
'T is true, the Tyrant screened and hid
   His rogues from justice[4]—*ditto* SID.
'T is true the Peer is grave and glib
   At moral speeches—*ditto* TIB.[5]
'T is true the feats the tyrant did
   Were in his dotage—*ditto* SID.

So far, I own, the parallel
'Twixt TIB and SID goes vastly well;
But there are points in TIB that strike
My humble mind as much more like
   Yourself, my dearest Lord, or him,
Of the India Board—that soul of whim!
Like him, TIBERIUS loved his joke,[6]
   On matters, too, where few can bear
   one;
E.g. a man cut up, or broke
   Upon the wheel—a devilish fair one!

and Castleses ought to erect a statue) was Romanus Hispo; *"qui formam vitæ iniit quam
postea celebrem miseriæ temporum et audaciæ
hominum fecerunt."*—TACIT. *"Annal."* i. 74.

3 They certainly possessed the same art of *insti-
gating* their victims, which the Report of the Secret Committee attributes to Lord Sidmouth's
agents:—"socius [says Tacitus of one of them]
libidinum et necessitatum, quo pluribus indiciis
inligaret."

4 *"Neque tamen id Sereno noxæ fuit,* quem
odium publicum tutiorem faciebat. *Nam ut
quis districtior accusator* velut sacrosanctus
erat."—*"Annal." lib.* iv. 36.—Or, as it is translated by Mr. Fudge's friend, Murphy:—"This
daring accuser had the *curses* of the *people,* and
the *protection* of the *Emperor. Informers,* in
proportion as they rose in guilt, *became sacred
characters.*"

5 Murphy even confers upon one of his
speeches the epithet "constitutional." Mr
Fudge might have added to his parallel, that Tiberius was a *good private* character:—*"egre-
gium vitâ famâque* quoad privatus."

6 "*Ludibria seriis permiscere solitus.*"

Your common fractures, wounds and fits,
Are nothing to such wholesale wits;
But, let the sufferer gasp for life,
   The joke is then worth any money;
And, if he writhe beneath a knife, —
   Oh dear, that 's something *quite* too
    funny.
In this respect, my Lord, you see
The Roman wag and ours agree:
Now as to *your* resemblance — mum —
This parallel we need not follow; [1]
Tho' 't is, in Ireland, said by some
Your Lordship beats TIBERIUS hollow;
Whips, chains — but these are things too
   serious
For me to mention or discuss;
Whene'er your Lordship acts TIBERIUS,
PHIL. FUDGE'S part is *Tacitus!*

September 2.

Was thinking, had Lord SIDMOUTH got
Any good decent sort of Plot
Against the winter-time — if not,
Alas, alas, our ruin 's fated;
All done up and *spiflicated!*
Ministers and all their vassals,
Down from CASTLEREAGH to CASTLES, —
Unless we can kick up a riot,
Ne'er can hope for peace or quiet!
What 's to be done? — Spa-Fields was
   clever;
   But even *that* brought gibes and mock-
    ings
Upon our heads — so, *mem.* — must never
Keep ammunition in old stockings;
For fear some wag should in his curst
   head
Take it to say our force was *worsted.*
Mem. too — when SID an army raises,
It must not be " *incog.*" like *Bayes's :*
Nor must the General be a hobbling
Professor of the art of cobbling;
Lest men, who perpetrate such puns,
   Should say, with Jacobinic grin,
He felt, from *soleing Wellingtons*,[2]
A *Wellington's* great *soul* within!
Nor must an old Apothecary
Go take the Tower, for lack of pence,

With (what these wags would call, so
   merry,)
   Physical force and *phial*-ence!
No — no — our Plot, my Lord, must be
Next time contrived more skilfully.
John Bull, I grieve to say, is growing
So troublesomely sharp and knowing,
So wise — in short, so Jacobin —
'T is monstrous hard to *take him in.*

September 6.

Heard of the fate of our Ambassador
In China, and was sorely nettled;
But think, my Lord, we should not pass
   it o'er
Till all this matter 's fairly settled;
And here 's the mode occurs to *me :* —
As none of our Nobility,
Tho' for their *own* most gracious King
(They would kiss hands, or — any thing),
Can be persuaded to go thro'
This farce-like trick of the *Ko-tou;*
And as these Mandarins *won't* bend,
   Without some mumming exhibition,
Suppose, my Lord, you were to send
   GRIMALDI to them on a mission:
As *Leg*ate, JOE could play his part,
And if, in diplomatic art,
The "*volto sciolto*" [3] 's meritorious,
Let JOE but grin, he has it, glorious!

A *title* for him 's easily made;
   And, by the by, one Christmas time,
If I remember right, he played
   Lord MORLEY in some pantomime; [4] —
As Earl of MORLEY then gazette him,
If *t' other* Earl of MORLEY 'll let him.
(And why should not the world be blest
With *two* such stars, for East and West?)
Then, when before the Yellow Screen
   He 's brought — and, sure, the very
    essence
Of etiquette would be that scene
   Of JOE in the Celestial Presence! —

3 The *open countenance*, recommended by
Lord Chesterfield.

4 Mr. Fudge is a little mistaken here. It was
not Grimaldi, but some very inferior performer,
who played this part of "Lord Morley" in the
pantomime, — so much to the horror of the distinguished Earl of that name. The expostula-
tory letters of the Noble Earl to Mr. Harris, upon
this vulgar profanation of his spick-and-span new
title, will, I trust, some time or other, be given
to the world.

1 There is one point of resemblance between
Tiberius and Lord C. which Mr. Fudge *might*
have mentioned — "*suspensa semper et obscura
verba.*"

2 Short boots, so called.

He thus should say: — " Duke Ho and
Soo,
" I 'll play what tricks you please for
you,
" If you 'll, in turn, but do for me
" A few small tricks you now shall see.
" If I consult *your* Emperor's liking,
" At least you 'll do the same for *my*
King."

He then should give them nine such grins,
As would astound even Mandarins;
And throw such somersets before
The picture of King GEORGE (God
bless him!)
As, should Duke Ho but try them o'er,
Would, by CONFUCIUS, *much* distress
him!

I start this merely as a hint,
But think you 'll find some wisdom in 't,
And, should you follow up the job,
My son, my Lord (you *know* poor BOB),
Would in the suite be glad to go
And help his Excellency, JOE; —
At least, like noble AMHERST'S son,
The lad will do to *practise* on.[1]

LETTER X.

FROM MISS BIDDY FUDGE TO MISS DOROTHY ——.

WELL, it *is n't* the King, after all, my
dear creature!
But *don't* you go laugh, now — there 's
nothing to quiz in 't —
For grandeur of air and for grimness of
feature,
He *might* be a King, DOLL, tho', hang
him, he is n't.
At first, I felt hurt, for I wisht it, I own,
If for no other cause but to vex Miss
MALONE, —
(The great heiress, you know, of Shan-
dangan, who 's here,
Showing off with *such* airs, and a real
Cashmere,[2]
While mine 's but a paltry, old rabbit-
skin, dear!)

But Pa says, on deeply considering the
thing,
" I am just as well pleased it should *not*
be the King;
" As I think for my BIDDY, so *gentille*
and *jolie*,
" Whose charms may their price in an
honest way fetch,
" That a Brandenburgh " — (what *is* a
Brandenburgh, DOLLY?) —
" Would be, after all, no such very
great catch.
" If the REGENT indeed " — added he,
looking sly —
(You remember that comical squint of
his eye)
But I stopt him with " La, Pa, how *can*
you say so,
" When the REGENT loves none but old
women, you know!"
Which is fact, my dear DOLLY — we,
girls of eighteen,
And so slim — Lord, he 'd think us not
fit to be seen;
And would like us much better as old —
ay, as old
As that Countess of DESMOND, of whom
I 've been told
That she lived to much more than a hun-
dred and ten,
And was killed by a fall from a cherry-
tree then!
What a frisky old girl! but — to come to
my lover,
Who, tho' not a King, is a *hero* I 'll
swear, —
You shall hear all that 's happened, just
briefly run over,
Since that happy night, when we
whiskt thro' the air!

Let me see — 't was on Saturday —
yes, DOLLY, yes —
From that evening I date the first dawn
of my bliss;
When we both rattled off in that dear
little carriage,
Whose journey, BOB says, is so like Love
and Marriage,

---

1 See Mr. Ellis's account of the Embassy.

2 See Lady Morgan's " France " for the anecdote, told her by Madame de Genlis, of the
young gentleman whose love was cured by finding that his mistress wore a *shawl* "*peau de
lapin.*"

"Beginning gay, desperate, dashing,
      down-hilly,
"And ending as dull as a six-inside
      Dilly!"[1]
Well, scarcely a wink did I sleep the
      night thro';
And, next day, having scribbled my letter
      to you,
With a heart full of hope this sweet fel-
      low to meet,
I set out with Papa, to see LOUIS DIX-
      HUIT
Make his bow to some half-dozen women
      and boys,
Who get up a small concert of shrill
      Vive le Rois —
And how vastly genteeler, my dear, even
      this is,
Than vulgar Pall-Mall's oratorio of hisses!
The gardens seemed full — so, of course,
      we walkt o'er 'em,
'Mong orange-trees, clipt into town-bred
      decorum,
And daphnes and vases and many a
      statue
There staring, with not even a stitch on
      them, at you!
The ponds, too, we viewed — stood
      awhile on the brink
   To contemplate the play of those pretty
      gold fishes —
"*Live bullion*," says merciless BOB,
      "which, I think,
   "Would, if *coined*, with a little *mint*
      sauce, be delicious!"[2]

But *what*, DOLLY, what, is the gay
      orange-grove,
Or gold fishes, to her that's in search of
      her love?
In vain did I wildly explore every
      chair
Where a thing *like* a man was — no lover
      sat there!
In vain my fond eyes did I eagerly cast
At the whiskers, mustachios and wigs
      that went past,
To obtain if I could but a glance at that
      curl, —
A glimpse of those whiskers, as sacred,
      my girl,
As the lock that, Pa says,[3] is to Mussul-
      men given,
For the angel to hold by that "lugs them
      to heaven!"
Alas, there went by me full many a
      quiz,
And mustachios in plenty, but nothing
      like his!
Disappointed, I found myself sighing out
      "well-a-day," —
Thought of the words of TOM MOORE's
      Irish Melody,
Something about the "green spot of
      delight"[4]
   (Which, you know, Captain MACKIN-
      TOSH sung to us one day):

---

1 The cars, on the return, are dragged up slowly by a chain.

2 Mr. Bob need not be ashamed of his cookery jokes, when he is kept in countenance by such men as *Cicero*, *St. Augustine*, and that jovial bishop, *Venantius Fortunatus*. The pun of the great orator upon the "*jus Verrinum*," which he calls bad *hog-broth*, from a play upon both the words, is well known; and the Saint's puns upon the conversion of Lot's wife into salt are equally ingenious: — *In salem conversa hominibus fidelibus quoddam præstitit* condimentum, *quo sapiant aliquid, unde illud caveatur exemplum.*" — "*De Civitat. Dei*," lib. xvi. *cap.* 30. — The jokes of the pious favorite of Queen Radagunda, the convivial Bishop *Venantius*, may be found among his poems, in some lines against a cook who had robbed him. The following is similar to *Cicero's* pun: —

   plus juscella Coci quam mea jura *valent.*

   See his poems, "*Corpus Poetar. Latin.*" tom. ii. p. 1732. — Of the same kind was *Montmaur's*

joke, when a dish was spilt over him — "*summum jus, summa injuria*;" and the same celebrated parasite, in ordering a sole to be placed before him, said, —

   eligi cui dicas, tu mihi sola *places.*

   The reader may likewise see, among a good deal of *kitchen* erudition, the learned *Lipsius's* jokes on cutting up a capon in his *Saturnal. Sermon.*" lib. ii. *cap.* 2.

3 For this scrap of knowledge "Pa" was, I suspect, indebted to a note upon Volney's "Ruins;" a book which usually forms part of a Jacobin's library, and with which Mr. Fudge must have been well acquainted at the time when he wrote his "Down with Kings," etc. The note in Volney is as follows: — "It is by this tuft of hair (on the crown of the head), worn by the majority of Mussulmans, that the Angel of the Tomb is to take the elect and carry them to Paradise."

4 The young lady, whose memory is not very correct, must allude, I think, to the following lines: —

   Oh that fairy form is ne'er forgot,
      Which First Love traced;
   Still it lingering haunts the greenest spot
      On Memory's waste!

Ah DOLLY, *my* "spot" was that Satur-
    day night,
  And its verdure, how fleeting, had
    withered by Sunday!
We dined at a tavern — La, what do
    I say?
  If BOB was to know! — a *Restaura-
    teur's*, dear;
Where your *properest* ladies go dine
    every day,
  And drink Burgundy out of large
    tumblers, like beer.
Fine BOB (for he's really grown *super-
    fine*)
  Condescended for once to make one
    of the party;
Of course, tho' but three, we had dinner
    for nine,
  And in spite of my grief, love, I
    own I ate hearty.
Indeed, DOLL, I know not how 't is,
    but, in grief,
  I have always found eating a wondrous
    relief;
And BOB, who's in love, said he felt the
    same, *quite* —
  "My sighs," said he, "ceased with
    the first glass I drank you;
"The *lamb* made me tranquil, the *puffs*
    made me light,
  "And — now that all 's o'er — why,"
    I'm — pretty well, thank you!"

To *my* great annoyance, we sat rather
    late;
  For BOBBY and Pa had a furious debate
About singing and cookery — BOBBY, of
    course,
  Standing up for the latter Fine Art in
    full force; [1]
And Pa saying, "God only knows which
    is worst,
  "The French Singers or Cooks, but I
    wish us well over it —

---

[1] Cookery has been dignified by the researches
of a *Bacon;* (see his "*Natural History*," *Receipts, etc.*) and takes its station as one of the Fine
Arts in the following passage of Mr. *Dugald
Stewart:* — "Agreeably to this view of the subject *sweet* may be said to be *intrinsically* pleasing, and *bitter* to be relatively pleasing; which
both are, in many cases, equally essential to those
effects, which, in the art of cookery, correspond
to that *composite beauty*, which it is the object
of the painter and of the poet to create. —
"*Philosophical Essays*."

"What with old LAÏS and VÉRY, I'm
    curst
  "If *my* head or my stomach will ever
    recover it!"

'T was dark, when we got to the Boule-
    vards to stroll,
  And in vain did I look 'mong the
    street Macaronis,
When, sudden it struck me — last hope
    of my soul —
  That some angel might take the dear
    man to TORTONI'S! [2]
We entered — and, scarcely had BOB,
    with an air,
  For a *grappe à la jardinière* called
    to the waiters,
When, oh DOLL! I saw him — my hero
    was there
  (For I knew his white small-clothes
    and brown leather gaiters),
A group of fair statues from Greece
    smiling o'er him, [3]
  And lots of red currant-juice sparkling
    before him!
Oh! DOLLY, these heroes — what crea-
    tures they are;
  In the *boudoir* the same as in fields full
    of slaughter!
As cool in the Beaujon's precipitous car,
  As when safe at TORTONI'S, o'er
    iced currant water!
He joined us — imagine, dear creature,
    my ecstasy —
  Joined by the man I'd have broken ten
    necks to see!
BOB wished to treat him with Punch *à
    la glace*,
  But the sweet fellow swore that my
    beauté, my *grâce*,
And my *je-ne-sais-quoi* (then his whiskers
    he twirled)
  Were, to *him*, "on de top of all Ponch
    in de vorld." —
How pretty! — tho' oft (as of course
    it must be)
  Both his French and his English are
    Greek, DOLL, to me.

---

[2] A fashionable *café glacier* on the Italian
Boulevards.

[3] "You eat your ice at Tortoni's," says Mr.
Scott, "under a Grecian group."

But, in short, I felt happy as ever fond
　　heart did;
And happier still, when 't was fixt, ere
　　we parted,
That, if the next day should be *pastoral*
　　weather,
We all would set off, in French buggies,
　　together,
To see *Montmorency* — that place which,
　　you know,
Is so famous for cherries and JEAN
　　JACQUES ROUSSEAU.
His card then he gave us — the *name*,
　　rather creased —
But 't was CALICOT — something — a
　　Colonel, at least!
After which — sure there never was hero
　　so civil — he
Saw us safe home to our door in *Rue
　　Rivoli*,
Where his *last* words, as, at parting,
　　he threw
A soft look o'er his shoulders, were —
　　" How do you do! " [1]
But, lord! — there 's Papa for the post
　　— I 'm so vext —
Montmorency must now, love, be kept
　　for my next.
That dear Sunday night! — I was charm-
　　ingly drest,
And — *so* providential! — was looking
　　my best;
Such a sweet muslin gown, with a flounce
　　— and my frills,
You 've no notion how rich — (tho'
　　Pa has by the bills)
And you 'd smile had you seen, when
　　we sat rather near,
Colonel CALICOT eying the cambric, my
　　dear.
Then the flowers in my bonnet — but,
　　la! it 's in vain —
So, good-by, my sweet DOLL — I shall
　　soon write again.
　　　　　　　　　　　　　B. F.

Nota bene — our love to all neighbors
　　about —
Your Papa in particular — how is his gout?

P.S. — I 've just opened my letter to say,
In your next you must tell me, (now
　　do, DOLLY, pray,

1 Not an unusual mistake with foreigners.

For I hate to ask BOB, he 's so ready
　　to quiz,)
What sort of a thing, dear, a *Branden-
　　burgh* is.

LETTER XI.

FROM PHELIM CONNOR TO ——.

YES, 't was a cause, as noble and as
　　great
As ever hero died to vindicate —
A Nation's right to speak a Nation's
　　voice,
And own no power but of the Nation's
　　choice!
Such was the grand, the glorious cause
　　that now
Hung trembling on NAPOLEON'S single
　　brow;
Such the sublime arbitrament, that
　　poured,
In patriot eyes, a light around his sword,
A hallowing light, which never, since the
　　day
Of his young victories, had illumed its
　　way!

Oh 't was not then the time for tame
　　debates,
Ye men of Gaul, when chains were at
　　your gates;
When he, who late had fled your Chief-
　　tain's eye,
As geese from eagles on Mount Taurus
　　fly,[2]
Denounced against the land, that spurned
　　his chain,
Myriads of swords to bind it fast again —
Myriads of fierce invading swords, to
　　track
Thro' your best blood his path of ven-
　　geance back;
When Europe's Kings, that never yet
　　combined
But (like those upper Stars, that, when
　　conjoined,
Shed war and pestilence,) to scourge
　　mankind,

2 See Ælian, *lib* v. *cap.* 29., — who tells us
that these geese, from a consciousness of their
own loquacity, always cross Mount Taurus with
stones in their bills, to prevent any unlucky
cackle from betraying them to the eagles —
διαπέτονται σιωπῶντες.

Gathered around, with hosts from every
shore,
Hating NAPOLEON much, but Freedom
more,
And, in that coming strife, appalled to
see
The world yet left one chance for lib-
erty! —
No, 't was not *then* the time to weave a
net
Of bondage round your Chief; to curb
and fret
Your veteran war-horse, pawing for the
fight,
When every hope was in his speed and
might —
To waste the hour of action in dispute,
And coolly plan how freedom's *boughs*
should shoot,
When your Invader's axe was at the
root!
No sacred Liberty! that God, who
throws,
Thy light around, like his own sunshine,
knows
How well I love thee and how deeply
hate
All tyrants, upstart and Legitimate —
Yet, in that hour, were France my native land,
I would have followed, with quick heart
and hand,
NAPOLEON, NERO — ay, no matter
whom —
To snatch my country from that damning doom,
That deadliest curse that on the conquered waits —
A Conqueror's satrap, throned within
her gates!

True, he was false — despotic — all you
please —
Had trampled down man's holiest liber-
ties —
Had, by a genius, formed for nobler
things
Than lie within the grasp of *vulgar*
Kings,
But raised the hopes of men — as eaglets
fly
With tortoises aloft into the sky —

To dash them down again more shatter-
ingly!
All this I own — but still [1]
. . . .

LETTER XII.
FROM MISS BIDDY FUDGE TO MISS
DOROTHY ——.

AT last, DOLLY, — thanks to a potent
emetic,
Which BOBBY and Pa, with grimace
sympathetic,
Have swallowed this morning, to balance
the bliss,
Of an eel *matelote* and a *bisque d'écre-
visses* —
I 've a morning at home to myself, and
sit down
To describe you our heavenly trip out of
town.
How agog you must be for this letter,
my dear!
Lady JANE, in the novel, less languisht
to hear
If that elegant cornet she met at Lord
NEVILLE'S
Was actually dying with love or — blue
devils.
But Love, DOLLY, Love is the theme *I*
pursue;
With Blue Devils, thank heaven, I have
nothing to do —
Except, indeed, dear Colonel CALICOT
spies
Any imps of that color in *certain* blue
eyes,
Which he stares at till *I*, DOLL, at *his* do
the same;
Then he simpers — I blush — and would
often exclaim,
If I knew but the French for it, "Lord,
Sir, for shame!"

Well, the morning was lovely — the
trees in full dress
For the happy occasion — the sunshine
express —

[1] Somebody (Fontenelle, I believe,) has said,
that if he had his hand full of truths, he would
open but one finger at a time; and the same
sort of reserve I find to be necessary with respect
to Mr. Connor's very plain-spoken letters. The
remainder of this Epistle is so full of unsafe matter-of-fact, that it must, for the present at least,
be withheld from the public.

Had we ordered it, dear, of the best
   poet going,
It scarce could be furnisht more golden
   and glowing.
Tho' late when we started, the scent of
   the air
Was like GATTIE'S rose-water, — and,
   bright, here and there,
On the grass an odd dew-drop was glittering yet,
Like my aunt's diamond pin on her
   green tabbinet !
While the birds seemed to warble as
   blest on the boughs,
As if *each* a plumed Calicot had for her
   spouse;
And the grapes were all blushing and
   kissing in rows,
And — in short, need I tell you, where-
   ever one goes
With the creature one loves, 't is *couleur de rose;*
And ah ! I shall ne'er, lived I ever so
   long, see
A day such as that at divine Montmorency !

There was but *one* drawback — at first
   when we started,
The Colonel and I were inhumanly
   parted;
How cruel — young hearts of such
   moments to rob !
He went in Pa's buggy, and I went with
   BOB;
And, I own, I felt spitefully happy to
   know
That Papa and his comrade agreed but
   so-so.
For the Colonel, it seems, is a stickler of
   BONEY'S —
Served *with* him of course — nay, I 'm
   sure they were cronies.
So martial his features ! dear DOLL, you
   can trace
Ulm, Austerlitz, Lodi, as plain in his face
As you do on that pillar of glory and
   brass,[1]
Which the poor DUC DE BERRI must
   hate so to pass !
It appears, too, he made — as most for-
   eigners do —

---

1 The column in the Place Vendôme.

About English affairs an odd blunder or
   two.
For example — misled by the names, I
   dare say —
He confounded JACK CASTLES with Lord
   CASTLEREAGH;
And — sure such a blunder no mortal hit
   ever on —
Fancied the *present* Lord CAMDEN the
   clever one !

But politics ne'er were the sweet fellow's
   trade;
'T was for war and the ladies my Col-
   onel was made.
And oh ! had you heard, as together we
   walkt
Thro' that beautiful forest, how sweetly
   he talkt;
And how perfectly well he appeared,
   DOLL, to know
All the life and adventures of JEAN
   JACQUES ROUSSEAU ! —
" 'T was there," said he — not that his
   words I can state —
'T was a gibberish that Cupid alone
   could translate; —
But " there," said he, (pointing where,
   small and remote,
The dear Hermitage rose), "there his
   JULIE he wrote, —
" Upon paper gilt-edged, [2] without blot
   or erasure;
" Then sanded it over with silver and
   azure,
" And — oh, what will genius and fancy
   not do? —
" Tied the leaves up together with *nom-
   pareille* blue !"
What a trait of Rousseau ! what a crowd
   of emotions
From sand and blue ribbons are con-
   jured up here !
Alas, that a man of such exquisite [3] no-
   tions
Should send his poor brats to the
   Foundling, my dear !

---

2 " *Employant pour cela le plus beau papier
doré séchant l'écriture avec de la poudre d'azur
et d'argent, et cousant mes cahiers avec de la
nompareille bleue.*"— " *Les Confessions,*" part
ii. *liv.* 9.

3 This word, " exquisite," is evidently a favorite of Miss Fudge's ; and I understand she was

"'T was here too perhaps," Colonel
CALICOT said —
As down the small garden he pensively
led —
(Tho' once I could see his sublime fore-
head wrinkle
With rage not to find there the loved
periwinkle) [1]
"'T was here he received from the fair
D'ÉPINAY
"(Who called him so sweetly *her Bear*,[2]
every day,)
"That dear flannel petticoat, pulled off
to form
"A waistcoat, to keep the enthusiast
warm!" [3]

Such, DOLL, were the sweet recollections
we pondered,
As, full of romance, thro' that valley we
wandered.
The flannel (one's train of ideas, how
odd it is!)
Led us to talk about other commodities,
Cambric, and silk, and — I ne'er shall
forget,
For the sun was then hastening in pomp
to its set,
And full on the Colonel's dark whiskers
shone down,
When he askt me, with eagerness, —
who made my gown?
The question confused me — for, DOLL,
you must know,
And I *ought* to have told my best friend
long ago,

not a little angry when her brother Bob committed a pun on the last two syllables of it in the
following couplet: —

" I 'd fain praise your Poem — but tell me,
how is it
When *I* cry out " Exquisite," *Echo* cries
" *quiz it* ? "

[1] The flower which Rousseau brought into
such fashion among the Parisians, by exclaiming
one day, "*Ah, voilà de la pervenche!*"

[2] " *Mon ours, voilà votre asyle — et vous*, mon
ours, *ne viendrez vous pas aussi ?* " — *etc.*

[3] " *Un jour, qu'il geloit très fort, en ouvrant
un paquet qu'elle m'envoyoit, je trouvai un petit
jupon de flanelle d'Angleterre, qu'elle me mar-
quoit avoir porté, et dont elle vouloit que je me
fisse faire un gilet. Ce soir, plus qu'amical, me
parut si tendre, comme si elle se fût dépouillée
pour me vêtir, que, dans mon émotion, je baisai
vingt fois en pleurant le billet et le jupon.*"

That, by Pa's strict command, I no
longer employ [4]
That enchanting *couturière*, Madame LE
ROI;
But am forced now to have VICTORINE,
who — deuce take her! —
It seems is, at present, the King's man-
tua-maker —
I mean *of his party* — and, tho' much
the smartest,
LE ROI is condemned as a rank Bona-
partist.[5]
Think, DOLL, how confounded I lookt
— so well knowing
The Colonel's opinions — my cheeks
were quite glowing;
I stammered out something — nay, even
half named
The *legitimate* sempstress, when, loud,
he exclaimed,
" Yes, yes, by the stitching 't is plain to
be seen
" It was made by that Bourbonite bitch,
VICTORINE ! "
What a word for a hero ! — but heroes
will err,
And I thought, dear, I 'd tell you things
just as they were.
Besides, tho' the word on good manners
intrench,
I assure you 't is not *half* so shocking in
French.

But this cloud, tho' embarrassing, soon
past away,
And the bliss altogether, the dreams of
that day,
The thoughts that arise, when such dear
fellows woo us, —
The *nothings* that then, love, are *every
thing* to us —
That quick correspondence of glances
and sighs,
And what BOB calls the " Twopenny-post
of the Eyes " —
Ah, DOLL ! tho' I *know* you 've a heart,
't is in vain

[4] Miss Biddy's notions of French pronunciation may be perceived in the rhymes which she
always selects for " *Le Roi.*"

[5] LE ROI, who was the *Couturière* of the
Empress Maria Louisa, is at present, of course,
out of fashion, and is succeeded in her station by
the Royalist mantua-maker, VICTORINE.

To a heart so unpractised these things to
explain.
They can only be felt, in their fulness
divine,
By her who has wandered at evening's
decline,
Thro' a valley like that, with a Colonel
like mine!

But here I must finish — for BOB, my
dear DOLLY,
Whom physic, I find, always makes
melancholy,
Is seized with a fancy for church-yard
reflections;
And, full of all yesterday's rich recollections,
Is just setting off for Montmartre — " for
there is,"
Said he, looking solemn, " the tomb of
the VÉRYS! [1]
" Long, long have I wisht as a votary
true,
" O'er the grave of such talents to
utter my moans;
" And, to-day — as my stomach is not in
good cue
" For the *flesh* of the VÉRYS — I 'll
visit their *bones!*"
He insists upon *my* going with him —
how teasing!
This letter, however, dear DOLLY,
shall lie
Unsealed in my drawer, that, if any
thing pleasing
Occurs while I 'm out, I may tell you
— good-by.

B. F.

Four o'clock.

Oh, DOLLY, dear DOLLY, I 'm ruined
for ever —
I ne'er shall be happy again, DOLLY,
never!
To think of the wretch — what a victim
was I!
'T is too much to endure — I shall die, I
shall die —
" My brain 's in a fever — my pulses
beat quick —

I shall die or at least be exceedingly
sick!
Oh! what do you think? after all my
romancing,
My visions of glory, my sighing, my
glancing,
This Colonel — I scarce can commit it to
paper —
This Colonel 's no more than a vile
linen-draper!!
'T is true as I live — I had coaxt brother
BOB so,
(You 'll hardly make out what I 'm writ-
ing, I sob so,)
For some little gift on my birth-day —
September
The thirtieth, dear, I 'm eighteen, you
remember —
That BOB to a shop kindly ordered the
coach,
(Ah! little I thought who the shop-
man would prove,)
To bespeak me a few of those *mouchoirs
de poche,*
Which, in happier hours, I have
sighed for, my love —
(The most beautiful things — two Na-
poleons the price —
And one's name in the corner embroi-
dered so nice!)
Well, with heart full of pleasure, I
entered the shop,
But — ye Gods, what a phantom! — I
thought I should drop —
There he stood, my dear DOLLY — no
room for a doubt —
There, behind the vile counter, these
eyes saw him stand,
With a piece of French cambric, before
him rolled out,
And that horrid yard-measure upraised
in his hand!
Oh! — Papa, all along, knew the secret,
't is clear —
'T was *a shopman* he meant by a
" Brandenburgh," dear!
The man, whom I fondly had fancied a
King,
And, when *that* too delightful illusion
was past,

---

1 It is the *brother* of the present excellent
Restaurateur who lies entombed so magnifi-
cently in the Cimetière Montmartre. The inscription on the column at the head of the tomb
concludes with the following words: — " *Toute
sa vie fut consacrée aux* arts utiles."

As a hero had worshipt — vile, treacherous thing —
  To turn out but a low linen-draper at
  last!
My head swam around — the wretch
smiled, I believe,
But his smiling, alas, could no longer
deceive —
I fell back on BOB — my whole heart
seemed to wither —
And, pale as a ghost, I was carried back
hither!
I only remember that BOB, as I caught
him,
  With cruel facetiousness said, " Curse
  the Kiddy!
"A stanch Revolutionist always I 've
thought him,
  " But now I find out he 's a *Counter*
  one, BIDDY!"

Only think, my dear creature, if this
should be known
To that saucy, satirical thing, Miss MA-
LONE!

What a story 't will be at Shandangan
for ever!
  What laughs and what quizzing she 'll
  have with the men!
It will spread thro' the country — and
never, oh! never
  Can BIDDY be seen at Kilrandy again!
Farewell — I shall do something desperate, I fear —
And, ah! if my fate ever reaches your
ear,
One tear of compassion my DOLL will
not grudge
To her poor — broken-hearted — young
friend,

            BIDDY FUDGE.

Nota bene — I am sure you will hear,
with delight,
That we 're going, all three, to see
BRUNET to-night.
A laugh will revive me — and kind Mr.
Cox
(Do you know him?) has got us the
Governor's box.

THE FUDGES IN ENGLAND;

BEING A SEQUEL TO THE

"FUDGE FAMILY IN PARIS."

PREFACE.

THE name of the country town, in England — a well-known fashionable water-ing-place — in which the events that gave rise to the following correspondence occurred, is, for obvious reasons, suppressed. The interest attached, however, to the facts and personages of the story, renders it independent of all time and place; and when it is recollected that the whole train of romantic circumstances so fully unfolded in these Letters has passed during the short period which has now elapsed since the great Meetings in Exeter Hall, due credit will, it is hoped, be allowed to the Editor for the rapidity with which he has brought the details before the Public; while, at the same time, any errors that may have been the result of such haste will, he trusts, with equal consideration, be pardoned.

THE FUDGES IN ENGLAND.

LETTER I.

FROM PATRICK MAGAN, ESQ., TO THE
REV. RICHARD ——, CURATE OF ——,
IN IRELAND.

WHO d' ye think we 've got here? — quite
    reformed from the giddy,
Fantastic young thing, that once made
    such a noise —
Why, the famous Miss Fudge — that de-
    lectable Biddy,
    Whom you and I saw once at Paris,
      when boys,
In the full blaze of bonnets, and rib-
    bands, and airs —
    Such a thing as no rainbow hath colors
      to paint;
Ere time had reduced her to wrinkles
    and prayers,
    And the Flirt found a decent retreat in
      the Saint.

Poor "Pa" hath popt off — gone, as
    charity judges,
To some choice Elysium reserved for the
    Fudges;
And Miss, with a fortune, besides ex-
    pectations
From some much revered and much pal-
    sied relations,
Now wants but a husband, with requisites
    meet, —
Age thirty, or thereabouts — stature six
    feet,
And warranted godly — to make all com-
    plete.
Nota bene — a Churchman would suit, if
    he 's *high*,
But Socinians or Catholics need not apply.

What say you, Dick? does n't this tempt
    your ambition?
    The whole wealth of Fudge, that re-
    nowned man of pith,

All brought to the hammer, for Church
    competition, —
    Sole encumbrance, Miss Fudge to be
    taken therewith.
Think, my boy, for a Curate how glori-
    ous a catch!
While, instead of the thousands of souls
    you *now* watch,
To save Biddy Fudge's is all you need do;
And her purse will meanwhile be the
    saving of *you*.

You may ask, Dick, how comes it that I,
    a poor elf,
Wanting substance even more than your
    spiritual self,
Should thus generously lay my own claims
    on the shelf,
When, God knows! there ne'er was
    young gentleman yet
So much lackt an old spinster to rid him
    from debt,
Or had cogenter reasons than mine to
    assail her
With tender love-suit — at the suit of his
    tailor.

But thereby there hangs a soft secret, my
    friend,
Which thus to your reverend breast I
    commend:
Miss Fudge hath a niece — such a crea-
    ture! — with eyes
Like those sparklers that peep out from
    summer-night skies
At astronomers-royal, and laugh with de-
    light
To see elderly gentlemen spying all
    night.

While her figure — oh! bring all the
    gracefullest things
That are borne thro' the light air by feet
    or by wings,

Not a single new grace to that form
    could they teach,
Which combines in itself the perfection
    of each;
While, rapid or slow, as her fairy feet
    fall,
The mute music of symmetry modulates
    all.

Ne'er in short was there creature more
    formed to bewilder
A gay youth like me, who of castles
    aërial
(And *only* of such) am, God help me !
    a builder;
Still peopling each mansion with lodg-
    ers ethereal,
And now, to this nymph of the seraph-
    like eye,
Letting out, as you see, my first floor
    next the sky.[1]

But, alas ! nothing 's perfect on earth —
    even she,
    This divine little gipsy, does odd things
      sometimes;
Talks learning — looks wise (rather pain-
    ful to see),
    Prints already in two County papers
      her rhymes;
And raves — the sweet, charming, ab-
    surd little dear !
About *Amulets*, *Bijous*, and *Keepsakes*,
    next year,
In a manner which plainly bad symp-
    toms portends
Of that Annual *blue* fit, so distressing to
    friends ;
A fit which, tho' lasting but one short
    edition,
Leaves the patient long after in sad in-
    anition.

However, let 's hope for the best — and,
    meanwhile,
Be it mine still to bask in the niece's
    warm smile ;
While you, if you 're wise, Dick, will
    play the gallant
(Uphill work, I confess,) to her Saint
    of an Aunt.

---

1 That floor which a facetious garreteer called
" *le premier en descendant du ciel.*"

Think, my boy, for a youngster like you,
    who 've a lack,
    Not indeed of rupees, but of all other
      specie,
What luck thus to find a kind witch at
    your back,
    An old goose with gold eggs, from all
      debts to release ye !
Never mind, tho' the spinster be rever-
    end and thin,
    What are all the Three Graces to her
      Three per Cents. ?
While her acres ! — oh Dick, it don't
    matter one pin
    How she touches the affections, so *you*
      touch the rents ;
And Love never looks half so pleased as
    when, bless him, he
Sings to an old lady's purse " Open,
    Sesame."

By the way, I 've just heard in my walks,
    a report,
Which, if true, will insure for your visit
    some sport.
'T is rumored our Manager means to be-
    speak
The Church tumblers from Exeter Hall
    for next week;
And certainly ne'er did a queerer or rum-
    mer set
Throw, for the amusement of Christians,
    a summerset.
'T is feared their chief " Merriman,"
    C—ke, cannot come,
Being called off, at present, to play
    Punch at home;[2]
And the loss of so practised a wag in
    divinity
Will grieve much all lovers of jokes on
    the Trinity;—
His pun on the name Unigenitus, lately
Having pleased Robert Taylor, the *Rev-
erend*, greatly.[3]

---

2 See the Dublin *Evening Post*, of the 9th of
this month (July), for an account of a scene
which lately took place at a meeting of the Synod
of Ulster, in which the performance of the above-
mentioned part by the personage in question
appears to have been worthy of all his former
reputation in that line.

3 " All are punsters if they have wit to be so ;
and therefore when an Irishman has to commence
with a Bull, you will naturally pronounce it a
bull. (A laugh.) Allow me to bring before you

'T will prove a sad drawback, if absent
　　he be,
As a wag Presbyterian 's a thing quite
　　to see;
And, 'mong the Five Points of the Cal-
　　vinists, none of 'em
Ever yet reckoned a point of wit one of
　　'em.
But even tho' deprived of this comical
　　elf,
We 've a host of *buffoni* in Murtagh
　　himself,
Who of all the whole troop is chief
　　mummer and mime,
As Coke takes the *Ground* Tumbling, *he*
　　the *Sublime ;* [1]
And of him we 're quite certain, so
　　pray come in time.

LETTER II.

FROM MISS BIDDY FUDGE, TO MRS.
ELIZABETH ——.

JUST in time for the post, dear, and
　　monstrously busy,
　　With godly concernments—and worldly
　　　　ones, too;
Things carnal and spiritual mixt, my dear
　　Lizzy,
In this little brain till, bewildered and
　　dizzy,
　　'Twixt heaven and earth, I scarce
　　　　know what I do.

First, I 've been to see all the gay fash-
　　ions from Town,
Which our favorite Miss Gimp for the
　　spring has had down.
Sleeves *still* worn (which *I* think is wise),
　　à la folle,
Charming hats, *pou de soie* —tho' the
　　shape rather droll.
But you can't think how nicely the caps
　　of *tulle* lace,
With the *mentonnières*, look on this poor
　　sinful face;

And I mean, if the Lord in his mercy
　　thinks right,
To wear one at Mrs. Fitz-wigram's to-
　　night.

The silks are quite heavenly : — I 'm
　　glad too to say
Gimp herself grows more godly and good
　　every day;
Hath had sweet experience — yea, even
　　doth begin
To turn from the Gentiles, and put away
　　sin —
And all since her last stock of goods
　　was laid in.
What a blessing one's milliner, careless
　　of pelf,
Should thus " walk in newness," as well
　　as one's self !

So much for the blessings, the comforts
　　of Spirit
I 've had since we met, and they 're
　　more than I merit ! —
Poor, sinful, weak creature in every re-
　　spect,
Tho' ordained (God knows why) to be
　　one of the Elect.
But now for the picture's reverse.— You
　　remember
That footman and cook-maid I hired last
　　December;
He, a Baptist Particular — *she*, of some
　　sect
Not particular, I fancy, in any respect;
But desirous, poor thing, to be fed with
　　the Word,
And " to wait," as she said, " on Miss
　　Fudge and the Lord."

Well, my dear, of all men, that Particu-
　　lar Baptist
At preaching a sermon, off hand, was the
　　aptest;
And, long as he staid, do him justice,
　　more rich in
Sweet savors of doctrine, there never
　　was kitchen.
He preached in the parlor, he preached
　　in the hall,
He preached to the chambermaids,
　　scullions and all.

the famous Bull that is called Unigenitus, referring to the only-begotten Son of God." — *Report
of the Rev. Doctor's Speech, June 20, in the
Record Newspaper.*

1 In the language of the play-bills, " Ground
and *Lofty* Tumbling."

All heard with delight his reprovings
of sin,
But above all, the cook-maid ;— oh, ne'er
would she tire —
Tho', in learning to save sinful souls from
the fire
  She would oft let the soles she was
  frying fall in.
(God forgive me for punning on points
thus of piety ! —
A sad trick I 've learned in Bob's heathen
society.)
But ah ! there remains still the worst of
my tale;
Come, Asterisks, and help me the sad
truth to veil —
Conscious stars, that at even your own
secret turn pale !

*   *   *   *   *   *   *

*   *   *   *   *   *   *

In short, dear, this preaching and psalm-
singing pair,
Chosen " vessels of mercy," as *I* thought
they were,
Have together this last week eloped;
making bold
To whip off as much goods as both ves-
sels could hold —
Not forgetting some scores of sweet
Tracts from my shelves,
Two Family Bibles as large as them-
selves,
And besides, from the drawer — I neg-
lecting to lock it —
My neat " Morning Manna, done up for
the pocket." [1]
Was there e'er known a case so distress-
ing, dear Liz?
It has made me quite ill : — and the
worst of it is,
When rogues are *all* pious, 't is hard to
detect
Which rogues are the reprobate, *which*
the elect.

1 " Morning Manna, or British Verse-book,"
neatly done up for the pocket," and chiefly intended to assist the members of the British Verse
Association, whose design is, we are told, " to
induce the inhabitants of Great Britain and Ireland to commit one and the same verse of Scripture to memory every morning. Already, it is
known, several thousand persons in Scotland,
besides tens of thousands in America and Africa,
are *every morning learning the same verse.*"

This man " had a *call*," he said — im-
pudent mockery !
What call had he to *my* linen and crock-
ery?

I 'm now and have been for this week
past in chase
Of some godly young couple this pair to
replace.
The enclosed two announcements have
just met my eyes
In that venerable Monthly where Saints
advertise
For such temporal comforts as this world
supplies; [2]
And the fruits of the Spirit are properly
made
An essential in every craft, calling and
trade.
Where the attorney requires for his
'prentice some youth
Who has " learned to fear God and to
walk in the truth; "
Where the sempstress, in search of employment, declares,
That pay is no object, so she can have
prayers;
And the Establisht Wine Company
proudly gives out
That the whole of the firm, Co. and all,
are devout.

Happy London, one feels, as one reads
o'er the pages,
Where Saints are so much more abundant
than sages;
Where Parsons may soon be all laid on
the shelf,
As each Cit can cite chapter and verse
for himself,

2 The *Evangelical Magazine.* — A few specimens taken at random from the wrapper of this
highly esteemed periodical will fully justify the
character which Miss Fudge has here given of it.
" Wanted, in a pious pawnbroker's family, an
active lad as an apprentice." " Wanted, as
housemaid, a young female who has been brought
to a saving knowledge of the truth." " Wanted
immediately, a man of decided piety, to assist in
the baking business." " A gentleman who understands the Wine Trade is desirous of entering
into partnership, etc. He is not desirous of
being connected with any one whose system of
business is not of the strictest integrity as in the
sight of God, and seeks connection only with a
truly pious man, either Churchman or Dissenter."

And the *serious* frequenters of market
and dock
All lay in religion as part of their
stock.[1]
Who can tell to what lengths we may
go on improving,
When thus thro' all London the Spirit
keeps moving,
And heaven 's so in vogue that each shop
advertisement
Is now not so much for the earth as the
skies meant?

P. S.

Have mislaid the two paragraphs — can't
stop to look,
But both describe charming — both Foot-
man and Cook.
She, " decidedly pious " — with pathos
deplores
The increase of French cookery, and sin
on our shores;
And adds — (while for further accounts
she refers
To a great Gospel preacher, a cousin of
hers,)
That " tho' *some* make their Sabbaths
mere matter-of-fun days,
She asks but for tea and the Gospel, on
Sundays."
The footman, too, full of the true saving
knowledge; —
Has late been to Cambridge — to Trinity
College;

1 According to the late Mr. Irving, there is
even a peculiar form of theology got up expressly
for the money-market. " I know how far
wide," he says, " of the mark my views of Christ's
work in the flesh will be viewed by those who are
working with the stock-jobbing theology of the
religious world." " Let these preachers," he
adds, " (for I will not call them theologians),
cry up, broker-like, their article." — "*Morning
Watch.*" — No. iii. 442, 443.
From the statement of another writer, in the
same publication, it would appear that the stock-
brokers have even set up a new Divinity of their
own. " This shows," says the writer in question, " that the doctrine of the union between
Christ and his members is quite as essential as
that of substitution, by taking which latter alone
the *Stock-Exchange Divinity* has been produced." — No. x., p. 375.
Among the ancients, we know the money-
market was provided with more than one presiding Deity. " *Deæ Pecuniæ* [says an ancient
author] *commendabantur ut pecuniosi essent.*"

Served last a young gentleman, studying
divinity,
But left — not approving the morals of
Trinity.

P. S.

I enclose, too, according to promise,
some scraps
Of my Journal — that Day-book I keep
of my heart;
Where, at some little items, (partaking,
perhaps,
More of earth than of heaven,) thy
prudery may start,
And suspect something tender, sly girl
as thou art.
For the present, I 'm mute — but, what-
e'er may befall,
Recollect, dear, (in Hebrews, xiii. 4,)
St. Paul
Hath himself declared, " marriage is
honorable in all."

EXTRACTS FROM MY DIARY.

Monday.

TRIED a new châlé gown on — pretty.
No one to see me in it — pity !
Flew in a passion with Friz, my maid; —
The Lord forgive me ! — she lookt dis-
mayed;
But got her to sing the 100th Psalm,
While she curled my hair, which made
me calm.
Nothing so soothes a Christian heart
As sacred music — heavenly art !

Tuesday.

At two a visit from Mr. Magan —
A remarkably handsome, nice young
man ;
And, all Hibernian tho' he be,
As civilized, strange to say, as we !

I own this young man's spiritual state
Hath much engrossed my thoughts of
late;
And I mean, as soon as my niece is gone,
To have some talk with him thereupon.
At present I naught can do or say,
But that troublesome child is in the way;
Nor is there, I think, a doubt that he
Would also her absence much prefer,

As oft, while listening intent to me,
　He 's forced, from politeness, to look
　　at her.

Heigho! — what a blessing should Mr.
　　Magan
Turn out, after all, a " renewed " young
　　man;
And to me should fall the task, on earth,
To assist at the dear youth's second birth.
Blest thought! and ah! more blest the
　　tie,
Were it Heaven's high will, that he and
　　I —
But I blush to write the nuptial word —
Should wed, as St. Paul says, " in the
　　Lord; "
Not *this* world's wedlock — gross, gal-
　　lant,
But pure — as when Amram married his
　　aunt.

Our ages differ — but who would count
One's natural sinful life's amount,
Or look in the Register's vulgar page
For a regular twice-born Christian's age,
Who, blessed privilege! only then
Begins to live when he 's born again.
And, counting in *this* way — let me see —
I myself but five years old shall be,
And dear Magan, when the event takes
　　place,
An actual new-born child of grace —
Should Heaven in mercy so dispose —
A six-foot baby, in *swaddling* clothes.

Wednesday.
Finding myself, by some good fate,
With Mr. Magan left *tête-a-tête,*
Had just begun — having stirred the fire,
And drawn my chair near his — to inquire
What his notions were of Original Sin,
When that naughty Fanny again bounced
　　in ;
And all the sweet things I had got to say
Of the Flesh and the Devil were whiskt
　　away !

Much grieved to observe that Mr. Magan
Is actually pleased and amused with Fan !
What charms any sensible man can see
In a child so foolishly young as she —
But just eighteen, come next May-day,

With eyes, like herself, full of naught
　　but play —
Is, I own, an exceeding puzzle to me.

LETTER III.

FROM MISS FANNY FUDGE, TO HER COUSIN, MISS KITTY ——.

STANZAS (INCLOSED)

TO MY SHADOW; OR, WHY? — WHAT?
　　　— HOW?

DARK comrade of my path ! while earth
　　and sky
　　Thus wed their charms, in bridal light
　　　arrayed,
Why in this bright hour, walkst thou
　　ever nigh,
　　Blackening my footsteps with thy
　　　length of shade —
　　　　Dark comrade, WHY?

Thou mimic Shape that, mid these
　　flowery scenes,
　　Glidest beside me o'er each sunny spot,
Saddening them as thou goest — say,
　　what means
　　So dark an adjunct to so bright a lot —
　　　　Grim goblin, WHAT?

Still, as to pluck sweet flowers I bend
　　my brow,
　　Thou bendest, too — then risest when
　　　I rise ; —
Say, mute, mysterious Thing ! how is 't
　　that thou
　　Thus comest between me and those
　　　blessed skies —
　　　　Dim shadow, HOW?

(ADDITIONAL STANZA, BY ANOTHER
　　HAND.)
Thus said I to that Shape, far less in
　　grudge
　　Than gloom of soul; while, as I eager
　　　cried,
Oh Why? What? How? — a Voice, that
　　one might judge
　　To be some Irish echo's, faint replied,
　　　　Oh fudge, fudge, fudge !

You have here, dearest Coz, my last
　　lyric effusion;
　　And, with it, that odious " additional
　　　stanza,"

Which Aunt *will* insist I must keep, as
　conclusion,
And which, you 'll *at once* see, is
　Mr. Magan's; — a
Most cruel and dark-designed ex-
　travaganza,
And part of that plot in which he and
　my Aunt are
To stifle the flights of my genius by
　banter.

Just so 't was with Byron's young eagle-
　eyed strain,
Just so did they taunt him; — but vain,
　critics, vain
All your efforts to saddle Wit's fire with
　a chain !
To blot out the splendor of Fancy's
　young stream,
Or crop, in its cradle, her newly-fledged
　beam ! ! !
Thou perceivest, dear, that, even while
　these lines I indite,
Thoughts burn, brilliant fancies break
　out, wrong or right,
And I 'm all over poet, in Criticism's
　spite !

That my Aunt, who deals only in Psalms,
　and regards
Messrs. Sternhold and Co. as the first of
　all bards —
That *she* should make light of my works
　I can't blame;
But that nice, handsome, odious Magan
　— what a shame !
Do you know, dear, that, high as on
　most points I rate him,
I 'm really afraid — after all, I — *must*
　hate him.
He is *so* provoking — naught 's safe from
　his tongue;
He spares no one authoress, ancient or
　young.
Were you Sappho herself, and in *Keep-
　sake* or *Bijou*
Once shone as contributor, Lord ! how
　he 'd quiz you !
He laughs at *all* Monthlies — I 've
　actually seen
A sneer on his brow at *The Court Maga-
　zine !* —

While of Weeklies, poor things, there 's
　but one he peruses,
And buys every book which that Weekly
　abuses.
But I care not how others such sarcasm
　may fear,
One spirit, at least, will not bend to his
　sneer;
And tho' tried by the fire, my young
　genius shall burn as
Uninjured as crucified gold in the fur-
　nace !
(I suspect the word " crucified " must
　be made " crucible,"
Before this fine image of mine is produ-
　cible.)

And now, dear — to tell you a secret
　which, pray
Only trust to such friends as with safety
　you may —
You know and indeed the whole country
　suspects
(Tho' the Editor often my best things
　rejects),
That the verses signed *so*, ☞, which you
　now and then see
In our County *Gazette* (vide *last*) are by
　me.
But 't is dreadful to think what provok-
　ing mistakes
The vile country Press in one's prosody
　makes.
For you know, dear — I may, without
　vanity, hint —
Tho' an angel should write, still 't is
　devils must print ;
And you can't think what havoc these
　demons sometimes
Choose to make of one's sense, and
　what 's worse, of one's rhymes.
But a week or two since, in my Ode
　upon Spring,
Which I *meant* to have made a most
　beautiful thing,
Where I talkt of the " dewdrops from
　freshly-blown roses,"
The nasty things made it " from freshly-
　blown noses ! "
And once when to please my cross Aunt,
　I had tried
To commemorate some saint of her *clique*,
　who 'd just died,

Having said he "had taken up in heaven
　　his position,"
They made it, he 'd "taken up to heaven
　　his physician!"

This is very disheartening;—but brighter
　　days shine,
I rejoice, love, to say both for me and
　　the Nine;
For what do you think?—so delightful!
　　next year,
　Oh, prepare, dearest girl, for the grand
　　news prepare—
I 'm to write in "*The Keepsake*"—yes,
　　Kitty, my dear,
　To write in "*The Keepsake*," as sure
　　as you 're there!!
T' other night, at a Ball, 't was my for-
　　tunate chance
With a very nice elderly Dandy to dance,
Who, 't was plain, from some hints
　　which I now and then caught,
Was the author of *something*—one
　　could n't tell what;
But his satisfied manner left no room to
　　doubt
It was something that Colburn had lately
　　brought out.

We conversed of *belles-lettres* thro' all the
　　quadrille,—
Of poetry, dancing, of prose, standing
　　still;
Talkt of Intellect's march—whether
　　right 't was or wrong—
And then settled the point in a bold *en
　　avant.*
In the course of this talk 't was that,
　　having just hinted
That *I* too had Poems which—longed
　　to be printed,
He protested, kind man! he had seen,
　　at first sight,
I was actually *born* in "*The Keepsake*" to
　　write.
"In the Annals of England let some,"
　　he said, "shine,
"But a place in her Annals, Lady, be
　　thine!
"Even now future '*Keepsakes*' seem
　　brightly to rise,
"Thro' the vista of years, as I gaze on
　　those eyes,—

"All lettered and prest, and of large-
　　paper size!"
How un*like* that Magan, who my genius
　　would smother,
And how we true geniuses find out each
　　other!

This and much more he said with that
　　fine frenzied glance
One so rarely now sees, as we slid thro'
　　the dance;
Till between us 't was finally fixt that,
　　next year,
　In this exquisite task I my pen should
　　engage;
And, at parting, he stoopt down and
　　lispt in my ear
These mystical words, which I could but
　　just hear,
　"Terms for rhyme—if it 's *prime*—
　　ten and sixpence per page."
Think, Kitty, my dear, if I heard his
　　words right,
　What a mint of half-guineas this small
　　head contains;
If for nothing to write is itself a delight,
　Ye Gods, what a bliss to be paid for
　　one's strains!

Having dropt the dear fellow a courtesy
　　profound,
　Off at once, to inquire all about him,
　　I ran;
And from what I could learn, do you
　　know, dear, I 've found
　That he' s quite a new species of liter-
　　ary man;
One, whose task is—to what will not
　　fashion accustom us?—
To *edit* live authors, as if they were
　　posthumous.
For instance—the plan, to be sure, is
　　the oddest!—
If any young he or she author feels
　　modest
In venturing abroad, this kind gentle-
　　man-usher
Lends promptly a hand to the interesting
　　blusher;
Indites a smooth Preface, brings merit
　　to light,
Which else might, by accident, shrink
　　out of sight,

And, in short, renders readers and critics
    polite.
My Aunt says — tho' scarce on such
    points one can credit her —
He was Lady Jane Thingumbob's last
    novel's editor.
'T is certain the fashion 's but newly in-
    vented;
    And quick as the change of all things
        and all names is,
Who knows but as authors like girls are
    presented,
    We girls may be *edited* soon at St.
        James's?

I must now close my letter — there 's
    Aunt, in full screech,
Wants to take me to hear some great
    Irvingite preach.
God forgive me, I 'm not much inclined,
    I must say,
To go and sit still to be preached at to-
    day,
And besides — 't will be all against
    dancing, no doubt,
Which my poor Aunt abhors with such
    hatred devout,
That so far from presenting young nymphs
    with a head,
For their skill in the dance, as of Herod
    is said,
She 'd wish their own heads in the plat-
    ter instead.
There again — coming, Ma'am! — I 'll
    write more, if I can,
Before the post goes,
        Your affectionate Fan.

                Four o'clock.

Such a sermon! — tho' *not* about dan-
    cing, my dear;
'T was only on the end of the world be-
    ing near.
Eighteen Hundred and Forty 's the year
    that some state
As the time for that accident — some
    Forty Eight: [1]

1 With regard to the exact time of this event,
there appears to be a difference only of about
two or three years among the respective calcula-
tors. M. Alphonse Nicole, Docteur en Droit,
et Avocat, merely doubts whether it is to be in
1846 or 1847. *"A cette époque,"* he says, *"les
fidèles peuvent espérer de voir s'effectuer la purification du Sanctuaire."*

And I own, of the two, I 'd prefer much
    the latter,
As then I shall be an old maid, and
    't won't matter.
Once more, love, good-by — I 've to make
    a new cap;
But am now so dead tired with this horrid
    mishap
Of the end of the world that I *must* take
    a nap.

LETTER IV.

FROM PATRICK MAGAN, ESQ., TO THE
REV. RICHARD——.

HE comes from Erin's speechful shore
Like fervid kettle, bubbling o'er
    With hot effusions — hot and weak;
Sound, Humbug, all your hollowest
    drums,
He comes, of Erin's martyrdoms
    To Britain's well-fed Church to speak.

Puff him, ye Journals of the Lord, [2]
Twin prosers, *Watchman* and *Record!*
Journals reserved for realms of bliss,
Being much too good to sell in this,
Prepare, ye wealthier Saints, your din-
    ners,
    Ye Spinsters, spread your tea and
        crumpets;
And you, ye countless Tracts for Sinners,
    Blow all your little penny trumpets.
He comes, the reverend man, to tell
To all who still the Church's part take,
Tales of parsonic woe, that well
    Might make even grim Dissenter's
        heart ache: —
Of ten whole bishops snatched away
For ever from the light of day;
(With God knows, too, how many more,
For whom that doom is yet in store) —
Of Rectors cruelly compelled
    From Bath and Cheltenham to haste
    home,
Because the tithes, by Pat withheld,
    Will *not* to Bath or Cheltenham come;
Nor will the flocks consent to pay
Their parsons thus to stay away; —
Tho' with *such* parsons, one may doubt
If 't is n't money well laid out; —

2 "Our anxious desire is to be found on the
side of the Lord." — *Record Newspaper.*

Of all, in short, and each degree
Of that once happy Hierarchy,
  Which used to roll in wealth so pleas-
    antly;
But now, alas! is doomed to see
  Its surplus brought to nonplus pres-
    ently!

Such are the themes this man of pathos,
Priest of prose and lord of bathos,
  Will preach and preach t' ye, till
    you're dull again;
Then, hail him, Saints, with joint ac-
    claim,
Shout to the stars his tuneful name,
Which Murtagh *was*, ere known to fame,
  But now is *Mortimer* O'Mulligan!

All true, Dick, true as you're alive —
I've seen him, some hours since, arrive.
Murtagh is come, the great Itinerant —
  And Tuesday, in the market-place,
Intends, to every saint and sinner in 't,
  To state what *he* calls Ireland's Case;
Meaning thereby the case of *his* shop, —
Of curate, vicar, rector, bishop,
And all those other grades seraphic,
That make men's souls their special
    traffic,
Tho' caring not a pin *which* way
The erratic souls go, so they *pay*. —
Just as some roguish country nurse,
  Who takes a founding babe to suckle,
First pops the payment in her purse,
  Then leaves poor dear to — suck its
    knuckle:
Even so these reverend rigmaroles
Pocket the money — starve the souls.
Murtagh, however, in his glory,
Will tell, next week a different story;
Will make out all these men of barter,
As each a saint, a downright martyr,
Brought to the *stake* — i. e. a *beef* one,
Of all their martyrdoms the chief one;
Tho' try them even at this, they'll bear it,
If tender and washt down with claret.

Meanwhile Miss Fudge, who loves all
    lions,
Your saintly, *next* to great and high
    'uns —
(A Viscount, be he what he may,
Would cut a Saint out any day,)

Has just announced a godly rout,
Where Murtagh's to be first brought out,
And shown in his tame, *week-day* state :—
" Prayers, half-past seven, tea at eight."
Even so the circular missive orders —
Pink cards, with cherubs round the bor-
    ders.

Haste, Dick — you're lost, if you lose
    time ; —
Spinsters at forty-five grow giddy,
And Murtagh with his tropes sublime
  Will surely carry off old Biddy,
Unless some spark at once propose,
And distance him by downright prose.
That sick, rich squire, whose wealth and
    lands
All pass, they say, to Biddy's hands,
(The patron, Dick, of three fat recto-
    ries !)
Is dying of *angina pectoris;* —
So that, unless you're stirring soon,
Murtagh, that priest of puff and pelf,
May come in for a honey-*moon*,
  And be the *man* of it, himself !

As for *me*, Dick — 't is whim, 't is folly,
But this young niece absorbs me wholly.
'T is true, the girl's a vile verse-maker —
  Would rhyme all nature, if you'd let
    her; —
But even her oddities, plague take her,
  But made me love her all the better.
Too true it is, she's bitten sadly
With this new rage for rhyming badly,
Which late hath seized all ranks and
    classes,
Down to that new Estate, " the masses;"
  Till one pursuit all tastes combines —
One common railroad o'er Parnassus,
Where, sliding in those tuneful grooves,
Called couplets, all creation moves,
  And the whole world runs mad *in
    lines*.
Add to all this — what 's even still
    worse,
As rhyme itself, tho' still a curse,
Sounds better to a chinking purse —
Scarce sixpence hath my charmer got,
While I can muster just a groat;
So that, computing self and Venus,
Tenpence would clear the amount be-
    tween us.

However, things may yet prove better: —
Meantime, what awful length of letter!
And how, while heaping thus with gibes
The Pegasus of modern scribes,
My own small hobby of farrago
Hath beat the pace at which even *they*
go!

LETTER V.

FROM LARRY O'BRANIGAN, IN ENGLAND,
TO HIS WIFE JUDY, AT MULLINAFAD.

DEAR JUDY, I sind you this bit of a letther,
By mail-coach conveyance — for want of
a betther —
To tell you what luck in this world I
have had
Since I left the sweet cabin, at Mullinafad.

Och, Judy, that night! — when the pig
which we meant
To dry-nurse in the parlor, to pay off
the rent,
Julianna, the craythur — that name was
the death of her [1] —
Gave us the shlip and we saw the last
breath of her!
And *there* were the childher, six innocent
sowls,
For their nate little play-fellow tuning
up howls;
While yourself, my dear Judy (tho'
grievin' 's a folly),
Stud over Julianna's remains, melancholy —
Cryin', half for the craythur and half
for the money,
"Arrah, why did ye die till we 'd
sowled you, my honey?"

But God's will be done! — and then,
faith, sure enough,
As the pig was desaiced, 't was high
time to be off.
So we gothered up all the poor duds we
could catch,
Lock the owld cabin-door, put the kay
in the thatch,

Then tuk laave of each other's sweet
lips in the dark,
And set off, like the Chrishtians turned
out of the Ark;
The six childher with you, my dear Judy,
ochone!
And poor I wid myself, left condolin'
alone.

How I came to this England, o'er say
and o'er lands,
And what cruel hard walkin' I 've had
on my hands,
Is, at this present writin', too tadious to
speak,
So I 'll mintion it all in a postscript,
next week: —
Only starved I was, surely, as thin as a lath,
Till I came to an up-and-down place
they call Bath,
Where, as luck was, I managed to make
a meal's meat,
By dhraggin' owld ladies all day thro'
the street —
Which their docthors (who pocket, like
fun, the pound starlins,)
Have brought into fashion to plase the
owld darlins.
Divil a boy in all Bath, tho' *I* say it,
could carry
The grannies up hill half so handy as
Larry;
And the higher they lived, like owld
crows, in the air,
The more *I* was wanted to lug them up
there.

But luck has two handles, dear Judy,
they say,
And mine has *both* handles put on the
wrong way.
For, pondherin', one morn, on a drame
I 'd just had
Of yourself and the babbies, at Mullina-
fad,
Och, there came o'er my sinses so plasin'
a flutther,
That I spilt an owld Countess right clane
in the gutther,
Muff, feathers and all! — the descint
was most awful,
And — what was still worse, faith — I
knew 't was unlawful:

---

[1] The Irish peasantry are very fond of giving
fine names to their pigs. I have heard of one instance in which a couple of young pigs were
named, at their birth, Abelard and Eloisa.

For, tho', with mere *women*, no very
 great evil,
T' upset an owld *Countess* in Bath is the
 divil!
So, liftin' the chair, with herself safe
 upon it,
(For nothin' about her was *kilt*, but her
 bonnet,)
Without even mentionin' "By your lave,
 ma'am,"
I tuk to my heels and — here, Judy, I
 am!

What 's the name of this town I can't
 say very well,
But your heart sure will jump when you
 hear what befell
Your own beautiful Larry, the very first
 day,
(And a Sunday it was, shinin' out
 mighty gay,)
When his brogues to this city of luck
 found their way.
Bein' hungry, God help me, and hap-
 penin' to stop,
Just to dine on the shmell of a pasthry-
 cook's shop,
I saw, in the window, a large printed
 paper,
And read there a name, och! that made
 my heart caper —
Though printed it was in some quare
 A B C,
That might bother a schoolmaster, let
 alone *me*.
By gor, you 'd have laughed, Judy, could
 you 've but listened,
As, doubtin', I cried, " why it *is !* — no,
 it *is n't :* "
But it *was*, after all — for, by spellin'
 quite slow,
First I made out " Rev. Mortimer " —
 then a great " O ; "
And, at last, by hard readin' and rackin'
 my skull again,
Out it came, nate as imported, " O'Mul-
 ligan ! "

Up I jumpt like a sky-lark, my jewel, at
 that name, —
Divil a doubt on my mind, but it *must*
 be the same.

" Masther Murthagh, himself," says I,
 " all the world over!
My own fosther-brother — by jinks, I 'm
 in clover.
Tho' *there*, in the play-bill, he figures so
 grand,
One wet-nurse it was brought us *both* up
 by hand,
And he 'll not let me shtarve in the
 inemy's land ! "

Well, to make a long hishtory short,
 niver doubt
But I managed, in no time, to find the
 lad out;
And the joy of the meetin' bethuxt him
 and me,
Such a pair of owld cumrogues — was
 charmin' to see.
Nor is Murthagh less plased with the
 evint than *I* am.
As he just then was wanting a Valley-de-
 sham;
And, for *dressin'* a gintleman, one way
 or t' other,
Your nate Irish lad is beyant every
 other.

But now, Judy, comes the quare part of
 the case;
And, in throth, it 's the only drawback
 on my place.
'T was Murthagh's ill luck to be crost,
 as you know,
With an awkward mishfortune some
 short time ago;
That 's to say, he turned Protestant —
 why, I can't larn;
But, of coorse, he knew best, an' it 's
 not *my* consarn.
All I know is, we both were good Cath-
 olics, at nurse,
And myself am so still — nayther bet-
 ther nor worse.
Well, our bargain was all right and tight
 in a jiffy,
And lads more contint never yet left the
 Liffey,
When Murthagh — or Morthimer, as
 he 's *now* chrishened,
His *name* being convarted, at laist, if *he*
 is n't —

Lookin' sly at me (faith, 't was divartin'
    to see)
" *Of coorse*, you 're a Protestant, Larry,"
    says he.
Upon which says myself, wid a wink
    just as shly,
" Is 't a Protestant? — oh yes, *I am*,
    sir," says I; —
And there the chat ended, and divil a
    more word
Controvarsial between us has since then
    occurred.
What Murthagh could mane, and, in
    troth, Judy dear,
What *I myself* meant, does n't seem
    mighty clear;
But the thruth is, tho' still for the Owld
    Light a stickler,
I was just then too shtarved to be over
    partic'lar : —
And, God knows, between us, a comic'-
    ler pair
Of twin Protestants could n't be seen
    any where.

Next Tuesday (as towld in the play-bills
    I mintioned,
Addrest to the loyal and godly intin-
    tioned,)
His Riverence, my mastĕr, comes forward
    to preach, —
Myself does n't know whether sarmon
    or speech,
But it 's all one to him, he 's a dead hand
    at each;
Like us Paddys in gin'ral, whose skill in
    orations
Quite bothers the blarney of all other
    nations.

But, whisht! — there 's his Riverence,
    shoutin' out " Larry,"
And sorra a word more will this shmall
    paper carry;
So, here, Judy, ends my short bit of a
    letther,
Which, faix, I 'd have made a much
    bigger and betther,
But divil a one Post-office hole in this
    town
Fit to swallow a dacent sized billy-dux
    down.
So good luck to the childer! — tell
    Molly, I love her;

Kiss Oonagh's sweet mouth, and kiss
    Katty all over —
Not forgettin' the mark of the red-cur-
    rant whiskey
She got at the fair when yourself was so
    frisky.
The heavens be your bed! — I will
    write, when I can again,
Yours to the world's end,
        LARRY O'BRANIGAN.

LETTER VI.

FROM MISS BIDDY FUDGE, TO MRS.
ELIZABETH ——.

How I grieve you 're not with us ! —
    pray, come, if you can,
Ere we 're robbed of this dear, oratorical
    man,
Who combines in himself all the multi-
    ple glory
Of Orangeman, Saint, *quondam* Papist
    and Tory; —
(Choice mixture ! like that from which,
    duly confounded,
The best sort of *brass* was, in old times,
    compounded) —
The sly and the saintly, the worldly and
    godly,
All fused down in brogue so deliciously
    oddly !
In short, he 's a *dear* — and *such* audi-
    ences draws,
Such loud peals of laughter and shouts
    of applause,
As *can't* but do good to the Protestant
    cause.

Poor dear Irish Church ! — he to-day
    sketched a view
Of her history and prospects, to *me* at
    least new,
And which (if it *takes* as it ought) must
    arouse
The whole Christian world her just rights
    to espouse.
As to *reasoning* — you know, dear,
    that 's now of no use,
People still will their *facts* and dry *fig-
    ures* produce,
As if saving the souls of a Protestant
    flock were
A thing to be managed " according to
    Cocker ! "

In vain do we say, (when rude radicals
hector
At paying some thousands a year to a
Rector,
In places where Protestants *never yet
were*,)
"Who knows but young Protestants
may be born there?"
And granting such accident, think, what
a shame,
If they did n't find Rector and Clerk
when they came!
It is clear that, without such a staff on
full pay,
These little Church embryos *must* go
astray;
And, while fools are computing what
Parsons would cost,
Precious souls are meanwhile to the
Establishment lost!

In vain do we put the case sensibly
thus; —
They 'll still with their figures and facts
make a fuss,
And ask "if, while all, choosing each
his own road,
Journey on, as we can, towards the
Heavenly Abode,
It is right that *seven* eighths of the travel-
lers should pay
For *one* eighth that goes quite a differ-
ent way?" —
Just as if, foolish people, this was n't, in
reality,
A proof of the Church's extreme liber-
ality,
That tho' hating Popery in *other* respects,
She to Catholic *money* in no way ob-
jects;
And so liberal her very best Saints, in
this sense,
That they even go to heaven at the
Catholic's expense.

But tho' clear to *our* minds all these
arguments be,
People can not or *will* not their cogency
see;
And I grieve to confess, did the poor
Irish Church
Stand on reasoning alone, she 'd be left
in the lurch.

It was therefore, dear Lizzy, with joy
most sincere,
That **I** heard this nice Reverend O'
something we 've here,
Produce, from the depths of his knowledge and reading,
A view of that marvellous Church, far
exceeding,
In novelty, force, and profoundness of
thought,
All that Irving himself in his glory e'er
taught.

Looking thro' the whole history, present
and past,
Of the Irish Law Church, from the first
to the last;
Considering how strange its original
birth —
Such a thing having *never* before been
on earth —
How opposed to the instinct, the law
and the force
Of nature and reason has been its whole
course;
Thro' centuries encountering repugnance,
resistance,
Scorn, hate, execration — yet still in existence !
Considering all this, the conclusion he
draws
Is that Nature exempts this one Church
from her laws —
That Reason, dumb-foundered, gives up
the dispute,
And before the portentous anomaly
stands mute; —
That in short 't is a Miracle ! — and,
once begun,
And transmitted thro' ages, from father
to son,
For the honor of miracles, *ought to go
on*.

Never yet was conclusion so cogent and
sound,
Or so fitted the Church's weak foes to
confound.
For observe the more low all her merits
they place,
The more they make out the miraculous
case,

And the more all good Christians must
deem it profane
To disturb such a prodigy's marvellous
reign.

As for scriptural proofs, he quite placed
beyond doubt
That the whole in the Apocalypse may
be found out,
As clear and well-proved, he would venture to swear,
As any thing else has been *ever* found
there : —
While the mode in which, bless the dear
fellow, he deals
With that whole lot of vials and trumpets and seals,
And the ease with which vial on vial he
strings,
Shows him quite a *first-rate* at all these
sort of things.

So much for theology : — as for the affairs
Of this temporal world — the light,
drawing-room cares
And gay toils of the toilet, which, God
knows, I seek,
From no love of such things, but in humbleness meek,
And to be, as the Apostle was, " weak
with the weak,"
Thou wilt find quite enough (till I 'm
somewhat less busy)
In the extracts inclosed, my dear news-
loving Lizzy.

EXTRACTS FROM MY DIARY.

Thursday.

LAST night, having naught more holy to
do,
Wrote a letter to dear Sir Andrew Ag-
new,
About the " Do-nothing-on-Sunday-
Club,"
Which we wish by some shorter name
to dub : —
As the use of more vowels and conso-
nants
Than a Christian on Sunday *really* wants,
Is a grievance that ought to be done
away,
And the Alphabet left to rest, that day.

Sunday.

Sir Andrew's answer ! — but, shocking
to say,
Being franked unthinkingly yesterday,
To the horror of Agnews yet unborn,
It arrived on this blessed Sunday
morn ! ! —
How shocking ! — the postman's self
cried " shame on 't,"
Seeing the immaculate Andrew's name
on 't ! !
What will the Club do? — meet, no
doubt.
'T is a matter that touches the Class De-
vout,
And the friends of the Sabbath *must*
speak out.

Tuesday.

Saw to-day, at the raffle — and saw it
with pain —
That those stylish Fitzwigrams begin to
dress plain.
Even gay little Sophy smart trimmings
renounces —
She who long has stood by me thro' all
sorts of flounces,
And showed by upholding the toilet's
sweet rites,
That we girls may be Christians without
being frights.
This, I own, much alarms me; for tho'
one 's religious,
And strict and — all that, there 's no
need to be hideous;
And why a nice bonnet should stand in
the way
Of one's going to heaven, 't is n't easy
to say.

Then, there 's Gimp, the poor thing —
if her custom we drop,
Pray what 's to become of her soul and
her shop?
If by saints like ourselves no more orders
are given,
She 'll lose all the interest she now takes
in heaven;
And this nice little " fire-brand, pluckt
from the burning,"
May fall in again at the very next turning.

Wednesday.

Mem. — To write to the India-Mission
Society;
And send £20 — heavy tax upon piety!

Of all Indian luxuries we now-a-days
boast,
Making "Company's Christians"[1] perhaps costs the most.
And the worst of it is, that these converts full grown,
Having lived in *our* faith mostly die in
their *own*,[2]
Praying hard, at the last, to some god
who, they say,
When incarnate on earth, used to steal
curds and whey.[3]
Think, how horrid, my dear! — so that
all 's thrown away;
And (what is still worse) for the rum
and the rice
They consumed, while believers, we
saints pay the price.

Still 't is cheering to find that we *do* save
a few —
The Report gives six Christians for Cun-
nangcadoo;
Doorkotchum reckons seven, and four
Trevandrum,
While but one and a half 's left at Coo-
roopadum.
In this last-mentioned place 't is the bar-
bers enslave 'em,
For once they turn Christians no barber
will shave 'em.[4]

To atone for this rather small Heathen
amount,
Some Papists, turned Christians,[5] are
tackt to the account.

1 The title given by the natives to such of
their countrymen as become converts.

2 Of such relapses we find innumerable instances in the accounts of the Missionaries.

3 The god Krishna, one of the incarnations of
the god Vishnu. "One day [says the Bhaga-
vata] Krishna's play-fellows complained to Ta-
suda that he had pilfered and ate their curds."

4 "Roteen wants shaving; but the barber
here will not do it. He is run away lest he
should be compelled. He says he will not shave
Yesoo Kreest's people." — *Bapt. Mission Society,* vol. ii. p. 493.

5 In the Reports of the Missionaries, the Roman Catholics are almost always classed along

And tho', to catch Papists, one need n't
go so far,
Such fish are worth hooking, wherever
they are;
And *now*, when so great of such converts
the lack is,
One Papist well caught is worth millions
of Blackies.

Friday.

Last night had a dream so odd and funny,
I cannot resist recording it here. —
Methought that the Genius of Matrimony
Before me stood with a joyous leer,
Leading a husband in each hand,
And both for *me*, which lookt rather
queer; —
One I could perfectly understand,
But why there were *two* was n't quite
so clear.
'T was meant however, I soon could see,
To afford me a *choice* — a most excel-
lent plan;
And — who should this brace of candi-
dates be,
But Messrs. O'Mulligan and Magan: —
A thing, I suppose, unheard of till then,
To dream, at once, of *two* Irishmen! —
That handsome Magan, too, with wings
on his shoulders
(For all this past in the realms of the
Blest,)
And quite a creature to dazzle beholders;
While even O'Mulligan, feathered and
drest
As an elderly cherub, was looking his
best.
Ah Liz, you, who know me, scarce can
doubt
As to *which* of the two I singled out.
But — awful to tell — when, all in dread
Of losing so bright a vision's charms,
I graspt at Magan, his image fled,
Like a mist, away, and I found but the
head
Of O'Mulligan, wings and all, in my
arms!

with the Heathen. "I have extended my labors,
[says James Venning, in a Report for 1831,] to the
Heathen, Mahomedans, and Roman Catholics."
"The Heathen and Roman Catholics in this
neighborhood [says another missionary for the
year 1832] are not indifferent, but withstand,
rather than yield to, the force of truth."

The Angel had flown to some nest divine,
And the elderly Cherub alone was mine !
Heigho !— it is certain that foolish Magan
Either can't or *won't* see that he *might*
    be the man;
And, perhaps, dear — who knows? — if
    naught better befall
But— O'Mulligan *may* be the man, after
    all.

N. B.

Next week mean to have my first scrip-
    tural rout,
For the special discussion of matters de-
    vout ; —
Like those *soirées*, at Powerscourt,[1] so
    justly renowned,
For the zeal with which doctrine and
    negus went round ;
Those theology-routs which the pious
    Lord Roden,
That pink of Christianity, first set the
    mode in ;
Where, blessed down-pouring ![2] from tea
    until nine,

---

1 An account of these Powerscourt Conver-
saziones (under the direct presidency of Lord
Roden), as well as a list of the subjects discussed
at the different meetings, may be found in *The
Christian Herald* for the month of December,
1832. The following is a specimen of the nature
of the questions submitted to the company : —
" *Monday Evening, Six o'clock, September* 24,
1832. — ' An examination into the quotations
given in the New Testament from the Old, with
their connection and explanation, viz.' etc.
Wednesday. — ' Should we expect a personal
Antichrist ? *and to whom will he be revealed ?'*
etc. — *Friday.* — ' What light does Scripture throw
on present events, and their moral character?
What is next to be looked for or expected ?' " etc.

The rapid progress made at these tea-parties
in settling points of Scripture, may be judged
from a paragraph in the account given of one of
their evenings, by *The Christian Herald :* —

" On Daniel a good deal of light was thrown,
and there was some, I think not so much, perhaps, upon the Revelations ; though particular
parts of it were discussed with considerable
accession of knowledge. There was some very
interesting inquiry as to the quotation of the Old
Testament in the New ; particularly on the point,
whether there was any ' accommodation,' or
whether they were quoted according to the mind
of the Spirit in the Old ; this gave occasion to
some very interesting development of Scripture.
The progress of the Antichristian powers was
very fully discussed."

2 " About eight o'clock the Lord began to
pour down his spirit copiously upon us — for they
had all by this time assembled in my room for the

The subjects lay all in the Prophecy
    line ; —
Then, supper — and then, if for topics
    hard driven,
From thence until bed-time to Satan was
    given ;
While Roden, deep read in each topic
    and tome,
On all subjects (especially the last) was
    at home.

LETTER VII.

FROM MISS FANNY FUDGE, TO HER COUSIN, MISS KITTY ——.

IRREGULAR ODE.

Bring me the slumbering souls of flowers,
    While yet, beneath some northern sky,
Ungilt by beams, ungemmed by showers,
They wait the breath of summer hours,
    To wake to light each diamond eye,
    And let loose every florid sigh !

Bring me the first-born ocean waves,
From out those deep primeval caves,
Where from the dawn of Time they 've
    lain —
THE EMBRYOS OF A FUTURE MAIN ! —
Untaught as yet, young things, to speak
    The language of their PARENT SEA
(Polyphlysbæan [3] named, in Greek),
Tho' soon, too soon, in bay and creek,
Round startled isle and wondering peak,
    They 'll thunder loud and long as HE !

Bring me, from Hecla's iced abode,
    Young fires —

    I had got, dear, thus far in my ODE,
Intending to fill the whole page to the
    bottom,
But, having invoked such a lot of fine
    things,
Flowers, billows and thunderbolts,
    rainbows and wings,

---

purpose of prayer. This down-pouring continued till about ten o'clock." — Letter from
Mary Campbell to the Rev. John Campbell, of
Row, (dated Fernicary, April 4, 1830,) giving an
account of her " miraculous cure."

3 If you guess what this word means, 't is
    more than I can : —
    I but give 't as I got it from Mr. Magan.

                    F. F.

Did n't know *what* to do with 'em, when
    I had got 'em.
The truth is, my thoughts are too full, at
    this minute,
Of Past MSS. any new ones to try.
This very night's coach brings my des-
    tiny in it —
    Decides the great question, to live or
        to die !
And, whether I 'm henceforth immortal
    or no,
All depends on the answer of Simpkins
    and Co. !

You 'll think, love, I rave, so 't is best
    to let out
    The whole secret, at once — I have
        publisht a Book ! ! !
Yes, an actual Book : — if the marvel
    you doubt,
    You have only in last Monday's *Cou-*
        rier to look,
And you 'll find "This day publisht
    by Simpkins and Co.
A Romaunt, in twelve Cantos, entitled
    " Woe Woe ! "
By Miss Fanny F——, known more
    commonly *so ☞.* "
This I put that my friends may n't be
    left in the dark,
But may guess at my *writing* by knowing
    my *mark.*

How I managed, at last, this great deed
    to achieve,
Is itself a " Romaunt" which you 'd
    scarce, dear, believe;
Nor can I just now, being all in a whirl,
Looking out for the Magnet,[1] explain
    it, dear girl.
Suffice it to say, that one half the expense
Of this leasehold of fame for long cen-
    turies hence —
(Tho' " God knows," as aunt says, my
    humble ambition
Aspires not beyond a small Second Edi-
    tion,) —
One half the whole cost of the paper
    and printing,
I 've managed, to scrape up, this year
    past, by stinting

---

1 A day-coach of that name.

My own little wants in gloves, ribands,
    and shoes,
Thus defrauding the toilet to fit out
    the Muse !

And who, my dear Kitty, would not
    do the same?
What 's *eau de Cologne* to the sweet
    breath of fame?
Yards of riband soon end — but the
    measures of rhyme,
Dipt in hues of the rainbow, stretch
    out thro' all time.
Gloves languish and fade away, pair
    after pair,
While couplets shine out, but the brighter
    for wear,
And the dancing-shoe's gloss in an even-
    ing is gone,
While light-footed lyrics thro' ages trip
    on.

The remaining expense, trouble, risk
    — and, alas !
My poor copyright too — into other hands
    pass;
And my friend, the Head Devil of the
    " *County Gazette* "
(The only Mecænas I 've ever had
    yet),
He who set up in type my first juvenile
    lays,
Is now set up by them for the rest of
    his days;
And while Gods (as my " Heathen
    Mythology" says)
Live on naught but ambrosia, *his* lot
    how much sweeter
To live, lucky devil, on a young lady's
    metre !

As for *puffing* — that first of all literary
    boons,
And essential alike both to bards and
    balloons,
As, unless well supplied with inflation,
    't is found
Neither bards nor balloons budge an
    inch from the ground; —
In *this* respect, naught could more pros-
    perous befall;
As my friend (for no less this kind
    imp can I call)

Knows the whole world of critics —
   the *hypers* and all.
I suspect he himself, indeed, dabbles
   in rhyme,
Which, for imps diabolic, is not the first
   time;
As I 've heard uncle Bob say, 't was
   known among Gnostics,
That the Devil on Two Sticks was a
   devil at Acrostics.

But hark ! there 's the Magnet just dasht
   in from Town —
How my heart, Kitty, beats ! I shall
   surely drop down.
That awful *Court Journal Gazette,
   Athenæum,*
All full of my book — I shall sink when
   I see 'em.
And then the great point — whether
   Simpkins and Co.
Are actually pleased with their bargain
   or no ! —

                    Five o'clock.

All 's delightful — such praises ! — I
   really fear
That this poor little head will turn giddy,
   my dear,
I 've but time now to send you two
   exquisite scraps —
All the rest by the Magnet, on Monday,
   perhaps.

FROM THE " MORNING POST."

'T is known that a certain distinguisht
   physician
   Prescribes, for *dyspepsia,* a course of
      light reading;
And Rhymes by young Ladies, the first,
   fresh edition
(Ere critics have injured their powers
   of nutrition,)
   Are he thinks, for weak stomachs, the
      best sort of feeding.
Satires irritate — love-songs are found
   calorific;
But smooth, female sonnets he deems
   a specific,
And, if taken at bed-time, a sure sop-
   orific.

Among works of this kind, the most
   pleasing we know,
Is a volume just published by Simpkins
   and Co.,
Where all such ingredients — the flowery,
   the sweet,
And the gently narcotic — are mixt *per*
   receipt,
With a hand so judicious, we 've no
   hesitation
To say that — 'bove all, for the young
   generation —
'T is an elegant, soothing and safe preparation.

Nota bene — for readers, whose object 's
   to sleep,
And who read, in their nightcaps, the
   publishers keep
Good fire-proof binding, which comes
   very cheap.

ANECDOTE — FROM THE " COURT JOURNAL."

T'other night, at the Countess of ***'s
   rout,
An amusing event was much whispered
   about.
It was said that Lord ——, at the Coun-
   cil, that day,
   Had, more than once, jumpt from his
      his seat, like a rocket,
And flown to a corner, where — heedless,
   they say,
How the country's resources were squan-
   dered away —
   He kept reading some papers he 'd
      brought in his pocket.
Some thought them despatches from
   Spain or the Turk,
   Others swore they brought word we
      had lost the Mauritius;
But it turned out 't was only Miss Fudge's
   new work,
   Which his Lordship devoured with
      such zeal expeditious —
Messrs. Simpkins and Co., to avoid all
   delay,
Having sent it in sheets, that his Lord-
   ship might say,
He had distanced the whole reading
   world by a day !

LETTER VIII.

FROM BOB FUDGE, ESQ., TO THE REV.
MORTIMER O'MULLIGAN.

Tuesday evening.

I MUCH regret, dear Reverend Sir,
　I could not come to * * * to meet you;
But this curst gout won't let me stir —
　Even now I but by proxy greet you;
As this vile scrawl, whate'er its sense is,
Owes all to an amanuensis.
Most other scourges of disease
Reduce men to *extremities* —
But gout won't leave one even *these.*

From all my sister writes, I see
That you and I will quite agree.
I 'm a plain man who speak the truth,
　And trust you 'll think me not uncivil,
When I declare that from my youth
　I 've wisht your country at the devil:
Nor can I doubt indeed from all
　I 've heard of your high patriot fame —
From every word your lips let fall —
　That you most truly wish the same.
It plagues one's life out — thirty years
Have I had dinning in my ears,
　" Ireland wants this and that and
　　t' other,"
And to this hour one nothing hears
　But the same vile, eternal bother.
While, of those countless things she
　wanted,
Thank God, but little has been granted,
And even that little, if we 're men
And Britons, we 'll have back again!

I really think that Catholic question
Was what brought on my indigestion;
And still each year, as Popery's curse
Has gathered round us, I 've got worse;
Till even my pint of port a day
Can't keep the Pope and bile away.
And whereas, till the Catholic bill,
I never wanted draught or pill,
The settling of that cursed question
Has quite *un*settled my digestion.

Look what has happened since — the
　Elect
Of all the bores of every sect,
The chosen triers of men's patience,
From all the Three Denominations,

Let loose upon us; — even Quakers
Turned into speechers and law-makers,
Who 'll move no question, stiff-rumpt
　elves,
Till first the Spirit moves themselves;
And whose shrill Yeas and Nays, in
　chorus,
Conquering our Ayes and Noes sonorous,
Will soon to death's own slumber snore
　us.
Then, too, those Jews! — I really sicken
To think of such abomination;
Fellows, who won't eat ham with chicken,
To legislate for this great nation! —
Depend upon't, when once they 've sway,
　With rich old Goldsmid at the head
　o' them,
The Excise laws will be done away,
　And *Circum*cise ones past instead o'
　them!

In short, dear sir, look where one will,
Things all go on so devilish ill,
That, 'pon my soul, I rather fear
Our reverend Rector may be right,
Who tells me the Millennium 's near;
Nay, swears he knows the very year,
　And regulates his leases by 't; —
Meaning their terms should end, no
　doubt,
Before the world's own lease is out.
He thinks too that the whole thing 's
　ended
So much more soon than was intended,
Purely to scourge those men of sin
Who brought the accurst Reform Bill in.[1]

However, let 's not yet despair;
　Tho' Toryism 's eclipst, at present,
And — like myself, in this old chair —
Sits in a state by no means pleasant;
Feet crippled — hands, in luckless hour,
Disabled of their grasping power;
And all that rampant glee, which revelled
In this world's sweets, be-dulled, be-
　deviled —

---

1 This appears to have been the opinion also
of an eloquent writer in the *Morning Watch.*
" One great object of Christ's second Advent, as
the Man and as the King of the Jews, is to *punish the Kings* who do not acknowledge that their
authority is derived from him, and *who submit to
receive it from that many-headed monster, the
mob.*" No. x., p. 373.

Yet, tho' condemned to frisk no more,
And both in Chair of Penance set,
There 's something tells me, all 's not o'er
With Toryism or Bobby yet;
That tho', between us, I allow
We 've not a leg to stand on now;
Tho' curst Reform and *colchicum*
Have made us both look deuced glum,
Yet still, in spite of Grote and Gout,
Again we 'll shine triumphant out!

Yes — back again shall come, egad,
Our turn for sport, my reverend lad.
And then, O'Mulligan — oh then,
When mounted on our nags again,
You, on your high-flown Rosinante,
Bedizened out, like Show-Gallantee
(Glitter great from substance scanty); —
While I, Bob Fudge, Esquire, shall ride
Your faithful Sancho, by your side;
Then — talk of tilts and tournaments!
Dam'me, we 'll —

.   .   .   .

'Squire Fudge's clerk presents
To Reverend Sir his compliments;
Is grieved to say an accident
Has just occurred which will prevent
The Squire — tho' now a little better —
From finishing this present letter.
Just when he 'd got to "Dam'me,
we 'll " —
His Honor, full of martial zeal,
Graspt at his crutch, but not being able
To keep his balance or his hold,
Tumbled, both self and crutch, and
rolled,
Like ball and bat, beneath the table.

All 's safe—the table, chair and crutch; —
Nothing, thank God, is broken much,
But the Squire's head, which in the fall
Got bumped considerably — that 's all.
At this no great alarm we feel,
As the Squire's head can bear a deal.

Wednesday morning.
Squire much the same — head rather
light —
Raved about "Barbers' Wigs" all night.

Our housekeeper, old Mrs Griggs,
Suspects that he meant "barbarous
Whigs."

LETTER IX.

FROM LARRY O'BRANIGAN, TO HIS WIFE JUDY.

As it was but last week that I sint you a
letther,
You 'll wondher, dear Judy, what this
is about;
And, throth, it 's a letther myself would
like betther,
Could I manage to lave the contints of
it out;
For sure, if it makes even *me* onaisy,
Who takes things quiet, 't will dhrive
you crazy.

Oh! Judy, that riverind Murthagh, bad
scran to him!
That e'er I should come to 've been
sarvant-man to him,
Or so far demane the O'Branigan blood,
And my Aunts, the Diluvians (whom not
even the Flood
Was able to wash clane from the
earth)[1]
As to sarve one whose name, of mere
yestherday's birth,
Can no more to a great O, *before* it, pur-
tend,
Than mine can to wear a great Q at its
end.

But that 's now all over — last night I
gev warnin',
And, masth'r as he is, will discharge him
this mornin'.
The thief of the world! — but it 's no
use balraggin';[2] —
All I know is, I 'd fifty times rather be
draggin'
Ould ladies up hill to the ind of my
days,
Than with Murthagh to rowl in a chaise,
at my aise,

---

1 "I am of your Patriarchs, I, a branch of one
of your antediluvian families — fellows that the
Flood could not wash away." — CONGREVE,
"*Love for Love.*"

2 To *balrag* is to abuse — Mr. Lover makes
it *ballyrag*, and he is high authority: but if I remember rightly, Curran in his national stories
used to employ the word as above. — See Lover's
most amusing and genuinely Irish work, the
"Legends and Stories of Ireland."

And be forced to discind thro' the same
   dirty ways.
Arrah, sure, if I 'd heerd where he last
   showed his phiz,
I 'd have known what a quare sort of
   monsther he is;
For, by gor, 't was at Exether Change,
   sure enough,
That himself and his other wild Irish
   showed off;
And it 's pity, so 't is, that they had n't
   got no man
Who knew the wild crathurs to act as
   their showman —
Sayin', " Ladies and Gintlemen, plaze
   to take notice,
" How shlim and how shleek this black
   animal's coat is;
" All by raison, we 're towld, that the
   nathur o' the baste
" Is to change its coat *once* in its lifetime,
   at laste;
" And such objiks, in *our* counthry, not
   bein' common ones,
" Are *bought up*, as this was, by way of
   Fine Nomenons.
" In regard of its *name* — why, in throth,
   I 'm consarned
" To differ on this point so much with
   the Larned,
" Who call it a ' *Morthimer*,' whereas
   the craythur
" Is plainly a ' Murthagh,' by name and
   by nathur."

This is how I 'd have towld them the
   rights of it all,
Had *I* been their showman at Exether
   Hall —
Not forgettin' that other great wondher
   of Airin
(Of the owld bitther breed which they
   call Prosbetairin),
The famed Daddy Coke — who, by gor,
   I 'd have shown 'em
As proof how such bastes may be tamed,
   when you 've thrown 'em
A good frindly sop of the rale *Raigin
   Donem*.[1]

But throth, I 've no laisure just now,
   Judy dear,
For any thing, barrin' our own doings
   here,
And the cursin' and dammin' and thun-
   d'rin' like mad,
We Papists, God help us, from Murthagh
   have had.
He says we 're all murtherers — divil a
   bit less —
And that even our priests, when we go
   to confess,
Give us lessons in murthering and wish
   us success !

When axed how he daared, by tongue or
   by pen,
To belie, in this way, seven millions of
   men,
Faith, he said 't was all towld him by
   Docthor Den ![2]
" And who the divil 's *he ?*" was the
   question that flew
From Chrishtian to Chrishtian — but not
   a sowl knew.
While on went Murthagh, in iligant
   style,
Blasphaming us Cath'lics all the while,
As a pack of desaivers, parjurers, vil-
   lains,
All the whole kit of the aforesaid mil-
   lions,[3] —
Yourself, dear Judy, as well as the rest,
And the innocent craythur that 's at your
   breast,
All rogues together, in word and deed,
Owld Den our insthructor and Sin our
   creed !

When axed for his proofs again and again,
Divil an answer he 'd give but Docthor
   Den.
Could n't he call into coort some *livin'*
   men?

---

1 Larry evidently means the *Regium Donum;*
—a sum contributed by the government annually
to the support of the Presbyterian churches in
Ireland.

2 Correctly, Dens — Larry not being very particular in his nomenclature.

3 " The deeds of darkness which are reduced
to horrid practice over the drunken debauch of
the midnight assassin are debated, in principle,
in the sober morning religious conferences of the
priests." — *Speech of the Rev. Mr. M'Ghee.* —
" The character of the Irish people *generally* is,
that they are given to lying and to acts of theft."
— *Speech of the Rev. Robert Daly.*

" No, thank you " — he 'd stick to Doc-
thor Den —
An ould gintleman dead a century or
two,
Who all about *us*, live Catholics, knew;
And of coorse was more handy, to call
in a hurry,
Than Docthor Mac Hale or Docthor
Murray !

But, throth, it 's no case to be jokin'
upon,
Tho' myself, from bad habits, is *makin'*
it one.
Even *you*, had you witnessed his grand
climacterics,
Which actually threw one owld maid in
hysterics —
Or, och! had you heerd such a purty
remark as his,
That Papists are only " *Humanity's car-*
casses,
" *Risen* " — but, by dad, I 'm afeared I
can't give it ye —
"*Risen from the sepulchre of — inac-*
tivity ;
" *And, like owld corpses, dug up from*
antikity,
" *Wandrin' about in all sorts of in-*
ikity ! ! " [1]
Even you, Judy, true as you are to the
Owld Light,
Would have laught, out and out, at this
iligant flight
Of that figure of speech called the Blath-
erumskite.
As for me, tho' a funny thought now and
then came to me,
Rage got the bether at last — and small
blame to me !
So, slapping my thigh, " by the Powers
of Delf,"

Says I bowldly " I 'll make a noration
myself."
And with that up I jumps — but, my
darlint, the minit
I cockt up my head, divil a sinse remained in it.
Tho', *saited*, I could have got beautiful
on,
When I tuk to my legs, faith, the gab
was all gone : —
Which was odd, for us, Pats, who,
whate'er we 've a hand in,
At laste in our *legs* show a sthrong under-
standin'.

Howsumdever, determined the chaps
should pursaive
What I thought of their doin's, before I
tuk lave,
" In regard of all that," says I — there
I stopt short —
Not a word more would come, tho' I
shtruggled hard for 't.
So, shnapping my fingers at what 's called
the Chair,
And the owld Lord (or Lady, I believe)
that sat there —
" In regard of all that," says I bowldly
again —
"To owld Nick I pitch Mortimer — *and*
Docthor Den;"
Upon which the whole company cried
out " Amen;"
And myself was in hopes 't was to what
I had said,
But, by gor, no such thing — they were
not so well bred:
For, 't was all to a prayer Murthagh just
had read out,
By way of fit finish to job so devout;
That is — *afther* well damning one half
the community,
To pray God to keep all in pace an' in
unity !

This is all I can shtuff in this letther,
tho' plinty
Of news, faith, I 've got to fill more —
if 't was twinty.
But I 'll add, on the *outside*, a line,
should I need it,
(Writin' " Private " upon it, that no
one may read it,)

<hr>

1 " But she (Popery) is no longer *the tenant*
of the sepulchre of inactivity. She has come
from the burial-place, walking forth a monster,
as if the spirit of evil had corrupted *the carcass*
of her departed humanity.; noxious and noisome, an object of abhorrence and dismay to all
who are not *leagued with her in iniquity.*" —
Report of the Rev. Gentleman's Speech, June
20, in the *Record* Newspaper.

We may well ask, after reading this and other
such reverend ravings, " *quis dubitat quin omne*
sit hoc rationis egestas ? "

To tell you how *Mortimer* (as the Saints
　　chrishten him)
Bears the big shame of his sarvant's dis-
　　misshin' him.

(*Private outside.*)

Just come from his riv'rence — the job is
　　all done —
By the powers, I 've discharged him as
　　sure as a gun!
And now, Judy dear, what on earth I 'm
　　to do
With myself and my appetite — both
　　good as new —
Without even a single traneen in my
　　pocket,
Let alone a good, dacent pound-starlin',
　　to stock it —
Is a mysht'ry I lave to the One that 's
　　above,
Who takes care of us, dissolute sowls,
　　when hard dhrove!

LETTER X.

FROM THE REV. MORTIMER O'MULLIGAN,
TO THE REV. ——.

THESE few brief lines, my reverend
　　friend,
By a safe, private hand I send
(Fearing lest some low Catholic wag
Should pry into the Letter-bag),
To tell you, far as pen can dare
How we, poor errant martyrs, fare; —
Martyrs, not quite to fire and rack,
As Saints were, some few ages back,
But — scarce less trying in its way —
To laughter, whereso'er we stray;
To jokes, which Providence mysterious
Permits on men and things so serious,
Lowering the Church still more each
　　minute,
And —injuring our preferment in it.

Just think, how worrying 't is, my friend,
To find, where'er our footsteps bend,
　　Small jokes, like squibs, around us
　　　whizzing;
And bear the eternal torturing play
Of that great engine of our day,
　　Unknown to the Inquisition — quiz-
　　　zing!

Your men of thumb-screws and of racks
Aimed at the *body* their attacks;
But modern torturers, more refined,
Work *their* machinery on the *mind*.
Had St. Sebastian had the luck
　　With me to be a godly rover,
Instead of arrows, he 'd be stuck
　　With stings of ridicule all over;
And poor St. Lawrence who was killed
By being on a gridiron grilled,
Had he but shared *my* errant lot,
Instead of grill on gridiron hot,
A *moral* roasting would have got.
Nor should I (trying as all this is)
　　Much heed the suffering or the shame—
As, like an actor, *used* to hisses,
　　I long have known no other fame,
But that (as I may own to *you*,
Tho' to the *world* it would not do,)
No hope appears of fortune's beams
Shining on *any* of my schemes;
No chance of something more *per ann.*
As supplement to Kellyman;
No prospect that, by fierce abuse
Of Ireland, I shall e'er induce
The rulers of this thinking nation
To rid us of Emancipation;
To forge anew the severed chain,
And bring back Penal Laws again.

Ah happy time! when wolves and priests
Alike were hunted, as wild beasts;
And five pounds was the price, *per* head,
For bagging *either*, live or dead;[1] —
Tho' oft, we 're told, *one* outlawed
　　brother
Saved cost, by eating up *the other*.
Finding thus all those schemes and
　　hopes
I built upon my flowers and tropes
All scattered, one by one, away,
As flashy and unsound as they,
The question comes — what 's to be
　　done?
And there 's but one course left me —
　　one.
Heroes, when tired of war's alarms,
Seek sweet repose in Beauty's arms.

1 " Among other amiable enactments against
the Catholics at this period (1649), the price of
five pounds was set on the head of a Romish
priest — being exactly the same sum offered by
the same legislators for the head of a wolf." —
Memoirs of Captain Rock, book i., chap. 10.

The weary Day-God's last retreat is
The breast of silvery-footed Thetis;
And mine, as mighty Love 's my judge,
Shall be the arms of rich Miss Fudge!

Start not, my friend, — the tender
    scheme,
Wild and romantic tho' it seem,
Beyond a parson's fondest dream,
Yet shines, too, with those golden dyes,
So pleasing to a parson's eyes —
That only *gilding* which the Muse
Can not around *her* sons diffuse; —
Which, whencesoever flows its bliss,
From wealthy Miss or benefice,
To Mortimer indifferent is,
So he can only make it *his*.
There is but one slight damp I see
Upon this scheme's felicity,
And that is, the fair heroine's claim
That I shall take *her* family name.
To this (tho' it may look henpeckt),
I can't quite decently object,
Having myself long chosen to shine
Conspicuous in the *alias*[1] line;
So that henceforth, by wife's decree,
    (For Biddy from this point won't
    budge)
Your old friend's new address must be
    The *Rev. Mortimer O'Fudge* —
The " O " being kept, that all may see
We 're *both* of ancient family.

Such, friend, nor need the fact amaze you,
My public life's calm Euthanasia.
Thus bid I long farewell to all
The freaks of Exeter's old Hall —
Freaks, in grimace, its apes exceeding,
And rivalling its bears in breeding.
Farewell, the platform filled with
    preachers —
The prayer given out, as grace,[2] by
    speechers,

Ere they cut up their fellow-crea-
    tures : —
Farewell to dead old Dens's volumes,
And, scarce less dead, old *Standard's*
    columns : —
From each and all I now retire,
My task, henceforth, as spouse and sire,
To bring up little filial Fudges,
To be M.P.s, and Peers, and Judges —
Parsons I 'd add too, if alas !
There yet were hope the Church could
    pass
The gulf now oped for hers and her,
Or long survive what *Exeter* —
Both Hall and Bishop, of that name —
Have done to sink her reverend fame.
Adieu, dear friend — you 'll oft hear
    from me,
  Now I'm no more a travelling drudge;
  Meanwhile I sign (that you may judge
How well the surname will become me)
    Yours truly,
      MORTIMER O'FUDGE.

LETTER XI.

FROM PATRICK MAGAN, ESQ., TO THE
    REV. RICHARD ———.
        ——————, *Ireland.*

DEAR DICK — just arrived at my own
    humble *gîte,*
I enclose you, post-haste, the account, all
    complete,
Just arrived, *per* express, of our late
    noble feat.

[*Extract from the " County Gazette."*]

This place is getting gay and full again.

. . . .

Last week was married, " in the
    Lord,"
The Reverend Mortimer O'Mulligan,
Preacher, in *Irish*, of the Word,
(He, who the Lord's force lately led
    on —
Exeter Hall his Ar*magh*-geddon,)[3]

---

1 In the first edition of his Dictionary, Dr.
Johnson very significantly exemplified the meaning of the word "alias" by the instance of Mallet, the poet, who had exchanged for this more
refined name his original Scotch patronymic,
Malloch. " What *other* proofs he gave [says
Johnson] of disrespect to his native country, I
know not ; but it was remarked of him that he
was the only Scot whom Scotchmen did not
commend." — *Life of Mallet.*

2 " I think I am acting in unison with the
feelings of a Meeting assembled for this *solemn*

object, when I call on the Rev. Doctor Hollo-
way to open it by prayer." — *Speech of Lord
Kenyon.*

3 The rectory which the · Rev. gentleman
holds is situated in the county of *Armagh !* — a
most remarkable coincidence — and well worthy
of the attention of certain expounders of the
Apocalypse.

To Miss B. Fudge of Pisgah Place,
One of the chosen, as "heir of grace,"
And likewise heiress of Phil. Fudge,
Esquire, defunct, of Orange Lodge.

Same evening, Miss F. Fudge, 't is
    hinted —
    Niece of the above, (whose "Sylvan
        Lyre,"
In our *Gazette*, last week, we printed),
    Eloped with Pat. Magan, Esquire.
The fugitives were trackt, some time,
    After they 'd left the Aunt's abode,
By scraps of paper, scrawled with rhyme,
    Found strewed along the Western
        road; —
Some of them, *ci-devant* curl-papers,
Others, half burnt in lighting tapers.
This clew, however, to their flight,
    After some miles was seen no more;
And, from inquiries made last night,
    We find they 've reached the Irish
        shore.

Every word of it true, Dick — the escape
    from Aunt's thrall —
Western road — lyric fragments — curl-
    papers and all.
My sole stipulation, ere linkt at the shrine
(As some balance between Fanny's *num-*
    bers and mine),
Was that, when we were *one*, she must
    give up the *Nine;*
Nay, devote to the Gods her whole stock
    of MS.
With a vow never more against prose to
    transgress.
This she did, like a heroine; — smack
    went to bits
The whole produce sublime of her dear
    little wits —
Sonnets, elegies, epigrams, odes, canzo-
    nets —
Some twisted up neatly, to form *allu-*
    mettes,
Some turned into *papillotes*, worthy to rise

And enwreathe Berenice's bright locks
    in the skies!
While the rest, honest Larry (who 's
    now in *my* pay),
Begged, as " lover of *po'thry*," to read
    on the way.

Having thus of life's *poetry* dared to dis-
    pose,
How we now, Dick, shall manage to get
    thro' its *prose*,
With such slender materials for *style*,
    Heaven knows!
But — I 'm called off abruptly — *another*
    Express!
What the deuce can it mean? — I 'm
    alarmed, I confess.

P.S.

Hurrah, Dick, hurrah, Dick, ten thou-
    sand hurrahs!
I 'm a happy, rich dog to the end of my
    days.
There — read the good news — and
    while glad, for *my* sake,
That Wealth should thus follow in Love's
    shining wake,
Admire also the *moral* — that he, the
    sly elf,
Who has fudged all the world, should be
    now fudged *himself!*

EXTRACT FROM LETTER ENCLOSED.

With pain the mournful news I write,
Miss Fudge's uncle died last night;
And much to mine and friends' surprise,
By will doth all his wealth devise —
Lands, dwellings — rectories likewise —
To his "beloved grand-niece," Miss
    Fanny,
Leaving Miss Fudge herself, who many
Long years hath waited — not a penny!
Have notified the same to latter,
And wait instructions in the matter.
            For self and partners, etc.

INDEX TO THE POEMS

INDEX OF FIRST LINES.